INTRODUCTION TO BIOPSYCHOLOGY

LEARN AND REVISE
BIOPSYCHOLOGY THROUGH COLOURING!

'A fun and relaxing way to consolidate learning'

THE BIOPSYCHOLOGY COLOURING BOOK

SUZANNE HIGGS
ALISON COOPER
JONATHAN LEE

sagepub.co.uk/biopsychcolouringbook

4TH EDITION

INTRODUCTION TO BIOPSYCHOLOGY

Andrew P. Wickens

Los Angeles | London | New Delhi
Singapore | Washington DC | Melbourne

Los Angeles | London | New Delhi
Singapore | Washington DC | Melbourne

SAGE Publications Ltd
1 Oliver's Yard
55 City Road
London EC1Y 1SP

SAGE Publications Inc.
2455 Teller Road
Thousand Oaks, California 91320

SAGE Publications India Pvt Ltd
B 1/I 1 Mohan Cooperative Industrial Area
Mathura Road
New Delhi 110 044

SAGE Publications Asia-Pacific Pte Ltd
3 Church Street
#10-04 Samsung Hub
Singapore 049483

Editor: Donna Goddard
Development editor: Martha Cunneen
Editorial assistant: Esmé Carter
Assistant editor, digital: Sunita Patel
Production editor: Rachel Burrows
Marketing manager: Camille Richmond
Cover design: Wendy Scott
Typeset by: C&M Digitals (P) Ltd, Chennai, India
Printed in the UK

Library of Congress Control Number: 2021931236

British Library Cataloguing in Publication data

A catalogue record for this book is available from
the British Library

ISBN 978-1-5297-1593-4
ISBN 978-1-5297-1594-1 (pbk)

CONTENTS

EXTENDED CONTENTS

PREFACE

The human brain is the most complex living object known in the universe. Although an average adult brain weighs only about a kilogram and a half, it contains in the region of 100 billion nerve cells which transmit tiny electrical signals. But this figure is small compared to the trillions of connections between the neurons. These are called synapses – tiny gaps mostly awash with neurotransmitters and chemicals. It is at these sites that the main information processing of the brain is believed to take place. Somehow, the electrical and chemical melee of this activity gives rise to the human mind with its remarkable capacity for behaviour, intentional thought and consciousness. How it achieves this remarkable feat is still largely a mystery, and the conundrum taxes the ingenuity of psychologists, neuroscientists and philosophers alike. Nonetheless, the number of ground-breaking scientific discoveries about the brain increases with every passing year. The aim of this book is to make this ever-growing knowledge both accessible and interesting to the curious person who may not have any previous knowledge of biological psychology. It is also hoped the book will take you on a journey that will fascinate, surprise and give you greater insight into your behaviour and that of others. If you are a student, it will even help you to pass your exams!

This is the new fourth edition and the book has come a long way since its first appearance in 2000. Originally entitled *Foundations of Biopsychology*, it is now entitled *Introduction to Biopsychology* to reflect a much broader scope. It also has a new publisher (SAGE) to spruce things up. When writing the first edition I was conscious of the need to stamp my own style on the book. There were a number of highly respected textbooks already available, and it was not always easy to avoid imitation. But, I hope, I succeeded in writing my own version, and in doing so provide a valuable text for students. One unique feature of the new book is the inclusion of a Key Thinker box in each chapter. I am a great believer in the usefulness of history to teach students about where biological psychology has come from and where it is heading – and these boxes hopefully get across some of the excitement of important discoveries about the brain and the personalities behind them. In addition, the book has individual chapters on degenerative disease and genetics. Looking at other texts, I discovered this is quite an unusual feature, but I feel both are necessary for showing some of the ways in which neuroscience is moving forward. The new edition of the book also has a companion website that is designed to encourage independent learning for students as well as providing a useful resource for lecturers. I would also add that I have tried out every chapter in a two-hour lecture setting – so I know they work in the classroom.

Despite all these improvements, I still like to believe the most important feature of *Introduction to Biopsychology* is its readability. When writing the first edition, I had been lecturing in Biopsychology and Neuroscience for over a decade. Nothing is worse that lecturing to a group of disinterested students. And this soon taught me that the art of good teaching lay in one's enthusiasm, and making the subject informative and structured in a way that enabled the content to be easily followed and understood. If the lecture followed some sort of narrative – then all the better. These are also the principles I have attempted to incorporate in each chapter of this book. Fortunately, tutor and student feedback has confirmed that my attempts provide an enjoyable and academically rigorous introduction to biopsychology. I hope it continues with this new edition.

Biological psychology is the study of how the brain produces behaviour, and is one of the most demanding subjects of all. A good knowledge of biological psychology requires more than a passing understanding of many other disciplines, including anatomy, physiology, biochemistry, pharmacology and genetics. Thus one might be excused for finding a simpler subject to study. But by doing this one would miss out on a subject that has no equal when it comes to providing powerful and insightful explanations of human nature. The Nobel laureate Gerald Edelman called the subject 'the most important one imaginable' because, in his view, 'at its end, we shall know how the mind works, what governs our nature and how we know the world'. And this is only one of the benefits, because as knowledge progresses, better treatments for a wide range of medical, behavioural and psychological problems will arise. Hence students should never lose sight of the great good which biopsychology can bring to our world.

The past decade or so has seen many exciting advances in biopsychology. For example, the widespread use of functional scanning techniques, such as fMRI, has allowed the cognitive processes of the mind to be visualized for the first time. This has led to a new discipline called Cognitive Neuroscience, which may one day have the power to expose your own private thoughts and emotions to scientific scrutiny. At the other end of the spectrum are advances in genetics, allowing the creation of transgenic animals, so that scientists can work out the function of individual genes and their impact on behaviour and disease. We are also at the beginning of the stem cell revolution, which will undoubtedly bring further remarkable advances. These examples not only help illustrate the broad canvas of biopsychology, they also show we are standing at the threshold of a new age in unravelling the mysteries of the brain. This is an exciting time to study biological psychology.

Inevitably, writing a book of this size will reflect the author's interests and biases. As you will see, this includes a smattering of history and philosophy, which are subjects close to my heart. However, I have also tried to include areas that are likely to be important for the brain scientist in the future. This is one reason why the final chapter is on genetics, which introduces some of the new developments taking place in molecular biology and brain science. Some may argue that the gap between molecular biology and behaviour is too great for it to be relevant to psychologists but I disagree. If you are to be student of the brain, then you must be prepared to expand your academic horizons in a wide variety of new ways. After all, biopsychology is a multidisciplinary subject, and this is one of the reasons why it is such a fascinating one. I hope this book can provide you with a thorough grounding in biopsychology and more. But most of all, I hope it gets across some of the excitement and wonder I feel when contemplating the brain. If this book helps you to pass an exam in biopsychology that is great. And if it stimulates you to go beyond its pages, and develop an ongoing fascination with the brain, then it will have been a greater success. I like to think that, for some of its readers, it will do just that.

Andrew Wickens
January 2021

ACKNOWLEDGEMENTS

PUBLISHER'S ACKNOWLEDGEMENTS

The author and SAGE would like to thank all the lecturers who reviewed this book's content to ensure it is as useful as possible:

Duncan Carmichael, Edinburgh Napier University

Mark Edwards, Australian National University

Andreas Kalckert, University of Skövde

Zoe Kolokotroni, Leeds Beckett University

Sanjay Kumar, Oxford Brookes University

Judith Schomaker, Leiden University

Lucy Troup, University of the West of Scotland

Sonia Tucci, University of Liverpool

AUTHOR'S ACKNOWLEDGEMENTS

The origins of this new edition of *Introduction to Biopsychology* came about through a meeting with Becky Taylor, a publisher with SAGE, in the refectory at the University of Central Lancashire in early 2018. Although I was in talks with another company at the time, I am grateful to Becky for recommending me to her colleagues, before she left SAGE to become a publishing consultant. As things transpired, I am very happy to have joined the SAGE family! I would also like to thank the Senior Commissioning Editor, Donna Goddard, for making me feel so welcome, and especially Martha Cunneen, who has been the Development Editor for my book. She has helped me every step of the way and been invaluable in reading my scripts and correcting them when necessary. This book has been significantly improved through her efforts. I would also like to thank Rachel Burrows, who has been responsible for overseeing the book through the latter stages of its production, and Audrey Scriven for her Herculean efforts in copyediting my manuscript. Last but not least, I am grateful to my girlfriend Kathy Wright for her continual support and friendship.

HOW TO USE THIS BOOK

LEARNING OBJECTIVES

After reading this chapter you should be able to:

- Explain what is meant by biological psychology and neuroscience.
- Outline the historical development of ideas concerning the brain.
- Describe the components of a nerve cell.
- Explain how the nervous impulse (action potential) is generated.
- Understand the importance of synapses and neurotransmitters.
- Elucidate the role of ion channels and second messengers in neural function.
- Depict the autonomic and somatic nervous systems.
- Describe the CNS, the main regions of the brain, and their behavioural significance.

Learning Objectives list everything you should achieve and understand by the end of the chapter.

afflictions such as behavioural disabilities, mental illness and with the prospect of much more effective treatments.

The brain may be complex, but it is continually giving up i bombardment of scientific attack. Arguably, there is no ical psychology which can give us greater insight into our potential to change people's lives for the better. For the stud this fascinating subject, this is an exciting time to become a

KEY TERMS: *neurons, synapses, neurotransmitters*

WHAT IS BIOLOGICAL PSYCH

To understand what is meant by biological psychology

Key Terms highlight the need-to-know terminology for the chapter.

KEY THINKER 1.1
SIR HENRY DALE

The concept of chemical synaptic neurotransmission is one of the fundamental keystones on which neuroscience is based. Indeed, without the knowledge of chemical neurotransmission, it would be impossible to understand how the nervous system and brain works. Sir Henry Dale is undisputedly one of the greatest British pharmacologists of the twentieth century, whose work not only identified acetylcholine as a neurotransmitter in the autonomic and somatic nervous systems, but was also pivotal in establishing the principles of chemical neurotransmission.

Dale was born in London in 1875 and later went to Trinity College, Cambridge, where he studied natural sciences. After medical training at St Bartholomew's hospital, Dale accepted an appointment in 1904 at the Wellcome Physiological Research Laboratories in London. This was an unusual choice, for the Wellcome was aimed primarily at developing new drugs (it had produced an antitoxin for diphtheria in 1894), and Dale's friends feared it would compromise his independence as a researcher. After starting his post, Dale was asked to examine the chemical constituents of a patristic fungus called ergot known to affect rye and other cereals. Although Dale was not attracted by the challenge he soon realized that ergot was a treasure trove of chemical substances. One of the first drugs he managed to extract from the fungus was ergotoxine which could be used to treat high blood pressure (it is now known to be an alpha-adrenergic blocker). Soon after, Dale discovered that ergot contained histamine – a chemical which he would show to be a naturally occurring substance in the

Key Thinker boxes spotlight the lives and work of important thinkers and researchers from history to share the story of their discoveries.

SPECIAL INTEREST 2.1

JOHN DALTON AND THE DISCOVERY OF COLOUR BLINDNESS

Despite coming from a poor Lake District family, John Dalton (1766–1844) became one of the great pioneers of modern physical science when he developed modern atomic theory – essentially the idea that matter is composed of small indestructible atoms with different sizes and masses, whose combination creates different chemicals and their reactions. However, Dalton also made contributions to many other subjects and gave the first account of colour blindness in 1794. It is said that he first realized he had a colour defect when he wore a bright scarlet robe to receive his PhD degree, thinking it was dark blue. Being a Quaker who always wore plain and unostentatious clothing, this was somewhat embarrassing! When Dalton began examining his own visual capabilities by viewing light passed through a prism, he discovered that while most people could distinguish six colours, he could see just two – blue/violet and yellow. Dalton's brother had the same affliction and he was to find a similar defect in 28 other people who were all male. Dalton believed his colour blindness was due to a blue colouring in the vitreous humour of his eyes, and specified that after his death they should be examined to prove his hypothesis. However, no blue colouring was found.

We now know that most types of colour blindness are inherited and caused by a faulty gene that makes the photopigments in the cones. The most common type of colour blindness which occurs in about 8% of males and 0.6% of females, is where the person cannot distinguish between red and green. There are two forms of this deficit: deuteranopia, where the person lacks the green photopigment, and protanopia, where the red pigment is missing. In both

Special Interest boxes bring biopsychology to life through fascinating discussions related to the chapter. Includes the discoveries of colour-blindness and synaesthesia, the memory of London cab drivers, and a look at why we laugh.

Further Reading provides suggestions for exploring the subject further to help build your bibliography for assignments.

FURTHER READING

Blumenfeld, H. (2011). *Neuroanatomy through clinical cases*. Sinauer.
A comprehensive textbook which uses clinical examples to help students learn more about the neuroanatomy and behavioural functions of the brain.

Carlson, N. R. (2016). *Physiology of behavior*. Allyn and Bacon. First published in 1977 and now in its 12th edition.
A classic textbook that provides an excellent introduction to biological psychology.

Clark, D. L., Boutros, N. N., & Mendez, M. F. (2018). *The brain and behavior: An introduction to behavioral neuroanatomy*. Cambridge University Press.
A good introduction to neuroanatomy for first-time students, which also relates brain structure to behaviour.

Diamond, M. C., Scheibel, A. B., & Elson, L. M. (2000). *The human brain colouring book*. HarperCollins.
This book provides a practical means of learning about the structure and function of the brain through a 'colouring-in' of its illustrations. It's very useful for students who find the various parts of the brain difficult to visualize.

Garrett, B. (2015). *Biological psychology*. SAGE.
This has become one of the author's favourite textbooks with its high-quality artwork and well-written text.

Kandel, E., Schwartz, J., Jessell, T., Siegelbaum, S., & Hudspeth, A. J. (Eds.). (2012). *Principles of neural science*. McGraw-Hill.
It has been said this book should be mandatory for someone who wants to become a neuroscientist. If you read its 1706 pages then I think you will have passed the apprenticeship!

MULTIPLE CHOICE QUESTIONS

Answer the questions below to test your understanding of this chapter's Learning Objectives. You'll find the answers at the end of the chapter.

1. What philosopher/scientist is famously credited with introducing the concept of 'the reflex' as a means of explaining the neural control of certain behaviours?

    a. Galen
    b. Descartes
    c. Cajal
    d. Henry Dale

2. What part of the neuron transmits the electrical flow of nerve impulse?

    a. dendrite
    b. cell body (soma)
    c. axon
    d. the synapse

3. The reason why there is a sudden shift in the electrical potential of the neuron (from about −70mV to about +50mV) in the first millisecond of an action potential is due to the influx of what ion into the cell?

    a. calcium
    b. chloride
    c. potassium
    d. sodium

4. Which of the following is not a neurotransmitter in the CNS?

    a. acetylcholine
    b. cortisol
    c. dopamine
    d. serotonin

Multiple Choice Questions at the end of the chapter test your comprehension of the chapter themes and learning objectives.

Online tools are available at **https://study.sagepub.com/wickens** to help you further test your understanding of brain and behaviour and revise key concepts and terms. Look out for the icon below

- **Drag and drop** – label diagrams for a fun and interactive way to revise the important brain and sensory systems.

- **Flashcard glossary** – check the definitions of key terms and hear the correct pronunciations.

ONLINE RESOURCES FOR LECTURERS

Visit **https://study.sagepub.com/wickens** to access the following resources available to support you in your teaching. All resources have been designed and formatted to upload easily into your LMS or VLE.

- **Instructor's Manual** – access further support when teaching each chapter, including ideas for seminar activities and discussions.
- **PowerPoint Slides** – save time and focus on your teaching by using these prepared, customisable slides for each chapter.
- **Image Bank** – visualize the learning experience for students by drawing on this bank of images, figures and tables from the textbook.
- **Test Bank** – test your students' understanding and help them prepare for assessments with this collection of 200 multiple choice and short answer questions.

AN INTRODUCTION TO BIOLOGICAL PSYCHOLOGY, BRAINS AND NERVE FUNCTION

LEARNING OBJECTIVES

After reading this chapter you should be able to:

- Explain what is meant by biological psychology and neuroscience.

- Outline the historical development of ideas concerning the brain.

- Describe the components of a nerve cell.

- Explain how the nervous impulse (action potential) is generated.

- Understand the importance of synapses and neurotransmitters.

- Elucidate the role of ion channels and second messengers in neural function.

- Depict the autonomic and somatic nervous systems.

- Describe the CNS, the main regions of the brain, and their behavioural significance.

GO ONLINE

Test your understanding of this chapter and visit **https://study.sagepub.com/wickens** to access interactive 'Drag and Drop' labelling activities and a flashcard glossary.

INTRODUCTION

An isolated human brain is a pinkish-grey mass of tissue which on first sight is not dissimilar in appearance to a giant walnut. If held in the palm of one's hand, it is deceptively heavy (an adult brain weighs about 3.5 pounds or 1.5 kilograms) and feels like hardened jelly to touch. It may not appear to be the most complex object in the universe, but the chances are that it is. Indeed, when holding a brain in our hands, or viewing it from afar, it is difficult not to be moved by what we have in our presence. This odd-looking structure once housed the mind of a human being – their memories, thoughts and emotions – their wishes, aspirations and disappointments – and their capability for consciousness, self-reflection and free will. Somehow this organ has enabled us to become the most dominant species on Earth with all of our many artistic, scientific, medical and technological achievements.

But what exactly is it that is so special about the human brain? Part of the answer is its great complexity. Like any other part of the body, the brain is composed of individual autono-mous cells, the most important being **neurons** which are specialized to receive, process and transmit information. Their main purpose is to communicate with each other, and they do so using a mechanism that is not dissimilar to an incredibly fast electrical on-off switch.[1] Although estimates vary (see Herculano-Houzel, 2009), the human brain contains in the region of one hundred billion neurons (100,000,000,000) – a figure so great that if you took a second to count every cell it would take over 3,000 years. Yet, what makes our brain really complex is the way the neurons are arranged and connected. Neurons rarely form connec-tions with each other on a one-to-one basis, but rather a single nerve cell may project up to between 5,000 and 10,000 others. This means that there are literally trillions of connections between neurons, and to make matters even more complicated, their points of contact are not physically continuous or joined but instead exist as **synapses** (these can be envisaged as miniscule gaps), which in the majority of cases rely on chemicals (or **neurotransmitters**) for communication. The number of synapses in the human brain is truly astronomical. In fact, Thompson in his textbook *The Brain* (1993) went so far as to say that the number of possible synaptic connections in the human brain is greater than the number of atomic particles that constitute the entire universe. If you don't fully understand this logic, don't worry, nor does the author of this book – but it is certainly a lot of connections! Yet one thing is for sure: as you read these very words, millions upon millions of tiny electrical signals are being rapidly sent through the neural fibres of your brain which is also awash with a huge variety of fleetingly formed chemical substances at the synapses.

One might be forgiven for thinking the brain is so complex that it defies comprehen-sion, but I hope this book will demonstrate otherwise – at least on a biological level. Neuroscience is one of the most rapidly expanding areas in modern science today, and an important part of this endeavour is psychobiology which attempts to understand how the brain's anatomy, physiology and neurochemistry give rise to human thought, emotion and

---

[1] It takes about 3–4 milliseconds (thousandths of a second) for a neuron to generate a nerve impulse (or action potential). Thus, neurons can achieve firing rates of up to 300–400 impulses per second.

behaviour. Progress is occurring at an ever-increasing pace. In addition, brain research has many potential benefits for us all, including greater insights into the causes of human afflictions such as behavioural disabilities, mental illness and degenerative diseases, along with the prospect of much more effective treatments.

The brain may be complex, but it is continually giving up its secrets to the unrelenting bombardment of scientific attack. Arguably, there is no other discipline than biological psychology which can give us greater insight into ourselves, as well as having the potential to change people's lives for the better. For the student beginning their study into this fascinating subject, this is an exciting time to become acquainted with your brain.

KEY TERMS: *neurons, synapses, neurotransmitters*

WHAT IS BIOLOGICAL PSYCHOLOGY?

To understand what is meant by biological psychology it is helpful to consider first the word 'psychology'. The term derives from the Greek words *psyche* ('mind') and *logos* ('reason'). Thus, 'psychology' literally means the reasoned study of the mind. Few psychologists, however, would unreservedly accept this definition today. The study of psychology first emerged in the nineteenth century as a branch of philosophy concerned with explaining the nature of thought through the technique of introspection (i.e. self-reflection). In fact, the first laboratory dedicated to psychological research was created by Wilhelm Wundt at the University of Leipzig in 1879. But the problem with introspection is that no matter how skilled the practitioner, its findings are subjective and unable to be verified by others. Because of this, a more experimental approach to psychology began to emerge in the early twentieth century that focused on overt behaviour which could be empirically observed and measured (Watson, 1913). This emphasis on experimentation and measurement has continued to the present day and many psychologists would now describe psychology as *the scientific or experimental study of behaviour and mental processes*.

Modern psychology has developed into a wide-ranging discipline concerned with understanding behaviour and mental processes from a variety of perspectives. As the name suggests, biological psychology is the branch of science that attempts to explain behaviour in terms of biology, and since the most important structure controlling behaviour is the brain, biopsychology is *the study of the brain and how it produces behaviour and mental processes*. Implicit in this definition is the assumption that every mental process, feeling and action must have a physical or neural basis in the brain. This is much the same as saying that the mind is the product of the brain's electrical and neurochemical activity. Although there are some philosophical grounds for questioning this viewpoint (Chalmers, 2010; Levine, 2001), even the most hardened cynic of materialism (i.e. the view that the mind is the result of physical processes) would find it hard to disagree that mind and brain are inextricably linked. This assumption is the foundation on which biological psychology is built. Yet the perplexing mystery of how the brain creates the mind remains unsolved (see Goldstein, 2020 for a recent account of how neuroscience is trying to tackle the problem).

To link the brain with behaviour, however, is a daunting task. Indeed, any attempt to do so must first require a very good understanding of the brain's biology. Traditionally, the two disciplines most relevant to the biological psychologist have been neuroanatomy (the study of the brain's neural architecture and pathways) and neurophysiology (the study of how neurons produce action potentials and neural information). However, in the last few decades the study of brain function has expanded greatly and attracted the interest of specialists from many other disciplines, including experts in biochemistry, molecular biology, genetics, pharmacology, psychiatry and artificial intelligence. Not all scientists working in these fields are necessarily interested in behaviour, although their discoveries can sometimes be of great interest to the biological psychologist. Consequently, in recent years, psychologists interested in the brain have become aquatinted with many other areas of biological science that lie outside the traditional domains of their subject. In addition, there is growing interest in how understanding the brain may relate to the philosophy of mind.

A number of different terms have been used to describe the study of brain and behaviour, and these terms at first can be confusing. For much of the twentieth century, the study of brain and behaviour was called physiological psychology because its investigators typically used 'physiological' techniques such as lesioning (the selective removal of small parts of the brain) and stimulation (using either electrical current or direct chemical administration) as their main experimental tools. This approach was complemented by examining human subjects who had suffered brain damage from accidents and stroke etc. – an area known as clinical neuropsychology. Although the terms 'physiological psychology' and 'clinical neuropsychology' are still heard today, there is a growing acceptance that they do not adequately cover many of the newer disciplines and techniques currently being used to examine the brain. Indeed, one notable major change that has taken place in brain research over the last few decades has been the use of computerized brain-scanning techniques to study the brain's activity – an area that has become known as cognitive neuroscience (a term invented by Michael Gazziniga and George Miller in the back of a New York taxi in the 1970s). Although some have suggested the terms 'biological psychology' or 'behavioural neuroscience' to describe today's brain research (Davis et al., 1988; Dewsbury, 1991), perhaps the most satisfactory is 'biopsychology' (Pinel, 2011). Whatever the arguments for and against these terms, they mean roughly the same thing: they attempt to give an appropriate name to the scientific discipline which relates brain function with psychology and behaviour. It is also important to note that biopsychology forms arguably the most important discipline within the much broader field of **neuroscience** – or what is generally regarded as the study of the nervous system in its entirety from molecules to behaviour (Cowan, 1978).

KEY TERMS: *neuroanatomy, neurophysiology, lesioning, stimulation, neuroscience*

ANCIENT HISTORICAL BEGINNINGS

Amongst the first people to realize that the brain was the organ of mind and behaviour were the ancient Greeks. The first person to recognize this appears to be Alcmaeon of Croton (c. 510–440 BC) and it was endorsed by the father of medicine, Hippocrates

(c. 460–370 BC). However not everyone agreed, including the most famous philosopher of antiquity Aristotle (348–322 BC) who believed the heart was the organ of sensation and that the brain merely served to cool blood! In fact the ancient Egyptians were so dismissive of the brain that during mummification they extracted it through the nose with an iron hook and threw it away, unlike other parts of the body which they stored in canopic jars for use in the afterlife. Throughout most of the ancient world, the human body was sacred and autopsies were prohibited – a situation that prevailed until the fourteenth century in Europe – and the first naturalistic drawings of the human brain were not undertaken until Leonardo da Vinci did so around 1480. Nonetheless, the ancient Greeks were aware of the basic form of the brain mainly through animal dissection, and they described its **ventricles** – a series of connected fluid-filled cavities that could be seen when the brain was sliced open. Because the ventricles stood out visually from the rest of the brain, it is perhaps not surprising they were used to formulate early theories about how the brain worked (Wickens, 2015, 2017a).

Figure 1.1   The ancient Egyptian hieroglyph for the brain as shown in the Edward Smith papyrus
Source: Said Carnot/Wikimedia Commons

One of the first writers to propose a theory of brain function based on the ventricles was the most important physician of the Roman Empire, Galen (c. 130–210 AD), who is also credited with performing the first experiments on the brain in a variety of animals including monkeys and pigs. From this work he also made many important anatomical discoveries including the cranial nerves that pass between the brain and the body (see later). Galen believed that the heart was the organ of the body that gave the spark of animation to the person because it contained a *vital spirit* necessary for life. This vital spirit was also transported to a large group of blood vessels at the base of the brain called the *rete mirabile* ('wonderful net')where it was mixed with air that had been inhaled through the nose, and transformed into *psychic pneuma*. This was then stored in the brain's ventricles and believed to provide the 'substance' of the mind. When needed for action, the pneuma was said to enter nerves resembling hollow tubes, which passed into the body where it pneumatically moved muscles to produce behaviour. Galen knew that the brain had four main ventricles. The first two are now called the lateral ventricles which form a

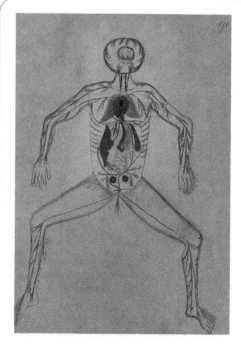

Figure 1.2   One of a series of five drawings found in a number of early medical manuscripts, possibly first drawn in Alexandria c. 300 BC. The insert shows the earliest depiction of the brain
Source: From Sudhoff 1908, plate 2. With permission from the University of Basel (Basel University Library, sign D II, fol 170)

symmetrical pair inside the two hemispheres of the cerebral cortex. Both of these feed into the third ventricle located close to the thalamus, that joins the fourth ventricle in the medulla via a narrow passage called the cerebral aqueduct (see Figure 1.3).

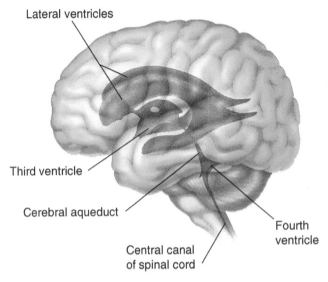

Figure 1.3 The ventricular system of the brain
Source: Garrett and Hough (2021)

Others who followed Galen extended his ideas and gave the ventricles different functions. For example, in the fourth century AD, Nemesius, the Bishop of Emesa, hypothesized that the lateral ventricles were the site of sensory and mental impressions; the third ventricle the site of reason; and the fourth ventricle the site of memory. This theory was also adopted by St Augustine (354–430 AD), who was one of the founding fathers of the Christian religion. With respected spiritual authority behind it, the ventricular concept of psychological function became the most popular theory in the brain's written history and was accepted uncritically for nearly 1,500 years. The first doubts only surfaced in the Renaissance when Vesalius (1543) in his great anatomical work *De humani corporis fabrica* showed that the human brain does not actually contain a *rete mirabile*. It seems that Galen, who had not been allowed to perform human dissection in Rome, had inferred its human existence by observing it in cattle and oxen (Wickens, 2015).

KEY TERMS: *lateral ventricles, third ventricle, fourth ventricle, cerebral aqueduct*

A NEW AGE OF REASON: DESCARTES

Descartes was a French philosopher and mathematician who more than any other person was responsible for the demise of the intellectual assumptions characterizing the Middle Ages. Indeed, his scepticism of all knowledge expressed in his famous quote *Cogito, ergo sum* ('I think, therefore I am'), which refers to Descartes' doubt of all things except his own mental existence, is widely seen as heralding a new age of reason. The importance of Descartes in the development of psychology lies largely with his attempt at resolving the mind–body problem. Descartes believed, as did many ancient philosophers, that mind and body are two entirely different things (a theory known as dualism), with the body composed of physical matter and the mind being non-physical and a separate entity from the material world. A problem with this position, however, lies in explaining how the soul-like mind can control the physical workings of the body. In his attempt to provide an answer, Descartes proposed that the mind and body interacted in the **pineal gland**. Descartes chose this organ because he believed the soul had to be a unified entity without different parts, and the pineal gland was one of the few structures in the brain that was singular (most other brain areas are bilateral). It also helped that the pineal gland intruded into the third ventricle which put it into contact with the cerebrospinal fluid. Descartes hypothesized that the soul was able induce 'minute movements' in the pineal gland, which caused the flow of animal spirits stored in the ventricles to enter the nerves of the body. In other words, the pineal gland provided the site where the soul could act upon the brain (Lokhorst and Kaitaro, 2001; Mazzolini, 1991).

Yet Descartes realized that a great deal of behaviour was mechanical without the need for mental intervention. He first developed this idea during a visit to the Royal Gardens in Paris as a young man. The gardens exhibited mechanical statues that moved and danced whenever they were approached, caused by hydraulic pressure-sensitive plates hidden under the ground. This led Descartes to speculate that the human body might work according to similar principles. From this premise, he developed the concept of the reflex which occurs, for example, when a limb is quickly moved away from a hot source such as a fire. To explain this response, Descartes hypothesized that a sensory nerve is composed of a hollow tube – which contains small threads or fibrils passing to the ventricles of the brain. Here, they pulled open valves in the ventricular walls that forced or 'reflected' the animal spirits to flow out through the nerves, back to the muscles of the affected limb, thereby causing its withdrawal. The important point was that this response was reflexive: the mind was not involved (although it felt pain and was aware of what had happened) and therefore not a *cause* of behaviour. This idea was truly revolutionary for its time.

Figure 1.4   Descartes and his illustration of the reflex from *L'Homme* (published in 1662)

Source: Anthonyhcole/Wikimedia Commons

Prior to Descartes, it was believed that a soul-like animating force (called the *psyche* by Aristotle) controlled all the actions of the human body, but Descartes appeared to show the body operated according to mechanical principles – not unlike the internal workings of a watch. Nor did it need a soul to make it operate once it had been put into motion. With remarkable foresight, Descartes not only proposed that functions such as digestion and respiration were reflexive, but also included (more controversially) some mental functions including the receipt of sensory input, emotions and memory. He based this idea partly on his observation that animals, which he believed had no soul, were capable of sensory processing along with emotion and memory. Thus, if these processes did not need the involvement of a soul-like force in animals, then why should humans be any different? In other words, they could be regarded as reflexive responses that belonged to the physical or mechanical world. The one exception for Descartes, however, was reasoning and thought, which he held was the exclusive property of the mind and uniquely human.

Descartes' theory laid the foundations for the modern development of physiology and psychology. Although his theory was based on a dualist view of the mind, it helped shift attention towards the practical problem of how reflexes might underlie behaviour without fear of contradicting religious dogma. In addition, it encouraged others to think more deeply about how the brain worked. But perhaps most importantly, Descartes provided a great impetus for experimental research – not least because some of his ideas could be tested. As we have seen, he believed that the nervous system controlling reflexes was a hydraulic system consisting of hollow tubes through which animal spirits flowed from the ventricles to the muscles. If this idea was correct, then it followed that muscles should increase in volume as they 'swelled' with spirit during contraction. When investigators tested this theory by flexing a person's arm in a container of water, however, no increase in its level occurred. Nonetheless, Descartes had paved a way for a scientific and non-secular approach to understanding human physiology that included the brain (Wickens, 2015, 2017a).

KEY TERMS: *dualism, pineal gland, reflex.*

THE DISCOVERY OF 'ANIMAL' ELECTRICITY

In 1791, the idea of animal spirit as the cause of nervous activity was challenged by the Italian Luigi Galvani who undertook a series of experiments on amputated frog legs which included stimulating the exposed ends of their severed nerves. Galvani found that he could induce the frog's leg to twitch in a number of ways (see Figure 1.5) as indeed shown in one famous case where during a thunderstorm, he connected a nerve stump to a long metallic wire that pointed to the sky and obtained strong muscular contractions in the detached leg (arguably the most dangerous experiment in the history of biopsychology!). But perhaps more importantly, he also found that similar movements were produced when he suspended the frog's leg between two different metals. Although he did not know it at the time, Galvani had shown that when dissimilar metals make contact through a salt solution an electrical current is produced. This was, in fact, the first demonstration of the battery later formally invented by Volta in 1800. These discoveries led Galvani to conclude that nerves are capable of conducting electricity. In other words, what had previously been regarded as some form of 'invisible spirit' was now conceived as being electrical in nature. Galvani called this intrinsic force 'animal electricity'. Its existence was finally proven beyond reasonable doubt in 1820 when the German Johann Schweigger invented the galvanometer (named in honour of Galvani) that measured the strength and direction of an electrical current. Thus, the twitching frog's legs marked the end of hydraulic theories of nervous action and the start of a new chapter in understanding how nerve cells work (McComas, 2011; Piccolino, 1997).

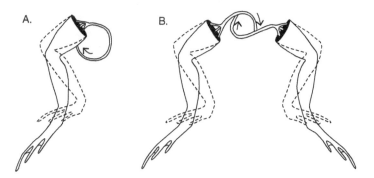

Figure 1.5 Two simple demonstrations (1794 and 1797 respectively) used to show the existence of animal electricity

In both instances muscular contraction occurs without any metallic involvement: (A) when an exposed nerve touches the muscle, the leg contracts; (B) when the right sciatic nerve touches the intact left sciatic nerve, then both legs contract.

Source: Wickens (2009). Images drawn by, and reproduced with permission from, Charlotte Caswell

One question that fascinated neurophysiologists during this time was the speed of the nervous impulse that flowed down the fibre (axon). Although the galvanometer could detect electrical activity, the nerve impulse appeared to be instantaneous and too fast to be measured. In fact, the famous physiologist Johannes Muller wrote somewhat despairingly in 1833 that the speed of the nerve impulse was comparable to the speed of light and would never be accurately estimated. However, Muller was soon proven wrong by the work of Hermann von Helmholtz – in the early 1850s – who managed to extract long motor nerves (some 50–60 mm in length) that were still attached to muscles taken from frog legs. Helmholtz recorded the delay between the onset of electrical stimulation and the resulting muscle twitch, and calculated the speed of the impulse to be about 90 feet (27 metres) per second or around 60 miles (96 kilometres) per hour. We now know that Helmholtz was fairly accurate with his estimation. Moreover, whilst the nerve impulse was fast, it was not comparable with the speed of light. In fact, neurophysiologists have now established that speed of nerve conduction varies depending on the type of **axon** (or nerve fibre), with the impulse being quicker in large diameter axons which are sheathed in an insulating layer of **myelin** (e.g. the fastest neuron can conduct action potentials at a speed of 120 metres per second or 432 km per hour), and slowest in small diameter unmyelinated axons (e.g. 35 metres per second).

KEY TERMS: *axon, myelin*

THE NOBEL PRIZE IN PHYSIOLOGY OR MEDICINE

As a student of biopsychology, the most coveted award you can aspire to achieving is the Nobel Prize in Physiology or Medicine. As a recipient of this award, you will have been judged to have made '*discoveries*' conferring '*the greatest benefit on mankind*', and will enjoy instant recognition, celebrity and unrivalled authority. At the time of writing, some 216 persons have been given this accolade in 'physiology or medicine', with about 50 of those individuals making contributions that can be considered relevant to neuroscience. Put simply, if one is ingenious enough to win the prize, then one will belong to a very select band of scientists whose fame will be eternal in the annals of physiology and medicine.

Alfred Bernhard Nobel was born in 1833 in Stockholm, Sweden. The son of an engineer, he moved in his childhood to Russia, where his father made a fortune making explosives and military equipment. At the age of 17, Nobel studied chemistry in Paris and worked for a time in the USA before returning to Sweden in 1859. In 1866, he invented nitro-glycerine. Unfortunately, an explosion at his factory was to kill Nobel's younger brother Emil and four other workers in 1864. In an attempt to make a safer explosive he invented dynamite in 1867. This was to establish Nobel's fame world-wide as it was widely used to blast tunnels, cut canals and build railways and roads. By the time Alfred Nobel died in 1896, he had made a massive fortune, and in his will left instructions that most of his money (which amounted to 94% of his total assets, or 31 million Swedish kronor) should be used to give prizes that honoured people from all over the world for outstanding achievements in physics, chemistry, medicine, literature and peace. Although the will was strongly contested, the first awards were made in 1901 on the fifth anniversary of Nobel's death.

The first Nobel Prize in Physiology or Medicine was awarded in 1901 to Emil Adolf von Behring, for his work on developing a vaccine against diphtheria. But the first person of interest to psychologists to become a Nobel Laureate was Ivan Pavlov in 1904. Despite this, his prize was in recognition of research on the physiology of digestion and not for his experiments which followed on the elucidation of conditioned reflexes. In fact, the first 'proper' brain researchers to obtain the award were Camillo Golgi and Santiago Ramón y Cajal, in 1906, for their work describing the neuroanatomy of the central nervous system. The award ceremony, however, was not without some acrimony, as during their acceptance speeches Golgi and Cajal gave opposing views on whether neurons were joined together or separated by synapses. Golgi, who believed that nerves were joined together in a reticulum, accused his rival of not having any 'firm evidence' to support his claims of neurons being independent units. However, it was Cajal who was correct. There have also been other controversies. For example, in 1949 Egas Moniz won the prize for introducing the frontal lobotomy to treat mental illness – a procedure that often resulted in many harmful side effects. Protests from over 250 scientists were also raised about the 2000 Nobel Prize (awarded to the neuroscientists Avrid Carlsson, Paul Greengard and Eric Kandel) for the non-inclusion of Oleh Hornkiewicz who has been noted for his work on Parkinson's disease. Another controversy was the omission of Rosalind Franklin in the 1962 award for the discovery of DNA. Although she was the first to take an X-ray picture of DNA, shown to Crick and Watson, without her permission, and vital in their deductions of determining the structure of the DNA molecule, Franklin is often forgotten for her work.

Table 1.1   Nobel Prize winners in areas related to Biopsychology and Neuroscience

Date	Nobel Laureate	Nationality	Area of work
1904	Ivan Pavlov	Russian	Digestion
1906	Camillo Golgi	Italian	Structure of the nervous system
	Santiago Ramón y Cajal	Spanish	
1914	Robert Barany	Austrian	Vestibular apparatus of the ear
1932	Charles Sherrington	British	Function of neurons
	Edgar Adrian	British	
1936	Henry Dale	British	Chemical nature of the nerve impulse
	Otto Loewi	German	
1944	Joseph Erlanger	American	Research on single nerve fibres
	Herbert Gasser	American	
1949	Egas Moniz	Portuguese	Lobotomy
	Walter Hess	Swiss	Functions of the hypothalamus
1961	Georg von Békésy	Hungarian	Functions of the cochlea
1963	Alan Hodgkin	British	Ionic basis of neural transmission
	Andrew Huxley	British	
	John Eccles	Australian	
1967	Ragnor Granit	Finnish	Visual processes of the eye
	Haldan Hartline	American	
	George Wald	American	
1970	Jules Axelrod	American	Release of neurotransmitters in the synapse
	Bernard Katz	German/British	
	Ulf von Euler	Swedish	
1973	Konrad Lorenz	Austrian	Ethology and animal behaviour
	Nikolaas Tinbergen	Dutch	
	Karl von Frisch	Austrian	
1977	Roger Guillemin	French	Discovery of neuropeptides
	Andrew Schally	Polish	
1979	Herbert Simon	American	Cognitive psychology
1979	Godfrey Hounsfield	British	Invention of CAT scanning
	Allan MacLeod	South African	
1981	David Hubel	Canadian	Visual cortex
	Torsten Wiesel	Swedish	Functions of the cerebral hemispheres
	Roger Sperry	American	
1986	Rita Levi-Montalcini	Italian	Discovery of neural growth factors
	Stanley Cohen	American	
1991	Erwin Neher	German	Ion channels in nerve cells
	Bert Sakmann	German	

(Continued)

Table 1.1   (Continued)

Date	Nobel Laureate	Nationality	Area of work
1994	Alfred Gilman	American	G proteins and their role in signal transduction
	Martin Rodbell	American	
1997	Stanley Prusiner	American	Discovery of prions
2000	Arvid Carlsson	Swedish	Discoveries related to synaptic neurotransmission
	Paul Greengard	American	
	Eric Kandel	American	
2003	Paul Lauterbur	American	The development of magnetic resonance imaging
	Sir Peter Mansfield	British	
2004	Linda Buck	American	The discovery of odorant receptors
	Richard Axel	American	
2007	Mario Capecchi	Italian	The genetic modification of stem cells
	Sir Martin Evans	British	
	Oliver Smithies	British-American	
2014	John O'Keefe	American-British	Brain mechanisms of spatial navigation
	May-Britt Moser	Norwegian	
	Edvard Moser	Norwegian	
2017	Jeffrey Hall	American	Discoveries concerning the molecular basis of circadian rhythms
	Michael Rosbash	American	
	Michael Young	American	

THE DISCOVERY OF THE NERVE CELL

Although Galvani had shown that nervous energy was electrical in nature, there was still much to learn about nerves and the nervous system. For example, up until the early nineteenth century there was no accurate idea of what a nerve looked like, other than they had some sort of body (sometimes called a globule) and long thin projections. In fact, many believed that nerves were joined together in much the same way as blood vessels are interconnected (i.e. through a system of connecting tubes) which was called a reticulum by neuroanatomists. These beliefs persisted despite the invention of the microscope in 1665 by Robert Hooke, who coined the word 'cell' after examining a slither of cork, and the subsequent work of Anton Von Leeuwenhoek, who used it to examine biological tissues. Unfortunately, the early microscopes did not reveal neural structure in great detail, and it wasn't until around 1830 when chromatic lenses were developed that they provided stronger and clearer magnification. Even so, there was the problem of how to prepare the tissue for microscopic work so that nerve cells could be distinguished from other types of material. Although by the 1800s, histologists had found new ways to stain nerve tissue, their methods stained all neurons indiscriminately. This meant that the only way to visualize a neuron was to remove it from the mass of tangled cells in which it was embedded. Since neurons were far too small to be seen with the naked eye, this proved extremely difficult and rarely successful.

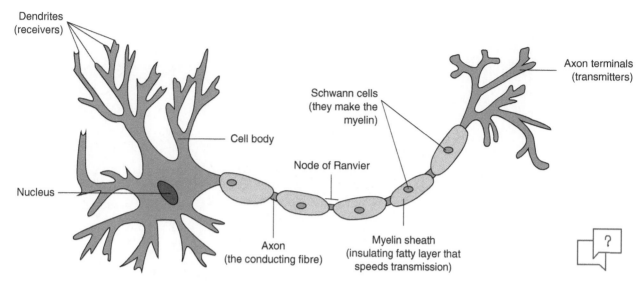

Dendrites (receivers)

Cell body

Nucleus

Schwann cells (they make the myelin)

Node of Ranvier

Axon terminals (transmitters)

Axon (the conducting fibre)

Myelin sheath (insulating fatty layer that speeds transmission)

Figure 1.6   The main components of a typical brain neuron
Source: Higgs et al. (2020); Quasar Jarosz/Wikimedia Commons

In 1875, however, a major breakthrough occurred when the Italian anatomist Camillo Golgi (1843–1926) discovered a new stain that allowed individual nerve cells to be observed. By serendipity, he found that when he exposed nervous tissue to silver nitrate, this caused nerve cells to turn black, enabling them to stand out in bold relief so they could be clearly be seen under a microscope. But more importantly, Golgi's technique only stained around 2% of the cells in any given slice of nervous tissue. This was a great advance as it made individual neurons and all their various components such as **dendrites** and **axons** more clearly observable (see Figure 1.6). This method soon proved indispensable for examining the wide variety of cells in the brain. Indeed, much of the basic terminology which we now use to describe nerve cells was introduced by anatomists around this time (c. 1880).

The person who put the Golgi stain to its greatest use, however, was the Spaniard Santiago Ramón y Cajal (1852–1934) who many regard as the father of modern neuroscience. Cajal not only improved upon Golgi's method by double staining to give more reliable results, but he also spent many hours peering down a microscope to describe and draw the neural anatomy of the brain with the technique. The number of his important neuroscience discoveries is probably unmatched by any other researcher. He showed, for example, that the brain contains a great variety of cells with different characteristics. Although some cells had short axons that projected to cells within the same structure (i.e. interneurons), others had long axons that formed pathways that projected to distant brain regions. Cajal further showed that the brain was not a random morass of nerve cells as had been widely assumed, but a highly organized structure with clearly defined regions and groups of nuclei composed of cell bodies (see Figure 1.7). Cajal even guessed the direction of information flow though neurons. For example, his observations led him to realize that neurons received much of their input via their dendrites (from the Greek *dendron* meaning tree) and that they sent information along their cable-like pathways called axons. Thus, he was one of the first to see that there is a preferred direction for transmission from cell to cell – something he called dynamic polarization (Finger, 2000).

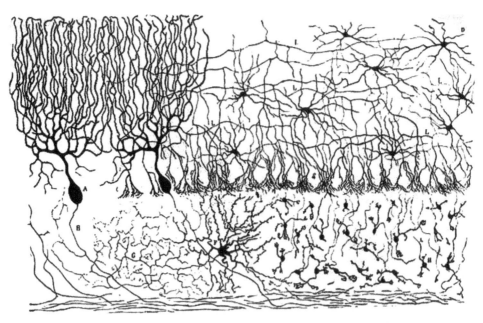

Figure 1.7   Cajal's depiction of neurons in the cerebellum using the Golgi stain
Source: Santiago y Ramon Cajal, public domain

Yet perhaps Cajal's most important contribution to neuroanatomy was his discovery that nerve cells were individual units which became known as **neurons** (a term first used by Wilhelm Waldeyer in 1891). Put another way, the nervous system was composed of cells much like any other part of the body. Previously, it had been believed that nerves were joined together in a network of tubes called a reticulum by Golgi who was a vociferous supporter of this theory. However, Cajal showed that nerve cells are not physically joined or connected. Rather, the axon terminals end very close to the neurons – normally by innervating their dendrites. In other words, each neuron is an individual unit that is not joined to its neighbours – and in some cases they can be seen to be separated by a small gap (see Figure 1.9). These points of contact were called 'synapses' in 1897 by the British neurophysiologist Charles Sherrington who derived the term from the Greek synapsis which means 'to clasp'. This discovery raised many new questions, not least how nerve cells sent information across the synapse, and how this transmission was able to generate a new electrical signal in the postsynaptic neuron.

Following Golgi's discovery many other staining techniques were developed that enabled investigators to examine nerve cells in more detail. For example, some techniques were able to selectively stain cell bodies, called the soma, whereas others highlighted the axons by staining their myelin covering – which allowed neural pathways in the brain to be traced. In other instances, staining techniques were combined with lesioning methods to provide useful information (e.g. neural pathways can be traced by staining degenerating axons that arise from a structure after it has been experimentally destroyed). By the turn of the century the study of neuroanatomy had become an established discipline. It also provided one of the foundation stones on which physiological psychology was based, for without knowledge of brain structure and organization, very little can be said about how it functions to produce behaviour (Rapport, 2005; Shepherd, 1991).

KEY TERMS: *cell, dendrites, axons, soma, interneurons.*

THE DISCOVERY OF CHEMICAL NEUROTRANSMISSION

One of the most important questions following Cajal's work concerned the nature of the message crossing the synapse from the presynaptic neuron (the neuron before the synapse) to the postsynaptic neuron (recipient neuron). From the time of Galvani, it was known that neurons transmitted messages using electrical energy, but how did this principle extend to synapses? For example, did an electrical current jump across the synapse, or was there another form of communication? As early as 1877 the German physiologist Emil Du Bois-Reymond had suggested that chemical transmission might be the answer. And in 1904, the Cambridge researcher Thomas Elliott lent support to this idea by showing that adrenaline stimulated the activity of bodily organs that were innervated by the body's autonomic nervous system. Indeed, Elliott made what is now regarded as the first clear statement about the feasibility of neurotransmission. Indeed, Elliott made what is now regarded as the first clear statement about the feasibility of neurotransmission by stating: 'Adrenaline might then be the chemical stimulant liberated on each occasion when the impulse arrives at the periphery.' But, arguably, the most important experiment to confirm chemical transmission was performed by Otto Loewi in 1921. According to Loewi's memoirs, this discovery began on the night of Easter Saturday when he awoke from a sleep and wrote down the details of an experiment that had come to him in a dream. Loewi then went back to sleep, but on waking again, was unable to decipher his notes. The next night he awoke at 3 am with the experiment back on his mind, and this time he immediately cycled to his laboratory to perform it (see Figure 1.8). Two hours later, the chemical nature of synaptic transmission had been established (Zigmond, 1999).

In his experiment, Loewi used frog hearts which are similar to our own in that they are innervated by two different autonomic nerves: the sympathetic branch that excites the heart and makes it beat more rapidly, and the parasympathetic branch (also called the vagus nerve) which slows it down. Loewi used two hearts: one with the sympathetic and vagus nerve intact, and the other with nerves removed. He then placed the intact heart in a fluid bath and stimulated its vagus nerve, causing its beat to slow down. Loewi

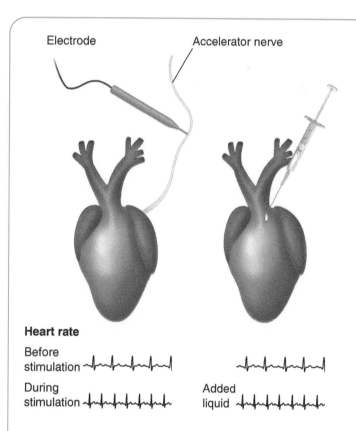

Electrode   Accelerator nerve

Heart rate

Before stimulation

During stimulation

Added liquid

Figure 1.8 Loewi's experimental set-up showing that nerves send messages by releasing chemical substances

Source: Garrett and Hough (2021)

collected the fluid surrounding this heart and applied it to the second one – and found that its intrinsic beat also began to decrease. This indicated that the fluid must contain a substance that had been secreted by the stimulated vagus nerve. Later analysis by Sir Henry Dale and his colleagues showed this chemical to be acetylcholine, which is now recognized as an important neurotransmitter in the peripheral and central nervous systems (Wickens, 2019a).

Although electrical synapses are known to exist, it is now accepted that the vast majority of nerve cells in the body, including the central nervous system, communicate by releasing neurotransmitters from their axon terminals into synapses. The series of events that produce this transmission can be described simply as follows:

1. The axon terminals of the 'first' or *presynaptic neuron* receive an electrical impulse called an **action potential** and in response they typically secrete a *neurotransmitter*.
2. This chemical diffuses into the synapse and binds to adjacent specialized sites on the 'recipient' *postsynaptic neuron* called **receptors**.
3. Receptor binding leads to changes in the *postsynaptic neuron*, which either directly or indirectly (i.e. via second messengers) cause the opening of ion channels in its cellular membrane. This, in turn, allows positively or negatively charged ions to enter the neuron, which increases (excites) or decreases (inhibits) its internal resting electrical voltage.
4. If the neuron is excited past a certain level (i.e. by about –15mV) at its axon hillock, the increase in voltage generates an action potential (nervous impulse) that is conducted down the axon to its terminals, leading to neurotransmitter release.

Much of the subsequent chapter discusses these steps in greater detail.

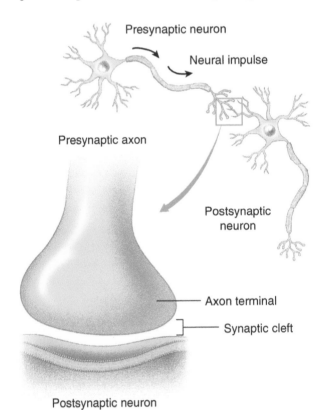

Figure 1.9 The synapse between a presynaptic and postsynaptic neuron
Source: Garrett and Hough (2021)

It is now recognized that the brain contains dozens of different neurotransmitters. The first to be confirmed was **acetylcholine** (Loewi was awarded a Nobel Prize for his discovery along with Sir Henry Dale in 1936). This was followed by **noradrenaline** in the 1940s, **dopamine** and **serotonin** in the 1950s, and gamma-Aminobutyric acid (GABA), **glutamate** and glycine in the 1960s. All of these chemicals are synthesized and stored in the nerve endings. In the 1970s, a new group of transmitter substances called neuropeptides composed of amino acids were discovered which included opiate-like substances (endorphins). These are synthesized in the cell body. More recently, it has been found that certain gases such as nitric oxide also have a neurotransmitter function. To make matters more complex, neurons do not necessarily release a single neurotransmitter as was once thought (known as Dale's Law) but secrete two or more substances together. Many of these 'secondary' chemicals act primarily as neuromodulators whose function is to 'modify' the effect of other neurotransmitters. These substances, which include the endorphins (natural opioid-like substances), prostaglandins and endogenous cannabinoids, tend to affect groups of neurons in a generalized diffuse manner (see Hyman, 2005).

Table 1.2   The main neurotransmitters found in the central nervous system

Neurotransmitter	Function
Acetylcholine	Transmitter at muscles; in brain, involved in learning, etc.
Monoamines	
Serotonin	Involved in mood, sleep and arousal, aggression, depression, obsessive-compulsive disorder, and alcoholism.
Dopamine	Contributes to movement control and promotes reinforcing effects of food, sex, and abused drugs; involved in schizophrenia and Parkinson's disease.
Norepinephrine	A hormone released during stress. Functions as a neurotransmitter in the brain to increase arousal and attentiveness to events in the environment; involved in depression.
Epinephrine	A stress hormone related to norepinephrine; plays a minor role as a neurotransmitter in the brain.
Amino Acids	
Glutamate	The principal excitatory neurotransmitter in the brain and spinal cord. Vitally involved in learning and implicated in schizophrenia.
gamma-Aminobutyric acid (GABA)	The predominant inhibitory neurotransmitter. Its receptors respond to alcohol and the class of tranquilizers called benzodiazepines. Deficiency in GABA or receptors is one cause of epilepsy.
Glycine	Inhibitory transmitter in the spinal cord and lower brain. The poison strychnine causes convulsions and death by affecting glycine activity.
Neuropeptides	
Endorphins	Neuromodulators that reduce pain and enhance reinforcement.
Substance P	Transmitter in neurons sensitive to pain.
Neuropeptide Y *Gas*	Initiates eating and produces metabolic shifts.
Nitric oxide	One of two known gaseous transmitters, along with carbon monoxide. Can serve as a retrograde transmitter, influencing the presynaptic neuron's release of neurotransmitter. Viagra enhances male erections by increasing nitric oxide's ability to relax blood vessels and produce penile engorgement.

Source: Garrett and Hough (2018)

The discovery of chemical transmission by Otto Loewi, Henry Dale and others, leading to the discipline of psychopharmacology, is one of the greatest scientific achievements of the twentieth century. It not only opened up new ways of understanding brain function, it also raised the possibility of modifying behaviour by the use of drugs that targeted the action of neurotransmitters. This advance has since been realized in many ways, with the development of drugs that can be used to treat various types of mental illness such as depression or schizophrenia, or neurodegenerative disorders such as Parkinson's and Alzheimer's disease. It is also now recognized that many of the drugs acting on the brain do so either by mimicking the action of a neurotransmitter at its receptor site (known as an **agonist**) or by blocking the receptor from working (known as an **antagonist**). In addition, histochemical advances have enabled neurotransmitters in nerve endings to be visualized, enabling chemical pathways in the brain to be traced and mapped out (Hökfelt, 2009; Snyder, 2009).

KEY TERMS: *presynaptic neuron, postsynaptic neuron, neurotransmitters, receptors, ion channels, agonist, antagonist*

NEURAL CONDUCTION

By the early part of the twentieth century, neurophysiologists knew that neurons were capable of generating electrical currents, but they did not know the finer details of how this energy was being created or conducted along the axon. The main difficulty lay in trying to record from the neuron during these events. Although physiologists had at their disposal recording electrodes with very fine tips, along with oscilloscopes and amplifiers that greatly magnified the tiny electrical charges, neurons were too small to enable this type of work to take place. This remained the case until 1936, when Oxford biologist John Z. Young discovered a neuron located in the body of a squid (*Loligo pealii*) which had an axon nearly 1 mm in diameter (about 100 to 1,000 times larger than a typical mammalian axon). Not only was this axon large enough to allow the insertion of a stimulating or recording electrode, but it could also be dissected from the animal and kept alive in a bath of salt for several hours. This allowed both the electrical and chemical properties of the neuron to be examined in great detail.

Almost everything we know about how neurons generate impulses has been derived from research on the giant squid axon. Because it is accepted that all nerve cells, no matter what size or type of animal they come from, work according to the same principles, the giant squid neuron has provided an invaluable means of understanding neural function. The use of this technique was largely pioneered by two physiologists at Cambridge University called Alan Hodgkin and Andrew Huxley,[2] who published their main findings in a classic landmark set of papers in 1952 (although important work was also undertaken by Kenneth S. Cole and Howard J. Curtis in America). Hodgkin and Huxley not only developed a technique enabling recording electrodes to be positioned inside and outside the neuron without causing it damage, but they also found a way of 'squeezing' cytoplasm from the axon so its chemical composition

---

[2]Huxley's grandfather was the famous biologist Thomas Huxley who was also known as 'Darwin's bulldog' for his support of evolutionary theory.

SIR HENRY DALE

The concept of chemical synaptic neurotransmission is one of the fundamental keystones on which neuroscience is based. Indeed, without the knowledge of chemical neurotransmission, it would be impossible to understand how the nervous system and brain works. Sir Henry Dale is undisputedly one of the greatest British pharmacologists of the twentieth century, whose work not only identified acetylcholine as a neurotransmitter in the autonomic and somatic nervous systems, but was also pivotal in establishing the principles of chemical neurotransmission.

Dale was born in London in 1875 and later went to Trinity College, Cambridge, where he studied natural sciences. After medical training at St Bartholomew's hospital, Dale accepted an appointment in 1904 at the Wellcome Physiological Research Laboratories in London. This was an unusual choice, for the Wellcome was aimed primarily at developing new drugs (it had produced an antitoxin for diphtheria in 1894), and Dale's friends feared it would compromise his independence as a researcher. After starting his post, Dale was asked to examine the chemical constituents of a patristic fungus called ergot known to affect rye and other cereals. Although Dale was not attracted by the challenge he soon realized that ergot was a treasure trove of chemical substances. One of the first drugs he managed to extract from the fungus was ergotoxine which could be used to treat high blood pressure (it is now known to be an alpha-adrenergic blocker). Soon after, Dale discovered that ergot contained histamine – a chemical which he would show to be a naturally occurring substance in the body and now recognized as a neurotransmitter.

But Dale's most important discovery came in 1913 when he identified a substance called acetylcholine in ergot. This chemical had effects on the body, mimicking the activation of the parasympathetic nervous system which included slowing heart rate and respiration. Dale would not only go on to prove that acetylcholine was a natural constituent of the body (he did this by obtaining 71 pounds of ox spleen tissue from the local abattoir from which he extracted one-third of a gram of acetylcholine), but would also show that it mimicked the drugs muscarine and nicotine at different sites of the body. Although this did not confirm chemical neurotransmission at the time, it was nevertheless strong evidence that different receptors for acetylcholine existed in the body. In fact, we now know that muscarinic receptors exist in the autonomic nervous system whereas nicotinic receptors are found at the neuromuscular junction. Both receptor types are also found in the brain.

In 1936, Dale won the Nobel Prize (along with Otto Loewi) for his work on the chemical transmission of the nerve impulse. At the time it still remained an open question whether chemical neurotransmission occurred in the central nervous system, with some, including the notably strident Australian John Eccles, believing it was electrical. This situation led to much hotly contested debate and argument at various scientific meetings in the 1940s and early 1950s in what has become known as 'the soup versus sparks debate'. Dale argued strongly for chemical neurotransmission and would be proven right in 1952, when Eccles himself provided irrefutable proof that his own theory was wrong (see Wickens, 2019b).

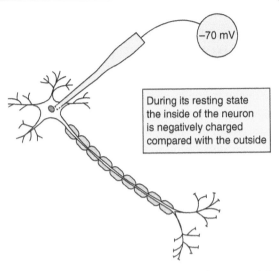

–70 mV

During its resting state the inside of the neuron is negatively charged compared with the outside

Figure 1.10   Measurement of the resting potential of the nerve cell using a micro-electrode

Source: Wickens (2009)

could be examined. This was an important step in allowing Hodgkin and Huxley to deduce how the neuron produced an electrical impulse (Wickens, 2019b).

One of the most important discoveries made by Hodgkin and Huxley (c. 1939) was that the giant squid axon exhibited a **resting potential** (Figure 1.10). That is, if a recording electrode was inserted into the neuron when it was at rest, and its voltage compared to that just outside the cell, a small but consistent difference between the two electrodes was found. Crucially, this voltage difference is around –70 millivolts (mV) with the interior of the neuron always negative compared to the outside. The difference is roughly one tenth of a volt or about 5% as much energy as exists in a torch battery. This may not appear to be very much, but it is a huge energy differential for a tiny nerve cell to maintain, and it is this voltage difference that holds the secret to understanding how it generates electrical current in the form of action potentials.

To explain why the voltage difference of –70mV occurs, it is important to understand that the intracellular and extracellular environments of the neuron, when it is at rest, are different in their concentrations of ions. An ion is simply an electrically charged atom, or particle, that has lost or gained an electron which gives it a positive or negative charge (see Figure 1.11). As any school pupil should know, an atom is composed of a nucleus containing positively charged (+) protons and neutrons, surrounded by tiny negatively charged (–) electrons that orbit around it. In the atom's normal state, the opposite charges of protons and electrons cancel themselves out, making it neutral. However, if the atom loses an electron, then it will have one less negative charge, and the result is it becomes a positively charged (+) ion. Alternatively, if the atom gains an extra electron it becomes a negatively charged (–) ion. Although only a few types of ion exist in the nervous system, they play a crucial role in the production of the nerve impulse. These include sodium ions (NA^+) and potassium ions (K^+) that have lost an electron and as a result become positively charged, and chloride (Cl^-) and organic anions (A^-) that have gained an electron and become negatively charged.

One of Hodgkin and Huxley's most important discoveries was that the concentrations of ions differed between the interior and exterior of the cell when it was at rest (see Wickens, 2015). For example, they showed positive sodium ions (NA^+) to be more highly concentrated outside the neuron than inside (at a ratio of around 14:1), along with negatively charged chloride ions (a ratio of around 25:1). In contrast, positive potassium ions (K^+) were found predominantly inside the neuron (at a ratio of around 28:1), as were negatively charged anions (which are actually large protein molecules confined to the inside of the neuron). When the positive and negative charges of the ion concentrations were added up by Hodgkin and Huxley it explained why the resting potential inside the neuron was about –70mV. In short, the intracellular fluid of the cell contains more negatively charged ions, whereas the extracellular fluid is dominated by positively charged (sodium) ions.

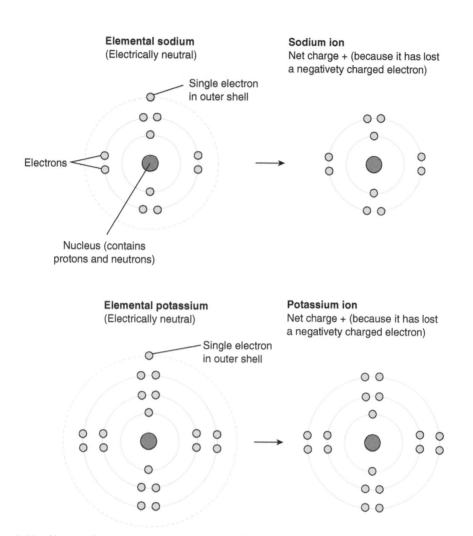

Figure 1.11 How sodium and potassium ions are formed
Source: Wickens (2009)

KEY TERMS: *resting potential, sodium ions (NA⁺), potassium ions (K⁺)*

Table 1.3 The concentration of ions inside and outside the axon when it is at rest expressed in millimoles (mM)

	Concentration of ions in axoplasm (mM)	Concentration of ions outside the cell (mM)
Potassium (K⁺)	400	10
Sodium (Na⁺)	50	450
Chloride (Cl⁻)	40	560
Organic anions (A⁻)	345	0

HOW DOES THE NEURON MAINTAIN ITS RESTING POTENTIAL?

Because of the uneven distribution of ions, a state of tension always exists between the inside and outside of the nerve cell. This occurs because positively charged ions are strongly attracted to negative ones, or vice versa (a force known as the electrostatic gradient), and because high concentrations of ions are attracted to areas of low concentration, or vice versa (a force known as the diffusion gradient). Consequently, when an unequal distribution of ion concentrations occurs between the interior and exterior of the cell, strong electrical and diffusion forces are produced. This means that the extracellular sodium ions will be attracted to inside of the nerve cell by electrostatic and diffusion forces, produced by the cell's negative resting potential and its relative lack of sodium. Similarly, the intracellular positively charged potassium ions will be attracted to the extracellular fluid, albeit more weakly, by diffusion forces.

If this is the case, then why don't ions simply pass down their respective electrostatic and diffusion gradients to correct the ionic imbalance and cancel the negative resting potential in the neuron? The secret lies with the nerve cell's outer coating, or membrane, which consists of a double layer of lipid (fat) molecules. This acts as a barrier to ion flow. However, embedded in the membrane are a number of specialized protein molecules that act as ion channels. These are tiny pores that can open to allow certain ions to flow into, or out of, the neuron. There are two main types of ion channel which we will discuss in more detail later: ligand-gated ion channels that are opened by ligands (i.e. chemicals) attaching themselves to receptors, and voltage-gated ion channels opened by voltage changes occurring inside the neuron. However, ion channels are also 'leaky'. In fact, when the neuron is at rest, the membrane is about 100 times more permeable to potassium ions than sodium – largely because potassium is more able to leak through its own channels. Thus, potassium moves in and out of the cell more freely than sodium.

This brings us to another important question: if ions are in constant motion across the neural membrane, how can it be that the resting potential of –70 mV is maintained? Clearly, if physical forces are simply left to operate, the flow of potassium to the extracellular fluid will quickly cause the resting potential inside the neuron to become neutral – and the flow of sodium towards the cell's interior, even at a slower rate of infiltration, will help to do the same. The answer is that the neuron maintains the intra- and extracellular balance of ions by a specialized protein located in its membrane which acts as a **sodium/potassium pump** – a molecule that transports three sodium ions out of the cell for every two potassium ions it takes in. This requires considerable energy with about 20% of the cells' energy spent on this pumping process (Dudel, 1978). Such is the importance of maintaining the negative resting potential. Without it, the neuron would be unable to generate action potentials.

KEY TERMS: *electrostatic gradient, diffusion gradient, ligand-gated ion channel, voltage-gated ion channel, sodium/potassium pump*

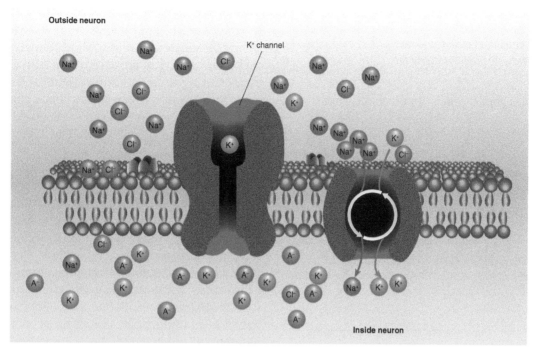

Figure 1.12 An illustration showing a potassium (K⁺) channel and a sodium/potassium pump
Source: Higgs et al. (2020), adapted from Garrett (2011)

THE ACTION POTENTIAL

It was established over a century ago by Emil du Bois-Reymond that the nerve impulse is a brief pulse of electrical excitation which flows down the axon. He called this the action current, which later became known as the action potential. But how does the neuron produce this electrical excitation in the first place? By undertaking a large number of experiments on the giant squid axon, Hodgkin and Huxley demonstrated that the electrical pulse was caused by the sudden back and forth movement of sodium and potassium ions, which act as tiny electrical charges, through their respective ion channels in the neural membrane (see Wickens, 2015). They also showed the triggering event for this process was initiated when the neuron's resting potential (–70 mV) became more positive by about +15 mV. That is, the resting potential has to increase to around –55 mV, otherwise known as its threshold potential. But what exactly causes this event to happen?

As we have seen, the neuron is like a tiny biological battery with the negative (–70mV) pole inside the cell and the positive one outside. And it goes to great lengths with the sodium-potassium pump to maintain this polarity. But this also puts the neuron's resting potential under strain – not least because of the electrostatic and diffusion pressures acting to force ions in and out of the cell. In fact, the cell's resting potential is not stable at –70 mV, even with the help of the sodium potassium pump. One reason for this lies with other neural input whose activity causes the release of neurotransmitter that constantly targets the receptors of the neuron. One effect of this receptor activation is the brief opening of tiny pores in the cell's membrane, called ligand-gated ion channels, which enables small amounts of ions to flow into

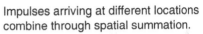
Impulses arriving at different locations combine through spatial summation.

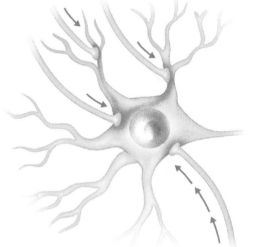

Impulses arriving a short time apart combine through temporal summation.

Figure 1.13   Spatial and temporal summation in the neuron

Source: Garrett and Hough (2021)

the cell – which then cause small changes to the neuron's resting potential. Some neurotransmitters such as glutamate make the resting potential more positive by increasing the membrane's permeability to positive ions, whereas others such as GABA make it more negative by allowing the influx of negative ions (see Hille, 2001).

Although a few molecules of neurotransmitter binding to a receptor will probably have a negligible effect on the cell's resting potential, it must be remembered that a neuron is likely to have thousands of receptors (and ion channels) spread over its dendrites and soma. A significant number of these receptors will also be subjected to both excitatory and inhibitory neurotransmitters impinging upon them at any moment. Consequently, the 'summation' of all this stimulation, at a given point in time, may produce a significant change in the cell's resting potential. In fact there are two types of summation: spatial summation where inputs from widely distributed neural sources impinge on the neuron at once, or temporal summation where a high frequency of inputs occur at a single or smallish location (see Figure 1.13). If the summation, spatial or temporal, causes the voltage inside the cell to become more positive it produces what is known as **excitatory postsynaptic potential** (EPSP). If the internal voltage of the cell becomes more negative it is called an **inhibitory postsynaptic potential** (IPSP).

KEY TERMS: *action potential, summation, excitatory postsynaptic potential, inhibitory postsynaptic potential*

The change in resting potential produced by the flow of ions into the cell following neurotransmitter stimulation normally begins in the dendrites, with the voltage change (i.e. an EPSP or IPSP) spreading down into the cell body. But how does a change in resting potential lead to an action potential? The answer lies with a specialized part of the neuron called the **axon hillock** located at the junction between the cell body and axon. Like the rest of the neuron, this area normally has a resting potential of around –70mV. But if the voltage at this site is increased to reach its threshold value of –55 mV, then a rapid sequence of events occurs that causes an action potential, or nerve impulse, to be produced and move down the axon.

As Hodgkin and Huxley showed, if a recording electrode is placed into the axon hillock during the formation of an action potential, it reveals some remarkable events (see Figure 1.14). Firstly, there will be a sudden increase in voltage from about –55mV to about +30mV in less than one thousandth of a second (msec)! This is

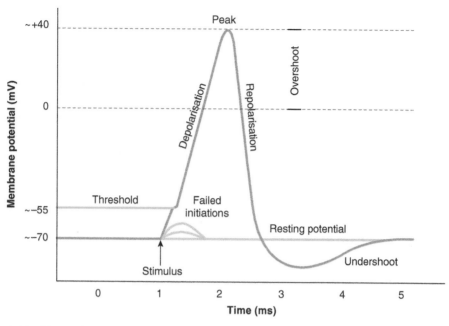

Figure 1.14   The action potential

Source: Higgs et al. (2020); Chris 73 and Diberri/Wikimedia Commons

known as depolarization (Chen & Lui, 2020). However, this huge reversal from negative to positive does not last long. Almost immediately, the voltage will show a sudden decline, falling from +30mV to –80mV, before returning to –70mV. This fleeting drop below the resting potential of –70mV is called the refractory period and during this interval the neuron is inhibited from firing again. But, since this whole process takes place in just 4 or 5 msecs, it means it is possible for a neuron to fire over a hundred times a second. The depolarization at the axon hillock is the origin of the nervous impulse that begins its journey down the axon.

It follows that the axon hillock is the critical site where the integration of excitatory and inhibitory postsynaptic potentials has to take place before an action potential can be generated. This response is 'all-or-nothing' as the neuron either fires or doesn't (e.g. there is no in-between or graded response). However, once the action potential is formed, it travels down the nerve fibre to reach the axonal endings where the stores of neurotransmitter are located ready to be released into the synapse. But here lies a physiological difficulty: axons are long spindly projections, and if the action potential passively moved down the fibre, its energy would decay before getting very far. Thus the axon must have some way of actively moving the charge down its length. The secret of how it does this lies with a fatty sheath called myelin which covers the axon and is not dissimilar to the rubber coating that surrounds an electrical cable. Unlike an electrical cable, however, the myelin contains short gaps along its length called nodes of Ranvier, and it is here renewal of the action potential takes place. At each node, the action potential is amplified back to its original intensity. In effect, the impulse 'jumps' down the axon. This process is called **saltatory conduction** (from the Latin *saltare* meaning 'to jump') and explains how the action potential can travel long distances without weakening. If you imagine a neural impulse going from a giraffe's brain to its back legs, then you will realize the necessity of such a process.

KEY TERMS: *axon hillock, depolarization, all-or-nothing response, saltatory conduction*

THE IONIC BASIS OF THE ACTION POTENTIAL

How does the neuron bring about the sudden change in depolarization (e.g. from –55 mV to around +30mV) to generate an action potential? The answer lies with the sodium and potassium ions – or rather, the opening and closing of their respective voltage-gated ion channels embedded in the neural membrane (Bean, 2007). As we have seen, large numbers of sodium ions exist in the extracellular fluid, and these are attracted to the cell's interior by strong electrical and concentration forces. Yet the cell's membrane acts as a barrier to sodium, and if ions infiltrate into the neuron, they are removed by the sodium-potassium pump. However this fine balance is changed when the threshold potential (–55mV) is reached. When this moment occurs, the membrane's sodium channels open, and and as if a door is thrown open, sodium ions flood into the cell propelled by electrostatic and concentration forces. It has been estimated that up to 100,000,000 ions can pass through a channel per second (although they only remain open for a fraction of this time), and it is this large influx of sodium (N^+) current into the cell that changes its negative resting potential into a positive depolarization (see Figure 1.15).

At the peak of this sodium flow (1 or 2 milliseconds after the ion channels have opened) the permeability of the membrane changes again. The neuron now closes the sodium channels and opens its potassium channels (in fact, these began to open just after the onset of the sodium influx). Because the inside of the cell at this point is now positively charged (around +30mV) due to the higher concentration of sodium, the positively charged potassium ions are pushed out of the neuron by electrostatic (as occurs with a magnet, two positive forces repel each other) and diffusion forces. This not only causes the cell's resting potential to become –70mV again, at which point the potassium channels close, but also the flow of potassium ions to the outside of the neuron is so strong, that its internal voltage drops further to about –80mV. This is called the refractory period and it is only after this event has occurred that the cell's resting potential returns to normal with the sodium-potassium pump restoring the ionic balance.

A similar pattern of ion movements in and out of the cell also occurs along the axon's length during saltatory conduction. As the electrical energy generated by the action potential spreads down the axon, it causes the opening of voltage-gated sodium channels in the nodes of Ranvier. This causes a sudden burst of sodium ions into the axon and a re-charging of the action potential. As this energy passes to the next node, there is an outflow of potassium ions at the node left behind restoring the axon's resting potential. As this cycle is repeated, the electrical signal is conducted down the full length of the axon without a loss of strength (Levitan & Kacmarek, 2015).

KEY TERMS: *voltage-gated ion channels, sodium channels, potassium channels*

NEUROTRANSMITTER RELEASE

When the action potential reaches the end of the axon, it passes through a large number of smaller axon branches ending in slightly swollen boutons otherwise known as synaptic

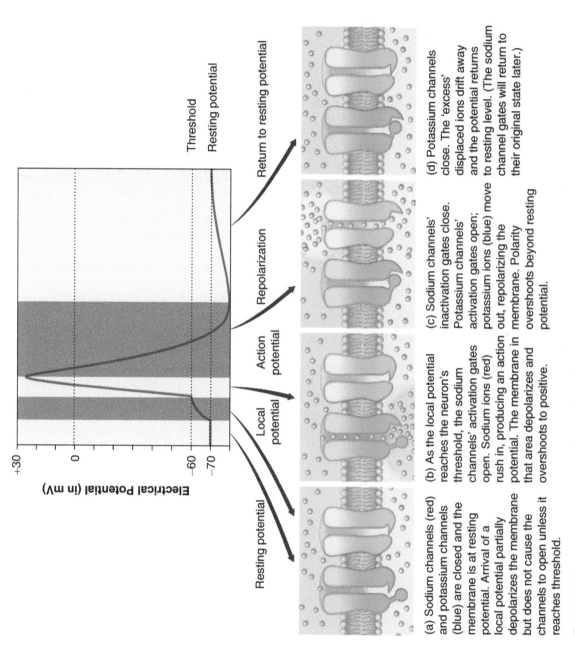

Figure 1.15   Ion movement and voltages during the nerve impulse

Source: Garrett and Hough (2021)

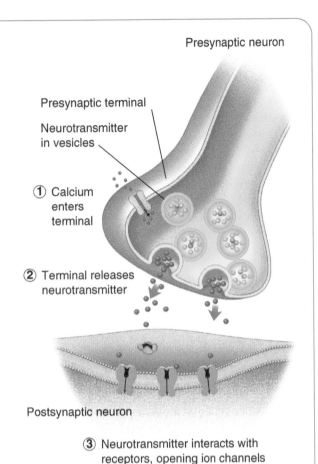

Presynaptic neuron

Presynaptic terminal

Neurotransmitter
in vesicles

① Calcium
enters
terminal

② Terminal releases
neurotransmitter

Postsynaptic neuron

③ Neurotransmitter interacts with
receptors, opening ion channels

Figure 1.16   The release of chemical
neurotransmitters across the synapse
Source: Garrett and Hough (2021)

terminals. Stored within these terminals are large numbers of **synaptic vesicles** each containing a few hundred molecules of neurotransmitter. As the action potential arrives at the terminal, it causes a different type of ion channel to open – namely the voltage-controlled calcium channel which allows positively charged calcium ions (Ca^{++}) to enter the bouton. This leads to a process known as **exocytosis** in which the vesicles fuse with the presynaptic membrane, releasing their contents into the synapse (Liang et al., 2017). In fact, vesicles are continually fusing with the axon terminal membrane resulting in the secretion of small amounts of neurotransmitter, although the action potential markedly speeds up this process. Consequently, the higher the number of action potentials, the greater the influx of calcium ions into the synaptic terminals with more neurotransmitter release.

The synaptic gap between neurons is around 50 nanometres across, which is equivalent to 0.00005 millimetres, and each neuron has anywhere between a few hundred to hundreds of thousands of synaptic connections (Caire et al., 2020). On one side is the presynaptic neuron with its axon ending, and on the other side is the postsynaptic neuron. When a neurotransmitter is released, it diffuses across the synapse, and binds to receptors on the postsynaptic neuron where it may exert several effects (see next section). But this is not the full story regarding the neurotransmitter's fate. Neurotransmitters must be quickly deactivated and broken down into inert chemicals, otherwise they will continue to exert a receptor effect, or block the receptor from receiving further input. Because of this, a number of processes have evolved to limit the life of a neurotransmitter in the synapse. One mechanism is to remove the transmitter from the synapse by means of a reuptake pump which recycles it back into the presynaptic axon terminal. This process is particularly important for the monoamine neurotransmitters such as noradrenaline, dopamine and serotonin. An understanding of reuptake also has important clinical implications, since drugs that block this process for either noradrenaline (e.g. Imipramine) or serotonin (e.g. Prozac) are useful in the treatment of depression and other types of mental illness (Stahl, 2013). Another important process involves chemical breakdown (i.e. enzymatic degradation). For example, acetylcholine is rapidly broken down into inert choline and acetate by the enzyme acetylcholinesterase (AchE) found in the synapse. Inhibitors of this enzyme have also been used to increase brain levels of acetylcholine in Alzheimer's disease. Another enzyme, this time present in axon terminals and glial cells, is monoamine oxidase (MAO) which degrades noradrenaline, serotonin and dopamine. Some antidepressant drugs such as Marsilid work by inhibiting this enzyme.

KEY TERMS: *synaptic vesicles, calcium channels, exocytosis, reuptake pump*

RECEPTORS

In 1905, the Cambridge physiologist John Langley first used the term '**receptor**' to refer to a site he believed must exist on muscle and neurons which were sensitive to chemicals released by the nervous system. We now know that Langley was correct and that neurotransmitters produce their effects by interacting with protein receptor molecules – many of which, but not all (see next paragraph), are found on the postsynaptic cell's membrane. The receptor and its neurotransmitter can be likened to a lock and key. In the same way it takes a specific key to turn a lock, a given neurotransmitter will only bind to its own type of receptor. Once this occurs, changes in the conformation of the receptor protein will initiate a series of events, typically leading to the opening of certain ion channels, with the subsequent ion flow instigating a change in the cell's internal voltage (i.e. an EPSP or IPSP). Interestingly, there are often several types of receptor for each neurotransmitter. For example, there are two different types of receptor for acetylcholine (muscarinic and nicotinic); two for noradrenaline (alpha and beta); five for dopamine (designated D-1 to D-5); and seven different classes with various subtypes for serotonin (designated 5HT-1 to 5HT-7). In effect, this means that a neurotransmitter can exert a different cellular response depending on the receptor it interacts with. This subject is of interest to neuropharmacologists who try to develop drugs with highly specific affinities for certain types of receptors in their attempts to better treat various conditions (see Feldman et al., 1997).

Table 1.4   Some of the main receptor subtypes found in the central nervous system

Neurotransmitter	Types of receptor
Acetylcholine (ACh)	Muscarinic and nicotinic
Dopamine (DA)	D-1, D-2, D-3, D-4 and D-5
gamma-Aminobutyric acid (GABA)	GABA-A and GABA-B
Glutamate	NMDA, APPA and kainate
Histamine	H-1, H-2 and H-3
Noradrenaline	Alpha (α) and beta (β)
Opioid	Mu (μ), delta (δ) and kappa (κ)
Serotonin (5HT)	5HT-1, 5HT-2, 5HT-3, 5HT-4, 5HT-5, 5HT-6 and 5HT-7

Although most receptors are located on dendrites, which make up most of the neuron's surface area, and to a lesser extent the cell body, they can also be found in some other places. For example, certain specialized receptors are found on the axonal endings, where they modulate neurotransmitter release, normally by a process called presynaptic inhibition. In this instance, stimulation of the receptor might cause less neurotransmitter to be released. GABA-A receptors, for example, are important in producing presynaptic inhibition, and when stimulated they reduce the inflow of calcium ions into the axon terminal, thereby slowing down exocytosis. Other types of

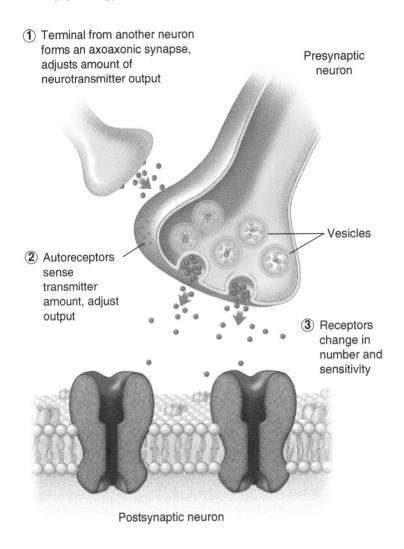

① Terminal from another neuron forms an axoaxonic synapse, adjusts amount of neurotransmitter output

Presynaptic neuron

Vesicles

② Autoreceptors sense transmitter amount, adjust output

③ Receptors change in number and sensitivity

Postsynaptic neuron

Figure 1.17   Regulating activity at the synapse
Source: Garrett and Hough (2021)

receptors are found at the axonal endings which react to neurotransmitters released by their own neuron. These 'feedback' receptors are called **autoreceptors** and they normally act to inhibit further neurotransmitter release. It is now known that a number of neurotransmitters have presynaptic autoreceptors that serve this function, including noradrenaline, dopamine, serotonin and GABA. To complicate matters further, receptors are not static entities but can change in number and sensitivity.

KEY TERMS: *receptors, acetylcholine, dopamine, noradrenaline, serotonin, presynaptic inhibition*

CHEMICAL EVENTS IN THE POSTSYNAPTIC NEURON

Whilst many types of neurotransmitter receptor exist in the central nervous system, they all alter the voltage of the neuron by opening ion channels in the neural membrane.

But how can receptor activity alter ion channels? There are two basic ways. In one situation, the receptor and ion channel form part of the same molecular unit. That is, the receptor is actually located on the ion channel and it directly influences its opening. These are called ionotropic receptors. In the other situation, the receptor and ion channels are separate entities which are not physically joined together. These are known as metabotropic receptors.

In the case of ionotropic receptors, the binding of the neurotransmitter to its receptor will directly cause a conformational change in the protein molecules making up the ion channel, thereby causing it to open for a brief period of time. However, metabotropic receptors are very different. Here, the receptor activates a type of specialized protein located on the inner aspect of the cell membrane called a **G-protein**, which acts as a molecular switch to instigate a cascade of intracellular chemical processes involving various enzymes and **second messengers**. One effect of these chemical events is to activate other effector proteins to open the ion channel.

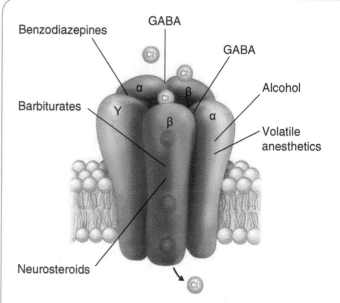

Figure 1.18   The GABA-A receptor complex
Source: Carolina Hrejsa/Body Scientific Intl. in Gaskin (2021)

An example of a ionotropic receptor, sometimes called a ligand-activated channel, is the GABA-A receptor (see Figure 1.18). This consists of a long polypeptide chain which is shaped in such a way that it forms five elongated units, arranged in the shape of a cylinder, that pass through the neural membrane. These units are tightly held together. However, if GABA binds to a receptor site on the surface of this complex, they briefly change their shape, which creates a channel that allows the influx of negative chloride ions (Cl^-) into the cell. The GABA-A receptor is also notable for having separate binding sites for barbiturates such as Pentobarbital, and benzodiazepines such as Valium, which increase the chloride current. Thus, both Pentobarbital and Valium enhance inhibitory activity in neurons with GABAergic receptors. Another example of a ligand-activated channel is the cholinergic nicotinic receptor found at the neuromuscular junction. This receptor also contains five units in the shape of a cylinder that pass through the membrane. When acetylcholine binds to part of this site, an influx of positively charged sodium ions (NA^+) enters the cell. A distinguishing feature of ligand-gated channels is the rapidity with which they open, and for this reason they are involved in the fastest forms of synaptic transmission which take only a few milliseconds to occur.

KEY TERMS: *ionotropic receptor, metabotropic receptor, G-protein, second messenger*

Most receptors in the brain are of the metabotropic variety – which includes muscarinic acetylcholine receptors, GABA-B receptors, and several types of monoamine receptors. In these cases, when a neurotransmitter binds to its receptor, it causes an alteration in the G-protein to which it is attached. There are many types of G-proteins with wide-ranging intracellular actions. One of the best known effects occurs when certain G-proteins increase the activity of an enzyme called **adenylate cyclase** that converts ATP, a substance used by the cell to provide energy, into cyclic adenosine monophosphate (cAMP) (see Figure 1.19). This chemical acts as a **second messenger** (the first messenger being the neurotransmitter) by diffusing through the cell's cytoplasm to open ion channels by the process of protein phosphorylation (a fancy term for changing the configuration or 'shape' of a protein). This mechanism is believed to underlie the action of noradrenergic beta receptors and dopaminergic D-1 receptors. It should also be noted that cAMP can affect many other chemical processes within the cell and not just those associated with ion channel function.

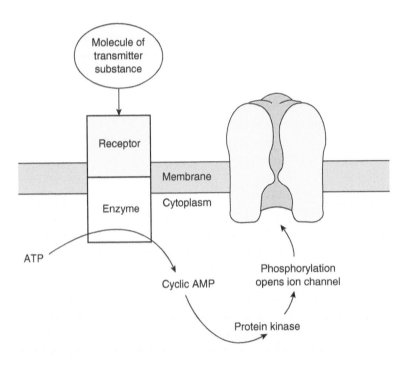

Figure 1.19   Diagram showing the main steps in the cAMP second messenger system
Source: Wickens (2009)

In recent years, much attention has focused on another second messenger system which involves G-protein stimulation of an enzyme called phospholipase C. This enzyme generates two second messengers: diacylglycerol (DAG) and inositol triphosphate (IP3). DAG activates the enzyme protein kinase C which can phosphorylate ion channel proteins, whereas IP3 acts to release stores of calcium ions within the cell which alters the excitability of the neuron. Some serotonergic receptors along with the histamine H-1 receptor use these second messenger systems. In addition to opening ion channels, certain types of second messenger can enter the cell's nucleus where they influence the activity of genes. Such a mechanism, for example, may allow changes in the physical alteration of dendritic synapses that underlie long-term memory.

Second messengers may at first sight appear to be a complex way of going about opening ion channels, but this process actually gives the cell far greater adaptability.

For example, activation of ionotropic receptors, such as GABA-A, typically results in the rapid depolarization of the cell in as little as 2 to 10 milliseconds. This may be ideal for a rapid response such as a muscle contraction or encoding of pain, but it shows little variation. In contrast, the slower action of second messenger systems involving metabotropic receptors can take from 20 milliseconds to over 10 seconds, and alter the function of several types of ion channel. In turn, this may allow the cell to alter its response in many different ways. For example, second messengers may be involved in changing the sensitivity of receptors, or adapting the neuron to the long-term exposure to certain drugs. Similar second messenger processes are also involved in learning and neural plasticity (Snyder, 2009).

KEY TERMS: *second messengers, cAMP, protein phosphorylation, phospholipase C*

GLIAL CELLS

It may come as a surprise to find out that neurons are not the most common type of cell in the human brain. In fact, this accolade goes to the **glial cells** which are around ten times more numerous than neurons, although they are about one-tenth of their size which means that they take up roughly the same volume. The first person to discover glial cells in the brain was the German pathologist Rudolf Virchow in 1846 who called them '*nevroglie*' (nerve glue) because they appeared to stick the neurons together. We now know that the brain and spinal cord contain several types of glial cell which provide vital functions for the maintenance, survival and normal activity of neurons.

The largest and most abundant type of glia cell is the astrocyte – so called because of its star-shape created by a radiating assemblage of many spindly extensions. Astrocytes supply structural support with their interweaving extensions providing scaffolding to anchor neurons, thus enabling them to maintain a regular blood supply. However astrocytes have a multitude of other functions. They control the ionic composition of the extracellular fluid, remove waste products, and deactivate neurotransmitters (e.g. some astrocytes contain monoamine oxidase). Others release growth factors involved in the formation and repair of nerve cells, or assist the transport of nutrients across the neural membrane. Astrocytes also act to increase the brain's activity by dilating blood vessels which allows greater amounts of oxygen and glucose to reach the neurons. They heal brain tissue by forming scar material – although they can give rise to tumours (gliomas) if they proliferate abnormally. There is still much to learn about astrocytes, with some studies showing that they can propagate intercellular calcium (Ca^+) waves over long distances allowing information exchange within glia networks (Metea & Newman, 2006), or release transmitters such as glutamate which can synchronize neuronal activity (Angulo et al., 2004).

Another function of astrocytes is to provide a covering for the blood vessels of the brain which forms the so-called blood–brain barrier. In the body, capillaries are 'leaky' because the endothelial cells that make up their walls contain gaps which allow a wide range of substances in and out of the blood. However, in the brain, the end feet of the astrocyte extensions cling to the outer surface of capillaries which help push the endothelial cells together. Thus, the brain's capillary walls are tightly compacted with their outer surface covered by astrocyte extensions. Although this still allows small molecules such as oxygen and carbon dioxide to enter the brain, along with lipid or fat-soluble substances (this includes nicotine, heroin and alcohol), it bars the entry of larger molecules and most toxins. This feature has to be taken into consideration when developing drugs to treat brain disorders. For example, the neurotransmitter dopamine which would be expected to have a beneficial effect in treating Parkinson's disease, does not cross the blood–brain barrier. Thus, doctors tend to prescribe L-dopa which can enter the brain where it is converted into dopamine.

A second type of glial cell is the oligodendrocyte which is smaller than the astrocyte with far fewer extensions (the Greek *oligos* means 'few'). This type of glial cell has a more

Table 1.5   Types of cell in the nervous system

Nervous system cell	Location	Subtype	Function
Neurons	Central and peripheral nervous system	Unipolar, bipolar or multipolar	To generate action potentials for sending and receiving information.
Neuroglia	Central nervous system	Astrocytes	Secure neurons to their blood supply. Regulate the external chemical environment of neurons by removing excess ions (such as potassium) and promote reuptake of neurotransmitters released during synaptic transmission. Form the blood–brain barrier.
		Microglia	Specialized macrophages capable of phagocytosis. Thus, they protect neurons from pathogens.
		Ependymal cells	Thought to be stem cells in the nervous system. Create and secrete cerebrospinal fluid (CSF) and circulate it by cilia activity. A role in reabsorption of CSF.
		Oligodendrocytes	Produce myelin to coat axons of neurons.
	Peripheral nervous system	Schwann cells	Produce myelin to coat axons of neurons. Protective role – phagocytotic and remove debris to allow growth and regrowth of neurons.
		Satellite cells	Regulate external chemical environment of neurons, particularly calcium ions. Thought to play a role in chronic pain as they are sensitive to injury and inflammation.

Source: Cook et al. (2021)

specific function: it provides the myelin that covers the axons of most nerve fibres in the brain and spinal cord. Myelination occurs because extensions of the oligodendrocytes wrap themselves around the axon to provide an insulated covering. This allows the axon to propagate electrical impulses much more efficiently. An autoimmune disorder that causes demyelination by attacking and destroying oligodendrocytes, resulting in the impaired flow of neural transmission throughout the central nervous system, is multiple sclerosis. In the peripheral nervous system, however, myelin is produced by the Schwann cell which is not attacked by the immune system.

A third type of glial cell is the microglial cells which as the name suggests are very small. Microglial make up about 15% of all glial cells and they provide the brain's main immune defence. In response to injury or infection, microglial cells multiply and migrate in large numbers to the sites of injury, where they engulf invading micro-organisms or infected neurons. They also help in the removal of debris from injured or dead cells. A fourth type of glial cells is that of ependymal cells which line the ventricles and the central canal of the spine. These play an important role in the production and regulation of the cerebrospinal fluid.

KEY TERMS: *glial cells, astrocyte, oligodendrocyte, blood–brain barrier, Schwann cell, microglial*

SPECIAL INTEREST 1.2

WHAT HAPPENED TO EINSTEIN'S BRAIN?

Albert Einstein was one of the greatest intellectual figures of the twentieth century. In one year alone (1905) at the age of twenty-six, whilst working in the Swiss Patent Office in Bern, he published four papers that were to profoundly change the way we understand the universe. One of these included his special theory of relativity with the famous equation $E = mc^2$ which showed that some aspects of Newton's mechanics were wrong. Einstein died in 1955 aged 76 from a ruptured aorta, and within 7 hours his brain had been perfused with a formalin solution (by injection into the internal carotid artery) and removed by pathologist Thomas Harvey. After being stored for several months the brain was photographed and measurements taken of its cerebral structures. The cerebral hemispheres were then cut into around 240 blocks of about 10 cm³, embedded in wax and kept in alcohol. However, close examination of the brain by Harvey revealed nothing unusual about its shape or structure.

Einstein's brain was soon forgotten and stored in two large jars housed in Dr Harvey's office for the next 20 years or so. In 1978, the brain was 'rediscovered' by journalist Steven Levy who brought it to the attention of the media. The discovery was of interest to the neuroscientist Marian Diamond at the University of California. Back in the 1960s, Diamond had shown that rats living in enriched environments had more cortical glial cells per neuron than those raised in impoverished environments. This indicated that active neurons required greater metabolic assistance from the supporting glia. Later work by Diamond also showed that the prefrontal cortex of humans has more glial cells per neuron compared to the parietal lobe – implying

(Continued)

that this frontal area was more active and evolved than other brain regions. But what about Einstein's brain? When Diamond examined it, she surprisingly found more glial cells in the left parietal cortex than in the frontal regions (Diamond et al., 1985).

Further examination of Einstein's brain by Sandra Witelson revealed other unique features. Most striking was the absence of a region called the parietal operculum – a ridge (or gyrus) in the parietal cortex located between the Sylvian fissure and the postcentral sulcus. Consequently, the Sylvian fissure and postcentral gyrus were partially joined in Einstein's brain – a feature that Witelson was unable to find in over 90 control brains. This resulted in the areas on either side of these sulci to be enlarged – presumably to compensate for the operculum's loss. In fact, Witelson found that the parietal lobes were 1 cm wider (an increase in size of 15%) in Einstein's brain compared to controls, and this enlargement was symmetrical in both right and left hemispheres. Because most people have a relatively larger right parietal cortex compared to the left, this meant that Einstein's left parietal lobe was significantly larger than normal (Witelson et al., 1999).

One can only speculate the extent to which Einstein's unique brain anatomy contributed to his ideas and in particular the theory of relativity. However, the parietal lobes are known to be involved in visuospatial cognition, including the manipulation of three-dimensional spatial images along with mathematical ability and imagery of movement – and all of these were highly characteristic of Einstein's thought. In fact, Einstein was famous for his highly visual thought experiments and it is said he came up with his theory of relativity after imagining what it must be like to ride a light beam. He also said that verbal language had little part to play in his thinking (Einstein, 1954). Interestingly, enlarged parietal cortices have also been reported for other famous thinkers, including the mathematician Gauss and the physicist Siljeström.

AN INTRODUCTION TO THE STRUCTURE OF THE NERVOUS SYSTEM

The complete network of all nerve cells in the human body is divided into two systems: the **central nervous system** (CNS) and **peripheral nervous system** (PNS) (see Figure 1.20). The CNS is composed of the brain and spinal cord and is referred to as 'central' because it integrates information from the entire body and coordinates physiological activity in return. Acting as the body's command centre, the highest levels of the CNS are also crucially involved in decision making – analysing sensory events and deciding how best to respond to changing events. In higher animals such as ourselves this goes beyond mere reflexes to involve cognition. The PNS has a simpler function: conveying sensory input from the tissues of the body or external environment to the spinal cord and brain, and relaying motor output back to the body's muscles and glands. Thus, without the PNS, the brain would have neither sensation nor the ability to instigate any movement of the body. The PNS is also divided into two main divisions: the **somatic nervous system** and the **autonomic nervous system**.

The somatic nervous system is primarily responsible for providing us with our main peripheral senses and producing muscle movement. Its sensory input derives from the skin, muscles, bones and joints (e.g. touch, pressure, temperature, pain etc.), and also from the ears, nose, tongue and skin (note the optic nerve and retina are

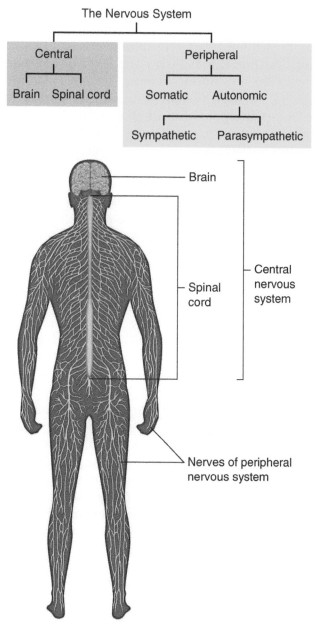

Figure 1.20 The overall organization of the nervous system

Source: Garrett and Hough (2021), adapted from Wilson, J. (2003). *Biological foundations of human behavior.* Wadsworth.

regarded as part of the CNS). The somatic nervous system also moves the skeleton by contracting skeletal muscles. For this reason it is also known as the voluntary nervous system since it allows us to undertake purposeful behaviour. The cell bodies of the somatic fibres controlling movement are mainly located in the spinal cord, although some exist in the brain stem which reach the periphery by the cranial nerves. All fibres of the somatic nervous system pass uninterrupted to reach their target structures, where they secrete the neurotransmitter acetylcholine onto nicotinic receptors. We shall discuss the role of this system in more detail when we examine motor behaviour in Chapter 4.

The autonomic nervous system is the part of the peripheral nervous system that controls the activity of involuntary muscle involved in essential visceral functions such as breathing, heart rate, blood pressure, kidney function, and digestion. Most of the time it acts below the level of conscious awareness. To provide this control, the autonomic nervous system is composed of two divisions: the **sympathetic nervous system** (SNS) and the **parasympathetic nervous system** (PNS) which act in opposition to each other (see Figure 1.21). The SNS increases the activity of autonomic structures in the body to prepare it for physical exertion, stressful anticipation or emergencies. Thus, the SNS will increase heart rate, blood pressure and respiration, whilst inhibiting digestion and diverting blood away from the skin to the skeletal muscles (this is why skin may go paler after a sudden fright). It will also stimulate the adrenal glands to secrete adrenaline and noradrenaline. This pattern of physiological activity which prepares the body for a threat or potential emergency, is sometimes called 'the fight-or-flight response'.

In contrast, the PNS reverses the effects of sympathetic activity, and also acts to conserve energy or maintain resting body function. Thus, the parasympathetic division generally responds with actions that do not require immediate reactions. For example, it is involved in digestion and relaxed body states that occur during sleep. The one part of the body that provides an exception to the relaxation rule, however, is the penis whose 'excitation' is under the control of the PNS. This is one reason why stress (i.e. SNS involvement) is generally not conducive to producing an erection.

The output fibres of the sympathetic nervous system are more complex than those of the somatic nervous system since they form pathways making up a chain of two neurons. These are called preganglionic and postganglionic nerve fibres. The cell bodies of the first link (the preganglionic fibres) are located in the spinal cord and brain stem, and their axons pass into the body, destined to reach clusters of other nerve cells and dendrites called autonomic ganglia. In effect, these are relay stations interposed between autonomic fibres originating in the CNS and the nerves innervating their target organs in the periphery. Consequently, axons arising from these ganglia create the second link (i.e. the postganglionic fibres). The neurotransmitter used at the junction between the preganglionic fibres and postganglionic cell bodies (i.e. in the autonomic ganglia) is acetylcholine which binds to nicotinic receptors. In turn, the postganglionic fibres project to the effector organs (smooth muscle, cardiac muscle and glands) where they secrete the neurotransmitter noradrenaline which binds to either alpha or beta noradrenergic receptors. The motor neurons of the parasympathetic division are different. Although the preganglionic fibre, like its sympathetic counterpart, secretes acetylcholine at a nicotinic receptor, the postganglionic fibre also releases acetylcholine (not noradrenaline), but this time at a muscarinic receptor which normally inhibits the activity of the effector organs (see McCorry, 2007).

KEY TERMS: *central nervous system, somatic nervous system, autonomic nervous system, sympathetic system, parasympathetic system, cranial nerves*

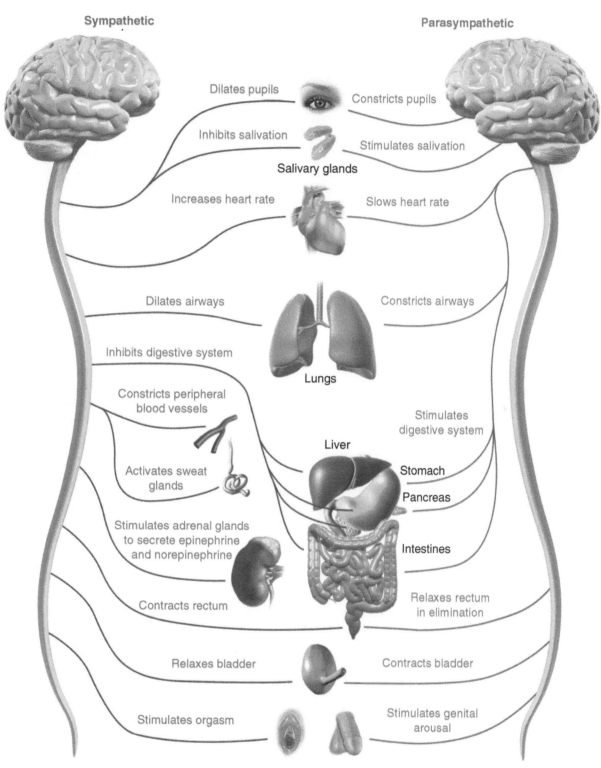

Figure 1.21 The autonomic nervous system. Please note that this simplified figure does not show the preganglionic and postganglionic components of the nerve pathways

Source: Garrett and Hough (2021)

THE ENDOCRINE SYSTEM

The endocrine system is a collection of ductless glands scattered throughout the body that secrete hormones (from the Greek *hormon* meaning to excite) into the bloodstream. More than 50 different hormones may be circulating through the body at any one time, released by such internal organs as the thyroid, thymus, adrenal glands, pancreas and gonads (testes and ovaries). Although hormones act as long-distance chemical messengers, each one is targeted toward certain organs and tissues, and between them they regulate a huge amount of bodily functions including metabolism, growth, tissue function, sexual maturation, sleep, and blood pressure (to name a few). Most of our endocrine glands are actually under the control of a pea-sized gland located on the underside of the brain in a bony hollow, just behind the bridge of your nose, called the **pituitary gland**. Although only weighing about 0.5 grams in humans, the pituitary is regarded as the master gland because of its controlling influence on other endocrine organs enabling it to exert a profound impact on many bodily activities. The pituitary gland is also under the control of the **hypothalamus**, to which it is attached by a thin stalk of tissue called the infundibulum. In fact, the pituitary consists of two main lobes: the anterior pituitary, or adenohypophysis, which is connected to the hypothalamus via a complex series of blood vessels, and the posterior pituitary (neurohypophysis) which receives neural connections and blood vessels from the hypothalamus through the infundibulum.

Hormone release from the anterior pituitary is regulated by the secretion of chemicals called **releasing factors** from the hypothalamus which include adrenocorticotropic releasing factor (CRF) and growth hormone releasing factor (GHRF). In response, the glandular cells of the anterior pituitary secrete a number of trophic hormones into the bloodstream, such as the adrenocorticotropic hormone (ACTH) that acts on the adrenal glands; the thyroid stimulating hormone targeting the thyroid gland; prolactin that acts on the mammary glands; and the follicle stimulating hormone and luteinising hormone affecting the ovaries and testes. Another substance secreted by the anterior pituitary is growth hormone which stimulates growth, cell reproduction and cell regeneration. The posterior pituitary stores and releases just two hormones: the antidiuretic hormone (vasopressin) involved in controlling water balance and blood pressure; and oxytocin which stimulates uterine contractions during labour and milk secretion during breastfeeding.

Table 1.6   The main effects of hormones in the body controlled by the pituitary gland

Hypothalamic hormones	Anterior pituitary gland	Function
Thyrotrophin RH	Thyroid Stimulating Hormone (TSH)	Stimulates thyroid gland to secrete thyroid hormones (thyroxine (T4) and T3)
		Regulates metabolic rate
Corticotrophin RH	Adrenocorticotrophic Hormone (ACTH)	Stimulates adrenal cortex to secrete glucocorticoid hormones
		Response to stress
Gonadotrophin RH	Luteinising Hormone (LH) Follicle Stimulating Hormone (FSH)	Stimulates gonads (see Figure 7.9) male ($\male$) and female ($\female$)
		LH: causes ovulation ($\female$) and release of testosterone ($\male$)
		FSH: regulates oogenesis ($\female$) and spermatogenesis ($\male$)

Hypothalamic hormones	Anterior pituitary gland	Function
Prolactin RH Prolactin IH	Prolactin	Stimulates milk production from breasts
Growth hormone RH Growth hormone IH (somatostatin)	Human growth hormone (hGH)	Stimulates growth of bones, muscles, cells in general
Hypothalamic nuclei	Posterior pituitary gland	Function
Supraoptic and paraventricular nuclei nerve impulses	Oxytocin	Mainly neuromodulator in brain. 'Bonding hormone' (orgasm, social recognition, pair bonding, anxiety, etc.). Role in childbirth and breast-feeding
Suprachiasmatic nucleus nerve impulses	Antidiuretic Hormone (ADH) (vasopressin)	Water retention, vasoconstriction □ raised blood pressure
	Intermediate pituitary gland	
Regulated by a number of different factors	Melanocyte Stimulating Hormones (MSH)	Production and release of melanin from melanocytes in skin and hair. Helps activation of regulatory T-cells in immune system (Namba et al., 2002)

Male = ♂; Female = ♀; RH = Releasing Hormone; IH = Inhibiting Hormone

Source: Cook et al. (2021)

The control of hormonal release by the pituitary gland works on the basis of negative feedback. That is, when blood levels of a given hormone begin to increase (e.g. cortisol), the pituitary gland detects the change and decreases the output of its controlling trophic hormone (e.g. ACTH). In practice however things are more complex, as the hypothalamus (and in some cases other brain regions) will also receive feedback about hormone levels and the effects they are having on the body. In response to all this information, the hypothalamus can also inhibit secretion of its own releasing factors, thereby regulating the pituitary's activity. The combination of the hypothalamus and pituitary gland working together means that the control exerted over hormone secretion is complex and finely tuned.

Both the endocrine and nervous systems work in tandem to provide integrated action. In general, the nervous system transmits messages that require immediate action, whereas the endocrine system is involved in slower, less immediate responses. In fact, some hormones may take minutes or even hours to reach their target, although they have a far longer duration of action. Despite this, hormones are very potent regulators of the body's physiology and effective in minute concentrations. Hence, a slight change in a hormone's concentration can have a significant impact on behavioural functioning.

KEY TERMS: *hormones, pituitary gland, hypothalamus, releasing factors, negative feedback*

INTRODUCTION TO THE CENTRAL NERVOUS SYSTEM

The **central nervous system** (CNS) consists of the brain and spinal cord and acts as the integrative control centre of the body. In particular, the brain exerts executive control over the peripheral nervous system and endocrine glands, and is the instigating

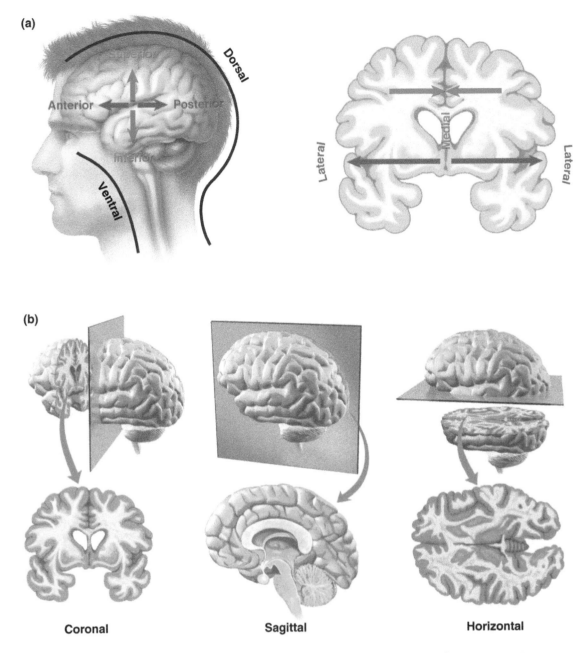

Figure 1.22   The main anatomical terms used to denote direction and orientation in the nervous system
Source: Garrett and Hough (2021)

organ of movement and emotion, along with thought and conscious awareness. An important prerequisite for understanding how the brain produces behaviour is a good understanding of its neuroanatomy. This includes knowing where the main brain regions are located, and the ways in which they are connected. This can be a daunting challenge for students. One problem is the terminology. Many Greek and Latin terms are used to describe parts of the CNS (although some areas are named after people such as Broca and Wernicke) and unfamiliar terms can be difficult to remember.

An added difficulty often occurs in trying to visualize the shape of brain structures and pathways. It may also be disconcerting that brain structures can rarely, if ever, be tied down to single behavioural functions. The brain is simply far too complex.

To make matters more demanding, anatomists tend to use specific terms to identify the precise direction or location of a certain region. This is not too dissimilar to an explorer who uses compass bearings to find their way around the environment. In the case of a brain the four main bearings are *anterior* (to the front), *superior* (to the top), *posterior* (to the back) and *inferior* (to the bottom). In addition, because the brain is three-dimensional, the terms *lateral* (to the side) and *medial* (to the middle) are also frequently used. Two other terms that students with an interest in anatomy will also encounter are *dorsal*, meaning towards the back, and *ventral*, meaning towards the stomach.

Another way of classifying the direction and orientation of the brain is to slice it into various planes. There are three ways of doing this. The *coronal* plane slices the brain vertically from side to side; the *sagittal* plane slices it vertically from the front to back; and the *horizontal* plane slices it between top to bottom. These three terms are now commonly used by cognitive neuroscientists who work with brain-scanning techniques.

If we take the emergence of primates as the starting point, then the evolution of the human brain has taken place over a period of some 70 million years. This is a long period of time, especially when one considers that human western civilization has only existed for around 3,000 years. The gradual process of evolution has resulted in new structures taking over the roles of older ones. However, this does not mean that the older brain regions have become redundant. Rather, they remain incorporated into the neural circuits of the brain and still have important functions. Consequently, the brain acts as a collective entity, whilst showing a hierarchy of function where newer structures are likely to be involved in more complex behaviours. Another feature of evolutionary development is the massive increase in size of the brain in relation to the body (cephalization). This trend is most noticeable in the cerebral cortex, which has become so large and complex in mammals, and especially humans, that it has developed ridges and fissures in order to increase its surface area. In fact, the cerebral cortex is not unlike a sheet of tightly screwed-up paper, and it this adaptation that allows a large surface area to be housed in a small space which also gives the cortex its distinctive wrinkly appearance.

KEY TERMS: *anterior, superior, posterior, inferior, dorsal, ventral.*

THE SPINAL CORD

The spinal cord is an extension of the medulla in the brain, about the diameter of a large pencil, that forms a cylinder of nervous tissue running down the back, which is enclosed and protected in a bony column of 31 flexible segments (vertebrae). From top to bottom, these segments are comprised of 8 cervical vertebrae, 12 thoracic, 5 lumbar, 5 sacral and 1 coccygeal. The spinal cord serves many functions: it helps us maintain an erect posture, and provides the point of attachment for the muscles in the back.

However, its three major roles for the biopsychologist are to relay sensory messages to the brain, send motor output to different parts of the body, and produce simple reflexive actions. One such reflex is the knee jerk response which a doctor may use to test the health of the nervous system.

The most striking feature of the spinal cord is its grey matter, which is largely formed by the cell bodies of neurons and white matter, which is comprised of myelinated axons. Forming a butterfly shape in the centre of the spinal cord, grey matter is composed of motor neurons which send their fibres out to innervate the muscles of the body, along with a large number of small interneurons that are entirely confined to the grey columns. Interneurons are located between sensory fibres passing in and motor axons going out, which enable sensory-motor coordination and reflexes to take place. Interneurons also allow communication between different segments of the spinal cord. The central grey core is surrounded by white matter composed of long myelinated axons that form pathways which ascend and descend the spinal cord. The white matter therefore forms the main motorways of the spinal cord. The routes ascending to the brain have their cell bodies located in the grey matter, whilst the descending pathways from the brain also terminate in the grey matter where they form synapses with motor neurons. There are a number of distinct columns in white matter including the posterior columns which convey touch and pressure information to the thalamus, and the more lateral corticospinal tracts that pass information all the way from the motor regions of the cerebral cortex.

Along the vertebrate's length are 31 pairs of spinal nerves which enter and leave the spinal cord on either side. In fact, these are ganglia containing large numbers of sensory, motor and autonomic fibres. Closer examination of these nerves show they form two branches or roots as they join the spinal cord. The dorsal root relays sensory information into the spinal cord, whereas the ventral root conveys motor output out and away from the spinal cord. The spinal cord also contains cerebrospinal fluid which is connected with the brain's ventricles. Samples of this fluid can be a useful diagnostic tool in determining various brain disorders.

KEY TERMS: *grey matter, white matter, posterior columns, corticospinal tracts, spinal nerves*

THE BRAIN STEM

As the spinal cord passes through the opening of the foramen magnum to enter the brain it enlarges to form the brain stem (see Figure 1.23). Although comprising less than 3% of the brain's weight, the brain stem is crucial for the maintenance of life. The oldest part is the **medulla oblongata** ('long marrow') which contains groups of nuclei necessary for vital functions such as breathing, heart rate, blood pressure, salivation and detecting toxins (vomiting). It also contains ascending and descending nerve pathways passing between the spinal cord and higher brain areas. Damage to the medulla is inevitably fatal.

Above the medulla lies the **pons** (Latin for 'bridge') which appears as a significant enlargement of the brain stem, largely as a result of it containing peduncles (fibre tracts) connecting the two cerebellar hemispheres. The pons is also the main site where ascending and descending fibre tracts cross from one side of the brain to the other, including the pyramidal tracts originating in the cerebral cortex. Like the medulla, the pons contains nuclei involved in autonomic functioning. Two important areas often regarded as pontine nuclei (although they also extend into the midbrain) are the **locus coeruleus** and **dorsal raphe** which are the origin of noradrenergic and serotonergic containing fibres in the forebrain respectively. The upper or dorsal pons also includes an area known as the tegmentum, from the Latin for 'covering', which includes many motor nuclei and secondary sensory cell groups, as well as the higher reaches of the **reticular formation** – a tubular net-like mass of grey tissue involved in generating sleep cycles and different levels of arousal including consciousness.

The pons serves further as a bridging point between the two hemispheres of the **cerebellum** and for relaying its connections to the rest of the brain. The cerebellum (which is discussed more fully in Chapter 4) is located towards the back of the neck, and is a conspicuous bulbous structure whose cortical surface is covered with finely spaced parallel grooves. Incredibly, the cerebellum contains in the region of 70 billion neurons (there are fewer than 1 billion in the brain stem) which is about 3.6 times more than found in the neocortex (a ratio that is also conserved across many different mammalian species). As might be expected the cerebellum is massively connected with the rest of the brain and spinal cord. Traditionally, the cerebellum has been linked with the coordination of muscular activity required for smooth automated movement, although more recently it has been implicated in some cognitive functions such as attention and language.

The brain stem (medulla and pons) also gives rise to the cranial nerves, which were first discovered by Galen back in the first century AD. There are 12 pairs of cranial nerves which connect the brain with various organs of the body – and 8 of these originate or terminate in the brain stem: 4 from the medulla (hypoglossal, spinal accessory, vagus and glossopharyngeal), and 4 from the pons (auditory, facial, abducens and trigeminal). Cranial nerves can be sensory, motor, or mixed (i.e. relay both sensory and

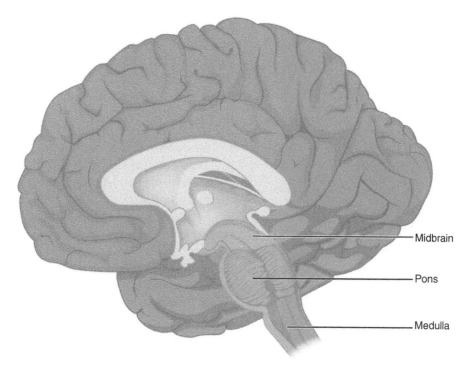

Figure 1.23   The areas of the brain stem
Source: Gaskin (2019); OpenStax College/CFCF/Wikimedia Commons

motor input), and also include autonomic sympathetic and parasympathetic fibres. In general, the brain stem's cranial nerves are involved in taste, hearing and balance – along with the reflexive action of chewing, swallowing, breathing, eye movements and facial expression. The vagus nerve (from the Latin '*vagus*' meaning 'wandering') is somewhat different: it has the most extensive distribution of any cranial nerve, projecting to organs in the abdomen and thorax including the heart, lungs and digestive system. A consideration of the cranial nerves provides an interesting insight into the functions of the brain stem.

KEY TERMS: *medulla oblongata, pons, reticular formation, cerebellum*

THE MIDBRAIN

The midbrain, also called the mesencephalon, is the name given to the region that forms the top part of the brain stem (see Figure 1.24). It is normally divided into the tegmentum, which is continuous with the pontine region below it, and the 'roof' which sits above. The tegmentum contains several nuclei with important motor functions associated with basal ganglia function, including the **red nucleus** and **substantia nigra**. But other areas of the tegmentum are more diffuse and these include the periaqueductal grey area, which lies around the passage connecting the third and fourth ventricles called the cerebral aqueduct, and the ventral tegmental area characterized by its dopaminergic neurons that project to regions of the forebrain. The ventral tegmental area is also recognized as an integral part of a network of structures in rewarding and reinforcing behaviour.

Several midbrain tegmental nuclei also contribute to the ascending reticular activating system (ARAS) which first forms in the brain stem. This collection of fibres passes primarily to the thalamus although there are important connections with the hypothalamus and cerebral cortex. This system is chemically complex and uses a number of neurotransmitters including acetylcholine, glutamate, noradrenaline and serotonin, as well as a neuropeptide called hypocretin. One of its main functions is to regulate the level of electrical activity that governs states of arousal in the cerebral cortex. This can be measured by an electroencephalograph (EEG).

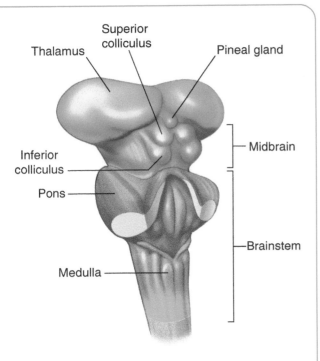

Figure 1.24   The midbrain
Source: Garrett and Hough (2021)

In lower animals such as fish and amphibians, the tectum is well developed which also serves as the main visual centre. This visual function is preserved in humans with the **superior colliculi** (colliculi is derived from the Latin meaning 'small hills') emerging as small bumps that protrude from the dorsal surfaces of the tectum. In humans, the upper layer of the superior colliculus receives input from the eye's retina, whilst its lower layers contain neurons involved in orienting the eyes to new stimuli. Located close to the superior colliculi are two smaller bumps called the **inferior colliculi**. These are involved in sound location and auditory processing. The tectum also gives rise to two cranial nerves: the oculomotor controlling the muscles of the eyeball, and the trochlear involved in eye movements.

> **KEY TERMS:** tegmentum, tectum, red nucleus, substantia nigra, ventral tegmental area, periaqueductal grey area, ascending reticular system, superior and inferior colliculi

THE FOREBRAIN

(A) THALAMUS AND HYPOTHALAMUS

Up to this point, the brain can be likened to a neural tube that has evolved and enlarged from the spinal cord. In fact, this is basically what happens during embryonic development. At first, the brain and spinal cord of every vertebrate animal begins as a tube that is one cell thick – and as it grows it starts to show three bulbous swellings called the primary brain vesicles. These can be observed in the embryo by the third week of gestation. From bottom to top these are called the hindbrain which becomes the brain stem, the mesencephalon which becomes the midbrain, and the forebrain. And, with further development, we see the forebrain 'mushroom out' so that it not only covers and surrounds much of the 'tubular' brain, but also adds greater complexity with the emergence of many new structures. In fact, the forebrain will develop into two main regions: the diencephalon, which literally means 'between-brain', and the telencephalon, or 'endbrain'.

The most important structures of the diencephalon are the **thalamus** and hypothalamus. The thalamus, from the Greek for 'inner chamber', consists of a symmetrical pair of egg-shaped structures that are separated along their midline by the third ventricle, and bounded laterally by the internal capsule – a band of white myelinated fibres which convey ascending and descending fibres between the cerebral cortex and lower regions of the brain and spinal cord. The thalamus contains some 30 or 40 different nuclei which can be divided into anterior, medial, lateral and ventral groups (see Clark et al., 2005). In general terms, the thalamus acts as a relay station for input destined for the cerebral cortex and forebrain. Although many of its nuclei have precise destinations (e.g. the lateral geniculate nuclei project to the visual cortex, the mediodorsal nucleus to the frontal cortex and limbic system, and so on), other thalamic nuclei have diffuse radiations that spread to widespread areas of cortex (e.g. the intralaminar nuclei) and appear to be involved in arousal and consciousness.

Located just underneath the thalamus is a small structure – roughly the size of a pea and making up less than 1% of the brain's weight – called the **hypothalamus** (*hypo* meaning 'below'). Despite its small size the hypothalamus is an extremely complex part of the brain containing many regions with highly specialized functions. Nonetheless, at the risk of over-simplification, the hypothalamus can be divided into four main regions: the preoptic area anteriorly; the medial zone which contains the majority of its nuclei; the lateral nuclei with its widespread projections to other areas of the brain; and the posterior hypothalamus which includes the **mammillary bodies**.

One of the major roles of the hypothalamus is to maintain **homeostasis**, i.e. to keep the body in a stable, constant condition, despite its continual exposure to physiological changes and external fluctuations. In order to do this, the hypothalamus responds to a wide variety of signals, both chemical and neural, and combines this information to instigate bodily responses to correct any imbalances. We have already noted how the hypothalamus is the main regulator of the pituitary gland and the endocrine system of the body – but it is also the most important region of the brain that controls the autonomic nervous system too. Clearly, the hypothalamic control over these two systems is vital for the maintenance of life, and this is shown by the fact that destruction of the hypothalamus will cause death (Stein & Stoodley, 2006). Yet our hypothalamus does much more than this as it also responds to stress, regulates our emotions and feelings, is importantly involved in sexual behaviour, causes sleep, and controls our daily circadian rhythms. And this list of behavioural functions is far from exhaustive.

KEY TERMS: *thalamus, lateral geniculate nucleus, mediodorsal nucleus, hypothalamus, preoptic area, mammillary bodies*

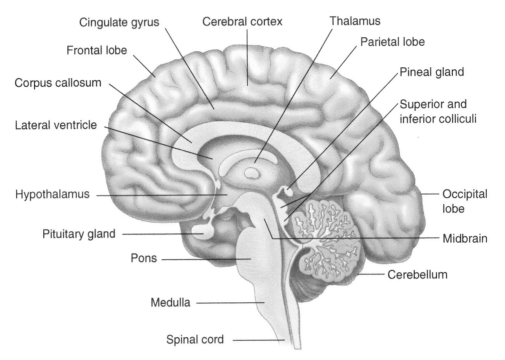

Figure 1.25   Sagittal view of the internal features of the human brain
Source: Garrett and Hough (2021)

(B) THE LIMBIC SYSTEM

Although the hypothalamus is part of the diencephalon, it is also regarded as an important component of the **limbic system** (see Figure 1.26). The word *limbus* comes from the Latin word for 'border' and was used by Paul Broca in 1878 to describe a great lobe of tissue on the underside of the cerebral cortex surrounding the thalamus and striatum, which appeared to separate the cortex from the brain stem. Because of its large size in lower animals, Broca believed the limbic lobe was involved in olfaction, but clearly this does a great injustice to this large part of the brain. Later, it was shown that this 'grand lobe' was composed of many integrated structures and called the limbic system by Paul MacLean in 1952. Although there is still considerable debate over which structures should be included in the limbic system, or whether it constitutes a system at all, there is little doubt that this brain region plays a major role in many behaviours. From the time of MacLean, the limbic system has been associated with producing drives, motivation and emotion – not least because it has been shown to be involved in feelings of pleasure, anxiety and fear. But according to some leading theorists, such as Joseph LeDoux, this theory is misleading since relatively few limbic areas have been shown to actually contribute to emotional behaviour, whilst one of its most important structures, the hippocampus, is much more strongly implicated in cognitive functions (LeDoux, 2012).

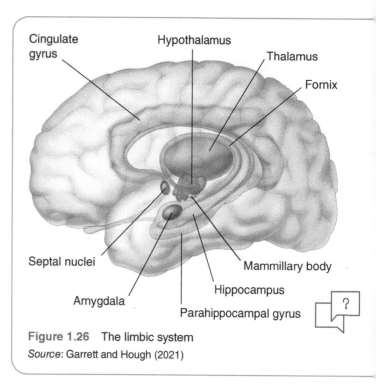

Figure 1.26   The limbic system
Source: Garrett and Hough (2021)

The complicated anatomy of the limbic system is not easy to visualize. One of its most conspicuous structures is the elongated **hippocampus**, which is actually an 'old' type of cortical tissue that consists of three laminae and makes up much of the medial temporal lobe. Surrounding most of the anterior hippocampus are the **entorhinal cortex** (which is the origin of the perforant pathway into the hippocampus), parahippocampal cortex and pyriform cortex. Another striking feature of the limbic system is the **fornix**, which is a long arching pathway that connects the posterior regions of the hippocampus with the mammillary bodies and hypothalamus at the front of the brain. The hypothalamus is a pivotal point in the limbic system because it projects via the anterior thalamus to the **cingulate cortex** which wraps itself around the upper part of the corpus callosum. The cingulate cortex also contains a large bundle of fibres called the cingulum which projects back into the hippocampus. Another important structure found in the limbic system is the **amygdala** which lies near the anterior tips of the hippocampus. This is another pivotal structure since it has two descending pathways to the hypothalamus (the ventral amygdalofugal pathway and stria terminalis) and another pathway that projects to the prefrontal cortex via the mediodorsal nuclei of the thalamus.

KEY TERMS: *limbic system, hippocampus, entorhinal cortex, fornix, cingulate cortex, amygdala.*

(C) THE BASAL GANGLIA

If we move laterally, or sideways, from the thalamus we come to several structures nestled under the cerebral cortex that form the **basal ganglia** (see Figure 1.27). Here, three large groups of interconnected nerve cells can be seen: the **caudate nucleus** which also has a tail that curls over the top of the thalamus; the **putamen** separated from the caudate by the fibres of the internal capsule; and the **globus pallidus** that lies medially to the putamen. The caudate nucleus and putamen are also referred to as the corpus striatum – a term coined by Thomas Willis in 1664 who noted that it had a distinct striated appearance of white and grey bands. Two other structures also regarded as components of the basal ganglia are the substantia nigra, which innervates the corpus striatum with dopaminergic neurons, and the subthalamic nucleus, which has reciprocal connections with the globus pallidus.

Traditionally, the basal ganglia have been regarded as part of the extrapyramidal motor system. This term refers to the fact that the output fibres of this system (which also includes the cerebellum and certain areas of the brain stem) do not cross in the pyramidal region of the medulla, unlike those passing down to the spinal cord from the motor cortex. The extrapyramidal system is involved in the automated control and coordinated regulation of motor action, including reflexes, allowing complex movements to be undertaken without 'thinking'. This system is also compromised in Parkinson's disease in which marked degeneration of the substantia nigra and its innervation of the striatum (i.e. the **nigral-striatal pathway**) occurs, which causes rigid paralysis, tremor and slow movement. The corpus striatum is also heavily innervated with fibres from motor areas of the cerebral cortex which release the neurotransmitter glutamate. In turn, the output fibres of both caudate and putamen project to, or pass through, the globus pallidus. From here, fibres travel back to the cerebral cortex via the ventral nuclei of the thalamus, with a smaller projection going to the substantia nigra.

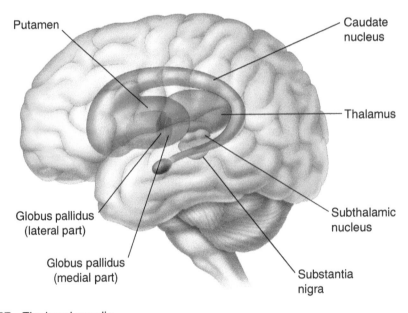

Figure 1.27   The basal ganglia
Source: Garrett and Hough (2021)

To make matters more complex, the caudate, putamen and globus pallidus also have a basal extension (known as the ventral striatum) closely linked to the limbic system and implicated in motivation and reward-related behavior. The ventral striatum, which includes the **nucleus accumbens**, is at the crossroads for several limbic pathways and receives input from the basolateral amygdala, hippocampal formation and prefrontal cortex. In turn, it projects to the lateral hypothalamus and brainstem regions via the ventral pallidus. Other structures associated with the ventral striatum include the olfactory tubercle, substantia innominata and basal nucleus of Meynert. There is much more to be learned about this mysterious part of the brain.

> **KEY TERMS:** *basal ganglia, caudate nucleus, putamen, globus pallidus, subthalamic nucleus, nigral-striatal pathway, nucleus accumbens*

(D) THE CEREBRAL CORTEX

The most striking feature of the human brain is made up of the two nearly symmetrical wrinkled cerebral hemispheres that form the **cerebral cortex** (cortex means 'bark' in Latin). Making up about half the weight of our entire brain, this remarkable structure has been estimated to contain some 16 billion neurons (Herculano-Houzel, 2009) whose cumulative axon length would measure over 150,000 km (Pakkenberg et al., 2003). The number of synapses in the cerebral cortex has been estimated at about 150 trillion, although these decrease with ageing (Nguyen, 2010). The appearance of the cerebral cortex is also somewhat deceptive: whilst only 2–3 millimetres thick it is highly folded, enabling its large area to fit inside the small confines of the skull. In fact, if the tissue was flattened out, its surface area would be similar in dimensions to a large newspaper (e.g. about 2.5 sq ft or 75 cm^2) (Nolte, 2008). Because of its folding, about two-thirds of the cortex is hidden from view in fissures (also known as sulci) which in turn help form the surface ridges (also known as gyri) that give the cerebrum is walnut-like appearance. The main fissures also make good surface landmarks from which to distinguish different regions of the cerebral cortex (see Figure 1.29). For example, all of the cortex anterior to the central sulcus, sometimes called the Rolandic fissure, comprises the **frontal lobe**, whereas the tissue posterior to it is the **parietal lobe**. Another sulcus called the parietal-occipital fissure separates the parietal lobe from the occipital lobe posteriorly. The other main region of the cerebral cortex is the **temporal lobe** which is separated from the frontal and parietal lobes by the lateral fissure (sometimes called the Sylvian fissure).

When stained appropriately and examined under a high-powered microscope, it can be seen that about 90% of the cerebral cortex is made up of six layers (this is known as **neocortex**) which is anatomically more complex than the primitive three-layered cortex (archicortex) found in parts of the limbic system. About two-thirds of neurons in the cerebral cortex are pyramidal cells – so called because of their pyramidal-shaped cell bodies. These neurons also have what are known as apical dendrites that extend from the apex of the pyramid cell to the cortical surface, and long axons that project inwards – some of which can travel some distance to other brain regions and the spinal cord. Despite this, there is considerable variation in the types of cells and their organization within the cerebral cortex. In 1909, Brodmann divided the cerebral cortex into 52 different regions based on their cellular differences (now known as

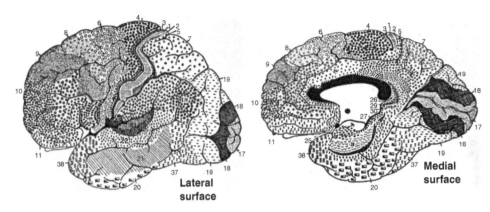

Figure 1.28 Brodmann's map of the cerebral cortex
Source: Looie496/Wikimedia Commons

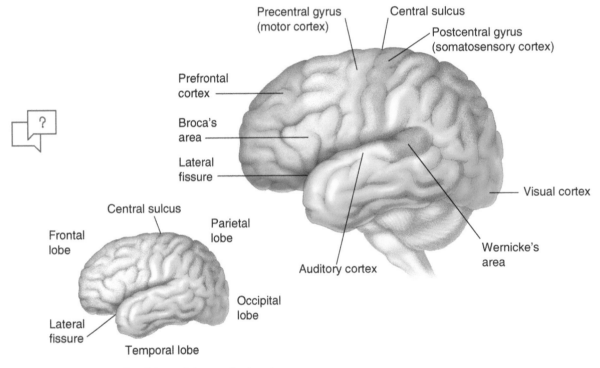

Figure 1.29 The lobes of the cerebral cortex
Source: Garrett and Hough (2021)

Brodmann's areas) and showed that this cortical organization was similar in all mammals. These anatomical differences probably reflect different behavioural or mental functions undertaken by the cerebral cortex.

The behavioural functions served by the cerebral cortex are extremely varied (see Kolb & Whishaw, 2015). For example, it contains the primary sensory areas that are the main regions that receive visual, auditory and somatosensory (touch) input from the senses. This information is relayed to the cortex by specific nuclei in the thalamus. In addition, the cerebral cortex contains a number of motor areas, including the primary motor cortex located in the precentral gyrus of the frontal cortex that governs voluntary action. The cerebral cortex also has several areas specialized for understanding and producing language. Yet, most of the human cerebral cortex is composed of the association cortex which integrates many different types of highly processed information. It is these areas which are predominantly involved in the higher functions of the brain including our abilities to plan and see the consequences of our actions and engage in various forms of abstract thought. It is also interesting to note that the right and left hemispheres show different types of cognition: the left is normally dominant for language and the right normally more specialized for spatial processing and emotion. The two cerebral hemispheres communicate with each other via a huge fibre bundle called the **corpus callosum** containing around 300 million axons. It is the largest white matter structure in the human brain and got its name from Galen who likened it to a callus or an area of paler thickened skin.

KEY TERMS: *frontal lobes, parietal lobes, temporal lobes, occipital lobes, Brodmann's areas, corpus callosum*

MONOAMINE PATHWAYS IN THE BRAIN

Examining the different anatomical parts of the brain provides one way of understanding its function, but there are also other ways of gaining important insights into its secrets. Another approach is to explore its neurochemistry. One of the great achievements of the twentieth century has been the discovery of chemical neurotransmission in the central nervous system – a fact only established for certain during the 1950s. This quickly led to the realization that the brain has a number of neurotransmitter systems with crucial behavioural roles. But how to locate these pathways? An important advance took place in the late 1950s when it was found that cells of the adrenal gland fluoresced if treated with a chemical called formalin and exposed to ultraviolet light. This florescent reaction took place because the adrenal cells contained monoamines (chemicals that have a single amine group in its molecule) such as adrenaline that reacted with the formalin. This simple discovery was a major breakthrough because some of the neurotransmitters utilized by the

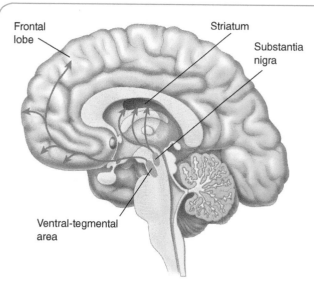

Figure 1.30 The main dopaminergic pathways of the brain
Source: Gaskin (2021)

brain are also monoamines, and the fluorescent technique provided a way of identifying their location. The first use of this method to map neurotransmitter systems in the brain was undertaken by Dahlstrom and Fuxe in 1964, who distinguished between noradrenaline (NA) and dopamine (DA) that fluoresced green, and serotonin (5-HT) which fluoresced as yellow. Their research also showed that all neurons containing these neurotransmitters had cell bodies originating from circumscribed areas of the upper brain stem or midbrain – with their axons forming diffuse pathways that projected throughout the forebrain (see Hökfelt, 2009).

The origin of most NA neurons in the brain is a small bluish nucleus in the pontine region of the upper brain stem called the locus coeruleus. In humans, this nucleus only contains around 24,000 neurons, although they project diffusely with their multiple bifurcating axons branching to millions of other cells, including those in the cerebral cortex, limbic system and thalamus. In fact, no other brain nucleus has such widespread projections (Sara, 2009). The function of this system is not fully understood although it is linked to attention, arousal and mood. The raphe nuclei, also situated in the pontine region, are a 5-HT counterpart to the locus coeruleus. Two **raphe nuclei**, the dorsal and the median, account for about 80% of 5-HT in the forebrain. Similar to the locus coeruleus, the raphe have relatively few neurons, but they give rise to many axons with widespread forebrain projections. Although the destination of the 5-HT axons largely overlap with NA (particularly in the limbic system), there are some places such as the basal ganglia where 5-HT predominates. Again, it is difficult to describe precisely the function of the 5-HT system, although it has been implicated in a wide range of behaviours. The selective serotonergic uptake blockers used to treat depression also work on this system.

The neurons that synthesize and release the neurotransmitter DA show some differences from the NA and 5-HT ones. Not only are there more dopaminergic neurons in the brain than for NA and 5-HT (e.g. there are over 40,000 DA cells), but they also give the impression of forming distinct pathways – although whether they do or not is a matter of some debate (see Figure 1.30). The pathway that has attracted most attention, largely because of its involvement in Parkinson's disease, is the nigral-striatal pathway which arises from the substantia nigra to the **striatum**. The substantia nigra is actually embedded in a midbrain region called the **ventral tegmental area** which is also the origin of two other major DA pathways: the mesolimbic pathway which projects primarily to the amygdala and nucleus accumbens, and the mesocortical pathway that projects to the frontal cortex (the 'meso' prefix here means 'middle' and refers to their origin in the midbrain). Both these pathways are involved in a wide range of behaviours. At the risk of being over simplistic, it is probably fair to say that the mesolimbic system is involved in emotion including motivation, reward and fear etc., whereas the mesocortical system is more concerned with cognitive skills including executive function, working memory and inhibitory control. It should be noted that there are several other DA pathways in the brain including one in the hypothalamus which controls the release of the hormone prolactin from the pituitary gland.

KEY TERMS: *monoamines, noradrenaline, dopamine, serotonin, locus coeruleus, raphe nuclei, substantia nigra*

SUMMARY

The study of the brain has a long history which stretches back to ancient Greece. One of the earliest theories of brain function was formulated by the Roman physician Galen (c. 130–200 AD) who believed that *animated spirit* (analogous to the soul) resided in the ventricles, with each ventricle having a different mental function. This theory remained in vogue for over 1,500 years, partly because it was compatible with Christian doctrine about the immortality and non-material nature of the soul. The first break with this tradition came with the French philosopher Descartes (1596–1650) who argued that much of our behaviour is not governed by spiritual forces, but is mechanical and reflexive. The gradual acceptance of this view enabled the neural reflex to become a legitimate subject for scientific study. Approximately 150 years later, in 1791, the Italian Luigi Galvani discovered that the 'force' in nervous tissue was not *spirit* but electricity – thereby refuting Galen's doctrine. Although the microscope had been invented in the seventeenth century, it was not until the nineteenth century with the development of more powerful instruments, along with neural staining methods, that the nerve cell was visualized. The first stain to allow individual neurons to be seen clearly was discovered by Camillo Golgi in 1875, and this enabled Santiago Ramón y Cajal to meticulously draw the structure of different brain regions and their interconnections. He also realized that axon endings are not physically joined to their recent cells – and these small gaps or points of contact were termed *synapses* by Charles Sherrington in 1897. At first the nature of the message that crossed the synapse was not known. However, in 1921, a famous experiment undertaken by Otto Loewi showed that synaptic transmission was chemical. At this point, little was known about how the nerve impulse was generated by the neuron. But in 1936, John Z. Young discovered a giant neuron in the body of the squid which could be implanted with a recording electrode. And it was this preparation which allowed Alan Hodgkin and Andrew Huxley to describe how the action potential was created in 1952.

To understand how a neuron can generate an electrical impulse or action potential, it is necessary to realize that the voltage *inside* the cell, when it is at rest, is negative compared to the *outside*. In fact, its resting potential is about –70Mv. The reason for this voltage difference lies with the distribution of **ions** (atoms that have lost or gained an electron that makes them positively or negatively charged) which are found inside and outside the neuron. More specifically, the inside of the neuron contains a large amount of negatively charged anions, along with positive potassium ions (K+) and the extracellular fluid contains a high solution of positive sodium (NA+) ions. This creates a state of tension with NA+ ions being strongly attracted to the inside of the cell by chemical and electrostatic forces. However, the neural membrane forms a barrier that partly stops the flow of ions in and out of the cell, with an NA+/ K+ pump also helping to maintain this balance. The neuron is also being bombarded by transmitters binding to receptors on its dendrites and soma, creating tiny voltage changes, and if these are sufficient to increase the resting potential at the axon hillock by about +15Mv, everything changes. This event causes ion channels to open, enabling NA+ ions to flow into the cell – which increases the internal voltage to about +30Mv in less than a thousandth of a second. This is the start of the action potential which passes down the axon by salutary conduction until it reaches the axon endings where the fusing of synaptic vesicles with the membrane causes exocytosis and **neurotransmitter** enters the synapse.

The adult brain is believed to contain around one hundred billion neurons and a truly extraordinary number (trillions) of synapses. The brain first develops as an extension of the spinal cord called the brain stem composed of the medulla and pons. Coursing through the brain stem and midbrain is a network of neurons making up the reticular system whilst towards the neck lies the cerebellum. Sitting above the pons, at the end of the brain stem, is the midbrain consisting of the tectum, tegmentum and **periaqueductal grey area**. The rest of the brain is known as the forebrain. This includes the thalamus, sited centrally, which acts as a relay station for information going to the cerebral cortex, and the hypothalamus which controls the pituitary gland and autonomic nervous system. The rest of the forebrain is made up of a number of inter-connected structures that include the basal ganglia consisting of the caudate nucleus, putamen, globus pallidus and substantia nigra. In addition, the limbic system, some of which lies nestled under the cerebral cortex, includes the cingulate gyrus, hippocampus, fornix, amygdala and hypothalamus. Finally, the most recent striking feature of the human brain is the cerebral cortex with its distinctive array of ridges (gyri) and fissures (sulci). The cerebral cortex has four main lobes (the occipital, parietal, temporal and frontal) that are involved in a wide range of higher cognitive functions that make us distinctly human. The two cerebral hemispheres are also joined by a huge fibre bundle called the corpus callosum.

GO ONLINE

TEST YOUR UNDERSTANDING OF THIS CHAPTER AND VISIT HTTPS://STUDY.SAGEPUB.COM/WICKENS TO ACCESS INTERACTIVE 'DRAG AND DROP' LABELLING ACTIVITIES AND A FLASHCARD GLOSSARY.

MULTIPLE CHOICE QUESTIONS

Answer the questions below to test your understanding of this chapter's Learning Objectives. You'll find the answers at the end of the chapter.

1. What philosopher/scientist is famously credited with introducing the concept of 'the reflex' as a means of explaining the neural control of certain behaviours?

   a. Galen
   b. Descartes
   c. Cajal
   d. Henry Dale

2. What part of the neuron transmits the electrical flow of nerve impulse?

   a. dendrite
   b. cell body (soma)
   c. axon
   d. the synapse

3. The reason why there is a sudden shift in the electrical potential of the neuron (from about −70mV to about +50mV) in the first millisecond of an action potential is due to the influx of what ion into the cell?

   a. calcium
   b. chloride
   c. potassium
   d. sodium

4. Which of the following is not a neurotransmitter in the CNS?

   a. acetylcholine
   b. cortisol
   c. dopamine
   d. serotonin

5. The central nervous systems consists of the:

    a. brain only
    b. brain and spinal cord
    c. brain, spinal cord and autonomic nervous system
    d. brain, spinal cord, autonomic nervous system and somatic nervous system

6. The hypothalamus is found in what major region of the brain?

    a. the limbic system
    b. the brain stem
    c. the striatum
    d. the occipital lobes

FURTHER READING

Blumenfeld, H. (2011). *Neuroanatomy through clinical cases.* Sinauer.
A comprehensive textbook which uses clinical examples to help students learn more about the neuroanatomy and behavioural functions of the brain.

Carlson, N. R. (2016). *Physiology of behavior.* Allyn and Bacon. First published in 1977 and now in its 12th edition.
A classic textbook that provides an excellent introduction to biological psychology.

Clark, D. L., Boutros, N. N., & Mendez, M. F. (2018). *The brain and behavior: An introduction to behavioral neuroanatomy.* Cambridge University Press.
A good introduction to neuroanatomy for first-time students, which also relates brain structure to behaviour.

Diamond, M. C., Scheibel, A. B., & Elson, L. M. (2000). *The human brain colouring book.* HarperCollins.
This book provides a practical means of learning about the structure and function of the brain through a 'colouring-in' of its illustrations. It's very useful for students who find the various parts of the brain difficult to visualize.

Garrett, B. (2015). *Biological psychology.* SAGE.
This has become one of the author's favourite textbooks with its high-quality artwork and well-written text.

Kandel, E., Schwartz, J., Jessell, T., Siegelbaum, S., & Hudspeth, A. J. (Eds.). (2012). *Principles of neural science.* McGraw-Hill.
It has been said this book should be mandatory for someone who wants to become a neuroscientist. If you read its 1706 pages then I think you will have passed the apprenticeship!

Kolb, B., Whishaw, I. Q., & Campbell Tesky, G. (2019). *An introduction to brain and behavior.* Worth.
Another excellent textbook covering brain and behaviour, with a greater emphasis on clinical neuropsychology than most others.

Pinel, J. P., & Barnes, S. (2017). *Biopsychology.* Allyn and Bacon.
An informative textbook on biopsychology which is nicely illustrated and clearly written. Now in its 10th edition.

Wickens, A. P. (2015). *A history of the brain: From stone age surgery to modern neuroscience.* *Psychology Press. An introduction to the history of neuroscience from antiquity to the present day.*

Wickens, A. P. (2019). *Key thinkers in neuroscience.* Routledge. *This book provides insight into the life and work of some 46 eminent brain scientists.*

THE VISUAL SYSTEM

2

LEARNING OBJECTIVES

After reading this chapter you should be able to:

- Describe the anatomical structure of the eye and retina.

- Depict the neural pathways from the retina to the visual cortex.

- Understand the concept of receptive fields.

- Explain how the cells of the visual cortex encode orientation, form and depth.

- Elucidate the theories of colour vision.

- Specify the types of visual processing undertaken by the parietal and temporal lobes.

- Characterize visual disorders such as agnosia and Bálint's syndrome.

- Appreciate the perplexing nature of the binding problem.

GO ONLINE

Test your understanding of this chapter and visit **https://study.sagepub.com/wickens** to access interactive 'Drag and Drop' labelling activities and a flashcard glossary.

INTRODUCTION

Most people would agree that vision, or rather the ability of the eyes to detect changes in patterns of light, is our most important sense. Arguably, vision, more than any other sense, provides us with our most detailed information regarding the world beyond our body surface. Consider for one moment what our visual system can do: we are able to detect shapes, follow movement, differentiate colours and judge distances – we can focus on nearby objects one second and see far into the distance the next – and if an object should unexpectedly appear in the corner of our eye, then we can turn our gaze towards it in a fraction of a second.

These skills are so effortless and reliable that it is tempting to think, especially in this age of cinematic films and television, that our eyes and brain are providing us with a faithful recording of the visual world. After all, 'seeing is believing'. However, our visual system is much more sophisticated than this – not least because we are constantly trying to interpret what we see. Unlike a camera which simply records a visual scene, our brain is continually striving to make sense of the infinite variety of images it is processing. Because of this, what we actually *perceive* is different from what the eyes *see*. This means what we perceive is a construction of reality manufactured by the brain. This can been seen, for example, if we look at Figure 2.1. In reality, the picture is no more than an assortment of five simple curved and straight lines, but once our brains find a meaning to the picture, we cannot help but perceive it in a different way.

Clearly our ability to process visual information is extremely complex, and it is often reported that about half of our cortex is devoted to visual analysis and perception. Although the visual system has been studied more than any other sensory system, the question of how the brain processes visual information, and constructs meaningful images from it, still remains one of the great challenges for modern biopsychology (see also Trenholm & Krishnaswamy, 2020).

Figure 2.1   A jumble of lines – until you realize that there is a picture there. But what is it?

(See the answer at the bottom of the page.[1])

WHAT IS LIGHT?

The stimulus for activating the visual system is light, which is a form of electromagnetic radiation generated by the oscillation of photons, that carry energy whilst having zero mass. Photons also act simultaneously as a wave and a particle. There are many forms of electromagnetic radiation, including gamma rays, ultraviolet light and radio waves, and all move at the speed of light, i.e.186,000 miles per second. Indeed, one might wonder why something travelling this fast does not hurt us! But what distinguishes each form of electromagnetic radiation is its wavelength – and light is no exception. In fact, light is simply a narrow band of the electromagnetic spectrum that has a wavelength ranging from about 380 to 760 nanometres (nm) (a nanometre is one billionth of a meter). Put another way, our visual system detects only a very small portion of the electromagnetic spectrum surrounding us.

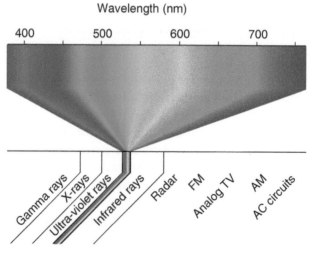

Figure 2.2   The electromagnetic spectrum
Source: Garrett and Hough (2018)

The two most important qualities we perceive from light are its colour and brightness. Colour is produced by the length of the light's wavelength. For example, the shortest wavelength detectable by the human eye is around 380 nm and this produces the

---

[1]Back view of a washerwoman showing her posterior and the soles of her shoes along with her bucket.

sensation of violet. As the length of the light waves increases the colour changes, approximating to violet, blue, green, yellow, and then red. Interestingly, other animals may be sensitive to different parts of the visual spectrum. Bumblebees and some birds, for example, can respond to much shorter violet wavelengths, whereas snakes can detect the longer infrared wavelengths. The brightness of a colour, however, is not related to its wavelength, but instead to the amplitude, or height, of its oscillation, which is due to the density of photons in the wave. Thus the more photons in the wave, the brighter the light (or colour) will appear to be.

Although we can detect white light, which is the complete mixture of all of the wavelengths of the visible spectrum, most of the time we see coloured things that are produced by objects or things that are reflecting a wide range of different wavelengths. In fact, we only see an object if the light striking its surface is partially absorbed, so that some of it is reflected back to us. If an object was to absorb all light hitting its surface it would appear to be black, and if the same object reflected all light, it would appear as a mirror surface of the light source. Therefore, it is the patterns of reflection and absorption, along with the many wavelengths they create, that allow us to see the shapes and surfaces of objects.

THE STRUCTURE OF THE EYE

The eye is the organ for sight whose main function is to detect changes in light wavelength and intensity, and transmit this information to the brain via the optic nerves. To a degree, the human eye can be likened to an old-fashioned camera since both are basically darkened chambers with a small aperture at the front to let in light, along with a focusing mechanism and a plate to receive the projected image at the back. In the case of a camera it is the photographic film which records the image, and with the eye it is the photoreceptors located at the back of the retina that do the same. Unlike the camera, however, the eye's photoreceptors transduce light into neural input so it can be processed by the brain.

If an eye was removed from its socket you would find it has a spherical shape, and for the most part is covered in a tough white tissue called the sclera, which we sometimes see as the 'the whites of our eyes'. The sclera does not completely cover the frontal surface, however, and it has a small round window called the cornea that enables light to enter the eye. The cornea acts as a simple fixed lens that gathers light and gives the eye some of its focusing power. Once light has passed through this transparent layer, it travels through the aqueous humour (aqueous means 'watery') to reach the pupil. The pupil is an aperture or gap that regulates the amount of light entering the next chamber of the eye, and its size is controlled by a ring of muscles called the iris, which also gives the eye its blue, green or brown colour. The iris is governed by the autonomic nervous system and can act in several ways: it not only enlarges the pupil if one moves from bright light into darkness (its diameter can change from 2- to 8 mm in this situation), but dilation can also occur during an arousing or threatening event. Behind the pupil is the lens, which brings visual images into sharp focus by acting as a fine adjustment to the cornea. This process, known as accommodation, is controlled by the cillary muscles that act to change the curvature of the lens – either by 'bending' it more, enabling vision of nearby objects, or by making it 'flatter', allowing vision of distant objects. After the lens, light passes through a clear gelatinous substance called the vitreous humour (vitreous means 'glassy') that helps maintain the shape of the eye, before it reaches the retina.

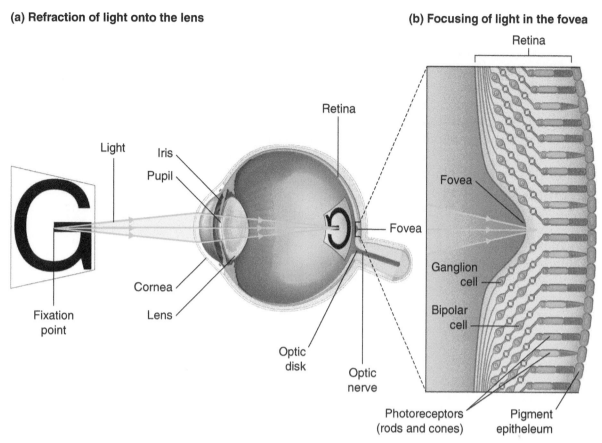

(a) Refraction of light onto the lens

(b) Focusing of light in the fovea

Figure 2.3   The structure of a human eye

Source: Garrett and Hough (2018), modified from Figure 26-1 in Kandel, E. R., Schwartz, J. H., Jessell, T. M., Siegelbaum, S. A., Hudspeth, A. J., & Mack, S. (2012). *Principles of neural science* (5th ed.).

KEY TERMS: *cornea, pupil, lens, cillary muscles, retina*

THE STRUCTURE OF THE RETINA

The neural processing of visual input begins with photoreceptors composed of rods and **cones** located at the back of the retina (see Figure 2.4). There are about 120 million rods and 6 million cones in each human retina, which are distributed differently, with rods located mainly in the periphery and cones in the central **fovea**. The rods and cones also deal with different types of light. The rods work most effectively in dim light and are mainly used for vision in dark conditions. This is why, for example, in order to see the dimmest lights such as faint stars in the sky, we often turn our heads slightly to one side so the light rays fall in part of the retina containing the rods. In contrast, the cones function best in bright light and provide us with vision of high acuity which allows us to see fine detail along with colour. Thus, where there are good lighting conditions, the eye focuses light onto our fovea where the cones are concentrated (Lamb, 2015).

Although the retina is only about 250 micrometers thick (about the size of a razor blade edge) it has several layers of cells (see Hoon et al., 2014). The rods and cones are located at the back of the retina and light has to pass through the overlying cells to reach them. This arrangement may appear to be odd as one might expect the overlying cells to interfere with the projection of the light's rays, but it seems that no visual disturbance occurs. The rods and cones contain special chemicals called photopigments (or opsin type proteins) that absorb light and transduce it into neural information. This is passed to the next layer of **bipolar cells** (so called because they have one axon and one dendrite). There are two types of bipolar cell: those which become depolarized, or increase activity, to visual information, and those that become hyperpolarized (i.e. they decrease activity) in response to input. In turn, the bipolar cells project to the **ganglion cells** whose cell bodies in the outer layer of the retina form axons making up the optic nerve that goes to the brain. The retina also contains horizontal cells that project laterally (i.e. sideways) which interconnect the photoreceptors; and various types of amacrine cell linking the bipolar and ganglion cells in much the same way. Although the function of these lateral cells is not fully understood, they are involved in modifying or inhibiting

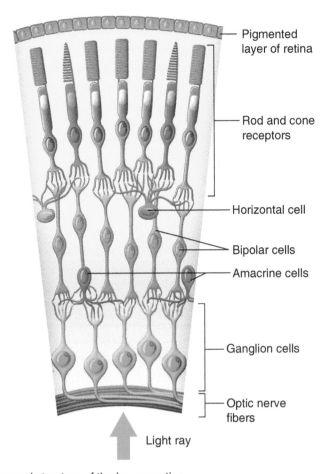

Figure 2.4   The neural structure of the human retina

Source: Garrett and Hough (2021), adapted from Dowling, J. E., & Boycott, B. B. (1966). Organization of the primate retina. *Proceedings of the Royal Society of London B*, 166, Fig. 23 on p. 104. Copyright 1966 by the Royal Society.

visual information reaching the ganglion cells, which is important in the creation of their receptive fields (see later). Thus, a considerable amount of neural processing takes place at the retina before reaching the optic nerve (Masland, 2001).

There are approximately 800,000 axons in each optic nerve, and as we have seen, over 120 million photoreceptors (rods and cones) in the retina. This means that a convergence of neural input takes place between the photoreceptors and each ganglion cell. In fact, the degree of convergence depends upon the location of the photoreceptor in the retina. In the periphery, several hundred photoreceptors (rods) may converge onto a single ganglion cell, but this figure is far less towards the centre of the retina where the cones are found. For example, a foveal ganglion cell may receive input from just one or two cones. This relationship helps explain the better acuity of foveal vision compared to peripheral rod vision. It is also relevant to note that because large numbers of rods feed into a single ganglion cell, all this 'extra' stimulation means that it is more likely to fire. This helps explain why rods are better at detecting changes in dim light.

KEY TERMS: *rods, cones, fovea, bipolar cells, ganglion cells*

Table 2.1   Summary of the response characteristics of the rods and cone systems.

	Rod System	**Cone System**
Function	Functions best in dim light, poorly or not at all in bright light	Functions best in bright light, poorly or not at all in dim light
	Detail vision is poor	Detail vision is good
	Does not distinguish colours	Subset distinguishes among colours
Location	Mostly in periphery of retina	Mostly in fovea and surrounding area
Receptive field	Large, due to convergence on ganglion cells; contributes to light sensitivity	Small, with one or a few cones converging on a single ganglion cell; contributes to detail vision

Source: Garrett and Hough (2018)

THE VISUAL PATHWAYS TO THE BRAIN

The axons of the ganglion cells form the optic nerve which leaves the retina at the blind spot, located just to the nasal side of the fovea. As the name suggests, an object focused in this area of the retina is not visible – although we are normally never aware of any visual loss since our eyes are continually moving and focusing objects on larger parts of the retina. The optic nerve transverses the lower surfaces of the brain until it reaches a point close to the pituitary stalk. Here, the two optic nerves converge to form the **optic chiasm** where some, but not all, of the axons pass to the opposite of side of the brain (see Figure 2.5). To be more precise: the axons arising from the nasal or nose side of the retina, which includes most of the fovea, cross to the opposite (contralateral) side of the brain, while the fibres from the outer or temporal side of the retina continue on the same (ipsilateral) side. Although all axons pass straight through the optic chiasma, the fibres that leave are referred to as the optic tract, each of which then ascends into the brain where they terminate in two peanut-sized clusters of neurons in the ventral part of the thalamus called the **lateral geniculate nucleus**. These nuclei then relay information via the **optic radiations** to the primary **visual cortex**, sometimes called the striate cortex because of its striped appearance, located in the cortical occipital lobes. It is also important to note that not all visual input from the eyes reaches the lateral geniculate nucleus since some of the optic nerve branches away before reaching the thalamus. This includes pathways to the **suprachiasmatic nucleus** (involved in circadian rhythms), the pretectum (pupillary reflexes) and the superior colliculus (saccadic eye movements).

KEY TERMS: *optic chiasma, lateral geniculate nucleus, optic radiations, visual cortex*

Each of the two lateral geniculate nuclei (the word *geniculate* means 'bent like a knee') contains six layers of cells and they receive both crossed (contralateral) and

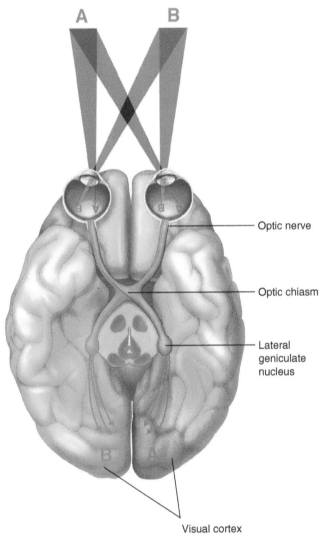

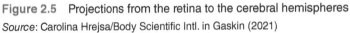

Figure 2.5   Projections from the retina to the cerebral hemispheres
Source: Carolina Hrejsa/Body Scientific Intl. in Gaskin (2021)

uncrossed (ipsilateral) input. At this stage, however, the visual information is segregated with each cell layer receiving input from a single eye. To make matters more complex, the top four layers of the lateral geniculate nucleus are composed of small neurons known as parvocellular cells which receive input predominantly from the fovea, and the last two layers contain bigger neurons known as magnocellular cells which get their input from the peripheral part of the retina (these cells will be discussed in more detail later). In addition, the lateral geniculate nucleus receives significant feedback from the primary visual cortex.

The axons leaving the geniculate nucleus form the optic radiations that project to the primary visual cortex – the primary region of the brain that receives, integrates and processes information from the eyes. The fact that the nasal optic nerve fibres have crossed at the optic chiasm, whilst the more temporal ones have continued on ipsilaterally, means that each visual cortex actually receives the same visual field from both eyes – and it is at this point the first preliminary analysis of the complete visual image takes place (see Figure 2.5). In the human brain, the primary visual cortex is about 1.5 mm in thickness, and composed of six main layers (similar to the rest of the cerebral cortex). The axons from the lateral geniculate nucleus terminate in its fourth layer, which is divided into sub lamina, one of which is called the stria of Gennari, which is a band of myelinated axons visible to the naked eye as a white strip and helps give the visual cortex its striated appearance. From here, neurons project to other layers directly above, or below, in the same column of the visual cortex.

The primary visual cortex is organized topographically – that is, if two adjacent points are stimulated on the retina, causing different ganglion cells to fire, then adjacent areas in the visual cortex will also be activated. In effect, this means that the layout of the photoreceptors in the retina is mapped out in the visual cortex – albeit in a peculiar way. The organization of the visual cortex is also heavily biased towards processing foveal information, although the fovea forms only a small part of the retina. Also, because axons from the nasal halves of each retina cross to the other side of the brain, each hemisphere receives information from the opposite side of the visual scene. In other words, if a person looks straight ahead, the left visual cortex receives information from the right visual field of each eye (A), and the right visual cortex obtains input from the left visual field of each eye (B). Thus, although each visual cortex receives input from *both* eyes, the left visual cortex only processes information from the right side of its world, and the right visual cortex only processes information from the left side of its world. To fully appreciate this arrangement, you will need to carefully study Figure 2.5.

After the visual cortex has undertaken the first stages of encoding, the information is passed to surrounding areas of the visual cortex, sometimes referred to as extrastriate areas. There are at least 30 other areas scattered through the cortex involved in higher visual processing which include largely separate pathways for colour and movement, along with specialized areas involved in reading, object recognition and spatial awareness. Although visual information can take a number of routes through the brain, including intra-hemispheric communication via the corpus callosum, two main pathways appear to be particularly important: one involving a ventral system coursing through the temporal lobe, and one involving a dorsal system passing through the parietal lobes. We will return to these pathways towards the end of the chapter.

KEY TERMS: *parvocellular cells, magnocellular cells, stria of Gennari, extrastriate cortex*

THE RECEPTIVE FIELDS OF RETINAL GANGLION CELLS

As we have seen, a retinal ganglion cell may receive converging information from a large number of rods, or maybe several cones. It follows, therefore, that a single ganglion cell will be sensitive to visual stimulation from a distinct small region of the retina where its cluster of photoreceptors are located. The part of the visual scene 'out there' detected by a group of photoreceptors that feed into a single ganglion cell is known as its **receptive field**. An examination of receptive fields has provided researchers with a powerful means of understanding how the visual system encodes information. To identify a ganglion cell's receptive field, however, is no easy task. First, a recording microelectrode is inserted into the optic nerve of an anaesthetized animal, close to a single ganglionic neuron, and then the eye is presented with a visual stimulus projected onto a screen facing the animal. The stimulus is moved around until the neuron (or rather electrode) picks up the neural activity of the visual input. This search may take hours, but once the receptive field is identified, its neural encoding can be mapped in fine detail.

Much of what we know about the receptive fields of retinal ganglion cells is due to the work of Stephen Kuffler at Johns Hopkins University, who pioneered this type of research in cats during the 1950s (e.g. Kuffler, 1953). One of Kuffler's most important discoveries was that ganglion cells were never 'silent'. Rather, they are continually generating action potentials with a background firing rate of around five impulses per second. But Kuffler was more interested in learning how ganglion cells respond to different types of stimuli, and to do this he explored their receptive fields with a fine spot of light. Using this technique, he found that each ganglion cell's receptive field was circular in shape and varied in size, with those in the fovea being small, and fields in the periphery being larger. He also found that ganglion cells either increased activity in response to visual stimulation or were inhibited by it.

However, Kuffler's most important discovery was that the receptive fields of ganglion cells actually contained both excitatory and inhibitory areas (see Figure 2.6) which were arranged in a centre-surround fashion. That is, the receptive field shape of ganglion cells consisted of a circular central area and an outer ring that surrounded it. Moreover, these areas responded with different types of neural activity to visual stimulation. For example, in some ganglion cells, a spot of light shone directly into the central region of its visual field greatly increased the background firing rate (an 'on' response), whereas light projected into its surround reduced it (an 'off' response). This was called a centre-on, surround-off ganglion cell. However, in other cells the effect was reversed, with illumination of the centre producing an 'off' response and stimulation of the surround an 'on' response. This was called a centre-off, surround-on ganglion cell.

When a light was shone over the whole receptive field, Kuffler found that the 'on' and 'off' responses tended to cancel each other out. The extent of this antagonistic effect depended on the relative proportions of the on-off regions that were stimulated. For example, if a spot of light was progressively made larger in the centre of an 'on'-centre receptive field, the firing rate of the cell increased until the centre was completely filled – at which point the response began to decline as the light encroached into the off-surround. As the surround became increasingly illuminated, however, it cancelled out the cell's

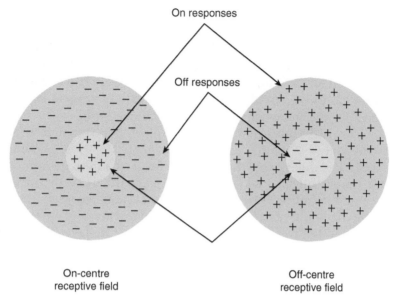

Figure 2.6   Retinal ganglion cell receptive fields showing the typical centre-surround arrangement
Source: Higgs et al. (2020)

on-response, returning it to its baseline level of firing. In other words, the ganglion cell shows a graded response to a light stimulus projecting on its receptive field.

According to some theorists, retinal ganglion cells can be divided into three categories: W-ganglion cells are excited by the rods and sensitive to movement; X-ganglion cells (which are the most common) have small receptive fields and encode colour with a sustained response; Y-ganglion cells respond to rapid eye movements and sudden changes in light intensity (Krüger, 1981). It should also be noted that a small number of retinal ganglion cells, despite being photosensitive, do not contribute to vision, but form the retinohypothalamic tract which governs circadian rhythms, or pass to areas in the brain stem involved in the pupillary light reflex.

KEY TERMS: *receptive field, centre-on, surround-off ganglion cell, centre-off, surround-on ganglion cell, antagonistic effect*

RECEPTIVE FIELDS IN THE VISUAL CORTEX

In the late 1950s and early 1960s, David Hubel and Tortsten Wiesel started to examine the receptive fields of neurons higher up in the visual system (see Hubel & Wiesel, 2005 for a historical overview of their research). More specifically they began by looking at the lateral geniculate nucleus and primary visual cortex. Using a similar procedure to that of Kuffler, they presented anaesthetized cats, who wore special contact lenses to keep their eyes open, with small spots of light, and then recorded the resultant changes in activity from single neurons. Their initial hope was that the receptive fields of brain cells would be similar to the circular on and off retinal ganglion cells identified by Kuffler. Although this proved to be true for the lateral geniculate nucleus, the small spots of light used by Kuffler were ineffective at stimulating neural activity in the visual cortex. In fact, it was only by accident when removing slides from their projection apparatus that they discovered a line passing over a particular location on the retina caused certain cortical cells to start firing. This led Hubel and Wiesel to discover that most cells in the visual cortex have elongated receptive fields which were particularly sensitive to the movement of edges (Barlow, 1982).

As mentioned, when Hubel and Wiesel examined the receptive fields of lateral geniculate neurons, they exhibited similar characteristics to those obtained from retinal ganglion cells. In other words, the receptive fields of all the neurons in the visual pathway from retina to thalamus were monocular and showed concentric on-off responses as found by Kuffler. But, when Hubel and Wiesel recorded from cells in the visual cortex, the shape and behaviour of the receptive fields were different. Beginning with neurons located in layer four of the visual cortex (the layer that receives input from the lateral geniculate nucleus), they found that maximal responses were produced by visual presentation of elongated bars or edges. Thus, cells in this layer of visual cortex showed an increase of activity when the stimulus presented to their receptive field was in the form of a straight line. However, for the cell to fire maximally, the stimulus had to be in a very precise location and orientation on the retina. In fact, this was because the receptive fields of cortical neurons were elongated (not concentric) although they still retained the antagonistic on-off regions. And, as might be expected, these brain cells only fired maximally when the line presented to the retina was orientated in such a way that it fell within the 'on' region of the receptive field. Hubel and Wiesel called these simple cells.

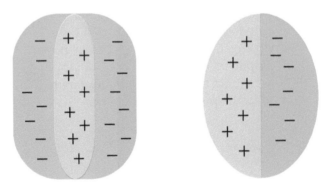

Figure 2.7   The receptive fields of cortical simple cells
Source: Higgs et al. (2020)

Why do simple cells in the visual cortex have oblong-shaped receptive fields? The answer lies with the way they receive their neural input from the lateral geniculate nucleus (see Figure 2.8). In short, each simple cell obtains information from an array of lateral geniculate neurons, which are 'wired' in such a way to receive input from oblong-shaped groups of retinal ganglion cells. Consequently, it follows that a line falling on the retina may stimulate many photoreceptors, yet only activate (or inhibit) a single cell in the cortex. Thus, visual processing is hierarchical with a convergence of input from basal arrays or collective groups of cells feeding into 'higher' individual neurons (Snowden et al., 2012).

KEY TERM: *simple cells*

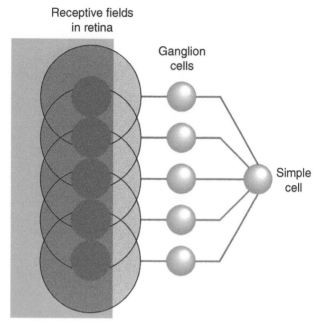

Figure 2.8   Hubel and Wiesel's explanation for responses of simple cells
Source: Garrett and Hough (2021)

COMPLEX AND HYPERCOMPLEX CELLS

Simple cells are not alone. When Hubel and Wiesel moved their recording electrodes up and down other layers of the visual cortex, they discovered two other types of cell which they called complex and hypercomplex. Complex cells are actually the most common type of cell in the primary visual cortex, and found mainly in layers two and three (which both receive input from layer four). Although complex cells have receptive fields which are orientation selective, they do not respond to stationary stimuli as do simple cells. Hence, to produce a sustained response, the stimulus must be moving across the receptive field. Some complex cells fire maximally when a line stimulus is moved into the receptive field from a particular direction, whereas others respond to line movement from any direction. Complex cells also have larger receptive fields than simple cells, and this combined with their motion selectivity means that a response is elicited over a vast range of stimulus positions. Hubel and Wiesel also suggested that complex cells are hierarchically organized from arrays of simple cells (Martinez & Alonso, 2003).

Hypercomplex cells have similar properties to complex cells, except they have an extra inhibitory area at the ends of their receptive field. This means that they respond best when the line is of a specific orientation *and* a certain length. In fact, if the line is too long and extends into the inhibitory part of the receptive field, then the firing rate of the cell declines (and for this reason they are sometimes called 'end-stopped'). Some hypercomplex cells also respond maximally to two line segments meeting at a particular point, suggesting that they may also act as angle detectors. However, it should be noted that the term 'hypercomplex' has now fallen out of fashion, as it is known that some simple and complex cells can also be end-stopped. Consequently, hypercomplex cells are now generally regarded as a subtype of simple and complex cells, with researchers preferring the terms 'simple end-stopped cells' and 'complex end-stopped cells' to describe their functional properties.

KEY TERMS: *complex cells, hypercomplex cells*

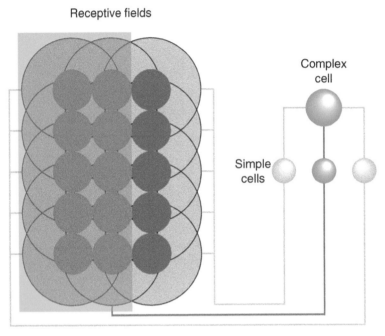

Figure 2.9   Hubel and Wiesel's explanation for responses of complex cells
Source: Garrett and Hough (2021)

THE ARRANGEMENT OF CELLS IN THE PRIMARY VISUAL CORTEX

Hubel and Wiesel's work also showed that the visual cortex is comprised of columns containing cells which all share similar properties. The idea that the cerebral cortex processed information in columns in which connections 'up and down' were more important that those going from 'side to side' had first been made by Vernon Mountcastle in the mid-1950s. However, Hubel and Wiesel's research gave the idea much greater support. For example, if a microelectrode is lowered into the cortex, perpendicular to its surface, not only will one find simple, complex and hypercomplex cells, but the central direction of their respective receptive fields will also be the same. In other words, all neurons in a particular column respond maximally to the same line orientation. Thus, if a simple cell is found to respond best to a 90° vertical line, the complex and hypercomplex cells in the same column will do likewise. These units were termed orientation columns.

As the recording electrode is moved sideways to the adjacent columns, another feature of the visual cortex is observed. In short, the preferred axis of orientation of the lines rotates in a clockwise or anticlockwise manner with each 0.05 millimetres of sideways movement producing a rotation of 10°. In other words, if the cells in one column are all 'tuned' to vertical stimuli, the cells in the next column will respond best to lines 10° from the vertical, and so on (although occasionally there are discontinuous jumps). A transverse of a 1 mm length of cortex is generally sufficient to detect every possible line orientation across 180°. And, although the cells in each 180° unit respond to many different receptor field orientations, all derive from the same part of the retina, showing that each 'block' of orientation cells is involved with processing visual information from the same part of the world (Hubel, 1995).

The columns of the visual cortex are also organized on the basis of ocular dominance or eye preference. Although we have two eyes, we only have one unified visual world. Hence, a convergence of retinal input must take place somewhere in the visual system. The first place where this occurs is the visual cortex. Indeed, it has been found that many cells in the visual cortex have binocular receptive fields (i.e. they respond to input from both eyes), although many show a preference for one of the eyes (i.e. they will fire more strongly when the 'favoured' eye is stimulated). The organization of ocular dominance in the visual cortex follows a pattern similar to that for orientation. Thus, if a microelectrode in lowered into a cortical column, all of its cells will respond best to input from the same eye. And as the electrode is moved laterally, the right-eye and left-eye preference alternates, with each band alternating every millimetre or so. When ocular dominance columns and orientation columns are combined, they form something that Hubel and Wiesel called a hypercolumn (Ts'o et al., 2009) (see Figure 2.10). A hypercolumn is essentially a 1 mm block of primary visual cortex containing both the ocular dominance and orientation columns for a particular region in visual space. In fact, this view of the visual cortex persisted into the 1980s when researchers discovered that there was another component to be incorporated into this unit – namely cytochrome blobs concerned with colour processing. These will be discussed later.

One might ask what the function is of the primary visual cortex which represents the first stage of higher visual processing in the brain. Although damage to the visual cortex will cause blindness in the part of the visual field (the area of blindness is called a scotoma), it is unlikely that our conscious perception of the visual world occurs in this part of the brain. Hubel and Wiesel's work suggests that the cells of the visual cortex simply act as feature detectors that respond to specific elements of the visual scene such as lines, edges, angles, motion and (as we will see) colour. Their research also indicates this raw visual input is analysed in a hierarchical fashion with increasing levels of complexity (e.g. simple, complex and hypercomplex cells). Presumably, this hierarchical processing continues as the visual information is analysed beyond the primary visual cortex (Risenhuber & Poggio, 1999).

KEY TERMS: *orientation columns, ocular dominance, hypercoloumn, scotoma*

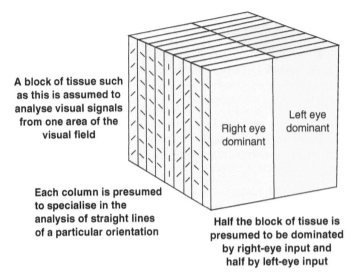

A block of tissue such as this is assumed to analyse visual signals from one area of the visual field

Right eye dominant

Left eye dominant

Each column is presumed to specialise in the analysis of straight lines of a particular orientation

Half the block of tissue is presumed to be dominated by right-eye input and half by left-eye input

Figure 2.10   A hypercolumn showing orientation and ocular dominance components
Source: Wickens (2009)

KEY THINKERS 2.1

DAVID HUBEL AND TORSTEN WIESEL

David Hubel was a Canadian who studied medicine after graduating in mathematics and physics. Taking up a residency in neurology in Montreal, he became interested in vision. After being drafted into the army, Hubel worked in an institute where he was given the task of recording from single cortical cells in the visual cortex of anaesthetized cats. He soon realized this would require him to develop a new type of tungsten electrode – a task that took him several months to achieve.

Torsten Wiesel was born in Sweden to a psychiatrist father. It was less than idyllic since the family lived in the grounds of the largest mental asylum in Scandinavia. Wiesel would later recall times when he could hear agonized screams from the nearby buildings housing the severely ill. After studying medicine, in 1955, Wiesel joined the laboratory of Stephen Kuffler to examine the receptive field properties of retinal ganglion cells. It was around this time that Hubel and Wiesel first met.

In 1958 Hubel also joined Kuffler's laboratory, thereby beginning one of the great collaborations in the history of neuroscience. Although keen to map the receptive fields of cells beyond the retina, Hubel and Wiesel experienced problems obtaining responses from the neurons of the visual cortex. That was until they made a lucky discovery, when a brisk discharge of a neuron was caused by repositioning a glass slide into a projector. At once Hubel and Wiesel realized the neuron was reacting to an edge or line. Those findings were published in 1959, and followed by the discovery of *simple* and *complex* cells (1962) and *hypercomplex* cells (1965). This also soon led Hubel and Wiesel to identify the presence of columns for *orientation* and *ocular dominance*. Another of their interests concerned the early development of the visual system, and the ages at which the visual cortex was modifiable through experience. Using animals with one eye sealed from an early age, they found this significantly altered the functioning of the binocular columns in the visual cortex that received input from the sighted eye. In some cases this abolished all later cellular activity from the deprived eye. However, this only occurred during early development. If the eye was sealed in adult animals, no long-term effects on vision or neural functioning were found.

Hubel and Wiesel's work appeared to show that visual processing is hierarchical. For example, the receptive fields of many retinal ganglion cells inputted onto a simple cell with a preferred line orientation. In turn, multiple aggregations of simple cells could input onto a complex cell. Presumably, this hierarchical processing continues as information is analysed beyond the visual cortex. Indeed, there is evidence to support this theory, with neurons in the temporal lobes responding to specific objects including faces. This raises an intriguing question: do we have a cell at the top of the hierarchy for everything in our visual world – such as a 'grandmother cell'? The answer to this perplexing question is probably no, and most researchers now accept that some sort of population encoding must take place instead.

Hubel and Wiesel's work was recognized in 1981 with the Nobel Prize. Sadly, by then the two men had stopped working together – a split Hubel felt was due to the increasing pressure to undertake administration and teaching. But both men continued working on vision. In 1983 Wiesel joined Rockefeller University, New York, to head its section on Neurobiology. He later became the president of the university and held this post until his retirement in 1998. Hubel remained at Harvard for the rest of his life, and in 1988 became president of the Society for Neuroscience.

AN ALTERNATIVE THEORY: POPULATION ENCODING

Although Hubel and Wiesel's hierarchical theory of visual processing lends itself to the idea that as one progresses from the retina, lateral geniculate nucleus and multiple areas of occipital cortex, the visual image becomes more elaborate and fully formed – perhaps even leading to a cell somewhere at the top of the hierarchy which is responsible for detecting a fully formed image (i.e. a so-called 'grandmother cell') – few believe this is actually the case (see Bowers, 2017). Not surprisingly, this has led researchers to consider alternative possibilities. The more likely explanation is that every sensory event elicits activity in a broad population of cells that is distributed across several cortical areas. Indeed, it has been found in experiments that even simple sensory stimuli can activate large populations of neurons. Thus, it is widely believed that visual information must be encoded in the spatiotemporal profile of large numbers of collective neuronal responses known as a population code. How these neurons function together to represent the sensory environment has now become a major question in neuroscience. A number of proposals have been made, and recent advances in multi-neuronal recording have enabled researchers to test the predictions of several population-coding theories. These include explanations involving population vectors, linear decoders and Bayesian inference (see Tanabe, 2013 for further information). Although it is almost certainly the case that information processing in the visual cortices, and for other senses, is mediated by the coordinated activity of large populations of neurons, the computational rules used by neurons to process information remain poorly understood. Clearly, there is still much to learn about the sensory encoding of neurons and how this information is integrated and recognized.

KEY TERMS: *population code*

INTRODUCTION TO COLOUR VISION

The world would be a lot less interesting without our rich experience of colour. It has been reported that we can perceive some 150 different basic hues or colours, with 100–150 levels of saturation (intensity) and 100–200 levels of lightness, which suggests that a human being can differentiate up to 4.5 million colours (Kernell, 2016). Remarkably, all these colours derive from a small part of the electromagnetic spectrum – from light wavelengths of around 400 nm which produces the sensation of blue, through to about 550 nm causing the sensation of green-yellow, and finally to around 650 nm that enables the detection of red. It is also fascinating to note that electromagnetic waves actually do not reflect or contain colour (they are simply waves of electricity and magnetism). Consequently, attributing colour to objects is ultimately produced by the visual system. And so as you look at the colours on this page you might like to contemplate that your brain is actually inventing them!

The first stage in colour vision begins with the cones in the retina (Solomon & Lennie, 2007). In fact there are three types of cone: the first absorbs light maximally in short wavelengths around 445 nm (blue); the second absorbs light at medium wavelengths at around 535 nm (green); and the third absorbs light at long wavelengths of about 570 nm (red). Despite this, cones show considerable overlap in their detection of wavelengths. For example, light in wavelengths of 600 nm will induce the greatest response from the red cones, but also produce a weaker reaction in the green ones. Thus, red-sensitive cones do not respond exclusively to long wavelengths of light – they just respond better – and the same principle holds for the other two cones (Baylor, 1987).

We are able to detect light and colour because the electromagnetic wave reaching our eyes is transduced by the cones into neural impulses by using photopigments, which are specialized unstable molecules embedded in their membrane that undergo a chemical change when they absorb light (see Luo et al., 2008). Or more precisely, the pigment changes its conformation or shape when it absorbs a photon. The rods manage this feat by using a photopigment called rhodopsin which is composed of two interconnected molecules: opsin (a protein) and retinal (derived from Vitamin A) that forms part of a **G-protein** coupled membrane receptor. The three types of cone photoreceptor are similar except their opsins are slightly different. Remarkably, each photoreceptor may have as many as 10 million photopigment molecules – and when exposed to light, the opsin and retinal molecules split, causing a series of chemical reactions, leading to a change

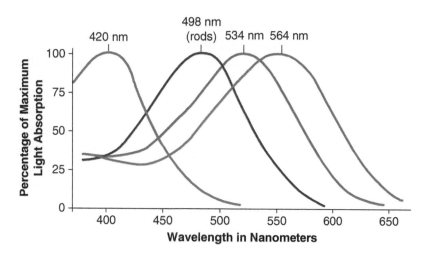

Figure 2.11   The relative absorption of light of various wavelengths by the rods and cones

Source: Garrett and Hough (2021), adapted from Bowmaker & Dartnall (1980). Visual pigments of rods and cones in human retina. *Journal of Physiology*, 298, 501–511. Copyright 1980, with permission from John Wiley & Sons, Inc.

in the cell's rate of firing. There are three forms of opsin found in cones, with each one maximally sensitive to a different wavelength of light or colour.

KEY TERMS: *rhodopsin, opsins*

THEORIES OF COLOUR VISION

The idea that our eyes contain receptors for different light wavelengths was first made by the British physicist Thomas Young in 1802. This was long before the visual characteristics of cones were discovered (Brown & Wald, 1964). Young made his claim on the basis that any colour can be produced, including white, if three different types of light are mixed in the right proportion – providing the wavelengths are separated far enough from each other. This led Young to propose that the retina must also contain three different receptors for colour, with their sensitivities being for blue, green and red (the so-called 'primary colours'). Young's theory was supported by Hermann von Helmholtz in the 1850s, and became known as the Young-Helmholtz or trichromatic theory of colour vision.

One problem with the trichromatic theory, however, was that it could not explain the effect of negative after-images. For example, if we stare at a red square against a white background for a few minutes, and then look at a blank card, we will see a green after-image of the square. Alternatively, staring at a blue square produces a yellow after-image, and staring at a black one produces a white effect. A similar type of relationship also exists for colour blindness. For example, the most common types of colour blindness are for red-green, and blue-yellow (there is no such thing as red-blue or green-yellow blindness). This shows that red-green and blue-yellow are linked in a way that cannot be explained by the trichromatic theory.

In 1870, the German physiologist Ewald Hering proposed an alternative explanation. Although agreeing that the colour spectrum could be created by mixing three primary colours, Hering did not believe yellow was derived from a mixture of red and green as the trichromatic theory held, but that it was also a primary colour along with red, green and blue. With four primary colours instead of three, Hering saw that the visual system now only required two types of colour detector – one responding to red or green, and the other to blue or yellow. Because each type of detector was hypothesized to produce two different colour sensations that acted to oppose each other (red-green, yellow-blue, and black-white), the theory was called the opponent theory of colour vision.

KEY TERMS: *trichromatic theory, opponent theory*

WHAT THEORY IS CORRECT?

On first sight, there is evidence to support the trichromatic theory. Not only is it confirmed by colour-mixing experiments (since three primary colours can be mixed to produce other colours), but also, more importantly, we now know that there are three types of retinal cones which respond to the wavelengths of light corresponding to blue, green and red. These are, of course, the three primary colours predicted by the trichromatic theory.

However, things are not quite that simple. One difficulty with the trichromatic theory is the discovery of ganglion cells in the retina that respond in a way that is consistent with Hering's theory. That is, they increase their activity to one colour, and decrease it to another. These are called dual-opponent colour neurons of which there are two basic types: those that produce opposite responses to red and green, and those responding the same way to blue and yellow. For example, one type of cell is excited by the colour of red and inhibited by green (R+, G–) or vice versa (R–, G+). And the other type of cell is excited by the colour blue and inhibited by yellow (B+, Y–) or vice versa (B–, Y+). These are, of course, exactly the type of responses predicted by the opponent-process theory (De Valois & De Valois, 1988).

Like other retinal ganglion cells, opponent cells have concentric receptive fields – except in their case the centres and surrounds are colour sensitive. For example, an opponent cell might be excited by green and inhibited by red in the centre of its receptive field, with an opposite response in the surrounding ring. Similarly, a ganglion cell may show the same response to blue and yellow. There is also a third type of ganglion cell, linked to cones, but which only detects black and white. In fact, recent work suggests that these may be more common that the other two types of cone in the retina (Sabesan et al., 2016).

Hence, both the trichromatic and opponent theories appear to be correct. If this is the case then the fundamental problem becomes one of explaining how the three types of cone (red, green and blue) combine to form the two types of ganglionic opponent cell with their receptive fields corresponding to red-green and blue-yellow. Or put simply, where does yellow come from? The answer to this question, proposed by Hurvich and Jameson (1957), lies with the neural 'wiring' that connects the cones and the ganglion cells (see Figure 2.12). Indeed, assuming this is the case, then the red-green opponent cell is easy to explain as it must receive input from both the red and the green cones. Thus, if the input from the red cones was excitatory, and input from the green cones inhibitory, then this would explain the R+, G– opponent cell. Similarly, a reversed system could account for the R–, G+ opponent cell. But, using the same logic, how can the blue-yellow opponent cell be explained when there is no cone for yellow?

Hurvich and Jamison argued that the blue-yellow opponent cell receives input from three sources, i.e. the blue, green, and red receptors. In this scheme, the input to the blue part of the opponent cell is simple as there is a corresponding cone for blue. In contrast, the yellow part of the opponent cell is derived from both the red and green receptor input. That is, we see yellow not because we have a specific photoreceptor for yellow – but because it is created by inputs arriving from the red and green cones. Therefore, when we detect the light wavelength corresponding to yellow (which falls between the red and green bands) this stimulates both red and green cones equally, and it this dual activation that causes the yellow part of the yellow-blue ganglion cell to produce its excitation or inhibition.

In order for ganglion cells to show opponent red-green and blue-yellow responses, the 'wiring' of the neural pathways linking the cones with opponent ganglion neurons must take place in the retina. It is believed this function is served by the horizontal cells that connect the cones with the bipolar cells, or by the multi-branched connections of the bipolar cells that synapse with the ganglion cells. Despite this somewhat complex explanation, the trichromatic and opponent theories, even when combined in this way, still cannot account for all the phenomena of colour perception. One serious problem with both these theories is **colour constancy** – the fact that the perceived colour of an object remains much the same under very different lighting conditions (e.g. we see a white cat as white despite wearing sunglasses). This indicates the colours we perceive are not necessarily determined by the exact wavelengths reaching our eyes after all (Foster, 2011; Krantz, 2009).

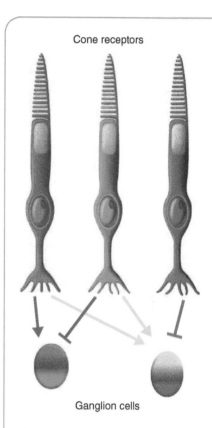

Cone receptors

Ganglion cells

Figure 2.12   Colour coding in the retina

Source: Garrett and Hough (2021), based on the findings of De Valois et al. (1966)

KEY TERMS: *dual-opponent colour neurons, colour constancy*

JOHN DALTON AND THE DISCOVERY OF COLOUR BLINDNESS

Despite coming from a poor Lake District family, John Dalton (1766–1844) became one of the great pioneers of modern physical science when he developed modern atomic theory – essentially the idea that matter is composed of small indestructible atoms with different sizes and masses, whose combination creates different chemicals and their reactions. However, Dalton also made contributions to many other subjects and gave the first account of colour blindness in 1794. It is said that he first realized he had a colour defect when he wore a bright scarlet robe to receive his PhD degree, thinking it was dark blue. Being a Quaker who always wore plain and unostentatious clothing, this was somewhat embarrassing! When Dalton began examining his own visual capabilities by viewing light passed through a prism, he discovered that while most people could distinguish six colours, he could see just two – blue/violet and yellow. Dalton's brother had the same affliction and he was to find a similar defect in 28 other people who were all male. Dalton believed his colour blindness was due to a blue colouring in the vitreous humour of his eyes, and specified that after his death they should be examined to prove his hypothesis. However, no blue colouringwas found.

We now know that most types of colour blindness are inherited and caused by a faulty gene that makes the photopigments in the cones. The most common type of colour blindness which occurs in about 8% of males and 0.6% of females, is where the person cannot distinguish between red and green. There are two forms of this deficit: deuteranopia, where the person lacks the green photopigment, and protanopia, where the red pigment is missing. In both cases, the person sees their world in shades of blue, yellow and grey. The reason why red-green colour blindness largely affects males is because the protan and deuta genes are located on the X chromosome that determines sex, of which men have one (XY) and women two (XX). Thus, women are rarely red-green blind because if one of their X chromosomes is defective, the other will compensate. This also means that red-green colour blindness is passed down from a colour-blind male through his daughters (who are normally unaffected) to his male grandchildren. The sons will be unaffected as they always receive his Y chromosome and not the defective X one. In fact, about 8% of women are carriers of these faulty genes.

There are other types of colour blindness although they are less common. These include tritanopia, where the retina lacks blue cones (here the person is unable to distinguish between blue and yellow), and achromatopia, where the person sees their world in much the same way as a black and white television picture. Tritanopia is not sex-linked as the defective gene occurs on chromosome 7 and so occurs equally in male and females. Tritanopia is found about once in every thousand people, and achromatopia once in every hundred thousand.

Returning to John Dalton, we know he suffered from a red-green colour defect – but was it deuteranopia or protanopia? In 1995, investigators from London and Oxford settled the issue (Hunt et al., 1995). They extracted DNA from Dalton's eyes which had been kept in the possession of the Manchester Literary and Philosophical Society, and discovered a faulty gene for the green pigment. Thus, Dalton was a deuteranope. He would not only have been gratified to learn that the answer to his visual defect had finally been solved some 150 years after his death, but it is also a quirk of fate that his atomic theory provides the chemical basis that made its analysis possible.

A CLOSER LOOK AT THE LATERAL GENICULATE NUCLEUS

As we have seen, the lateral geniculate nucleus, located in the thalamus, is the first higher forebrain region to receive information from the optic nerve. In humans, it consists of six layers of cells receiving input from one eye only that can be distinguished by their neural input and shape. From bottom to top, layers 1, 4 and 6 obtain axons from the nasal part of the contralateral eye, and layers 2, 3 and 5 get projections from the outer part of the ipsilateral eye. Although this arrangement is hard to visualize, it means that each lateral geniculate nucleus only processes information from the opposite side of the visual world. In addition, the upper four layers of the lateral geniculate nucleus contain small neurons called parvocellular cells, while the lower two layers have neurons called magnocellular cells.

The parvocellular cells pick up fine detail (i.e. they have high spatial resolution) and are sensitive to colour, with concentric receptive fields showing the same opponent red-green and blue-yellow responses as found with ganglion cells. In fact, about 80% of parvocellular cells show this response with the rest having no colour preference. In contrast, the magnocellular cells are colour blind but have receptive fields with directional specificity. Or put another way, unlike parvocellular cells which give a sustained response to a visual stimulus, magnocellular neurons respond rapidly but briefly to stimuli. In other words, parvocellular cells are better suited to analysing stationary objects, whereas magnocellular neurons respond best to movement. Interestingly, there is evidence to show that magnocellular cells are underdeveloped in many dyslexics who have difficulty reading (Stein, 2014).

This type of findings have been confirmed by examining the visual capabilities of monkeys after lesions of the lateral geniculate nucleus. For example, damage to the magnocellular layers has little effect on visual acuity or detecting colour, but impairs the monkey's ability to view moving stimuli. Damage to the parvocellular layers has little effect on motion perception, but impairs fine pattern vision and colour perception. This shows that parvocellular cells are essential for highly focused vision which enables detailed analysis of the shape, size and colour of objects to take place, whereas the magnocellular cells process information that analyses the movement of objects (Livingstone & Hubel, 1988). As we shall see, the segregation of parvocellular and magnocellular information is also maintained in the visual cortex and secondary visual areas.

Interestingly, the retina only provides about 20% of the total neural input to the lateral geniculate nucleus, with the greatest contribution being provided by the visual cortex, and to a lesser extent the brain stem including the pons, medulla and tectum. Presumably, the input from the cortex represents some sort of feedback mechanism that sharpens the visual image in some way, or perhaps blocks irrelevant information. A reciprocal pathway involved in this process passes back to the visual cortex (Briggs & Usray, 2011). It is also believed that the brain stem's input can 'turn off' the visual signal during eye movements – presumably so we do not see the world jump when our eyes move (Noda, 1975). This is known as saccadic suppression (Krekelberg, 2010).

KEY TERMS: *lateral geniculate nucleus, parvocellular cells, magnocellular cells*

COLOUR PROCESSING IN THE CORTEX

Although Hubel and Wiesel had established the importance of simple and complex cells for pattern recognition and movement, how the visual cortex processed colour was less clear. Interestingly, colour-sensitive cells in the upper layers of the visual cortex had been detected, but they were relatively rare and made up about 10% of all cells. Moreover, their location seemed to occur at random making it difficult to study them in a systematic way. However, in the late 1970s a way of identifying colour-processing cells was unexpectedly discovered when Wong-Riley (1979) stained the visual cortex with a mitochondrial enzyme called cytochrome oxidase. Mitochondria are tiny organelles inside the cells that produce energy – and it was found that when they were stained in the brain, darkened clusters of cells called **cytochrome blobs** appeared in the visual cortex. In fact, these emerged as peg-like dark columns that gave the visual cortex a polka-dot appearance. Closer inspection showed that they were about 0.2 mm in diameter and passed through all layers of the visual cortex except layer 4. But, importantly, it was found that the cells in these blobs were sensitive to colour. Indeed, their responses were similar to those obtained from the parvocellular cells of the lateral geniculate nucleus, i.e. they had round receptive fields that responded to either red-green or blue-yellow (Livingstone & Hubel, 1984).

The discovery of cytochrome blobs has led to much research and some degree of controversy. It might be predicted from what we already know about the visual pathways that the colour-processing parvocellular cells will project to the blobs, whereas the magnocellular cells will project to the areas in-between (known as interblob regions). Indeed, this occurs, although the situation is not entirely simple. While most (about 70%) of the parvocellular axons from the lateral geniculate nucleus pass into the blob regions, some also project to interblob areas. Therefore a small percentage of cells in the interblob regions are also sensitive to colour, although it appears this only occurs when they define edges or borders (Leventhal et al., 1995). To make matters more complex, the high-resolution magnocellular cells also send some of their axons into the blob regions. Despite this overlap, it is fair to say that colour is predominantly processed by the parvocellular-dominated blobs, and detailed pattern recognition by the magnocellular-dominated interblob regions – at least in primates and other higher animals such as cats.

KEY TERM: *cytochrome blobs*

THE MODULAR STRUCTURE OF THE VISUAL CORTEX

The discovery of cytochrome blobs also led to a revision of ideas concerning the structure of the visual cortex. Hubel and Wiesel had previously established that the visual cortex was organized into blocks of orientation columns (with simple, complex and hypercomplex cells) accompanied by other columns for eye preference. Into this unit the colour-processing blobs could now be placed (see Figure 2.13). One term that has been used to describe this type of complex is the **cortical module** – a term introduced by Vernon Mountcastle in 1957 who realized that the somatosensory cortex was composed of columnar units which functioned as its main units of information processing. In fact, this type of anatomical organization has been found to be highly characteristic of the whole cortex. Columnar organization also reflects the local neural 'wiring' of the cerebral cortex, with connections 'up' and 'down' within the thickness of the cortex being much more extensive than connections that spread from side to side.

In the case of the visual cortex as envisaged by Hubel and Wiesel, the module consists of two ocular dominance units, each receiving input from each eye, along with two colour-processing blobs. In addition, each module contains the full range (in fact twice over) of orientation columns that cover every orientation across 180°. Thus, it can be seen that each cortical module has several important functions including the analysis of pattern, colour, luminance, movement and depth.

According to Hubel, each module in the human visual cortex is a 2 mm × 2 mm chunk of tissue and contains the neural machinery to deal completely with some particular area of the visual field – an area that can be spacially small as in the fovea, or much larger as occurs in the peripheral retina (Hubel, 1995, pp. 130–131). According to Hubel's calculations there are some 500 to 1,000 of these modular components in the primary visual cortex dedicated to processing a small part of the visual world – each of which are receiving around 10,000 neural inputs (mainly from the lateral geniculate nucleus) whilst sending out 50,000 axonal projections to other areas of the brain. This rich profusion of output fibres is a sure indication that visual processing gets even more complex as we go further away from the visual cortex. It should be pointed out, however, that since Hubel's calculations, the results of other studies have led to different conclusions. Therefore the described organization of the visual cortex should perhaps be considered a work in progress rather than the final word.

KEY TERMS: *cortical module, ocular dominance units, colour-processing blobs, orientation columns*

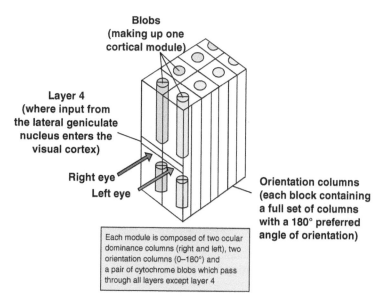

Figure 2.13   Hubel's model of the modular structure of the visual cortex
Source: Wickens (2009)

PROCESSING BEYOND THE PRIMARY VISUAL CORTEX

Hubel and Wiesel had concentrated most of their efforts in exploring the primary visual cortex located in the calcarine sulcus of the occipital lobes, but it had been known since the work of Karl Brodmann in the early 1900s (see Chapter 1) that the visual cortex contained other areas based on differences in their cell morphology. Brodmann labelled these areas 17 (i.e. the primary visual cortex), and two other regions, areas 18 and 19, that came to be recognized as the visual association cortex (sometimes called the extrastriate cortex). Because area 17 receives input directly from the lateral geniculate nucleus it also known as visual area 1 (V1). In turn, areas 18 and 19 became V2 and V3 respectively. It was also clear that axons from V1 fed into to area V2, which projected to V3. Apparently, each visual area elaborated on the processing of the preceding one. In support of this, the cells at each successive stage were found to have larger receptive fields which suggested they re-analysed the same features at progressively more complex levels.

This 'simple' three-stage view began to change in the late 1960s and 1970s when Semir Zeki, and others, traced the connections between different regions of the visual cortex (see Zeki, 1993). One technique was to follow the degeneration of fibres caused by discrete lesions of the visual cortex. It revealed that areas 18 and 19 were more complex than previously thought, since there were other visual areas beyond their boundaries. For example, in addition to the major outflow from V1 to V2 to V3, Zeki found a path that branched from V2 to a region close to the inferior (ventral) temporal cortex. He labelled this V4. Closer examination showed it was the origin of a visual pathway that went deeper and more anteriorly into the inferior temporal lobes. Another area to be discovered that lay outside the visual cortex was V5 which also become known as the middle temporal area (MT). Importantly, the flow of its output then appeared to turn more dorsally and became destined for the posterior parietal cortex. Since then the number of visual areas in both the temporal lobes and parietal lobes has greatly increased to around 30.

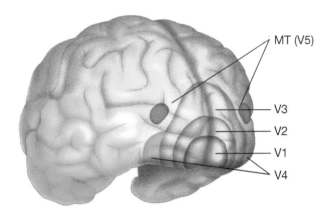

Figure 2.14   A simplified diagram showing the striate cortex (V1) and the extrastriate cortices (V2, V3, V4 and V5/MT)

Source: Gaskin (2021)

Evidence also showed that the visual input continues to be segregated as it is processed by the higher visual areas – a process that can be said to begin in the lateral geniculate nucleus with its division of parvocellular and magnocellular cells. For example, in humans, V2 is a large strip of tissue some 6 to 8 millimetres wide that surrounds the V1 cortex. When the V2 area is stained with cytochrome oxidase, it reveals regions of high and low activity arranged in parallel thin and thick stripes that are interrupted by unstained inter-stripe regions (Livingstone & Hubel, 1988). Closer examination reveals that these anatomical differences reflect three different functions: (1) the thick stripes receive input from the geniculate magnocellular cells via layer 4 of V1 and are specialized for processing movement; (2) the thin stripes receive their input from the blobs and process colour; (3) the pale stripes obtain input from the extrablob areas involved in orientation and form. These last two systems, therefore, process parvocellular information.

At this point the three streams of visual information diverge and travel into different areas of the brain – although the complexity of the pathways and the number of areas involved in processing make it difficult to follow the processing with precision (Van Essen et al., 1992). Nonetheless, one route passes from the thick stripes of V2 to V3, with this pathway involved in pattern recognition (Boynton & Hegdé, 2004). Another route passes from the thin stripes of V2 to V4 which continues the colour processing (Gegenfurtner, 2003). Interestingly, it has been found that patients with damage to region V4 suffer from a form of colour blindness known as cerebral achromatopsia in which they can only see shades of grey. If the damage is bilateral, then such patients cannot even imagine colours or remember the colours of objects they saw before their brain insult occurred. However, if damage is unilateral, patients only lose colour vision in half of the visual field. Both V3 and V4 send fibres into the inferotemporal cortex.

A third route passes from the thick stripes of V2 (and V3) to V5 which is important for the processing of movement. Indeed, over 90% of neurons in V5 are sensitive to the movement of shapes and objects (Zeki & Shipp, 1988). Damage to area V5 can also produce a rare condition known as cerebral akinetopsia which impairs a person's ability to perceive motion. For example, one patient (known as LM) reported that when they attempted to pour coffee, the fluid appeared to be frozen (Zihl et al., 1983). Moreover, their inability to see movement in a speaker's mouth made it difficult for them to follow a conversation. Although people with V5 damage can see objects at rest perfectly, when they move it often leads to them vanishing. This makes certain everyday tasks, such as crossing the street, highly dangerous. It is believed that the input conveying movement passes from V5 into the posterior parietal lobe (see Zihl & Heywood, 2015).

KEY TERMS: *Visual areas V1, V2, V3, V4 and V5, temporal lobes, middle temporal area, parietal cortex*

THE DORSAL ('WHERE') AND VENTRAL ('WHAT') PATHWAYS OF VISUAL PROCESSING

If one follows the division of parvocellular (detail and colour vision) and magnocellular (movement vision) processing through the hierarchical different stages of visual cortex, it appears to separate into two distinct systems – one (parvocellular) going to the temporal lobes and the other (magnocellular) to the parietal lobes. In 1982, a seminal article was published by Leslie Ungerleider and Mortimer Mishkin which became one of the most cited papers in the field of visual neuroscience that also emphasized these two pathways. Largely based on their own behavioural findings, Ungerleider and Mishkin proposed that visual processing in primates occurs along two cortical routes. These are (1) a dorsal pathway passing through the parietal lobes that processed information concerning the spatial location of objects, and (2) a ventral pathway coursing through the temporal lobes which encoded the visual recognition of objects. In effect, Ungerleider and Mishkin had proposed an anatomical and functional distinction for two separate visual systems in the brain that were specialized for asking 'where is something?' and 'what is something?'.

The main evidence for Ungerleider and Mishkin's position was derived from experiments where the visual discrimination abilities of monkeys were examined by the use of lesions or single cell recording. Although it had been known since the work of Klüver and Bucy in the 1930s that monkeys with temporal lobes lesions (particularly of the inferotemporal cortex) were visually impaired at recognizing previously familiar objects (say a cup and saucer), they had no obvious visual problems if they were allowed to pick these up and handle them. As was noted by the neuroscientist Karl Pribram (cited by Goodale & Milner, 2004), monkeys with temporal lobe lesions, trained for months to no avail to learn a pattern discrimination task, could nevertheless snatch flies out of the air with great dexterity. In contrast, monkeys with parietal lesions revealed a different problem. They could recognize objects known to them prior to surgery, but were unable to reach or grasp for them accurately afterwards. In other words, parietal lesioned monkeys could not use their vision to guide movements with any degree of precision. These animals also showed impairments when having to recall the spatial location of a hidden object in order to obtain a reward.

Although Ungerleider and Mishkin's theory received support, there were other possible interpretations. For example, Goodale and Milner (1992) proposed that the main function of the dorsal pathway is not so much to encode the spatial configuration of an object and its relations – but to visually guide motor actions. For example, if someone throws you a ball, you are likely to try catching it. But you don't plan the catch, or think about it. You just do it. This action, Goodale and Milner would claim, is a function of the dorsal visual pathway. Moreover, because we perform many of our actions without 'thinking', they also suggested that the dorsal pathway is largely automatic and unconscious. In contrast, Goodale and Milner propose that the ventral pathways are involved in choosing a goal, and in recognizing (or memorizing) visual objects. These are believed to be essentially perceptual cognitive processes that are available to conscious decision making and interpretation. The destination of both pathways would appear to be the prefrontal cortex known to be involved in executive functions such as **working memory** (see Chapter 10 for further discussion of executive function).

However we choose to construe the function of the two vision systems passing through the dorsal (parietal) and ventral (temporal) lobes, they nonetheless appear to largely reflect the division of visual input that first diverged in the lateral geniculate nucleus. In short, the magnocellular system dominates in the dorsal stream (i.e. action, movement and spatial mapping) whilst the parvocellular dominates in the ventral stream (i.e. perceptual recognition of objects and things). This distinction has also been confirmed in several human studies using brain-scanning techniques (Ungerleider & Haxby, 1994). Despite this, recent evidence is beginning to show that things may be more complex since a great deal of object information, especially related to shape, size and viewpoint, may actually be represented by both ventral and dorsal pathways. This suggests that the two systems are much more closely intertwined that first envisaged (Konen & Kastner, 2008; Rossetti et al., 2017). There is also accumulating evidence that the lower visual areas, even V1, rather than being simple detection areas, may have a far greater involvement in higher cognitive functions than first believed (Muckli, 2010).

KEY TERMS: *dorsal pathway, parietal lobes, ventral pathway, temporal lobes*

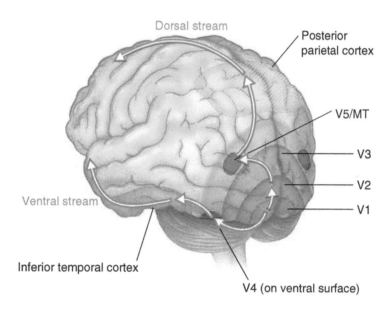

Figure 2.15 The ventral 'what' and dorsal 'where' streams of visual processing
Source: Carolina Hrejsa/Body Scientific Intl. in Gaskin (2021)

VISUAL AGNOSIA: SEEING WITHOUT RECOGNIZING

One disorder that lends support to the 'where' (spatial understanding) and 'what' (object recognition) dichotomy of visual processing is visual agnosia. This is a relatively rare condition characterized by an inability to recognize or name familiar objects by vision, although if the agnostic went to an optician to have a standard eye test they would be found to have essentially 'normal' sight (presuming they could name the letters!). Consequently, a person with agnosia may be unable to name a given object when it is shown to them visually (say a chair), but be able to recognise it when presented in another sensory mode (e.g. by touch). The term 'agnosia' is derived from the Greek meaning 'lack of knowledge' and was first coined by Sigmund Freud in 1891. However, a more important contribution was made by Lissauer in 1890 who proposed that this type of condition should be divided into two types: 'apperceptive' and 'associative'. This distinction came from his belief that visual recognition must involve two processes: (1) perceptual integration (apperception) in which sensory data is organized into a meaningful 'whole', and (2) association where the percept is linked with stored knowledge (memory) so its meaning can be established.

An example of apperceptive agnosia (which is very rare) is the case of Dr P, the character after which Oliver Sacks named his book *The Man who Mistook his Wife for a Hat* (1985). Dr P was a well-educated music teacher unable to recognize the faces of his students by sight, although he could identify them when they spoke. He was also impaired at recognizing a wide range of objects. For example, when Sacks gave Mr P a glove, he recognized it had five appendages and guessed it might be a purse-like cloth container. Despite prompting, he was unable to discern it as a glove. Similarly, when Sacks presented him with a red rose, Dr P described it as 'a convoluted red form with linear green attachment', but could not guess what it was until asked to smell it. But perhaps the most striking example of his deficit came at the end of his examination when Dr P, looking for his hat, tried to pick up his wife's head!

In apperceptive agnosia, basic vision is intact, but the person cannot combine the visual elements into a meaningful percept. Thus, while they can make out contours, edges, colour, motion etc., the apperceptive agnostic has trouble forming the overall picture and categorizing its individual parts. This can be demonstrated by asking them to copy simple letters, shapes and line drawings. Often, the apperceptive agnosia is unable to make even the most rudimentary approximation of their shape (see Figure 2.16). They are also impaired at matching simple shapes. This form of agnosia is associated with bilateral damage to the secondary areas of the visual cortex and adjoining regions of the parietal cortex. In other words, apperceptive agnosia is caused by damage to the early stages of the 'where' pathway as it begins to course through the parietal lobes.

A less severe and more common form of the deficit is associative agnosia. Someone with this condition, for example, typically has no difficulty in copying a line drawing, yet they may be unable to recognize what they have drawn, or be able to draw the object from memory. Therefore, an associative agnostic can 'see' objects – but not know what they are. The extent of this deficit can vary greatly. In some cases the associative agnostic will not be able to determine the exact instance of a previously known object (e.g. robin), but be capable enough to extract enough information to recognize its main category (e.g. bird). In other instances they may be unable to assess its important attributes (e.g. whether it is tame or dangerous). The brain sites responsible for associative agnosia are found on the occipital-temporal lobe border, especially where the visual cortices border the inferotemporal part of lobe. In other words, associative agnosia is associated with damage to the 'what' pathway that courses through the temporal lobes.

KEY TERMS: *visual agnosia, apperceptive agnosia, associative agnosia*

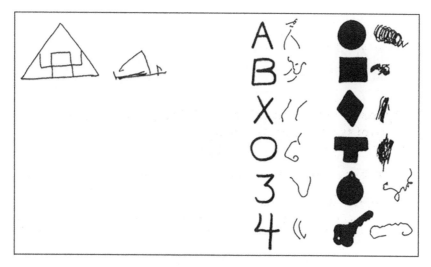

Figure 2.16   Examples of drawings made by patients with apperceptive and associative agnosia

Source: Wickens (2009), from Banich, M. T. (2004). *Cognitive neuroscience and neuropsychology* (2nd ed.), p. 195 and Rubens, A. B. & Benson, D. F. (1971). Associative visual agnosia. *Archives of Neurology*, 24, 305–316.

OTHER VISUAL DEFICITS ASSOCIATED WITH PARIETAL AND TEMPORAL LOBE DAMAGE

Evidence showing the parietal cortex's involvement in the spatial aspects of vision, including the analysis of motion, and grouping the positional relationships of objects with each other, has come from **Bálint's syndrome**. This rare condition occurs when there is extensive bilateral damage to the posterior regions of the parietal lobes which leads to three main types of visual impairment. One is a difficulty in shifting gaze to a new stimulus, fixing a stare, or being able to follow movement. This is known as **ocular apraxia** and it results in a person being unable to make a systematic scan of their visual scene, or focusing on a particular object. Instead, their eyes tend to 'wander' around so that objects come into view and are then replaced by other stimuli. Although a person with Bálint's syndrome will recognize what they see, they will have difficulty assessing *where* that object is located in their visual world. A second deficit is an inability to reach for objects under visual guidance. This is known as optic ataxia and it causes a person to fumble or misreach for objects, and be unable to point accurately at a visual stimulus. However, perhaps the most dramatic deficit in Bálint's syndrome is a person's inability to see the totality of their visual scene. Instead the individual will have a very narrow visual attention field causing them to see only one object at a time (e.g. if presented with a razor and toothbrush they might be able to see one – but not both together). This is called simultanagnosia (see Figure 2.17) and it means, in effect, that a Bálint's patient can only focus on a tiny part of their visual world at any one moment. For example, if a person is shown a rural scene, they may be able to see a tree, a river, a house, a field and a cow, but also be unable to integrate these into a unified whole.

The temporal lobes are specialized for determining what objects are (object recognition), colour processing and fine detail. One interesting deficit sometimes observed in

When asked to describe this picture, an individual with this syndrome could describe the handlebars, the car and the helmet but could not perceive why the girl was trying to flag down the car.

Figure 2.17   An illustration of simultanagnosia

Source: Wickens (2009), from Banich, M. T. (2004). *Cognitive neuroscience and neuropsychology* (2nd ed.), p. 244

patients with damage to the temporal lobes is an inability to recognize faces (Corrow et al., 2016). This is called **prosopagnosia** and like the broader form of visual agnosia there are two types: apperceptive and associative. In apperceptive prosopagnosia, people cannot make any sense of facial features or make same–different judgements when presented with pictures of different faces. In addition, they are unable to recognize both familiar and unfamiliar faces, but may guess people's identity on the basis of things such as clothing, hairstyle, skin colour or voice. For example, Damasio et al. (1990b) reported the case of a 60-year-old woman, with normal visual acuity, who suffered a bilateral stroke to the border of the occipital and temporal lobes and was unable to recognize the faces of her husband or daughter – despite being able to identify them by their voices. A person with this type of prosopagnosia may even be unable to recognize their own face, and there are reports of them bumping into a mirror and saying 'excuse me', mistaking their own image for another person (Klein & Thorne, 2007).

Associative agnosia is less severe. An associative prosopagnosic may be able to determine whether photos of people's faces are the same or different, and guess their age and gender. Clearly, therefore, they can make use of some face information. They also usually describe the emotion the face is expressing. However, they may not be able to identify the person, remember them as a friend, or provide a name or occupation.

Interestingly, in recent years a third type of prosopagnosia has been recognized. This is developmental prosopagnosia, a lifelong condition that first manifests itself in early childhood, and cannot be attributed to acquired brain damage. It runs in certain families and may have a genetic cause (Dalrymple et al., 2012).

The development of functional scanning techniques in recent years has been important for identifying the brain regions involved in face processing along with establishing the areas of damage in those with prosopagnosia. This condition is caused by lesions in various parts of the inferior occipital areas, the anterior temporal cortex and an area at the base (or underside) of the inferotemporal lobe called the fusiform face gyrus (Brodmann's area 37). First identified by Sergent et al. (1992), this area, especially on the right side, appears to be specifically activated by faces, but not other types of visual stimuli (Kanwisher et al., 1997). Interestingly, the fusiform face gyrus is underdeveloped in children and does not fully develop until adolescence – although clearly young infants can recognize faces. Nonetheless, having an area of the brain devoted to the processing of faces shows just how special faces are in our visual world. And we are not alone in the animal kingdom, since a number of mammals have also been shown to have brain regions involved in face recognition. For example, in sheep, cells have been found in the temporal cortex that respond selectively to the faces of horned sheep, unhorned sheep, sheepdogs, wolves and even their own shepherd (Kendrick & Baldwin, 1987).

KEY TERMS: *Bálint's syndrome, optic apraxia, optic ataxia, simultanagnosia, prosopagnosia, fusiform face gyrus*

SUBCORTICAL VISUAL SYSTEMS

The visual pathway from retina to cortex, and beyond, is not the only system devoted to vision in the brain. In fact, about 10% of the retinal ganglion cells branch away from the optic nerve before reaching the lateral geniculate nucleus and pass to subcortical regions. One important destination is the midbrain tectum located at the top of the brain stem. In many lower species such as fish, reptiles and birds, the tectum provides the highest site for visual analysis, and this region in primates, which is dominated by the superior colliculus, still remains functionally important. The superior colliculus is involved in the control of automatic reflexes and orienting movements of the head and eyes – especially when new stimuli appear in the visual field. In addition, the superior colliculus helps to co-ordinate **saccadic eye movements**, i.e. sudden automatic and rapid movements of the eyes that allow us to explore changing visual scenes and to continually bring new images onto the fovea (Furlan et al., 2015).

Although it is clear that the superior colliculi visual system is far older in evolutionary terms than the one passing to the cortex, they are closely connected. In fact, the superior colliculus receives extensive input from the primary and secondary areas of the visual cortex. In return, the superior colliculus projects to the pulvinar of the thalamus – another area with strong reciprocal connectivity with the visual cortex, and known to be involved in promoting synchronized oscillatory activity underlying visual processes. The superior colliculus also projects to the lateral geniculate nucleus, and is the origin of two large descending pathways which travel to the brain stem and spinal cord (May, 2006).

There is also some evidence that the superior colliculus may make an important contribution to automatic visual processes of which we have no conscious awareness. This has come from the remarkable discovery of **blindsight** which was first shown in a patient known as DB by Weiskrantz et al. (1974). DB was a patient who had much of their right primary visual cortex surgically removed following a tumour. It has long been known that damage to the visual pathways from retina to visual cortex produces blindness in the visual field opposite to the side of the brain where the lesion has occurred, and DB was no exception as the surgery appeared to leave him totally blind in his left visual field. Despite this, DB was accurate at pointing to the position of markers on a wall, deciding whether a stick was horizontal or vertical, and distinguishing between 'X' and 'O'. Yet DB protested he was guessing and unable to see the visual stimuli (see Weiskrantz, 2010 for an interesting account). This type of residual vision in people who are blind is more common than one might expect, being found in around 20% of subjects with visual cortex damage.

It is now known that there are two types of blindsight. Type 1 blindsight refers to the ability to guess above chance levels about aspects of a visual stimulus without any conscious awareness of the stimuli. Type 2 blindsight occurs when subjects claim to have a feeling that there has been a change within their blind area, especially regarding movement, but without being able to form a visual representation (Weiskrantz, 1997). Although many investigators believe that blindsight is dependent on the superior colliculus, perhaps through its innervation of the non-damaged parts of the visual cortex, there are other possible explanations (Fendrich et al., 2001). For example, it could be that blindsight is caused by stray light passing from the blind visual field into the sighted one, thereby giving a clue to the target's location. Or perhaps small islands of functional visual cortex surrounding the damaged areas remain (Gazzaniga et al., 1994). Another possibility is that blindsight is due in some way to the functioning of the lateral geniculate nucleus. Nonetheless, whatever the cause, blindsight challenges the common belief that our perceptions must enter consciousness to affect behaviour. Clearly, a considerable amount of visual processing takes place below conscious awareness. Further work into blindsight should provide important insights into which visual processes are necessary for conscious vision and which are not (Ajina & Bridge, 2017).

KEY TERMS: *superior colliculus, saccadic eye movements, blindsight*

THE GREAT MYSTERY

As we have seen, one of the distinguishing features of visual processing in the brain is the breaking down and segregation of visual input. Although this process begins in the retina, it is most noticeable in the lateral geniculate nucleus where visual input is divided into two channels – the parvocellular, involving colour and high resolution vision, and the magnocellular, involving movement. As these two paths of information pass to the primary visual cortex (area V1) they divide into three streams responsible for colour, pattern recognition and movement. Although the visual processing gets significantly more complicated thereafter, the segregation of function remains, with a dorsal pathway passing through the parietal lobes concerned with spatial vision and a ventral pathway passing through the temporal lobes involved in object recognition. The astute student following these arguments might then ask: where does all this information get joined together into one complete whole? The simple answer is we do not know!

How the brain manages to combine its sensory input into one complete whole is known as the binding problem. In fact, our conscious experience of the world is both spatially and temporally bound. As you read this book, you may be sitting in your room with your computer by your side, with a cup of coffee on the table, with the window partially closed by some curtains. In other words, you are experiencing a spatial configuration of your world that is all meaningfully bound together. And if now someone knocks on your door, you shift your orientation to the sound and get up to see who the visitor is. Everything then changes in visual appearance, but your brain copes easily with the temporal changes which remain bound together. However, this example just refers to visual binding. Imagine frying an egg. The colour, shape, size and texture of the egg are bound together to form an integrated experience of a yellow and white-shaped blob in the frying pan. But in addition the auditory sensation of the sizzling is bound together with the smell of the egg in order to create a multimodal perceptual experience of seeing, hearing and smelling. We just don't bind visual input, we also combine all our sensory modalities into one unified whole every instant of our conscious lives.

Some philosophers have suggested that we have some sort of theatre inside our head where all this information is projected onto an inner screen which has been disparagingly dubbed the Cartesian theatre by Daniel Dennett. This possibility, however, is very unlikely. There is probably no single place where information is bound together in this way, or a site in the brain where there is an internal screen – not least because it would imply the existence of another spectator or homunculus (little man) watching it. Nonetheless, neuroscientists have speculated where the visual input, especially from the dorsal and ventral streams, might all come together in the brain. Several suggestions have been made including the prefrontal cortex (Cola-Conde et al., 2004), the superior temporal gyrus (Baizer et al., 1991) and the posterior parietal cortex (Driver & Mattingly, 1998). An even more complex idea is to view visual binding as a distributed process perhaps involving as many as 32 areas of cortex with over 300 connecting pathways (Van Essen et al., 1992). With such questions unanswered, it is an exciting time to be a biopsychologist!

KEY TERMS: *the binding problem, Cartesian theatre, homunculus*

SUMMARY

Vision, or our ability to detect different wavelengths of light, is arguably our most important sense, with about one-third of the human brain directly or indirectly devoted to its analysis. Our visual processing begins with our eyes. Light passes through the transparent cornea, into the aqueous humour, and the aperture of the pupil (controlled by the iris, which gives the eyes their colour) which regulates the amount of light entering the eye. Behind the pupil lies the lens which acts to bring visual images into clear focus onto the retina and whose shape is controlled by the ciliary muscles. Light then passes through the vitreous humour and is projected onto the retina, which contains the photoreceptors of the eye. There are two types of photo-receptor: the rods, which are found predominantly in its periphery and involved in the detection of light intensity, and the cones, found in the fovea and involved in detailed (acute) vision and colour detection. There are three main types of cone roughly sensitive to blue, green and red wavelengths of light. It is estimated that each retina has in the region of 120 million rods and 6 million cones. From the retina, information from the rods and cones passes to the bipolar cells and then ganglion cells forming the optic nerve. There are about 800,000 axons in each optic nerve, which pass on the underneath of the brain before joining the optic chiasm. This is a crossing-over point where about two-thirds of axons from the nasal side of the retina cross to the opposite side of the brain. These pass to the lateral geniculate nucleus of the thalamus. From here, neurons project via the optic radiations to the **primary visual cortex** (sometimes called V1) in the occipital lobe. Information is then passed to several other visual areas within the occipital lobes (e.g. V2 to V7) which all appear to have specialized functions concerned with either feature detection, motion or colour.

The nature of the information processed by the visual system was examined by Stephen Kuffler in the 1950s, who recorded the electrical activity of ganglion cells in the cat's optic nerve by passing a small spot of light across their receptive fields. He found that the receptive fields were concentric, consisting of a circular central area surrounded by a ring. These zones also produced different types of neural activity in response to visual stimulation. In some cells, light shone in the central region increased its rate of firing (an 'on' response), whereas light falling in the surround inhibited firing (an 'off' response). In other cells, the situation was reversed with stimulation of the centre producing an 'off' response, and stimulation of the surround producing an 'on' response. This work was extended by Hubel and Wiesel who examined cells in the primary visual cortex. This research showed that the visual cortex contained three types of cell – called simple, complex and hypercomplex – which had elongated receptive fields and were sensitive to lines, angles and movement. Hubel and Wiesel also showed that the visual cortex contained orientation columns with each having simple, complex and hypercomplex cells that fired to lines of the same angle. These orientations rotated in a clockwise manner by about 10° in adjacent columns – so that approximately each 2 mm of visual cortex contained enough columns to detect every line orientation over 360°. A more complex processing unit called a cortical module was later shown to exist. Each contains a block of orientation columns that covers all line angles over 360°, two blocks of ocular dominance columns with a preference for input from each of the eyes, and a pair of cytochrome blobs which are involved in colour processing. It is believed that the human primary visual cortex may contain around 2,500 of these modules, with each one processing a small part of the visual world at the retinal level. From the primary visual cortex (sometimes called region V1), information is passed to a number of secondary visual areas (including regions V2, V3, V4 and V5). Although the pathways are anatomically complex, it appears that processing for colour, motion and orientation is largely independent at this stage. Visual information is then channelled either through the dorsal pathway of the parietal lobes (the 'where' pathway) or the ventral pathway of the temporal lobes (the 'what' pathway).

GO ONLINE

TEST YOUR UNDERSTANDING OF THIS CHAPTER AND VISIT
HTTPS://STUDY.SAGEPUB.COM/WICKENS TO ACCESS INTERACTIVE
'DRAG AND DROP' LABELLING ACTIVITIES AND A FLASHCARD GLOSSARY.

MULTIPLE CHOICE QUESTIONS

Answer the questions below to test your understanding of this chapter's Learning Objectives. You'll find the answers at the end of the chapter.

1. The amount of light reaching the retina is controlled by which of these?

   a. cornea
   b. pupil
   c. retina
   d. sclera

2. What is the first terminus in the brain for the majority of fibres making up the optic nerve?

   a. optic chiasma
   b. Deiter's nucleus
   c. lateral geniculate nucleus
   d. visual cortex

3. In what part of the brain did Hubel and Wiesel find *simple*, *complex* and *hypercomplex* cells?

   a. lateral geniculate nucleus
   b. superior colliculus
   c. primary visual cortex (area V1)
   d. all of the above, although most were found in V1

4. How many types of opponent cells encoding colour are found in the optic nerve?

   a. one (black-white)
   b. two (red-green, blue-yellow)
   c. three (red-green, blue-yellow, red-blue)
   d. four (red-green, blue-yellow, red-blue, green-yellow)

5. The dorsal (*where is it?*) and ventral (*what is it?*) visual pathways pass through what parts of the cortex?

   a. cingulate and limbic
   b. occipital and hippocampal
   c. insular and frontal
   d. parietal and temporal

6. The patient DB who demonstrated blindsight had damage to which area?

   a. visual cortex
   b. lateral geniculate nucleus
   c. superior colliculus
   d. retina

FURTHER READING

Bruce, V., Green, P. R., & Georgeson, M. A. (2003). *Visual perception: Physiology, psychology and ecology*. Psychology Press.
A well-written, colourful textbook that covers the physiology of the visual system and its involvement in perception.

Farah, M. J. (2004). *Visual agnosia*. MIT Press.
Describes how brain damage can result in disorders of object recognition, and its implications for understanding visual processing.

Hubel, D. H., & Wiesel, T. N. (2005). *Brain and visual perception: The story of a 25-year collaboration*. Oxford University Press.
A book that includes all of Hubel and Wiesel's main academic papers. Although technical, each chapter contains a foreword which provides useful and interesting information for the student.

Kernell, D. (2016). *Colours and colour vision*. Cambridge University Press.
An excellent textbook which is easy to read.

Mather, G. (2016). *Foundations of perception*. Psychology Press.
A colourful and well-written textbook on perception with seven excellent chapters specifically on vision.

Milner, A. D., & Goodale, M. A. (2006). *The visual brain in action*. Oxford University Press.
A book that examines the two main pathways that process vision beyond the visual cortex (i.e. the dorsal and ventral streams) and their relevance for human perception and behaviour.

Palmer, S. E. (1999). *Vision science: Photons to phenomenology*. MIT Press.
A substantial textbook of over 800 pages devoted to the science of vision that covers all the major topics from early neural processing in the eye, to high level functions such as memory, imagery and awareness.

Snowden, R., Thompson, P., & Troscianko. T. (2012). *Basic vision: An introduction to visual perception*. Oxford University Press.
An excellent textbook. All students will benefit from reading this book.

Tovee, M. J. (2008). *An introduction to the visual system*. Cambridge University Press.
A concise yet surprisingly detailed overview of the visual system which is easy to read and highly informative.

Valberg, A. (2005). *Light vision colour*. John Wiley.
Although this book covers the fundamentals of vision, it also includes recent developments in vision science and addresses some advanced issues.

MULTIPLE CHOICE ANSWERS - 1. B | 2. C | 3. C | 4. B | 5. D | 6. A

3

SENSORY SYSTEMS OTHER THAN VISION

LEARNING OBJECTIVES

After reading this chapter you should be able to:

- Appreciate the functional anatomy of the ear and the neurobiological processing of sound information (audition).

- Explain how the nose encodes smell (olfaction) and how this is processed by the brain.

- Explain how the tongue encodes taste (gustation) and how this is processed by the brain.

- Elucidate the receptor basis, neural pathways and brain regions involved in the sense of touch, proprioception and somatosensory function.

- Understand the neurobiological and chemical basis of pain.

- Characterize the pharmacological action of morphine and the behavioural roles of the endogenous opiates.

GO ONLINE

Test your understanding of this chapter and visit **https://study.sagepub.com/wickens** to access interactive 'Drag and Drop' labelling activities and a flashcard glossary.

INTRODUCTION

Although vision is often said to be our most dominant sense, it is not the only one playing a vital role in our lives. For example, cast your mind back to when you woke this morning. Perhaps you were woken by the sound of an alarm clock and you pulled the covers back to get out of the bed. Downstairs in the kitchen you made a cup of coffee and put some bread in the toaster. Most of us will be familiar with this scenario and it shows from the first moment of our day, different senses provide us with a constant stream of information about the world. The alarm clock elicits sound (the sense of audition), our movements are guided by tactile sensations (touch), the coffee has a nice smell (olfaction), and the toast provides a pleasant taste (gustation).

These senses give such a veritable richness to our lives that it is easy to overlook the fact that they originally evolved to help us survive in a dangerous world. Without audition we could not hear the hissing of a kettle, and the loss of olfaction and gustation would make us unable to smell a gas leak or detect rancid food. Losing our sense of bodily feedback leads to uncoordinated movement. And, of course, the pain of picking up a hot knife alerts us to hazard and possible injury. Clearly, we are dependent on our senses to provide experience about the world necessary for our wellbeing.

Although it is often said that humans have five senses, we have more. The skin, for example, in addition to touch, senses heat and cold (thermoception) and feels itching and tickling. The ear contains organs that provide us with a sense of balance (the vestibular sense), while the skeletal muscles and joints of the body contain receptors for pressure and movement (proprioception). We should also not forget that some animals have other senses (e.g. bats can detect objects by reflected sound), or exhibit superior ones to ours (e.g. a bloodhound's sense of smell is 10 million times more sensitive than a human's).

Because our knowledge of the world is dependent on our sensory faculties, this area of study is an important one, for it allows us to understand how the brain makes sense of its external world, and is able to process feedback from the internal workings of the body.

SOUND AND THE SENSE OF HEARING (AUDITION)

Unlike light which can move through a vacuum, the transmission of sound requires a medium such as air or water that gives rise to vibrations. When an object is struck such as a tuning fork, it vibrates and sets up movements in the surrounding air molecules causing them to condense and expand. This also creates a wave with alternating increases and decreases in air pressure which moves away from the source of vibration. We detect this as sound. The speed of these air waves is relatively slow as they travel at about 0.2 miles or 0.32 kms per second in air (about 740 miles or 1190 kms per hour) which is much slower than light at 186,000 miles (or nearly 300,000 km) per second. This is why a clap of thunder will often occur several seconds behind a flash of lightening. The velocity of sound also differs according to the medium in which it travels: it moves faster in solids and slower in gases such as air.

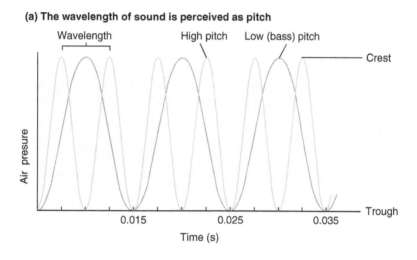

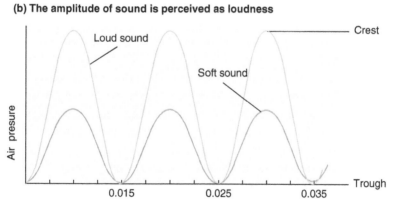

Figure 3.1   The wavelength (pitch) and amplitude (loudness) of sound waves
Source: Wickens (2009)

We can depict a 'perfect' sound wave graphically as a sine wave (i.e. one with a smooth periodic oscillation) in which the compressed pressure is represented by the crest, and the decompression by the trough. This type of wave is the simplest pattern of pressure pulsations generated by a pure tone, and a closer examination of this wave reveals two characteristics that are essential to our perception of sound: namely the wavelength's frequency and its amplitude. The wavelength is the distance between two consecutive crests (or troughs) and this is constant for a particular tone. Since the wave also moves, it has a frequency – that is, the number of waves that pass at a given point in a given time. This is normally expressed as hertz (Hz), or cycles per second. We use this property to measure the pitch of a sound, with shorter wavelengths providing tones of higher frequency. Thus, the highest note on a piano (C) produces a wave that moves at about 4,186 Hz, while the lowest note (A) has a frequency of around 27 Hz. Humans with good hearing can detect sounds in a range of 20 to 20,000 Hz. However, we are most sensitive to 2,000 to 4,000 Hz frequencies, i.e. the range within which most conversation occurs.

The amplitude of the wavelength is the change from maximum to minimum pressure, or put simply the height of the wave. We use this feature of the wave to determine the intensity of the sound (i.e. loudness). In general, if the amplitude of a wavelength increases, we hear this as a rise in volume. The range of intensities that humans can detect is very large, and typically reported in terms of logarithmic units called decibels (named in honour of Alexander Graham Bell). With the decibel scale, a difference of 10 dB corresponds to a 1 log unit (or factor of 10) change in sound intensity. Therefore, an increase in intensity of a sound from 10 to 20 dB corresponds to a 10-fold intensity difference, while an increase from 10 to 30 dB represents a change in intensity by a factor of 100. The loudest sound that can be heard without pain is approximately 1 million times, or 120 dB, greater that the threshold sound we can hear. This is roughly the difference between hearing a jet plane take off from a distance of 30 metres to the listening of a barely audible tone of 1,000 Hz.

Although a tuning fork should produce a pure tone, most sounds in our everyday world consist of combinations of many different frequencies. It may come as a surprise to learn that whilst musical notes may sound 'pure', they rarely are. Rather, they are composed of a large number of different harmonic frequencies that are present in varying amounts. It is these extra frequencies that give musical instruments their own distinct qualities. Indeed, if we were to remove all the harmonics, leaving only the fundamental sound wave, any two instruments (say a trombone and a piano) playing the same note would sound identical. To complicate matters, instruments can also play different notes together to form chords. In this case, to understand the sound wave produced, one must take the sine functions for all the notes and add them together. For example, if you play the notes C, E and G (the chord of C) you will produce a highly complex sound wave with many crests and troughs of variable size, and whilst it is no longer a sine wave, there is still a repeating pattern to it. Next time you listen to your favourite band or piece of music you might want to contemplate the nature of the sound waves entering your ears. They are having to decipher some very complex wave patterns (Schnupp et al., 2011).

KEY TERMS: *wavelength frequency and amplitude, hertz*

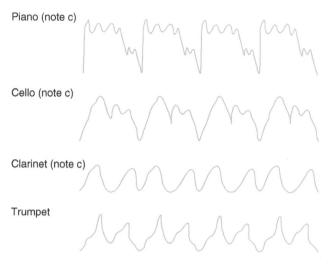

Figure 3.2   Complex sound waves for four musical instruments
Source: Wickens (2009)

THE PHYSIOLOGY OF THE EAR

The ear is the organ of hearing, and in mammals it also provides the main organ of balance. The ear has three main components, i.e. the outer, middle and inner, all of which serve a different function in transforming pressure waves (normally propagated in air) into sound. Put simply, the outer ear 'collects' the pressure waves, the middle ear acts as a mechanical transformer of these waves into physical events, and the inner ear transduces the sound-induced mechanical energy into neural energy (Brownell, 1997).

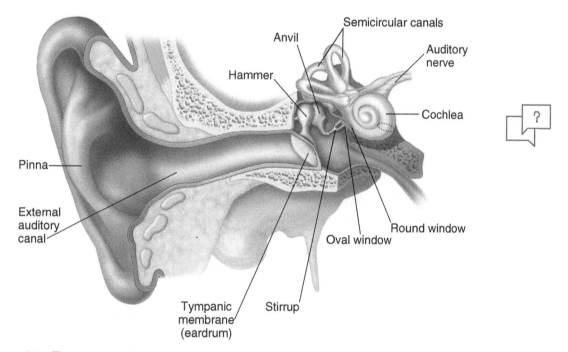

Figure 3.3   The outer, middle and inner ear
Source: Garrett and Hough (2021)

Hearing begins with the external ear, composed of the fleshy pinna whose distinct shape helps direct sound waves into the auditory canal. In many animals, the pinna is able to move and provides an effective sound gathering device. In humans, the pinna is immobile (although a few people can wriggle their ears slightly), but still provides an important function as its damage can cause people to have difficulty locating the source of sound. A depression in the pinna leads to the auditory canal, a tube some 3 cm long and 0.6 cm wide, through which sound waves travel to a thin covering called the tympanic membrane (the ear drum). Because of its physical shape, the auditory canal improves the detection of sounds in the range of 3,500 Hz, which is close to the midpoint of human hearing. The tympanic membrane is the boundary between the inner and middle ears, and shaped like a cone with its apex pointing into the ear. It is sent into vibratory motion when struck by sound waves, and transfers the energy to the bones of the middle ear. Apparently, the membrane making up the eardrum is extremely sensitive and we can detect sounds if it moves by as little as the diameter of a hydrogen atom (Hudspeth, 1983).

The small air-filled cavity behind the tympanic membrane forms the middle ear and it contains the three smallest bones in the body, known collectively as the ossicles. Individually, these are the malleus (Latin for hammer), incus (anvil) and stapes (stirrup). These bones resemble a series of three levers and are set into motion by the vibrations of the tympanic membrane. The end result is that the stapes will hit the **oval window** of the **cochlea**. It may appear to be a complicated arrangement having three small bones to transmit sound, but they exist because the middle ear cavity contains air, which it gets from the Eustachian tubes connected to the mouth, while the inner ear is filled with fluid. Air offers less resistance to movement than fluid, and consequently if pressure waves were to strike the oval window through the medium of air, most of the energy would be reflected back, making the inner ear less sensitive to sound. Because the ossicles are made of bone, they greatly amplify the vibrations, thereby overcoming the resistance difference. Interestingly, the muscles attached to the ossicles can tighten the joints to increase their sensitivity to quiet sounds or slacken them to soften loud sounds.

The oval window is in effect the entrance to the inner ear, which is sometimes called the labyrinth because of its highly intricate structure of interconnecting chambers and passages. Although this part of the ear contains the three **semicircular canals** which play an important role in maintaining balance (these will be discussed in the next chapter), the most important part of the middle ear for hearing is the cochlea (from the Greek word for snail), a hollow spiral-shaped bony chamber that coils around for about two and half turns. Resembling a snail's shell, it measures about 4 mm in the human ear, but if uncoiled would extend to about 40 mm. The opening of the cochlea can be seen to contain three membrane fluid-filled chambers or canals. These are the scala vestibuli (the upper passage), scala media (middle passage) and scala tympani (tympanic ramp).

KEY TERMS: *pinna, tympanic membrane (ear drum), ossicles, cochlea, scala vestibuli, scala media, scala tympani*

Closer examination of the cochlea's opening shows that the stapes and its oval window is actually adjacent to a fluid pathway called the scala vestibuli. If we now follow the tube-like chamber of the scala vestibuli into the cochlea through its turns, to its apex, we will come to a very small opening called the helicotrema. In fact, this is where the scala vestibuli joins the scala tympani, and one can follow this tiny passage through its turns back to the opening of the cochlea where there is another membrane wall called the round window. Thus, although the scala vestibuli and scala tympani appear to be separate, they are joined and therefore share the same fluid.

As we have seen, the bone-encased cochlea receives its sound input from the stapes tapping on its oval window located at the entrance of the scala vestibuli. At this point, the pulsations on the membrane of the oval window create a pressure wave in the fluid of the scala vestibuli which moves into the cochlea and through the helicotrema into the scala tympani. Since the fluid in these chambers is virtually incompressible, the pressure is transmitted to the scala tympani's round window which flexes outward with each sound wave. In fact, the only way that waves can be generated in the inner ear is because of this relief point, i.e. when the oval window is pushed in, the round window is pushed out and vice versa (Figure 3.4).

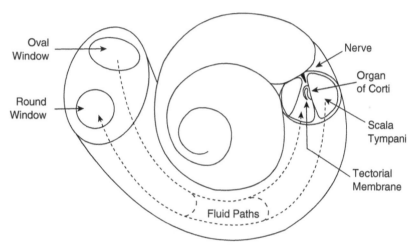

Figure 3.4   The cochlea and its inner anatomy
Source: Dicklyon and Fred the Oyster/Wikimedia Commons

However, lying interposed between the scala vestibuli and scala tympani is the cochlear canal which houses a further chamber called the scala media (see Figure 3.5). This contains an essential structure for hearing which runs along its coiled floor called the **basilar membrane** – a stiff structural protrudence forming the base of the **organ of Conti** which contains hair-like outgrowths where the auditory receptors picking up the vibrations in the inner ear are located. The pressurized waves in the fluid compartments of the scala vestibuli and scala tympani therefore have a very important consequence: their forced pressure motions lead to the moving of the basilar membrane's hairs in the scala media (Pickles, 2013).

KEY TERMS: *helicotrema, round window, basilar membrane, organ of Conti*

(a) The middle ear–tympanic membrane and ossicles—and the inner ear–the cochlea. (b) A section of the cochlea. (c) The organ of Corti.

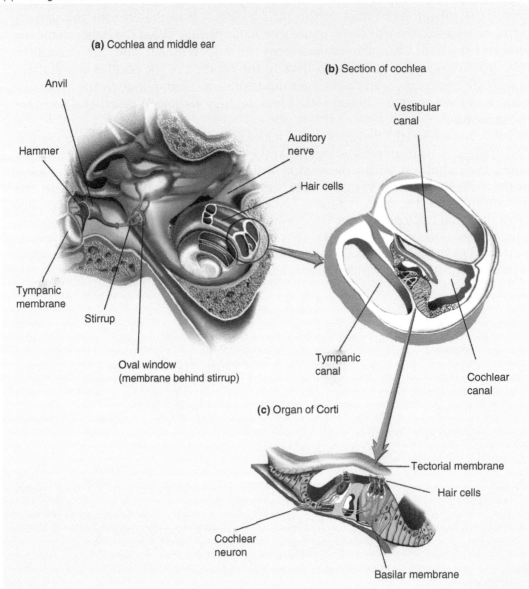

Figure 3.5   The structures of the middle and inner ear
Source: Garrett (2015)

THE TRANSDUCTION OF SOUND INTO NEURAL ENERGY

The stiff mattress of the basilar membrane holds the intricate organ of Corti which acts as the cochlear's sound-transformational device, by turning pressure changes into neural input. If one looks closely at the organ of Conti they will see it consists of four rows of specialized sensory cells resembling fine hairs that protrude up into the scala media from a bed of supporting cells. When the stapes knocks on the oval window, the pressure changes in the scala vestibuli and scala tympani also cause a wave-like movement along the basilar membrane which ripples into the deeper recesses of the cochlea. The mechanical properties of the basilar membrane also change as it extends into the cochlea: it is narrow and relatively stiff near the oval window, and wider and more flexible towards the cochlea's apex. As a result, the part of the basilar membrane showing the greatest movement will depend on the frequency of the vibration: low sounds producing most displacement near the apex, while high sounds produce greater displacement near the base.

The organ of Conti contains two different sets of sensory hair cells. There is a single row of about 3,500 inner hair cells that run along the medial aspect of the basilar membrane, and around 12,000 outer hair cells which form three rows more laterally. The less numerous inner hair cells are the most important for hearing, with their axons making some 95% of the fibres of the auditory nerve that project to the brain. In contrast, the more numerous outer hair cells act to increase the cochlea's sensitivity by mechanically amplifying low-level sound.

How do these hair cells transduce pressure into neural energy and produce action potentials? The answer lies with lots of very fine finger-like protrusions, called cilia, which are found on the upper surface of hair cells that extend upwards to an outer fibrous covering called the tectorial membrane (tectorial means 'cover'). As pressure waves enter the cochlea, the motion causes the basilar membrane and tectorial membranes to flex, and this forces fluid to flow past the cilia making them move laterally (right and left). This also leads to the transduction of sound pressure into neural energy (Moller, 2000). Under resting conditions the cilia are connected to their neighbours by fine filaments known as tip links. Normally these links are taut, but when displaced by the flexing of the basilar and tectorial membranes, their potassium channels become exposed. This allows potassium ions to move into the hair cells, causing their partial depolarization, which then opens excitatory calcium channels adding to the influx of positive current. However, unlike other nerve cells, the hair cell itself does not create an action potential. Rather, the influx of calcium triggers neurotransmitter (thought to be glutamate) release directly into the synapse, which then triggers action potentials in the neurons making up the cochlear (auditory) nerve.

KEY TERMS: *sensory hair cells, cilia, tectorial membrane*

THE ASCENDING AUDITORY PATHWAYS

The brain receives sound information from the auditory nerve (or cochlear nerve) which is a branch of the eighth cranial nerve (the other main branch arises from the ear's vestibular system). This emerges from the cochlea as the spiral ganglion, composed of highly specialized bipolar cells that have a single main dendrite feeding into a centralized cell body and transmitting axon. There are around 50,000 bipolar cells in each human spiral ganglion. Of these, the vast majority receive input from the inner hair cells protruding from the basilar membrane. Clearly, these are the most important for the transmission of sound information to the brain. The remainder of the spiral ganglion's bipolar cells obtain input from the outer hairs.

The axons of the bipolar cells leave the cochlea, forming a nerve trunk which in humans is about an inch long. This travels up into the brain through the bony posterior cranial fossa to enter the medulla oblongata. Here the axons synapse with the neurons of the **cochlear nuclei** located in the upper part of the medulla. At this point, the projection is ipsilateral with fibres from the right ear arriving at the right cochlear nucleus and vice versa. However, this arrangement is made more complex because the auditory nerve now splits, with one branch going to the dorsal (upper) part of the cochlear nucleus, and the other innervating its ventral (lower) part. This division segregates auditory input: fibres passing to the dorsal cochlear nucleus conveying high-frequency sounds, and those to the ventral region low-frequency sounds. After the cochlear nucleus, most fibres pass to the opposite side of the brain. Two ascending pathways now become conspicuous (see Figure 3.6). These are the ventral acoustic stria which passes through the trapezoid body to the superior olivary complex located in the tegmentum of the pons, and the dorsal acoustic stria (sometimes

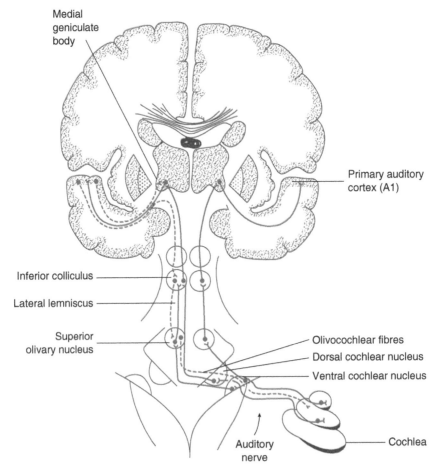

Figure 3.6   The auditory pathway and auditory cortex
Source: Higgs et al. (2020); Barnes (2013)

called the stria of von Monakow) ascending in the lateral lemniscus that terminates in the **inferior colliculi** close to the superior colliculi. The inferior colliculi is the largest nucleus of the human auditory system which is anatomically complex, containing more than ten times the number of neurons than there are axons in the auditory nerve (Batra, 2014). In turn, the inferior colliculi gives rise to a pathway to the medial geniculate nucleus in the thalamus. From here, there is an orderly projection of fibres to the primary **auditory cortex** situated in the upper or superior gyrus of the temporal lobes (Webster, 1992).

In addition to this ascending system originating in the ear's cochlea and ultimately passing all the way through the medulla and midbrain to the temporal lobes, there is a pathway that goes in the opposite direction. This descending nerve pathway originates in the auditory cortex and projects via the medial geniculate nucleus and inferior colliculi to the superior olivary complex in the brain stem. In turn, this forms the olivocochlear bundle whose fibres synapse on the inner and outer hair cells of the cochlea. It appears this pathway has an inhibitory effect on the hair cells which may function to reduce the responses of these cells to non-essential information. Apparently, this feedback inhibition sharpens the perception of pitch and is important for the suppression of background noise when attention is being concentrated on a particular sound (Plack, 2014).

> **KEY TERMS:** *cochlear nuclei, superior olivary complex, inferior colliculi, medial geniculate nucleus, auditory cortex, olivocochlear bundle*

THE PERCEPTION OF PITCH

Our ability to hear pitch – or being able to distinguish differences between the high and low tones of a sound – is essential to hearing. Without this faculty our sonic world would be a blur, lacking the capability to hear different words or make sense of music. But how are we able to tell apart one type of sound wave from another? Although this is a simple question, it has not always been easy to answer. Traditionally, two main theories have arisen: place theory and frequency theory. The place theory was first proposed by Hermann von Helmholtz in 1863, who argued that we detect differences in sound because certain points on the basilar membrane vibrate maximally to sound waves of a particular frequency. More specifically, Helmholtz compared the membrane to a piano and the membrane's hair cells to piano strings, each tuned to vibrate to a particular frequency – a system which he believed was so precise that it enabled us to distinguish around 5,000 different pitches. Helmholtz also pointed out that the basilar membrane is narrow and stiff (like a high string on a piano) near the oval window, and wide and floppy (like a low string) at the other end. This spatial difference, he argued, then allowed each sound frequency arriving at the ear to activate a different set of neurons in the auditory nerve.

However, not all investigators accepted place theory. In 1886, shortly after the telephone was invented, William Rutherford proposed the frequency theory. Rutherford's work had led him to believe that sound waves cause every individual hair cell in the ear to be stimulated to some extent. Thus, pitch was more likely to be encoded by the *pattern* of neural activity in the auditory nerve, and not *subsets* of neurons. To give a very simplistic hypothetical example, the neurons of the auditory nerve could be imagined to fire at the same frequency as the vibrations rippling through the basilar membrane. Hence, if the ear encoded a tone of 1,000 Hz, then the auditory nerve neurons might fire at the same rate (e.g. 1,000 times a second).

Early evidence supported frequency theory. For example, Wever and Bray (1930) attached a recording electrode to the auditory nerve of an anaesthetized cat, and found the frequency and amplitude of neural responses were similar to the sounds arriving at the ear. However, there was a problem with the frequency theory because there is a limit to how many times a neuron can fire. In fact, the highest rate of firing a neuron can achieve is around 1,000 impulses per second – yet we can detect tones up to 20,000 Hz. To resolve this difficulty, Wever and Bray devised an explanation involving the 'volley principle'. This proposed that at higher frequencies the neurons of the auditory nerve do not fire in synchronization, but rather in a quick and rapid pulse-like succession. In effect, the neurons 'take turns' at firing. The idea is similar to the way in which a group of soldiers can achieve constant fire with single shot rifles, i.e. they can only maintain a constant volley if one group is shooting, while another group is reloading. But, even with this ingenious explanation, the volley principle was still found wanting since it could only explain neural frequency codes up to 4,000 Hz.

In the 1950s, evidence began to support the place theory, largely though the research of a Hungarian communications engineer called Georg von Békésy, who would win the Nobel Prize in Physiology for his work in 1961 – some of it involving work on cochleas from deceased elephants and humans. By stimulating the oval window of the middle ear with an electronically powered piston, von Békésy was able to observe the movement of the cochlear basilar membrane (using a technique involving strobe photography and the movement of silver flakes). Von Békésy showed that a sound of a given frequency caused the basilar membrane to bulge in a wavelike manner, which began at the base of the cochlea and moved inwards towards its apex. He also found that the sound's frequency determined the exact site on the membrane where the peak of the bulge took place. A high-pitched sound produced the highest bulge at the base, whilst lower bass frequencies caused the peak to move towards the apex. However, very low frequencies did not produce this effect. Instead, a broad bulge that covered the entire basilar membrane was caused by deep bass sounds which made it vibrate at the frequency of the incoming sound.

Von Békésy's research therefore showed that both the frequency and place theories are correct to some extent. Pitch produced by sounds of low frequency does indeed appear to be coded by rate of firing in the auditory neurons as Rutherford first thought – although this only occurs for a limited part of the sound spectrum. But for most of the sounds we hear, pitch is coded by the place at which the basilar membrane is vibrated by its greatest degree. This, presumably, is then encoded by a specific set of neurons. Exactly where the transition occurs from frequency to place processing is not known for sure. It is likely, however, that the frequency code works below 400 Hz, the place code works above 4,000 Hz, and both codes (perhaps using the volley principle) work together in varying degrees to represent the frequencies in between (Yost, 2009).

Because the cilia of the hair cells at the base of the cochlea are displaced by high-frequency sounds, and those further up at the apex by low-frequency sounds, this means the basilar membrane along its length encodes auditory information from high to low. In other words, the basilar membrane represents sound in a tonotopic way. This tonotopic representation is further maintained in the cochlear nucleus, inferior colliculus, medial geniculate nucleus and auditory cortex. The discovery of the basilar membrane's tonotopic map has also enabled the development of **cochlear implants** – electronic devices implanted in the inner ear to allow people with deafness to hear. They work essentially by attaching a miniature microphone to the outside of the ear which encodes the frequencies of incoming sounds. It then relays the information to a speech processor just beneath the skin. From there, the signal travels through a wire that is threaded through the cochlea to the appropriate places on the basilar membrane, thereby allowing the person to perceive sound with different pitches (i.e. it works on the principle of place analysis). Although cochlear implants do not restore full normal hearing, and their effectiveness varies between individuals, most recipients of cochlea implants are able to successfully engage in face-to-face conversation and can also use a telephone.

KEY TERMS: *place theory, frequency theory, basilar membrane, tonotopic representation, cochlear implants*

THE PERCEPTION OF LOUDNESS

In physical terms, loudness is caused by changes in the amplitude of a sound wave. But how is this encoded in neural terms? In his classic work on the cochlea, Békésy found that although pitch determined the distance the bulge in the basilar membrane travelled, loudness was produced by the height and expanse of the bulge. In other words, by increasing the loudness of a sound, the basilar membrane was displaced over a much larger area and with increasing vigour. This indicated that loudness might be encoded by the auditory nerves in two ways. Firstly, as the sound stimulus gets more intense, the basilar membrane vibrates with greater amplitude, and this might be expected to cause higher rates of depolarization in the hair cells thereby increasing the number of nerve impulses in the auditory nerve. Secondly, the greater expansive movement of the basilar membrane would be expected to cause a larger number of neurons to fire. Although there have been some objections (e.g. Relkin & Doucet, 1997), research supports the involvement of both these mechanisms working together to produce the neural encoding for loudness.

THE LOCALIZATION OF SOUNDS

A vital requirement for survival for most animals is being able to locate the source of a sound. If we close our eyes, it is likely we will determine quite accurately where certain sounds are originating from – whether they are coming from right or left, front or back, above or below. This ability is largely dependent on the sound reaching each of our ears at slightly different times. For example, if someone sounds a horn to our right, it is easy to picture the sound waves reaching the right ear before the left. In addition, our head will act as a barrier to make the distance to the left ear greater. Consequently, the sound waves reaching the right ear will be slightly out of phase with those on the left (see Figure 3.7). This is called the interaural time difference. Although this gap is normally less than one-tenth of a second (it is maximal when the sound source is 90° to our gaze, and minimal if in front or behind us), it is sufficient for the brain to locate the sound.

Another feature of the sound stimulus used to judge its location is the interaural intensity difference. Because sound waves get weaker as they travel through air, a horn sounded to our right will result in less intense sound waves reaching our left ear. This, again, will be accentuated by our head which will impede the sound waves reaching the left. In many instances, our head creates such an impenetrable barrier, or sound shadow, for our opposing ear, that the only way for it to detect sound is to have it reflected back from a nearby surface. Obviously, this produces a further weakening of the sound's intensity.

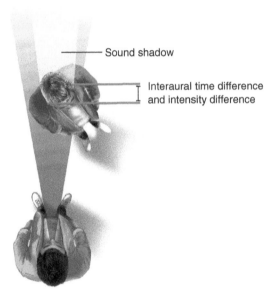

Figure 3.7   Differential intensity and time of arrival as cues for sound localization
Source: Garrett and Hough (2018), from 'Navigation in Fog', *Scientific American*, July 3, 1880, p. 3.

Since the auditory system makes use of interaural differences in both time and frequency, an obvious question to ask is what's the most important factor in locating the source of a sound? The answer depends on the pitch of the sound wave. For example, low-frequency (bass) sounds tend to wrap themselves around our head and reach our far ear with almost the same intensity as our closer ear. Thus, low-frequency sound waves travel around our head without significant reductions in intensity, which means that our ears have to rely on interaural time differences to locate sound. In contrast, high-frequency (treble) sounds tend to be reflected by our head before getting to our opposite ear. Consequently, the main cue used to locate high frequencies is the interaural intensity difference.

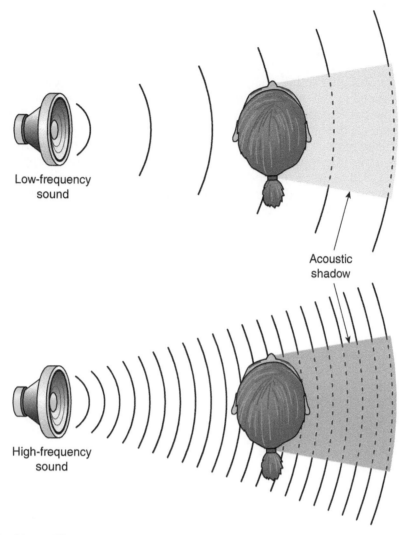

Figure 3.8   Phase differences as a cue for sound localization. Note that now low-frequency sounds produce far less of a sound shadow than high-frequency sounds.

Source: Garrett and Hough (2018)

Although several brain areas are involved in the coding of binaural cues, the most important is the first brain area to receive input from both ears – namely the superior olive located in the pons. This nucleus has two regions responsive to binaural cues: the medial superior olive which encodes latency differences, and the lateral superior olive which does the same for intensity. Recordings taken from single neurons in these areas show they respond best when the two ears receive the same sound at slightly different times, or at slightly different intensities. In fact, some neurons in the medial olive respond more intensely when the left ear receives sound first, and others respond this way if the right ear receives the sound first. A similar type of processing occurs for intensity differences reaching the neurons in the lateral olive. Thus, neurons in both these regions detect a wide range of binaural differences in latency and intensity, and it is these responses that allow us to localize a sound's source (Hudspeth, 2000).

KEY TERMS: *interaural time difference, interaural intensity difference, superior olive*

THE AUDITORY CORTEX

The first stage of higher sound analysis takes place in the auditory cortex. In humans this lies embedded in the upper part of the posterior temporal lobe, hidden from view in a fold known as Heschl's gyrus, just inside the lateral fissure. This region contains two main areas: (1) the primary auditory cortex (area A1) receiving projections from the medial geniculate nucleus, and (2) the associative or secondary auditory cortex (area A2), which also receives innervation from the medial geniculate nucleus, but gets most of its input from A1. Although the ascending auditory system crosses in the brain at several points as it passes upwards, the auditory cortex still gets most of its input bilaterally. Hence, a sound from the right-sided ear is registered and processed predominantly (but not exclusively) by the left primary auditory cortex, and vice versa. Despite this, there is a bias, since it has been shown that tones presented separately to either ear produce greater activation in the left auditory cortex compared to the right (Devlin et al., 2003).

The primary auditory cortex (A1) is also tonotopically organized for pitch or pure tones (see Figure 3.9). That is, cells with similar tone preferences lie in columns close to each other with an orderly progression of frequency bands as one moves across the cortex (Moerel et al., 2014). More specifically, the anterior end of the cortex contains cells that encode for deep (bass) sounds, whilst its posterior regions process high-frequency sounds. This has been demonstrated by extracellular single cell recording (Philips et al., 1994) and brain-scanning techniques (Talavage et al., 2014). These cortical neurons also respond to the onset of a particular tone (an 'on' response), the termination of a tone (an 'off' response), or sometimes both 'on-off' responses. In addition to the pitch detecting neurons, which make up the majority of cells in the cortex, there are others responding to more complex sounds, including noise bursts, clangs or clicks. Some also encode the duration of a sound, or respond best to moving sounds (Coren et al., 2004).

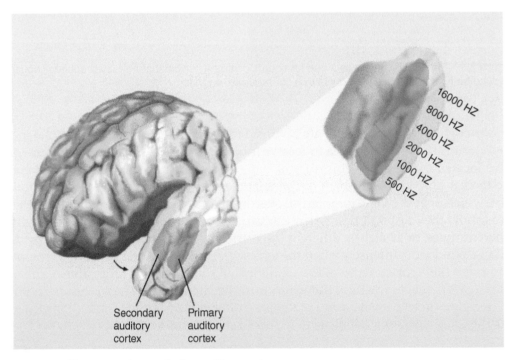

Figure 3.9   The tonotopic map in the auditory cortex
Source: Garrett (2015)

The neural responses to sound in A2 are more varied. These neurons generally do not respond to simple pure tones, but fire in sustained ways to complex patterns of sounds, or those which have been learned. In animals these can include species-specific vocalizations of various types. In humans, there are also regions of A2 specialized for analysing speech and musical sounds (Zatorre et al., 2002). More specifically, neurons in A2 are especially sensitive to changing trajectories of a sound's frequency that incorporate many different components (Chong et al., 2019). Such sounds are likely to convey complex and meaningful information such as speech or the events of social interaction. A2 cells are also more likely to fire in response to higher 'top-down' cognitive influences as occurs when someone is directing attention (Banich & Compton, 2018). It is also interesting to note that whereas electrical stimulation of the human auditory cortex during surgery typically produces simple sound sensations such as ringing and tones, stimulation of adjacent areas can produce complex auditory hallucinations.

Two main streams of auditory processing take place beyond the auditory cortex and its phonological network – one passing dorsally through the parietal lobe concerned with recognizing the spatial location of sounds in the visual scene, and the other going ventrally through the temporal lobe involved in sound recognition and analysis of its specific auditory components (Kaas & Hackett, 2000). This latter pathway may also be involved in converting auditory events into audio-visual concepts. These two pathways are not dissimilar to the '*where*' (dorsal route) and '*what*' (ventral route) systems which operate for vision (see Chapter 2).

KEY TERMS: *Heschl's gyrus, primary auditory cortex (A1), medial geniculate nucleus, secondary auditory cortex (A2)*

THE SENSE OF SMELL (OLFACTION)

Smell (olfaction) and taste (gustation) are sometimes referred to as the chemical senses since they depend on the nose and mouth respectively to detect chemical compounds. In the case of smell, the chemicals must exist in an airborne or vaporous state, whereas for taste they need to be soluble in water (see later). The chemical senses were the first to evolve in animals (remember the earliest life arose in a sea of chemicals) and are consequently found in the most primitive of organisms. Despite this, the chemical senses still provide important functions for higher creatures including ourselves. Apart from its obvious pleasurable qualities, taste provides a means of evaluating whether food is safe to consume. Alternatively, smell is used by many animals to help obtain a mate, mark territory, identify others of the same species, and find food. Although smell and taste are often considered to be poorly developed in humans, they remain important determinants of our behaviour, and may be much more influential than we realize. For example, mothers can recognize their babies by smell (Porter et al., 1983) and male body odour can significantly affect the mate choices of females (Wedekind et al., 1995). It has also been claimed, and widely stated, that females living together can synchronize their menstrual cycles on the basis of olfactory cues (McClintock, 1971), although this has been denied by others (Clarke et al., 2012). A certain smell such as a perfume can also conjure up vivid memories and emotions from the past – a response that can be used in therapy to help people with dementia recall things about their lives (Afif & Kim, 2018).

KEY TERMS: *chemical senses, olfaction*

THE SMELL PATHWAYS FROM NOSE TO BRAIN

In humans, the receptors for smell are found in a small patch of mucus-covered membrane, about 3×3 centimetres (roughly the size of a postage stamp), called the **olfactory epithelium** located in the roof of each nasal cavity (Figure 3.10). Curiously, because this site lies at the top of the nasal cavities where they turn into the respiratory passageways, the olfactory receptors are not in the most effective position to be stimulated by air currents. This is why we often sniff the air to increase its flow across the olfactory epithelium. Each olfactory epithelium contains about 5 million neurons (actually specialized endings of the olfactory nerve) whose dendrites extend into the mucus layer on the epithelial surface, where they terminate in bulbous knobs from which protrude around 10–20 specialized long hairs or cilia. This arrangement not only increases the sensory surface area of the olfactory epithelium, but because they are also covered by a thin coat of mucus which flows constantly (it is replaced about every 10 minutes), the cilia are immersed in a solvent for odour molecules. Interestingly, the olfactory bipolar cells are constantly being replaced every 30 days or so. This rapid turnover is unusual and no other type of neuron in the nervous system is known to be replaced so quickly (Graziadei, 1977).

The size of the olfactory epithelium is an indicator of an animal's olfactory sensitivity. For example, the surface area of the human olfactory epithelium is around 9 cm², whereas in certain dogs it can be as large as 170 cm². The effectiveness of a larger olfactory epithelium is largely due to it containing a far greater number of receptors for detecting smells. The German Shepherd Dog, for instance, not only has some 100–150 cilia per bipolar cell that project into the mucus layer of the olfactory epithelium, but this greater area also provides some 224 million receptors compared to just 10 million for humans (Wenzel, 1973). With an ability to smell between 10,000 to 100,000 times better than people, it has been estimated that some dogs can detect odours in parts per trillion (Walker et al., 2006).

Each bipolar olfactory neuron also has an ascending output axon that passes away from the olfactory epithelium and through a series of tiny holes in the cribriform plate lying at the base of the cranium, called the olfactory foramina. Lying just above the cribriform plate is the **olfactory bulb** situated at the anterior base of each cerebral hemisphere. The olfactory bulb, which is regarded as a forebrain structure, is anatomically complex. When reaching the olfactory bulb, the bipolar fibres target a mitral cell which has a triangular body and is named after its resemblance to a bishop's mitre. In the human brain, there are around 50,000 mitral cells and each receives input from around 250 axons. The mitral cells are also bundled together in clumps forming a dense accumulation of synapses and dendrites known as olfactory glomeruli

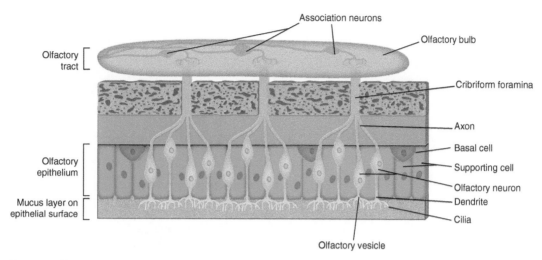

Figure 3.10 The olfactory epithelium
Source: Cook et al. (2021)

(a glomerulus is a cluster of nerve endings). There are around 1,000 glomeruli in each olfactory bulb, and each receives information from a particular type of olfactory receptor responsible for encoding a certain smell. Hence, different types of odorants activate different groupings of glomeruli.

The olfactory bulb also contains other neuron types, including tufted cells which arise from the glomeruli and granule cells which inhibit mitral cells so that only highly excited olfactory impulses are transmitted. This inhibition is important in olfactory adaptation – as occurs when we quickly become habituated to a new smell. The granule cells also receive input from other brain areas such as the limbic system, and this may help modify our reaction to smell under certain conditions. For example, the aroma of certain foods is perceived differently depending on whether we are hungry or have just finished eating.

KEY TERMS: *olfactory epithelium, olfactory bulb, olfactory glomeruli*

From the olfactory bulb, the axons of mitral and tufted cells pass into the olfactory tract which runs under the frontal cortex, before dividing into the lateral olfactory stria and medial olfactory stria. The olfactory tract is unique among sensory cranial nerves since it does not proceed directly to the brain stem or thalamus (although the thalamus does receive a projection from the olfactory tubercle – see Courtiol and Wilson 2015). Instead, it passes directly to higher areas of the forebrain. More precisely, the lateral olfactory stria projects to the primary olfactory cortex, located in the medial aspects of the limbic temporal lobe which includes the olfactory tubercle along with the piriform cortex and **periamygdaloid cortex** – the latter areas making up an ill-defined region which surrounds the **amygdala** (see Figure 3.11). From here, olfactory information is dispersed to the entorhinal cortex (sometimes called the association olfactory cortex), amygdala and hippocampus (Nagappan et al., 2017). In contrast, the medial olfactory stria, which is not well developed in humans, projects to structures lying

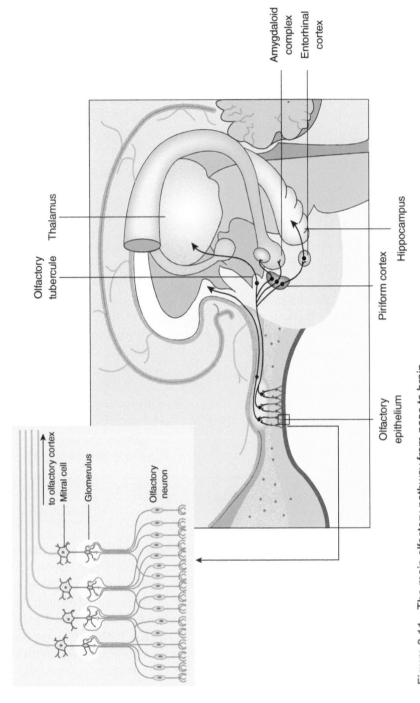

Figure 3.11 The main olfactory pathway from nose to brain

Source: Higgs et al. (2020), adapted from the Open University Course SD329: Sensation and Perception (2003)

close to the anterior hypothalamus, of which the most important is the septal nuclei (sometimes known as the medial olfactory area) which is found below the rostrum (snout) of the corpus callosum. This pathway is believed to be involved in producing emotional responses that are elicited by olfactory stimuli (Purves et al., 2008).

KEY TERMS: *auditory cortex, piriform cortex, periamygdaloid cortex, amygdala, lateral and medial olfactory stria*

SPECIAL INTEREST 3.1

SYNAESTHESIA: THE MERGING OF THE SENSES

The word 'synaesthesia' means joined sensation, being derived from the Greek *syn* (together) and *aisthesis* (perception), denotes a condition where a sensation in one modality will cause an involuntary sensation in another. So, for example, colours may be perceived by hearing sounds. Although synaesthesia can take many forms and may sometimes involve all the main senses, it most commonly occurs when letters, numbers or tones are seen as certain colours (e.g. the number 8 may be seen as purple, or the tone G-sharp perceived as green). These perceptions are also highly specific to each individual. Although synaesthesia was first described by the philosopher John Locke in 1690, who reported the case of a blind man who experienced the colour scarlet when hearing a trumpet, and given further credence by Sir Francis Galton in 1883, many researchers remained sceptical until the neurologist Richard Cytowic rekindled interest when he published *The Man Who Tasted Shapes* in 1993, which described the case of his friend Michael Watson. The first time that Cytowic became aware that Watson was a synaesthete took place when the two men had dinner. When making the sauce for the meal, Watson confided that tastes produced shape sensations that swept down his arms to his fingertips, and in some cases these taste shapes were experienced all over his body. When cooking the meal, Watson had intended the taste of the chicken to have 'a pointed shape', but to his dismay it had come out 'all round'.

How common is synaesthesia? Estimates vary with Cytowic giving a figure of 1 in 20,000 people, although others believe it may be as high as 1 in 200 (Ramachandran & Hubbard, 2001). Part of the problem in assessing its prevalence is that estimates have typically relied on synaesthetes reporting themselves, a problem exacerbated by the likelihood that significant numbers of people may have the condition but don't realize it, believing they are normal. One well-controlled study suggests it occurs in 1% of the population, equally between males and females, with the most common variant being the colouring of days (Simner et al., 2006). There also appears to be a positive family history of the condition in around one-third of cases (Baron-Cohen et al., 1996) which has led to speculation that, at least in some instances, synaesthesia has a genetic basis. It has also been claimed there is a tendency for people with synaesthesia to be left-handed and autistic (Baron-Cohen et al., 2013). A number of gifted people are also believed to have been synaesthetic, including the poet Arthur Rimbaud, the physicist Richard Feynman, and the painter Wassily Kandinsky whose work was sometimes intended to evoke sounds in those who viewed it. Another synaesthete is the British artist David Hockney who perceives music as colour.

(Continued)

The most popular theory of synaesthesia proposes that during early development, the brain of a synaesthete becomes cross-wired in such a way that extra neural links are formed between areas serving different senses. If this is true, then one might expect to find more sensory brain areas at work in the brain of a synaesthete. One study that examined this question was undertaken by Paulesu et al. (1996), who set up a positron emission tomography (PET) study that measured cerebral blood flow in six female synaesthetes who were asked to name what colours they sensed when hearing words and tones. Both the synaesthetes and controls exhibited increased activity in the main language areas that border the Sylvian fissure. However, the synesthetes showed far greater and more extensive activation of the visual association areas, including the posterior temporal cortex, and the junction between the parietal and occipital cortex. Other studies have suggested that grapheme-colour synaesthesia might be due to cross-activation of a grapheme-recognition region near Wernicke's area and a colour area called V4 in the visual cortex (Ramachandran & Hubbard, 2003). However, as the research has progressed, it appears that a network of at least six overlapping brain areas (both motor and sensory) rather than a single brain region or connection underlie synaesthesia, which includes the intraparietal sulcus and inferior temporal cortex (Rouw et al., 2011; Weiss & Fink, 2009).

THE DISCOVERY OF OLFACTORY RECEPTORS

It has long been known that humans can recognize thousands of different smells, along with an appreciation of odour that has been deeply rooted in many cultures (Philpott et al., 2008). The fact that we are sensitive to such a large number of odours has long interested researchers and posed a challenge for those who believed there must be a way of categorizing these into a meaningful classification. This was attempted, for example, by the great Swedish botanist Linnaeus, who is famous for his classification of animals and plants. In 1752, Linnaeus grouped odours into seven classes: (1) aromatic, (2) fragrant, (3) musky, (4) garlicky, (5) goaty, (6) repulsive and (7) nauseous. This classification was expanded by the Dutch physiologist Hendrik Zwaardemaker in 1895 who added two more classes (tobacco-like and perfume-like), along with various subclasses for each primary smell. However, these attempts at classification never gained widespread support – partly because they did not explain the underlying physical nature of the odour, or the reason for the differences between them. By the early part of the twentieth century, researchers had established that odours were likely to be chemical in nature, but remained puzzled since similar chemical substances often produced different smells (or that different chemicals could evoke similar smells). In 1949, the Scottish scientist Robert Moncrieff proposed it was the size and shape of the chemical molecule, and not its chemical composition, which was the important coding feature of an odorant. This also implied that odorous, airborne chemicals had to have a molecular configuration that fitted into a specialized receptor, presumably located in the olfactory epithelium.

During the 1960s, the British biochemist John Amoore studied the molecular structure of over 600 odorant compounds and concluded that the molecule's three-dimensional shape determined its smell (Amoore et al., 1964). That is, molecules with similar sizes and shapes produced the same type of smell. Indeed, by noting the shape and size of a given molecule (say, a spherical molecule with a diameter of six angstroms[1]) Amoore was able to predict its smell (in this case musk). Amoore also categorized odorous molecules into seven groups, with each one producing a 'primary' odour.[2] This suggested the nose contained seven basic types of receptor, with each one sensitive to a primary odorant which fitted neatly into its site. This was called the **stereochemical theory of olfaction**. However, the theory soon proved problematic because many molecules did not conform to Amoore's predictions. Yet some support for stereochemical theory came from studies of **anosmia** where people have lost the ability to detect certain smells (Boesveldt et al., 2017). Several dozen different types of anosmia are known to occur with some types being quite common (e.g. one person in ten is insensitive to the smell of cyanide, and one in a thousand cannot detect butyl mercaptan which has a strong skunk odour). The simplest explanation is that the anosmic lacks the receptor for the smell they cannot detect. But if this is true, then it implies the olfactory system must contain many more types of receptor than Amoore first envisaged.

More recent biochemical and molecular research has indeed discovered that the olfactory system does have many more (e.g. hundreds) different receptors. The first step towards this breakthrough came when Jones and Reed (1989) identified a specific **G-protein** in the sensory neurons of the olfactory epithelium. This was important because G-proteins are directly linked to receptor molecules in the cellular membrane, where they stimulate the synthesis of the second messenger cAMP inside the cell (see Chapter 1). Following this, Linda Buck and Richard Axel (see the *Key Thinker* box) were able to use the genes responsible for G proteins to track down olfactory receptor genes. In fact, they would discover that human DNA has around 400 functional genes each encoding for individual receptors in the olfactory epithelium. Buck and Axel have also shown that axons from neurons expressing each type of odorant receptor project to the same segment of the olfactory bulb. Thus, the encoding of different smells becomes segregated at this first stage of olfactory processing.

Despite Buck and Axel's pioneering research, there are still many unanswered questions concerning olfaction. One such puzzle is our amazing sensitivity to smell. Remarkably, by varying the components of 128 odour molecules, Bushdid et al. (2014) have estimated that humans can distinguish a trillion different smells. Clearly, we cannot have a different receptor for each smell. Nor can an individual neuron with its own specialized odorant receptor produce the variety of signals required to distinguish between so many smells. Consequently, olfactory discrimination, or its finer aspects, must take place elsewhere in the system – perhaps in the brain. However, just how it does this remains a mystery.

KEY TERMS: *stereochemical theory of olfaction, anosmia, G-protein*

---

[1]An angstrom is a unit of length used to measure very small distances. One angstrom is equal to 10^{-10} m (one ten-billionth of a meter or 0.1 nanometres).

[2]Amoore's groups were camphoraceous, musky, floral, pepperminty, etheral, pungent and putrid.

KEY THINKER 3.1

LINDA BUCK

Linda Buck is a Nobel Prize laureate for her work on olfaction, which showed that the cells of the human nose not only contain receptors for smell, but they are also encoded by a family of over 1,000 different genes, with each one specifying a receptor able to detect only a few odours. Buck was raised in Seattle, Washington, by a mother of Swedish ancestry and an electrical engineer father with a penchant for inventing things. Encouraged to think independently and be ambitious, Buck attended the nearby University of Washington. Although setting out to major in Psychology with a view to becoming a psychotherapist, she turned to medical biology – graduating with a BSc in Psychology and Microbiology in 1975. Her PhD examined the functions of white blood cells, and in 1980 she moved to Columbia to begin postdoctoral work looking at the proteins found on cell surfaces that help the immune system recognize self from non-self. This led to a breakthrough when Buck discovered that some of these proteins accumulated inside cells – a finding requiring her to learn more about the molecular biology. To this end, she moved into the laboratory of Richard Axel, a well-known pioneer of recombinant DNA technology, skilled in creating new genetic sequences, isolating genes, and inserting this material into other genomes. Such recombinant engineering could also produce clinically useful proteins from genes inserted into 'factory' cells, and it resulted in a group of five patents (known as the 'Axel patents') that proved highly lucrative for Columbia – earning it some $790 million in revenues until they began to expire in 2000.

In her new role, Buck would also team up with Eric Kandel, who was known for his work with the sea-slug *Aplysia* (see Chapter 9). This research would show that an Aplysia neuron (known as R15) found in its abdominal ganglion expressed a gene that produced neuropeptides involved in egg-laying. However, as this work drew to a close in 1985, Buck came across a paper that was to change her life. It addressed the question of how odours are detected by the nose. The problem was simple: how are animals able to detect an enormous number of different smells estimated to number 10,000 or more? There was also the problem of how nearly identical chemicals can generate very different odour perceptions. Buck was hooked by the problem and joined forces with Axel to try locating odorant receptors in the nose's epithelium tissue. Although this would take her more than five years to accomplish, the results of that work led to a major breakthrough. It showed there was a multigene family in the rat that coded for over 100 different odorant receptors – each able to detect a unique smell. Subsequent work showed that humans have around 400 (or so) odorant receptors which are derived from the largest known gene family in our DNA.

In 1991, Buck moved to Harvard. The next step was to understand how the odorant receptors were organized in the olfactory epithelium. To locate these receptors, Buck used a technique called 'in situ hybridization', which used DNA probes to identify specific receptors. This work showed that each olfactory sensory neuron expressed only one type of receptor. From this, Buck was able to estimate that the olfactory epithelium contained in the region of 5 million receptors. Each odorant receptor was also distributed over the entire olfactory epithelium.

Her initial results in 1991 had indicated that each odorant receptor only detected one type of smell, but this situation turned out to be more complicated when she began exposing murine olfactory neurons to a series of odorants using calcium imaging to visualize their responses. This work showed that a smell (e.g. orange, nut-like etc.) could activate different types of receptor, and a single receptor could be activated by a handful of different odorants at varying intensities. It was apparent, therefore, that the nose was using a combinational code, which Buck likened to the colours on a patchwork quilt, with different odours being recognized by different combinations of odorant receptors (patches). This theory also helped explain why changing the structure of an odour, even slightly, could alter its smell.

In 2004, Buck and Axel won the Nobel Prize 'for their discoveries of odorant receptors and the organization of the olfactory system'. Over the course of some 25 years, Buck has transformed our understanding of smell and opened up new ways of showing how genes are linked to the transmission of sensory information. Her work has also demonstrated the enormous power of molecular biology to help solve fundamental problems in neuroscience. Linda Buck is, at present, one of only three women to have won a Nobel Prize for neuroscience research (the other two are Rita Levi-Montalcini and May Britt-Moser) and hopefully will prove an inspiration for many more women to follow in her footsteps.

THE SENSE OF TASTE (GUSTATION)

Humans evolved as omnivores, enabling them to eat a variety of food of both plant and animal origin. Consequently, early on in their evolutionary development, humans depended on a sensitive system of taste recognition which could distinguish between new sources of food or potential poisons (Breslin, 2013). The sensation of taste is produced when a substance in the mouth reacts chemically with a taste receptor. Although the main organ for taste is obviously our tongue, a few taste receptors can also be found on the soft palate, the inner surface of the cheeks, and even the epiglottis of the larynx. Scattered all over the tongue's upper surface are small, nipple-like protrusions called papillae which give the tongue its slightly abrasive feel. Each of these has from one to several hundred taste buds, with each one containing some 50 to 150 taste receptors. There are about 10,000 taste buds on the human tongue, although this number can vary from 500 to 20,000, each of which is a globular structure consisting of three types of cell: supporting cells, taste cells, and basal cells. Supporting cells provide the structural support and basal cells are the site of origin for new taste buds. The sensory taste cells are visually distinct since they give rise to microvilli, sometimes called gustatory hairs, that protrude through a taste pore (or gap) at the surface of the taste bud, where they become bathed by saliva. It is here, within the microvilli, that transduction of taste information into neural input takes place. The taste bud cells are not neurons and nor do they have axons to carry gustatory information to the brain. Nonetheless, these cells contain ion channels which change their electrophysiological properties, causing neurotransmitter to be released onto nerve fibres at the bottom of the taste bud (Chaudhari & Roper, 2010). Taste cells have a short lifespan and are constantly replaced every few weeks or so (Barlow, 2015).

Although the number of different chemicals that form the basis of our tastes is endless, we appear to be only capable of recognizing a few basic taste sensations. Traditionally, these have been divided into four categories: sour, salty, bitter and sweet. Young babies generally have a marked innate preference for sweet substances while rejecting bitter ones – a useful bias since most toxins are also bitter tasting. This taste preference appears to be well developed before birth since it also occurs in premature infants (Goldson & Kelly, 2008). More recently, a fifth primary taste sensation has been identified called 'umami', meaning 'delicious' in Japanese, which is described as having a 'meaty' or 'savoury' flavour (Kurihara & Kashiwayanagi, 1998). This taste appears to help us select protein in our diet. All of these sensations are created by a different group of chemicals: for example, the taste of sour is produced by acids, or more specifically their hydrogen ions; salty tastes are produced by metal ions (inorganic salts); and bitter ones, produced by alkaloid compounds. In contrast, the taste of sweetness is elicited by many organic substances, including sugars and some amino acids.

It was once thought, and is sometimes still stated in school textbooks, that our sensitivity to these tastes varies in distinct regions across the tongue. In short, the traditional picture, apparently derived from the German psychologist D.P. Hänig (who was a student of Wilhelm Wundt) in 1901, is that the tip of the tongue contains receptors for sweetness, the sides have receptors for saltiness and sourness, and the posterior part of the tongue preferentially detects bitterness (Figure 3.12). The modern picture, however, is that this beguiling idea is simply wrong (see Bartoshuk, 1978

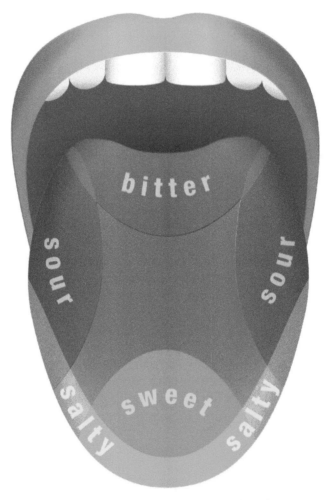

Figure 3.12   The taste zones of the tongue as drawn by Hänig (1901)
Source: Gaskin (2021)

for a historical account), and was disproved by the work of Virginia B. Collings who showed all parts of the tongue are responsive to each of the basic tastes (Collings, 1974). Moreover, most if not all taste buds can respond, at least to some degree, to two, three or even four types of tastes (Nowlis & Frank, 1977). This appears to be due to the taste buds having different thresholds for detecting the concentration of certain chemicals. At concentrations just above the threshold, most taste buds tend to be sensitive to one basic taste, but as the concentrations of the taste stimuli are increased, the taste buds become less selective (Bear et al., 1996). Consequently, many substances produce a mixture of taste sensations (e.g. lemonade can be broken down into sweet, sour and bitter sensations) and some even change flavour as they flow through the mouth. Saccharin, for example, is tasted as sweet initially, but leaves a bitter aftertaste at the back of the tongue. These types of findings indicate that our sensation of taste is as much to do with the brain as it is with the tongue.

For a chemical to be tasted it must be dissolved in saliva and diffuse into the taste bud, where it stimulates the taste receptors located on the gustatory hairs. In response to this stimulation, the hair cells generate excitatory potentials that summate in unison to trigger action potentials in the next cell in the chain – namely the sensory neurons lying at the base of the taste bud. These sensory neurons form components for three cranial nerves that go to the brain. A branch of the facial nerve (cranial nerve VII) called the chorda tympani transmits impulses from taste receptors from the anterior two-thirds of the tongue, whereas the glossopharyngeal nerve (cranial nerve IX) relays information from the posterior tongue. Taste impulses from the few taste buds in the epiglottis and pharynx are conducted by the vagus nerve (cranial nerve X). In general, damage to the glossopharyngeal nerve impairs the detection of bitter substances, whereas injury to the facial nerve reduces the sensitivity to sweet, sour and salt.

KEY TERMS: *papillae, taste buds, gustatory hairs, facial, glossopharyngeal and vagus nerves*

All three cranial nerves project to the **nucleus of the solitary tract** – a cluster of nerve cell bodies forming a vertical column of grey matter embedded in the upper part of the brain's medulla. This nucleus is also involved in a wide range of other autonomic functions including cardio-respiratory and gastrointestinal processes. From here, the fibres conveying taste information take one of two main routes into higher areas of the brain (Figure 3.13). The main pathway ascends via a bundle of heavily myelinated white fibres called the medial lemniscus to the ventral posterior thalamus. This might be considered a curious place for taste information to be sent as this thalamic area is also the main relay for somatosensory information that carries touch, pain and temperature from the face and mouth. However, it also means that taste information reaches several areas of the cortex – the most conspicuous being the primary gustatory cortex which contains the anterior insula (in the insular lobe) folded deep within the lateral sulcus. This is located in the parietal lobe close to the part of the somatosensory cortex receiving touch information from the tongue and pharynx (Simon et al., 2006). The second route from the solitary nucleus goes directly to the amygdala and **hypothalamus** located in the limbic system. This is likely to give taste its emotional significance including pleasure and aversion (Oliveira-Maia et al., 2011).

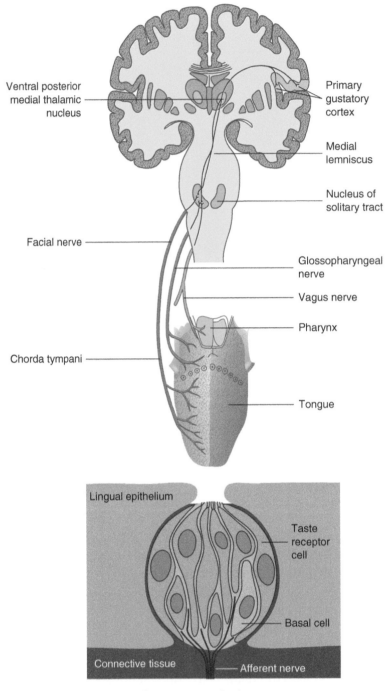

Figure 3.13   The main taste pathways from tongue to brain
Source: Higgs et al. (2020); Barnes (2013); NEURO tiker, Wikimedia Commons

It should also be noted that our sense of taste is strongly influenced by smell. This is nicely demonstrated by the likely probability that most of us, including young children, will not be able to distinguish eating an apple from an onion if our eyes are covered and our nose plugged. Moreover, as we eat, many foods release volatile chemicals which reach the back of the throat and into the retronasal passage – the tube that connects the nose and throat. A subset of odour receptors then interprets the aromas of the food, adding to our perception of taste. Further important components of many taste sensations include texture and temperature. Even pain cannot be ruled out as a gustatory sensation as some hot spicy foods include capsaicin (the main ingredient in chillies and peppers) that produces its fiery burning sensation by acting on nociceptors (Frias & Merighi, 2016).

> **KEY TERMS:** *nucleus of the solitary tract, medial lemniscus, ventral posterior thalamus, gustatory cortex, insula, amygdala, hypothalamus*

THE SOMATOSENSORY SYSTEM

The somatosensory system is the part of our nervous organization involved in the detection and relay of information concerning touch, pain, temperature and movement which arises from the stimulation of receptors in the skin, muscles and joints (Hayward, 2018). This sensory information can be divided into two types: cutaneous, which includes touch, pressure, pain and temperature; and proprioceptive, which provides largely unconscious feedback about joint and muscle position from within the body itself (Proske & Gandevia, 2012). Without these senses, we would not be able to experience sensation from our skin, or monitor the location of our body parts as we move. We would also not be able to detect harmful events occurring to our bodies without the sensation of pain. Unlike all the other senses discussed so far, the stimuli processed by the somatosensory system are diverse and cannot be specified along any single dimension or type of receptor. This is also shown by the fact that different types of somatosensory information can travel along separate spinal pathways to the brain. Hence, it is more accurate to regard somatic sensations as a grouping of different but related senses (Nelson, 2001). The next section will examine the skin's cutaneous senses, while proprioception is discussed more fully in Chapter 4.

> **KEY TERMS:** *somatosensory system, cutaneous senses, proprioceptive senses*

THE CUTANEOUS SENSES

For many of us, the sense of touch provides our most intimate contact with the world. Traditionally, the cutaneous senses have been grouped into four broad categories: pressure, pain, warmth and cold – a classification first devised by the Austrian-German physiologist Max von Frey in the late nineteenth century. Von Frey also proposed that each of these senses was due to stimulation of a specific type of receptor with their own specialized nerve fibres, which projected to different sites in the spinal cord and brain. Although we now know that the skin does indeed contain specialized receptors (see below), the processing of somatosensory information by nerve fibres is not as simple as von Frey imagined.

The most abundant type of cutaneous receptor in the skin is that of free nerve endings, sometimes called naked endings, although they occur in many other types of tissue including muscles, joints, blood vessels and the heart. As their name suggests, they are the fine specialized extensions of dendrites, which appear as multi-branched endings, that resemble in some respects the roots of a plant. Most, although not all, are partially ensheathed by Schwann cells and therefore myelinated. Free nerve endings are not easy to categorize since they come in slightly different forms and have different rates of adaptation and stimulus preference. But since the work of von Frey, these nerve endings have been known to be sensitive to pain, thereby acting as nociceptors (from the Latin *nocere* meaning 'to hurt'). However, free nerve endings also respond to many other types of stimuli, including *mechanical* stimuli (painful pressure, squeezing or cutting) and temperature (i.e. **thermoreceptors**). Some free nerve endings only respond to one type of stimulus, whereas in other instances they are polymodal. Indeed, most nociceptors respond to heat and cold, mechanical stimuli, and chemicals associated with tissue damage or disease. One type of free nerve ending, for example, is known to signal temperature changes at low levels of activity and pain at higher intensities.

KEY TERMS: *free nerve endings, nociceptors, thermoreceptors*

The skin also contains other types of sensory receptors where the nerve ending is encased in a specialized capsule (see Figure 3.14). Most of these act to detect changes in the movement of the skin which are known as mechanoreceptors (Abraira &

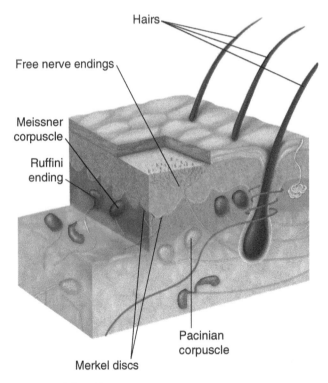

Figure 3.14   The receptors of the skin
Source: Garrett and Hough (2021)

Ginty, 2013). There is a wide variety of these receptors. Merkel discs, for example, are found in the upper layers of the skin and are slow adapting which allows them to detect continuous touch against the skin. They also encode light types of touch that allows the location of a stimulus to be pinpointed. Meissner corpuscles are even more sensitive to touch, being encapsulated myelinated nerve endings, which react rapidly to a pressure stimulus. Being highly sensitive to touch, they are found abundantly in the fingertips, eyelids, tip of the tongue, lips, nipples, clitoris and penis. Because Merkel discs are slowly adapting receptors and Meissner corpuscles are rapidly adapting receptors, our skin is able to encode information relating to how we are touching something and how long it is touching our skin. Another type of mechanoreceptor is the cylindrical-shaped Pacinian corpuscle, some of which are visible to the naked eye, which encode changes in rapid movement and stretch along with vibration. It has been speculated that their vibrational function may also be used to detect differences in surface texture such as rough and smooth. Pacinian corpuscles also have the largest receptive field on the skin's surface with their central region being especially sensitive. Two other types of somatosensory receptor with encapsulated endings are Krause's end-bulbs and Ruffini's corpuscles (Johnson, 2001). Both of these are mechanoreceptors involved in sensing pressure, although they also appear to be sensitive to temperature, with the former encoding cold and the latter hot.

All of these cutaneous receptors are found at the endings of elongated dendrite fibres that belong to sensory neurons whose cell bodies lie in the dorsal (grey) roots of the spinal cord. In turn, their axons, otherwise known as fibres, ascend in the white tracts of the spinal cord, with many passing directly to the brain. In fact, four different types of fibre are recognized, defined by their axon diameter. This is significant because axon diameter determines the speed of the nervous message – the larger the diameter, the faster the impulse. In addition, myelinated axons are faster than unmyelinated. The smallest fibres are called C-fibres. These are around 1 micron (μm) in diameter, unmyelinated, and conduct action potentials at around 1 metre per second (m/s). The next smallest are the A-delta fibres (Aδ) which are 2–4 μm in diameter, myelinated, and have a speed of about 5–30 m/s. The remaining two types of fibre are A-beta and A-alpha. Both are myelinated with large diameters of 10 μm and 15 μm respectively. This allows them to conduct action potentials at fast rates of 35–55 m/s and 80–120 m/s. Closer examination also reveals that these fibres convey different types of information. In short, most types of pain and temperature information are relayed by small diameter C and Aδ nerve fibres, whilst light touch, stretch and pressure are encoded by the larger beta and alpha fibres (Kaas, 2012).

The differences in fibre diameter mean that various types of cutaneous information arrive in the spinal cord at different times. For example, if we accidentally hit our fingers with a hammer, the pain impulse will be carried along the C-fibres and take about a second to reach our spinal cord. This is some 100 times slower that the muscle feedback necessary to move our fingers conveyed by the A-fibres which reaches our spinal cord in only 10 milliseconds. Why such a difference? In fact, it makes perfect sense. The priority must be to move our hand away from the painful stimulus – and the sensation of pain can wait until after the event.

KEY TERMS: *mechanoreceptors, Merkel discs, Meissner corpuscles, Pacinian corpuscles, Krause's end-bulbs, Ruffini's corpuscles*

THE MAJOR ASCENDING SOMATOSENSORY PATHWAYS

All the cutaneous, joint and visceral afferent input composed of myelinated A-delta, A-beta and A-alpha fibres, along with the unmyelinated C fibres, join to form spinal nerves, which enter the spinal cord via its dorsal roots. There are 31 pairs of spinal nerves innervating the cord along its entire length at regular intervals, and it is estimated there are 2–2.5 million afferent fibres in human adult dorsal roots on each side (Schoenen & Grant, 2004). In addition to all this somatosensory information, these sensory spinal nerves also contain axons from the muscle spindles embedded in the muscles (see next chapter) and input from the autonomic nervous system.

All the axons passing through the dorsal roots make synapses in the grey matter of the spinal cord – from which the second-order neurons then take one of two main routes. The largest pathway, which in humans occupies over a third of the spinal cord at high cervical levels, is the dorsal-column medial-lemniscus system (Figure 3.15). This system is primarily involved in the transmission of cutaneous information regarding fine touch, pressure and proprioception. As its name suggests, it begins in the posterior white matter of the spinal cord called the **dorsal columns**. These columnar tracts can be seen on both sides of the spinal cord and there are segregated paths with the gracile fasciculus carrying sensory information from the lower half of the body (entering the spinal cord at the lumbar level), and the cuneate fasciculus relaying information from the upper half of the body (upper limbs, trunk and neck) that enters the spinal cord at the cervical level. Both these tracts provide a fast direct highway to the medulla where they project to the dorsal column nuclei which contains the nucleus gracilis and nucleus cuneatus. At this point, the output from the dorsal column nuclei crosses to the other side of the brain, where the axons ascend in a highly conspicuous white pathway called the medial lemniscus. This passes to the ventral posterior thalamus from where information reaches the primary (SI) and secondary (SII) regions of the somatosensory cortex, located in the postcentral gyrus of the parietal lobe (Kaas, 2012).

The anterolateral system (Figure 3.15) provides a second major ascending somatosensory pathway, involved mainly in the transmission of noxious stimulation and pain. This pathway begins in the substantia gelatinosa of the spinal dorsal horns, but unlike the dorsal column system, axons then cross to the opposite side of the spinal cord, where they form a major white ascending tract of fibres called the anterolateral system. It is actually comprised of three pathways. In humans, the largest is the **spinothalamic tract** which passes directly to the ventral posterior nuclei of the thalamus (i.e. the same thalamic nuclei that receives input from the lemniscus system) and somatosensory cortex. The two other anterolateral pathways are derived mainly from C-fibres. These are the **spinoreticular tract** which passes to the reticular formation, important in arousal, and the **spinotectal tract** which reaches the midbrain. It can be seen, therefore, that pain processing takes a somewhat different route through the CNS to that of cutaneous information, although there is some overlap (Kaas, 2012).

KEY TERMS: *dorsal-column medial-lemniscus system, medial lemniscus, ventral posterior thalamus, anterolateral system, spinothalamic, spinoreticular and spinotectal tracts*

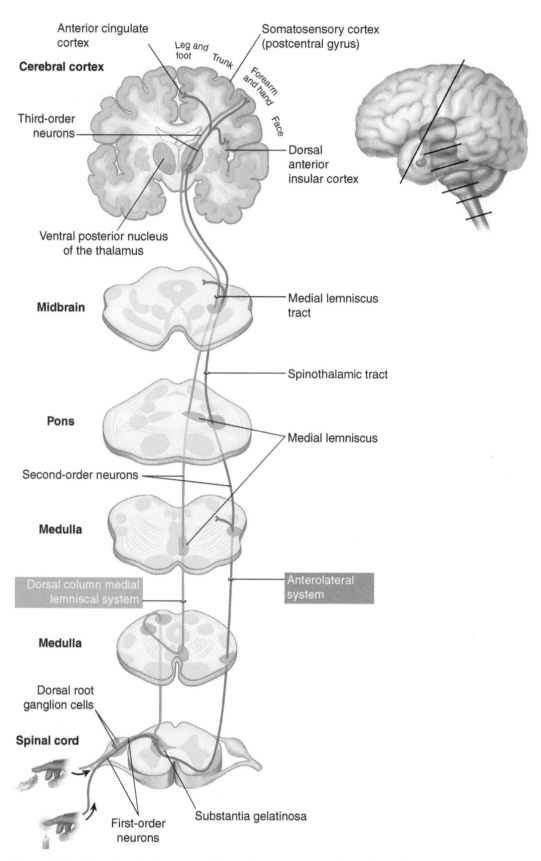

Figure 3.15   The dorsal column medial lemniscus system and anterolateral system

Source: Carolina Hrejsa/Body Scientific Intl. in Gaskin (2021)

THE SOMATOSENSORY CORTEX

The primary **somatosensory cortex** (SI) lies in the postcentral gyrus of the parietal cortex, just posterior to the fissure called the central sulcus that separates the frontal and parietal lobes (see Pleger and Villringer, 2013). It appears as a strip of cortex, running from ear to ear across both hemispheres. This region was first mapped by Wilder Penfield in the 1930s who pioneered the use of brain surgery to treat patients with severe epilepsy. The problem facing Penfield was not so much to identify the tissue where the seizures originated, but to make sure its removal would not have adverse effects such as speech loss or paralysis. To do this, Penfield stimulated the brain with a mild electric current in conscious patients prior to surgery – a technique that caused no discomfort. One aim was to identify the functionally important language and motor areas (the location of which can vary considerably between individuals) so they could be avoided during surgery. When Penfield applied stimulation to the postcentral gyrus he found the patients typically reported somatosensory sensations such as tingling from parts of the body. After scrutinizing his findings, Penfield realized the somatosensory cortex was topographically organized. That is, spatially adjacent regions of the body were correspondingly mapped in the cortex. For example, the brain areas receiving input from the legs and trunk were in the upper part of the somatosensory cortex, whilst areas receiving input from the hands and face were in its lower parts. Penfield also found that the body map of the somatosensory cortex was somewhat distorted, with the greatest proportion of its tissue in receipt of information from the bodily organs capable of making the most sensitive tactile discriminations. The areas of the somatosensory cortex devoted to processing information from the hands and parts of the face were particularly large (Catani, 2017).

Microelectrode investigations have shown that the somatosensory cortex has four distinct areas – each of which contains a separate representation of the body (Kaas, 2012). These anatomical areas were first discovered by Korbinian Brodmann in 1909 who identified them by their differing cell types. He named them 1, 2, 3a and 3b. They were later found to have different behavioural functions. Areas 3a and 3b receive information from the thalamus. The former processes cutaneous input and the latter proprioceptive muscles and joint information. In turn, area 3b is the main source of neural input to somatosensory areas 1 and 2. The projection from 3b to 1 primarily relays texture information; the projection to area 2 emphasizes size and shape (Viaene et al., 2011).

All areas of SI project to the adjacent secondary somatosensory area (S2) which lies posteriorly in the parietal operculum. This area, first discovered by Edgar Douglas Adrian in 1940, receives input from the left and right somatosensory cortices, so it combines input from both sides of the body. Neuroimaging studies have found that S2 is responsive to light touch, pain, visceral sensation and tactile attention (Eickhoff et al., 2008). In addition, neurons in this area are sensitive to tactile forms of stimulation that have become associated with reward (Pleger et al., 2008). S2 also has strong connections with the hippocampus which is known to be important for learning and memory (Burman, 2019).

In humans, damage of the somatosensory cortex reduces the sensitivity of touch and impair sensory discrimination – especially on the opposite side of the body.

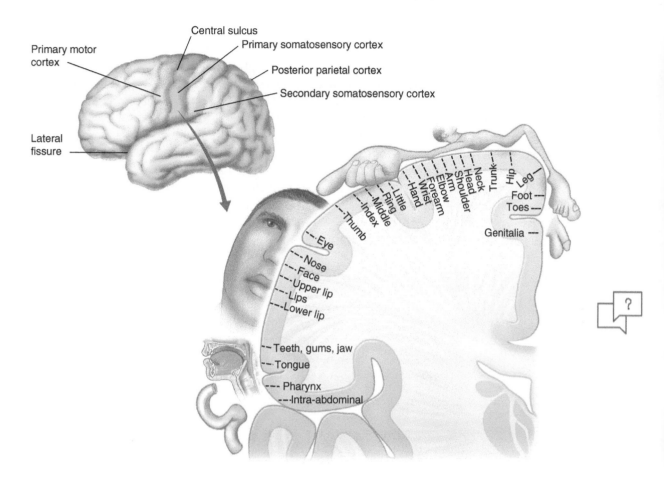

Figure 3.16   The primary and secondary somatosensory areas

Source: Garrett and Hough (2018), adapted from Penfield and Rasmussen (1950) © 1950 Gale, a part of Cengage Learning, Inc

One of the first extensive studies to assess the effects of somatosensory damage was undertaken by Josephine Semmes who tested World War II soldiers with missile wounds to the head (Semmes, 1960). Her findings were somewhat surprising since damage anywhere in the right hemisphere could produce somatosensory deficits, whereas a lesion in the left hemisphere had to include the somatosensory cortex. However, research on patients who had received cortical excisions for seizures did not support this finding (Corkin et al., 1970). For example, in one study which examined over 120 patients on a range of tasks, it was found that somatosensory deficits only occurred when the postcentral gyrus was damaged, whatever the hemisphere, with lesions outside this area producing little effect (Corkin et al., 1970). The difference between the results of Semmes and Corkin has never been satisfactorily explained, although it should be borne in mind that the former study examined patients with large wounds to the brain, whereas the latter looked at those with small surgical excisions. Damage to the somatosensory cortex following stroke has been shown to impair the ability to discriminate object size and texture. Also decreased or lost on the opposite side of the body is the ability to discriminate the position and movement of body parts and the control of fine movements. There may be a decrease, but not a total loss of pain sensation (Nolte, 2008).

Damage to the somatosensory cortex can also cause two types of tactile agnosia. The first is **astereognosis**, where the person is unable to recognize an object by touch, despite having some cutaneous sensation. Although astereognosis is traditionally associated with the somatosensory cortex it is now recognized that posterior parietal lesions can also produce this impairment (Knech et al., 1996). The second is **asomatognosia**, which refers to the loss of knowledge about one's own body or even bodily condition. This may lead the patient to ignore or even deny ownership of a body part such as an arm contralateral to the brain lesion. For example, a patient with asomatognosia might use a right hand to follow their paralyzed left arm to the shoulder, but still deny the left arm belongs to them. A related condition is anosognosia, where there is an unawareness or denial of a serious illness. Like astereognosis, both these conditions can also be associated with damage to the right parietal lobe although it generally include secondary areas of the somatosensory cortex (Kolb & Whishaw, 2015).

KEY TERMS: *somatosensory cortex, secondary somatosensory cortex, astereognosis, asomatognosia, anosognosia*

THE PHENOMENON OF PAIN

The cutaneous senses also detect pain. As we all know, this provides an unpleasant sensation, typically resulting from noxious stimulation which is an indicator of harm occurring to our body. Thus, pain serves as an important signal of danger, and our attempts to avoid it provide one of our best defences against injury. Despite this, the relationship of pain with harm is not straightforward. For example, some fatal diseases do not produce pain, and there are other conditions such as toothache that can cause excruciating discomfort, yet have little risk for the individual. The amount of pain experienced by a person is also strongly influenced by their psychological state. Indeed, pain can be ignored in times of battle, sporting endeavour and passion – or enhanced by anticipation, fear and anxiety. But one thing is certain, the experience of pain, especially if prolonged, is always distressing to the individual, often depriving their body and mind of vigour, and causing health decline. Sadly, chronic pain is not uncommon. In fact one recent study has estimated that chronic pain affects between one-third and one-half of the population of the UK, corresponding to just under 28 million adults, and this figure is likely to increase with an increasingly ageing population (Fayez et al., 2016). One only needs to walk into a chemist to realize that pain is big business.

The importance of detecting noxious stimulation can be seen in a rare condition called congenital analgesia, where individuals are unable to feel pain. These people are not only at greater risk of injuring themselves through burning, bruising and lacerations, but because of their cumbersome heavy movement unchecked by normal painful feedback, they often have inflamed worn joints along with damaged muscle tissue. A striking account of congenital analgesia is given by Melzack and Wall (1988) in their book *The Challenge of Pain*. Miss C was an intelligent young student at McGill University in Montreal, but experienced no pain when parts of her body were subjected to strong electric shock, scolding hot water, or prolonged exposure to ice.

Inserting a stick up her nose, pinched tendons, or histamine injected under the skin also failed to elicit responses. And just as remarkable, Miss C showed no changes in blood pressure, heart rate or respiration when subjected to these ordeals.

Miss C's insensitivity to pain caused her to suffer from many medical problems. As a young girl she bit off the end of her tongue, and as she grew older developed damage to her knees, hip and spine requiring orthopaedic operations. Miss C also developed 'Charcot joint' where her ankles, knees, wrists and elbows became deformed and swollen – a problem that arose because of her inability to shift her body weight properly when moving, sitting and sleeping. Another consequence of Charcot's joint is the occurrence of infections in the inflamed tissue surrounding the damaged joints. Sadly, this was to occur with Miss C whose infections became so severe that they extended into the bone marrow where they could not be controlled by antibiotics. Miss C died at the age of 29 years from massive infection.

KEY TERM: *congenital analgesia*

THE RECEPTOR BASIS OF PAIN

As we have seen earlier, the main receptors responsible for detecting noxious stimulation are the free nerve endings which are found in the skin and many other organs of the body. These transduce a variety of cutaneous stimuli into neural impulses, and if stimulated at high intensities they typically function as pain detectors or nociceptors (Dubin & Patapoutian, 2010). Although the free nerve endings appear to be anatomically similar, they can functionally be divided into three different types: (1) mechanical nociceptors that respond to potentially damaging pressure or touch, (2) temperature nociceptors that respond to potentially damaging extremes of heat and cold, and (3) chemical nociceptors that respond to noxious chemicals (Koop & Tadi, 2020). This last type of free nerve ending reacts not only to externally applied chemicals, but also to substances released from bodily organs. These include potassium ions and histamine released from the skin itself (especially following damage), serotonin from cells in the blood, and substance P from nerve endings. Some of these chemicals, especially histamine, enhance the process of inflammation which increases the sensitivity of nociceptors.

A further subdivision of nociceptors can be made on the basis of whether they are are unimodal (responding to only one type of pain sensation) or polymodal (responding to a variety of stimuli). In general, unimodal nociceptors have a much lower threshold for stimulation and provide a rapid response to noxious stimuli, although they only produce a transient or short-lasting neural signal. In contrast, polymodal nociceptors require a higher threshold to be activated and produce a more sustained neural response (Smith & Lewin, 2009).

Information arising from the nociceptors travels to the spinal cord via two types of axon: lightly myelinated polymodal C fibres which conduct action potentials at rates of 1–2 metres per second (m/s), and myelinated unimodal Aδ fibres which conduct neural impulses at faster speeds of 15–30 m/s. These two types of fibres are also associated with different sensations of pain with the Aδ fibres producing short duration 'pricking' pain, whereas the C fibres generate longer lasting 'burning' pain sensations. The difference in the conduction times of these two fibre types also helps explain why pain often seems to occur in two different phases: a painful stimulus will typically cause a sharp localised pain (sometimes called fast pain), followed by a less intense and diffuse pain (called slow pain). Despite this, if there is a prolonged stimulation of a C fibre, there can be a progressive build-up of neural activity in the spinal cord which can greatly increase the sensitivity to pain (Fields, 1999).

KEY TERMS: *nociceptors, histamine, polymodal C fibres, unimodal Aδ fibres*

Table 3.1   The four main types of afferent fibre conveying touch and pain

Fibre	Name	Diameter (µm)	Speed (m/s)	Function
Aα	A-alpha	13–20	80–120	Proprioception (skeletal muscle)
Aβ	A-beta	6–12	35–75	Mechanoreceptors of skin
Aδ	A-delta	1–5	15–30	Sharp pain and temperature
C	C	0.2–1.5	1–2	Burning pain, itching and temperature

BRAIN REGIONS INVOLVED IN PAIN

To understand the psychobiology of pain, it is necessary to be familiar with the anterolateral system (see above) which conveys noxious information from the periphery to the brain. It has three main sites of termination: the somatosensory cortex, reticular formation and midbrain. Researchers have also tended to divide the anterolateral pathways into lateral and medial systems. The former is the main route conveying pain information to the ventral-posterior thalamus and somatosensory cortex. The medial system is different since it innervates the medullary-pontine reticular formation and tectum. It is also far older in evolutionary terms since it is present in fish and amphibians which have no lateral system. In humans, the reticular component ascends to the thalamus, in what is called the spinothalamic tract, which innervates the intradmedian nucleus of the thalamic intralaminar nuclei – and not the ventral-posterior thalamus. This is significant since the thalamic intralaminar nuclei project diffusely throughout the cerebral cortex, including the medial frontal cortex and temporal lobe, cingulate cortex and limbic system. These nuclei are also involved in the synchronization of neural activity which determines the general level of arousal and consciousness (Saalmann, 2014). Thus, whereas the lateral system has a fairly precise site of termination in the somatosensory cortex, the medial system has a very diffuse set of destinations.

These two systems have different roles in the processing of pain-related information. Put simply, the lateral pathways are involved in detecting the location of pain in the body, whereas the medial pathways are concerned with its affective-motivational, or aversive, aspects (Kulkarni et al., 2005). Several lines of evidence support this claim. For example, damage to the somatosensory cortex in humans has little effect on reducing the sensitivity to pain, although it may impair the ability to localize it (Bushnell et al., 1999). In other words, the unpleasant feeling of pain must be produced elsewhere. This conclusion is also supported by the classic work of Penfield and Boldrey (1937) who showed that electrical stimulation of the primary somatosensory cortex rarely produced pain sensations.

So which brain regions give rise to the unpleasant sensation of pain? The key structures are the aforementioned spinothalamic tract and medial thalamus (Cassanari & Pagni, 1969; Yen & Lu, 2013). Indeed, one of the most effective surgical operations for the relief of chronic pain is removal of the medial thalamus. It has been reported that around two-thirds of patients report effective pain relief without any somatosensory deficits after its surgical excision (Jeanmonod et al., 1993). Interestingly, the medial thalamus projects to the frontal cortex and **cingulate cortex**, and both these areas can also be surgically removed for the relief of pain. Although patients with frontal and cingulate lesion report are still able to feel pain, it does not seem to bother them for its aversive quality has been removed.

Further support for the distinction between the lateral and medial systems has come from electrophysiological research. For example, it has been shown that most neurons in the posterior nuclei of the thalamus, which projects to the somatosensory cortex, do not selectively respond to noxious stimulation from the periphery. Rather, they respond to a broad range of stimuli (they are sometimes called wide dynamic range neurons) from mild touch to pain. These neurons are also particularly sensitive to changes in stimulus intensity. In contrast, a high percentage of neurons in the medial thalamus respond only to painful stimulation when applied to the skin, and these are further modified by the emotional state of the animal (Price, 2002). Thus, the medial thalamus (or spinothalamic tract) is associated with the emotional qualities of pain.

The brain areas involved in pain have also been examined using functional brain-scanning techniques. A study using PET was undertaken by Rainville et al. (1997) who exposed their subjects to painful stimuli by immersing their hands in hot water, while also using hypnosis to alter the perceived unpleasantness of the task. The results revealed significant changes in pain-evoked activity in the cingulate cortex consistent with the perceived emotional unpleasantness, but not the somatosensory cortex. These findings support the idea that the medial thalamus–cingulate cortex connection is important for the suffering experience of pain – whereas the somatosensory cortex does not have this emotional role. Despite this, it should be pointed out that brain-scanning studies have highlighted the fact that many other brain regions are involved in processing pain. In fact, overall, there appears to be an extensive cortical network, including somatosensory, insular and cingulate areas as well as frontal and parietal areas involved in pain perception. In other words, there is no pain centre, but instead a complex network of brain regions which has been termed *a pain matrix* (Apkarian, 2011; Morton et al., 2016). Although the areas of the brain making up the pain matrix are viewed by some as the means by which the intensity and unpleasantness of a noxious event are transformed into a conscious percept of pain, others have proposed that the matrix reflects a system that is instead involved in detecting, orienting attention towards, and reacting to the occurrence of salient sensory events (Legrain et al., 2011). Whether this is the case or not, it remains the case that some areas of the brain are more important than others for the experience of pain – but establishing this likely fact is far from easy because so many areas appear to be involved (Peyron et al., 2000).

A. Brain areas functionally related to pain processing.

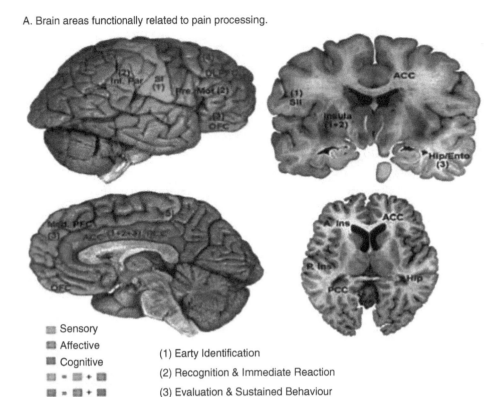

■ Sensory
■ Affective
■ Cognitive
■ = ■ + ■
■ = ■ + ■

(1) Early Identification
(2) Recognition & Immediate Reaction
(3) Evaluation & Sustained Behaviour

B. Example of functional MRI response to painful stimulation.

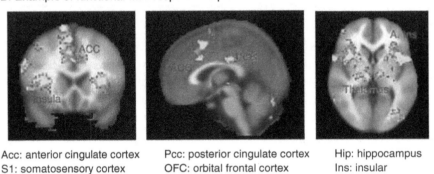

Acc: anterior cingulate cortex   Pcc: posterior cingulate cortex   Hip: hippocampus
S1: somatosensory cortex   OFC: orbital frontal cortex   Ins: insular

Figure 3.17   The main areas of the brain involved in pain
Source: Borsook et al. (2007)

KEY TERMS: *anterolateral system, medial system, spinothalamic tract, intralaminar nuclei of the thalamus, medial thalamus, frontal cortex, cingulate cortex, pain matrix*

THE PUZZLING PHENOMENA OF PHANTOM LIMB PAIN

In 1866, after treating injured soldiers in the American Civil War, the eminent neurologist S. Weir Mitchell coined the term 'phantom limb' which referred to a condition where a person after having the amputation of a limb still continued to experience sensations from that lost bodily organ. However, he was not the first to describe this phenomenon. In 1797, at the battle of Santa Cruz, Lord Nelson had his right arm shattered by gunfire which required amputation. Afterwards, he complained of intense phantom limb pain, most notably from his fingers digging into his palm. For Nelson, this was proof of his non-material soul which he reasoned had survived the loss of his amputated body part. The pain was clearly hard to explain from a physical perspective, and perhaps for this reason S. Weir Mitchell was wary of publishing his observations in a reputable medical journal for fear of ridicule. Instead, he wrote his article as a short story under a pseudonym (Melzack, 1992).

We now know that 80–90% of amputees have phantom limb experiences and pain which can last for years or even decades. Such sensations are typically reported following the amputation of an arm or a leg, but may also occur following the removal of a breast, a tooth, or an internal organ. It has even been reported that around 60% of men who have had to have their penis amputated for cancer will experience a phantom penis (Ramachandron & McGeoch, 2007). To the amputee, the phantom limb is very real. For example, they may feel a lost arm swinging in co-ordination with the other when walking, or have a gesticulating hand during conversation. Alternatively, a phantom leg may bend when getting into bed, or feel upright whilst standing. Such a limb may also become hot or cold, feel sweaty or have an irritating itch – and there are even instances of phantom eyes, breasts or penises with erections. Unfortunately, in most cases phantom limbs are accompanied by pain. Often described as cramping, burning, crushing or shooting, the pain may also sometimes be 'caused' by distortion of an appendage such as a badly twisted foot, or fingernails penetrating the flesh of the palm. This type of pain can be more debilitating that the loss of the limb itself. Sadly, it is notoriously difficult to treat. One approach which may lessen the pain up to 50% is deep brain stimulation (Bittar et al., 2005). Another helpful innovation is the mirror box developed by Vilaynur Ramachandron where the subject is able to see the reflected image of their good hand making movements, so it appears as if the phantom limb is moving. By using this type of artificial visual feedback it is possible for the patient to 'move' the phantom limb and unclench it from painful positions. Although the use of mirror therapy has been shown to be effective in some cases, there is still no widely accepted theory of how it works (Barbin et al., 2016).

What causes phantom limb pain? The obvious explanation is it arises from the exposed nerve endings of the amputated limb, which continue sending nerve impulses to the brain. However, we now know this theory is incorrect for the simple reason that paraplegic patients who have no sensation below a spinal cord lesion can still experience phantom limb pain. An alternative theory proposed by Tim Pons (Pons et al., 1991) is that the defunct parts of the somatosensory cortex caused by the amputation start to reorganize themselves and begin responding to stimulation from other parts of the body. As we have seen, the somatosensory cortex contains a topographic map of the body in which the face is represented next to the hand, and the feet next to the trunk. Thus, if redundant parts of the somatosensory cortex reorganize to process new sensation from other body regions, we might predict that touching the face will produce phantom limb sensations in the hand, or stimulation of the trunk will cause foot sensations. In fact, this is exactly what was found by Ramachandran who used Q-tips to probe the body surface of amputees (Ramachandran & Blakeslee, 1998). It is also interesting to note that Ramachandran also found a patient who felt orgasms in his phantom foot during sexual activity. A closer examination of the somatosensory map shows the genital region does indeed lie next to the foot, and not at the bottom of the trunk as might be expected.

THE GATE THEORY OF PAIN

The sensation of pain can be modified by a number of factors. For example, everyone learns from experience that rubbing a knock or injury will diminish its painfulness. There are also many recorded cases where the excitement of a sporting event, or intense experience of being in a dangerous situation, has suppressed the pain of a serious injury. This was observed by army surgeon Henry Beecher during the World War II (Beecher, 1959). He found that upon reaching hospital, only one in three injured soldiers complained of enough pain to require an analgesic. Yet the men were not in a state of shock, and readily felt pain as shown by their protestations when given an inept injection. Even the wounded were often surprised at the lack of their own discomfort. To explain their indifference, Beecher argued that psychological factors were reducing the pain's impact. In this instance, any pain experienced by a wounded soldier on the battlefield was being compensated by the relief and great joy of being removed from life-threatening danger. A similar injury, say caused by a car accident occurring to a bank manager on his way to work, would likely have a very different effect.

Although several theoretical frameworks have been used to account for pain (see Moayedi & Davis, 2013), perhaps the most influential one, which also explains how cutaneous stimulation and emotion can affect pain sensitivity, was proposed by Canadian psychologist Ronald Melzack and British physiologist Patrick Wall in 1965. Their basic idea, known as the gate theory of pain, did not explain pain as a simple noxious sensation that is passed directly from the nerve endings to the brain. Rather, they saw it as input that is modified by operation of a gate-like mechanism in the substantia gelatinosa of the spinal cord. This area found in the dorsal horns contains a large number of interneurons (small neurons confined to the grey matter) that receive input from the small $A\delta$ and C fibres which convey pain information, and the larger fibres conveying touch, or non-pain, input.

But why should the interneurons of the substantia gelatinosa receive two very different types of cutaneous information? The answer according to Melzack and Wall is that it allows the activity in one set of fibres to affect neural transmission in the other. For example, they proposed that when the small $A\delta$ and C fibres relaying noxious input are stimulated, they excite the interneurons of the substantia gelatinosa. However, touch input from the larger fibres has the opposite effect by inhibiting the interneurons. Consequently, if the large touch fibres are activated at the same time as the $A\delta$ and C fibres, their action would dampen the excitability of the interneurons – or 'close the gate' to pain impulses reaching the ascending tracts in the white matter. This gating mechanism, of course, explains why rubbing an injured area is effective at diminishing the sensation of pain.

Melzack and Wall also used a similar argument to explain how the emotional or psychological state of the person could reduce the sensation of pain. In short, they proposed there is a second pathway which descends from the brain to the interneurons of the substantia gelatinosa – where it exerts a similar type of effect as the neurons conveying touch from the periphery. In effect, therefore, this pathway allows certain areas of the brain to open or close the gating mechanism, thereby increasing or lessening the flow of noxious stimulation into the central nervous system.

If this theory is correct, then there must be areas of the brain that are actively involved in suppressing pain and where electrical stimulation would have therapeutic analgesic effects. One region where this type of effect occurs is the periaqueductal grey area, a region that occupies a column of brain stem that stretches about 14 mm in length which surrounds the cerebral aqueduct connecting the third and fourth ventricles. In fact, the pain relief from this type of stimulation is so effective that it enables surgical procedures to take place without anaesthesia (Basbaum & Fields, 1978). The periaqueductal grey area produces this effect by means of a pathway that passes to the **nucleus raphe magnus** (one of several raphe nuclei located in brain stem) and regions of the adjacent ventromedial medulla. From here, a tract travels down in the dorsolateral columns of the spinal cord to its substantia gelatinosa. In support of gate theory, stimulating the periaqueductal grey area markedly inhibited these dorsal horn cells to noxious skin stimuli, while leaving their responses to gentle tactile stimulation unaffected (Mayer, 1979). It is also interesting to note that lesions of the periaqueductal grey area reduce the analgesic effects of systemic morphine.

Although gate control theory has been modified in some minor ways since it was first proposed in 1965, it has stood the test of time. Indeed, the theory has been characterized as 'an excellent first approximation of the neural mechanisms underlying the transmission of nociceptive information' (Price, 1988). But perhaps the most important contribution of gate theory has been to provide a theoretical framework for over half a century of pain research. Although it is now considered to be oversimplified, gate control theory is currently the only theory that most accurately accounts for the physical and psychological aspects of pain (Mendell, 2014).

KEY TERMS: *gate theory of pain, interneurons, periaqueductal grey area, nucleus raphe magnus*

THE ENDORPHINS

For over 5,000 years, opium derived from the seeds of the *Papaver somniferum* poppy has been used to treat pain and other medical conditions. The main active analgesic ingredient of opium is morphine (making up about 12% of its weight) which was first isolated in 1805 by the German chemist Friedrich Sertürner and was the first ever isolation of an active pharmacological agent from a plant. Morphine revolutionized medical practice, especially after the drug company Merck began marketing it commercially in 1827. The main reason was its remarkable capacity to produce deep and long-lasting analgesia without significantly affecting basic sensations such as touch or consciousness.

The opiates also began to attract further attention during the early 1970s when evidence indicated that similar substances might occur naturally in the brain. One reason was their high potency. For example, a 5–10 mg injection of morphine every four hours is often sufficient to control serious pain. However, other opiates are far more powerful with some producing analgesia in humans at doses that are a small fraction of a milligram. Such potency is difficult to explain unless the drug is able to fit perfectly into a specialized receptor site. Another factor hinting at the existence of receptors was the discovery of drugs that could block opiate action. For example, an injection of **naloxone** can reverse the effects of a potentially fatal heroin overdose within 30 seconds – an effect hard to explain without postulating the existence of opiate receptors. But why should the central nervous system be equipped with receptors for a substance derived from the opium poppy? The obvious reply is that the brain and spinal cord must be using their own opiate-like substances.

In the early 1970s, researchers began to use radioligand binding techniques to hunt for opiate receptors. In this procedure, tissue likely to contain opiate receptors was homogenized into a pulp, and then centrifuged to obtain neuronal membranes. This material was then immersed in a solution containing an opiate drug 'tagged' with a radioactive tracer. After drying, it was then possible to see if any of the drug had fixed itself to the tissue, presumably to opiate receptors, by measuring the radioactive emissions. Using this method, opiate receptors were found widely distributed throughout the brain and parts of the spinal cord (Pert & Snyder, 1973). Later, research would identify three different types of receptor: mu (μ), kappa (κ) and sigma (σ). Morphine, importantly, was shown to bind to the mu receptor.

The discovery of these receptors encouraged researchers to look for opiate substances in the body. These were duly found by pharmacologists as the University of Aberdeen in 1975. Initially called enkephalins, the term endorphins became more popular – a term derived from the word combination *endogenous* and *morphine*. Several classes of endorphin were to be identified, although the most important behaviourally is β-endorphin which is found in neurons of the hypothalamus, as well as the pituitary gland for circulation in the bloodstream. The endorphins also had another surprising characteristic: they were peptides composed of short chains of amino acids connected by peptide bonds. Unlike most other conventional neurotransmitters which are synthesized in the axon terminals by a series of specialized enzymes, peptides are formed in the cell body and have to be transported along the axon to the nerve ending.

The endorphins have since become implicated in a wide variety of behaviours which are centred around their capacity to inhibit pain and cause euphoria. Thus, endorphins are released in response to adversity and pleasure. For example, endorphin levels can be increased in those who engage in long-distance running and other forms of strenuous exercise. This probably explains the resistance of many athletes to great discomfort and their reports of euphoric happiness. Endorphins have also been found to increase in the placental bloodstream of pregnant women close to childbirth. There is also good evidence showing that endorphins play an important role in love and sexuality, including the pleasurable sensation of orgasm (Khajehei & Behroozpour, 2018). The list goes on: elevated endorphin levels have been found in subjects listening to music, laughing, meditating, food starvation (i.e. anorexia) and even eating chocolate (see Levinthal, 1988).

KEY TERMS: *naloxone, opiate receptors, endorphins, peptides*

SUMMARY

The auditory system provides us with our sense of hearing. Sound is transduced into neural input after it passes through the outer and middle parts of the ear. The latter contains three small bones called the malleus, incus and stapes which act to vibrate the oval window leading into the inner ear which contains the coiled cochlea. Housed within the cochlea is the organ of Conti sitting on the basilar membrane. The movement of its hair cells leads to neural impulses being sent to the cochlear nuclei located in the medulla via the eighth cranial nerve. The ascending auditory pathways in the brain are crossed at all levels. Two pathways from the cochlear nucleus are particularly important. One passes via the trapezoid body to the superior olivary complex in the tegmental area of the pons which is involved in sound location. The other ascends in the lateral lemniscus to the inferior colliculi from where a pathway extends to the medial geniculate nucleus in the thalamus and primary auditory cortex in the temporal lobes. This system is involved in auditory recognition and understanding.

Olfaction (smell) and gustation (taste) are chemical senses because both the nose and the tongue contain receptors that detect chemical stimuli. Neurons from the olfactory epithelium of the nose pass to the olfactory bulb lying below the ventromedial frontal cortex. The majority of its neurons then travel to the primary olfactory cortex located in the medial aspects of the limbic temporal lobe, including the piriform cortex, amygdala and **entorhinal cortex**. In contrast, taste information from the tongue passes to the solitary nucleus in the upper medulla, and then ascends to the ventral posterior medial thalamus before reaching the primary gustatory cortex. This is located close to the part of the somatosensory cortex that receives sensory afferents from the tongue and pharynx.

The somatosensory system is a complex network of sensory neurons and neural pathways that respond to changes at the surface of or inside the body. These include sensations from the skin involving touch, pressure, pain and temperature (the **cutaneous senses**) and feedback from the position of the joints and muscles (the **proprioceptive senses**). Somatosensory input is processed by two main pathways: the **dorsal-column medial-lemniscus pathway**, concerned primarily with touch, and the **anterolateral pathway** which encodes information regarding noxious stimulation (pain) and temperature. The first passes through the dorsal columns of the spinal cord to the dorsal column nuclei composed of the cuneate nucleus and gracile nucleus. Here, paths cross to the other side of the brain, forming the medial lemniscus passing to the ventral posterior thalamus and then the somatosensory cortex located in the parietal lobe's postcentral gyrus. The anterolateral pathway takes a different route, crossing to the other side of the spinal cord where it forms three tracts whose destinations are: (1) the **reticular formation** and then medial and intralaminar nuclei of the thalamus, (2) the tectum, and (3) the ventral posterior thalamus and somatosensory cortex. The emotional suffering aspect of pain appears to predominantly involve the reticular pathway. Pain is also modified by the operation of 'gates' in the **substantia gelatinosa** of the spinal cord that act to dampen or enhance the pain input relayed by C fibres and Aδ fibres. These are also controlled by other types of touch fibre, or descending pathways from the periaqueductal grey area and nucleus raphe magnus located in the brain stem.

MULTIPLE CHOICE QUESTIONS

Answer the questions below to test your understanding of this chapter's Learning Objectives. You'll find the answers at the end of the chapter.

1. In what part of the ear would you find the organ of Conti?

   a. The cochlea
   b. The Eustachian tube
   c. in the middle ear
   d. next to the tympanic membrane

2. Where would you find the olfactory bulb?

   a. in the nose
   b. at the base of the frontal lobes
   c. in the hypothalamus
   d. in the primary olfactory cortex

3. Which of the following areas of the brain has a topographical or map-like representation of the body?

   a. the amygdala
   b. the thalamus
   c. the somatosensory cortex
   d. the cingulate cortex

4. Which of the following is not a major brain target of the ascending anterolateral system?

   a. the cerebellum
   b. the somatosensory cortex
   c. the reticular formation
   d. the thalamus

5. According to gate theory, the interneurons that are able to inhibit the flow of pain into the CNS are found where?

   a. the nucleus raphe magnus
   b. the grey matter of the spinal cord
   c. the periaqueductal grey area
   d. the white matter of the spinal cord

6. What type of chemical class do endorphins belong to?

   a. amino acids
   b. catecholamines
   c. monoamines
   d. neuropeptides

FURTHER READING

Goldstein, E., & Brockmole, J. (2016). *Sensation and perception*. Wadsworth.
Nicely produced textbook with detailed chapters on all the senses and supported by clear colour illustrations.

Harris, J. (2014). *Sensation and perception.* SAGE.
Has well-written chapters on hearing, taste, smell, touch and pain, along with proprioception. Also, provides a good overview of some of the more general issues involving perception.

Hawkes, C. H., & Doty, R. L. (2018). *Smell and taste disorders.* Cambridge University Press.
Above all, the first two chapters provide an excellent introduction to the neuroanatomy of olfaction and gustation, although the chapters on clinical disorders also make interesting reading.

Hertenstein, M. J., & Weiss, S. J. (Eds.). (2011). *The handbook of touch: Neuroscience, behavioral and health perspectives.* Springer.
A detailed book which is likely to include all you need to know about the somatosensory system (and more).

McMahon, S., Koltzenburg, M., Tracey, I., & Turk, D. C. (Eds.). (2013). *Wall & Melzack's textbook of pain.* Elsevier. Contains 76 chapters written by various experts.
The sections on the neurobiology of pain and its treatment are detailed and excellent.

Pickles, J. O. (2013). *An introduction to the physiology of hearing.* Academic Press.
A fine introduction for the biopsychology student which describes the basic anatomy and physiology of all stages of the auditory system – and much more besides.

Wall, P. (2002). *Pain: The science of suffering.* Columbia University Press.
A wide-ranging examination of pain which also highlights the fact that it is a behaviour whose manifestations differ among individuals, situations and cultures.

Wolf, J. M., Kluender, K. R., Levi, D. M., Bartoshuk, L. M., Herz, R. S., Klatzky, R. L., & Merfeld, D. M. (2019). *Sensation and perception.* Sinauer.
Written by experts in each of the five senses who convey the excitement of the field to students by emphasizing human sensory and perceptual experience and its basic neuroscientific underpinnings.

Yost, W. A. (2013). *Fundamentals of hearing: An introduction.* Academic Press.
An excellent introduction to how the ear encodes auditory information and is processed by the brain. Now in its fifth edition which is testament to its popularity.

4

THE CONTROL OF MOVEMENT

LEARNING OBJECTIVES

After reading this chapter you should be able to:

- Describe the physiology of muscles and transmission at the neuromuscular junction.

- Explain what is meant by proprioception.

- Depict how reflexes work – both monosynaptic and polysynaptic.

- Appreciate the importance of the vestibular system for movement.

- Define the differences between the pyramidal and extrapyramidal systems of the brain.

- Characterize the motor functions of the spinal cord, cerebellum and basal ganglia.

- Appreciate the higher roles of the cerebral cortex in movement.

- Describe what is known about the initiation of movement.

GO ONLINE

Test your understanding of this chapter and visit **https://study.sagepub.com/wickens** to access interactive 'Drag and Drop' labelling activities and a flashcard glossary.

INTRODUCTION

The human brain processes an enormous amount of sensory information – gathering and analysing input from the environment and receiving feedback from the internal state of its own body. However, no matter how much information is analysed, it is of little use unless it can be acted upon. Indeed, one characteristic of all creatures, from the simplest single cellular organism to the most complex, is the ability to generate movement. For higher animals this is necessary not only to control the automated functions of the body such as respiration, heart rate and digestion (which is largely undertaken by the smooth muscles of the viscera), but also to move the skeletal muscles that operate the bones in order to produce reflexes and purposeful behaviour.

Trying to understand how the brain and spinal cord control muscle activity presents a considerable challenge. For example, imagine an everyday apparently simple behaviour such as walking. How does the central nervous system decide which joints need to be moved, when they should bend, and by how much? In fact, every single muscle movement has to be correct for force, speed and position. And then more remarkably, how is all this muscle activity coordinated to produce what, after all, is a complex movement of typically long duration which also incorporates the senses of vision and balance?

Our capacity for movement appears almost miraculous, and one only has to observe the motions made by the most technologically sophisticated but cumbersome robots to gain an insight into the great dexterity of even the simplest creatures who propel themselves, swim, fly and run. But this is perhaps being unfair to robots, since human movement is the result of a long process of evolution which has taken place over millions of years. This can be recognized by noting the increasing levels of complexity we observe, from simple spinal reflexes to more complex patterns of behaviour controlled by the brain, including higher cognitive processes governed by the cerebral cortex.

Clearly, by attempting to understand how the brain produces movement the biopsychologist will be getting to the heart of what causes human behaviour. But it should also be remembered that a greater appreciation of movement neurophysiology may lead to better treatment and rehabilitation for those people who have suffered injury or movement disorders following disease or stroke.

MUSCLES

There would be no movement without muscles (incidentally, the word muscle comes from the Latin *musculus* meaning 'little mouse' – so called because of the imagined resemblance of some muscles under the skin to mice). The body contains three different types of muscle: skeletal attached to bones; smooth found in the walls of visceral organs such as blood vessels, gland cells, gut and bladder; and cardiac that forms the bulk of the heart. In this chapter we will only be concerned with the action of skeletal muscles, sometimes called 'striated muscle' because of their striped appearance, that are controlled by the somatic nervous system. The human body contains over 600 different types of skeletal muscle making up about 50% of its weight, and these are responsible for posture, locomotion and voluntary movement. In contrast, the smooth and cardiac muscles are governed by the autonomic nervous system, and certain hormones, and these concern the involuntary functioning of the body's organs. Although smooth and cardiac muscle can function in the absence of neural input (e.g. the heart has its own pacemaker cells that create rhythmic impulses for pumping), this does not occur with skeletal muscle, which always requires neural stimulation from a motor neuron for it to contract. Skeletal muscle contracts rapidly and fatigues quickly.

The most important function of skeletal muscle is to bend the joints of the skeleton that allow the limbs to move. To do this, the muscle must be attached to a pair of bones. In fact, regardless of how complex a movement may be, skeletal muscles work only one way: by contraction or pulling on a joint. It follows, therefore, that at least two muscles, or sets of muscles, have to be used to move a bone into one position and then back. Consequently, joints are operated by two sets of muscles whose effects oppose or antagonize each other. This can be seen, for example, in the arm, which consists of an upper bone called the humerus, and lower bones called the ulna and radius, that join at the elbow joint (see Figure 4.1). The biceps (the flexion muscles) connect the upper and lower bones at the *front* of the joint, and when they contract the elbow is made to bend. In contrast, the triceps (the extensor muscles) run along the *back* of the upper and lower arm bones, and when they contract the limb becomes straightened out. This means the flexion and extensor muscles have to be finely co-ordinated, with the contraction of one being counter-balanced by relaxation of the other. In fact, it is unusual for a movement to involve a single pair of antagonistic muscles. Even the simple movement of the elbow requires the integrated action of many different muscles, and this principle holds true for nearly all other types of joint and movement.

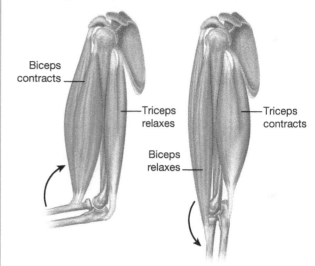

When the biceps muscle contracts, it flexes the arm (left); contracting the triceps muscle extends the arm.

Biceps contracts

Triceps relaxes

Biceps relaxes

Triceps contracts

Figure 4.1   The flexion and extension muscles of the upper arm

Source: Garrett and Hough (2021), based on Starr and Taggart (1989)

If a skeletal muscle is examined closely under a microscope, one will see it consists of muscle cells (also known as myocytes) which appear as long thin fibres that are enclosed by a specialized outer membrane called the sarcolemma (see Mukund & Subramaniam, 2019). Muscle fibres are in turn composed of hundreds, and sometimes thousands, of small contractile threads called **myofibrils** which run the entire length of the cell. These are made up of two proteins, actin and myosin, that form repeating units in the muscle called sarcomeres which give the muscle its striated appearance. The actin and myosin can be likened to interlocking fingers able to slide over each other following a nerve impulse. By doing this, they cause the myofibrils to shorten (in some cases by as much as 30–60% of their length) with their combined activity forcing the contraction of a much larger skeletal muscle. Interestingly, the length of muscle cells can vary enormously, with the largest being found in the Sartorius muscle of the thigh reaching over 30 cm in length, and the smallest in the stapedius muscle of the inner ear which is less than 1 mm.

KEY TERMS: *skeletal, cardiac and smooth muscle, antagonism, myocytes, sarcolemma, myofibrils*

THE NEURAL INNERVATION OF MUSCLE

Skeletal muscles are controlled by motor neurons whose cell bodies lie in the ventral horn of the spinal cord, or in some cases the brain via its cranial nerves. Every muscle is served by at least one motor neuron, called an **alpha motor neuron**, which typically gives rise to hundreds of tiny multi-branching axonal endings that innervate a large number of muscle fibres (Stifani, 2014). Consequently, when the motor neuron depolarizes, it causes all of its target muscle fibres to contract at the same time. Alpha motor neurons are amongst the largest in the body, with their axons conducting impulses rapidly – often at speeds of more than 120 metres per second (or over 400 km/h). Hence, the brain can move the big toe in just a few hundredths of a second. The number of fibres innervated by a single axon of a motor neuron varies depending on the type of muscle. For example, the ocular muscles of the eye receive about 1 axon for every 10 muscle fibres, while some muscles of the hand may have a motor neuron for every 100 muscle cells, and this number can rise to 1 axon per 2,000 cells for the large muscles of the trunk and leg. In general, muscles that are innervated by large numbers of motor neurons are involved in fine and dextrous movement, in contrast to those involved in less flexible responses.

The synapse lying between the axon endings of the motor neuron and muscle fibre is called the **neuromuscular junction** (Slater, 2017). Closer examination of this site shows that as the motor axon reaches the muscle, it divides into many fine unmyelinated branches, with each one ending in swollen protrusions called synaptic knobs (see Figure 4.2). In turn, these knobs fit into 'pits' located on a specialized part of the muscle fibre's postsynaptic membrane called the motor end plate. When a nerve impulse reaches the axonal ending, the synaptic knobs release the neurotransmitter **acetylcholine** that binds to postsynaptic nicotinic receptors. These receptors increase the permeability of the muscle fibre membrane (the sarcolemma) to sodium and potassium ions, which causes a small depolarization (i.e. a voltage increase) in the fibre called an end plate potential. This form of synaptic transmission is fast as it takes only 0.5 to 0.8 msec for a neural impulse to initiate an end plate potential, and reliable as its generation nearly always instigates an action potential in the muscle fibre (in contrast, most other neurons require the summation of many inputs for this to occur). The high sensitivity of muscle fibres to acetylcholine is due to the large and highly folded surface area of the motor end plate, which contains thousands of synaptic knobs and is packed full of receptors.

KEY TERMS: *alpha motor neuron, neuromuscular junction, acetylcholine, nicotinic receptors, end plate potential*

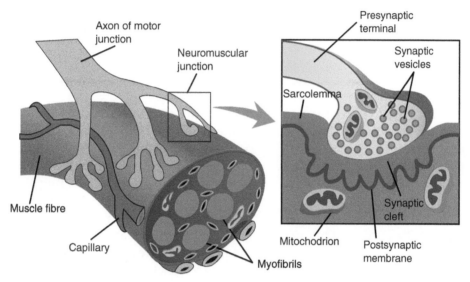

Figure 4.2   The neuromuscular junction
Source: Higgs (2020)

How then does the action potential of the motor neuron trigger muscle contraction? The answer lies with an organelle called the sarcoplasmic reticulum – essentially an intricate network of tubes and sacs that extend through each individual muscle fibre, which can be seen wrapping around, but not contacting, the myofibrils. These structures are also storage sites for large numbers of excitatory calcium ions ($Ca2^+$). As the action potential stimulates the muscle fibre, a cascade of calcium ions is released from the sarcoplasmic reticulum into the muscle cell. These ions bind to the myofibril filaments and create a molecular reaction that causes changes in the shape of the actin and myosin bonds, setting into motion muscle contraction.

KEY TERMS: *sarcoplasmic reticulum, calcium ions, myofibril filaments*

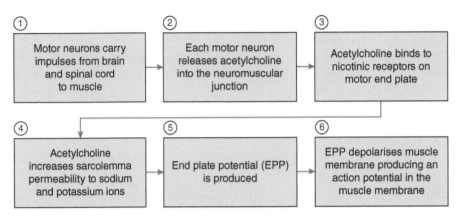

Figure 4.3   Summary of events in muscle contraction

DISORDERS THAT AFFECT THE NEUROMUSCULAR JUNCTION

Certain diseases also affect the neuromuscular junction. One such condition is myasthenia gravis – an illness where the immune system attacks and destroys the nicotinic cholinergic receptors (Trouth et al., 2012). Although new nicotinic receptors are made to replace the loss, they do not fully correct the damage. Consequently, the cholinergic impulse is less efficiently translated into a muscle contraction, resulting in muscle weakness and fatigue. The course of this illness is somewhat variable and may ultimately be fatal in about 10% of cases. It normally begins in the facial muscles causing drooping of the eyelids, along with weakness of the throat and tongue, resulting in chewing and swallowing difficulties. As the disorder progresses it can affect the limbs, making physical exertion impossible, leading to muscle wasting in the later stages of the disease. One of the main treatments for this disorder uses drugs such as physostigmine and neostigmine that inhibit the enzyme **acetylcholinesterase** (AchE). This enzyme acts to break down acetylcholine in the neuromuscular junction after it has been released from the presynaptic nerve fibres – so if it is inhibited, then the pharmacological action of acetylcholine is extended. Unfortunately, physostigmine and neostigmine have no effect on slowing down the progression of the underlying disease, and treatment may have to be supplemented by immunosuppressive agents such as corticosteroids. The prevalence of myasthenia gravis is about 1 in 25,000 and is more common in females than males. One person to have suffered the disease was Aristotle Onassis, who married Jacqueline Kennedy, the widow of the assassinated American President John F. Kennedy.

Another condition associated with the neuromuscular junction is Duchenne muscular dystrophy. This is produced by a mutation on the sex-linked X chromosome that causes the absence of the structural protein dystrophin. The result is morphological abnormalities of the neuromuscular junction, leading to an abnormal gait and atrophy of the leg muscles, which are accompanied by muscle pain, tenderness, weakness and swelling. It affects 1 in 3,600–6,000 males and frequently causes death by the age of 30 (Sinha et al., 2017).

It should come as no surprise that a large number of poisons also interfere with transmission at the neuromuscular junction. One of the best known is curare which is a mixture of toxins derived from a woody vine found in the Amazon region of South America. First encountered by Europeans when Sir Walter Raleigh came across it in his expedition up the Orinoco in 1595, the drug is still used today by certain Amazonian tribes who use it to coat darts normally shot from a blowpipe to bring down small prey (Wickens, 2015). The main active ingredient in curare is the alkaloid δ-tubocurarine which is a potent antagonist at cholinergic nicotinic receptors. Consequently, if nicotinic receptors are blocked by δ-tubocurarine, skeletal muscles can no longer be activated by motor neurons and the result is paralysis.

A number of snake venoms also act on the neuromuscular junction both presynaptically and postsynaptically. Those venoms affecting the release of acetylcholine from the presynaptic membrane are called β-neurotoxins and those affecting the postsynaptic membrane are called α-neurotoxins. The majority of β-neurotoxins act by inhibiting the release of acetylcholine into the synapse, which creates a neuromuscular blockade with the victim helpless from muscle weakness and paralysis. One such neurotoxin is called crotoxin which is used by certain types of rattlesnake. Postsynaptic neurotoxins, in contrast, tend to exert their effects by blocking cholinergic nicotinic receptors. One such poison is α-bungarotoxin which is found in the venom of the banded krait found in South Eastern Asia – one of the most deadly snakes in the world. Because of its high affinity for nicotinic receptors, however, this toxin has become a useful experimental substance for visualizing the molecular structure of the receptor. Other animals that use venom with agents that block nicotinic receptors include cobras and several types of sea snake (Ferraz et al., 2019).

It may be of interest to note that nicotine, which is derived from the dried leaves of the tobacco plant, not only acts as an agonist (stimulant) at cholinergic nicotinic receptors (both at the neuromuscular junction and in the brain), but is also highly poisonous. In fact, a dose of 60 mg is often given as the lethal dose (Koob & Le Moal, 2006). Smokers avoid poisoning by ingesting tiny doses since a cigarette typically contains around 12 mg of nicotine. Nonetheless, even at small doses, nicotine taken into the body by smoking may act on the neuromuscular junction to produce fine tremor, decreased muscle tone, and a reduction in the strength of skeletal reflexes.

KEY TERMS: *myasthenia gravis, acetylcholinesterase, Duchenne muscular dystrophy, curare, nicotinic receptors, α-bungarotoxin*

PROPRIOCEPTION

It is often said we have five senses: sight, hearing, taste, touch and smell. Perhaps it is because we tend to be consciously aware of these senses that we attach so much importance to them. But one often overlooked sense, which often operates below conscious awareness (and is mentioned in the last chapter), is proprioception – a term first introduced by Charles Sherrington in 1905 who derived it from the Latin *proprius*, meaning 'one's self'. Sometimes described as our kinaesthetic or sixth sense, proprioception provides us with internal information about the position of our limbs and other body parts in space, along with the speed and force of their movements (Proske & Gandevia, 2012). It is therefore the part of the nervous system that keeps track of, and controls, the different parts of the moving body. Thus, it is indispensable for creating the normal, easeful, graceful movement that we all take for granted. Because proprioception is involved with movements of the joints and limbs, it is generally considered to be a crucial component of the motor system.

It is tempting to think that movement simply results from a series of commands originating in the brain or spinal cord, which instruct the muscles how to move. However, things are not so straightforward since practically all movement also depends on large amounts of sensory input feeding back from the peripheral senses organs. For example, the motor control areas of our spinal cord and brain require sensory feedback to assess if the intended movement is being executed as planned, and whether new adjustments are necessary to finely tune the tension, contraction and coordination of the muscles. Without such proprioception the brain cannot 'feel' what the body is doing, and the movement has to be executed using a less efficient conscious approach. A memorable account illustrating the importance of proprioception is found in Oliver Sacks' (1985) book *The Man who Mistook his Wife for a Hat*. In a chapter entitled 'The Disembodied Lady', Sacks describes Christina, a young athletic woman, who when given antibiotics prior to gallstone surgery, lost all sense of proprioception. Causing such a severe collapse of muscle tone and posture, Christina was unable to move, sit, speak or even change facial expression. Although her movement would return it was never normal – not least because she was only able to move the parts of her body that she could consciously guide by sight. This made her actions clumsy, laborious and slow. As Christina put it, it was as if her body had lost all *sense of itself*.

Proprioception depends on many organs and receptors in the body. These include muscle spindles, Golgi tendon organs, and joint receptors which monitor stretching, tension, pressure and velocity. The visual system provides further sensory input to increase the accuracy of movement, whilst the skin's tactile receptors contribute information about different forces acting on the body. Another important component of proprioceptive feedback is provided by the vestibular system – a fluid-filled set of chambers in the inner ear that keeps the head and body properly oriented and balanced. It is a remarkable feat of the brain, and to a lesser extent the spinal cord, that all of these senses are continually monitored in an unconscious and automated fashion, providing us with posture, balance and finely tuned movement.

KEY TERMS: *proprioception, vestibular system*

FEEDBACK FROM MUSCLES (MUSCLE SPINDLES)

Embedded within the layers of most skeletal muscles, lying parallel and squashed within their fibres, are proprioceptor units called **muscle spindles**. These consist of a cluster of slender strands called intrafusal fibres contained within a fluid-filled capsule. Wrapped around the middle section of the capsulated spindle are large diameter and fast acting axons (known as Ia sensory fibres) that send muscle information to the spinal cord. The muscle spindle also receives input from the spinal cord via a gamma motor neuron that induces it to contract – although this is a separate phenomenon from the contraction of the surrounding muscle. The muscle spindle has two functions: (1) to provide information to the central nervous system on the state and position of the muscles, and (2) to initiate reflex contraction of the muscle when it becomes stretched. Because of this, muscle spindles are sometimes referred to as stretch receptors.

The importance of stretch receptors can be seen when a heavy weight is placed in a person's hand. At first the arm will begin to drop from the elbow and the biceps of the upper arm will be forced to stretch. As this movement occurs, the muscle spindles in the biceps will extend, and this information is relayed to the spinal cord. This input then causes what is known as an alpha motor neuron projecting to the biceps to fire, producing contraction of its muscles and enabling the arm to resist the stretch. In this way, the biceps make an automated reflexive movement to the force of the weight.

The ability to adjust muscle tone rapidly in response to such sudden shifts in muscle length is a basic prerequisite for smooth movement – and the stretch reflex is vital in this regard for maintaining muscle tone and posture. It also has to take place quickly which explains why this reflex is controlled by the spinal cord and not by the brain (Stifani, 2014).

The best-known example of the stretch reflex is the patellar tendon reflex, or knee jerk, which is routinely used by doctors to assess the condition of the nervous system. When the doctor strikes the tendon of the patient's knee, the extensor muscle running along the thigh (the quadriceps) becomes stretched (see Figure 4.4). The quadriceps muscle spindles then relay input to motor neurons in the spinal cord, which react by sending nerve impulses along their axons back to the stretched muscle. The result is a compensatory muscle contraction and

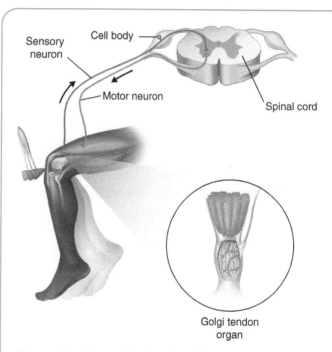

Figure 4.4   The patellar tendon reflex
Source: Garrett and Hough (2021)

sudden leg extension. This type of reflex is also called a monosynaptic reflex because only one synapse, located in the spinal cord, is encountered along the route from receptor (muscle spindle) to effector (leg muscle). Thus, the sensory neuron from the muscle spindle directly synapses with the motor neuron.

We have mentioned above that muscle spindles are also innervated by a gamma motor neuron. But why should this occur when it is the alpha motor neurons that cause the muscle to contract? The answer is that the muscle spindles have to contract with the surrounding muscle fibres, otherwise they would become 'flaccid' – an event that would cause them to stop signalling to the spinal cord. If this happened the spinal cord would have no way of knowing the length of the muscle or the weight acting on it. As a result, during the initiation of muscle contraction, both alpha motor neurons (which directly cause the muscle shortening) and gamma motor neurons (which innervate the spindles) are activated simultaneously. In this way, a small contraction of the muscle spindle occurs at the same time as the muscle fibres are contracting. Hence, the spindle matches the length of the muscle, and its Ia sensory fibres provide continuous feedback to the spinal cord.

KEY TERMS: *muscle spindles, gamma motor neuron, alpha motor neuron, patellar tendon reflex, monosynaptic reflex*

THE GOLGI TENDON REFLEX

Although muscle spindles provide the spinal cord with information relating to a muscle's length and degree of stretch, they do not provide feedback concerning the muscle's tension or force of contraction. In fact, this information is provided by another type of proprioceptive receptor called the Golgi tendon organ located on the collagen fibres that form the tendons (i.e. the connective material that attaches muscle to bone). There are hundreds of Golgi tendon organs in each muscle and each one is attached to about 10–15 muscle fibres. Consequently, these organs are excited when the muscle contracts following alpha motor neuron stimulation, or is stretched by a load. This information is relayed to the interneurons within the spinal cord by Ib sensory fibres. In turn, the interneurons form inhibitory synapses with alpha motor neurons.

The way the Golgi tendon organ feedback works to compensate for muscle tension is not too different from the way muscle spindles work. In fact, the Golgi tendon reflex can be regarded as the inverse of a stretch reflex, since it acts as a protective feedback mechanism to control the tension of an active muscle by causing relaxation before the tendon tension becomes too dangerous. For example, if a heavy weight is placed in our hand, the Golgi tendon organs respond to the muscle tension by sending excitatory input to the spinal cord's interneurons, which then inhibit the alpha motor neurons projecting back to our muscles. This reduces the amount of contraction being applied to the muscle, causing it to relax and lengthen. In this way, the muscle avoids damage, or in a worst case scenario, being ripped away from the bone. But just as important, this mechanism also helps maintain our steady control over the muscle tension essential for most of our movements (Nichols, 2018).

In addition to muscle length and tension, the spinal cord and brain also receive proprioceptive input regarding mechanical pressure, position and movement from mechanoreceptors in the ligaments and tissues surrounding the joints. There are four types of mechanoreceptors embedded in ligaments (Pacinian corpuscles, Meissner's corpuscles, Merkel nerve endings and Ruffini corpuscles) and they rapidly transmit sensory information regarding joint position. These receptors are not particularly well understood.

KEY TERMS: *Golgi tendon organs, interneurons, mechanoreceptors*

POLYSYNAPTIC REFLEXES

So far, we have examined two types of spinal reflex: the patellar tendon reflex, which involves one synapse (monosynaptic), and the Golgi tendon reflex, requiring the mediation of at least one interneuron and at least two synapses (polysynaptic). The latter polysynaptic reflexes underpin just about every kind of human movement (Stifani, 2014). A further example of a polysynaptic reflex is where a person abruptly pulls their hand away from a painfully hot surface – also known as a flexion reflex. In this situation, pain receptors in the fingers send input to the spinal cord via an axon that synapses with several interneurons located within its grey matter. At this point, the neural input can take several routes through the spinal cord, with the end result being a complex and co-ordinated response involving several muscles. This is not only slower than the monosynaptic reflex (due to the involvement of the extra interneurons) but also more complex behaviourally. For example, the interneurons excite the alpha motor neurons serving the flexor muscles of the arm (biceps) and those of the hand and fingers, whilst inhibiting the alpha motor neurons innervating the extensor muscles (triceps). The result is that the hand is quickly pulled away from the painful stimulus.

All polysynaptic reflexes involve reciprocal inhibition involving the combined action of agonist and antagonistic muscles – a reaction first recognized by Charles Sherrington in 1891. As discussed earlier, joints require two sets of muscles in order to move. For instance, the biceps cause the arm to bend (flex) whilst the triceps enable it to straighten (extend). Consequently, for the arm to move away from a painful stimulus, the biceps (flexor muscles) need to be excited by the alpha motor neurons, whilst the triceps (extensor muscles) must be inhibited. If this reciprocation did not occur there would be a muscle 'stand-off' with paralysis. Reciprocal inhibition, therefore, mediated by spinal cord interneurons, enables the flexor muscles to be excited whilst acting to inhibit the extensors (or vice versa).

Reciprocal inhibition also occurs in the crossed extensor reflex. For example, if we step on a sharp nail, our leg will not only be withdrawn from the painful stimulus – but our opposite leg will support the weight suddenly shifted onto it. This shows that flexion of the stimulated limb is always accompanied by an opposite reaction in the contralateral limb. It is also a type of reflex which allows the movement of our limbs to be co-ordinated. In fact, the spinal interneurons mediating reciprocal inhibition, in addition to receiving direct input from receptors such as muscle spindles and free nerve endings, also communicate with other segments of the spinal cord and brain. This allows the sensory and motor neurons involved in reflexes to enter and leave the spinal cord at different levels, and for the higher centres of the brain to be involved in reflexive action. For example, when picking up a scalding cup of tea, the brain may inhibit the flexion reflex if it decides that such an action might actually have worse consequences than getting burned.

KEY TERMS: *polysynaptic reflex, flexion reflex, reciprocal inhibition, crossed extensor reflex*

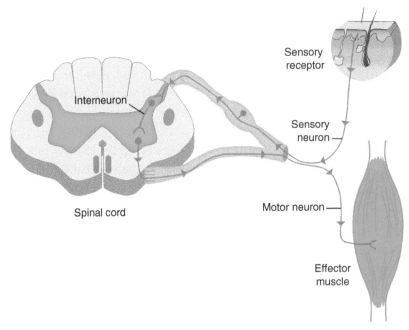

Figure 4.5   A simplified diagram of the spinal polysynaptic reflex
Source: Cook et al. (2021)

HEAD MOVEMENT AND THE VESTIBULAR SYSTEM

An important component of proprioception is our sense of balance, which is governed by the vestibular system in our inner ear (Holstein, 2012). This is particularly important for complex postural activities such as walking, running and riding a bicycle. It is also necessary to stabilize the fixation of our eyes to allow a still image on the retina when our head moves. Without this system we would be unable to maintain a correct head position, or adopt proper postural balance in a limitless variety of body manoeuvres and positions involving vision. Even when we are completely motionless, the vestibular system remains at work signalling the relentless pull of gravity on our bodies.

The most striking anatomical feature of the vestibular system is the **semicircular canals** which consist of three looping interconnected 'D-shaped' fluid-filled tubes that are positioned in three planes. These provide a mechanism that allows a representation of all angular or rotational head movements to be monitored. In fact, the semicircular canals will detect movement when we nod our head up and down, shake it left to right, or tilt it from side to side. They manage to do this because during head movement, the liquid (called endolymph) inside the corresponding canal to the plane of motion will, after a short lag period, move in the same direction as the head movement. This fluid shift then acts to deform specialized vestibular hair cells lying at the base of each canal, and whose movement leads to the initiation of action potentials in the vestibulocochlear nerve.

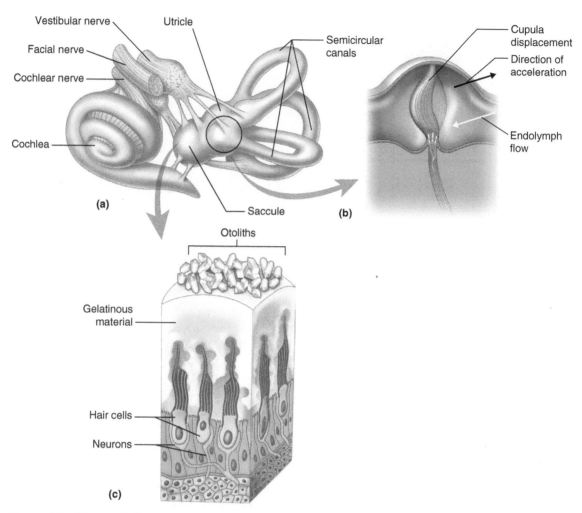

Figure 4.6   The vestibular organs

Source: Garrett and Hough (2021); (a) Iurato (1967); (b) Based on Goldberg and Hudspeth (2000)
© 2000 McGraw-Hill; (c) Based on Martini (1988)

Adjacent to the semicircular canals are two bulbous swellings, the utricle and saccule, which provide information about our head's position relative to our body, as well as its acceleration during movement. Like the semicircular canals, the utricle and saccule are filled with endolymph and contain hair cells for detecting motion, and these are embedded in a gelatinous mass called a cupula which contains small stones of calcium carbonate. When our head is tilted, or our body's position is changed with respect to gravity, the displacement of the stones cause the hair cells to bend. For this reason, the utricle and saccule are sometimes called the otolith organs (from the Greek *ot* meaning 'ear', and *lithos* meaning 'stone'). The hair cells of the utricle and saccule are also oriented differently. In the utricle they are roughly parallel to the ground when our head is upright, whereas those in the saccule are vertical. Because of this arrangement, the hairs inside the utricles are more sensitive to the magnitude and direction of head movements that occur in a horizontal plane (as happens in an accelerating car), whilst the saccules respond to vertical acceleration (as happens when ascending in an elevator). This information is also being continually fed back to our brain. Interestingly, it appears that the calcium stones (otoconia) are not replaced during our lifetime, and this might explain why balance inevitably worsens with time, or why patients after head-injury never quite regain their former balance function (Hain, 2019).

KEY TERMS: *vestibular system, semicircular canals, utricle, saccule, cupula*

HIGHER ORDER REFLEXES INVOLVING THE VESTIBULAR SYSTEM

The vestibular hair cells within the semicircular canals and otolith organs synapse with neurons that form the vestibular nerve. This pathway actually combines nerve fibres encoding sound information from the cochlea nucleus and it forms the eighth cranial nerve, or auditory nerve. The vestibular nerve passes to the vestibular nuclei which are located in both the medulla and pons. There are four vestibular nuclei (lateral, medial, superior and inferior) and the vestibular fibres terminate in one or more of these cell groups. In general, the utricle and saccule innervate the lateral and inferior nuclei, whereas the semicircular canals supply input to the superior and medial nuclei.

The outputs of the vestibular nuclei divide into ascending and descending pathways (Bronstein et al., 2014). The lateral vestibular nucleus, also known as Deiter's nucleus, gives rise to a tract which projects to the spinal cord on the same side. This is involved in regulating muscle tone. The medial vestibular nucleus, however, gives rise to several tracts – some innervating the upper, or cervical, spinal cord, and others ascending to brain stem nuclei such as the abducens nucleus, oculomotor nucleus, and the midbrain's trochlear nucleus, which are involved in automated eye movements including saccades. A tract also passes to the inferior peduncle which reaches the fastigal nucleus of the contralateral **cerebellum**.

The vestibular nucleus co-ordinates postural adjustments of the head and body. To give an example, imagine someone slipping on ice with their feet flying off the ground. This sudden movement will cause changes of fluid pressure in the semicircular canals – leading to activity in the cranial nerve and vestibular nucleus. In response, the vestibular nucleus will correct the situation. By innervating the motor neurons located in the upper spinal cord controlling the neck muscles, the position of the head will be brought upwards, and by exerting a powerful excitatory influence on the extensor muscles of the trunk and limbs, increased muscle tension in the arms and legs will help break the fall and right the body to its correct orientation. Thus, the vestibular nucleus simultaneously controls and integrates the action of the head, trunk and limbs that are losing their balance (Bronstein et al., 2014).

KEY TERMS: *vestibular nerve, vestibular nuclei, Deiter's nucleus, fastigal nucleus, cerebellum*

THE CENTRAL CONTROL OF MOVEMENT

A large number of structures in the central nervous system contribute to movement. These are also hierarchically organized, with lower areas tending to control simple reflexes and higher regions involved in more complex behaviours. The most basic behaviours are produced by the spinal cord. We have already seen how the spinal cord produces simple monosynaptic and polysynaptic reflexes, but it also contains neural circuits that govern more complex reflexes. These include groups of neurons, called central pattern generators, that control rhythmical activities such as walking, running and swimming. For example, electrical stimulation of the lumbar region in paraplegic humans with an upper severance of the spinal cord has been shown to induce stepping movements of the legs and rhythmical bending of the knees (Dimitrijevic et al., 1998). Similarly, the vigorous scratching movements produced by a dog in response to a flea are caused by patterns of interneurons in the spinal cord. In 1910, Sherrington showed this reflex is composed of two parts: the scratching motion and an adjustment for maintaining balance. The scratching motion involves a series of alternating knee, ankle and hip movements which use a total of 19 muscles, while a further 17 muscles stop the dog falling over. Remarkably, a decerebrate animal was able to follow an 'artificial electrical flea' all over its body and scratch in the appropriate places.

But, of course, the brain is the most significant structure for controlling movement and behaviour. Although it is an oversimplification, four main areas of the brain have long been known to be involved in producing and controlling movement: these are parts of the brain stem, the cerebellum, the **basal ganglia** and frontal areas of the **cerebral cortex** (Latesh, 2008). In addition, the **thalamus** occupies a pivotal position within all this motor circuitry. It is perhaps fair to say that the highest levels of the motor system are responsible for purposeful action, especially in terms of reaching locations and goals, whereas the lowest levels help transform these plans into smooth co-ordinated movement. This can also be seen in the case of infant development when at birth the most active part of the brain is the brain stem, which is then followed by increased cerebellar activity at around six months when the child expands their motor skills (crawling, walking, lifting their head). Over the next few years much of this behaviour becomes more cognitive-dependent and is taken over by the basal ganglia and cerebral cortex. Nonetheless, all of these brain regions act as an integrated unit (Kobesova & Kolar, 2014).

KEY TERMS: *central pattern generators, brain stem, cerebellum, basal ganglia, thalamus, cerebral cortex*

Another way of understanding the brain's motor systems is to recognize they are connected to the spinal cord in one of two ways. That is, motor commands reach the spinal cord by either the **pyramidal system** or the **extrapyramidal system**. Traditionally, the pyramidal system has been associated with voluntary or purposeful action under the control of higher cognition, whilst the extrapyramidal system is more involved with postural, reflexive or stereotypical forms of movement – or what can be regarded as the involuntary and automatic control of the body's musculature. Although this division of function is too simplistic, not least because both systems have integrated roles and other functions, it still serves as a useful generalization.

The pyramidal system originates in the cerebral cortex – most notably in a strip of tissue called the **motor cortex** which is found in the precentral gyrus of the frontal cortex. Contributing to the motor cortex are the premotor cortex and supplementary motor area – also located in the frontal cortex (see later in the chapter). All these regions are the origin of the corticospinal tract – a massive white bundle of over

(a)

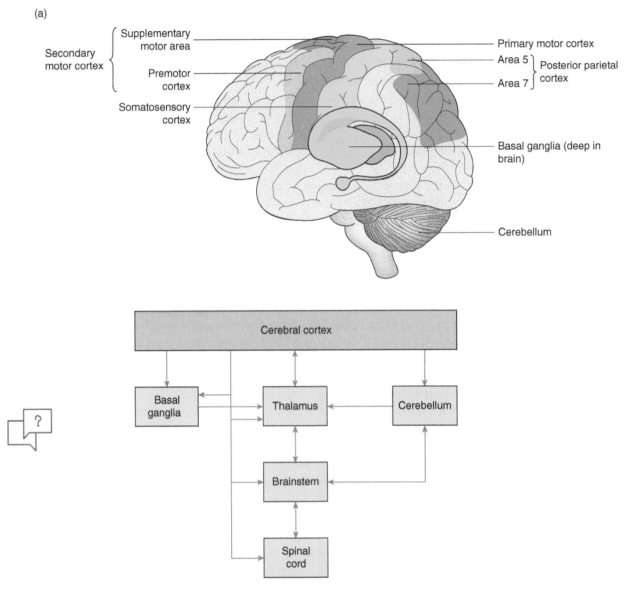

Figure 4.7   A simplified scheme showing the main movement areas of the brain

Source: Higgs et al. (2020)

1 million myelinated axons that passes down through the internal capsule close to the lateral aspects of the thalamus, into the spinal cord. Before reaching the spinal cord, however, about 80% of its axons will cross (decussate) to the opposite side of the body in the pyramidal decussation located in the pons. Here, the lateral corticospinal tract is formed, descending in the lateral funiculus of the spinal cord. The remaining uncrossed axons make up the anterior corticospinal tract, also reaching the spinal cord where they cross in the segment in which they terminate. Thus, the pyramidal system is completely contralateral (Afifi & Bergman, 2005).

The extrapyramidal system is composed of all the motor regions and pathways of the brain whose output does not contribute to the pyramidal system (de Oliveira-Souza, 2012). It is also different because most of its fibres (although there are exceptions)

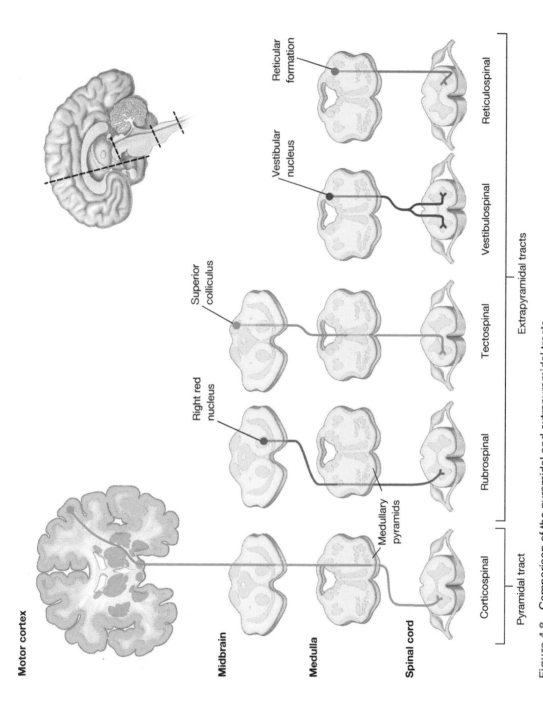

Motor cortex

Midbrain

Medulla

Spinal cord

Right red nucleus

Superior colliculus

Vestibular nucleus

Reticular formation

Medullary pyramids

Corticospinal

Rubrospinal

Tectospinal

Vestibulospinal

Reticulospinal

Pyramidal tract

Extrapyramidal tracts

Figure 4.8   Comparison of the pyramidal and extrapyramidal tracts

Source: Carolina Hrejsa/Body Scientific Intl. in Gaskin (2021)

do not cross over to the opposite side of the spinal cord (see Figure 4.8). One of the most important regions of the extrapyramidal system is the brain stem, which is the origin of several pathways to the spinal cord including the vestibulospinal tract and the reticulospinal tracts which start from the medulla and pons. Other descending extrapyramidal pathways include the rubrospinal tract (originating in the red nucleus) and the vestibulospinal tract (originating in the vestibular nucleus). Another significant contributor to the extrapyramidal system is the cerebral cortex which gives rise to the corticpontocerebellar tract. Originating from widespread areas of the cortex, its 19 million fibres or so project onto nuclei situated in the pons. Here, second-order neurons enter the middle cerebellar peduncle to innervate the cerebellum. Another important extrapyramidal pathway arising from the cerebral cortex is that of the corticostriate fibres which innervate the striatum which forms part of the basal ganglia. Both the cerebellum and basal ganglia give rise to a number of complex and multisynaptic pathways, which although having no direct link with the spinal cord, are nevertheless integrated with other movement areas that do – including the brain stem motor areas of the cerebral cortex.

KEY TERMS: *pyramidal and extrapyramidal systems, motor cortex, premotor cortex, supplementary motor areas, corticospinal tract, corticpontocerebellar tract, corticostriate fibres*

THE BRAIN STEM

The brain stem which, connects the spinal cord to the expanded forebrain, consists of the medulla oblongata, pons and midbrain. It also contains a central core of descending and ascending projections called the **reticular formation** that has many diffusely connected cell groups and receives sensory input. In particular, nuclei in the medulla along with those in the lower pontine regions have a wide range of reflexive motor functions, including respiration and cardiovascular function, eye movements and postural adjustment. We have already seen how the vestibular nuclei act to maintain the balance and stability of the head as the body moves, but there are also other brain stem nuclei and pathways to the spinal cord that contribute to movement. The most conspicuous of these are the reticulospinal tracts which arise from reticular nuclei in the medulla and pontine regions. There are two of these pathways: the ventral originating from the pontine reticular formation, and the dorsal from the medulla, and they descend in separate columns of the spinal cord. They terminate on interneurons where they work in tandem to control the flexor and extensor muscle reflexes controlling posture, locomotion and reaching. The reticulospinal tracts also receive input from extrapyramidal motor areas of the cerebral cortex, basal ganglia and cerebellum.

Two other descending pathways from the upper brain stem are the rubrospinal tract arising from the red nucleus, and the tectospinal tract (also called the colliculospinal tract) from the superior colliculus. The large **red nucleus** (which is actually pale pink in colour) receives input from the motor cortex and cerebellum. Although its spinal projections indicate it is involved in arm movements, there is evidence that the red nucleus is involved in the learned blink response following classical conditioning –

since lesions abolish the conditioned, but not the unconditioned, component of this response (Holstege, 1991). The tectospinal tract projects to the neck where it coordinates postural movements of the head and eyes.

The brain stem is also the origin for cranial nerves III through to XII, which are controlled by distinct cranial nuclei or local circuits of neurons. These are involved in a variety of reflexes, including chewing, facial expression, hiccupping, yawning and swallowing – along with those regulating respiration and heart rate. In addition, other areas of the brain stem, especially its upper midbrain parts, contain more complex patterns of reflexes that underlie many types of species-typical behaviour, such as those mediating aggression, threat displays, mating rituals, and grooming. For example, stimulation of the **periaqueductal grey area** can provoke defensive responses characterized by freezing immobility, escape behaviour, jumping, and increases in blood pressure (Deng et al., 2016).

Although the brain stem has a surprisingly diverse role in producing movement, it is entirely reflexive in nature. Consequently, without any involvement from higher brain regions, the brain stem can give no meaning to any given motor act. This is illustrated by Leonard (1998) who has pointed out that an animal with an isolated brain stem detached from the rest of the brain will walk on a treadmill and show no obvious deficit in locomotion. But when such an animal reaches an obstacle or wall, instead of circumventing it, they will walk head-first into the barrier and continue with stereotypical walking movements regardless. Thus, without the rest of the brain to guide behaviour, the brain stem's walking reflex becomes a purposeless act.

> **KEY TERMS:** *reticular formation, reticulospinal tract, rubrospinal tract, tectospinal tract, red nucleus, periaqueductal grey area*

THE CEREBELLUM: FIRST APPEARANCES

The **cerebellum** (Latin for 'little brain') lies at the back of the brain stem, partially underneath the occipital and temporal lobes. It is well developed in humans and roughly the size of two fists. Although the human cerebellum only weighs about 150 grams (about 10% of the brain's weight), it contains over 50% of its neurons, which some have estimated at 69 billion (Azevedo et al., 2009). This means there are about 3.6 times more neurons in the cerebellum than in the neocortex – a ratio that is conserved across many different mammalian species (Herculano-Houzel, 2009). The cerebellum also receives around 200 million input fibres from other areas of the brain (Llinás et al., 2004) and it projects to most other areas of the motor system – although curiously it has no direct connections with the basal ganglia. In terms of appearance the cerebellum is distinct with its surface exhibiting many small fissures and ridges (see Figure 4.9). This enables it to have a much larger surface area than would otherwise be the case. If we could unfold and flatten a human cerebellum it would measure about 100 cm × 100 cm which is about 40% of that of the cerebral cortex (Afifi & Bergman, 2005).

The cerebellum has two hemispheres and these are connected by a vertically oriented midline ridge called the vermis (from the Latin for 'worm'). Amongst the surface fissures of the cerebellum, two are large and conspicuous: these are the

Midsaggital section of cerebellum

Superior view of an 'unrolled' cerebellum

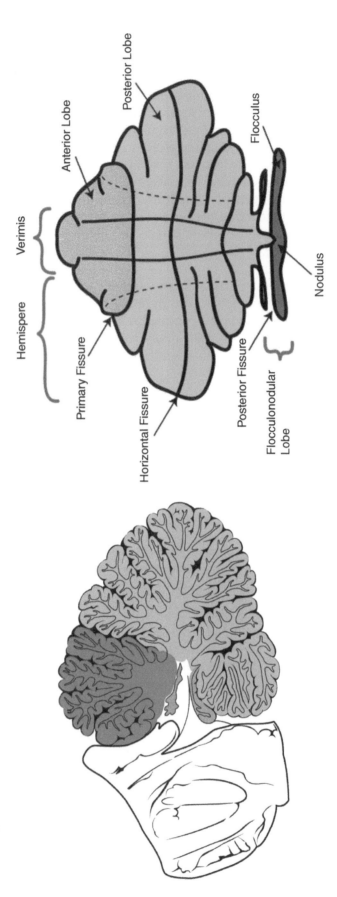

Posterior Lobe

Anterior Lobe

Flocculus

Verimis

Hemispere

Primary Fissure

Horizontal Fissure

Posterior Fissure

Nodulus

Flocculonodular Lobe

Figure 4.9   Major regions of the cerebellum

Source: OpenStax College/CFCF/Wikimedia Commons; https://commons.wikimedia.org/wiki/File:1613_Major_Regions_of_the_Cerebellum-02.jpg

anterior lobe and posterior lobes which are separated by the primary fissure. In addition, the posterolateral fissure, hidden on the underside of the cerebellum, separates the posterior lobe from the flocculonodular lobe. To complicate matters, the cerebellum can also be divided into lateral zones parallel with the vermis. Adjacent to the vermis is the intermediate zone and this is flanked by the lateral hemispheres which are noticeably large in humans. Unlike the aforementioned lobes, there are no clear visually identifiable borders between the lateral zones. Yet these lateralized areas receive different types of input. In brief, the vermis receives information from the vestibular system; the intermediate zone from the spinal cord; and the lateral zone obtains input from the pontine nuclei which relay output from the cerebral cortex. And, as might be expected, these three longitudinal cerebellar regions are associated with different functions. The vermis deals with balance, the intermediate zone with the spinal control of muscle tone for posture and locomotion, and the lateral zone (which sends output to the ventrolateral thalamus and primary motor cortex) with the planning of movement. More recent work is also beginning to show that these three areas can be further subdivided into different functional modules (Cerminara & Apps, 2011).

KEY TERMS: *cerebellum, vermis, anterior lobe, posterior lobe, primary fissure, posterolateral fissure flocculonodular lobe, intermediate zone, lateral hemispheres*

THE NEURAL STRUCTURE OF THE CEREBELLUM

The neuroanatomy of the cerebellum is beautifully organized. If sliced open, perpendicular to its surface, the internal structure of the cerebellum will appear as three layers, cut by many folded convolutions called folia. The three layers comprise: (1) an outer cortex of grey matter packed tight with cell bodies which contains almost all of the cerebellum's neurons; (2) a middle layer of white myelinated axons; and (3) an inner grouping of three clusters of grey cells known as deep nuclei. These are the dentate nucleus, the interposed nuclei (made up of the emboliform and globus nucleus) and the fastigial nucleus. These three groupings of cells provide the sole output by which the cerebellum communicates with the rest of the brain. Sometimes grouped with these nuclei are the vestibular nuclei (mentioned earlier in the chapter) which are considered to be functionally equivalent to the cerebellar nuclei despite being found in the medulla.

The outer grey cerebellar cortex is the place where most of the neural processing takes place. This too can be divided into three layers. The thick innermost granule cell layer is made up of huge numbers of small tightly packed neurons called granule cells. These are among the smallest neurons in the human brain and it has been estimated that there are around 50 billion of them. The middle layer is narrower and comprises the soma of Purkinje cells which have large distinctive flask-shaped cell bodies. They also have profusely branching dendrites which enter the outer molecular cell layer. Here, they are joined by a huge array of parallel fibres which penetrate the dendritic trees at right angles. This outermost layer of the cerebellar cortex also contains two types of inhibitory interneuron, stellate cells and basket cells, which synapse onto the dendrites of the Purkinje cells (Wright et al., 2016).

In addition to these cells, three types of axon also play an important role in cerebellar function (see Figure 4.10). The first of these are the mossy fibres (which get their name from the appearance of their knotty synaptic terminals) that form excitatory synapses with the granule cells. These arrive from many brain areas, but most noticeably from the pontine nuclei and spinal cord. In fact, granule cells receive all of their input from mossy fibres, although they outnumber them by about 200 to 1. In turn, the thin unmyelinated axons of the granule cells rise vertically, past the Purkinje cells, to the molecular layer where they split into two, making a distinctive 'T' shape. Each branch then travels horizontally to form a parallel fibre. In humans, these run for about 3 mm coursing through the Purkinje dendritic trees where they form many synapses. In contrast to the granule cells, the Purkinje cells receive their input from so-called climbing fibres which derive from the inferior olivary nucleus on the opposite side of the medulla. Interestingly, whilst the inferior olivary nucleus receives input from the spinal cord, brain stem and cerebral cortex, its output is exclusively directed to the cerebellum. Although each Purkinje cell receives input from exactly one climbing fibre, this single fibre 'climbs' the dendrites of the Purkinje cell, winding around them, and making a total of up to 300 synapses as it goes (Wright et al., 2016).

In turn, the Purkinje cell sends its axons to the cerebellum's three output structures – namely the deep cerebellar nuclei. Each pair of deep nuclei (the cerebellum has two hemispheres) is also associated with a corresponding region of the cerebellum. In short, the dentate nuclei receive input from the lateral hemisphere; the interposed nuclei receive input from the paravermal zone, and the fastigial nuclei from the vermis. In turn, the fastigial nuclei send their axons to the vestibular nucleus and other

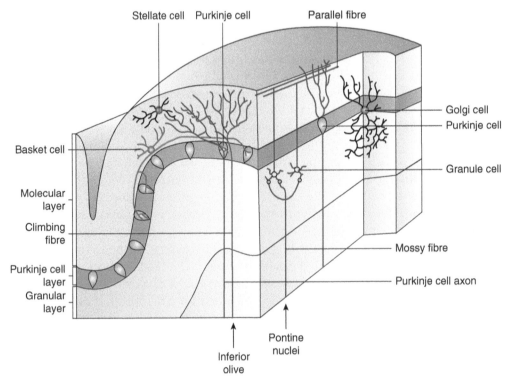

Figure 4.10   A schematic cross-section through the cerebellum
Source: Higgs et al. (2020); Ramnani (2006)

motor nuclei in the brain stem; the interposed nuclei innervate the red nucleus; and the dentate nucleus projects to the premotor and prefrontal areas of the cerebral cortex via the ventrolateral thalamus. The cerebellum is therefore at a pivotal point in a number of multisynaptic circuits involved in motor control.

> **KEY TERMS:** *dentate nucleus, interposed nuclei, fastigial nucleus, dentate cells, Purkinje cells, stellate cells, basket cells, mossy fibres, inferior olivary nucleus, parallel fibres, climbing fibres*

THE FUNCTIONS OF THE CEREBELLUM

One way of understanding what the cerebellum does is by examining the effects of its damage. In humans, cerebellar lesions reduce the fluidity of coordination which makes movements appear robot-like (Bastian, 2011). This is most noticeable in tasks requiring a series of rapid actions as occurs during dancing, playing a musical instrument or undertaking sporting activities. Although a person with injury of the cerebellum may be able to make individual movements, they are often unable to link them together into a continuous smooth sequence. For example, imagine we are to throw a baseball with our right hand. We may think this a straightforward movement. But if we act it out, it's not so simple. The chances are, as our right arm retreats to throw, we will shift our body weight to our right leg, stretch out our left arm for balance, and move our head towards our throwing arm. And all of this occurs before the ball is propelled forward. However, a person with cerebellar damage will be slow to make these bodily adjustments, resulting in a cumbersome and jerky action. This is known as asynergia. In addition, there may also be 'intentional' tremor during the movement (this is different from the 'resting tremor' seen in Parkinson's disease which disappears during movement). Other possible signs of cerebellar damage include the undershooting or overshooting of the intended arm and leg position, a tendency toward falling, weak muscles, and an unsteady, wide-based walking gait called **ataxia** (Bastian et al., 1996).

The type of deficit following cerebellar damage will depend on which parts are affected. For example, injury to the vermis will cause disturbances in posture and balance, lesions to the intermediate zones will tend to produce limb rigidity, and damage to the lateral lobes is likely to impair the timing of ballistic movements – rapid and automated movements of the limbs requiring high velocities and accelerations over a short period of time. A good example of a ballistic movement is a golf swing. For instance, once a golfer begins their swing, the stroke will be completed – no matter what type of sensory feedback they receive during the action. This shows the cerebellum is especially crucial in the execution of rapid co-ordinated responses.

The cerebellum controls the coordination of movement, enabling it to be smooth, quick and free of tremor. Yet how it performs this function is not fully understood. There are several hypotheses (see Kozio et al., 2014; Manto et al., 2012), although one popular theory is that the cerebellum assesses the rate of movement required for a particular action to take place, and then calculates the time necessary for the limbs to reach their intended position (Bastian et al., 1996). When we make a ballistic movement, it is often so rapid that our brains cannot rely on sensory feedback to guide or stop the movement. Consequently, the cerebellum must be able to anticipate the distance that the limb needs to travel, and the point at which the movement has to be terminated. One way it may do this is by timing the duration of the rapid muscle movements which is also integrated with proprioceptive feedback keeping track of the limbs. This also implies the cerebellum contains an internal 'model' of the intended ballistic movement, and it uses this representation to correct for small errors during its execution.

The cerebellum is also involved in motor learning. This has been clearly demonstrated in situations where cerebellar damage disrupts the acquisition and retention of classical conditioning. One such procedure occurs when an eye is made to blink following a puff of air. If a neutral stimulus, such as a tone, is sounded just prior to a puff of air to the eye, then human subjects will soon begin closing the eye when the tone is sounded. However, this may not occur if someone has damage to the cerebellum. The problem is not one of an impaired motor response as the subject is still able to blink their eyes to air puffs – rather the difficulty lies in predicting that the tone always precedes the event (Daum et al., 1993).

Prior to the 1990s the behavioural role of the cerebellum was widely believed to be purely motor-related. But more recently, especially with the use of functional imaging techniques such as fMRI, this view has changed, and there is far greater awareness of a cerebellar involvement in cognition, language, attention and mental imagery (Klein et al., 2016; Rapoport et al., 2000). This is perhaps not surprising as brain-scanning studies have also revealed that more than half of the cerebellar cortex is interconnected with association regions of the cerebral cortex (Buckner et al., 2011). It is possible, therefore, that the timing or anticipatory function of the cerebellum is related not just to the planning of movement, but to many types of non-motor cognition as well (Doya, 1999). These skills include reasoning, linguistic processing, shifts of attention, imagining movements, and even the regulation of emotion.

KEY TERMS: *asynergia, ataxia, classical conditioning*

THE BASAL GANGLIA

The basal ganglia (see Figure 4.11 and Figure 1.27 in Chapter 1) refers to a group of extrapyramidal cell groups and pathways that lie buried underneath the folds of the cerebral hemispheres (Lanciego et al., 2012). They are comprised of the **caudate nucleus** (meaning 'tail') and **putamen** (meaning 'nut' or 'shell'), along with the **globus pallidus** ('pale globe') which is divided into internal and external segments (Steiner & Tseng, 2016). Although the caudate and putamen appear to be separated by the large white tract of fibres making up the internal capsule, which relays information from the cortical motor regions to the lower brain and spinal cord, they are interconnected and work as a functional unit. Together they form a large neural mass, with a volume of around 10 cm³ in the human brain, called the corpus striatum (meaning 'striped body' because of the white myelinated axons that run through it). The caudate and putamen have also evolved more recently than the globus pallidus, and because of this are sometimes called the neostriatum (new striatum). Other nuclei associated with the basal

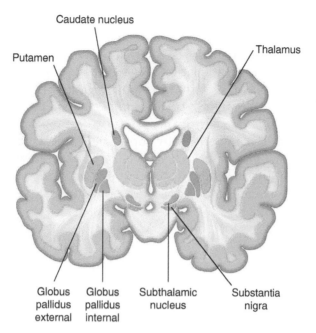

Caudate nucleus

Putamen

Thalamus

Globus pallidus external   Globus pallidus internal   Subthalamic nucleus   Substantia nigra

Figure 4.11 The location of the basal ganglia
Source: Carolina Hrejsa/Body Scientific Intl. in Gaskin (2021)

ganglia including the subthalamic nucleus located in the diencephalon, and the black pigmented **substantia nigra** found in the tegmentum of the upper brain stem. The latter is divided into two parts – a dorsal region called the pars compacta and a ventral region called the pars reticulata. It is interesting to note that none of these five structures receive direct inputs from, or send direct outputs to, the spinal cord (Latesh, 2008).

KEY TERMS: *caudate nucleus, putamen, globus pallidus, subthalamic nucleus, substantia nigra*

One way of understanding the functional anatomy of the basal ganglia is to view it as a network of parallel loops that is closely connected with the cerebral cortex (Simonyan, 2019). Indeed, most regions of the cerebral cortex involved in movement, including the primary motor cortex, secondary motor areas and parietal association areas, project with excitatory **glutamate** fibres to the striatum. The cortical inputs to the caudate and putamen, however, are not identical. To be more precise, the caudate nucleus receives projections from the multimodal association cortices and the frontal areas involved in eye movements, whereas the putamen receives input from the premotor and motor cortices of the frontal cortex, and the primary and secondary somatosensory cortices of the parietal lobes. Interestingly, the caudate and putamen have distinct patches called striosomes, which are 'islands' of tightly packed cells embedded in a less dense matrix background. The neurons in the striosomes also receive different types of input than those in the matrix. Although their functional significance remains largely unknown, it indicates that the corticospinal projection consists of multiple parallel pathways that serve different functions (Purves et al., 2008).

The striatum is the main hub of the basal ganglia. In turn, the cell bodies of the striatum, which are predominantly GABAergic medium spiny neurons, have a very specific output destination – namely the internal segment of the globus pallidus. The pallidal cell bodies of this region are also GABAergic and project to the ventroanterior and ventrolateral thalamus. Both these thalamic regions help convey input to the frontal cortex, including its premotor cortex, supplementary motor area, and primary motor cortex. Another component of this system is the substantia nigra pars compacta which innervates the striatum with dopaminergic fibres. This neural circuit is often referred to as the *direct route* and its main effect on movement is excitatory, since activation of the striatum causes inhibition of the globus pallidus, which acts to release it of its inhibitory control over the thalamus and motor cortex.

The direct pathway

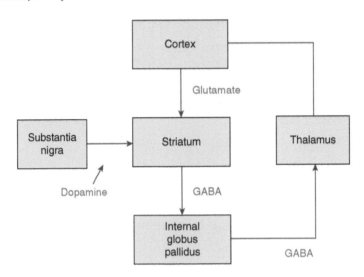

The indirect pathway

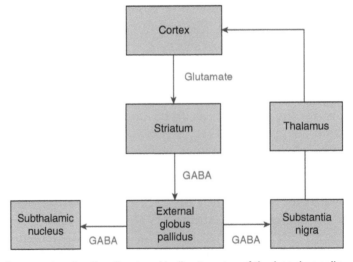

Figure 4.12   Flow diagram showing the direct and indirect routes of the basal ganglia

There is, however, is a second way in which the striatum can influence the motor areas of the cerebral cortex – and this is through a series of pathways called the *indirect route*. This is similar to the first circuit, except that input from the striatum now passes to the external segment of the globus pallidus. Like its internal counterpart, this contains GABAergic neurons, but their axons have two main outputs. One is to the subthalamic nucleus which feeds back to the internal segment of the globus pallidus. The other passes to the substantia nigra pars reticulata which projects to the motor nuclei of the thalamus (as does the internal globus pallidus). Both these 'extra links' are important, for the indirect route has effects on movement that are opposite to that produced by the direct route. That is, when this route is activated by the striatum its action on the globus pallidus is inhibitory. Hence, it will inhibit the motor areas of the cerebral cortex. Both the direct and indirect routes form large multisynaptic loops connecting the striatum and cerebral cortex. Emerging evidence suggests that these pathways may actually be composed of hundreds of 'mini-circuits' that are involved in a vast range of different functions or behaviours (Simonyan, 2019).

The anatomy of the basal ganglia is actually more complex than just described. For example, the striatum also receives input from the centromedian and intralaminar thalamus which relays it with information from the reticular formation. In addition, the striatum receives a dopaminergic innervation from the substantia nigra pars compacta – a pathway whose degeneration causes Parkinson's disease. It is also worth noting that both the neostriatum and globus pallidus extend downwards to form the ventral striatum and pallidum which are not regarded as motor structures of the basal ganglia. Embedded in this region are the **nucleus accumbens** and the somewhat mysterious **basal nucleus of Meynert** and substantia innominata. The ventral striatum receives limbic input from the cingulate cortex, along with information from the temporal lobe and frontal cortex. In turn, the ventral striatum completes the loop to the frontal and cingulate cortices via the mediodorsal thalamus. This pathway is involved in emotion, motivation and reward (Daniel & Pollmann, 2014).

KEY TERMS: *internal and external segments of the globus pallidus, ventroanterior and ventrolateral thalamus, subthalamic nucleus, substantia nigra pars reticulata, ventral striatum and pallidum*

THE FUNCTIONS OF THE BASAL GANGLIA

The basal ganglia have long been recognized as part of the brain's motor control system, not least because their damage is associated with a number of movement disorders, including Parkinson's disease and Huntington's disease (see Chapter 13). It is also apparent that basal ganglia damage can produce two opposite kinds of motor disturbance which appear to reflect abnormal function of either the excitatory 'direct' pathway leading to positive symptoms, or the inhibitory 'indirect' pathway leading to negative symptoms. Positive symptoms, which are a common feature of Huntington's disease, are characterized by exaggerated motor responses involving too much force. These include the presence of involuntary jerking or writhing movements (chorea) and strong muscle contraction, leading to abnormal posture (**dystonia**). In contrast, negative symptoms, which are symptomatic of Parkinson's disease, include impoverished or slow movement (**akinesia**) and muscle weakness. Damage to the striatum can also cause depression and slowness of thought accompanied by general apathy and forgetfulness which is sometimes called subcortical dementia.

One of the problems facing people with Parkinson's disease is a difficulty in initiating movement – suggesting that the basal ganglia may be involved in setting in motion behavioural action. However, electrophysiological recording from the brain during movement does not support this theory (Deecke & Kornhuber, 1978). For example, recordings taken from cells in the putamen and globus pallidus show that they do not become active until *after* a movement has been initiated by the motor areas of the cerebral cortex (Latesh, 2008). Thus, the striatum probably does not initiate movement (this is left to the cerebral cortex), but once an action has begun, it backs up the cerebral motor plan with fine adjustments. The precise nature of this control remains unclear. One possibility is that the striatum determines the sequencing of movements – which is supported in the case of patients with Parkinson's who typically have far greater difficulty performing a series of movements than individual ones. An alternative theory is that the striatum acts to disinhibit certain areas of the cerebral motor cortex from producing competing responses, whilst allowing the appropriate movement to occur (Schroll & Hamker, 2013). Or put another way, the striatum acts to select one pattern of motor action from the large number of possible options stored in the cerebral cortex (see Yanagisawa, 2018). A third idea is that the striatum backs up cortical planning by generating the right amount of force for a particular movement to occur by acting on the direct and indirect pathways to the globus pallidus – an effect that is not dissimilar to the way the accelerator and the brake pedal work in a car (Mink, 1999). If this is the case, the basal ganglia can be likened to a volume control whose output determines whether a movement will be weak or strong (Yin, 2014).

Another way in which the basal ganglia may improve the fluency of movement is by making 'large' postural adjustments to the body that leave the cortical motor regions 'free' to produce finer movements. That is, the basal ganglia may be responsible for making gross body movements, whereas the cortex controls actions involving the fingers, hands and face. Supporting this idea is the fact that people with basal ganglia damage often show marked postural dysfunction and have difficulty making normal gross movements of the limbs. It has been suggested that the pathway for postural movement does not involve the cortex, but rather the substantia nigra. In turn, the substantia nigra projects to brainstem areas such as the pedunculopontine nucleus involved in gait and posture (Pahapill & Lozano, 2000).

Despite its key role in regulating movement, it is becoming increasingly clear that the striatum serves many more behavioural roles. Not only has it been implicated in the learning of motor actions and physical skills, but striatal circuitry is also involved in cognition, memory and emotion-related patterns of action. In addition to its role in the learning and generation of motor habits, the striatum also appears to be also involved in habits of thought. Indeed, according to Graybiel and Grafton (2015), the striatum is a site where motor skills and thought habits meet. As these authors note, understanding how the learning repertoires of thought and action are combined is an important goal for future work.

KEY TERMS: *chorea, dystonia, akinesia*

THE MOTOR AREAS OF THE CEREBRAL CORTEX

In 1870, Gustav Fritsch and Eduard Hitzig, using a dog as their subject, and working on a table in the bedroom of Hitzig's house in Berlin, were the first to show that electrical stimulation of a small region of the frontal cortex triggered a number of bodily movements, including those of the face, neck and paws. Fritsch had first become interested in exploring this possibility when treating soldiers' wounds in the battlefield during the Prussian–Danish War (1864). He noted that if he accidentally touched part of the exposed brain when attempting to dress severe head wounds, it caused violent twitching on the opposite side of the body (Wickens, 2015). What Fritsch had identified, confirmed by his dog experiments, was the primary motor cortex – an area which in humans exists as a strip of precentral gyrus tissue in the posterior frontal cortex (this and several other motor areas are shown in Figure 4.14). This was mapped by the Canadian Wilder Penfield during the 1930s and 1940s using electrical stimulation of the cortex in conscious and fully awake humans prior to surgery for seizures – work that famously demonstrated the motor cortex was topographically organized for body layout (see Key Thinker 4.1 below). In short, it contained a point-to-point map of the body or what was referred to as a motor homunculus ('little man'). Consequently, if the motor cortex was stimulated along its length (from top to bottom), it produced movement of the feet, legs, body, arms and head. The amount of tissue given over to controlling each part of the body was also related to the precision of its movement. For example, a large proportion of the motor cortex controls the small muscles of the face and hands, but little of it moves the trunk and legs.

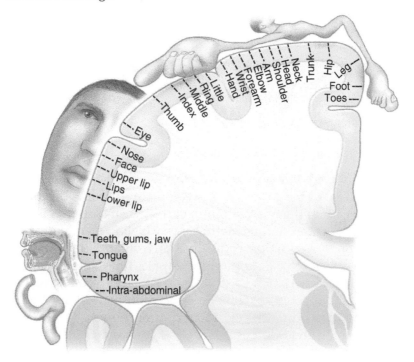

Figure 4.13   The primary motor cortex

Source: Adapted from *The cerebral cortex of man*, Penfield and Rasmussen © 1950 Gale, a part of Cengage Learning, Inc. in Gaskin (2021)

As Penfield explored the primary motor cortex he also realized it was surrounded by other motor areas that had an important influence on its functioning. In particular, stimulation of these 'secondary' areas typically produced more complex movements such as body turning or extension of the whole arm. These regions included two large areas anterior to the motor cortex called the **supplementary motor cortex** and the **pre-motor area** (both were grouped together by Brodmann as area 6). Another important region that influences the motor cortex is the **somatosensory cortex** which lies posteriorly, just across the central sulcus, in the parietal lobe. This area, as discussed in the previous chapter, receives touch and proprioceptive input from the body. Penfield also stimulated the somatosensory cortex and found it was also organized in a homuncular topographical arrangement. The somatosensory cortex and the primary motor cortex are closely linked, and their interaction demonstrates the importance of sensory feedback for the precise control of skilled movement (Wei et al., 2018).

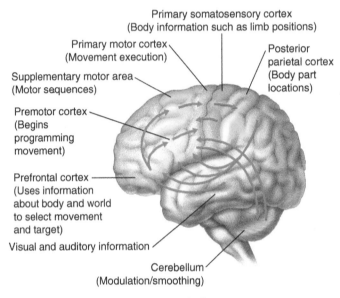

Figure 4.14   The motor areas of the cortex and cerebellum
Source: Garrett and Hough (2021)

As might be expected with so many cortical areas involved in the initiation of movement, the nature of the pathways between these regions is complex. But at the risk of oversimplification, the primary motor cortex receives its main input from the supplementary motor cortex and premotor areas, which in turn receive most of their input from the frontal association cortex and prefrontal cortex. The latter part of the brain is known to receive and integrate diverse information from the parietal, temporal and occipital association cortical areas, which provides it with highly processed visual input, along with paralimbic association cortical areas (Haber, 2016). This information is then transmitted to the primary motor cortex via multiple motor-related routes. In addition, the primary motor cortex and its surrounding areas receive input from the ventrolateral area of the thalamus which is the main route by which the basal ganglia (and cerebellum) is able to influence cortical processing.

The most striking output of the primary motor cortex, along with its surrounding areas, is the corticospinal tract. This is sometimes called the great voluntary motor pathway and it contains around one million fibres which project into the grey matter of the spinal cord. Because some 80% of fibres in the corticospinal tract cross, or decussate, in the pyramidal region of the medulla, this pathway is generally referred to as the pyramidal system. The majority of axons cross to the opposite side of the brain stem where they form the lateral corticospinal tract and primarily target the neurons that move the arm and legs. The axons that remain ipsilaterally form the ventral corticospinal tract and they move the trunk of the body. The primary motor cortex contributes about 40% of all corticospinal tract fibres, and the remainder arise from the premotor and supplementary motor areas and parietal lobes (Fitzgerald et al., 2012).

Although the cerebral cortex has direct access to the spinal cord via the corticospinal tract, it also affects movement in many other ways. For example, the primary motor cortex is the origin of the corticobulbar tract which projects to the medulla and synapses on the motor neurons of the cranial nerves innervating the face and tongue. In addition, there are cortical fibres that terminate on brainstem nuclei such as the red nucleus (the origin of the rubrospinal tract), pontine nuclei (from where information can reach the cerebellum) and vestibular nuclei. All of these make up important components of the extrapyramidal system. In addition, as we have seen earlier in the chapter, widespread areas of the motor cerebral cortex project to the caudate nucleus and putamen which form the striatum.

KEY TERMS: *motor cortex, precentral gyrus, supplementary motor cortex, premotor cortex, corticospinal tract, corticobulbar tract*

KEY THINKER 4.1

WILDER PENFIELD

Wilder Penfield was born in 1891 and followed the occupation of his father as a doctor, because 'it seemed to be the best way to make the world a better place'. After winning a Rhodes Scholarship in 1914, enabling him to study at Oxford, Penfield came under the influence of Charles Sherrington, who inspired a lifelong fascination into the mysteries of the brain. Later, he moved to the National Hospital in London where his abiding interest in epilepsy began. Returning to Canada in 1928, he took up a position as a surgeon in Montreal. A few months later, his sister Ruth was diagnosed with a tumour deep in her brain – a growth he attempted to remove with a radical operation. Unfortunately, he was unsuccessful and his sister died three years later. By now, his driving mission was to establish an institute where experts could work together in understanding and treating epilepsy. With an award of $1.2 million from the Rockefeller Institute, Penfield founded the Montreal Neurological Institute in 1934.

Epilepsy afflicts about 1% of the population. Although in most cases a cause cannot be found, there are instances when the seizures are attributable to scar tissue in the brain arising from head trauma. This can often be removed in an operation. However, one of the difficulties facing surgeons is removing the tissue in a such a way that it does not cause other serious impairments. In particular, a surgeon must be mindful about whether the operation could lead

(Continued)

to paralysis or aphasia. To avoid this, Penfield began electrically stimulating the exposed brain in fully awake patients prior to surgery. Requiring only a local scalp anaesthetic, this allowed him to remove tissue with greater confidence. The aim was simple: if the stimulation caused a sudden limb movement or vocalization, then this area had to be spared. But in most instances, the patient was unresponsive to stimulation, showing it could be removed safely.

The Montreal procedure, as it became known, was a major advance in the treatment of epilepsy, and it gave some fascinating insights into the workings of the human brain. The first report of this came in 1937 when Penfield and Edwin Boldrey analysed the results from their first 163 operations. Their stimulation had targeted the deep fissure, called the central sulcus, that separates the frontal and parietal lobes. Although this area had been shown to contain isolated motor regions in a dog by the German physicians Fritsch and Hitzig (c. 1870) and monkey by Beevor and Horsley (1890), Penfield showed that the precentral (frontal) part of the gyrus contained a complete map or topographic representation of the human body from which movements could be elicited. The postcentral gyrus of the parietal cortex was also found to contain a similar map – although stimulation in this region produced a tingling sensation in the body. In fact, Penfield had discovered the somatosensory cortex which receives sensory, tactile and proprioceptive feedback from the skin and muscles of the body (see Chapter 3).

By the time Penfield retired at the age of 70, he had been awarded numerous honours, including the accolade of being the greatest living Canadian despite being American by birth. Penfield spent much of his retirement considering philosophical issues in books such as *Mystery of the Mind* (1975), which he wrote in his eighties. Penfield still had some surprises, admitting that as a young man he had believed the neurological processes of the brain would one day fully explain the mind, but as he got older, he changed his opinion. As Penfield pointed out, the conscious willing to do or believe in something had never been invoked in a person by electrically stimulating their brain. Or as he put it: 'There is a switchboard operator as well as a switchboard.' In fact, Penfield had come to believe that brain and mind are two different things – a dualistic view associated with Descartes. Penfield died at the age of 85, just three weeks after completing his autobiography *No Man Alone* – a book espousing his belief in teamwork as a means of improving surgery and understanding the mysteries of the brain.

THE FUNCTION OF THE PRIMARY MOTOR CORTEX

The location of the primary motor cortex puts it in an ideal position to be accessed by conscious thought which is presumably involved in directing voluntary, goal-directed behaviour. It is also activated by massive neural input from a large number of other cortical and subcortical areas (Rizzolatti & Kalaska, 2013). Thus, we might expect primary motor cortex damage to cause serious motor deficits and paralysis – not least because of its major contribution to the corticospinal tract. However, motor cortex injury in humans produces less disability than might be expected. For example, lesions of this brain area can occur as a result of a stroke to part of the middle cerebral artery. Although this may initially produce flaccid muscle tone and paralysis, most patients show considerable recovery, including the ability to walk again and reach for objects. In fact, the most likely long-term deficit involves an inability to make fine dextrous movements of the fingers such as those required for buttoning clothes, writing or typing. Damage to the primary motor cortex may also impair the ability to grip objects, or move a single limb precisely, which will reduce the speed, accuracy and strength of a person's movement (Mendoza & Foundas, 2008). In addition, these deficits may disrupt the elicitation of smooth integrated muscle synergies that help produce complex or skilled patterns of motor behaviour (Capaday et al., 2013).

Lesions of the primary motor cortex, therefore, do not abolish voluntary movement. On first sight this may appear somewhat surprising, but it should not be forgotten that several other cortical regions store motor programs for action and are capable of instigating movement. These secondary areas also contribute to the corticospinal tract and presumably they can compensate to some degree for the effects of primary cortex damage. It is also known that the motor cortex can reorganize itself following injury, with unaffected parts taking over the role of the injured tissue (Jaillard et al., 2005).

Deficits in fine or dextrous movement also occur in animals after motor cortex and corticospinal tract lesions, although a certain amount of recovery also takes place. This was shown, for example, by Lawrence and Kuypers (1968) who bilaterally lesioned the corticospinal tracts in rhesus monkeys. Within a day or two of their operation, the animals could stand upright, hold the bars of their cage, and move freely. After six weeks, they ran, climbed and reached for food. Yet their manual dexterity remained poor. The monkeys were unable to manipulate their fingers when picking up small pieces of food. And, once they had food in their hands, they were not able to release it from their grasp, leading them to use their mouth to pry their hands open. Curiously, they had no difficulty releasing their grip when climbing the bars of their cage, indicating that this eating behaviour may be controlled by a different pathway or brain region.

The primary motor cortex, therefore, regulates the speed, force and agility of movements, especially those requiring the precise or fine actions of dextrous body parts such as the fingers. It was once thought that the primary motor cortex controlled fine movement by its sequential action on individual muscles. However, we now know that this is not the case. In fact, if a single neuron is identified in the primary motor cortex, and its axon followed down in the corticospinal tract to the spinal cord, one will find that it does not control a single muscle in the body, but instead it projects to many motor neurons, sometimes at different spinal levels. Hence a single neuron in the primary motor cortex innervates a number of muscles (Lemon, 2008).

It is also becoming clear that large numbers of cells in the primary motor cortex are involved in even the simplest movement. For example, in one study, the firing rates of cells in the motor cortex were examined as monkeys learned to move their arm to one of eight possible locations (Georgopoulos, 1994). It was found that individual cells in the motor cortex would fire most vigorously to a 'preferred' location, although the cell would often show some increased activity over a wider spatial area. In fact, the best way to predict the direction of the arm was to pool the information from many neurons. That is, when the activity of several hundred neurons was examined, it provided a much better indication of the direction of the reaching arm. In other words, movement in the primary motor cortex is encoded by populations of neurons rather than by single cells (Ebner et al., 2009). A similar example of *population coding* was also discussed in Chapter 2 regarding object recognition by the visual system.

THE CONTRIBUTION OF OTHER CORTICAL AREAS TO MOVEMENT

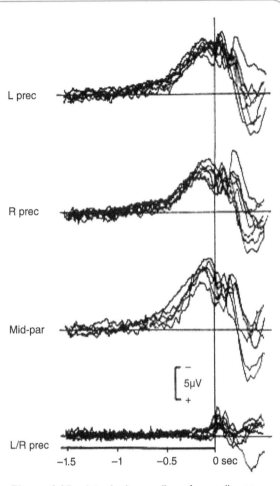

L prec

R prec

Mid-par

$5\mu V$

L/R prec

−1.5   −1   −0.5   0 sec

Figure 4.15   A typical recording of a readiness potential

Source: Lüder Deecke/BotMultichill/Wikimedia Commons

The cerebral motor areas consist not only of the primary motor cortex with its famous homuncular map, but also the supplementary motor area (SMA) and premotor cortex. Both these regions are richly interconnected and integrate information arriving from other cortical areas – especially from the **prefrontal cortex**. In turn, much of this feeds into the primary motor cortex (Chouinard & Paus, 2006). The supplementary and premotor areas were shown to have a motor function in humans by Penfield, who found that electrical stimulation of these regions often gave rise to complex bilateral postural movements such as a raised hand before the face, or movement of all four limbs (Penfield & Rasmussen, 1950). Electrical stimulation of the SMA also frequently elicited an urge to make a movement, or anticipate that one was about to happen (Chauvel et al., 1996; Penfield & Welch, 1951). Since this pioneering work, it has become clear that the supplementary and premotor regions play a crucial role in initiating actions. Some of the strongest evidence for this has come from the discovery of an EEG measure called the readiness potential (Kornhuber & Deeke, 1965), which is a ramp-like build-up of electrical activity that reliably precedes intentional voluntary action by about a second. This potential consists of an early component emerging at about 1,000 milliseconds (msecs) prior to movement from the SMA and premotor cortex, and a later component (about 300 msecs before action) originating from the motor cortex (Hallett, 2016).

The SMA and premotor cortex have also been examined by the use of functional scanning techniques which allow brain activity to be observed while the subject is planning or performing an action. Although it is now a bit dated, one of the most instructive of these studies was undertaken by the Danish investigator Per Roland (1993), who used single-photon emission computer tomography to track brain activity in the form of regional blood flow during the performance of various hand movements. When subjects were asked to perform a simple reflexive tapping movement of the right index finger, increased blood flow was directed to the opposite (left) primary motor cortex and somatosensory cortex. However, when subjects were asked to perform a much more complicated set of 16 movements involving the mental plan of sequencing several fingers, increased blood flow occurred bilaterally in the SMA (and parts of the prefrontal cortex). And perhaps even more intriguing, when subjects were asked to mentally rehearse (i.e. imagine) the movements, this also increased blood flow in the SMA. In fact, the SMA's involvement in the mental imagery of behavioural action has now become a well-documented effect (Iseki et al., 2008).

Another demonstration illustrating the different roles of the SMA and primary motor cortex was provided by Gerloff et al. (1997) who used a technique called transcranial magnetic stimulation (TMS). This uses a magnetic force as a non-invasive form of stimulation to induce small electrical currents in the brain by holding a magnetic field generating coil next to the head – a procedure causing the neurons under its influence to produce a disruptive burst of action potentials. Subjects were trained to produce a complex sequence of 16 movements involving all 4 fingers on an electric piano. When TMS was applied over the part of the primary motor cortex representing the hand, sequence responding was disrupted – typically causing the movement to be halted in mid-flow, or the wrong key to be pressed. The subjects, however, perceived the problem as a temporary loss of coordination and explained the mistake as the finger suddenly jerking in the wrong direction. In contrast, when the TMS targeted the SMA, the jerk was delayed, occurring some three key presses after the stimulatory pulse. But now the explanation was different, with the subjects attributing the mistake to losing track of the sequence, or forgetting the order of the key presses. From this, it appears that the stimulation of the SMA interferes with the conscious intention of the movement. Without this action plan, the subject realizes something is amiss, but is unable to say what. But with a simple error of execution (motor cortex) the behaviour can be more easily explained as a simple mistake (Gazzaniga et al., 2002).

Whilst the SMA seems to plan and sequence movements guided by internally generated stimuli (or intentions), the premotor cortex does the same for externally guided movements. For example, Roland et al. (1980) found that motor tasks involving sensory-guided movements, such as following verbal instructions, caused more blood flow to the premotor cortex than SMA. Similarly, in another experiment where subjects had to make sequential finger movements, self-imagined actions enhanced blood flow to the SMA whereas movements made in response to a computer-generated tone caused increased activity in the premotor areas (Jenkins et al., 2000). Clearly, most movements are guided by both mental intention and external stimulus events, and the connections between the SMA and premotor cortex co-ordinate movement planning.

KEY TERMS: *supplementary motor cortex, premotor cortex, prefrontal cortex, readiness potential, transcranial magnetic stimulation*

SPECIAL INTEREST 4.1

MIRROR NEURONS AND IMITATION

Human babies are good at imitation. Within the first week of life, a baby is capable of mimicking a parent if they stick their tongue out in a playful gesture (Anisfeld, 1996). This behaviour is not as simple as it first seems. If we consider how imitation occurs, it is clear this requires the observer not only to carefully watch the act, but also somehow recreate it. This is an

(Continued)

exceptional skill for a newborn baby. Although imitation is important for social interaction, its role in human development may be more profound. Many psychologists believe that imitation allows us to develop empathy – that is, to put ourselves in the place of others and 'read' their minds. Humans are strongly empathetic: if we see someone cry we are likely to feel sad, and when we observe laughter we often become happy. In 1903, the German Theodore Lipps noted that the perception of another individual's emotional expression automatically activates the same emotion in the perceiver. According to Lipps we don't have to consciously think about empathy, we do it automatically.

An important discovery in recent years has been the identification of brain neurons involved in imitation. These were first discovered in monkeys by Giacomo Rizzolatti at the University of Parma in 1996. Initially, Rizzolatti was examining the role of the premotor cortex in planning movements by recording from neurons that fired when a monkey performed a hand action such as gripping an object or picking up a peanut. But during this work, Rizzolatti realized many of these neurons also became active when the monkey observed another monkey, or even a human, perform the same action. For example, the neurons did not fire at the sight of an object (e.g. peanut), but at a whole behavioural action involving the peanut. In other words, the cells were selective in their firing. Put simply, these neurons fired when the monkey executed a specific action (e.g. picking a raisin from a tray) and again if the animal watched the same action in another individual. These were dubbed 'mirror neurons' (Gallese et al., 1996; Rizzolatti et al., 1996).

The next big question was whether mirror neurons existed in the human brain. To examine this, Rizzolatti undertook a PET study measuring blood flow in subjects lying in a brain scanner who had to observe and mimic an experimenter handling various objects (see Rizzolatti et al., 2001). The results showed that imitation was associated with increased activity in the left hemisphere's lateral frontal lobe which included the premotor region and Broca's area. The discovery of mirror neurons in Broca's area raised great interest, as it led to speculation that our capacity to communicate with language may have evolved from the mirror neuron system.

Since then, brain imaging of mirror neurons has become one of the most popular subjects in cognitive neuroscience, with the observation of film, rather than direct action, providing the choice research method. In 2010, a meta-analysis of 139 fMRI and PET mirror neuron experiments by Caspers et al. (2010) showed that three main regions of the human brain were involved in mirroring behaviour: (1) the frontal cortex, including the lateral premotor cortex and adjacent supplementary motor area; (2) the inferior parietal lobe; and (3) the posterior middle temporal gyrus which borders on the occipital lobes. This work has been confirmed in monkeys, which has enabled Rizzolatti to trace the neural inter-connectivity of these regions with standard anatomical techniques. According to Rizzolatti, this has shown that certain areas in the temporal lobe pass information to the frontal cortex, along two major pathways through the parietal lobes. One of these pathways is involved in recognizing the agent of the motor act, while the other is concerned with the details of the hand grip or body movement.

THE CONSCIOUS INTENTION TO ACT

Intentional voluntary action is fundamental to human existence, and most of us navigate our lives with the implicit belief we all have conscious free will which enables us to perform predetermined acts and take responsibility for our behaviour. This was also the famous dualist view of Descartes in the seventeenth century who held that when a person makes a conscious decision to act, this mental event produces the neural events which cause movement. This theory is one we can all relate to – for we do seem to have an internal private stream of mental activity inside our heads, capable of making conscious decisions and undertaking deliberate action. But there is a fundamental problem with this theory as Descartes was aware. Put simply, how can the mind (which Descartes regarded as a non-physical thing) initiate the physical neural events in the brain that instigate behavior? This is known as the interaction problem.

Although there is no solution to this central philosophical question, there is evidence that Descartes may have been wrong to suppose our conscious intentions cause behaviour. This issue has been examined in a series of studies by Benjamin Libet (see Libet, 2004). In the late 1950s, Libet was given the opportunity of experimentally stimulating the somatosensory cortex in subjects prior to surgery. It had been known since Penfield that that an electrical stimulus applied to the somatosensory cortex could induce a touch sensation that appeared to arise from a corresponding part of the body or skin. Libet's main concern at first was to establish the minimum amount of stimulation which would produce a conscious tactile sensation, and this led him to make a surprising discovery – namely that an electrical stimulus elicited no reportable experience unless the train of stimulation exceeded 0.5 seconds. Libet concluded that neuronal adequacy for conscious sensation is only achieved after half a second of continuous stimulation to the somatosensory cortex.

These results had several implications, not least that consciousness is a slow process which lags half a second (or 500 msecs) behind the events of the real world! In fact, 500 milliseconds is a long time in terms of brain activity. For example, it takes just 2–3 milliseconds for a neuron to generate an impulse which means it is feasible that an excited cell could transmit over 100 action potentials per second. It only takes about 15 milliseconds for somatosensory stimuli to reach the brain, and a reaction time to a simple stimulus (say pressing a button to light onset) may be as little as 200 milliseconds. Therefore the time lag of 500 milliseconds seconds for a conscious experience to emerge is remarkably slow. At the very least this amount of time is likely to involve the activity of many thousands, if not millions of neurons.

Further work was performed by Libet in the 1970s. It was known that stimulating the somatosensory cortex blocked touch sensations arising from the skin. So, if consciousness took half a second to build up, then it should be possible to impede touch sensation by stimulating the cortex up to half a second later. In fact, this is exactly what Libet found. Tactile sensation was not felt by the person, even if it took place some 300–500 milliseconds after the cortical stimulation.

In 1977, Libet turned his attention to the question of how long it took someone to make a decision to perform an intentional act. To do this, subjects had to watch a small clock hand that completed each full revolution in 2.5 seconds. While fixated on the clock, the subject was asked to flex their wrist at a time of their choosing. The subject then reported the position of the clock hand at the time when they first became aware of the will to move. Libet called this subjective judgement 'W' (for will). At other times, subjects had to judge the position of the hand when they actually moved. Libet called this judgement 'M' (for movement).

Libet also measured two other parameters: the electrical (EEG) activity over the cortical motor areas of the brain, and the electrical activity of the muscles involved in the wrist movement. To examine the motor areas, Libet used an EEG measure called the readiness potential (as discussed earlier) which is a build-up of electrical activity with a characteristic shape that reliably precedes voluntary action. By recording the muscle activity involved in the wrist movement, Libet was also able to time the onset of movement relative to the readiness potential. As expected, Libet found that the 'will to act' came before the wrist movement. However, he also found a consistent temporal relationship between the subjective experience and the brain event (readiness potential). In short, the readiness potential (i.e. neural preparation to move) always preceded conscious awareness of the intention to move by 300–500 milliseconds. Thus, the brain is preparing the movement even before the subject is consciously aware of deciding to move!

These results have been confirmed by others. For example, Lau et al. (2006) asked subjects to make finger movements at the time of their own choosing whilst watching a red light that moved around a clock face at about 2.5 seconds per revolution. The subjects were also asked to pay attention to the instant when they decided to make their movement. The conscious decision made by the subject to act typically occurred some 0.2 seconds prior to the action. However, their brain activity, as measured by fMRI, revealed that the SMA was exhibiting increased excitation some 2 or 3 seconds before this conscious awareness arose. These findings lead to the somewhat unpalatable conclusion (for some anyway) that the neural activity responsible for the decision to act begins well before a person is consciously aware of making that decision (Matsuhashi & Hallet, 2008).

KEY TERMS: *free will, the interaction problem, neuronal adequacy, the readiness potential*

SUMMARY

Skeletal movement is the result of muscle contraction. The body contains three types of muscle, i.e. smooth, cardiac and striated, with the latter producing movement of the skeletal bones and posture. The human body contains over 600 striated muscles which make up around 50% of its weight. Muscles are composed of long thin muscle cells that contain numerous smaller cylindrical fibres called myofibrils. These contain sliding filaments of actin or myosin which gives the myofibril, and ultimately the muscle fibre, its ability to contract. All skeletal muscles are innervated by alpha motor neurons whose cell bodies are located in the ventral horn of the spinal cord. The synapse between the alpha motor neuron and its muscle cell is known as the neuromuscular junction which uses acetylcholine (ACH) as its neurotransmitter. When ACH binds to the nicotinic receptors at the **motor end plate** it initiates a series of chemical events in the muscle cell that cause it to contract.

The spinal cord can act by itself through monosynaptic and polysynaptic reflexes – the latter of which can produce quite complex patterns of behaviour. But mostly, the neural circuitry of the spinal cord is under the control of the brain, which contains two main systems: the pyramidal and the extrapyramidal. The pyramidal system originates in the cerebral cortex and its axons enter the corticospinal tract. En route about 80% of these fibres cross to the contralateral side of the brain in the pyramidal decussation before reaching the spinal cord. Its remaining fibres also cross – but only when they reach the spinal segment in which they terminate. The extrapyramidal system is, in effect, all the brain's remaining motor nuclei and pathways. Its most conspicuous descending pathways include: the reticulospinal tract originating from several reticular nuclei; the rubrospinal tract arising from the red nucleus; and the vestibulospinal tract from the vestibular nuclei. Most, but not all, of the extrapyramidal pathways pass down into the spinal cord without crossing over to its contralateral side.

A number of brain areas are responsible for producing and regulating movement. These include the cerebellum which is highly intricate in its neural circuitry, and important for enabling movement to be smooth, quick, and free of tremor. Another important region is the basal ganglia – a set of interconnected structures that include the **striatum** (caudate nucleus and putamen), globus pallidus and substantia nigra. The basal ganglia are closely associated with the motor areas of the cerebral cortex, and probably involved in correcting the force of movements and making postural adjustments of the body. This is shown in the case of basal ganglia damage (e.g. Parkinson's disease) where people show gross postural dysfunction and have difficulty initiating movement. A number of regions in the cerebral cortex are involved in producing movement and these include the prefrontal cortex, premotor cortex, supplementary motor cortex and primary motor cortex (the latter being the main source of fibres projecting into the corticospinal tract). The primary motor cortex is also topographically organized containing a point-to-point representation of the body. The cortical motor areas, especially the supplementary motor area and premotor cortex, are important for the conscious planning and initiation of purposeful action.

GO ONLINE

TEST YOUR UNDERSTANDING OF THIS CHAPTER AND VISIT HTTPS://STUDY.SAGEPUB.COM/WICKENS TO ACCESS INTERACTIVE 'DRAG AND DROP' LABELLING ACTIVITIES AND A FLASHCARD GLOSSARY.

MULTIPLE CHOICE QUESTIONS

Answer the questions below to test your understanding of this chapter's Learning Objectives. You'll find the answers at the end of the chapter.

1. What is the neurotransmitter that is always released at the neuromuscular junction?

   a. acetylcholine
   b. dopamine
   c. GABA
   d. noradrenaline

2. The main function of muscle spindles is to act as which of the following?

   a. cutaneous (touch) receptors
   b. nociceptors (pain) receptors
   c. stretch receptors
   d. fast-twitch fatiguable fibres

3. In humans, damage to the cerebellum is most likely to produce which of the following?

    a. an inability to initiate purposeful or voluntary movement
    b. flaccid muscle paralysis
    c. flexed limbs which are adducted and internally rotated
    d. movements that are slow, uncoordinated and robot-like?

4. The substantia nigra pars compacta projects to what part of the forebrain?

    a. caudate and putamen
    b. globus pallidus
    c. internal capsule
    d. premotor cortex

5. Which of the following brain areas contributes extensively to the pyramidal tracts?

    a. cerebellum
    b. precentral gyrus (cerebral cortex)
    c. striatum
    d. all of the above

6. The readiness potential is recorded from which part of the brain?

    a. caudate nucleus
    b. cerebellum
    c. globus pallidus
    d. motor areas of the cortex

FURTHER READING

Berthoz, A., & Weiss, G. (2002). *The brain's sense of movement*. Harvard University Press.
Somewhat technical, but it does review a lot of material on how the brain is able to maintain balance and co-ordinate movement.

Broussand, D. M. (2013). *The cerebellum: Learning, movement, language and social skills*. Wiley-Blackwell.
A clearly written overview of the physiology and function of the cerebellum as it relates to learning, plasticity, and neurodegenerative diseases.

Ferrari, P., & Rizzolatti, G. (2015). *New frontiers in mirror neuron research*. Oxford University Press.
This book provides a comprehensive overview of the latest advances in mirror neuron research which is accessible to both experts and students.

Ito, M. (2011). *The cerebellum: Brain for an implicit self*. FT Press.
The author (who has undertaken pioneering work on the cerebellum) advances a detailed and fascinating view of a wide range of cerebellar functions – much of it beyond its traditional role in body movement.

Latash, M. L. (2008). *Neurophysiological basis of movement*. Human Kinetics Pub.
A comprehensive textbook covering all levels of the motor system, from muscle contraction to brain function, movement disorders and current theories of motor control and coordination.

Latash, M. L. (2012). *Fundamentals of motor control*. Academic Press.
This book focuses on how the nervous system produces purposeful, coordinated movements in its interaction with the body and environment through conscious and unconscious thought.

Leonard, C. T. (1998). *The neuroscience of human movement*. Mosby.
A well-written account with excellent material examining the role of the central nervous system in the control of movement.

Libet, B. (2004). *Mind time: The temporal factor in consciousness.* Harvard University Press.
A historical account of Libet's own research which is also interesting in regard to how the brain comes to produce purposeful action.

Steiner, H., & Tseng, K. Y. (Eds.). (2016). *Handbook of basal ganglia structure and function.* Academic Press.
A book of over a thousand pages providing everything you will need to know about the structural and functional aspects of the basal ganglia, highlighting clinical relevance.

MULTIPLE CHOICE ANSWERS - 1. A | 2. C | 3. D | 4. A | 5. B | 6. D

5

HUNGER AND EATING DISORDERS

LEARNING OBJECTIVES

After reading this chapter you should be able to:

- Understand the concept of homeostasis.

- Explain the bodily states of absorption and fasting.

- Describe the importance of the glucostatic theory of hunger.

- Elucidate the dual set-point model of hunger and eating.

- Understand the importance of the hypothalamus in feeding behaviour.

- Outline the role of neuropeptides in hunger and satiety.

- Explain the role of leptin in appetitive behaviour and controlling body weight.

- Describe the causes and biological underpinnings of obesity and anorexia nervosa.

GO ONLINE

Test your understanding of this chapter and visit **https://study.sagepub.com/wickens** to access interactive 'Drag and Drop' labelling activities and a flashcard glossary.

INTRODUCTION

Hunger is a compelling motive, and the need, or desire, to eat, one of the most important determinants that shape our daily routines and activities. We obviously share our basic reliance on food for energy and sustenance with other animals. Yet for humans, eating behaviour is much more than the simple replenishment of nutrients. Indeed, one only has to contemplate the wide variety of food-related information in our world, including TV programmes, magazine articles, advertisements and the fascination with newfangled diets, to realize the central importance of eating in our everyday existence.

The complexity of this behaviour is also seen when we begin to examine the biological basis of hunger and eating. It is tempting at first to explain hunger as a simple physiological response to declining levels of nutrients, with important roles for peripheral mechanisms (i.e. stomach and liver) monitored and governed by regions in the brain stem and hypothalamus.

Yet it is clear our eating behaviour cannot be adequately explained this way. Instead, eating and hunger are the products of a highly intricate psychobiological system interacting with myriad social and cultural factors that are not linked to any obvious nutrient deficiency. We can demonstrate this by the simple observation that we often eat not in response to direct hunger pangs, but in anticipation of eating. Indeed, there is little doubt we visit our favourite restaurant not because of low glucose levels, or any other nutrient deficiency, but because the overall experience is *pleasurable*. Moreover, most of us become hungry at set meal times showing that time of day and/or the effects of conditioning often dictate when we eat.

The quest to understand the psychobiological mechanisms of eating has become an important area of research in recent years, not least because of the high prevalence of disorders and illnesses relating to this behaviour which have become serious public health issues. It is estimated that around 1.25 million people suffer from an eating disorder in the UK, which includes anorexia nervosa and bulimia, and this figure is dwarfed by the numbers of people who are overweight or obese. We live in an age where all of these disorders have become more common, with obesity likely to increase alarmingly over the coming years. The impetus will increasingly be on the psychologist to explain the determinants of appetite, satiety and body weight, along with developing more effective treatment options.

HOMEOSTASIS

In 1865, in his major work on the scientific method entitled *Introduction to Experimental Medicine*, the French physiologist Claude Bernard wrote 'The stability of the internal environment (the *milieu intérieur*) is the condition for the free and independent life'. In other words, he was pointing out that the body's internal milieu (i.e. the desirable conditions for cells to function) has to remain constant despite large fluctuations in the external environment. This basic requirement of the body was coined **homeostasis** by the American physiologist Walter Cannon in 1932, who derived the word from the Greek *homos* ('same') and *stasis* ('standing still'). To appreciate the importance of homeostasis, one must realize that in order to survive, living organisms must always maintain the physiological and chemical balance of their bodies within very fine limits. For example, human beings are warm-blooded and have to keep their body temperature at about 37°C regardless of whether they live in the Antarctic or the tropics. In fact, a change in core body temperature of just a few degrees will alter the rate of chemical reactions taking place in our cells, leading to organ failure and death. Thus, it is essential that the body is able to regulate its temperature homeostatically within a narrow margin.

But how does our body manage this heat regulation? Clearly, there must be mechanisms that not only detect alterations in temperature, but also instigate the physiological reactions necessary to correct any deviation from 37°C. Such adaptive responses, for example, include increased perspiration to cool the body, and shivering to provide warmth. These responses also point to certain important features that must be common to all homeostatic systems: (1) there is a set-point or optimal level that the system tries to maintain; (2) there are bodily receptors, such as thermoreceptors, that detect changes in the variable; (3) there is a centralized control centre which constantly analyses the body state and decides what action needs to be taken; and (4) there is a way of switching off the corrective responses when the set-point value has been reached again. This inhibition is typically called the negative feedback response.

On closer inspection, therefore, homeostatic systems are not as simple as they first appear. It is also obvious there must be many homeostatic processes operating in the body which work to the same principles. These include, for example, those governing the body's water content, its oxygen and carbon dioxide levels, and its concentration of various ions, minerals and hormones. In addition, levels of many nutrients obtained from food and drink are maintained in a similar manner. For example, the concentration of glucose in the blood needs to be between 60 and 90 milligrams per 100 cubic centimetres of blood. If it falls below this range, then hypoglycemia is likely to result with coma and death, whereas increased levels of glucose produce hyperglycemia with increased excitability.

Traditionally, hunger has been regarded as homeostatic process, i.e. dependent on a bodily feedback mechanism to the brain signalling a deficiency of some nutrient, say glucose, below a given set-point (see Figure 5.1). Similarly, satiety has often been viewed as an event occurring when certain nutrient levels increase above a desirable level (as determined by the system's set-point) enabling hunger to be switched off. If we accept this homeostatic model, which seems to make intuitive sense, then eating is the response by which the energy or nutrient source is replenished – and this will prompt the negative feedback response to stop hunger. As we shall see, such analogies still dominate much biopsychological thinking about eating behaviour, despite their obvious simplicity and limitations.

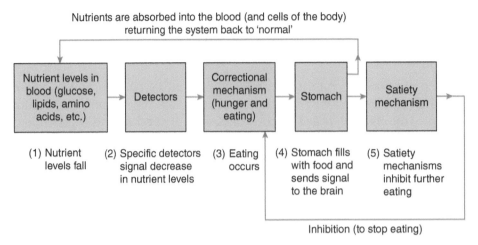

Figure 5.1   A hypothetical outline of a homeostatic system that controls eating

KEY TERMS: *homeostasis, set-point, receptors, control centre, negative feedback*

THE PROCESS OF DIGESTION

Food is any substance that is consumed to provide nutritional support for an organism which is usually of plant or animal origin. In terms of its constituents, therefore, this means food is a collection of proteins, fats and carbohydrates, along with a small amount of essential vitamins and minerals. These large insoluble foodstuffs have to be broken down into simple molecules through the act of digestion (Figure 5.2). This process begins in the mouth where food is mashed and mixed with saliva which turns starch-like substances into sugars. The softened and moistened material is then swallowed to reach the stomach, where it is mixed with gastric juices containing hydrochloric acid and pepsin to produce a semi-fluid mixture called chyme. Depending on the amount and contents of the meal, it will normally take the stomach somewhere between 40 minutes and 2 hours to turn the food into this mixture. The chyme then passes into the small intestine where absorption into the blood occurs. The upper part of the small intestine is particularly important as it contains the **duodenum** which receives a duct from the **pancreas gland**. This gland secretes several digestive enzymes as well as two hormones essential for digestion, called **insulin** and **glucagon** (see next section). The remainder of the small intestine, which is about 600 cm in length in humans, absorbs the chyme's nutrients – mainly glucose, amino acids and lipid (fats). The glucose and amino acids enter the blood stream and pass to the liver via the hepatic portal system, whereas the emulsified fats and fat-soluble vitamins are absorbed into the lymphatic system. Here, they will be eventually transported to the venous circulation.

KEY TERMS: *digestion, chyme, duodenum, pancreas gland, insulin, glucagon*

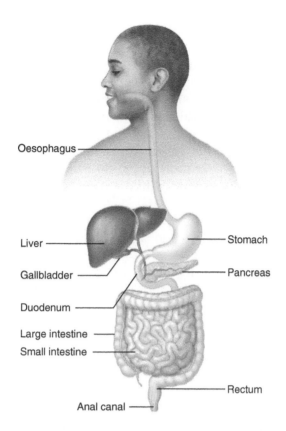

Figure 5.2 The digestive system
Source: Garrett and Hough (2021)

ABSORPTION AND FASTING

It is not uncommon to eat a large meal that contains more energy than is immediately needed by the body. For example, imagine going to a restaurant for a three-course meal that includes a starter, main course and dessert. On top of this, you may have several alcoholic drinks, followed by coffee and a complementary chocolate sweet at the end. This substantial meal not only contains far more nutrients than your body actually needs – but, if all its glucose was absorbed straight into the bloodstream unchecked, it would cause hyperglycemia and most likely have fatal consequences. Thus, it is crucial for the body to store the nutrients quickly following absorption to stop their levels rising dangerously in the bloodstream. But, just as important, the body must be able to release the stored nutrients, or the energy derived from their transformation, in the periods between feeding. These two bodily states are known respectively as the **absorptive** and **post-absorptive phases** and are controlled by different physiological processes (see Figure 5.3).

The absorptive phase of metabolism starts during a meal. When a person begins eating, the hormone insulin is released from the pancreas gland even before the glucose enters the blood. This response occurs because the pancreas gland is stimulated by the parasympathetic vagus nerve that conveys gustatory (taste) signals from the mouth. The insulin then acts to lower blood glucose levels by circulating in the blood where it facilitates glucose transport across the cellular membranes. In effect, insulin enables glucose to enter the body's cells where it can be safely stored and used to produce energy. The only exception to this rule is the brain, where glucose is transported across neural and glial membranes by insulin independent glucose transporter proteins. In addition to facilitating glucose absorption, insulin has three other mechanisms of regulating nutrient levels during absorption: (1) it converts excess blood glucose into glycogen which is stored by the liver and muscles; (2) it facilitates the transport of amino acids into cells allowing protein synthesis to occur; and (3) it facilitates the transport of fats into adipose cells enabling fat storage.

After nutrients have been absorbed into the blood, the post-absorptive phase of the metabolism takes over. The main signal instigating this phase is believed to be a drop in blood glucose that is detected by the brain. This causes sympathetic stimulation of the pancreas gland which halts insulin secretion. At this point, the pancreas gland now releases the hormone glucagon which has an opposite effect to insulin – causing the liver to convert glycogen back into glucose via a process called glycogenolysis. If the fasting period is prolonged, however, glucagon will also begin to break down the body's fat stores into fatty acids which are normally used for energy. In addition, the liver will act to convert some of the fat-based glycerol into glucose. This latter process is important for the brain since it cannot utilize fatty acids or glycerol for energy, and has to rely on glucose provided by the liver during starvation (or the post-absorptive period). A normal adult will require 200g of glucose per day, two-thirds of which is specifically required by the brain to cover its energy needs.

KEY TERMS: *absorptive phase, post-absorptive phase, insulin, glucagon, glycogenolysis, glycerol*

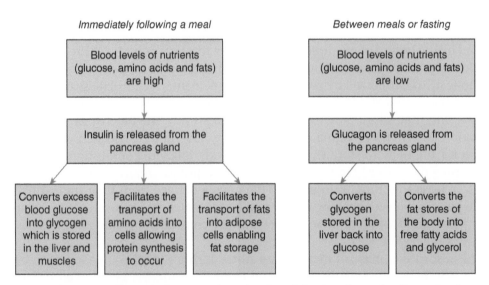

Figure 5.3 Flow chart of metabolic events that take place following absorption (immediately following a meal) and post-absorption (between meals)

DOES AN EMPTY STOMACH SIGNAL HUNGER?

A deceptively simple question, with no easy answer, is what causes hunger. One common belief is that hunger is caused by empty movements of the stomach. Common sense tells us we feel satiated when our stomach is distended, and we often attribute hunger pangs to the gastric sensations produced by our empty stomach. An experimental test of this idea was undertaken by W. B. Cannon in 1912 who persuaded his research student A. L. Washburn to swallow a balloon that was inflated to 8 cm in diameter in his stomach – a procedure that took several weeks of daily training before it could be accomplished. The balloon was then connected by a tube to a water-filled glass U-tube, and when a stomach contraction occurred, it caused an increase in the water level, producing an upward mark on a moving piece of paper. It was found that Washburn's reported hunger pangs were nearly always accompanied by stomach contractions (Cannon & Washburn, 1912). In fact, in his Harvey Lecture, given in 1911, Cannon was confident enough to assure his audience (erroneously) that hunger is solely due to stomach movements.

Further evidence linking an empty stomach with hunger came from a study of a patient called Mr V, who had accidentally swallowed acid when aged nine years that caused his oesophagus to fuse shut. This person was fitted with a gastric fistula (essentially a small tube some half an inch in diameter) which allowed him to inject food directly into his stomach after he had chewed it in a normal manner. The fistula also provided a useful opportunity for researchers to directly examine Mr V's gastric movements, and for food to be placed in the stomach without his knowledge – manipulations that confirmed stomach contractions were often associated with feelings of hunger (Carlson, 1912).

More evidence confirming the importance of gastric cues in hunger and satiety came from the discovery of stretch receptors in the stomach wall whose activity increases in proportion to the volume of the stomach (Paintal, 1954). Indeed, we now know that that as food enters the stomach, it expands and activates stretch receptors which send impulses via the vagus nerve to the **medulla oblongata** (including the nucleus of the solitary tract and adjacent area postrema) which in turn cause a reflex whereby hydrochloric acid is secreted into the stomach. There is also evidence that stomach distension changes the rate of firing in cells in several areas of the brain including the midbrain, hypothalamus, amygdala and hippocampus (Spetter et al., 2014).

As might be expected, experiments with laboratory animals also implicate gastric factors in feeding behaviour. For example, preloading the stomach of a rat with food in order to produce stomach distension produces a significant reduction in eating. Alternatively, removing food from a rat's stomach after it has just eaten a large meal will induce hunger. It has been reported that such an animal will consume almost exactly the same amount of food, or amount of calories, that has just been taken out (Deutsch and Gonzalez, 1980). These findings suggest that animals, and humans, are able to monitor the volume of food, and its caloric value in their stomachs, and use this as a feedback signal to govern hunger and satiety (Mazzawi et al., 2019).

KEY TERMS: *stretch receptors, vagus nerve, medulla oblongata, stomach distension*

LIMITATIONS OF THE STOMACH DISTENSION THEORY

But can hunger exist without stomach pangs? The answer to this question is clearly yes. For example, Tsang (1938) removed the stomach from seven rats and connected the oesophagus directly to the small intestines. After one day's fasting the gastrectomized rats were just as motivated (i.e. hungry) as normal to learn a maze task in order to receive a food reward. Thus, it is clear there are other factors besides the mechanical signalling of an empty or full stomach that instruct the brain to initiate or terminate eating. This has also been supported in human studies. For example, a full gastrectomy, or removal of the entire stomach, which necessitates the oesophagus to be connected directly to the duodenum, is sometimes undertaken in patients with stomach cancer. Nonetheless, these patients still experience hunger, and whilst they tend to eat smaller meals they still maintain proper regulation of food intake. In fact, such patients are often emphatic in reporting that the sensation of hunger is just as same as when their stomachs were intact (Jeon et al., 2010; Wangensteen & Carlson, 1931).

Further support showing that the stomach is not necessary for hunger has come from experimental studies that have lesioned the vagus nerve which conveys the stretch receptor neural input from the stomach to the brain. In this case, the operation has little effect on hunger, although the vagal-lesioned animals tend to overfill their stomach (Gonzalez & Deutsch, 1981). But, in this case, how does the brain know about the nutrient state of the body? The most likely explanation is that the relatively unaffected regulation of eating for vagal-lesioned rats occurs because the gut also releases chemical factors that govern food intake.

Evidence for this position was provided by Koopmans (1981) who transplanted an extra stomach into rats in which the main blood vessels of the implanted organ were connected to the circulatory system of the recipient. Koopmans found that when he injected food into the extra stomach, the animal became satiated and stopped eating. Since the transplanted stomach had no neural connections with the brain, and because absorption did not occur from the stomach, this proved that chemical messengers from the gut were being released in response to food intake. We now have ample evidence to show that the stomach, and many other parts of the digestive system, do indeed release a number of different chemical substances in response to food that informs the brain of its nutrient status (see below). Thus, distension of the stomach is only one of the signals informing the brain of its nutrient status.

KEY TERMS: *gastrectomy, vagus nerve*

THE NUTRIENT SIGNALS RELAYING HUNGER INFORMATION

Further evidence that a blood-borne chemical factor is involved in satiety was provided by Davis et al. (1971). Clearly, if the blood contains a post-absorptive substance that signals whether an animal has eaten, then the transfusion of blood from a well-fed rat should reduce hunger (or eating) in a food-deprived one. And this is exactly what was found. For example, the intake of milk by hungry fasted rats was some 50% below normal after their blood had been transfused with that of satiated rats. This effect could not be explained by the transfusion itself, because it was found that hunger was only suppressed when well-fed rats donated the blood. In fact, to be most effective, the blood had to be taken from the donors 45 minutes after their meal, which is about the time it takes for appreciable amounts of nutrients and hormones to accumulate in the blood after eating.

The obvious place to begin looking for a blood-borne chemical that signals hunger and satiety is in food itself. But what macronutrients influence hunger? There are several candidates. Since our food is mainly a combination of carbohydrates (sugar and starches), lipids (fat) and protein (amino acids), it is likely that one of these products of digestion, or their circulating metabolites, could provide the brain with important nutrient information. It is also feasible that all of these substances are involved, and this has led to the glucostatic, lipostatic and aminostatic theories of hunger and satiety, which emphasize the importance of glucose, fat and proteins respectively (see Carreiro et al., 2016). The basic idea follows the principle of homeostasis: when the brain detects a deficiency in one of these nutrients, craving or the sensation of hunger is produced, and when levels are restored to a given set-point, the result is satiety.

KEY TERMS: *carbohydrates, lipids, proteins*

THE GLUCOSTATIC THEORY

Glucose is an obvious contender for the most important metabolic signal mediating hunger and satiety. Following a meal, carbohydrates are broken down into smaller molecules, which ultimately means much of our digested food enters the bloodstream as glucose (a simple sugar which is our body's preferred source of fuel). This substance is not only used for immediate energy expenditure, but can also be stored for longer-term use. Our brain also requires a constant supply of glucose, so any drop in the level of this sugar will have significant consequences for its function. It should come as no surprise therefore that there is evidence associating blood glucose with hunger. For example, it has long been known that injections of glucose into hungry animals suppresses eating, whereas insulin administration which lowers blood glucose levels causes them to start feeding (Mayer, 1953). In experiments where blood glucose is monitored, it has been reported that baseline levels tend to be relatively constant (e.g. they rarely fluctuate by 2%) until about 10 minutes before a meal when they drop by about 8% (Campfield & Smith, 1990). These researchers also found that an injection of glucose at the point when glucose levels were beginning to drop would postpone eating, although curiously this effect does not occur some 3–4 minutes prior to eating.

In 1953, Jean Mayer proposed the glucostatic theory of hunger. According to this theory, an increase in blood glucose concentration results in increased feelings of satiety, whereas a drop in blood glucose causes the opposite effect of producing hunger. Although on first sight this idea sounds highly plausible, the simple version of this

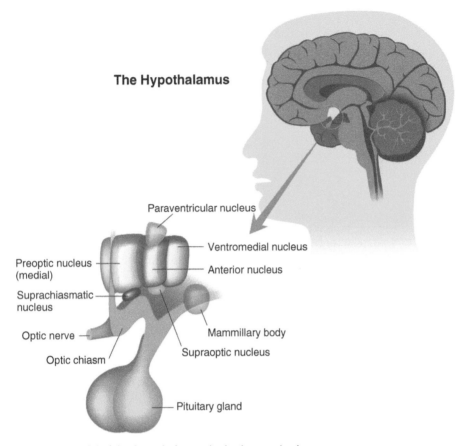

Figure 5.4 The nuclei of the hypothalamus in the human brain
Source: © Alila Medical Images/Alamy Stock Photo

theory faces a serious difficulty. The problem is that people with diabetes who are unable to produce insulin, and as a result have high levels of blood glucose, experience hunger – and sometimes ravenously so. Thus, if glucose is the metabolic signal for appetitive behaviour, there must be a more complex mechanism at work than its concentration in the bloodstream.

To surmount this problem, Meyer proposed the brain contains specialized cells called glucostats which measure the rate at which glucose is utilized to provide energy. More specifically, he believed the glucostats did this by comparing the difference between levels of glucose in the arterial blood glucose entering the brain (which has to be relatively constant), and the 'used' blood in the venous circulation. A significant discrepancy would, according to Mayer, result in hunger. Soon after proposing his theory, Mayer and Marshall (1956) identified the possible existence of glucoreceptors in the brain after injecting mice with gold thioglucose – a substance that mimics glucose and is taken up into cells, but is neurotoxic and causes them to die. When the brains were examined, damage was found to be strongly localized to the **ventromedial hypothalamus** (see Figure 5.4). But just as important for supporting the theory, after injecting mice with gold thioglucose, Mayer found his animals would began to eat huge quantities of food and became obese.

KEY TERMS: *glucose, glucostatic theory of hunger, diabetes, glucostats, ventromedial hypothalamus*

A CLOSER LOOK AT GLUCOSTATIC RECEPTORS

Confirmation of glucostatic detectors, or glucoreceptors, came from the finding that some neurons in the ventromedial hypothalamus are sensitive to changing levels of glucose. That is, glucose injections into this hypothalamic region altered the activity of its neurons (Anand et al., 1964). Increased uptake of radioactivity in the ventromedial hypothalamus also occurred after gastric injections of D-glucose-^{14}C in rats (Panksepp, 1972). Despite this, the role of these glucose sensitive cells in hunger and satiety is contentious. For example, if these cells control food intake, then infusions of glucose into the ventromedial hypothalamus should reduce food intake in hungry animals, but this does not happen (Epstein et al., 1975). Alternatively, the administration of 2-deoxyglucose (a glucose analogue that causes glucose deprivation) might be expected to stimulate eating. But, again, this does not occur. Such findings have led investigators to propose that hypothalamic glucoreceptors are more likely to be involved in producing homeostatic responses to blood glucose levels. Indeed, it has been shown that glucoreceptor activity is able to stimulate pancreatic glucagon secretion through the sympathetic nervous system in response to falling glucose levels (Borg et al., 1995). This appears to show that hypothalamic glucose sensitive cells are not involved in hunger, but in the metabolic control that enables the brain to instigate compensatory responses for energy deficits when glucose levels fall (Routh et al., 2014).

Another place where glucoreceptors have been found is in the liver. This was first proposed when it was discovered that glucose injected into the hepatic portal vein (the main blood vessel from the intestines to the liver) stopped hungry animals from eating (Russek, 1971). Evidence linking the liver with glucose detection also came from Stricker et al. (1977) who injected rats with insulin to lower blood glucose and induce hunger. The animals were then given the sugar fructose. Although this type of sugar is metabolized by the liver, it does not cross the blood–brain barrier. Thus, these rats should have had high glucose passing through in the liver, but low glucose levels in the brain. If glucose receptors in the brain are an important determinant of hunger, then these animals should have remained hungry. But when presented with food, they showed no signs of hunger.

The liver, therefore, would appear to provide the brain with an important signal regarding the availability of glucose. This would make sense since the liver is the first organ of the body to receive nutrients from the small intestine and ideally positioned to monitor food intake. There is also evidence to show that hepatic glucoreceptors provide input to a number of brain regions including the **nucleus of the solitary tract** in the medulla, and the hypothalamic arcuate nucleus (Bentsen et al., 2019). Moreover, some animal studies have shown that administration of glucose into the hepatic portal vein increases neural activity in the ventromedial hypothalamus, whilst decreasing the firing rate of cells in the lateral hypothalamus (Shimizu et al., 1983). Despite this, the evidence for an important hepatic involvement in glucose sensing in human appetite is far from proven and it must be more fully elucidated (Donovan & Bohland, 2009).

If glucose was the sole determinant of hunger and satiety, then it might be expected that stopping neural feedback from the hepatic system by vagotomy would disrupt eating behaviour. The evidence relating to this point is somewhat mixed with some studies showing that such animals still exhibit relatively normal patterns of eating

(Kodamo et al., 2010). This shows that other biological mechanisms, therefore, must compensate for the loss of information from the liver. Nonetheless, other studies have reported weight loss (14–30%) in animals with vagal lesions (e.g. Mordes et al., 1979) which has led some to suggest the use of vagotomy to treat obesity (Neergaard, 2007). However, overall, the evidence suggests that the liver and its monitoring of blood glucose is only one component of the peripheral system that provides feedback to the brain regarding the nutrient status of the body (Chan & Sherwin, 2014).

KEY TERMS: *glucose receptors, ventromedial hypothalamus, liver, nucleus of the solitary tract, arcuate nucleus*

THE ROLE OF NEUROPEPTIDES IN PRODUCING SATIETY

One of the most important advances in appetite research over the last 50 years has been the discovery that **neuropeptides** produced by the gut and intestines are involved in feeding behaviour. Neuropeptides are small chains of amino acids, which are synthesized in the cell body at the ribosomes, and are typically packed into vesicles and transported down the axon to the nerve endings ready to be released (this is unlike most other neurotransmitters that are synthesized in the endings themselves). Neuropeptides are also found in many regions of the brain where they are frequently involved in the long-lasting modulation of synaptic transmission. However, those produced by the gut and intestinal system act on surrounding tissues including nerves and ganglia, or are transported in the blood as hormones.

The first gut hormone to be linked with appetitive behaviour was cholecystokinin, or CCK (from the Greek *chole* meaning 'bile'). Discovered by Ivy and Oldberg in 1928, CCK was found to elicit gallbladder contraction after release by cells of the duodenum in response to the presence of fat or protein. Later, CCK was shown to stimulate pancreatic secretion and control emptying of the stomach. However, a significant breakthrough took place in the early 1970s when CCK administration was found to cause a reduction in food intake in rats in a dose-dependent manner (Gibbs et al., 1973). This was the first time a duodenal or gastrointestinal hormone had been found to have this type of effect, and its suppressant action on appetite was soon extended to humans (Kissileff et al., 1981). In fact, some studies showed that CCK could produce a 60% reduction in food intake – depending on the dose and other circumstances. Because of the important implications of CCK's therapeutic potential for eating disorders, considerable attention has been focused on the study of this hormone (Smith, 2012).

CCK acts on specialized receptors distributed throughout the gastrointestinal system and brain. There are two types of receptor: CCKa and CCKb. The CCKa variety are predominantly found in the stomach, intestines and liver, where they induce contraction of the gallbladder, reduce gastric acid secretion and increase bile acid production. In addition, CCKa receptors are found on the vagal afferent nerves which project to the solitary nucleus and hypothalamus. This vagal feedback is believed to provide the main signal to the brain informing it of satiety. Support for this idea comes from the finding that cutting the vagus nerve to the brain eliminates the satiety-inducing effect of CCK injections (Bray & York, 1979). In contrast, the CCKb receptors are mainly located in the brain, including the solitary nucleus and the ventromedial, periventricular and arcuate nuclei of the hypothalamus (Beinfeld & Palkovits, 1981). These receptors are sensitive to CCK which can cross the blood–brain barrier in the vicinity of the hypothalamus (Lopez et al., 2007). Somewhat surprisingly, CCK receptors are also found in other brain regions, including the periaqueductal grey area, amygdala, hippocampus and cerebral cortex. Here, they appear to induce anxiety (Skibicka & Dickson, 2013) or have effects on learning and memory (Reisi et al., 2015).

Since the discovery of CCK, a number of other peptides have been found that also suppress hunger. One of these is the 36 amino acid peptide YY (PYY) that is released from the ileum and colon in response to feeding. The peripheral administration of PYY inhibits the feeding of primates, and this satiating effect also occurs when it is injected into the brain (Woods & D'Alessio, 2008). Another important neuropeptide is the small 14 amino acid bombesin which is found in several peripheral tissues and provides a further source of negative feedback that inhibits eating (Yamada et al., 2000). Two related bombesin-type peptides called gastrin-releasing factor and neurmedin are also produced by the mammalian stomach and intestines. Again, the plasma levels of these peptides rise after food

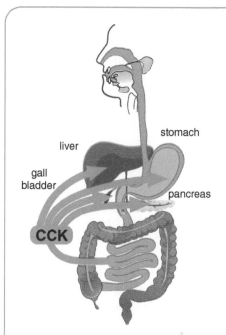

Figure 5.5   The effects of cholecystokinin on the gastrointestinal tract

Source: McortNGHH/Wikimedia Commons

intake and suppress appetite (Merali et al., 1999). Since gastrin-releasing factor and neurmedin do not cross the blood–brain barrier, they most likely produce their effects on the vagus nerve, or other neural connections from the stomach.

KEY TERMS: *neuropeptides, cholecystokinin, peptide YY, bombesin*

GHRELIN AND THE STIMULATION OF HUNGER

Another important advance was the discovery of ghrelin by Kojima et al. (1999). This is a peptide produced by the stomach and gastrointestinal tract and first shown to cause growth hormone release from the pituitary gland (the word 'ghrelin' being derived from the term *GH releasing peptide*). But soon after this, ghrelin was found to regulate food intake and body weight by its action on the brain (Tschöp et al., 2000). At present, it is the only gastrointestinal peptide known to stimulate appetite, and for this reason it has attracted much attention. In the early stages of ghrelin research, a theory emerged proposing it acted as a 'hunger hormone' signalling the need to increase nutrient intake. This was supported by the finding that blood levels of ghrelin in humans rise significantly with hunger sensations, and then decline quickly after a meal (Cummings et al., 2001; Tschöp et al., 2001). Ghrelin also enhances the sensation of subjective hunger and increases food intake when injected into healthy human volunteers (Wren et al., 2001). Animal studies have backed up this evidence. For example, injecting ghrelin directly into the brain's ventricles caused rats to eat more and gain weight four times faster than controls (Kamegai et al., 2001).

The daily blood levels of ghrelin naturally increase at times when eating is most likely to occur. Moreover, ghrelin is also one of the few neuropeptides which is able to directly enter the brain (Kojima & Kangawa, 2005). This occurs in the vicinity of the ventromedial hypothalamus where the blood–brain barrier is specialized to allow the passage of certain peripheral hormones and nutrients. Close by is the arcuate nucleus which *is* a crucial hypothalamic region for monitoring the body's nutrient levels. The arcuate nucleus not only contains high numbers of ghrelin receptors, but also projects to the paraventricular nucleus and **lateral hypothalamus** (see below). These pathways also use peptides to transmit neural messages, including one called **neuropeptide Y** which is orexigenic (i.e. it stimulates appetite), and another called α-melanocyte stimulating hormone which suppresses appetite.

Neuropeptide Y has generated much interest. This small amino acid is closely related to peptides found in the pancreas gland and gut, and first localized to the CNS during the early 1980s. When injected into the ventricles of the brain, close to the hypothalamus, NPY produces a vociferous, frantic and prolonged increase in food intake (Clark et al., 1984). The feeding response to NPY is so marked that rats injected with this peptide will press a lever hundreds of times for food reward, consume food made bitter with quinine, and endure painful electric shocks to their tongue in order to drink milk (Jewitt et al., 1992). As might be expected, the production of NPY is stimulated by ghrelin (Arora, 2006) whilst drugs which that NPY abolish the food intake induced by ghrelin administration (Nakazato et al., 2001).

The cell bodies of NPY neurons located in the ventromedial part of the arcuate nucleus in the hypothalamus are also notable for another characteristic – they synthesize a peptide called agouti-related peptide (AGRP) which is released by their axon terminals. Similar to the orexigenic effects of NPY, AGRP stimulates eating behaviour. In one study it was found that an injection of a small amount of this substance into the brain's ventricles of a rat produced an increase in food intake which lasted six days (Lu et al., 2001). This makes it one of the most potent stimulators of feeding behaviour known. It is also interesting to note that in humans, certain variants of the gene that produce AGRP have been consistently associated with resistance to fatness, whilst transgenic mice over-expressing this gene are ubiquitously hyperphagic and obese (Iinytska & Argyropoulus, 2008).

Although ghrelin has become known as the 'hunger hormone' it has other behavioural functions. For example, ghrelin promotes slow-wave sleep in humans and influences circadian rhythms. In animal studies, ghrelin infusions into the ventral tegmental area increase the amount of dopamine in the nucleus accumbens – a response with rewarding and pleasurable effects. Ghrelin also acts on the hypothalamic-pituitary-adrenal axis where it has a mood-enhancing effect. It may even promote long-term potentiation in the hippocampus to help consolidate memory. Clearly, ghrelin has a host of biological functions which researchers are only just beginning to fully elucidate (Muller et al., 2015).

KEY TERMS: *ghrelin, arcuate nucleus, blood–brain barrier, neuropeptide Y, α-melanocyte stimulating hormone, agouti-related peptide*

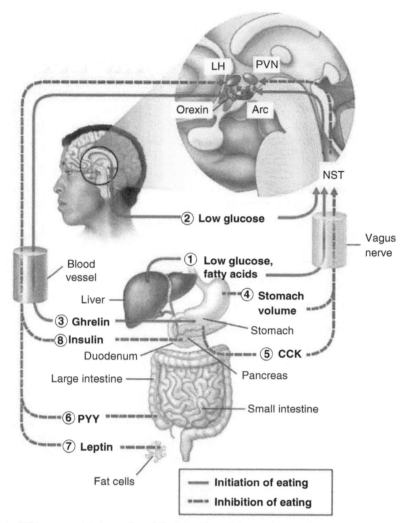

Note: PVN = paraventricular nucleus; LH = lateral hypothalamus; Arc = arcuate nucleus; NST = nucleus of thr solitary tract; PYY = paraventricular nucleus; CCK = cholecystokinin.

Figure 5.6 Hunger control signals and brain centres
Source: Garrett and Hough (2021)

ANDREA PRADER AND HEINRICH WILLI

Although Andrea Prader and Heinrich Willi would not have regarded themselves as neuroscientists (they were both paediatricians working at the Children's Hospital in Zurich), they were the first to describe a rare syndrome (along with internist Alexi Labhart) which showed that feeding behaviour has important genetic antecedents. First described in 1956, after both men had realized there was a group of children with a similar group of symptoms, Prader-Willi syndrome (PWS) is a developmental disorder with serious consequences for adult

(Continued)

behaviour and health. In fact, unbeknown to them, an account resembling the disorder had already appeared in *The Pickwick Papers* by Charles Dickens (1836).

PWS arises in infancy when weak muscle tone, feeding problems and stunted growth become apparent. But the most striking behavioural feature occurs between the ages of two and four, when the child begins to have a ravenous and insatiable desire for food. At this point, with their excessive food intake, caregivers may have to resort to installing locks on food stores and refrigerators where food is kept. Despite this restriction, a lifetime obsessive interest in food is likely to develop – a situation not helped when the individuals complain of hunger despite regularly consuming large meals. Not surprisingly, obesity and type 2 diabetes are serious health concerns. This is exacerbated by the likelihood that those with PWS will have a reduced metabolic rate and require fewer calories than others. Other symptoms of PWS include unusual facial features (a prominent nasal bridge, narrow forehead and down- turned mouth) and poor motor coordination. Learning disabilities and immature sexual development are also common.

Most cases of PWS (about 70%) are caused by the deletion of several genes from the long arm of chromosome 15 which is inherited from the father – an event that occurs during the early stages of foetal development. Although we normally inherit two copies of this chromosome (one from each parent) which would normally protect us from the harmful effects of such genetic deletions (this is because we have a 'good' chromosome to mitigate against the effects), this does not happen in those with PWS. Rather, for some reason, the mother's genes are 'switched off'. Called genomic imprinting, the turning off of one parent's gene (which is thought to occur during the formation of an egg or a sperm cell) will have adverse consequences if there is a serious problem with the other parental chromosome – and this is exactly what happens in PWS.

Although PWS has serious neurobiological consequences, several of its symptoms are linked to dysfunction of the hypothalamic-pituitary-axis, including the marked hyperphagia (excessive eating) and slow sexual maturation. The release of several hormones is also affected including the sex hormones, growth hormone and oxytocin. The latter may be due to a reduction of oxytocin-containing cells in the hypothalamic paraventricular nucleus (Swaab et al., 1995). This is important since oxytocin is known to be involved in suppressing appetite, and its low hypothalamic levels, likely to be key for causing insatiable hunger. Indeed, restoring oxytocin levels in children with PWS is showing promise in normalizing feeding behaviour (Miller et al., 2017). Another feature of PWS is high plasma ghrelin levels, indicating that impaired gut signalling may also be contributing to the increased hunger (Purtell et al., 2011).

BRAIN STEM REGIONS GOVERNING FOOD INTAKE

The most basic level of the CNS for governing nutrient intake is the brain stem which is capable of controlling ingestion, digestion and food absorption. The medulla, for example, contains the nucleus of the solitary tract which obtains input from the vagus nerve conveying information from the stomach, intestines, pancreas and liver. Nearby is the area postrema capable of sensing circulating chemical messengers in the blood (it also acts as a vomiting centre). The solitary nucleus also receives information from the seventh cranial (facial) nerve which conveys input from taste receptors of the tongue and is involved in assessing the palatability of food. In turn, the medulla contains numerous cell groups that govern the parasympathetic nervous system directing the various processes of digestion. The best known is the dorsal motor nucleus of the vagus nerve (DMN) which provides the main source of vagal motor efferents innervating the gut and stomach. In fact, the solitary nucleus, area postrema and DMN are collectively known as the dorsal vagal complex. As well as its descending influence, information from the solitary nucleus reaches a large number of other brain regions, including the hypothalamic paraventricular nucleus and central nucleus of the amygdala – as well as an assortment of other nuclei in the brain stem (Bradley, 2007).

Evidence showing that the brain stem exerts some degree of control over food intake has come from studies with rats where the forebrain, including the hypothalamus, is severed from the brain stem. Although these decerebrate animals only have a functioning brain stem, they retain posture, groom, and ambulate when provoked. A decerebrate rat also consumes food, discriminates taste and stops eating when satiated. Whilst reflexively swallowing liquid food when put in its mouth, it will stop ingestion if the taste is aversive or poisonous. Nor is the decerebrate rat 'fooled' by non-food substances. All of these behaviours show that the brain stem contains regions that maintain the basic reflexes of satiety. Yet the animal does not show increased appetite if food deprived, indicating that higher areas of the brain, such as the hypothalamus, are required for this behaviour. Nor does a decerebrate animal have the ability to seek food, or modify dietary intake on the basis of learning (Grill & Kaplan, 2002).

KEY TERMS: *nucleus of the solitary tract, area postrema, dorsal motor nucleus of the vagus nerve, dorsal vagal complex*

THE HYPOTHALAMUS AND FEEDING BEHAVIOUR

The **hypothalamus** has long been recognized as a key structure in the regulation of feeding behaviour. As early as 1839, it was shown by the Austrian neurologist Alfred Fröhlich that hypothalamic tumours in humans were associated with eating dysfunction and obesity. This effect was attributed to hormonal imbalances resulting from damage to the nearby pituitary gland. But later on in the early part of the twentieth century, with the invention of stereotaxic surgery and lesioning, researchers began to realize that the crucial part of the brain for producing obesity lay not with the pituitary gland, but with the nearby regions of the hypothalamus including the ventromedial hypothalamus (VMH). This was shown, for example, by Hetherington and Ranson in the late 1930s, who found that VMH excisions in rats caused excessive eating (**hyperphagia**) and weight gain. This type of effect was not produced by hypophysectomy (i.e. removal of the pituitary).

The VMH was not the only area to be linked with appetitive behaviour. Anand and Brobeck (1951) reported that lesions to the lateral hypothalamus (LH) caused **aphagia** in rats with the complete cessation of eating and drinking, and that such animals would soon die of starvation unless force-fed despite having food and water freely available. The importance of the hypothalamus in feeding was confirmed by other studies. For example, electrical stimulation of the LH produced compulsive eating in animals that had been satiated, whereas stimulation of the VMH inhibited food intake in hungry animals. All these findings clearly implicated the hypothalamus in the initiation and termination of feeding. In 1954, a theory based on this notion was proposed by Eliot Stellar who argued that the VMH acted as the brain's satiety centre, and the LH as its hunger centre (Stellar, 1954).

This theory, which became known as the dual-centre set-point theory, viewed the VMH and LH as the control centres regulating hunger and feeding (see Figure 5.7). Both these structures are in an ideal position to integrate information from other brain regions, and were known to receive feedback from the gut and liver. And, as mentioned previously, the VMH had been shown to contain glucostats by Mayer in 1956. The close anatomical proximity of the VMH and LH also encouraged the idea that these two structures interacted with each other. Put simply, the theory held that when the VMH was neurally or hormonally informed of food intake, it inhibited the LH feeding centre causing satiation. In contrast, when the LH was instructed of declining nutrient availability, especially of a decline in glucose below a certain set-point, it inhibited the VMH, thereby causing hunger. The theory also had the benefit of fitting nicely into a homeostatic framework of feeding. At the time it seemed the only problem was to identify the signals and receptors that initiated hunger and satiety, and determine how they were integrated in the hypothalamus.

KEY TERMS: *hypothalamus, ventromedial hypothalamus, hyperphagia, lateral hypothalamus, aphagia, dual-centre set-point theory*

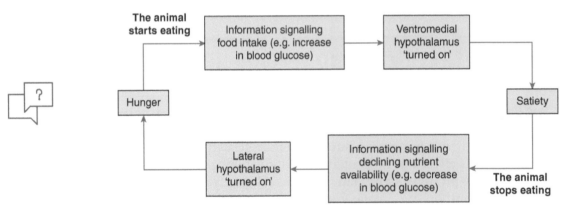

Figure 5.7   The dual-centre set-point model of feeding

A CLOSER LOOK AT VENTROMEDIAL HYPOTHALAMIC LESIONS

The dual-centre set point model was soon subject to criticism. The ventromedial hypothalamus had come to be viewed as the satiety centre because its removal caused animals to become ravenous and eat continually. But on closer inspection, things were more complicated. Although VMH lesioned rats ate vast amounts at first, often doubling their body weight within a few weeks, this period of weight gain did not last. Instead, the food intake soon declined with the animal returning to patterns of normal feeding. Following this, a new body weight was maintained at a higher level, with food intake only slightly increased. Thus, it was apparent that the lesioned rat underwent a phase of weight gain, followed by a static phase where it maintained its new weight with a relatively normal satiety response to eating. In terms of the dual-centre set-point model, this finding made little sense because these animals become satiated despite having no VMH (Wagner, 1999).

Lesions of the VMH were also found to produce a number of metabolic and physiological changes. Perhaps the most important was the finding that VMH lesions caused rats to have high levels of insulin which promoted eating and fat deposition. Indeed, if VMH lesioned rats were made to eat exactly the same amount of food as controls, they still gained weight in comparison – presumably because of their increased insulin levels. Supporting this interpretation, pancreas gland removal in these animals largely prevented the VMH lesioned induced hyperphagia and obesity. Thus, rather than inducing overeating, VMH lesions appeared to be changing the level of the body's insulin secretion which caused the animal to adopt a new 'set point' for its body weight (Woods & Stricker, 2013). More recently, it has also been shown that VMH damage makes rats overproduce a chemical called **leptin** (see later), which also causes them to overeat leading to marked weight gain (Satoh et al., 1997). The function of the VMH, therefore, would appear to be more closely allied with controlling aspects of the body's feeding metabolism than satiety.

Interestingly, there are also other notable characteristics produced by VMH lesions. For example, once these animals have stabilized their weight, they are very finicky – much preferring to eat palatable food (e.g. food with extra fat or sugar) compared to their normal 'dry' laboratory food. And if these animals are given food that is slightly stale, or made to taste bitter by the addition of quinine, they eat far less of it than controls (Peters & Gunion, 1980). Thus, the removal of the VMH causes an exaggerated reaction to palatability which can actually result in underfeeding. Nor are these animals prepared to work for food rewards. Typically, they will show a lethargic response if required to perform a task such as pressing a lever to obtain food.

KEY TERMS: *ventromedial hypothalamus, insulin, leptin*

A CLOSER LOOK AT THE LATERAL HYPOTHALAMUS

As we have seen, **lateral hypothalamus** lesions lead to profound aphagia or a disinclination to eat – an effect that was interpreted to show that this brain region acted as a hunger centre. This was supported by the finding that electrical stimulation of the LH stimulated eating. However, this theory soon ran into problems – not least when it found that the aphagia could be reversed. Although rats with bilateral LH lesions initially do not consume food, they can be coaxed back to eating by being fed through a tube into their stomach. And after several weeks of this, they restart eating, especially if given palatable food such as biscuit crushed in milk. In such instances, the rat will typically eventually return to its 'normal' regime of dry rat chow and water (Teitelbaum & Epstein, 1962).

The idea of the lateral hypothalamus as a feeding centre came under further critical scrutiny when other types of deficit were noted after its removal. For example, LH lesioned rats did not move around or even right themselves when placed on their sides, and were also unresponsive to sensory stimuli and seemingly under-aroused (Marshall et al., 1971). The reason for these deficits only became clearer in later studies when it was realized that the LH was a site that contained large numbers of so-called fibres of passage, i.e. fibres that passed through its confines (without making contact) en route to other destinations. The most conspicuous of these were noradrenergic and dopaminergic fibres which formed part of the median forebrain bundle (see Chapter 12). It was no surprise that when these pathways were selectively lesioned, sensorimotor deficits were produced along with aphagia and weight loss resembling the effects of LH damage (Ungerstedt, 1971).

Despite this, the LH remains a pivotal structure for feeding behaviour (see Stuber & Wise, 2016). For example, experiments that have destroyed all the cell bodies in the LH without damaging fibres of passage by the use of neurotoxins such as kainic acid still cause marked aphagia in experimental animals (Stanley et al., 1993; Winn et al., 1984). Confirmation that the LH is involved in hunger and food intake has also come from studies that have injected neurotransmitters into it, with **glutamate** receptor activation inducing feeding and **GABA** agonists suppressing it. Thus, the modulation of neurotransmission within the LH can generate feeding responses similar to those observed following electrical stimulation or lesions (Qualls-Creekmore & Münzberg, 2018).

But perhaps the most exciting development concerning our understanding of the LH has come from the discovery that a subset of its neurons produces the neuropeptides orexin A and orexin B which stimulate feeding behaviour (de Lecca et al., 1998; Sakurai et al., 1998). Indeed, when these peptides are infused into the brain's ventricles of experimental animals they cause rapid and prolonged eating – a characteristic that led to them being called orexins (from the Greek word for appetite). One of the unique features of the LH's orexinergic projections is that they innervate the remainder of the hypothalamus including the arcuate nucleus and paraventricular area. They also have extensive projections to many other brain regions including the locus coeruleus and raphe. The importance of these peptides to eating was confirmed when it was reported that levels of orexins increased in the LH during periods of fasting and hypoglycemia (Liu et al., 2001). Moreover, increased glucose levels are able to completely inhibit the firing of orexin neurons in the LH (Burdakov et al., 2005). As might be predicted, the LH's orexin neurons are partly under the control of neuropeptide Y releasing neurons arriving from the arcuate nucleus (Niimi et al., 2001).

Although initially believed to be primarily involved in the stimulation of food intake, it is now recognized that orexins are involved in a wide range of behavioural functions. In particular, they are involved in arousal and regulate the sleep–wake cycle (see Chapter 7). The orexins have also been linked with the mood states of happiness and sadness, and their levels shown to change in major depression, stress and anxiety disorders (Grafe & Bhatnagar, 2018). Other functions attributed to orexins include stress, cognition, addiction and pain (Tsujino & Sakurai, 2013). It should come as no surprise that drugs that can affect orexin systems are generating a lot of interest from pharmaceutical companies.

KEY TERMS: *lateral hypothalamus, fibres of passage, medial forebrain bundle, glutamate, GABA, orexins*

THE INFLUENCE OF LEARNING ON EATING BEHAVIOUR

So far in this chapter, one might be excused for thinking that hunger is a homeostatically controlled process governed by a decline of blood glucose, or some other nutrient variable, acting on the hypothalamus. Similarly, it is tempting to regard satiety as a response resulting from a cacophony of chemical and neural signals reaching our brain about the quantity of food passing through our stomach. However, we do not have to look far to realize our eating behaviour is not as physiologically determined as it first appears. For example, one of the factors that often causes hunger is time of day. Indeed, most of us not only eat at fixed times, but become hungry in anticipation of an approaching meal. And other animals behave in a similar way. For example, as early as 1927, Richter showed that rats given one meal a day came to anticipate their feeding time with increased running in activity wheels. The importance of learning in feeding behaviour was also nicely demonstrated by Weingarten (1983) who used a classical conditioning procedure to present a light and tone to rats every time they were given a meal of evaporated milk. Animals were fed this way 6 times every day over a period of 11 days. Following this conditioning regime, the rats were given unlimited access to food to produce overeating and satiation. Although these animals soon became well fed, they nonetheless began eating again when suddenly re-presented with the light and tone. Clearly, these rats were not consuming food to restore an energy deficit. Rather, they were eating because they had been conditioned to do so.

This finding should not surprise us. When an animal is regularly provided with food, it exhibits gastrointestinal reflexes, sometimes called anticipatory or cephalic phase responses, controlled by the autonomic nervous system (and not by the absorptive effects of ingested nutrients). These reflexes include, for example, the secretion of saliva, gastric juices and insulin in response to the smell and taste of a meal, which in turn help prepare the body to digest, metabolize and store the food. The secretion of these substances which help to stimulate hunger can also be conditioned to external events such as time of day, or the sight of a bakery selling fresh bread (i.e. conditioned stimuli). And it is possible that satiety may also be conditioned in a similar way. For example, it has been proposed by Booth (1990) that events at the end of a meal may become associated with the bodily changes during this time, such as the release of glucagon which may underpin a conditioned satiety response.

The effects of learning also influence the choice of foods we eat. For example, few of us would find squid cooked in its own ink, fried grasshoppers or sheep eyes very appetising, yet these are delicacies eaten in other parts of the world. The great difference in diet in different cultures demonstrates that we what we eat is a large result of upbringing and/or food availability. Our learning of food preferences begins at a surprisingly early point in life for it has been shown that flavours from the mother's diet during pregnancy are transmitted to amniotic fluid or breast milk. This influences food choices later on. For example, one study has shown that infants who had been exposed to the flavour of carrots in either amniotic fluid or breast milk behaved differently in response to that flavour in a food base at around six months of age than did non-exposed control infants (Mennella et al., 2001). It appears that the crucial period for this type of effect occurs when a child transitions from a purely milk-based diet to a more varied solid-food diet (Ventura, 2017). The dietary regime of the child's first 1,000 days – defined as the period from conception to 2 years old – is also now known to be a critical period for later obesity (Woo Baidal et al., 2016).

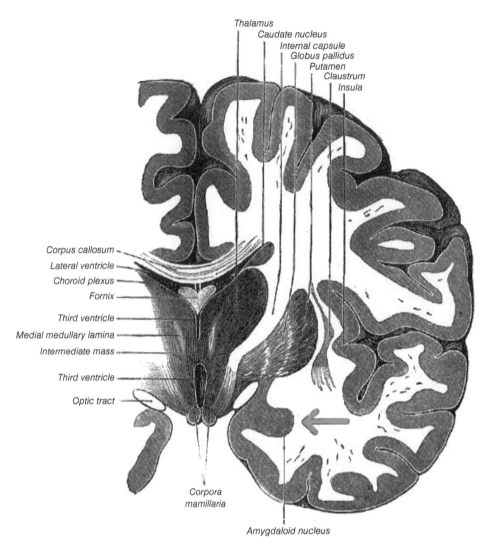

Thalamus
Caudate nucleus
Internal capsule
Globus pallidus
Putamen
Claustrum
Insula

Corpus callosum
Lateral ventricle
Choroid plexus
Fornix

Third ventricle
Medial medullary lamina
Intermediate mass

Third ventricle

Optic tract

Corpora
mamillaria

Amygdaloid nucleus

Figure 5.8   The location of the amygdala
Source: Quibik/Wikimedia Commons

Although there are undoubtedly many brain areas involved in learning about the
pleasurable and aversive aspects of food, some are more important than others. For
example, Holland and Petrovich (2005) trained food-deprived rats to consume food
in a conditioning procedure, not unlike the one used by Weingarten (see above),
in which visual and auditory cues were paired with food. After training, their cues
were able to elicit eating, even when the rat was satiated and not hungry. This cue-
potentiated eating, however, was abolished by lesions of the basolateral amygdala
(see Figure 5.8) – a region with connections to a circuit involving the lateral hypothalamus and medial prefrontal cortex. These researchers also examined the expression
of certain immediate early onset genes in these brain areas which are involved in
protein synthesis (a common response in learning when new neural connections
have to be made). The early onset genes in the basolateral amygdala, medial frontal

cortex and lateral hypothalamus were selectively activated by the conditioning procedure. Holland and Petrovich concluded that cue-potentiated feeding is mediated by the frontal and amygdala neurons that directly target the lateral hypothalamus.

> **KEY TERMS:** *gastrointestinal reflexes, conditioned stimuli, basolateral amygdala, lateral hypothalamus, medial prefrontal cortex*

SENSORY-SPECIFIC SATIETY

Another stimulant of increased food intake is temptation, especially when we are given the choice of different types of foodstuff. For example, most of us will choose a sweet dessert after a large meal at a restaurant – a response showing that the palatability of food, and not the amount of prior consumption, can cause us to eat greater amounts. A related type of behaviour occurs when we experience a decline in pleasantness of a food as it is eaten relative to a food that has not been eaten – a phenomenon called **sensory-specific satiety** (Rolls et al., 1981). This can often be observed when people are offered a standard buffet with a variety of foods. In this situation, people are much more likely to snack on a larger amount of food because of the greater choice. Sensory-specific satiety can also be examined experimentally. In one study, subjects were given a four-course lunch with either a different food in each course (sausages with bread and butter, banana, and chocolate dessert) or four courses of just one of these foods. The results revealed a 44% increase in overall food consumption when exposed to the meals with a variety of foods (Rolls et al., 1984).

The same phenomenon occurs in animals. Adding a small amount of a sweetener to standard laboratory rat food produces a significant increase in its consumption, and a rise in the animal's body weight over several weeks. The addition of bitter-tasting quinine has the opposite effect. And as with humans, an effective way of increasing food intake in laboratory animals is to feed them a highly varied diet. For example, rats given bread and chocolate along with normal chow increased their food intake by 60%, and this led to a 49% increase in weight gain after only 120 days of feeding (Rogers & Blundell, 1980).

Sensory-specific satiety shows we tend to get 'bored' with a single type of food if consumed over a long period of time. Clearly, this desire for greater choice is beneficial as it encourages us to have a diet with a greater range of nutrients. But there can be a downside to this as well, not least because in our modern world people are faced with a great variety of food that can stimulate their hunger leading to excess weight and obesity. Nonetheless, the potential dieter can also make use of this knowledge. Since eating monotonous meals results in long-term sensory-specific satiety, a dieter can use this strategy for reducing food intake and aiding weight loss (Raynor et al., 2006).

The causes of sensory-specific satiety are surprisingly complex and more than just a form of simple habituation where a response to a stimulus decreases after repeated or prolonged presentation (Wilkinson & Brunstrom, 2016). Sensory-specific satiety has also been shown to have a neural basis in the hypothalamus and frontal cortex. For example, Edmund Rolls identified neurons in the lateral hypothalamus that ceased to respond to a substance on which a monkey had been fed to satiety, but became activated again when presented with a different food. A similar type of changeable response was also found in the orbitofrontal cortex where neurons sensitive to food-related sights, tastes and odours have been identified (Rolls, 1999). In humans, functional imaging studies have confirmed that parts of the orbitofrontal cortex show increased activity in response to pleasant food which reduces with satiety (O'Doherty et al., 2000). The orbitofrontal cortex is likely to play an important role in this type of satiation since it is a site where multimodal representations of food are established which include taste, texture, olfactory and visual components. In building this representation, the orbitofrontal cortex relies on a number of other brain structures relaying food-related information including the hypothalamus, amygdala, insula and olfactory cortex (Rolls, 2006).

KEY TERMS: *sensory-specific satiety, habituation, orbitofrontal cortex*

THE PROBLEM OF OBESITY

Few would dispute we are living through a global obesity epidemic (Hruby & Hu, 2015). The statistics are hugely worrying. The World Health Organization (WHO, 2020) has estimated that obesity has nearly tripled worldwide since 1975. In 2016 more than 1.9 billion adults were overweight, and of these over 650 million fulfilled criteria for obesity. In percentage terms this means roughly 39% of all adults worldwide are overweight with 13% being obese. The figures are even more alarming for children who will most likely face a lifetime of weight-related problems. According to the WHO, 41 million children under the age of 5 were overweight or obese in 2016 with this number rising to over 340 million children and adolescents aged 5–19 (WHO, n.d.). As the WHO notes, obesity affects virtually all age and socioeconomic groups and threatens to overwhelm both developed and developing countries alike. Indeed, contrary to conventional wisdom, the obesity epidemic is not restricted to industrialized societies, for over 115 million people suffer from obesity-related issues in developing countries. Nonetheless, the statistics for industrialized countries tend to be worse. In England, the National Health Service (NHS, 2019) has estimated that 20% of children are obese, with the figure being twice as high in the most deprived areas of the country compared to the least deprived areas. This number rises to 29% for adults – a figure that has grown from 23% in 2003 (Department of Health, 2003). And already, according to data provided by the NHS online in 2020, it is estimated that the majority of adults in England can be classified as overweight. However, obesity is the main concern with its incidence still increasing. According to some estimates it is predicted that if the current trend continues, up to 48% of men and 43% of women in the UK could be obese by 2030, adding an additional £2 billion per year in medical costs for obesity-related diseases (Wang, McPherson et al., 2011).

Although obesity is a complex condition, where there is a wide range of biological and social factors that play a part in causing the individual to be overweight, there is little doubt that the so-called obesogenic environment – a term coined to refer to our present social world with all its encouragements to make people eat unhealthily and not do enough exercise – has been a major contributor to the obesity epidemic (Swinburn et al., 1999). One only has to look around at our public places and high streets to see they are dominated by shops selling highly processed and calorific sugar-laden food such as burgers, sugary drinks, pasties and sweets, and at home we are bombarded by food advertising on TV and other media. All in all, there is little doubt that the temptations for unhealthy eating confronting us today are far greater than they have ever been. Indeed, the NHS has estimated that only 18% of children and 29% of adults consume the recommended five or more portions of fruit and vegetables per day.

Although several methods are used to assess the amount and location of fat in the body, the most commonly used measure is the body mass index (BMI), calculated by dividing body weight by height squared. A BMI of 25 is overweight, whereas a BMI of over 30 is regarded as obese. Severe obesity occurs when the BMI reaches 35 to 40, with an estimate greater than 40 regarded as morbidly obese. It should be noted, however, that the BMI is far from perfect and many regard it as a rather poor indicator of percentage of body fat (Frank, 2015). One reason is because it is unable to differentiate dangerous intra-abdominal fat around the waistline from potentially less harmful fat in other areas of the body. Nonetheless, the BMI provides a convenient rule of thumb and is widely used for its simplicity. The BMI is also favoured by the life insurance industry who were also instrumental in it gaining acceptance (Nutall, 2015).

The health costs of being overweight and obese are considerable. Over 2,000 years ago, the health risks of obesity were noted by Hippocrates who wrote that 'persons who are naturally very fat are apt to die earlier than those who are slender', and modern evidence supports his claim. In England alone, it is estimated that obesity is responsible for more than 30,000 deaths each year, and on average it deprives an individual of an extra 9 years of life. Obesity also increases the risk of developing a whole host of diseases. For example, obese people are at increased risk of certain cancers (including being 3 times more likely to develop colon cancer); more than 2.5 times more likely to develop high blood pressure (a risk factor for heart disease); and 5 times more likely to develop type 2 diabetes. In addition, excessive eating raises the level of cholesterol which is a leading cause of strokes and heart attacks. The cost of this to the taxpayer is considerable. In fact, the National Audit Office has estimated the direct and indirect annual costs of obesity for the NHS Service in England to be in the region of £6.1 billion (2014–2015). They also note that the annual expenditure on the treatment of obesity and diabetes is greater than the amount spent on the police, the fire service and the judicial system combined (Public Health England, 2017).

KEY TERMS: *obesity, obesogenic environment, body mass index*

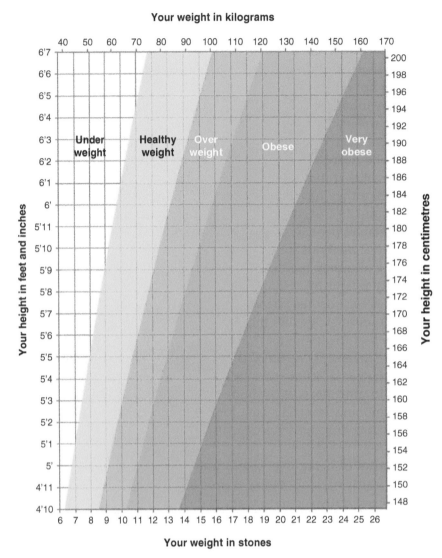

Figure 5.9 Body mass calculation chart

Source: NHS (Crown Copyright)

THE CAUSES OF OBESITY

At first sight, the causes of obesity seem simple enough: it develops when the body's energy intake exceeds energy expenditure over time (usually many years) leading to the accumulation of excess of fat. Considering that the recommended NHS guideline for the daily energy intake of calories for young men is 2,500 and 2,000 for women, it is readily seen how such limits can be easily breached in our modern world. However, the causes of obesity are more complex than simple calorie consumption since it doesn't account for many other factors that influence our weight – including how much we exercise and how our bodies metabolize food energy. Clearly, the problem of obesity is a classic nature–nurture issue, in which genetic factors linked with metabolism and other biological predispositions interact with environmental risk factors such as unhealthy diets and inactive lifestyles. Thus, the causes of obesity are multi-factorial with genetic and environmental factors influencing each other (Jackson et al., 2020). In general, it appears that severe obesity at a young age is likely to be caused by major genes that control energy balance, whilst obesity occurring later in life is more likely to have a strong environmental component with some influence from minor genes (Wilding, 2006).

The idea of there being an innate or genetic cause of obesity was first proposed by Von Noorden in 1907. One way of examining this issue is to look for the concordance of obesity in twins, especially when they have been raised in different families. For example, in one study which examined the body weight of 540 adopted Danish twins, it was found that the weight of the adults was closer to that of their biological parents than their adopted ones (Stunkard et al., 1986). Identical twins are not only more similar in weight and obesity compared to fraternal ones, but have very similar weights across their life span (often within 4 kg of each other). It has also been reported that children with two obese parents have an approximate 70% chance of being overweight compared to 40% for children with one obese parent and 10% when neither parent is obese (Logue, 1986). A comparison of such studies has suggested a body weight heritability estimate of about 60–70% for identical twins and 30–40% for non-identical twins (Plomin et al., 2013; Silventoinen et al., 2010).

Metabolism is also important. During each decade of life, the average adult will consume around 10 million calories, yet only gain a few pounds. This type of metabolic efficiency appears to be largely genetic. For example, Bouchard et al. (1990) took 12 pairs of identical twins with no history of weight problems, and overfed them daily by 1,000 calories for a period of 100 days. During this time they consumed an extra 84,000 calories, causing them to gain around 8 kgs of extra weight. Although there was a high variability between twin pairs (e.g. one pair gained 4 kgs and another pair gained 12 kg), the differences within each pair were small. Again, these results show that weight gain has a significant inherited component.

With the sequencing of the human genome (see Chapter 14), and the development of modern technology aimed at detecting genetic variations in obese individuals, a large number of genes have been identified that regulate weight (Choquet & Meyre, 2011). At least 12 genes have now been recognized where a genetic mutation is known to be linked to weight gain (Thaker, 2017). These monogenetic causes of obesity, however, are relatively rare and mainly linked to severe early onset obesity accompanied with endocrine disorders. Other genes linked with weight come in different versions or alleles. One such gene with several different variations is the so-called fat mass and obesity gene (FTO) located on chromosome 16. It has been reported that a common variant of this gene causes individuals to weigh on average some 1.2 kilograms (2.6 lb) more than those without this allele. Those unfortunate enough to carry two copies of this allele (16% of the subjects) weighed 3 kilograms (6.6 lb) more and had a 1.67-fold higher rate of obesity than those with no copies (Frayling et al., 2007).

Most cases where there is a predisposition towards obesity, however, are 22polygenetic – caused by the cumulative contribution of a large number of genes whose effect is amplified in a 'weight-gaining' environment which disturbs the normal homeostatic mechanisms involved in eating. Indeed, it is hard to see how the recent rapid increase in obesity over the last few decades could not have an important environmental component. Central to this problem is our increasing reliance on diets with

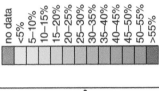

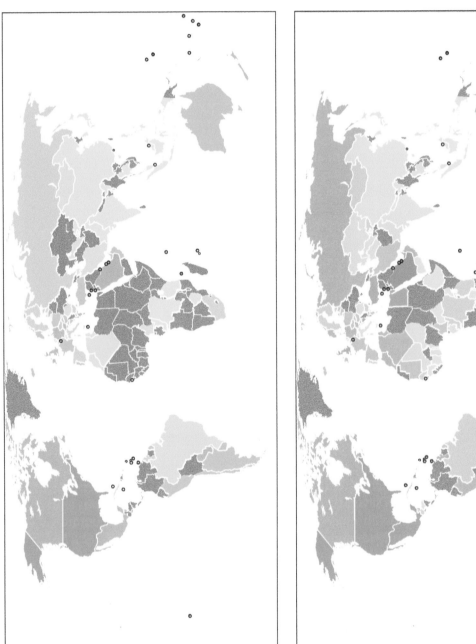

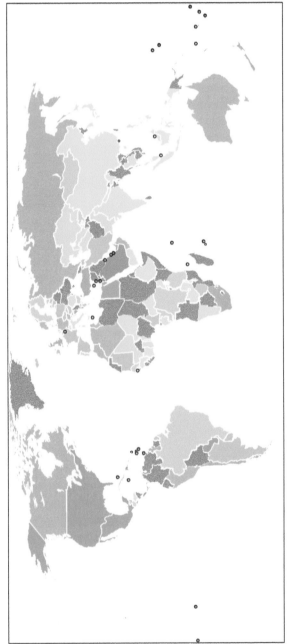

Figure 5.10   World obesity prevalence among males (left) and females (right) in 2008

Source: Lokal_Profil/Wikimedia Commons

a high caloric and fat content. In westernised countries, marked changes in diet have occurred over the last 50 years, especially with the increased consumption of energy-rich food and drinks. To give an example: before 1900, sugar was a rare treat, but since then, the average per-person consumption of sugar in the US has increased from 4–6 pounds per year to about 150–170 pounds today (Meldrum et al., 2017). This type of food also produces a less powerful satiety response and has led to a dramatic increase in portion sizes (Young & Nestle, 2002).

The problem is compounded by food marketing that makes these diets more attractive. There is little doubt that we live in a time where there is a huge variety of different foods available which can encourage overeating through the process of sensory-specific satiety. In the UK, spending on junk-food advertising is nearly 30 times what government spends on promoting healthy eating (O'Dowd, 2017), and there is little doubt this expenditure works – with one study, for example, showing that watching TV food commercials could increase caloric intake by up to 71% (Blass et al., 2006). In fact, new rules in the UK banning the advertising of high fat, salt and sugar food and drink aimed at the under-16s came into effect on 1 July 2017, and more legislation will almost certainly follow.

The problem of obesity is exacerbated by the marked decline of physical activity that has taken place over recent years. In the UK it has been estimated that the average individual now walks about 25 miles (40 km) less per week than they did in 1950. Moreover, the use of labour-saving devices, and increased sedentary leisure-time pursuits such as television and computer games, have also contributed to the decline in physical activity (Wilding, 2006). Indeed, it may come as no surprise to learn that in both children and adults, there is a significant correlation between television viewing time and the risk of obesity (Vioque et al., 2000). Nor is this a western phenomenon, for it has been estimated that at least 30% of the world's population get insufficient exercise (WHO, 2009). Clearly, our urban environment with its reliance on labour-saving devices, along with the emphasis on computers and various modes of transport, discourages many of us from taking up an acceptable level of physical activity.

KEY TERMS: *obesity, nature–nurture, monogenetic and polygenetic causes, alleles, the fat mass and obesity gene*

SPECIAL INTEREST 5.1

CAN CALORIE RESTRICTION HELP YOU LIVE LONGER?

We all want to live longer and healthily, but is this possible? The answer may be yes, and the secret known for nearly a century: it is calorie restriction (CR) which is basically reduced feeding without malnutrition. CR was first performed on rats by the American physiologist

(Continued)

Clive McCay in the 1930s. He believed animals would not show ageing decline as long as they were continuing to grow – encouraging him to attempt slowing the growth of rats by feeding them with just enough to maintain health. To do this, McCay kept the animal at a constant weight for between 1 to 4 months, before allowing a small weight gain of 10 g by increasing the amount of food. Consequently, the deprived rats remained small and continued to grow throughout their life. After 18 months, when normal rats had been fully grown for more than a year, the deprived animals were about one-quarter size, and none had reached their full adult weight. However, the most important finding was the difference in lifespans between the two groups: the CR rats lived nearly 50% longer (on average 820 days) compared to controls (483 days). Also striking was the healthy demeanour of the CR rats which by the age of 1,000 days (at which time all the controls had died) exhibited the appearance of much younger animals. They remained active, had glossy sleek coats, and performed well on maze tasks which measured their intelligence.

These findings have been confirmed in a wide variety of species, including nematode worms, water fleas, spiders, fish and rodents. Although the most effective results on longevity and fitness are obtained when animals are placed on CR after weaning, beneficial effects can also occur when food deprivation is started in adulthood. Since CR can be effective *after* the animal has fully grown, this indicates that the cause of its anti-ageing effect must lie with the diet itself. One explanation is that CR works by reducing free-radical damage to the cells of the body (Wickens, 2001). Free radicals are chemicals that contain an unpaired outer electron, which are byproducts created when oxygen is broken down in cellular energy metabolism. Although highly reactive, these chemicals only exist for a few milliseconds. Nonetheless, during this time they can react with other biological molecules and cause considerable damage to the cell. This is also a popular theory of why we age (Wickens, 1998).

Could CR be beneficial for humans? Although no long-term investigations have been performed yet, evidence indicates that CR in humans might lower insulin, core body temperature, DNA damage, and the chances of cancer (Taormina & Mirisola, 2014). Long-term food restriction has been performed on primates, however, and in the late 1980s two parallel studies began to assess the effects of CR on rhesus monkeys. One of these was undertaken at the National Institute on Aging (NIA) involving 121 monkeys, and the other at the University of Wisconsin Madison (UW) with 76 animals. The NIA study found no significant survival effect (or reductions in cancer, heart disease and diabetes), whereas the UW study reported a significant positive impact of CR on survival and longevity. In fact, their data show that the male monkeys gained an extra two years of life and the female monkeys almost six years. The reasons for the different outcomes of the two studies are being investigated – and there are many factors to be considered, including diet composition, feeding regimens, and the genetic background of the animals. Nonetheless, the overall evidence suggests a beneficial effect for CR (Mattison et al., 2017).

THE DISCOVERY OF LEPTIN

One of the biggest breakthroughs in obesity research, concerning the ways in which our adipose tissue signals the brain to regulate food intake, has come from the discovery of leptin which was first isolated in the early 1990s. One of the puzzles facing researchers up to this time was how people were able to maintain relatively constant body weights across much of their adult lives despite large fluctuations in their energy intake. This appeared to indicate that the brain had some mechanism that

Figure 5.11   A normal mouse and an *ob/ob* mouse placed together
Source: Higgs et al. (2020); photo courtesy of The Jackson Laboratory, Bar Harbor, ME USA, www.jax.org

governed an 'ideal' body weight which it also defended or maintained in times of food scarcity or abundance. But until the 1990s, the physiological mechanism by which the body set its own weight was unknown. Many suspected body weight was largely inherited, not least because it was established that certain genes had an effect on controlling body weight in experimental animals. This was shown as early as 1950 when a genetic mutation occurred in a colony of mice housed at the Jackson Laboratory in Bar Harbour, USA, which caused them to weigh up to three times heavier than normal (Ingalls et al., 1950). This gene was designated as *obese* (*ob*), and because the Bar Harbour mice carried two copies (it was a recessive gene), they were called **ob/ob** mice (see Figure 5.11). Not only did these mice eat large amounts of food, but they also had a low body temperature and metabolism. Like obese humans, they were also more susceptible to diabetes. But how could a mutation in *ob* genes set in motion the biological events that caused these changes?

During the early 1970s, it became apparent the *ob/ob* mice were overweight because they lacked a blood-borne satiety chemical. This discovery was made by Coleman (1973) who joined *ob/ob* mice with normal lean ones in a parabiotic preparation. In this technique, two mice are surgically joined along flank incisions that ran from forelimb to hind limb, enabling their vascular networks to conjoin. The results of this procedure caused the *ob/ob* mice to eat less and lose weight. But how could this be explained? The most likely explanation was that the blood of the normal mouse contained a weight-regulating substance that was encoded by the normal *ob* gene, and absent or abnormal in the *ob/ob* mice.

To determine the nature of this substance it was necessary to first identify the position of the *ob* gene in the genome and then determine its amino-acid sequence. The *ob* gene was located on chromosome 6 in mice (see Coleman, 1978), and then cloned and sequenced in the laboratory of Jeffrey Friedman (Zhang et al., 1994). This work revealed that the *ob* gene produced a 167 amino acid protein called leptin (from the Greek *Leptos* meaning 'thin') which was produced by the body's adipocytes (fat cells). This substance could then reach the brain by being secreted into the blood.

The discovery of leptin showed that adipose tissue was not an inert energy store, but it could also function as an active endocrine gland. Since the amount of body fat determined the levels of leptin in the blood (i.e. the greater the fat, the greater the leptin level), this meant that this substance provided a chemical signal which the brain could use to monitor body weight. Not only was leptin missing in *ob/ob* mice, but when injected into these animals, it also caused a marked decrease of food intake leading to a drop in body weight. Indeed, a daily injection of leptin over the course of two weeks caused the mice to lose 30% of their body weight (Halaas et al., 1995). The cause of overeating and increased weight in the *ob/ob* mice therefore lay with their deficiency in the leptin protein.

However, leptin administration not only changed feeding behaviour in *ob/ob* mice, it also reduced food intake in normal animals. Thus it became clear that leptin was more than a chemical signalling weight, it was an important determinant of appetite and satiety. The mechanism by which leptin exerts appetitive effects has now been studied in some detail (Bouret et al., 2004). Leptin crosses the blood–brain barrier and acts on receptors (called ObRs) located in several areas of the hypothalamus known to be crucial for feeding (Li, 2011). One important area is the arcuate nucleus. Here, leptin inhibits the synthesis and release of neuropeptide Y (NPY) into the paraventricular nucleus (Wang et al., 1997). Consequently, the normal appetite-stimulating (orexigenic) effect of NPY is reversed. Alternatively, animals who are deficient in leptin produce higher levels of NPY, and this appears to be an important contributor to overeating and weight gain (Schwartz & Seeley, 1997). Leptin also has much the same effect on agouti-related peptide which is released from the same neurons that secrete NPY.

Yet this is not the only action of leptin in the arcuate nucleus, for it controls the activity of two other neuropeptides involved in appetite and energy homeostasis. One of these has the unlikely sounding name of cocaine and amphetamine regulated transcript (CART). This substance increases in times of food deprivation, whilst decreases of this peptide lead to satiety (Kristensen et al., 1998). Leptin also controls α-melanocyte-stimulating hormone (αMSH) which appears to exerts its main suppressant effect through the activation of melanocortin 4 receptor (MC4R) located in the hypothalamic paraventricular nucleus. The net effect of leptin on both these neuropeptides together is a suppression of appetite and feeding, increased autonomic activity and thermogenesis (Friedman, 2019; Seoane-Collazo et al., 2020).

KEY TERMS: *leptin, ob/ob mice, parabiotic preparation, arcuate nucleus, neuropeptide Y*

LEPTIN AND OBESITY

The discovery of leptin, along with evidence showing that it reduced the weight of *ob/ob* mice by decreasing food intake, led to speculation concerning its involvement in human obesity. For example, are obese humans like *ob/ob* mice with homozygous mutations in their *ob* genes? The answer to this question is that it is possible – although cases of obesity arising from mutations of the *ob* gene with complete leptin deficiency are extremely rare. So far, only a few people world-wide have been found with these *ob* genes mutations. The first report on congenital leptin deficiency was published by Montague et al. (1997) who described a boy and girl from the same family believed to be carrying *ob* mutations. Although their weight was normal at birth, the children became seriously obese after a couple of years. And by the age of 8 years, the girl weighed 86 kg (190lbs) with 57% body fat compared to the normal range of 15–25%. The treatment of the girl with genetically produced (recombinant) leptin started when she was 9 years old, and within 2 weeks weight loss was observed. After just 1 year of treatment her body fat had decreased by 15.6 kg. Her eating habits also changed and her constant hunger disappeared.

It is now well established that the vast majority of obese humans are not leptin deficient and don't have mutations in their *ob* genes. In fact, they typically have high circulating leptin levels (in contrast to *ob/ob* mice who have lower levels) and are either resistant or tolerant to its weight-reducing effects (Kelesidis et al., 2010). Thus, if leptin plays a role in human obesity, the most likely mechanism is a reduced sensitivity to this hormone, rather than decreased secretion. Nonetheless, attempts have also been made to treat obesity with subcutaneous injections of leptin (Heymsfield et al., 1999). The results showed that only a small percentage (about 5%) of individuals experienced weight loss after 24 weeks of treatment. Thus, leptin does not appear to be the panacea for obesity as some had initially hoped.

It should be remembered that the primary function of leptin is its regulation of body weight and adipose tissue, and that levels of this hormone do not change acutely following a meal (Ahima, 2008). In fact, in humans, there is a circadian secretion of leptin secretion over the course of the day with low basal levels between 0800 and 1200 hours, which rise progressively to peak between 2400 and 0400 hours. Nonetheless, diet-induced weight loss causes a decrease in plasma leptin concentrations – and this decrease may play an important role in stimulating hunger when the body is subjected to low energy reserves. Thus, leptin may be an important contributor to the high failure rate of dieting. Consequently, there is still much clinical interest in the possibility of leptin treatment for weight loss maintenance (Kelesidis et al., 2010).

Table 5.1   Summary of feeding signals involved in hunger and satiety

STIMULUS	SIGNAL SOURCE	PATHWAY
START MEALS		
1. Glucose, fatty acids	Detected in liver as nutrients in blood are depleted.	Signal travels via vagus nerve to NST, then to arcuate nucleus in hypothalamus.
2. Glucose (in brain)	Low level detected by glucose receptors in the brain.	Detection occurs within the pathway, in hypothalamic and brain stem centres.
3. Ghrelin	Peptide released by stomach during fasting.	Circulates in bloodstream to arcuate nucleus.
END MEALS		
4. Stomach volume	Stretch receptors in stomach detect increased volume from food.	Signal travels via vagus nerve to NST, then to arcuate nucleus in hypothalamus.
5. CCK (and other nutrient indicators)	Stomach and intestines release peptides that aid digestion, signal brain of nutrient's presence.	CCK and others initiate activity in vagus to NST and hypothalamus; some may circulate in blood to brain.
LONG TERM		
6. PYY	Released by intestines.	Travels in bloodstream to arcuate nucleus; inhibits NPY neurons.
7. Leptin	Released by fat cells.	Travels in bloodstream to arcuate nucleus; inhibits NPY neurons.

(Continued)

Table 5.1   (Continued)

STIMULUS	SIGNAL SOURCE	PATHWAY
8. Insulin	Released by pancreas.	Travels in bloodstream to arcuate nucleus; inhibits NPY neurons.
9. Orexin	Released by neurons from the lateral hypothalamus.	Released in the arcuate nucleus; activates NPY neurons and inhibits POMC neurons.

Note: CCK = cholecystokinin; NPY = neuropeptide Y; NST = nucleus of the solitary tract; PYY = peptide $YY_{3.36}$

Source: Garrett and Hough (2018)

ANOREXIA NERVOSA AND BULIMIA

The eating-disorder charity Beat has estimated that around 1.25 million people in the UK are affected by what they regard as a mental health problem that involves disordered patterns of eating behaviour. These disorders can take many forms, and in some cases they are ill-defined (see Hay et al., 2017). Nonetheless, the two most common are generally recognized as anorexia nervosa and bulimia. The term 'anorexia' means loss of appetite and was first used by the English physician Sir William Gull in 1873. Although the term has remained, it is not an accurate description of the disorder as people with anorexia still experience hunger. Rather, anorexia is characterized by a persistent reduction of food intake which produces a body weight significantly lower than what is acceptable for a person's height and age. In extreme cases an anorexic may have a body mass index of less than 15, with a body weight some 60–70% of what is considered normal. People with anorexia are invariably obsessed with being thin and fearful of becoming fat – a preoccupation that is often accompanied by a deformed perceptual self body image and distorted attitudes regarding their condition (Mölbert et al., 2018). Compelled to eat small amounts of food, they may also undertake self-induced vomiting, excessive exercise, or use laxatives to minimize their weight. Anorexia is not uncommon. Predominantly aged affecting young females, it reaches a peak incidence of 1 in 100 among adolescents between 15 and 19, although anorexia can occur much earlier (even in 10 year olds) and is sometimes found in females over 40. About 0.4 per cent of young women are affected in a given year, and it is reported to be 10 times more common in females than males (Smink et al., 2014). The effects on health include a loss of menstruation, lowered blood pressure, sleep disturbances, and metabolic abnormalities including excess secretion of **cortisol** and decreased thyroid function. Anorexia nervosa has the highest mortality rate of any psychiatric disorder in the USA, with an annual death rate of 5.6%, which is 12 times higher than that found in control women (Rosling et al., 2011). One well-known person with anorexia was the singer Karen Carpenter who died from this condition in 1983. Despite its seriousness, no medication has yet been approved for its treatment.

Bulimia was first described by British psychiatrist Gerald Russell in 1979. It is characterized by bouts of binge eating where individuals consume large amounts of food in a short space of time. Consequently, it is not unusual for people with bulimia to gorge themselves with thousands of calories, which is followed by self-induced vomiting or the use of laxatives to purge themselves of the food they have just consumed. Although about 40% of people with anorexia engage in binge eating, many individuals with bulimia do not develop anorexia. Thus, bulimia qualifies as an eating disorder in its own right. It is found in some 1–2% of females aged 16 to 35 years, and is less common in males.

The causes of anorexia and bulimia are poorly understood. Since people with anorexia are by definition underweight, a number of biological abnormalities are bound to exist as a result of their under-nutrition. It therefore becomes difficult to know whether these represent causal factors, or are a secondary consequence of excessive dieting. For a long time, there was evidence to show that grey matter volume and cortical thickness were lower for patients with anorexia (both during the illness and after recovery) than in controls, although some more recent evidence has indicated that such abnormalities normalize with weight gain (Frank et al., 2019). One brain structure suspected of being involved in anorexia nervosa is the hypothalamus along with the pituitary gland (Warren, 2011). Evidence linking this brain region with anorexia has come from the finding that many as 25% of females with anorexia show a loss of menstruation and low levels of reproductive hormones before significant weight loss occurs. In addition, the high cortisol levels which are often found in these anorexics is a result of increased secretion of corticotropin releasing factor (CRH) under the control of the hypothalamic-pituitary axis. Nonetheless, it remains that in most individuals, both menstruation and cortisol tend to normalize with clinical recovery, which casts doubt on their etiological involvement (Misra & Klibanski, 2014; Misra et al., 2006).

KEY TERMS: *anorexia nervosa, bulimia, cortisol, corticotropin releasing factor, hypothalamic-pituitary axis*

Some individuals have been shown to have decreased levels of noradrenergic metabolites in their urine and CSF which points to reduced noradrenaline levels in the brain. These metabolites also tend to remain low after recovery from anorexia (Kaye et al., 1985). This is noteworthy since injections of noradrenaline into the hypothalamus, especially the paraventricular nucleus, causes animals to eat, whilst low levels have the opposite effect (Wellman, 2000). Low levels of noradrenaline are also linked to dysphoric mood – a common characteristic of people with anorexia even after recovery (Ferguson & Piggot, 2000). Evidence from animal studies shows that overactive α2-adrenoceptors may contribute to hunger and hedonic binge eating (van Gestel et al., 2014).

Evidence also shows a disturbance of dopaminergic and serotonergic systems in anorexia nervosa (see Phillipou et al., 2014). For example, several PET studies have reported reduced numbers of dopamine receptors in the anterior ventral striatum – an area containing the **nucleus accumbens** known to be important for the rewarding effects of food (Kaye et al., 2013). Individuals with anorexia also tend to show elevated levels of the serotonergic metabolite 5-HIAA which persists into the recovery phase of their illness (see Figure 5.12). However, perhaps the most striking feature of serotonergic dysfunction concerns receptors – for a number of studies have shown that anorexia tends to show an increased 5-HT_{1A} binding, but a reduced 5-HT_{2A} binding in various cortical brain areas, including the frontal cortex, hippocampus, amygdala, cingulate cortex and parts of the parietal lobe (Bailer & Kaye, 2011). Abnormal serotonergic function is known to be linked to anxiety disorders and obsessive compulsive personality, both of which are highly characteristic of individuals prior to developing anorexia (Kaye et al., 1998). It is interesting to note that antidepressants which block the reuptake of serotonin such as fluoxetine (Prozac) have been shown to be of some use in the treatment of anorexia and bulimia. Other brain areas currently implicated in anorexia with functional brain-scanning techniques include the left-sided medial orbitofrontal cortex and right insula (Frank, 2015; Kaye et al., 2011).

KEY TERMS: *noradrenaline, paraventricular nucleus, dopamine, serotonin, nucleus accumbens, 5-HT1A and 5-HT2A receptors*

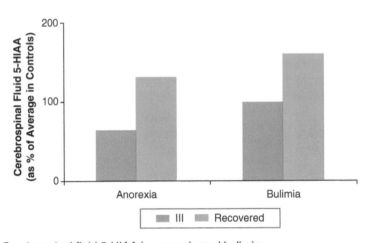

Figure 5.12   Cerebrospinal fluid 5-HIAA in anorexia and bulimia

Source: Garrett and Hough (2021), adapted from Figure 1 of Kaye, W., Gendall, K., & Strober, M. (1998). Serotonin neuronal function and selective serotonin reuptake inhibitor treatment in anorexia and bulimia nervosa. *Biological Psychiatry*, *44*, 825–838. Copyright, 1998. Used with permission from Elsevier.

SUMMARY

Hunger and satiety are influenced by biological and psychological variables. Traditionally, physiological accounts of appetitive behaviour have regarded it as a homeostatic process in which the body attempts to maintain various levels of essential nutrients (glucose, fats, proteins, etc.) within narrow and strict limits. However, it is also clear that psychological factors play an equally important role in eating as shown by the fact we often feel hungry in anticipation of being fed. Digestion involving the mouth, stomach and small intestine is the process by which large insoluble food molecules are broken down, enabling them to be used by the body. This requires absorption which takes place in the small intestine where nutrients, including glucose, enter the general circulation (after reaching the liver) along with emulsified fats that are transported into the lymphatic vessels. During a meal, the pancreas gland releases insulin which allows the circulating glucose to enter the body's cells, but in the periods between eating, the pancreas secretes glucagon which converts glycogen in the liver into glucose, whilst enabling stores of fatty acids to form glycerol. A large number of peripheral mechanisms play a role in keeping the brain informed of the nutrient status of the body. These include neural signals from the vagus nerve which conveys stretch information from the stomach, and glucoreceptors in the liver, along with various neuropeptides secreted into the blood including cholecystokinin (a hunger suppressant) and ghrelin (which increases hunger).

Many brain areas are involved in eating behaviour, but most attention has focused on the hypothalamus. It has long been known that lateral hypothalamus (LH) lesions produce aphagia (cessation of eating) whilst ventromedial hypothalamus (VMH) damage causes hyperphagia (excessive eating and weight gain). These observations led to the dual-centre set-point theory which viewed the LH as the eating centre of the brain and the VMH as its satiety centre. This theory is now known to be far too simple and most likely fundamentally incorrect. Although the LH appears to have a role in food intake, so do many other regions of the hypothalamus, including the arcuate nucleus (where many nutrient substances pass through the blood brain barrier) and paraventricular nucleus (PVN). Injections of neuropeptide Y into the PVN produce markedly excessive eating, which in turn stimulates a class of neuropeptides known as the **orexins** which project to various hypothalamic nuclei and other brain areas involved in appetitive behaviour.

Eating disorders are common. It is estimated that around 1.25 million people suffer from an eating disorder in the UK which includes anorexia nervosa and bulimia – both of which can have serious effects on health and fatal consequences. But these figures are dwarfed by the large numbers of people who are overweight or obese. Already in the UK, and other parts of the developed world, the majority of adults can be classed as overweight, and it is predicted that if the current trend continues, up to 48% of men and 43% of women in the UK could be obese by 2030. The discovery of leptin in the early 1990s, which is secreted by the body's fat cells, provided new insights into the regulation of body weight and eating behaviour. As fat levels accumulate, so does the circulating leptin which provides the brain with a signal concerning the size of its fat stores. Leptin is also known to affect appetite by acting on the arcuate nucleus of the hypothalamus where it affects the release of several neuropeptides including neuropeptide Y. Although there are a few cases where leptin deficiency has been shown to cause obesity, it is now well established that the vast majority of obese humans are not leptin deficient or don't have mutations in their ob genes. Rather there is a complex interplay of other factors including other types of gene, metabolism, learning, and exposure to an obesogenic environment.

GO ONLINE

TEST YOUR UNDERSTANDING OF THIS CHAPTER AND VISIT HTTPS://STUDY.SAGEPUB.COM/WICKENS TO ACCESS INTERACTIVE 'DRAG AND DROP' LABELLING ACTIVITIES AND A FLASHCARD GLOSSARY.

MULTIPLE CHOICE QUESTIONS

Answer the questions below to test your understanding of this chapter's Learning Objectives. You'll find the answers at the end of the chapter.

1. The main function of insulin is to:

   a. speed up stomach contractions
   b. enable the absorption of nutrients through the small intestine
   c. break down protein
   d. enable glucose to enter body cells

2. The dual-centre set-point model of hunger attributed the 'hunger centre' and the 'satiety centre' to which respective brain regions?

   a. basolateral amygdala and orbitofrontal cortex
   b. lateral hypothalamus and ventromedial hypothalamus
   c. dorsomedial hypothalamus and paraventricular hypothalamus
   d. basolateral amygdala and dorsomedial hypothalamus

3. What was the first gut hormone to be linked with appetitive behaviour?

   a. cholecystokinin
   b. ghrelin
   c. neuropeptide Y
   d. leptin

4. Where would you find the arcuate nucleus?

   a. brain stem
   b. midbrain
   c. hypothalamus
   d. basal forebrain

5. Sensory-specific satiety occurs when:

   a. one gets 'bored' eating the same food over a period of time
   b. one gets 'conditioned' to terminate eating
   c. one becomes satiated after eating a small sweet dessert before their main meal
   d. one becomes nauseous after eating a certain food

6. Which of the following is a characteristic of Prader-Willi syndrome?

   a. insulin deficiency
   b. a ravenous desire to eat
   c. low body weight despite high calorie intake
   d. glucose intolerance

FURTHER READING

Brownell, K. D., & Walsh, T. (Eds.). (2018). *Eating disorders and obesity*. The Guilford Press.
A comprehensive but highly focused book with 108 well-written chapters by various experts which is indispensable for anyone interested in eating disorders.

Dickson, S. L., & Mercer, J. G. (Eds.). (2016). *Neuroendocrinology of appetite*. John Wiley.
A book which concentrates on the chemical basis of feeding behaviour including hormones, neuropeptides and transmitter systems.

Le Magnen, J. (2012). *Neurobiology of feeding and nutrition*. Academic Press.
Written by a renowned expert, this book discusses the neural and endocrine basis of appetitive behaviour.

Legg, C. R., & Booth, D. (2002). *Appetite: Neural and behavioral basis.* Oxford University Press.
Examines the psychology and neurobiology of appetite in relation to food, drugs, sex and gambling in an attempt to find common denominators between them.

Leng, G. (2018). *The heart of the brain: The hypothalamus and its hormones.* The MIT Press.
Not a book on eating and satiety per se, but very informative on the hypothalamus, and has relevant chapters on obesity and appetite.

Pirke, K. M., & Ploog, D. (Eds.). (2012). *The psychobiology of anorexia nervosa.* Berlin and Heidelberg.
A very useful book which provides the latest research concerning the psychobiology of anorexia nervosa.

Pirke, K. M., Vandereycken, W., & Ploog, D. (Eds.). (2012). *The psychobiology of bulimia nervosa.* Berlin and Heidelberg.
This book provides the latest research concerning the psychobiology of bulimic disorders.

Ritter, R. C., Ritter, S., & Barnes, C. D. (Eds.). (2012). *Feeding behavior: Neural and humoral controls.* Academic Press.
All 11 chapters of this book are highly relevant to the material covered in this chapter.

Smith, G. P. (Ed.). (1998). *Satiation: From gut to brain.* Oxford University Press.
A detailed account of the physiological and hormonal mechanisms underlying satiety.

Yeo, G. (2018). *Gene eating: The story of human appetite.* Orion Spring.
An entertaining, informative and easy to read book which discusses the science of obesity and dieting.

6

EMOTIONAL STATES

LEARNING OBJECTIVES

After reading this chapter you should be able to:

- Describe how the autonomic nervous system works.

- Compare the James–Lange and Cannon–Bard theories of emotion.

- Explain how cognitive factors are involved in emotion.

- Appreciate the importance of the hypothalamus and limbic system in emotion.

- Understand the neural basis of aggression.

- Describe how the amygdala is involved in fear responding.

- Elucidate the role of the frontal cortex in emotion.

- Understand the concept of anxiety and its drug treatment.

INTRODUCTION

The term **emotion** is derived from the Latin *emovere*, meaning 'to move' or 'disturb'. It is an apt word as emotions do indeed prompt action and signal that something significant is happening to us. They also create a feeling – love, elation, happiness, fear, anger, joy and surprise to name a few – that colours our perception and drives us into action. Emotions are at the heart of what it means to be alive and human, and it is hard to imagine the dull grey world that would exist without them. However, for psychologists, emotions are also an enigma – not least because there is no consensus on what they are or even how they arise.

Over 2,000 years ago, Plato wrote that emotions are to be distrusted as they arise from the lower part of the mind which prevents rational thought. As we all know, emotions often do seem to arise involuntarily, triggering strong physiological reactions, and producing thoughts and behaviours that can be difficult to control. Thus, Plato was possibly close to the truth when regarding emotions as the antithesis of reason.

Later, Charles Darwin pointed out that many of our emotions occur in other animals which shows they evolved to serve important functions. His theory is supported by the finding that the expression of most emotions is universal across all cultures. Although the subject is plagued with conceptual difficulties, most would accept that an emotion has four components: (1) a cognitive appraisal of an arousing event; (2) physiological changes in the viscera; (3) an increased readiness to act; and (4) a subjective sense of feeling.

There is perhaps no more powerful determinant of human behaviour, and clearly attempting to understanding emotions has many benefits, not least because affective disturbances cause anxiety and stress, and underpin nearly all behavioural problems and illnesses. By understanding the biological nature of emotion, we not only gain a far deeper insight into our own human nature, we are also in a stronger position to help those who are suffering with emotional problems.

THE AUTONOMIC NERVOUS SYSTEM AND EMOTION

The most obvious sign of emotional arousal involves changes in the **autonomic nervous system** (ANS) such as a pounding heart, increased respiration or 'butterflies' in the stomach. Autonomic means 'self-governing' and for the most part our ANS operates beyond voluntary or conscious control. This system uses motor nerves to control the viscera or internal organs of the body, and it also innervates several endocrine organs including the adrenal glands. These glands, which sit just above the kidneys, are composed of the inner adrenal medulla which secretes **adrenaline**, and the outer adrenal cortex, which releases a glucocorticoid hormone called **cortisol**. As we saw in Chapter 1, the ANS is comprised of two divisions: the **sympathetic nervous system** (SNS) and the **parasympathetic nervous system** (PNS). The first of these prepares the body for dangerous or stressful situations – a pattern of responses called the '**fight-or-flight response**' by the famous physiologist Walter Cannon in the 1920s. SNS activity increases respiration, heart rate and blood pressure to ensure the bodily organs obtain the necessary levels of oxygen and blood sugar. It also shunts blood away from skin to the muscles to aid vigorous exercise (this is why the skin goes paler after a shock) and stimulates sweat glands to cool the body. As the SNS comes into play, it also inhibits non-essential functions such as digestion. These reactions prepare the person for a potential or actual emergency that requires a sudden energy output.

In contrast, the PNS promotes relaxation and becomes more active during resting and non-stressful conditions. It is primarily concerned with conserving body energy and this is seen when the PNS diverts blood away from skeletal muscles to the gut where it assists digestion. The one exception to this general rule, however, concerns the active role of the PNS in regulating sexual arousal. For this reason, the PNS has sometimes been called the feed-and-breed system. But in general, the PNS and SNS have antagonistic effects. Hence, the SNS increases heart rate, respiration, sweat gland activity etc., whereas PNS activity returns it to normal. To provide this type of autonomic balance, it is necessary for the motor branches of both systems to innervate the same body organs.

Although the ANS has evolved over millions of years to control the functions necessary for life, and to handle fight-or-flight situations, it has also become intimately linked with producing emotion states. Thus, emotions are closely allied with physiological responses. It may also come as a surprise to realize that the autonomic changes underlying both positive emotions (e.g. happiness and love) and negative ones (e.g. anger and fear) are similar. Indeed, both love and fear can produce a rapid heartbeat, increased respiration, enlarged pupils and fluttery feelings in the stomach. While it is not clear whether all aspects of autonomic activity are the same in these disparate emotions (see later), there is little doubt it plays a pivotal role in all of our major emotional states. This physiological involvement in emotion has most likely evolved to add greater emphasis to behaviours where either attraction or avoidance from threat is necessary. Emotions also help to make these events more memorable (Anderson & Phelps, 2001; Tyng et al., 2017) indicating, if nothing else, that they are important for our survival as Darwin maintained.

KEY TERMS: *autonomic nervous system, adrenaline, cortisol, sympathetic and parasympathetic systems, fight-or-flight response*

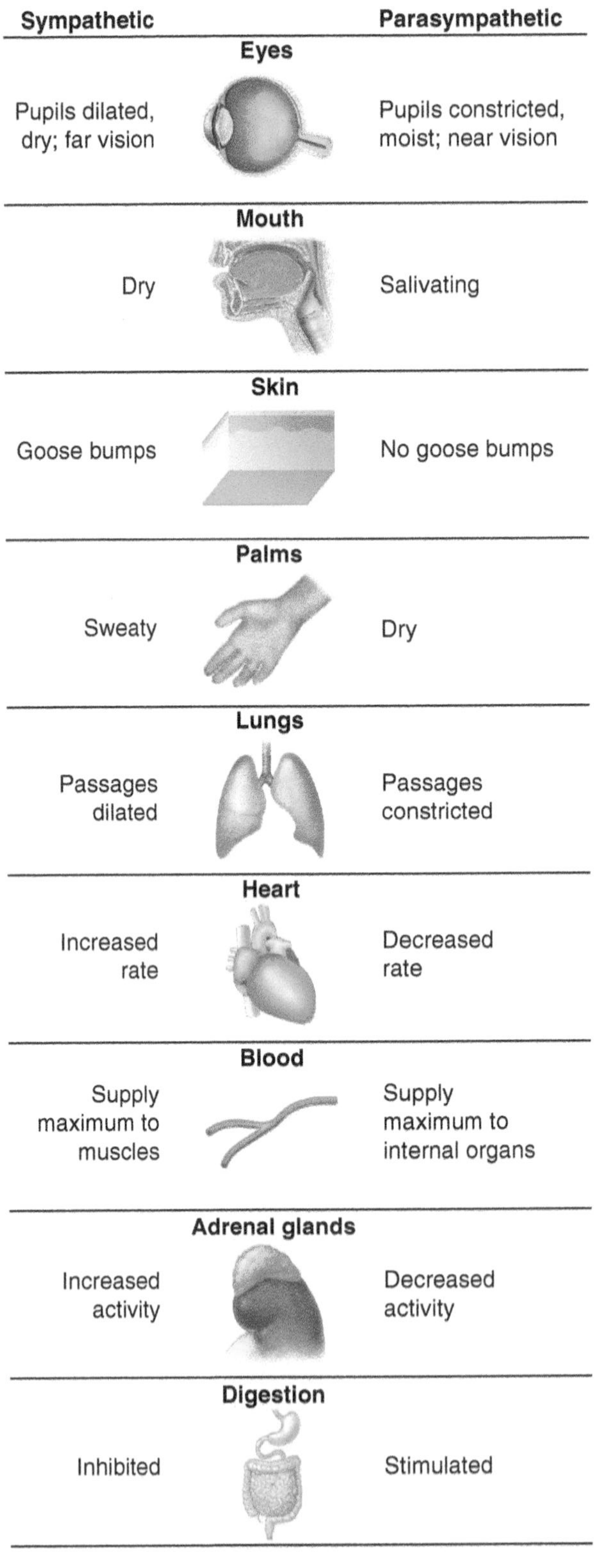

Sympathetic		Parasympathetic
Eyes		
Pupils dilated, dry; far vision		Pupils constricted, moist; near vision
Mouth		
Dry		Salivating
Skin		
Goose bumps		No goose bumps
Palms		
Sweaty		Dry
Lungs		
Passages dilated		Passages constricted
Heart		
Increased rate		Decreased rate
Blood		
Supply maximum to muscles		Supply maximum to internal organs
Adrenal glands		
Increased activity		Decreased activity
Digestion		
Inhibited		Stimulated

Figure 6.1   Comparison of sympathetic activity during emotional arousal with parasympathetic activity during relaxation

Source: Garret and Hough (2021), created by Epicstudios, inc

THE JAMES–LANGE THEORY OF EMOTION

At first sight, identifying the cause of an emotion seems straightforward. If we are walking in a field and suddenly see a snake, the chances are we will feel an emotion (fear) and react by breathing more deeply and increasing our heart rate. These responses will allow us to more effectively move away from the danger. In this scenario there appears to be a clear chain of events: (1) we see a snake, (2) we feel emotion, (3) we react physiologically, and (4) we flee. However, around the turn of the century the American psychologist and philosopher William James and Danish physiologist Carl Lange, in separate papers, advocated an alternative theory (see Lang, 1994). Instead of saying we run away because of fear (as the above example suggests) they proposed we become afraid *because we run*. Thus, they held that the physiological changes and behavioural action come before the emotion is experienced. If this is true, then the conscious sensation of an emotion only arises once we receive feedback from the ANS (see Figure 6.2).

This is now known as the James–Lange theory of emotion and it can be briefly summarized as follows: a stimulus is processed by the appropriate part of the brain, such as the visual or auditory cortex which assesses its relevance. If the stimulus is emotionally significant, information is passed to the ANS which instigates components of the fight-flight response. The resulting bodily arousal is then detected by the conscious part of the brain, which interprets the emotional nature of the physiological state it is experiencing. Emotional experience results therefore from the physiological arousal that precedes it. Running away from a fearful stimulus such as a snake, with a pounding heart and gasping for breath, will cause us to be afraid.

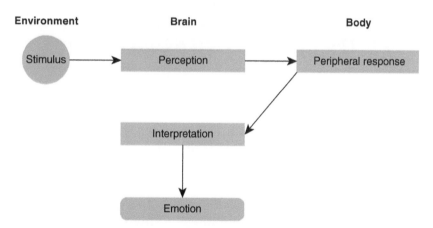

Figure 6.2   Schematic representation of the James–Lange theory
Source: Higgs et al. (2020)

The main problem with this idea is that emotions such as love and hate 'feel' very different. How can we possibly decide what emotion we are experiencing from our bodily reactions? The answer according to the James–Lange theory is that a different set of physiological responses underpins every emotion. This is similar to saying that each affective response has its own unique set of **visceral changes** associated with the internal organs of the body – and it is this reaction which the brain interprets as emotion. In support of this idea, James argued that it was impossible to feel an emotion without experiencing the body response that comes before it. He also pointed out that people can sometimes feel anxious, angry or depressed without knowing why, indicating that bodily states can be independent from cognitive or conscious analysis.

One way the James–Lange theory has been tested was by examining emotional responding in men who have become paraplegic and quadriplegic (paraplegic refers to paralysis below the waist whilst quadriplegic refers to all four limbs). If the theory is correct, then reduced sensation from the body to the brain should decrease the intensity of emotion. This prediction was tested by Hohmann (1966) who measured the emotional reactions of 25 World War II veterans who had suffered spinal wounds that led them to lose sensation from various parts of the body. Some had low-level lumbar damage where most of the spinal cord was intact, whereas others had cervical or thoracic damage causing most body sensation to be lost. Hohmann interviewed his subjects and included questions about their emotions including fear, anger, grief and sentimentality. His findings revealed those with lumber damage appeared to show normal emotional responding, whereas those with higher level spinal damage (i.e. with little peripheral sensation) spoke of intense mental emotions with little bodily involvement. For example, one subject described his experience of anger: 'It just doesn't have the heat to it that it used to. It's a mental kind of anger.' Although these findings confirm visceral feedback is an important component of emotion, they also demonstrate that a mental form of emotional responding can occur without physiological arousal – something which the James–Lange theory does not predict.

KEY TERMS: *James–Lange theory, visceral changes*

WALTER CANNON'S VIEWS ON EMOTION

The James–Lange theory remained popular until the 1920s when Harvard physiologist Walter Cannon compiled evidence against it (see Dror, 2013). In one experiment, Cannon (1927) kept cats alive and healthy after surgically removing their sympathetic nervous systems. Although this abolished all signs of physical arousal in the animals (including sympathetic vascular reactions and adrenal gland secretion), it had no effect on their emotional behaviour. For example, the cats exhibited the typical signs of rage in response to a barking dog, and displayed normal fear and pleasure. Similar effects were found in animals with complete transections of the spinal cord. Cannon also noted that many automatic responses such as smooth muscle contraction or adrenaline release took time to develop, and were too slow to provide a signal for the brain to generate an emotional experience. According to his estimates, it took around 0.8 seconds for autonomic arousal to occur – which was about the same time as it took a person to react mentally. Thus, Cannon reasoned the physiological response must occur at the same time, or possibly lag slightly behind, the beginnings of the mental interpretation. Hence, the feeling of emotion was not dependent on physiological changes in the body, and even if the autonomic responses took place, Cannon believed they were neither changeable nor sensitive enough to provide the physiological basis for different types of emotion as the James–Lange theory held.

Further evidence against the James–Lange theory came from studies where humans were injected with adrenaline. This produced physiological reactions resembling excitement and strong fear which included heart palpitations, trembling, sweating, shortness of breath and drying of the mouth. Yet despite the elicitation of these highly arousing effects, the injection did not cause the participants to experience fear or any other strong emotion. Instead, they were able to interpret their bodily reactions objectively without experiencing them as emotional. The one exception to this occurred, however, after the adrenalin was injected following a discussion (concerning sick children or dead parents) that had caused emotional reactions in a participant. Here, the adrenaline injection reinforced the intensity of the emotional mood (Cannon, 1927).

This evidence has led to an alternative theory which has become known as the Cannon–Bard theory of emotion (Figure 6.3) (we will talk about the work of Bard in the next section). In contrast to the James–Lange theory which saw emotion resulting from a chain of events leading from physiological arousal to emotional feeling, Cannon proposed that physiological and mental responses occur simultaneously but independently of each other. In other words, emotion did not entail physiological feedback. Rather, emotionality was an intrinsic function of the brain and it led to two events: the stimulation of the ANS to produce physiological arousal, and the conscious interpretation of the emotional event. This meant that the initiation of autonomic arousal and cognitive analysis involved two separate routes. The coordinating brain structure responsible for this divergence, Cannon believed, was the **thalamus** – which sent input to the spinal cord (to trigger visceral changes) whilst at the same time relaying sensory information to the cerebral cortex (Dror, 2013).

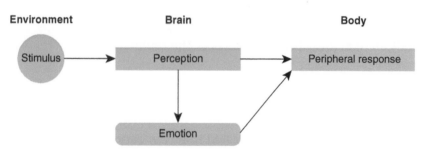

Figure 6.3   Schematic representation of the Cannon–Bard theory
Source: Higgs et al. (2020)

It is also apparent the Cannon–Bard theory does not accept the idea that emotions have their own individual pattern of body activity as the James–Lange theory maintained. In fact, Cannon held that the general nature of the autonomic arousal was the same for all emotion; moreover, that this feedback wasn't even necessary for an emotion to be experienced. Thus, according to the Cannon–Bard theory, if we see a snake, we run away because we have a mental sensation of fear that will be closely tied to, but still independent of, bodily arousal.

KEY TERMS: *Cannon–Bard theory, physiological arousal, conscious interpretation, thalamus*

THE WORK OF PHILIP BARD

Cannon's theory was developed by his doctoral student Philip Bard during the 1930s. Bard was interested in identifying the brain areas involved in producing emotion. This led him to show that decorticated animals (i.e. cats deprived of their cerebral cortex) became highly emotional and aggressive, responding with exaggerated hissing and snarling to the slightest provocation (e.g. having their tail touched). This behaviour showed all the usual autonomic features associated with emotional arousal such as increased heart rate and blood pressure etc. However, the emotional response was not entirely normal as it was never directed to the threatening stimulus, and the rage quickly subsided when the threat was removed. Bard referred to this as sham rage. His work suggested that the cerebral cortex did not necessarily produce emotional behaviour, but was important in directing it to the appropriate situation (Bard, 1934).

But why did loss of the cerebral cortex cause rage? Bard's explanation was that the cortex acted to inhibit emotion and aggression governed by lower levels of the brain. Hence, its removal caused a loss of inhibition in the areas responsible for producing the rage reaction, thereby causing them to become overactive. This was also in accordance with several other observations. For example, surgeons and dentists had long known that some patients show a strong emotional response, such as crying, laughter and aggression, during the early stages of anaesthesia when the neural activity in the cerebral cortex is becoming inhibited. Another interesting behaviour was observed in patients with paralysis on one side of the body due to motor cortex damage (hemiplegia). Although hemiplegic patients exhibit paralysis of the face muscles, there are instances when involuntary smiling can occur in response to a happy event. These findings indicate that areas below the level of the cerebral cortex are involved in producing emotional responses.

Bard showed that sham rage could be elicited by brain lesions all the way down to the level of the **hypothalamus**. However, if the hypothalamus was removed, rage did not occur, although some uncoordinated components of the behaviour were still observed. Thus, the hypothalamus appeared to be the critical structure associated with the expression of emotional behaviour. On this evidence, Bard concluded that the control of rage behaviour lay in the antagonistic relationship between the cerebral cortex and hypothalamus. In short, although an intact cortex was necessary for receiving sensory stimulation and directing the emotional response properly, the coordinated pattern of emotional behaviour, including reflex movements and autonomic responses, depended on the integrity of the hypothalamus. Since Bard, it has been increasingly recognized that the hypothalamus exerts much of its influence over neural networks in the brain stem and reticular formation which has been dubbed the 'emotional brain stem' (Venkatraman et al., 2017).

KEY TERMS: *decorticated animals, sham rage, hypothalamus*

HYPOTHALAMIC STIMULATION AND AGGRESSION

Around the same time as Bard was investigating the behavioural effects of decortica-tion, Walter Hess in Switzerland was pioneering the technique of electrical stimulation of the brain with permanently implanted electrodes in freely moving animals. He was to examine the functions of several brain regions with this method and win a Nobel Prize for his work in 1949. Hess obtained some of his most important results by stimulating the hypothalamus which produced a wide range of visceral responses. Indeed, he found that stimulation of the posterior hypothalamic nuclei caused strong sympathetic activation, whilst stimulating its anterior regions resulted in parasym-pathetic activity. However, Hess's most famous experiments took place in the 1940s when he stimulated the ventral and posterior areas of a cat's hypothalamus. Providing the right intensity of current was used, electrical stimulation of these regions imme-diately turned a good-natured cat into an aggressive one – with hissing, growling, spitting, and the bristling of hair along its back. The experimenters were not immune from this aggression, for if they strayed too close, the cat would lurch at them. Con-sequently, Hess's laboratory assistants carried a towel at these moments in order to protect themselves (Wickens, 2019b). Thus, unlike the rage produced by decortica-tion, stimulation of the hypothalamus elicited an aggressive and threatening attack that was directed *towards* an object. Almost as dramatic was the effect when the stim-ulation was turned off with the cat quickly returning to its normal calm state.

These findings supported the Cannon–Bard theory of emotion. Despite its small size, the hypothalamus was clearly an important centre for control of the autonomic nervous system governing the bodily arousal associated with emotional states. It was also apparent that the hypothalamic stimulation caused certain types of species-specific emotional behaviour (fighting or fleeing) to be elicited. Viewed in terms of the Cannon–Bard model, it made sense to regard the hypothalamus as an emotional centre that received input from the thalamus and cerebral cortex, which then translated this mes-sage into the physiological response. Cannon also believed that the hypothalamus had a pathway back to the cerebral cortex, which informed the conscious part of the brain about the emotion it was experiencing.

KEY TERMS: *electrical stimulation, ventral and posterior hypothalamus*

THE COGNITIVE-AROUSAL THEORY

An alternative theory of emotion was proposed by Schachter and Singer (1962). This is called the **cognitive-arousal theory** and it argues that when we become aware of our body's physiological arousal, we seek to understand cognitively what is causing this to happen (see Figure 6.4). By doing this, we generally attribute our emotion to the prevailing environmental conditions. Evidence supporting this theory was pro-vided by a classic experiment. Schachter and Singer told subjects they intended to evaluate the effects of vitamin A injections on visual skills. However, unknown to the participants, they received either a placebo injection, or one containing **adrenaline** that caused sympathetic arousal. In addition, some subjects were given accurate details about the physiological effects of their injection, whilst others were misinformed or not given information at all. After the injection, subjects were put into a room containing a confederate (an actor employed by the experimenters) who asked the participants to complete a questionnaire. Unknown to the subjects, the confederate had been instructed to act euphorically, or in an insulting way, in this situation. For example, they either started laughing at the questions and folded the sheets into paper aeroplanes, or became annoyed and screwed the paper up into balls which were angrily thrown across the room.

When the subjects were later questioned about their experiences of the study, it was found that the group given adrenaline and misinformed about its effects reported stronger feelings of euphoria or anger than subjects correctly informed about the drug. That is, the individuals who had been made physically aroused, but unaware it was due to adrenaline, attributed their bodily state to the environmental conditions. This led to emotions that matched the 'emotion' of the confederate. In contrast, the informed and placebo groups experienced little emotional change in response to the confederate's acting.

So what does this study tell us about emotion? Firstly, it supports the idea that one basic state of physiological arousal may underlie different types of emotion (e.g. anger or happiness) as proposed by Cannon and Bard. It also shows sympathetic activity is an important source of feedback which allows the individual to interpret what is happening to them. In other words, a bodily sensation such as a rapid heartbeat may serve as a signal to trigger emotion, although it is up to the person to decide what type of emotion is being experienced. This lends some degree of support to the James–Lange theory which emphasized the vital role of visceral responses in determining emotion, but only to a degree as Schachter and Singer believe that emotion is primarily a cognitive process. In short, the key to understanding different emotions would appear to lie with cognitive interpretation of the internal body state *and* the events of the external situation. For this reason the theory is called the two-factor theory of emotion.

Supporting the two-factor theory is evidence showing that our cognitive interpretation of physical states can sometimes be 'fooled' into associating them with the wrong emotion. For example, in one study, young men were asked to walk over a 450-foot-long suspension bridge over the Capilano Canyon in British Columbia (Dutton & Aron, 1974). This experience proved scary for most subjects as the bridge had low handrails, swayed easily, and was suspended 230 feet above a ravine made up of rocks and rapids. After the crossing, each man was interviewed by an attractive female researcher. In one condition, this took place immediately after the crossing when the participants were still highly aroused by the experience. In another condition, the interview took place 10 minutes later when the subjects were calmer. After the interview, the female researcher gave each subject her telephone number and informed them they could phone later to learn more about the study. The researchers predicted that if the men found the woman attractive, they would be more likely to phone if they were physiologically aroused in her presence. And that was what occurred: 65% of men in the aroused condition phoned the interviewer compared to 30% in the 'calm' condition.

It should be noted that several criticisms have been made of Schachter and Singer's study – with the most serious being that it has been hard to replicate. The main problem seems to be that it is much more difficult to induce euphoria in subjects with the help of a confederate than it first appears (Marshall & Zimbardo, 1979). In addition, a sizeable number of subjects are seemingly insensitive to adrenalin injections.

KEY TERMS: *cognitive-arousal theory, adrenaline, two-factor theory of emotion*

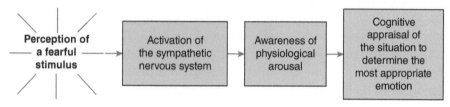

Figure 6.4   The Schachter-Singer theory of emotion
Source: Wickens (2009)

DOES THE SAME PATTERN OF AROUSAL UNDERLIE ALL EMOTIONS?

A significant feature of the Cannon–Bard theory, also supported by Schachter and Singer, is the idea that one basic state of physiological arousal underpins all emotion. However, this is not necessarily supported by other studies which show different patterns of arousal underlying various types of emotion. A classic study in this regard was undertaken by Ax (1953) who measured 14 different physiological responses with body electrodes in subjects made to feel fear and anger. Those in the fear condition, for example, received small but increasing electric shocks to their little finger. When the subjects complained about this, the experimenter expressed surprise and then pretended to check the wiring of the recording equipment before exclaiming there was a dangerous, high voltage, short-circuit! Not surprisingly this scared the participants. In contrast, those in the anger condition were told the technician undertaking the polygraph measurements had been previously sacked for incompetence, but was now re-employed. The bogus technician was then offensive to the participants during the procedure – a rouse that successfully caused them to become angry. Indeed, self-reports from the subjects after the study confirmed they had experienced the appropriate emotions. Yet the two groups not only differed in their emotions, they also differed in regard to several physiological measures; e.g. increases in pulse rate, blood pressure and face temperature were more marked in the anger group. Furthermore, those who had been made fearful produced physiological effects similar to those brought on by injections of adrenalin, whereas the effects of anger were similar to the arousal produced by both adrenalin and noradrenaline. In another study, Daniel Funkenstein (1955) reported the adrenal glands release adrenaline in response to fear, but secrete noradrenaline during anger.

The American psychologist Paul Ekman has also identified distinct patterns of autonomic activity with different emotions. In one experiment (Ekman et al., 1983) subjects were asked to make a facial expression for each of six emotions (anger, fear, sadness, happiness, surprise and disgust), or to imagine re-enacting a past emotional experience. During these conditions a number of physiological variables were recorded. The results showed a different pattern of autonomic arousal with each emotion. For example, increased heart rate was found in response to anger and fear, but a rise in body temperature only occurred with anger. In another study, by Collet et al. (1997), the same basic six emotions were induced by showing subjects a series of six emotionally loaded slides, whilst six autonomic parameters were recorded which included skin conductance (basically a measure of sweating), blood flow and temperature. Again, a different pattern of autonomic activity distinguished the emotions.

Nonetheless, this area of research is fraught with problems of interpretation. One is the difficulty of knowing whether the physiological differences are due to the nature of the emotion or its intensity (e.g. anger may produce a more severe emotion than imagined fear). There may also be considerable variation in an individual's physiological response to an emotional event. Hence, a person with mild hypertension might show a greater rise in blood pressure than, say, respiration. This makes it difficult to say with certainty whether alternate types of autonomic arousal produce different emotions, and even if autonomic activity helps differentiate some emotions, it may not differentiate *all* emotions (Stemmler, 2004).

THE FACIAL FEEDBACK HYPOTHESIS

So far we have emphasized the importance of autonomic arousal as the key physiological mediator of emotion. However, it is feasible that feedback from other parts of the body not controlled by the autonomic system, such as the skeletal muscles, may also influence the emotional experience. Indeed, one of the ways in which this has been demonstrated is in the case of facial expressions. According to Keltner and Ekman (2000) there are seven facial expressions which are innate: anger, contempt, disgust, fear, happiness, sadness and surprise. Clearly, these serve important functions by playing a role in social communication, and providing clues about the person's feelings, but they also appear to be involved in producing an emotional state. One way this has been tested is by asking subjects to perform movements of the face corresponding to a particular emotion, without informing them of what they are mimicking. To do this, subjects can be asked to follow a set of instructions such as 'pull your eyebrows down and together, raise your upper eyelids and tighten your lower eyelids, narrow your lips and press them together' (Ekman & Friesen, 1978). This facial expression, unknown to the actor, will resemble anger. Another strategy is to ask subjects to clench a pen between their teeth to mimic a smile, or hold a pen between their lips to simulate a frown.

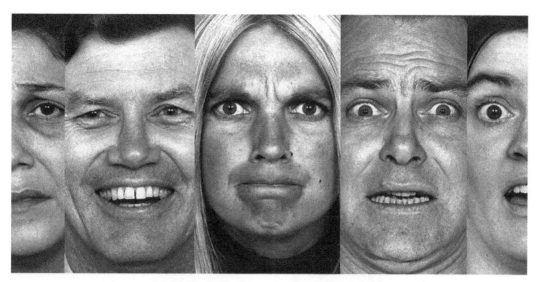

Figure 6.5   Some emotional expressions posed using Ekman's instructions
Source: Paul Ekman Group

Experiments using these types of procedure have revealed that facial feedback can influence a person's emotion. For example, when subjects were asked to judge a series of cartoons, the ones who had been biting a pen between their teeth to mimic smiling rated them as funnier compared to those who were 'frowning' (Strack et al., 1988). Alternatively, when subjects performed happy, angry or neutral movements of the face whilst watching neutral or emotionally charged slides, they reported feeling happier or angrier when making the appropriate facial expression (Rutlidge & Hupka, 1985). One would suspect that proprioceptive information from the muscles is important for producing this effect, although somewhat surprisingly forehead temperature has also been consistently found to discriminate reliably between positive and negative emotions (Adelmann & Zajonc, 1989). More recently, the technique of functional infrared thermal imaging of the face has been shown to be an accurate method by which to measure emotional autonomic responses – a technique that can distinguish emotions induced by interpersonal communication, including those involving potentially threatening or attractive events (Kosonogov et al., 2017).

These emotional responses may well be universal. For example, the elicitation of emotional experience was studied in the Minangkabau of West Sumatra who live in a social system where each person is identified with their mother's lineage, and where there is a strong proscription against public displays of negative emotion (Levenson et al., 1992). Forty-six Minangkabau men were instructed to contract their facial muscles into the prototypical configurations of five different emotions, and these were compared with subjects from the United States. The two groups were found to be similar, both in terms of autonomic activity and the reports of subjective emotional experience. Whilst much evidence suggests that physiological states cause emotion, facial feedback theory suggests that peripheral signals from the face might be a significant factor too.

Some unusual evidence supporting the facial feedback theory has come from women who have had injections of the botulinum toxin (Botox) to remove frown lines. These women are unable to frown normally due to paralysis of their corrugator muscles, and they report less negative mood, which has led to the idea that Botox treatment might be useful as a treatment for depression (Lewis & Bowler, 2009). Although one might suspect that this effect is psychological in nature, this may be oversimplifying matters, for when these women attempt to initiate angry expressions, they produce less activation of the amygdala than women who had not received the Botox treatment (Hennenlotter et al., 2009). As we shall see later, the amygdala is a key brain structure for the elicitation of emotion.

KEY TERMS: *facial feedback, proprioception*

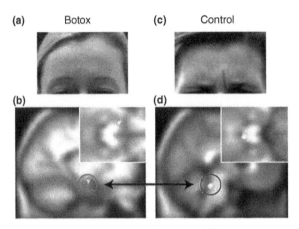

Figure 6.6   Disabling corrugator muscle reduces the amygdala's response to anger
Source: Garrett and Hough (2021); adapted from Hennenlotter et al. (2009). By permission of Oxford University Press.

INTRODUCTION TO THE LIMBIC SYSTEM

As the early work of Bard and Hess showed, the hypothalamus is a crucial collection of nuclei for the behavioural expression of emotion, but it does not act alone since the hypothalamus forms an integral part of a much larger circuit called the **limbic system** (see Figure 6.7) (Wickens, 2017d). Historically, the existence of the so-called limbic lobe (from the Latin word *limbus* meaning border) was first conceptualized by Paul Broca in 1878 who described a ring of tissue separating the cerebral cortex from the rest of the brain. This grey mass most noticeably included the **hippocampus** and cingulate gyrus. However, Broca minimized the limbic lobe's importance at the time by stressing its involvement in smell and animal instincts. Consequently, Broca did not believe the limbic lobe was particularly important for human behaviour because its 'brute force' was held in check by the cerebral cortex where intelligence and moral behaviour resided. Later, the limbic lobe was shown to be more complex than Broca had envisaged, with other nuclei and pathways including the **amygdala**, **septum** and fimbria-fornix. Partly for this reason, the limbic lobe was rechristened the limbic system in 1949 by Paul MacLean, who also referred to it as the *visceral brain* – a description which now associates this brain area with deep inward feelings and emotion (Wickens, 2019b). Other brain structures closely connected with the limbic system include the anterior thalamus, medial temporal lobe, nucleus accumbens and orbitofrontal cortex (see Rajmohan & Mohandras, 2007), but pivotal within its circuitry is the hypothalamus.

MacLean had been inspired by the neurologist James Papez who began linking several limbic regions with emotional behaviour in 1937. Basing his ideas on Cannon and Bard's distinction between the behavioural expression of emotion (involving the hypothalamus) and the subjective 'feeling' of emotion (requiring the cerebral cortex), Papez emphasized the importance of a circuit for this model that linked several brain regions. Beginning in the hypothalamus where the bodily reactions of emotion were

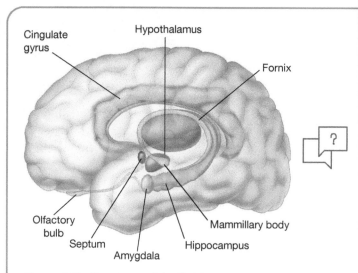

Figure 6.7   Structures of the limbic system
Source: Carolina Hrejsa/Body Scientific Intl. in Gaskin (2021)

made manifest, he argued that input for higher processing passed to the anterior thalamus (via the mammillary bodies) and then cingulate cortex. At this point, one route passed to the frontal cortex where the emotion was made available for cognitive processing and became conscious, and another back to the hypothalamus via the hippocampus and fornix. This latter route, now known as the Papez circuit, was believed to link the behavioural expression of emotion with a subjective feeling.

The importance of the limbic system was also emphasized by MacLean in 1952 who proposed it formed one of the three major evolutionary divisions of the brain (see Figure 6.8). Tracing brain evolution from reptiles to mammals, Maclean argued this long journey over the course of vertebrate evolution had caused the human brain to contain three functionally distinct regions, arranged in a hierarchy, that echoed its ancestral origins (this is sometimes called the triune brain). These were (a) the old reptilian brain which consisted of the brain stem responsible for vital life functions and stereotyped action, (b) the old mammalian brain comprising the limbic system involved in primitive instincts such as exploration, feeding, aggression, sexuality and emotion, and (c) the new mammalian brain, or neocortex, concerned with higher cognitive functions. MacLean also hypothesized that the limbic system and cerebral cortex reciprocally interacted, with the former responsible for what we 'feel' and the latter determining what we 'know'.

KEY TERMS: *limbic system, hippocampus, cingulate cortex, septum, fimbria-fornix, Papez circuit, the triune brain*

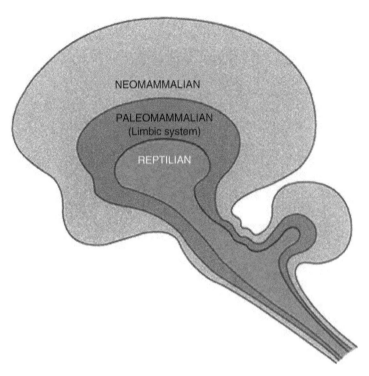

Figure 6.8   MacLean's triune (evolutionary) theory of the brain
Source: Wickens (2009); MacLean (1990)

AN INTRODUCTION TO THE AMYGDALA

Some of the best evidence for the limbic system's involvement in emotional behaviour came in the late 1930s when Heinrich Kluver and Paul Bucy discovered that bilateral removal of the temporal lobes, including the amygdala and parts of the hippocampus, dramatically reduced fear in rhesus monkeys. Normally these animals in the laboratory are highly aggressive towards their handlers. However Klüver and Bucy found they became docile and exhibited no fear or rage following lesioning, and also showed other bizarre behaviours. They frequently masturbated or made indiscriminate attempts to mate with other male and female monkeys, and were obsessed with touching things and seemingly unable to recognize objects unless they placed them in their mouths (Klüver & Bucy, 1938). This constellation of symptoms became known as Klüver-Bucy syndrome.

In their initial experiments, Klüver and Bucy's lesions had destroyed large areas of the temporal lobes, but to identify the brain areas responsible for the taming effect, they set about making smaller and more selective lesions. Their research soon showed that a nut-shaped mass of grey matter called the amygdala (from the Greek word for almond) was the crucial structure for the reduction of aggression. They concluded that the amygdala, therefore, acted as a brain centre for producing fear.

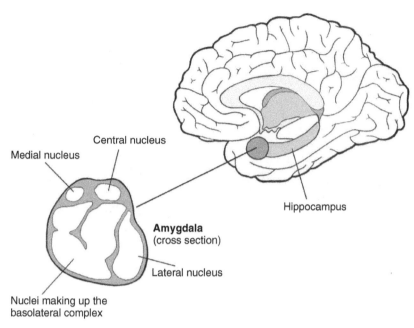

Figure 6.9 The amygdala

Source: Wenzel (2017); image drawn by, and reproduced with permission from Charlotte Caswell

The amygdala is comprised of a group of nuclei located in the frontal part of the temporal lobes anterior to the hippocampus. Although containing over a dozen nuclei, it can be divided into three main cell groupings. (1) The basolateral group are the amygdala's 'deep' nuclei that form reciprocal connections with the parietal, cingulate, insular and prefrontal cortex. This complex also contains the lateral nucleus which receives fibres from cortical areas specifically involved in vision, audition, touch and pain. Lying inwards from the basolateral region are (2) the centromedial nuclei which obtain input from older parts of the brain including the olfactory bulb, upper brain stem and hypothalamus. In turn, the centromedial nuclei feed into the striaterminalis – a compact fibre bundle that runs into the bed nucleus of the stria terminalis. From here there is an outflow of projections to the ventral hypothalamus, septum and brain stem. Interestingly, the stria terminalis is sexually dimorphic, being twice as large in males than in females. The third amygdala region (3) is the central nucleus. Deriving its input largely from the basolateral and centromedial groups, it forms the amygdalofugal pathway projecting to the preoptic and lateral hypothalamus as well as several brainstem nuclei. Some of its axons even reach the cervical spinal cord (Wickens, 2017b).

In most instances, removal of the amygdala reduces fear. Apparently, rats with bilateral amygdala lesions are so fearless that they will not only approach a sedated cat, but climb over its back and head. Garrett (2015) even reports that one rat even nibbled on the sedated cat's ear which provoked an attack – following which, the rat climbed straight back! However, it is also the case that amygdala lesions do not always lessen aggression or emotion. For example, Bard and Mountcastle (1948) reported increased rage and emotion in cats following amygdala removal. Why lesions of the amygdala can lead to differing behavioural effects is debatable. One reason may lie with its structural complexity. Because the amygdala contains over 20 separate cell groups or nuclei, it is possible that researchers have produced different patterns of damage. Indeed, slight variations in the size and location of lesions are

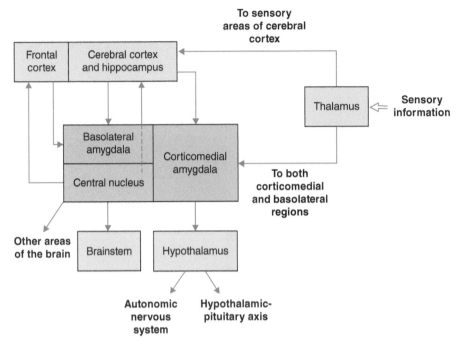

Figure 6.10   The main anatomical connections of the amygdala
Source: Wickens (2009)

likely to produce discrepant results – especially as the amygdala has both excitatory and inhibitory effects on aggression and these regions lie in close proximity together. Another reason may lie with the experience of the animal. For example, Rosvold et al. (1954) lesioned the amygdala in the most dominant and aggressive monkey of a group of eight, and found that this animal quickly dropped to the bottom of its social dominance hierarchy, but when a similar lesion was made in the third most dominant monkey, there was no decline in aggressive behaviour or status. A possible explanation is that the effects of amygdala lesions are dependent upon the monkey's experience. In other words, the aggressive monkey may have learned to become successful at fighting, and its lesion disrupted the neural basis of this behaviour more than it did in its less dominant rival. Thus, the animal's previous learning may have a bearing on how the amygdala lesion manifests itself.

KEY TERMS: *Klüver-Bucy syndrome, amygdala, basolateral and centromedial nuclei, central nucleus, stria terminalis, amygdalofugal pathways*

SPECIAL INTEREST 6.1

THE STIMULATION OF THE AMYGDALA IN HUMANS

As we saw in Chapter 3, Penfield pioneered the technique of electrically stimulating the brain in conscious humans as a prelude to the surgical treatment of seizures. One site which he came to recognize as being involved in temporal lobe epilepsy (sometimes called a complex partial seizure) is the amygdala. Although this type of epilepsy does not normally lead to a grand mal seizure with its characteristic full loss of consciousness and violent muscle contractions, it nonetheless causes a semi-unconscious state or 'absence' which can be accompanied by automated behaviours (e.g. the person repeatedly buttons their clothes, or drums their fingers on a table). In rare instances seizures lead to behavioural episodes of violence. Such seizures are also often preceded by visual and olfactory hallucinations or feelings of *deja vu*. When symptoms are particularly severe or debilitating, the amygdala can be removed as a treatment for this form of epilepsy (Kullmann, 2011).

Electrical stimulation of the amygdala in humans often elicits feelings of fear or anxiety as well as autonomic reactions indicative of fear. The response may be so intense that the person lets out a terrifying scream as if they are experiencing the most extreme terror (Gloor, 1990). There also appears to be a functional difference between the two amygdalae. For example, in one study, electrical stimulations of the right amygdala induced negative emotions, especially fear and sadness, whereas stimulation of the left amygdala induced either pleasant (happiness) or unpleasant (fear, anxiety, sadness) emotions (Lanteaume et al., 2007).

In some instances stimulation of the amygdala can cause violent behaviour. This was dramatically shown by Vernon Mark in a patient called Julia S who suffered from temporal lobe epilepsy as a teenager, which sometimes led to unprovoked and highly aggressive outbursts. When Julia reached the age of 22 years, her surgeons decided to operate by removing both amygdalae. However, there was a small twist: prior to the final operation, Mark performed a procedure whereby he stimulated one of Julia's amygdalae with implanted electrodes that were activated from a radio transmitter some distance away. Mark did not inform Julia when the stimulation was to occur (Julia and her parents had agreed to this beforehand). Although Mark stimulated several electrodes, there was only one that elicited rage, and he stimulated this site on two occasions. On the first occasion, Julia was sitting on a bed. Following stimulation, she grimaced and retracted her lips which resembled a primate threat display. Then she lurched and violently attacked the wall with her fists. On the second occasion, Julia's amygdala was stimulated when she was singing and playing a guitar. After five seconds of stimulation, she stopped, stared blankly, and was unresponsive to questioning. Then, suddenly, she violently smashed her guitar against the wall (Mark & Ervin, 1970). It appears that Julia's predisposition to violent attacks may have been a factor in her behaviour, since electrical stimulation of the amygdala does not cause aggression or even anger in most individuals (Langevin, 2012).

THE AMYGDALA AND FEAR

An animal's ability to experience fear, or sense potential danger before it strikes, is essential for survival. Not surprisingly, one effect of fear is to trigger the fight-or-flight response which biologically prepares the organism to flee from threat or defend itself against attack. Fear also causes an unpleasant feeling which in humans leads to anxiety and panic. Although these emotions may be the evolutionary key to survival in nature, they can also have negative effects in humans, especially if levels of fearfulness and anticipated fear (anxiety) become excessive and chronic. As we shall see later in the chapter, anxiety can be debilitating and give rise to serious mental health problems.

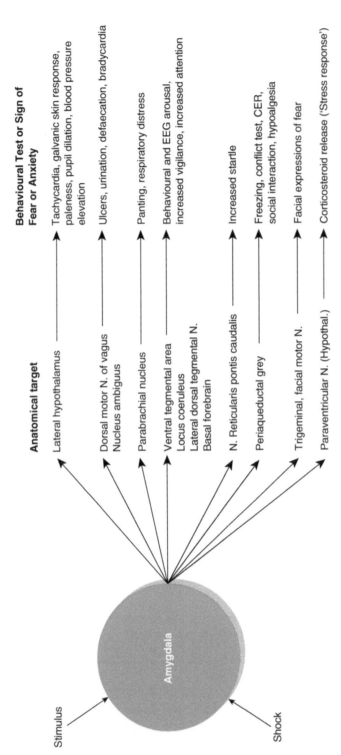

Figure 6.11 The amygdala projections to areas of the brain responsible for coordinating fear responses

Source: Higgs et al. (2020); adapted from Davis (1992)

More is probably known about the brain mechanisms underlying fear than any other emotion. This is because fear is easily recognized and elicited in other animals under experimental conditions. For example, fear can be produced through classical conditioning in which an animal, say a rat, is presented with a tone stimulus that is paired with an aversive event such as an electric shock. After a few pairings, the animal will typically begin to show fearful behaviour when the tone is sounded. Typically, the rat will freeze, startle easily, increase its heart rate and respiration, and show frantic signs of escape behaviour. When these responses are produced by the tone alone (without the shock) the pattern of behaviour is known as a conditioned emotional response (CER) – a term first introduced by Estes and Skinner (1941) although this type of methodology derives from Pavlov. Importantly, the strength of this reaction can also be quantified using physiological and behavioural measurements which have allowed the neural circuitry of fear to be understood in some detail.

Studies of the CER have revealed the amygdala plays an important role in the behavioural expression of fear. For example, Bruce Kapp and his colleagues presented rabbits with two tones, one of which was followed by electric shock (Kapp et al., 1979, 1984). Prior to conditioning, neurons in the amygdala did not respond to either of the tones, but after conditioning, there was an increased response to the tone signalling the shock. The rabbits also showed signs of fear in this situation with increased heart rate and arousal. This anticipatory response, however, was abolished by lesions to the amygdala's central nucleus. At this point, the animal no longer appeared to be afraid of the sounding of the tone that signalled the likelihood of shock.

The central nucleus is the main output pathway of the amygdala – and it projects to a wide variety of brain areas involved in the expression of CERs. For example, its projections to the periaqueductal grey area of the midbrain initiate freezing, whilst those to the pontis caudalis of the reticular formation potentiate startle (LeDoux, 1995). The central nucleus of the amygdala also importantly innervates the hypothalamus, which as we have seen above, exerts control over the autonomic nervous system, essential for producing many other behavioural manifestations of fear. Lesions of the central nucleus, therefore, abolish many behavioural components of the CER (LeDoux, 2003).

Other amygdala nuclei are involved in learning about fearful events. The basolateral amygdala, in particular, puts it in a prime position to associate a wide range of stimuli with threat and danger since it receives input from higher brain areas including the cerebral cortex (Phelps & LeDoux, 2005). Evidence linking the basolateral amygdala with fear conditioning was shown by Killcross et al. (1997). Using a procedure whereby a rat could avoid the aversive consequences of a tone by pressing a lever, they found that animals with central nucleus lesions were able to learn this escape response – unlike those with lesions of the basolateral amygdala who continued to receive the punishing electric shocks. More recent evidence shows that the basolateral amygdala interacts with the hippocampus to form long-term memories. Thus, during emotional reactions, these two brain regions interact to translate the emotion into particular outcomes (Lane & Nadel, 2002; Yang & Wang, 2017).

Emotion has a significant impact on learning and memory (Tyng et al., 2017) and this has also been supported from studies that have examined the phenomenon of long-term potentiation (this is covered more fully in Chapter 9). For example, if a pathway entering the amygdala, say from the thalamus, is stimulated with a brief burst of electrical current (which triggers thousands of nerve impulses over a few seconds), neurons in the **lateral amygdala** will show increased excitatory activity for several minutes, or even for hours afterwards. Moreover, these neurons will be more likely to fire if the stimulation is repeated again. It has been shown that a similar LTP effect can be produced in amygdala neurons by a tone signalling shock (this is also conveyed to the amygdala by a pathway from the thalamus) but not by a neutral tone (Rogen et al., 1997). Thus, it is also clear there has to be a 'fearful' or punishing association for this response to occur. These results show the lateral amygdala is involved in emotional conditioning, and helping the animal evaluate (i.e. learn) the significance of fearful associations with events in its environment (Dityatev & Bolshakov, 2005; Kim & Cho, 2017).

> **KEY TERMS:** *fear, conditioned emotional response, central nucleus, basolateral amygdala, long-term potentiation, lateral amygdala*

FEAR INVOLVES A SUBCORTICAL ROUTE

How does auditory input conveying information about a tone signalling a punishing electric shock reach the amygdala? The first stage of this journey is clear: the auditory nerves convey sound information from the ears to various areas of the brain, including the brain stem (olive nucleus, trapezoid body etc.), thalamus and then primary **auditory cortex** (see Chapter 3). In turn, it is known that the auditory cortex has connections with the amygdala (McDonald, 1998). Thus, one might expect this route is important in the acquisition of CERs. Yet things were not so simple when LeDoux et al. (1984) examined the effects of auditory cortex lesions on these types of CER task. In fact, this did not abolish the learning of a CER involving tone stimuli – but lesions to the medial geniculate nucleus (part of the thalamus) did impair such responding. A closer examination of the medial geniculate nucleus, using the neuroanatomical tracing chemical wheat germ agglutinin, showed that it too had a pathway which passed to the amygdala. Thus, auditory input does not necessarily have to be processed by the cerebral cortex before reaching the amygdala. Rather, there is an alternative subcortical route – and this is the one primarily responsible for producing conditioned emotional responses. The cortical and the thalamic routes to the amygdala have respectively been called the 'high' and 'low roads' (LeDoux, 1998).

The fact that the medial geniculate nucleus has priority over the auditory cortex in fear-linked behaviour makes a lot of sense. When faced with a dangerous situation, animals require an immediate alarm mechanism which allows them to respond as quickly as possible to the event. The thalamic input to the amygdala provides this prioritized response. It takes around 12 milliseconds for a sound stimulus to reach the amygdala via the medial geniculate nucleus, and at least twice as long via the auditory cortex. This arrangement, therefore, enables fear processing to begin in our amygdala before we are aware of what is happening. Because failing to respond to danger is, for most animals, likely to prove fatal, it is safer to react first than waste time analysing

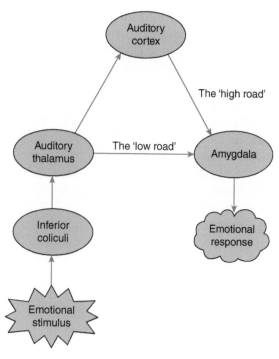

Figure 6.12   The 'low' and 'high' roads to the amygdala
Source: Wickens (2009)

the event. Thus, reflexive emotional responses are evolution's solution to danger, and the subcortical route to the amygdala allows a 'react first, think later' response to take place (LeDoux, 1998).

The cortical route to the amygdala is still important, however, since it enables us to form a more accurate cognitive understanding of the fear-provoking stimulus. Cortical analysis allows us to interpret what is happening to us and make decisions based on previous experience. The amygdala also receives input from the hippocampus that informs us about the location of dangerous environments. For example, Phillips and LeDoux (1992) found that hippocampal lesions had no effect on a rat's ability to learn a CER. That is, these rats readily became conditioned to associate a tone with punishment. But when the same animals were placed back in the apparatus where they had been conditioned, they did not seem to recognize it as the environment where the CER training had taken place. Consequently, they showed no fear. This was in contrast to the unlesioned rats who exhibited signs of nervousness.

LeDoux has also examined the output pathways from the amygdala involved in producing behavioural fearful responses. As we have seen, the lateral amygdala projects to the central nucleus which acts as a conduit for its main output. Indeed, LeDoux et al. (1988) were to show that all the components of the CER are mediated by different outputs of the amygdala's central nucleus. Thus lesioning the central pathway to the periaqueductal grey area of the midbrain interfered with the freezing response, whereas severing the pathway to the **lateral hypothalamus** abolished the increase in blood pressure; and a lesion made to the bed nucleus of the stria terminalis, which projects to the ventromedial hypothalamus, was later shown to stop the release of stress hormones involved in fear, including adrenocorticotropic hormone and corticosterone (Kim & Gorman, 2005).

The role of the amygdala in fear conditioning has also been examined in humans. In one experiment a 54-year-old woman known as SP, who had undergone an amygdalotomy for epilepsy, was shown a blue card which was always paired with a mild electric shock to the wrist that followed some ten seconds after its initial presentation (Phelps et al., 1998). Unlike normal subjects, SP did not develop an anticipatory galvanic skin response, or GSR (a measure of skin conductance caused by sweating), to the presentation of the blue square. Despite this, SP was clearly capable of producing GSRs, since she did so at the moment of receiving the shock. Afterwards, SP expressed surprise at the results, for she had quickly come to realize she would be shocked following the presentation of the blue square – which she confessed was an unpleasant experience. These results show there is a dissociation between the conscious knowledge of the events taking place, and the accompanying unconscious conditioned responses. Thus, the amygdala is necessary for the implicit or automated expression of emotional learning, but not its conscious or cognitive aspects (Gazzaniga et al., 2009).

KEY TERMS: *auditory cortex, medial geniculate nucleus, high and low roads of fear processing, periaqueductal grey area, lateral hypothalamus, galvanic skin response*

KEY THINKER 6.1

JOSEPH LEDOUX

Joseph LeDoux was born in Eunice, Louisiana. His father had been a travelling rodeo performer in his teens, before becoming a butcher. However, his son was not interested in riding horses or becoming a cowboy. Nor was he attracted by the prospect of selling meat – although as a young boy given the task of digging his fingers around in the soft flesh of a cow's brain to remove the bullet which had dispatched the animal, LeDoux contemplated what the animal's mind must have experienced in the moments before death. Taking a Major in Business Administration, LeDoux came across Psychology – where one of his courses was taught by Robert Thompson whose research interests concerned the neural basis of classical conditioning. Turning to psychology, LeDoux began his PhD in 1974 in New York under the tutelage of Michael Gazzaniga, where he started work with split-brain patients (see Chapter 10). Here, LeDoux became interested in the ways in which the dominant left hemisphere was able to deal with the unconscious 'disconnected' behaviours of the right hemisphere (as occurs, for example, when the right hemisphere is given a command to stand, and the left hemisphere – not knowing the reason, confabulates an explanation – such as having to stretch the legs). This would also be the start of his interest in emotion.

Following his PhD, LeDoux began experimenting with animals using some of the approaches learned under Thompson. More specifically, he decided to make use of the conditioned emotional responding (CER) technique in which he could reliably elicit several 'fearful' physiological reactions in rats including increased blood pressure and sudden 'freezing' of behaviour. Using this approach, LeDoux mapped out the brain's neural networks that allow a conditioned acoustic stimulus such as a tone to produce these behaviours. Using several different approaches, including neural tracing and electrical recording of single cells, one nucleus stood out as a vital component in this response – the amygdala. In fact, LeDoux would not only show that the amygdala receives fear input well before the higher cerebral cortex has time to analyse it, but would also demonstrate that all the components of the CER are mediated by different outputs of its central nucleus.

Because the amygdala is the site where information about the tones and shocks are processed, it is reasonable to propose it is the place where the neural basis of fearful learning occurs. The discovery that long-term potentiation (LTP) occurs in the amygdala provided support for this hypothesis. Moreover, LeDoux has shown that the acquisition of conditioned fear in rats is blocked by the infusion of glutamate antagonists into the amygdala, which prevents the formation of LTP. Fear conditioning has also been shown to increase the levels of calcium inside amygdala neurons through glutamate activation of NMDA receptors – a cellular change that activates various protein kinases, in turn stimulating gene expression and protein synthesis, resulting in the long-term consolidation of memory.

In recent years, LeDoux has attempted to address some of the broader theoretical issues concerning emotion – especially how the conscious feeling of fear comes about. His views on this subject are somewhat controversial. For many psychologists, emotions are produced by circuits within the limbic system, but LeDoux disagrees, contesting that much of the limbic system is not involved in emotion at all. He also believes that whilst the amygdala may contribute to the expression of behavioural fear responses, it is too simple to regard it as the brain's fear centre.

With over 30 years' research into emotion, and being the author of popular books including *The Emotional Brain*, LeDoux has been instrumental in founding the field of affective neuroscience. He has also undoubtedly done much to make the amygdala a household word. In addition, he is one of the few neuroscientists who is a lead singer and guitarist of a rock band (called *The Amygdaloids*). His song writing is also influenced by his work. On the first track of his band's album, *Heavy Mental*, LeDoux sings 'Why do we feel so afraid? Don't have to look very far. It's all in a nut – in your brain'.

PERCEIVING FEAR IN OTHERS

The human amygdala is also involved in recognizing fearful facial expressions in others. This was shown by Breiter et al. (1996) who presented subjects with pictures of fearful, happy or neutral faces. Using fMRI, the researchers found the amygdala showed increased activation in response to the fearful expressions. This effect even persists when the pictures are presented subliminally. For example, Whalen et al. (1998) undertook a study where very brief presentations of fearful and happy faces were 'masked' by neutral faces. Although most subjects reported seeing the latter, the fMRI signal intensity was significantly higher in response to the masked fearful faces than the others. These findings have been confirmed by others. In a meta-analysis of 385 PET and fMRI studies examining predictors of amygdala stimulation, a much higher probability of activation for fear (and disgust) was consistently reported than for happiness (Costafreda et al., 2008).

Brain-scanning studies have also shown the amygdala is involved in the formation of emotional memory associated with fear. In one study, Cahill et al. (1996) had subjects watch a set of twelve neutral films, or highly emotionally arousing ones such as scenes of violent crimes. Three weeks later, the experimenters asked the subjects to recall the films. The results showed that increased glucose utilization in the right amygdala during presentation was strongly correlated with recall, i.e. the films that initially caused the most amygdala activation were the ones best remembered. Evidence suggests that this type of effect critically depends on the role of the basolateral amygdala (BLA). In particular, it appears that the BLA is able to directly influence several memory systems via its glutamatergic projections to other brain regions, including the hippocampus or dorsolateral striatum, or indirectly through activation of the hypothalamic-pituitary-adrenal axis, which in turn leads to the release of adrenal stress hormones that stimulate memory structures of the brain (Goodman et al., 2017).

Further support for the amygdala's involvement in emotional memory has come from patients with Urbach-Wiethe disease. This is a rare, recessively inherited disorder (there have only been around 400 reported cases since its discovery in 1929) which causes bilateral calcification and degeneration of the amygdala and anterior-medial temporal lobes. Subjects with this condition have been shown to have difficulty remembering emotionally arousing stories, but have no problem recalling neutral ones (Adolphs et al., 1997). This deficit is specific for recognizing fear. For example, a 30-year-old woman with Urbach-Wiethe disease known as S.M. was unable to recognize fearful or angry facial expressions portrayed in pictures, but could identify the emotions of happiness and sadness (Adolphs et al., 1994). Another patient (A.P.) could not recognize vocal expressions of fear, although they were able to detect those of joy, anger and sadness (Buchanan et al., 2009).

KEY TERMS: *fearful facial expressions, emotional memory, basolateral amygdala, Urbach-Wiethe disease*

AUTISM AND THE AMYGDALA

First conceptualized by Leo Kanner in 1943, autism is a lifelong disorder which often begins to manifest itself in early childhood. Its chief characteristic is an inability to communicate and relate emotionally or feel empathy towards others. Individuals with autism often seem to be in their own self-centred world and uninterested in others (the word autism is derived from *autos* meaning 'self'). Consequently, many have difficulty engaging in the give and take of everyday interaction. This awkwardness can even sometimes be observed in the first few months of life when an autistic baby may avoid eye contact with their parents or resist attention and affection. Such behaviour is likely to continue into adulthood and affect the person's ability to form relationships. Another cardinal sign of autism is poor use of language. About half of all children with autism never develop functional speech, and those who do may use language in unusual ways – unable to combine words into sentences, or repeat the same phase over and over. In some cases their tone of voice may be 'robot-like' with little inflexion, and accompanied by impoverished facial movements and gestures. A good portrayal of this type of severely impaired person with autism is Dustin Hoffman's character in the 1988 movie *Rain Man*.

Today, most clinicians prefer to use the term autistic spectrum disorders which refers to a wider range of symptoms of varying severity, extending from people who are severely affected and cannot speak or look after themselves, to higher functioning individuals including people with Asperger's syndrome (who typically exhibit relatively normal language and intelligence). It is estimated that autistic spectrum disorders affect more than 2% of children (Kogan et al., 2018) and are four times more common in boys than girls. The cause of autism is unknown, although genetic factors are likely important as the condition is some 50 times more frequent in the siblings of affected persons than controls. In a meta-analysis of twin studies, the heritability estimate for autistic spectrum disorders was stated to be between 64% and 91%, with the impact of the environment having relatively little effect on the condition (Tick et al., 2016). Many also believe autism has its origins in foetal development. Not only is there an increased frequency of complications in pregnancy and childbirth in mothers who give birth to autistic children, but there is also evidence that foetal exposure to toxins, metabolic disorders or viral infections can lead to autism (Fletcher-Watson & Happé, 2019; Gardener et al., 2009).

Abnormalities in certain brain structures have been found in autistic individuals. Post-mortem examinations, for example, have shown that some severely autistic brains have a smaller brain stem with the near absence of the nucleus that controls facial expression and the superior olive which processes auditory input (Rodier, 2000). Others have reported that the cerebral cortex can be bigger in autistic brains – a trait that most likely reflects immature development (Piven, 1997). However, the brain region that has attracted the most attention is the amygdala. Studies have shown that children with autism (7.5–12.5 years of age) have a larger amygdala than other children, although this difference disappears by adolescence (Schumann et al., 2004). Aberrant patterns of amygdala activity have also been detected in autistic brains (Dichter, 2012). For example, in an fMRI study where subjects had to view and recognize faces, amygdala activation in adults with autism (aged from 18 to 44) remained elevated long after subjects without autism had habituated to the task (Kleinhans et al., 2009). It has also been found that the amygdala in individuals with autism has weak functional connections with the visual cortex, which is also important in the encoding of facial expressions, gaze and other emotional cues (Fishman et al., 2018). These recent studies are beginning to place the focus of interest on the amygdala's connectivity in order to provide a greater elucidation of its multiple behavioural roles.

KEY TERMS: *autism, autistic spectrum disorders, Asperger's syndrome, amygdala*

INTRODUCTION TO THE FRONTAL LOBES

A major region which is richly connected with the limbic system, including the hypothalamus and amygdala, is the frontal lobes (see Figure 6.13). These are well developed in humans and comprise almost one-half of the cerebral cortex (Damasio, 1991). It has long been known that damage to the frontal lobes can produce a bewildering variety of symptoms. We have already seen (Chapter 4) that the posterior part of the frontal lobes adjacent to the central sulcus is the site of the primary motor cortex, but as we move anteriorly (forwards) to the prefrontal cortex the functions of this brain region become more diverse. As we shall see in Chapter 10, these include the ability to plan, see the consequences of one's action, initiate action and reason abstractly. The frontal lobes are also associated with emotion, and in particular the restraint of inappropriate behaviour. Yet the functions of the frontal lobes remain enigmatic. Despite being highly evolved in humans and taking up much of the cortical mantle, individuals with prefrontal damage typically exhibit little intellectual impairment on IQ tests (Tranel et al., 2008). Moreover, their behaviour, at first sight at least, appears not to be affected in any obvious way – a situation that led some early investigators to regard the frontal lobes as functionally insignificant (Szczepanski & Knight, 2014).

Table 6.1   Some of the behavioural functions ascribed to the frontal lobes

Restraint	Initiation	Cognition
Judgement	Curiosity	Working memory
Concentration	Drive	Sequencing
Foresight	Personality	Insight
Inhibiting socially unacceptable behaviour	Mental flexibility	Seeing the consequences of one's actions
Perseverance	Motivation	Abstract thought

The anterior and greatest expanse of the frontal lobes is taken up by the prefrontal cortex (a name first proposed by Rose and Woolsey in 1948). In humans, the prefrontal cortex is divided into three main regions: (1) the dorsolateral prefrontal cortex lying on the outer surface of the frontal lobes, receiving input from the adjacent motor areas and other regions of the cerebral cortex; (2) the orbitofrontal cortex at the base of the frontal lobes, which gets its name from the orbits or bones of the eye sockets that lie just underneath it; and (3) the medial frontal cortex lying deep and centrally in the frontal lobes with its close association with the anterior cingulate cortex. Both the orbitofrontal region and the medial frontal cortex reciprocally connect with regions of the limbic system, including the cingulate cortex, hippocampus, lateral hypothalamus and amygdala. All of these connections play a critical role in the generation and regulation of emotion.

The prefrontal cortex also increases in size with evolutionary development. According to Brodmann (1912) it constitutes 29% of the total cortex in humans and 17% in chimpanzees. For dogs and cats the respective figures are 7% and 3.5%. Although the use of these comparisons has pitfalls, the increased size of the prefrontal cortex in humans is nonetheless striking. It is also interesting to note that in humans, the frontal lobe only fully develops around the late 20s, marking the cognitive maturity associated with adulthood (Giedd et al., 1999).

KEY TERMS: *frontal lobes, prefrontal cortex, dorsolateral prefrontal cortex, orbitofrontal cortex, medial frontal cortex, anterior cingulate cortex, limbic system*

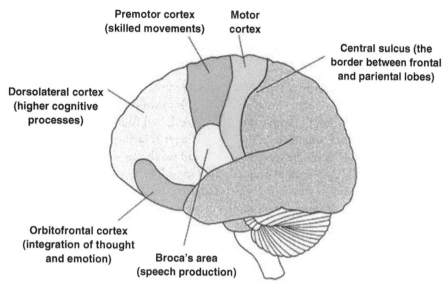

Figure 6.13 The main regions of the frontal lobes
Source: Wickens (2009)

THE REMARKABLE CASE OF PHINEAS GAGE

Phineas Gage is perhaps the most famous person to have survived brain damage, and whilst his accident happened in 1848, it remains a topic of scientific debate today. One reason for the interest in Gage is that he not only survived a massive wound to his brain which attracted public and medical interest at the time, but it also dramatically affected his emotions, personality and intellect. Prior to the mid-1800s, higher psychological function was widely believed to be relatively unaffected by brain damage. However, as Gage's story shows, even the most unique human traits are dependent on the brain. His case was also one of the first to spark an interest in the frontal lobes (Macmillan, 1996).

Gage was a foreman of a railway construction gang employed in New England. Their main task was to flatten the ground enabling new rail tracks to be laid. This necessitated rock to be removed from the path with dynamite. Although a straightforward task, it was dangerous since a hole had to be bored into the rock to be filled with explosives. A fuse was then inserted into the dynamite with sand poured on top to protect the mixture. Gage's job was to tamp down the sand using a large rod. On the morning of September 13th, 1848, Gage accidentally dropped his tampering iron onto the rock before the sand had been laid, creating a spark which ignited the blasting powder. This sent the tampering iron through his left cheek bone and out the top of his head. The force of the explosion caused the iron rod (which was 3 feet 7 inches long, 1¼ inches in diameter, and weighed over 13 pounds) to land some 30 metres behind him.

Gage was thrown to the ground and lost consciousness, but was alert and rational a few minutes later. He was taken on a cart to a nearby hotel and soon able to walk without assistance. One of the town's physicians, John Harlow, was summoned, and found Gage sitting upright and answering questions about his accident (see Harlow, 1848). Although 'the pulsations of the brain' could be seen through a wound that looked like an 'inverted funnel', he seemed unaffected by the trauma. The immediate danger to Gage was infection which required the wound to be cleaned and drained on a regular basis. Within a few months the wound had healed and he returned home.

However, Gage was never re-employed again by the railroad company. Although he had regained his physical strength, and suffered no obvious motor, speech or memory impairment, his personality was undergoing a dramatic change. Prior to the accident, Gage had been regarded as a responsible, hard-working and conscientious individual, who his bosses had described as the most efficient and capable person in their employ. Following the accident, Gage became childish, selfish, impatient and disrespectful. He was frequently rude to others and inclined to become angry or over-react. Previously energetic and polite, he was now erratic and unpredictable. Gage also had trouble forming and executing plans, yet was emotionally unconcerned about the consequences of his actions. As John Harlow put it: 'The equilibrium or balance, so to speak, between his intellectual faculties and animal propensities, seems to have been destroyed.'

Following Gage's accident, he managed to hold down a number of short-term jobs, including being exhibited as a freak in Barnum's American Museum in New York. In 1860, some 12 years after his accident, Gage began to suffer from epileptic seizures. He died at the age of 38. Although no autopsy was performed on the brain, his body was exhumed in 1867 and the skull sent to Dr John Harlow. He estimated that the tampering iron had passed through the left anterior part of the frontal lobes including the orbitofrontal cortex (see Figure 6.14). The skull was preserved in a museum at Harvard Medical School, where it is still on show, and re-examined using the technique of magnetic resonance imaging in the 1990s (Damasio et al., 1994). This analysis showed that the rod had severely damaged the frontal lobes of both hemispheres, with the lesion being especially marked in the left orbitofrontal cortex.

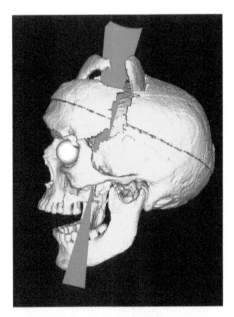

Figure 6.14   Reconstruction of the damage to Phineas Gage's brain

Source: Van Horn, J. D., Irimia, A., Torgerson, C. M., Chambers, M. C., Kikinis, R., & Toga, A. W. (2012). Mapping connectivity damage in the case of Phineas Gage. *PLoS ONE*, 7(5): e37454. https://doi.org/10.1371/journal.pone.0037454

EGAS MONIZ AND THE DEVELOPMENT OF PSYCHOSURGERY

Harlow's account of Gage's accident remained largely forgotten until the Scotsman David Ferrier reintroduced it, along with his own work on the frontal lobes, in his Goulstonian Lectures of 1878 (Wickens, 2015). But in the wake of this talk, it also became apparent that many cases of frontal lobe injury did not lead to obvious behavioural and personality changes. Such inconsistent effects led to much uncertainty regarding the role of the frontal cortex in human behaviour, with some even claiming the prefrontal cortex was cognitively 'silent' and not essential for normal functioning. However, this viewpoint changed in 1935 when John Fulton and Carlyle Jacobsen transformed a volatile and highly aggressive chimpanzee called Becky into a tamed docile animal after a bilateral frontal lobe lesion. This finding was to have far-reaching consequences. On hearing about this work, the Portuguese neurologist Egas Moniz realized similar lesions could be used to treat emotionally disturbed patients. Within three months, Moniz had persuaded neurosurgeon Almeider Lima to perform a frontal lobotomy on a female patient suffering from severe depression and paranoia. The operation involved holes being drilled into the skull, with pure alcohol injected into the white matter of the prefrontal area to destroy the pathway with the thalamus (the main subcortical relay to the frontal lobes). According to Moniz, the operation was a great success and a 'clinical cure'.

Moniz refined his surgical technique by designing a 'leucotome' which was an instrument with a retractable steel wire loop. After inserting it into the brain, the steel loop was opened and then twisted to cut out cores of tissue. In 1936, Moniz reported the results of this procedure with his first group of patients, stating it had produced full recovery in seven patients and a favourable outcome in seven more. The remaining six patients showed little improvement. A year later, Moniz gave an account of several more patients he had treated using a technique where he cut six cores of white matter from each hemisphere. Again, he reported favourable results. His outcomes with mentally ill and emotionally disturbed patients deemed incurable were so remarkable that many other physicians began to adopt his psychosurgery.

After this work, Moniz supervised only a small number of lobotomies. Nonetheless, the treatment seemed to improve life for patients who had previously suffered from intractable psychiatric illness. In 1949, Moniz was awarded the Nobel Prize in Physiology or Medicine (the first Portuguese to win such an award). However, tragedy would soon strike, when in the same year, at the age of 76, Moniz was shot four times by one of his paranoid patients which left him a paraplegic. Despite the accolades, it has since become clear that Moniz was less than thorough in his evaluation of patients, and provided little verifiable evidence regarding their improvement. Other doctors that examined his patients described the improvements as slight, and one even called the procedure 'pure cerebral mythology' (Valenstein, 1986).

KEY TERM: *frontal lobotomy*

THE RISE AND FALL OF PSYCHOSURGERY

In 1936, within a year of Moniz's first operation, the first lobotomy was performed in the United States by psychiatrist Walter Freeman and neurosurgeon James Watts. Because the procedure was primarily used to treat mental symptoms it became widely known as psychosurgery. Their first patient was suffering from agitated depression, and after six 'cores' of the prefrontal cortex were removed, they became more relaxed and no longer fearful and anxious. Encouraged by their success, Freeman and Watts operated on more patients. Freeman also pioneered new psychosurgical techniques, and in 1938 introduced a procedure where holes were drilled into the side of the skull, allowing the insertion of a thin knife. The fibres between the frontal cortex and thalamus were then cut by sweeping the instrument up and down. In 1948 Freeman went on to invent a more controversial method. This was the transorbital lobotomy which involved a leucotome being placed beneath the upper eyelid and driven through the lower cranium with a mallet (a procedure that became known as 'ice pick' surgery). Because this method cut fewer fibres than the standard lobotomy, it was believed to produce less side effects. Due to its simplicity, the transorbital lobotomy was performed on some 50,000 patients in the USA during the 1940s and 1950s (Culliton, 1976). In some cases it was even administered in a physician's office. Freeman undertook or supervised more than 3,500 of these operations before he retired in 1970.

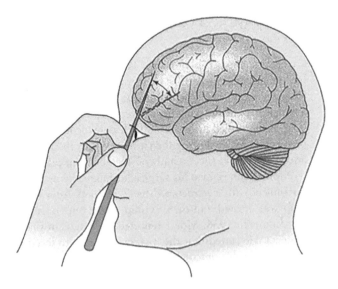

Figure 6.15   Ice pick surgery

Source: Wickens (2009), adapted from W. Freeman (1949) *Proceedings of the Royal Society of Medicine*, 42 (suppl.), 8–12

The ethical justification of psychosurgery along with its safety has always been a matter of controversy. Indeed, criticism and public debate prompted the formation of national commissions to evaluate the effectiveness of psychosurgical procedures and encourage legislation. Despite this, the outcomes were often reported as favourable. For example, a survey in England and Wales from 1942 to 1954 showed that 10,365 patients had undergone some form of psychosurgery, with a follow-up study examining 9,284 of these patients revealing that 41% had greatly improved, while 28% were minimally improved. Only 2% had become worse with 4% mortality. Severely depressed patients had the best outcome with 63% showing benefits compared to 30% with schizophrenia (Tooth & Newton, 1961). Today, about a third of patients show significant improvement after the operation (Mashour et al., 2005).

Nonetheless, it was also becoming clear by the 1960s that psychosurgical operations were having adverse effects on patients that often went unreported. In particular, patients were frequently listless, apathetic and lacking spontaneity. Emotions tended to be dampened, which led to patients having no social inhibitions or concern for others. It also became clear that patients had difficulty solving problems, following instructions and making plans. Consequently, many psychiatrists questioned whether the risks or drawbacks of surgery were worthwhile. Fortunately, by the early 1960s, the use of effective antidepressants and major tranquilizers greatly reduced the need for psychosurgery, and more recently the use of deep brain stimulation has also lessened the need. Some countries have banned psychosurgery altogether, whilst in the UK only two centres (University of Wales Hospital in Cardiff, and Ninewells Hospital in Dundee) perform psychosurgical procedures – largely for depression, obsessive compulsive disorder and anxiety. Even so, fewer than 100 such operations are generally carried out each year.

KEY TERMS: *psychosurgery, transorbital lobotomy*

THE ROLE OF THE ORBITOFRONTAL CORTEX IN EMOTION

The region of the frontal lobes most implicated in emotional behaviour, as we have seen, is the orbitofrontal cortex (see Figure 6.16). This area, sometimes called the ventromedial prefrontal cortex, lies above the orbits of the eyes, and is the part of the frontal lobes which receives input from the mediodorsal thalamus. As might be expected, it is highly interconnected with limbic structures including most conspicuously the amygdala, although other areas include the hypothalamus and parts of the medial temporal lobe including the entorhinal cortex and hippocampus. Another close association is formed with the cingulate gyrus (a curved fold of cortical tissue lying above the corpus callosum). The orbitofrontal cortex also projects to the periaqueductal grey and ventral tegmentum of the midbrain, and brainstem nuclei that control autonomic functions (Hurley et al., 1991). Whilst it is often said that the orbitofrontal cortex is among the least understood regions of the human brain, it is nonetheless clearly important in emotional decision making and assessing the importance of reward or punishment (Barbas, 2007; Kringelbach, 2005). It also plays a key role in formulating goals for action (Rolls & Grabenhorst, 2008).

A modern day informative case study of a person with extensive bilateral damage of the orbitofrontal cortex, caused by surgery to remove a tumour, has been provided by Eslinger and Damasio (1985). At the time of the operation, the subject was

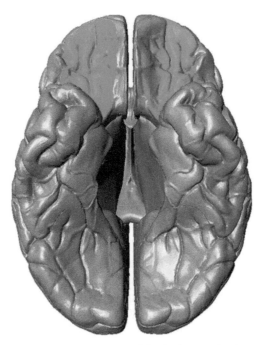

Figure 6.16   The orbitofrontal cortex (shown in red) in the human brain
Source: Was a bee/Wikimedia Commons

35-year-old man (known as EVR) who was married with two children and employed as a financial officer. In the months after the operation, EVR lost his job, went bankrupt and was divorced by his wife. He married a prostitute but was divorced again within two years. Eslinger and Damasio tested EVR during this period on a number of psychological measures. EVR had a high IQ of 125, and showed above-normal comprehension of complex social and political issues. He was also capable of sound social judgement when given hypothetical 'moral dilemma' tests that required him to make a decision about whether a certain behaviour in a given imagined situation was right or wrong. He provided sensible answers to these types of problem which he justified with sound logic.

However, EVR's personal behaviour did not follow the same rules when he was confronted with real-life problems. For example, he had great difficulty in making the simplest of decisions, including which toothpaste to buy, food to eat or clothes to wear. Previously regarded as respectable and likable, EVR was now described by his friends as irresponsible, disorganized, obsessive and lazy. Despite this, EVR showed little concern about such criticism. The lack of emotional reactivity was also shown experimentally when EVR failed to exhibit the normal increased autonomic skin conductance in response to arousing visual images. His skin conductance remained 'flat' when he was shown pictures of a horribly mutilated car accident victim, whereas subjects without bilateral damage showed increased arousal and emotional distress. At the end of the testing session, EVR admitted that he had not experienced the kind of feeling he thought he should have (Neafsey, 1993).

These results help show how orbitofrontal cortex damage causes the individual to be emotionally flat and apathetic. In fact, Antonio Damasio has termed EVR's deficit acquired sociopathy since it resembled the behaviour of a psychopath, i.e. an individual who is intelligent, but has poor self-control, no sense of remorse, and responds inappropriately in many social situations. Psychopaths also show impaired skin conductance responses which reveal a lack of anxiety (Damasio et al., 1990a). To account for this behaviour, Damasio has proposed a theory which implicates the orbitofrontal cortex in learning about punishing or aversive events that can occur in social situations (Damasio, 2000). When the orbitofrontal cortex is damaged, it is unable to provide an emotional warning signal for behaviours that most of us are likely to recognize as having adverse consequences (e.g. the desire to tell your boss he is an idiot). The emergence of enduring antisocial personality changes in individuals who experience such damage has since been shown to be most marked in those with bilateral or predominantly right-sided damage to the orbitofrontal cortex and its connected regions (de Oliveira-Souza et al., 2019).

Damasio's theory of acquired sociopathy was supported by a study of risk taking in patients with frontal lobe damage by Bechara et al. (1997), who administered a task where participants had to choose cards from one of four packs. Turning over 'reward' cards in two of the decks led to a gift of $100, whereas the other decks only had a reward value of $50. However, in the high-reward conditions there was also a greater penalty if certain punishment cards were picked (a loss of $1250) compared with the low-reward deck (less than $100). Subjects with frontal lobe damage preferred picking cards from the high-reward packs despite the harsh penalties. Damasio has likened these subjects to children who can't resist pinching a sweet even when they know it will lead to punishment. Interestingly, by the 50th card, subjects without damage were showing an anticipatory skin conductance response when having a 'hunch' associated with a 'risky' pack, but this was absent in those with orbitofrontal damage. Thus, subjects without frontal lobe damage often have 'feelings' about what is right or wrong that help guide their behaviour – an instinct lacking in individuals with damage. This behaviour is not unlike that shown by EVR who could rationally decide whether something was right or wrong when given a hypothetical problem, but not implement this knowledge in real life.

KEY TERMS: *orbitofrontal cortex, mediodorsal thalamus, amygdala, hypothalamus, hippocampus, cingulate gyrus, acquired sociopathy*

AN INTRODUCTION TO ANXIETY AND STRESS

Fear and anxiety are closely related. Anxiety produces a feeling of uneasiness and worry which is distinct from fear by the lack of an immediate external threat, i.e. anxiety comes from within us, and fear from the outside (LeDoux, 1998). Thus the sight of a snake in long grass may elicit fear, but anticipation that a snake may be hiding in the grass causes anxiety. Because anxiety is essentially fearful anticipation, it can often occur in situations that are not inherently dangerous, causing an emotional over-reaction to a potential risk. Indeed, as the American psychologist David Barlow has noted, anxiety is essentially 'a future-oriented mood state in which one is not ready or prepared to attempt to cope with upcoming negative events' (Barlow, 2000). Despite this, anxiety is an important necessity of life – acting as a brake against antisocial, careless or misguided behaviour by increasing apprehension and caution. Both anxiety and fear share a similar biological basis with increased activation of the sympathetic nervous system. The physiological arousal produced by fear, however, is more intense (i.e. the body is prepared for a fight-or-flight situation), whereas anxiety produces less arousal, but a response that is normally more prolonged. Nonetheless, severe anxiety can be severely debilitating to an individual who is unable to cope with a situation that causes persistent worry, dread and even terror.

A closely related phenomenon to anxiety is stress. Although difficult to define, most people view stress as similar to anxiety, which again arises from the individual's perception of danger and threat. A straightforward definition was provided by one of the great pioneers of stress research, Hans Selye, who explained it as: 'the rate of all the wear and tear caused by life.' Yet whichever way one looks at it, stress is a condition that places unpleasant demands on the individual and causes a state of physical and mental disequilibrium. Despite this, the impact of stress depends very much upon the individual. For some people, the daily routines of daily life can be stressful, whereas for others, the most dangerous of activities may not be enough to satisfy them. But regardless of personal limits, there is little doubt that stress can have a significant bearing on our mental wellbeing and health.

It has been known since the pioneering work of Hans Selye in the 1940s and 1950s that prolonged stress has a predictable effect on the organism (see Jackson, 2014). Selye performed hundreds of experiments, mainly with rats, examining the impact of various long-term stresses on the organ systems of the body. No matter what type of stressor he used, Selye observed a consistent physiological reaction which he called the general adaptation syndrome. This consists of three stages. When the animal is first exposed to the stressor the initial response is an alarm reaction, which is essentially the fight-or-flight response produced by the sympathetic nervous system. This primes or mobilizes the body's resources to cope with a threatening situation. It is also accompanied by increased secretion of adrenaline and noradrenaline from the adrenal medulla. However, this is only a short-term response. If the stressor is prolonged, the animal will enter the resistance stage. Because it cannot maintain the high level of physiological arousal produced by the alarm reaction, it will now modify its metabolism to produce a new homeostatic balance. One consequence is that the hypothalamus will begin stimulating the release of adrenocorticotropic hormone (ACTH) from the anterior pituitary gland – which enters the circulation where it will cause the secretion of glucocorticoid hormones from the adrenal cortex (see Figure 6.17). There are several glucocorticoids, including hydrocortisone, corticosterone and cortisol which exert various metabolic effects on the body. But in general, they act to increase the tone of the sympathetic nervous system, whilst converting fats and proteins into sugars to help the increased energy needs of the body. The glucocorticoid hormones also reduce the 'non-essential' functioning of the body's systems. Most noticeably, this includes the immune system which slows down antibody formation and decreases white blood cell formation.

If the stressor is prolonged or frequently repeated, the organism will be unable to maintain this increased level of energy expenditure, and its physiological resources

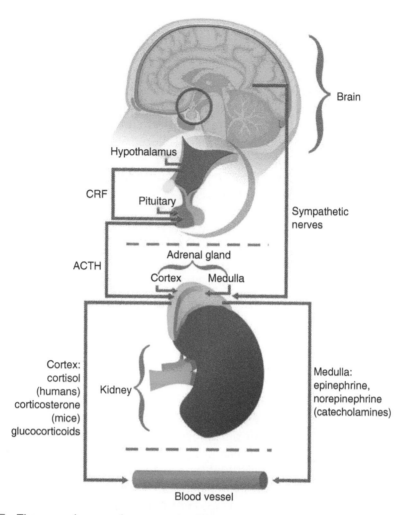

Figure 6.17   The neuro-hormonal response to stress

Source: Campos-Rodríguez, R., Godínez-Victoria, M., Abarca-Rojano, E., Pacheco-Yépez, J., Reyna-Garfias, H., Barbosa-Cabrera, R. E., & Drago-Serrano, M. E. (2013). Stress modulates intestinal secretory immunoglobulin A. *Front. Integr. Neurosci.*, 7, 86. doi: 10.3389/fnint.2013.00086

will slowly but surely become depleted. At this point, the body is unable to maintain its normal everyday function and the organism will enter the *exhaustion stage*. This will not only lead to the body's immune system becoming seriously weakened, but cause other bodily functions to become impaired, along with reduced strength and energy. One consequence of this decline is an increased susceptibility to illnesses such as stomach ulcers, cardiovascular disease and depression. Any additional stressors which the organism would have previously coped with may now result in serious ill health, despondency and even death.

KEY TERMS: *stress, general adaptation syndrome, adrenal medulla, adrenocorticotropic hormone, glucocorticoid hormones, adrenal cortex*

ANXIETY DISORDERS

A certain amount of **anxiety** is a necessary part of everyday life. Anxiety stops us being rude to the boss, speeding on motorways and lying in bed all day. It is also a powerful reason for making students go to lectures and study for their exams. Unfortunately, for some, anxiety can become so intense or misplaced that it loses its adaptive value and instead causes mental problems and ill health. In clinical practice, anxiety disorders are common with around 33% of the population likely to suffer from an anxiety disorder at some point in their lives (Bandelow & Michaelis, 2015). Not only are such disorders associated with immense health care costs and a high burden of disease, but they are also highly comorbid with other anxiety disorders and other mental disorders such as depression.

Anxiety disorders can take many forms. One highly persistent and debilitating illness is generalized anxiety disorder in which the patient has unfocused worry and anxiety that is not connected to recent stressful events, although it can be aggravated by certain situations. This condition has a lifetime prevalence of about 5% and a probable 12-month prevalence of between 1–2% (Tyrer & Baldwin, 2006). Like most other anxiety disorders it is twice as common in females as it is in males.

The most common type of anxiety disorder, however, is generally regarded to be that of simple phobias, which affects some 15% of the population (Eaton et al., 2018). These are called 'simple' not to minimize their importance, but because they involve a clearly defined dreaded object (e.g. snakes or spiders) or situation (e.g. heights). An equally if not more debilitating type of fear occurs in social phobia where the person is highly anxious about engaging in social interaction. This occurs in males and females equally and may have a prevalence as high as 3%. A related condition is panic disorder whose symptoms include attacks of intense terror that are accompanied by choking, palpitations and shortness of breath. These symptoms can be so extreme that the person thinks they are going to die, and in some cases extend to a fear of public places or agoraphobia. The incidence of panic disorder is around 1%.

KEY TERMS: *anxiety, generalized anxiety disorder, simple phobias, panic disorder, agoraphobia*

OBSESSIVE COMPULSIVE DISORDER

Another often chronic and potentially disabling condition is obsessive compulsive disorder (OCD), characterized by the intrusion of powerful obsessive thoughts that lead to patterns of ritualistic and compulsive behaviour. The most common type of compulsion is a fear of germs and hand washing, which is typically accompanied by obsessive thoughts about dirt and contamination. Individuals with this type of OCD may wash their hands hundreds of times each day, resulting in raw and blistered skin, and be fearful of touching the most common everyday objects. A compulsion to check lights, doors, locks or electric switches for hours before leaving the house is another frequent type of OCD. In some cases this can give rise to odd rituals. For example, Rapoport (1989) reports the case of a person who had to take 74 steps in a specific zigzag pattern before they could enter their front door. And there are others who roll about on the grass and touch various trees before entering their house. Although this behaviour can be embarrassing for the individual, the obsessive thoughts are so powerful that they are compelled to perform them at whatever cost. OCD is classified as an anxiety disorder because of the anxiety that is felt if the intrusive thoughts are not acted upon. The disorder is also surprisingly common. It is estimated that more than 2% of the population will suffer from OCD, making it more common than schizophrenia, manic depression or panic disorder (Ruscio et al., 2010; Stein et al., 2019).

Clinical trials in recent years have shown that drugs that affect the neurotransmitter **serotonin** (5-HT) can significantly improve the symptoms of OCD. The first of these drugs to be discovered (in the early 1980s) was the 5-HT uptake blocker, clomipramine. This was followed by drugs with a similar action including fluoxetine (Prozac) and fluvoxamine. Large-scale studies have shown that about 50% of patients enjoy a beneficial response to these drugs (Kellner, 2010). The discovery of clomipramine was also important since it indicated that OCD could be due to 5-HT dysfunction. However, the nature of this abnormality remains unclear. Although some people with OCD have higher levels of the 5-HT metabolite 5-HIAA in their CSF, indicating overactivity of 5-HT in the brain, this is not always found. The fact that drug treatment often requires several weeks to become effective suggests that changes in the sensitivity of certain 5-HT receptors may be a more important causal factor (van Dijk et al., 2008).

There is evidence that the anatomical basis of the disorder involves the **basal ganglia** and frontal cortex. More specifically, this involves pathways from frontal regions which project to the striatum and then travel back through direct and indirect routes via the thalamus to the frontal regions. This circuitry has been corroborated by brain-scanning studies which show that resting blood flow and glucose metabolism are abnormally increased in the frontal orbital cortex and caudate nucleus of individuals with OCD (van der Straten et al., 2017). It is further increased when OCD patients are exposed to phobic stimulation such as skin contact with dirty objects (Baxter, 1995). As we saw in the previous chapter, the striatum has long been implicated in movement, and the frontal cortex in emotion and planning. Thus the involvement, and dysfunction, of these two brain regions in OCD make a great deal of sense – especially as they both receive 5-HT innervation from the raphe nuclei. More recently, other brain regions have been implicated in OCD including the cingulate cortex and anterior temporal cortex including the amygdala (Milad & Rauch, 2012; Moreira, Marques, et al., 2017).

KEY TERMS: *obsessive compulsive disorder, serotonin, clomipramine, 5-HIAA, basal ganglia, frontal cortex*

ANXIOLYTIC DRUGS

Human beings have frequently turned to chemical substances to help them cope with the stresses of life, and there has always been a need for effective sedatives and hypnotics to aid relaxation and sleep. In centuries past, alcohol, opium and bromides were some of the substances that served this purpose, and in the early twentieth century these agents were replaced by barbiturates. Despite their benefits as sedatives and anti-epileptic agents, these barbiturates were potentially dangerous as they could easily produce fatal overdoses, especially when taken with alcohol. Two famous stars who committed suicide with these drugs were Judy Garland and Marilyn Monroe. In the late 1950s and early 1960s, however, a new class of drug was developed by Roche Pharmaceuticals that was safer than the barbiturates. They were also dubbed as true anxiolytics. These were called **benzodiazepines** (BZPs) and they included chlordiazepoxide (Librium) first marketed in 1960, and diazepam (Valium) which appeared in 1962.

These drugs had notable advantages over the barbiturates – especially in the treatment of anxiety. Lethal overdosing was uncommon, and once the user had become tolerant to their initial sedative action they produced few side effects. In the early days of their use, it was also claimed that they did not produce addiction or withdrawal symptoms, although this was later found to be untrue. In fact, these drugs are now recognized as highly addictive and are only prescribed with great caution by doctors (Brett & Murnion, 2015; Schmitz, 2016). But perhaps the most fascinating characteristic of these drugs for psychopharmacologists was their apparent specific targeting of reducing anxiety symptoms. In most instances, after taking benzodiazepine medication, the patient's fears, restlessness and somatic symptoms of anxiety faded and often disappeared. They were seemingly 'true anxiolytics', and within a decade after their introduction had become the most prescribed drug in the world. The extent of their popularity can be seen by annual prescription figures for the UK, which rose from 3 million in the early 1960s, to reach 18 million prescriptions in 1972, to over 30 million by 1979 (Beaumont, 1991). At the height of their use in the late 1970s, it was estimated that one in five women and one in ten men were regularly taking these drugs.

During the 1970s, doctors began to realize that benzodiazepines were not as safe as they first appeared, with a large number of people unable to stop their use. Long-term users of these drugs often experienced physical withdrawal symptoms such as fear, insomnia and muscle tremor when trying to stop their use. Psychological dependence where the person felt unable to cope with the pressures of life without the regular use of these drugs was a further problem. Consequently, there has been a significant curtailing in the prescribing of these agents and a sharp decline in their use. Despite this, there is still a surprisingly high amount of benzodiazepine use in the UK and across the world. For example, Davies et al. (2017) have estimated that the mean percentage of registered patients prescribed benzodiazepines in England is around 0.69%, which yields a total of 296,929 people who have used the drug long term. In other words, more than a quarter of a million people in England are taking highly dependency-forming hypnotic medications far beyond their recommended periods of usage.

Benzodiazepines have also been shown to reduce the symptoms of anxiety in animals. This can be demonstrated by use of a **conflict test** (Bourin, 2015). In this situation, a rat is trained to press a lever in an operant box for a food reward. Following training, the animal is put back into the box and an intermittent tone is introduced. If the lever is pressed during its presentation, the dispension of food will be accompanied by a mild electric shock. Normal rats soon show signs of 'nervousness' during the tone presentation and stop pressing the lever. However, if animals are injected with a benzodiazepine, they continue for longer to press the lever for a food reward. Since benzodiazepines neither increase hunger nor suppress pain, it appears they are acting on the conflict itself, i.e. they make the animal less 'anxious' about being punished.

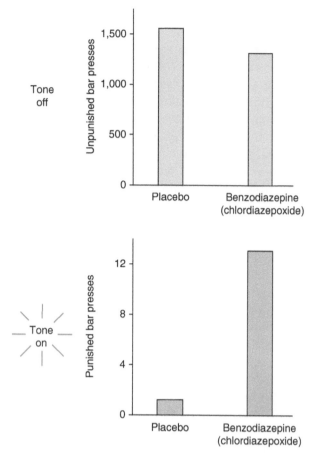

Figure 6.18   The effects that benzodiazepines have on punished responding (as recorded by the number of bar presses) in a conflict test

Source: Wickens (2009)

Similar results are obtained with barbiturates and alcohol – except these drugs cause sedation, with a depression of responding in both unpunished (tone-off) and punished (tone-on) conditions. This doesn't occur with benzodiazepines (except at very high doses), indicating that they exert a genuine anxiolytic effect (Cryan & Sweeney, 2011).

KEY TERMS: *barbiturates, anxiolytics, benzodiazepines, chlordiazepoxide, diazepam, conflict test*

THE NEUROCHEMICAL BASIS OF ANXIETY

The discovery of benzodiazepines led to attempts to understand how they worked on the brain. It soon become apparent that they had a different pharmacological mechanism of action from other agents that caused sedation. Early experiments in the 1960s showed that benzodiazepines had an inhibitory effect on motor neurons which passed out of the spinal cord to the body's skeletal muscles. It was known that the neurotransmitter released by the fibres travelling in the spinal cord that terminated onto the output motor neurons was gamma aminobutyric acid (**GABA**). Thus, benzodiazepines were suspected of potentiating the action of GABA. This was an intriguing finding because at the time GABA had not been proven to exist as a brain neurotransmitter. In fact, GABA is now recognized as the most common inhibitory neurotransmitter throughout the central nervous system (Obata, 2013).

During the 1970s, it was found that benzodiazepines have their own specific receptor in the brain. In fact, the benzodiazepine receptor was a site on the much larger GABA-A receptor complex. As we saw in Chapter 1, the GABA-A receptor is an example of an ionotropic receptor consisting of five elongated proteins arranged in a shape of a cylinder that passes through the membrane. These proteins form a closed chloride channel. However, when GABA binds to the receptor, it causes a change in the shape of the proteins forming the ion channel, which allows negatively charged chloride ions to flow into the neuron. This creates a local hyperpolarization, or inhibitory postsynaptic potential (IPSP), which helps inhibit the neuron from firing (Nutt & Malizia, 2001).

It might be expected that benzodiazepine receptors act in a similar fashion, i.e. by opening the chloride channels. In fact, research shows that benzodiazepines do not affect chloride conductance by themselves. Rather, they potentiate or facilitate the effects of GABA on chloride permeability. That is, if the benzodiazepine receptor is stimulated along with the GABA-A receptor, there is a greater flow of negative chloride ions into the neuron than if the GABA-A receptor is stimulated by itself. The likeliest explanation for this is that the chloride ion channel remains open for longer. Whatever the mechanism, the result is more pronounced neural inhibition. This facilitatory action is known as allosteric modulation. Interestingly, both alcohol and barbiturates have a similar effect on GABA-A receptors by an allosteric mechanism.

Benzodiazepine receptors are found throughout the brain, with highest numbers located in the cerebral cortex, basal ganglia and cerebellum (Abadie et al., 1992). There are also functionally important benzodiazepine receptors in the amygdala which are believed to be crucially involved in mediating the anxiolytic effects of these drugs (Griessner et al., 2021). But this also begs the question of why should the brain have benzodiazepine receptors in the first place? These drugs, after all, are synthetic and man-made. The likely answer is that the brain must make its own kind of endogenous substance that resembles the benzodiazepine molecule in some way. A number of substances have been found in the brain that bind to benzodiazepine receptors including the β-carbolines, and most noticeably a peptide called diazepam-binding inhibitor. However, the functions of these substances, despite much research since the 1990s, have proven surprisingly elusive (Christian et al., 2013).

KEY TERMS: *GABA, GABA-A receptors, allosteric modulation, diazepam-binding inhibitor*

THE MODERN DRUG TREATMENT OF ANXIETY

Because of the addictive potential and side effects associated with the use of benzodiazepines, attempts were made to develop alternative drugs for the treatment of anxiety. One of the earliest to be marketed was buspirone (BuSpar) first introduced into clinical practice in 1986. This drug was shown to be an effective anxiolytic, especially for generalized anxiety disorders, but with fewer side effects than the benzodiazepines and little addictive potential (see Wilson & Tripp, 2019). Interestingly, buspirone does not bind to benzodiazepine or GABA receptors. Rather, it was found to have a strong affinity for serotonin 5HT1a receptors, where it acts as a partial agonist (although it also has a weak affinity for serotonin 5HT2 receptors and acts as a weak antagonist on dopamine D2 autoreceptors). The key to its effectiveness, however, was believed to be at the 5HT1a receptor (Howland, 2015). This is also supported by the fact that 5HT1a receptors are found in high concentrations in the hippocampus and amygdala where they reduce neural excitability, as well as the dorsal raphe which leads to reduced serotonin release in the forebrain, including the striatum and cerebral cortex. Not surprisingly, the discovery of buspirone led drug companies to search for new serotonergic agonists which became known collectively as second-generation anxiolytics.

More recent second-generation anxiolytics include mirtazapine (Remeron), which increases synaptic serotonin and noradrenaline by blocking postsynaptic 5-HT2 and 5-HT3 receptors along with auto-inhibitory alpha-2 receptors, and the noradrenaline reuptake inhibitor reboxetine (Edronax). Another anxiolytic agent is vortioxetine (Trintelix) which acts as a full 5-HT1A receptor agonist and uptake inhibitor. Despite their potential in treating anxiety disorders, it is fair to say that all of these agents have become more widely used as antidepressants. In fact, the most common agents used nowadays to treat anxiety appear to be the selective serotonin reuptake inhibitors (SSRIs) which block the reuptake of this neurotransmitter in the synapse leading to increased levels of serotonin in the brain. Other commonly used prescriptions (see Murrough et al., 2015) include the combined serotonin and noradrenaline reuptake inhibitors, and the tricyclic antidepressants (these are discussed more in Chapter 11). Nonetheless, the therapeutic effects of all these drugs are thought to be related to the serotonergic stimulation of 5-HT1 receptor subtypes (Outhoff, 2010).

KEY TERMS: *buspirone, mirtazapine, reboxetine, vortioxetine, selective serotonin reuptake inhibitors*

SUMMARY

Although there is no current scientific consensus on their definition, emotions are an important determinate of our behaviour. They create a feeling which signals that something significant is happening to us, and this often propels us to take immediate action. When we experience emotion a number of bodily changes typically take place which resembles the fight-or-flight response governed by the sympathetic division of the autonomic nervous system (ANS). These changes may include, for example, a rapid heartbeat, increased respiration, dilated pupils and sweaty palms. The relationship between the physiological response and the subjective experience of the emotional event, however, is a matter of conjecture. The James–Lange theory holds that every type of emotion is associated with its own specific set of physiological changes that are instigated in the body before they are subjectively experienced or felt. In contrast, the Cannon–Bard theory proposes that we are capable of experiencing an emotion before the accompanying bodily changes take place. This theory also holds that all emotions, from fear to pleasure etc., have the same underlying physiological response. The Schachter–Singer theory also proposes that there is only one basic physiological response – but holds that we determine the nature of our emotion by combining a cognitive appraisal of both our body state and environmental situation. None of the above theories are wholly convincing – partly because some emotions appear to be associated with different types of physiological response, and also because some emotions appear to be appraised at an unconscious level before they reach consciousness. It is also the case that autonomic arousal doesn't underlie all emotions as shown by the importance of feedback from the facial muscles.

The main area of the brain that has become associated with emotional behaviour is the limbic system – a term (or concept) invented by Paul MacLean in 1954, which was based on an earlier formulation by Paul Broca who originally coined the term 'limbic lobe'. One of the most important and pivotal areas of the limbic system is the hypothalamus. Situated just above the pituitary gland, this tiny mass of cells regulates the autonomic nervous system as well as governing the release of many hormones throughout the body. In the 1930s, work by Philip Bard showed that lesions of the hypothalamus eliminated rage (e.g. hissing and snarling) in cats, whereas lesions of the **cerebral cortex** tended to elicit this type of behaviour. These results indicate that the cerebral cortex helps inhibit the hypothalamus in its expression of emotional behaviour. Another important area of the limbic system for emotion is the amygdala. This region was first highlighted in the late 1930s, when Klüver and Bucy showed that lesions of the amygdala eliminated aggression and fear in rhesus monkeys. Electrical stimulation of this structure has also been shown to induce fear and aggression in humans (e.g. the case of Julia). However, the most extensive work on the amygdala has been undertaken by Joseph LeDoux and his colleagues who have shown that the amygdala receives fear input well before the higher cerebral cortex has had time to analyse it, and that all the behavioural components of conditioned emotional responding are mediated by the different outputs of its central nucleus. The amygdala also has reciprocal connections with the frontal lobes which are involved in assessing the emotional significant of events and determining the appropriate response. This was most dramatically seen in the case of Phineas Gage, a railway worker, who in 1848 suffered a horrifying accident when an iron rod was blown through the front of his brain. Although Gage was regarded as an exemplary worker, in the years after the accident he became 'gross, profane, coarse and vulgar' and unable to inhibit his behaviour. Psychosurgery involving the frontal lobe and its pathways has also been used to dampen emotion and treat severe forms of mental illness including depression and obsessions.

Although anxiety and stress are a necessary part of life, they can also result in mental distress and illness. Estimates show that a third of the population are likely to suffer from an anxiety disorder at some point of their lives. The most common type of anxiety complaint is phobias which can take many forms, such as simple phobias relating to a specific object (e.g. snakes, spiders and needles), or generally more debilitating forms such as agoraphobia or social phobia. Other often-chronic conditions include generalized anxiety, post-traumatic stress disorder and obsessive compulsive disorder – the latter occurring when a person feels compelled to undertake specific rituals such as washing their hands or checking the lock before leaving the house. A number of anxiolytic drugs have been developed to treat these types of conditions, including the benzodiazepines which act on the GABA-A receptor.

The addictive potential of the benzodiazepines, however, has led to the development of a number of second-generation anxiolytics such as **buspirone** and **mirtazapine** which are safer. In addition, the **selective serotonergic reuptake inhibitors** (normally used to treat depression) have been shown to be effective at relieving anxiety.

GO ONLINE

TEST YOUR UNDERSTANDING OF THIS CHAPTER AND VISIT HTTPS://STUDY.SAGEPUB.COM/WICKENS TO ACCESS INTERACTIVE 'DRAG AND DROP' LABELLING ACTIVITIES AND A FLASHCARD GLOSSARY.

MULTIPLE CHOICE QUESTIONS

Answer the questions below to test your understanding of this chapter's Learning Objectives. You'll find the answers at the end of the chapter.

1. What two neurotransmitters are used by the sympathetic and parasympathetic nervous systems?

   a. dopamine and noradrenaline
   b. dopamine and acetylcholine
   c. noradrenaline and acetylcholine
   d. serotonin and noradrenaline

2. According to the James–Lange theory of emotion which of these statements is correct?

   a. visceral (body) feedback tells the brain which emotion it is experiencing
   b. the conscious brain interprets the emotion before any body change takes place
   c. all emotions are dependent on the release of adrenaline
   d. the Papez circuit governs emotional responding

3. Which of the following structures does not belong to the limbic system?

   a. hypothalamus
   b. hippocampus
   c. amygdala
   d. basal ganglia

4. According to Joseph LeDoux, which of the following brain structures is crucial for the 'act first, think later' reaction of the amygdala to a fearful or dangerous event?

   a. frontal cortex
   b. hypothalamus
   c. cingulate cortex
   d. auditory thalamus and inferior colliculus

5. According to Antonio Damasio, damage to the orbitofrontal cortex produces which one of these outcomes?

   a. acquired sociopathy
   b. memory loss for emotional events
   c. increased anxiety in social encounters
   d. a greater likelihood of aggression

6. Benzodiazepines exert their pharmacological effect in the brain by acting on what type of receptor?

   a. cholinergic
   b. dopaminergic
   c. GABAergic
   d. serotonergic

FURTHER READING

Adolphs, R., & Anderson, D. J. (2018). *The neuroscience of emotion: A new synthesis.* Princeton University Press.
An accessible book that emphasizes the importance of examining the biological roots of emotion in both animals (including insects) and humans.

Amaral, D. G., & Adolphs, R. (Eds.). (2016). *Living without an amygdala.* The Guilford Press.
This volume presents research on rats, monkeys, and humans, and reports on fascinating cases of people living without an amygdala, whether due to genetic conditions, disease or other causes.

Barrett, L. F., Lewis, M., & Haviland-Jones, J. M. (Eds.). (2016). *Handbook of emotions.* The Guilford Press.
Although this handbook is wide-ranging, it includes useful chapters on the biological and neuroscientific underpinnings of emotions.

Damasio, A. R. (2000). *The feeling of what happens: Body, emotion and the making of consciousness.* Vintage.
Drawing on his experience with brain-damaged patients, Damasio shows how the awareness of emotion is central to self-awareness.

Davidson, R. J., Schere, K. R., & Goldsmith H. H. (Eds.). (2002). *Handbook of affective states.* Oxford University Press.
Consisting of 59 chapters written by various experts, and over a thousand pages in length, this is a comprehensive and surprisingly lucid overview of research into the psychobiology of emotion.

Joseph, R. (2012). *Limbic system: Amygdala, hypothalamus, septal nuclei, cingulate, hippocampus.* Cosmology Science Publishers.
An introductory anatomical text that provides an overview of the main structures of the limbic system and its behavioural correlates.

Keltner, D., Oatley, K., & Jenkins, J. M. (2018). *Understanding emotions.* John Wiley and Sons.
A well-written book aimed at general psychology students, but contains a useful chapter on the brain mechanisms of emotion.

LeDoux, J. (1998). *The emotional brain: The mysterious underpinnings of emotional life.* Weidenfeld and Nicolson.
A readable account, based partly on LeDoux's own research, that explores the underlying brain mechanisms underlying emotion.

Panksepp, J. (2004). *Affective neuroscience: The foundation of human and animal emotions.* Oxford University Press.
A book that shows the similarity between human and animal emotions, and how they can be understood in terms of the neurochemistry and neurobiology of the brain.

Sapolsky, R. M. (2004). *Why zebras don't get ulcers.* Freeman.
A well-written and interesting account of the body's stress response and its importance for physical and psychological wellbeing, which also covers Sapolsky's work on glucocorticoids and the hippocampus.

Whalen, P. J., & Phelps, E. A. (Eds.). (2009). *The human amygdala.* The Guilford Press.
A book that captures the exciting progress made in understanding the amygdala over the past decade, with an emphasis on understanding its function and dysfunction.

MULTIPLE CHOICE ANSWERS - 1. C | 2. A | 3. D | 4. D | 5. A | 6. C

7

SLEEP AND CIRCADIAN RHYTHMS

LEARNING OBJECTIVES

After reading this chapter you should be able to:

- Describe the EEG brain waves associated with waking and sleep states.

- Compare the characteristics of slow wave and REM sleep.

- Explain the functions of sleep.

- Understand the effects of sleep deprivation.

- Elucidate the neurological basis of sleep.

- Understand the nature of circadian rhythms.

- Explain the functional role of the suprachiasmatic nucleus.

- Describe how the pineal gland and melatonin are involved in circadian rhythms.

GO ONLINE

Test your understanding of this chapter and visit **https://study.sagepub.com/wickens** to access interactive 'Drag and Drop' labelling activities and a flashcard glossary.

INTRODUCTION

The urge to sleep when tired is an extremely powerful one. We spend around one-third of our lives asleep – that is, roughly twenty-five years of an average life in a state of inertia where our responsiveness to external stimuli is diminished and normal consciousness is suspended. Sleep occurs in all mammals, and the vast majority of vertebrates as well, which surely proves that whatever it does, it serves a crucial purpose. And as we all know, the need for daily sleep is never far away. We crave sleep if deprived of it, and animal studies have shown that forced prolonged sleep deprivation has adverse health effects which can ultimately lead to death.

But why do we sleep? On first sight, sleep appears to be a simple form of rest or recuperation. Yet on closer inspection, it is apparent there is more to sleep than this. Sleep produces a highly characteristic state of brain arousal which consists of two very different stages called slow wave sleep and rapid eye movement sleep. These states don't simply happen when we close our eyes, but are actively generated by neuronal and chemical systems found in the oldest parts of the brain (e.g. the brain stem and hypothalamus). Sleep is therefore not a simple passive winding-down in response to tiredness, but an organized set of brain states with a purpose. In the case of rapid eye movement sleep, the brain's neural activity can be greater than occurs during wakefulness. Sleep states are also complex as they affect every level of biological organization, from genes and intracellular mechanisms to networks of cell populations and physiological systems. In turn, these changes impact on our autonomic functions, behaviour and cognition.

But why the brain has evolved to periodically lapse into this semi-comatose state is an enigma. Indeed, the function of sleep has been described as one of the most persistent and perplexing mysteries in biology (Frank, 2006), and one researcher went so far as to say the only thing we can say for sure is that sleep overcomes sleepiness (Horne, 1988). Obviously, there is much more to sleep than this, although proving the point is not easy. On top of this, we have the tantalizing puzzle of dreaming, which accompanies certain stages of sleep to add further interest to the mystery.

HANS BERGER AND THE DISCOVERY OF THE EEG

The modern history of sleep research begins with the invention of the **electroenceph-alogram** (EEG) by the German psychiatrist Hans Berger in 1929. This apparatus, which records electrical brain activity by means of electrodes, or small metal discs, placed on the scalp, was developed in secret during the latter part of the 1920s. In fact, during its development Berger gave talks on telepathy as a diversionary tactic to disguise his true research, and only tested the prototype apparatus on his son. The EEG electrodes detect the very small voltages of neurons firing beneath the skull, and these are ampli-fied thousands of times to increase the electrical signals. Berger's first EEG apparatus was crude and consisted of two fine silver wires inserted under the patient's scalp connected to a galvanometer whose activity he could photograph in bursts of three seconds (Wickens, 2015). Today, almost a century later, high-resolution EEG recording can be performed by using up to 256 electrodes which are evenly spaced around the scalp (typically via a cap or net). These provide a signal that is digitalized, processed (filtered) and stored by high-performance computers.

It might have been expected that this procedure, with each electrode recording the small voltage changes produced by many tens of thousands of neurons in its vicinity, would produce a random and disorganized mess of activity, but this was not the case. Instead, Berger showed that the electrical activity of the brain, as recorded on the surface of the cerebral cortex, was regular and wave-like. In other words, the electrical activity had a regular 'beat' indicating that large numbers of neurons were firing together in a synchronized pattern. Berger also identified two different types of activity which occurred during waking – called alpha waves and beta waves (see Figure 7.1). Beta waves were the most common, characterized by low amplitude and very irregular (desynchronized) waves varying between 13 and 30 cycles (Hz) or 'beats' per second. This pattern occurred when subjects were aroused or engaged in some mental activity. During periods of rest and relaxation however the waves slowed down (8–12 Hz), producing a more synchronized 'high amplitude' pattern of alpha waves.

The publication of Berger's *On the Electroencephalogram of Man* in 1929 opened up a new chapter in brain research, allowing its internal electrical activity to be moni-tored and measured for the first time. Sadly, Berger never received the recognition he deserved for his invention. By the late 1930s there was interest in the EEG, and plans

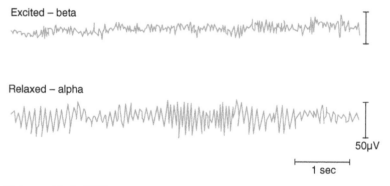

Figure 7.1   Alpha and beta EEG waves
Source: Wickens (2009)

were made for him to visit the United States, but this was also the time when the Nazis were coming to power in Germany. According to some biographies, Berger was hostile to the Nazi regime and forced to retire from university life in 1938. However, more recent evidence in 2005 suggested a different picture, with Berger actively serving on Nazi committees that imposed sterilizations on those with mental retardation and other illnesses (Zeidman et al., 2013). Whatever the truth of the matter, suffering from depression and later institutionalized, Berger hung himself in 1941.

KEY TERMS: *electroencephalogram (EEG), alpha waves, beta waves*

THE DISCOVERY OF REM SLEEP

Nathaniel Kleitman established the world's first sleep laboratory at the University of Chicago in 1925, but despite his innovation the study of human sleep was not a major research area. This changed in 1950 when a PhD student called Eugene Aserinsky joined the laboratory. At the time, Kleitman had noticed that slow rolling movements of the eyes occurred in infant sleep, along with intermittent pauses, and he gave Aserinsky the task of finding out more. To do this, Aserinsky began recording eye movements and EEG during the night from his 6-year-old son. This was the first time a continuous measurement of sleep had been made throughout the night – partly because nobody had suspected sleep changed significantly after its onset, and because a full night's recording would generate more than half a mile of paper. However, Aserinsky soon got a surprise when he noticed periods in his son's sleep where the eyes darted around under their lids and the EEG became highly active and desynchronized. At this point, it resembled a pattern normally seen when a person was awake.

At first, Aserinsky suspected there was a fault with his equipment. In 1952, however, he began a series of studies with a more reliable EEG machine, running more than 50 sleep sessions on two dozen subjects. The results supported his initial observations, i.e. sleeping subjects showed periods in their EEG which resembled the type of brain waves found during waking – and these were accompanied by jerky eye movements. But adding to the puzzle, Aserinsky and Kleitman (1953) found that when they woke subjects up during this form of sleep, they reported having been dreaming. Together they had discovered a new sleep state. The findings were published in a short article where the new type of sleep was called rapid eye movement sleep (REM).

Another person working in Kleitman's laboratory was William Dement. His observations would lead to another unexpected discovery about sleep – namely that it follows several repetitive EEG cycles throughout the night, in which REM sleep is interspersed with periods of more sedate sleep. More precisely, Dement showed that when we fall asleep, our brain waves start to slow down and become more synchronized. This was known as **slow wave sleep** (SWS). Dement not only found that SWS had an EEG rhythm that was slower and more regular than that occurring in the waking state, but it also slowed down over time. Closer inspection of the EEG showed that this type of sleep could be divided into four stages (stages 1–4), and its wave slowing lasted for a period of around 90 minutes. It was only at this juncture that the first signs of REM sleep suddenly appeared.

A CLOSER LOOK AT SLOW WAVE SLEEP

If we could observe someone fall asleep, we would notice a brief transitory period identified by the appearance of theta waves in the EEG that are slightly slower (4–7 Hz) than the alpha ones (8–12 Hz) which were in evidence when the person was relaxed but awake. This is generally classified as stage 1 slow wave sleep, although if the person is woken at this point, they will report being awake but drowsy. But this period only lasts a few minutes and as sleep progresses, stage 2 sleep is reached in which the person is now 'fully' asleep. This stage is characterized by a greater amount of theta activity which now dominates the EEG, although this is also interrupted with some new features. This includes 0.5 second bursts of 12–15 Hz activity called sleep spindles along with large waves that occur about once a minute called K-complexes. It has been suggested that sleep spindles may perhaps serve a gating function which prevents external stimuli from reaching the cortex and waking the sleeper (Dang-Vu et al., 2010), whilst K-complexes appear to be beneficial for mem-

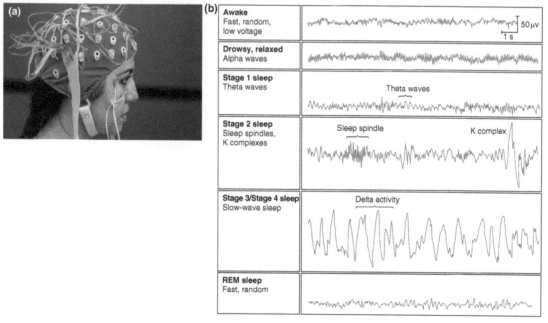

Figure 7.2   (a) Woman undergoing an EEG (b) Brain waves measured by EEG are associated with different stages of sleep

Source: Gaskin (2021), from Hauri, P. (1982). *Current concepts: The sleep disorders.* Upjohn.

ory storage (Caporro et al., 2012). When stage 3 is reached, the number of sleep spindles declines and the EEG shows the first signs of very slow (1–4 Hz) high amplitude waves called delta waves. Marking the start of deep sleep, it proceeds into stage 4 which is the most difficult state to be woken from. This final stage is similar to the previous one, except delta waves now form more than 50% of the brain waves in the EEG. Drawings showing the rough features of the EEG waves associated with waking and sleep are shown in Figure 7.2.

A number of physiological changes also take place during SWS. For example, the energy consumption of the brain as measured by cerebral blood flow will decline to about 25% of its waking value by the fourth stage of sleep (DiNuzzo & Nedergaard, 2017). The brain appears to have become not only more 'restful' at this point, but also less responsive to external stimuli, and if the person is woken from their slumber they can be groggy and confused. The body also shows signs of resting, with the sleeper only moving sporadically by changing their body position once every 10 or 20 minutes. This is accompanied by increased parasympathetic activity with decreased heart rate, blood pressure, respiration and body temperature. Night terrors and sleepwalking are also behaviours that can occur during the later stages of sleep.

KEY TERMS: *theta waves, sleep spindles, K-complexes, delta waves, deep sleep*

A CLOSER LOOK AT REM SLEEP

After about 40 minutes of deep sleep (slow wave stages 3 and 4), a dramatic change takes place in the EEG. At this point, the sleeper moves rapidly back through the SWS stages in reverse order to enter a state where the EEG begins to show a highly desynchronized state. Here, the brain waves are faster and smaller with less amplitude – not dissimilar in appearance to the beta waves that characterize arousal and waking. Indeed, if oxygen consumption and blood flow are measured in the cerebral cortex at this point, they are found to be similar to when the person is awake. At this point, the person is in REM sleep, and the brain has left its slow wave resting state behind.

With the onset of REM sleep, a new set of physiological changes takes place in the body. For example, there is a loss of muscle tone with signs of paralysis, accompanied by periodic (or phasic) 'twitches' of the eye muscles, fingers and toes. Because the activity of the body and brain are so different at this point (i.e. the brain appears to be awake, yet the body is largely paralyzed) this sleep state was called 'paradoxical' by Michel Jouvet in 1967. Increased sympathetic activation with periods of cardiac acceleration, raised but fluctuating blood pressure, and variable changes in respiration also occur in REM sleep, although body temperature falls to its lowest point (Somers et al., 1993). Despite this, penile erection in males and increased vaginal blood flow in females show evidence of increased parasympathetic activity. Yet overall the body remains still and in a state of muscular paralysis called atonia.

However, the most intriguing feature of REM sleep is the occurrence of **dreaming**. Dement and Kleitman (1957) found that when people were woken up during REM sleep, 80% of them reported dreaming, although only 20% did so in SWS. This also probably helps explain the lack of muscle tone in REM sleep, since it acts as a brake to stop the dreamer acting out their dreams. REM and SWS are also associated with different types of dreaming. REM sleep produces dreams that typically follow a narrative, or storyline, with vivid or intense situations that on waking may appear bizarre or illogical, whereas SWS dreams, which are far less frequent, involve the repetition of ideas that do not progress (Hobson, 1989). Nightmares where the person feels 'trapped' also tend to occur in SWS. However, dreams are quickly forgotten, and subjects who are woken only minutes after the end of an REM episode rarely remember them (Koulack & Goodenough, 1976). Although there is considerable inter-individual variability in dream-recall frequency, all people have dreams, but because these are quickly forgotten, some individuals claim not to do so (van Wyk et al., 2019).

KEY TERMS: *REM sleep, atonia, dreaming*

THE SLEEP CYCLE

What happens after we have gone through the stages of SWS and a subsequent period of REM sleep? The answer is we go into SWS again (unless we wake up). Consequently, as first shown by William Dement, periods of SWS and REM sleep repeat in cycles throughout the night. The typical average length of the sleep cycle in an adult is 90 minutes and about 50–60 minutes in infants. This is called a **sleep cycle** and because people sleep on average for around 6–8 hours per night, the majority of adults will undergo four of five sleep cycles during this time (see Figure 7.3). Most will be spent in SWS which takes up around 80% of our sleeping time with the remainder in REM. The relative proportions of SWS and REM in each cycle also change as sleep progresses through the night. Although the REM periods roughly occur at regular 90-minute intervals, the time spent in REM sleep will increase from about 20 minutes (in the first sleep cycle) to around 40 minutes in the last. Thus, as sleep progresses, the relative time spent in SWS declines. In addition, SWS gets shallower, with stages 3 and 4 dropping out of the cycle, so that by the end of the night, sleep may consist entirely of stage 2 SWS (stage 1 is a transitional stage between waking and sleep). All mammals show sleep cycles although their length varies considerably. For example, in rats the sleep cycle lasts about 12 minutes, in cats about 30 minutes, and in elephants up to 120 minutes (Tobler et al., 1992).

KEY TERM: *sleep cycle*

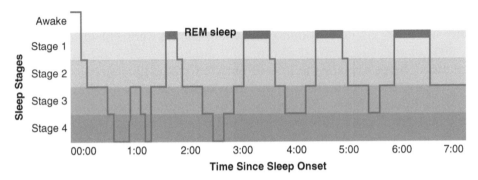

Figure 7.3   Time spent in various sleep stages during the night
Source: Garrett and Hough (2021)

SLEEP IN OTHER ANIMALS

Mammals, birds, some reptiles and even the cuttlefish (*Sepia officinalis*) have been shown to exhibit both slow wave and REM sleep (Rattenborg et al., 2017), whilst of rest and recuperation are observed in insects and even single-celled organisms. But mammals in particular have evolved the most highly variable sleeping patterns (Campbell & Tobler, 1984). For example, the champion sleeper amongst mammals is the two-toed sloth which sleeps on average 20 hours a day (or more than 80% of its life), although its close cousin the 3-toed sloth only sleeps for 17 hours a day (Martin, 2002). At the other end of the spectrum are cows, elephants, horses and deer which sleep for around 3 to 4 hours each day. The kangaroo sleeps for about 1.5 hours which appears to be the minimum for mammals. Humans sleep for around 8 hours a day, the chimpanzee about 9–10 hours and the gorilla 12 hours. Birds also sleep with mammalian-like patterns of SWS and REM. Pigeons sleep for about 10 hours a day, with only 40 minutes in REM sleep, made up of brief periods. They also repeatedly open their eyes during sleep, presumably to look out for predators. However, when pigeons sleep in groups they open their eyes less, indicating the group as a whole may be sharing surveillance (Borbély, 1986).

Some reptiles sleep, although in the few studies where their brain waves have been recorded, the patterns differ from those of mammals and birds. For example, high amplitude spikes have been recorded in the brain of the South American caiman during apparent sleep or behavioural quiescence (Lavie, 1996). Similar activity has been found in turtles and tortoises. But whether this is true sleep remains debatable, especially as it is difficult to distinguish this state from the torpor that affects cold-blooded animals at low temperatures (Borbély, 1986). Until recently, most researchers believed that cold-blooded animals only showed periods of rest and activity and not the sleep states characteristic of warm-blooded animals. However this view may be changing. For example, Leung et al. (2019) recorded brain activity in zebra fish while they slept in an agar solution that immobilized them, along with observations of heart rate, eye movement and muscle tone – and observed neural signatures corresponding to SWS and REM sleep. These researchers note that the vertebrate brain may well have begun to evolve sleep processes well over 450 million years ago.

Regardless of sleep, all forms of life appear to show periods of rest and activity which follow some kind of circadian rhythm. For example, the fruit fly remains immobile

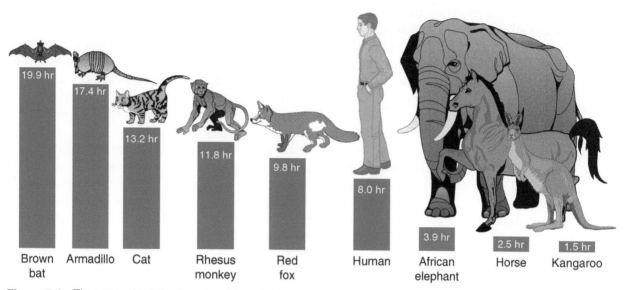

Figure 7.4   Time spent in daily sleep for different animals

Source: Garrett and Hough (2021), based on data from Campbell, S. S. & Tobler, I. (1984). Animal sleep: A review of sleep duration across phylogeny. *Neuroscience and Biobehavioral Reviews*, 8, 269–300.

for periods lasting up to 7 hours around the same time each day, and they generally rest in a preferred location (Shaw et al., 2000). Another example is the giant marine snail *Aplysia californica*. When kept in an aquarium, this simple animal moves around the tank during the day and spends much of its time searching for food. At sunset, however, it withdraws to a corner and remains stationary. Even the most primitive multicellular organisms with an organized nervous system, such as jellyfish, have been shown to have regular rest periods that superficially resemble sleep (Kavanau, 2006).

WHY DO WE SLEEP?

The question of why we sleep may be a simple one, but it has no fully satisfactory answer. From a Darwinian perspective, sleep must have bestowed some advantage, otherwise it would not have evolved – and this evolutionary hypothesis is surely borne out by the fact that sleep is essential for all higher forms of life. The importance of sleep is also shown by some of the ingenious ways it is produced. A good illustration is the bottlenose dolphin which has to regularly break the water's surface to breathe. These animals have evolved to sleep with one eye open at a time, which allows the two sides of the brain to take turns at sleeping. In this way, there is always one hemisphere awake to guide behaviour – an ability that allows dolphins to sleep under water without drowning (Lyamin et al., 2007). Similar forms of unihemispheric sleep are also believed to occur in whales, porpoises and seals.

Evolutionary pressures have undoubtedly shaped sleeping habits. Lions, for example, have most likely evolved a rest pattern that allows them to sleep for long uninterrupted periods because they have little threat from other predators. In contrast, grazing animals such as zebras need to be more vigilant and they sleep for shorter periods of time. Other species may have evolved sleep patterns as an adaptive response to conserve energy rather than to avoid danger. In support of this idea, it is known that small animals with high metabolic rates (e.g. rodents) tend to sleep for longer than larger animals with slower metabolic rates (e.g. horses and cows). In other cases, the pattern of sleep may have been determined by the amount of time the animal spends searching for food and eating. That is, sleep may impose a rest on animals at a certain time of day (e.g. at night) when they would not be very efficient at finding food. But evolution aside, it still remains that sleep must provide some essential biological need to justify its universal occurrence in the animal kingdom (Joiner, 2016).

Most functional theories of sleep fall into one of two categories: those highlighting tissue restoration, and those emphasizing its importance for **neuroplasticity** (e.g. learning and memory). The first theory suggests the body needs regular periods in which to rest and recuperate (Benington & Heller, 1995). In other words, the implication here is that being awake impairs the functioning of the body in some way, and sleep provides a period of repair which helps restore the body back to an optimal physiological state. Support for this idea has come from the discovery that **growth hormone**, which is released from the pituitary gland, takes place during the first hour of slow wave sleep (Weitzman et al., 1981). This hormone not only promotes growth in children, but has an anabolic function in adults, including the increased uptake of amino acids into cells which stimulates protein and ribonucleic acid (RNA) synthesis. This activity is particularly marked in the brain (Seibt et al., 2012). In addition, many genes that regulate metabolism are enhanced during sleep compared to wakefulness (Zielinski et al., 2016), including those that contribute to the synthesis and maintenance of myelin and cell membranes (Cirelli et al., 2004). Despite this, the restorative role of growth hormone in sleep is conjectural because its release can be suppressed without altering the normal course of sleep (Lavie, 1996). It has also been argued that if the primary function of sleep was to synthesize proteins, then larger animals would require more sleep – when the reverse is true (Assefa et al., 2015).

Another restorative theory is that sleep is necessary to conserve energy (Berger & Philips, 1995). Thus, the lower metabolic rate of sleep may allow biological processes occurring during sleep to be completed at a lower energy cost compared to waking. Although this may be true for SWS, the theory is challenged by the occurrence of REM sleep, which is characterized by increased brain activity, metabolism and energy use. It has also been argued that the amount of body energy saved during sleep relative to wakefulness is relatively small, making it unlikely that this is the main function of sleep (Assefa et al., 2015).

A recent idea is that sleep is necessary to 'wash away' waste and toxic chemicals. In 2012, a team led by Maiken Nedergaard at the University of Rochester discovered that cerebrospinal fluid is able to flow through the brain, controlled by astrocytes that create channels for its passage. This allows it to collect disused proteins and other debris, which are then drained into the same ducts used by the lymphatic system in a process called glymphatic flow (Lliff et al., 2012). Nedergaard also showed that glympahtic flow increases significantly when animals such as mice enter sleep. This correlated with a twofold faster clearance of waste products in sleeping mice compared to awake ones (Xie et al., 2013). Although the research was primarily interested in the removal of amyloid (a waste product associated with Alzheimer's disease), this type of clearance may remove other chemicals. Thus sleep may be a cleansing mechanism for the brain (Benveniste, 2018).

KEY TERMS: *evolutionary hypothesis, tissue restoration, neuroplasticity, growth hormone, glymphatic flow*

THE EFFECTS OF SLEEP ON LEARNING AND MEMORY

One of the more consistent findings regarding the function of sleep is that it benefits the retention of memory (Rasch & Born, 2013). This includes a sleep facilitation of enhancing memories by protecting them from interfering stimuli, and a second role whereby sleep aids the process of memory consolidation (Stickgold et al., 2001; Walker & Stickgold, 2004). Some of the best experimental evidence for this mnemonic involvement has come from studies that have used procedural motor-based tasks. In one study, by Walker et al. (2002), the effects of sleep were examined on a task where subjects had to learn a rapid sequential series of five finger-thumb tapping movements with their non-dominant hand (see Figure 7.5). They were trained either in the morning or evening, and retested 12 hours later, following a period of being awake or sleeping. The subjects who had trained in the morning showed no improvement in speed when retested after 12 hours of being awake, but those who experienced a night of sleep afterwards exhibited a 20% improvement by the next morning. This motor-skill learning effect was most marked for subjects that had practised the task during the evening, and even greater in those who had managed three nights of sleep before having their performance tested again.

Participants learned a motor skill task and were retested twice at 10-hr intervals. There was no statistically significant improvement for individuals who remained awake during the interval (a, Retest 1), but performance improved following sleep (a, Retest 2, and b, Retest 1 and Retest 2).

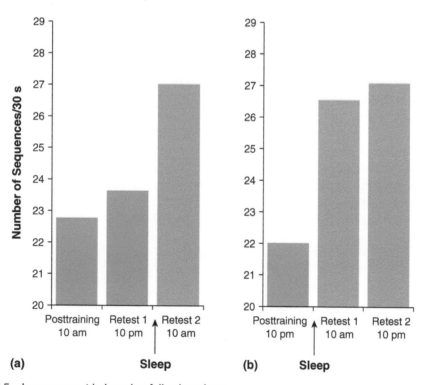

Figure 7.5 Improvement in learning following sleep

Source: Garrett and Hough (2021), adapted from Walker, M. P., Brakefield, T., Morgan, A., Hobson, J. A., & Stickgold, R. (2003). Practice with sleep makes perfect: Sleep-dependent motor skill learning. *Neuron*, 35, 205–211, with permission from Elsevier.

The effects of sleep have also been tested on a visual discrimination task where subjects had to detect hidden or 'masked' stimuli (Stickgold et al., 2000). Detection performance showed maximal improvement 48–96 hours after training if accompanied by a period of sleep – even without any additional practice. However, subjects deprived of sleep for 30 hours after training, and then tested after two full nights of recovery sleep, showed no significant improvement. When the sleeping patterns of the trained subjects were analysed, they revealed that the memory consolidation had two components, both of which required a combination of both slow wave and REM sleep. Overnight improvement was correlated with the percentage of slow wave sleep during the first quarter of the night, and the percentage of REM sleep in the last quarter of the night – with these two parameters explaining 80% of the variance in the performance (Stickgold et al., 2000).

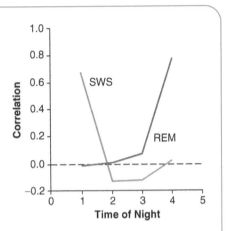

Figure 7.6   Correlations of slow wave and REM sleep with overnight task improvement

Source: Garrett and Hough (2021), adapted with permission from Stickgold et al. (2001). © 2001 American Association for the Advancement of Science. Reprinted with permission from AAAS.

These results support a basic finding that has become well established in sleep research – namely that REM sleep tends to increase after learning, whilst REM deprivation interferes with memory storage (Sara, 2017). But why this occurs is a matter of conjecture. For example, some researchers believe that REM sleep may facilitate learning and memory by helping to refresh the autonomic patterns of activation underlying consolidation – perhaps by increasing synaptic strength in certain pathways (Li et al., 2017; Seibt & Frank, 2019) or by reactivating the memories themselves (Wamsley & Stickgold, 2011). On the other hand, Crick and Mitchison (1983) proposed that REM sleep is a memory eraser which eliminates or reduces memories of unwanted behaviours. Whilst each theory has its adherents, both ideas are compromised by the finding that some individuals show a complete absence of REM sleep through brain damage. One such subject was an Israeli soldier (known by the initials YH) who suffered a brain wound from Egyptian shrapnel at the Suez Canal in the early 1970s. Although this injury prevented both REM sleep and dreaming, it apparently had no adverse effects on his memory. In fact, immediately after sustaining his injuries YH completed his high school studies and was accepted at law school, from which he graduated successfully (Lavie, 1996).

KEY TERMS: *memory consolidation, REM deprivation*

SLEEP ACROSS THE LIFE SPAN

Another way to consider the function of sleep is to examine how it changes across the lifespan. Although we all know that newborn infants sleep a great deal (e.g. around 16 to 18 hours a day), it may come as a surprise to find out that about 50% of this is made up of

REM. And this proportion is even greater in premature infants (e.g. babies born after 30 weeks of gestation) who spend about 80% of their sleep in REM (Grigg-Damberger & Wolfe, 2017). However, infant REM shows some differences from that of an adult – with no motor paralysis and the occasional facial expression associated with crying, anger and rejection. Another common response in sleep at this stage is laughter (Trajanovic et al., 2013) which may include the infant's first smile (Davies, 2018). As the child ages, the time spent in REM decreases, falling from 50% of sleep time at three months to about 25% at one year, which is similar to that of young adults. Despite this, infant sleep cycles will typically be shorter (e.g. 60 minutes) compared to those of older children (90 minutes).

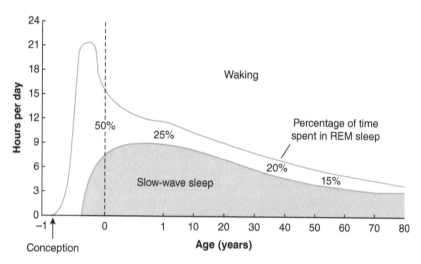

Figure 7.7   The duration and pattern of sleep as a function of age
Source: Wickens (2009)

The fact that high levels of REM sleep occur in the first year of life has led to much speculation that it has an important role in neural growth and brain maturation. Indeed, an early theory by Roffwarg et al. (1966) proposed that REM sleep plays a role in the development of the nervous system – not unlike the effects of physical exercise on the growth of muscle. More specifically, he argued that REM sleep ensures the cerebral cortex receives 'stimulation' which is crucial to the development of nerve cells during a critical period. At the time, this theory was supported by Hubel and Wiesel's classic work which had reared kittens in total darkness from birth that led to impaired vision and degeneration of cells in the visual cortex. However, neural maturation is not the only probable benefit of REM sleep for the infant. For example, it has been suggested that infants are able to process sensory stimuli and even learn about contingencies in their environment during sleep, which also plays an important role in allowing children to make the transition from reflexive to cortically mediated behaviour (Tarullo et al., 2011). Despite this, some have claimed that there is no obvious relationship between REM sleep and later outcomes pertaining to cognitive, psychomotor and temperament development (Ednick et al., 2009).

The maturation of the sleep cycle takes place by early adolescence, at which point most people will sleep between 6 and 8 hours each night – with REM making up a quarter of this time. But as ageing takes place, the time we spend sleeping tends to decline, falling to around 4–6 hours by the age of 50. This is accompanied by a marked reduction of SWS, particularly stages 3 and 4, which by age 60 is about half of what it was at 20.

By the age of 90, SWS will have declined further, perhaps disappearing altogether – a change that may be partly responsible for the decline in cognitive abilities that can accompany getting older. Indeed, poor sleep quality in old age has been shown to increase the risk of dementia (Kang et al., 2017). In contrast to the decline of SWS, REM shows little change with ageing, decreasing by approximately 0.6% each decade between the ages of 19 and 75. Remarkably, according to one study, it even shows a small increase when aged 76 to 85 (Floyd et al., 2007).

KEY TERMS: *REM sleep, neural maturation*

SPECIAL INTEREST 7.1

SLEEP HABITS IN FAMOUS PEOPLE

'Early to bed, early to rise, makes a man healthy, wealthy and wise' is a well known proverb. But is it really true? In fact, there are many famous people whose sleeping habits have not followed this advice. Napoleon was one who needed little sleep. He slept for about 2 hours during the night, after which he would get up to work until 5 am, before returning to bed for another 2 hours. He was also quoted as saying that 5 hours of sleep are enough for a man, 6 hours for a woman, and 7 hours for a fool.

Although nobody would agree with his misconceived sexist beliefs today, he was not alone in his unusual sleeping habits. Another leader, Winston Churchill, worked until 3 or 4 am and was up again by 8 am (although he always took a 2-hour nap in the afternoon); and it was famously documented that Margaret Thatcher only slept for a few hours each night. Nor was she alone amongst politicians. Donald Trump allegedly sleeps 3–4 hours per night, Angela Merkel 4 hours and Boris Johnson 5 hours. But perhaps the strangest short sleeper was Leonardo da Vinci, who followed a polyphasic sleep pattern with a 20-minute nap every 4 hours. On the other hand, there have been others who needed longer. Ronald Reagan slept until 9 in the morning, a practice he even maintained on the day of his inauguration, and Albert Einstein enjoyed spending 10 hours a day in bed where he 'discovered' crucial aspects of his relativity theory. The swimmer Michael Phelps, who is the most decorated Olympian of all time with a total of 28 medals, is another endorsing the importance of sleep. Whilst training he used to place his bed in a chamber that mimicked an altitude of about 9,000 feet so that it decreased the available oxygen and made his body work harder to get the oxygen to his muscles.

What then are the norms for sleeping in human beings? According to Empson (1993), surveys show that adults sleep on average of 7½ hours with a standard deviation of about 1 hour. This means that about two-thirds of the population can be expected to sleep between 6½ and 8½ hours per night. In addition, another 16% regularly sleep over 8½ hours and 16% sleep under 6½ hours. However, individuals who regularly sleep less than 5 hours (and in some cases as little as 2 hours each night) represent a sizeable minority. For example, Jones and Oswald (1968) verified in a sleep laboratory the cases of two middle-aged Australian men who claimed they only needed 2–3 hours of sleep per night. Their sleep was found to contain relatively more stages of 3 and 4 SWS, and extra REM which occurred soon after the sleep onset. Another short sleeper was Miss M, a 71-year-old retired nurse who only slept for about an hour each day (Meddis, 1977). Although this lack of sleep is unusual, others have been reported with similar patterns.

Nonetheless, all people sleep – despite claims to the contrary. For example, Oswald and Adam (1980) reported the case of a man who claimed he had not slept for 10 years following a car accident (for which he had been awarded £12,000 compensation). When examined in a sleep laboratory, the man remained awake for the first few nights, but on the fifth day fell asleep and snored loudly until his wife woke him 2½ hours later. According to Oswald this man was a short sleeper who had attempted to make a profit out of his alleged disability. However, the best evidence showing the necessity of sleep comes from the very rare genetic condition called fatal familial insomnia. This progressive and fatal disease typically strikes in middle age, and results in an almost a total inability to sleep. It is caused by damage to the thalamus and also gives rise to serious attention and memory deficits. Death typically occurs within 18 months after the onset of the disease.

THE EFFECTS OF SLEEP DEPRIVATION IN HUMANS

There have been numerous attempts to keep humans awake for long time periods to determine the behavioural effects of sleep deprivation. One of the first studies to do this was by Patrick and Gilbert (1896) who kept three people awake for a period of 90 hours. The results showed that the subjects were not seriously affected by the ordeal, although there was a deterioration of reaction time, memory and sensory responsiveness along with a decline in body temperature. A more famous example of sleep deprivation is the case of Peter Tripp, a disc jockey who in 1959 attempted to stay awake for 200 hours as a publicity stunt to raise money for charity. During this time he made radio broadcasts from a glass booth in New York's Times Square and was constantly supervised to prevent sleeping. Three days into the experience, Tripp became emotional and abusive, and after five days was slurring his speech and hallucinating the presence of people who weren't there. He described cobwebs on people's faces and had a terrifying moment when he apparently saw a spider crawling around his shoes. By the end of his ordeal, believing he was being drugged, he refused to co-operate with his helpers. Delusional and paranoid, Tripp stopped the stunt after 201 hours of being awake. At this point, Tripp's EEG brain waves were indistinguishable from those of a sleeping person, and he fell into a deep sleep that lasted 24 hours (Dement, 1976; Martin, 2002). Following this, he began to think he was an imposter of himself and continued to believe this for some time afterwards. It is now known that Tripp was using amphetamine to keep him awake during the ordeal which may have contributed to his psychotic episodes.

A few years later, in 1965, a 17-year-old student from San Diego called Randy Gardner challenged the world sleep deprivation record of 260 hours (10 days and 20 hours) that was at the time given as the world record in the *Guinness Book of Records*. It still remains the best scientifically documented record for the longest period of time a human has intentionally gone without sleep whilst not using stimulants of any kind.[1] Gardner was constantly under the scrutiny of two observers, and for the last five days observed by William Dement. During his attempt, Gardner experienced blurred vision, irritability and memory problems. On the fourth day he began to experience mild hallucinations, and after nine days was unable to fully concentrate or complete sentences. By this time, his EEG no longer showed the normal patterns of alpha waves associated with being awake, but these symptoms showed considerable fluctuation, and on the last night he went to an amusement arcade for several hours where he played Dement at a penny basketball game. About one hundred games were played and Gardner won every single game! After breaking the record, Gardner gave a coherent and impeccable account of himself at a national press conference. He then slept for 15 hours, followed by another night's sleep of 10.5 hours, after which he showed no adverse effects from the ordeal (Boese, 2007).

The results of these two examples show that the effects of prolonged sleep deprivation can vary significantly and may depend to some extent on personality factors and age. Nonetheless, lapses of concentration, irritability, and episodes of disorientation with hallucinations are all possible consequences. Also puzzling is the way these changes fluctuated over the deprivation period. Indeed, the performance of another sleep-deprived subject was described as being 'like a motor that after much use misfires, runs normally for a while, then falters again' (quoted in Breedlove et al., 2007). A different perspective has been given by Horne (1978), who has reviewed over 50 studies where humans have been deprived of sleep for varying lengths of time. His main conclusion is that sleep deprivation impairs the performance of complex mental tasks (but not simple ones) which require high amounts of concentration. This has been supported by more recent studies showing that sleep deprivation adversely affects executive tasks and working memory, along with learning tasks involving the hippocampus (Krause et al., 2017). Physiologically, sleep deprivation has wide-ranging effects, including increased blood pressure, elevated levels of stress hormones, aching muscles, and tremors. It also appears to be linked to an increased risk of Type 2 diabetes and a lowering of immunity (Kushida et al., 2005).

Researchers have also examined the effects of sleep deprivation by waking subjects every time they enter REM sleep, or in some cases slow wave sleep stages 3 and 4. The results from these experiments have been variable, with deficits in some studies but not others (Bonnet & Arand, 1996), but more reliable is the finding that REM duration tends to be increased by mental effort and learning. For example, the REM sleep of college students increases during exam time when they are likely to be spending more time learning new information (Smith & Lapp, 1991). A lack of REM sleep in humans is also associated with enhanced emotional reactivity (Rosales-Lagarde et al., 2012). The importance of REM sleep is further highlighted by the tendency of the brain to make up for lost REM sleep after periods of deprivation (known as REM rebound). For example, if a subject is woken up every time they enter the REM state, they often show a 50%, or so, rebound increase of REM next time they sleep. And typically, complete sleep recovery occurs after two or three sleep periods (Jay et al., 2007).

One might be tempted to conclude that REM sleep serves an essential purpose. But, as mentioned earlier, the case of YH. who as a young man in the Israeli army suffered

---

[1]The Guinness World Record stands at 449 hours (18 days, 17 hours), held by Maureen Weston, of Peterborough, Cambridgeshire, in April 1977, in a rocking-chair marathon.

a shrapnel injury to the brain which abolished his capacity for REM sleep, casts doubt on this (Lavie et al., 1984). When YH. was closely examined, he showed no REM sleep in three of his eight night sleeps, and for the remaining five nights the average time spent in REM was six minutes. This did not seem to produce any ill effects (Lavie, 1996). Another example that casts doubt on the importance of REM sleep comes from subjects who take tricyclic antidepressant drugs to treat depression. These drugs significantly reduce the occurrence of REM sleep, but they do not appear to have any adverse cognitive effects for their users.

KEY TERMS: *sleep deprivation, REM rebound*

THE EFFECTS OF SLEEP DEPRIVATION IN ANIMALS

Although sleep deprivation in humans does not appear to produce any obvious life-threatening effects, the same is not true for captive or laboratory animals. One of the earliest studies to examine this was performed by Russian scientist Marie de Manacéine in the late nineteenth century who deprived puppies of sleep by keeping them constantly active. They all died within four or five days (Martin, 2002). The puppies also showed a decline in body temperature, which is a consistent finding from other such studies. A more standard method of inducing sleep deprivation in the laboratory rat is by use of a carousel apparatus, which consists of two separate chambers in a Plexiglas cylinder that share a rotating turntable as a floor (Rechtschaffen et al., 1983). A rat is placed in each chamber, with food and water, with both animals attached to electrodes that record EEG and body temperature. One of the rats is destined to be sleep deprived and the other its control. When EEG recordings show that the 'to be deprived' rat is beginning to sleep, the floor automatically begins to rotate, forcing the 'dozing' rat to walk backwards or fall into a shallow pool of water. However, during the periods when the deprived rat is awake, and the floor is motionless, the control animal can snatch periods of sleep. In this way the control animal gets exactly the same amount of exercise as the deprived rat, but gains more sleep.

A simpler variation of this method is the flowerpot technique which is designed to allow SWS but prevent REM sleep. A laboratory rat is positioned on top of an upside-down flowerpot which is placed in a large bowl of water. While in SWS the rat retains muscle tone, so it can sleep on top of the flowerpot, but when entering REM sleep, the subsequent muscle atonia will cause the animal to fall into the water and wake (Mehta et al., 2018).

Both procedures are effective at producing sleep deprivation. The carousel apparatus, for example, reduced the amount of sleep by 87% in the deprived condition and by 31% in the control (Rechtschaffen et al., 1989). But the most striking effects using this procedure are the physiological consequences for the animal. Although there are few obvious effects in the first week, after this period the deprived rats start showing a marked deterioration. The rats stop grooming which gives their fur a matted dishevelled appearance, and despite eating significantly more they lose weight. Curiously, their metabolic rate increases whilst body temperature declines. There is also a reduction in the release of anabolic hormones. If sleep deprivation is continued, the animals die within two to three weeks of the ordeal (Rechtschaffen et al., 1983).

What is the cause of death in these animals? Surprisingly, there is no obvious answer. For example, when various body organs such as brain, liver, spleen, stomach, thyroid and thymus are examined, they appear to be normal. There is, however, an increase in the size of the adrenal glands and release of **cortisol** in the final few days before death in the deprived rats, accompanied by a drop in core body temperature. This latter temperature effect is not fatal since rats kept warm with increased external heating still died from the sleep deprivation. A more likely cause of death is an increase of body metabolism which might explain why the deprived rat needs to eat more. This, in turn, may increase the amount of oxidative stress, leading to the overproduction of free radicals – unstable and highly reactive by-products of oxidative metabolism that cause damage to cells and also cause aging (Villafuerte et al., 2015). Despite this, if the animals are removed from the apparatus when close to death and allowed to sleep, they quickly recover their well-being. They also show a huge increase in REM sleep, which can be ten times greater than normal.

Sleep deprivation also produces a decline in the body's immune defences. In support of this, it has been found that rats subjected to severe sleep deprivation have lymph nodes heavily infected with dangerous bacteria that have migrated there from the intestines (Everson & Toth, 2000). There is also reliable evidence that the overall functioning of the immune system is seriously compromised by sleep deprivation. Indeed, even moderate sleep loss in humans lasting some two or three days produces a marked decline in the production of interlukin-2, which in turn affects the ability of lymphocytes and natural killer cells to fight off invading bacteria and viruses (Irwin, 2015).

KEY TERMS: *carousel apparatus, flowerpot technique, adrenal glands, cortisol, oxidative stress*

BRAIN MECHANISMS OF SLEEP

Until the late 1930s it was assumed that sleep was a passive process that occurred when the brain became deprived of sensory stimulation. Put simply, deprive the brain of sensory input and the animal will fall into a resting state (i.e. sleep). The onset of sleep in humans was therefore attributed to the gradual decay in the level of stimulation reaching the brain that occurs over the course of the day. One of the first to examine this idea was the Belgium neurophysiologist Frédéric Bremer, who in 1937 made a complete transaction of the upper brain stem of cats, called a *cerveau isolé* preparation, which cut the forebrain from its base to eliminate most of the sensory input reaching the cerebral cortex (see Figure 7.8). In this state, the lesioned cat was unresponsive to external stimuli although it could breathe unaided. But more importantly, it also appeared to be permanently asleep, with its cortical EEG exhibiting slow, large and synchronized waves characteristic of SWS. This led Bremer to propose that sleep was caused by a shutdown of sensory input.

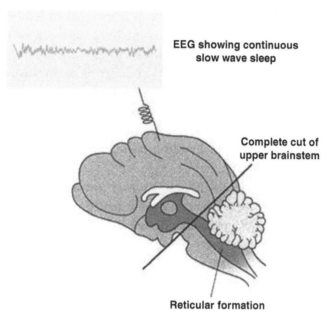

EEG showing continuous
slow wave sleep

Complete cut of
upper brainstem

Reticular formation

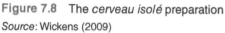

Figure 7.8 The *cerveau isolé* preparation
Source: Wickens (2009)

However, Bremer soon discovered a problem with his theory. When he made a cut at the lower end of the brain stem where it joined the spinal cord (called *encéphale isolé*) he found that the cat exhibited short sleep–wake cycles as well as a hypervigilant state when awake. Yet they were still being deprived of sensory input (the main difference between the *cerveau* and *encéphale isolé* preparations is that the former does not sever input from the trigeminal nerve which provides tactile information from the head and face). This new finding did not support the sensory deprivation theory of sleep, but instead implied that waking and sleep were being generated within the brain, and the mechanism for producing sleep and wakefulness was located somewhere between the two transections in the brain stem.

This brainstem area was not well understood at the time, although it was known to contain a complex meshwork of cells and fibres called the **reticular formation** (*reticulum* means 'net') that ran through its central core (Yeo et al., 2013). A major advance would come with the work of Giuseppe Moruzzi and Horace Magoun when they showed it was able to regulate the neural excitability of the cerebral cortex. They referred to this system as the ascending reticular formation (also known as the ascending reticular activating system) and hypothesized it was important for generating sleep (see the Key Thinker box below). Further support for their hypothesis came from Lindsley et al. (1949) who lesioned the upper part of the reticular formation but spared the pathways conveying sensory input to the cortex. The result was a comatose animal exhibiting EEG activity characteristic of deep sleep. Clearly, a lack of sensory input reaching the cortex could not explain sleeping. Rather, it was the reticular formation which governed the active control of sleep.

KEY TERMS: *upper brain stem, lower brain stem, reticular formation, ascending reticular activating system*

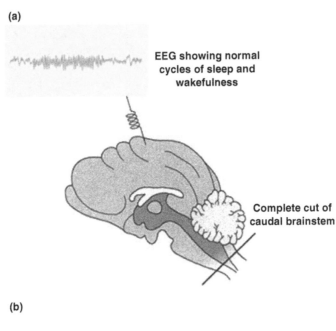

(a)

EEG showing normal
cycles of sleep and
wakefulness

Complete cut of
caudal brainstem

(b)

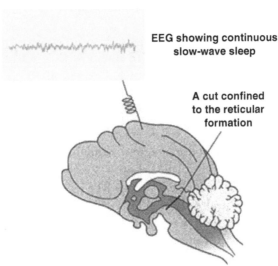

EEG showing continuous
slow-wave sleep

A cut confined
to the reticular
formation

Figure 7.9   Two other types of brain stem lesion and their effects on sleep
Source: Wickens (2009)

KEY THINKER 7.1

GIUSEPPE MORUZZI AND HORACE MAGOUN

Giuseppe Moruzzi and Horace Magoun are famous for their 1949 landmark paper which hypothesized the existence of an *ascending reticular formation* – a network of neurons originating in the core of the brain stem, and whose fibres project to the forebrain, including the intralaminar nuclei of the thalamus – which in turn forms extensive reciprocal pathways with widespread regions of the cerebral cortex. The importance of this system lies in its regulation of wakefulness and sleep states, although it has also been implicated in many other functions including motor function, learning and memory, emotion and motivation.

The son of a physician, Moruzzi began studying medicine at the University of Parma in 1927, where he studied under Antonio Pensa who had been a pupil of Camillo Golgi. His interest in neuroanatomy was reflected in his first research paper examining the granular layer of the cerebellum. After graduating in 1933, Moruzzi would spend a year in Brussels working in the laboratory of the noted sleep researcher Frédéric Bremer. This was a period when the neurophysiology of sleep was poorly understood, although Bremer's theory, which viewed sleep as a passive process occurring when sensory information was turned off from reaching and activating the cerebral cortex, dominated thinking. Moruzzi could never have realized that one day he would perform an experiment that convincingly refuted this theory.

Magoun was born in Philadelphia and grew up on Rhode Island where his father was an Episcopal clergyman. Graduating in biology, Magoun began his PhD at Northwestern University in Chicago under the guidance of leading neurophysiologist Stephen Ranson. Here, Magoun became proficient at stereotaxic surgery – a procedure enabling precise lesioning and electrode placements to target any structure in the brain. This instrument was to have a big impact on the development of biological psychology, and Magoun would use it extensively to explore the hypothalamus.

Moruzzi's and Magoun's paths crossed in 1948 when Moruzzi (who had served as a medic in the Italian army) arrived in Chicago on a Rockefeller scholarship. The two men decided to examine the function of the cerebellum. Their intent was to electrically stimulate one of its major output pathways – namely the *superior cerebellar peduncle* – which they expected to alter EEG activity in the precentral gyrus of the motor cortex. However, to their surprise, it produced a highly aroused pattern of EEG throughout the cerebral cortex. Although puzzled, they came to realize that their stimulation was inadvertently activating the brain's *reticular formation* which was causing the cortical arousal via the thalamus.

The reticular formation is a complex mesh of cells and fibres that runs through the brain stem's central core, but there was little evidence at this time to show it had functional connections with the cerebral cortex. Nonetheless, when Moruzzi and Magoun placed their electrode placements into the reticular formation, they found their stimulation closely mimicked the EEG response obtained from the cerebral peduncles. Their initial work had clearly been a fortuitous mistake.

One important implication of Moruzzi and Magoun's findings was that it contradicted Bremer's theory of sleep which held that sleep arose through sensory deprivation. Instead, it showed that the reticular formation acted as the brain's arousal centre which actively implemented the stages of waking and sleep. The result of the collaboration between Moruzzi and Magoun was published in the 1949 inaugural volume of *Electroencephalography and Clinical Neurology*. We now know that the ascending reticular formation is not only involved in sleep and wakefulness, but is important for consciousness. Thus the cerebral cortex requires input from the brain stem to maintain awareness. Without the ascending reticular formation we would be psychologically dead.

THE ASCENDING RETICULAR ACTIVATING SYSTEM

The human **reticular formation** was first recognized as an anatomical entity by Auguste Forel in 1877. We now know it is composed of a large number interconnected nuclei whose fibres form a central core ascending through the medulla oblongata, pons, and parts of the midbrain. In fact, its diffuse aggregations of neurons extend from the spinal cord all the way up to the hypothalamus and thalamus. The reticular formation is one of the oldest parts of the brain and serves numerous physiological functions – many of which are essential for survival. These include autonomic and reflexive motor control, pain modulation, simple learning and species-specific behaviours. As we have seen, it also governs states of sleep, wakefulness and consciousness. It manages this feat via projections in the ascending reticular activating system (ARAS) which controls the level of cortical arousal, as is recorded by the EEG (Jones, 2011).

But, how does the ARAS manage to control the excitability of the cortex? The answer, in part, lies with a type of reticular neuron which receives input from multiple sensory sources. These also have long diffusely branching axons that innervate widespread regions of the forebrain. Although some pass straight to the cerebral cortex (especially its frontal regions), their major destination is the **thalamus**, especially its reticular nucleus and intralaminar nuclei, which in turn project widely throughout the cerebral cortex. These two regions of the thalamus therefore have a nonspecific arousal effect by 'alerting' or 'activating' the cerebral cortex as a whole (Wickens, 2017e). Damage to these ascending brainstem fibres can result in loss of consciousness and coma, even in the absence of any damage to the cerebral hemispheres.

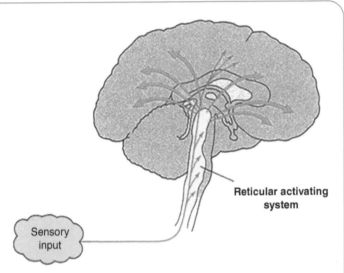

Reticular activating system

Sensory input

Figure 7.10   The ascending reticular formation
Source: Wickens (2009)

Anatomically the human ARAS is intricate and complex, with at least 20 different reticular nuclei capable of affecting cortical arousal (Nieuwenhuys, 2011). As we shall see below, it also contains a large number of neurotransmitter systems. The pathway to the thalamus consists primarily of cholinergic neurons, whereas the direct cortical pathways (and those to the hypothalamus) are composed primarily of monoamine neurotransmitters including dopamine, noradrenaline and serotonin. In turn, the ARAS is modulated by other regions of the brain. In particular, the orexin neurons of the lateral hypothalamus have been shown to be important in coordinating its activity (Chokroverty & Montagna, 2009).

KEY TERMS: *reticular formation, ascending reticular activating system, thalamus, reticular nucleus, intralaminar nuclei*

IDENTIFYING THE RETICULAR AREAS INVOLVED IN SLEEP

The first attempts to link specific regions of the reticular formation with sleep took place in the late 1950s and early 1960s. A leading pioneer was Frenchman Michel Jouvet (see Jones, 2018) who coined the term paradoxical sleep after discovering that muscle paralysis is a feature of REM sleep. Jouvet also went on to show that REM sleep was dependent on the pontine region of the upper brain stem. More precisely, he found that electrical stimulation of the pons in cats induced periods of REM sleep (Jouvet, 1962), and that its associated eye movements arose when a burst of neural activity known as ponto-geniculo-occipital (PGO) waves began in the pons and spread to the occipital cortex via the thalamus. It was no surprise, therefore, when Jouvet found that bilateral damage of the pontine region caused a marked decrease for REM sleep in cats (Jouvet, 1967).

The next step was to identify the most important areas of the pontine region for generating REM sleep. At this point, Jouvet was assisted by the new development of histofluorescent techniques (see also Chapter 1) that allowed monoamines to be visualized along with their pathways. Two transmitter systems mapped in this way were those using **noradrenaline** and **serotonin**. Although fibres containing these neurochemicals were found to innervate large areas of the brain, including the cerebral cortex, limbic system and basal ganglia, their site of origin was traced back to two small structures located in the pons. The site of noradrenaline containing fibres was a small purple nucleus called the **locus coeruleus** in the upper pons, and the site of serotonin fibres was a cluster of cell groups called the **raphe nuclei** which lay distributed near the midline of the brain stem.

These new techniques also allowed the raphe and locus coeruleus to be lesioned with precision, and it soon led them to be implicated in sleep. For example, raphe lesions caused insomnia in cats (Jouvet & Renault, 1966), and the raphe was further linked with sleep when it was found that p-chlorophenylalanine, which blocked serotonergic synthesis, caused a significant reduction of SWS. In contrast, the locus coeruleus was more closely linked with REM sleep. For example, lesions of the pons, which included the locus coeruleus, abolished REM but not slow wave sleep (Jouvet & Delorme, 1965), whereas its electrical stimulation produced an EEG pattern that closely resembled the brain waves found in REM sleep. From these early studies, Jouvet proposed that noradrenaline plays a role in producing REM sleep whilst serotonin brings about slow wave sleep. In fact, Jouvet went as far as to call the locus coeruleus the REM-executive (Jouvet, 1972).

KEY TERMS: *paradoxical sleep, noradrenaline, serotonin, locus coeruleus, raphe nuclei, REM-executive*

A CLOSER LOOK AT THE NEUROBIOLOGY OF REM SLEEP

Although the locus coeruleus was identified as the key structure for generating REM sleep, this was shown to be problematic by subsequent research. Most worryingly, precise lesions of the locus coeruleus using the neurotoxin 6-hydroxydopamine did not abolish REM sleep (Hartmann et al., 1971). Nonetheless, it was clear that some areas lying close to the locus coeruleus were involved in REM sleep. For example, Jouvet (1979) lesioned an area just below the locus coeruleus called the subcoeruleus area which had axons that travel down to the magnocellular nucleus located in the medulla oblongata. As a result of this surgery, the cat entered REM sleep without any loss of muscle tone. Thus, this area is the one that causes muscle paralysis in REM sleep and stops us acting out our dreams.

Further evidence against the locus coeruleus REM theory came from drug studies. One might have expected noradrenergic drugs to promote REM sleep. However, this was not the case. Instead, it was found that cholinergic agonists had this type of effect. Moreover, cholinergic muscarinic antagonists and monoamines (including some noradrenergic agents) inhibited REM sleep. Indeed, Jouvet had himself provided some of this data by showing that REM sleep was blocked by atropine (a cholinergic muscarinic antagonist) and enhanced by the cholinesterase inhibitor physostigmine which increased levels of acetylcholine.

As research continued, it became clear that the crucial area for the production of REM sleep lay not in the locus coeruleus, but in the nearby medial pontine reticular formation. Because this region contains some very large neurons it is sometimes referred to as the **gigantocellular tegmental field** (GTF). This collection of neurons not only provides a major component of the ascending reticular activating system, but as suggested by the drug studies mentioned above, its neurons are cholinergic. It has not only been shown that injections of cholinergic agonists into this pontine region help initiate REM sleep and extend its duration (McCarley et al., 1995), but also that levels of acetylcholine increase in the GTF during REM sleep (Kodama et al., 1990).

Further confirmation that the medial pontine region is involved in REM sleep has come from single cell recording studies. This has revealed that neurons in this area of the brain stem tend to be 'quiet' during waking and slow wave sleep, but show increased activity prior to REM sleep, which is followed by a high rate of discharge throughout the REM period (McCarley et al., 1995). As might be expected, lesions of this region disrupt REM sleep while leaving slow wave sleep intact (Jones, 1979).

The situation is actually more complex than this for it is now known that the GTF receives cholinergic projections from two nearby areas in the pons, called the laterodorsal tegmental nucleus (LDT) and pedunculopontine tegmental nucleus (PPN) which are sometimes grouped together as the peribrachial area (Torterolo et al., 2011). Although the LDT and PPN exercise important regulatory control over the GTF, they also give rise to their own ascending projections which reach the thalamus. It has been shown that 'REM-on' cells exist in the LDT and PPN which only fire during REM sleep (Steriade et al., 1990). Kainic acid lesions of these two areas also significantly reduce the amount of REM sleep (Webster & Jones, 1988). The importance of the LDT and PPN in REM sleep is further emphasized by the fact that both receive projections from the raphe and locus coeruleus. In fact, serotonin from the fibres of the dorsal raphe suppresses the neural activity of the LDT and PPN.

What then is the role of the locus coeruleus and raphe in sleep? One way this question has been addressed is to measure the firing rates of their neurons with microelectrodes during sleep and wakefulness (see Figure 7.11). This has shown that neural activity in the raphe and locus coeruleus is highest during waking, and becomes significantly lessened during sleep – especially during REM sleep (Hobson et al., 1975). In marked contrast, the neurons in the pontine GTF, LDT and PPN regions have all shown activity increases when REM sleep occurs. These findings have led to the reciprocal interaction model of REM sleep, which proposes that the cholinergic LDT and

PPN neurons become excited, as activity in the raphe and locus coeruleus declines (McCarley & Hobson, 1975). If this is the case, then the raphe and locus coeruleus instigate REM sleep by their disinhibition of the ascending cholinergic neurons arising from the LDT and PPN. How might this work? One idea is that the active LDT and PPN stimulate the production of REM sleep by 'turning on' neurons in the GTF, whilst inhibiting those in the raphe and locus coeruleus (see McCarley, 1995). More recently, several other brainstem structures, along with an important role for GABA and glutamate, have been implicated in the control of the pontine REM switch, which has increased the level of this model's complexity further (Fuller et al., 2007).

KEY TERMS: *magnocellular nucleus, medial pontine reticular formation, gigantocelluar tegmental field, peribrachial area, reciprocal interaction model*

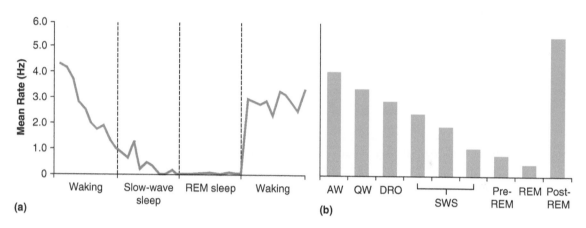

Figure 7.11   Firing rates in brainstem centres during waking and sleep

(a) Activity in the locus coeruleus; (b) activity in the raphe nuclei: AW = alert waking; QW = quiet waking; DRO = drowsy; SWS = slow wave sleep; pre-REM = 60 seconds before REM; post-REM = first second after REM ends

Source: Garrett and Hough (2021); (a) Copyright 1981 by the Society for Neuroscience; (b) From Trulson, M. E. et al. (1984). Activity of serotonin-containing nucleus centralis superior (Raphe Medianus) neurons in freely moving cats. *Experimental Brain Research*, 54, 33–44, fig. 2. © 1984. With kind permission from Springer Science and Business Media.

THE NEUROBIOLOGY OF SLOW WAVE SLEEP

An important clue to the neurobiological correlates of sleep had, in fact, been discovered many years before modern experimental techniques were brought to bear on the problem. The person to make this discovery was the great Viennese neurologist Constantin von Economo who during the 1920s examined the brains of people that had succumbed to the sleeping sickness **Encephalitis lethargica**. This illness mysteriously appeared in 1917 and it would cause the deaths of over 5 million people over the next decade (see Sacks, 1990). Whilst the illness had varying effects, in about one-third of cases patients fell asleep for extended periods from which they could rarely be woken. Some slept for 20 hours or more per day, waking only briefly to be fed. When von Economo examined the brains of these victims he found widespread damage that included the posterior hypothalamus. In cases where the person was hyperactive and unable to sleep, damage was more specific to the anterior hypothalamus (Hoffman & Vilensky, 2017). Subsequent animal work confirmed that large posterior hypothalamic lesions produce a prolonged sleep-like state (Nauta, 1946), whereas lesions to the pre-optic-anterior hypothalamus caused insomnia (McGinty & Sterman, 1968). These findings reveal the hypothalamus as an important sleep centre.

One hypothalamic area that plays an important and pivotal role in sleep is the ventrolateral preoptic nucleus (VLPO) which is a small cluster of neurons situated in the anterior hypothalamus. This area, sitting just above the optic chiasm, was first recognized experimentally for its involvement in sleep when Sherin et al. (1996) identified a group of neurons in the VLPO that express Fos protein more intensely during sleep, but not wakefulness (Fos protein is a chemical that increases with neuronal depolarization). It has since been shown that VLPO cells increase their activity when the animal sleeps (Szymusiak et al., 1998), whilst lesions of this brain region produces insomnia in experimental animals with decreases of total sleep by up to 50% (Lu et al., 2000).

Much attention has focused on the neurochemistry of VLPO neurons which use the inhibitory neurotransmitters GABA and galanin. The projections of the VLPO are also widespread, innervating many components of the ARAS including the locus coeruleus, raphe, periaqueductal grey matter, parabrachial nucleus and lateral hypothalamic area (Sherin et al., 1998). In fact, this system is sometimes referred to as the extended VLPO. But perhaps more importantly, a dense cell cluster in the VLPO also projects to the tuberomammillary nucleus – a loose constellation of some 120,000 neurons scattered in and around the posterior third of the hypothalamus. This region is innervated by orexin containing neurons originating in the lateral hypothalamus

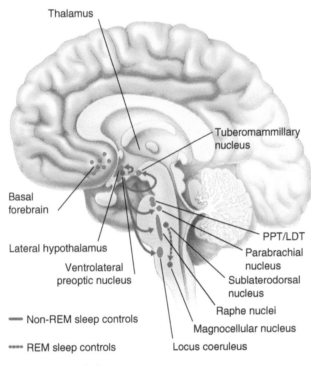

Figure 7.12   Brain mechanisms of sleep
Source: Garrett and Hough (2021)

(this system is discussed in the next section), whilst also being the sole source of histamine releasing neurons in the human brain – a neurotransmitter that normally has excitatory effects on target neurons – some of which are involved in wakefulness and sleep (see Thakker, 2011). For example, histamine projections extend throughout the brain, including the sleep-promoting anterior hypothalamus, and the arousal-promoting parts of the pontine region (Scammell et al., 2019). In addition, there is histamine innervation of the cerebral cortex which is believed to be involved in cortical activation and behavioural arousal (Gallopin et al., 2000). It has also been shown that administration of histamine agonists facilitates wakefulness whilst antihistamines induce both slow wave and REM sleep (España & Scammell, 2011).

> **KEY TERMS:** *Encephalitis lethargica, posterior and anterior hypothalamus, ventrolateral preoptic nucleus, tuberomammillary nucleus, histamine*

The GABA and galanin containing neurons of the VLPO are especially important for suppressing histamine activity in the tuberomammillary nucleus, helping to reduce cortical arousal which is an important requisite for sleep. It is also noteworthy that the

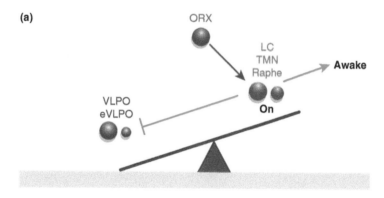

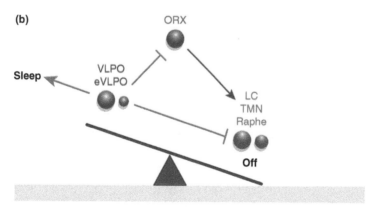

Figure 7.13   The 'flip-flop' switch theory of sleep. In (a) the VLPO areas are turned off by the LC, TMN and raphe which produces arousal. In (b) the VLPO areas turn off the orexin system and LC, TMN and raphe which produces sleep.

VLPO = ventrolateral preoptic nucleus; eVLPO = extended ventrolateral preoptic nucleus; ORX = orexins; LC = locus coeruleus; Raphe = raphe nuclei; TMN = tuberomammillary nucleus

Source: Higgs et al. (2019), adapted with permission of Wiley, from Saper et al. (2005). Homeostatic, circadian, and emotional regulation of sleep. *Journal of Comparative Neurology*, 493(1). Permission conveyed through Copyright Clearance Center, Inc.

VLPO receives reciprocal input from the locus coeruleus, raphe and other hypothalamic areas. The pivotal position of the VLPO within the brain circuitry that governs wakefulness and sleeping has led it to be compared to a 'flip-flop' switch (see Figure 7.13) that turns sleep on and off (Saper et al., 2010). The theory can be described very simply as follows: when the VLPO becomes active, it inhibits the orexin system, as well as the locus coeruleus, raphe and tuberomammillary nucleus, which produces a decrease in behavioural arousal leading to SWS (see Figure 7.13b). In contrast, when the VLPO is inhibited, these systems and structures are 'set free' from their inhibitory effects, causing an increase in behavioural arousal with waking and alertness (Figure 7.13a) (Schwartz & Roth, 2008).

KEY TERMS: *'flip-flop' switch, GABAergic inhibition*

NARCOLEPSY AND THE DISCOVERY OF OREXINS

Narcolepsy is a neurological disorder where people suffer frequent and intense attacks of sleepiness that can last from 5 to 30 minutes, thereby making them prone to falling asleep at dangerous or inappropriate times. However, the condition is more complex than this. About 70% of people with narcolepsy also suffer from cataplexy – a sudden loss of muscle tone that causes the body to collapse without loss of consciousness. In fact, about a third of people with narcolepsy experience at least one cataplexic attack each day, and these can also be triggered by strong emotions such as laughter, anger and sexual arousal. Other symptoms include sleep paralysis where the person is unable to move or speak for several minutes in the transition between waking and sleep. This state may also be accompanied by vivid and frightening dreams known as hypnagogic hallucinations which can also occur when the person is dozing or falling asleep.

The cause of narcolepsy lies with an abnormaility of REM sleep. More specifically, a narcoleptic attack occurs when the person falls directly into REM sleep – instead of the normal SWS phase that usually initiates the onset of sleeping. Thus, narcolepsy is due to the sudden intrusion of REM sleep into wakefulness, and cataplexy results from the inhibition of the motor systems (atonia) associated with this state. In effect, the brain does not pass through the normal sleep cycle, but goes directly into (and out of) REM sleep. This causes changes in the length of REM sleep and the ordering of SWS periods. As a result, nighttime sleep does not include as much deep sleep, leading to excessive sleepiness during the day. Despite this, many people with narcolepsy also suffer from insomnia for extended periods of time.

A major advance in narcolepsy research occurred in the early 1970s when scientists found that certain genetic strains of dogs, including Labrador Retrievers and Doberman Pinschers, exhibited sudden motor inhibition (cataplexy) with short REM sleep onset latencies. Hence, they provided an ideal animal model of narcolepsy. Canine narcolepsy turned out to be a recessive genetic condition (i.e. the dog had to inherit a copy of the mutant gene from both parents). Although most cases of human narcolepsy are not inherited (only about 10% of cases show a family history), scientists nonetheless set out to identify the gene responsible for canine narcolepsy. After a ten-year search they located it on chromosome 12 (Lin et al., 1999). Curiously, the only gene known to lie within this region was called HCRTR2, which was responsible for making a receptor for a class of neuropeptides called **orexins** (sometimes called hypocretins) which had first been discovered just a year earlier. Obtaining their name from the Greek *orexis*, meaning 'appetite', these neuropeptides were initially found to stimulate eating (see Chapter 4) but the lack of the orexin receptor turned out to be crucial for narcolepsy. For example, when mice were bred without the orexin gene (these are called knockout mice – see Chapter 14), they exhibited increased amounts of REM sleep and cataplexy (Chemelli et al., 1999). The suspicion that orexin dysfunction was involved in human narcolepsy was confirmed when paticipants with the disorder were found to have significantly fewer orexin neurons in their hypothalamus compared to those for controls (Thannickal et al., 2000). Around 90% of narcoleptics with cataplexy also have a low concentration of orexin peptides in their cerebrospinal fluid (Kumar & Sagili, 2014).

The orexin neurons are now known to be important regulators of sleep. These peptides are only produced in small neuronal populations within the **lateral hypothalamus** (and nearby perifornical area). Although there are only some 10,000 to 20,000 orexin-secreting neurons in the human brain, they have extensive projections, including the cerebral cortex and cell groups of the pontine brain stem. These neurons are most active during wakefulness and in bouts of motor activity (Lee et al., 2005) and it is believed they also act as a 'finger' on the 'flip-flop' switch in the VLPO that regulates sleep and waking (Saper et al., 2005). The lack of these neuropeptides in the brains of people with narcolepsy helps explain why this 'switch' is faulty – thereby making them more vulnerable to sudden bouts of sleepiness.

KEY TERMS: *narcolepsy, cataplexy, atonia, orexins, hypocretins, lateral hypothalamus*

AN INTRODUCTION TO CIRCADIAN RHYTHMS

The rotation of the Earth causes predictable changes in environmental light and temperature, and all land animals co-ordinate their action with these daily patterns. In effect, these responses, whether physical, mental or behavioural, follow what are known as circadian rhythms (from the Latin *circa* meaning 'about' and *dies* meaning 'a day'). The most conspicuous daily rhythm is the sleep–wake cycle, but less obvious is the fact that every physiological and biochemical activity in the body also follows a circadian rhythm (see Lemmer, 2009). For example, body temperature fluctuates by about 3°F during our 24-hour day, reaching its peak in the late afternoon and dropping to its lowest value in the early hours of the morning. The drop in evening body temperature is an indicator that it is time for sleep. Hormones are also released in regular and orchestrated circadian patterns. Peak levels of **melatonin** are released late in the evening, and growth hormone in the early part of the night. In contrast, cortisol and **testosterone** are released mostly in the morning around waking, and **adrenaline** during the late afternoon. Even birth and death appear to follow a circadian rhythm with around one-third of natural births occurring around 3 am, whereas death is more likely at 5 am (Groves & Rebec, 1992).

On first sight the existence of circadian rhythms may not appear to be too surprising. After all, it is easy to imagine they are caused in some direct way by the world around us. Thus, for example, one might assume that as daily temperature increases, so our body temperature passively follows a similar pattern. However this simple type of relationship does not hold. In fact humans and other organisms, including insects, bacteria and even plants, are equipped with internal clocks that time and control their own circadian rhythms. Consequently, even the simplest organism is able to predict the external changes that are about to take place in the world – and then use such information to synchronize and entrain its behaviour and physiology with its environment (Panda et al., 2002).

The first recorded experiment to demonstrate the existence of circadian rhythms was performed in 1729 by the French astronomer Jean-Jacques d'Ortus de Mairan, who showed that a heliotrope plant opened its leaves during the day and closed them at night. But when the plant was shut away in a dark cupboard, or kept in constant temperature conditions, de Mairan found it still continued to open and shut its leaves in synchronization with the light and dark cycles outside. Clearly, the plant appeared to have its own innate clock. Later, in 1832, the Swiss botanist Augustin de Candolle noted another characteristic of circadian rhythms in plants: when placed in the dark, plants were often not very accurate in their timing. In fact, some opened and shut their leaves every 22 hours. This was the first demonstration of a 'free-running' rhythm – or a rhythm that is not quite in synchronization with the outside world. It also suggested that the plant was only able to keep accurate time by 'resetting' its clock using some type of external time cue in its environment. Indeed, stimuli such as light and temperature are now recognized as important regulators of circadian rhythms which are collectively known as zeitgebers (from the German for 'time-givers').

One of the most fascinating examples of an internal rhythm has been found in *Hantzschia virgata* – microscopic golden brown algae which live in the tidal sands of Cape Cod. These tiny organisms produce energy by photosynthesis, and every day when the tide goes out, they rise to the surface of the sand to bathe in sunlight. However, moments before the tide returns they move back down into the safety of the sand. This behaviour is not generated by the tide, but by their own internal clock. For example, when these algae were transferred to a laboratory some 27 miles away from the beach, they continued to rise and burrow at times that corresponded to the Cape Cod tides. Perhaps even more remarkable is the fact that the tides follow a lunar cycle (a lunar day is 24.8 hours in length) and there are two tides each day. Thus, the algae show what is known as a bimodal lunar-day rhythm (Palmer, 1975).

> **KEY TERMS:** *circadian rhythms, melatonin, growth hormone, cortisol, testosterone, adrenaline, free-running rhythm, zeitgebers*

FREE-RUNNING RHYTHMS IN HUMANS

What is the evidence for humans having **biological clocks** with their own time-keeping mechanism? To prove such clocks exist, it is necessary to show that internally generated circadian rhythms still operate in the absence of time cues. This is not as simple as it first appears. The problem with using humans in these types of study is that it is extremely difficult to separate them from time-linked zeitgeber information. Even in the confines of a laboratory with constant light and temperature, there are many subtle time cues such as the sounds of the outside world, or people coming and going, that provide information about the time of day. How then does one go about cutting off *all* time cues from a subject? One way is to keep them isolated deep in underground rooms, or caves, separated from all temporal variables in the outside world.

The first experiments using this type of isolation were undertaken in the early 1960s by German physiologist Jürgen Aschoff, who built a 'time-free environment' in a basement under a Munich hospital which was able to house small groups of subjects. This was later replaced by a NASA-funded facility at Andechs in Bavaria. One of Aschoff's most important discoveries was that the free-running circadian rhythm of sleep and waking is close to 25 hours. That is, subjects kept in conditions without external cues would tend to go to sleep 1 hour later each day and wake 1 hour later. A similar rhythm also occurred for temperature along with urinary sodium and potassium excretions. However, the sleep–waking rhythm was more variable, sometimes lengthening to 28 hours or shortening to 22 hours. In these instances the sleeping cycle would 'break free' or uncouple from the other circadian rhythms of the body – an effect Aschoff called 'internal desynchronization' (Aschoff, 1967).

One of the most famous isolation experiments, however, was endured by the French geologist Michel Siffre in 1972, when he lived for 6 months in a carefully prepared cave, 100 feet below the ground in Texas. During this period Siffre was cut off from all forms of time-related information from the outside world, and the cave temperature was maintained at a constant 70°F. Although linked to the surface by a telephone, any conversation was kept to a minimum. Siffre had a stockpile of food which was the same as had been used on the Apollo 16 space mission, and 780 one-gallon jugs of water. Before sleeping, Siffre attached himself to equipment that recorded his sleep cycles, as well as his heart rate, blood pressure and muscle activity. He then instructed the operators at the surface by phone to switch off the lights. Siffre also saved his beard cuttings, regularly recorded his body temperature, and had his urine samples tested.

The results from this enforced isolation confirmed what Aschoff had shown. For example, Siffre's sleep–waking cycle tended to free-run between 25 and 32 hours which caused him to sleep at a later time each day. This also had the effect of lengthening the duration of his day. In fact, Siffre had reached his 151st sleep–wake cycle on the last (179th) day of the experiment. Consequently, in some psychological sense, Siffre had 'lost' 28 days. His temperature rhythm was more stable, however, and ran on a 25-hour cycle with little fluctuation. This meant his body temperature went in and out of synchronization with the sleep–wake cycle (an unusual situation since we normally go to sleep when our body temperature is beginning to drop). Not surprisingly, this experience had emotional and psychological effects on Siffre, who by the 80th day of his ordeal was suffering from depression, failing memory and poor manual dexterity (as shown by an inability to thread beads onto a string). And at this point the experiment was to continue for another 100 days! Long after the confinement had ended, Siffre complained of 'psychological wounds' that he did not 'understand' (Foer & Siffre, 2008; Siffre, 1975).

Like plants and other animals, light has been shown to be an important zeitgeber of circadian rhythms in humans. The Harvard biologist Charles Czeisler has even shown that the circadian clock can be reset in patients without sight – an effect that most likely occurs through non-visual photoreceptors (Münch & Bromundt, 2012). However Czeisler is better known for his work showing that the use of artificial light can be used in isolation experiments to manipulate the length of circadian rhythms. In another set of studies, Czeisler forced his subjects to go to bed four hours later each day, thus making them live by a 28-hour clock. This caused the daily rhythms of temperature and hormones in his subjects to rise and fall on an average cycle of 24 hours and 11 minutes – which is significantly shorter than the 25 hours that is more commonly reported (Czeisler et al., 1999).

KEY TERMS: *biological clocks, sleep–waking rhythm*

THE DISCOVERY OF THE CIRCADIAN CLOCK

If the sleep–wake cycle is under the control of a circadian pacemaker then where does it exist? One of the first scientists to address this question was Carl Richter who focused his attention initially on the endocrine glands of the body. However removing the main endocrine glands had little effect on altering the circadian rhythms of laboratory animals. Consequently, Richter turned to the brain – lesioning many different parts and testing their effects on circadian patterns of locomotion, feeding and drinking. Remarkably, he would undertake over 200 experiments over a period of 20 years in order to locate the endogenous pacemaker. Yet only one structure reliably disrupted circadian behaviour, and this was located in the anterior hypothalamus (Richter, 1967). Because this region was small and anatomically complex, he was unable to go further with his investigations.

In 1972, two research teams identified a small cluster of neurons in the anterior hypothalamus called the **suprachiasmatic nucleus** (SCN), where lesions disrupted a variety of circadian rhythms. This included the release of corticosterone (Moore & Eicher, 1972), and cycles of drinking and locomotion (Stephan & Zucker, 1972). Around the same time, the SCN was also found to have its own pathway conveying visual input, called the retinohypothalamic tract, which branches off from the optic nerve close to the optic chiasm. Lesioning this pathway did not impair vision, but it did abolish the synchronization of behaviour with external light–dark cycles. Similarly, lesioning of the SCN disrupted circadian rhythmicity. In particular, it altered the normal sleep pattern, making it more random, although it did not change the length of time spent sleeping, or the relative proportion of REM and SWS. These experiments confirmed that the SCN exhibited two properties required of a circadian clock: (1) lesions of the SCN abolished a range of circadian rhythms, and (2) lesions of the retinohypothalamic tract abolished entrainment of the clock to visual input.

So why did it take so long to discover the SCN? One reason is that it is extremely small. In humans, each nuclei is comprised of approximately 10,000 tightly packed neurons that are confined in a space of about 0.3 mm^3. Further, the SCN also contains some of the smallest neurons to be found in the human brain, and these can only be identified with specialized staining techniques (Weaver, 1998), and in rodent brains the size of this nucleus is even smaller. It is not surprising, therefore, that Richter with his relatively crude lesioning techniques was unable to narrow down his search for this tiny structure.

KEY TERMS: *anterior hypothalamus, suprachiasmatic nucleus, retinohypothalamic tract*

A CLOSER LOOK AT THE SUPRACHIASMATIC NUCLEUS

One special characteristic of the SCN is that it generates its own intrinsic circadian pattern of electrical activity. If microelectrodes are implanted in a rat's SCN, for example, the activity of its neurons shows a pattern of electrical activity that is highest during the day and lowest at night. Moreover, the neurons continue to show this rhythmical activity even when a fine rotating knife cut is made around the SCN, which isolates it from the rest of the brain. This operation abolishes circadian rhythmicity in other brain areas, but not the SCN (Inouye & Kawamura, 1979). Clearly, certain pathways from the SCN must be providing circadian timing information to other areas of the brain.

It is also possible to keep slices of brain tissue containing the SCN in a saline bath for a few hours, and record the electrical activity of its neurons *in vitro*. This type of research shows that the SCN neurons exhibit activity patterns which are synchronized to the light–dark cycle the animal kept when alive (Bos & Mirmiran, 1990). As with other findings, the discharge of the SCN neurons is higher during the day compared to night. Similar results are obtained when animals are injected with 2-deoxyglucose – a radioactive form of inert glucose that is taken up by neurons but not metabolized. Since the more active neurons will accumulate 2-deoxyglucose, this radioactive substance provides a useful way of identifying regional differences in brain activity. This technique reveals that the SCN is metabolically more active during a 12-hour light phase of a circadian cycle, and no other brain region exhibits such a pronounced rhythm (Schwartz & Gainer, 1977).

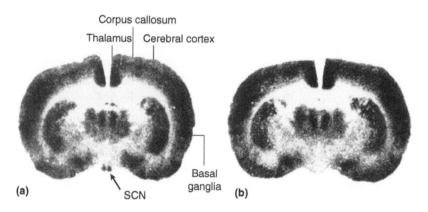

Figure 7.14 The suprachiasmatic nucleus

Source: Garrett and Hough (2021), reprinted with permission from Schwartz, W. J. & Gainer, H. (1977). Suprachiasmatic nucleus: Use of 14C-labeled deoxyglucose uptake as a functional marker. *Science*, 197, 1089–1091. Copyright 1977 American Association for the Advancement of Science. Reprinted with permission of AAAS

Further support for the SCN as the brain's circadian clock has come from transplantation studies. In 1988 researchers at the University of Oregon discovered a strain of hamsters (now called tau mutation hamsters) with a circadian rhythm of around 20 hours. This was shorter than usual. It also raised an intriguing question: what would happen if the SCN of these hamsters were transplanted into normal animals? Would the recipient show a circadian rhythm characteristic of the donor or recipient? Working with foetal tissue containing the SCN, Ralph et al. (1990) found that when they transplanted the tissue from tau hamsters into the brains of normal animals, a circadian pattern of around 20.2 hours was produced, but when the procedure involved the transplantation of the SCN from normal animals into the mutant hamsters, the 24-hour circadian period was restored.

So how does the 'ticking' of the biological clock come about in the SCN? In fact, the evidence suggests that each individual neuron in the SCN has its own timing mechanism. For example, Welsh et al. (1995) removed the SCN from rats and dissolved all its neural connections by using an enzyme called papain which breaks down proteins into smaller peptides and amino acids. The isolated cells were then placed on top of an array of microelectrodes so that their intrinsic electrical activity could be measured. Unlike the individual neurons *in situ* within the SCN, the isolated neurons had their own independent rhythm – although no two cells showed exactly the same pattern. In other words, all showed circadian rhythmicity, but their periods of peak activity occurred at different times of the day.

KEY TERMS: *2-deoxyglucose, transplantation studies*

THE MOLECULAR MECHANISMS OF BIOLOGICAL CLOCKS

As we have seen, simple organisms such as algae and plants exhibit circadian rhythmicity, yet they do not have a nervous system. This suggests that biological clocks may actually be intrinsic to all sorts of cells. But if so, where are they located within the cell? The answer lies with specialized genes whose protein products provide a rhythmicity to the cell's biological activity. An exciting breakthrough into identifying these genes was made in the early 1970s, when researchers bred three strains of fruit fly with genes that exhibited abnormal circadian rhythms (Konopka & Benzer, 1971). In fact, all three strains of fly were found to have mutations in a single gene which was called the ***period (per)*** gene. This so-called clock gene was responsible for generating 24-hour patterns of circadian activity in normal flies. But, per^s mutants had 19-hour rhythms, per^1 mutants had 29-hour rhythms, and per^0 mutants had no apparent rhythm at all.

When the *per* gene was cloned, it was shown to produce a large protein of more than 12,000 amino acids called PER. This protein was found in many tissues of the fly's body, although a small group of cells in its brain had large amounts that exhibited a 24-hour rhythmical pattern of expression. The discovery of the *per* gene and its protein PER was a major breakthrough as it allowed the molecular basis of circadian rhythms to be examined. Although initially found in flies, clock genes have also been found to exist in mammals. In turn, this has paved the way for understanding how SCN neurons generate their own intrinsic rhythmical activity.

The molecular basis of circadian rhythmicity in SCN neurons is now understood in some detail (Breedlove et al., 2007). It has been shown that clock genes synthesize certain proteins in SCN neurons that accumulate to a level whereby they inhibit their own production. As a result the levels of these proteins fall until the cycle starts up once again. Although the exact molecular details need not concern us (these involve the transcription of clock genes leading to the formation of two proteins called Per and Cry), the important point is that the whole cycle takes around 24 hours to complete (Hastings et al., 2018). This is believed to provide the basic molecular motor that operates in every SCN cell which underlies their circadian patterns of electrical excitability. In addition, the SCN is also one of the few areas in the brain to have electrical synapses. These are functionally important for they provide a mechanism by which its collection of neurons are able to synchronize their activity with each other (Long et al., 2005).

Understanding the molecular basis of circadian rhythmicity in cells also enables us to more fully appreciate how light is able to influence the SCN. More precisely, light stimulates fibres in the retinohypothalamic tract, which releases glutamate onto SCN neurons. This causes a cascade of chemical events inside the cell which initiates a new cycle of protein production that resets the molecular clock. And in this way, the SCN is able to fine-tune its electrical activity with the day–night cycle. The retinohypothalamic tract is also of interest for another feature: it receives input from photoreceptors in the retina which use a unique photopigment called melanopsin that transduces light into neural energy. But remarkably, this photopigment is not used for visual perception. Instead, it is used in the regulation of circadian rhythms. Even transgenic mice that have been bred to lack rods and cones, and are blind in every other respect, are still able to reset their SCN clock by using this alternative photopigment (Freedman et al., 1999).

KEY TERMS: *clock gene, period (per) gene, electrical synapses, melanopsin*

THE SUPRACHIASMATIC NUCLEUS AND MELATONIN

How does the intrinsic neural activity of the suprachiasmatic nucleus influence the circadian rhythmicity of other physiological systems and behaviour? After the discovery of the SCN in the early 1970s, attention focused on its control of a tiny structure called the **pineal gland**. This endocrine gland, first named by the Roman physician Galen who likened its shape to a pine cone, had also intrigued philosophers – not least when Descartes speculated that it might be the brain site for the 'principal seat of the soul'. A more realistic view of the pineal gland arose in the 1960s when it was found to secrete the hormone melatonin (so called because it stimulates the darkening skin pigment melanin). The release of melatonin also follows a circadian pattern which is under the direct control of light. In rats, for example, the light from a candle flame is sufficient to inhibit its release. Although humans are less sensitive, they nonetheless show their strongest suppressant response to light in the short-wavelength portion of the spectrum between 446 and 477 nm that appears blue (West et al., 2011).

The pineal gland is a richly vascular organ and is said to have a rate of blood flow only second to that of the kidney (Clark et al., 2005). In fish, amphibians and many reptiles, the pineal gland also contains photoreceptor cells sensitive to light similar to those in the eye, and is located on the dorsal surface of the brain where it can detect diffuse illumination through the cranium. The pineal gland of mammals does not have photoreceptors. Instead, it contains secretory cells called pinealocytes. It is also located differently in mammals. In humans, it is found near the centre of the brain, tucked in a groove separating two halves of the thalamus, within a recess of the third ventricle where it is bathed in cerebrospinal fluid.

Innervated by the SCN, which is sensitive to light, the pineal gland synthesizes melatonin which is released in a circadian rhythm with levels beginning to rise some two to three hours before habitual bedtime, and reaching a peak in the hours after midnight before dropping to negligible amounts during the day (Lewy et al., 1980). One effect of melatonin in humans is to lower body temperature, causing a reduction of arousal which may be an important trigger for sleep. It is also interesting to note that as we get older, the pineal gland shows signs of calcification and produces less melatonin (Wickens, 1998). This may be one reason why elderly people sleep less (Pandi-Perumal et al., 2005).

The SCN's control of melatonin synthesis depends on neural pathways with several components (see Figure 7.15). The process begins when visual input from the retinohypothalamic tract activates the SCN. In response, output fibres from the SCN terminate in the paraventricular hypothalamus, which in turn projects to the thoracic part of the spinal cord. At this point, the preganglionic and postganglionic fibres of the superior cervical ganglion (which is in fact the only ganglion of the sympathetic nervous system that innervates the head and neck) feed back to the pineal gland (Moore, 1996). During darkness, the fibres of the superior cervical ganglion release noradrenaline. Through a series of chemical steps this stimulates the formation of serotonin in the pineal gland which, in turn, is made into melatonin by an enzyme called N-acetyltransferase.

KEY TERMS: *suprachiasmatic nucleus, pineal gland, melatonin, pinealocytes, paraventricular hypothalamus, superior cervical ganglion, N-acetyltransferase*

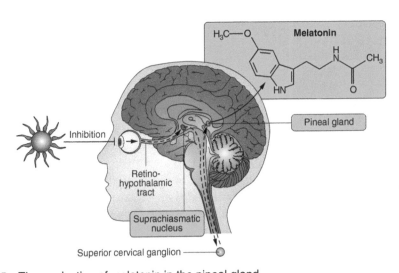

Figure 7.15   The production of melatonin in the pineal gland

Source: Birgit, C.P., et al. (2009). Circadian sleep–wake rhythm disturbances in end-stage renal disease. *Nature Reviews Nephrology*, 5(7), 407–416. With permission from Springer Nature. In Gaskin (2021)

Melatonin appears to be a crucial modulator of most, if not all of the body's circadian rhythms. Two types of melatonin receptor (MT^1 and MT^2) are found in the brain, and they also occur in high numbers in the SCN. Melatonin acts on these receptors to inhibit the electrical activity of SCN neurons and to 'reset' its circadian clock around dusk (Zee & Manthena, 2007). In addition, melatonin not only helps to regulate the sleep–wake cycle (its evening secretion leads to drowsiness), it also helps to synchronize the activity of many other hormones with sleeping, including the release of hormones from the pituitary gland including growth hormone, gonadotropin releasing hormone (which is important in the formation of testosterone and oestrogen) and prolactin. There is also a close relationship between melatonin and cortisol rhythms (Zisapel et al., 2005).

The output pathways of the SCN also innervate the subparaventricular zone of the hypothalamus (SPZ). This region connects with other hypothalamic regions, including the preoptic areas and dorsomedial nuclei. The SPZ is also important in generating sleep–wake and activity rhythms with lesions disrupting several aspects of circadian rhythmicity, including sleep patterns, feeding and locomotor activity. It also projects to the orexin-containing neurons located in the ventrolateral preoptic area of the hypothalamus, which as we have seen earlier act as an important switching 'flip-flop' mechanism for initiating sleep. The SPZ is also becoming increasingly recognized as a pivotal structure in the control of several important circadian rhythms (Wu et al., 2018).

KEY TERMS: *melatonin receptor, subparaventricular zone of the hypothalamus*

DISRUPTED CIRCADIAN RHYTHMS: JET LAG AND SHIFT WORK

There are many instances where the body's circadian rhythms can become desynchronized with the external world. An obvious example occurs when we fly across several time zones, which causes so-called jet lag. This can be disorientating in all sorts of ways. Imagine flying from London to San Francisco. The flight is about 11 hours and spread across 8 time zones. If you set off from London at noon you would arrive in San Francisco at 11 pm (your time) but 5 pm (US time). Thus your bodily rhythms would be 6 hours out of synchronization with the external world. Nor do matters improve when you fly home. For example, if you set off from San Francisco at noon on another 11-hour flight, you would arrive in London at about 5 am *the next day*. Although jet lag can occur after flights in both directions, the adjustment of body rhythms to new time zone shifts is more difficult flying east (Aschoff et al., 1975). This was also confirmed in a study that looked at American servicemen who were transferring to Germany. It was found it took 8 days to fully adjust their circadian clocks to their new environment, whereas it only took 3 days when returning to the USA (Wright et al., 1983). This difference is probably because our natural body clock runs on a daily rhythm of 25 hours and so can better adjust to longer days.

The most common symptoms of jet lag are disturbed sleep patterns which are out of synchronization with the new environment. In addition, a traveller will typically feel fatigued and listless, with increased irritability and a decline in their powers of concentration. Headache, a loss of appetite, anxiety, and a general feeling of malaise often add to the difficulties. This is a global and common problem. In 2007 it was estimated that over 31 million US residents flew overseas, with about 12 million travelling to Europe and 7 million to Asia. And these figures do not include military or government flights. Those travelling for business were reported to take an average of 4.5 trips in the year (Eastman & Burgess, 2009).

Although the effects of jet lag are relatively harmless for most travellers, this may not necessarily be true for those who fly on a regular basis. For example, it has been shown that flight attendants who operate on international flights, compared to those on domestic services, have elevated cortisol levels (Cho et al., 2000). Even more worryingly, the brains of female flight cabin crew with at least five years of regular flying experience have been shown to have shrunken right temporal lobes accompanied by slower reaction times and poorer memory (Cho, 2001). There is also an increased risk of cancer in flight attendants who frequently fly across many time zones (Pukkala et al., 2002). This has been confirmed in mice subjected to experimentally induced chronic jet lag who show accelerated malignant tumour development and reduced survival times (Filipski et al., 2004). Other potential sequelae of jet lag include cardiovascular disease and Type 2 diabetes (Hampton et al., 1996).

A number of strategies can be used to help travellers more quickly readjust their internal clock to the external environment after a long haul flight. One technique is to expose the person to bright light which helps shift the biological clock. Light exposure during the early part of the night will delay the clock, making them sleep at a later time next day, whilst light exposure in the morning, especially if it occurs a couple of hours before the person wakes, advances the clock and makes them sleep earlier. Another important regulator of circadian rhythms is melatonin, which begins to be released in the evening, with levels remaining high during the night. Several studies have now shown that if one takes melatonin during the early evening at one's arrival destination, it is possible to more quickly shift the body's circadian rhythm into phase with the new conditions (Arendt, 2009). Melatonin has even been shown to synchronize circadian rhythms and improve sleep in some blind people who cannot use light as a zeitgeber (Skene, Lockley & Arendt, 1999).

Another instance where circadian rhythms become disrupted is in shift work (James et al., 2017). This practice is more common than many people imagine. According to the European Working Conditions Survey, some 21% of the workforce are engaged in a form of shift work. It has also been estimated that 20% of American workers rotate shifts, sometimes working at night and sometimes during the day. This pattern of work may also pose significant health risks for the individual. Working at night not only leads to sleepiness, but also increases the risk of accidents. Indeed, one study of hospital nurses found that those on night shifts made five times as many serious diagnostic errors, and doubled their risk of a car accident when driving home after work (Rogers, 2008). Shift workers are also at increased risk of a multitude of chronic health concerns, including cardiovascular disease, metabolic disturbances and some cancers (Wang et al., 2011). In addition, shift work increases the risk of a number of stress-related problems such as ulcers, cigarette smoking and poorer pregnancy outcomes (Klein & Thorne, 2007).

KEY TERMS: *desynchronized, jet lag, melatonin, shift work*

SUMMARY

We spend about one-third of our lives asleep (roughly 25 years of an average life) yet nobody is absolutely sure why we sleep! This is all the more puzzling when one considers that mammals, birds, reptiles, amphibians, and some fish, show sleep patterns. Despite all the uncertainty, it is likely that sleep evolved to aid tissue restoration which combats the wear and tear of living, or to maintain the plasticity of the brain which is essential for learning and memory. The modern investigation of sleep began with the development of the EEG by Hans Berger in the 1920s, enabling the electrical rhythms of the brain to be observed for the first time. This would eventually lead Kleitman and Aserinsky in 1954 to show that the brain has two basic sleep states – slow wave sleep (SWS) and rapid eye movement sleep (REM). SWS has a number of stages in which brain activity 'slows down' and is accompanied by a physiological relaxation of the body. It is normally followed by a period of REM sleep with faster and desynchronized EEG rhythms which coincides with dreaming and a loss of muscular tone. The period of SWS followed by REM sleep is called a sleep cycle and it lasts for around 90 minutes. There are around four to five sleep cycles in an average night's sleep. As sleep progresses through the night, the REM periods tend to get longer and the bouts of SWS get shorter, with stages 3 and 4 showing the greatest reduction.

Sleep is an active process, and not a passive response to sensory deprivation as was once believed, which was attributed to the ascending reticular formation (a system linking the brain stem with the thalamus and cerebral cortex) by Moruzzi and Magoun in 1949. The most important area of the brain stem for generating sleep and wakefulness is now recognized as the medial pontine region. This area includes the locus coeruleus (the origin of forebrain noradrenergic fibres), the raphe nuclei (the origin of forebrain serotonergic fibres) and the gigantocellular tegmental field (the origin of forebrain cholinergic fibres). This latter region, which is under the cholinergic control of the nearby peribrachial area, has been shown to be particularly important in the production of REM sleep. The creation of SWS is also dependent on the anterior hypothalamus – an area of the brain which was first highlighted during the sleeping sickness epidemic of the early twentieth century. Of particular importance is the anterior-preoptic hypothalamus which contains a small cluster of neurons called the ventrolateral preoptic nucleus (VLPO). This region projects to the tuberomammillary nucleus which is the sole source for extensively projecting histamine neurons in the human brain, and the lateral hypothalamus that is the origin of sleep-promoting orexin fibres (which have also been shown to be involved in narcolepsy). The pivotal position of the VLPO, especially in regard to the brain stem and cerebral cortex, has led it to be likened to a 'flip-flop' switch that is able to regulate sleep and wakefulness.

The hypothalamus also contains the suprachiasmatic nucleus which is controlled in part by light input from the retinohypothalamic tract that governs the body's circadian rhythms, mainly through its influence on the pineal gland which secretes the hormone melatonin. The suprachiasmatic nucleus also contains so-called clock genes that are able to regulate its own intrinsic electrical activity though the synthesis of specialized proteins. Circadian rhythms can be disrupted by jet lag and shift work which may have serious health consequences in the long term.

MULTIPLE CHOICE QUESTIONS

Answer the questions below to test your understanding of this chapter's Learning Objectives. You'll find the answers at the end of the chapter.

1. When we are awake, the EEG normally shows which sort of activity?

   a. alpha waves
   b. beta waves
   c. both alpha and beta waves
   d. theta waves

2. As the sleep cycle progresses over the course of an average night, does the amount of time spent in REM sleep:

   a. decrease
   b. not change much
   c. increase
   d. become zero (i.e. REM eventually drops out of the sleep cycle)?

3. Giuseppe Moruzzi and Horace Magoun are famous for discovering which one of the following?

   a. the ascending reticular formation
   b. the 'flip-flop' switch in the hypothalamus
   c. orexins
   d. melatonin

4. Where in the brain do histamine neurons originate?

   a. gigantocellular tegmental field
   b. lateral hypothalamus
   c. locus coeruleus
   d. peribrachial area

5. The suprachiasmatic nucleus influences the release of melatonin by its effect on what structure?

   a. pineal gland
   b. pituitary gland
   c. thyroid gland
   d. hypothalamus

6. In humans, a surge of melatonin release occurs in which part of the day?

   a. about an hour after the person falls asleep
   b. morning
   c. afternoon
   d. evening

FURTHER READING

Dunlap, J. C., Loros, J. J., & DeCoursey, P. J. (2003). *Chronobiology: Biological timekeeping.* Freeman. *A textbook that provides a thorough overview of biological rhythms from molecular mechanisms to physiological systems in humans and other animals.*

Empson, J. (2001). *Sleep and dreaming*. Harvester and Wheatsheaf.
A concise and well-written account, accessible for undergraduate students, which includes information on the electrophysiology and neurophysiology of sleep, along with sleep disorders.

Foster, R., & Kreitzman, L. (2005). *Rhythms of life*. Profile Book.
A popular science book that provides an ideal introduction for students, with sections on genes and molecular biology. Another useful book by the same authors is Circadian rhythms: A very short introduction (Oxford University Press).

Kroger, K. (2007). *The sleep of others and the transformation of sleep research*. University of Toronto Press.
An engaging history of sleep research from antiquity to the present.

Kryger, M. H., Roth, T., & Dement, W. C. (Eds.). (2016). *Principles and practice of sleep medicine* (6th ed.). Saunders and Co.
A thorough academic text of over 1600 pages and 171 chapters written by various authors. Despite its title, this contains just about all you need to know about the biopsychology of sleep.

Lavie, P. (1996). *The enchanted world of sleep*. Yale University Press.
A highly enjoyable and thought-provoking overview of what we know about sleep and dreaming, including an examination of the brain centres involved in sleep regulation.

Leschziner, G. (2019) *The nocturnal brain: Nightmares, neuroscience and the secret world of sleep*. Simon & Schuster.
A book that follows in the tradition of Oliver Sacks which interweaves bizarre real-life stories with cutting-edge neurological science.

Mendelson, W. (2017). *The science of sleep: What it is, why we need it, and how it works*. Ivy Press.
Although this is a concise book with only eight chapters, it is very readable and a great introduction for students.

Moorcroft, W. H. (2013). *Understanding sleep and dreaming*. Springer.
A book that is suitable for psychology undergraduates and provides an informative and relevant account of sleep, including its characteristics, functions, physiology and disorders.

Walker, M. (2018). *Why we sleep: The new science of sleep and dreams*. Penguin.
A top ten Sunday Times bestseller, this book provides a wide-ranging introduction to sleep, which examines creatures from across the animal kingdom as well as human studies.

8

SEXUAL DEVELOPMENT AND BEHAVIOUR

LEARNING OBJECTIVES

After reading this chapter you should be able to:

- Understand the biological principles of sexual development.

- Appreciate some of the genetic and hormonal factors that can affect sexual identity.

- Explain how sex hormones affect the developing brain.

- Describe the types of effect sex hormones can have on later adult behaviour.

- Compare the differences in brain structure and cognition between males and females.

- Explain what digit ratio can tell us about behaviour.

- Outline the most important brain areas for male and female sexual behaviour.

- Appreciate the complex biological basis of sexual orientation.

GO ONLINE

Test your understanding of this chapter and visit **https://study.sagepub.com/wickens** to access interactive 'Drag and Drop' labelling activities and a flashcard glossary.

INTRODUCTION

Although sexual behaviour satisfies no vital tissue need, and nor is it necessary for our individual survival, from an evolutionary perspective it is the most crucial thing we do, as it guarantees the continuation of the species. Considering the origins of life began on Earth over 300 million years ago, and *Homo sapiens* are the end result of a long lineage of different species, it is not surprising therefore that the drive to reproduce (which requires sexual activity) is a very powerful one.

It is also a behaviour with many manifestations and complexities. Not only has evolution gone to great lengths to develop two different sexes, but it also requires they come together in an act of courtship to engage in sexual intercourse. In addition, most higher animals provide their offspring with territorial protection and assistance to ensure that they reach adulthood when they can look after themselves. It is easy to take this activity for granted, but if one thinks about it more carefully, sexual behaviour must be largely programmed into the brain as a result of past evolutionary pressures. Moreover, sexual development provides a vitally important determinant of human behaviour. Our sexual gender, for example, is arguably the single most important influence that affects how we think about ourselves and behave. Because of this, elucidating the biological basis of sexual development and how it comes to shape our conduct is important.

The subject, however, poses a unique challenge, especially when it comes to understanding human sexuality with all its prejudices and taboos. But the challenge is a necessary one for explaining who we are, and why we behave in certain ways. It is often overlooked that the most important sexual organ of the body is the brain, and the biopsychologist has a vital role to play in explaining how it produces sexual behaviour, along with providing insights into its dysfunction.

WHY HAVE SEX?

The obvious answer to this question, as any undergraduate student will be quick to tell you, is that it is highly enjoyable! But as true as this answer is, we must ask why sexual behaviour has evolved in the first place. On first sight the answer appears to be simple: sexual behaviour is necessary for the survival of the species. But again, this is not an entirely satisfactory answer because reproduction without sex, or asexual reproduction, is also possible. Indeed, many plants produce seeds that are clones of themselves, and most single-celled organisms (e.g. bacteria) replicate by dividing into two. Some other creatures reproduce by parthenogenesis – namely a mode of asexual reproduction in which offspring are produced by females without the genetic contribution of a male. Female greenfly, for example, give birth to 'virgin' young for several generations, and there are fish, including some sharks, which are all-female. Certain reptiles also reproduce without sex. In fact, there are about fifty species of lizard and one species of snake (the brahminy blind snake which is native to Africa and Asia) that reproduce solely through parthenogenesis (MacCulloch et al., 1997).

Since these animals can reproduce successfully, why go to the bother of inventing sexual reproduction? Sex is all the more puzzling when one considers it is not without its risks: it can cause harmful genetic mutations, result in sexually transmitted diseases, and prove hazardous during the establishment of territory, courtship and copulation. Indeed, most aggression in the animal kingdom is linked to these behaviours. Yet sexual behaviour is the norm in nature. Why?

The main reason for the evolution of sex lies with the great variety of gene combinations that it manufactures compared to asexual reproduction. With sexual reproduction, each parent transmits a random and unique set of genes, comprising about half of its genome, to each of its progeny. Because the array of genes in every sperm and egg is different, when randomly mixed together, this guarantees that each offspring will be genetically unique from its parents, or its brothers and sisters – unless it has an identical twin which develops from the same egg. Thus, sexual reproduction allows a couple to produce an infinite number of genetically discrete offspring. This constant shuffling of genes, and the large number of different individuals it creates, produces 'variation' in the population that is of great evolutionary advantage to the species. For example, if all of us were genetically identical, we would be equally vulnerable to the same viruses, diseases, or other threats to our survival. A species with many genetically different individuals, however, is more likely to survive a catastrophe. Variability between individuals also means some will become better suited to their environments than others, and these will be the ones more likely to survive, mate, and pass on their genes. In this way, the survival of the fittest (a term first coined by Herbert Spencer in 1864) ensures a species is able to adapt optimally to its own ecological niche. Hence sexual reproduction greatly assists the process of evolution.

KEY TERM: *parthenogenesis*

SEXUAL DEVELOPMENT AND DIFFERENTIATION

Almost every human body cell contains 23 pairs of **chromosomes** which accommodate the 30,000 or so **genes** we inherited from our parents at conception. One exception is the gametes, otherwise known as the sperm and ovum (egg), which only have 23 single chromosomes. Hence, it is only when the sperm and ovum come together during fertilization that the chromosomes become paired again – thereby creating a new genetic entity. Remarkably, we all start life as this single miniscule cell that is smaller than the head of a pin (the human ovum measures just 0.1 mm in diameter). Even more astonishing, encoded in the DNA of our first chromosomes are the genetic instructions that will turn the egg into an adult composed of more than 35 trillion cells. And there is another surprising fact: males and females only differ in terms of a single chromosome! Thus, all genetically normal humans, regardless of gender, share 22 pairs of chromosomes with only one extra pair showing a difference (always numbered as the 23rd pair). These are the sex chromosomes and they come in two forms: X and Y (see Figure 8.1).

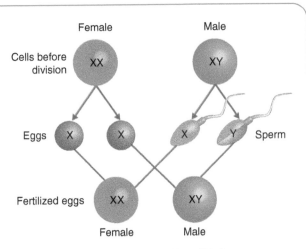

Figure 8.1   Female and male X and Y chromosomes

Source: Garrett and Hough (2021)

If the fertilized egg, or zygote, inherits two X chromosomes (XX) it will normally develop into a female. If it inherits X and Y chromosomes (XY) then a male is most likely. Because males can carry both types of chromosome, it is therefore the father that determines the genetic sex of the fertilized egg.

Following conception, the fertilized egg divides, growing in size until there are around 50 cells in a tiny ball called a blastocyst at around 4 days. This structure then grows more quickly, becoming a sphere with a tiny heart beating at around 21 days. It is not until the sixth week of foetal development, however, that the first sex differences emerge. Up to this point, males and females are identical, and despite their different XY and XX chromosomes, have the capability to develop into either sex. In other words, at this stage, the foetus contains precursor tissue for making either the testes or ovaries (also called gonads). This precursor gonadal tissue is connected to two tubular structures which are named after their discoverers: the Wolffian duct which has the potential to develop into the internal reproductive organs of the male (the epididymis, vas deferens and seminal vesicles), and the Müllerian duct capable of forming the female ones (Fallopian tubes, uterus and inner vagina). But of course, only one of these ducts will develop. The event that initiates this change occurs in the sixth week of gestation when a gene known as **SRY** (the sex region of chromosome Y) produces a protein called testis-determining factor. This causes the gonadal tissue to develop into testes. There is no female equivalent of this substance, and in its absence the differentiation of the ovaries will begin around the seventh week of gestation.

Experimental evidence showing the importance of the Y chromosome for male sexual development was provided by Koopman et al. (1991), who took a segment of the Y chromosome containing the SRY gene from a mouse embryo, and injected it into a fertilized egg containing two X chromosomes (i.e. female). Following this, at 14 days, the embryo began developing testes, and the genetic 'female' mouse developed into a male. Similarly, if the SRY gene is not present on the Y chromosome, the primitive gonadal tissue becomes ovaries, resulting in the development of a female.

The differentiation of gonadal tissue into testes or ovaries is the stage where a difference between the sexes can be observed. It also marks the point when the genetic influence on foetal sexual development wanes, and hormonal influences take over. The testes and ovaries play a critical role at this stage because they produce hormones that instigate the changes that ultimately lead to the sex of the individual. In males, the testes produce two hormones: **testosterone** and Müllerian duct-inhibiting substance. Testosterone acts on the Wolffian duct system to develop the internal male sex organs, whilst Müllerian duct-inhibiting substance prevents the female genitalia from forming. While the ovaries do not secrete sex hormones at this stage (the foetal ovary is inactive until late in development, although it produces small amounts of oestrogen at about 12 weeks), the lack of endocrine stimulation causes the Wolffian system to degenerate. Consequently, the Müllerian system will begin developing into the female sexual organs.

The external genitalia, which in the male includes the penis and scrotum, and the vagina, labia and clitoris in females, appears at about 8–12 weeks of gestation. Moreover, the same principles of hormonal organization hold as for internal development. That is, the release of testosterone by the testes causes the external male sex organs to be formed, whilst its absence stimulates the development of the female genitalia. At this stage, testosterone is also turned into a more potent androgen called 5-alpha-dihydrotestosterone by an enzyme called 5-alpha-reductase which is critical for the differentiation of the penis and scrotum. In fact, without dihydrotesterone, the foetus will not develop as a male, and the immature genitalia will form into a female pattern. Once the differentiation of the external genitalia has taken place (at around 18 to 22 weeks of pregnancy) the foetus can be observed to be either male or female.

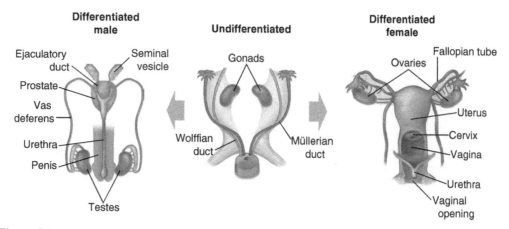

Figure 8.2   Development of male and female internal sexual organs

Source: Garrett and Hough (2021), adapted from Crooks, R. & Baur, K. (1999). *Our sexuality* (7th ed.). Cengage Learning. Fig. 3.2, p. 46.

KEY TERMS: *chromosomes, genes, gametes, sperm, ovum, zygote, Wolffian duct, Müllerian duct, SRY, testis-determining factor, testosterone, 5-alpha-dihydrotestosterone*

THE ADRENOGENITAL SYNDROME

The normal sexual development of the foetus, as we have just seen, depends on the differentiation of precursor tissue into testes or ovaries. It is this change that enables the proper hormonal environment for the internal and external sex organs to develop. But what if something goes wrong at this stage? What happens, for example, if the female foetus is exposed to high levels of testosterone around the sixth week of gestation when differentiation of the sex organs is taking place? In fact, this type of event can occur as a result of several recessive genetic conditions that cause mutations of genes encoding for enzymes mediating certain biochemical steps of development. One such condition is called congenital adrenal hyperplasia (CAH), which most commonly occurs when the foetal adrenal glands fail to produce an enzyme called 21-hydroxylase which is involved in making cortisol (a steroid hormone). As a result the adrenal glands secrete high levels of male steroids or **androgens**. A similar situation can also arise when the mother uses anabolic steroids during the early stages of pregnancy. In both cases, the high androgen exposure produces masculinization of the female genitalia. Consequently, the baby girl may have ambiguous genitalia with a small penis surrounded by skin folds resembling a poorly formed scrotum. Despite this, the internal sexual organs including the ovaries are normal because the adrenal androgens are released too late in development to affect Wolffian system formation. In other words, adrenal hyperplasia produces a female with ovaries, but a genital appearance of the opposite sex.

In the past, children with CAH were often left untreated and reared as boys. Unfortunately, problems of sexual development would arise in adolescence when puberty didn't occur. Today, such individuals are likely to be raised as girls, and treated with a corticosteroid hormone such as hydrocortisone to restore normal levels of androgens. In some cases this medical procedure may even be initiated when the baby is in the womb (Nimkarn & New, 2010). In other instances, surgical correction of the genitalia, especially the vaginal opening, may take place in the first year of life. Nonetheless, girls with CAH have been found to exhibit a tendency for stereotypically perceived 'masculine' behaviours in childhood and are often described as 'tomboys' (Dessens et al., 2005). They also show enhanced ability on cognitive tests that normally favour males, such as spatial puzzles (Berenbaum, 2001).

It has been reported that females with CAH also show a higher than average level of sexual interest in other women. Money et al. (1984) questioned 30 young adult women with adrenogenital syndrome. When asked to describe their sexual orientation, 37% described themselves as bisexual or lesbian, 40% heterosexual and 23% refused to disclose their sexuality. These findings indicate that high prenatal androgen levels in females may bias them towards bisexuality or homosexuality. But one can also see that this is far from inevitable with the most likely outcome being heterosexuality. Despite this things may not be so simple, as it is also claimed that there are increased rates of bisexual/lesbian fantasies and experiences in heterosexual CAH women (Dittmann et al., 1992), and that they have a greater likelihood not to have an exclusively heterosexual orientation compared with females from the general population (Daae et al., 2020). Due to the age of many of the leading studies on CAH, and with broader thinking around sex and gender moving on since they were conducted, you may need to think critically when considering their findings.

KEY TERMS: *congenital adrenal hyperplasia, androgens*

ANDROGEN INSENSITIVITY SYNDROME

Although increased amounts of androgens in foetal development have little effect on changing the sexual appearance of males, a decrease in these hormones or reduced sensitivity to them can produce femininity. One such condition is androgen insensitivity syndrome which is where testosterone – and other androgens – have no biological action on the developing embryo. This most commonly occurs when the testosterone receptor, whose gene is found on the X chromosome, is insensitive to the binding of sex hormones. The result is a failure of androgens to affect sexual foetal development.

Prior to this stage, however, the gonads still express the SRY gene which leads to the formation of the testes. However, because the bodily tissues are not sensitive to the androgens produced by the testes, the male develops external female genitalia (e.g. labia and clitoris). Consequently, the baby appears to be a female at birth. Yet because the foetus had continued to secrete Müllerian duct-inhibiting substance, causing the internal female sexual organs to degenerate, there are no fallopian tubes or uterus. The result is a person with some, or all, of the physical traits of a female – but the genetic makeup of a male. One famous person born with androgen insensitivity syndrome is the widely acclaimed American jazz singer and actress Eden Atwood who was born with XY chromosomes and two testes.

A newborn baby with androgen insensitivity syndrome will often be mistaken for a girl unless the testes have descended into the labia (which is not usual). Hence, these children are normally raised as females and their condition not recognized until puberty (when the lack of menstruation is one key sign). Even so, the person may develop feminine breasts in adolescence because some of their testosterone has metabolized into oestrogen. Furthermore, they have a vagina and typically show an interest in the opposite sex (although without ovaries and a uterus they are infertile). In many cases of testicular feminization, physicians recommend the child should be raised as a girl, since neither surgery nor hormonal treatment can create a functioning penis or alter the feminine appearance of the body (Masters et al., 1995). This does not generally present a problem as the great majority of these individuals regard themselves as female anyway. They typically dress as women, are sexually attracted to males, and their underlying genetic condition often remains unsuspected by others including close friends.

A similar outcome occurs in individuals who have a defect in the enzyme called 5-alpha-reductase. This chemical, as we have seen above, is involved in turning testosterone into dihydrotesterone which masculinizes the external genitalia of the foetus. Without this enzyme, however, the foetus develops external female genitalia, making the newborn baby appear as a girl. They are also typically raised at females – despite having an internal male-like genital anatomy. One consequence of this is that the testes, which tend to be hidden in the vagina, may secrete testosterone during puberty. This can occasionally lead to a surprising turn of events with the girl now seemingly turning into a boy – with a small phallus growing to form a penis and partially fused labia developing into a scrotum with testes. This masculinization may be completed by a male-like torso. Nonetheless, androgen-insensitive individuals are typically female in behaviour, have a strong childbearing urge, and are reportedly female-like in sexual orientation (Hines et al., 2003).

KEY TERM: *androgen insensitivity syndrome*

SEX CHROMOSOME ABNORMALITIES

Although we normally inherit a pair of sex chromosomes (XX or XY), there are instances when this does not occur. The most common instance is Turner's syndrome – a female-only disorder affecting about 1 in every 2,500 baby girls. This arises when the egg is fertilized by a sperm without an X chromosome. Consequently, only one maternal X chromosome is left (X0). Whilst the formation of the ovaries begins normally, their proper development requires both X chromosomes, and by birth they appear as abnormal streaks of connective tissue. Despite this, the baby shows normal external female genitalia. In fact, it is only at puberty when the non-functioning ovaries manifest themselves that the problems begin with stunted growth, absent menstruation, and lack of breasts. There can also be webbing of the neck and cardiac abnormalities. Many of these difficulties, however, can be corrected with medical treatment. For example, human growth hormone injections during childhood may increase adult height, and oestrogen replacement therapy can promote development of the breasts and hips (Bondy, 2007). Girls with Turner's syndrome typically have normal intelligence with good verbal skills, but are weaker in arithmetic and visuospatial skills (Mazzocco et al., 2006). Gender identity is nearly always female (Money & Ehrhardt, 1972). The male version of Turner's syndrome (Y0) does not exist because embryos with this combination are soon aborted.

There are also genetic conditions where females inherit extra copies of the X chromosome, including triple (XXX), tetra (XXXX) and even penta (XXXXX) syndromes (Printzlau et al., 2017). The most common is the triple X syndrome which affects about 1 in 1,000 females. Whilst females with the triple X inheritance may be taller than average, there are typically no other unusual physical features. Sexual development is normal and the female is able to conceive healthy children, despite having a greater chance of menstrual cycle irregularities and a premature menopause. There is a slight risk of learning disabilities and delayed speech and language skills. Nonetheless, it has been estimated that 90% of those affected are not diagnosed as they have either no or only a few symptoms (Tartaglia et al., 2010). In cases of tetra and penta inheritance, however, there are far greater difficulties, with an increased likelihood of decreased intelligence (IQ scores typically in the range of 20 to 75) and multiple physical malformations including upward-slanting eye slits, heart defects, and small hands with incurving fifth fingers.

A male-related genetic condition is Klinefelter's syndrome where an extra X chromosome (XXY) is inherited. This disorder occurs in about 1 in every 700 live births and increases the feminine characteristics of the male, although this is not usually noticed until adulthood. The main problem with the extra X chromosome is that it causes abnormal development of the testes with low plasma testosterone concentrations, but raised luteinizing hormone and follicle stimulating hormone levels. This leads to a high oestrogen to testosterone ratio. As adults, these males are often tall with poor muscular definition and enlarged breasts. In addition, they can be infertile with low sexual desire or impotence. Testosterone therapy may be successful at reversing some of these difficulties, although the individual still usually remains infertile. Intelligence is usually normal, but problems with reading skills and speech are not uncommon.

Males can also be born with an extra copy of the Y chromosome (XYY). The only developmental abnormality of this inheritance appears to be an increased possibility of having high testosterone levels, which may increase height and muscle mass, although this is far from inevitable. In the past this condition has been highly controversial, with some researchers associating it with males who have a mental disability or criminal and violent tendencies. This has been allegedly supported by evidence showing that whilst XYY inheritance only occurs in about one in 1,000 births, these individuals may make up 2–3% of the inmates of mental or penal institutions (Emery & Mueller, 1992). However, these statistics are likely to be misleading. For one thing, XYY syndrome is associated with a slightly increased risk of learning disabilities and delayed development of speech and language skills. Some affected males can have impaired motor skills and clumsiness which increases the chance of being diagnosed with attention-deficit/hyperactivity disorder. This condition is likely to adversely affect social interaction, especially in adolescence. Thus, whilst males with XYY syndrome have a greater risk of behavioural and emotional difficulties compared with unaffected peers, this may well have social causes (Stochholm et al., 2012). It should also be remembered that the majority of XYY individuals are neither delinquent nor aggressive, nor have a mental disability. They live their lives without any problem, unaware they have an extra Y chromosome.

KEY TERMS: *Turner's syndrome, Klinefelter's syndrome*

THE EFFECTS OF HORMONES ON THE DEVELOPING BRAIN

In the developing foetus, circulating androgens not only shape the development of the internal and external reproductive organs, but also act on the brain where they organize the neural circuits for later sexual behaviour. A classic study to show this was undertaken by Phoenix et al. (1959), who examined female sexual behaviour in guinea pigs that had been exposed to high testosterone levels during early development.

During ovulation, an adult female guinea pig will typically show lordosis, i.e. a mating position that includes lowering the forelimbs and raising the hind quarters to signal sexual receptivity. Lordosis is under hormonal control, and can also be induced by giving the female a priming dose of oestrogen for a few days, followed by progesterone. This procedure mimics the hormonal state of ovulation and makes the guinea pig sexually receptive a few hours later. When Phoenix et al. (1959) attempted to induce lordosis this way, in females that had been given testosterone during the first few days of life, this behaviour did not occur. In other words, the early exposure to testosterone had abolished an adult form of female sexual behaviour.

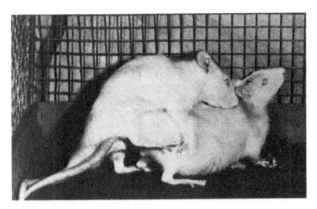

Figure 8.3   A female rat mounting a male

Source: Garrett and Hough (2021), from *Sex-hormone-dependent brain differentiation and sexual functions*. In G. Dörner (Ed.), *Endocrinology of sex* (pp. 30–37). J. A. Barth. Copyright 1974 Gunther Dörner. Used with permission.

The testosterone injection presumably had exerted a masculinizing influence on the brain, which later affected behaviour as an adult. In other words, the testosterone had altered the structure of the developing brain, making it less sensitive to the lordosis-inducing effects of oestrogen and progesterone. However, this only occurred if the testosterone was administered during the first ten days of life. Once this period had passed, testosterone exposure had no effect on later lordosis. A somewhat similar effect occurs when a female rat is given testosterone during a certain critical period, which leads to increased sexual interest and mounting attempts on other rats as adults (Gorski, 1974). Critical periods of development occur in many animals, including humans, although their actions, timing and duration will depend on the species (Hines, 2006).

So what is the situation regarding males? Male rats do not normally exhibit lordosis, but interestingly, if male rats are castrated at birth, they do show lordosis behaviour when administered female sex hormones as adults (Phoenix et al., 1959). These castrated rats also do not show male sexual behaviour as adults, even when given injections of testosterone to stimulate this type of activity. This demonstrates that the neural circuits governing sexual responses in rats are organized early in development, although the effects on adult sexual behaviour do not occur until much later. In fact, thousands of studies of non-human mammals have documented the contribution of gonadal steroids, particularly testosterone, to sexual differentiation of the brain and of behavior (Arnold, 2009).

It can be seen, therefore, that sex hormones such as testosterone have two fundamentally different types of effect. One is an organizational effect that determines gender and primes certain neural circuits for adult sexual behaviour – events often taking place within a critical period. But once adult sexual development is complete, these hormones exert a different type of influence – namely activational effects where they stimulate certain behaviours such as lordosis. These two effects are not entirely separate, for as we have seen, whether a hormone is able to exert an activational effect on behaviour is dependent on the way the brain has been 'organized' earlier. A number of activational effects have been linked with testosterone, including aggression, courtship, rough-and-tumble play, mood and cognition (Becker et al., 2002, Celec et al., 2015).

Attempts have been made to see whether early androgen exposure in primates produces effects similar to those found in rodents. Although primate behaviour is much more complex, there appears to be a hormonal influence at work. Young et al. (1964) reported on two prenatally androgenized female infants whose mothers were treated with daily testosterone from gestational days 40 through 90. The female infants exhibited masculinized juvenile behaviour as early as six weeks of age. Similar findings were reported by Goy et al. (1988) who showed female monkeys given prenatal androgens engaged in more rough-and-tumble play than normal. Thus, prenatal androgens appear to masculinize juvenile behaviours in rhesus monkeys (Thornton et al., 2009). The situation with humans is less clear due to the ethical difficulties of experimental manipulation (Hines et al., 2015). But as we have seen above, females exposed to high levels of testosterone in early development as a result of adrenogenital syndrome are often described as 'tomboys', and show an increased sexual preference for the same sex.

KEY TERMS: *lordosis, organizational effect, activational effects*

ADULT SEXUAL DEVELOPMENT

At birth, apart from the differences in sexual anatomy, human males and females are physically quite similar, and remain so until puberty when their secondary sex characteristics begin to develop. This is the final stage of sexual development and it transforms the young person into an adult capable of sexual intercourse and reproduction. One of the most striking changes during this period is the adolescent growth spurt which results in both sexes growing taller. In males, this is determined by the maturation of the testes, leading to increased testosterone production that helps build skeletal and muscle mass. There is also the growth of pubic hair, a deepening of the voice, and sperm production. In females, the release of ovarian sex hormones promotes breast growth, a fuller figure, and maturity of the external genitalia and uterus. At some point in female puberty, the first signs of menstruation also occur. This marks the point when pregnancy should become possible, although it often takes another year before the release of mature ova from the ovaries finally occurs.

The critical event responsible for puberty is the release of sex hormones from the gonads – namely, testosterone synthesized by the testes, and oestrogen and progesterone from the ovaries (see Figure 8.4). These events are triggered by the **hypothalamus** and **pituitary gland**. When a child reaches puberty, the hypothalamus begins to secrete **gonadotropin releasing hormone** (GnRH) which diffuses through the hypophyseal portal blood vessels into the anterior pituitary gland. In response, the pituitary releases two gonadotropins called **luteinizing hormone** and **follicle stimulating hormone** into the circulation. The only known physiologic effects of these gonadotropins are on the ovaries and testes. For males, luteinizing hormone causes the Leydig cells of the testes to manufacture testosterone, whereas the same hormone in females stimulates oestrogen production. In males, follicle stimulating hormone stimulates sperm

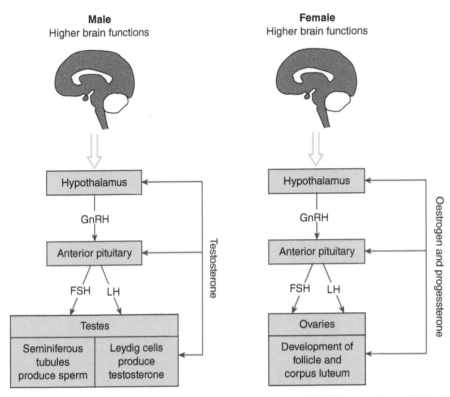

Figure 8.4 Flowchart showing how the hypothalamic-pituitary axis influences the activity of the testes and ovaries

Source: Wickens (2009)

formation, whilst in females it causes the secretion of progesterone. On average, in adult males, levels of testosterone are some seven to eight times greater than those found in females (Torjesen & Sandnes, 2004).

KEY TERMS: *hypothalamus, pituitary gland, gonadotropin releasing hormone, luteinizing hormone, follicle stimulating hormone*

THE MENSTRUAL CYCLE

The menstrual cycle (from mensis meaning 'month') is the regular periodical change that occurs in the human uterus and ovaries which makes pregnancy possible. Or put another way, the cycle is required for the production of an oocyte (i.e. an immature egg cell or ovum), and for the preparation of the uterus for pregnancy. Unlike most other species where the female is only sexually receptive and able to conceive during a specific period known as oestrus (this is when ovulation occurs), human females along with certain other primates can be sexually receptive at any point in their reproductive cycle. The human menstrual cycle also differs from the oestrus cycle because of menstruation – the process by which the lining of the uterus is discarded at the end of the cycle. Despite this, both the oestrus and menstrual cycles are controlled by hormones released by the pituitary gland.

The menstrual cycle has three main phases, known as follicular, ovulatory and luteal (see Figure 8.5). By convention, the first day of the menstrual cycle begins with menstruation where the uterine wall is discarded (usually lasting for a few days). This marks the start of the follicular phase. During this time, the hypothalamus secretes GnRH which causes the pituitary gland to release luteinizing hormone (LH) and follicle stimulating hormone (FSH). The latter exerts the more important effect at this stage as it stimulates the development of a protective sac that surrounds the unfertilized (ovum) egg in the ovary called a follicle. The follicle also produces oestrogen. As many as 20 follicles may start to develop at the beginning of each cycle, although only one usually reaches maturity, and this will secrete increasing amounts of oestrogen. And as the oestrogen level increases, the FSH concentration will fall, until a level is reached, usually around the 12th day of the cycle, when the pituitary's release of FSH is switched off. At this point the pituitary begins to secrete large amounts of LH instead.

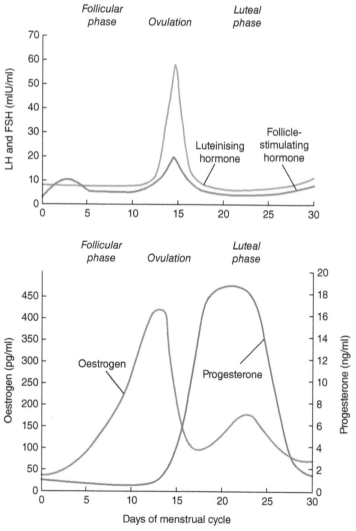

Figure 8.5 The menstrual cycle
Source: Wickens (2009)

By this stage of the cycle, the follicle has grown to form a large bulge in the lining of the ovary. However, the sudden surge in circulating LH now causes the walls of the follicle and ovary to rupture, releasing the matured egg into the upper sections of the fallopian tubes in a process called **ovulation**. At this point the egg can be fertilized by a male sperm, but the time frame for this event is relatively short since the egg is only viable for about 12–24 hours, and most sperm can only exist in the female for about a day (although some 'super' sperm may survive up to 72 hours). Thus, there is a period of around three days in every cycle when pregnancy can take place as the egg moves down the fallopian tubes into the uterus.

Following ovulation, the ruptured follicle remains in the ovary and forms a yellow mass of tissue called the corpus luteum. This begins to secrete progesterone, and to a lesser extent oestrogen, which initiates the luteal phase of the menstrual cycle. The main function of progesterone ('pro-gestation') is to build up the lining of the uterus with blood – essentially nourishment for the implantation of the egg should it be fertilized. Increased progesterone eventually turns off hypothalamic GnRH release leading to a rapid decline of LH and FSH. If fertilization of the egg occurs, progesterone levels remain high and the womb's lining will continue to develop, but if fertilization fails to take place, the corpus luteum will shrink and reduce its hormonal secretion. Because the lining of the uterus cannot be maintained without progesterone, it will dissipate over several days causing menstruation.

Most women have menstrual cycles that last 28 days, although they can range from 20 to 40 days, and these will continue until the menopause. On average, therefore, a non-childbearing female will undergo around 400 menstrual cycles in her lifetime. It has been estimated that a human female begins life with approximately 400,000 primary follicles, which is actually a significant reduction from around the 7 million which are present by the sixth month *in utero*. Thus relatively few follicles (around one-fiftieth) are utilized in the lifetime of a female. Most birth-control pills prevent pregnancy by interfering with the normal development of the follicle. The widely used combination contraceptive pill, for example, which contains oestrogen and progesterone, works in two ways: the oestrogen suppresses the release of FSH, thereby blocking the development of the follicle, whilst the progesterone inhibits the secretion of LH, stopping the release of ova from the ovary.

KEY TERMS: *menstrual cycle, oocyte, oestrus, follicle, oestrogen, ovulation, corpus luteum, progesterone*

TESTOSTERONE AND AGGRESSION

Numerous studies have shown a positive relationship between testosterone levels and aggression – whether it relates to anger, verbal aggressiveness, competition, dominance or physical violence (Batrinos, 2012). Indeed, for the majority of animals, including humans, the male is recognized as the most aggressive sex – especially in young adulthood when androgen levels are at their highest. One of the earliest studies to show the effects of androgens on aggression was undertaken by Allee et al. (1939) who injected testosterone into low ranking hens and found this increased their aggressive behaviour, leading them to rise in dominance, sometimes to the top position in their group. This was accompanied by their comb size increasing (a male characteristic), crowing (which is rare in hens), and a sexual interest in other hens. A masculization effect has also been observed in female rhesus monkeys given testosterone injections over an eight-month period. These monkeys became so aggressive, they replaced the males in the top position of the social hierarchy (Joslyn, 1973). In contrast, reduced testosterone can decrease aggressive behaviour. We have long known this, for humans have been castrating domestic animals for thousands of years to make them more manageable, and the anti-aggressive effects of castration have been shown in several studies (Takeshita et al., 2017).

Despite this, the relationship between testosterone and aggression in humans is not a straightforward one. One of the first studies to examine this issue was undertaken by Kreuz and Rose (1972) who found that prisoners that had committed violent crimes during their adolescence had higher testosterone levels. In another study, it was reported that 10 out of 11 inmates with the highest testosterone had committed violent crimes, whereas 9 out of 11 who had committed non-violent crimes had the lowest testosterone levels (Dabbs et al., 1987). However, others have questioned whether testosterone levels correlate with aggressive behaviour. For example, Archer (1994) reviewed ten studies in which aggressive and non-aggressive groups were compared for androgen levels, finding only a weak correlation in the region of +0.3. A similar finding was reported by Dabbs and Morris (1990) who measured testosterone in 4,462 US military veterans. Although those with levels in the top 10% had shown more antisocial behaviour including assault, the overall correlative relationship was relatively small. The tendency to produce aggressive behaviour in this study was also more pronounced in the men from lower socio-economic groups.

It is often overlooked that environmental events may have an important bearing on testosterone levels. This can be seen, for example, in species that live in social groups with dominance hierarchies. Whilst the highest ranked individuals in such groups (e.g. alpha males) are indeed often the ones with greater levels of testosterone, this does not mean the dominant animals are always strongly androgenic. For example, Rose et al. (1975) found that a monkey's testosterone level before it was placed into a new social group did not correlate with the rank they would later attain, but once the social groups were established and the dominance ranking stabilized, a significant rise in testosterone (as much as tenfold) could be found in the dominant male. The most important cause of this rise was success in aggressive encounters. Conversely, a defeated monkey may show a fall in testosterone of some 10–15% within 24 hours, and this androgen can remain depressed for several weeks (Monaghan & Glickman, 1992).

Similar findings have also been reported for humans. In men participating in a wide range of sports, testosterone often increases for a couple of hours after victory and decreases following a loss (Archer, 2006; Wood & Stanton, 2012). Increases in testosterone have also been found in chess players and laboratory contests of reaction time (Mazur & Booth, 1998). Changes in testosterone also apparently occur during vicarious experiences of winning and losing among fans at sporting events (Bernhardt et al., 1998). To give an example, prior to the 1994 World Cup soccer final between Brazil and Italy (which Brazil won 1–0) testosterone levels were taken from a small group of both fans. The levels rose in 11 of the 12 Brazilian fans by an average of 27.6%, and decreased by 26.7% in the Italian fans (Fielden et al., 1994). Nor are such changes limited to sporting contests. A sample of 57 male voters in the 2008 US presidential elections showed that saliva testosterone remained stable in voters who had won, but dropped in those which had voted for the loser (cited in Wood & Stanton, 2012).

When trying to make sense of these findings, it may be more meaningful to view testosterone as a hormone that encourages dominance, i.e. to enhance one's status over other people. Although dominant behavior is sometimes aggressive with an intent to inflict harm on another person, this is not always the case, especially in the case of humans who often seek to assert their superiority over others without any intent to cause physical injury. Thus, it may be the case that testosterone is related primarily to dominance among men and not aggression. Indeed, nearly all primate studies that have linked testosterone to aggression may just as easily be interpreted as supporting the dominance theory (Mazur & Booth, 1998).

TESTOSTERONE AND SEXUAL BEHAVIOUR

There is also a link between testosterone and sexual behaviour. Male rat sexual behaviour has been intensively studied over the past hundred years (Shulman & Spritzer, 2014). To give an example of this knowledge, during a typical sexual interaction, the male performs ten to twelve intromissions[1] and then a prolonged intromission in which they ejaculate. And typically a male rat can ejaculate six to seven times within four hours of contact with a receptive female. Another finding to emerge from research is the undermining effects of castration on sexual activity. For example, if an adult male rat is castrated, it exhibits a marked decline in sexual activity and little interest in a receptive female. Reproductive interest is restored, however, by the administration of testosterone (Becker et al., 2002). Despite this, there is a caveat. Whilst a certain threshold level of testosterone is needed to stimulate sexual activity, increasing it above normal does not necessarily increase sexual activity. Or put more simply, testosterone concentration, in the rat at least, does not predict sexual activity (Damassa et al., 1977). Nonetheless, testosterone is released by sexual stimuli and events. For example, male rats reflexively release testosterone when they smell a female in anticipation of sexual activity, or during mating and ejaculation. Testosterone levels return to baseline, however, within 1.5 hours after exposure to a receptive female (Shulman & Spritzer, 2014). It is also recognized that testosterone release is affected in humans by sexual events and situations (Goldey & van Andrews, 2014).

For humans and primates, the relationship between testosterone and sexual activity is more complex. Male primates are typically able to maintain sexual behaviour for some years after castration, although it does eventually cause a decrease in activity and interest. The situation appears to be similar in humans with a gradual waning of sexual motivation, but there is also great variability between individuals. Some castrated males quickly become impotent, whilst others show relatively normal sexual function for years, or even decades, after the operation (Money & Ehrhardt, 1996). Historical accounts of eunuchs who were employed as harem guards, or young men castrated for their opera-singing abilities, point to a similar conclusion (Heriot, 1955). Reliable reports

---

[1]The act of inserting the penis into the vagina during intercourse.

also confirm that castrated men are capable of both erections and orgasms (Kinsey et al., 1948). Thus it would appear that testosterone loss is not crucial for male copulatory behaviour.

It is even questionable whether testosterone enhances libido. In one double-blind-placebo study, the raising of testosterone in young men did not significantly increase the frequency of sexual intercourse, or other aspects of sexual desire and behaviour (O'Connor et al., 2004). Despite this, testosterone is still capable of influencing sexual behaviour. For example, when hypo-gonadal men with abnormally low levels of testosterone are given hormone replacement therapy, they often report increases in sexual activity, along with increased frequency of sexual thoughts and fantasies (Davidson et al., 1979). This effect may not be specific to males since the adrenal glands in females also produce small amounts of testosterone, and females who have injections of androgens have reported a heightened sexual desire. This has also led to pharmaceutical companies marketing testosterone for the treatment of low sexual desire in women (Cappelletti & Wallen, 2016). It is also interesting to note that females can show a greater increase in salivary testosterone after sexual activity than males (see Figure 8.6).

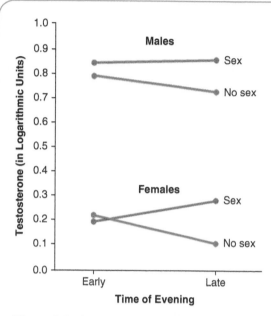

Figure 8.6 Relationship between sexual behaviour and salivary testosterone levels in men and woman

Source: Garrett and Hough (2021), from Dabbs, Jr., J. M. & Mohammed, S. (1992). Male and female salivary testosterone concentrations before and after sexual activity. *Physiology and Behavior*, 52, 195–197, Fig. 1. © 1992 Reprinted with permission from Elsevier Science.

SEXUAL DIMORPHISM IN THE CENTRAL NERVOUS SYSTEM

Charles Darwin first coined the term **sexual dimorphism** which refers to the differences in physiology and appearance of males and females – with the exception of their sexual organs. These include secondary sex characteristics and differences in the nervous system that may affect behavioural and cognitive differences. Whilst it has long been known that sex hormones exert important effects on early development, it was not until the early 1970s, when sex differences in the synaptic connections of the rat **medial preoptic hypothalamus** were discovered, that researchers realized dimorphism extended to the brain (Raisman & Field, 1973). Raisman and Field's discovery that the female preoptic area contained significantly more synapses than the male was also hormone dependent, for when males were castrated soon after birth their synapse numbers increased to female levels. Alternatively, testosterone given to young females resulted in a decrease of synapses to male levels.

Sexual dimorphism was also reported in zebra finches and canaries by Nottebohm and Arnold (1976) who identified two brain nuclei that control bird song (called the robustus archistriaum and high vocal centre). These were up to six times larger in male birds. Again, this structural difference was due to the early effects of sex hormones. When researchers exposed a young female zebra finch to testosterone, it caused the bird-song nuclei to grow much larger in adulthood, making them sing more like a male. The song nuclei also grew larger in the male during the spring when testosterone levels were higher.

A further important discovery was of a small nucleus embedded in the preoptic area of rats which was up to five times larger in males (Gorski et al., 1978). This was called the **sexually dimorphic nucleus** (see Figure 8.7) and its size was also found to be dependent on early androgen exposure. Males castrated at birth had smaller dimorphic nuclei, while females given androgens at birth developed a much larger nucleus. However, the size of the sexually dimorphic nuclei could only be altered during the first 10 days after birth. If male rats were castrated after this period, or females given androgens, the size of the nucleus remained unchanged. Interestingly, the sexually

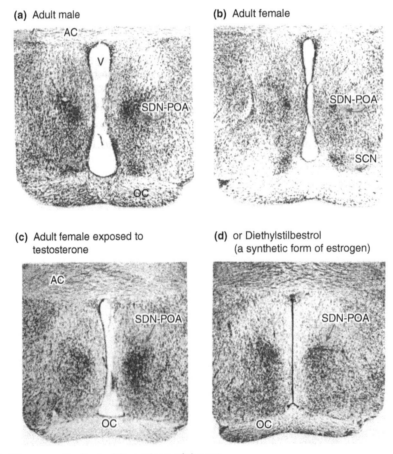

Figure 8.7   The sexually dimorphic nucleus of the rat

Source: Garrett and Hough (2021), from Gorski, R. A. (1974). The neuroendocrine regulation of sexual behavior. In G. Newton & A.H. Riesen (Eds.), Advances in psychobiology (Vol. 2) (pp. 1–58). Wiley. Reprinted with permission of John Wiley & Sons, Inc.

dimorphic nucleus has been found to be larger in the males of all mammals. In the case of humans, the preoptic area is more complex since it contains four small nuclei, otherwise known as the **interstitial nuclei of the anterior hypothalamus** (INAH 1–4). These nuclei appear to be the human equivalent of the rat's sexually dimorphic nucleus. It has been shown that whilst the INAH-1 and INAH-4 do not show any size difference between the sexes, the remaining two nuclei, particularly INAH-3, are larger in males (Allen et al., 1988). In fact, the INAH-3 is about 40% larger in males than females. There is also evidence that INAH-3 may influence sexual orientation as it has been shown to be significantly smaller in homosexual men than heterosexual men (LeVay, 1993). The implications of this finding are discussed later in the chapter.

How then does testosterone affect the development of the nervous system? The answer may come as a surprise. Although many neurons in the CNS have receptors for testosterone and other steroids, unlike the effects of neurotransmitters (whose main function is to affect the electrical excitability of the neuron), activation of sex steroid receptors initiates a cascade of chemical events inside the neuron. These then act on the nucleus to affect the transcription of certain genes. More precisely, in certain areas of the brain (including the hypothalamus and limbic system) testosterone enters the cell, where it is transformed by an enzyme called aromatase into estradiol. This sets into action a number of chemical steps leading to gene transcription. Elsewhere in the body, testosterone is transported into the cytoplasm of target tissue cells where it is reduced to 5α-dihydrotestosterone (DHT) by the enzyme 5α-reductase. This structural change allows it to move into the nucleus and bind directly to specific nucleotide sequences of the chromosomal DNA. Here sex steroids may influence cell numbers by stimulating the formation of trophic factors that promote the growth of cell size, dendritic branches and possibly synaptic numbers – or conversely by altering the incidence of programmed cell death (Pfaff et al., 2002).

KEY TERMS: *sexual dimorphism, medial preoptic hypothalamus, sexually dimorphic nucleus, interstitial nuclei of the anterior hypothalamus, INAH-3, aromatase, estradiol, 5α-dihydrotestosterone*

SPECIAL INTEREST 8.1

THE SMELL OF SEX: THE VOMERONASAL ORGAN

The vomeronasal organ (VNO) is a tiny duct with a cluster of receptors located in the soft tissues of the nose just above the roof of the mouth. Whilst hardly discernible in humans, it is well developed in other species, including most mammals, where it has neural connections with the hypothalamus and amygdala. The main role of the VNO is to detect pheromones – odour signals conveying information about the sexual condition of an individual, to other members of its group. This organ, for example, plays a crucial role in the male sexual behaviour of the golden hamster. If a male hamster is anaesthetized and placed in a lordosis position, other males will give it a cursory examination. But if the hindquarters of this hamster are smeared with a vaginal discharge, then the males will try mating with it. The pheromone responsible for producing this behaviour is called *aphrodism* and it requires an intact VNO to produce its stimulatory effect on the mating response.

(Continued)

Pheromones also play an important part in female sexual behaviour. If female mice are housed together, their oestrus cycles will lengthen and stop. This is called the *Lee-Boot effect* and it may have evolved to help conserve reproductive energy in the absence of males when ovulation is unlikely to lead to pregnancy. However, if the urine of a male is introduced into the female group, they will start oestrus cycling again (known as the *Whitten effect*). The presence of an unfamiliar male can also terminate the pregnancy of a recently impregnated female (the *Bruce effect*). This is likely to be advantageous for the female because the new male, by taking over his predecessor's territory, has shown himself to have 'better' genes that will likely produce fitter offspring. Both the Whitten and Bruce effects are caused by pheromones from the urine of adult males. The urine of a castrated male has no effect, showing that this pheromone requires the presence of testosterone.

But what about human behaviour? Although some researchers believe the human VNO is non-functional (Rodriguez, 2004), it still remains that pheromones can influence our behaviour. For example, when groups of females live together, their menstrual cycles tend to become synchronized. The chemical responsible for this effect may derive from the armpits, because when an extract from this region was swabbed onto women three times a week, their menstrual cycles began synchronizing with that the donor (Russell et al., 1980). Pheromones also play a role in human sexual attraction. For example, both men and women have reported heightened sexual interest when using aftershave or perfume laced with a synthesized pheromone (see McCoy & Pinto, 2002). It has also been found that women tend to prefer the smells of men who are most genetically dissimilar to themselves especially when they are in the most fertile part of their menstrual cycle (Wedekind et al., 1995). This type of preference makes sense since it would increase the beneficial effects of genetic diversity including a greater protection against a wider range of diseases. PET scans have also revealed that these types of sexually linked pheromones activate the anterior hypothalamic area (Savic et al., 2001).

SEX DIFFERENCES IN HUMAN BRAIN STRUCTURE

It has long been known that males tend to have larger brains than females. For example, the average brain volume for men is around 1260 cc compared to 1130 cc for women – although there is substantial individual variation (Allen et al., 2002). This finding has been confirmed using meta-analysis (Ruigrok et al., 2014), and also in a study that compared 2,750 female and 2,466 male brains (Ritchie et al., 2018). Across all ages total brain size is consistently reported to be about 10% larger in males – a difference that works out at about 23 billion cortical neurons for adult males and 19 billion for adult females. One reason for this difference might be because males are more likely to have larger bodies. Although there is some truth in this, with the larger muscle mass presumably requiring more neural control, this may not be the full story. For example, brain structures commonly reported to be different between the sexes include the caudate nucleus, amygdala, hippocampus, and cerebellum – all known to have a relatively high density of sex steroid receptors (Giedd et al., 2012). Thus, the sex difference in brain size may largely be due to the higher secretion of sex steroids during early development.

It is sometimes said a larger brain signifies greater intelligence but this a myth. For example, elephants have the largest brain of any land mammal, weighing around 11–13 pounds (roughly 5–7 kilograms), which is four times the size of the human brain, yet few would accept elephants are more intelligent than humans. What is more important for intelligence is the complexity of the brain and not its size. And on this point, there is evidence that females have more complex brains, at least in some respects. For example, whilst males show a greater total volume of brain tissue (Luders et al., 2003), if we examine the *relative proportions* of grey matter and white matter, a different picture emerges. It is estimated that men have 6.5 times more grey matter (made up of active neurons) in the brain than women, but women have around 10 times more myelinated white matter, which is involved in communication between different regions (Zaidi, 2010). This situation also results in female brains having neurons that are more tightly packed together than male brains. It has also been reported that women have greater white tract complexity (Ritchie et al., 2018).

Although it is now clear there are many morphological differences between male and female brains, some may be more important for cognition than others. For example, one major region of the cerebral cortex, the inferior-parietal lobe, is significantly larger on the left side in men (Frederikse et al., 1999). In women this asymmetry is reversed. The left inferior-parietal lobe is known to be involved in understanding spatial relationships along with mathematical abilities, and was shown to be abnormally large in Albert Einstein's brain (see Chapter 1). This structure difference may help explain why men tend to perform well on the Mental Rotations Test (MRT) which requires the subject to rotate complex 3-D shapes in their mind. Curiously, for women, having relatively larger amounts of grey matter in the parietal lobe was associated with poorer performance on the MRT (Koscik et al., 2009).

In contrast, females who tend to show better verbal skills than men, especially with regard to verbal fluency and verbal memory tasks, have also been shown to have larger brain areas associated with language. For example, one MRI study has found 23% more volume in Broca's area (involved in speech production) and 13% more volume in Wernicke's area (involved in speech comprehension) in females compared

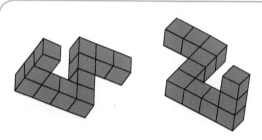

Figure 8.8   A spatial rotation task (in which the subject has to determine whether the two shapes are the same or different)

Source: Garrett and Hough (2021)

to males (Schlaepfer et al., 1995). A more recent analysis has shown much larger grey matter volumes in Broca's area in females compared to males which occurs bilaterally (Kurth et al., 2017). Moreover, the authors of this paper hypothesized that the observed larger grey matter volumes in females may be explained by a denser network of interwoven nerve fibres and glia, and increased dendritic arborization. Similarly, the greater size of Wernicke's area in females, which was found to be 18% larger in females compared with males (Harasty et al., 1997), has been attributed to its anatomical complexity (Jacobs et al., 1993).

Another brain area that has attracted a great deal of interest in sex-difference research is the huge bundle of white matter that connects the two cerebral hemispheres called the **corpus callosum**. In 1982 it was reported that the posterior part of the corpus callosum, called the **splenium**, which joins the occipital and parietal regions, was significantly larger and shaped differently in females (Lacoste-Utamsing & Holloway, 1982). Although this finding was confirmed by others, it proved controversial – not least when a thorough meta-analysis of 49 studies was published which found no significant differences in the size of the corpus callosum (Bishop & Wahlsten, 1997). Nonetheless, part of the dispute appears to lie in the fact that whilst men have bigger brains than women, the size of the corpus callosum remains much the same (which means it is relatively bigger in females). However, a more recent study that measured the midsagittal corpus callosum cross-sectional area from 316 MRI scans of normal subjects, which importantly controlled for brain size and age, reported that females have a significantly larger corpus callosum after all. This was also particularly pronounced in young adults (Ardekani et al., 2013). It appears that while male brains have more connections within a single hemisphere, female brains are more connected between the two hemispheres. Thus, females have greater inter-hemispheric connectivity and lateralization (Ingalhalikar et al., 2014).

If females do indeed have a larger corpus callosum, then one might expect that their brains will show a greater tendency to process verbal language simultaneously over both hemispheres of the brain. Some evidence for this possibility has come from the finding that males who have suffered a stroke to the left cortex are more likely to exhibit serious and longer lasting language deficits compared to females with the same type of damage (Levy & Heller, 1992). This has also been supported by some studies that have examined brain activity with functional brain scanning techniques. For example, Shaywitz et al. (1995) compared the sexes on several language tasks with fMRI, and found that brain activity in males was predominantly left hemispheric. Yet some degree of caution should be exercised when considering these findings. A meta-analysis study covering 14 functional imaging studies, providing data on 377 men and 442 women, showed no difference in the bilateral representation of language areas in men and women (Sommer et al., 2004).

KEY TERMS: *inferior-parietal lobe, corpus callosum, splenium*

SEX DIFFERENCES IN COGNITION

If men and women have different brains, then one might expect them to show variation in the solving of cognitive tasks. Indeed, there is support for this idea (Andreano & Cahill, 2009; Halpern, 2011) which extends to a variety of tasks. A consistent finding is a male superiority in spatial ability. One way of testing this is the Mental Rotations Task (see Figure 8.8) where subjects have to mentally visualize and manipulate a three-dimensional object. The male superiority on this type of task is around 20% and consistent across different cultures (Peters et al., 2007). It also appears that men and women solve these problems differently since brain-imaging studies show that men tend to use their parietal lobes in such tasks, whereas women utilize the frontal cortex (Hugdahl et al., 2006). Males have also been reported to perform better on other spatially based tasks including maths and science tests, reading a map, solving a maze or visuospatial problems, and judging velocity (Halpern, 2004, 2011). Despite this, there is much individual variability between the sexes. Around a quarter of adult women, for example, do better than men on the visual-spatial questions of an IQ test (Kimura, 1992). It should also be noted that some have questioned whether the cognitive differences between the sexes are really as pronounced as they first appear (Hirnstein et al., 2019).

Testosterone is an important determinant of spatial ability. For example, men with low levels of testosterone caused by pituitary dysfunction often perform poorly on spatial tests. Conversely, females with congenital adrenal hyperplasia who have relatively high levels of testosterone show superior performance (Resnick et al., 1986), as do females with an androgynous or masculine appearance (Peterson, 1976). Despite this, the relationship between testosterone and spatial ability is not as simple as it first appears (see Figure 8.9). In a study that tested spatial abilities in adult men of different ages, better performance was associated with medium levels of testosterone (Yonker et al., 2006). In other words, men with average testosterone levels were superior to those with high levels. Thus, the association between testosterone and spatial abilities is curvilinear (Celec et al., 2015; Gouchie & Kimura, 1991).

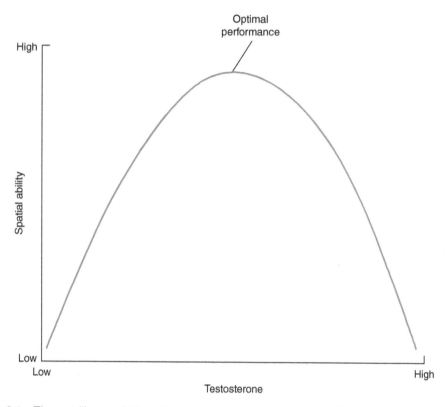

Figure 8.9 The curvilinear relationship between testosterone and spatial ability
Source: Wickens (2009)

In contrast, studies have shown that women tend to outperform males on tasks of verbal ability (see Kurth et al., 2017). This difference can be observed with a simple verbal fluency test whereby subjects are told to write down as many words beginning with a given letter (say 'A') in a certain time period. Although females do not have a larger vocabulary than males, it is claimed they often outperform them on this task (Kimura, 1999). In a more recent study that looked at 200 adults aged 18 to 70 years, which examined two types of verbal fluency (testing for semantic words or emotional words), a significant difference was found only for emotional verbal fluency (Gawda & Szepietowska, 2013). However, again, there is a great deal of overlap between men and women on these types of tests, and results vary considerably across different studies. Women also tend to perform better on tests of perceptual speed where they have to match items, or tasks requiring them to remember whether an item has been mis-placed from a picture or array (visual memory). Another female superiority occurs in colour naming. Females are typically able to name a series of colour patches or circles faster than males, and this effect is found in primary school children, as well as university undergraduates (Kimura, 1999).

Although it is impossible to prove empirically, it may well be that sex differences in human cognition have an evolutionary basis which first arose when humans were hunter-gatherers (e.g. c. 10,000 years ago). During this time, males and females would have most likely had different roles. The males were hunter-gatherers, travelling long distances away from their home base, which would have required good navigational and spatial skills. In contrast, the females stayed in one place, forming social groups and looking after children – a situation more conducive to developing verbal skills. Thus, it is tempting to speculate that the demands of these two situations somehow led to a change in these respective abilities in males and females (Kimura, 1999). However, there are those who disagree with this theory. For some researchers, many cognitive abilities are more importantly modulated by environmental, cultural and learning influences (Jäncke, 2018). Indeed, this appears to be borne out by some fairly recent findings showing that cognitive sex differences are changing in some tasks and decreasing in others (Miller & Halpern, 2013).

DIGIT RATIO: AN INDICATOR OF PRENATAL TESTOSTERONE

It has been known since the late nineteenth century that males tend to have a longer ring finger (the 4th digit) compared to the index (2nd digit). This relationship (index finger length divided by ring finger length) produces what is known as a low digit ratio. In contrast, females are more likely to have a digit ratio of around 1.0 meaning the two fingers are the same length. In 1998, the evolutionary biologist John Manning measured index and ring finger lengths in 800 males and females, ranging from 2 to 25 years, and confirmed males tend to have a lower 2D:4D (on both hands). This was consistent across all ages and remained unchanged over time. It appears that this difference is a result of foetal development, for digit ratios are established by the 13th week of gestation, and governed by the same homeobox or *Hox* genes that control the formation of our testes and ovaries (Garn et al., 1975). Moreover, this finger difference first manifests itself when the foetus is being exposed to high levels of testosterone. Manning has also shown that males with the low 2D:4D ratios continue to exhibit higher testosterone levels along with increased sperm counts (another indicator of testosterone) as adults. In contrast, higher levels of luteinizing hormone and oestrogen are related to higher 2D:4D ratios which is more common in females (Manning et al., 1998).

As we saw earlier, there is evidence that sex hormones exert organizational effects upon the brain during foetal development which masculinizes or feminizes certain later behaviours. This is particularly true for the later part of the first trimester, which is the time when digit ratio is formed, and a critical period for sexual differentiation of the body and brain. The implication from Manning's work was that a low 2D:4D ratio could act as a marker for a uterine environment high in testosterone and low in oestrogen. Conversely, a high 2D:4D ratio could be a marker for a uterine environment low in testosterone and high in oestrogen. If this was indeed the case, then one might expect to find a wide range of behavioural differences between individuals with high and low digit ratios (Manning, 2002).

Since Manning's discovery, work on digit ratio has become a major area of research in biopsychology (see Valla & Cici, 2011; Voracek & Loibi, 2016). Although some are keen to 'debunk' the idea that finger length can reveal anything meaningful (Leslie, 2019), digit ratio has nonetheless become linked with a wide range of behavioural and cognitive traits, whilst also being recognized as an important determinant of health and sexuality (Manning, 2002, 2007). Low digit ratio, for example, has provided an indicator of sexual orientation. This was shown by Manning et al. (2007) who took self-reported finger measurements from 255,166 participants in a BBC internet survey designed to investigate the relationship between digit ratio and sex, ethnicity and sexual orientation. The results revealed that heterosexual males had a lower 2D:4D ratio across all ethnic groups. However, male homosexuals and bisexuals tended to have a higher (more female-like) 2D:4D digit ratio. No significant relationship between digit ratio and sexual orientation was found for women, although there was a trend for a lower 2D:4D ratio in female homosexuals – a finding that has since been confirmed in other studies (Grimbos et al., 2010).

Research also shows a relationship between digit ratio and performance on many cognitive tasks. For example, in a sample of 134,317 men and 120,783 women, it was found that men performed better than women on a mental rotation task, and this effect was most pronounced in men with low 2D:4D digit ratios (Peters et al., 2007). There is also an inverted U-shape relation between digit ratio and mathematical ability (i.e. subjects with either high and low digit ratios perform more poorly in mathematics exams while those with intermediate digit ratios do better) (Sánchez et al., 2014). The situation regarding verbal fluency is less clear. Although there is evidence that women with high 2D:4D digit ratios exhibit superior verbal fluency performance compared to males (Burton et al., 2005), this effect is apparently not robust or associated with hormone levels (Miller & Halpern, 2013).

Digit ratio also provides an indicator for health and several psychological disorders. For example,

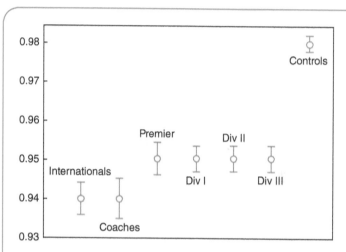

Figure 8.10 Digit ratios of professional soccer players

Source: Wickens (2009), from Manning, J. T. (2001). Second to fourth digit ratio and male ability in sport: Implications for sexual selection in humans. *Evolution and Human Behaviour*, 22, 61–69. Reproduced by permission of Professor Manning.

Martin et al. (1999) showed that a low digit ratio in men is correlated with higher levels of depression. There is also a higher incidence of ADHD and autism spectrum disorders, including Asperger's syndrome, in low ratio males (Martel et al., 2008). In terms of health, a low digit ratio increases the risk for prostate cancer (Manning, 2002) whereas a high digit ratio increases the risk of breast cancer in females (Muller et al., 2012). However, a low 2D:4D ratio may have benefits as well. A tendency for low 2D:4D ratios has been found in professional soccer players, which is most pronounced for international players, and in elite male musicians from a British symphony orchestra. There is even an association (apparently) between a low digit ratio and having a longer penis in males! (See Choi et al., 2011.)

KEY TERM: *low digit ratio*

KEY THINKER 8.1

CHARLES BROWN-SEQUARD

The male testes have long been associated with sexual vigour, youthfulness and longevity. In ancient Greece and Rome, concoctions made from goat and wolf testes were used as aphrodisiacs, and similar practices still occur today in some places of the world. The relationship between sexual vigour and youthfulness has also fascinated humans – not least because it is obvious, especially to old frail men, that the period of youth coincides with peak sexual performance. But can sexual vigour and youthfulness be linked to the testes? One person who believed so was Charles Brown-Séquard (1817–1894). The imposing 6'4'' bearded French professor was author of over 500 research papers including pioneering work on the adrenal glands. For most of his life Brown-Séquard had been a prolific researcher, but as he approached his seventieth birthday he became aware of a decline in his concentration and work. This was accompanied by tiredness and a waning of his muscular strength. Despite being recently married with a young wife, he also became impotent with a declining sexual interest. Worried about his lack of vitality, he set about ways of rejuvenating himself.

Brown-Séquard believed the testes, or rather the seminal fluid that contains the sperm, had invigorating properties, so he started testing the effects of such extracts on himself. In his first attempt, he ground up the testicles of a young dog and passed the mixture through filter paper. He then put the residue in distilled water and injected it into his leg. The procedure seemed to have a beneficial effect, and after a few injections Brown-Sequard felt stronger and rejuvenated. He repeated the procedure twice more with extracts taken from guinea pigs. The health benefits appeared to be so impressive that, in 1889, at the age of 72, Brown-Séquard made the bold step of presenting his findings to a prestigious group of scientists at the *Société de Biologie* in Paris.

Although the talk only lasted 15 minutes, it had a dramatic impact. This was largely due to Brown-Séquard explicitly describing the effects of his experiences, including a confession of having paid his wife 'a visit' which he had not done for a long time. He claimed his extract led to rejuvenation and prolonged life. The talk provoked much debate in scientific circles, and not surprisingly was reported in a sensational fashion by the national press. Consequently, he soon become the world's foremost advocate for the existence of 'internal secretions' or what we now know as hormones. In this belief about hormones, Brown-Séquard was to be proven correct – but in regard to his views on testicular extracts and rejuvenation, history was to treat him less kindly. Within a year of his talk, over a thousand physicians world-wide were testing his elixir in clinical trials, but few replicated the findings. Brown-Séquard was also an easy target for ridicule and his professional reputation quickly became tarnished by the episode. With his health beginning to deteriorate, his wife left him for a younger man, and despite keeping up his injections, he died from a stroke at the age of 77. But why was Brown-Séquard so mistaken in his views? The likeliest answer is that he was fooled by a *placebo effect*, i.e. he was expecting his elixir to work, and his optimism led him to incorrectly exaggerate its benefits. This was further compounded by the lack of a control group (preferably it should also be *double-blind* where neither the subjects nor the experimenter know who is receiving a particular treatment) which is an essential experimental requirement for drug studies.

THE NEUROLOGICAL BASIS OF SEXUAL BEHAVIOUR

While the brain is undoubtedly the most important organ for our sexual behaviour, some of the basic reflexes that play an integral role in our reproductive acts are controlled by the spinal cord. For example, stimulation of the genitals in some animals, such as dogs, elicits sexual responses such as penile erections, pelvic thrusting and ejaculations even when the brain is severed from the spinal cord (Hart, 1967). Similar responses have also been observed in paraplegic men. In 1960, John Money questioned paraplegic males with lesions of the spinal cord and found that 20% were able to engage in coitus, 65% could achieve a full erection, and 20% could manage partial erections. Many of these men were also capable of ejaculation although they could not 'sense' the orgasm mentally.

One key brain region for sexual behaviour is the hypothalamus. This area not only controls the release of LH and FSH from the pituitary gland, leading to the release of the sex hormones from the testes and ovaries, but is also involved in acts of sexual intercourse. In the case of male sexual activity, the **medial preoptic area** (MPA) plays an important role. As we have already seen (Gorski et al., 1978) the MPA contains the sexually dimorphic nucleus which is bigger in male brains. This structure has been linked with the act of male sexual intercourse, since lesions of this area impair the ability of male rats to copulate, but it does not affect female sexuality (Heimer & Larson, 1967). Electrical stimulation of this region also facilitates sexual behaviour in male rats (Davidson, 1980), whilst mating behaviour can be reinstated in castrated males by small implants of testosterone into the MPA (Breedlove et al., 2007). One way the MPA exercises its influence over sexual behaviour is by its control over the **periaqueductal grey area** (PGA). This is an area that contains neural circuits for producing complex reflexes and species-typical patterns of behaviour including those necessary for copulation (Carere et al., 2007).

In females, the ventromedial hypothalamus (VMH) is more strongly implicated in sexual behaviour. Lesions of the VMH in rats abolish the ability of the female rat to perform lordosis, as do injections of drugs into the VMH which block progesterone receptors (Ogawa et al., 1994). Tiny implants of oestrogens into this region of the hypothalamus will also increase female receptivity towards males (Becker et al., 2002). A model that explains the neural circuitry underlying lordosis behaviour has been proposed by Pfaff and Schwartz-Giblin (1988). According to their theory, lordosis is initiated when the male shows interest in the female which leads to stimulation of her rump. This sensory information is relayed to the VMH. Providing the VMH has been primed with oestrogen and progesterone, it will trigger the command for producing lordosis, by acting on the PGA and midbrain reticular formation – areas that have motor neurons responsible for controlling the deep back muscles that are involved in producing the postural changes of lordosis. A multisynaptic pathway then passes down to the spinal cord where the behavioural reflexes are put into motion.

There is also some evidence from human studies to show that the hypothalamus is involved in sexual activity. For example, one 50-year-old male patient with a tumour of the left hypothalamic region developed erectile and ejaculatory difficulties and a sexual preference for children (Miller et al., 1986). There have also been attempts, controversially, to lesion the hypothalamus for the treatment of sexual deviancy. Roeder et al. (1972) lesioned the VMH in ten patients with issues ranging from paedophilic homosexuality to intractable exhibitionism. The results showed that sex drive was diminished or abolished in all his cases. Perhaps a more reliable indicator of hypothalamic function and sexuality, however, comes from neuroimaging studies. For example, Ferretti et al. (2005) found increased activation of the hypothalamus following sexual arousal elicited by pornographic pictures and during ejaculation.

Other regions of the limbic system have also been implicated in sexual behaviour. One area is the septal region which is found just below the anterior part of the corpus callosum and tucked in-between the horns of the two lateral ventricles. This was demonstrated by the American psychiatrist Robert Galbraith Heath (a somewhat notorious figure known for his 'therapeutic' attempts to convert gay men into heterosexuals), who undertook experiments electrically stimulating various brain sites in a sample of 54 patients with a range of conditions including schizophrenia. He found that feelings of sexual arousal and a subjective 'pleasurable response' were elicited by stimulation of the septal region in all patients. Remarkably, Heath then developed a device that allowed his patients to self-stimulate their own brain. He reported that septal self-stimulation elicited orgasm and a compulsion to masturbate (Heath, 1972).

The amygdala has also been linked with sexual behaviour. Classic work by Klüver and Bucy (1938), for example, showed that amygdala lesions in monkeys produced hypersexuality with indiscriminate attempts at mating. There have also been sporadic accounts of similar behaviour in humans following amygdala damage. For example, Terzian and Ore (1955) reported a case of a man who underwent bilateral removal of the temporal lobes, including the amygdala, for intractable epilepsy, which resulted in hypersexuality. This was manifested as frequent exhibitionism, homosexual and heterosexual advances toward others, and habitual masturbation. Although the symptoms of human Klüver-Bucy syndrome can vary, it typically results in greater sexual interest and increased masturbation (Lilly et al., 1983).

The cerebral cortex should not be underestimated for its involvement in many aspects of sexual activity. For example, Beach (1940) found a decrease in male copulation in rats following cortical damage, with lesions involving 60% of its tissue abolishing the behaviour completely. However cortical damage did not alter female sexual activity. One cortical region implicated in human sexual behaviour is that of the frontal lobes. It is known that disinhibited sexual behaviour can be a consequence of frontal lobe damage, especially if it involves the orbitofrontal region (Baird et al., 2007). Inappropriate sexual behaviour in a geriatric population was also found to be associated with right frontal lobe strokes (Bardell et al., 2011), while sexual automatisms characterized by rhythmic pelvic movements and handling of the genitalia have been reported in patients with seizures arising from the same part of the brain. Brain-scanning studies have also provided interesting information (see Ruesink & Georgiadis, 2017). For example, activation of numerous frontal regions, including the right prefrontal cortex, anterior cingulate cortex and orbitofrontal region, has been observed during sexual arousal involving masturbation-induced orgasm (Karama et al., 2002).

KEY TERMS: *medial preoptic area, periaqueductal grey area, ventromedial hypothalamus, septal region*

WHAT DETERMINES A PERSON'S SEXUAL ORIENTATION?

We all have sexual preferences, whether for members of the opposite sex, same sex, or both. But what causes our sexual orientation? As might be expected there are many theories, although most fall into three main groups: those emphasizing genetic factors; those stressing hormonal activity; and those focusing on the importance of learning and environment. Of course, all of these factors need not be mutually exclusive. Genetic and hormonal factors are closely associated, and there is probably a complex interaction of all these factors in varying degrees throughout our early development and life to influence our sexual predisposition (Bailey et al., 2016; Bogaert & Skorska, 2020).

One way of gauging the genetic influence on sexuality is by comparing the concordance between identical twins (who share the same genes) and fraternal twins (who share around 50% of their genes). An early study which looked at 85 male twins where homosexuality was present, reported a 100% concordance rate for identical twins compared to 10% for fraternal twins (Kallmann, 1952). However more recent studies have reported estimates of around 50% for identical twins – whether male or female. Bailey and Pillard (1991), for example, found that 52% of monozygotic twins and 22% of dizygotic were concordant for homosexuality. Similar figures occurred for females, with 48% of identical twins both exhibiting lesbi-anism, compared to 16% for fraternal (Bailey et al., 1993). Although these results suggest a genetic influence on the development of homosexuality, it is not marked, and there are just as many instances of identical twins where one is homosexual and the other heterosexual.

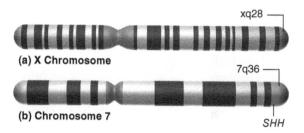

(a) The X chromosome, showing the Xq28 region. (b) Chromosome 7, indicating region 7q36 and the relative location of the SHH gene.

xq28 —

(a) X Chromosome

7q36 —

(b) Chromosome 7   SHH

Figure 8.11   Possible locations of the genes for male homosexuality

Source: Garrett and Hough (2018), based on data from 'Genetic and Environmental Effects on Same-Sex Sexual Behavior: A Population Study of Twins in Sweden', by N. Långström, Q. Rahman, E. Carlström, and P. Lichtenstein, 2010, *Archives of Sexual Behavior*, 39, 75–80.

The search for genes that may underlie homosexuality has led to researchers concentrating on the X chromosome. It is known that gay men tend to have more gay relatives on their mother's side of the family than on the father's side, and since it is only the mother who contributes X chromosomes to her offspring, then it follows that this chromosome could in theory provide the key genetic influence for the family effect. Hamer et al. (1993) performed a linkage analyses of 110 families of gay men, and found a correlation between homosexual orientation and the inheritance of certain polymorphic markers on the X chromosome in a region designated as Xq28. This was present in 64% of the twins tested. However this has not been confirmed by others. In a more thorough study, Mustanski et al. (2005) performed the first genome-wide scan of sexual orientation in men that examined 456 individuals from 146 families. They found no linkage to Xq28; instead their work suggested that many gay men may share a stretch of DNA on chromosome 7 in the 7q36 region.

For early researchers, one of the favoured biological explanations for homosexuality was the possibility of altered levels of sex hormones, but studies revealed no deficit or excess of sex hormones in gay men (Meyer-Bahlburg, 1984). The situation with women may be more complex since higher testosterone levels have been claimed to have been found in some 'butch' lesbians (Singh et al., 1999). Whether there is hormonal influence at work organizing the brain during foetal development is a different issue, and some believe it plays an important role (Balthazart, 2011). As we have seen earlier, exposure to androgens during early development in females, which can produce the androgen-ital syndrome, leads to a greater probability of adult lesbianism. The situation may be reversed for gay males. For example, gay men are more likely to have a high 2D:4D digit ratio which is indicative of lower prenatal testosterone levels. There is also evidence showing that male laboratory animals exposed to low levels of testosterone early in life show a greater sexual preference for their own sex as adults (Adkins-Regan, 1988).

It might come as a surprise to find out that probably the most reliable indicator of sexual orientation comes from the order in which a child is born in their family. In the 1990s, the Canadian Ray Blanchard noted that gay men tended to have older brothers, but not older sisters or younger brothers. He showed that for each extra male child born to a mother, the probability of a homosexual offspring was increased by 30% (Blanchard, 2001). In other words, the more older brothers a male has, the greater probability he will be gay. This effect is so strong that it is estimated that one gay man in seven owes his sexual orientation to birth order (Cantor et al., 2002) and the effect still occurs if they are reared apart from his family (Bogaert, 2006). The likeliest explana-tion for this birth effect lies with the mother's immune system. With each male birth, the mother develops increasing amounts of antibodies to male-specific proteins in the brain – and these somehow in turn alter the structure of her son's brain. Interestingly, it is claimed this birth effect is only seen in boys who are right-handed (Blanchard, 2008).

BRAIN STRUCTURE AND HOMOSEXUALITY

If there is a biological basis to homosexuality, one might expect to find a variation in brain structure between heterosexuals and gay individuals. In the early 1990s, a difference of this type was shown for the third interstitial nuclei of the anterior hypo-thalamus (INAH) by the neuroscientist Simon LeVay (who is himself openly gay). As we saw earlier in the chapter, the INAH are located in the preoptic hypothalamic area. They are also sexually dimorphic with INAH-2 and INAH-3 being larger in the male. However, LeVay found that INAH-3 was twice as large in heterosexual males (N = 6) compared to a group of homosexuals (N = 19). Or put another way, the size of INHA-3 in homosexual men was similar in size to that of heterosexual women. Although the role of the INAH in human sexuality is unknown, LeVay suggests that homosexuality may, in part, be due to the 'feminisation' of the NIHA-3 (LeVay, 1993, 2016).

The significance of this discovery remains uncertain. Whilst the INAH are believed to be analogues of the sexually dimorphic nuclei found in lower species, and whose size is influenced by early androgen exposure (Gorski et al., 1978), it is possible that the smaller INAH-3 in homosexual men could have occurred after early development. It may be, for instance, that the sexual experience of homosexual men has affected the size of their INAH-3. Thus, its smaller size could be the result of homosexuality rather than its cause. However, even if the size of INAH-3 resulted from low androgen levels during foetal development, it seems improbable that such a tiny brain structure could act as the sole determinant of one's sexuality.

It should also be noted that not all researchers have confirmed LeVay's findings. For example, Byne et al. (2001) found while the volume of the INAH-3 was slightly smaller in gay men, there was no difference in the number of neurons within the nucleus based on sexual orientation. Others have also argued that there are a number of conceptual and methodological flaws in these studies (Mbugua, 2003).

A second brain structure showing a size difference between gay and heterosexual men is the bed nucleus of the stria terminalis which forms part of a pathway connecting the amygdala with the hypothalamus. The size of this nucleus is larger in males than in females (Chung et al., 2002; Zhou et al., 1995). Interestingly, while it appears to be the same size in male heterosexuals and homosexuals, it is smaller and contains fewer neurons in transgender women (Kruijver et al., 2000). Transgender people do not identify with the sex/gender they were assigned at birth (in the case of this study, male), and may undergo transition to change their gender socially, legally and/or medically (for instance, through hormone therapy).

The **suprachiasmatic nucleus**, located in the anterior hypothalamus and involved in the production of circadian rhythms, has also been found to be larger in gay men. In one study, it was 150% larger in the brains of gay men that had died from AIDS compared to a group of heterosexuals. It also contained twice as many cells that secrete the neuropeptide vasopressin (Swaab & Hofman, 1990). On first sight this appears to be a puzzling difference, although the key to understanding its significance may lie with the finding that the suprachiasmatic nucleus also regulates the reproductive cycle in female rats. Furthermore, blocking the effects of testosterone in male rats during the prenatal period increased the number of vasopressin-secreting cells in the suprachiasmatic nucleus as adults. Interestingly, they also preferred the company of a sexually active male rather than a receptive female in oestrous (Swaab & Hofman, 1995).

KEY TERMS: *interstitial nuclei of the anterior hypothalamus, bed nucleus of the stria terminalis, suprachiasmatic nucleus, vasopressin*

SUMMARY

Reproduction is a complex behaviour, which for most species requires the coming together of male and female in an act of sexual intercourse. It also involves courtship, territorial ownership and parental assistance. In humans, a fertilized egg develops into either a male or female embryo depending on the **sex chromosomes**. Nearly every cell in the human body contains 23 pairs of chromosomes (basically tightly coiled DNA) with the sexes differing in just one pair: males having **XY** and females **XX** chromosomes. At around six weeks of gestation, the **SRY gene** on the Y chromosome produces a chemical that causes the foetal gonadal tissue to develop into testes. In turn, this tissue starts to secrete androgens (including testosterone) which begin the masculinization process of the foetus. Without this hormonal influence, the foetus will form ovaries at about the 12th week of gestation causing it to develop as a female. These hormonal actions are known as organizational effects. Another type of organizational effect takes place at puberty, when increased testosterone in males, and increased oestrogen and progesterone in females, cause the adult secondary sex characteristics to appear. During adulthood, the sex hormones continue to influence sex-related activity by exerting activational effects on behaviour. In males, androgens increase levels of aggression and competitiveness. In females, oestrogen and progesterone are secreted in a monthly pattern known as the menstrual cycle which prepares the womb for a fertilized egg (should it occur). It appears that testosterone increases sexual libido in both males and females.

Although male and female brains appear similar, they are sexually dimorphic in some areas. For example, the third interstitial nuclei of the anterior hypothalamus (INAH-3) is significantly bigger in male brains compared to female brains. There are also differences in brain regions involved in cognition, with men tending to have a better developed left parietal lobe, and women exhibiting more fully formed language regions including Wernicke's area, along with a relatively larger corpus callosum. These differences may help explain why men tend to be superior on tasks involving spatial memory, whereas women are superior on verbal and dexterity tests. Another difference between men and women occurs in the case of digit ratio, which has been shown to be linked to prenatal androgen exposure. Digit ratio has also been correlated with a large number of behavioural and cognitive traits, and found to be an important determinant of health and sexuality.

Although the neurobiological basis of sexual behaviour is not fully understood, the hypothalamic medial preoptic area has been implicated in male sexual behaviour, and the **ventromedial hypothalamus** in female sexual behaviour. This latter brain region has also been shown to be important for lordosis in female rats which is mediated by neural circuits in the periaqueductal grey area. Other brain areas implicated in various sexual activities include the **septum**, **amygdala** and frontal cortex. Sexual orientation in humans is affected by many variables, including genetic inheritance, hormonal exposure during foetal development, birth order and the effects of experience. There is also some evidence to show a neurobiological brain difference between heterosexual and gay men. In particular, gay men have been shown to have a smaller third interstitial nuclei of the anterior hypothalamus, but a larger suprachiasmatic nucleus with an increased number of vasopressin secreting cells. Transgender women have been shown to have a small bed nucleus of the stria terminalis which connects the amygdala and hypothalamus.

GO ONLINE

TEST YOUR UNDERSTANDING OF THIS CHAPTER AND VISIT HTTPS://STUDY.SAGEPUB.COM/WICKENS TO ACCESS INTERACTIVE 'DRAG AND DROP' LABELLING ACTIVITIES AND A FLASHCARD GLOSSARY.

MULTIPLE CHOICE QUESTIONS

Answer the questions below to test your understanding of this chapter's Learning Objectives. You'll find the answers at the end of the chapter.

1. Congenital adrenal hyperplasia occurs in foetal development when the adrenal glands produce high levels of which of the following?

    a. 21-hydroxylase
    b. adrenaline
    c. cortisol
    d. androgens

2. What condition is caused by the inheritance of an extra x chromosome (XXY)?

    a. Klinefelter's syndrome
    b. congenital adrenal hyperplasia
    c. testicular feminization syndrome
    d. Turner's syndrome

3. In humans, what are the sexually dimorphic nuclei otherwise known as?

    a. habenular nuclei
    b. mammillary bodies
    c. interstitial nuclei of the anterior hypothalamus
    d. septal nuclei

4. According to John Manning, in general, what is distinctive about male hands?

    a. they have a larger right thumb
    b. their ring finger is longer than the index finger
    c. their index finger is longer on their right hand
    d. the length of their index finger correlates with their testosterone levels

5. According to Roy Blanchard, what is male homosexuality due to?

    a. genetic causes
    b. having a dominant father
    c. the number of older brothers in the family
    d. structural differences in the anterior hypothalamus

6. In the rat, where have neural circuits for lordosis behaviour been found?

    a. hypothalamus
    b. amygdala
    c. bed nucleus of the stria terminalis
    d. periaqueductal grey area

FURTHER READING

Becker, J. B., Berkley, K. J., Geary, N., Hampson, E., Herman, J. P., & Young, E. A. (Eds.). (2007). *Sex differences in the brain: From genes to behavior*. Oxford University Press.
This book contains some very useful chapters on the neurobiology and behavior of sex differences in both humans and animals.

Becker, J. B., Breedlove, S. M., & Crews, D. (Eds.). (2002). *Behavioral endocrinology*. MIT Press.
Excellent textbook with a number of relevant chapters written by various experts, including several that cover hormonal influences on sexual behaviour, and others examining the effects of hormones on brain development and cognition.

Bullough, V. L. (1994). *Science in the bedroom: A history of sex research*. Basic Books.
From the first serious sex study ever undertaken (in France in 1830 with a group of prostitutes) to the latter-day work of Masters and Johnson, this is a very general but interesting account of the historical development of sex research.

Diamond, J. (1997). *Why is sex fun? The evolution of human sexuality*. Basic Books.
Takes an evolutionary approach to explain why humans might have sex without any intention of procreating, or why the human penis is proportionately larger than in other animals.

Halpern, D. (2011). *Sex differences in cognitive abilities*. Psychology Press.
The most up-to-date account of recent research findings and theories on cognitive sex differences which is accessible and useful for students and experts alike.

LeVay, S. (2016). *Gay, straight, and the reason why: The science of sexual orientation*. Oxford University Press.
Written by a leading researcher, this is a very readable account which argues sexual orientation results primarily from an interaction between genes, sex hormones and brain organization.

LeVay, S., & Valente, S. M. (2006). *Human sexuality*. Palgrave Macmillan.
An undergraduate textbook, illustrated in full colour with CD-ROM, that takes a multidisciplinary approach to understanding human sexuality.

Manning, J. T. (2002). *Digit ratio: A pointer to fertility, behavior and health*. Rutgers University Press.
Shows how the relative lengths of our 2nd and 4th fingers, which is determined by prenatal exposure to testosterone, predict a wide variety of behaviours and health issues.

Money, J., & Ehrhardt, A. K. (1996). *Man & woman, boy and girl*. Aronson.
A book that is still relevant which traces the development of gender from conception to maturity, with an emphasis on understanding the interaction between hormonal and environmental influences.

Shansky, R. M. (Ed.). (2015). *Sex differences in the central nervous system*. Elsevier.
Written by various experts, this book offers a comprehensive examination of the current state of sex differences research, from both the basic science and clinical research perspectives.

MULTIPLE CHOICE ANSWERS - 1. D | 2. A | 3. C | 4. B | 5. C | 6. D

9

LEARNING AND MEMORY

LEARNING OBJECTIVES

After reading this chapter you should be able to:

- Appreciate the work of Karl Lashley and his quest to find the engram.

- Understand the importance of Hebbian cell assemblies.

- Describe how experience may alter the physiology and neurochemistry of the brain.

- Explain how habituation occurs in *Aplysia*.

- Understand the importance of long-term potentiation.

- Elucidate the role of the hippocampus in memory consolidation.

- Describe the characteristics of temporal lobe and diencephalic amnesia.

- Explain the neurobiological basis of cognitive mapping.

GO ONLINE

Test your understanding of this chapter and visit **https://study.sagepub.com/wickens** to access interactive 'Drag and Drop' labelling activities and a flashcard glossary.

INTRODUCTION

Learning and memory are inseparable. Learning is the acquisition of new information, whilst memory is the capacity for storing and retrieving this material. Obviously, there can be no learning without memory, although some types of stored information can be innate such as instincts and basic reflexes.

But for all intents and purposes our memory is derived from experience and learning. It is easy to take our capacity to learn and remember for granted, although without these truly remarkable abilities, we would be mentally and psychologically dead. Learning and memory constitute the mental glue that links our present to our past and future, and without them we would have no personal history or even awareness. If we lacked memory we would not be able to recognize our family, friends, objects, possessions or ourselves. And nor would we be able to think, use language or perceive things around us. To put it bluntly, without learning and memory we would be nothing but a body without a conscious mind. For this reason, memory has been described as the most extraordinary phenomenon in the natural world (Thompson & Madigan, 2005).

The question of how the brain acquires new information, stores it, and retrieves it when necessary, has been the subject of much speculation that goes back to Aristotle. Yet it is also a problem at the forefront of modern psychology and neuroscience, especially as a complete understanding requires an account of brain function on many different levels: from genes, protein synthesis, synaptic activity and neurotransmitter release, to the neural basis of conditioning, and the physiology of many different brain structures.

Our knowledge of how the brain learns and remembers has grown substantially over recent years which reflects the importance of the challenge. Not only does an elucidation of learning and memory provide valuable insights into how the brain works, and has the potential to help those with memory disorders such as dementia – but for the curious it also offers an intellectual adventure that promises to reveal the inner secrets of the mind's existence and how we have come to be who we are.

WHAT DOES A MEMORY IN THE BRAIN LOOK LIKE?

If we pause for a moment to consider how the brain learns and remembers new information, then we begin to confront a puzzle that is as complex and challenging as anything in science. For example, imagine a typical event in our life – say, for example, somebody asking our name. A remarkable thing about this is that we will seem to remember our name, and the experience of being asked, *immediately*. We are so used to our ability to remember the events in our life as they happen, that it is easy to overlook that the memory of such an experience must have involved some incredibly quick and relatively permanent change in the structure of our brain. Indeed, how else could we remember what we have just seen and heard? When considered in this way, it reveals our brains must be in some form of rapid and continual flux if we are to have immediate recall. And perhaps even more remarkable, someone calling our name has probably altered the electrical and chemical activity of millions of neurons, arranged in networks, throughout many areas of the brain. However, even this type of analysis does the brain's capacity for learning and memory an injustice. For as Rose (2003) points out, memories are living processes, which become transformed and imbued with new meanings each time we recall them. Thus, returning to our example, we not only remember somebody calling our name – but there is also an overall meaning and situational context to the memory which allows us to understand how it relates to what went before, and after.

But what is the nature of the underlying biological change in the brain that provides us with the capacity to learn and remember? Neuroscientists have tended to answer this question in one of two ways: (1) by asking how memories can be encoded at the neural level, and (2) by identifying the brain structures dedicated to learning and remembering. The first question attempts to explain how memory is represented within the mix of chemical molecules, ions, proteins and lipids that make up a nerve cell. This type of explanation, for example, may view memory as resulting from the creation of new **synapses** or dendrites (which will require genetic control of protein synthesis), or from changes in the sensitivity of neurotransmitter receptors or their associated second messenger systems. As we shall see in this chapter, both these forms of plasticity have provided plausible explanations of how neurons encode and store new information.

The second question concerns the warehousing of memories in the brain, i.e. where are the main brain sites where memories are localized? The problem of memory storage appears on first sight to be a more straightforward task for the psychologist than trying to understand the molecular changes taking place in neurons. However, the history of research into this area has been complicated and controversial. Part of the problem lies with the fact that whilst the changes taking place within an individual neuron may be relatively simple, the sheer number of cells involved in learning and memory makes exact localization impossible. Indeed, even the simplest memory trace (if such a thing actually exists) in humans will probably involve huge numbers of neurons and numerous brain structures. Even if we assume that this network exists, and is responsible for memory, there are other problems with the warehousing concept. For example, it not only supposes there are dedicated brain areas for memory storage, but also implies that memories are acted upon by other cognitive processes. In other words, memories are somehow transferable from one part of the warehouse (or brain region) to another.

Although a digital computer works in this way, and such concepts may help the psychologist provide models of memory, there is actually little evidence to show that the brain works in this manner (Eichenbaum & Cohen, 2001).

THE WORK OF KARL LASHLEY

Karl Lashley was one of the founders of neuropsychology (the branch of psychology concerned with how the brain governs a person's cognition and behavior). He was also one of the first scientists to search for the site of memory storage in the brain (Wickens, 2019b). In fact, he spent most of his research career, spanning over 40 years, trying to discover the neuroanatomical basis of memory in the brain, or what he called the **engram**. Lashley had been a student of J. B. Watson, and when he began his research in the 1920s, psychologists were strongly influenced by the work of the Russian physiologist Ivan Pavlov who had identified a form of learning known as classical conditioning (see Figure 9.1). This type of learning occurs when an animal associates a stimulus with a particular event which leads to a new behaviour. For example, when Pavlov presented food to a hungry dog, it produced salivation. Since this response was reflexive and not learned, he called salivation an *unconditioned response*, but if he repeatedly paired a tone (an *unconditioned stimulus*) with the presentation of the food, Pavlov discovered that the tone alone would come to elicit salivation. In Pavlovian terminology, the salivation is now a *conditioned response*, and the tone has become a *conditioned stimulus*. This situation also shows the dog has learned something new: namely the tone predicts a reward and delivery of food. At the time, many psychologists were interested in Pavlov's work because they also believed that human learning followed the same principles of classical conditioning. Indeed, J. B. Watson with assistant Rosalie Rayner showed that human behaviour (e.g. fear) could be shaped by classical conditioning in a famous (though ethically dubious) experiment involving a 9-month-old infant called Little Albert in 1920.

Lashley was more interested, however, in understanding the neurobiology of classical conditioning. Considered in neuroanatomical terms, it made sense to regard the stimuli as events processed by the sensory areas of the cerebral cortex, and the conditioned response to be produced by its motor regions. Thus, Lashley hypothesized that the neural basis of learning must involve the growth of new connections linking the sensory regions of the cerebrum with its motor areas. A useful analogy here is to think of the brain as an old-fashioned telephone switchboard with new connections being made between the caller (sensory area) and receiver (motor area).

It was against this intellectual backdrop that Lashley set about trying to discover the engram. He reasoned the most likely site for the storage of stimulus-response connections (i.e. memory) would be the association areas of the cerebral cortex. Further, if learning took place in the cortex, and resulted from new pathways being formed between sensory and motor areas, then a knife cut between these two areas following conditioning should impair the performance of the learned response. To test this hypothesis, Lashley trained rats to run through mazes and then made knife cuts to the cortex. For each rat, he made a cut in a different location. He reasoned that if he could find a location where a cut impaired the animal from correctly re-negotiating the maze, this would be evidence for the engram. However Lashley found no single cut, or combination of cuts, that abolished the maze performance.

In a second set of experiments, he removed 'chunks' of the cerebral cortex. Firstly, he ran rats through a maze with eight 'incorrect' alleys, until they could successfully negotiate the apparatus on ten consecutive trials without error. Then he made cortical lesions of various sizes. He found that lesions that removed 10 to 20% of cortical tissue had a negligible effect on maze performance, but a large lesion (e.g. 50%) caused significant impairment. Even so, the rat was still able to relearn the maze with further training. But, for Lashley, the most important finding was that the exact site of the lesion was unimportant. Cortical lesions of equal size produced similar behavioural effects regardless of where they were located. It was as if memory was stored everywhere – or no site in particular.

On the basis of these findings Lashley concluded that memories for maze tasks were stored diffusely throughout the cerebral cortex. He called this the principle of mass action. He also proposed that all parts of the association cortex play an equal role in

Figure 9.1   An illustration showing how classical conditioning occurs
Source: Salehi.s/Wikimedia commons

memory storage – a principle he termed **equipotentiality** (Lashley, 1950). Although some areas of the cortex appeared to be more involved in certain types of learning than others (e.g. the occipital lobes were important in tasks requiring the discrimination of visual patterns), Lashley nevertheless found that no single region was crucial. Indeed, no matter what area of the cortex was removed, the animal could relearn the task. From these experiments, Lashley concluded the brain functioned as a holistic whole. There was no specific region responsible for storing the engram (Wickens, 2019b).

KEY TERMS: *engram, classical conditioning, stimulus-response connections, mass action, equipotentiality*

WAS LASHLEY CORRECT?

Lashley's work raises a number of fundamental questions. Not least is the issue of whether a cognitive ability such as memory can be localized to a specific brain area, or whether the brain acts as some sort of holistic device where mental functions are integrated and distributed throughout all its regions. Lashley was not the first to address this question (see Wickens, 2015). In the early nineteenth century, the founder of phrenology, Franz Joseph Gall, proposed that the cerebral cortex had at least 27 different areas with localized functions (see Chapter 1). This notion, however, was discredited by others, most notably the French physiologist Pierre Flourens, whose much more scientific approach, based on lesioning, showed that behavioural functions were not localized in discrete areas of the brain. But the issue is an important one. Or put more specifically: is the human brain composed of a set of highly specialized components, each carrying out a specific aspect of human cognition, or is it more of a general-purpose device, in which each component participates in a wide variety of cognitive processes? Even today the controversy still remains a central puzzle of brain science. Lashley's concepts of mass action and equipotentiality clearly support the view of the cortex as a general-purpose device, yet it is also clear that some areas of the cerebral cortex, especially in humans, do indeed have specialized abilities. These include Broca's and Wernicke's areas which serve language functions, and the motor cortex with its topographical map of the human body (see Chapter 4). There is also evidence that the frontal, parietal, temporal and occipital lobes may all have different roles to play in cognition and behaviour. The paradox of specialized regions and distributed functions has yet to be satisfactorily resolved (Kanwisher, 2010; Ross, 2010).

Part of the problem regarding Lashley's own research, however, may lie in his choice of an alley way maze task which he used to examine the rat's learning and memory. Put simply, it can be argued that maze learning is inappropriate for studying localization of function, since the task may require the creation of many types of engram spread throughout the cerebral cortex. For example, as the rat learns to run through the maze, it might utilize different types of sensory information (i.e. vision, olfaction, proprioception etc.), or various strategies (i.e. run left then right etc.), to perform the task. Thus, whilst each engram could be localized, the maze task may be so complex and draw upon so many different abilities that the full memory is stored throughout the cortex. This also implies the maze task can be learnt in many different ways. If so, it might explain why an animal can relearn the maze task following the removal of large parts of the cortex. It simply adopts a new learning strategy based on different cues.

Another criticism of Lashley is his assumption that the cerebral cortex is the only site of learning and memory. To some extent this bias was due to the initial influence of Pavlov, who believed that the cerebrum was the site of stimulus-response connections. In addition, because his work largely predated the use of modern surgical techniques, Lashley was unable to make accurate lesions to many subcortical regions of the brain. In fact, he performed his lesions by cutting the cortex under direct vision and removing it with a suction pump. Nevertheless, it is now clear that a number of other structures do have a role to play in learning, memory and cognition. These include, for example, the cerebellum which is involved in learning motor actions, and the hippocampus, which plays a vital role in memory consolidation and retrieval (see later).

THE CONTRIBUTION OF DONALD HEBB

Donald Hebb (1904–1985) was one of the most influential psychologists of our time. Not only did he extend the work done by Lashley (he obtained his PhD at Harvard University under Lashley's guidance in 1936), but also his ideas have continued to exert a major influence on cognitive psychology and neuroscience (Wickens, 2019b). Hebb's (1949) most famous work is *The Organisation of Behavior* in which he sought a new way of explaining mental function, including attention, perception and thinking, that went beyond the current behaviourist thinking of his time dominated by concepts of conditioning and the psychology of Skinner (Brown, 2020). In contrast, Hebb wanted to develop a theory consistent with what was known about the brain and neural biology. As we have seen, the dominant view, endorsed by Lashley, was that behaviour arose from stimulus-response reflexes. In other words, behaviour arose from a series of neurons arranged in direct one-way pathways, which could be activated by a specific stimulus – much like a knee jerk when the patellar tendon is tapped by a doctor. However Hebb believed this idea was far too simple to explain brain function.

One of Hebb's most important innovations was to replace the simple reflex with a neural circuit that contained an assembly of cells – an idea that had first been introduced by the Spaniard Rafael Lorente de Nó in the 1930s. Thus, instead of viewing the reflex as a one-way chain of neural events that automatically led from stimulus to response, Hebb placed a 'loop' in the middle of the neural chain which greatly increased the number of neurons. The reflex arc was now circular (i.e. a cell assembly) and not linear. This concept had two important advantages over the simple reflex. Firstly, cell assemblies could be autonomous and continuously active; i.e., once activated by a stimulus, they could remain in a self-generating excited state. Secondly, and perhaps more important, Hebb realized that such reverberatory activity could provide the neural basis for learning and memory. For example, it could be envisaged that initial learning induced increased electrical activity in cell assemblies which lasted for some hours after the event. This, in effect, could be responsible for short-term memory. However, if this reverberatory activity occurred for long enough, then it could produce structural changes in the cell assembly's neurons, thereby providing the basis for permanent or long-term memory.

The most likely site for structural change, according to Hebb, was the synapse. Indeed, a synapse that is 'strengthened' as a result of learning is now called a **Hebbian synapse**. In his book *The Organization of behavior* (1949, p. 62), Hebb used italics to describe his rule: *'When an axon of cell A is near enough to excite a cell B and repeatedly or persistently takes part in firing it, some growth or metabolic change takes place in one or both cells such that A's efficiency, as one of the cells firing B, is increased'*. This rule can perhaps be put more simply: co-activation of two neurons will strengthen their synaptic connection, increasing the probability that if the presynaptic one fires the postsynaptic one will do so also.

This was an important theoretical development that helped illustrate how memory could be stored in a diffuse and distributed network, and it also explained how individual neurons might be modified to encode and store memory. In short, changes in the sensitivity of receptors, or perhaps increases or decreases in the readiness of a neuron to release neurotransmitter, could provide a viable mechanism for learning and neural plasticity. Hebb's theory also explained how memories could be formed and recalled. In short, if synaptic connections were strengthened in a cell assembly, then this change could act as memory – which would be elicited again by further stimulation of the circuit. With remarkable foresight, Hebb even reasoned that if such cell assemblies worked together to form phase sequences, then they could even form streams of thought.

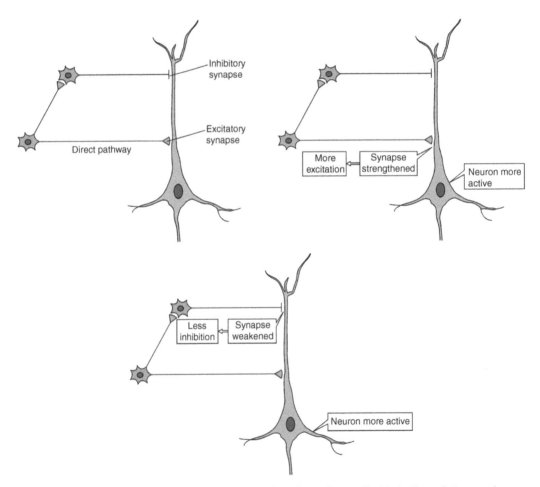

Figure 9.2   An illustration of Hebb's law showing how it can be applied to both excitatory and inhibitory synapses.

Source: Higgs et al. (2020)

Although Hebb's ideas concerning cell assemblies and synaptic plasticity were theoretical, they have become important concepts in neuroscience and psychology. In particular, Hebb's statement of his rule has become one of the most quoted sentences in neuroscientific literature. Indeed, some of the strongest evidence for the Hebbian synapse and its involvement in learning and memory came in 1973 with the discovery of *long-term potentiation* which will be discussed later in the chapter. Hebb's theories have also been particularly influential in neural network programming and artificial intelligence (Cooper, 2005).

> **KEY TERMS:** *cell assemby, reverberatory activity, short- and long-term memory, the Hebbian synapse*

THE EFFECTS OF EXPERIENCE ON THE BRAIN

Hebb's theory emphasized the importance of synaptic changes for neural plasticity. However, in the 1960s, researchers also discovered that other types of structural change in neurons – most notably in the size and complexity of dendrites – could occur as a result of experience and learning. This largely came about by examining the brains of young animals reared in stimulating and enriched environments. In fact, Hebb had initiated this line of research, and wrote about it in *The Organization of Behavior* when he reported that his daughters' pet rats, which were allowed to explore his home, were superior to laboratory ones when it came to learning maze tasks.

This also raised the question of whether an intelligent rat could be distinguished from a less bright one on the basis of their brain structure and neurochemistry. During the mid-1950s, Rosenzweig et al. (1958, 1972) set out to examine this question by raising rats for various lengths of time in impoverished or enriched environments. In the impoverished condition, the animals lived alone in small cages placed in quiet rooms which were lit with low-level illumination. The enriched rats, in contrast, were placed in large groups, and lived in big cages furnished with a variety of toys, runways and objects. A new object was placed in the cage each day to add further novelty. At the end of a given period (between 30 days and several months), the animals were sacrificed, and a histological examination of the their brains was undertaken to determine whether any changes had taken place.

The results showed that the enriched conditions caused rats to have a thicker and heavier cerebral cortex which was most marked for the occipital areas. In addition, the enriched cortices contained greater levels of **acetylcholinesterase** (AChE), an enzyme that is responsible for breaking down **acetylcholine**. In fact, because acetylcholine is broken down almost immediately after being released, AChE was a more reliable marker of increased acetylcholine levels in these brains. But the most striking discovery was the difference in the shape of the neurons taken from different parts of the cerebral cortex. Rats reared in the enriched environment had more spines on their dendrites. Because these spines contain high numbers of receptors, this indicated that the number of synapses were increasing with greater experience. This prediction, along with evidence showing the synapses were also larger, was later confirmed by electron microscopy (Turner & Greenough, 1983, 1985). For example, the enriched rats were shown to have about 9,400 synapses per neuron in their occipital cortex, compared to about 7,600 for deprived animals. Thus, the enriched environment had caused an increase of over 20% more synapses in the visual areas of the brain.

Although these findings may not surprise us today, they generated considerable interest, and even scepticism at the time. This was because many believed the brain's neurophysiology was fixed by adulthood, with learning having no effect on changing the shape of neurons. The discovery that neurons could be structurally changed by experience altered the way investigators viewed the brain. As Hebb had envisaged, researchers then began to realize that enriched environments promoted better learning, and could provide useful therapy for people with brain injuries. Indeed, it is now accepted that environmental enrichment is more effective than either formal training or physical exercise in the recovery of learning capacity after a physical injury (Will et al., 2004). Evidence also shows that early deprivation can lead to a large number of short- and long-term consequences, including alterations in brain structure and function, resulting in changes at cellular and molecular levels, and a plethora of psychological and behavioural impairments (Nelson et al., 2019).

KEY TERMS: *impoverished or enriched environments, acetylcholinesterase, acetylcholine, dendrites, receptors, synapses*

LEARNING IN SIMPLE NERVOUS SYSTEMS: *APLYSIA*

Some of the most important advances in understanding the neural basis of learning have come from research on the relatively simple nervous systems of invertebrates (animals without backbones). These creatures have many advantages for the neuroscientist. Firstly, their nervous systems contain far fewer neurons than vertebrates – although the biochemical and biophysical properties of the nerve cells remain the same. Secondly, invertebrate neurons are relatively large and can be seen with a microscope. Thirdly, most of the neurons have fixed locations, allowing them to be easily identified. And perhaps most importantly, invertebrates are capable of several forms of learning. While a number of invertebrates have been utilized in neurobiological research, including crayfish, lobsters, flies and nematode worms, the most important and extensively studied is a giant reddish-yellow sea slug called *Aplysia californica*. This mollusc inhabits the Californian and Mexican sea floor, and is sometimes seen grazing on seaweed at low tide. It has few predators, due to its unpalatable taste, and releases a dark purple toxic fluid when threatened. *Aplysia californica* can reach 30 centimetres in length and weigh 7 kg (15 lb) making it easy to handle in the laboratory. But this is relatively small compared to the closely related *Aplysia vaccaria*, also known as the Californian black sea hare, which can weigh up to 15.9 kg or grow to the size of a small dog. These creatures are sometimes called sea hares because their posterior chemosensory tentacles stick up like ears (Moroz, 2011).

Aplysia californica has a simple nervous system with around 20,000 neurons, most of which are organized into bundles of nerve fibres called ganglia. Amongst these are the head ganglia that control functions such as locomotion, feeding and mating, and the abdominal ganglion involved in circulation, respiration, excretion and egg-laying.

Figure 9.3 *Aplysia californica* emitting an ink cloud
Source: Genny Anderson/Wikimedia Commons

These nerve bundles also contain some of the largest nerve cells to exist in nature (only egg cells are larger) which are easily identified based on their colour, size, electrical properties, and their position in the ganglia. Consequently, they are well suited for electrophysiological and molecular investigations, and these advantages have yielded several fundamental discoveries concerning the neurobiology of learning and memory (Akhmedov et al., 2014).

Although *Aplysia* first attracted interest in the 1940s, it was not until 1970, when three papers were published in the prestigious journal *Science* by Eric Kandel and his colleagues, that this simple mollusc caught the attention of neuroscientists (see Kandel, 2016). Kandel could not have guessed that this work would lead him to win a Nobel Prize some 30 years later (Wickens, 2019b). One type of learning investigated in these papers was habituation – a behavioural response where the animal learns to ignore a stimulus. For example, nearly all living organisms will show a startle response when they are confronted by an unexpected stimulus event. But if the stimulus is presented repeatedly and/or turns out to be harmless, then the startle reaction will diminish and eventually not be elicited at all. In other words, the animal will have habituated to the event. Habituation is also exhibited by humans. The ticking of a clock which fades away or an unusual smell which soon disappears upon entering a new house are two simple examples. Whilst habituation is a simple form of non-associative learning, it must nevertheless depend on changes taking place within the nervous system. Kandel and his colleagues set out to understand how and where this learning occurs in *Aplysia*.

Kandel examined the process of habituation in *Aplysia* by measuring its gill-withdrawal reflex (GWR) which is controlled by the neurons of its abdominal ganglia.

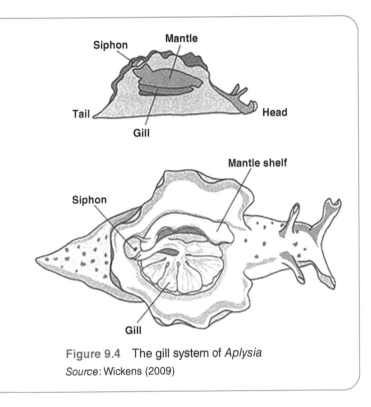

Figure 9.4   The gill system of *Aplysia*
Source: Wickens (2009)

Aplysia is somewhat unusual as it has a large gill (responsible for extracting oxygen from water) on its back or dorsal surface (Figure 9.4). The gill is also connected to a siphon that expels the deoxygenated water. Being the main organs of respiration, both are vital, delicate and sensitive organs, and if touched, *Aplysia* will vigorously retract them into a protective cavity, which is then quickly covered by a large fleshy pad called the mantle shelf.

To induce habituation, Kandel used a calibrated jet of water as a weak stimulus applied repeatedly to the siphon. This initially produced a strong GWR, but with repeated presentation, the strength of the mantle's retraction became less pronounced, until it disappeared. The strength of this response was found to be dependent on the amount of stimulation. For example, the effects of a single short training period (ten bursts of water) lasted for several minutes, but when *Aplysia* was subjected to multiple training sessions, the habituated response lasted several weeks. Kandel also discovered that *Aplysia* was capable of two other simple forms of learning which would also later become the focus of much research (but are not discussed any further here). These were dishabituation where the habituated response is 'unlearned' by administering a new stimulus to the head or tail, and sensitization whereby the strength of the GWR is increased by a noxious stimulus.

KEY TERMS: *Aplysia, habituation, gill-withdrawal reflex, dishabituation, sensitization*

THE NEURAL BASIS OF SHORT-TERM HABITUATION IN *APLYSIA*

To explain the process of habituation, it was necessary to first identify the neural circuitry underlying the GWR. In order to do this, a slit was made in *Aplysia*'s neck, exposing the nerves of the **abdominal ganglion**, which then allowed Kandel to record from, and stimulate, the neurons controlling the reflex. Using this technique, the siphon was found to contain twenty-four **sensory neurons** responding to tactile information. In turn, the siphon's sensory cells innervated a cluster of six central **motor neurons** that were responsible for retracting the gill. Although the neural circuitry is actually much more complex than this (e.g. the sensory neurons also receive input from other neurons, whilst projecting to other types of cell including different sets of excitatory and inhibitory interneurons (see Figure 9.5b)), for the sake of simplicity, we will just consider the direct neural circuit of sensory cells and motor neurons described here. In this circuit, habituation must take place. The important question is where and how?

To answer this question, Kandel and his colleagues inserted electrodes into the abdominal sensory and motor neurons to record their impulses and to see if this activity correlated with habituation of the GWR. The siphon's sensory neurons did not show any decline in activity with repeated stimulation. Thus, the activity of these nerve cells did not explain habituation. However the postsynaptic motor neurons controlling gill retraction *did* show a decline in responsiveness with habituation – producing fewer nerve impulses from each siphon stimulation. In other words, the activity of the motor neurons correlated with the decline of the GWR.

There were two possible explanations. Either the motor neurons were becoming fatigued and less able to invoke a response, or there were changes taking place at the synapses between sensory and motor neurons. The first possibility could be ruled out when electrical stimulation of the motor neurons was found to always produce the same amount of muscle contraction, regardless of how many impulses they had previously received. Clearly, these neurons were not getting 'tired' with repetitive firing. Therefore, the main event underlying habituation was taking place at the synapses between sensory and motor neurons.

But what was happening here? Again, there were two possibilities: either the sensory neurons were releasing less neurotransmitter with each impulse, or the receptors located on the motor neuron were becoming less responsive to the transmitter. Although both are feasible forms of neuroplasticity, the former turned out to be true in this instance. In short, it was shown that fewer molecules of transmitter were being

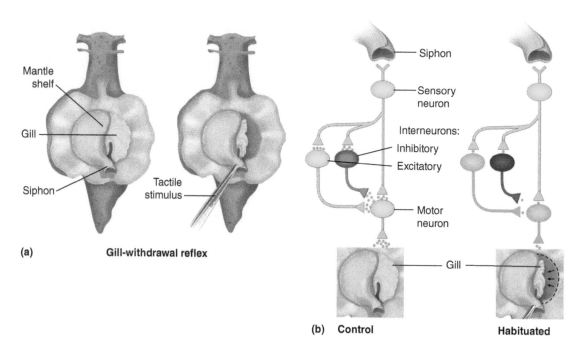

(a)   **Gill-withdrawal reflex**

(b)   **Control**   **Habituated**

Figure 9.5   The neural and biochemical stages underlying habituation of the gill-withdrawal reflex in *Aplysia*.

Note: for the sake of simplicity only the main axon from the sensory neuron is discussed in the text.

Source: Liana Bauman/Body Scientific Intl. in Gaskin (2021)

released from the siphon's sensory neurons with each action potential (see Figure 9.5). Thus, each tactile stimulus was causing a decrease in the amount of excitatory transmitter (now known to be **glutamate**) from the terminals of the sensory neurons, which in turn produced less stimulation of the motor neurons innervating the gill. In short, glutamate transmission was depressed between the sensory and motor neurons. More recently, it has been shown that this glutamatic decrease is actually caused by less calcium ions entering the axon terminals of the sensory neurons (Gover & Abrams, 2009). And to complicate matters further, both excitatory and inhibitory interneurons also have a role to play in this response (see Figure 9.5).

KEY TERMS: *abdominal ganglion, sensory and motor neurons, glutamate, calcium ions*

LONG-TERM LEARNING IN *APLYSIA*

Although short-term habituation in *Aplysia* (which can last 30 minutes) can be explained by a transient reduction in glutamate release from sensory neurons, longer-term habituation (which lasts several days) can also be produced by modifying the experimental protocol. In fact, a depressed GWR can be maintained up to three weeks if more intense and prolonged stimulation procedures (e.g. five days of training) are used (Carew et al., 1972). This longer type of learning also requires protein synthesis since it is blocked by the administration of the protein synthesis inhibitor anisomycin when infused into the abdominal ganglion (Castellucci & Schacher 1990). Since protein synthesis is a necessary prerequisite for producing new structural features such as synapses, receptors or dendrites, this indicates that long-term habituation must involve such modifications. Indeed, these have been observed. For example, Bailey and Chen (1983, 1988) examined the siphon's sensory neurons with light and electron microscopy. When these investigators stimulated the siphon over several successive days to produce habituation, they found this reduced the number of presynaptic terminals (called variccosites) on the sensory neurons by about 35%. In addition, the active zone region of these terminals containing the transmitter vesicles was smaller.

These were exciting findings as similar forms of neural change most likely underlie learning and memory in higher organisms. However they also raised many more uestions – not least those surrounding the synthesis of new proteins. This is a complex process requiring the transcription of genes in the nucleus (e.g. the means by which a segment of DNA is copied into RNA), and the assembly of proteins in the cytoplasm (see Chapter 14). These molecular processes, however, were impossible to examine in the *in vivo* or intact *Aplysia*. Consequently, Kandel and his colleagues were forced to develop a much simpler *in vitro* preparation. This involved extracting a single sensory neuron with its recipient motor cell from *Aplysia*, which was then kept alive and manipulated for several hours in an organ bath. This was a technique that would allow the molecular basis of learning in *Aplysia* to be explored in great detail.

The molecular basis of long-term habituation in *Aplysia* has turned out to be surprisingly complex (Esdin et al., 2010; Glanzman, 2009). Nonetheless, in some types of learning, it has been shown that stimulation of the siphon's sensory neurons produces the second messenger cAMP which then activates an enzyme called protein kinase (PKA). This enzyme has many effects inside the cell including altering the shape of a protein called CREB (an abbreviation derived from cAMP response element binding protein). This intracellular messenger passes to the nucleus where it causes the transcription of certain genes. Although the nature of the genes activated by CREB is poorly understood, they are believed to stimulate the synthesis of proteins in the cell that form new synaptic terminals and synapses between the sensory and motor neurons. It is likely that several genes are involved in this process which create a variety of proteins (Kandel, 2012; Kandel et al., 2014).

KEY TERMS: *protein synthesis, transcription of genes, cAMP, protein kinase, CREB*

LONG-TERM POTENTIATION

As we saw earlier, over 50 years ago, George Hebb speculated that long-term memory must involve structural changes in neurons, brought about by 'reverberating' activity in neural circuits which took place after the initial learning event. He also believed the most likely site for structural change in this scenario was the **synapse**. This led him to formulate a rule which stated if a presynaptic and postsynaptic neuron were both simultaneously active, then the synapse between them would be strengthened as a result. Evidence supporting this idea was lacking until the early 1970s when Timothy Bliss and Terje Lomo described a phenomenon called long-term potentiation (LTP). In their initial experiment (Bliss & Lomo, 1973) they anaesthetized a rabbit and exposed its **hippocampus**. They then stimulated a pathway entering the hippocampus from the adjacent entorhinal cortex called the perforant pathway with a burst of high-frequency electrical impulses (see Figure 9.7). At the same time,

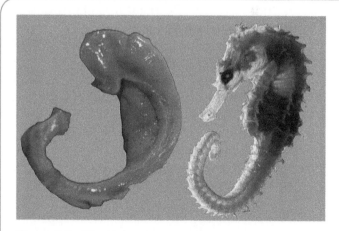

Figure 9.6 The hippocampus is derived from the Greek word for seahorse

Source: Laszlo Seress/Anthonyhcole/Wikimedia commons

Bliss and Lomo recorded the electrical potentials from the postsynaptic hippocampal cells receiving the perforant input (i.e. the granule cells of the dentate gyrus). As expected, they found increased neural excitation in response to this stimulation.

Following a delay of some hours, Bliss and Lomo then stimulated the perforant path with pulses of low intensity current. To their surprise, they found a huge increase in the firing of the recipient granule cells, with the amplitude of the responses increased

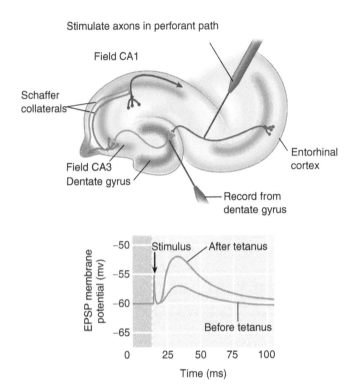

Figure 9.7   How long-term potentiation is examined

Source: Amanda Tomasikiewicz/Body Scientific Intl. in Gaskin (2021)

by 200–300%. Clearly, their initial burst of high-frequency stimulation had modified the granule neurons in some way, i.e. it appeared to have caused an increase in the strength of the synapses between the perforant path and granule cells. In effect, this now produced a stronger electrical response in the post-synaptic neurons – an effect that can last up to several weeks depending on the initial stimulus parameters. LTP can also be induced in other areas of the brain, especially those which have been implicated in learning and memory, including the amygdala and cerebellum. Some researchers even believe that LTP may occur at all excitatory synapses in the mammalian brain (Malenka & Bear, 2004).

Soon after Bliss and Lomo's discovery, a way of examining LTP in slices of hippocampal tissue kept alive in an oxygenated saline bath was developed. This allowed the microelectrodes to be positioned with great precision, and provided a far better model for understanding LTP. It soon became apparent that the increased postsynaptic activity produced by a train of impulses (or a tetanus) is generally detectable within five minutes, and reaches a plateau after an hour. And depending on the stimulus parameters used, the maintenance of LTP is likely to last for several days (Nicoll, 2017).

But can the increased potentiation of synapses and neurons in a glass dish really tell us anything meaningful about learning and memory at the behavioural level? One of the first researchers to address this issue was Richard Morris who examined the effects of the glutamate antagonist called APV – a drug known to abolish LTP development in the hippocampus. When Morris tested the effects of APV on the performance of rats to learn a spatial memory task, known to be dependent on hippocampal functioning (see later in the chapter), he found it significantly impaired the animals' performance. Further, when hippocampal slices were taken from animals after testing, LTP could not be induced in the brains of APV-treated rats (although it could be produced in rats that had swum the maze without the drug treatment). This was evidence that glutamate mediation of LTP was required for at least some types of learning and memory (Morris et al., 1986). Indeed, this has been confirmed in many other studies since, using a variety of different behavioural tasks including radial mazes and one-trial avoidance (Izquierdo et al., 2008).

> **KEY TERMS:** *long-term potentiation, hippocampus, perforant path, glutamate antagonist*

THE CHEMICAL BASIS OF LONG-TERM POTENTIATION

The nature of the intracellular events responsible for producing LTP is a major research question. It is now known that the first stage of LTP (at least in the hippocampus) involves the release of glutamate from the perforant path's axon terminals, which binds to receptors on the dentate cells (see Figure 9.8). In fact, there are two types of glutamate receptor: the AMPA receptor and NMDA receptor. The release of glutamate initially activates the AMPA receptor which causes a moderate depolarization of the neuron. At this stage, the NMDA receptor is unresponsive to the effects of glutamate because its receptor-ion channel complex is blocked by magnesium ions. This odd feature, in effect, stops excitatory calcium (Ca^{2+}) and sodium (Na+) ions flowing into the neuron. However these magnesium ions become displaced once the cell becomes depolarized following AMPA activation. At this point, the Ca^{2+} and Na+ ions surge into the neuron causing a delayed but much larger depolarization of the dentate cell (Lüscher & Malenka, 2012).

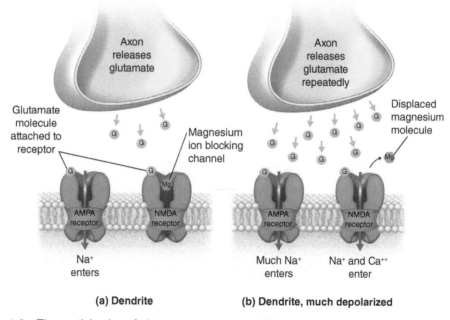

(a) Dendrite   **(b) Dendrite, much depolarized**

Figure 9.8   The participation of glutamate receptors in LTP
Source: Garrett and Hough (2021)

The flow of Ca²⁺ ions into the cell is crucial for the generation of LTP. Indeed, drugs that stop Ca²⁺ ions from entering the cell prevent LTP, whilst those that increase Ca²⁺ flow enhance LTP (Teyler & DiScenna, 1987). The importance of intracellular calcium lies in its ability to activate a number of enzymes. One of these is called calmodulin (an abbreviation for calcium-modulated protein) which stimulates the activity of an enzyme called CaMK11. The activity of this biological catalyst continues long after the Ca²⁺ influx has ceased and is vital for the generation of LTP (Lisman et al., 2012). CaMK11 appears to act as a switch that changes the strength of the AMPA receptors, thereby increasing the neuron's sensitivity to glutamate – which generates larger neural response to stimulation (O'Connor et al., 2005).

To make matters more complex, there is also evidence that LTP is accompanied by an enhanced release of glutamate from the presynaptic neurons. The cause of this increased glutamate release is due to a gas called nitric oxide, which is released by the hippocampal dentate cells and acts as a retrograde messenger to inform the presynaptic neuron to release more glutamate (Bon & Garthwaite, 2003). Although the nitric oxide signal is transient and brief, the increase in neurotransmitter is long term (Hardingham et al., 2013).

LTP also leads to structural changes in neurons. If the duration of potentiation is long-lasting, the postsynaptic neurons start to develop increased numbers of dendritic spines which are the main site for AMPA and NMDA receptors. This modification, therefore, increases the number of synapses (Bailey et al., 2015). There is also evidence of LTP-induced neurogenesis (growth of new nerve cells) in the hippocampus, with these additional neurons integrating themselves into the already pre-existing neural networks. These are believed to underlie the new memory of the event (Jacobs et al., 2000; Kee et al., 2007). Much research has been undertaken into this area, with many other chemical mediators and pathways being implicated in LTP; however this is an area too complex to be discussed here (see Adams & Dudek, 2005; Nihonmatsu et al., 2020; Vickers et al., 2005).

KEY TERMS: *glutamate, AMPA and NMDA receptors, calmodulin, CaMK11, nitric oxide, neurogenesis*

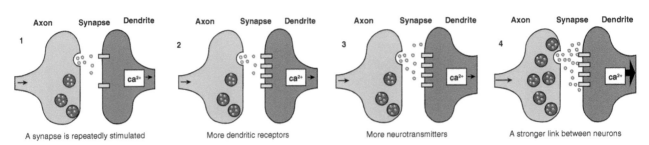

Figure 9.9   A simplified account of the main changes that can result from LTP
Source: Tomwsulcer/Wikimedia Commons

AN INTRODUCTION TO HUMAN MEMORY AND AMNESIA

Whilst it is important to understand the molecular neurobiology of learning and memory, using experimental models such as *Aplysia* and LTP, this type of knowledge tells us little about the organization of memory in the human brain. Nor does it explain how our day-to-day memories are encoded, consolidated or retrieved. Traditionally, psychologists have focused on such questions by experimenting on human subjects (Ebbinghaus, 1885), or by examining the memory deficits of those affected with brain damage. Indeed, it has long been known that damage to certain areas of the brain in humans, especially the medial temporal lobe, can lead to memory impairments, including an inability to learn new knowledge or to recall previously learned information. In fact, the inability to form new memories, or recall facts, information and experiences, is known as **amnesia** (from the Greek *a* meaning 'without' and *mnesis* meaning 'memory'). It is generally accepted there are two types of amnesia: **anterograde amnesia** and **retrograde amnesia**. The former refers to an inability to acquire new information, whereas the latter refers to an inability to recall previously learned information (Ortega-de San Luis & Ryan, 2018). In the case of retrograde amnesia, recent memories are normally more vulnerable to amnesia than older ones, and this is known as Ribot's (1881) law of regression.

Traditionally, case studies of notable individuals with memory loss have played a significant role in defining the characteristics of amnesia, and highlighting the brain regions most important for memory. One of the earliest reports linking amnesia with brain damage came in 1899 when Vladimir Bekhterev exhibited the brain of a patient with memory loss at a medical meeting in St Petersburg. This showed a discoloration and softening of the temporal lobes and hippocampus. Similar cases were also reported in the early twentieth century, although most were by German doctors who did not publish their findings in English. Further support linking the temporal lobes with memory came from Wilder Penfield who pioneered the use of electrically stimulating the brain in conscious patients prior to surgery for the treatment of epilepsy. During this work, Penfield found that stimulation of the temporal lobes often caused visual and auditory flashbacks which sometimes included vivid memories of past experiences.

But the most important case study of amnesia is undoubtedly that of a patient who during his lifetime was only known to the wider public by his initials HM. First reported by Scoville and Milner (1957), Henry Molaison (whose name was only made public after his death in 2008) was born in 1926 and grew up in a working-class town in Connecticut. By all accounts, HM enjoyed good health and a normal childhood until the age of nine when he had a bicycle accident that rendered him unconscious for several minutes. It is likely this incident led to the start of his seizures which began at the age of ten. By his mid-twenties, HM was experiencing multiple seizures every day. In 1953, the neurologist and surgeon William Scoville (a man who, if some accounts are to be believed, was a brash character known for his reckless behaviour – see Rolls, 2005) identified the **medial temporal lobes** (Figure 9.10) as the origin of the seizures. With the authorization of HM's family, in August 1953, Scoville bilaterally removed the tissue he believed was causing the seizures. It is hard to believe today that HM was fully conscious during the procedure. After administering a local anaesthetic to the scalp, Scoville bored two holes into HM's skull above the eyes, and pushed the frontal lobes up with a spatula to gain access to the medial regions of the temporal lobes. By using a knife and suction pump to remove tissue, Scoville removed about the size of a tennis ball from each hemisphere. In effect, HM had received a bilateral excision of the anterior two-thirds of his hippocampus, along with adjacent regions of the entorhinal cortex, parahippocampal region and amygdala. According to one report of the event, it was immediately apparent that the procedure had caused HM immediate memory difficulties and loss (Rolls, 2005).

KEY TERMS: *amnesia, anterograde amnesia, retrograde amnesia, medial temporal lobes, hippocampus*

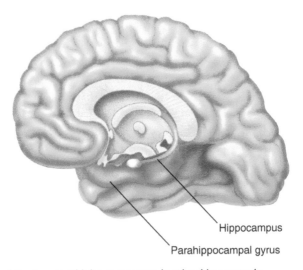

Hippocampus

Parahippocampal gyrus

Figure 9.10   Some of the temporal lobe structures involved in amnesia

Source: From Garrett and Hough (2021), adapted with permission from 'Remembrance of Things Past', by D. L. Schacter and A. D. Wagner, *Science*, 285, 1503–1504. Illustration: K. Sutliff. © 1999 American Association for the Advancement of Science. Reprinted with permission from AAAS.

A CLOSER LOOK AT HM'S MEMORY DEFICIT

HM's amnesia was so severe that he forgot the events of his daily life almost as soon as they occurred. For example, when HM met someone new, he soon had no recollection of them after they had left his company. Nor did he recognize them again. This included the psychologist Suzanne Corkin who first met HM in 1962 and tested him repeatedly three times a year up until 2008. His amnesia even extended to comprehending the death of his parents. When his father died in 1967, HM continued to enquire about his whereabouts for several years afterwards. Similarly, when his mother died at the age of 94 in 1981 (causing HM to be taken into residential care), he vaguely told acquaintances she may have left him. He also grieved each time when told of her death. Unable to remember things following his surgery, HM tended to guess he was around 33 years old (he was actually 27 when he had his operation), and this belief led to shock when he saw his aged reflection in a mirror. It also meant that HM was unable to recognize later pictures of himself (Rolls, 2005). Although HM forgot most of his life experiences after his 1953 operation, he nonetheless retained much of what he had learned before that. He knew the personal details of his parents and relatives and enjoyed recalling historical facts learned at school. HM also had a good vocabulary, normal language skills and an above-average IQ (Corkin, 1984, 2013).

Early tests with HM showed he had a relatively normal short-term memory which enabled him to remember information for brief periods of time. Hence, he could memorize a string of seven numbers forward and five numbers backward, repeat sentences, and perform mental arithmetic (Milner et al., 1968; Scoville & Milner, 1957). However, if HM was distracted from his task, then everything was forgotten. Although his capacity for short-term retention meant he could hold intelligent conversations, read books and engage in his favourite pastime of solving crossword puzzles, he was aware of his condition and apologetic for his memory loss. He was once reported as saying, 'Right now I am wondering. Have I done or said anything amiss? You see, at this moment everything looks clear to me, but what happened just before? That's what worries me. It's like waking from a dream. I just don't remember' (Milner, 1970). Clearly HM's inner psychological world was affected by his amnesia, and this may have been exacerbated by his poor ability at estimating periods of time, especially beyond 20 seconds. It has been suggested this caused HM to experience his days as periods that barely lasted a few minutes. If this is true, then it may have been that the last 55 years of his life seemed no more than a few months (Rolls, 2005).

Despite this, HM's memory loss for factual or semantic information was not totally complete since he occasionally had 'islands' of somewhat confused memory. For example, he remembered certain aspects of the space shuttle disaster several years after the event, although much of it was inaccurate and confabulated. He also acquired some post-operative facts about the names and faces of a few famous people. But overall, he was severely impaired when asked to recognize these well known individuals. HM also sometimes guessed correctly he was being tested at the Massachusetts Institute of Technology. Despite all his difficulties, HM was a cheerful and sweet man, much beloved by those who knew him, which was in no small part to his 'endearing nature, his sense of humour and his willingness to be helpful' (Ogden & Corkin, 1991).

TASKS THAT HM COULD PERFORM

Despite HM's severe inability to memorize information, there were some exceptions to his anterograde amnesia. For example, in 1965 Brenda Milner tested HM on a mirror drawing task. This required him to trace around the outline of a complex geometric shape (a star) which was hidden from direct view and only observable by use of a mirror. At first, most subjects find this task difficult since there is a 'mismatch' between the visual feedback and the required movement of the hands, but with practice they become more proficient. And this was also true of HM, who over the course of ten practice trials improved his accuracy at drawing around the shape. Moreover, he maintained this ability over several days of testing – despite claiming not to recognize the apparatus on each occasion, and having to be told what to do anew.

HM also showed evidence of learning when given a cue or prompt to help him recall past information. This is known as priming. In one experiment, HM was given a task where he was presented with a series of fragmented drawings, one at a time, which progressively provided more detail, until it was obvious what the picture was. When normal subjects are given this type of task, they recognize the fragmented picture more quickly the second time around – and this was also true of HM, even when the pictures were presented hours later (Milner et al., 1968). A similar improvement also occurred with verbal material. When HM was shown a word such as 'Define', and later given the prompt 'Def', he typically remembered the original correct word (Ogden & Corkin, 1991).

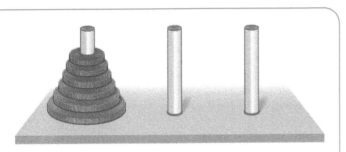

Figure 9.11   The Tower of Hanoi problem
Source: Garrett and Hough (2021)

Another task that HM could perform was the Tower of Hanoi problem (see Figure 9.11). In its simplest version, the subject is presented with a board containing a line of three wooden spindles, with the left-sided one holding three disks arranged on top of each other in descending size. The objective is to move each disk, one step at a time, from the left- to the right-sided spindle, without placing a large disk on top of a smaller one. For the three-spindle task, the quickest solution is seven moves, but HM was able to perform a five-disk version of this puzzle (which requires a minimum of thirty-one moves) in only thirty-two moves (Cohen & Corkin, 1981).

Somewhat surprisingly, HM was also able to draw a detailed map of the topographical layout of his house which he had moved into some five years after his operation. It is well established that the hippocampus is involved in spatial memory and one might have expected HM's sense of spatial mapping to be severely impaired. However, Corkin had an interesting explanation for HM's topographical drawing skills. She hypothesized that he 'was able to construct a cognitive map of the spatial layout of his house as the result of daily locomotion from room to room' (Corkin, 2002). It would appear, therefore, that the procedural act of moving through the rooms of his residence helped HM learn the layout of his spatial environment.

KEY TERMS: *mirror drawing task, priming, Tower of Hanoi problem*

WHAT HAVE WE LEARNED FROM HM?

HM died in 2008 at the age of 82 years. His brain was removed and taken to the University of California, San Diego, where it was cut into over 2,400 microscopically wafer-thin slices in a procedure that lasted 53 hours (Worth & Annese, 2012). The goal was to create an archive of anatomical slides and histological data, that would enable a digital reconstruction of HM's brain damage. During his life, HM's generosity in helping researchers had led to over 2,000 research papers, and his brain data bank would allow these publications to be reassessed in light of this new information. The results of this endeavour were published by Annese et al. (2014). Surprisingly, they reported that half of HM's hippocampus had survived the 1953 surgery, although there was extensive damage to the surrounding temporal lobe tissues. There was also a lesion in the prefrontal cortex above the left eye, most likely caused by Scoville during the operative procedure. All of this showed that the wider extent of damage in HM's brain was more extensive than had been believed, making it hard to identify a single specific region, or even grouping of regions, underlying his memory deficits. The digital atlas of HM's brain was made available on the Internet free of charge in 2014.[1] As Corkin (2013) notes in her book *Permanent Present Tense*, even after his death, HM still continues to make groundbreaking contributions to science.

There is little doubt that over the course of his last 55 years, HM had greatly helped us to understand the neuroanatomical basis of human memory. But what has it taught us? For one thing, we can deduce that the medial temporal lobes, including the hippocampus, are not the site where memories are actually stored, since HM could accurately recall his earlier years. Instead, it would appear, therefore, that this part of the brain is involved in laying down memories in other parts of the cortex. The storage of memories is known as consolidation. Another lesson to be learned from HM is that there are multiple memory systems in the brain. This is seen most clearly in the case of his short-term memory which allowed him to understand conversations and read books etc. It also enabled him to exist in 'the here and now'. Consequently, this type of memory must have a different neural substrate than the memories that are consolidated into the permanent or long-term memory by the medial temporal lobes.

But as we have seen, work with HM has shown that not all forms of long-term storage are dependent on the medial temporal lobes. If we examine more closely the type of tasks that HM could perform (mirror drawing, priming etc.), they all appear to have had an automatic quality which was not dependent on conscious awareness. Interestingly, a distinction of this type has been made before. For example, in 1911, the French philosopher Bergson noted there was a difference between the memory needed for motor performance and that involving conscious thought. Similarly, the English philosopher Gilbert Ryle in 1949 made the distinction between *knowing how* and *knowing that*. Ryle noted that one type of memory allows us to do things that we do not need to think about, whilst the other is a type of memory that is needed for conscious self-introspection.

In psychology, this idea has typically taken the form of a division between **procedural memory** and **declarative memory**. In short, procedural memory enables us to know how to do things, including motor skills (e.g. riding a bicycle), whereas declarative memory consists of a store of facts and events that can be recalled or 'declared' into conscious thought (Squire, 1992, 2004). HM would also appear to support such a distinction, for he showed procedural learning (as shown by his ability to find his way around the layout of his new house), but was unable to learn new factual information (Cohen & Squire, 1980). This latter impairment includes the inability to mentally re-experience specific events from his personal past (episodic memory) and recall

---

[1]https://www.thebrainobservatory.org/project-hm/

language-based knowledge of the world (semantic memory). If Cohen and Squire are correct, then declarative memory depends on the medial temporal lobes, including the hippocampus (see also Moscovitch et al., 2006). Procedural memory, however, would appear to have a different neuroanatomical basis – perhaps involving the cerebellum and striatum (Doyon et al., 2009; Penhune & Steele, 2012).

KEY TERMS: *consolidation, short- and long-term memory, procedural and declarative memory, episodic and semantic memory*

IMAGING THE HUMAN BRAIN AND MEMORY

One of the most important advances in neuroscience over recent years has been the emergence of brain-scanning techniques such as functional magnetic resonance imaging (fMRI). This is a technique that allows the activity of the brain to be directly observed (typically by measuring blood flow) whilst a subject normally performs some task. Although the historical development and use of these techniques are explored more fully in the next chapter, it is suffice to say here that they have been used to monitor the operations of many brain regions involved in a wide variety of memory tasks. And they are providing crucial new insights into the functions of the hippocampus, and other regions with which it is connected (see Emad-ul-Haq et al., 2019, for a recent review).

One consistent finding from such studies is the hippocampal involvement in encoding new information. A standard way of testing this is to employ a task where subjects are presented with a list of items that require some sort of decision. For example, Ranganath et al. (2004) presented their subjects with lists of words – from which they had to say whether each item was animate or inanimate. In addition, a decision had to be made on whether the items were large or small. When making both these decisions, the subject's brains were scanned by fMRI. At a later point in the experiment, and outside the scanner, the subjects were given a list of words again and asked to decide whether they had seen them before. The results showed that the successful recollection of items could be predicted by how much activation occurred in the hippocampus during the encoding stage. This finding has been replicated by several other research groups (Kim et al., 2011; Spaniol et al., 2009).

The hippocampus has also been shown to be involved in the retrieval of information. For example, in a similar type of study where participants were asked to memorize lists of words, Eldridge et al. (2000) scanned the brain at the stage of remembrance. The results showed that the hippocampus was only activated when the subject correctly recalled a word, but not by those words previously seen by the subject which had been forgotten. Nor was there increased hippocampal activity for words that were recognized as new. In short, the hippocampal activity was specific for the successful retrieval of information (Gazzaniga et al., 2009).

In addition to encoding and retrieval, the hippocampus also makes associations between stimuli and events. Henke et al. (1997) presented subjects with pictures illustrating a person and a house. Subjects were asked to judge whether the person was a likely resident or visitor of that house. For example, in one instance, the subjects were shown an elegant lady and a sophisticated sitting room that was an appropriate match. Another instance showed a dishevelled man and a large mansion representing an unlikely scenario. Thus, the task encouraged the subject to make an association between the person and the house. As a control group, subjects were shown pictures in which they had to make a 'non-associative decision' about gender (male or female) and a house (exterior or interior view). The results showed greater levels of neural activation in the medial temporal lobes when the subjects associated the person and the house. This type of encoding is believed to support stronger learning and memory.

There is also some evidence that certain regions of the hippocampus serve different memory roles. In a review of 52 PET studies, Lepage et al. (1998) showed that the anterior parts of the hippocampus are more activated when encoding new information, whilst the activity of the posterior hippocampus is correlated with memory retrieval. In another study supporting a much broader division of function in the medial temporal lobes, Gabrieli et al. (1997) presented subjects with drawings of common objects and animals. A day later, subjects were shown a list of words and asked to identify which ones previously described the drawings. This retrieval task was found to elicit greater activation of the parahippocampal cortex. In the second part of the study, subjects were asked to memorize colour pictures of indoor and outdoor scenes. When re-presented with a selection of these scenes, along with some new ones, it was the latter scenic pictures (requiring new encoding) that increased hippocampal activity. This was most pronounced in the subiculum. Despite this, it should be noted there is considerable disagreement over the possibility of specialized regional functions of the hippocampus with regard to encoding and retrieval. Some researchers have been unable to confirm this relationship (Greicius et al., 2003), whilst others argue that the dorsal (or posterior) hippocampus is implicated in memory and spatial navigation, whereas the ventral (or anterior) hippocampus mediates anxiety-related behaviours (Strange et al., 2014).

KEY TERMS: *encoding and retrieval of memory, anterior and posterior hippocampus*

SPECIAL INTEREST 9.1

THE HIPPOCAMPI OF LONDON TAXI DRIVERS

Finding our way around our environment is something we all take for granted. Yet it is a remarkable skill which requires spatial and working memory along with cognitive mapping. The most important brain area for this ability is the hippocampus – not least because it is well established that lesions of this structure markedly impair performance on a variety of spatial tests. There is also evidence that the size of the hippocampus correlates with spatial ability. For example, birds that store food, requiring them to later recall the locations of the storage sites, have a larger hippocampus than non-hoarders (Sherry et al., 1992). A related example occurs with North American meadow voles where the male has a territory several times larger than the female and a correspondingly larger hippocampus. In contrast, male and female pine voles that travel over equal distances have equal-sized hippocampi (Jacobs et al., 1990).

(Continued)

Even the seasons can determine hippocampus size. For example, over the autumn–winter season, the mass of the hippocampus declines by 29% in the common shrew and in 34% in the pygmy shrew (Yaskin, 2011). This is a rapid morphological change showing the hippocampus is able to react surprisingly quickly to ecological events.

The size of the human hippocampus has also been shown to be affected by navigational experience. This has been demonstrated by Eleanor Maguire and her colleagues at University College London, who examined the hippocampi of 16 right-handed London taxi drivers with MRI. These men had been driving taxis for a mean of 14.3 years, and had been required to pass an examination which tested their ability to navigate some 24,000 streets in the city to get a licence – a level of proficiency taking most drivers two years to accomplish. Maguire found this driving experience increased the size of the hippocampus. For example, the posterior part of the hippocampus was significantly larger in taxi drivers compared to controls – although the anterior part of the hippocampus was smaller (Maguire et al., 2000). Maguire also found the volume of the right-sided hippocampus was significantly correlated with the number of years spent as a taxi driver, although the left-sided hippocampus did not show this relationship. This finding was also in accordance with an earlier study by Maguire et al. (1997) who had asked London taxi drivers to recall complex routes around the city. She found this led to increased activity in the right hippocampus, but not the left.

Taxi drivers, along with other types of experts, frequently show cognitive abilities that exceed the normal limits of short-tem or working memory (Ericsson & Kintsch, 1995). In a study that explored the ability of Finnish taxi drivers to serially recall street names, it was found this skill was dependent on them having greater amounts of pre-learned and task-specific knowledge. In turn, this allowed them to encode information (by a process called 'chunking') in a much more efficient way (Kalakoski & Saariluoma, 2001). Again, this ability appears to be hippocampal-dependent, since it has been shown that increased hippocampal size predicts more rapid learning of a cognitive map in humans (Schinazi et al., 2013).

KORSAKOFF'S SYNDROME

The hippocampus and medial temporal lobes are not the only brain areas associated with memory and amnesia. One of the most common forms of amnesia seen in clinical practice is Korsakoff's syndrome, named after the Russian physician Sergei Korsakoff who first described the condition in 1889. Korsakoff's syndrome is mainly found in alcoholics and develops as a result of thiamine (vitamin B1) deficiency due to a poor diet, and long-term reliance on alcohol (see Figure 9.12). As we shall see, this form of amnesia is associated with damage to certain regions of the thalamus and hypothalamus, along with some degree of generalized brain shrinkage (Arts et al., 2017).

The first signs of Korsakoff's syndrome often appear as Wernicke's encephalopathy. This is characterized by a triad of symptoms: (1) ocular disturbances including double vision which can be accompanied by rapid involuntary movements of the eye known as nystagmus; (2) confusion where the person may have problems recognizing friends and surroundings; and (3) an unsteadiness of balance and poor motor co-ordination (ataxia). Other symptoms can include stupor, epileptic seizures, and a progressive loss of hearing. Wernicke's encephalopathy is a serious condition and if left untreated may lead to death through infection, hepatic failure or coma. Fortunately, it is reversed with thiamine and glucose infusion – although this generally does not stop the deterioration of memory and personality that progresses into Korsakoff's syndrome. Approximately 80–90% of individuals with Wernicke's encephalopathy will develop this type of amnesia – the symptoms appearing as the encephalopathy begins to lessen (Sullivan & Fama, 2012).

Korsakoff's syndrome leads to a long-term memory impairment, especially with regard to learning new information (anterograde amnesia). For example, a Korsakoff's patient may take weeks or months to learn the names of doctor and nurses, or the location of their hospital bed. They also perform poorly in laboratory experiments. If presented with a list of eight paired associate words such as *man-hamster*, and asked to recall the second word (*hamster*) when *man* is presented again, it may take the Korsakoff amnesic some 30 or 40 trials to learn this association compared to only 3 or 4 trials for a normal subject (Butters, 1984). However, the cognitive deficits are more extensive than this (Oscar-Berman, 2012). For example, Brand et al. (2003) tested Korsakoff patients on a battery of several neuropsychological tests and found impairments on the speed of mental processing, executive function and the cognitive estimation of size, weight, quantity and time. In some instances the responses were bizarre with an estimation of 1 hour for a shower and 15 tons for the weight of a car!

Another abnormality sometimes found in Korsakoff's syndrome is retrograde amnesia, which refers to memory loss for events preceding the onset of the disease. Although this type of amnesia is generally mild, and the loss most noticeable for the months leading up to their illness, in some cases the memory impairment goes back many years. This may even lead to the patient 'living in the past', convinced that their life and the world around them are unchanged since the onset of the condition. A good example of this is the case of Jimmie G, given in Sacks (1985) who could remember nothing of his life since the end of World War II (this was in the early 1980s). Consequently, he still believed Roosevelt was president. This type of memory difficulty may also lead to confabulation whereby the person with Korsakoff's amnesia makes up stories about themself, or invents plausible answers to questions which upon verification are found to be totally false. Whilst this is an attempt to replace the memories which have become irreversibly lost, the problem is exacerbated by the Korsakoff patient's lack of insight into their condition – which can lead them to believe there is nothing wrong with their memory. It appears that retrograde amnesia is largely due to damage in a circuit that links the **dorsomedial thalamus** and **prefrontal cortex** (Verstichel, 2000).

There are some notable differences between the symptoms of amnesia caused by temporal lobe damage and Korsakoff's syndrome. Although both are characterized by an inability to learn new information, the temporal lobe amnesiac typically does not engage in confabulation or suffer from general confusion. Another difference occurs with affective responding. An individual with Korsakoff's is often emotionally flat and apathetic (e.g. they may stare at a blank TV screen without switching it on) whilst a person with temporal lobe amnesia typically shows normal emotions. But perhaps the most interesting difference occurs with forgetting. Although people with Korsakoff's syndrome take a relatively long time to learn new information, they forget at normal rates. This is in contrast to those with damage to the medial temporal lobes who forget very rapidly (Huppert & Piercy, 1979).

KEY TERMS: *Wernicke's encephalopathy, nystagmus, ataxia, retrograde amnesia, confabulation, dorsomedial thalamus, prefrontal cortex*

THE NATURE OF THE BRAIN DAMAGE IN KORSAKOFF'S SYNDROME

Historically, Korsakoff's syndrome has been associated with damage to the diencephalon which includes the hypothalamus and thalamus. This type of damage was first described by Hans Gudden in 1896, who noted discolouring of the mammillary bodies which form part of the posterior hypothalamus, and then confirmed by Eduard Gamper in 1928 who had studied the brains of 16 Korsakoff patients. However, the picture became more complicated when Victor et al. (1971), after studying 80 Korsakoff brains, identified damage to the dorsomedial thalamus as a more reliable feature of the illness. Today, with the help of brain-scanning techniques, many other atrophied brain regions have become implicated in the disease, including other areas of the thalamus, periaqueductal grey area, cerebellum and frontal lobes (Arts et al., 2017; Caulo et al., 2005). In addition, there is often damage to the walls of the third ventricle, and the floor of the fourth ventricle close to the pons and medulla (Kril & Harper, 2012).

The widespread damage in Korsakoff's syndrome makes identifying the site of the memory loss difficult to locate. Nonetheless, evidence points to infarctions of the mammillothalamic tract as an important location (Yoneoka et al., 2004). This pathway originates from the mammillary bodies, and fibres of the fornix, and projects to various nuclei of the anterior thalamus. These nuclei also receive input from the cerebral cortex which is integrated and re-directed back to the cortical areas known as association areas (i.e. regions other than primary motor and sensory areas). Such areas are believed to be key substrates for higher cognition, including memory, executive function, language, and attention (Jung et al., 2017).

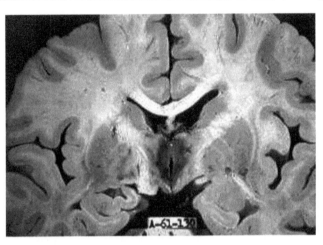

Figure 9.12   Korsakoff's syndrome is caused by a lack of thiamine (vitamin B1). Note the darkened diencephalon region which shows atrophy in the centre of the brain

Source: Higgs et al. (2020)

Another thalamic area linked with amnesia is the dorsomedial thalamus which receives its input predominantly from the striatum and innervates the frontal lobes. Although animal experiments have confirmed the involvement of the dorsomedial thalamus in memory and other cognitive tasks (Mitchell & Chakraborty, 2013), the most dramatic human evidence linking this thalamic structure with amnesia has come from an ex-American airforce technician known as NA (Squire & Moore, 1979). In 1960, when aged 22, NA suffered a fencing foil injury to the brain. In fact, the accident occurred when NA was building a model aeroplane in the company of a friend who was larking about behind him with the weapon.

When NA turned suddenly, he was stabbed through the right nostril – the foil passing up through the cribriform plate and entering the left side of the brain.

Although the extent of the damage appeared to be relatively small, with the hippocampus completely spared, the injury caused NA to suffer from a type of anterograde amnesia which caused him to quickly forget verbal information, although the memory loss was less severe for nonverbal memories such as faces. Like HM, NA was unable to provide much information about his life following his accident, but had almost normal recall for events up to that point (Squire, 1987). In 1979, Squire and Moore performed a CAT scan on NA and found the foil had damaged the left-sided dorsomedial thalamus. This initial report indicated that the injury was highly localized with little damage elsewhere. However, a later MRI study showed that damage had also occurred to the intralaminar nuclei of the thalamus, and had most likely interrupted the trajectories of the mammillothalamic tract and postcommissural fornix (Squire et al., 1989). Which of these regions is most crucial for producing NA's amnesia remains unclear. Nonetheless, all are located in the diencephalon.

> **KEY TERMS:** *diencephalic amnesia, mammillary bodies, mammillothalamic tract, association areas, dorsomedial thalamus*

MEMORY CIRCUITS IN THE BRAIN

So far, we have noted two distinct regions of the brain associated with memory: the hippocampus (medial temporal lobes) and diencephalon. It should come as no surprise, therefore, to discover these two areas are anatomically connected. In 1937, James Papez described a brain circuit (called the **Papez circuit**) that linked the hippocampus with the diencephalon. More specifically, the circuit consists of the hippocampus which projects to the mammillary bodies via a long arching pathway called the **fornix** (from the Latin for 'arch'). From here, as we have already seen, a tract projects to the anterior thalamic nuclei. Papez completed the circuit by recognizing a thalamic pathway feeding into the cingulate gyrus (which lies immediately above the corpus callosum) which projected back to the hippocampus. Although Papez believed this circuit was involved in emotion (see Chapter 6), one might also expect it to be involved in learning and memory. Today, a modified version of the Papez circuit is preferred by memory researchers. As Aggleton (2014) notes, the anterior thalamic nuclei are a pivotal point in this circuit since these are densely and reciprocally interconnected with the retrosplenial cortex – an area lying just behind the posterior part of the corpus callosum. In addition, it is now known the anterior thalamic nuclei and retrosplenial cortex both project to the hippocampal formation with their fibres terminating in the **subiculum**. All of these sites are believed to form an interconnected system for the encoding or retrieval of declarative memory under the predominant control of the hippocampal formation (Mitchell et al., 2018; Vann et al., 2009).

Despite this, there is some uncertainty regarding the Papez circuit hypothesis as stated. If this circuit was involved in memory processing, then we would expect an important mnemonic role for the fornix, which in humans is the largest outflow of the hippocampus containing around a million fibres. Its main target is the mammillary bodies, although it should be noted the fornix also projects to the septum, as well as having direct connections with the anterior thalamus. Yet evidence linking the fornix with memory is not convincing. For example, Squire and Moore (1979) reviewed 50 instances of fornix lesions and found evidence of mild amnesia in only three cases. Another study of 10 patients who had cysts surgically removed from the fornix showed some intellectual deficits and memory impairments on tests of recall – but not recognition (Aggleton et al., 2000). These findings suggest that the connection between hippocampus and mammillary is not an important one for memory processing (Aggleton, 2014).

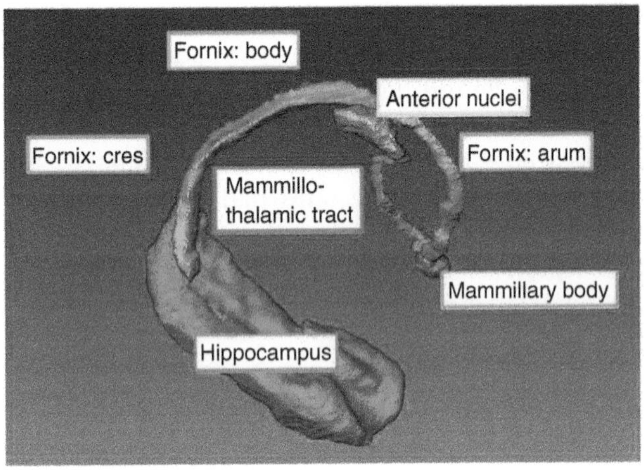

Figure 9.13 Some of the key structures making up the Papez circuit

Source: Mori, S. & Aggarwal, M. (2014). In vivo magnetic resonance imaging of the human limbic white matter. Front. *Aging Neurosci*. 6,321. doi: 10.3389/fnagi.2014.00321

Although the most conspicuous pathway leaving the hippocampus is the fornix, there is a second route by which hippocampal output can gain access to other brain regions. This is via the **parahippocampal gyrus** which is cortical tissue lying just below the hippocampus proper. This area receives extensive converging input from the association areas of the cerebral cortex, especially from the prefrontal cortex, parietal cortex and temporal cortex. in turn. The hippocampus gyrus relays this information to the hippocampus via the perforant pathway which originates in the subiculum (as we saw earlier, this pathway is involved in long-term potentiation) in turn. The hippocampus, the hippocampus completes the loop by sending projections back to the cortical regions through the **entorhinal cortex**. Thus, it mediates two-way communication between the cortex and hippocampus (Eichenbaum, 2002).

This diffuse circuit is likely to be important for the consolidation and recall of memory – with the parahippocampal gyrus also undertaking extensive mnemonic information processing of its own. For example, fMRI studies show that the parahippocampal gyrus is active when we learn about topographical or configurational information such as images of landscapes or cityscapes, but it is not involved with identifying individual objects within those scenes (Bohbot et al., 2015). The parahippocampal gyrus has also been associated with many other cognitive processes, including episodic memory and understanding the context of a situation (Aminoff et al., 2013).

KEY TERMS: *Papez circuit, mammillary bodies, fornix, cingulate gyrus, retrosplenial cortex, subiculum, parahippocampal gyrus, perforant pathway, entorhinal cortex*

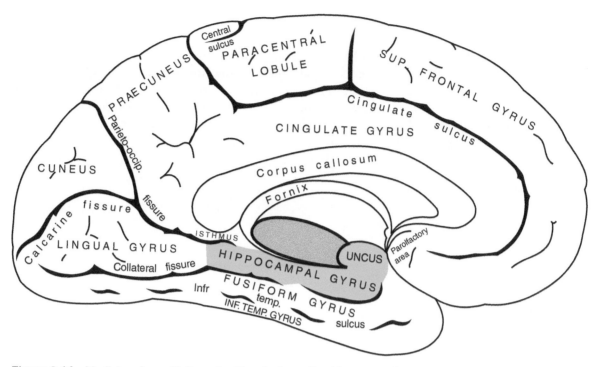

Figure 9.14   Medial surface of left cerebral hemisphere. Parahippocampal gyrus shown in orange
Source: Gray; Mysid; was_a_bee/Wikimedia Commons

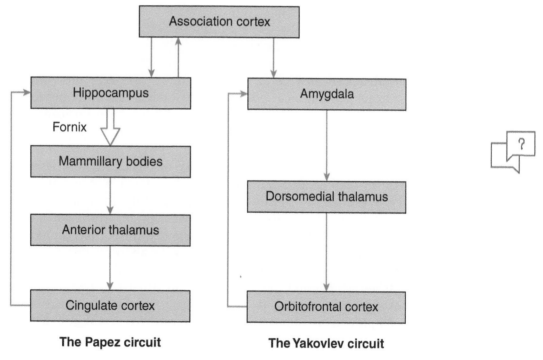

Figure 9.15   The Papez and Yakovlev circuits
Source: Wickens (2009)

Interestingly, the dorsomedial thalamus, which as we have seen has also been implicated in amnesia, lies outside the Papez circuit. Instead, it forms part of a different system that includes the amygdala, orbitofrontal cortex and cingulate gyrus. This is known as the anterior temporal system (sometimes called the Yakovlev circuit). Animal research indicates that parts of this system are important for learning about fearful events, although its role in humans is less clear since neuroimaging studies have implicated it in object and face recognition, conceptual identity, and salience (Ranganath & Ritchey, 2012). The orbitofrontal cortex is also involved in episodic and working memory (Duarte et al., 2010; Ross et al., 2013).

KEY TERMS: *dorsomedial thalamus, anterior temporal system, Yakovlev circuit*

A CLOSER LOOK AT THE HIPPOCAMPAL INVOLVEMENT IN SPATIAL MEMORY

One of the key findings from animal research is that hippocampal damage leads to deficits in tasks that require spatial memory and cognitive mapping of the environment. That is, the hippocampus enables different locations as well as the spatial relationships between these locations to be remembered – an ability enabling the animal to navigate through its environment without getting lost. Much of the impetus for this discovery came from the work of John O'Keefe at the University of London. O'Keefe pioneered a technique where he could record the electrical activity of single hippocampal cells as rats explored and moved around their environment. To his surprise, he found that some neurons only fired when the animal was in a certain location. That is, these neurons remained 'quiet' until the animal reached an exact geographical point – when the cell abruptly became active and fired rapidly. But as the animal moved away, the neuron returned to its resting state. O'Keefe called these neurons **place cells** since they only fired when the rat was in a specific place (O'Keefe & Dostrovsky, 1971).

O'Keefe also demonstrated that the activity of place cells was dependent on the configuration of cues located outside the testing arena. For example, O'Keefe and Conway (1978) trained rats to run a T-maze where only one of the arms always contained food. The maze was surrounded by a black curtain which had a distinct object or cue hanging on each of its four sides. Importantly, the curtain could also be moved around the apparatus, so that the cues changed location relative to the T-maze, but remained in the same configuration to each other. On all trials, the arm containing the food was always pointed towards the corner situated between the light and the card. To make sure the rats learned the spatial location of the arm relative to these cues (and not a simple response bias), the starting position was changed from trial to trial.

The experiment showed that place cells only became active when the animal was in a specific location in relation to the cues. If the curtain was moved around shifting the configuration of the cues with it, the place cell still fired – but only if the rat was in the same relative position to the cues. In other words, the place cells did not fire at a specific internal site in the maze – rather, it was the animal's position relative to its outer environment that was crucial. The importance of the external cues was also highlighted when they were removed. If any two cues were taken off the curtain, the place cells continued to fire, but if three cues were removed, they stopped. The important stimulus for activating the place cell was therefore the spatial configuration of the cues. This indicated the hippocampus was forming a cognitive map of its environment, which it continuously formed and updated to guide direction and goal location (O'Keffe & Nadel, 1978).

Some of the strongest support for the cognitive mapping theory has come from Morris et al. (1982) who developed a spatial memory task which required rats to swim a water maze (Figure 9.16). The 'maze' is a large circular tank of water which is made murky and opaque with the addition of milk. Hidden just below the surface, out of view, is a small escape platform. On their first trial, rats are placed into the water and allowed to swim around until they 'bump' into the platform – onto which they inevitably climb. It is important to realize that the rats cannot see the platform, and can only learn its location by assessing its position in relation to the spatial configuration of cues outside the tank. Morris found the intact rats learned the task very quickly (within one or two trials). In contrast, the hippocampal lesioned ones were unable to learn the platform's location after 40 days of training. The failure of the hippocampal lesioned rats to perform this relatively easy task provides strong support for the cognitive mapping theory.

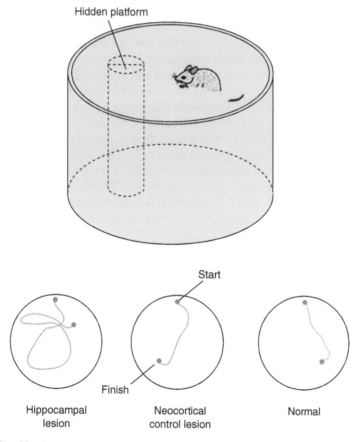

Figure 9.16   The Morris water maze

Source: Wickens (2009) from R.G.M. Morris et al. (1982) Examples of routes taken after training by rats in water maze, *Nature*, 297, 681–683

The Morris water maze has now become a standard behavioural test in brain research because of it precision for testing spatial memory (Nunez, 2008). Although many different-sized pools have been used, they all produce the same type of result, with video-tracking devices now routinely used to measure the escape path and distance travelled in finding the platform. Although initially seen as a pure test of hippocampal function, the water maze is increasingly being used to test many other parameters, including the effects of ageing, drug abuse, and the involvement of neurotransmitter systems in memory function. Adaptations of the maze also provide a valuable animal model for acquired traumatic brain injury which is frequently accompanied by persistent cognitive symptoms, including executive function disruptions and memory deficits (Tucker et al., 2018).

KEY TERMS: *spatial memory, cognitive mapping, place cells, water maze*

KEY THINKER 9.1

JOHN O'KEEFE

For students who come from a humble educational background, John O'Keefe may be an inspiration. O'Keefe was born in Harlem, New York (1939), to Irish immigrant parents – neither of whom had completed elementary education. Growing up in the Bronx, O'Keefe's father worked as a bus mechanic, and his mother a welder in the shipyards during the WW2. Although O'Keefe showed academic promise, he left school at 16 with poor grades and became an office worker. However, he soon grew bored and began an evening course in aeronautical engineering at New York University while working during the day. It would be a stepping stone to him enrolling full-time to study for a degree, opting to major in Psychology with a minor in Philosophy. Graduating in 1963, O'Keefe moved to McGill University in Montreal to do his PhD under the guidance of pain expert Ronald Melzack. At the time, Melzack had received a large grant to build an electrophysiological laboratory, and O'Keefe used the new equipment to develop techniques for recording from single cells in the rat's amygdala. Soon after obtaining his doctorate in 1967, O'Keefe took up a research position at University College, London – and fell in love with London and British culture.

In 1970 O'Keefe began his first studies with the hippocampus, and as with so many new breakthroughs, this development was more a case of good fortune than design. Interested in motor activity, he attempted to implant a microelectrode in the thalamus, but missed and inserted it into the hippocampus instead. He was immediately struck by the correlation of the theta rhythmicity of the hippocampal neurons (theta activity occurs when the cell fires in oscillations that have a frequency of 4 to 7 hertz) when the rat moved around its environment.

Around this time, an Israeli graduate student called Jonathan Dostrovsky joined O'Keefe's laboratory. Together they recorded from hippocampal cells whilst the rat was engaged in a variety of basic behaviours – including eating, drinking, grooming and exploring. They soon realized the hippocampus contained a type of cell that produced theta activity whenever the rat moved into a certain location. It wasn't until some months later, 'on one electrifying day', that O'Keefe recognized these cells were responding to the configuration of landmark cues in their environment, allowing the rat to encode its location. O'Keefe published the results in a three-page paper (O'Keefe & Dostrovsky, 1971) where he introduced the term *place cells*. Around the same time, an old acquaintance called Lynn Nadel, who had fled his postdoctoral fellowship in Prague after the Russian invasion of Czechoslovakia in 1968, also joined O'Keefe's laboratory. Together they would write the influential *The Hippocampus as a Cognitive Map* (1978) which provided strong arguments for the hippocampus being responsible for creating spatial reference maps of its environment to enable navigation.

By the late 1970s, O'Keefe had begun to realize that place cells were utilizing two types of information. The first was the spatial cues, or landmarks, which provide the three-dimensional map of our external world. This was easy to demonstrate in experiments that manipulated the configuration of external cues in maze tasks (e.g. O'Keefe & Conway, 1978). But just as important, in order to successfully navigate through this spatial layout, the hippocampus would also have to compute other things such as distance. However, how it managed this feat was not clear until the Norwegian husband and wife team of May-Britt and Edvard Moser (who had worked with O'Keefe in 1996) found the answer in 2005. The answer lay with a type of neuron in the medial entorhinal cortex called a **grid cell** which fired at highly regular equidistant points as the animal moved. It was as if a grid had been drawn on the floor with the cell firing each time it passed through the centre of a new grid. In short, the grid cells appeared to provide a coordinate system by which distances could be measured for spatial navigation.

In 2014, John O'Keefe along with May-Britt and Edvard Moser were awarded the Nobel Prize 'for their discoveries of cells that constitute a positioning system in the brain'. In announcing the award, the Nobel Assembly commented that O'Keefe and his colleagues had not only solved a problem that had fascinated philosophers and scientists for centuries, but had also opened up a new paradigm for exploring many other cognitive process including memory, thinking and planning.

MEMORY TASKS INVOLVING PRIMATES

The use of primates offers another way of investigating the brain areas involved in learning and memory, and one providing a better approximation of human function. Because primates have good visual acuity, like humans, researchers have often tested their memory by using visual discrimination tasks. This can be undertaken with a delayed response task where the monkey is presented with a tray containing two food wells – one of which is covered by a distinctive object (the sample). If the animal removes the object, then it will find a reward (e.g. a banana chip) in the well underneath. Following this, the tray is removed from sight (accomplished by lowering a screen) and is presented again after a period of time with two test objects: the original sample and a new unfamiliar object. In the delayed matching to sample task, the animal has to remember the previously chosen object. There is, however, an alternative version where the monkey must displace the new object to obtain the reward. This is known as the delayed non-matching to sample procedure. It appears that monkeys learn to perform the non-matching version of the task quicker than the matching one because of their tendency to preferentially attend to novel stimuli (Mishkin & Delacour, 1975).

One person who pioneered this type of research was Mortimer Mishkin (see Wickens, 2019b). Mishkin's early work with the delayed non-matching to sample task produced some unexpected findings, especially regarding the hippocampus.

For example, Mishkin (1978) lesioned the hippocampus or the amygdala in macaque monkeys, and found neither operation produced a marked impairment on delayed non-matching. In fact, both groups performed at about 90% correct after a two-minute delay. But when Mishkin combined the hippocampus and amygdala lesion, performance fell to near chance. This finding is noteworthy because HM's operation also involved removal of the amygdala and hippocampus, as well as the surrounding medial temporal lobe. On first sight, therefore, Mishkin's work implied that both the hippocampus and amygdala were necessary for memory. Indeed, as we have seen in this chapter, there is evidence that these two structures form part of different memory circuits in the brain. Mishkin reasoned both circuits had to be damaged for severe amnesia to occur in monkeys and humans.

This theory, however, is no longer the favoured one (see Meunier & Barbeau, 2013 for an historical account of the issues). Since Mishkin's work, it has been recognized that lesions to several other areas within the medial temporal lobes, as well as the frontal cortex, also impair memory on the delayed non-matching to sample task. These areas include the prefrontal cortex, parahippocampal region, inferotemporal cortex and mediodorsal thalamus (Rodriguez & Paule, 2009). However, the crucial region appears to be the rhinal cortex (see Figure 9.17) which

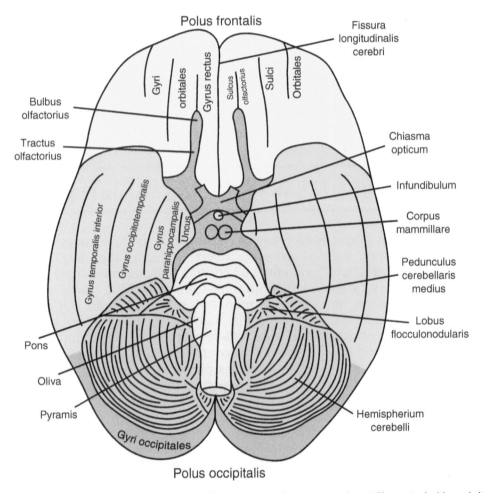

Figure 9.17   Basal view of a human brain. Note that the rhinal cortex is not illustrated although it is located in the region of the posterior parahippocampal gyrus

Source: NEUROtiker/Wikimedia Commons

is an area of cortex on the medial underside of the temporal lobes surrounding the rhinal fissure that contains the entorhinal and **perirhinal cortex**. In fact, rhinal cortex lesions disrupt delayed non-matching performance as much as Mishkin's hippocampal-amygdala lesion. It is also likely that the rhinal area was damaged by Mishkin's combined lesions (Meunier et al., 1993), and this area would also have been destroyed by Scoville's operation on HM in 1953. The question of whether the hippocampus is actually important for performance on delayed non-matching tasks has now become unclear, since some researchers have found little impairment after damage (Murray & Mishkin, 1998) whilst others report significant deficits (Zola et al., 2000). It should also be noted that lesion studies do not provide all the data needed to understand a cognitive function such as memory. For example, electrical recording has shown that neurons in the dorsolateral prefrontal cortex show sustained excitatory activity during the delay period (Funahashi et al., 1989) as well as those in the medial posterior parietal cortex (Daniel et al., 2016).

The delayed non-matching to sample procedure is also regarded as an animal test of **working memory**. In humans, this refers to a limited capacity form of memory able to hold information in a short-term buffer, which allows it to be available for further cognitive processing (see also next chapter). So, for example, when stopping our car to ask a pedestrian the way to the theatre, we may hold the directions in mind (e.g. turn left, then right at the traffic lights) whilst implementing the turns in their correct sequence. In the case of delayed non-matching tasks, the requirement of having to learn a new cue from trial to trial qualifies it as a test of working memory (Rodriguez & Paule, 2009). Working memory is an important human ability and one which deteriorates rapidly in dementia such as Alzheimer's disease (Huntley & Howard, 2010). It follows, therefore, that the delayed non-matching to sample task also provides a useful animal model of dementia, and one that has already proven useful for the development of drugs with clinical promise to treat the disease (Jackson et al., 1995; Prendergast et al., 1997).

> **KEY TERMS**: *delayed matching to sample and delayed non-matching to sample tests, rhinal cortex, working memory*

SUMMARY

There is no learning without memory, although some information can be innate as in the case of instincts and basic reflexes. The search for the engram (the anatomical site of memory storage) was initiated in the 1920s by Karl Lashley who made knife cuts to the **cerebral cortex** in rats after they had learnt to run through a maze. Lashley found his animals were able to relearn the maze task after receiving large lesions, leading him to conclude that memories for negotiating mazes were stored diffusely throughout the cerebral cortex. He called this the principle of mass action. Lashley also believed that all parts of the cortex played an equal role in memory storage – a principle he termed equipotentiality. His work was supported, in part, by Donald Hebb, who theorized that learning and memory must involve large groups of neurons, or cell assemblies, which 'reverberated' for some time after the event. In turn, this led to structural change at synapses which provided a hypothetical substrate for long-term memory. Evidence of increased electrical activity in neurons after learning has come from the discovery of long-term potentiation, whilst a detailed account of the synaptic changes that accompany habituation and sensitisation has come from an examination of the gill-withdrawal reflex in **Aplysia**. Both long-term potentiation and learning in *Aplysia* have also been subject to molecular investigation, which has highlighted the importance of intracellular changes that lead to protein synthesis. Research examining the effects of rats reared in enriched environments has also shown that this can produce a number of changes in the brain, including increased numbers of dendritic spines, synapses, and higher levels of the enzyme acetyl-cholinesterase which breaks down the neurotransmitter acetylcholine.

A brain structure that appears to be crucial for learning and memory in humans is the hippocampus. This was dramatically shown in the case of Henry Molaison (HM) who underwent bilateral removal of the medial temporal lobes in 1953 for the treatment of epilepsy. Following the operation, HM suffered from a profound anterograde amnesia which caused him to forget factual knowledge almost immediately, although he could keep things in his mind for a brief period (i.e. short-term memory) when concentrating on the material. Although HM could remember much of his childhood and adolescence, he suffered from some degree of retrograde amnesia for events that took place in the years leading up to his surgery. Despite this, HM was capable of learning certain tasks (e.g. mirror drawing, priming etc.) showing that the medial temporal lobes are not necessarily involved in all types of memory. This has also led to the idea that the hippocampus is necessary for declarative memory (or 'knowing what' information which can be 'declared' into consciousness), but not 'knowing how' skills otherwise called procedural memory. Studies of the hippocampus in animals, especially by John O'Keefe, have also shown it to be essential for cognitive mapping and spatial memory. Another region of the brain implicated in human amnesia is the **diencephalon**, which includes the mammillary bodies and dorsomedial thalamus. Damage to both these areas occurs in Korsakoff's syndrome associated with chronic alcohol abuse. The location of brain sites implicated in amnesia points to two main memory pathways in the brain: the Papez circuit and the Yakovlev circuit. The former includes the hippocampus, fornix, mammillary bodies and cingulate gyrus, and the latter includes the amygdala, dorsomedial thalamus and frontal cortex. Research using delayed matching to non-sample tasks in primates has further identified other areas in the medial temporal lobes involved in memory processing which include the rhinal cortex. In addition, the delayed matching to non-sample task provides a useful animal model of working memory (an important component of human cognition) which can be used to test drugs that have the potential to treat dementia such as Alzheimer's disease.

GO ONLINE

TEST YOUR UNDERSTANDING OF THIS CHAPTER AND VISIT HTTPS://STUDY.SAGEPUB.COM/WICKENS TO ACCESS INTERACTIVE 'DRAG AND DROP' LABELLING ACTIVITIES AND A FLASHCARD GLOSSARY.

MULTIPLE CHOICE QUESTIONS

Answer the questions below to test your understanding of this chapter's Learning Objectives. You'll find the answers at the end of the chapter.

1. Which part of the brain did Lashley believe the memory trace (engram) for maze learning in rats was stored in?

    a. hippocampus
    b. visual cortex
    c. diffusely throughout the cerebral cortex
    d. nowhere! (Because his lesions had no long-term effect on maze learning he concluded the engram did not exist.)

2. According to Donald Hebb, the formation of the memory trace involves which of the following?

    a. neural circuits called cell assemblies
    b. reverberatory activity
    c. structural changes at the synapse
    d. all of the above

3. Bliss and Lomo first demonstrated long-term potentiation in the hippocampus by stimulating what pathway?

    a. perforant path
    b. Schaffer collaterals
    c. fornix
    d. the cingulum

4. Which of the following best describes the extent of HM's bilateral brain damage which occurred as a result of Dr Scoville's operation in 1953?

    a. hippocampus only
    b. hippocampus and fornix
    c. hippocampus and mammillary bodies
    d. hippocampus, amygdala and adjacent cortex

5. Who invented the water maze (submerged platform) task as a means of testing spatial memory?

    a. Donald Hebb
    b. Richard Morris
    c. John O'Keefe
    d   Eric Kandel

6. According to O'Keefe and Nadel (1978) the role of the hippocampus is to provide animals with which of the following?

    a. working memory
    b. long-term memory
    c. a cognitive map
    d. none of the above

FURTHER READING

Andersen, P., Morris, R., Amaral, D., Bliss, T., & O'Keefe, J. (Eds.). (2006). *The hippocampus book*. Oxford University Press.
With 16 chapters written by various experts, this contains everything you will need to know about the hippocampus.

Bourtchouladze, R. (2002). *Memories are made of this*. Weidenfeld and Nicolson.
Described on the inside cover as 'a brilliant work of popularisation', this book may be the place to start for the student who wants a simple but broad introduction to the biopsychology of memory.

Corkin, S. (2013). *Permanent present tense: The man with no memory, and what he taught the world.* Allen Books.
The story of Henry Molaison and what he has taught us about memory from a researcher who worked with him for nearly five decades.

Dubai, Y. (2004). *Memory from A to Z: Keywords, concepts, and beyond.* Oxford University Press.
A surprisingly useful, detailed and innovative book consisting of over 130 entries which (largely but not exclusively) concern topics that relate to the neuroscience of memory.

Eichenbaum, H. (2012). *The cognitive neuroscience of memory: An introduction.* Oxford University Press.
A clear and accessible textbook which covers amongst other things separate chapters on the brain systems for procedural, declarative and emotional memory.

Eichenbaum, H., & Cohen, N. J. (2004) *From conditioning to conscious recollection: Memory systems of the brain.* Oxford University Press.
An informative book covering historical issues, cellular plasticity, the neurobiology of declarative memory, and other specialized memory systems of the brain.

Kandel, E. (2006). *In search of memory: The emergence of a new science of mind.* Norton and Co.
Although this is an autobiography of Eric Kandel, it is also much more, and can be read as an interesting and accessible introduction to the biology of memory.

Rudy, J. W. (2014). *The neurobiology of learning and memory.* Sinauer.
A textbook which covers the foundations of synaptic plasticity, molecular biology, and the neuroanatomy of memory systems in the brain, and provides a decent introduction for the student of neuroscience.

Squire, L. R., & Kandel, E. R. (1999). *Memory: From mind to molecules.* Scientific American Library.
A well-written and richly illustrated text that provides a good overview of research into the neural mechanisms underlying learning and memory.

Wickens, A. P. (2019). *Key thinkers in neuroscience.* Routledge.
Has individual chapters discussing many of the key thinkers covered in this chapter, including Karl Lashley, Donald Hebb, Brenda Milner, Eric Kandel, Mortimer Mishkin, Timothy Bliss and John O'Keefe.

MULTIPLE CHOICE ANSWERS - 1. C | 2. D | 3. A | 4. D | 5. B | 6. C

10

LANGUAGE AND COGNITION

LEARNING OBJECTIVES

After reading this chapter you should be able to:

- Explain the involvement of the main brain areas responsible for language.

- Describe the different types of aphasia.

- Specify the causes of dyslexia.

- Understand the Wernicke–Geschwind model of language.

- Appreciate hemispheric differences and the importance of split-brain studies.

- Describe the historical development and use of functional brain-scanning techniques.

- Understand what is meant by executive function and working memory.

- Outline what is known about how the brain processes musical information.

GO ONLINE

Test your understanding of this chapter and visit **https://study.sagepub.com/wickens** to access interactive 'Drag and Drop' labelling activities and a flashcard glossary.

INTRODUCTION

One of the greatest challenges facing psychologists is to understand the biological nature of mental activity such as language, cognition and self-awareness. Put simply, the question can be rephrased as how can the neural machinery of the brain, with its billions of neurons, give rise to the mental processes that create the human mind? Although this issue has fascinated philosophers since the time of Descartes in the seventeenth century, who was the first to recognize that many of our mental processes were mechanical or reflexive in nature, scientists have been restricted by the limited methodologies that could tackle such questions.

In fact, until fairly recently (e.g. the mid-1970s) the neuroscientific investigation of cognition, including language, was largely dependent on examining individuals with brain damage such as stroke or other types of injury. This type of approach was also reliant on neuropsychological testing when the person was alive, and post-mortem analysis to locate the brain damage after death. Although this had some success – not least in the discovery of the main language centres of the brain during the nineteenth century – it also proved limited in many other respects, especially in explaining the underlying neural processes involved in cognition.

This situation has changed, however, with the development of non-invasive functional brain-scanning techniques such as positron emission tomography (PET) and functional magnetic resonance imaging (fMRI). Both permit the neural activity of the brain to be directly observed in a conscious living person. These techniques have allowed researchers to study just about every type of thought process, and to visualize the activation of multiple brain areas that take place during such mental events. They have also given rise to a new academic field known as cognitive neuroscience which is primarily concerned with integrating cognitive science (an area that borrows largely from computer science which views the brain as an information-processing system) with biopsychology.

There has been meteoric growth in this type of research, and no doubt it will continue to provide new insights into the mental activity of the brain over the coming years as its sophistication develops.

THE FIRST DISCOVERIES LINKING LANGUAGE WITH THE BRAIN

One of the unique things that distinguish us from other creatures is our ability to use language. Of course, all higher animals are capable of communication, but humans are the only ones who use a powerfully complex, creative and abstract system of sounds that enables them to express their thoughts and feelings in speech as well as writing. It is believed our language first began to evolve around 50,000–150,000 years ago, at the very dawn of our existence as modern *Homo sapiens*, and it would be impossible to imagine human existence without it. Our ability to use language is remarkable in many ways. For example, during a simple conversation we speak around 180 words a minute from a vocabulary of between 60,000 to 120,000 words. Although this is an impressive number, even more important is our ability to utilize an extensive knowledge of linguistic rules including those governing the sequencing of words and their form (i.e. grammar and syntax). In fact, this rule system provides us with the potential to make an infinite number of word sequences (and meanings) from a finite number of sounds. Human language is also unique for its ability to refer to abstract concepts, imagined or hypothetical events, and situations that took place in the past or are likely to happen in the future. The richness and complexity of human language has undoubtedly provided the keystone that underpins cultural evolution and enabled knowledge to be written down for prosperity. However, language is much more than mere communication for it also provides a system for representing knowledge in the brain and a vehicle for thought. In fact, it has been said that the main use of language is to transfer thoughts from one mind to another mind (Gleitman & Papafragou, 2005). It is therefore no surprise that language has been described as the greatest of all human achievements (Ornstein, 1988).

One of the most enduring debates in the history of neuropsychology has been the question concerning localization of function (Wickens, 2015). In short, can certain behavioural and mental functions such as memory and language be localized to discrete regions of the brain, or does the brain act in a more holistic way with no specialized areas for any particular faculty? Up until the nineteenth century, the main consensus was for the latter – not least because many held that the mind was unitary and undividable – but this view began to change when it was discovered that the brain housed specific regions for language. The first brain area to be implicated in this way was that of the **frontal lobes**. These attracted interest in the 1820s when a French doctor, Jean-Baptiste Bouillaud, examined over a hundred individuals with speech disturbances and found all of them had suffered injury to the frontal cortex. Bouillaud's observations led him to conclude that this type of damage stopped the person from speaking clearly, although they could express themself with gestures and writing, and were able to comprehend others. A dramatic case was reported in 1861 when Bouillaud's son-in-law, Simon Aubertin, came across a man who had shot away part of his left frontal cranium in a failed suicide attempt. The injury had also exposed the brain, and during the course of his examination, Aubertin found if he pressed a spatula against the exposed brain whilst the man was speaking, his speech was immediately halted. However, when the compression was lessened, his speech resumed (Finger, 1994).

Despite this, there was a general reluctance by investigators at the time to accept that a complex psychological function such as speech could be localized to a specific brain region. This was partly because localization of function seemed to support the popular fad of phrenology which had been ridiculed and discredited. However, another problem was that many individuals were known who had substantial frontal lobe damage *without* any form of language impairment. And to confound the matter further, the French doctor Gabriel Andral during the 1830s identified a number of instances where language deficits occurred in patients that appeared to have *no* frontal lobe damage whatsoever.

A general acceptance of a speech centre in the frontal lobes would have to wait for stronger evidence. This was provided by Paul Broca, who became interested in the subject of language localization after hearing Aubertin give a talk in 1861. Soon after this, one of Broca's patients called Leborgne, who had been interned at the Bicêtre Hospital for over 20 years because of his inability to speak (although he could utter the simple expression 'Tan'), died after succumbing to gangrene. Despite his muteness, Leborgne had been reasonably intelligent and capable of understanding spoken and written language. Six days after Leborgne's death, Broca performed an autopsy. His findings would have a profound effect on neuropsychology for he found a large cavity about the size of a chicken's egg located towards the back of the frontal lobes in the left hemisphere – a site that Bouillaud and Aubertin had long argued was involved in the articulation of language.

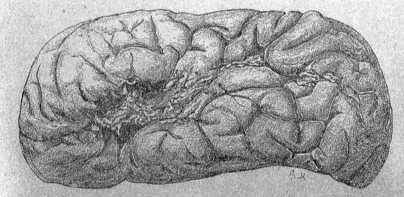

Prenons d'abord le premier cas, le cas Leborgne; il s'agit, sans aucune discussion possible, d'une Aphasie de Broca, le malade n'a

Fig. 1 — Hémisphère gauche du cerveau de Leborgne, première autopsie de Broca. Dessin fait sur la photographie de la pièce actuellement conservée au Musée Dupuytren. On voit que, en outre de la lésion de la troisième frontale, le ramollissement existait tout le long de la scissure de Sylvius et siégeait par conséquent aussi dans la zone de Wernicke.

plus à sa disposition que la syllabe *tan*, il est hémiplégique à droite, c'est un aphasique typique.

Voyons les données de l'autopsie;

Figure 10.1   A drawing of Leborgne's brain

Source: Travaux et mémoires/Pierre Marie. Credit: Wellcome Collection. Attribution 4.0 International (CC BY 4.0).

Broca referred to the loss of speech suffered by Leborgne as *aphemie* (aphasia) and stressed it had been caused by a stroke to the posterior part of the frontal cortex. Yet this was only the beginning of his discoveries, for Broca was to identify eight more individuals with aphasia who all had left-sided damage of the frontal lobes by 1863. Describing the consistency of his findings as 'remarkable', there was little doubt in Broca's mind that language articulation was localized in the brain. Today, this region–which is located just anterior to the part of the primary motor cortex that governs the movement of the vocal cord and mouth–is called **Broca's area**.

KEY TERMS: *language, localization of function, frontal lobes, Broca's area*

BROCA'S APHASIA

The term **aphasia** literally means a complete loss of speech (*a* meaning without; *phasia* meaning speech). But it is more accurate to regard aphasia as a disturbance in the production and/or comprehension of speech following brain damage. It is rarely (as in the case of Leborgne) the complete loss of language use. Nonetheless, the symptoms can vary considerably, from getting a few words mixed up to having difficulty with all forms of communication (speaking, listening, writing and reading). Around 85% of aphasia cases are due to cerebrovascular accidents (stroke) with the remainder caused by head injuries, tumours and disease (Martin, 2006). It is also important to note that not all people with speech disturbances are aphasiac. For example, an inability to speak through deafness, paralysis of the speech muscles, or lack of motivation to communicate does not constitute aphasia. Although aphasia affects a person's ability to communicate it does not normally affect their intelligence.

Broca's aphasia (sometimes called 'expressive aphasia') is characterized by language that is slow, laboured and lacking grammar. Whilst the person may have a large vocabulary, their speech tends to be composed of simple nouns, verbs and adjectives (not unlike the type of language once used to write a telegram). Their speech also suffers from abnormal prosody, i.e. it lacks the rhythm, intonation and inflection of normal language. Another characteristic of Broca's aphasia is difficulty in finding the 'right word'

Asked to tell the story of Cinderella
(previously shown picture version of the story to facilitate recall)

Cinderella...yes...now...busy me (*gestures dusting, Ironing etc.*....)...la la la...happy...
no sad...two erm sss...sss...sisters...bad...bad sisters... dance...fff fairy god dance swoosh
(*gestures magic wand*)...Cinderella...pr...pr...priz ch... no too hard (*therapist: 'Prince Charming'*)...
Yes him...lovely...dancing...happy happy...oh no...time time...run shoe...Cinderella...
shoe...mine...mine OK... lovely happy...the end...hard work (*laughs*)

(underline indicates extra stress)

Figure 10.2   Non-fluent Broca's type aphasia
Source: provided by Mandy Galling, Reg RCSLT, Guild Community Healthcare NHS Trust

(anomia) which can cause long pauses during speech. To make matters worse, the person is also likely to have articulation difficulties making their speech difficult to understand. Not surprisingly, this can cause someone with Broca's aphasia to become frustrated when attempting to communicate with others. Despite this, simple automated expressions such as 'hello', or emotional outbursts including swearing, are often unaffected. In some cases, a person with Broca's aphasia may even be able to sing old and well-learned songs without difficulty (Yamadori et al., 1977).

How can we best explain the deficit in Broca's aphasia? One clue comes from the observation that these patients often have difficulty carrying out a simple command such as being asked to stick out their tongue (oral apraxia), yet have no problem licking their lips after eating a sugary doughnut (which also requires them to stick out their tongue). This reveals the person is unable to proactively produce the correct motor responses for articulating speech. Indeed, a closer examination of the anatomical site of Broca's area shows it to be next to the primary motor cortex (which governs voluntary actions) where it lies adjacent to the part that is responsible for mouth and face movements. Thus, Broca's aphasia is in part due to the patient's inability to properly move their tongue and mouth muscles in order to produce fluent vocalization.

But there is more to Broca's aphasia than this. In addition to difficulties expressing themselves, individuals with Broca's aphasia can have trouble with language comprehension in certain ways. This occurs, for example, with complex instructions. So, for instance, they may be unable to follow a command such as 'Put the cup on top of the fork and place the knife inside the cup'. Another problem arises in understanding sentences where there is an unusual word order or a degree of ambiguity. Thus, a patient is likely to understand who is doing the chasing in 'The mouse was chased by the cat', but will have difficulty with 'The boy was chased by the girl'. Obviously, a mouse cannot chase a cat, although it is possible a boy could chase the girl. The question of whether such comprehension deficits are due to syntactic processing, or a failure of verbal working memory, is the focus of much research at present (Rogalsky et al., 2008).

KEY TERMS: *aphasia, Broca's aphasia, prosody, anomia, articulation difficulties, primary motor cortex*

WERNICKE'S APHASIA

In 1874, a 26-year-old German neurologist called Carl Wernicke published a short monograph describing another type of language impairment, which became known as **Wernicke's aphasia**. The symptoms were different from those of Broca's aphasia and not caused by frontal lobe damage. Instead, they were associated with lesions to a left-sided region of the **temporal lobes**, adjacent to Heschl's gyrus, which is also the site of the primary auditory cortex (see Chapter 3). Unlike Broca's aphasia, damage to Wernicke's area does not interfere with the rhythm and grammar of speech. Hence, these patients articulate their words and sentences fluently, making it sound quite normal to a casual non-attending listener, but if one listens carefully to the words, they will soon realize it is largely devoid of meaning. In fact, Wernicke's aphasia produces speech largely composed of inappropriate words (paraphasias) or ones that do not exist (**neologisms**). For example, in reply to the question 'Where do you work?', one subject was quoted as saying 'Before I was in the one here, I was in the other one. My sister had the department in the other one' (Geschwind, 1972). Alternatively, when Kertesz (1979) asked a patient to name a toothbrush and a pen, they responded with 'stoktery' and 'minkt.'

Required to tell the therapist about trip to visit his daughter and a meal out

Claire?...yes...well...I was will...miner...mineral water...of my 'pitch' on stonework 'make' and 'ww' and 'wiker' of 'wenner'. December and London...on 'minter' of 'minder' and 'si' or 'risher'...I was 'madge'

(Targets very difficult to interpret. Items In quotation marks show broad phonological approximation)

Figure 10.3   Fluent Wernicke's aphasia

Source: provided by Mandy Galling, Reg RCSLT, Guild Community Healthcare NHS Trust

Damage to Wernicke's area also produces a serious deficit in language comprehension. This varies depending on the amount of brain damage and its location, producing an impairment which may range from regularly missing certain details of a conversation, to being unable to understand even the simplest spoken and/or written information (Brookshire, 2007). This makes it difficult to engage in meaningful conversation with a person with Wernicke's aphasia, and to make matters worse they are often unaware of their difficulties (Mesulam et al., 2015). The use of inappropriate words produces a disjointed and confused form of speech known as jargon aphasia. In addition, reading and writing are impaired in Wernicke's aphasia. There are even some subjects who, if given a book, will go through the motions of reading it aloud, only to recite utter nonsense (Springer & Deutsch, 1989). Yet a person with Wernicke's aphasia will still normally follow the non-verbal rules during a conversation by pausing and taking turns to speak, nodding their head in appropriate places, and being sensitive to tone of voice and facial expressions.

How can we best understand the underlying deficit in Wernicke's aphasia? According to Wernicke, the impairment is caused by a lesion that stops sound input being linked with its meaning which was stored deeper in the brain. The fact that Wernicke's area lies in close proximity to the primary auditory cortex supports this contention – for it would appear to be an excellent location to serve translating sounds into verbal coding. For this reason, Wernicke's aphasia is known as sensory or receptive aphasia. Moreover, the location of Wernicke's area which lies in a gyrus at the junction of the temporal lobe with parietal and occipital regions, gives it access to widespread regions of the brain that are necessary for different types of interpretation. One important brain region for verbal comprehension is the parietal cortex which contains a network of areas known to be important for integrating different types of sensory information and has several regions that are necessary for language processing (see Banich & Compton, 2018).

KEY TERMS: *Wernicke's aphasia, temporal lobes, primary auditory cortex, paraphasias, neologisms, jargon aphasia, receptive aphasia, parietal cortex*

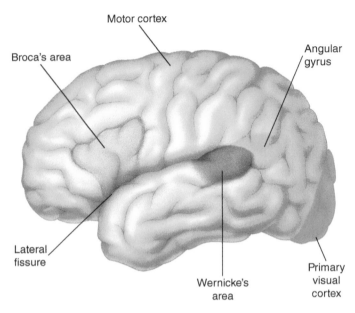

Figure 10.4   Language-related areas of the cortex
Source: Garrett and Hough (2018)

ALEXIA AND AGRAPHIA

In 1891, the French doctor Jules Dejerine reported the case of a 63-year-old man called Monsieur S, who woke one morning to realize he could not read his newspaper. When examined by Dejerine, he was unable to recognize letters or words (a condition known as **alexia**) or write to dictation (**agraphia**), yet he had no problem recognizing objects and people, or comprehending speech. When Monsieur S died nine months later, a brain autopsy revealed damage to the **angular gyrus** (see Figure 10.4). This is a site located in the parietal lobe close to Wernicke's area and its border with the occipital lobes. Dejerine concluded the lesioned angular gyrus had prevented Monsieur S from translating the appearance of written information into the appropriate mental sounds and meanings (Glynn, 1999).

A year later, Dejerine found another individual, this time named Monsieur C, who was a 68-year-old Parisian fabric designer. Monsieur C had experienced a transient attack of body numbness, following which he was unable to recognize words or letters, yet he still retained the ability to write fluently, either spontaneously or to dictation. Nor had there been any change to his handwriting. His alexia, however, produced some odd patterns of behaviour. For example, he could copy words out correctly, and providing they were large enough for him to trace his finger around, he could deduce their meaning. He was also able to recognize words when the individual letters were spoken out aloud (e.g. c-a-t), but still could not visually read a single word (Bub et al., 1993).

Close examination of Monsieur C revealed he was blind in the right visual field of both eyes – indicating that his brain lesion lay somewhere in the left visual cortex (see Chapter 2). This was confirmed at autopsy. But just as important to explaining his alexia was the discovery of damage to the posterior portion of the corpus callosum which carries visual information between the two hemispheres. Although Monsieur C could see words and letters with his right intact visual cortex, he was unable to cross this information over to the angular gyrus in the language-dominant left hemisphere, where presumably the meaningful reading took place. This type of deficit, which involves a lesion to a pathway, has since been called a **disconnection syndrome** (Geschwind, 1965). The result was that Monsieur C could see written words, but not recognize them from their visual characteristics. His ability to copy out written information probably occurred because of intact connections between the right visual cortex and the motor areas that control hand movement. In other words, copying involved an alternative route through the brain which did not involve the left-sided angular gyrus. These two syndromes demonstrate that multiple processes are involved in reading and writing (Sheldon et al., 2008).

KEY TERMS: *alexia, agraphia, angular gyrus, disconnection syndrome*

THE WERNICKE-GESCHWIND MODEL

Wernicke not only described the type of aphasia that bears his name, but in 1874 he also formulated a neurological model which attempted to explain how language was processed by the brain. This theory was later elaborated in the 1880s by Ludwig Lichtheim. According to Wernicke, the comprehension and production of speech were undertaken in a series of interconnected localized regions located in the cerebral left hemisphere. These regions are illustrated in Figure 10.5. When listening to speech, his model proposed that a progression of brain activity began in the **auditory cortex** which passed to **Wernicke's area**. This acted as a phonological lexicon – a sort of buffer where the meanings of words were understood. Wernicke did not believe the word meanings were literally stored here. Rather, he thought that word meanings (or concepts) were distributed throughout the cortex, including the areas surrounding Wernicke's area, and linked extensively by association fibres. In turn, the output of Wernicke's area passed to Broca's area which he believed held the motor programs controlling the muscle movements necessary for speech. In effect, Wernicke had invented the first neuropsychological theory of language, and it would soon gather considerable support.

The neurological model for reading was much the same except now the process began in the visual cortex and the words were translated into verbal codes by the angular gyrus. In turn, this information was passed to Wernicke's area for comprehension. It was also a simple step to explain how pure thought and cognition could generate verbal responses. In this instance, no sensory input from the ears and eyes is needed. Instead, mental activity, presumably generated by the association areas of the cerebral cortex, interacts with Wernicke's area directly (and possibly Broca's area too).

Wernicke's and Lichtheim's model remained influential, but was elaborated further by Norman Geschwind in 1965. Geschwind's insight was to realize that several types of aphasia could be predicted from the model – especially when a 'disconnection' occurred in a pathway between two regions where language processing took place. An obvious site was the one that linked Wernicke's with Broca's area. This pathway is called the **arcuate fasciculus**. Interestingly, this connection was only discovered in the early part of the twentieth century by the anatomist Constantin von Monakow (Catani & Mesulam, 2008) although Wernicke had predicted the consequences of its damage. In fact, he reasoned this would not affect language comprehension as Wernicke's area remained intact, nor would it impair speech production as Broca's area was intact. The nature of the deficit, therefore, would be a specific type of aphasia where the person was unable to repeat words and sentences fluently.

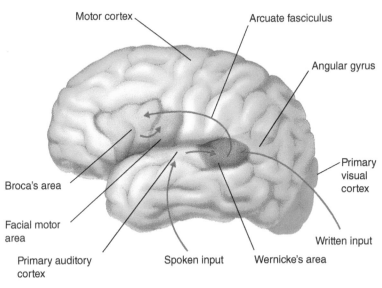

Figure 10.5   The Wernicke–Geschwind model of language

Source: Garrett and Hough (2021), adapted from 'Specializations of the Human Brain', by N. Geschwind, *Scientific American*, 241(9), 180–199

As Geschwind (1967) was to show, Wernicke turned out to be accurate in his predictions. People with arcuate fasciculus damage are able to comprehend language and produce fluent speech, but are impaired in repeating certain words and sentences. This is now known as **conduction aphasia**. The deficit is particularly marked if the person is asked to repeat words that denote abstract concepts. For example, someone with conduction aphasia may be able to repeat words such as 'bicycle' and 'elephant', but not 'myth' or 'carburettor'. This appears to occur because concrete words can generate a visual image which passes to Broca's area via a different pathway (presumably from the occipital lobes). Geschwind's contribution to our understanding of aphasia has led to the overall scheme being called the Wernicke–Geschwind model of language processing.

KEY TERMS: *auditory cortex, Wernicke's area (phonological lexicon), Broca's area (motor program store), arcuate fasciculus, conduction aphasia, Wernicke–Geschwind model*

OTHER TYPES OF APHASIA

There are other types of aphasia which can be understood in terms of the Wernicke–Geschwind model. The severest is global aphasia where the person loses the ability to comprehend language and articulate it meaningfully. Although patients with global aphasia may be able to verbalize a few short utterances, their overall production ability is very limited (Manasco, 2014). Consequently, speech typically deteriorates into unintelligible jargon aphasia. A person with global aphasia will also be severely impaired at reading and writing. This type of aphasia, therefore, combines many of the symptoms associated with Broca's and Wernicke's forms. Global aphasia occurs after widespread damage to the left cerebral cortex, especially the area lying around the upper Sylvian fissure (sometimes called the lateral sulcus) which separates the parietal and temporal lobes. In addition, there may be damage to the thalamus and basal ganglia. Most cases of global aphasia are caused by strokes to the middle cerebral artery which serves large areas of the left hemisphere. Despite this, people with global aphasia who normally have an intact right hemisphere can communicate as they express feelings and wishes through facial, vocal and other physical gestures.

Another type of aphasia is transcortical sensory aphasia. This is similar to Wernicke's aphasia as it is characterized by fluent but unintelligible speech, and poor comprehension. Yet people with this type of aphasia can repeat words and non-words spoken to them, and even identify grammatical errors in spoken language. Sadly, this ability is compromised by the probability of them having little understanding of what they are

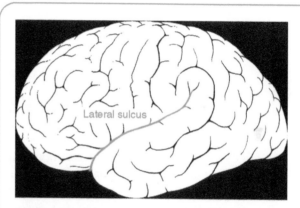

Figure 10.6   The Sylvian fissure (shown here as the lateral sulcus)

Source: Jimhutchins/Wikimedia Commons

saying. In everyday social interaction this may lead to echolalia where the person continually repeats words or phrases spoken to them (Manasco, 2014). Transcortical sensory aphasia is produced by damage to the cortex surrounding Wernicke's area, especially at the temporal lobe-parietal lobe borders, which leaves the arcuate fasciculus intact. It is believed this disrupts the flow of information from the area decoding phonological information (e.g. Wernicke's area) to the areas responsible for determining the meaning of the sound (Boatman et al., 2000).

In contrast, transcortical motor aphasia has more similarities with Broca's aphasia. A person with this impairment will have difficulties initiating speech, and produce non-fluent and dysprosodic language which is full of grammatical errors. Like Broca's aphasia, speech is typically composed of short utterances containing only one or two words. Despite this, a transcortical motor patient will have good language comprehension, and be able to repeat words and name objects (Brookshire, 2007). This is because they have an intact arcuate fasciculus. This form of aphasia is associated with damage to the **supplementary motor cortex** adjacent to the primary motor cortex, and the

dorsolateral frontal cortex which lies just above Broca's area. However, in most cases, Broca's area is spared from damage. The lesioned areas are probably responsible for the initiation of speech (supplementary motor areas) and the ongoing control of speech (dorsolateral frontal cortex).

A much rarer language disorder is anomic aphasia (sometimes called deep dysphasia) where the person has difficulty finding the right word, and will often substitute this with related but inappropriate ones. For example, when asked to repeat the words 'kite or shell', the person may respond with 'balloon' and 'kernel' (Martin, 2006). Although verbal comprehension is good in this type of aphasia, the substitution of alternative words in their speech makes it difficult to understand. Patients with this type of aphasia often forget the word just presented to them, although they may retain its meaning. The anatomical basis for this type of aphasia is not well established. It possibly involves a disconnection between Wernicke's area and Broca's area, but one involving a pathway other than the arcuate fasciculus (Heilman, 2006).

KEY TERMS: *global aphasia, Sylvian fissure, transcortical sensory aphasia, transcortical motor aphasia, supplementary motor cortex, dorsolateral frontal cortex, anomic aphasia*

A REVALUATION OF THE WERNICKE-GESCHWIND MODEL

The model of language processing developed by Wernicke and Geschwind was a major achievement that stimulated research and guided the diagnosis of aphasia and other speech problems. Despite this, the theory is only accurate up to a point, and some researchers now even regard it as obsolete (Tremblay & Dick, 2016). Although Broca's aphasia is more often associated with a frontal stroke, and Wernicke's aphasia with damage to the temporal lobes, the effects of such lesions are rarely as predictable as the Wernicke–Geschwind model makes out. Indeed, people with Wernicke's aphasia nearly always have some degree of motor speech abnormality, and those with Broca's aphasia show comprehension deficits (O'Sullivan et al., 2019).

Another problem lies with evidence showing that damage to Broca's and Wernicke's areas does not necessarily produce the effects that are expected. For example, lesions confined to Broca's area itself do not generally lead to long-lasting language impairments (Mohr et al., 1978); nor do those individuals with Broca's aphasia always have damage to Broca's area (Dronkers et al., 2004). In fact, slow destruction of the Broca's area by brain tumours can leave speech relatively intact, suggesting its functions are able to shift into nearby brain areas (Plaza et al., 2009). The situation regarding Wernicke's area is even more confusing – not least because it is anatomically difficult to localize and define (Dronkers et al., 2004). Some, for example, identify Wernicke's area with the anterior part of Brodmanns area 22 (or the posterior superior temporal gyrus) which has been consistently implicated in auditory word recognition by functional brain-imaging experiments (DeWitt & Rauschecker, 2013), whereas others believe it extends into quite large areas of the partial lobe (Mesulam, 1998). It may well therefore be the case that a clear anatomically unified Wernicke's area does not actually exist.

It has also long been apparent that the brain contains several other important areas for language which are not accounted for by the Wernicke–Geschwind model. This was recognized in the 1950s by Wilder Penfield who stimulated various regions of the cerebral cortex with an electrical current in fully awake humans (see Chapter 4). Penfield was able to elicit verbal responses from several areas that did not correspond to Broca's and Wernicke's speech zones which included the supplementary motor area located on the midline surface of the frontal cortex. Interestingly, electrical stimulation of Broca's area produced mouth movements rather than vocalization (Penfield & Roberts, 1959).

The mapping of brain regions involved in language was also pursued by George Ojemann and his colleagues who electrically stimulated the cerebral cortex of their subjects during the naming of pictures – a procedure that readily causes naming errors to occur. In a classic study which examined 117 patients, Ojemann found naming errors arose from stimulation of many cortical areas (Ojemann et al., 1989). More importantly, this work also demonstrated that language representation in the brain is organized in mosaic-like areas of 1 to 2 cm^2 which vary in size and location between individuals. Although these mosaics are usually spread across large regions of the temporal and frontal lobes, their exact locations differ between individuals – and some only have them in one cortical region. Moreover, the correspondence of these sites with Wernicke's or Broca's areas is weak. In the main, Ojemann's mapping work has shown that the most important regions involved in language comprehension and production are found either side of the Sylvian fissure (Ojemann, 2010).

Researchers testing brain-damaged patients have arrived at broadly similar conclusions. For example, a common deficit of left hemisphere damage is difficulties in word retrieval and naming pictures. However, this problem is associated with widespread damage over a wide area of the left hemisphere and not any particular location (McCarthy & Warrington, 1990). The severity of the naming deficit is also increased with the size of the lesion, especially if it involves the temporal lobe, whilst many other language deficits including articulation, word fluency, and comprehension are associated with multiple sites throughout the cerebral cortex (Hécaen & Angelergues, 1964). Moreover, most areas involved in language are multi-functional (see Figure 10.7). This is not a prediction of the Wernicke–Geschwind model.

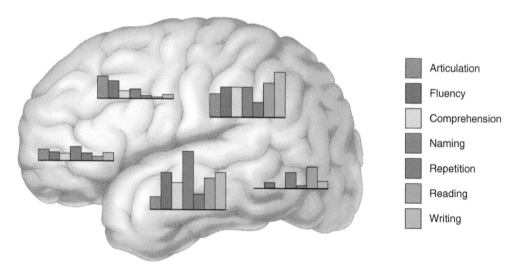

Articulation

Fluency

Comprehension

Naming

Repetition

Reading

Writing

Figure 10.7 Language functions are more widely distributed than originally thought
Source: Garrett and Hough (2018), based on Hécaen and Angelergues (1964)

The Wernicke–Geschwind model also fails to take into account the role of subcortical regions in language processing. Both Wernicke and Broca's areas have reciprocal connections with the thalamus, whose damage can produce symptoms of aphasia including mild comprehension deficits, whilst stimulation of the pulvinar region of the thalamus arrests speech in a similar way to that which occurs for the cerebral cortex (Ojemann, 1975). In addition, it is known that neural circuits linking different cortical regions with the **striatum** (e.g. the caudate nucleus and putamen) regulate speech production and syntax. The basal ganglia are important for sequencing movements, and damage to these regions produces language that is slow, without rhythm, and monotonous (Chan et al., 2013).

In recent years there has been a shift away from localization models emphasizing brain regions, to ones that advocate a role for networks in the brain which are not specialized for language or indeed any other single cognitive domain. This has led to the development of network-based models which are composed of parallel and interconnected streams involving both cortical and subcortical areas. One such model has been proposed by Hickok and Poeppel (2007), who argue that speech processing takes place in two interacting networks which have been designated the 'dorsal' and 'ventral' streams. The ventral stream is bilaterally organized from the temporal pole to the basal occipitotemporal cortex and responsible for speech comprehension, whilst the dorsal stream is left hemisphere dominant, passing from the posterior superior temporal lobe to the inferior frontal cortices. These models are attracting a lot of attention and also likely to fundamentally change our understanding of the functional neuroanatomy of language in the future (Nasios et al., 2019; Saur et al., 2008).

> **KEY TERMS:** *supplementary motor cortex, Sylvian fissure, pulvinar, striatum, network-based models*

DYSLEXIA

Dyslexia (from *dys* meaning 'bad', and *lexia* meaning 'reading') is characterized by slow and inaccurate word recognition resulting in an inability to read correctly, despite the person most likely having normal intelligence, motivation and schooling. Although dyslexia can be acquired through brain injury, in most cases it is a developmental disorder that manifests itself when the child begins to read. It is also the most common learning disability of childhood, affecting 7% of children (Peterson & Pennington, 2012), although it is estimated that 20% of the general population have reading difficulties of some kind. Whilst dyslexia has traditionally been seen as mainly affecting boys, this may be because they tend to attract greater clinical interest – not least because they are more likely to have other types of behavioural problem such as attention-deficit hyperactivity disorder. Some evidence even suggests that dyslexia is equally common in females (Handler & Fierson, 2011). Longitudinal studies show that dyslexia is a persistent and chronic condition which is not caused by delayed development (Morken et al., 2017). Despite this, some experts believe dyslexia should be considered as a different way of learning that has both benefits and disadvantages (Schneps, 2015).

Officially, there are no diagnostic subtypes of dyslexia, but some experts find it helpful to categorize dyslexia into phonological and surface forms. Phonological dyslexia is where the reader is unable to make the sound of a word – a deficit that makes reading unfamiliar or unusual words very difficult. In effect, this involves having difficulty breaking words down into smaller units, making it hard to match sounds with their written form. In the case of surface dyslexia the reader is slow to visually recognize words, but can do so if given time to read out the letters one by one. Thus, individuals with this form of dyslexia have difficulties reading words, but not individual letters. It is important to realize that surface dyslexia does not involve an eyesight problem. Rather it is caused by a difference in the way a person's brain recognizes letters and words (or numbers). In the early 1970s, a distinction between phonological and surface processing led to the dual-route theory of reading (Marshall & Newcombe, 1973) which postulated that two cognitive routes are involved in reading aloud: one involving a process where the reader can 'sound out' a written word, and the other lexical where words are recognized by their visual features. Despite the usefulness of the phonological/surface distinction, most experts, although not all (see Zoubrinetzky et al., 2014), regard dyslexia as a central phonological impairment (Vellutino et al., 2004). For example, when a group of people with dyslexia were given a battery of tests, ten had auditory deficits and two had a visual function problem, but all showed a phonological impairment (Ramus et al., 2003).

So what causes dyslexia? One clue comes from the finding that reading difficulties tend to run in families which implies a genetic component. Research shows that as many as 65% of children with dyslexia have a parent with the disorder. Twin studies also show a higher concordance rate for reading disability in monozygotic twins (68%) compared to dizygotic twins (38%) (DeFries & Alercón, 1996). Despite this, the genetic basis of dyslexia is complex, with no single gene being responsible for the disorder, or any following a simple Mendelian pattern of inheritance. Like all behaviourally-defined disorders, the aetiology of dyslexia is almost certainly multifactorial, involving numerous genes and environmental risk factors. In fact, at least six different chromosomes are known to exist which contain genes that affect reading ability. Some of these genes have been shown in animal models to influence neuronal migration and axon guidance during early development (Peterson & Pennington, 2012).

Investigators have long been interested in identifying the neurobiological hallmarks of dyslexia. A breakthrough took place in 1979 when Galaburda and Kemper found neural abnormalities in the **planum temporale** during a post-mortem analysis. The planum temporale corresponds to part of Wernicke's area, along with some of the adjacent auditory cortex, which in most individuals is larger in the left hemisphere (Geschwind & Levitsky, 1968). This difference in the size of the planum temporale arises in the human foetus and is detectable by the 31st week of gestation (Chi et al., 1977). Galaburda and Kemper found the planum temporale not only to be the same size across both hemispheres in their dyslexic subject, but also to contain immature neurons which had not reached their correct destinations. These findings were confirmed by Larsen et al. (1990) who examined a group of people with dyslexia using MRI brain scanning and found that 70% of their brains showed symmetry compared with only 30% of the controls. Other neural features found in the brains of individuals with dyslexia included abnormal migration patterns and clusters of displaced cells called ectopias, found primarily along the left-sided

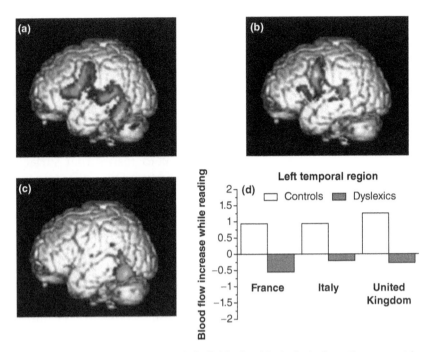

Figure 10.8   Activation of language areas in individuals with dyslexia from three countries. Here (a) shows activation due to reading in control subjects; (b) shows activation due to reading in dyslexics; (c) indicates the area significantly less activated in dyslexics than in control subjects; and (d) shows that dyslexia is associated with the same deficiency in individuals from Italy, France and the UK.

Source: Garrett and Hough (2021), from Paulesu et al. (2001). Dyslexia: Cultural diversity and biological unity, *Science*, 291, 2165–2167. Reprinted with permission of AAAS.

Sylvian fissure through the temporal and parietal lobes (Galaburda, 1993). These findings pointed towards an early developmental failure in the brains of at least some of these subjects.

However, it is far too simple to view dyslexia as an exclusive planum temporale dysfunction. In fact, our understanding of dyslexia has been greatly enhanced by the development of brain-scanning techniques, and these have revealed functional abnormalities of a distributed language network that courses through the left hemisphere (Démonet et al., 2004; Shaywitz & Shaywitz, 2005). In particular, reduced neural activity has been reported in two localized areas: a temporoparietal region that roughly equates to the planum temporal, and an occipitotemporal region which encompasses the basal temporal cortex including the fusiform gyrus and part of the middle temporal gyrus (Chai et al., 2016). The planum temporale is known to be critical for phonological processing and phoneme-grapheme conversion, whilst the temporal regions are involved in whole word recognition (Jobard et al., 2003). Both these language-processing networks also extend anteriorly into the inferior frontal cortex close to Broca's area. Interestingly, PET imaging studies have found that dyslexia exhibited by English, French and Italian readers shows roughly the same areas of brain dysfunction – notably in the middle temporal gyrus and middle occipital gyrus (see Figure 10.8c) (Paulesu et al., 2001).

KEY TERMS: *dyslexia, phonological dyslexia, surface dyslexia, dual-route theory of reading, planum temporale, distributed language network, temporoparietal and occipitotemporal regions*

SUBCORTICAL ABNORMALITIES IN DYSLEXIA

Neural abnormalities associated with dyslexia have also been found in some subcortical sites. One such region is the **cerebellum**. Not only have functional imaging studies shown that cerebellar involvement is an important component of learning to read in children (Stoodley & Stein, 2011), but structural differences in the cerebellum have also been reported in dyslexics, including reduced amounts of grey matter in certain areas and differences in symmetry (Stoodley, 2014). Another subcortical brain structure where abnormalities have been found is in the **lateral geniculate nucleus**. For example, Galaburda and Livingstone (1993) found that neurons in the magnocellular layers of the lateral geniculate nucleus were smaller and more variable in size and shape than were normal in dyslexic brains. This is an intriguing finding as the magnocellular system is the part of the visual pathway that is specialized to encode movement (see Chapter 2). Moreover, it is also the system that controls the eye movements (i.e. saccadic eye movements and fixations) involved in reading – a finding that led to the magnocellular deficit theory of dyslexia (Stein, 2001). However, whilst some dyslexics have complained that small letters appear to blur and move around when they are trying to read which implies a dysfunction of the magnocellular system, most researchers have not found saccadic eye movement or fixation abnormalities in dyslexia. It is perhaps fair to say that the magnocellular theory of dyslexia is at present somewhat contentious (Stein, 2019).

KEY TERMS: *cerebellum, lateral geniculate nucleus, magnocellular system*

SPECIAL INTEREST 10.1

WHAT IS THE REAL NATURE OF THE MIND?

We may have split the atom, sent humans to the moon and formulated quantum physics, but many deep mysteries remain. And perhaps the most mysterious of all is the mind–body problem which has taxed philosophers ever since the time of ancient Greece. Put simply, the mind-body problem is the difficulty of understanding how our subjective mental experience can be explained by the physical states of our brain. At the heart of the matter is the appearance that mind and brain are different types of thing. Of course, it is possible to define a brain: it is the assemblage of structures, neurons and synapses which a neuroscientist explores. But what about the mind? It is a very different thing entirely with its ability to sense, feel, act freely and think.

Descartes set the agenda for our modern-day conception of the mind–body problem in the seventeenth century when he argued the mind is composed of a mental substance which is very different from the material substance of the body. This view is called dualism and it

(Continued)

rests on the assumption that two different types of substance exist in our world: the physical (*res extensa*) and the mental (*res cogitans*). Physical substances are 'extended' in space, and include particles which can be observed and measured. Mental substances, in contrast, cannot be examined for they do not have any material basis or fixed location. This type of explanation is still very popular and versions of it are endorsed by all the world's great religions – most of which also argue for an eternal soul. But, of course, it's not a position accepted by many neuroscientists, not least because an acceptance of a spiritual entity controlling our behaviour through the brain would make a mockery of any scientific explanation. The theory of dualism also flounders on the problem of interaction, i.e. how can the immaterial mind interact with a physical body such as the brain? This does not seem likely.

An alternative to dualism is monism – the position that only one type of substance exists in our world. This view is also consistent with materialism or the idea that physical matter is the fundamental substance in nature. Like dualism, materialism goes back to the ancient Greeks, but one famous scientist who endorsed it was Francis Crick (1994) who co-discovered the structure of DNA. In his book *The Astonishing Hypothesis*, he takes a materialistic view of the mind by stating that consciousness is 'no more than the behavior of a vast assembly of nerve cells and their associated molecules'. This position is also supported by the philosophers Patricia and Paul Churchland who endorse a strong from of reductionism called 'eliminative materialism'. This holds not only that all processes attributable to the mind will one day be explainable in terms of neurobiology, but that doing this will also require us to invent a new vocabulary to avoid the problem of misleading commonsense explanations (folk psychology). However not many philosophers accept this. As you read this book, you'll be aware of the sights, smells and sounds around you. These sensory qualities, called 'qualia', are subjective and private. For many philosophers, it is inconceivable that the neural structure of the brain, as we know it, can create the red hue of a rose or the aroma of a freshly baked pizza. In fact, this has been dubbed the 'hard problem' of consciousness by David Chalmers, and even the most optimistic bunch of neuroscientists will admit they have no way of solving it.

There is, however, a third alternative which has been termed 'property dualism' by some and 'non-reductive materialism' by others. A more scientific term might be 'emergence'. This idea goes back to Spinoza who was a monist believing in only one substance, but one that could have different attributes or properties. Although Spinoza believed the single substance was God, many would contend it makes more sense to view it as a fundamental material substance of some sort. If we accept this, then it is compatible with the idea that the mind is an emergent property of neural activity. This can also lead to a position where the mental properties of the brain have their own existence, but cannot be explained in terms of lower-level physical events. This type of idea has been endorsed by some philosophers, notably Donald Davidson and John Searle, although others such as Jaegwon Kim have argued that this also gives rise to a form of dualism where the problem of downward mental causation remains.

AN INTRODUCTION TO THE CORPUS CALLOSUM

Experimental proof that the two hemispheres of the cerebral cortex serve very different mental functions was dramatically shown in the 1960s when the behaviour of patients who had undergone a **commissurotomy** was closely examined. This operation involves the severing of the **corpus callosum** which is the large white fibre bundle that can be seen when the brain is sliced open through its sagittal plane. It is the largest tract of fibres in the human brain, containing some 300 million neurons, whose myelinated axons connect widespread regions of the two cerebral hemispheres. Although the corpus callosum appears uniform, it actually contains four main parts composed of different nerve tracts. From front to back these are the rostrum, the genu, the trunk (or main body) and the **splenium**. The corpus callosum has long fascinated researchers. It was first described by the Roman physician Galen who called it a *callus* (callous) meaning hard or thickened skin. The callous body was later depicted by Thomas Willis in his book *Cerebri Anatome* (1664) who proposed the 'spirits' of the brain resided there. The corpus callosum in his view was a conduit allowing spirits to move between the cerebral cortices. It was not until the late eighteenth century that the French anatomist Félix Vicq d'Azyr realized the corpus callosum was composed of nerve fibres. He also introduced the term 'commissure' to denote a fibre pathway.

A new era in the investigation of the corpus callosum began in the 1930s when the American surgeon Walter Dandy severed the corpus callosum in patients to allow him better access to brain tumours. Surprisingly, the patients did not appear to suffer any intellectual, mental or motor deficits. Further operations were undertaken by William Van Wagenen in 1940 who performed a partial or complete commissurotomy on 24 epileptic patients in an attempt to reduce the spread of epileptic seizures. These patients were examined extensively on a wide range of neurological and psychological tests in the years afterwards by the psychologist Andrew Akelaitis. His findings, again, revealed that the patients suffered little impairment – either in terms of cognitive impairment, personality change or emotional responsiveness. Considering the striking prominence of the corpus callosum in the brain, these results were surprising. This led Karl Lashley to quip in 1951 that the only known function of the corpus callosum was to keep the hemispheres from sagging!

KEY TERMS: *corpus callosum, commissurotomy, rostrum, genu, splenium*

THE FIRST STUDIES WITH SPLIT-BRAIN PATIENTS BY SPERRY AND GAZZANIGA

In the 1960s, a clearer picture of corpus callosum function began to emerge with the work of Roger Sperry (who would win a Nobel Prize for his work in 1981) and research student Michael Gazzaniga. Working at the Californian Institute of Technology in Pasadena, Sperry had taken an experimental interest in the corpus callosum of cats and monkeys during the 1950s. But in 1960, he was given an opportunity to test human patients that had received corpus callosum excisions from the neurosurgeon Joseph Bogen (see Wickens, 2019b). Colloquially known as split-brain patients, Sperry and Gazzaniga began examining the isolated functions of the two hemispheres by delivering visual information specifically to each individual cortex. This task is far from simple, as the optic nerve from each eye projects to both hemispheres (as can be seen in Figure 2.5). As can be seen, input from the right visual field of the eye crosses to the left visual cortex, and that from the left visual field goes to the right visual cortex (the crossing takes place in the optic chiasma). The remaining input from the eye, however, does not pass through the optic chiasma, but passes ipsilaterally (same side) to the visual cortex (see also Chapter 2).

To project visual input into one cortex only, Sperry and Gazzaniga designed a task where they asked split-brain subjects to stare at a point in the middle of a screen (see Figure 10.9), following which they briefly flashed visual stimuli to either side of the fixation point (i.e. the words fork and spoon). By doing this, they were able to project stimuli into either the right or left visual fields of the eyes. The exposure time was long enough for subjects to perceive the stimulus, but sufficiently brief so the eyes did not have time to move. Stimuli presented to the left visual field therefore passed to the right hemisphere, and stimuli in the right visual field went to the left hemisphere.

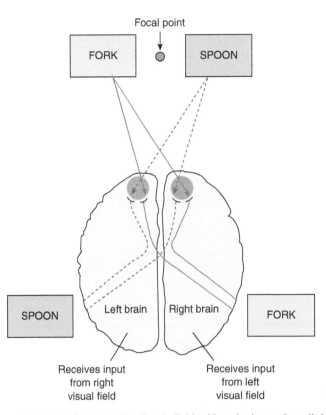

Figure 10.9 The presentation of visual stimuli to individual hemispheres in split-brain subjects
Source: Wickens (2009), adapted from Brown, T. S. & Wallace, P. M. (1980). *Physiological psychology*, p. 520

A second task developed by Sperry and Gazzaniga presented tactile (touch) information to the two hemispheres. They did this by blindfolding split-brain patients, and asking them to identify objects placed in their right or left hands. In humans, the somesthetic pathways that convey the bodily sensations of touch, pressure and pain to the brain, unlike the visual system, cross completely from one side of the body to the opposite hemisphere. Thus, a blindfolded split-brain subject who is asked to hold an object in their right hand will be sending information to their left hemisphere. In this instance, the right hemisphere will have no access to somesthetic input, whether it be from the eyes, hands or corpus callosum. Armed with these two tasks, Sperry and Gazzaniga had a method by which they could examine the cognitive and behavioural functions of the two hemispheres (see Gazzaniga, 1970).

The first subject tested by Sperry and Gazzaniga was a World War II paratrooper known as WJ who had been hit over the head with a rifle butt behind enemy lines – an injury leading to frequent seizures. It soon became clear from WJ, along with other split-brain subjects, that the left hemisphere was specialized to understand language. For example, when a written word was presented to the right visual field so it reached the left hemisphere, split-brain patients could read it out aloud and understand its meaning, but when the same word was presented to the right hemisphere it elicited no verbal response, with subjects often reporting they had seen noth-

Figure 10.10   A patient with a severed corpus callosum identifying objects by touch
Source: Garrett and Hough (2018)

ing or maybe just a brief flash of light. When pictures of common everyday objects were presented to the left hemisphere, the person could name the object. But when flashed to the left visual field the same person could neither name nor describe it (Sperry, 1964). These results confirmed what Broca had demonstrated a hundred years previously, i.e. the left hemisphere was dominant for language and speech.

The right hemisphere, however, was not without its linguistic abilities. For example, a split-brain patient who heard a verbal description of an object was able to feel an array of several objects with their left hand (controlled by the right hemisphere) and pick up the specified item. Similarly, when an object name was flashed to the right hemisphere (e.g. 'fork'), the left hand selected the target from a range of objects hidden behind a screen. However, in this case the subject typically reported that they had not seen anything, and could not describe what they had picked up. In fact, in one experiment where different object names were flashed simultaneously to both hemispheres (e.g. 'keyring'), it was found that patients would typically pick up the object presented to their right hemisphere (e.g. 'ring'), but name the object given to the left hemisphere (e.g. 'key'). The subjects were astonished to find they had misnamed the object when it was brought into full view.

Prior to this research, it had been widely believed that the right hemisphere lacked linguistic competence, but Sperry and Gazzaniga demonstrated that the right hemisphere could understand simple speech and recognize certain words, despite being unable to verbalize a response to confirm this knowledge. This effect was also observed in a patient who was blindfolded and given a toothbrush to hold in their left hand. In this instance, the right hemisphere recognized the object because the person made the gesture of brushing their teeth when asked what it was, but was unable to name the toothbrush (unless it was placed in the right hand). Interestingly, the right hemisphere controlled left hand was also able to write, or arrange letter blocks to spell out three- or four-letter words. Some researchers have suggested that right hemispheric language ability is approximately the same as that found in a 6-year-old child (Zaidel, 1985).

KEY TERMS: *split-brain patients, optic chiasma, visual field, right and left hemispheres*

RIGHT HEMISPHERE SPECIALIZATIONS

Although the right hemisphere has a limited ability to recognize language and read, Sperry and Gazzaniga soon discovered it was specialized for some functions not shared by the left. One skill was an ability to arrange coloured blocks to match a pictured design. For example, if a split-brain subject was given several coloured blocks and asked to arrange them to a certain pattern, this task could only be accomplished by the left hand (right hemisphere). The left hand was also able to copy simple pictures such as a cube or a house with a fair degree of accuracy, unlike the right hand which was poor at drawing. The left hand was also superior at learning finger mazes, completing jigsaws, solving spatial puzzles and sorting shapes into categories. And when geometric patterns, drawings or faces were presented to the right hemisphere, the left hand was able to point to the correct picture in a recognition test. The 'right hemisphere' was even able to recognize its own self in a photograph along with those of family and friends. Prior to this groundbreaking work, the right hemisphere had been regarded as the minor hemisphere – but Sperry and Gazzaniga had now revealed it to have a unique and specialized form of intelligence for spatial abilities. Subsequent research has also shown that certain aspects of mental imagery are differentially specialized, with the right hemisphere being superior for mental rotation and the left better for generating mental images (Farah, 1989; Sack & Schuhmann, 2012).

The right hemisphere is also superior, compared to the left, at recognizing emotion or responding emotionally to situations. For example, if a picture of a nude figure is presented to the right hemisphere, the split-brain subject may report that they have not seen anything, whilst at the same time blushing and showing embarrassment. This shows that recognition has taken place, although the verbal left side of the brain will often be puzzled by the emotional reaction and try to explain it in some way (Springer & Deutsch, 1989). The same degree of emotion, however, is not elicited when the stimulus is projected to the left hemisphere. More recently it has been shown that split-brain patients recognize both positive (happy) and negative (sad) facial expressions with the right hemisphere. Thus, this side of the brain is superior at recognizing the mood of an individual (Prete et al., 2015).

The emotional involvement of the right hemisphere was not entirely a surprise, for it had also been observed previously in certain individuals who had suffered brain damage. For example, in the 1950s Kurt Goldstein reported that patients with damage to their left hemisphere tended to exhibit feelings of despair, hopelessness and anger – or what he termed a **catastrophic-dysphoric reaction** (Goldstein, 1952). In contrast, those with right hemisphere damage were more likely to be indifferent to their injury. One study that looked at 150 people with unilateral brain injury, found that 62% with left hemispheric damage exhibited highly emotional responses to their plight compared to 10% with right-sided injuries (Rasmussen & Milner, 1977). These results show that when the left cortex is damaged, the right hemisphere recognizes the loss and responds with a strong emotional reaction; but this emotional reaction does not take place when damage occurs to the right hemisphere, which leaves the left hemisphere to make a more rational and detached interpretation of the situation.

KEY TERMS: *right hemisphere, spatial abilities, emotion, catastrophic-dysphoric reaction*

DO SPLIT-BRAIN SUBJECTS HAVE DUAL CONSCIOUSNESS?

Split-brain research shows that the two cerebral hemispheres control different aspects of cognition and action – the left hemisphere being superior for language and analytical thought, whereas the right is better on visuospatial tasks and emotional thinking. In some instances this can even lead to the two hemispheres acting in a contradictory manner. For example, in one task where a split-brain patient was asked to arrange a group of blocks to make a pattern with their right hand (i.e. testing the ability of their left hemisphere), it was found that the left hand (right hemisphere) persistently tried to take over the task. In this particular instance, Gazzaniga (1970) had to wrestle with the patient's right hand to stop it solving the problem. A similar situation can arise when a split-brain patient tries to read a book whilst holding it in their left hand. Although the left hemisphere may be interested in the book, the person often finds themself putting it down. The reason is presumably because the right hemisphere (which controls the left hand) can't read and sees little point in holding the book. Gazzaniga has also described a patient who would sometimes pull their trousers down with one hand, only to immediately pull them up with their other hand! In fact, all of these examples show the presence of what is known as the alien hand syndrome – a neurological disorder in which the hand of an afflicted individual appears to have a mind of its own.

Sperry believed that alien hand syndrome shows the human brain to have two separate minds, with each hemisphere experiencing its own private mental world of sensations, perceptions, memories and ideas (Sperry, 1974). In other words, each hemisphere has its own unique consciousness or awareness. If this is true, then a split-brain patient has two separate conscious minds. As one might guess, this is a controversial theory. For one thing, alien hand syndrome is not only found in split-brain patients, but can occur in people with tumours, aneurysms, stroke and dementia (Panikkath et al., 2014). Moreover, there are alternative explanations. For example, Munévar (2012) has pointed out that two cortical areas are particularly important in the planning and execution of movement – namely the supplementary motor area and premotor cortex. Both these regions are believed to formulate a series of different strategies or plans for any one specific action before it is performed. These pre-behavioural plans are also unconscious and bilaterally organized. If this is the case, then it is probable that their final unitary expression would be disrupted in a split-brain patient.

Looked at from this perspective, there is then no need to attribute each hemisphere with a separate mind (see also Rosen, 2018).

Back in the 1960s, Sir John Eccles (who won a Nobel Prize for his work in synaptic physiology) pointed out that since the right hemisphere cannot communicate its awareness by language, it most likely acts as a non-conscious automaton (Eccles, 1965). Thus, for Eccles, consciousness resides in the left hemisphere and is dependent on language. However, there are difficulties with this theory, not least because people who have suffered massive damage to the left hemisphere, or are aphasic, do not lose conscious awareness. But an alternative possibility has been proposed by Gazzaniga & LeDoux (1978) who believe the left hemisphere contains 'an interpreter' that attempts to understand the totality of what is happening to the individual. For example, in one experiment a split-brain subject was presented with two pictures: the right hemisphere was shown a winter landscape with snow, and the left hemisphere a chicken's claw (see Figure 10.11). After seeing both pictures, the subject was given an array of new pictures and asked to choose one that went with the first presentation. Gazzaniga found the two hemispheres selected appropriate pictures – the subject's left hand (right hemisphere) pointing to the shovel, and the right hand (left hemisphere) to a chicken. However, when the subject was asked why they had chosen the shovel, the left hemisphere replied by saying that it could be used to clean out the chicken house. This is despite the fact that the left hemisphere had no way of knowing why the right hemisphere had chosen the shovel. According to Gazzaniga this shows that the left hemisphere has an interpreter which 'tries to bring order and unity to our conscious lives' even when it has incomplete information (Gazzaniga, 1989).

The left hemisphere interpreter theory is a beguiling concept. It assumes that both hemispheres contain specialized modules for performing a wide range of mental functions. These are not organized hierarchically (there is no overall controller

Figure 10.11   A split-brain patient engaged in the task described in the text

Source: Garrett and Hough (2021), Gazzaniga (2002), based on an illustration by John W. Karpelou, BioMedical Illustrations

as such), but operate in a parallel and distributed system. Gazzaniga also believes that decision-making, judgement, perception, and just about every other cognitive and emotional action in the brain take place unconsciously – and what we recognize as consciousness arises in the left hemisphere through an appraisal process which he calls 'post-hoc rationalization'. Thus, the interpreter is the part of the brain that pulls all the information together to provide meaning to our reactions. It is, in effect, creating a theory to justify what it has just experienced (Gazzaniga, 2011).

> **KEY TERMS:** *alien hand syndrome, supplementary motor area, premotor cortex, consciousness, left hemisphere interpreter theory*

THE WADA PROCEDURE

Another method used to assess hemispheric function is the Wada test named after the Canadian-Japanese physician Juan Wada in the late 1940s. This procedure was first discovered when Wada had to treat a young man with a serious bullet wound to one side of the brain causing him to experience repetitive seizures. In his desperation to help the patient, Wada injected a short-acting anaesthetic (sodium amytal) into the carotid arteries of the neck that carry blood to the brain. Because the right and left arteries feed their own respective hemispheres, Wada knew a single injection would anaesthetize one side of the brain to temporarily shut down its function, whilst leaving the other hemisphere unaffected. The procedure was a therapeutic success, but it soon became apparent that Wada's test had other uses. In particular, it could be used to help neurosurgeons locate the dominant cerebral hemisphere for language prior to brain surgery – information that could help the surgeon minimize the potential adverse consequences of their procedure (Loring & Meador, 2019).

If sodium amytal is injected into the left or dominant hemisphere, it typically produces an immediate arrest of verbal communication within 30 seconds which lasts for around 5 minutes. This is also often accompanied by a state of confusion, although the patient retains some degree of consciousness (Meador et al., 1997). In contrast, if the anaesthesia is injected into the right or non-dominant hemisphere, language function is relatively intact and the patient is able to converse and answer questions. In the vast majority of patients, the Wada technique reveals language to be localized in the left hemisphere. However, this is not always the case, and in some people, language may be localized to the right hemisphere or be equally distributed across both cortices (Arora et al., 2009).

One of the most interesting findings revealed by the Wada test is that the cerebral dominance of language has a tendency to be different in right and left handers (see Figure 10.12). For example, Rasmussen and Milner (1977) tested 262 patients with the Wada technique, and found that 96% of right-handed people had language strongly lateralized to the left hemisphere. In left handers this percentage dropped to about 70%. This, of course, left a sizeable minority where language was not predominantly left hemispheric. In fact, Rasmussen and Milner found that in the remaining subjects, about

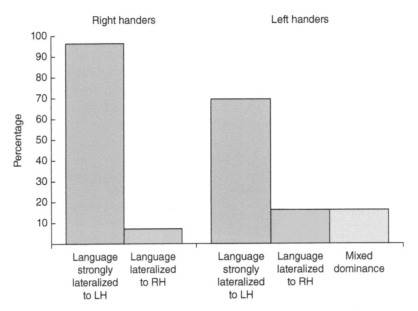

Figure 10.12   The hemispheric investigation of language in right and left handers
Source: Wickens (2009)

15% of left handers had language lateralized to the right hemisphere, and another 15% showed mixed cerebral dominance. Because it is known that around 90% of people are right handed, a simple calculation shows that over 90% of the population will have a left hemispheric dominance for language, with the remaining 10% showing a right-sided specialization or bias.

KEY TERMS: *the Wada test, right and left handers*

MICHAEL GAZZANIGA

Michael Saunders Gazzaniga is best known for his work on split-brain patients, for his interpreter theory, and for being one of the founders of cognitive neuroscience – a term he coined in the back of a New York taxi in the late 1970s. The son of a well-known surgeon, Gazzaniga was a gifted student who won a place at Dartmouth College, a private Ivy League university, where his older brother Alan was a star football player. Here, Gazzaniga took an interest in psychology and brain science, and during his third year came across a *Scientific American* article on the work of Roger Sperry. At the time, Sperry was undertaking nerve-growth experiments. Keen to expand his horizons, Gazzaniga wrote to Sperry asking if he would take him on as an intern. But after getting the job, Gazzaniga was introduced to a completely new field of research – the role of the corpus callosum. In fact his first task was to find a way of temporarily anaesthetizing one side of a rabbit brain. Smitten with the work,

Gazzaniga gave up his intention to pursue medicine after obtaining his BA in 1961 (despite his father's disappointment) and returned to Sperry's laboratory.

The question of corpus callosum function in humans was one of the great puzzles for brain research in the early 1960s. Although small groups of patients had undergone a commissurotomy for the treatment of seizures, this operation had apparently not affected their thought, emotion or behaviour. But during the 1950s, Sperry began showing otherwise when he trained commissurotomized cats on various tasks such as maze learning, with eye patches used to train individual hemispheres. His work showed the corpus callosum was involved in the inter-hemispheric communication of information.

In 1962, the surgeon Joseph Bogen began performing human split-brain procedures, and offered Sperry the chance to test his patients. Gazzaniga was given the assignment. His first patient was a former paratrooper (WJ) who had become epileptic after being hit over the head with a rifle. Using specialized procedures to project visual and tactile information to a single hemisphere, it soon became clear his two cortices had different functions. For example, if a word was presented to the left hemisphere, WJ could understand its meaning, but the same word to his right hemisphere elicited no response. Despite this, the right hemisphere was not without its linguistic abilities. For example, when an object name (e.g. spoon) was flashed to the right hemisphere, WJ's left hand could select it from a range of objects hidden behind a screen, but he could not describe what he had picked up. This seminal work was published in 1962, and Gazzaniga would go on to test ten other split-brain patients. Although Sperry sometimes sat in on the testing, Gazzaniga was the 'chief operating officer' who designed and ran the studies. Yet after obtaining his PhD in 1965, there was no place for him in Sperry's laboratory. He would take a number of positions before settling in New York. With limited access to split-brain patients, much of his work would now focus on the unconscious processing of information in patients with other types of brain damage.

Sperry had come to view each hemisphere as having its own specialized mind. However, Gazzaniga would arrive at a different conclusion – attributing the left hemisphere with *an interpreter* that attempts to make sense of its experiences. According to Gazzaniga the interpreter 'tries to bring order and unity to our conscious lives' even when it has incomplete information. The interpreter theory also argues that both hemispheres contain specialized modules for performing a wide range of mental functions which operate in a parallel and distributed system. These also operate unconsciously – and what we recognize as consciousness only arises afterwards in the left hemisphere through a process called 'post-hoc rationalization'.

But perhaps Gazzaniga's most lasting legacy to neuroscience will turn out to be an event in the back of a New York taxi cab during the late 1970s, when he and the psychologist George Miller came up with the term *cognitive neuroscience* en route to a dinner. Neither man remembers, or is willing to say, which of them first used the term, but it took hold. Since then, Gazzaniga has helped found the Cognitive Neuroscience Society (in 1994) along with the *Journal of Cognitive Neuroscienc*e. His long experience with brain-damaged patients has also led him to speculate on some of the wider questions about human behaviour, such as moral responsibility, free will, and consciousness. He has also written a highly regarded textbook on cognitive neuroscience and several books accessible to a lay audience.

HANDEDNESS

A remarkable fact about human beings is that 90% of the population have a preference for using their right hand – a characteristic consistent across all cultures, and known to have been in existence since humans started making stone tools around 2 million years ago (Faurie and Raymond, 2004). Like most minority groups, prejudices against left handers abound. A measure of this bias can be seen by the way the word 'left' has evolved in our language. In English the word stems from the Anglo Saxon *lyft* meaning 'weak'. Similar sentiments are also expressed in French where left (*gauche*) means 'clumsy', and in Italian where *mancino* means 'dishonest'. In Latin, the word for left is *sinister* which signifies evil. If this is not bad enough, the world of human objects strongly favours right handers. For example, scissors, knives, coffee pots, power tools, golf clubs and guitars are made for right handers, as indeed is the book you are reading.

There are many explanations for why handedness has arisen (see McManus, 2019 for an interesting historical account). One popular idea is that it was better for ancient warriors to hold shields in their left hand to protect the heart, thereby enabling the right hand to become more skilled. A female version of this idea supposes it was better for mothers to hold babies in their left hand, so they could be soothed by their heartbeat. Both claims are probably unsound because most animals exhibit some form of right-left bias. It is more likely that right-handedness evolved with the lateralization of language in the left hemisphere. One possibility is that right-handedness arose because of an association between vocalization and the use of supporting manual gestures (Corballis, 2003). With such a clear anatomical bias for the left hemisphere, it is not surprising that researchers have tried to find a specific cortical feature that is associated with handedness. Although left handers have been shown to have differences in the shape and depth of their central sulcus (Sun et al., 2012) and the gyrification pattern of Heschl's gyrus (Marie et al., 2015), no significant cortical area correlates of handedness were found in a large study involving 106 left-handed subjects and 1960 right-handed subjects by Guadalupe et al. (2014). Functional imaging studies have also been inconclusive in linking the activity of certain brain regions such as the motor cortex with handedness (Hatta, 2007).

It is clear that handedness develops before birth. In a study of 224 foetuses, aged from 4 to 9 months, it was found that 94.6% sucked their right thumb in the womb (Hepper et al., 1991). More recently it has been shown that 39% of infants aged 6 to 14 months and 97% of children aged 18 to 24 months demonstrate a clear hand preference (Nelson et al., 2013). These preferences are believed to be largely genetic although the inheritance pattern is not simple and much more needs to be discovered (McManus, 2019). Indeed, whilst left-handedness runs in families (Medland et al., 2009) and its concordance is greater in monozygotic twins than dizygotic twins (Ooki, 2014), the heritability of handedness has been estimated at only 24% (Medland et al., 2006). Nonetheless, researchers have searched for the genes underlying handedness and four important genetic loci have been identified (Wiberg et al., 2019). Three of these loci are in genes encoding proteins involved in brain development.

Although the vast majority of left handers are perfectly normal, as a group they suffer a higher incidence of language disorders such as autism and dyslexia (Brandler &

Paracchini, 2014) along with mental illnesses such as schizophrenia (Hirnstein & Hugdahl, 2014). Despite this, it is often said they are more creative, intelligent, and gifted in art and music. In terms of intelligence, there is little support for these claims. For example, after combining the results of two large-scale studies, it was shown that left handers had an average IQ of 99.5, which was only half a point less than right handers. However, a survey of 17 professional orchestras in the UK found that 13% of the musicians were left handed, which was greater than expected by chance (McManus, 2002). Evidence also shows left handers perform significantly better than right handers in musical memory tasks (Smit & Sadakata, 2018). Although few studies have looked at artists, it appears that right and left handers view the world slightly differently. For example, when Canadian and British subjects were asked to indicate whether the face portrait on their coinage pointed left or right (it points to the right) the left handers were more accurate. This may be because right handers tend to draw heads facing to the left, and left handers to the right (McManus, 2002).

THE DEVELOPMENT OF BRAIN-SCANNING TECHNIQUES

Until the mid-1970s, researchers interested in identifying the neural basis of language and other aspects of cognition were generally forced to rely on neuropsychological testing of subjects with brain damage, along with a post-mortem assessment of their lesions. This was far from ideal, especially as many of these subjects had suffered diffuse brain damage as a result of stroke or head trauma. It also made the identification of regions contributing to thought and cognition problematic – not least because by the time the patient came to autopsy, some recovery of function had often taken place. Fortunately, researchers are no longer stuck with this situation due to the development of non-invasive brain-imaging techniques.

The origins of non-invasive scanning began with Wilhelm Roentgen's discovery of X-rays in 1895 which allowed doctors to see inside the human body for the first time. However, the technique was of little use to brain researchers since X-rays could not distinguish between different types of soft tissue. In fact, for most of the twentieth century, the only way investigators could use X-rays to visualize the brain was to make the major blood vessels visible through a procedure known as cerebral angiography. This involved injecting a radioactive dye into the carotid artery and observing its perfusion into the brain tissue by taking a series of X-ray photographs. The pictures, called angiograms, could then be used to identify vascular damage or tumour location (as revealed by the displacement of blood vessels). This technique works because the injected dye absorbs X-rays differently than the surrounding brain tissue.

Things changed in the late 1960s and early 1970s when a British electrical engineer working for EMI called Godfrey Hounsfield and a South African mathematician called Allan Cormack, working independently, came up with a method by which X-rays could be adapted to detect hundreds of different density levels by the use of highly specialized computer algorithms. Its outcome would lead to the development of computerized axial tomography (CAT). This procedure worked by passing a large

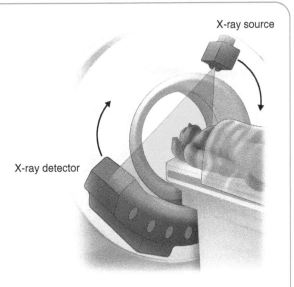

X-ray source

X-ray detector

Figure 10.13   Computed tomography scanning procedure

Source: Garrett and Hough (2021)

number of narrow beam X-rays through a body organ such as the brain with a ray gun that moved around the body part or the person's head. Providing a contrast medium or dye was injected into the person that could diffuse throughout the tiny blood vessels of the brain, then it was possible to take pictures of the soft tissue – since the amount of absorbed radiation could now be shown to vary from region to region. In fact, it is the differing density of the blood vessels that basically forms the image. The amount of radiation picked up by the X-ray detectors was then processed using a form of tomographic reconstruction to produce a series of three-dimensional cross-sectional images of the brain. Thus, a CAT scan can be likened to looking at a single slice of bread within a whole loaf.

Hounsfield presented the world's first CAT images at Imperial College, London, in April 1972, and began a new chapter in the history of medicine and biopsychology. For his work, Hounsfield would win the Nobel Prize with Cormack in 1979, and a knighthood in 1981. The first clinical CAT scanners were installed between 1974 and 1976, and had become commonplace by about 1980. These greatly facilitated doctors' ability to assess the location and extent of various types of brain damage. Not only were CAT scans effective in identifying tumours and stroke damage, but they also visualized the ventricles which stood out in black due to the cerebrospinal fluid's low density. This proved useful as enlarged ventricles are an indication of brain atrophy and degeneration.

Today, the use of CAT scanning has become an indispensable tool in all areas of medicine, with an estimated 80 million scans performed in the United States alone during 2015 (see Figure 10.14 for some images taken from CAT scanning). The main technological advance has been in the speed of image collection. The first CAT scanner developed by Hounsfield took several hours to acquire the raw data for a single scan, and took days to reconstruct a single image. More recent multi-slice CAT systems can collect up to four slices of data in about 350 microseconds, and reconstruct a 512×512-matrix image from millions of data points in less than a second. Thus, an entire brain can be scanned in five to ten seconds. Despite this, CAT scans have some restrictions for the neuroscientist. In particular, the pictures produced by CAT scans only have limited detail as white and grey matter have similar radioactive densities (Irimia et al., 2019). In addition, CAT scans have only a relatively low resolution, being unable to discriminate two objects that are less than 5 mm apart (Gazzaniga, 2011). Thus, at present, CAT scans reveal the gross features of the brain, but do not resolve its finer structure as well, although this situation is likely to improve over the next decade or so (Pelc, 2014).

KEY TERMS: *cerebral angiography, computerized axial tomography*

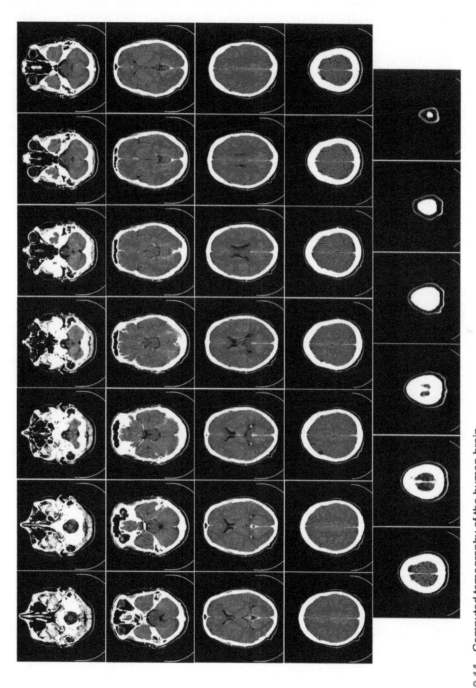

Figure 10.14 Computed tomography of the human brain

Source: Mikael Häggström/Wikimedia Commons

POSITRON EMISSION TOMOGRAPHY (PET)

The development of CAT was soon followed by positron emission tomography (PET) which appeared during the late 1970s (Shukla & Kumar, 2006). The first PET scanner to create three-dimensional pictures of the brain was built by Michael Phelps and Edward Hoffman at Washington University in 1975. The historical roots of PET are somewhat different from those of CAT (see Portnow et al., 2013). Instead of using X-rays to visualize the body, PET requires the ingestion of short-lasting radiopharmaceuticals that emit subatomic particles known as positrons. These are positively charged electrons (electrons are normally negatively charged) that are naturally created when neutrons are broken down in the nucleus of the atom – although the positrons used in PET are artificially produced in a machine called a cyclotron. When injected into the body, the emitting positrons of the radioactive substance travel a short distance before they are attracted by the negative charge of surrounding electrons. The result is a collision between the positron and electron which annihilate each other – generating two high-energy photons that leave the impact site 180° apart. These photons are then detected by an external scanner from which a three-dimensional representation of the chemicals' distribution in the body (or brain) can be digitally generated (see Figure 10.15 for the type of tomograms produced by this method).

One great advantage of PET is that different substances can be used for different imaging purposes depending on what the neuroscientist wants to measure. In fact, several hundred molecules have now been produced with positron emitters for this type of research. To give an example, a researcher interested in Alzheimer's disease might use a radiopharmaceutical such as florbetapir F18 to detect amyloid plaques in the cerebral cortex – a procedure that would allow them to make an early diagnosis of Alzheimer's disease (Fleisher et al., 2011). This is a capability that is beyond CAT. Similarly, if a dopaminergic anatagonist such as raclopride is made radioactive, it can be used to determine the location and number of receptors in individuals with illnesses such as Parkinson's and Huntington's disease, tardive dyskinesia, and schizophrenia (Elsinga et al., 2006).

But for many neuroscientists, the importance of PET lies in its ability to observe the activity of the brain. For example, the use of oxygen-15 which can be injected into an arm vein, provides a way of observing regional blood flow in the brain which can be used as a measure of mental activity. The procedure rests on two principles: the brain requires energy to work, and the regions of the brain most involved in mental activity will be the ones using up most energy. Since the brain's energy in the form of oxygen (and glucose) is provided by blood, the assumption is that the rate of flow to any region will be proportional to the level of neural activity. Alternatively, the researcher may choose to measure brain activity by injecting the glucose analogue fluoredeoxy-glucose, which will accumulate in the most active regions of the brain. The first functional imaging experiments of the brain using PET appeared in the early 1980s. A standard technique is to examine the brain at rest, and then again when it is engaged in some form of mental activity. By subtracting the difference in regions of blood flow or glucose uptake between these two states, a map of the brain regions responsible for the task can be visualized over a period of time.

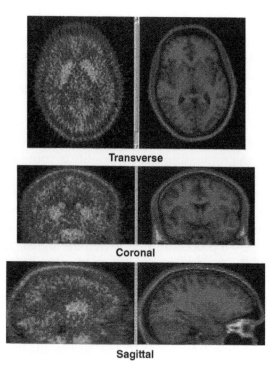

Figure 10.15 Positron emission tomography

Source: Grachev, I.D., Doder, M., Brooks, D.J., & Hinz, R. (2014). An in vivo Positron Emission Tomography Study of Adenosine 2A Receptor Occupancy by Preladenant using 11C-SCH442416 in Healthy Subjects. *Journal of Diagnostic Imaging in Therapy*. 1(1): 20–48. CC BY-SA 2.0.

Unfortunately, PET has several drawbacks. Firstly, PET equipment is expensive. A cyclotron costs well over a million dollars and requires dedicated staff to operate it (Saha, 2005). Adding to the expense, PET does not image the brain tissue itself, so the results have to be displayed overlaid on a brain image produced by another means such as CAT. The risk of radiation exposure is also higher than other scanning methods which limits repetitive testing. Although PET can be a powerful tool for measuring cellular-level metabolic changes in the brain, the speed of producing visual images is not ideal. In fact, PET scanning cannot detect changes during mental activity or behaviours that are briefer than 45 seconds (Bischoff-Grethe and Arbib, 2001). Despite this, PET remains useful, especially in the clinical diagnosis and understanding of neural degeneration, movement disorders and neuropsychiatric conditions (see Slough et al., 2016).

> **KEY TERMS:** *positron emission tomography, positrons, cyclotron, oxygen-15, regional blood flow, fluorodeoxyglucose*

MAGNETIC RESONANCE IMAGING (MRI)

During the 1970s, another type of scanning technique emerged that would have an even greater impact on neuroscientific research. This was **magnetic resonance imaging** (MRI) which provides detailed pictures of the inner organs of the human body without the use of potentially harmful ionizing radiation. This has proven one of the most important developments in the history of medicine. MRI is based on a phenomenon, first discovered in the 1940s, that occurs when atomic nuclei are placed in a strong magnetic field. That is, they will align themselves in an orderly manner in the force fields, and in doing this, can absorb radio waves which makes them resonate (spin). When these atomic nuclei are removed from the magnetic force, however, they return to their previous energy level and emit radio waves. These discoveries had important implications in physics: by varying the intensity of the radio waves, and measuring the energy released by the resonating nuclei, scientists could determine the types of atoms that made up a given substance.

It would be many years before this technique was used in medicine. The break-through came when the American chemist Paul C. Lauterbur, in the 1970s, was able to generate anatomical images by fluctuating the strength of the magnetic field passing through biological tissue – a procedure that varied the signals from its different con-stituent atoms. Around the same time, the British scientist Peter Mansfield developed the mathematical formulae that turned MRI into a useful rapid imaging technique (both men would win the Nobel Prize in Medicine for their achievements). Following this, it would not take long for the American Raymond Damadian to construct the first whole-body MRI scanner called 'Indomitable' in 1977. One of the great benefits of MRI was its high resolution (see Figure 10.16), and by the late 1980s detailed brain images were being produced that were superior to those obtained from CAT. In most cases, measuring the spin of hydrogen nuclei provided the best pictures, and this suited neuroscience since the brain is 78% water. Moreover, because grey matter (cell bodies), white matter (axons), cerebrospinal fluid and bone all differ in water content, these tissues were readily distinguished by MRI (Chow et al., 2017).

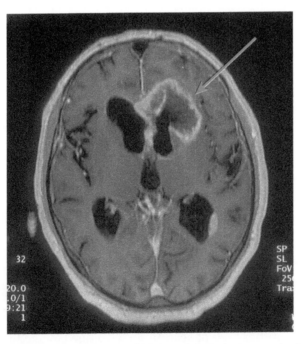

Figure 10.16   A magnetic resonance image which has detected a tumour (red arrow)
Source: Filip em/Wikimedia Commons.

Following the development of the first MRI scanners, researchers began to adapt it for measuring brain activity. This breakthrough was achieved by Seiji Ogawa in 1990 who discovered that oxygenated and deoxygenated blood emit different MRI signals. In fact, haemoglobin (which transports oxygen in the blood) has magnetic properties, and as it passes through capillaries, where it loses some of its oxygen, its magnetic force changes. This alters the intensity of the signals measured by MRI. Ogawa called it blood oxygen level dependent contrast (BOLD). Two years later, Ogawa found a way of detecting this difference in the brain. Thus, functional magnetic resonance imaging (fMRI) was born, which enabled investigators to visualize blood flow changes coursing through different areas of the human brain – a change (which as we also saw for PET) is proportionally related to energy use. But in the case of fMRI, when an area of the brain is active, its amount of oxygenated blood to deoxygenated blood will increase. Thus, by measuring this change, a picture of the brain activation can be derived (see Figure 10.17a and b).

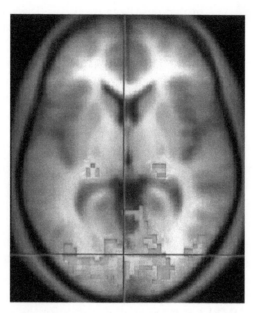

Figure 10.17(a)   An fMRI image with yellow areas showing increased activity (i.e. increased blood flow) compared with a control condition
Source: Open Stax/Wikimedia Commons

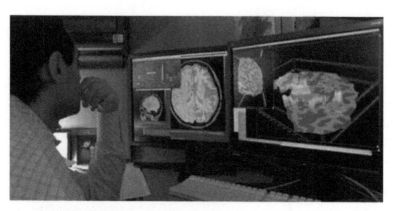

Figure 10.17(b)   A researcher checking fMRI images.
Source: US Department of Health and Human Services: National Institute of Mental Health/Wikimedia Commons.

MRI has several advantages over other scanning techniques that have made it highly valuable in medical diagnosis and research. Firstly, it does not involve potentially harmful radiation, which allows an individual to be scanned repeatedly without risk. Secondly, the spatial resolution of the MRI image is far superior to other methods, and it can detect structures smaller than 1 mm in diameter.

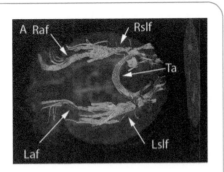

Figure 10.18   A diffusion tensor image revealing fibres connecting frontal, parietal, temporal and occipital areas

Source: Garrett and Hough (2018); courtesy of Aaron Filler, MD, PhD

Thirdly, by varying the magnetic gradients and radio frequency pulse parameters, MRI scanners can generate images based on a wide variety of different atoms or contrast mechanisms. Although most MRI images are designed to use the properties of hydrogen, other atoms can be 'tuned in' to produce different pictures if the pulse parameters are changed. Indeed, an important variant of MRI is called diffusion tensor imaging (Figure 10.18) which measures the movement of water molecules. Because water flows along the length of an axon, this technique is useful for three-dimensional imaging of myelinated axons, including the various tracts that connect cortical and subcortical regions. It has been used in a wide variety of ways, including an assessment of brain connectivity in patients with various disorders such as multiple sclerosis, epilepsy, Alzheimer's disease and schizophrenia (Alexander et al., 2007; Soares et al., 2013).

It is no exaggeration to say that fMRI has revolutionized our study of the brain. According to one estimate, since its first use over a quarter of a century ago, fMRI has given rise to 40,000 published papers (Eklund et al., 2016). It has become so popular that the method can even claim to have given rise to a new branch of psychology called cognitive neuroscience whose aim is to understand the neural mechanisms underlying cognitive processes (Glover, 2011). For the brain researcher, fMRI has many benefits. One is that the images can be collected every two seconds (the time frames for PET are much longer) which allows patterns of activity to be observed sequentially. Moreover, fMRI has good spatial resolution, with activity detectable in cortical areas as small as 1.6 mm (Slotnick, 2013). Although at present the MRI scanner is a luxury item for most university departments, there is also hope that they will become small enough to be portable and cost a few thousand dollars – a situation that cannot be envisaged for PET.

Despite this, fMRI has its limitations (Turner, 2016). Perhaps the biggest drawback is that fMRI can only measure blood flow in the brain. Thus, it cannot home in on the activities of individual nerve cells (neurons) which are critical to fully understanding mental function. In fact, according to some estimates, even the fastest fMRI is around one thousand times too slow to track neural activity (Slotnick, 2013). Nonetheless, fMRI remains one of our most powerful techniques and its data are likely to be subject to more sophisticated analysis in the future (Specht, 2020).

KEY TERMS: *magnetic resonance imaging, blood oxygen level dependent contrast, functional magnetic resonance imaging (fMRI), diffusion tensor imaging, cognitive neuroscience*

EXECUTIVE FUNCTION

One research area where brain-scanning techniques have advanced our neurobiological understanding of cognition is that of executive function. The term is not easily defined and is best understood as an umbrella term for a variety of cognitive processes and sub-operations (Elliott, 2003). These include a set of mental skills that involve attention, working memory, flexible thinking, and behavioural self-control. It has also been said that executive function is 'the co-ordinated operation of various processes to accomplish a particular goal in a flexible manner' (Funahashi, 2001). This is a useful way of understanding executive function – for if one considers the ability to create a plan and follow it through (say cooking a meal or arranging the daily shopping), then it will become readily apparent that the task will normally require us to adapt flexibly, sequence or prioritize decisions, and interact in a socially astute manner. Because of its multifaceted nature, an executive function therefore typically involves more than one mental skill to achieve its goal. This also means that when we come to examine the neural correlates of executive functions, it is unlikely we will be able to link one particular type of function with a specific brain area (Banich & Compton, 2018). Nonetheless, research into the biological basis of executive functions has increased markedly over recent years with the advent of brain-scanning techniques – and one area that has been consistently implicated in this type of cognition is that of the frontal lobes (Miller & Cummings, 2017; Wickens, 2017c).

Evidence supporting the involvement of the frontal lobes in executive function had come initially from patients with brain damage. For example, it had long been known that patients with damage to the **prefrontal cortex** (located in the most anterior part of the lobe) showed impaired judgement, poor organization, planning and decision-making, as well as behavioural disinhibition and impaired intellectual abilities (Kolb & Whishaw, 2015; Szczepanski & Knight, 2014). The advent of neuroimaging studies confirmed this relationship and led to a situation, according to Elliott (2003), where 'executive function' and 'frontal lobe function' become interchangeable terms. However, one frontal lobe region became recognized as more involved in executive functioning than the others, and this was the dorsolateral prefrontal cortex (DLPFC) – an area located in the lateral and dorsal parts of the prefrontal convexity, which roughly corresponds to Brodmann's areas 9 and 46 (see Figure 10.19). The DLPFC is unique because it is a part of the human brain that undergoes a prolonged period of maturation until adulthood (Gogtay et al., 2004). It is also involved in higher thought processes including task switching, memory updating, and response sequencing, monitoring and manipulation (Curtis & D'Esposito, 2003; Fuster, 2004).

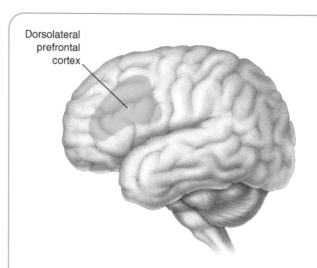

Dorsolateral prefrontal cortex

Figure 10.19   The dorsolateral prefrontal cortex
Source: Garrett and Hough (2021)

One idea that has attracted considerable interest is the possibility that the DLPFC may play a central role in executive function because of its involvement in **working memory** (Banich & Compton, 2018). Working memory is a form of short-term memory that is able to hold multiple pieces of information in the mind where it can then be manipulated. In effect, it provides a cognitive system for monitoring and handling thought content that operates in a wide variety of tasks. Our modern concept of working memory derives largely from the work of Alan Baddeley who proposed a model which divided it into discrete mental components (Baddeley, 1986; Baddeley & Hitch, 1974). In short, the theory proposed that working memory utilized three main systems: the phonological loop, the visuospatial sketchpad and the central executive. The phonological loop stores sound information (i.e. language) and maintains it in our memory by continuously working it in a rehearsal loop. The visuospatial sketchpad does the same for our visual and spatial information. And in command of these two systems is the executive control centre which directs information between our phonological and visuospatial systems. In 2000, Baddeley extended the model by adding a fourth component, the episodic buffer, which holds information not covered by the other two memory loops (such as semantic knowledge and musical information).

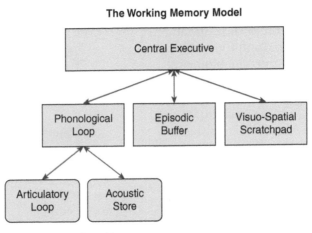

Figure 10.20   Baddeley's model of working memory

Source: Cheese360/Wikimedia Commons

Over the last 20 years or so, thousands of neuroimaging studies have been undertaken to examine the mental processes and neural correlates of working memory (Shulman, 2013). There is little doubt the DLPFC monitors and manipulates items for updating working memory (Barbey et al., 2013), but the wealth of evidence has also led to some confusion. Early studies indicated that verbal working memory included a storage component involving the left-sided posterior parietal cortex, and a sub-vocal rehearsal mechanism controlled by Broca's area (and the premotor and supplementary motor areas). In contrast, spatial working memory was dependent on a network of predominantly right-hemisphere regions involving areas in the posterior parietal and occipital cortex (Smith & Jonides, 1998). In both processing loops, the DLPFC activity exerted 'on-line' processing which integrated the cognitive information. However, this theory is now regarded as being far too simple. For example, a meta-analysis of over 60 neuroimaging studies by Wagner and Smith (2003) revealed that much larger areas of the brain are involved in working memory than first envisaged, with activation spread widely throughout the cerebral cortex. And perhaps more difficult to explain, not every task involving executive function or working memory apparently involves the DLPFC. For some researchers these types of finding reveal the limitations of neuroimaging studies (Shulman, 2013).

KEY TERMS: *executive function, frontal lobes, prefrontal cortex, dorsolateral prefrontal cortex, working memory, verbal and spatial working memory*

MUSIC AND THE BRAIN

All human societies produce music and it clearly has a powerful influence on our moods and feelings (Peretz, 2006). Its origins are also interesting because unlike the development of writing, which arose around 3500 BC in the West, music appears to have emerged across all human groups much further back in time. In 1995, a bone flute used by Neanderthals, dating from between 43,000 and 82,000 years old, was discovered in Slovenia (Turk et al., 1995). If this dating is accurate, then music predates the emergence of *Homo sapiens*. We also have an innate appreciation of music since infants as young as two months will turn toward pleasant sounds and away from dissonant ones (Weinberger, 2004). Adults and young infants also have similar music-listening abilities. Indeed, if an infant sits on a parent's lap watching a puppet show, whilst a simple melody plays from a speaker nearby, a wrong note or musical error will generally evoke an orientation reaction to the offending sound. Experiments like these have shown that babies can recognize differences in tone, melody, key and rhythm, and in some cases their ability is better than that of adults (Trehub, 2001). This is a remarkable skill. Music, like all sounds, unfolds over time. Thus, our ability to appreciate music must depend on working memory mechanisms that allow a stimulus to be maintained 'on-line' so that one element in a sequence can be related to another that occurs later.

Our unique competence at appreciating and playing music begs the question of its function. In *The Descent of Man*, Darwin speculated that singing was most likely to have arisen through natural selection – perhaps serving an important role in courtship – but there are other possibilities, including its tendency to bring people together in groups and create social cohesion, both of which would have survival benefits (Huron, 2001). It has also been proposed that musical vocalizations preceded the development of language (Mithen, 2005) although this is disputed by Pinker (1997) who insists music is just entertainment without any evolutionary adaptive function. Or as he memorably puts it: 'Music is auditory cheesecake. It just happens to tickle several important parts of the brain in a highly pleasurable way, as cheesecake tickles the palate.'

Described as the art of thinking in sounds (Combarieu, 1910), music differs from language in several ways. Most noticeably, music is not concerned with comprehending the meaning of individual sounds, but rather with the distributed arrangement of tones, their duration and the intervals between them. Traditionally, music has also been regarded as a right hemispheric function of the brain which is distinct from language – although as we shall see, this is an oversimplification. Nonetheless,

Figure 10.21   Maurice Ravel
Source: Nagualdesign/Wikimedia Commons

one of the first studies to support this idea was undertaken by Henschen (1926), who described 16 patients with music agnosia who were tone deaf and unable to repeat simple melodies or rhythm. Despite their musical impairment, none of these patients had any language problems – a situation that led Henschen to conclude that language and music functions were located in opposite sides of the brain.

Further support for this idea has come from patients with severe aphasia following left hemisphere damage, many of whom can hum a tune, or even sing the words of a learned song. A famous example of this type of preserved ability comes from the French composer Maurice Ravel, who in 1933, suffered a left hemispheric stroke. Despite being aphasic, most of his musical abilities remained intact. For example, Ravel could recognize melodies, play scales and recite his old compositions. He could also spot the tiniest mistakes in music when he listened to an orchestra. Yet the stroke had finished Ravel's musical career for he was no longer able to read or write music. Speaking of his proposed opera *Jeanne d'Arc*, Ravel confided to a friend, 'This opera is here, in my head. I hear it, but I will never write it. It's over. I can no longer write my music'.

The use of brain-scanning techniques has revealed that musical abilities, including melody, harmony, rhythm or singing, depend on different parts of the brain (Peretz & Coltheart, 2003). In general, it has further emphasized the importance of the right hemisphere for listening to pitch and tonal patterns, and the left for rhythm and recognizing the meaning of musical pieces (Andrade & Bhattacharya, 2003). An important area for music appreciation is the right-sided auditory cortex which increases its activity when the subject listens to a melody, or mentally imagines a familiar tune (Halpern & Zatorre, 1999). In one study that presented listeners with random sounds, increased activation of **Heschl's gyrus** and the planum temporale was observed (both lie adjacent to the auditory cortex) in both hemispheres, but when the pitch was varied to produce a melody, there was greater activation of the right auditory cortex which then extended into the nearby superior temporal gyrus (Patterson et al., 2002). This study and others have shown that there is a hierarchy of sound processing in which the centre of brain activity moves away from the primary auditory cortex into the surrounding temporal cortex as the music proceeds.

In contrast, the ability to perceive and produce rhythm is more dependent on the left hemisphere (Peretz & Zatorre, 2005). For example, Pflug et al. (2019) have found that the left auditory cortex is preferentially involved in tapping a fast complex rhythm compared to the right. Other areas that have been shown to be involved in rhythmic tasks include the left premotor and parietal areas and the right cerebellar anterior lobe (Sakai et al., 1999). The left-sided inferior frontal region, including Broca's area, should also not be overlooked for its musical capabilities, for these parts of the brain can detect wrong notes in a piece of music (Maess et al., 2001).

Music also exerts an effect on the pleasure systems of the brain. This was shown by Blood and Zatorre (2001) who asked subjects to select a favourite piece of music (among the choices were Samuel Barber's Adagio for Strings and Rachmaninoff's Piano Concerto No. 3) and undergo a PET scan when listening to their selection. The music, especially at emotionally high points, increased blood flow in the nucleus accumbens, amygdala and orbitofrontal cortex. All these three brain regions are known to be involved in pleasurable emotions, including those linked to biologically important stimuli such as food and sex. Considering that music is not necessary either for biological survival or reproduction, this is a remarkable finding.

A hotly debated topic is whether trained musicians show differences in their brain structure compared to non-musicians. The first indication of this possibility came when it was reported there is a right-ear (left hemispheric) dominance in musicians, but left-ear (right hemisphere) dominance in non-musicians (Bever & Chiarello, 1974). This was confirmed in a brain-imaging study that examined timbre, chord and pitch tasks in trained and untrained musicians (Mazziotta et al., 1982). The authors speculated that the left-sided dominance in musicians might be related to an analytical process, i.e. they interpret music more deeply than non-musicians. In another study, Schlaug et al. (1995) measured the size of the planum temporale in the left hemisphere, reporting it was twice as large in musicians with perfect pitch compared to those of controls. The corpus callosum has also been shown to be 10 to 15% thicker in musicians who began studying music before the age of seven (Lee et al., 2003). This finding may help explain why trained musicians tend to use much larger areas of the cerebral cortex to process music than non-musicians.

KEY TERMS: *music, music agnosia, right-sided auditory cortex, Heschl's gyrus, planum temporale, corpus callosum*

SUMMARY

Language provides us with a complex, creative and powerful system of communication, and a vehicle for thought, which makes us uniquely human. The first brain region to be linked with spoken language was Broca's area, named after Paul Broca who undertook an autopsy on a patient in 1861 who had been unable to utter meaningful speech for over 20 years. This revealed a large area of damage to the posterior part of the left frontal lobe, which is situated close to the part of the **motor cortex** that controls the musculature of the face, mouth and vocal cords. People with Broca's aphasia generally exhibit language that is slow, laboured, and lacking grammatical structure or inflection, although verbal comprehension is relatively intact. Later, in 1874, Carl Wernicke described another type of aphasia where patients speak grammatically correct speech, but whose content is largely devoid of meaning. This type of aphasia is also accompanied by severe comprehension defects. It is now known as Wernicke's aphasia and associated with damage to a region of the left temporal lobe (superior temporal gyrus) which also contains the primary auditory cortex. The arcuate fasciculus provides a pathway from Wernicke's area to Broca's area, and its damage causes conduction aphasia characterized by an inability to repeat abstract, or non-words. An understanding of aphasia also led to the highly influential Wernicke–Geschwind theory. This multi-stage model proposes that verbal comprehension for both verbal and written information takes place in Wernicke's area – and its verbal coding can be passed to Broca's area if a verbal output (i.e. speech) is required. Although it has proven very useful, it is now accepted that the Wernicke–Geschwind model only provides us with a somewhat simplified account of language comprehension and production.

In general, the cerebral left hemisphere is predominantly involved in language, and the right hemisphere with visual-spatial skills and emotion. Evidence supporting this idea was provided by Roger Sperry and Michael Gazzaniga during the 1960s, who began examining split-brain patients that had undergone a commissurotomy (i.e. a severing of their corpus callosum) that stops the two cerebral hemispheres from communicating with each other. It was found that if a written word was presented to the left hemisphere, split-brain subjects typically had no problem reading it, but they would not see the word when presented to the right. However, the right hemisphere was superior at copying drawings or completing jigsaws. In addition, pictures presented to this hemisphere were more likely to elicit an emotional response than the left. Despite this, there are exceptions to the rule that language is lateralized. For example, studies using the Wada test, where either one of the hemispheres can be temporarily anaesthetized, have shown that whilst 95% of right-handed people have language strongly localized to the left hemisphere, this figure drops to about 70% in left handers. Furthermore, about 15% of left handers have language lateralized to the right hemisphere, and the remaining 15% show mixed dominance.

Since the 1970s the study of the brain has been revolutionized by the development of brain-scanning techniques. These include computerized axial tomography (CAT), positron emission tomography (PET) and magnetic resonance imaging (MRI). The last two methods have also allowed the activity of the brain to be observed and measured in real time. They have also led to a new branch of scientific investigation called cognitive neuroscience which attempts to understand the neurobiological processes that underlie cognition. One area where brain-scanning techniques have been extensively used is in the case of executive function including working memory. Although this work has shown the involvement of the dorsolateral frontal cortex in working memory, much uncertainty remains regarding its exact role and its interaction with other brain regions. Brain-scanning techniques have also investigated how the brain processes music which has shown it to be a predominantly right hemispheric function – although not exclusively so.

GO ONLINE

TEST YOUR UNDERSTANDING OF THIS CHAPTER AND VISIT HTTPS://STUDY.SAGEPUB.COM/WICKENS TO ACCESS INTERACTIVE 'DRAG AND DROP' LABELLING ACTIVITIES AND A FLASHCARD GLOSSARY.

MULTIPLE CHOICE QUESTIONS

Answer the questions below to test your understanding of this chapter's Learning Objectives. You'll find the answers at the end of the chapter.

1. Broca's area is located in which of the following?

    a. prefrontal cortex
    b. posterior frontal cortex close to the motor cortex
    c. Heschl's gyrus
    d. temporal lobe adjacent to the auditory cortex

2. Wernicke's aphasia is usually characterized by which of the following?

    a. meaningless speech, although it sounds grammatically correct
    b. slow, laborious and non-fluent ('telegram') speech
    c. an inability to read fluently
    d. an inability to use (and repeat) abstract words, but not concrete ones

3. If objects are placed in the left hand of a split-brain subject who is blindfolded, which of the following will happen?

    a. they will be unaware that anything is happening
    b. they will unconsciously try to place the object in their right hand
    c. they will be able to name the object and recognize its function
    d. they will be aware of something in the hand, but unable to name it

4. Which of the following scanning techniques uses blood oxygen level dependence (BOLD) to measure brain activity?

    a. computerized axial tomography (CAT)
    b. positron emission tomography (PET)
    c. functional magnetic resonance imaging (fMRI)
    d. diffusion tensor imaging

5. What part of the brain has been most implicated in executive function?

    a. frontal cortex
    b. parietal lobes
    c. temporal lobes
    d. the areas either side of the Sylvian fissure

6. When listening to a melody, what area of the brain is likely to show the greatest activation?

    a. dorsolateral frontal cortex
    b. right-sided Broca's area
    c. right-sided arcuate fasciculus
    d. right-side auditory cortex and adjacent temporal lobe

FURTHER READING

Banich, M. T., & Compton, R. J. (2018). *Cognitive neuroscience.* Cambridge University Press.
An accessible introduction to the field of cognitive neuroscience which is comprehensive, insightful and well written.

Feldman, J. A. (2008). *From molecule to metaphor: A neural theory of language*. MIT Press.
A book that integrates recent findings from biology, computer science, linguistics, and psychology, to offer a new novel way of understanding language. This is possibly the direction that the neuroscience of language is heading towards.

Gazzaniga, M. S. (2016). *Tales from both sides of the brain: A life in neuroscience*. HarperCollins.
An interesting autobiography which tells the story of Gazzaniga's work with spilt-brain patients, and others with brain damage, and his attempt to make sense of their deficits.

Gazzaniga, M. S., Ivry, R. B., & Mangum G. R. (2019). *Cognitive neuroscience: The biology of mind*. Norton.
A classic accessible textbook which claims boldly to have revolutionized the teaching of psychology by unifying cognitive psychology, behavioural neurology, and behavioural neuroscience.

Hickok, G., & Small, S. L. (Eds.). (2015). *Neurobiology of language*. Academic Press.
The definitive reference on the neurobiology of language which includes 100 chapters written by various experts in their field.

McManus, C. (2002). *Right hand, left hand*. Weidenfeld and Nicolson.
A fascinating book that tries to understand the asymmetry of the world we live in, including why most people are right handed and exhibit hemispheric differences.

Obler, L. K., & Gjerlow, K. (1999). *Language and the brain*. Cambridge University Press.
A little dated, but still a useful book which provides an introduction to the neurobiological basis of language, focusing predominantly on individuals with brain damage.

Pinker, S. (2015). *The language instinct*. William Morrow.
A readable account that argues language is an instinct that is hard-wired into the brain and programmed through the process of evolution.

Shulman, R. G. (2013). *Brain imaging: What it can (and cannot) tell us about consciousness*. Oxford University Press.
A book that critically looks at the present limits of brain-imaging studies and cognitive neuroscience.

Springer, S. P., & Deutsch, G. (2001). *Left brain, right brain: Perspectives from cognitive neuroscience*. Freeman.
An award-winning book that is perfect for psychology undergraduates interested in the lateralization of function in human brains.

Ward, J. (2014). *The student's guide to cognitive neuroscience*. Psychology Press.
An excellent textbook on cognitive neuroscience.

MULTIPLE CHOICE ANSWERS - 1. B | 2. A | 3. D | 4. C | 5. A | 6. D

11

THE BIOLOGICAL BASIS OF MENTAL ILLNESS

LEARNING OBJECTIVES

After reading this chapter you should be able to:

- Understand the classification of affective disorders.

- Explain how antidepressant drugs work.

- Describe the monoamine theory of depression.

- Appreciate the different types of antidepressant drug.

- Explain how antipsychotic drugs work.

- Understand the dopaminergic theory of schizophrenia.

- Outline the types of brain damage that can be found in schizophrenia.

- Specify the genetic and environmental contributions to schizophrenia.

GO ONLINE

Test your understanding of this chapter and visit **https://study.sagepub.com/wickens** to access interactive 'Drag and Drop' labelling activities and a flashcard glossary.

INTRODUCTION

The term 'mental illness' has no precise definition, although in the main, it is a label for disorders that are treated by medical practitioners called psychiatrists. Although mental illnesses can arise through physical injury to the brain, including tumours, infection and vascular disease, in the vast majority of cases, they are conditions in which the symptoms appear to be largely in the person's mood or thinking, and where there is no sign of biological damage. Because of this, some experts in the field, such as the late eminent psychiatrist Thomas Szasz, have argued that psychiatric disorders are not true illnesses and should not be treated by medical doctors.

But, this is a this is a controversial view, and a more balanced one holds that mental illnesses arise from a complex interaction of biological, social and personal factors, which may lead to neurochemical or physiological changes in the brain, even if they cannot be reliably identified. Whatever one's opinion, it cannot be disputed that the effects of mental illness, which include depression, mania, schizophrenia and various anxiety disorders, are severely debilitating.

Mental health problems are also surprisingly common. According to the mental health charity Mind, in the UK, about one person in four will seek help for a mental health problem, and only a few will be referred to a psychiatrist (Mind, 2020). This makes mental health problems only surpassed in frequency by common colds, bronchitis and rheumatism, and, if anything, their incidence appears to be rising. A survey of 16 European countries found that 27% of adults (which equalled 82 million people) were affected by at least one mental health disorder in a 12-month period, although only about a quarter of these sought medical help (Wittchen & Jacobi, 2005; Wittchen et al., 2011).

A biopsychologist with an interest in brain and behaviour has a special role to play in understanding the causes of mental illness – and one likely to have benefits in developing more effective treatments. This makes the challenge an exciting one with a real possibility of helping millions of people.

AN INTRODUCTION TO DEPRESSION

Everybody from time to time feels depressed (or what the *Oxford Dictionary* defines as a state of 'low spirits or vitality') in response to adversity, loss or perceived misfortune. Thus depression, whether experienced as feelings of glum sadness or utter abject misery, is an emotion known to everyone. These feelings play an important role in human existence, not least because depression along with happiness will form part of the process by which our brains register and process punishment and reward. However, there are some people where depression becomes severely maladaptive. In such instances there may be no obvious reason for the depression to occur (endogenous depression) or its severity may be out of proportion to the events that triggered it (reactive depression). Whilst these states are often of short duration, with the sufferer experiencing no more than a few serious periods of depression during a lifetime, in some cases they can be long-lasting or even permanent. In such instances, the treatment may well require hospitalization. It is difficult to say exactly at what point depression becomes a mental illness, although when it becomes so severe that the sufferer is continually unable to feel happy, plagued by negative thoughts, often thinks about suicide, and cannot function properly at work or in social relationships, then the problem is clear for all to see.

In everyday language, depression is normally described as a state characterized by feelings of sadness or gloom, but in clinical cases there is much more to the disorder. Clinical depression, or what is more commonly called a major depressive disorder, can exhibit a constellation of symptoms, which according to the DSM-5[1] must involve a depressed mood or loss of interest and pleasure in almost all activities, which impairs normal functioning for at least two weeks. The symptoms fall under four headings: emotional, cognitive, motivational, and physical. Not only is the clinically depressed person likely to feel sad, tearful and miserable (emotional symptoms), but they are also likely to experience negative thoughts including low self-esteem and a sense of helplessness (cognitive symptoms). This may be accompanied by energy loss where even the simplest chore can prove daunting (motivational symptoms), which is not helped by sleep disturbances, appetite loss, sexual difficulties, and various aches and pains (physical symptoms). Clinical depression may cause such general apathy that sufferers are unable to wash, cook, or look after themselves. In other instances, depression may be associated with high anxiety (sometimes referred to as neurotic depression) or delusional behaviour (psychotic depression).

Depression is classified by most psychiatric classification systems as a 'mood' or affective disorder (see Figure 11.1). But depression is not the only type of mental illness where the person's mood is the main underlying problem. In the case of mania (also known as manic syndrome) there is heightened euphoria, elevated arousal, exuberance and increased energy, which can also give rise to serious behavioural abnormalities such as drug misuse, anxiety or even violence. In many cases, although not all, the individual will also experience bouts of depression, which frequently follow the manic episode in a predictable or cyclical pattern – a condition otherwise known as manic depression. Because of this possible polarity, affective disorders are divided into two

---

[1]*The Diagnostic and Statistical Manual of Mental Disorders* (DSM) is published by the American Psychiatric Association and is one of the most widely used classification systems used to diagnose mental illness.

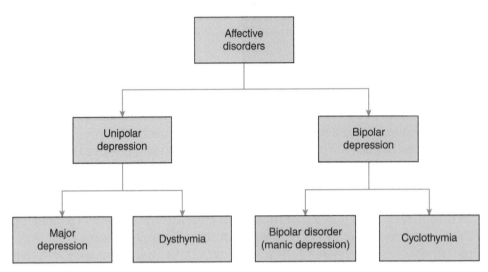

Figure 11.1   Types of depression
Source: Wickens (2009)

categories: unipolar depression, where the person only suffers from periods of sadness and despondency (although a rare form of unipolar disorder involves just mania), and bipolar depression, where the person has alternating periods of depression and mania. There is good evidence, both from genetics and the way these conditions respond to different drugs, that unipolar and **bipolar depression** have a different biological basis (Cuellar et al., 2005).

Another type of affective disorder is dysthymia which is also called persistent depressive disorder. This can be regarded as a milder, albeit long-lasting version of unipolar depression, and is diagnosed in individuals who experience a depressed mood for at least two years. Although the symptoms are similar to those associated with major depressive disorder, they tend to interfere less with day-to-day functioning (Schramm et al., 2020). Similarly, psychiatrists have recognized a milder form of bipolar illness called cyclothymia (sometimes known as bipolar II). This is a condition that tends to exhibit hypomania which is a period of mood and behaviour that is elevated above normal.

Mood disorders are by far the most common type of mental illness. It has been estimated that 5% of the population will be affected by depression at any one point in time (Klein & Thorne, 2007), and three out of ten people will suffer a mood disorder in their lifetime (Kessler, 2012). Depression also occurs twice as frequently in women as in men, although the reasons for this difference are not clear (Salk et al., 2017). Some believe it represents a biological difference in susceptibility to depression, whilst others point to social factors, with women being more inclined to seek help, or finding themselves in menial life situations with reduced opportunities. Clinical depression can begin at any age, although most people are likely to develop their first depressive episode between the ages of 30 and 40, with a second peak of incidence occurring between the ages of 50 and 60 (Eaton et al., 1997). The treatment of depression is a huge economic burden for society. In 2010, the cost of mood disorders in Europe was 113 billion euros – a figure representing roughly 1% of the total European gross domestic product. This includes both healthcare costs and those associated with patients' production losses (Gustavsson et al., 2011).

Although bipolar illness is less common, affecting around 1% of the population (Moreira, Van Meter, et al., 2017), in many ways it is a more serious problem. Bipolar illness is one of the most unpredictable psychiatric conditions of all, and tends to be a life-long problem requiring continual treatment. Not only does the person experience severe bouts of depression, where the risk of suicide is high, but they will also alternate the down times with periods of euphoria, high energy levels, poor judgement, and compulsive behaviour with little regard for the consequences. Consequently, around a third of people with bipolar disorder have financial, social or work-related problems due to the illness (Anderson et al., 2012). Bipolar illness occurs equally in both sexes, and a 2000 study by the World Health Organization found its prevalence and incidence were very similar across different cultures of the world (Ayuso-Mateos, 2000).

KEY TERMS: *major depressive disorder, affective disorder, mania, manic depression, unipolar and bipolar depression, dysthymia, cyclothymia*

THE DEVELOPMENT OF ANTIDEPRESSANT DRUGS

The origin of antidepressant therapy can be said to have begun with a highly toxic substance called hydrazine which was used towards the end of World War II as a propellant by which to fire the German V2 rocket. After the war, large stocks of hydrazine were given to pharmaceutical companies who sought ways of finding a clinical use for it. Two drugs derived from hydrazine in the early 1950s were isoniazid and iproniazid – both of which were found to be effective in the treatment of tuberculosis. However, it also became apparent that iproniazid was making a number of patients feel happier and more optimistic. In 1956, the American psychiatrist Nathan Kline began testing iproniazid on hospitalized patients with various types of mental illness, establishing that it significantly improved mood in those with severe depression. Within a year, iproniazid was being marketed as an antidepressant under the trade name of Marsilid, making it the first clinically proven drug to treat depression (López-Muñoz & Alamo, 2009).

Before then only two main medical treatments for depression had been feasible: electroconvulsive therapy (ECT) or a lobotomy. Fortunately Marsilid, and the other drugs that soon followed it, greatly reduced the need for these harsh procedures. Indeed, within a few months of its introduction, Marsilid was being administered to a huge number of patients. But Marsilid not only provided a much needed treatment for depression, it was also an indispensable research tool for neurobiologists and pharmacologists interested in understanding the biological basis of the illness. If they could appreciate how Marsilid and other antidepressant drugs worked on the brain, then this knowledge would help explain the neurochemical causes of depression.

How then does Marsilid exert its effects? The first clue came in 1952 when the biochemist Albert Zellar discovered it inhibited an enzyme called monoamine oxidase (MAO). This enzyme is located in the nerve terminals and glia, where it breaks down and inactivates monoamine neurotransmitters, including noradrenaline,

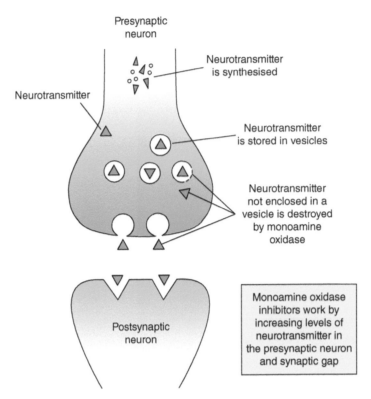

Presynaptic
neuron

Neurotransmitter
is synthesised

Neurotransmitter

Neurotransmitter
is stored in vesicles

Neurotransmitter
not enclosed in a
vesicle is destroyed
by monoamine
oxidase

Postsynaptic
neuron

Monoamine oxidase
inhibitors work by
increasing levels of
neurotransmitter in
the presynaptic neuron
and synaptic gap

Figure 11.2   The mechanism by which monoamine oxidase inhibitors exert their biochemical effects
Source: Wickens (2009)

dopamine and serotonin. By inhibiting MAO, Marsilid therefore caused higher levels of monoamines to build up in the nerve terminals, with a subsequent increased release into the synapse (see Figure 11.2). This finding had important implications. If Marsilid was producing its antidepressant effect by *increasing* the secretion of monoamines into the synapse, this suggested that depression was caused, in the first place, by *reduced levels* of these neurotransmitters. Thus, MAO inhibitors such as Marsilid appeared to be working by correcting a neurochemical deficit.

Further evidence to support this theory came from the drug reserpine. This chemical was first isolated in 1951 from the snakeroot plant (*Rauwolfia serpentina*) which had been used in India for hundreds of years to treat insanity as well as fever and snake bites. Although reserpine was effective for treating high blood pressure, it also caused depression in a number of patients. What was responsible for this mood-altering effect? In the early 1960s it was found that reserpine depleted the brain of monoamines. More specifically, reserpine caused these neurotransmitters to 'leak out' from protective synaptic vesicles in the nerve terminals, where they became exposed to MAO (see Figure 11.3). Thus, reserpine had an opposite neurochemical effect to Marsilid: it produced depression and depleted the brain of monoamine neurotransmitters (Hillhouse & Porter, 2015). It therefore provided strong reinforcement for the monoamine theory of depression.

Although MAO inhibitors are still used in clinical practice (see Fiedorowicz & Swartz, 2004) they tend to be chosen only when other treatments have failed. In fact, they now make up less than 10% of all prescriptions for depressive disorders. One reason for this is because these drugs produce several side effects, caused by their interactions with foodstuffs that contain tyramine. These include cheese, red wine, chocolate

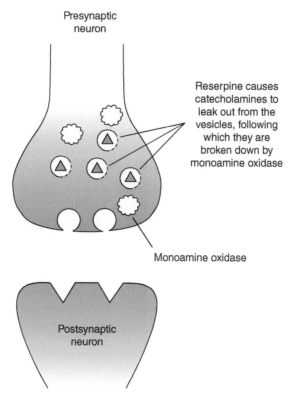

Presynaptic
neuron

Reserpine causes
catecholamines to
leak out from the
vesicles, following
which they are
broken down by
monoamine oxidase

Monoamine oxidase

Postsynaptic
neuron

Figure 11.3   The mechanism by which reserpine exerts its biochemical effects
Source: Wickens (2009)

and beer. Tyramine is also a powerful elevator of blood pressure and is metabolized by
the liver. MAOIs interfere with this metabolism, causing hypertensive effects, leading
to severe headaches, increased body temperature, and even intracranial bleeding. In
some cases these effects have proven fatal. Patients taking MAOIs, therefore, have to
be careful with their diet. But, perhaps most serious of all, MAOIs can be lethal when
taken in overdose – which is especially problematical since seriously depressed people
may be inclined to attempt suicide. It is therefore not surprising that the heyday for
these drugs was between the years 1957 and 1970.

KEY TERMS: *iproniazid, Marsilid, monoamine oxidase, MAO inhibitors, reserpine*

THE DISCOVERY OF THE TRICYCLIC ANTIDEPRESSANTS

Marsilid was not the only antidepressant to be discovered in the 1950s. This was a time
when antipsychotic drugs were also being developed, and one such compound, initially
called G22355, was synthesized by the Ciba-Geigy Drug Company in Switzerland.

It was tested by the psychiatrist Roland Kuhn working in Germany. Although he found G22355 to be ineffective as a treatment for schizophrenia, it nevertheless made his patients feel happier. The antidepressant effects of the compound were confirmed when given to a group of 40 patients with depression in 1955 (Kuhn, 1958). It was then called imipramine and launched in 1957 under the brand name Tofranil – quickly becoming the most popular antidepressant in the world. It was also structurally different from the MAOIs. In fact, imipramine and other antidepressants of the same class are known as tricyclic antidepressants (TADs) because their molecular structure contains a chain of three rings. These drugs would not lose their popularity until the emergence of the selective serotonergic blockers in the late 1980s.

Curiously, imipramine did not inhibit MAO, and its pharmacological action was not discovered until 1961, when Julius Axelrod, working at the National Institute of Mental Health in Baltimore, made a vital new discovery. He showed that most mon-oamine neurotransmitters are removed from the synapse through a reuptake process that returns them back into the nerve terminals. Axelrod was one of the first scientists to work with a radioactive version of **noradrenaline** which allowed its distribution and metabolism in the body to be monitored. When he administered noradrenaline into rats he found it accumulated in the sympathetic nerves of the body. This implied that noradrenaline was being taken up by the sympathetic nerves. The important question

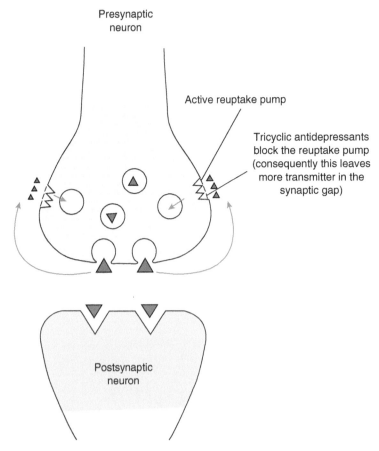

Figure 11.4   The mechanism by which the tricyclic antidepressants exert their pharmacological effects

Source: Wickens (2009)

though was how? Axelrod's answer was that noradrenergic neurons have a reuptake pump that causes the neurotransmitter, when released, to be taken back up into nerve endings. This removed noradrenaline from the synapse and helped in its recycling. Similar reuptake pumps were later discovered for serotonin and dopamine. Axelrod would receive a Nobel Prize for his work in 1970.

In 1961, Axelrod showed that Tofranil exerted its pharmacological effects by inhibiting the reuptake of noradrenaline (although it was later shown to block serotonin reuptake as well). Tofranil did this by binding to the uptake pump and impairing its function. Inhibiting the removal of noradrenaline from the synapse caused the synaptic concentration of noradrenaline to become elevated, which also enhanced neurotransmission. The functional effect was similar to that produced by the MAO inhibitors (e.g. increased noradrenaline in the synapse), although the pharmacological mechanism was different.

Following the appearance of Tofranil in 1958, a number of tricyclic compounds were introduced into clinical practice. Although Axelrod had emphasized their role in blocking noradrenaline reuptake, they also inhibited serotonin, and to a lesser extent dopamine. In fact, Tofranil blocked noradrenergic and serotonergic reuptake in almost equal measure. The tricyclic antidepressants also have effects on other neurotransmitter systems. For example, they often act as an antagonist at histamine receptors and cholinergic muscarinic receptors (Gilman, 2007). These two effects are also believed to be beneficial as they produce a sedative effect. Unfortunately, the tricyclic antidepressants also act as sodium channel blockers and calcium channel blockers, which is less desirable since these can cause cardiac dysfunction in high dosage.

KEY TERMS: *imipramine, Tofranil, tricyclic antidepressants, noradrenaline, reuptake pump*

THE EFFECTIVENESS OF THE TRICYCLIC ANTIDEPRESSANTS

There is little doubt that tricyclic drugs are effective in treating depression. In general, studies have shown, providing they are given over a period of several weeks, that they improve the symptoms of depression in around 60–70% of patients compared to 35–40% for placebo (Arroll et al., 2005; Lickey & Gordon, 1991). Although it is now dated, a major multicentre trial of the effects of imipramine and other antidepressant treatments was carried out by the Medical Research Council (1965) in the UK. This study showed that electroconvulsive therapy (ECT) was the most effective treatment after four weeks, but both ECT and imipramine improved about two-thirds of patients when the period of treatment extended to twelve weeks. The improvement rates for the MAO inhibitor phenelzine and placebo were half of this figure. More recent meta-analysis of antidepressant efficiency in clinical care,which included 522 trials comprising 116,477 participants, showed that all antidepressants (a total of 21 were examined) were more effective than placebo (Cipriani et al., 2018).

Although the tricyclics are generally safer than MAO inhibitors, they still produce side effects (Coupland et al., 2018). For example, their anti-cholinergic actions in the peripheral nervous system can lead to a dry mouth, constipation, blurred vision and dizziness. Tricyclics may also act on the heart to cause irregular heartbeats and hypotension, with the latter sometimes making the person feel faint. Headaches and fine muscular tremors are also experienced. But the most worrying aspect of these drugs is that they are dangerous when taken in excess. During the 1990s, tricyclic overdose was one of the commonest causes of dug poisoning in accident and emergency units (Kerr et al., 2001), and some two decades on, the death rates from tricyclic antidepressants remain a concern. Of particular note is the tricyclic compound amitriptyline which accounts for about 40% of all deaths from all antidepressant treatment.

NEWER ANTIDEPRESSANTS

Although the tricyclic antidepressants block monoamine reuptake, as we have seen, they exert a significant effect on other neurochemical systems which may lead to serious side effects. Consequently, researchers have sought to develop more selective and safer antidepressive compounds. In fact, a large number of 'second-generation' antidepressants were developed over the years that were neither MAO inhibitors nor tricyclics. But perhaps the most significant advance came when the Eli Lilly pharmaceutical company developed fluoxetine (sold under the brand name Prozac) which appeared in Europe in 1986 and the USA a year later. Within a few months Prozac was outselling all other antidepressants and it became the second most prescribed drug in the USA (it is now the 29th). The situation in the UK was similar, where annual prescriptions hit the 3 million mark (Greenfield, 2000). Fluoxetine also had a simple pharmacological profile: it was a highly selective serotonin reuptake inhibitor (SSRI) without any appreciable effect on noradrenaline (or dopamine) inhibition at therapeutic doses. In the wake of fluoxetine, a number of other SSRIs have been developed including sertraline, paroxetine and citalopram.

Although it is not clear whether the SSRIs are superior to the tricyclic antidepressants in terms of their efficacy, they are safer (especially in overdose), tolerated well, and have a broad range of other uses including the treatment of panic disorder, obsessive-compulsive behaviour, bulimia, and alcohol withdrawal. The SSRIs have also gained a reputation for making patients 'feel good about themselves' which helps to increase productivity and self-esteem. Despite this, the SSRIs can cause nausea, gastrointestinal problems, insomnia and headaches. Another common problem is sexual dysfunction, including anorgasmia in women and delayed ejaculation in men (Bahrick, 2008). More worryingly, there are some cases where the SSRIs have been implicated in agitated behaviour, self-harm, and even suicide (Fergusson et al., 2005).

Although the SSRIs remain the first choice for the treatment of depression, the last few decades have seen the introduction of other types of antidepressant. In 1997, the first commercially available selective noradrenergic reuptake inhibitor (NRI) was marketed by Pfizer called reboxetine (brand name Edronax). Approved for use in many countries worldwide (although not the USA), its effectiveness remains controversial, with one meta-analysis study showing it to be no more effective than a placebo (Cipriani et al., 2009). Another important development took place in 1993 with the introduction of venlafaxine (brand name Effexor) which was a selective **serotonin**-noradrenaline reuptake inhibitor. Although this sounds similar to a tricyclic antidepressant, it belongs to a class of drugs known as the phenylethylamines. Not only has it fewer severe side effects than the tricyclics, but there are claims it may be more effective than the SSRIs for major depression (Smith et al., 2002). It is also able to treat generalized anxiety disorder, panic disorder, social phobia and chronic pain. However, according to some, the claims for reboxetine are highly exaggerated (Eyding et al., 2010). Nonetheless, the prospects are good for the development of novel and more effective antidepressants over the coming years (Holtzheimer & Nemeroff, 2006).

> **KEY TERMS:** *fluoxetine, Prozac, selective serotonin reuptake inhibitor, noradrenergic reuptake inhibitors, reboxetine, venlafaxine, serotonin-noradrenaline reuptake inhibitors*

THE MONOAMINE THEORY OF DEPRESSION

The discovery of effective antidepressant drugs which acted to increase the synaptic concentrations of noradrenaline and serotonin by inhibiting MAO or the blocking of reuptake, led to the **monoamine theory of depression** (a monoamine is simply a chemical with a single amine group in its molecule). This theory was first formulated in the mid-1960s by Joseph J. Schildkraut, who proposed depression was the result of a 'relative deficiency' of monoamine neurotransmitters, particularly noradrenaline, at synaptic sites in the brain. He also argued that heightened emotion or mania was caused by an increased release of the same neurotransmitter. Although others were making a case for serotonin, Schildkraut's argument proved the most influential at the time. As a result of his hypothesis, noradrenaline became one of the most intensively studied neurotransmitters in the brain (see Healy, 1997).

One way of testing the monoamine theory was to look for biochemical abnormalities in the body fluids of depressed patients. If the idea was correct, then one would expect to find a decrease in noradrenaline levels or its major metabolites (i.e. break down products). Most studies, however, were unable to demonstrate this relationship. For example, noradrenergic function can be assessed by measuring MHPG (3-methoxy-4-hydroxyphenlglycol) taken from the cerebrospinal fluid (CSF) which is a metabolite derived in large part from the brain. Contrary to the predictions of the monoamine theory, there was great variability in the levels of MHPG, with some depressed patients showing low levels and others high levels (Ashton, 1992). Similarly, no changes in brain concentrations of noradrenaline, or its metabolites, were reliably found post mortem in people who had suffered depression or committed suicide (Slaby, 1995). And paradoxically, MHPG in the body fluids of patients undergoing successful treatment for depression often became reduced – a finding not easy to reconcile with the idea that antidepressant administration leads to an increased turnover of noradrenaline.

We now know that one of the weaknesses with Schildkraut's theory was that it underestimated the importance of serotonin. Indeed, CSF studies that have examined the serotonergic metabolite 5-HIAA (5-hydroxyindoleacetic acid) have found reduced

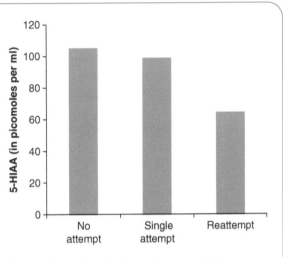

Figure 11.5   Serotonin levels and suicide

Source: Garrett and Hough (2021), based on data from Roy, DeJong, and Linnoila (1989)

levels in certain groups of depressed patients – especially those with a suicidal predisposition (Chatzittofis et al., 2013). However, this finding is far from consistent, and there is great variability with some depressed individuals even showing high levels of 5-HIAA (Asberg, 2006; Asberg et al., 1976). Moreover, low 5-HIAA concentrations often persist after clinical recovery in depressed patients, which casts doubt on the role of serotonin in depressed mood (Gjerris et al., 1987). In short, no simple association between low CSF 5-HIAA and depressive illness appears to exist, although there may be a subgroup of depressed patients with a disturbance of serotonin function.

Another way of assessing serotonergic function is to measure the uptake of this substance in blood platelets. In fact, serotonin was first isolated from blood (it was named *serotonin* to indicate its origin from blood serum) where it exerts a vasoconstrictor effect. Blood platelets also have a serotonergic uptake mechanism. Thus, they provide a relatively simple model of serotonergic function. A number of studies that have taken platelets from depressed patients report a reduced uptake of serotonin, along with decreased numbers of uptake sites (Maes & Meltzer, 1995). But again, there is considerable variability in the findings with some depressed patients showing opposite results (Parakh et al., 2008). Clearly, there is much inconsistency regarding the monoamine theory, especially in the way it was formulated by early investigators (Delgado, 2000; Healy, 1997). Despite this, it would seem that the administration of SSRIs does increase the extracellular levels of serotonin (Stanford, 1996).

KEY TERMS: *monoamine theory of depression, metabolites, MHPG, cerebrospinal fluid, 5-HIAA*

THE RECEPTOR SENSITIVITY HYPOTHESIS OF DEPRESSION

During the 1970s, the focus of attention with regard to the monoamine theory began to move away from neurotransmitter and metabolite levels, to alterations in the sensitivity of receptors. The main reason for this development was the problem of explaining the time delay it took for antidepressants to start having their therapeutic effects. For example, the pharmacological inhibition of MAO, or the blocking of reuptake by tricyclic compounds, takes place almost immediately, yet it generally takes around two to three weeks before these drugs begin alleviating the symptoms of depression. This indicated that it was not the direct pharmacological action of the antidepressant causing mood improvement, but a secondary change taking place in the monoaminergic neurons themselves. The likeliest site for this change was that of the neurotransmitter receptors.

Monoaminergic neurons have both presynaptic and postsynaptic receptors. The former are also called **autoreceptors** and they are normally located near the transmitter secreting axon terminals (although some types are also found on the cell body). On first sight, it may appear odd that neurons have their own presynaptic autoreceptors – but they have an important function. Put simply, they provide a mechanism for monitoring the concentration of neurotransmitter in the synapse, and when levels increase they provide a feedback signal that inhibits further release from the neuron. In this way, autoreceptors regulate the amount of neurotransmitter secreted into the synapse. The best understood types of autoreceptors are the noradrenergic alpha-2 receptor and the serotonergic 5-HT1A and 5-HT1B receptors (Langer, 2008).

One explanation for the time lag of antidepressant therapy is that continued exposure to the drug produces a gradual change in autoreceptor function (see Figure 11.7). For example, during the first days of treatment with a tricyclic antidepressant, alpha-2 autoreceptors will compensate for an increase of synaptic noradrenaline, by inhibiting its further release. Thus, they cancel out the initial effects of drug treatment. But with repeated drug administration, the autoreceptors begin losing their inhibitory capability, with the result that more neurotransmitter is released. This may happen in one of two ways: either the autoreceptors become insensitive to the higher synaptic levels of noradrenaline (i.e. desensitization), or the autoreceptors become fewer in number in a process called down-regulation. Whatever the mechanism, the effect is much the same: the loss of inhibitory control by the autoreceptors causes the presynaptic neuron to gradually release more neurotransmitter over the first few weeks of treatment.

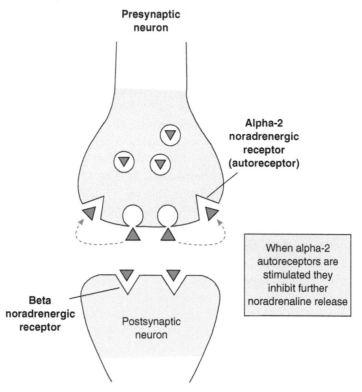

Figure 11.6   How autoreceptors affect presynaptic transmitter release
Source: Wickens (2009)

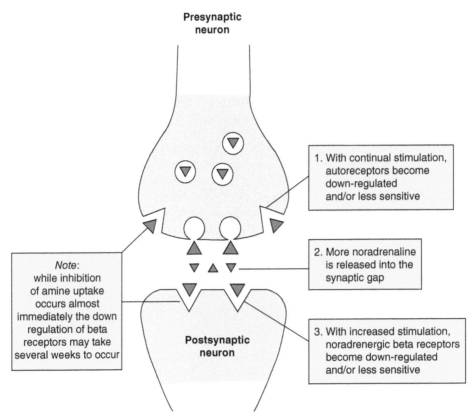

Figure 11.7 The time lag from presynaptic uptake blockade to postsynaptic receptor down-regulation

Source: Wickens (2009)

But what about the receptors located on the postsynaptic neurons? After all, these are the main target for the released neurotransmitter. The main type of noradrenergic receptors found postsynaptically are called beta receptors, and like the autoreceptors, with increased transmitter exposure they also become less sensitive (or maybe down-regulated) which reduces their function. Similarly, in the case of tricyclic antidepressants which affect serotonin, it is known that their postsynaptic receptors (e.g. 5-HT2 receptors) also become desensitized. In fact, it is believed that most antidepressants, whether MAO inhibitors, tricyclics, 5-HT uptake blockers or the newer generation of compounds, produce their gradual beneficial effects by the desensitization (and perhaps down-regulation) of both presynaptic and postsynaptic receptors.

This theory also suggests that the biochemical cause of depression may lie with receptor abnormalities instead of there being a simple deficiency of neurotransmitter release. A proposal of this type was made, for example, by Sulser et al. (1978) who argued that depression is due to over-sensitive noradrenergic receptors, and a similar case can also be made for serotonin (Carr & Lucki, 2011). Looked at this way, effective antidepressant treatment acts to desensitize these receptors. However this explanation also has other ramifications. For example, it is known that receptor desensitization occurs through a process known as phosphorylation which involves alterations in the shape of intracellular receptor proteins involved in signal transduction. In turn, this can alter the internal functioning of the cell in many ways, including changes in the opening of ion channels, sensitivity of second messenger systems (e.g. cAMP), and even the activity of protein kinases which provide signalling input to the nucleus. This has made it very difficult to pin down exactly how antidepressant drugs are working on the neurons of the brain (Rantamäki & Yalcin, 2019).

> **KEY TERMS**: *autoreceptors, alpha-2 receptor, serotonergic 5-HT1A and 5-HT1B receptors, desensitization, down-regulation, postsynaptic beta and 5-HT2 receptors.*

THE PERMISSIVE THEORY OF DEPRESSION AND MANIA

Since evidence implicates both noradrenaline and serotonin in depression, this raises the possibility that both transmitters might be involved in mood dysfunction. Hence, it might be that depression results from an imbalance of noradrenergic and serotonergic systems rather than a dysfunction of just one. This idea is not a new one. In 1957, Brodie and Shaw suggested that the brain's noradrenergic and serotonergic systems act in a way that is not unlike the sympathetic and parasympathetic divisions of the autonomic nervous system. They proposed that the noradrenergic system of the brain is primarily involved in mediating vigilance and arousal, whereas the serotonergic system is more concerned with restful states and relaxation. Brodie and Shaw also suggested that depression may be related to decreased noradrenergic activity (reduced arousal) in combination with an increased serotonin sensitivity.

A more popular variation of this idea is the permissive hypothesis, first proposed by Prange et al. (1974) (see Figure 11.8). This argues that low levels of serotonin 'permit' a deficiency of noradrenaline to produce depression, or an excess of noradrenaline to cause mania. Or put more simply, low levels of serotonin will cause dysregulation of the noradrenergic system. In support of this theory, it is known that L-tryptophan (a precursor of serotonin) reduces mania, whereas the effects of antidepressant drugs can be reversed by drugs such as p-chlorophenylalanine which depletes the brain of serotonin. According to the permissive hypothesis, therefore, antidepressant drugs are effective because they reinstate serotonin's ability to correctly regulate noradrenaline, thus restoring the critical balance that controls emotional behaviour. If this theory is correct then depression is not so much caused by neurotransmitter depletion, or receptor sensitivity, but by the imbalance of neurotransmitter systems involving serotonin.

In support of this idea, there is good evidence showing the brain's noradrenergic and serotonergic systems are closely related both anatomically and functionally. For example, the **locus coeruleus**, whose neurons are the main source of noradrenergic fibres to the forebrain, and the **dorsal raphe** which provides the forebrain with serotonin, are located close together in the upper pons (see Figure 11.9). The dorsal raphe also receives noradrenergic fibres from the locus coeruleus, whilst serotonergic drugs, especially 5-HT2

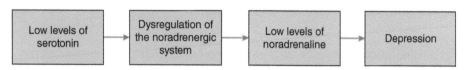

Figure 11.8 The permissive theory of depression
Source: Wickens (2009)

agonists, change the firing rate of the locus coeruleus (Mongeau et al., 1997). In addition, the projections of the locus coeruleus and raphe show a great deal of overlap in the forebrain, especially in the limbic system and cerebral cortex. The permissive hypothesis is also supported from studies showing that SSRI administration increases noradrenaline concentrations in some brain areas, including the frontal cortex and striatum (Goodnick & Goldstein, 1998). Thus drugs that enhance serotonin activity increase noradrenergic activity as well.

KEY TERMS: *permissive hypothesis, locus coeruleus, dorsal raphe*

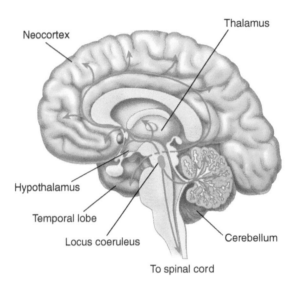

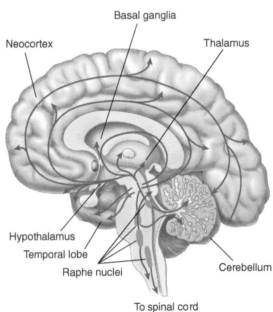

Figure 11.9   The forebrain's noradrenergic and serotonergic systems: (top) the forebrain's noradrenergic system originating in the locus coeruleus; (bottom) the forebrain's serotoergic system originating in the raphe nuclei

Source: Gaskin (2021)

SPECIAL INTEREST 11.1

ORGASMS AND YAWNING: WHAT IS THE CONNECTION?

There may not appear to be an obvious connection between yawning and having an orgasm, but the selective serotonergic reuptake inhibitors (SSRIs) have shown otherwise. One well-known side effect of the SSRIs is the likelihood of sexual dysfunction. These drugs have been reported to reduce sexual desire, cause impotence, and make it difficult for men and woman to reach orgasm (anorgasmia). It is estimated that sexual dysfunction occurs in some 30–50% of patients taking SSRIs, and may even be as high as 80% (Das et al., 2012). But one of the most unusual side effects of the SSRIs is spontaneous orgasm during the act of yawning. This phenomenon was first reported by McLean et al. (1983), who described two patients (a male and female) that orgasmed during a yawn, and two others (again male and female) who had intense sexual desires when yawning. The drug in this instance was the tricyclic compound clomipramine which exerts its main effect on blocking serotonin receptors. However, since this initial report, there have been many further examples of yawning-induced orgasm after SSRI administration, including fluoxetine (Prozac), sertraline and bupropion, and apparently this embarrassing behaviour can be reversed by the serotonergic antagonist cyproheptadine (Cohen, 1992). In some instances, the SSRI-linked orgasm may occur without yawning. For example, Pasick (2000) reported the case of a woman who experienced a three-hour sudden spontaneous orgasm while shopping. She said the experience was pleasurable but also socially awkward, and stopped taking her medication. Although the 'yawning orgasm' is believed to be rare, it could be more common than is currently thought because patients are too embarrassed to report their experiences (Segraws, 2008).

This brings us to an intriguing question: why do we yawn? The scientific study of yawning is known as chasmology and the subject has become a popular one in recent years (see Seuntjens, 2010). Yawning is a surprisingly complex stereotypical reflex behaviour, involving the simultaneous inhalation of air and the stretching of the eardrums which is followed by an exhalation of breath. It apparently occurs in all mammals, birds and reptiles – and can even be observed in the 12-week-old human foetus. It is often assumed yawning is a response to lowered levels of oxygen; i.e. when people become sleepy, tired or bored, they breathe more slowly, and as carbon dioxide builds up in the blood, yawning helps to increase oxygen; intake. But psychologist Robert Provine has cast doubt on this idea by showing that the inhalation of air containing different concentrations of oxygen and carbon dioxide has no effect on yawning (Provine et al., 1987). Another idea is that yawning may paradoxically make us more alert or ready for actions. Support for this theory comes from observations that paratroopers have been noted to yawn during the moments before they exit their aircraft, and athletes sometimes yawn just before a race (Hooper, 2007).

But most puzzling is that yawning is contagious. About 55% of people will yawn within five minutes of seeing someone else doing it, and this even occurs in blind people if they hear others yawn. Contagious yawning also occurs in many animals and can take place between members of different species – although apparently not in tortoises (Wilkinson et al., 2011). In humans, the contagious effect of yawning first manifests itself between the first and second years of life (Provine, 1989). This has led to speculation that it may be a left-over response from a time in our evolutionary past when it acted to co-ordinate the social behaviour of the group. However this is far from certain and yawning remains one of the great mysteries of human and animal behaviour (Provine, 2005).

THE HYPOTHALAMIC-PITUITARY-ADRENAL AXIS AND DEPRESSION

Depression is more than a mental disorder. People suffering from clinical depression often show a number of hormonal irregularities, including elevated levels of the 'stress' glucocorticoid hormone **cortisol**, whose secretion is controlled by the hypothalamic-pituitary-adrenal axis. This hormone is produced when the paraventricular hypothalamus secretes corticotrophin releasing factor (CRF) into the hypophyseal portal system – a system of small blood vessels that connects it with the anterior pituitary gland. In response, the pituitary releases adrenocorticotropic hormone (ACTH) into the circulation which targets the adrenal glands sitting just above the kidneys, causing it to secrete cortisol. As its blood levels rise, the cortisol will also act back on the hypothalamic-pituitary-adrenal axis to suppress the CRF and ACTH release (this is known as negative feedback). There are also glucocorticoid receptors in other regions of the brain, including the amygdala and hippocampus, both of which influence the hypothalamus, with the amygdala facilitating CRF releaseand the hippocampus inhibiting it (Sapolsky, 2004).

Almost every cell in the body contains receptors for cortisol, and this steroid can therefore have lots of different actions depending on which sort of cells it acts upon. However, a crucial function of cortisol is to maintain the correct chemical balance of the body in the face of change and adversity. Cortisol increases the production of blood glucose to provide greater energy during periods of acute or prolonged stress. It also acts to speed up the body's metabolism for energy needs, although it can inhibit

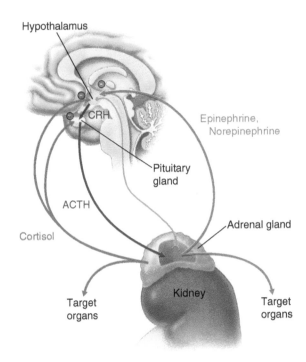

Figure 11.10   The hypothalamus-pituitary-adrenal axis
Source: Garrett and Hough (2018)

the immune system at the same time which leads to a decrease in inflammatory reactions. Cortisol plays a vital role in the body, and the effects of its deficiency can be seen in Addison's disease with its symptoms of weight loss, muscle weakness, fatigue and low blood pressure, along with psychological problems including memory disturbances, apathy and depression.

Not surprisingly, many individuals with depression show elevated cortisol levels because their mood condition is highly stressful, but there is more to increased cortisol secretion in depression than first meets the eye, because it has been shown there is a dysfunction of the hypothalamic-pituitary-adrenal axis in a subset of people with depression (Varghese & Brown, 2001). Evidence supporting this idea has come from the dexamethasone test. Dexamethasone is a synthetic glucocorticoid, and its administration will normally suppress ACTH release from the pituitary – causing decreased cortisol secretion from the adrenal cortex. This occurs because the dexamethasone mimics high levels of cortisol in the blood which 'fool' the pituitary into switching off ACTH secretion. However, in some depressed individuals, this dexamethasone suppression does not occur. For example, in an analysis of over 150 studies, it was found that non-suppression occurred in 43% of persons with major depression, and in 67% of those with psychotic depression (Arana et al., 1985). Studies have also reported a positive correlation between dexamethasone non-suppression and the number of depressive episodes, with a normalization of the response often occurring as the mood symptoms resolve.

One area of the brain that contains a high concentration of glucocorticoid receptors is the **hippocampus**. This is a relevant finding because animal studies have shown that the hippocampus is sensitive to chronic stress, and that an over-secretion of glucocorticoids can contribute to its degeneration (Conrad, 2008). This has also led to the idea that depressed people who exhibit dexamethasone non-suppression may have reduced numbers of hippocampal glucocorticoid receptors that detect cortisol, or they become less sensitive to the feedback signal, which lessens the impact of negative feedback (Varghese & Brown, 2001). It has also been shown that effective antidepressant treatment increases the activity of genes involved in the formation of proteins that make up hypothalamic glucocorticoid receptors. In one study, it was found that five weeks of treatment with desipramine produced a 25% increase in the number of glucocorticoid receptors in the hypothalamus, and that this increase paralleled the clinical improvement of depression (Reul et al., 1993, 1994). Thus, antidepressants may exert part of their effect by helping to restore the normal functioning of the hypothalamic-pituitary-adrenal axis (Bao & Swaab, 2019).

A further involvement of the hypothalamus in depression is shown by circadian rhythm dysfunction, with peaks of hormone release such as melatonin and cortisol occurring at the wrong time of day or with reduced amplitude. In particular, this can cause people with depression to experience sleep disturbances, including insomnia and early morning awakenings (Boyce & Barriball, 2010). Researchers have also found that the patterns of gene expression associated with regulating circadian rhythms were much weaker and often disrupted in the brains of patients at post-mortem who had been suffering from a major depressive disorder (Li et al., 2013). It is not surprising, therefore, that many people with depression who are experiencing disruption to their circadian rhythms feel physically unwell in addition to their mental anguish.

KEY TERMS: *cortisol, hypothalamic-pituitary-adrenal axis, CRF, ACTH, Addison's disease, dexamethasone test, hippocampus, glucocorticoid receptors*

THE GENETICS OF DEPRESSION

Genetic factors play an important role in the aetiology of depression (Flint & Kendler, 2014). For example, when one identical twin has depression, the probability of the other twin also experiencing the illness is about 50% compared with 20% for fraternal twins. These types of difference are also maintained when the twins have been separated from their biological parents and reared in separate environments. The heritability of depression is also seen in family studies, with the relative risk of major depression being two to five times greater in the relatives of depressed patients than in the relatives of controls (Stoudemire, 1998). There is also sex difference at work in these figures. For example, a Swedish twin study estimated the heritability of depression for men at 29% and 42% for women (Kendler et al., 2006). Overall, the heritability of depression is judged to be around 38% (Flint & Kendler, 2014).

These types of finding have led to a search for the genes or polymorphisms (unique sections of DNA within a gene) that may cause depression. Although no single gene has been unequivocally linked with depressed mood, a number of chromosomal locations have been identified that appear to increase its susceptibility. For example, in one study that examined patients with early onset major depression disorder, seven genes were found to be exclusive to men, nine were exclusive to women, and only three were shared by both sexes (Zubenko et al., 2002). These findings indicate that depression is likely to be influenced by several genes, with increased vulnerability resulting from a highly complex interaction between multiple genetic interactions and environment.

One gene that has been linked with depression is the SLC6A4 gene located on chromosome 17 which encodes the protein for the serotonin uptake pump. In particular, a small region of this gene (in its promoter region) known as the 5-HTTLPR polymorphism appears to be important (Bleys et al., 2018). This was nicely demonstrated by Caspi et al. (2003), who tracked the progression of depression in a cohort of 847 New Zealanders on an every-other-year basis for 26 years. One of the variables examined was the number of stressful life events that had taken place between the ages of 21 and 26 (these included employment, financial, health and personal stressors). In addition, Caspi et al. grouped the subjects according to the types of polymorphism they carried for the 5-HT transporter. In fact, there are two alleles (or gene variants) called 'short' and 'long' that refer to the length of the DNA sequence found in each gene. Although both genes produce the same 5-HT uptake protein, the 'long' polymorphism makes more of it. In effect, this means the 'long' allele leads to a more efficient transcription of the gene, resulting in greater numbers of protein molecules (and presumably receptors) which in turn increases the efficiency of serotonin uptake activity.

Caspi et al. found that 17% of their group had a pair of short alleles, 51% had one short and one long allele, and 31% had a pair of long alleles (individuals inherit an allele from each parent – see Chapter 14). It was also apparent that the subjects with two short alleles were more likely to suffer a major depressive episode and experience thoughts of suicide than people with two long alleles. The individuals with mixed genes fell between these two extremes. However the most interesting finding arguably concerned the stressful life events. It was evident in those with the short alleles that the greater the number of stressful life events in the five years leading up to their diagnosis, the higher the probability of developing a major depressive disorder. In contrast, the number of stressful life events made no difference in those with two copies of the long allele.

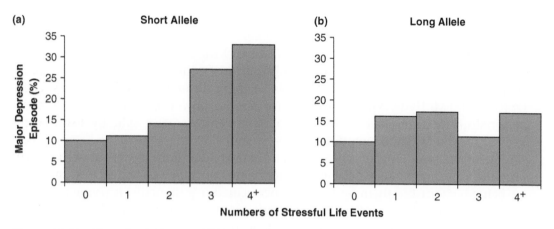

Figure 11.11   The role of stress and the serotonin transporter gene in depression
Source: Garrett and Hough (2018), from Caspi et al. (2003), fig. 3, p. 389. © 2003. Reprinted by permission of AAAS.

This study has been widely used to show that a susceptibility to depression requires the right set of environmental events for it to be expressed, but there is more here, since not only has the short-armed 5-HT gene has been linked with reduced grey matter in the amygdala and cingulate cortex (Pezawas et al., 2005). Moreover, individuals individuals carrying this polymorphism also show an exaggerated amygdala response to fearful facial expressions (Hariri et al., 2002). These findings lend support to the idea that the way in which an individual responds to aversive and stressful events is influenced by their genetic makeup.

These findings, however, must be viewed with some caution. A meta-analysis study that undertook a statistical integration of 14 published reports showed that while stressful life events led to a higher risk of depression, there was no effect of the 5-HTTLPR genotype on depression, and no gene-by-environment interaction with stressful life events (Risch et al., 2009). Data analysed from a sample of several hundred thousand individuals have confirmed these findings (Border et al., 2019). This, of course, does not mean there is no relationship between serotonin and depression. But as Ockenburg (2019) has argued, it is perhaps unlikely that a single genetic variation of the 5-HTTLPR gene (or any other gene for that matter) will have such a massive impact on whether or not an individual develops depression or indeed any other form of mental illness.

SCHIZOPHRENIA: AN INTRODUCTION

If we are asked to imagine a stereotypical mental illness, it is likely something resembling **schizophrenia** will come to mind. Schizophrenia belongs to a group of disorders known as the psychoses which are characterized by the affected individual losing touch with reality – either through distortions in perception or intellectually understanding their world. It can also be one of the most devastating illnesses for its victims. Although the first description of what we now recognize as schizophrenia was made by the German psychiatrist Emil Kraepelin in 1896, who called it 'dementia praecox' (early dementia), the actual term 'schizophrenia' was invented by Eugen

Bleuler in 1911, who derived it from the Greek *schizio* meaning 'split' and *phreno* meaning 'mind'. By adopting this term, Bleuler was emphasizing the fragmented and incoherent thought processes as the key feature of the illness. However, the term has sometimes been confused (at least in the layperson's mind) with multiple personality syndrome where the person exhibits two or more different personalities – such as Dr Jekyll and Mr Hyde. A person with schizophrenia, however, does not have different personalities. Instead, their single personality is overpowered or 'split' by disturbances to their mental function, emotions and behaviour.

One of the symptoms of schizophrenia is bizarre delusions. A person with schizophrenia, for example, may believe they are being controlled by others (e.g. messages are being broadcast to them by radio), or persecuted (e.g. someone is trying to poison them). In some individuals the whole personality may become deluded, causing them to believe they are someone else (e.g. Napoleon or Jesus) or they have a divine mission to fulfil. Such delusions may be accompanied by auditory hallucinations with voices telling the person what to do, along with tactile and olfactory disturbances. Even if the person is free of delusions and hallucinations, the continuity of their thought is often fragmented, making their speech and behaviour incomprehensible. They are also likely to have abnormal emotions with increased excitability, blunted effect, or feelings that most would consider strange or inappropriate. Bouts of excitement or agitation (i.e. nervously pacing up and down and talking in repetitive rhymes), or being lethargic and catatonic, can also occur.

The clinical picture of schizophrenia just described is a standard one, but it may well be that there are different types of schizophrenia with their own sets of characteristics. Indeed, many now regard schizophrenia as a spectrum disorder that includes a group of related mental disorders which share some symptoms (Makin, 2015). Consequently, schizophrenia is a difficult disorder to define precisely. One useful distinction, however, is to divide the symptoms of schizophrenia into two categories, i.e. positive and negative. Positive symptoms are those that reflect over active brain function such as hallucinations, delusions, confused thinking and exaggerated emotions. Negative symptoms are those that arise from under-aroused brain activity which include poverty of thought or speech, blunted affect and social withdrawal. Some types of schizophrenia are characterized by positive symptoms, others by negative symptoms, and some by a mixture of the two (Peralta et al., 1992). It should also be noted that many people with schizophrenia suffer from other mental disorders, including depression, obsessive compulsive disorder, panic attacks and substance abuse (Spaulding et al., 2017).

KEY TERMS: *schizophrenia, psychoses, positive and negative symptoms*

THE EPIDEMIOLOGY OF SCHIZOPHRENIA

Estimates of the incidence (the number of new occurrences over a given period) and prevalence (the number of actual cases at a given point) of schizophrenia depend on the criteria for diagnosis and the population surveyed. Nonetheless, the annual incidence of schizophrenia has been cited as 15.2 per 100,000 persons with a lifetime prevalence risk of about 0.7% (McGrath et al., 2008). Yet it is also likely that another 2–3% of the population will show some borderline or related symptoms (Perälä et al., 2007). The incidence of schizophrenia is slightly higher for men, who also tend to have an earlier age of onset than women (18 and 25 years respectively), and a more severe illness including more hospital admissions. An earlier age of onset also makes it more likely that cognitive deficits will be present (Kar & Jain, 2016). Despite this, a sizeable number of schizophrenic cases also occur after the age of 40. A study by the World Health Organization showed that the incidence of schizophrenia was similar across ten countries which included both developed and third world states (Jablensky et al., 1992). However, others disagree with this assessment and argue that schizophrenia does not distribute itself equally across all cultures and countries – not least because it is more prevalent in urban regions (Messias et al., 2007).

In most cases the severity of schizophrenia shows considerable fluctuation over time with periods of remission, but it can be more permanent and this chronic form of the illness is characterized by a preponderance of negative symptoms, including lack of drive, social withdrawal and emotional apathy. In a 15-year follow-up of 82 schizophrenic patients, it was found that 12% fully recovered after a single episode of psychosis, and another 30% had psychotic episodes interspersed with good mental health. Another third (33%) exhibited repeated and increasingly severe psychotic periods with negative symptoms, while 11% experienced one single psychotic episode with no long-term recovery (Wiersma et al., 1998). These findings also lend further support to the idea that schizophrenia is not a single illness, but a group of related disorders (Lysaker et al., 2018).

Among psychiatric illnesses, schizophrenia is one of the most disabling, taking up a disproportionate share of mental health services. Patients with schizophrenia occupy about 25% of all psychiatric hospital beds and make up 50% of all admissions to mental institutions. In 2004–5, the total cost of treating schizophrenia was estimated to be £6.7 billion for England alone (Mangalore & Knapp, 2007) and around $39 billion annually in the United States – a figure that is about half the cost of all other mental disorders combined (Uhl & Grow, 2004). There are also enormous emotional costs to patients, families, and society at large. In fact, the combined economic and social costs of schizophrenia place it among the world's top ten causes of disability, and this statistic holds true for both developed and developing countries (Musser & McGurk, 2004). However schizophrenia does not just affect mental health: patients with schizophrenia die 12 to 15 years before the population average, with this mortality difference showing signs of increasing in recent years (Saha et al., 2007).

THE DISCOVERY OF ANTIPSYCHOTIC DRUGS

Prior to the early 1950s, there were no effective drugs to treat schizophrenia. Anyone unfortunate enough to be suffering from a psychosis was probably given a barbiturate to make them sleep, or an insulin injection to impart a 'revitalizing' shock to the brain. Although such measures were desperate attempts by well-meanng psychiatrists to help their patients, they were ineffective. Consequently many schizophrenics were housed in institutions, often for long periods of time, in sterile and boring environments. They had little chance of recovery. In fact, estimates show the number of patients kept in mental institutions was rising by about 10–15% for each year in the first part of the twentieth century (Snyder, 1986). There was a desperate need to develop more effective treatments for schizophrenia and other types of mental illness.

As with the development of antidepressants, the discovery of the first antipsychotics were somewhat fortuitous. In 1933, the French pharmaceutical company Rhône-Poulenc began to develop antihistamine compounds for use in a range of conditions, including nausea and allergies. It was soon found, however, that many of these drugs produced marked sedation. This was of interest to a French surgeon called Henri Laborit who believed that an antihistamine drug with the right properties could be an effective pre-anaesthetic agent when given prior to surgery. This led to the synthesis of chlorpromazine in 1950 which had strong calming properties without causing a loss of consciousness. Chlorpromazine also came to the attention of two French psychiatrists, Jean Delay and Pierre Deniker, who began the first clinical trials with the drug in 1952. After treating 38 psychotic patients with daily injections of chlorpromazine, without the use of other sedating agents, they reported remarkable results with benefits that went beyond simple sedation. Hallucinations and delusions disappeared, with their patients showing more logical thought processes. Agitated schizophrenics were calmed, whereas catatonic patients became more active which allowed them to engage more effectively in psychotherapy (Preskorn, 2007).

Chlorpromazine appeared to be a 'true' antipsychotic drug, and was marketed for the treatment of schizophrenia in 1954 under the trade name Thorazine. Its introduction has been labelled as one of the great advances in the history of psychiatry for chlorpromazine was the first drug to be marketed to treat a specific mental illness. It also had an immediate impact, and within a few years the number of people in mental institutions began to show a marked decline. For example, in the US the number of people being treated in hospitals and institutions for mental illness was around 375 per 100,000 of the population, but after 1954 this number fell by about 50% over the next ten years. Although there were other factors at work, and the fall was not as dramatic in Europe, there is little doubt that Thorazine heralded a new dawn in psychiatry.

Chlorpromazine belongs to a class of drugs known as the phenothiazines (a class of drug first synthesized as dyes in the late 1800s), and it led to the development of many other phenothiazine compounds with useful antipsychotic properties. However, it soon became clear that these agents were not the only ones that improved the symptoms of schizophrenia. In Belgium, the pharmacologist Paul Janssen, after reasoning that a treatment for amphetamine intoxication would most likely provide a cure for paranoid schizophrenia, discovered haloperidol (Haldol) which was first synthesized in 1958. This drug belonged to a class of compounds known as the butyrophenones, and it was effective at treating schizophrenia with fewer side effects. It replaced Thorazine in terms of popularity and still remains today the most commonly used drug to treat schizophrenia (López-Muñoz & Alamo, 2009).

KEY TERMS: *chlorpromazine, Thorazine, phenothiazines, haloperidol, butyrophenones*

ORIGINS OF THE DOPAMINE THEORY OF SCHIZOPHRENIA

How then do chlorpromazine and haloperidol act to improve the symptoms of schizophrenia? In the late 1950s, research began to show that both drugs exerted their main pharmacological effects by reducing **dopamine** activity in the brain. Evidence to support this idea came from the drug reserpine. As we have already seen above, reserpine was known to deplete the brain of monoamines which often led to depression. But reserpine had also shown some promise as an antipsychotic, although it was not as effective as chlorpromazine which also had fewer side effects. Interestingly, reserpine, chlorpromazine and haloperidol all produced Parkinson-like side effects, such as rigidity and tremor, in high doses. This was an important clue that all these drugs had a similar mode of pharmacological action.

In 1960, the focus turned to dopamine when Oleh Hornykiewicz in Vienna made the seminal discovery that the brains of those with **Parkinson's disease** lacked this neurochemical. This indicated that antipsychotic drugs might produce their rigidity and tremor by reducing dopamine activity, and if this was the case then it implied that psychosis was being caused by the overactivity of this neurotransmitter in the brain. In effect, this was the origin of the **dopamine theory of schizophrenia** which would prove to be the most influential and enduring hypothesis that has guided thinking about this illness ever since (Howes & Kapur, 2009).

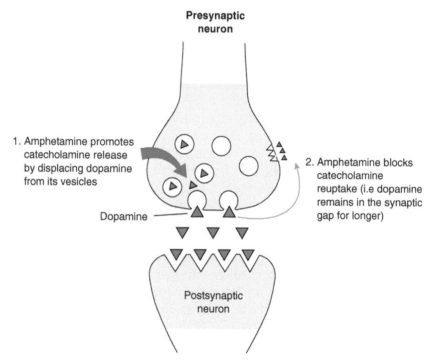

Figure 11.12   The mechanism by which amphetamine exerts its pharmacological effects
Source: Wickens (2009)

Support for the involvement of dopamine in schizophrenia came from the psychostimulant **amphetamine**. When taken in high amounts, amphetamine produces a number of side effects, including restlessness, confusion and agitated behaviour. Moreover, overdoses can cause a psychosis which includes hallucinations, delusions and paranoia similar to schizophrenia. In the late 1950s it was found that amphetamine caused the release of catecholamines, particularly noradrenaline and dopamine, from nerve terminals in the brain (see Heal et al., 2013; Snyder, 1973). In other words, increased catecholaminergic transmission could induce psychotic behaviour – an effect opposite to that being produced by reserpine, chlorpromazine and haloperidol. It also become clear that the behavioural effects of amphetamine could be blocked most effectively by dopaminergic antagonists (Kellendonk et al., 2009).

> **KEY TERMS:** *dopamine, reserpine, Parkinson's disease, dopaminergic theory of schizophrenia, amphetamine*

HOW DO ANTIPSYCHOTIC DRUGS WORK?

It was expected that chlorpromazine and haloperidol would have pharmacological effects similar to those for reserpine, i.e. by depleting the brain of dopamine. However, in 1963 Arvid Carlsson and Margit Lindqvist showed otherwise. When they injected mice with chlorpromazine, they found it did not reduce the levels of catecholamines, including dopamine. In fact the reverse was true, at least in the short term, as the level of dopaminergic metabolites increased – a finding showing that chlorpromazine was somehow increasing the release of dopamine (which was then being broken down to produce its metabolites). Thus, despite similar behavioural effects, reserpine and chlorpromazine were having different neurochemical effects on the brain (Carlsson & Lindvist, 1963; Curzon, 1990).

To account for these results, Carlsson and Lindqvist proposed what was then a radically new theory. In effect, they argued that chlorpromazine acted as a 'false' neurotransmitter, which bound to the dopamine receptor – but in doing so it then blocked the dopamine molecules from binding to the site (see Figure 11.13). Carlson and Lindqvist also hypothesized that if dopamine was unable to reach its receptors, its neurons would respond by increasing the release of dopamine in an attempt to compensate for the deficit at the postsynaptic receptors (this assumed, of course, that the dopaminergic neurons received information from the postsynaptic receptors, informing them of the reduced dopamine stimulation). The net result of this receptor blockade by chlorpromazine would therefore be an increased release of dopamine from the presynaptic neurons, which would then be broken down in the synaptic cleft, causing the increased level of metabolites (Baumeister, 2013).

Although this was an interesting idea, it could not be proven in the early 1960s. There was no way of identifying receptors at this time, let alone establishing whether they could be 'blocked'. Nonetheless, Carlsson and Lindqvist were shown to be correct in the 1970s when a technique called radioligand binding was developed.

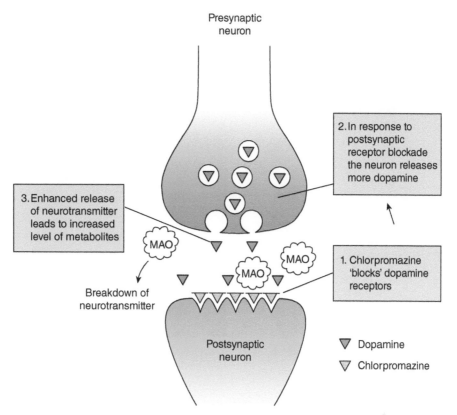

Presynaptic
neuron

2. In response to postsynaptic receptor blockade the neuron releases more dopamine

3. Enhanced release of neurotransmitter leads to increased level of metabolites

MAO

MAO

MAO

1. Chlorpromazine 'blocks' dopamine receptors

Breakdown of
neurotransmitter

Postsynaptic
neuron

▽ Dopamine

▽ Chlorpromazine

Figure 11.13   The Carlsson and Lindqvist theory of how chlorpromazine and haloperidol produce their pharmacological effects
Source: Wickens (2009)

In this procedure, a radioactive tracer is added to a neurotransmitter or drug thought to bind to certain receptors, which is then rinsed through specially prepared brain tissue. This causes the tissue to emit a small amount of radioactivity. In fact, this emission is derived from the drug bound to the tissue's receptors, and the level of radioactivity can be measured to allow an estimate of the receptor numbers. This procedure, for example, showed that the highest amount of dopamine receptors were found in the striatum (Creese et al., 1976).

Following the development of this technique, the effects of chlorpromazine and haloperidol on displacing radioactive dopamine were examined in a procedure known as competitive binding. This technique rests on the assumption that if there are drugs that block dopamine receptors, then they should be able to compete with the dopamine in the radioligand binding procedure. Thus, blocking should then result in less radioactivity being emitted from the dopamine receptor. Indeed, this is what occurred when chlorpromazine was washed through striatal tissue along with radioactive dopamine. In fact, chlorpromazine not only blocked the effects of dopamine, but the clinical potency of a wide range of antischizophrenic drugs was also found to correlate with their ability to displace dopamine. The more effective a given drug was at treating schizophrenia, the better it was at blocking dopamine receptors (Snyder, 1986).

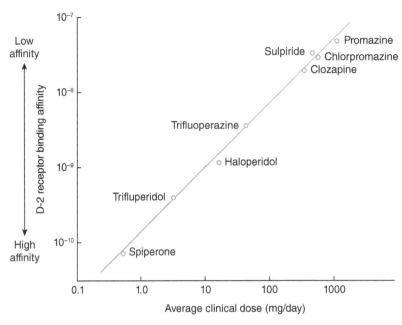

Figure 11.14 Graph showing the correlation between the clinical potencies of antipsychotic drugs and their ability to block the D-2 dopamine receptor

Source: Wickens (2009)

However haloperidol was an exception to this rule. The competitive binding technique showed that haloperidol was weak at binding with dopamine receptors in the striatum. Nor did its rather poor ability to bind with striatal dopamine receptors match its potency at treating schizophrenia. Nonetheless, it was clear that haloperidol bound to striatal tissue and other dopaminergic areas in the brain. How could this puzzling finding be explained? The answer became clear when it was discovered there was more than one type of dopaminergic receptor in the brain (Kebabian & Calne, 1979). During the early 1980s, the brain was shown to contain two types of dopamine receptor which were called D-1 and D-2. It was also found that while chlorpromazine bound with equal affinity to both D-1 and D-2 receptors, haloperidol only bound to D-2 receptors. This not only explained the discrepant results obtained with competitive binding, it also indicated that antipsychotic drugs worked by blocking D-2 receptors. Taking this discovery one step further, it also implicated the D-2 receptors in the aetiology of schizophrenia (Nord & Farde, 2010).

It should be noted that the last two decades have seen exciting advances taking place in the field of receptor pharmacology with the discovery of three more dopamine receptor subtypes (called D-3, D-4 and D-5). The D-3 and D-4 receptors have generated interest because they are structurally similar to the D-2 receptor. However, unlike the D-2 receptors which are found in large amounts in the striatum, D-3 and D-4 receptors are found mainly in the limbic system, particularly the nucleus accumbens and olfactory tubercle. Both chlorpromazine and haloperidol have varying affinities for all these receptors (Missale et al., 1998).

KEY TERMS: *dopamine receptors (D-1, D-2, D-3, D-4, D-5), radioligand binding, competitive binding*

ARVID CARLSSON

Carlsson's list of achievements is remarkable. These include the discovery of dopamine as a chemical neurotransmitter in the brain, revealing its involvement in the pathophysiology of Parkinson's disease and schizophrenia, and for identifying dopamine receptor blockade as the pharmacological mechanism of antipsychotic drugs. Carlsson was born in Uppsala, Sweden, to parents who were both historians. He began his medical studies in 1941, at the University of Lund, but because of World War II, served some of his time in military service. Towards the end of the conflict, he became one of the first medics to examine the emaciated prisoners from Nazi concentration camps, some of whom had reached Sweden. After medical training, Carlsson took an unpaid position in a pharmacology laboratory where he examined the action of the convulsant pentylenetetrazol. It would lead to his first paper in 1946.

In 1954, he received an invitation to work at the National Health Institute in Bethesda, Maryland. This was a period when psychopharmacology was undergoing a revolution with the first drugs purposively developed to treat mental illness. Carlsson's task was to examine the antipsychotic agent reserpine, which he showed inhibited the storage of serotonin in blood platelets. Returning to Lund to become a professor of pharmacology, he continued his work with reserpine, showing that it depleted noradrenaline (NA) levels in the brain. Curiously, he also found that L-Dopa was able to quickly reverse reserpine's sedative effects – an effect that was independent of its action on NA. Somewhat puzzled, Carlsson turned his attention to dopamine (DA) – at the time, a recently discovered brain chemical which was believed to be involved in the formation of NA. It was an inspired decision because he found that reserpine not only depleted the brain of DA, but that this also correlated with reserpine's behavioural action. It was the first indication that dopamine might serve a neurotransmitter role in the brain – an idea that was supported when Carlsson discovered there was actually more DA in the brain than NA. It was also found predominantly in the striatum – an interesting finding because reserpine was known to produce Parkinson-like side effects. It did not take long for Carlsson to propose that a loss of dopamine in the striatum might be a cause of Parkinson's disease – a far-reaching claim which turned out to be correct. This finding would also lead to the treatment of Parkinson's disease with L-Dopa in the mid-1960s, which at the time was probably neuroscience's greatest achievement (and perhaps still is).

During the early part of the 1960s, Carlsson, working with Margit Lindqvist, turned his attention towards understanding the pharmacological action of the antipsychotics chlorpromazine and haloperidol. Although both produced reserpine-like side effects, including sedation and immobility, Carlsson found that neither depleted the brain of DA. In a bold leap of imagination, he proposed that chlorpromazine and haloperidol exerted their effects by blocking DA receptors. Although it would take years to prove, Carlsson's theory was found to be the correct explanation. This idea would also provide the basis for the dopamine hypothesis of schizophrenia.

Two other discoveries by Carlsson can also be mentioned. Firstly, in the late 1960s, he showed that tricyclic antidepressants blocked not only the reuptake of NA, but 5-HT as well. This led him to develop the first 5-HT uptake inhibitor (Zimelidine) which became the forerunner of

(Continued)

many more selective drugs such as Prozac. Secondly, in the early 1970s, research began to point to the possibility of presynaptic receptors on the axon endings of neurons. Carlsson confirmed this by showing that DA synthesis and release could be altered by certain DA receptor agonists and antagonists. In 1975, Carlsson used the term *autoreceptors* to refer to this specialized presynaptic receptor – a word that has become widely adopted. We now know that autoreceptor function plays a significant role in the pharmacological action of many antidepressant drugs. In 2000, Carlsson was the recipient of the Nobel Prize (along with Eric Kandel and Paul Greengard) for his work concerning signal transduction in the nervous system.

DOPAMINE PATHWAYS AND SCHIZOPHRENIA

Although the human brain has relatively few dopaminergic neurons, which total around 400,000 in number (Schultz, 2007), they have extensive projections to several regions of the forebrain (Yetnikoff et al., 2014). In 1964, Annica Dahlström and Kjell Fuxe mapped the brain's noradrenergic cell groups (which they labelled A1–A7) and dopaminergic cell groups (A8–A15). The two largest dopamine systems reaching the forebrain were shown to originate from the **ventral tegmental area** (A10) and substantia nigra pars compacta (A9), both located in the midbrain. The ventral tegmentum (A10) actually gives rise to two pathways: the mesocortical pathway which innervates the prefrontal cortex, and the mesolimbic pathway which projects to the ventral striatum including the nucleus accumbens and olfactory tubercle (the prefix 'meso' which means 'middle' in Greek, simply refers to the midbrain). The A9 pathway passes to the dorsal striatum and is better known as the nigrostriatal pathway. This provides the striatum with about 80% of the brain's dopamine. Following this discovery, those interested in schizophrenia tended to focus on the mesocortical system which was believed to be involved in cognition, and the mesolimbic system implicated in emo-

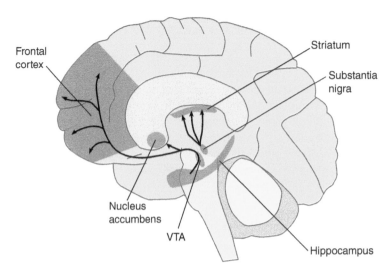

Figure 11.15   The major dopaminergic pathways of the brain
Source: NIDA/Quasihuman/Wikimedia Commons

tion. The nigrostriatal pathway, known for its involvement in the control of voluntary motor function and learning new motor skills, did not seem to be a promising candidate for understanding schizophrenia. In fact, this system was shown to be involved in many of the troublesome side effects of antipsychotic medication, including tardive dyskinesia – a disorder characterized by involuntary and repetitive body movements, including grimacing and sticking out the tongue.

One popular theory has viewed schizophrenia as arising from an imbalance of the mesolimbic and mesofrontal pathways (Davis et al., 1991). This idea proposes that negative symptoms occur as a result of decreased dopaminergic activity in the frontal system, whereas the positive symptoms arise from an overactive limbic system. Evidence for this has come from PET scanning which shows reduced blood flow, or hypofrontality, in the frontal cortex of people with schizophrenia when they undertake cognitive tasks such as the Wisconsin Card Sorting Task (Prentice et al., 2008). Although hypofrontality is not observed in all people with schizophrenia, it is found in a significant number – perhaps as many as 50%

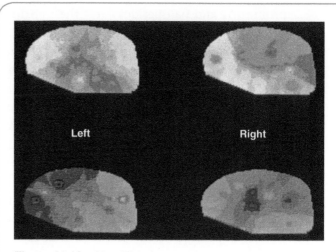

Figure 11.16   Blood flow in normal brains (upper images) and schizophrenic brains (lower images) during the Wisconsin Card Sorting Task (the blue colouring shows a lower level of perfusion)

Source: Garrett and Hough (2021), from 'Physiologic Dysfunction of Dorsolateral Prefrontal Cortex in Schizophrenia: I. Regional Cerebral Blood Flow Evidence', by D. R. Weinberger, K. F. Berman, and R. R. Zec, 1986, *Archives of General Psychiatry*, 43, 114–124

(Hill et al., 2004). The reduced blood flow to the frontal cortex appears to involve dopamine, since amphetamine increases blood flow in the prefrontal cortex and improves Wisconsin Card Sorting performance (Brisch et al., 2014; Daniel et al., 1991).

The mesolimbic system with its association with emotion and reward has also been regarded as a prime candidate for an involvement in schizophrenia. Recently, however, advances in neuroimaging techniques have led to the somewhat unanticipated finding that dopaminergic dysfunction in schizophrenia is greatest within the nigrostriatal pathways, implicating the dorsal striatum in the pathophysiology of schizophrenia (Weinstein et al., 2017). For example, studies involving PET scanning have allowed the radio-labelling of dopamine precursors to enable the measurement of its uptake and conversion in dopamine neurons. This then gives an index of dopamine synthesis capacity. Meta-analysis of studies using these type of measures shows that there is a robust increase in striatal dopamine synthesis and release in psychosis (McCutcheon et al., 2019). Furthermore, and possibly even more important, the striatal dopaminergic hyperactivity in schizophrenia is associated with the psychotic symptoms of the illness (Howes et al., 2012). These findings are beginning to change our concepts of the nature of dopaminergic dysregulation in schizophrenia (McCutcheon et al., 2019).

KEY TERMS: *ventral tegmental area, substantia nigra pars compacta, mesolimbic and mesocortical systems, nigrostriatal pathway, tardive dyskinesia, hypofrontality*

PROBLEMS WITH THE DOPAMINE THEORY

As we have seen, amphetamine, which causes the release of dopamine, can induce a psychotic episode similar to that which occurs in schizophrenia, whilst chlorpromazine and haloperidol exert their antipsychotic effects by blocking dopamine receptors. These data therefore imply that schizophrenia is caused by excess dopaminergic activity, but not all the evidence supports this somewhat simple idea. For example, one might predict that the brains of schizophrenics will contain increased levels of dopamine and its metabolites; however, this is not the case. Although there is variation in the results, most studies of dopamine metabolites, such as homovanillic acid (HVA) in the cerebrospinal fluid, have not found higher levels in psychotic patients (Markianos et al., 1992). Similarly, there is little consistent evidence showing increased levels of dopamine, or its metabolites in the brain at post-mortem (Cross et al., 1986).

An alternative version of the dopaminergic theory proposes there is hyperactive dopamine transmission in schizophrenia – perhaps caused by a greater proliferation of dopamine brain receptors. Indeed, a number of post-mortem studies have shown an elevation of D-2 receptors in the striatum of patients with schizophrenia (Seeman & Kapur, 2000). Increased D-2 receptor numbers have also been reported from brain-scanning studies (Jaskiw & Kleinman, 1988) which have also identified increased numbers of D-3 and D-4 receptors in the limbic and cortical areas of schizophrenic brains (Jardemark et al., 2002). But again, there is much inconsistency in the findings. One difficulty is that the therapeutic use of antipsychotic drugs leads to an upregulation of dopamine receptors. Thus, it is possible that many studies that have measured receptors have been biased because of previous drug treatment. Although some studies have reported increased numbers of D-2 receptors in unmedicated patients with schizophrenia that had been drug-free for some time before testing, this has not always been confirmed. An explanation has been provided by Kestler et al. (2001), who in an extensive review of the literature have concluded there are moderate increases in dopamine receptors in some, but not all, groups of schizophrenia.

Another problem with the dopamine hypothesis is that antipsychotic drugs block receptors within a day or two, although it takes several weeks for clinical benefits to occur. This improvement is reflected in an initial rise in HVA levels, followed by a gradual decline. Thus, it is likely the blockade of dopaminergic receptors is not the final mechanism by which these drugs work. In this regard it is interesting to note that the main enzyme involved in the synthesis of dopamine, tyrosine hydroxylase, is significantly increased in certain brain areas of those with schizophrenia, indicating an increased capacity for production of dopamine (Howes et al., 2013).

KEY TERMS: *hyperactive dopamine transmission, tyrosine hydroxylase*

THE DISCOVERY OF ATYPICAL ANTIPSYCHOTICS

Another problem for the dopamine theory is that around 30–40% of patients with schizophrenia do not respond favourably to the traditional antipsychotic drugs. This is despite the likelihood that these patients have a pharmacological blockade of their dopamine receptors which exceeds 90%. The ineffectiveness of standard antipsychotics for some patients led researchers to look for new agents (sometimes called atypical or second-generation antipsychotics). One drug to emerge was clozapine (sold under the brand name of Clozaril). Synthesized in 1958 as a tricyclic antidepressant, clozapine was first used to treat schizophrenia in the early 1970s when it gained a high reputation for improving the symptoms of those who were resistant to standard medication (McKenna & Bailey, 1993). Although withdrawn from clinical practice due to it causing a dangerous drop in the number of white blood cells, which compromised immunity in some patients, it was reintroduced back into psychiatric use in 2002 (with the proviso that patients' blood cell count be regularly monitored). Since then, it has been shown to be twice as effective as haloperidol, with the greatest benefits in those who had been drug resistant. In one study which compared 15 antipsychotic drugs, clozapine was ranked first and clearly superior to all other antipsychotics (Leucht et al., 2013). Many patients treated with clozapine show significantly greater improvement than control subjects on positive symptoms after six weeks of treatment – a benefit that is still enhancing the quality of life at one year (Rosenheck et al., 1999).

Clozapine's pharmacological action has also led to a re-evaluation of the dopamine theory of schizophrenia. Whilst it binds to a wide range of receptors, including those for serotonin, histamine, noradrenaline and acetylcholine, it has a relatively small effect on dopaminergic receptors. In fact, it only has a short-lived binding effect on D-1 and D-2 receptors (Tauscher et al., 2004), although it is significantly more potent at D-4 receptors (Sanyal & Van Tol, 1997). However, clozapine is a potent antagonist of serotonergic 5-HT2A receptors, and this action is believed to be the important one by which it exerts its antipsychotic effects (Meltzer et al., 2003). This has expanded our understanding of schizophrenia. The 5-HT2A receptor has a wide distribution throughout the brain, but high concentrations are found in the cerebral cortex where they are believed to be involved in a wide range of higher cognitive processes (Zhang & Stackman, 2015). Activity at the 5-HT2A receptor has also been shown to enhance both glutamate and dopamine release (Aghajanian & Marek, 1999a). According to Stahl (1996) some 85–90 % of 5-HT2A receptors are blocked by a therapeutic dose of clozapine that simultaneously blocks 20% of dopamine D-2 receptors.

The discovery of clozapine was a major breakthrough in the treatment of schizophrenia. It is not only acting as a prototype for newer antipsychotic compounds, but also opening up new ideas concerning the biological basis of the illness. Clozapine has, for example, been shown to preferentially stimulate dopamine release in the frontal cortex compared to the striatum (Youngren et al., 1999). This may also explain why clozapine produces so few extrapyramidal side effects. The discovery of clozapine may even help us understand how hallucinations occur. Hallucinations are, of course, among the hallmarks of schizophrenia. Interestingly, functional scanning of

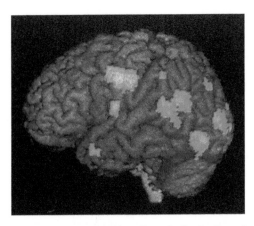

Figure 11.17   Brain activation during visual and auditory hallucinations in a schizophrenic which highlights both language areas and the occipital cortex

Source: Garrett and Hough (2021), from Silbersweig et al. (1995). A functional neuroanatomy of hallucinations in schizophrenia. *Nature*, 378, 176–179. Reprinted by permission of Nature, copyright 1995.

people with schizophrenia has shown that several visual areas of the brain are active during visual hallucinations (Figure 11.17). In the case of hearing voices (auditory hallucinations) this activity shifts to Wernicke's area and other language-related sites (Silbersweig et al., 1995). One drug which famously produces marked visual and auditory hallucinatory activity is lysergic acid diethylamide (LSD), and it probably is not incidental that it exerts a pharmacological effect that is in some ways opposite to that of clozapine – namely by stimulating the 5-HT2A receptor.

> **KEY TERMS:** *atypical and second-generation antipsychotics, clozapine, 5-HT2A receptors, hallucinations, lysergic acid diethylamide*

THE GLUTAMATIC THEORY OF SCHIZOPHRENIA

Although high doses of amphetamine can induce the positive symptoms of schizophrenia, two other drugs which are apparently even better at mimicking psychotic behaviour, as they produce both positive and negative effects, are phencyclidine and ketamine (Sawa & Snyder, 2002). Phencyclidine, otherwise known as PCP or 'angel dust', is a drug that has been used recreationally for its mind-altering effects, but can trigger visual and auditory hallucinations, delusions, paranoia, high anxiety and agitated behaviour. In addition, severe depression and a sense of isolation can also be manifested. These effects may also persist for several weeks after the drug is taken. Interestingly, phencyclidine and ketamine have no direct effects on dopamine receptors. Rather, they act as antagonists at the glutamate N-methyl-D-aspartate (NMDA) receptor. **Glutamate** is an excitatory neurotransmitter primarily involved in sending 'fast' signals to other cells. It is also the most abundant neurotransmitter in the CNS, being used at around 40% of all synapses in the brain (Alexander, 2009). It is even possible that every brain neuron expresses glutamate receptors which are predominantly located on dendrites and dendritic spines (Moriyoshi et al., 1991). High amounts of NMDA receptors are found in the cerebral cortex, including the circuits that regulate dopamine release. This has led to the proposal that the dopaminergic deficits in schizophrenia may be secondary to underlying glutamatergic dysfunction (Javitt, 2010).

The glutamate theory of schizophrenia is based on the idea of there being abnormal glutamate activity in the brain, particularly in the **prefrontal cortex**, due to impaired functioning of the NMDA receptor (Moghaddam & Javitt, 2012). In turn this produces an increase in glutamate release which has far-reaching effects (Homayoun & Moghaddam, 2007). For example, prefrontal glutamatergic neurons project to the ventral tegmental area (VTA) where they form synapses with dopaminergic neurons that project back to the prefrontal cortex. The administration of NMDA antagonists into the prefrontal cortex has been shown to inhibit this pathway, which is believed to contribute to the negative and cognitive symptoms of schizophrenia (Svensson, 2000). However, this is not the only dopaminergic system affected by prefrontal glutamatic activity, since a pathway also synapses with GABA-secreting neurons in the VTA that project to the nucleus accumbens. Importantly, infusions of phencyclidine into the prefrontal cortex increase dopamine release in the nucleus accumbens – an effect that may be responsible for producing positive symptoms (Howes et al., 2015; Uno & Coyle, 2019). It is also interesting to note that the effects of phencyclidine can be reversed by antipsychotic drugs and clozapine (Kargieman et al., 2012).

Further support for the glutamate theory has come from an autoimmune disorder called anti-NMDA receptor encephalitis which is caused by antibodies that attack a subunit of NMDA receptor (Warren et al., 2018). This leads to NMDA dysregulation and downregulation. The disorder most commonly presents itself with agitation and aggression, abnormal speech, catatonia, seizures, and psychosis-inducing delusions and hallucinations. In addition, the cognitive deficits shown by those with anti-NMDA receptor encephalitis are very similar to those found in schizophrenia. In fact, in one study, it was reported that 6.5% of patients fulfilling the diagnostic criteria for schizophrenia were actually NMDA receptor-antibody positive (Zandi et al., 2011).

KEY TERMS: *phencyclidine, ketamine, N-methyl-D-aspartate (NMDA) receptors, glutamate, prefrontal cortex, ventral tegmental area, nucleus accumbens, anti-NMDA receptor encephalitis*

EVIDENCE FOR BRAIN DAMAGE IN SCHIZOPHRENIA

In many schizophrenic individuals there is brain tissue loss with a significant decrease in both the grey (cell bodies) and white matter (myelinated fibres). For example, Honea et al. (2005) reviewed 15 voxel-based morphometry (VBM) studies which included 390 patients with a diagnosis of schizophrenia and 364 healthy controls (VBM is a computational technique using MRI that allows investigation of structural differences in brain anatomy using parametric statistics). They found grey and white matter deficits in 50 brain regions in the schizophrenic brain – with abnormalities in the left superior temporal gyrus and left medial temporal lobe being most consistent. Some of these regions showed functional deficits as well. Schobel et al. (2009) used a high-resolution variant of fMRI to examine the brain in subjects with schizophrenia. This revealed a decrease of cerebral blood volume in the dorsolateral prefrontal cortex, but increased flow in the orbitofrontal cortex and CA1 subfield of the hippocampus. This latter finding was also significant since it predicted the course of the disorder. In those who were at the beginning of their illness, the extent of the increased hippocampal activity was able to predict a full-blown schizophrenia illness with 70% accuracy. Given the importance of the hippocampus in memory and cognition, this abnormality might be responsible for some of the deficits in thought and reasoning that are so characteristic of schizophrenia.

One of the most common findings in schizophrenia is an enlargement of the two lateral **ventricles** located in each of the cerebral hemispheres (see Figure 11.18). For example, Weinberger and Wyatt (1982) examined the CAT scans of 80 chronic patients and found the size of the ventricles to be twice as large compared to those of controls. Although others have not reported such big differences, there is still often an increase in volume (Sayo et al., 2012). This, in turn, causes a reduction in brain volume which is around 2% (Hajima et al., 2013). The enlargement of the ventricles is specific to schizophrenia, as shown by studies of monozygotic twins who are discordant for the illness. In such cases, the affected twin is the only one to show increased ventricle size (Torrey et al., 1994). Ventricular enlargement does not appear to be related to the length of the illness or duration of drug therapy (McDonald et al., 2002), but it is correlated with the severity of the negative symptoms (Andreasen, 1988). The mechanism underlying ventricular enlargement is not known, although an abnormality in the function of the ependymal cells which line the ventricles has been established (Eom et al., 2020).

Brain-imaging techniques have revealed other types of damage in schizophrenia. For example, a technique called diffusion tensor imaging using MRI has also been used to assess the integrity of white matter (myelinated pathways) in the brains of people with schizophrenia. This technique, which measures the diffusion of water molecules, has shown that the white matter tends to be more disorganized (i.e. less neatly aligned) in a number of brain regions, including the prefrontal cortex and temporal lobes (Burns et al., 2003). In other words, the neural connectivity between several large cortical regions is likely to be dysfunctional in schizophrenia (Ellison-Wright & Bullmore, 2009).

KEY TERMS: *dorsolateral prefrontal cortex, orbitofrontal cortex, hippocampus, lateral ventricles, diffusion tensor imaging*

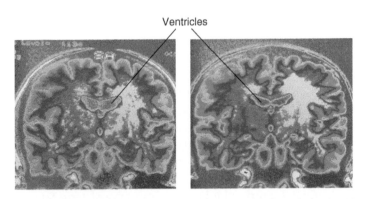

Ventricles

Figure 11.18   In two identical twins, the lateral ventricles are larger in the one with schizophrenia (on the left).

Source: Garrett and Hough (2021), © 1990 Massachusetts Medical Society. All rights reserved.

TWO TYPES OF SCHIZOPHRENIA?

During the 1980s, British psychiatrist Timothy Crow proposed that there are two distinct types of schizophrenia, each with their own pathology which he called type 1 and type 2 (Crow, 1985). Type 1 schizophrenia, characterized by positive symptoms including hallucinations and delusions, is associated with dopaminergic dysfunction (e.g. increased numbers of D-2 receptors) and responds well to conventional drug therapy. This form of schizophrenia also has a good long-term prognosis. In contrast, type 2 schizophrenia is characterized by a greater incidence of negative symptoms, associated with structural brain damage, and responds poorly to standard antipsychotic treatment. This is more likely to result in a permanent (chronic) condition, where there is a greater intellectual and cognitive dysfunction, and poorer chances of recovery.

Table 11.1   Positive versus negative symptoms

Aspect	Type I (positive)	Type II (negative)
Characteristic symptoms	Delusions, hallucinations, etc.	Poverty of speech, lack of affect, etc.
Response to antidopaminergic drugs	Good	Poor
Symptom outcome	Potentially reversible	Irreversible?
Intellectual impairment	Absent	Sometimes present
Suggested pathological process	Increased D_2 dopamine receptors	Cell loss in temporal lobes

Source: Garrett and Hough (2018), from Crow (1985), with permission of Oxford University Press

A study that used factor analysis (a statistical technique that reduces a large number of variables into fewer numbers or factors) has supported Crow's model by confirming that many cases of schizophrenia fit into this type of classification system (Lenzenweger, 1988). However, there are also some difficulties with Crow's model. For example, many patients show a mixture of positive and negative symptoms, and the latter do not always correlate with the extent of brain damage. Moreover, there are some with predominantly positive symptoms with ventricular enlargement or other evidence of brain abnormality, and to confound the issue further, type 1 and type 2 symptoms can change with time. One study which examined the progress of 52 hospitalized schizophrenic patients over a 25-year period, found that positive symptoms gradually changed into more pronounced negative ones such as social withdrawal and blunted affect (Pfohl & Winnokur, 1983). There may also be a third type of schizophrenia (disorganized syndrome) which is characterized by symptoms such as an impaired capacity to sustain coherent discourse and inappropriate affect. This raises the possibility that Crow's schizophrenic types, rather than representing two different illnesses, are really the two ends of a continuum. Nonetheless, Crow's classification remains useful (Jablensky, 2010).

KEY TERMS: *type 1 and type 2 schizophrenia*

THE GENETICS OF SCHIZOPHRENIA

There is considerable evidence to show genetic inheritance is a significant contributor to the development of schizophrenia. For example, a large number of studies published over the last century or so have reported that the concordance for identical twins is around 40–60% whereas the rate for non-identical twins is 10–20% (Cardno et al., 1999; Fisher, 1971). Further, while the lifetime risk in the general population is just below 1%, this rises to 17% in those with one schizophrenic parent, and nearly 50% when both parents are affected. The incidence is around 5% in second-degree relatives, and 2% in first cousins or third-degree relatives (Gottesman, 1991). But these figures may be an underestimate. In the case of identical twins being discordant for schizophrenia, it has been shown that 54% of the non-affected twins will also show some symptomatology or a related spectrum disorder (Heston, 1970). Importantly, the heritability of schizophrenia still persists in individuals born to psychotic parents but adopted into new families at an early age (Kety et al., 1968). Thus, the children of schizophrenics are more likely to become psychotic, even if they have been reared away from the parents in different environments.

Although schizophrenia has a genetic component, it is clear the pattern of inheritance is complex and does not follow a Mendelian single-gene pattern of expression (see Chapter 14). Rather, it is likely schizophrenia has multiple genetic causes with each gene increasing the predisposition for the illness. Recent genome-wide studies have identified more than 70 genes suspected of playing a role in producing schizophrenia (Hosak, 2013), although the total number of genetic variants is believed to be much larger (Wray & Visscher, 2010). Consequently, it is probable that the development of schizophrenia involves the cumulative effects of multiple genes, with most of these only having a small effect by themselves. It follows, therefore, that the more of these genes one inherits, the greater the likelihood of developing schizophrenia.

Recently, there has been a lot of interest in the contribution of chromosome 22 to producing schizophrenia. A large missing part in one of the long arms of this chromosome produces a condition called 22q11.2 deletion syndrome. This occurs in around 1 in 4,000 live births, making it one of the most common genetic deletion syndromes, which is associated with cardiac and kidney dysfunction, cleft palate and intellectual disability. However, interestingly, about 25% of individuals develop psychotic symptoms which makes 22q11.2 deletion syndrome one of the strongest known risk factors for schizophrenia (Owen & Doherty, 2016). The most likely mechanism is the exclusion of one or more genes in the depleted region. But which ones? Attention has focused on the gene coding for catechol O-methyltransferase (COMT) which is an enzyme involved in the synthesis of dopamine. In one study that followed a group of 24 patients with 22q11.2 deletion syndrome, who were also known to carry a distinct polymorphism in their remaining COMT gene, it was found that seven went on to develop schizophrenia in their teenage years. These individuals showed the lowest COMT activity (indicating low dopaminergic activity) along with a smaller prefrontal cortex which correlated with poor IQ and language skills (Gothelf et al., 2005). Although not all studies have found a link between schizophrenia and the COMT gene, this remains an exciting finding and one that awaits further research (Armando et al., 2012).

KEY TERMS: *chromosome 22, 22q11.2 deletion syndrome, catechol O-methyltransferase, dopamine*

ENVIRONMENTAL FACTORS

Whilst genes play a significant role in the aetiology of schizophrenia, they only impart a certain vulnerability to developing the illness. Whether they become manifested appears to depend on adverse life events experienced by the individual. This has led to the vulnerability model which argues that environmental stresses interact with one's genetic predispositions, and when this combination reaches a critical threshold, the symptoms of the disorder appear (Zubin & Spring, 1977). This is much the same as saying that schizophrenia – and other psychiatric disorders – arise in certain individuals because they are genetically more predisposed to react badly to aversive life situations. Since the genetic vulnerability between individuals varies, this will also lead to different outcomes. For example, at one extreme are a small group of individuals who will become schizophrenic even under the relatively normal physical and psychological stresses of life. At the other extreme are those who will not become schizophrenic under any circumstances, or will do so only under the severest of stressful life events (Davis et al., 2016; Garrett, 2015).

One study highlighting the importance of vulnerability was the Finnish Adoptive Family Study of Schizophrenia (Tienari et al., 1985, 1994) which followed a group of children taken away from mothers with schizophrenia (high risk) who were compared with a group of low-risk subjects. The chances of developing schizophrenia were greater in the high-risk subjects, and most marked for those raised in a dysfunctional family environment. However, of course, there were instances when high-risk subjects did not develop schizophrenia despite exposure to a difficult environment, and there were instances when children raised by schizophrenic parents remained mentally healthy. The genetic variance in susceptibility to schizophrenia appears to be the key factor. Nor is family upbringing the only stress factor for schizophrenia. The illness is more common in the lower social classes and large urban areas. In fact, racial minorities living in big cities like London are twice as likely to develop schizophrenia if residing in areas where there are small numbers of fellow minority populations. These findings indicate that social isolation is another significant factor in schizophrenia (Boydell & Murray, 2003).

The risk of schizophrenia can also be greatly increased by prenatal events, or those taking place around the time of birth. Some of the strongest evidence has implicated foetal exposure to virus infections as a key factor for developing the illness. For example, in the northern hemisphere there is a small but significant risk that people with schizophrenia will be born in late winter and early spring. This effect has been observed in several studies, some with more than 50,000 schizophrenic patients as subjects (Bradbury & Miller, 1985). The risk is greater at higher latitudes and disappears in the tropics (Kendell & Adams, 1991). Infections are likely to be the cause of this effect because at northern latitudes, viral epidemics are more common in autumn. For children born in late winter and spring, this corresponds to the second trimester of pregnancy – a crucial time in the development of the brain. The virus that has been most implicated in this effect is influenza, not least because there is also a rise in schizophrenia cases some four to six months after a new outbreak (Sham et al., 1992). But perhaps even more convincing is evidence from Brown et al. (2004) who found

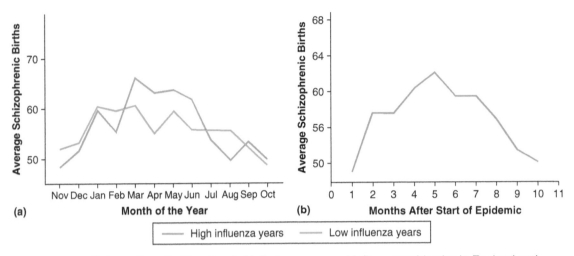

Figure 11.19   Relationship of schizophrenic births to season and influenza epidemics in England and Wales (1939–1960)

Source: Garrett and Hough (2021), from Sham, P. C. et al. (1992). Schizophrenia following pre-natal exposure to influenza epidemics between 1939 and 1960. *British Journal of Psychiatry*, 160, 461–466. Copyright 1992. Reprinted with permission of the publisher.

a sevenfold increased risk for schizophrenia when influenza antibodies were present in the mother. They also estimated that influenza infections account for 14% of all schizophrenia cases.

One curious risk factor for schizophrenia is the age of the father. There is an increased risk of schizophrenia in males, but not females, if the father's age at the time of conception exceeds 25 years. This risk increases by two-thirds when the parental age reaches 50 (Miller et al., 2010). The reasons for this are unknown, although it is possible that more mutations occur in paternal sperm cells as the father ages (Malaspina et al., 2001). The offspring of older fathers are also at an increased later risk of intellectual disability and autism spectrum disorders, whilst the offspring of young mothers are at an increased risk for substance use problems and attention deficit hyperactivity disorder (McGrath et al., 2014).

KEY TERMS: *vulnerability model, genetic variance, second trimester of pregnancy, influenza*

SUMMARY

Mental health problems are common. The most prevalent psychiatric disorder is depression which affects some 5% of the population. This condition can be a debilitating illness with low mood and a wide range of other behavioural effects. The first effective antidepressant to be developed was iproniazid (Marsilid) which increased levels of noradrenaline (NA) and serotonin (5-HT) in the brain by inhibiting the enzyme monoamine oxidase. Soon after its introduction in 1957, another effective antidepressant called impramine (Tofranil) was discovered which was a tricyclic compound. This drug also increased NA and 5-HT levels, but by blocking their respective reuptake pumps.

These findings, along with evidence linking reserpine with depression, led to the monoamine theory which proposed that depression was due to reduced levels of NA (and possibly 5-HT) at brain synapses. This idea provided a useful working hypothesis, although it is now known to be far too simple. One difficulty with the theory is that it takes some two to three weeks of antidepressant drug treatment before depression improves, although the uptake blockade is almost immediate. The cause of this delay appears to lie with the neurotransmitter receptors, including the alpha autoreceptors located on presynaptic neurons which control NA release. In addition, serotonergic receptors have also been implicated in this process. It is possible, therefore, that the cause of depression lies more with receptor sensitivity than with levels of neurotransmitter. An alternative theory is known as the permissive hypothesis which views depression as a result from an imbalance of 5-HT and NA brain systems. In 1987 the first selective serotonergic reuptake inhibitor (SSRI) called fluoxetine (Prozac) was marketed, which soon became the most popular antidepressant in the world. Since then there has also been the development of second-generation antidepressants, including specific NA reuptake inhibitors and 5-HT/NA uptake inhibitors.

Schizophrenia is a serious mental illness characterized by bizarre delusions, hallucinations, fragmented thought processes, and inappropriate emotions. This illness, which affects just under 1% of the population, has a strong genetic origin as shown by twin and adoption studies. It appears that the genetic influence manifests itself by predisposing the individual to become more vulnerable to 'stressful' environmental events. These events may also occur prenatally, including foetal influenza exposure, which can have a significant impact on the later development of the illness. The first successful antipsychotic drug was chlorpromazine (Thorazine) which became available in 1954, and this was followed by haloperidol (Haldol) in the early 1960s. Both drugs produced Parkinson's-like side effects (e.g. tremor and slow movement) which indicated they depleted the brain of dopamine (DA). This led to the idea that schizophrenia was caused by increased DA activity – a theory supported by the ability of the dopamine stimulant amphetamine to induce psychotic symptoms. The dopamine theory of schizophrenia was modified somewhat when it was discovered that chlorpromazine and haloperidol do not deplete the brain of DA. In fact, their pharmacological mode of action, discovered in the early 1970s, showed both drugs to be dopamine antagonists. Their antipsychotic effect also correlated with their potency at blocking D-2 dopamine receptors. Some studies, but not all, have shown increased numbers of DA receptors in the brain, raising the possibility that there are different types of this disorder (e.g. type 1 and type 2). A number of newer antipsychotic drugs have been developed, including clozapine which has little effect on D-2 receptors but blocks serotonergic 5-HT2 receptors. Clozapine is a prototype for the development of newer antipsychotic drugs, as well as stimulating new ideas about the biological basis of schizophrenia. A relatively new idea is the glutamate theory of schizophrenia which holds there is a deficiency in glutamate activity at the NMDA receptor and especially in the prefrontal cortex.

GO ONLINE

TEST YOUR UNDERSTANDING OF THIS CHAPTER AND VISIT HTTPS://STUDY.SAGEPUB.COM/WICKENS TO ACCESS INTERACTIVE 'DRAG AND DROP' LABELLING ACTIVITIES AND A FLASHCARD GLOSSARY.

MULTIPLE CHOICE QUESTIONS

Answer the questions below to test your understanding of this chapter's Learning Objectives. You'll find the answers at the end of the chapter.

1. Which of the following is not an example of an affective disorder?

   a. unipolar depression
   b. mania
   c. bipolar disorder
   d. schizophrenia

2. Which enzyme normally acts to break down excess amounts of synaptic catecholamines?

   a. adenylate cyclase
   b. cAMP
   c. monoamine oxidase
   d. adenosine triphosphate

3. What type of drug is fluoxetine (Prozac)?

   a. a selective serotonergic uptake blocker
   b. a monoamine oxidase inhibitor
   c. a tricyclic antidepressant
   d. a selective noradrenergic uptake blocker

4. Which of the following is an effective and widely used antipsychotic drug?

   a. reserpine
   b. haloperidol
   c. imipramine
   d. dexamethasone

5. How did Carlsson and Lindqvist (1963) explain the pharmacological action of chlorpromazine?

   a. it inhibited monoamine oxidase
   b. it blocked the reuptake of dopamine
   c. it blocked the release of dopamine
   d. it blocked dopamine receptors

6. Which of the following receptors has been most importantly implicated in the action of clozapine?

   a. the D-2 receptor
   b. the NMDA receptor
   c. the 5-HT2 receptor
   d. the NA beta receptor

FURTHER READING

Abel, T., & Nickl-Jockschat, T. (Eds.). (2016). *The neurobiology of schizophrenia*. Academic Press.
Written by various experts, this is a thorough overview of schizophrenia ranging from its genetic basis and neurochemistry (including the current status of the dopamine theory) to anatomical and functional aspects of brain involvement.

Charney, D., Nestler, E. J., Sklar, P., & Baxbaum, J. D. (Eds.). (2013). *Neurobiology of mental illness.* Oxford University Press.
A wide-ranging textbook with large sections on mood disorders and schizophrenia written from various neurobiological perspectives.

Cowen, P. J., Sharp, T., & Lau, J. Y. F. (Eds.). (2013). *Behavioral neurobiology of depression and its treatment*. Springer.
Relevant and informative chapters on the neurobiology of depression along with existing and novel treatments.

Gotlib, I. H., & Hammen, C. L. (Eds.). (2014). *Handbook of depression*. The Guilford Press.
A book that covers a lot of material, but with good chapters on the biology of depression and associated mood disorders.

Kasper, S., & Papadimitriou, G. N. (Eds.). (2009). *Schizophrenia: Biopsychological approaches and current challenges*. CRC Press.
Although written for experts, the selection of chapters on the neurobiology of schizophrenia are highly informative.

Lopez-Munoz, F., & Alamo, C. (Eds.). (2011). *Neurobiology of depression*. CRC Press.
Contains a number of chapters written by various experts that focus on the neural circuits of the brain that underlie depression.

McKenna, P. J. (2007). *Schizophrenia and related syndromes*. Routledge.
A very useful and readable overview of the many facets of schizophrenia research, including a good chapter on the importance of neurodevelopment.

Panksepp, J. (Ed.). (2003). *Textbook of biological psychiatry*. John Wiley.
A broad-ranging textbook, but the four chapters on the neurobiology and treatment of affective disorders and schizophrenia will prove very useful for the undergraduate student.

Ritsner, M. (Ed.). (2011). *Handbook of schizophrenic spectrum disorders. Volume 1: Conceptual issues and neurobiological advances*. Springer.
Provides the most up-to-date information on the origins, onset and outcomes of schizophrenic spectrum disorders.

Stahl, S. M. (2013). *Essential psychopharmacology*. Cambridge University Press.
An excellent textbook which focuses primarily on the neuropharmacological actions of drugs that are commonly used to treat mental illness, including antidepressants and antipsychotics.

12

DRUGS AND ADDICTION

LEARNING OBJECTIVES

After reading this chapter you should be able to:

- Outline how intracranial self-stimulation was discovered by Olds and Milner.

- Appreciate the importance of the medial forebrain bundle in drug use.

- Explain how dopamine is involved in reward.

- Elucidate how opiate substances such as heroin act on the brain.

- Understand the concept of addiction.

- Appreciate how pharmacological and environmental factors contribute to drug tolerance.

- Understand the importance of sensitisation and incentive salience.

- Specify the pharmacological effects of commonly used 'abused' drugs.

GO ONLINE

Test your understanding of this chapter and visit **https://study.sagepub.com/wickens** to access interactive 'Drag and Drop' labelling activities and a flashcard glossary.

INTRODUCTION

Human beings are hedonists. We spend a good part of our lives trying to obtain the things that give us pleasure – sex, chocolate, cake, watching football, or maybe even reading a good book. In this pursuit many of us also turn to the intoxicating and pleasurable properties of drugs, whether those are alcohol, cigarettes, caffeine, or illicit substances.

Humans have been taking psychoactive agents since the dawn of civilization. The use of the coca plant can be traced back 7,000 years, opium 6,000 years, and the consumption of alcohol goes back so far it has become lost in the mists of time. But the oldest recorded substance appears to be arecoline, a chemical found in the betel nut, which was chewed 13,000 years ago in Timor (Sullivan & Hagen, 2002). Drug taking is therefore as old as civilization itself.

Yet as we all know, drugs are not without their dangers. A serious risk is addiction – sometimes described as a compulsive engagement with rewarding stimuli despite having adverse consequences – which can arise from using commonly used drugs such as nicotine and alcohol. Addiction affects people in all societies and often becomes a major medical problem with its unhealthy lifestyles leading to physical and psychiatric illness. There are also the enormous societal costs of compulsive drug use, including family and community breakdown, increased crime and reduced productivity. And at the centre of this problem is the individual whose self-destructive behaviour is often highly resistant to treatment.

The neuroscientist has a vital role to play in the challenge of addiction, not least in explaining why certain drugs act on the brain to produce dependence, and in helping to develop better medical therapies to treat the problem. This will benefit us all. Few of us will go through life without developing an unhealthy dependence on certain drugs or pleasurable pursuits. In fact, according to the UK charity Action on Addiction, one in three people are addicted to something which can lead to compulsive and harmful use.

THE DISCOVERY OF PLEASURE SYSTEMS IN THE BRAIN

The existence of neural systems in the brain responsible for mediating pleasure and reward were first discovered by James Olds and a research student called Peter Milner at McGill University in the early 1950s. At the time, Milner was finishing his PhD in the laboratory of George Hebb, and Olds (a social psychologist with an interest in motivation) had just joined the department. In a joint project, Olds and Milner began to examine whether electrical stimulation of brain areas that increased arousal could improve learning. The inexperienced Olds performed his first stereotaxic operation by attempting to implant an electrode into a rat's reticular formation. Keen to test his animal, Olds discovered that if he placed it into a large open box and stimulated the electrode with a weak electric current, the rat would show a strong inclination to return and remain in the exact location where it had received stimulation. This unexpected finding only made sense if the rat was finding the stimulation pleasurable, but Olds and Milner were in for another surprise. When the location of the electrode placement was examined after all the behavioural testing, they found it was not placed in the reticular formation, but in a region close to the hypothalamus called the septal area. In fact Olds in his first attempt at stereotaxic surgery had missed the reticular formation by about 4 mm – a considerable distance for a rat's brain (Wickens, 2019b).

But was the electrical stimulation really acting as a reward? To examine this possibility further, Olds and Milner trained their rat to run through a T-maze, where the choice of the two goal arms had different consequences. In one of the arms, Olds and Milner administered brain stimulation before the food was reached, whilst in the other arm the animal was allowed to consume the food unperturbed. The question was: what arm would the rat choose when given a free choice? Olds and Milner found the rat always chose the arm where it had received stimulation. Despite being hungry, the animal would stop at the stimulation point and ignore the food that was just inches away.

Following this discovery, Olds and Milner soon developed a more efficient way of testing for the effects of brain stimulation by constructing

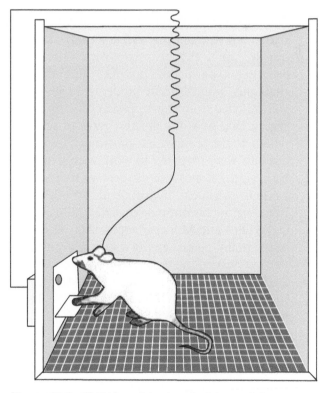

Figure 12.1   Experimental set-up for intracranial self-stimulation

Source: Wickens (2009)

an operant box in which a rat was able to stimulate itself (self-stimulation). By pressing its lever, the rat could now receive a small burst of electrical current which flowed through its electrode via a lead that passed through the chamber's ceiling (see Figure 12.1). Thus, the animal had full control over the stimulation it received, and clearly it would not self-stimulate in this situation if this was not pleasurable. But more important for the experimenters was that the rewarding properties of the stimulation could be quantified by counting the number of bar presses the rat was prepared to make. As Olds later recounted, the first animal tested in this procedure ended all doubts that the self-stimulation was highly rewarding. The rat responded every second or so, and when the current was terminated, it continued to press the lever for several minutes before giving up. Olds and Milner had in fact invented a new research paradigm enabling the reward systems of the brain to be mapped and closely examined (Olds & Milner, 1954). It would lead to many thousands of research papers by different groups in the decades afterward.

KEY TERMS: *septal area, operant box, self-stimulation*

THE MEDIAL FOREBRAIN BUNDLE

One of the first objectives for Olds and Milner was to identify the brain sites giving rise to self-stimulation, and it soon became apparent these were distributed throughout the brain. The areas from which the highest rates of response were obtained (e.g. around 500 bar presses per hour) included the septum, amygdala and anterior hypothalamus, whereas more moderate levels of responding (e.g. 200 bar presses per hour) were elicited from the hippocampus, cingulate gyrus and nucleus accumbens. But the region that gave the greatest rates of self-stimulation was the **lateral hypothalamus** which could produce bar-pressing rates exceeding 1,000 presses per hour. Moreover, animals were prepared to work with extreme vigour, and ignore basic drives such as hunger, thirst and sleep to receive its rewarding effects. In fact, one rat with an electrode in the lateral hypothalamus made 2,000 responses per hour for 24 consecutive hours before becoming exhausted (Olds, 1958).

As Olds and Milner mapped their electrode placements, it became clear that most of the brain regions giving rise to self-stimulation formed part of a large multisynaptic pathway called the **medial forebrain bundle** (MFB) (see Figure 12.2). This is essentially a collection of over 50 fibre bundles that interconnect the forebrain and the midbrain in both directions (Coenen et al., 2018). It has also been likened to a major highway joining the two coasts of a continent (Graham, 1990). If we extend this analogy further, then the central hub of this highway would appear, on first sight at least, to be the lateral hypothalamus. Although the lateral hypothalamus is an important cellular region in its own right, it also contains many fibres of passage (perhaps up to 10 million) which pass through without making synaptic contact. Most of these make up the central conduit of the MFB. The major areas connected by these fibres include the **limbic system**, **striatum** and frontal cortex of the forebrain, and the **ventral tegmental area** (VTA) and **periaqueductal grey area** (PGA) of the midbrain.

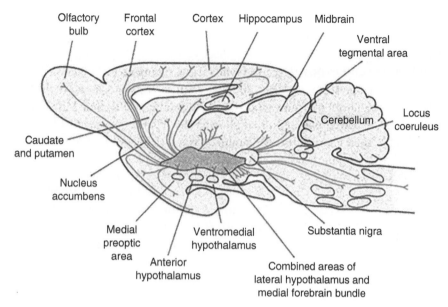

Figure 12.2   The medial forebrain bundle
Source: Wickens (2009)

The pivotal location of the lateral hypothalamus in the circuitry of the MFB initially led Olds to believe it was the main centre that governed reward and reinforcement. This was consistent with the idea that the MFB acted to collect information from all the various brain sites involved in pleasurable activities such as eating, drinking, aggression and sexual behaviour, and to channel this to the lateral hypothalamus where the rewarding event took place. However this theory was disproven when it was found that large lesions of the MFB did not always abolish self-stimulation, and that the lateral hypothalamus could be lesioned without significantly affecting self-stimulation from other MFB sites. Despite this, one part of the MFB was shown to be necessary for self-stimulation – namely the pathway from the hypothalamic region to the midbrain (Olds & Fobes, 1981).

KEY TERMS: *lateral hypothalamus, medial forebrain bundle, limbic system, striatum, frontal cortex (forebrain), ventral tegmental area, periaqueductal grey area (midbrain)*

IDENTIFYING THE IMPORTANCE OF DOPAMINE IN REWARD

When Olds and Milner first made their seminal discoveries, little was known about the neurotransmitter systems in the MFB, although **noradrenaline** (NA) and **dopamine** (DA) were suspected of being involved in reward – not least because the antagonists reserpine and chlorpromazine diminished hypothalamic self-stimulation, whereas amphetamine facilitated it. These findings took on a new significance when researchers began to map out the brain's catecholamine pathways in the 1960s. The breakthrough had occurred when it was discovered that adrenal gland cells treated with formaldehyde and exposed to ultraviolet light fluoresced. This reaction occurred because the catecholamines combined with formaldehyde produce light-emitting chemicals. The method was applied to brain sections by Dahlstrom and Fuxe in 1964. These researchers also realized they could distinguish between NA and DA (which fluoresced as different hues of green), allowing their pathways to be mapped in the brain under ultraviolet light.

One of the main findings to emerge from this work was that the catecholamine pathways of the brain arose from cell groups in the midbrain and upper brain stem. There are two main NA pathways. The dorsal tegmental tract arises from the **locus coeruleus** with its fibres distributed through the forebrain, whilst the ventral tegmental tract originates from several brainstem nuclei and goes to the hypothalamus. In contrast, the DA cell groups arise from the ventral tegmental area (VTA) and **substantia nigra**. These form the mesolimbic pathway projecting to the nucleus accumbens and amygdala, the mesocortical pathway to the frontal cortex, and the nigral-striatal pathway innervating the striatum. Importantly, all of these pathways were found to make up a significant part of the MFB which indicated that the catecholamines were involved in reward and pleasure.

During the 1970s, it became clear that DA was the most important catecholamine underlying the rewarding effects of self-stimulation. This idea had originated when it was found that the dopaminergic antagonists chlorpromazine and haloperidol reduced self-stimulation from electrodes placed in many areas of the MFB. But this idea gained further credibility when it also became apparent that high rates of self-stimulation were obtainable from the VTA, and that this effect depended on the integrity of its ascending DA pathways. Indeed, when researchers lesioned these pathways using 6-hydroxydopamine (a highly selective neurotoxin for DA neurons), self-stimulation of the VTA was significantly reduced (Philips & Fibiger, 1989; Wise, 2005).

KEY TERMS: *noradrenaline, dopamine, locus coeruleus, ventral tegmental area, substantia nigra, 6-hydroxydopamine*

CHEMICAL SELF-STIMULATION

Some of the strongest evidence linking DA with reward has come from experiments where animals self-inject with drugs (chemical self-administration). Much like the electrical self-stimulation procedure, animals can also learn how to bar press for a chemical injection that passes directly into their bloodstream by means of a catheter. This technique was first developed by Weeks (1962) who found that rats would quickly learn to press a lever in an operant box for an intravenous injection of morphine. Soon after this, Thompson and Schuster (1964) performed the first intravenous self-administration experiments using morphine with rhesus monkeys – obtaining similar patterns of behaviour.

The chemical self-stimulation procedure has proven very useful for examining how addictive drugs work on the brain and why they can lead to dependence. This is because many of the substances that animals self-administer are also the ones abused by humans (Belluzzi & Stein, 2001; Panlilo & Goldberg, 2007). For example, animals will self-administer opiates such as morphine and heroin, the major stimulants including cocaine and amphetamine, the depressants ethanol and barbiturates, and certain hallucinogens such as marijuana and phencyclidine. The two exceptions to the rule appear to be nicotine and LSD (Griffiths et al., 1980). The drugs self-administered by humans and animals are not only similar but have also been reported consistently for many species, including rats and mice, monkeys, cats, dogs, and even pigs.

The self-administration of drugs by animals also frequently resembles the pattern of use shown by humans. For example, the self-injection of amphetamine and cocaine in monkeys often leads to alternating periods of drug intake and abstinence. During drug-taking periods, which can last for a few days, there is an increase in responding with little eating or sleep. This is followed by a 'down' period when the animal terminates its drug use and exhibits little behavioural activity. A similar type of pattern can occur in humans with unlimited access to cocaine and amphetamine. Indeed, it is not uncommon for addicts who use intravenous amphetamine to repeatedly inject the drug for three to six days, during which time the user remains continuously awake. Following a 'run' the user becomes so exhausted and unable to get more pleasure from the drug that they sleep instead. This may last 12 to 18 hours, following which the user may feel so lethargic and depressed that they begin a new bout of drug taking (Hancock & McKim, 2017).

Such free access to cocaine can have fatal consequences. In one study where monkeys were allowed unlimited access to cocaine, all the animals suffered from convulsions and died within 30 days (Deneau et al., 1969). To avoid this problem in self-administration studies, researchers typically have to use a procedure where access to the drug is limited to several hours per day. This type of self-administration procedure also works well with rats. For example, George Koob trained rats to self-administer cocaine for either one hour each day (short access) or six hours each day (long access). The animals that self-administered for six hours a day were found to show symptoms resembling cocaine dependence, including an escalation of the dose over time, and increased administration when the cocaine was made available again (Koob & Le Moal, 2006).

KEY TERMS: *chemical self-administration*

THE NEUROPHARMACOLOGY OF COCAINE AND AMPHETAMINE

Cocaine is a naturally occurring alkaloid derived from the leaves of the coca plant (*erythroxylum coca*) native to the slopes of the Andes in South America. Its leaves have been chewed for thousands of years and used by the local Indians to prevent fatigue and increase energy in their harsh mountainous conditions. But as a drug of abuse, it is a white powder that is commonly snorted, smoked, or injected into a vein. In pharmacological terms, cocaine acts as an indirect-acting agonist by blocking the presynaptic reuptake of dopamine, thereby increasing its concentration in the synapse. Cocaine exerts a similar effect on NA and 5-HT systems (Ciccarone, 2011). Interestingly, it also has an anaesthetic action which blocks sodium channels and prevents the generation and conduction of nerve impulses (Knuepfer, 2003). For this reason cocaine can be used as a local anaesthetic in dentistry (novocaine is chemically related to cocaine). Coca leaves were also one of the original ingredients in the popular drink Coca-Cola (Pendergrast, 2013).

Strictly speaking, **amphetamine** (α-methylphenethylamine) was discovered by Barger and Dale in 1910, and first synthesized by Gordon Alles in 1927 (Heal et al., 2013). But today, the term 'amphetamine' more commonly refers to a group of synthetic drugs which includes amphetamine sulphate (Benzedrine), dextroamphetamine sulphate (Dexedrine) and methamphetamine (known on the street as *meth* or *crystal*). Unlike cocaine, all these compounds resemble the chemical structure of DA and NA. They also have a different mode of action. Instead of blocking reuptake, amphetamines are taken up into the endings of catecholaminergic neurons where they cause the release of DA and NA from their storage vesicles (Robertson et al., 2009). Thus, whilst cocaine and amphetamine exert different pharmacological effects, they both enhance catecholaminergic neurotransmission.

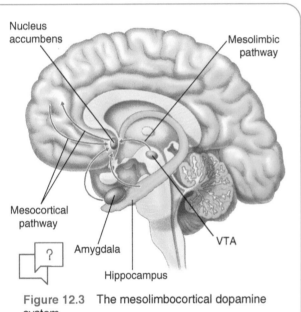

Figure 12.3 The mesolimbocortical dopamine system

Source: Garrett and Hough (2018)

As we have seen, cocaine and amphetamine are highly reinforcing, leading to compulsive use in self-administration paradigms. What then accounts for this effect? The evidence shows that DA is the most important neurotransmitter for this reinforcing action. For example, a number of DAergic drugs can be used as substitutes for amphetamine and cocaine in the self-stimulation paradigm, including the D-2 receptor agonists apomorphine and bromocriptine (Koob & LeMoal, 2006; Norman et al., 2011). DA receptor antagonists also modulate cocaine self-administration, showing a dose-dependent biphasic effect. For example, selective antagonists for both D-1 and D-2 receptors increase cocaine self-administration in response to lower doses of antagonist, but decrease self-administration in response to higher doses (Baik, 2013).

One brain structure that has been shown to be particularly important for the reinforcing effects of cocaine and amphetamine in animal studies is the **nucleus accumbens**. This is located in the ventral medial striatum and it receives dopamine input from the mesolimbic pathway originating in the VTA (Willuhn et al., 2010). Combined with the dopaminergic pathway to the frontal cortex this is sometimes called the mesolimbocortical dopamine system (see Figure 12.3). The nucleus accumbens is an important brain region for mediating a variety of behaviours associated with reward (see Salgado & Kaplitt, 2015) and often regarded as the main pleasure centre of the brain (Berridge & Kringelbach, 2015). Indeed, just about all drugs abused by humans increase dopamine levels in this brain region (Adinoff, 2004; Di Chiara & Imperto, 1988). As might be expected, an intravenous injection of amphetamine and cocaine causes significant DA release in the nucleus accumbens – an effect that does not occur in other dopaminergic regions (Fibiger et al., 1992). Animals will also self-administer dopamine agonists into the nucleus accumbens (Carlezon et al., 1995). This type of drug-taking behaviour is greatly reduced by lesions of the nucleus accumbens, but not the frontal cortex or striatum (Baik, 2013; Koob & Goeders, 1989).

KEY TERMS: *cocaine, indirect-acting agonist, dopamine, amphetamine, nucleus accumbens, mesolimbic pathway*

SPECIAL INTEREST 12.1

LAUGHTER, LIKE COCAINE, TICKLES THE NUCLEUS ACCUMBENS

Few would deny that laughter is an essential part of life. Most babies laugh out loud for the first time when they are only three or four months old, and this reaction is largely innate since children who are born blind and deaf still retain the ability to laugh (Gervais & Wilson, 2005). As adults, we laugh around 17 times a day, although this figure can vary from 0 to over 80 depending on the individual (Martin & Kuiper, 1999). Laughter is odd: sometimes we laugh at the most mundane and ordinary things in life, and at other times when nervous, embarrassed or disappointed, yet nobody is quite sure why we laugh. Most likely, laughter serves several functions (Provine, 2001). It may reduce stress and help release pent-up negative emotions such as anger or anxiety. This is seen when a well-timed joke eases the tension in a difficult situation. Laughter may also allow people to view a problem or issue with a new perspective. Sick humour, for example, might allow us to confront issues that we would not normally want to contemplate. Certainly laughter helps strengthen social bonds as it is a sign that we are feeling comfortable and relaxed in our surroundings, and a vital component of children's play. And for some mysterious reason we laugh when being tickled, yet can't tickle ourselves! Despite this, we should not lose sight of the fact that we laugh because it is pleasurable. One might predict, therefore, that laughter will have a neural basis by stimulating the pleasure systems of the brain.

One of the first studies to address this issue was undertaken by Mobbs et al. (2003), who used fMRI to visualize the brain activity of 16 subjects presented with 84 cartoons that were rated as very funny or not funny (the latter had the written cues omitted). It was found that the funniest cartoons activated the mesolimbic dopaminergic reward system. More specifically, activity in the nucleus accumbens correlated with how funny the subject thought the cartoon was –

(Continued)

the funniest jokes causing more activation of the nucleus accumbens than the boring ones. But several other brain areas were also stimulated by the humorous jokes, including the amygdala, the left frontal cortex including Broca's area, and the motor cortex – the latter most likely responsible for producing the physical movement of laughter (Fried et al., 1998).

Since the pioneering study by Mobbs et al., the study of humour and laughter (known as gelotology) has become an important research area. It is now recognized that humour affects a large brain network, including the superior and basal temporal lobes, striatum and amygdala. In addition, parallel activation of frontal areas appears to be important for the recognition of facial expressions involved in humour (Hennenlotter et al., 2005). Another area attracting interest is the anterior cingulate cortex. For example, Caruana et al. (2015) have stimulated this region in humans and found areas where laughter was produced with mirth (amusement) and other areas where only smiling was produced. The authors conclude that the anterior cingulate cortex is involved in both the affective and motor aspects of laughing.

The finding that funny cartoons activate the same circuits in the brain as addictive drugs such as cocaine helps explain our unique 'addiction' to humour. But, laughter does more than just make us feel good by stimulating our nucleus accumbens. There is evidence that it can reduce feelings of pain, boost the immune system, decrease cortisol levels and lower blood pressure (Martin, 2001). Long-lived persons also typically have a great sense of humour (Perls et al., 1999). Thus laughter is not only a sure sign of happiness – but is arguably better than any drug.

SENSITIZATION AND INCENTIVE SALIENCE

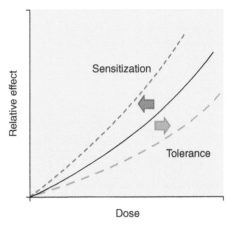

Figure 12.4 Change in dose response curve with tolerance and sensitization

Source: Higgs et al. (2020)

An interesting effect of stimulant use, which occurs with both cocaine and amphetamine, is behavioural sensitization. This is where repeated use of these drugs causes a progressively greater and more enduring behavioural response, which is the opposite of drug tolerance to be discussed later (see Figure 12.4). For example, when laboratory rats are given stimulants at low doses, this causes increased motor activity. With repeated administration this activity becomes more intense and new stereotyped behaviours emerge, such as licking, gnawing and sniffing. These behavioural effects are highly persistent and can occur a year after the last drug exposure in rats (Paulson et al., 1991). The chronic administration of cocaine also lowers the threshold for convulsions. Although sensitization is most associated with the use of cocaine and amphetamine, it can occur with other drugs of abuse including nicotine, ethanol, phencyclidine, MDMA, and even morphine (see Steketee & Kalivas, 2011).

Drug sensitization is believed to be an important mechanism underlying the development of addiction, leading to increased cravings and compulsive use of these drugs. This idea has led to the incentive sensitization theory of addiction (Robinson & Berridge, 1993) which proposes that compulsive drug-taking behaviour develops from a long-lasting sensitization of the mesolimbic DA pathway. One consequence of this enhanced DA activity is that the addict becomes 'sensitized' to drug-related stimuli – a phenomenon called incentive salience. This makes drug-associated stimuli difficult for addicts to ignore and amplifies their motivation for taking drugs, leading to strong cravings which gain control over voluntary behaviour. It is also interesting to note this theory does not associate the stimulation of DA in the nucleus accumbens with reward or pleasure. Rather, DA is involved in making stimuli associated with drugs or other rewards such as food and sex more salient, and in doing so it triggers desire. Looked at in this new light, the nucleus accumbens is involved in the processing of positive and desirable stimuli (Berridge & Robinson, 2016; Smith et al., 2011). A related view of nucleus accumbens function emphasizes its importance in integrating the cognitive and emotional information involved in action selection (Floresco, 2015). This view of the nucleus accumbens, therefore, holds that it is too simple for it to be regarded as a simple pleasure centre.

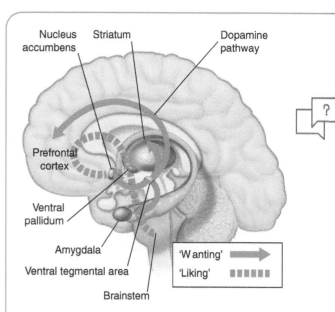

Figure 12.5   Brain areas involved in wanting and liking
Source: Carolina Hrejsa/Body Scientific Intl. in Gaskin (2021)

Berridge and Robinson (2016) also highlight the distinction between *wanting* and *liking* in the motivation for drug taking. In essence, they define *wanting* as strong cravings leading to drug-seeking behaviour – a type of motivation which occurs when the addicted person is exposed to the environmental cues (objects, places, people etc.) associated with drug taking. This craving is believed to involve sensitization and incentive salience associated with DA functioning of the mesolimbic and mesocortical pathways – including the VTA, nucleus accumbens, amygdala and frontal cortex. In contrast, *liking* is the pleasurable sensations or the euphoric 'high' of drug taking. According to Berridge and Robinson this is associated with several 'hedonistic hotspots' in the brain (Adinoff, 2004). Although these hotspots include the nucleus accumbens and prefrontal cortex (as well as the insular and orbitofrontal cortex), they do not believe this type of euphoric sensation simply involves increased DA activity. Instead, the pleasure of drug taking, Berridge and Robinson argue, is more likely to be dependent on neural systems involving opioid and endocannibinoid transmitters (see later).

KEY TERMS: *behavioural sensitization, incentive sensitization theory of addiction, incentive salience*

GLUTAMATE IS ALSO INVOLVED IN SENSITIZATION

The incentive sensitization theory of addition shows that sensitization involves several brain regions, and is also influenced by drug experience (Vanderschuren & Kalivas, 2000). There is also little doubt that DA is involved in the process of sensitization. For example, studies which have measured the extracellular concentration of DA in the nucleus accumbens using microdialysis, have shown there is a synaptic increase of this neurotransmitter when sensitization is produced after repeated cocaine and amphetamine injections (Singer et al., 2017). In other words, as behavioural sensitization develops, this is accompanied by the release of greater amounts of DA in the nucleus accumbens.

However, dopamine is not the only neurotransmitter associated with behavioural sensitization. In recent years, the focus has shifted to the involvement of **glutamate** in the mesolimbic system (Batten et al., 2018). Glutamate-containing fibres reach the VTA and the dopaminergic axon terminals of the nucleus accumbens from the prefrontal cortex, amygdala and hippocampus. Being an excitatory neurotransmitter, glutamate increases the activity of neurons in the VTA, which causes DA release in the nucleus accumbens. In addition, glutamate facilitates DA transmission in the nucleus accumbens by acting on glutamic AMPA receptors located on the DA terminals (see Tzschentke & Schmidt, 2003). Thus this important dopaminergic pathway is under higher control, with glutamate exerting an important modulatory effect on its expression (Tecuapetla et al., 2010). This glutamate involvement is also likely to be important for the development of sensitization.

KEY TERMS: *sensitization, glutamate*

AN INTRODUCTION TO OPIATE DRUGS

Ask the average person what is the most dangerous addictive drug, and the probable reply will be **heroin** – a substance often seen as the ultimate evil, synonymous with destitute behaviour and crime. About two-thirds of people who begin taking heroin will become dependent on it (Warburton et al., 2005), and a fair percentage of these will turn to crime in order to fund their habit. Heroin addicts who inject the drug also run a high risk of health problems, including hepatitis, AIDs, and fatal overdose which occurs in around 2% of users annually (Robson, 1999). Although not everyone fits this bleak picture, there are many users who do. Indeed, a Home Affairs Select Committee in 2004 reported there were 250,000 heroin addicts in the UK who fuelled drug crime worth some £20 billion per year – a typical addict spending some £8,000 on the drug in this period (Ashton, 2002). As if this was not bad enough, a 33-year study of 581 male heroin addicts, found that 49% were dead by the end of the study, with an average death age of 46 years (Hser et al., 2001). About 25% of these had died of drug overdose, and 20% from homicide, suicide or an accident. A further

15% of this sample had chronic liver disease. Half of the survivors in this group were still using heroin, and those who had managed to abstain for five years or more still returned to its use at certain times. This shows that heroin addiction is most probably a lifelong condition (Garrett, 2015).

Heroin belongs to a class of drugs known as opiates which refers to any substance that has properties similar to opium – whether it is natural or synthetic (the latter chemicals are sometimes referred to as opioids). Derived from slitting the seed capsules of the poppy *Papaver somniferum*, opium is a thick milky liquid that is dehydrated to produce a putty-like substance. It also has a long history of human use. The Babylonians cultivated poppies and isolated opium at the end of the third millennium BC, and called it the plant of joy. It is also mentioned in the Ebers papyrus (c. 1500 BC) where it is recommended for crying children (Crocq, 2007). Opium was widely used in Britain from the sixteenth century, where it treated a wide range of ailments up until the nineteenth century. In fact the demand for opium was so great that it was largely responsible for Britain's wars against China in 1839–42 and 1856–58, which led to the annexing of Hong Kong in 1842 and 1860 as part of the war repatriations.

The main psychoactive agent in opium, making up about 12% of its weight, is morphine. First isolated by Friedrich Serturner in 1803, who named it after Morpheus, the Greek god of sleep, morphine is ten times more potent than raw opium, and was found to be a powerful analgesic, especially after the invention of the hypodermic needle in the 1850s. It is hard to imagine a more important drug for the relief of pain in current medicine. In 1874, a new opiate was synthesized in St Mary's Hospital, London, by the chemist C. R. Alder Wright, who called it diacetylmorphine. This was subsequently produced commercially as heroin (from the word *heroisch* meaning 'heroic' or 'strong') by the German Bayer drug company who marketed it as a cough suppressant. Because of its high lipid solubility which allows it to rapidly pass the blood–brain barrier into the CNS, heroin is some ten times more potent than morphine when injected into the blood. There is little point in taking heroin orally because it is broken down into morphine by the liver, thus losing much of its potency.

KEY TERMS: *heroin, opiates, opium, morphine, diacetylmorphine*

THE ROUTE TO OPIATE ADDICTION: TOLERANCE AND WITHDRAWAL

Most people who become addicted to opiates follow a pathway that takes them from smoking heroin (or sometimes snorting) to regular intravenous injections. Smoking heroin – a practice known as chasing the dragon – is undertaken for its pleasant sedating qualities. However, even at this early stage, tolerance to the drug can rapidly occur with regular use. Drug tolerance refers to a situation where there is a decreasing response to a repeated dose of the drug, which often causes the individual to administer a higher dose to obtain the original pleasurable or beneficial effects. Opiate drugs are particularly renowned for their ability to induce tolerance, and it is not unusual for a user to increase their consumption tenfold after three or four months, resulting in a dosage that may have proven fatal first time around. Despite this, tolerance does not occur at the same rate for all of heroin's effects. For example, the constriction of the pupils only partially disappears with continued opiate use, and the constipating effects of these drugs rarely change (Hancock & McKim, 2017).

As the user becomes tolerant to the pleasant sedating effects of smoking heroin, this may encourage them to inject the drug. Once heroin enters the brain, it is converted to morphine and binds rapidly to opioid receptors (Volkow, 2014). This typically produces a surge of euphoria accompanied by a warm flushing of the skin, a dry mouth, and a heavy feeling in the extremities. After the initial effects wear off, the user will often be drowsy for several hours in a dreamy state, with depressed breathing and clouded mental function. In his book *Junky* William Burroughs described the feeling as being similar to floating without an outline in a bath of warm salt water.

However, of course, this increased usage is likely to lead to further drug tolerance which inevitably encourages the user to up their dosage. In the case of heroin, it is not unusual for a first-time user to use between 5 and 20 mg a day, while an established addict might require several hundred mg per day. But this leads to other problems – not least the risk of physical dependence where the body adapts to the chronic exposure to the drug. In turn, dependence leads to an increased likelihood of withdrawal symptoms when the drug effects start to wear off. The symptoms of opiate withdrawal include restlessness, muscle aches, insomnia, vomiting, cold skin ('cold turkey') and restless legs. These normally peak 24–48 hours after the last dose of heroin and subside after about a week, although they can last for longer in some individuals. For most addicts, the best 'cure' for these unpleasant withdrawal symptoms is a further 'fix' of the drug which will provide some relief. This, of course, is a strong motive for further use. Unfortunately, such repeated heroin use can result in heroin use disorder – a chronic relapsing illness that goes beyond physical dependence which is characterized by uncontrollable drug-seeking, regardless of the consequences (National Institute on Drug Abuse, 2018).

KEY TERMS: *drug tolerance, physical dependence, withdrawal symptoms, heroin use disorder*

THE BRAIN SITES OF OPIATE ADDICTION

Opiate drugs are self-administered intravenously by laboratory animals, showing they have reinforcing and pleasurable effects. In one study, when rhesus monkeys were given a choice of self-administering either cocaine or morphine, it was found they tended to inject themselves with both drugs, but at different times of the day – a combination that often had eventual fatal consequences for the animal (Deneau et al., 1969). Like humans, when allowed free access to morphine or heroin, monkeys increase their dose over time with few or no periods of abstinence or withdrawal. A ten-fold increase of heroin over a time span of 90 days is not uncommon (Griffiths et al., 1980). Moreover, when the opiates are discontinued, this leads to an abstinence syndrome where the animal presses the lever almost continuously in an attempt to receive further injections (Negus & Rice, 2009). Lever pressing for small doses of heroin will persist long after its availability has been discontinued (Gerak et al., 2009).

Both morphine and heroin work as agonists at opioid receptors. These sites, which were first discovered in the early 1970s (see Snyder & Pasternak, 2003), belong to a family of proteins known as G protein-coupled receptors. Three different types of opioid receptor are found in the brain and spinal cord – and these are mu (μ), delta (δ) and kappa (κ). Morphine and heroin are agonists for the μ-receptor, but have relatively little effect on the κ and σ subtypes (Koob & Bloom, 1988). The μ-opioid receptors exist mainly on axon terminals in the **substantia gelatinosa** of the spinal cord and the midbrain's periaqueductal grey region – both being crucially involved in pain processing. But in addition, μ-opioid receptors are located in the VTA, nucleus accumbens, amygdala and cerebral cortex. This distribution also shows that μ-opioid receptors have a close association with the dopaminergic systems of the brain which is likely to account for their pleasurable effects. Consequently, these neural systems are also most likely to underlie opiate addiction (De Vries & Shippenberg, 2002).

Although the neural circuitry underlying opiate addiction is complex (see Kosten & George, 2002), μ-receptors are located on GABAergic interneurons in the VTA, which synapse with the dopaminergic containing neurons to the nucleus accumbens. The result of this interneuron inhibition is an excitation of the DA neurons. As might be expected, rats will readily self-administer an opioid receptor agonist into the VTA, showing that these μ-receptors are critically involved in reinforcement (Le Merrer et al., 2009). A second mechanism appears to involve μ-receptor inhibition on the presynaptic terminals of the DA neurons in the nucleus accumbens (Gaskin, 2021; Margolis et al., 2014) which also lead to increased DA release (see Figure 12.6). In addition to feelings of pleasure, opioid μ-receptors in the nucleus accumbens are involved in positive social reward (Trezza et al., 2011) and have been implicated in encoding environmental stimuli and events (Simmons & Self, 2009). These social-based experiences may also be a factor in encouraging relapse during periods of opiate abstinence

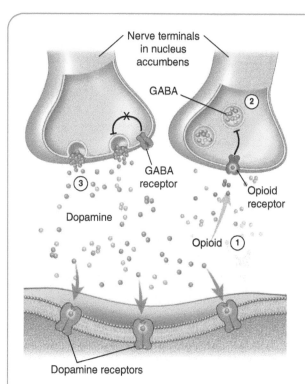

Figure 12.6 How opiate mu receptors stimulate dopamine release in the nucleus accumbens.
(1) Opioids such as morphine bind to opioid receptors located on GABAergic neurons. (2) GABAergic neurons are therefore inhibited and their inhibitory effect on dopaminergic neurons in the nucleus accumbens is removed. (3) This results in an increase of dopamine release in the nucleus accumbens.

Source: Amanda Tomasikiewicz/Body Scientific Intl. in Gaskin (2021)

Some of the strongest evidence supporting μ-opioid receptor involvement in addiction, however, has come from the development of genetic strains of knockout mice which lack the μ-opioid receptor. The experimental investigation of these animals reveals they receive no analgesic benefits from morphine. Nor do they self-administer and become physically dependent on this drug (Matthes et al., 1996). Even more remarkable, the reinforcing properties of alcohol, cannabinoids and nicotine are also strongly diminished in these mice (Kieffer & Gavériaux-Ruff, 2002). A closer examination of μ-opioid receptor knockout mice has allowed the identification of several genes that are associated with mu receptor signalling. Although the functions of these are uncertain, they are expressed in a complex neural network including the nucleus accumbens, amygdala, prefrontal cortex and hippocampus (Contet et al., 2004).

> **KEY TERMS:** *mu (μ), delta (δ), and kappa (κ) receptors, substantia gelatinosa, periaqueductal grey region, GABAergic interneurons, nucleus accumbens, knockout mice*

OPIATE TOLERANCE

Perhaps the most remarkable characteristic of opiate drugs is the rapidity by which tolerance occurs to most of their behavioural effects. As we have seen, a decrease in pharmacologic response following repeated or prolonged drug administration is one of the most distinctive aspects of heroin use, and this increased tolerance is associated with its high addictive potential – not least because abstinence can lead to the emergence of withdrawal symptoms. Although marked tolerance develops to the analgesic, euphorigenic and sedative effects of opiates, it also occurs with respect to the amount needed to kill (i.e. its lethal dose). For example, a long-term and experienced opiate user might be able to self-administer 2 grams of morphine intravenously over a period of 2–3 hours without a significant change in their blood pressure or heart rate (Koob & LeMoal, 2006). The lethal dose of morphine in a non-tolerant individual, however, is much less: about 200 milligrams. And for some individuals it might even be as low as 60 mg (Christiansen, 2020).

What causes drug tolerance? The answer to this question is complicated because different types of tolerance exist – some of which are biological and others behavioural. We will examine the biologic ones first. When a drug is administered over a long period of time, a number of adaptive bodily changes are likely to occur. These may include, for example, an upregulation of various enzymes involved in the metabolism of the drug, resulting in a smaller amount of that drug reaching its action site. This is called dispositional tolerance and it enables the body to become more efficient at metabolizing a drug and eliminating it. Dispositional tolerance, for example, is readily seen at work in people who regularly consume alcohol, because their drinking will increase levels of the enzyme **alcohol dehydrogenase** in the stomach and liver, which speeds up its metabolism. Another form of tolerance occurs when the effectiveness of a drug on its site of action is reduced. For example, this type of effect may occur when receptors become desensitized when regularly exposed to a high level of some substance. Indeed, acute desensitization of mu opioid receptors is thought to be the initial step in the development of tolerance to opioids (Allouche et al., 2014). This is otherwise known as pharmacodynamic tolerance (Dumas & Pollock, 2008).

One brain structure that has been implicated in the pharmacodynamic tolerance to opiate drugs is the locus coeruleus. As we have seen in the previous chapter, the locus coeruleus is the major noradrenergic nucleus of the brain, which gives rise to fibres that innervate extensive areas of the forebrain. It is also a chemical system that appears to regulate cortical arousal. The neurons of the locus coeruleus are strongly inhibited by opiates such as heroin, but show a 'rebound' increase in neural activity when such drugs are discontinued. Thus the noradrenergic neurons of the brain nucleus become hyperactive during opiate withdrawal (Ivanov & Ashton-Jones, 2001). The importance of this effect is demonstrated by the finding that clonidine (an α_2-noradrenergic agonist) which inhibits neural activity in the locus coeruleus, is effective at suppressing withdrawal symptoms in opiate users. This drug is now widely used to help detoxify heroin users (Gowing et al., 2016).

But the locus coeruleus is not the only brain area responsible for producing withdrawal symptoms. For example, Koob et al. (1992) made rats physically opiate dependent by implanting them with morphine pellets. The researchers then injected the opiate antagonist methylnaloxonium into various brain areas to see if this would trigger withdrawal symptoms such as shaking, teeth chattering, and startle responses. Although the area that gave rise to the most severe withdrawal symptoms was the locus coeruleus, several other areas also produced these behaviours, including the periaqueductal grey area, amygdala, anterior hypothalamus, and raphe magnus. The last structure is not the same as the dorsal raphe, mentioned elsewhere in this book, but the site of a descending pathway to the spinal cord involved in regulating the sensation of pain.

> **KEY TERMS:** *lethal dose, dispositional tolerance, pharmacodynamic tolerance, locus coeruleus, clonidine*

THE INTRACELLULAR BASIS OF OPIATE TOLERANCE

A breakthrough in opiate research occurred in the early 1970s, when a type of tumour cell (called a neuroblastoma-glioma hybrid) was discovered that expressed μ-opiate receptors which reacted to morphine (Klee & Nirenberg, 1974). One benefit of this discovery was it enabled the intracellular aspects of opiate receptor function to be explored using cell culture techniques (i.e. where cells are grown under controlled conditions). This led to the discovery that opiate receptors were coupled with G proteins – a family of proteins which transmit signals from chemical events outside a cell to its interior. G proteins also serve many functions. One important effect that followed activation of the μ-opiate receptors was the inhibition of an intracellular enzyme called **adenylate cyclase**, which in turn, reduced the formation of the second messenger cAMP (cyclic adenosine monophosphate). In turn, this caused an inhibition of sodium channels which reduced the flow of positive ions (NA+) into the cell – an effect that would be expected to depress the excitability of cells such as neurons. Another effect of cAMP was to activate protein kinase A – an enzyme capable of modifying the shape of other proteins (known as phosphorylation). This step is a critical one for many biochemical processes that take place inside the cell.

The neuroblastoma-glioma hybrid cell model also allowed the intracellular basis of morphine tolerance to be examined. When these cells were bathed in solutions of morphine, they responded by inhibiting cAMP, but this was temporary since after just two days of this morphine exposure, the cAMP levels returned to pretreatment levels (Sharma et al., 1975). Yet the situation was not quite normal, for when the morphine was removed

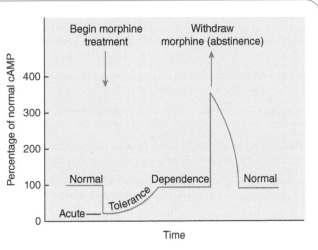

Figure 12.7   The effects of morphine on cAMP

Source: Wickens (2009), from Feldman, R. S. et al. (1997). *Principles of neuropharmacology*, p. 540

from the cell culture medium, the cAMP rebounded above control levels (see Figure 12.7), resulting in the opening of sodium channels and causing the flow of positively charged ions into the cell. If we extrapolate what is happening in this model to the locus coeruleus of an addict (remember both cells contain μ-opiate receptors) then we can make some useful deductions. The initial opiate exposure will cause neural inhibition but be short-lived, with the activity of locus coeruleus neurons soon returning to normal. This is a form of neural tolerance. But, when a period of opiate abstinence occurs a rise in cAMP will occur, thereby increasing locus coeruleus activity. This change is likely to contribute to some of the withdrawal symptoms that are common in opiate addiction (e.g. increased startle reactions, autonomic arousal, anxiety etc.).

The locus coeruleus is not the only brain area where these types of intracellular changes are taking place. Another key structure is the nucleus accumbens where the upregulation of the cAMP pathway is a common response to long-term exposure to drugs including opiates, cocaine and alcohol (Muntean et al., 2019). When these drugs are administered to laboratory animals, DA concentrations in the nucleus accumbens rise, leading to an increase in intracellular levels of cAMP – a step leading to an upregulation of adenylate cyclase and protein kinase A. But this is not the only effect. There is also an increase in the production of the cAMP response element-binding protein (CREB), which is a transcription factor that affects the expression of genes in the nucleus of the cell. The consequences of this are complex and not fully understood, but one effect of CREB activity in the nucleus accumbens is the production of dynorphin – a peptide with opiate-like effects. This is released from axons of the nucleus accumbens projecting to the VTA where it causes inhibition. The induction of dynorphin by CREB, therefore, dampens the activity of the brain's dopaminergic reward circuit, which helps to produce tolerance by making further use of the drug less rewarding (Muschamp & Carlezon, 2013; Nestler, 2004).

KEY TERMS: *G proteins, adenylate cyclase, cAMP, protein kinase A, nucleus accumbens, cAMP response element-binding protein, dynorphin*

BEHAVIOURAL TOLERANCE

It may come as a surprise to find out that dispositional and pharmacodynamic factors do not fully account for opiate tolerance and withdrawal. This is because the effects of a drug can also be influenced by learning and conditioning while intoxicated through a process commonly known as behavioural tolerance. In other words, the drug user's experience can significantly affect the potency of a substance on the body. One important factor in this regard is the environment, or context, in which the drug is taken (Siegel, 1976). This was nicely demonstrated in a study by Siegel et al. (1982) who administered either heroin or saline to laboratory rats housed in distinctively different testing cages. The heroin was injected over a period of 30 days in increasing doses to produce drug tolerance. At the end of this regime, the rats were given a final 'high' heroin dose that should have proved lethal for most of the animals. For half of the group, the last heroin injection was given in the same testing cage as with all previous injections, but for the other half of the animals, the injection was administered in a new and distinctly different cage. In fact, this new cage would prove to be much more lethal, causing significantly more deaths (96% of the group) compared to those rats where the high dose was given in the usual testing environment (64%). The only plausible explanation was that there was something about the new cage that caused the rat to lessen their tolerance to the effects of heroin and thereby causing it to be more lethal.

This type of effect also occurs in humans. When Siegel (1984) interviewed ten former heroin addicts from a methadone facility in New York, whose medical records showed hospitalization for heroin overdose, he found that unusual circumstances had surrounded the drug event in a number of the survivors. This included two instances where heroin administration had taken place in locations in which the addicts had never injected before. Since then a number of case reports have supported the idea that a new location, or context, can increase the risk of overdose (Siegel, 2016). An interesting insight into this effect was provided by Meissner et al. (2002) who compared blood morphine levels in overdose victims with those of automobile drivers arrested for opiate intoxication. He found there was a considerable overlap in the blood morphine levels of the two groups, with some automobile drivers having higher blood opiate levels than the fatalities. Although this is not conclusive, it illustrates that opiate concentrations in fatal cases are often less than might have been expected (Darke & Zador, 2014).

This type of contextual effect is not specific to opiates. For example, Le et al. (1979) examined the effects of repeated alcohol injections in rats over a period of several days. The alcohol caused a significant drop in body temperature in the early days of testing which normalized over subsequent days. Although the rats had quickly developed tolerance to the hypothermic effect of alcohol, when the animals were administered alcohol in a different room, this tolerance was lost, and a decrease in body temperature occurred similar to that which had happened at the start of the study.

How can these effects be explained? Siegel has proposed that behavioural tolerance comes about through a form of Pavlovian conditioning whereby the individual learns an association between two stimuli (see Figure 12.8). Pavlov, of course, most famously demonstrated this type of learning when he paired a bell (an unconditioned stimulus) with food which elicited salivation in a dog (an unconditioned response). With subsequent pairings of these two events, Pavlov found the bell would come to elicit salivation by itself without any food presentation. In effect, the dog had learned that the bell (which has now become a learned or conditioned stimulus) predicted food delivery, and in response it salivated (now a conditioned response). According to Siegel, drug tolerance comes about through a similar although not identical process. More specifically, Siegel argues that the environmental cues that regularly accompany the use of the drug start to act as conditioned stimuli which elicit conditioned responses. Strictly speaking, therefore, one might expect all the drug paraphernalia surrounding drug use (e.g. the washrooms, needles, white powder etc.) to begin producing conditioned responses similar to the intoxicating effects of the drug (e.g. sweating, lacrimation and excitement). But Siegel's interpretation of this situation is somewhat different, for he proposes instead that drug-related conditioned responses act to reduce the drug's impact on the body – or what he calls a compensatory conditioned response. It is, in effect, a learned form of drug tolerance.

KEY TERMS: *behavioural tolerance, contextual effect, Pavlovian conditioning, compensatory conditioned response*

Pavlovian conditioning

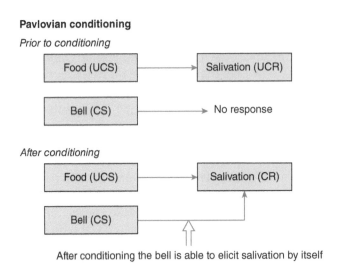

How Pavlovian conditioning, which associates drug-related stimuli with heroin use, may explain drug tolerance with repeated administration

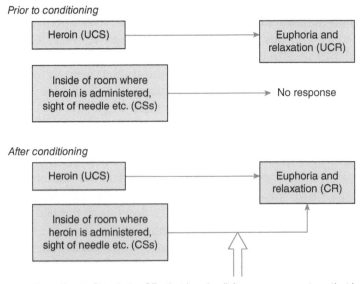

Figure 12.8 How compensatory conditioning may produce drug tolerance

Source: Wickens (2009)

CONDITIONED WITHDRAWAL

As with tolerance, behavioural factors can also play an important role in modifying the severity of withdrawal symptoms. Indeed, it has long been known that detoxified opiate addicts who have been in a drug-free state for some length of time may succumb to strong cravings and withdrawal symptoms when talking about drugs in group therapy, or upon returning to neighbourhoods where they had previously taken drugs. The American psychiatrist Wikler (1948) labelled this phenomenon conditioned withdrawal, arguing that environmental stimuli can acquire the ability through conditioning to trigger the symptoms of opiate withdrawal. He also believed this effect was an important reason why many people re-establish drug use after long periods of abstinence.

Evidence has confirmed that withdrawal symptoms can be elicited by environmental stimuli. In one study where abstinent opiate users had just completed a 30-day treatment programme in a therapeutic community, it was found that several physiological responses such as respiration, skin temperature and heart rate, along with strong cravings, occurred when subjects watched a drug-related video. And similar responses occurred when handling drug paraphernalia or performing a 'cook-up tie-off procedure' (Childress et al., 1986). For many addicts, these sorts of behaviour are in themselves pleasurable, and they help explain why drug use is often associated with various rituals and routines. An example of this phenomenon is the 'needle freak' who by the act of injection alone, or the administration of inert substances such as water, derives strong feelings of pleasure.

If conditioned withdrawal symptoms can be elicited by an environment where previous drug taking has taken place, then we might expect a novel environment to have the opposite effect. Indeed, this appears to be the case. For example, Krank and Perkins (1993) injected rats with increasing doses of morphine over a period of ten days. After the injection regime, the rats were given an injection of the opiate antagonist naloxone to trigger withdrawal symptoms. The results showed that the animals injected in their normal environment (in this case an operant chamber) exhibited significantly more withdrawal symptoms.

The neural circuitry underlying conditioned withdrawal has been shown to be similar to that involved in addiction. In one study, Frenois et al. (2005) attempted to identify the brain regions that are activated when opiate-dependent rats were re-exposed to stimuli that had previously been paired with morphine. To do this, they placed their dependent animals back into a Y-maze which had compartments with distinct visual and tactile cues, and then measured the extent of withdrawal by examining c-fos expression. C-fos is a gene that is expressed by active neurons which can be detected by using immunohistochemical techniques. The results showed that c-fos activation was most marked in a limbic circuit known as the extended amygdala which includes the VTA, nucleus accumbens, the bed nucleus of the stria terminalis, and the hippocampus.

Another way of examining conditioned withdrawal is to use a conditioned place preference procedure. Put in very simple terms, an animal is more likely to return to a location where pleasurable drug effects have been experienced (or conversely, less likely to revisit one where unpleasant experiences have taken place). This type of procedure was used by Dejean et al. (2017) who subjected opiate dependent rats to one of two compartments: one which was always paired with naloxone that precipitated

a) Conditioning with neutral substance (saline) in one compartment

b) Conditioning with drug in opposite compartment

c) Place preference testing

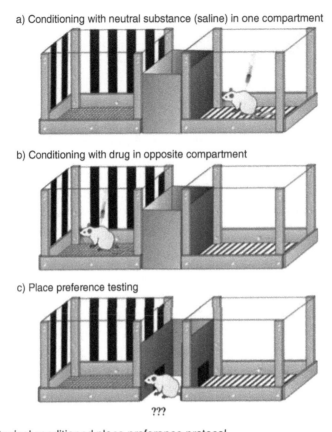

???

Figure 12.9   A typical conditioned place preference protocol

Source: from 'Conditioning of Addiction', by M. Foster Olive and Peter Kalivas. In *Addiction Medicine: Science and Practice*, A. Johnson Bankole, Ed., 2011. Reprinted by permission of Springer. In Gaskin (2021)

withdrawal, and one where a saline injection was given causing no withdrawal. After conditioning, the rats were given a free choice of compartment, and not surprisingly they exhibited a preference for the one where saline was administered. But the most interesting finding concerned the effects of the two environments on the neural activity of the nucleus accumbens since both compartments were found to be associated with specific neural signatures in the nucleus accumbens – the aversive one with a 80Hz gamma oscillation, and the saline one with a 60Hz gamma oscillation. The nucleus accumbens would appear to be involved in encoding both the pleasant and unpleasant aspects of place conditioning.

> **KEY TERMS:** *conditioned withdrawal, extended amygdala, conditioned place preference procedure*

DRUG ADDICTION IN VIETNAM VETERANS

An impressive illustration of the importance of environmental setting on drug taking can be seen in the case of US servicemen serving in the Vietnam War (1955–1975). At the time, Indochina was the source of cheap and plentiful heroin which was sold in an easy-to-use smokable form – and this proved attractive to many Americans. During the late 1960s and early 1970s, it was estimated that around 35% of enlisted men were using heroin in Vietnam, and 20% were showing signs of dependence. This situation had not gone unnoticed in the United States, where President Nixon expressed concern that the heroin-addicted Vietnam veterans would exacerbate the domestic drug problem on their return. Yet his fear, for the most part, did not materialize. The situation was well documented by Lee Robins, professor of social science is St Louis, who interviewed 617 enlisted men before their return from Vietnam in 1971, and again three years later (see Robins et al., 2010). This revealed a surprisingly low rate of heroin use by veterans in the 8–12 months after their return to the United States. In fact, only 10% reported any heroin use, 2% said they used heroin more than once weekly, and fewer than 1% admitted being addicted (a rate confirmed by urine analysis). A follow-up study two years later showed much the same levels of addiction. In effect, some nine out of ten soldiers who used heroin in Vietnam had quickly eliminated their addiction when back home.

These findings were important because they contradicted the prevailing belief at the time, which viewed heroin addiction as a permanent and irreversible condition. However, they also illustrated the importance of environmental setting on drug use, and the key factors that influence the development and maintenance of substance addiction, such as availability, the process of delivery, social norms and life circumstances. In a nutshell, while in Vietnam the US soldiers were placed in an unpleasant and distressing setting, cut off from their friends and family, with easy access to drugs. Back in the US they were in a very different setting, and able to resume everyday living without the need for heroin (Hall & Weier, 2017). Thus, when the context changed, so did the habit.

OTHER COMMONLY ABUSED DRUGS

ALCOHOL

Most of us enjoy drinking alcohol, although we may not be fully aware of its dangers. According to a health survey undertaken by the National Health Service (NHS) in 2018, 82% of adults had drunk alcohol in the past year, with 49% drinking it at least once a week. These figures, however, hide a more worrying statistic, for around 20% of the population are estimated to drink alcohol at high-risk levels – a habit that is a major cause of serious illness, including cancer and cardiovascular disease (Beard et al., 2017). There is also the risk of dependence. In England alone, there are over half a million people who can be regarded as suffering from alcoholism, more commonly called alcohol use disorder, where the individual is unable to control their drinking – a situation which often leads to dire consequences – yet only around 18% of alcoholics receive treatment (Public Health England, 2016).

However, it would be a mistake to think this is the only group who are putting their health at risk. Alcohol misuse is the biggest risk factor for death, ill health and disability among 15–49-year-olds in the UK, and the fifth biggest risk factor across all ages (Burton et al., 2017). In 2017, this amounted to some 7,697 alcohol-related deaths (Office for

National Statistics, 2017). In response to these numbers, in 2018, the NHS issued new guidelines regarding alcohol consumption, recommending that men and women consume no more than 14 units a week (one unit is 10 millilitres of pure alcohol). This is roughly six pints of beer or seven glasses of wine. Yet according to a Mori survey commissioned by the charity Drinkaware, around 3.5 million middle-aged men are still drinking more than 14 units per week with an average intake of 37 units per week (equivalent to 16 pints of 4% beer). The problem is also a world-wide one. According to the World Health Organization, over 3 million deaths each year result from the use of alcohol which represent 5.3% of all deaths (WHO, 2018).

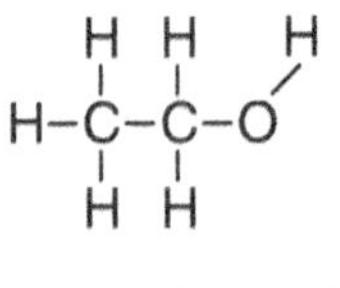

Figure 12.10   The molecular structure of ethanol
Source: Jü/Wikimedia Commons

In chemistry, 'alcohol' refers to any chemical where the molecule contains one or more hydroxyl groups attached to a chain of carbon atoms. Hence, there are different types of alcohol. But the one we drink is called ethanol (or ethyl alcohol) which is produced by the distillation and fermentation of sugar (obtained from plant products) by yeast. Ethanol is a small molecule, comprised of a small chain of saturated carbon atoms bound with hydrogen and oxygen. It is also soluble in both water and fat, allowing it to cross cell membranes and the capillaries that make up the blood–brain barrier. Once absorbed, alcohol becomes distributed fairly uniformly through the tissue and fluid compartments of the body, including the brain.

KEY TERMS: *alcohol use disorder, ethanol, blood–brain barrier*

THE NEUROPHARMACOLOGY OF ALCOHOL

How alcohol affects cellular function in the nervous system, and the neural mechanisms by which it influences behaviour, is complex and not fully understood. Because of its high lipid solubility, alcohol was once believed to exert its main pharmacological effect by dissolving in the outer cellular neural membrane – a mode of action that is similar to that for some anaesthetics (see Ingólfsson & Andersen, 2011). In turn, this was thought to increase the fluidity of the membrane (which is composed of two layers of lipid molecules) which then altered the function of its embedded proteins. One type of membranous protein is that of the ion channels that allow the transport of positive and negatively charged particles in and out of the neuron. Indeed, alcohol has been shown to decrease the influx of calcium ions (Ca^{2+}) into axonal endings which reduces neurotransmitter release, and also decrease the flow of sodium ions (Na^+) into the dendrites and cell body, thereby causing a reduction of neural excitability (Feldman et al., 1997).

It is also clear that alcohol can act directly on the receptor sites of several neurotransmitters. One important receptor in this regard is the GABA-A receptor (see Figure 1.18) whose activation leads to an increased flow of negative chloride (Cl^-) ions into the cell. GABA is the most abundant inhibitory neurotransmitter in the brain, and the GABA-A receptor is composed of five protein molecules that form an ion channel that passes through the neural membrane. This collection of proteins also has binding sites for barbiturates and benzodiazepines. But interestingly, one of the protein sub-units making up the GABA-A receptor (the δ-subunit) appears to respond to alcohol. Evidence for this has come from a novel benzodiazepine drug called Ro15–4513 which has been shown to antagonize many low-to-moderate dose alcohol actions in mammals (Linden et al., 2011). This drug appears to work by binding to a 'pocket' on the ⊠-subunit (Wallner & Olson, 2008). Although the efficacy of Ro15–4513 as an alcohol antagonist was not found to be high enough for clinical development, the mechanisms of its action for elucidating the action of alcohol remain of interest.

Another important neurotransmitter in the pharmacology of alcohol is glutamate – the most common excitatory neurotransmitter in the brain. For example, certain behavioural effects of alcohol in animals can be mimicked by the administration of N-methyl-d-aspartate (NMDA) receptor antagonists (Banerjee, 2014). As we saw in Chapter 9, the NMDA receptor is unusual, because in order for its associated ion channel to open, an amino acid glycine needs to be displaced. However, it appears that alcohol prevents glycine from executing its normal role, which results in less excitatory calcium ions (Ca^{2+}) entering the neuron. This leads to reduced excitation of the neuron. It is interesting to note that the increased activity at the GABA-A receptor, and decreased action at the NMDA receptor, have similar inhibitory or depressive effects on neural function.

Alcohol appears to produce its pleasurable effects by acting on the mesolimbic pathway (Ma & Zhu, 2014). For example, it has been found that low doses of alcohol in rats cause DA release in the nucleus accumbens, but not other dopaminergic regions of the brain (Hendler et al., 2013). Low doses of alcohol also increase the firing rate of neurons in the VTA, perhaps by its inhibitory action on GABA interneurons, or possibly by increasing the release of opioid peptides. Both these actions would also cause DA release in the nucleus accumbens. Moreover, alcohol consumption can be blocked by injecting low doses of either DA antagonists or glutamate antagonists directly into the nucleus accumbens (Hodge et al., 1997; Rassnick et al., 1992). Despite this, lesions of the mesolimbic DA system do not completely abolish alcohol-reinforced behavior, indicating that DA is an important, but not essential, component of alcohol reinforcement (Gilpin & Koob, 2008).

KEY TERMS: *ion channels, GABA-A receptors, Ro15–4513, glutamate, NMDA receptor, dopamine, nucleus accumbens*

NICOTINE

Of all the substances with addictive potential, tobacco must rank as the one that causes the most harm world-wide. According to statistics compiled by the WHO, over 1.1 billion people in the world habitually smoked tobacco in 2015 (WHO, 2017). Although this habit is declining in many western and affluent countries, it is increasing in poorer parts of the world, often abetted by intensive tobacco marketing. It is estimated that 6,000 billion cigarettes are smoked every year with more than 8 million people dying from their use. Cigarette smoke contains over 4,500 different compounds, and its inhalation is the leading cause of lung cancer, with more than 8 in 10 cases being directly related to this drug habit. Smoking is also a major contributor to other cancers, heart disease, bronchitis and emphysema. If this level of global tobacco consumption continues, then it is probable that 1 billion people will die from its use during the twenty-first century (Mishra et al., 2015). But one doesn't have to be a smoker to suffer from its adverse effects. Passive smoking has also been implicated in adverse health problems which cause some 1.2 million deaths annually – thousands of which are children. In recognition of the dangers, the UK government banned smoking in July 2007 from all indoor public places, including pubs, shopping centres and nightclubs.

The main psychoactive and addictive ingredient in tobacco is nicotine, which was first isolated from tobacco leaves in 1828 by Wilhelm Posselt and Karl Reimann. Making up about 2–3% of the dried leaf's weight, nicotine is a strong alkaloid (a class of natural substances which contain at least one nitrogen atom), which in its pure form is a clear liquid with a strong characteristic odour. When heated in a cigarette, nicotine 'rides' on small particles of tar, and when these reach the lungs, the nicotine is absorbed through the mucus membranes and carried to the heart. Nicotine is highly toxic and about 60 mg injected directly into a vein would normally be sufficient to kill a person. The average cigarette contains about 8–9 mg of nicotine, but most is burnt off, which means the typical smoker will only absorb around 1 mg in the course of taking 10 puffs per cigarette (Hancock & McKim, 2017). Nicotine reaches the brain in about 8 seconds after the smoke is inhaled, which is almost as fast as an intravenous injection. It remains in the brain for some time with about 50% of the dose taking 20 to 40 minutes to be redistributed to the body. The average smoker will administer some 70,000 puffs of nicotine into their lungs (and brain) every year (Gossop, 2017).

Nicotine is an agonist at certain receptors for acetylcholine. There are two types of cholinergic receptor – muscarinic and nicotinic – and as the name suggests, nicotine binds to the latter. These receptors are found throughout the body, including the neuromuscular junction where they are involved in muscle contraction (this is why smoking can cause tremor and increase the strength of reflexes). They are also present in the ganglia of both the sympathetic and parasympathetic branches of the autonomic nervous system. Here, nicotine in doses encountered in tobacco smoking stimulates the heart rate and blood pressure and constricts the blood vessels in the skin. The latter effect may help explain a smoker's 'cold touch'. Nicotine also acts on the adrenal glands to cause the secretion of adrenaline and noradrenaline.

But the pleasurable and ultimately addictive effects of nicotine occur in the brain. Nicotine receptors are located primarily on the presynaptic terminals of nerve fibres, where they affect neurotransmitter release (Benowitz, 2009). These receptors are found in the brain stem, thalamus, striatum and cerebral cortex, where the action of nicotine increases arousal and alertness. In addition, nicotinic receptors are located on DA neurons in both the ventral tegmental area (VGA) and nucleus accumbens, where they form part of the brain's reward circuitry. In common with other drugs of abuse, nicotine increases neural firing in the VTA and the release of DA in the nucleus accumbens (Fu et al., 2000; Pidoplichko et al., 2004). One curious consequence of smoking is that nicotine only stimulates the DA neurons for a few minutes, yet DA levels in the nucleus accumbens remain elevated for much longer. It is believed this effect occurs because nicotine has a long-term potentiating effect on excitatory glutamate neurons in the VTA, which enhances DA transmission to the nucleus accumbens. Smoking a cigarette may only take a few minutes, but the effects on excitatory glutamate neurotransmission are much longer (Mansvelder & McGehee, 2002).

KEY TERMS: *nicotine, acetylcholine, muscarinic and nicotinic receptors, presynaptic terminals, ventral tegmental area, nucleus accumbens, glutamate*

CAFFEINE: THE WORLD'S MOST POPULAR DRUG

Caffeine is the most widely used psychoactive drug in the world, and found in our most popular beverages and food, which includes coffee, tea, fizzy drinks and chocolate. More than 80% of the world's population, regardless of age, gender and culture, consume some form of caffeine on a daily basis. In the case of coffee, which is the most popular source of dietary caffeine, it is estimated that around 2.25 billion cups are drunk every day (Heckman et al., 2010). The British are amongst the world's heaviest users, with a typical adult consuming around 400 mg of caffeine per day mainly in the form of tea and coffee (Nehlig, 1999). Although caffeine is found in the beans, leaves or fruit of more than 60 different plants, where it acts as a natural pesticide, the coffee bean provides the main source of this drug. By drinking a standard cup of instant coffee one will normally ingest around 80 mg of caffeine, which can increase up to 150 mg in percolated coffee. Tea usually contains less caffeine (40 mg) although this figure can be highly variable. Another common source of caffeine is fizzy drinks which often contain more than 60 mg per can.

Caffeine belongs to a class of drugs known as the methylxanthines. There are other types of methylxanthine besides caffeine, but only two others occur naturally: theophylline (found in tea) and theobromine (found in chocolate). All methylxanthines are regarded as minor stimulants that increase alertness and reduce mental tiredness (Smith, 2002). At higher doses, caffeine does not have a mood-elevating effect (like other stimulants), but instead causes restlessness, tenseness and insomnia – a condition sometimes referred to as caffeinism. Although it is widely regarded as harmless, the abstinence of caffeine can cause withdrawal symptoms in regular users. including a headache, physical tiredness and mental drowsiness. For this reason, some have argued that caffeine is a 'model drug of abuse' (Holtzman, 1990).

Caffeine has a complex pharmacological action. Early research attributed its psychoactive effect to an inhibition of the enzyme phosphodiesterase which acts to break down the second messenger cyclic adenosine monophosphate (cAMP), but this requires very high doses of caffeine. Consequently, it is now believed that caffeine in the amount we ingest from a cup of coffee produces its effects by blocking adenosine receptors (Ballesteros-Yáñez et al., 2018). **Adenosine** is a neurotransmitter-modulator in the brain which is involved in a variety of cellular and metabolic processes. Two of its functions, for example, are to regulate the delivery of oxygen to cells and dilate the cerebral blood vessels. Adenosine is also an inhibitory neurotransmitter. There are four types of adenosine receptor (A_1, A_{2a}, A_{2b} and A_3), with caffeine blocking the A_1 and A_2 subtypes (McLelland et al., 2016). These receptors are located presynaptically where they act to inhibit neurotransmitter release from axon terminals. By antagonizing these receptors, caffeine enhances neurotransmitter release. Adenosine receptors also have a close relationship with DA receptors. In fact, A_1 receptors colocalize with D-1 receptors, and A_{2A} with D-2 receptors in joint receptor complexes (Fuxe et al., 2010). The A_{2A} and D-2 units, which are believed to be more important for caffeine's behavioural effects, are found in the striatum and nucleus accumbens where caffeine acts to increase the release of DA (Ferré, 2010, 2016). Although this increase of DA is not particularly marked, it is sufficient to have mild pleasurable effects. This hypothesis is supported by the finding that caffeine can potentiate the behavioural effects of cocaine and amphetamine in experimental animals

(Derlet et al., 1992). The latest research suggests that caffeine, when injected into the nucleus accumbens, can have both rewarding and aversive effects – depending on the site of injection (Yee et al., 2020).

KEY TERMS: *caffeine, methylxanthines, cAMP. adenosine*

KEY THINKER 12.1

PAUL GREENGARD

Paul Greengard was born in New York in 1925, the son of a father who had been a relatively successful vaudeville singer and dancer. After attending public schools, Greengard joined the Navy at the age of 17 to serve as an electronics technician in World War II. After three years of service, he began studying mathematics and physics in which he graduated in 1948. Deciding to pursue medical physics, an area then in its infancy, Greengard went to Johns Hopkins to undertake his first research with the neurophysiologist H. K. Hartline. However, in his second year, Greengard took an interest in neurochemistry and cell biology. The impetus for this came after he heard a talk by Alan Hodgkin describing his work with Andrew Huxley on the ionic basis of the nerve impulse. After hearing this, Greengard was convinced there was little more to discover in neurophysiology, and he turned to the biochemical basis of nerve function. Following his PhD in 1953, he spent some time in England (a country he liked), but the lack of equipment and central heating led him back to the United States, where he became a biochemist for the drug company Geigy in New York. He later became professor of pharmacology at Yale in 1968.

Prior to joining Yale, Greengard had taken a year's sabbatical working in the laboratory of Earl Sutherland. This was to prove highly formative. In the mid-1950s, Sutherland had been interested in how the pancreatic hormone glucagon breaks down glycogen in the liver to provide glucose for energy. He discovered that glucagon activated enzymes known as the adenylate cyclases, which led to the formation of cyclic adenosine monophosphate (cAMP). In effect, cAMP mimicked the action of glucagon. Or put another way, cAMP acted as a 'second messenger' inside the cell, following its activation by glucagon (the first messenger). The discovery of second messengers would win Sutherland a Nobel Prize in 1971.

This was the major biochemical breakthrough that Greengard had been waiting for, and he set about the ambitious task of finding second messengers in the nervous system. He chose to look for them in the superior cervical ganglion (SCG), a ganglion of the sympathetic nervous system that innervates parts of the head. Greengard soon found that electrical stimulation of the SCG increased the levels of cAMP in its neurons as did the application of dopamine (DA). The implication was that DA was exerting its intracellular effects through the formation of cAMP. The next step was to look for cAMP in the brain, and in 1971 Greengard reported adenylate cyclase and cAMP activity in tissue from the striatum exposed to dopamine. But this was not all. Soon after, another second messenger, called cyclic guanosine monophosphate (cGMP), was discovered. And in 1979 Greengard described a third messenger stimulated by calcium, which formed calmodulin – a substance that regulated many cellular functions. Greengard had provided convincing evidence for the role of second messengers in neural function involving synaptic transmission.

In his later career, Greengard turned his attention to intracellular signalling molecules involved in drug abuse. One protein discovered in his laboratory was called dopamine and cAMP-regulated phosphoprotein (DARPP-32). This molecule is activated by dopaminergic and glutamatergic (NMDA) receptor stimulation, and it acts to alter the shape of a large number of other proteins in the cell, thereby altering their function. This includes proteins involved in voltage-gated ion channels, ion pumps and gene expression. DARPP-32 is found predominantly in the striatum and nucleus accumbens. Moreover, a number of drugs have been shown to affect the phosphorylation of DARPP-32, including most drugs of abuse, such as cocaine, marijuana, nicotine, alcohol and LSD. It is believed that drugs targeting DARPP-32 could well turn out to have important therapeutic benefits in the future.

Greengard won the Nobel Prize in 2000, and with the winnings set up an annual award to encourage women to take up biological research, named in honour of his mother (The Pearl Meister Greengard Prize). Greengard had moved to Rockefeller University in 1983 where he worked until his death in 2019 at the age of 93. Old age had not slowed him down, and when asked about his work he replied 'It's more fun understanding the brain than doing a crossword puzzle. It's the same kind of cognitive challenge, but it's much more fun and you feel you're doing something worthwhile'. During his career, Greengard published close to a thousand important research papers – a truly remarkable record.

CANNABIS

Cannabis is the most commonly used illicit drug in the UK and many other countries. In 2013, the United Nations Office on Drugs and Crime estimated that between 128 and 232 million people worldwide used cannabis – which is some 2.7–4.9% of the global population between the ages of 15 and 65 (World Drug Report, 2013). There are probably some 15 million users in the UK, and it is a drug that divides public opinion. In 1969, a Gallup poll reported that only 12% of the American population favoured the legalization of cannabis. In 2010 the number was 46%, and by 2013 this had risen to 58% (Garrett, 2015). Such changing attitudes have made cannabis difficult to legislate. Indeed, partly because of its widespread use, and ineffective legislative control, cannabis was reclassified in the UK from a Class B drug under the Misuse of Drugs Act (1971) to Class C in 2004, but this was short-lasting as it was restored back to its Class B status in 2009. Although its personal use is often overlooked by the police, possession can nevertheless incur a penalty of up to three months' imprisonment and/or a fine at a magistrates' court. On a criminal indictment, the penalty can be up to five years' imprisonment and/or an unlimited fine.

Cannabis and its many derivatives, including hashish and marijuana, are derived from the *Cannabis sativa* plant, otherwise known as hemp. One of humanity's oldest non-food plants, the plant originated in central Asia where it was used in Neolithic times. Curiously, there is little evidence that it was first grown for its intoxicating properties. Rather, the plant was cultivated for fibre, seed, oil and medicine, and in ancient China it was used to make paper. The recognition of cannabis as a mind-altering drug appears to have been a relatively recent development, and most likely this discovery was made by Napoleon's soldiers advancing into North Africa in the late eighteenth century, who introduced marijuana smoking on their return (Booth, 2003).

Figure 12.11   A marijuana plant
Source: Fransvanswieten/Wikimedia Commons

The effects produced by smoking marijuana (the crushed dried leaves of the cannabis plant) include relaxation, increased sociability, euphoria and relief of anxiety. It can also provide a heightened awareness of colour and aesthetic beauty. At higher doses cannabis may cause short-term memory loss, disjointed thinking, confusion and perceptual distortions, although the latter are rarely as severe as those produced by other hallucinogenic drugs such as LSD (Iversen, 2003). Whilst the use of cannabis is perceived by many as relatively harmless, the adverse effects can be serious, including cognitive deficits, risks to mental health, and work absenteeism (Lorenzetti et al., 2016). Another problem is compulsive use and addiction. It has been estimated that the chances of becoming addicted to cannabis are around 8.9% (Lopez-Quintero et al., 2011). Although this is lower than for cocaine, alcohol and nicotine, the clinical need for treatment of cannabis addiction is substantial, and in Europe cannabis accounts for more first-time entrants into drug treatment services than any other illicit drug (Curran et al., 2016). It is also interesting to note that functional neuroimaging studies often reveal subtle differences in brain activity between chronic cannabis users and controls during performance of cognitive tasks – showing that this form of drug use can have serious long-term effects (Bloomfield et al., 2019; Zehra et al., 2018).

There are over 60 psychoactive agents in cannabis, but the most potent is delta-9-tetrahydrocannabinol (THC). First isolated by Raphael Mechoulam in 1964, this substance is highly lipid soluble which means that it dissolves in fats instead of water. Because of this, cannabis was once believed to exert its main pharmacological effects by dissipating into the outer lipid bilayer membrane of nerve cells. This view changed in the early 1990s when cannabinoid receptors were discovered in the body and brain (Matsuda et al., 1990). Two types of cannabinoid receptor exist called CB_1 and CB_2. The latter are mainly found in peripheral tissues such as the spleen and immune system, although they also occur in neuroglia (Wilson & Nicoll, 2002). However, it is the CB_1 receptor that has attracted the most attention, for it is one of the most ubiquitous receptors in the brain, and found in large amounts in the basal ganglia, cerebellum, hippocampus and cerebral cortex (Herkenham et al., 1991). It also shows an affinity for being localized on the presynaptic terminals of GABAergic neurons (Mackie, 2006). In terms of its biochemistry, the CB_1 receptor is attached to a G-protein which inhibits the intracellular enzyme adenylate cyclase. In turn, this reduces the flow of calcium ions into the axonal endings. The net result of activating the CB_1 receptor, therefore, is to inhibit neurotransmitter release. Structurally, the CB_1 receptor also has some similarities with opiate receptors and can be blocked by the opioid antagonist naloxone (Navarro et al., 2001). And as might be expected, THC exerts its psychological effects via its agonist actions on the CB_1 receptors (Lu & Mackie, 2016).

The identification of cannabinoid receptors not surprisingly led to a search for endogenous cannabis-type substances in the brain, and the first such substance to be discovered was called anandamide from the Sanskrit word for bliss (Devane et al., 1992). But since then a number of other cannabinoids have been discovered, including 2-Arachidonoylglycerol (2-AG) which is an endogenous agonist for the CB_1 receptor. Unlike other neurotransmitter substances, endocannabinoids are synthesized from lipid molecules found in the neural membrane. There is no evidence that anandamide or other endogenous cannabinoids are stored in synaptic vesicles like traditional neurotransmitters. Instead, they are synthesized in situ when needed (Mackie, 2006).

One of the more surprising findings to emerge from cannabinoid pharmacology is that the endocannabinoids can function as retrograde synaptic messengers (see Figure 12.12). That is, they are released from postsynaptic neurons and travel backward across synapses, where they can activate CB_1 receptors on presynaptic axons – thereby producing either short- or long-term changes in synaptic transmission. This effect is known to occur in the brain's DAergic systems (Wenzel & Cheer, 2018). For example, it has been shown that anandamide and 2-AG are released from DA

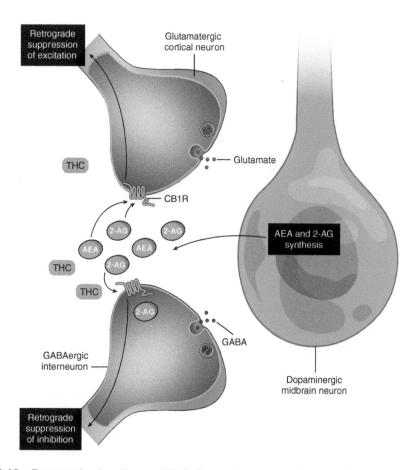

Figure 12.12   Retrograde signalling and THC. Dopamine neurons in the nucleus accumbens release endocannibinoids (AEA, 2-AG). These endocannibinoids travel back to presynaptic neurons and inhibit their ability to release neurotransmitters (e.g. GABA and glutamate) by binding to CB1 receptors. THC (grey rectangles) mimics the effects of endocannibinoids by binding to the same receptors. This results in the removal of GABA's inhibitory effects on dopamine neurons, explaining the rewarding properties of marijuana.

Source: from Bloomfield et al. (2016). The effects of Delta9-tetrahydrocannabinol on the dopamine system. *Nature*, 539(7629), 369–377. With permission from Springer Nature. In Gaskin (2021)

neurons in the nucleus accumbens which then cross back to the presynaptic sites where they inhibit the release of GABA and glutamate by binding to CB_1 receptors. This results in the removal of GABA's inhibitory effects on the axon terminals, leading to an increased release of DA in several regions of the brain including the nucleus accumbens (Bloomfield et al., 2016). This dopaminergic action is likely to be the mechanism by which cannabis produces its euphoric and pleasurable effects, leading to cravings and what has been termed a loss of executive control over excessive salience for cannabis (see Zehra et al., 2018).

KEY TERMS: *THC, cannabinoid receptors, adenylate cyclase, anandamide, 2-AG, retrograde synaptic messengers, nucleus accumbens*

THE HALLUCINOGENS

The hallucinogens are a diverse group of drugs that alter a person's awareness of their surroundings as well as their own thoughts and feelings. Sometimes described as 'psychedelic drugs' (a term invented by the British psychiatrist Humphrey Osmond to denote *mind revealing*), the hallucinogens are most noted for producing profound changes in consciousness and perceptual or – in rare instances – true hallucinations where perceptions are created entirely by the mind. The hallucinogens can be classified in various ways (see Garcia-Romeu et al., 2016), although the simplest is to divide them into classic hallucinogens such as lysergic acid diethylamide (LSD) and dissociative drugs such as phencyclidine that produce a sense of detachment or a disconnection from one's self and environment.

LSD has been described as the prototypical psychedelic (Carhart-Harris et al., 2016). It was first synthesized by the pharmacologist Albert Hoffman in 1938, whose aim was to develop new medicinal agents from a fungus known as ergot (*Claviceps purpurea*) which grows on rye and other cereals. Ergot was interesting because it had been known to cause outbreaks of St Anthony's fire (ergotism) in the Middle Ages, when people ate bread infected with this fungus – a condition leading to painful seizures, spasms, and mental disturbances such as mania and psychosis. Another serious complication was gangrene, a type of tissue death affecting the hands and feet caused by restricted blood flow to the limbs. In fact it was the potential medical ability of ergot to constrict blood vessels that interested Hoffman, and he set about developing and testing new derivatives of an ingredient called lysergic acid which was responsible for this effect. Hoffman first synthesized LSD in 1938, but it wasn't until 1943 when he spilled a small amount on his skin and began feeling peculiar that he took an interest. A few days later he self-administered LSD by ingesting what he believed was a very small dose (0.25mg). In fact, it was about ten times the amount required for a fullblown LSD experience. As a result, Hoffman became the first person to undergo an LSD trip (Hoffman, 2005).

Today, LSD usually comes on small squares of paper and is taken orally, with its effects beginning within 60 minutes and lasting up to 12 hours. The effects are

Figure 12.13   Albert Hoffman in 2006
Source: Stepan/Wikimedia Commons

difficult to describe because they are highly subjective and vary depending on the context, mood and expectations of the user. Nonetheless, it is probably fair to say that LSD's primary effects are visual. Colours appear more vivid, lights brighter, and stationary objects become distorted or move, leaving trails in their wake. When the user closes their eyes, they may experience a kaleidoscope of changing patterns. Strong emotions that may shift suddenly from well-being to extreme fear may also occur. It is sometimes said LSD does not produce true hallucinations but only distortions of things that already exist, but this is not true when LSD is taken in high doses. During the 1970s, Ronald Siegel at the University of Los Angeles trained subjects to encode their LSD experiences by using a series of letters and numbers which tracked images, colours and movement as quickly as they occurred (Siegel & Jarvik, 1975). This showed that, at higher doses, subjects could be swept up into their own hallucinations and enter an imaginary world where events unfolded with animated figures and panoramic scenes. After the LSD experience, the user may feel that their mind has expanded past its normal boundaries, enabling them to have new insight into spiritual matters (McGreal, 2012; Schmid & Liechti, 2018).

KEY TERMS: *hallucinogens, lysergic acid diethylamide (LSD), phencyclidine*

THE NEUROPHARMACOLOGY OF HALUCINOGENIC DRUGS

LSD has a molecular structure with some similarities to serotonin (5-HT). In 1954, Wooley and Shaw showed that LSD inhibited the action of 5-HT on the constriction of blood vessels, indicating it was a 5-HT antagonist. The next break-through came when LSD was shown to strongly inhibit the cells of the **dorsal raphe** (Aghajanian et al., 1968). This was significant because the raphe is the main source of serotonergic fibres in the forebrain. In effect, therefore, LSD depletes the forebrain, including the cerebral cortex, of 5-HT. Since 5-HT acts predominantly as an inhibitory transmitter, the loss of this inhibition was believed to mark-edly increase neural activity – an effect also bolstered by locus coeruleus activity freed from its normal inhibition by the raphe (Passie et al., 2008). One important effect of all these changes was increased activity in the reciprocal thalamocortical connections, especially those between the **thalamus** and **primary visual cortex**. Increased activity in these pathways has been shown to be correlated with subjective hallucinations (Liechti, 2017).

The neuropharmacology of LSD has turned out to be even more complex, largely because it binds to a variety of different receptors with varying degrees of antagonism and agonism. For example, LSD has a marked agonist effect on the 5-HT_{1A} receptor located in the raphe, locus coeruleus and cerebral cortex – an effect responsible for the raphe inhibition mentioned earlier. In addition, LSD binds to other 5-HT_1 receptors, including the 5-HT_{1B}, 5-HT_{1D} and 5-HT_{1E} subtypes, whose function is not so well understood. Despite this, the main hallucinogenic effect of LSD is believed to be due to its effects on the 5-HT_2 receptor, found predominantly in the cerebral cortex, where it acts as a partial 5-HT_2 agonist. It has long been known that the hallucinatory potency of many dugs correlates significantly with their ability to bind to 5-HT_2 receptors (Glennon et al., 1984; Titeler et al., 1988). But more recently, the focus has shifted to the 5-HT_{2A} receptor (Liechti, 2017), not least because the hallucinatory effects of LSD (and psilocybin) in healthy volunteers are reversed by the 5-HT_{2A} receptor antagonist ketanserin (Preller et al., 2017; Vollenweider et al., 1998).

Yet this may not be the full story. As mentioned, LSD is a partial agonist, which means that it binds to the 5-HT_{2A} receptor – but only has a partial effect in activating it. There remains a possibility, therefore, that LSD requires the presence of other, unknown, neurochemicals to exert a full agonistic effect (Aghajanian & Marek, 1999a). To make matters more complex, this might even mean that LSD acts as a partial antagonist by preventing the 5-HT_{2A} receptor from being activated by a full agonist of some sort.

The dissociative hallucinogens are structurally different, making up a large drug family which includes phencyclidine, ketamine and nitrous oxide (Morris & Wallach, 2014). Phencyclidine was first developed in the 1950s as a general anaes-thetic, but was discontinued because it produced serious side effects, although it is still used in veterinary practice. Ketamine is also occasionally used as an anaes-thetic, and was extensively used for surgery in the Vietnam War. Both drugs can also produce amnesia and catalepsy, along with a sense of detachment where perception of the outside world becomes dream-like or unreal. This has led some users to report being able to watch themselves as if viewing a movie, or even out-of-body experiences (Simeon, 2004). While not necessarily true of all dissociative anaesthetics, the key mechanism of the action of PCP and ketamine is that they act as antagonists at the N-methyl-d-aspartate (NMDA) glutamate receptor (Lodge & Mercier, 2015). PCP and ketamine have also been reported to have a high affinity for the 5-HT$_2$ and dopamine D-2 receptors which may also help explain some of their hallucinogenic effects (Kapur & Seeman, 2002).

KEY TERMS: *dorsal raphe, thalamocortical connections, thalamus, primary visual cortex, 5-HT$_1$ receptors, 5-HT2 receptor, partial 5-HT$_2$ agonist, 5-HT$_{2A}$ receptor, ketamine, dissociative hallucinogens, N-methyl-d-aspartate (NMDA) glutamate receptor*

SUMMARY

Drug addiction is one of the biggest problems facing society today. The discovery that the brain contains neural systems that mediate responses to pleasurable and rewarding events was made by James Olds and his research student Peter Milner in 1954, who found that rats would work voluntarily (i.e. press an operant lever) to self-stimulate their brains with an electrical current. A large array of brain sites was found to give rise to this type of behaviour with most contributing to the medial forebrain bundle (MFB), a large bi-directional multisynaptic pathway that connects regions of the forebrain with the midbrain. Initially, it was thought the lateral hypothalamus was the final common terminus for the MFB's reward messages. But this view changed when it was recognized that dopamine containing neurons in the ventral tegmental area (VTA), including those in the mesolimbic pathway projecting to the nucleus accumbens and those in the mesofrontal pathway to the prefrontal cortex, were most important. Evidence supporting the role of dopamine in reward has also come from experiments where animals self-administer drugs. Both rats and monkeys will work at lever pressing to receive an injection of cocaine and amphetamine which increases dopamine turnover in certain areas of the brain. This effect can be blocked by injections of dopaminergic antagonists into the nucleus accumbens. Further support for the pivotal role of the mesolimbic system in reward has come from an understanding of how opiate drugs work. The rewarding effects of these drugs appear to be dependent on opiate receptors located on GABA interneurons in the ventral tegmental area (VTA). These reduce the inhibition on tegmental dopamine neurons, causing transmitter release in the nucleus accumbens. Many other drugs of abuse are also known to influence, at least in part, the same dopaminergic reward pathways of the brain, including alcohol, nicotine and marijuana.

A well-documented effect of psychostimulant use is behavioural sensitization, whereby repeated exposure to these drugs produces a progressively greater and enduring behavioural response. This effect is likely to be an important mechanism underlying the development of addiction, leading to increased cravings and compulsive use. It has also led to the incentive sensitization theory which proposes that addictive drug-taking behaviour develops from a long-lasting sensitization of the mesolimbic dopamine pathway. In contrast, the opiates such as heroin and morphine lead to marked drug tolerance whereby increasing amounts of the drug are needed to produce the original effect. This can result in physical dependence with addicts compelled to continue drug use in order to avoid the unpleasant effects of withdrawal symptoms. Tolerance is a complex biobehavioural process which has both biological causes (e.g. dispositional and pharmacodynamic drug adaptations) and those involving learning. According to Siegel, behavioural tolerance comes about because environmental cues produce conditioned compensatory responses (similar in some ways to classical conditioning) that lessen the effects of the drug. This also shows that the environment is an important determinant of drug use – which was also seen in the case of US servicemen returning from the Vietnam War. It was estimated that about a third of servicemen used heroin in Vietnam, with many showing physical dependence. But on their return to the US, and away from the horrors of war, few veterans continued their drug habit.

Although most drugs of abuse work at some level on the mesolimbic dopamine system, their neuropharmacological effects vary. Alcohol has complex actions which include exciting the GABA-A receptor and inhibiting glutamate. Nicotine has a specific agonist effect at the cholinergic nicotinic receptor, whereas caffeine is an antagonist at adenosine receptors. Cannabis acts on endogenous cannabinoid receptors (CB_1 and CB_2). The CB_1 receptor is ubiquitous in the brain where it is primarily involved in controlling neurotransmitter release. Interestingly the endogenous cannabinoid 2-AG can function as a retrograde synaptic messenger. The pharmacological mechanism of LSD is complex as it works on a variety of serotonergic receptors. Its main hallucinatory effect would appear to be linked to its affinity for the serotonergic $5\text{-}HT_{2A}$ receptor where it acts as a partial agonist.

GO ONLINE

TEST YOUR UNDERSTANDING OF THIS CHAPTER AND VISIT HTTPS://STUDY.SAGEPUB.COM/WICKENS TO ACCESS INTERACTIVE 'DRAG AND DROP' LABELLING ACTIVITIES AND A FLASHCARD GLOSSARY.

MULTIPLE CHOICE QUESTIONS

Answer the questions below to test your understanding of this chapter's Learning Objectives. You'll find the answers at the end of the chapter.

1. What is the main pharmacological mechanism by which cocaine works?

    a. it blocks the reuptake of dopamine
    b. it acts as a direct agonist at D-2 receptors
    c. it facilitates the release of noradrenaline and dopamine
    d. it acts as an antagonist at dopaminergic autoreceptors

2. The nucleus accumbens receives dopaminergic input from which area of the brain?

    a. frontal cortex
    b. lateral hypothalamus
    c. striatum
    d. ventral tegmental area

3. Which of the following drugs is well known for its ability to produce behavioural sensitization?

    a. alcohol
    b. amphetamines and cocaine
    c. heroin
    d. LSD

4. What type of chemical is cAMP?

    a. a first messenger
    b. a second messenger
    c. a G protein
    d. an enzyme involved in the synthesis of dopamine

5. Which of the following receptors has a subunit which is sensitive to alcohol?

    a. cannabinoid CB_1
    b. dopaminergic D-2
    c. GABA-A
    d. serotonergic $5\text{-}HT_2$

6. LSD is believed to work primarily on which neurotransmitter system of the brain?

    a. dopaminergic
    b. GABAergic
    c. noradrenergic
    d. serotonergic

FURTHER READING

Advokat, C. D., Comaty, J. D., & Julien, R. M. (2018). *Julien's primer of drug action*. Worth.
The fact that this book is now in its 14th edition is testament to its excellence.

Brick, J., & Erickson, C. J. (1999). *Drugs, the brain, and behavior: The pharmacology of abuse and dependence*. Haworth Press.
A fairly simple introduction to the addictive drugs with basic neuroanatomy and pharmacology, but may be useful for the first-time student.

Erickson, C. K. (2007). *The science of addiction: From neurobiology to treatment*. Norton.
An accessible and concise overview of the biological basis of addiction, written primarily for caregivers working with drug users.

Frankenberg, F. (2014). *Brain-robbers: How alcohol, cocaine, nicotine, and opiates have changed human history*. Praeger.
A nicely written book that approaches addictive substances from a historical perspective.

Grilly, D. M., & Salamone, J. (2011). *Drugs, brain and behavior*. Pearson.
A well-established textbook that provides a broad introduction to psychopharmacology.

Hancock, S., & McKim, W. A. (2017). *Drugs and behavior: An introduction to behavioral pharmacology*. London.
Sadly, this is now prohibitively expensive for a textbook, although it remains very good. Older and much cheaper editions (written by McKim) are still very worthwhile.

Koob, G. F., Arends, M. A., & LeMoal, M. (2014). *Drugs, addiction, and the brain*. Academic Press.
This textbook includes scholarly chapters on each type of recreational drug, along with theories of addictions, aimed primarily at the neuroscientist.

Kuhn, C., Swartzwelder, S., & Wilson, W. (2014). *Buzzed: The straight facts about the most used and abused drugs from alcohol to ecstasy.* Norton.
A straightforward and accessible introduction to how drugs produce their effects on the body.

Meyer, J. S., & Quenzer, L. F. (2018). *Psychopharmacology: Drugs, the brain, and behavior.* Sinauer.
A textbook that provides a comprehensive overview of psychopharmacology, which shows how the mechanisms of psychoactive drugs affect brain and behaviour.

Preedy, V. R. (Ed.). (2016). *Neuropathology of drug addictions and substance misuse: Volumes 1–3.* Academic Press.
An excellent resource. The first volume covers the foundations of tobacco, alcohol, cannabinoids and opiates; the second covers the stimulants and hallucinogens; and the third covers more general drug processes. Each volume is a detailed tome of over 1,000 pages and written by various experts.

13

DEGENERATIVE DISEASES OF THE NERVOUS SYSTEM

LEARNING OBJECTIVES

After reading this chapter you should be able to:

- Describe the history, pathology and potential causes of Alzheimer's disease.

- Explain the amyloid theory of plaque formation.

- Appreciate the importance of cognitive reserve and the benefits of mental exercise.

- Describe the history, pathology and potential causes of Parkinson's disease.

- Understand how L-Dopa therapy works.

- Describe the history, pathology and genetic causes of Huntington's disease.

- Explain what is known about the role of the Huntingtin protein.

- Explain how infectious agents may cause neurodegenerative disease.

GO ONLINE

Test your understanding of this chapter and visit **https://study.sagepub.com/wickens** to access interactive 'Drag and Drop' labelling activities and a flashcard glossary.

INTRODUCTION

We live in a fortunate age in terms of life expectancy. In ancient Greece and Rome the average length of life was around 20 to 30 years, and by the end of the nineteenth century it had yet to reach 50 years. Today, life expectancy in the UK is 79.6 years for men and 83.2 years for women (2018 figures), with these ages likely to increase over the coming decades.

Although many of us can look forward to a high quality of life in our later years, there are drawbacks for some – not least for those who end their days with a degenerative brain disease. Already, neurodegenerative diseases, including dementia, are the leading cause of disability in the elderly, typically resulting in a significant decline of mental capacity and independence.

The most common form of dementia is Alzheimer's disease – an incurable and progressive illness that destroys people's lives by impairing memory, cognition and ultimately their self-awareness. Around 20% of people over 80 years suffer from this illness, and its complications now make it the fourth most common form of death in the western world. This is a disease to fear as we get older, and even if we avoid it, the economic burden of looking after its victims is one we will all have to bear. According to the Alzheimer's Society, the cost of dementia to the UK is currently £34.7 billion a year – and two-thirds of this sum is paid by the afflicted family, either in unpaid care or private nursing. It is a healthcare burden of epidemic proportions (Dharmarajan & Gunturu, 2009).

However, dementia is not the only neurodegenerative disorder of later life. Two others are Parkinson's disease and Huntington's disease, both primarily characterized by disabilities of movement that will cause the sufferer to become helpless and moribund. Moreover, some neurodegenerative diseases are not necessarily related to ageing. These include multiple sclerosis and motor neurone disease, and the fact they can occur in young adults perhaps makes them even more tragic.

Although there are no cures for any of these, they are the focus of a great deal of research, and the field has become one of the fastest growing areas in neuroscience. Work on neurodegenerative disease was not a major focus in brain science 40 years ago. But today, the field has advanced with cutting-edge research, and is likely to gain momentum in the coming years. The goal is truly an exciting one: to develop better treatments, or even cures, that might one day reverse the symptoms of these insidious conditions.

THE DISCOVERY OF ALZHEIMER'S DISEASE

Alzheimer's disease is named after a German doctor, Alois Alzheimer, who was born in 1864. He received his medical training at various universities in Germany, and in 1888 began his medical career in a Frankfurt hospital where he became senior physician. A man of striking appearance with a scar running from his left eye to his chin from a sabre duel incurred as a young man (this is never shown in his pictures), Alzheimer was also a heavy cigar smoker who left a trail of cigar stubs on his rounds (Wickens, 2015). It was in Frankfurt, in 1901, that a middle-aged women called Auguste D was admitted to hospital. Her disorder had started with unreasonable anger and aggression towards her husband, followed by memory decline leading to paranoid delusions and auditory hallucinations. Within a few years this had progressed into severe dementia and dystonia (abnormal posture). The relatively young age of Auguste D and her rapid demise made the illness an unusual one, and when she died in 1906 Alzheimer examined her brain. To visualize the brain tissue for microscopic analysis, he used a newly developed silver impregnation method that stained nerve fibres. It produced striking results. Most notably he found that a high number of neurons in the cerebral cortex contained tangles of fine fibres within their cytoplasm, now known as **neurofibrillary tangles**, along with tiny starch-like particle discs called **neuritic plaques**. Curiously, there was little blood vessel damage, which at the time was thought to be the main cause of dementia. Alzheimer presented his findings at a small conference in 1906, and published a paper of the talk in 1907.

It is probable that Alzheimer thought he had described nothing more than a very unusual case of dementia. But in 1910, the renowned psychiatrist Emil Kraepelin, in his authorative *Textbook of Psychiatry* (a book which provided the foundation for all the main classification system in psychiatric use today), wrote that Alzheimer had discovered a rare form of dementia associated with middle age which was different from the types of senile dementia found in later life. To back up his arguments, Kraepelin pointed to the importance of neurofibrillary tangles and plaques in the brains of its victims, along with the very rapid progression of its symptoms. However we now know that Kraepelin was wrong. Alzheimer's disease is not a rare form of senility only occurring in middle age, but a senile dementia that more frequently afflicts the elderly. There has been considerable debate over whether Kraepelin was sincere in his belief that it was a 'new' disease, as the neurofibrillary tangles and plaques observed by Alzheimer had been seen in demented brains before. Nor were its clinical features, including the rapid deterioration of personality and memory, particularly unusual. Whatever the truth of the matter, his misconception of Alzheimer's disease as a 'presenile' dementia would not be fully exposed for another 50 years or so (see Wickens, 2015).

For most of the twentieth century, therefore, Alzheimer's disease was regarded as a rare form of highly aggressive dementia, while memory loss in elderly people was generally attributed to vascular damage in the brain or a 'hardening of the arteries'. This view only began to change in the late 1960s when researchers realized that many elderly demented patients were free of significant vascular disease, yet exhibited plaques and neurofibrillary tangles (Blessed et al., 1968). Moreover, the number of neuritic plaques and neurofibrillary tangles at autopsy often correlated with the severity of the dementia. These findings indicated that Alzheimer's disease was much more widespread in the elderly than had previously been believed. As this became more apparent, it was recognized as the most common senile affliction of the elderly and a prominent cause of their death (Katzman, 1976).

THE EPIDEMIOLOGY OF ALZHEIMER'S DISEASE

The likelihood of developing Alzheimer's disease increases in older age groups. Between 40 and 65 years of age, the illness occurs in around 1 per 1000 people, and rises to about 1 in 50 people aged 65 to 70. From then on, its prevalence increases markedly so that it is found in around 1 of every 20 people between the ages of 70 and 80 years, and 1 in 5 of the over 80s (figures from the Alzheimer's Society of Great Britain). It can be seen, therefore, that the disease is not common below 65 years, but then becomes increasingly more frequent, so that by the age of 80 years, it is affecting some 20% of people. At the estimated rate of prevalence, there were about 1 million people with dementia in the UK in 2020. This number is set to increase to over 2 million by 2051. One reason for this dramatic increase will be the number of people who are living over the age of 80 – who are already the fastest growing segment of our population.

The projected increases in the elderly, and prevalence of Alzheimer's disease, are similar in other industrialized countries. For Europe as a whole, it has been estimated that the number of people aged over 80 years old will rise from 18.8 million in 2005 to 34.7 million in 2030, which will inevitably mean more people with Alzheimer's disease (Niu et al., 2017). The situation in the United States is just as bad where 4.5 million are afflicted with the disorder, and this will grow to 16 million by 2050. But Alzheimer's disease is not confined to wealthy countries. In 2005, Alzheimer Disease International commissioned a group of experts to determine the rates of dementia for every WHO region of the world. They estimated that 24.2 million people lived with dementia, with 4.6 million new cases arising every year (Ferri et al., 2005). By 2015, there were approximately 29.8 million people worldwide with Alzheimer's disease – a number that is likely to reach 34 million by 2025. Alarmingly, the global prevalence of dementia is predicted to double every 20 years through to 2040 (Mayeux & Stern, 2012). These are huge figures.

Despite this, Alzheimer's disease is not the only type of dementia to afflict the elderly. In fact, there are more than 60 disorders that can cause dementia, with Alzheimer's disease making up less than two-thirds of all cases. About 20% of people suffering from dementia have vascular or multi-infarct dementia caused by occlusions in the blood supply of the brain (Rizzi et al., 2014). These infarcts build up over time, increasing the severity of the dementia in a step-like manner. Another 10% of people have Lewy body dementia which is characterized by tiny 'sunflower-shaped' protein deposits in the brain that cause inflammation and degeneration. Other disorders that can produce dementia include frontotemporal dementia (an umbrella term for a group of illnesses that affect the frontal and temporal lobes), encephalitis and traumatic brain injury. As we shall see later in the chapter, dementia also occurs in Parkinson's and Huntington's disease.

THE CLINICAL COURSE OF ALZHEIMER'S DISEASE

Whilst the symptoms of Alzheimer's disease vary from person to person, they are often divided into three stages (Förstl & Kurz, 1999). Before these occur, however, the preclinical stage of Alzheimer's disease is somewhat inconspicuous with no reliable symptoms enabling an early diagnosis to be made. Despite this, some researchers believe that there is some gradual decline of cognitive function where the person becomes increasingly forgetful and absent-minded, which has been termed 'mild cognitive impairment' (Arnáiz & Almkvist, 2003). But at some point this weakening cognitive loss becomes severe enough to compromise the activities of daily living – and this denotes the first dementia stage. The main initial symptom of dementia is a marked decline in declarative memory for factual information and events. Although this can sometimes be viewed by relatives and friends as a normal and even amusing consequence of getting older, the sufferer may be aware of the problem and keep memo pads and notes to aid recall. Nonetheless, their decline begins to seriously interfere with work and social relationships, and they may become easily confused or disoriented when walking outside. Despite this, the person usually manages to live independently. Mood swings, personality changes and a general lack of energy or spontaneity can feature at this stage, although these changes are generally not marked.

In the second stage, the person's forgetfulness develops into severe memory loss. Speech and comprehension become slower, and they may have a short attention span leading them to easily lose the flow of their thoughts. Although the patient may be able to undertake simple chores such as dressing, more complicated tasks such as cooking or organizing the weekly shop will need the assistance of others. As the sufferer becomes more incapacitated, they can also become anxious, easily upset, unpredictable and restless – behaviours that are challenging for their carers. Daily routines become increasingly disorganized and the person unable to comprehend what is happening to them. Despite this, they may still have a reasonable recall of old cherished memories, although quickly forgetting things that have just recently happened.

By the final stage of the disease the person becomes severely disoriented and confused. Long-term memory deteriorates, with the person often losing their self-identity or ability to recognize others including close relatives. This may be confounded by a variety of visual problems, including loss of visual acuity, colour vision and agnosia. The person is now dependent on their carers, and to make matters worse they may develop neurological disturbances and language loss. Although some patients can become very demanding, suspicious and aggressive (this may be exacerbated by hallucinations and delusions), most are moribund and apathetic. During this stage, personal hygiene is ignored, mobility is difficult, and incontinence common. Sufferers may be unable to feed themselves, or will even lose the basic reflexes of chewing and swallowing. By the end, the bedridden victim is susceptible to pneumonia and infection which often contribute to their death (Förstl & Kurz, 1999). On average, a person with Alzheimer's lives four to eight years after diagnosis, but can live as long as twenty years depending on other factors.

Mild cognitive impairment

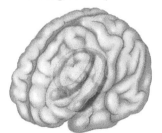

Duration: 7 years
Disease begins in medial
temporal lobe
Symptoms: Short-term
memory loss

Mild Alzheimer's

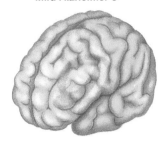

Duration: 2 years
Disease spreads to lateral
temporal & parietal lobes
Symptoms: Reading problems,
poor object recognition, poor
direction sense

Moderate Alzheimer's

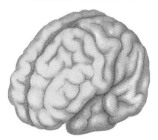

Duration: 2 years
Disease spreads to frontal lobe
Symptoms: Poor judgment,
impulsivity, short attention

Severe Alzheimer's

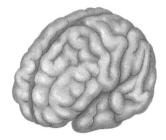

Duration: 3 years
Disease spreads to occipital lobe
Symptoms: Visual problems

Figure 13.1   A possible progression of Alzheimer's disease
Source: Carolina Hrejsa/Body Scientific Intl. in Gaskin (2021)

PATHOLOGICAL FEATURES OF ALZHEIMER'S DISEASE

Examination of the Alzheimer's brain at post-mortem typically shows a number of distinct abnormalities (Figure 13.2). On first inspection there is often a noticeable shrinkage of the cortical ridges or gyri with a widening of the fissures which is most obvious in the temporal and parietal lobe regions (Wenk, 2003). This shrinkage is caused by a loss of neurons in certain regions of the cerebral cortex – a pathological change that also causes an enlargement of the lateral ventricles. In fact, this can result in a ventricular volume of between 40 and 120 ml in Alzheimer's disease, compared to 20 to 30 ml in normal elderly individuals (Tomlinson, 1984). The use of structural MRI has greatly increased our knowledge of the brain atrophy accompanying Alzheimer's disease, with the hippocampus and surrounding areas of the temporal lobe consistently showing a cell loss of 30 or 40% (Burton et al., 2009; Galton et al., 2001). If anything, this degeneration is even more marked in the **entorhinal cortex**, which is the origin of an important neural pathway (the perforant pathway) into the hippocampus.

This is one of the first brain regions to show degeneration, with some studies showing a 60% loss of neurons during the early stages of the disease (Gomez-Isla et al., 1996). It has been proposed that atrophy in this region is the start of a process that is followed by neural loss in the hippocampus, amygdala and parahippocampal gyrus. This leads to degeneration of the posterior cingulate cortex which then becomes generalized to the temporal lobes and neocortical association areas (Rathakrishnan et al., 2014). Another site that shows the signs of early degeneration is the locus coeruleus (Braak et al., 2011).

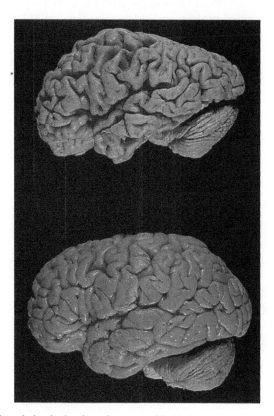

Figure 13.2   An Alzheimer's brain (top) and a normal brain
Source: Hersenbank/Wikimedia Commons

However, the true defining pathological hallmarks of Alzheimer's disease can only be observed with tissue staining and light microscopy. One distinguishing feature is senile plaques which are dense roughly spherical deposits found outside the cell, containing cellular debris and a protein called β-amyloid (see Figure 13.3). These vary in size from tiny grit-like deposits (10μm) to clumps that may be far bigger than a brain neuron. Although a small number of senile plaques can be found in healthy aged brains, they are abundant in Alzheimer's disease where they form in grey cortical matter and the hippocampus, and in the later stages of the disease they can spread to the striatum, cerebellum and brain stem (DeTure & Dickson, 2019). Senile plaques are often surrounded by clumps of degenerating axons and inflammation, indicating that their presence is toxic to brain cells.

The other main distinguishing pathological feature of Alzheimer's disease is neurofibrillary tangles (NFTs) which develop in the cytoplasm of neurons (see Figure 13.3). These resemble tiny bundles of knotted string (technically they are paired helical filaments) which are derived from **tau** – a protein that forms part of an elongated structure called a microtubule which forms the internal skeleton of the cell. In the early stages of the disease, NFTs are found in the entorhinal cortex and temporal lobes, but as the degeneration progresses they can be observed throughout the brain. Nonetheless, they are most pronounced in the cerebral cortex (DeTure & Dickson, 2019). Two other pathological features of Alzheimer's (although not necessarily specific to the disease) are granulovacuolar degeneration, where degenerating neuron cell bodies show bubble-like structures containing a dark pigment, and abnormal aggregations of protein called Lewy bodies (see later).

KEY TERMS: *lateral ventricles, entorhinal cortex, senile plaques, β-amyloid, neurofibrillary tangles, tau, microtubule, granulovacuolar degeneration, Lewy bodies*

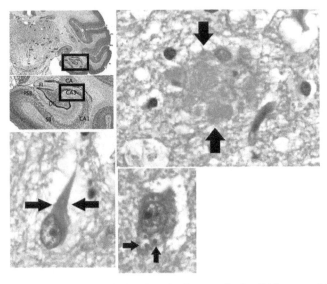

Figure 13.3   Histopathologic images of Alzheimer's disease, in the CA3 area of the hippocampus, showing an amyloid plaque (top right), neurofibrillary tangles (bottom left), and granulovacuolar degeneration bodies (bottom centre)

Source: Mikael Häggström and brainmaps.org. Creative Commons Attribution 3.0 License Neurofibrillary tangles – annotated, by Mikael Häggström, Public Domain Granulovacuolar degeneration – annotated, by Mikael Häggström, Public Domain Amyloid plaque – annotated, by Mikael Häggström, Public Domain

THE CHOLINERGIC THEORY OF ALZHEIMER'S DISEASE

In the mid-1970s, a significant breakthrough occurred in Alzheimer's research when it was found that an enzyme called choline acetyltransferase (CAT) was reduced at post-mortem by up to 90% in the cerebral cortex and hippocampus. CAT is involved in the synthesis of **acetylcholine** and its loss showed a marked decline of this transmitter was occurring in the disease (acetylcholine cannot be measured directly since it is broken down immediately on release). This finding was important because acetylcholine had long been linked with memory processes (see Hasselmo, 2006). The drug scopolamine, for example, which is derived from the poisonous deadly nightshade plant, blocks muscarinic cholinergic receptors and produces memory deficits in humans similar to those found in senile dementia (Drachman & Leavitt, 1974). Such findings led to the cholinergic hypothesis – which proposed that Alzheimer's disease resulted from a reduced synthesis of acetylcholine in the cortex and hippocampus (Francis et al., 1999). This theory also presumed that drugs able to correct this acetylcholine deficiency might provide an effective treatment for memory (Martorana et al., 2010). The cholinergic hypothesis was an important milestone which advanced the field of Alzheimer's disease research by moving it from the realm of descriptive neuropathology to a new focus on synaptic neurotransmission (Hempal et al., 2018).

One consequence of this new approach was a greater interest in the cholinergic pathways that innervate the cerebral cortex and hippocampus. These derive from the nucleus basalis of Meynert and septal diagonal band complex respectively – areas found in a complex of subcortical nuclei called the **basal forebrain**, which is not easy to define, but lies anterior to the striatum and just underneath the medial frontal cortex (Ballinger et al., 2016). This led to the discovery that the loss of cholinergic neurons located in the nucleus basalis of Meynert is particularly severe – there being around 500,000 cholinergic neurons in the healthy adult, but less than 100,000 in those with advanced Alzheimer's (Schliebs & Arendt, 2006). In addition, there is a strong correlation with the loss of these neurons and the severity of dementia (Wilcock et al., 1982).

The cholinergic theory also led to the first generation of drugs to treat Alzheimer's disease aimed at restoring the normal levels of acetylcholine. The most effective way of doing this was to administer a **cholinesterase inhibitor** such as Tacrine and Donepezil. These drugs inhibit the enzyme acetylcholinesterase which acts to break down acetylcholine after it is released into the synapse (Figure 13.4). When the breakdown

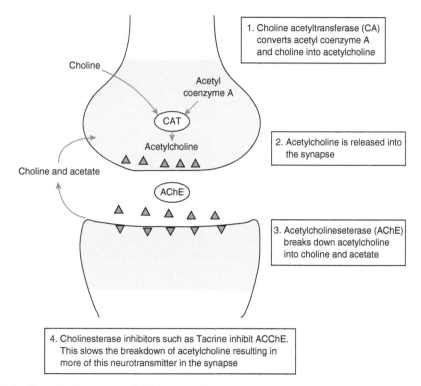

Figure 13.4   How cholinesterase inhibitors work

Source: Wickens (2009)

of acetylcholine is inhibited, levels of this neurotransmitter can build up and exert a longer duration of action (Ferreira-Vieira, 2016). Several cholinesterase inhibitors have now been shown to partially ameliorate cognitive deficits, enhance the quality of life, and diminish the caregiver burden for patients with mild to severe Alzheimer's (Sharma, 2019). But unfortunately, these drugs only have beneficial effects for around one to three years, and they do not slow down the progression of the disease. This simple fact indicates that the cholinergic deficiencies in Alzheimer's may not be the prime cause of the disorder, but a secondary consequence of something more fundamental and widespread (Chen & Mobley, 2019).

> **KEY TERMS:** *choline acetyltransferase, acetylcholine, nucleus basalis of Meynert, septal diagonal band complex, basal forebrain, cholinesterase inhibitor*

THE AMYLOID CASCADE THEORY

The hallmarks of Alzheimer's disease are the presence of amyloid plaques and neurofibrillary tangles (NFTs) in the brain, and by the 1980s most investigators believed these had a fundamental role in causing the illness. But before this could be proven, researchers would have to understand how plaques and tangles were formed – and whether they could cause neural degeneration. This type of reasoning led to the amyloid cascade theory (see Selkoe & Hardy, 2016) which many believe is the key to unlocking how Alzheimer's disease occurs (see Figure 13.5). Put simply, it proposes amyloid deposition is the initial pathological event in Alzheimer's disease leading to the formation of senile plaques, and then to neurofibrillary tangles, neuronal cell death, and ultimately dementia (Reitz, 2012).

It has been known since the time of Alzheimer that senile plaques contain a substance called amyloid (meaning starch-like) which had been first identified by the father of modern pathology, Rudolf Virchow. Now called beta amyloid (Aβ), this is actually an aggregate of protein that can assemble into different forms. It has also become the most investigated amino acid chain (peptide) in neuroscience. Intensive efforts to isolate and identify this protein culminated in 1984 when it was found that amyloid consisted of a chain of either 40 or 42 amino acids (Glenner & Wong, 1984). This was an important breakthrough since the purification of amyloid, and determination of its chemical structure, enabled the cloning of the DNA that controlled amyloid production. This was accomplished in 1987 when researchers from four different laboratories sequenced the gene for amyloid. This revealed that amyloid was a fragment of a much larger 695 amino acid protein, now known as the beta amyloid precursor protein (β-APP).

Interestingly, the β-APP protein occurs in many tissues and not just the brain. Its primary function is not known, although it is concentrated in the synapses of neurons (Priller et al., 2006). β-APP is a molecule that spans the cellular membrane, with a short chain of amino acids jutting into the cell and a longer tail projecting out. The part of protein making up the crucial Aβ molecule is composed of amino acids 597 through to 636, which are the 28 amino acids just outside the cell and the first 12 amino acids within the membrane. But why was the β-APP protein broken down? The answer is that the β-APP protein has a short life, and when it has served its biological purpose, it is removed from the membrane by being 'cut' into smaller units by enzymes called **secretases** (Thrap & Sarker, 2013).

Early work indicated that the β-APP molecule was cut in one of two ways. The first produced a form of soluble Aβ containing a chain of 40 amino acids. It was initially assumed this type of Aβ was a normal by-product of β-APP metabolism. The second form of Aβ was cut in such a way that it left it with two extra amino acids. This type of Aβ was insoluble, and it was the amyloid found in the plaques where it accumulated into hardened sheets. Not surprisingly, many researchers assumed this was harmful to neurons. It also led to the first version of the amyloid cascade theory which viewed the insoluble Aβ molecule as the initiating event in the formation of plaques, neurofibrillary tangles and subsequent cell death in the brain.

However, things have not turned out to be so straightforward and this chain of events is no longer widely believed. If the amyloid cascade theory was true, then one might expect the number of plaques to correlate with the severity of the illness, but this is not always the case (Dickson et al., 1995). Somewhat unexpectedly, it also became apparent that the amount of the soluble Aβ was a far better predictor of cognitive decline and synapse loss (Lue et al., 1999; McLean et al., 1999) which could reach a 70-fold higher level in the brains of people with Alzheimer's compared to those of controls. A decade of studies since has confirmed these findings and shown that the soluble oligomeric forms of Aβ (an oligomer is a molecular complex of chemicals that consist of a few repeating units) are much more likely to be involved in the pathophysiology of Alzheimer's disease (Larson & Lesné, 2012). This has greatly complicated the overall picture. It is believed that at least four types of oligomeric Aβ are formed – each of which may have differential effects on neuronal and synaptic survival.

KEY TERMS: *beta amyloid (Aβ), beta amyloid precursor protein (β-APP), secretases*

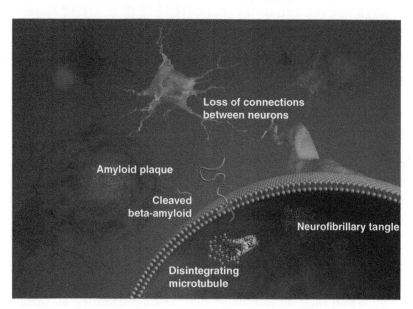

Figure 13.5   The amyloid hypothesis. Beta-amyloid plaques are formed when the extracellular portion of the APP (blue), the precursor protein for Aβ is cleaved by the enzymes β secretase (red) and presenilin (green). This causes the release of Aβ strands (orange) that accumulate into plaques in extracellular space. Neurofibrillary tangles inside the neuron are caused by the phosphhylated tau protein, which dissociates from microtubules causing them to disintegrate. The tau protein then aggregates into neurofibrillary tangles.

Source: from the National Institute on Aging, Progress Report on Alzheimer's Disease 2004–2005. In Gaskin (2021)

PROBLEMS WITH THE AMYLOID THEORY

Despite its popularity, the amyloid cascade theory has its critics (Makin, 2018). One of the main problems is that drug treatments aimed at reducing the amount of amyloid in the brain have been shown to be ineffective in treating the progression of the disease (Ricciarelli & Fedele, 2017), a situation that has led to great despondency in the pharmaceutical industry (*New York Times*, 2018)[1]. Another worrying problem is that according to some reports, NFTs arise in the brain before the formation of the amyloid plaques (Duyckaerts et al., 2009), or at the very least, the development of amyloid plaques and NFTs occurs independently and not necessarily in overlapping parts of the brain (Armstrong, 2011). The number of NFTs also correlates well with the severity of the dementia (Serrano-Pozo et al., 2011). These findings have led some researchers to propose that the NFTs (caused by the tau protein breaking away from the microtubule) are the main instigator of Alzheimer's disease (Maccioni et al., 2010). This has resulted in two camps: the baptists supporting the amyloid theory ('bap' being an abbreviation of *beta amyloid protein*), and the taurists advocating the importance of NFTs. But it may well be that neither is correct, with plaques and NFTs being the products of some more fundamental abnormal process rather than the cause of the degeneration (Reitz, 2012).

KEY TERMS: *baptists, taurists*

THE GENETICS OF ALZHEIMER'S DISEASE

One important advance arising from the identification of the β-APP protein was the locating of its associated β-APP gene on chromosome 21 (Tanzi et al., 1987). This proved of great worth because it opened the way up for understanding its role in the formation of β-amyloid. In addition, it was known that people who inherit an extra copy of chromosome 21 develop Down's syndrome – a disorder where high numbers of plaques and NFTs also occur in the brain, which invariably causes Alzheimer-like symptoms if the person lives past 50. The linkage to chromosome 21 also enabled researchers to look for individuals that carried mutations in the β-APP gene. Although it was clear that the vast majority of Alzheimer's cases were not caused by a single gene mutation, researchers were nonetheless aware of very rare instances where the disease did run in families, and during the 1990s, a family was found where each person with Alzheimer's had a mutation in their β-APP gene (Goate et al., 1991). Such discoveries were not common, however, and over the next 10 years or so, fewer than 20 families worldwide would be identified who carried the same β-APP mutation (Blacker & Tanzi, 1998). Despite its rarity, all instances of this

---

[1]As this book goes to press, a drug called aducanumab which reduces the build up of amyloid, has just been approved by the US authorities. So the situation regarding treatments aimed at amyloid now appears much more positive.

mutation were found to cause a form of Alzheimer's with an early mean age of onset of between 45 and 66 years. It is now known there are at least 20 slightly different types of mutation that can occur in the β-APP gene and all lead to early dementia (Tanzi, 2012). In recent years the linkage of chromosome 21 with Alzheimer's disease has become more complex, with the discovery that the β-APP gene is not the only gene on this particular chromosome involved in the formation and deposition of amyloid (Wiseman et al., 2018).

The linkage of the β-APP gene with early onset Alzheimer's led to a search of other chromosomes. This bore fruit in 1995 when a gene located on chromosome 14 called presenilin-1 was linked with an inherited form of Alzheimer's (Sherrington et al., 1995). Soon after, a presenilin-2 gene was traced to chromosome 1 which accounted for further familial cases (Levy-Lahad et al., 1995). Both genes appeared to produce their adverse effects by altering the processing of the β-APP protein (Borchelt et al., 1997). The mean age of onset of Alzheimer's with those carrying mutations of the presenilin-1, which is the most common inherited type of the disease (making up over 50% of familial cases), was found to be about 45 years. It was slightly higher for those with the presinilin-2 gene at 52 years (Blacker & Tanzi, 1998).

The vast majority of Alzheimer cases (>95%) are, however, of later onset and do not follow a familial pattern of inheritance. Like many other psychiatric and neurological disorders, the genetics of late-onset Alzheimer's disease are more complex, with environmental factors coming into play. Whilst no genetic mutations have been identified that directly cause one to inherit late-onset Alzheimer's, there are genes that can alter the risk of developing the illness (Bekris et al., 2010). The best known is the **apolipoprotein E gene** (ApoE) located on chromosome 19. This gene comes in three possible forms or alleles (designated 2, 3 and 4) and we inherit two versions – one from each of our parents. This means that we can carry one of six possible ApoE combinations (2:2, 2:3, 2:4, 3:3, 3:4 and 4:4). Of particular interest is the 4:4 combination which is over-represented in both early and late-onset forms of Alzheimer's disease (Strittmatter et al., 1993). It has been shown that the mean age of onset of the disease for individuals with two Apo-E-4 alleles is below 70 years. In contrast, it is between 80 and 90 years for those inheriting two ApoE-3 alleles (this is the most common combination), and over a 100 years for those with two ApoE-2 alleles (Roses, 1995).

Apolipoproteins are a large family of proteins, encoded by multiple genes, that are found in blood plasma. They are believed to have an important role in the transport of lipids such as cholesterol. This protein is also found in the glial cells of the brain where it is suspected of being involved in the repair, growth and maintenance of myelin and neuronal membranes (Avramopoulous, 2009). The wide diversity of apolipoproteins and their functions has made their involvement in Alzheimer's difficult to establish, but there is little doubt that the Apo-E-4 combination is a risk factor for the disease. This is seen by the fact that the Apo-E-4 combination is present in 20–30% of the general population, but 45–60% of patients with Alzheimer's (Blacker & Tanzi, 1998). Nonetheless, it must be noted that many people with Alzheimer's disease do not have Apo-E-4 genes, and many who do have them do not necessarily develop the disease.

How might a lipoprotein have such a bearing on the risk of developing Alzheimer's disease? Some lines of evidence support the idea that ApoE may affect the formation of amyloid. For example, mice that lack the gene for ApoE do not show amyloid deposition in their brains, whereas transgenic mice that overexpress the ApoE-4 gene exhibit increased numbers of amyloid plaques (Price et al., 1998). It has also been shown in laboratory studies that the protein derived from the ApoE-4 gene promotes amyloid formation more readily than its ApoE-3 form (Evans et al., 1995). However, there may be other reasons. For example, it has been shown that normal carriers of the ApoE-4 gene have lower cerebral blood flow (Thambisetty et al., 2010), and in another study infants with the ApoE-4 gene combination were shown to have reduced growth in their temporal and parietal cortices – areas of the brain that show later degeneration in Alzheimer's (Dean et al., 2014). There is clearly much more to learn about the genetics of Alzheimer's disease, with recent estimates putting its heritability at around 70% (Bellenguez et al., 2020).

> **KEY TERMS:** *β-APP gene, Down's syndrome, presenilin-1 and presenilin-2 genes, apolipoprotein E gene, alleles*

Table 13.1   Known genes for Alzheimer's

Gene	Chromosome	Age of onset (years)	Percentage of cases
APP	21	45–66	<0.1
Presenilin 1	14	28–62	1–2
Presenilin 2	1	40–85	<0.1
ApoE4	19	>60	>50

Source: Garrett and Hough (2018)

COGNITIVE RESERVE AND THE BENEFITS OF MENTAL EXERCISE

We might be forgiven for believing we can do little to offset the inevitable development of Alzheimer's in later life, yet this appears not to be the case, for convincing evidence has shown that the chances of developing dementia can be significantly reduced by education and the capacity for mental exercise. But why should these protect us against Alzheimer's disease? One theory is that it builds a **cognitive reserve** which increases the brain's resilience to later neural degeneration. The origins of this idea first arose when Katzman et al. (1988) undertook a post-mortem study examining the brains of 137 nursing home residents (average age 85.5 years) whose mental status had already been evaluated. It unexpectedly revealed there were some participants whose brains had extensive Alzheimer's disease pathology, yet no manifestations of the illness. These subjects also had heavier brains with more neurons (taken from a cross-sectional area of the cerebral cortex) compared to those of age-matched controls. This pointed to the possibility that these incipient Alzheimer individuals had escaped the neural degeneration because of their greater brain size – in other words, they had a greater 'brain reserve' to fight the illness.

Around the same time as this discovery, David Snowdon and his colleagues at the University of Minnesota were beginning to show that mental exercise was a critical factor in building up resistance to dementia. Snowdon persuaded 678 Notre Dame convent nuns, aged from 75 to 106, to take part in a study where they underwent rigorous mental and physical testing once a year, as well as allowing investigators full access to their convent and medical records. The nuns also agreed to donate their brains at death. As Snowdon (2001) recounts in his book *Aging with Grace*, a breakthrough occurred when the diaries of 93 sisters that had been written some 60 years earlier (just prior to their religious vows) were discovered. When these were examined, Snowdon realized that the nuns who had expressed the richest vocabulary, sentence construction and ideas were more likely to have aged successfully without dementia. In contrast, the nuns whose essays put them in the bottom third on a linguistic ability scale had increased their risk of a dementing illness.

Several other longitudinal studies have shown that mental exercise can provide protection against dementia. The most extensive are the Lothian Birth Cohort (LBC) studies of 1921 and 1936. On 1 June 1932, almost every child attending a Scottish school and born in 1921 took the same general mental ability test (known as the Moray House Test No. 12). This exercise was repeated on 4 June 1947 for every Scottish school pupil born in 1936. The purpose of these tests was to establish how childhood intelligence relates to cognition and mental health in old age. The LBC studies are unique since they are the only attempts to date of any country to measure the intelligence of a complete year of birth in its population. The cohorts have been followed up at multiple times since recruitment, and one of the main findings to emerge is that childhood intelligence is strongly correlated with intelligence in old age. Intelligence is therefore a highly stable trait (Deary et al., 2013). Moreover, the studies have also shown that lower childhood mental ability is associated with an increased risk of late-onset dementia (Whalley et al., 2000). This appears to be closely related to the integrity of white matter tracts in the brain which is a good predictor of healthy cognitive aging (Penke et al., 2010).

Another population-based cohort study by Huang et al. (2018) has reported findings from a large group of American male and female high school students who completed a variety of cognitive tests in 1960, and who were then followed up later to assess levels of dementia. The results showed that 2.9% of men and 3.3% of women had developed dementia at the time of testing. But perhaps more interesting was the finding that poorer mechanical reasoning was associated with dementia in men, and poorer word memory in adolescence associated with increased odds of dementia in women. These findings have led to calls for greater specialized educational intervention to build up cognitive reserves in individuals who are at risk for Alzheimer's (Russ, 2018).

Another lifestyle factor that provides protection against mental decline is physical exercise. For example, Yaffe et al. (2001) measured cognitive performance in 5,925 women aged over 65 years and asked them to record their weekly physical exercise. Increased physical activity was found to protect mental decline when intelligence was assessed some six to eight years later. A similar finding was reported by Laurin et al. (2001), who used data from 9,008 randomly selected men and woman aged over 65 years that had been interviewed about their general health and screened for dementia. When a large number of these subjects (N = 4,615) were followed up five years later, the amount of exercise was the most important factor in determining a person's risk of cognitive decline. This was most significant for those engaging in high levels of physical activity which was defined as exercise three or more times a week at an intensity greater than walking.

It is becoming clear that exercise exerts its neuroprotective effect through a wide variety of biological indices. This includes the production of antioxidant enzymes which reduces tissue-damaging free radicals, and a wide range of growth factors that help maintain healthy neural function (Chen et al., 2016). But even more remarkable is that physical exercise can lead to new brain growth. For example, Colcombe et al. (2006) found that an aerobic programme increased the volume of grey and white cortical matter in subjects over the age of 60 years, whilst Pereira et al. (2007) reported that a three-month aerobic exercise regimen led to an increase in cerebral blood flow and neurogenesis in the dentate gyrus of the hippocampus. In another study, aerobic exercise increased the size of the anterior hippocampus by about 2%, which led to improvements in spatial memory – an effect that was positively correlated with greater serum levels of brain-derived neurotrophic factor (Erickson et al., 2011). An increase in brain-derived neurotrophic factor with exercise has even been found in some patients with Alzheimer's disease (de Melo Coelho et al., 2014).

KEY THINKER 13.1

JEAN MARTIN CHARCOT

If there is one person responsible for creating the medical discipline of neurology, it is surely Jean-Martin Charcot. Born in 1825, the son of a working-class Parisian carriage builder, Charcot would rise from his humble beginnings to become the most famous doctor in France. Yet his rise was not meteoric for he would spend ten years working routinely in several Parisian hospitals – one of which was Le Salpêtrière. At its peak, it had been the largest asylum in Europe with over 8,000 inmates. But by the mid-nineteenth century, Le Salpêtrière had fallen into ruins. Nonetheless, Charcot saw in it a unique opportunity to inspect a large population of patients, most of whom had been committed for life, suffering from a 'pandemonium of human infirmities'. In 1862 Charcot became its chief, and with Alfred Vulpian set about classifying his patients' disabilities and organizing them into wards. A small stout man with a big head and bull neck, Charcot's authoritative command soon led him to be known as the Napoleon of Salpêtrière.

Charcot was meticulous in undertaking clinical examinations of his patients, which he recorded using detailed notes. He also set up a pathology laboratory to perform autopsies. His objective was to correlate the symptoms of his patients with their neurological abnormalities at death. This became known as the anatomo-clinical method, and in the hands of Charcot was to prove a very effective means of identifying new conditions, and greatly aiding understanding of those already known.

One of Charcot's most important contributions to medical knowledge was his description of *la sclérose en plaques* (multiple sclerosis) in 1868. Charcot was not the first to observe this illness, nor to show it was characterized by hardened and discoloured plaques that were scattered throughout the white matter of the brain and spinal cord. But he was the first to show that patients with sclerotic plaques always exhibited intentional tremor (produced during deliberate movement), whereas a similar behavioural disorder but without the plaques produced a resting tremor. In fact, Charcot had found a way of distinguishing between *la sclérose en plaques* and *paralysis agitans* (which he would later call *La maladie de Parkinson* in 1869). This discovery would lead to far more accurate descriptions of multiple sclerosis and Parkinson's disease – both of which had previously been confused.

The methods used by Charcot to correlate clinical symptoms with pathological anatomy also led to the discovery of motor neurone disease (otherwise known as amyotrophic lateral sclerosis).

During the 1860s, Charcot had begun examining the symptoms of two groups of patients: those with spasticity and those with atrophied muscles. After performing a number of autopsies, he realized these two groups had different types of spinal cord damage. The patients with spasticity had degeneration of the lateral columns, whereas those with muscular dystrophy had damage to the anterior horns. But as Charcot undertook more autopsies he found a small number of patients who exhibited both spasticity and dystrophy along with lateral column and anterior horn damage. Charcot had identified a new disorder, characterized by a rapidly progressive wasting disease beginning in mid-life and usually fatal within a few years. Motor neurone disease has struck down a number of famous people since, including the baseball player Lou Gehrig, the composer Dmitri Shostakovich, and the actor David Niven. The physicist Stephen Hawking was another victim, although his illness was a rare form with an unusually slow progression.

All of this was not overlooked by the French government, who awarded Charcot 200,000 francs in 1881 to create the world's first professorship devoted to neurological disease at the University of Paris. This was the moment when clinical neurology became a distinct area of medical specialization. Although Charcot's reputation would be later tarnished by his investigations into hysteria (see Wickens, 2015), his anatomo-clinical method had shown how it was possible to discover new neurological diseases, that hitherto had been confused or even unsuspected. Charcot had laid the foundations for modern neurological classification. He also achieved fame for his teaching – the notes of which would form a large body of work published in nine volumes between 1877 and 1890. Charcot died suddenly in 1893, at the age of 67, after spending a day walking in the countryside of Burgundy.

THE DISCOVERY OF PARKINSON'S DISEASE

In 1817, a London doctor called James Parkinson published a 66-page treatise entitled *Essay on the Shaking Palsy* which described a new medical condition that today bears his name. His account of the disorder, also known as *paralysis agitans*, was based on just six individuals – three of whom he observed at a distance in the street. Despite this, it is said that Parkinson described the condition with a vividness and insight that has never been surpassed (Sacks, 1990). Among the symptoms of **Parkinson's disease** were a resting tremor which could be so violent that it shook the floors of the room, **bradykinesia** (slow and impoverished movement), and **akinesia** (the loss or impairment of voluntary action). Parkinson also described the course of the disease which often led from a single tremor in one of the limbs to a loss of muscle tone and paralysis, causing the victim to become bedridden and helpless. Although these symptoms had been observed before (one can even find a good description of the disease in Shakespeare's *Henry IV*), they had been attributed to alcohol abuse or old age. Parkinson was the first to group the symptoms of tremor and paralysis into a specific neurological disease. Despite this, however, his essay had little impact for nearly half a century, and it did not become better known until Charcot began referring to *La Maladie de Parkinson* in the 1860s.

Parkinson was not an eminent person of his times. Trained as a surgeon, he spent his working life as a parish physician and warden of his church. He also had a secretive subversive side. The early nineteenth century was a time when the American colonies broke away from Britain to found a new political system based on equality, and the French Revolution had shown that monarchies could be overthrown. In the

Figure 13.6   Two sketches showing a man with Parkinson's disease
Source: Anetode/Wikipedia Commons

spirit of the times, Parkinson supported political reform in England. To this end, he belonged to several radical societies, and wrote political pamphlets under the pseudonym 'Old Hubert' that were highly critical of the government. Parkinson was even subpoenaed and examined under oath by the prime minister concerning knowledge of an alleged conspiracy to assassinate King George III in 1784. Although there is no evidence Parkinson was involved in this plot, he only agreed to testify after being assured he would not be forced to incriminate himself. It is also curious that no drawings or pictures of James Parkinson are known to exist.

KEY TERMS: *Parkinson's disease, resting tremor, bradykinesia, akinesia*

THE EPIDEMIOLOGY OF PARKINSON'S DISEASE

Parkinson's disease is the second most common neurodegenerative disorder after Alzheimer's disease, and it affects some 6.1 million people globally (2016 figures). Its prevalence also appears to be rising since there were only 2.5 million people with the disease in 1990 – a change that cannot be attributed solely to the increasing numbers of older people since (Dorsey et al., 2018). Parkinson's disease is primarily an illness of later life with the mean age of onset being between 55 and 65 years (Samii et al., 2004).

It occurs in around 1% of the population in western countries, with a slightly higher percentage of people affected in Europe (1.6%). This rises from 0.6% at age 60–64 years to 3.5% at age 85–89 years (De Rijk et al., 1997). In the UK, it is estimated that about 145,000 people have the disorder and it is some 1.5 times more common in men than in woman. The lifetime risk of being diagnosed with Parkinson's in the UK is 2.7% which is equivalent to about 1 in every 37 people developing the illness at some point in their life (parkinsons.org.uk). But certain disabilities of movement such as tremor and dystonia (which alone are not sufficient for a Parkinson's diagnosis) are more common than this, with one study showing that 15% of those aged 65–74, 30% of those aged 75–84, and over 50% of 85-year-olds have at least two motor impairments (Bennett et al., 1996). In rare cases, Parkinson's disease can also occur in younger individuals. Juvenile Parkinson's disease (with an onset before the age of 20) and early Parkinson's disease (21–40 years) make up around 5% of all cases.

THE CLINICAL COURSE OF PARKINSON'S DISEASE

The first symptoms of Parkinson's disease are often innocuous. In some cases the disorder may begin as a slight tremor in a hand, or a slight postural flexion of the neck (Figure 13.6). Although symptoms typically start on one side of the body, they inevitably spread to the other side within a year or so. As this occurs, a shaking tremor of certain parts of the body becomes more pronounced when the person attempts to move. There is also a general slowness of movement that is not helped by inflexible or rigid muscles which can cause a stiffness of the limbs and trunk, making it difficult for the person to maintain their balance and walk. This often results in the person developing a stooped head-down shoulders-drooped stance, with their walking characterized by small shuffling steps. There may also be a problem when beginning to walk forward, or perhaps a tendency to freeze in mid-stride. But it is not just movement that is affected. Curiously, a loss of smell (anosmia) is one of the most noticeable symptoms of Parkinson's and may appear several years before the disease is diagnosed. A person with Parkinson's can often be recognized by their blank facial expression (sometimes called facial masking) along with declining changes in the volume and quality of their voice. Many of these symptoms vary in severity from day to day, or even moment to moment (Sveinbjornsdottir, 2016).

In the later stages of the disease a number of secondary symptoms can appear. These include drooling saliva from the mouth, constipation, a difficulty in swallowing, incontinence, and excessive sweating. As the disease progresses, not only is their depression and anxiety likely to become more pronounced, but there may also be signs of subcortical dementia (a dementia primarily affecting areas below the cerebral cortex) with slow memory recall and a decline in intellectual capacity. In the end stages of the disease, especially without treatment, there will be almost complete invalidism, with postural muscle strength so weak that the person will find it difficult even to move their head. Before the introduction of effective drug therapy the average survival time for a patient with Parkinson's disease was around 8–10 years. Today, with treatment, life expectancy is not greatly reduced compared to that of the general population (Golbe & Leyton, 2018).

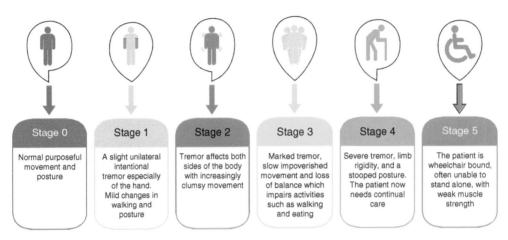

Figure 13.7 The stages of Parkinson's disease

Source: adapted from Wickens (2009), from Graham (1990)

THE PATHOLOGICAL FEATURES OF PARKINSON'S DISEASE

The underlying cause of Parkinson's disease was first discovered by Herbert Ehringer and Oleh Hornykiewicz in 1960, when they measured at post-mortem the levels of the then newly discovered neurochemical **dopamine** in patients who had died with basal ganglia dysfunction. In all the cases where Parkinson's disease had been present, they found a marked loss of dopamine (90%) in the **caudate nucleus** and **putamen** which are otherwise known as the striatum (see Figures 4.11 and 4.12 in Chapter 4). It was clear, therefore, that dopamine loss was involved in the pathophysiology of the disease. In 1964, Arvid Carlsson and his colleagues showed that dopamine in the caudate and putamen was derived from neurons arising from a small, darkly pigmented nucleus in the midbrain called the substantial nigra pars compacta. It soon become apparent that Parkinson's disease was due to marked degeneration of this nigral-striatal pathway (see Goetz, 2011), and that the loss of substantia nigra pigmentation was positively correlated with the neuronal loss of dopaminergic neurons (Dickson, 2018).

The involvement of the substantia nigra in Parkinson's disease had been suspected by some researchers, but many were also sceptical that damage confined to such a small brain area could produce such a devastating disease. However, further examination of the substantia nigra in Parkinson's disease not only showed a marked loss of its cells, but also revealed that the first behavioural signs of Parkinsonism did not appear until around 80% of the neurons had been lost (Bernheimer et al., 1973). In addition, the neurons of the substantia nigra were found to contain large numbers of **Lewy bodies** – tiny spherical structures within the cytoplasm of the cell that contained a core of α-**synuclein** (a neuronal protein of unknown function) surrounded by filamentous material (Dauer & Przedborski, 2003). Whether these are involved in the neurodegenerative process still remains uncertain (Parkkinen et al., 2011).

In the later stages of the disease, the loss of dopamine becomes more extensive. For example, dopamine levels in the ventral striatum, frontal lobes and hippocampus may decline by up to 50% (Agid et al., 1987). This is significant because whilst the extent of nigral-striatal degeneration correlates with the degree of motor impairment, the dopamine loss elsewhere correlates with the severity of affective and intellectual impairment (McNamara et al., 2002). In addition, it is likely that non-dopaminergic systems become impacted by the degeneration which plays a significant role in the later stages of the disease (Lang & Obeso, 2004). There is also an increasing deposition of Lewy bodies in many regions of the Parkinson's brain, including the basal forebrain, the amygdala and the medial temporal lobe, leading eventually to their formation in the cerebral cortex (Dickson, 2018).

KEY TERMS: *dopamine, caudate nucleus, putamen, substantial nigra pars compacta, Lewy bodies, α-synuclein*

THE FIRST EFFECTIVE DRUG TREATMENT: LEVODOPA (L-DOPA)

The discovery that Parkinson's disease was caused by nigral-striatal degeneration and dopamine depletion had important implications. If a way of replenishing the lost dopamine could be found, then an effective treatment for the disorder might be achieved. Unfortunately, the administration of dopamine proved ineffective because it did not cross the blood–brain barrier, and was quickly broken down in the blood by the enzyme dopa decarboxylase. However, in 1967, researchers discovered that large

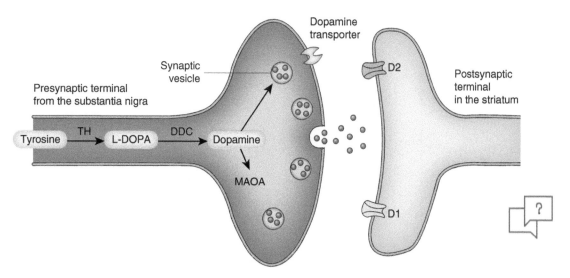

Figure 13.8 The synthesis pathway of L-Dopa. Levodopa (L-Dopa) is metabolized to dopamine by the enzyme dopa-decarboxylase (DDC). The dopamine is then packed into vesicles or metabolized by the enzyme monoamine oxidase A (MAO A)

Source: Higgs et al. (2020); Youdim et al. (2006). The therapeutic potential of monoamine oxidase inhibitors. *Nature Reviews Neuroscience*, 7(4), 295–309. Reprinted with permission from Nature: Springer.

oral doses of the amino acid L-dopa (also known as levodopa) had beneficial effects in relieving Parkinson's symptoms (Cotzias et al., 1967). This drug acts as a precursor substance involved in the synthesis of catecholamine neurotransmitters. Moreover, because of the high dosage that was administered, it enabled a large amount of L-dopa to pass into the brain where it was taken up by axon terminals within the caudate nucleus and putamen to increase dopamine production. This proved to be a dramatic turning point in the management of Parkinson's disease (Fahn, 2015). Later, L-dopa was combined with a dopa decarboxylase inhibitor, such as carbidopa, which allowed the dose of L-dopa to be reduced with its side effects lessened.

L-dopa has become one of the most successful therapies in neurology, with the potential to transform someone who is as rigid as a stone into a person that can walk and function again. Around 70% of patients with Parkinson's disease show at least a 50% improvement with L-dopa treatment, and in some cases the benefits can be immediate and dramatic. But typically, treatment is started with low doses of L-dopa, which are increased over several months, producing a gradual improvement with time. Slowness of movement and muscle tone improve first, with tremor becoming less troublesome as treatment progresses. Although some minor motor disabilities may remain, many Parkinson's patients will enjoy functional independence. Today, L-dopa still remains the most effective drug treatment and has been called the gold standard of Parkinson's disease therapy (Mercuri & Bernardi, 2005).

Unfortunately, L-dopa is not a cure or a panacea. The first problem to arise is often a decline in the effectiveness of L-dopa after several years of treatment (see Figure 13.9) which requires a higher dose to be administered. This will increase the risk of side effects such as nausea, fidgeting or psychosis. Another distressing problem is the 'on-off' responses to the drug, where periods of immobility and tremor begin to increase or occur in unpredictable ways. In some cases, the off response can happen so abruptly

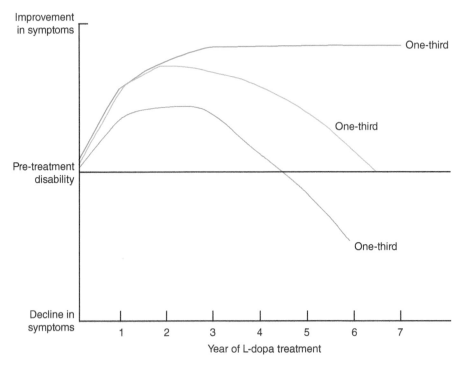

Figure 13.9 Possible outcomes of L-dopa therapy
Source: Wickens (2009)

that the person becomes 'frozen' in mid-movement. Another side effect is involuntary movements of the face, hands and limbs which is known as **dyskinesia**. It has been reported that these types of side effects occur in 80% of patients who have been given high doses of L-dopa for six or more years (Lees, 1986). Because of this problem, some doctors advise patients to take 'L-dopa holidays' in the hope that this will prolong the effectiveness of the drug. Alternatively, the patient is given a cocktail of drugs including dopamine agonists and cholinesterase inhibitors to supplement the L-Dopa. Nonetheless, L-dopa remains very much at the forefront of therapy and is likely to be used in combination with various new strategies such as gene therapy or transplantation in the future (Nagatsu & Sawada, 2009).

KEY TERMS: *L-dopa, 'on-off' responses, dyskinesia*

THE GENETICS OF PARKINSON'S DISEASE

Until recently, Parkinson's disease was believed to arise sporadically without significant genetic involvement. Support for this position came from twin studies which typically revealed a low concordance rate of Parkinson's disease (e.g. around 10–20%) in both monozygotic and dizygotic pairs (Golbe, 1995). This is not the pattern of results expected of a genetic disorder where greater concordance in identical twins is the norm (see next chapter). Nonetheless, it is now known that in around 5–10% of cases, an early onset form of the disease has a genetic origin. In a study examining 161 pairs of twins with late-onset Parkinson's disease (beginning after 50 years old) the concordance was 15.5% for monozygotic twins and 11.1% for dizygotic twins, but when the same analysis was undertaken for early onset Parkinson's, the concordance was 100% for identical twins compared to 17% for non-identical ones (Langston, 2002). Although the concordance rate for early onset Parkinson's disease is not always 100%, it is inevitably high. For example, if a member of a twin pair is diagnosed with the disease before the age of 51, the chances of an identical twin also developing the disorder are six times greater than for a non-identical twin (Tanner et al., 1999).

Worldwide, there are a few families where Parkinson's disease is inherited as an autosomal dominant disorder. That is, individuals who inherit a certain mutation within their genes will go on to develop the illness at some point in their lives. The first family to be identified where Parkinson's disease was clearly inherited came from the Italian province of Salerno and consisted of 45 affected members across four generations (Golbe et al., 1990). Known as the Contursi kindred, the individuals who developed the disease did so at an early age (mean age 46.5 years), and showed marked nigral degeneration and Lewy body formation at post-mortem. The mutation that causes this familial disease was found to be located on chromosome 4. In its unmutated state, the gene produces a small protein of just 140 amino acids called α-synuclein (Polymeropoulos et al., 1996). A change of a single base pair (from guanine to adenine) at position 53 is sufficient to produce a faulty protein.

The biological function of α-synuclein is not known, although it appears to be localized in the presynaptic membrane where it is likely to be involved in neurotransmitter release (Moore et al., 2005). Although α-synuclein is widely found in the brain, high amounts occur in the substantia nigra (Mori et al., 2006), and as we have already mentioned, it is a major component of Lewy bodies. One possibility is that the mutated form of α-synuclein accumulate into 'lumps' that are deposited in the cytoplasm which are toxic to the neuron (Fujiwara et al., 2002). In support of this idea, there is evidence that α-synuclein is not broken down and cleared away from neurons efficiently. This process normally uses the protein ubiquitin which 'tags' obsolete proteins, in order to provide a signal for another class of enzymes called proteosomes to begin the process of amino acid dismantling. It has been suggested this process may be faulty in Parkinson's disease, with a build-up of defective proteins taking place in dopaminergic neurons (Cookson, 2003). If this is the case, then treatments aimed at proteolytic clearance of extracellular α-synuclein might provide an exciting new therapeutic approach against Parkinson's disease (Park & Kim, 2013).

Since the discovery of the α-synuclein gene, a number of other genes have also been linked to Parkinson's disease. The best researched is the Parkin gene located on chromosome 6. This gene causes a recessive form of the disorder, which means that a defective copy of the gene has to be inherited from each parent for the illness to be inherited. In fact, this gene is the most common one in early onset Parkinson's disease. In a study of 73 families with Parkinson's disease that occurred before the age of 45 years, 49% were found to have the parkin mutation (Lucking et al., 2000). The normal parkin protein appears to play a role in transporting defective proteins to proteosomes, and presumably this process is defective in those with the mutated gene (Hattori & Mizuno, 2017).

Although there is little evidence supporting a direct (dominant or recessive) genetic involvement in late-onset Parkinson's disease, recent genome-wide association studies (see next chapter) have identified a large number of genes that appear to indicate susceptibility (Corti et al., 2011). A genome-wide association analysis is one that involves rapidly scanning genetic markers across complete sets of DNA, or genomes, to find variants specific to the disease (see next chapter). Many of the genes discovered in such association studies have either been implicated in **mitochondria** function, which are the intracellular organelles involved in energy production (Scorziello et al., 2020), or have been genes that are responsible for making substances that remove unwanted cellular proteins.

> **KEY TERMS:** α-synuclein, ubiquitin, proteosomes, Parkin gene, genome-wide association studies, mitochondria

ENVIRONMENTAL INFLUENCES IN PARKINSON'S DISEASE

Although genes play a key role in early onset forms of Parkinson's disease, environmental factors are likely to have a greater influence when it has a later onset. However, identifying these influences has proven elusive, and is hampered by a lack of understanding of what is happening during the long prodromal (gestation) period of the illness (Chen & Ritz, 2018). Despite this, there is no shortage of potential environmental risk factors. Viral infection is one such example, which on certain occasions has been linked with Parkinson's disease. This was shown in the great sleeping sickness pandemic that appeared during the winter of 1916–1917 in Europe, which then spread around the world affecting some 5 million people. Known as encephalitis lethargica, and presumed to be caused by a viral infection, the illness often caused the person to fall into a sleep-like coma, with many dying without regaining consciousness (see also Chapter 7). Post-mortem examination of their brains showed inflamed meninges and a reddish discolouration of the brain stem, with damage most evident in the hypothalamus and substantia nigra (Hoffman & Vilensky, 2017). Although some made a full recovery from the illness, many would later succumb to severe Parkinson-like symptoms. The story of those who fell into a coma but continued to survive is told in the 1990 film *Awakenings* starring Robert DeNiro and Robin Williams.

Exposure to certain toxins is another risk factor. Again, a tragic example can illustrate how this can arise. During the early 1980s, doctors in North California became suspicious when a group of relatively young people developed Parkinson's disease. Closer detective work revealed they had all used a synthetic form of heroin, bought from the same dealer which was contaminated with a poison called MPTP (Langston et al., 1983). The victims' loss was the experimenters' gain, for MPTP proved to be a selective neurotoxin for the substantia nigra. This also provided researchers with an effective means of mimicking the effects of Parkinson's disease in laboratory animals. But the most pressing matter was explaining how it caused nigral degeneration. It soon become clear that MPTP was oxidized into MPP+ which is a free radical – a highly reactive and toxic chemical. Normally formed in chemical reactions involving the breakdown of oxygen in cellular metabolism, free radicals only exist for a few millionths of a second, but the accumulation of free radical 'hits' over time inflicts damage on biological tissues and is believed to be an important cause of ageing (Wickens, 2001). In the case of MPP+, it was found to be taken up into the cells of the substantia nigra where it accumulated in the mitochondria. The result was a depletion of **ATP** (the cells' main source of energy), with a further cascade of damaging free radical reactions causing neuron death (Schapira, 1994).

It is troubling to realize that there are chemicals in the environment that resemble MPP+ which include various pesticides such as paraquat. And a number of studies have shown an association between areas of high pesticide use and Parkinson's disease (Hatcher et al., 2008). In one such investigation, Wang, Costello et al. (2011) focused on pesticide use in California's heavily agricultural central valley, and showed that exposure to these substances in the workplace substantially increased the risk for developing Parkinson's disease. This was most marked when people were exposed to three different types of pesticides all together (ziram, maneb and paraquat). The association between pesticide toxins and Parkinson-like behaviours has also been supported in animal experiments. For example, daily injections of the pesticide rotenone for 6–10 days in rats is sufficient to induce a 45% loss of dopaminergic neurons in the substantia nigra, along with striatal dopamine depletion, and motor symptoms such as bradykinesia, postural instability and rigidity (Cannon et al., 2009). There is also a greater risk of Parkinson's in those exposed to heavy metals such as lead and mercury, and people who have used certain illicit substances such as amphetamine and cocaine (Ball et al., 2019).

One of the more controversial risk factors implicated in Parkinson's disease is head injury. Although some large-scale studies have not found an association (Kenborg et al., 2015), others have shown that a mild traumatic brain injury including concussion can increase the chances of developing Parkinson's disease by more than 50%. For example, Gardner et al. (2015) examined the medical records of 325,870 veterans, half of whom had suffered a mild, moderate or severe head injury. Within 12 years, 1,462 veterans were diagnosed with PD, and 949 of them were those that had received an injury to the head. After adjusting for age and other factors, it was shown that mild brain injury increased the risk of Parkinson's by 56%, and this rose to 83% when the injury was rated as severe. It is also interesting to note that in animal models, brain inflammation (which can be a consequence of head trauma) has been shown to produce Parkinson-like effects (Taylor et al., 2016).

On a more positive note, some environmental factors may help protect against Parkinson's disease. One is smoking tobacco which has been estimated to decrease the risk of Parkinson's by 50% (Fratiglioni & Wang, 2000). This effect has been attributed to a more effective removal of free radicals from the brain (Calne & Langston, 1983). Another beneficial effect comes from drinking coffee which may reduce the chances of Parkinson's by 80% (Ross et al., 2000). As we saw in the previous chapter, coffee is an adenosine antagonist, so the reasons for this protective effect are not clear. Nonetheless, there has been some clinical success in treating Parkinson's with adenosine receptor antagonists (Hickey & Stacy, 2012).

KEY TERMS: *encephalitis lethargica, neurotoxin, free radical, ATP, head injury*

NEW PROSPECTS FOR PARKINSON'S DISEASE

In recent years, a major advance in the treatment of Parkinson's disease has been deep brain stimulation (DBS) (Figure 13.10). Previously, if patients had failed to respond to drug treatment, or the symptoms had become crippling and severe, their doctor may have recommended a brain lesion – typically a thalamotomy (thalamus) or pallidotomy (globus pallidus). Although this was a last resort, these operations could reduce rigidity and enhance the patient's ability to move. Fortunately, this has now been superseded by DBS, which uses permanently implanted electrodes connected to a pulse generator that delivers an electrical current to the brain. The generator is normally implanted in the upper chest and programmed externally by the patient using a special magnetic wand. DBS of the motor thalamus was first used in 1986 (Benabid et al., 1987), but the preferred target now is the subthalamic nucleus (STN), a relatively small group of cells that lie between the thalamus and the midbrain (Kocabicak et al., 2012). This type of stimulation results in significant and sometimes remarkable improvement of all the main motor symptoms of the disease, with sustained long-term benefits and improved quality of life (Groiss et al., 2009). Although it is not a cure and does not stop Parkinson's from progressing, it is usually beneficial in the later stages of the illness (the mean duration before initiating DBS in Parkinson's is about 13 years). Curiously, it is not clear how the procedure works. The subthalamic nucleus receives input from the globus pallidus and in turn innervates the striatum – which then forms a looped neural circuit back to the subthalamic nucleus. It is possible the procedure works by normalizing the abnormal oscillatory neural activity in this circuit which arises in the striatum (Groiss et al., 2009).

The ultimate aim, of course, is to find ways of slowing, stopping or even reversing the symptoms of Parkinson's disease, and there are high hopes that some of these objectives will be achieved over the next 20 years (Brundin & Wyse, 2019). One of the first attempts to reverse Parkinson's was by the transplantation of tissue into the brain to replenish the 'lost' dopamine. These experimental techniques were instigated in the early 1980s when researchers took tissue from the adrenal glands (which produces small amounts of dopamine) and placed it in the striatum (see Lindvall, 1989). However the benefits of this procedure were not impressive. Another approach to transplantation involved the use of foetal tissue which had yet to develop into mature brain cells. It was hoped that this tissue, when implanted into the striatum, would form new neural connections with the host dopaminergic cells. Ethical issues aside, the grafts survived well and increased dopamine production, but the

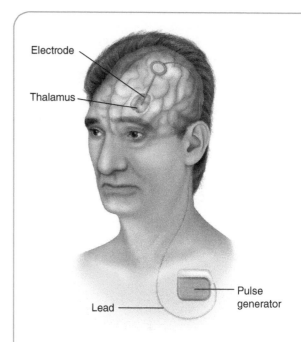

Figure 13.10   Deep brain stimulation

Source: Amanda Tomasikiewicz/Body Scientific Intl. in Gaskin (2021)

results of this procedure were highly variable and did not fully reverse symptoms or stop the disease from progressing (Freed et al., 2011).

The technique of foetal transplantation has now been superseded by the use of neural grafts composed of **stem cells**. These are basically 'blank' or undifferentiated cells which have the potential to turn into virtually any tissue in the human body, including nerve cells. Stem cells form in the embryo at a very early age (in humans they form in the blastocyst stage of embryonic development at around days 5–14), and they can be removed at this point and grown in the laboratory. In animal models, it has been shown that stem cells can be turned into fully functional dopamine neurons (this is discussed more fully in the next chapter). Such findings are tremendously exciting. As yet, no human studies using stem cell therapy in Parkinson's disease have been published, although the first clinical trials have started to take place (Fan et al., 2020). Clearly, they hold great promise for the future and there is genuine hope that stem cells will enter the clinic in the short- to medium-term future (Stoker, 2018).

KEY TERMS: *deep brain stimulation, subthalamic nucleus, transplantation, stem cells*

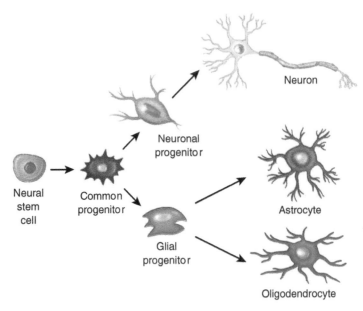

Figure 13.11   Neurogenesis using stem cells
Source: Amanda Tomasikiewicz/Body Scientific Intl. in Gaskin (2021)

SPECIAL INTEREST 13.1

THE SECRETS OF LONGEVITY

According to the *Guinness Book of World Records*, the oldest person to have ever lived is Jeanne Louise Calment who died when she was 122 years and 164 days old. Born in the Provence town of Arles, France, on February 21, 1875, she outlived 17 presidents, and recalled selling crayons in her father's shop to Vincent Van Gogh. But what was it about Jeanne that allowed her to live to such a great age? One notable feature of her life was that she rarely had to work since her family owned a wealthy drapery business. Consequently, she enjoyed a relatively stress-free and leisurely lifestyle with much of it spent playing tennis, cycling, swimming, roller-skating, and going to the opera. These activities would also continue well into her later years, with Jeanne taking up fencing at the age of 85 and riding a bicycle until she was 100. It also appears that Calment had good longevity genes with her father living to 94 and her mother to 86. After her husband died in 1943 (she had one daughter) Calment lived on her own until she was 110 when she entered a care home. Here she was spritely until a fall one month away from her 115th birthday. After surviving the subsequent hip operation she became the oldest person to have survived a surgical procedure. When asked about the secret of her longevity, Calment attributed it to a regular glass of port, taking care of her skin with olive oil, and good humour ('I've only one wrinkle – and I'm sitting on it!'). She would also take an afternoon nap for two hours. But not all of her habits were healthy ones. Jeanne was an occasional smoker of Dunhill cigarettes (including one before going to bed) and only quit at the age of 117 when she became too embarrassed to ask for a light because of her failing eyesight. She also loved chocolate, often eating a kilogram a week until her doctor persuaded her to give it up at the age 119 years. Always having been small in stature, she was just 137 cm tall (4 ft 6 in) in her final years (Allard et al., 1998).

The gerontologist Bernard Jeune has compared Jeanne Calment with 18 other people across the world who have been reliably verified to have reached at least 115 years of age. Whilst the lives of these individuals differ in many ways, they share a few common traits. For example, it helps to be female (only two were male), most smoked a little or not at all, and none had been obese. Another striking feature of Jeanne Calment and her fellow centenarians was their will to live and sense of humour. And a recurring theme in the relatives' descriptions of all these centenarians was that they were strong personalities who were able to combine strength of will with friendliness. It is also interesting to note all avoided dementia – at least until shortly before their death. They did not fear death and were seemingly reconciled with the fact their lives would soon end (Jeune et al., 2010).

The world's largest research study of centenarians is the New England Centenarian Study (NECS) which began in 1995. Led by Thomas Perls, the programme includes some 1,600 subjects along with their siblings (now in their 70s and 80s) and children. One key finding has been that exceptional longevity is a result of a combined influence of lifestyle and genetic factors. Although human twin studies suggest only 20–30% of genetic variation for longevity is inherited, the genetic influence is much higher in centenarians, and especially marked in those over 106 years. But unless we are blessed with such genes and want to become a centenarian, the best advice is to laugh, stay lean, remain active and reduce stress. And controversially, if you are a woman, have children after the age of 35 years (Perls et al., 1997).

THE DISCOVERY OF HUNTINGTON'S DISEASE

Another neurodegenerative disorder that primarily affects the striatum (caudate nucleus and putamen) is **Huntington's disease** – named in honour of George Huntington (1850–1916) who first described the condition in 1872. Huntington came from a family of doctors on Long Island, New York, and encountered the illness as a young boy. He was to recollect: 'Driving with my father … we suddenly came upon two women, mother and daughter, both tall, thin, almost cadaverous, both bowing, twisting, grimacing. I stared in wonderment, almost in fear. What could it mean?' (Wexler, 1996). Huntington would also observe the disease again, just after graduating with his medical degree, when returning home for a few months to help in the family practice. This gave him an opportunity to closely observe the affliction and examine the patient's medical records. In February 1872, Huntington reported his findings to a conference in Ohio, with a short paper of the talk entitled 'On Chorea' appearing two months later (*chorea* is now an outdated term meaning 'dance'). Although Huntington's paper was mostly concerned with Sydenham's chorea (a disorder linked to rheumatic fever in children), at the end, in seven short paragraphs, he described the 'heredity chorea' that existed on Long Island. It seems that Huntington thought of the disease as nothing more than a medical curiosity, but others, including the renowned physician Sir William Osler, realized its discovery had profound implications.

The real importance of Huntington's paper lay in the way he had described its inheritance. For example, Huntington had written: 'When either or both parents have shown manifestations of the disease ... one or more of the offspring almost invariably suffer from the disease, if they live to an adult age. But if by any chance these children go through life *without it*, the thread is broken, and the grandchildren and great-grandchildren of the original shakers may rest assured that they are free from the disease.' Although Huntington was unaware of the existence of genes (Mendel's laws of genetics were not to become widely known until 1900 – see next chapter), he was accurately describing a disease caused by a genetic mutation and inherited in an autosomal dominant fashion. Clearly, he was fortunate in being able to draw on medical records spanning a 78-year period from his family practice, but it was his insight into its inherited causation that was the key factor in generating interest in the new disorder. After publishing his paper, Huntington made no other scientific contribution to medicine, and did not even practise neurology (Finger, 1994).

The disease had undoubtedly existed before it was described by Huntington. In fact, a summary of the symptoms had been outlined by Charles Oscar Waters in a medical textbook of 1842. It also seems likely that Huntington's disease was around in 1630 when King Charles I allowed the Church to increase its persecution of non-believers – an edict that encouraged the hunting of witches. Anybody at the time suffering from Huntington's disease with its strange jerking movements would have most likely incited fear and misunderstanding, and it is thought some afflicted families fled to America to escape the persecution. They may not have been entirely successful however, for at least seven individuals in the Salem witch trials of New England are believed to have come from families with Huntington's disease, and one woman was convicted of witchcraft and hanged in 1653 (Finger, 1994).

THE EPIDEMIOLOGY OF HUNTINGTON'S DISEASE

Huntington's disease is a rare but ultimately fatal disorder which affects around 10 people per 100,000 in European and American populations. It is less common in African and Japanese groups, but can be significantly higher in certain countries, such as Venezuela, where families with Huntington's disease have become established in remote areas (Paradisi et al., 2008). In the UK there are between 6,500 and 8,000 people with the disorder. The disease, which affects men and woman in equal proportion, usually begins between the ages of 35 and 50, with an average onset of symptoms beginning around 40 years old. One consequence of this late onset is that many people with the disease will have had children by this time, thereby putting them at risk for the illness. Tragically, the severity of the disease progresses steadily without remission, typically causing death within 15–20 years. In about 10% of cases, Huntington's disease has a juvenile onset, beginning before the age of 20, which is associated with muscle rigidity rather than chorea, and complicated by seizures and intellectual disability. Whilst Huntington's disease is normally inherited, new mutations can sporadically arise, and although once considered rare, it is now estimated that these may account for 10% of cases (Dayalu & Albin, 2015).

THE CLINICAL MANIFESTATIONS OF HUNTINGTON'S DISEASE

Huntington's disease is comprised of three main types of abnormality: motor, cognitive and emotional. The first overt signs are often clumsiness, excessive fidgeting, or jerky movements, although personality changes, mood swings and bizarre behaviours may be noticed first by family and friends. Whatever the initial symptoms, the most distinctive feature of the disease is involuntary and abrupt abnormal movements, which occur in the trunk, fingers, feet and face (Quinn & Schrag, 1998). As these symptoms worsen, sudden and flailing movements of the arms and upper body may take place, causing the person to writhe and jerk, or making them lurch and stumble. These startling behaviours can be accompanied by slurred speech, nystagmus (abnormal eye movements), grimacing and jaw clenching. Because of the high amount of energy used up by this almost constant and sometimes painful movement, along with difficulties in eating (swallowing becomes a problem as the mouth and diaphragm muscles lose control), the sufferer may become underweight, making them prone to infection and other illnesses. During the final stages of the disease, the choreic movements diminish and become replaced by Parkinsonism-like symptoms such as rigidity and paralysis. This often causes the victim to become bedridden and require constant care (Eggers et al., 2018).

Cognitive impairment is also a feature of Huntington's disease. This may first appear as a slowing of thought processes or a dimming of intellect, which leads to a functional decline and loss of autonomy where the sufferer becomes easily confused or forgetful. Despite this, language is normally preserved in the Huntington's patient, as is the ability to recognize other people or everyday objects (a deficit that occurs in the later stages of Alzheimer's disease). As we will see, the reason for this difference lies in the location of the pathophysiology – Alzheimer's being a dementia associated with cortical degeneration, whereas Huntington's disease is an example of dementia caused by subcortical damage (Zakzanis, 1998).

A wide variety of personality changes can accompany the progression of Huntington's disease which include irascibility, hostility, impulsiveness, anxiety and social withdrawal. Alcohol abuse is another frequent manifestation of the illness, and in some instances, serious psychiatric complaints such as obsessive compulsive behaviour, or psychotic thought, add to the patients' difficulties (Roos, 2010). This also often makes caring for Huntington's patients very difficult. Mood disorders are also common, including both depression and manic episodes (Mendez, 2000). It may come as no surprise to learn that patients with Huntington's have a risk of suicide that is ten times higher than occurs in the general population (Kachian et al., 2019).

THE PATHOLOGICAL FEATURES OF HUNTINGTON'S DISEASE

The most striking change that takes place in the brains of people with Huntington's disease is degenerative cell loss in the caudate nucleus and putamen (neostriatum), along with the presence of granular deposits in the cytoplasm of their nerve cells (Hersch et al., 2011; Sieradzan et al., 1999). This degeneration causes the almost total obliteration of the striatum in the advanced stages of the disease, leading to a loss of brain weight of up to 25–30% (Roze et al., 2011). A grading system (1–5) for describing the progression of striatal neuropathology was developed by Vonsattel et al. (1985) which attempts to parallel the clinical course of the disorder. But as the striatum degenerates, significant cell loss also takes place in other areas of the brain (Rüb et al., 2015), including the cerebral cortex where the pyramidal cells located in layers III, V and VI are seriously affected (Rosas et al., 2008).

The striatum contains several different types of neurons, but the most vulnerable to degeneration are the medium spiny neurons – a special type of GABAergic inhibitory cell which makes up some 95% of all neurons within the striatum. These cells, which express high numbers of dopamine receptors, also form the output fibres of the striatum that project to the **globus pallidus** and **substantia nigra**. Hence, there is marked degeneration of these important output pathways in Huntington's disease (Vonsattel et al., 1985). The striatum also contains interneurons which use acetylcholine and somatostatin as their

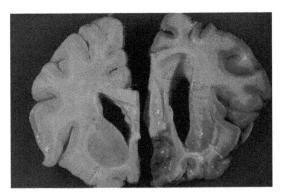

Figure 13.12   Loss of brain tissue in Huntington's disease. Left, a section from a normal brain; right, a section from a person with Huntington's disease. The enlarged lateral ventricle in the diseased brain is due to a loss of neurons in the caudate nuclei (arrows).

Source: Garrett and Hough (2021), courtesy of Robert E. Schmidt, Washington University

neurotransmitters. Although there is a significant loss of cholinergic interneurons, the ones using somatostatin appear relatively spared (Ferrante et al., 1987).

How might this pattern of changes produce the symptoms of chorea which are typical of Huntington's disease in its early and intermediate stages? One possibility is that choeric movement is produced by excess dopamine activity in the striatum (Chen et al., 2013). Put simply, the loss of the GABA striatal output lessens its inhibitory control over the substantia nigra, and without this inhibition the nigral neurons release more dopamine into the striatum, causing excessive and unregulated movement. Support for this idea has come from studies showing that drugs that increase dopamine (such as L-dopa) exacerbate the symptoms of Huntington's disease, whereas substances that reduce dopaminergic tone can be beneficial during the choreic movement phase (Mochel & Haller, 2011). In fact, a significant advance in treating Huntington's disease has been the discovery of a drug called Tetrabenazine which decreases the dopamine content in presynaptic vesicles and significantly reduces chorea (Huntington Study Group, 2006). At the time of writing, Tetrabenazine is the only drug formally approved for treatment of Huntington's chorea by a regulatory agency.

KEY TERMS: *caudate nucleus, putamen, medium spiny neurons, GABAergic, globus pallidus, substantia nigra, dopamine, Tetrabenazine*

THE CAUSE OF HUNTINGTON'S DISEASE

Huntington's disease is caused by the inheritance of a single mutated gene that follows an autosomal mode of inheritance. Put simply, if a person inherits the gene, they will inevitably develop the disorder at some point later in their life. Because a son or daughter inherits around half of their genes from their mother and half from the father, in a randomized order, it follows that if one parent carries the gene, then there will be a 50% chance they will pass it on to their offspring. One of the great tragedies of Huntington's disease is that it does not normally manifest itself until middle age. By then, a carrier, not knowing whether they harbour the mutated gene, is likely to have had children. Until the 1990s there was no way of knowing if someone was a carrier, but today the Huntington's gene can be identified from a simple blood test. In the UK testing is only available at Regional Genetics Clinics, and pretest counselling is an essential requirement to allow a patient an adequate opportunity to reflect on what will be an irrevocable decision (Craufurd et al., 2015). However, whether a prospective carrier wants to know if they have an incurable, fatal and extremely distressing disorder which causes mental anguish and physical degeneration is another matter. Indeed, only about 10–15% of people who are at risk for Huntington's have been tested since the procedure became available, and that percentage has not changed much over time (Anderson et al., 2019).

TRACKING DOWN THE HUNTINGTON'S GENE

The story of how the gene responsible for causing Huntington's disease was discovered is a fascinating one. It can be said to start with the legendary folk singer Woody Guthrie, who as a young man in the 1930s rode freight trains across America and lived with the downtrodden of the Great Depression. These experiences inspired him to write a number of songs that were later covered by artists such as Bob Dylan and Bruce Springsteen. However, Woody Guthrie was also struck down by Huntington's disease, diagnosed in 1952, which would progress for the next 15 years until he passed away in 1967. Following his death, Guthrie's ex-wife Marjorie set up an organization with the objective of providing services for families of those afflicted with Huntington's disease, as well as promoting education and research. This helped raise greater awareness of the then relatively unknown disorder, and it led to further developments. In 1968, Marjorie Guthrie met Milton Wexler, a Californian psychiatrist whose wife suffered from the disease. Together they lobbied Congress for assistance, leading to the creation of a federal Huntington's Disease Commission in 1976 – an organization that drew together various experts in the field and set a new agenda for research.

One of the objectives of the Commission was to discover where the Huntington's gene was located in the genome. This would be a major advance that would enable diagnostic testing for the illness, and provide greater understanding of the disease itself. The task was formidable, however, because Huntington's is a rare disorder, and the only way this gene could be identified was to screen a large groups of patients with a marker that 'tagged' the gene or nearby chromosomal area. Fortunately, the Commission made a crucial breakthrough when they discovered the world's largest group of Huntington's sufferers in an isolated community on the shores of Lake Maracaibo in Venezuela. Over a hundred people with Huntington's lived there – all descendants of a woman who had brought the disease to the area in the 1860s.

In 1981, Nancy Wexler (Milton's daughter) led the first research expedition to Lake Maracaibo. The work involved collecting blood samples from those people with the illness and compiling their family trees. The team sent 570 samples back to the US. One scientist to test the blood samples was a young Canadian molecular biologist called James Gusella. His approach to narrowing down the location of the gene was to use restriction enzymes. These can be likened to molecular scissors that cut DNA into various fragments. The fragments can then be radioactively labelled and used as probes – as they will attach themselves to the complementary bases of the DNA obtained from the blood samples (see Chapter 14). The hope was to discover a probe that consistently bound to the genetic samples provided by those with the illness. Although this may not necessarily locate the gene, geneticists knew that genes that lie close together on the same chromosome tend to get inherited together. For example, the genes that cause haemophilia and red-green colour blindness are located close together on the X chromosome, and both conditions tend to be co-inherited. Thus, Gusella was hoping to find a DNA probe that could be used to track the rough location of the Huntington's gene through a family tree. Such a genetic marker would tell the investigator with a reasonable degree of certainty whether a person carried the gene and where on the chromosome it lay.

Gusella had predicted it would take at least 100 probes, each from a different part of the genome, to discover a DNA fragment that was co-inherited with the mutated gene. In fact, he only got as far as his twelfth probe before he discovered one. This marker was located near the end of the short arm of chromosome 4 (Gusella et al., 1983). Its discovery was such an extraordinary piece of good fortune that it earned Gusella the nickname 'Lucky Jim' among his colleagues. For the first time, it allowed a reliable diagnosis of Huntington's disease to be made from a simple blood test, but perhaps even more importantly, researchers also now knew where the gene lay in the genome, from which they could start to untangle its precise structure, and understand how it produced its devastating effects.

It would be another ten years before the precise location of the gene and its structure were determined. But it would be worth the wait. This task was accomplished in 1993 when the Huntington's Disease Collaborative Research Group (a group of over 50 investigators from ten different research institutions) published their findings. This showed that the gene was relatively large and contained over 300,000 base pairs. However, the most striking thing about the Huntington's gene was the nature of its mutation. In all Huntington's sufferers, the gene contained a nucleotide triplet CAG – that is, a sequence of the bases comprising cytosine (C), adenine (A) and guanine (G). In normal healthy people, this triplet was repeated between 15 and 34 times (the average number of repeats being 20). In those with Huntington's disease, however, the triplet typically occurred between 37 and 66 times. The researchers also found a correlation between the number of repeats in the defective gene and the age of onset of the disease. The more CAG repeats in the gene, the earlier the illness would be manifested (Huntington's Disease Collaborative Research Group, 1993; Langbehn et al., 2010).

KEY TERMS: *Huntington's gene, chromosome 4, nucleotide triplet CAG*

THE HUNTINGTIN PROTEIN

The protein produced by the Huntington's gene was called **huntingtin** (htt). Unfortunately the sequencing of its amino acids provided few clues about its function since it did not resemble any other known protein. To make matters more confusing, the normal htt protein was found to be ubiquitous and expressed throughout the body (Gutekunst et al., 1999). Another odd feature of the protein is that it has no fixed size. As we have seen above, the protein contains a repeated sequence of CAGs, and this combination of bases produces the amino acid glutamine. The normal htt protein contains an elongated stretch of some 6–35 sequential glutamines in its structure, but in Huntington's disease there are over 36 glutamines and sometimes many more. It appears that this extra glutamine causes the htt protein to become misfolded, leading to toxic aggregates in the brain. The rate by which the protein aggregates (or forms clumps) is believed to be proportional to the length of glutamine expansion (Schulte & Littleton, 2011).

The function of htt remains unclear, although there are some clues. Immunohistochemical studies have shown that htt is found in the membrane of synaptic vesicles, and is also closely associated with microtubules, i.e. the fine tubes involved in intracellular transport along axons (Hoffner et al., 2002). This finding indicates that htt might help transport certain chemicals or organelles in the cell, or perhaps be involved in the exchange of substances across intracellular membranes such as synaptic vesicles or mitochondria (Caviston & Holzbaur, 2009).

There is evidence that htt is also a transcription factor – able to enter the cell's nucleus, bind to DNA, and control the expression of certain genes. This may explain why abnormal clumped fragments of the mutated htt protein are often found in the nucleus. One of htt's targets appears to be the gene controlling the production of brain-derived neurotrophic factor (BDNF) – a protein that plays an important role in neuronal survival and growth (Bathina & Das, 2015). It is believed that the abnormal htt protein impairs this transcription process, causing a marked decrease of BDNF (Zuccato et al., 2003). BDNF has also been shown to be synthesized by neurons in the cerebral cortex, from where it is transported to the cells of the striatum by cortical axons. This type of axonal movement is disrupted by the abnormal version of htt (Gauthier et al., 2004).

There is also some evidence that htt may be involved in the transcription of the gene which produces a protein called p53. This protein is important for suppressing cancer and it must be tightly regulated, otherwise self-inflicted programmed cell death called apoptosis can occur. The abnormal htt protein has been found to increase levels of p53 in transgenic mice especially bred with the Huntington's gene (Bae et al., 2005). These researchers also showed that increased p53 production led to malfunctions of the mitochondria. The mitochondria act as tiny 'batteries' within the cytoplasm that provide the cell's energy, although it is increasingly being recognized that these organelles can be transported along microtubules and that they also regulate intracellular calcium homeostasis. They are also an important source of damaging free radicals. All these activities have been implicated in Huntington's disease (Carmo et al., 2018).

KEY TERMS: *huntingtin, glutamine, transcription factor, brain-derived neurotrophic factor, mitochondria*

THE ROLE OF GLUTAMATE IN HUNTINGTON'S DISEASE

Several crucial unresolved questions concerning Huntington's disease remain – not least the sequence of events that leads to neurodegeneration and cell death. One neurotransmitter suspected of being involved in the degenerative process is gluta-mate. This is the most abundant excitatory neurotransmitter in the CNS, and one area which receives massive glutamatic innervation is the striatum which is derived from widespread regions of the cerebral cortex (Bunner & Rebec, 2016). This so-called corticostriatal system was implicated in Huntington's disease during the early 1970s when researchers found that certain glutamate-like substances such as kainic acid and quinolinic acid acted as neurotoxins. Moreover, when injected into the striatum, they produced a profile of neural damage similar to that found in Huntington's disease, i.e. these drugs caused marked degeneration of the GABAergic spiny neurons and cholin-ergic interneurons, whilst sparing the dopaminergic fibres (Coyle & Schwarcz, 1976). This led to the excitotoxicity hypothesis of Huntington's disease which proposes that striatal neurodegeneration is caused by an excess of excitatory glutamate neurotrans-mission, or by the overactivation of glutamate receptors (Ferrante et al., 1993).

Closer examination of the mechanisms by which glutamate, kainic acid or quinolinic acid acted as neurotoxins has shown they produced their effects by over-stimulating N-methyl-d-aspartate (NMDA) receptors. These are located primarily on the medium spiny neurons of the striatum. More precisely, the overstimulation of these neurons led to an increase of excitatory calcium ions ($Ca+^2$) entering the cell, which in turn caused damage to the mitochondria as well as producing a cascade of enzymatic reactions that destroy the neuron (André et al., 2010).

As might be expected, the number of NMDA receptors are reduced in the stria-tum of those with Huntington's disease, although the main interest has focused on glutamate uptake. Obviously, if glutamate is not removed efficiently from the syn-apse, then its build-up could trigger an excitotoxic cascade. The human brain has five specific transport proteins involved in glutamate removal, which are located mainly on astrocytes, although specific neuronal glutamate transporters also exist (Estrada-Sánchez & Rebec, 2012). These have been the focus of much attention in transgenic animal models of Huntington's, with evidence now linking the mutated htt gene with dysfunctional glutamate activity in the brain (Behrens et al., 2002). In particular, it appears that an impairment of astrocytic glutamate uptake is an important element in the pathophysiology of neurodegeneration (Malik & Willnow, 2019).

If glutamate plays a role in Huntington's disease, then a pharmacological blockade of this neurotransmitter might be useful in preventing or slowing down its progression. A number of glutamate antagonists such as amantadine, remacemide, riluzole and ketamine have been tested in clinical trials. Although some of these have improved chorea and motor function, they are also associated with serious side effects, including confusion, memory problems, agitation and hallucinatory disturbances (Coppen & Roos, 2017). Therefore, there is a pressing need to develop safer and more effective anti-glutamatergic agents in Huntington's disease – not least because they may help slow down the excitotoxicity (Anglada-Huguet et al., 2017).

KEY TERMS: *glutamate, corticostriatal system, excitotoxicity hypothesis, N-methyl-d-aspartate (NMDA) receptors*

AUTOIMUNITY AND DEGENERATITVE DISEASE

Some types of neurodegenerative disease can arise from autoimmune processes whereby the immune system mistakenly attacks its own body. In fact, there are over 80 types of autoimmune disease that affect humans, and some of these cause damage to the nervous system. One example is myasthenia gravis, a rare long-term condition which causes muscle weakness. This especially affects the muscles involved in controlling the eyes, eyelids, facial expression, chewing, swallowing and speaking. Whilst it can affect any age group, the symptoms most often begin in women under 40 and men over 50 (Trouth et al., 2012). In the majority of cases, this illness comes about through circulating antibodies which attack the nicotinic acetylcholine receptors located on the motor end plate of skeletal muscles. In turn, this reduces the number of receptors which causes a deterioration of neuromuscular transmission (Graus & De Baets, 1993). In severe cases, up to 80% of the receptors can be destroyed or damaged which necessitates the patient being hospitalized. Fortunately, improvements in treatment have decreased the mortality of this illness (Christensen et al., 1998).

Another illness widely believed to involve autoimmunity is multiple sclerosis. This is a disorder that primarily affects the motor system which produces many varied symptoms, including muscle weakness, tiredness and loss of coordination. Consequently, the illness often leads to walking and balance difficulties. It has been known since the time of Charcot that multiple sclerosis causes a deterioration of myelin (the fatty sheath that covers axons) which slows or eliminations the nerve impulse, thereby reducing the strength of muscle contraction and movement. As the disease progresses, unmyelinated neurons die, leaving areas of sclerosis or hardened scar tissue in the white matter of the spinal cord, optic nerve, brain stem, basal ganglia, and tracts close to the lateral ventricles (Kornek & Lassmann, 2003). Evidence supporting the idea that multiple sclerosis arises from autoimmunity comes from studies where foreign myelin has been injected into the brains of animals (Wekerle, 1993). This produces symptoms such as demyelination that are similar to those of the illness – presumably because the foreign myelin triggers the production of antibodies against the host's myelin. In addition, lymphocytes (T-cells) that are reactive to and destroy myelin proteins have been found in the blood of patients with multiple sclerosis (Fletcher et al., 2010).

Yet why the immune system attacks the myelin is another question. One possibility is that the immune system has been sensitized by an earlier viral infection. Indeed, some studies have found antibodies against the Epstein-Barr virus (the cause of glandular fever) in multiple sclerosis patients (Wagner et al., 2000). Multiple sclerosis has also been hypothesized to be the result of an aberrant immune response, possibly triggered by delayed exposure to a common virus infection such as mumps or measles during adolescence (Hernán et al., 2001). The viral theory of multiple sclerosis is not proven, however, and it remains somewhat contentious (Bager et al., 2004; Virtanen & Jacobson, 2012).

KEY TERMS: *autoimmune disease, myasthenia gravis, multiple sclerosis*

INFECTIOUS DEGENERATIVE DISEASE

As we have seen, some viral infections such as encephalitis lethargica can lead to neurodegenerative disease. Viruses are basically small packets of DNA enclosed in a protective case of protein. But unlike a bacterium, a virus is unable to replicate itself. Consequently, a virus can only reproduce by entering another cell, commandeering its nucleus, and reprogramming it to copy the viral genes and manufacture its proteins. The virus particles then emerge from the host cell to spread infection. As the recent Covid-19 pandemic has tragically demonstrated, viruses pose a great threat to our existence – and partly because of this we have evolved a sophisticated immune system involving the formation of antibodies to protect ourselves from them and other infectious agents. Despite this, there are certain degenerative diseases that can be virally transmitted between individuals.

The first transmissible neurodegenerative disease to be identified was an extremely rare illness called kuru. This disease was discovered during the early 1950s, when researchers encountered a small tribe of people in the eastern highlands of Papua New Guinea called the Fore (the word kuru is derived from the Fore word meaning 'to shake'). The women and children of this group were particularly vulnerable to this illness, which caused a rapid deterioration of motor function, with paralysis and death typically occurring within a year. Another characteristic feature of the Fore was that they practised cannibalism. Deceased family members were traditionally cooked and eaten which was believed to free the spirit of the dead. Custom also held that the women and children ate the internal organs, including the brain – and of course it was them who developed the illness. In the early 1960s, the American Carleton Gajdusek took tissue from a kuru victim and injected it into a chimpanzee. The animal soon showed the deteriorating signs of trembling and motor dysfunction. When the brain was examined it showed marked degeneration similar to that found in kuru (Gajdusek et al., 1967).

Kuru is not the only transmissible neurodegenerative disorder. In 1913, Hans Creutzfeldt described another rare fatal illness that led to impaired motor coordination and memory loss. A few years later, Alfons Jakob described four more patients with the same symptoms. The disorder is now known as Creutzfeldt-Jakob disease (CJD) and its main pathological feature is the occurrence of holes (or vacuoles) in the neural cell bodies which gives the brain the appearance of a sponge. For this reason it is also called spongiform encephalopathy. In 1968, Gajdusek was able to transmit this illness to a monkey with brain tissue taken from a 59-year-old man who had died from the disease. CJD was clearly caused by an infectious agent of some type. Gajdusek would go on to win the Nobel Prize in Physiology or Medicine for his work on infectious diseases in 1976.

At first, it was believed that kuru and CJD were caused by viruses. In 1972, a young neurologist called Stanley Prusiner set about trying to learn more about the infectious agents by purifying the infectious material of scrapie – a transmissible degenerative disorder that affected sheep. By the early 1980s, his work had shown that the infectious agent lacked any nucleic acid and only consisted of protein. It was also 100 times smaller than any known virus and triggered a process in the brain which caused normal proteins to fold abnormally. Prusiner called it a **prion**. In effect, prions are misfolded proteins with the ability to transmit their misfolded shape to normal variants of the same protein (Scheckel & Aguzzi, 2018). The discovery of prions would lead to Prusiner winning the Nobel Prize in 1997.

It would not be long before a prion disorder hit the news. In 1986, a disease of cows, called bovine spongiform encephalopathy (BSE), appeared in the UK. Otherwise known as mad cow disease, its symptoms included poor balance and motor abnormalities, changes in behaviour including aggression, and weight loss. It would reach epidemic proportions in 1992–1993 when around 1,000 new infections were reported each week. Linked to meat and bonemeal that contained infected meat, the emergence of this new form of disease was particularly worrying as it was able to jump species (sheep to cow), raising the possibility it could infect humans. This fear was realized in 1996 when a new variant of CJD was reported in the UK (Will et al., 1996). As of 2018, a total of 231 cases of CJD have been reported globally. Fortunately, in the UK, efforts to prevent the disease by not allowing any animal older than 30 months to enter the animal feed supply have led to its eradication (Casalone & Hope, 2018).

SUMMARY

Alzheimer's disease is the most common form of dementia and occurs in around 5% of people over 65 years and 20% of people over 80. Post-mortem examination of the Alzheimer's brain typically shows a marked loss of neurons in the cerebral cortex and hippocampus, accompanied by a profusion of neuritic plaques composed of tiny clumps of extracellular material called amyloid, along with intracellular twisted fibres called neurofibrillary tangles. The Alzheimer's brain also shows a number of neurochemical changes, including a significant decrease of the enzyme choline acetyltransferase (CAT) involved in the synthesis of acetylcholine. One explanation for the loss of neurons in Alzheimer's disease is that an abnormal form of amyloid is deposited in the brain which causes a cascade of events resulting in degeneration. Evidence supporting the amyloid cascade theory derives from studies showing that mutations in the gene which produce amyloid are responsible for some types of early onset Alzheimer's disease. Despite this, most cases of Alzheimer's disease are not inherited and have a late onset (i.e. occurring after 65 years). Although certain alleles of the APO-E gene have been shown to predispose people to late-onset Alzheimer's disease, lifestyle factors are also believed to play an important role. One form of protection against Alzheimer's disease may be to build up cognitive reserve – that is, forming new synaptic connections in the brain through increased mental use or exercise. In addition, people with physically active lifestyles appear to be better protected against dementia in later life.

Parkinson's disease and Huntington's disease are both disorders that primarily affect the **basal ganglia**, including the **striatum** (caudate nucleus and putamen). Parkinson's disease is caused by degeneration of a heavily pigmented nucleus in the midbrain called the substantia nigra pars compacta, which innervates the striatum with dopamine fibres. Consequently, there is a marked loss of dopamine in the striatum. This can be partly restored by the drug L-Dopa, which provides a highly useful treatment for the illness. In a few cases, Parkinson's disease can be inherited from mutations in certain genes on chromosomes 4 and 6, which produce the proteins α-synuclein and parkin respectively. But mainly, Parkinson's disease has no clear genetic basis which has raised speculation that environmental insults or toxins must play at least some role in its aetiology. One way of understanding how toxins may lead to substantia nigra degeneration has come from examining the drug MPTP, which produces the free radical MPP+. This is believed to cause nigral cell loss by damaging mitochondria which provide the neuron with its energy. In contrast, Huntington's disease is an autosomal dominant genetic disorder – meaning, if a person inherits a copy of the mutant gene they will inevitably develop the illness at some point in their life. This illness is associated with marked degeneration of the striatum (not the substantia nigra) and to some extent other brain areas, including the cerebral cortex. The gene responsible for the disease is found on chromosome 4, and the mutation is caused by an increased number of a nucleotide triplets containing the bases CAG. This produces the amino acid glutamine. In normal subjects this triplet is repeated 20–35 times, but in those with Huntington's the CAG repeat occurs many more times. The greater the repeat number, the sooner the disease begins to manifest itself. The normal gene is known to produce a protein called huntingtin which is found throughout the body and whose function is unknown. How its mutation leads to neural degeneration is not clear – although an involvement in disrupting the release or uptake of glutamate (known to be a potential neurotoxin) in the corticostriatal pathways is suspected.

There are many other types of degenerative disease that affect the nervous system. These diseases include amyotrophic lateral sclerosis which is a group of rare neurological diseases that mainly involve the nerve cells of the spinal cord responsible for controlling voluntary muscle movement. Other degenerative diseases include myasthenia gravis and multiple sclerosis. The former is known to be an autoimmune disease where antibodies attack the nicotinic receptors located in the neuromuscular junction. Multiple sclerosis is also widely believed by many to be an autoimmune disease, although there is much uncertainty over this possibility. In very rare cases degenerative diseases can be contagious. In the case of humans, this has been shown with kuru and Creutzfeldt-Jakob disease – the latter being a group of rare diseases called transmissible spongiform encephalopathies. These can also affect animals. One example is the so-called mad cow disease, which is a form of bovine spongiform encephalopathy.

GO ONLINE

TEST YOUR UNDERSTANDING OF THIS CHAPTER AND VISIT HTTPS://STUDY.SAGEPUB.COM/WICKENS TO ACCESS INTERACTIVE 'DRAG AND DROP' LABELLING ACTIVITIES AND A FLASHCARD GLOSSARY.

MULTIPLE CHOICE QUESTIONS

Answer the questions below to test your understanding of this chapter's Learning Objectives. You'll find the answers at the end of the chapter.

1. Which of the following is a pathological characteristic of Alzheimer's disease?

    a. Hirano bodies
    b. Lewy bodies
    c. neuritic plaques and neurofibrillary tangles
    d. spongiform encephalopathy

2. Which of the following proteins has been most implicated in the pathogenesis of Alzheimer's disease?

    a. adenylate cyclase
    b. amyloid and tau
    c. brain-derived neurotrophic factor
    d. glutamine

3. Parkinson's disease is primarily caused by degeneration to which brain structure?

    a. cerebellum
    b. hippocampus
    c. substantia nigra
    d. thalamus

4. There is a major loss of which brain neurotransmitter in Parkinson's disease?

    a. acetylcholine
    b. dopamine
    c. glutamate
    d. serotonin

5. Which brain region shows the most marked loss of neurons in Huntington's disease?

    a. cerebellum
    b. frontal and temporal lobes
    c. red nucleus
    d. striatum

6. Which of the following excitatory neurotransmitters has been most associated with neurotoxicity and brain degeneration in Huntington's disease?

    a. dopamine
    b. GABA
    c. glutamate
    d. acetylcholine

FURTHER READING

Budson, A. E., & Kowall, N. W. (Eds.). (2013). *The handbook of Alzheimer's disease and other dementias*. Wiley-Blackwell.
An extensive broad-ranging review of dementia with a useful section on neurodegeneration.

Campbell, D. (2019). *Parkinson's disease: Advanced research and clinical care*. Foster Academics.
Includes useful information on the latest developments in Parkinson's disease, although the chapters on care are of limited use.

Jucker, M., Beyreuther, K., Haass, C., Nitsch, R., & Christian, Y. (Eds.). (2010). *Alzheimer: 100 years and beyond*. Springer.
A diverse book with a historical focus, but with all the latest developments concerning the pathology of Alzheimer's disease.

Martin, C. R., & Preedy, V. R. (Eds.). (2020). *The neuroscience of Parkinson's disease.* Academic Press.
A two-volume set which covers everything you need to know about Parkinson's disease, including genetics, molecular biology, neurobiology and treatment.

Palfreman, J. (2016). *Brain storms: The race to unlock the mysteries of Parkinson's disease.* Ebury Publishing.
A professor of journalism who was diagnosed with Parkinson's disease chronicles the history of how scientists have worked to understand the illness and provide more effective treatments.

Rüb, U., Vonsattel, J. P. G., & Heinsen, H. (2015). *The neuropathology of Huntington's disease: Classical findings, recent developments and correlation to functional neuroanatomy.* Berlin: Springer.
This is possibly the best book on the neuroscience of Huntington's disease which also has a historical focus.

Schapira, A., Wszolek, Z. K., Dawson, T. M., & Wood, N. (Eds.). (2017). *Neurodegeneration.* Wiley-Blackwell.
A useful textbook written by various experts which presents a clinically oriented guide to the diseases caused by neurodegeneration.

Visser, T. J. (Ed.). (2011). *Huntington's disease: Etiology & symptoms, diagnosis & treatment.* Nova Science.
Detailed account of the pathology of Huntington's disease as well as a good review of the role of the huntingtin protein.

Walsh, A. (Ed.). (2019). *Handbook of Parkinson's disease.* Wisepress.
A comprehensive guide to Parkinson's disease with updated chapters that feature discoveries and breakthroughs in the diagnosis and management of the illness.

Wexler, A. (1995). *Mapping fate.* University of California Press.
A moving account of one family's fight against Huntington's disease. It also contains useful information on how the gene for Huntington's disease was discovered.

MULTIPLE CHOICE ANSWERS 1. C | 2. B | 3. C | 4. B | 5. D | 6. C

14

GENES AND BEHAVIOUR

LEARNING OBJECTIVES

After reading this chapter you should be able to:

- Understand Darwin's theory of natural selection.

- Explain the laws of genetic inheritance.

- Appreciate the structure and function of deoxyribonucleic acid (DNA).

- Describe how genes produce proteins.

- Understand the inheritance of single gene disorders.

- Appreciate the complexities of genetic and environmental interaction.

- Outline the main methods used to assess the effects of multiple genes on behaviour.

- Appreciate some of the ways transgenic animals have been used in neuroscience.

- Understand stem cells and their future potential in brain research.

GO ONLINE

Test your understanding of this chapter and visit **https://study.sagepub.com/wickens** to access interactive 'Drag and Drop' labelling activities and a flashcard glossary.

INTRODUCTION

According to a recent estimate, our bodies contain in the region of 37.2 trillion cells (Bianconi et al., 2013), each of which is a tiny self-governing entity that functions as the smallest and most basic unit of life. But an even more astonishing fact is that just about every cell (red blood cells, sperm and ova excepted) contains two copies of the genome – that is, a set of instructions for making a human being, as well as providing the central hub controlling the activity of each cell.

The human genome has evolved over many millions of years, creating 23 paired chromosomes composed largely of deoxyribonucleic acid (DNA) that encodes around 25,000 genes.[1] Just about every gene is a blueprint for making an individual protein – a large specialized molecule with a complex chemical configuration which has many vital roles to play in the body. For example, proteins form the structural machinery of our cells, serve as enzymes, act as receptors and transporter molecules, and some even function as neurotransmitters. Estimates show about two-thirds of our genes are expressed in the brain, which is another way of saying the human brain uses far more proteins than any other part of the body. It follows therefore that our genetic inheritance must have a significant bearing on the development and function of the brain, influencing to some extent how we think, feel and behave.

Attempts to understand whether genetic or environmental factors are more important in determining our behaviour have provided one of the great challenges in modern psychology. However there is more to genetic research than the question of nature and nurture. The functioning of our genes can 'go wrong', leading to debilitating illnesses and degenerative disease, yet in our quest to better understand our inheritance, modern-day technology has also allowed us to identify and manipulate genes and even create new transgenic animals. This has not only greatly widened the scope of experimentation into the genetic underpinning of behaviour, but also led to a better appreciation of inherited disease. The use of molecular genetics is becoming an increasingly important field in neuroscience and one with many potential benefits, not least because the development of new techniques such as gene therapy or the use of stem cells offers the promise of intervention into many illnesses that may one day help relieve the suffering of millions.

---

[1]According to the distinguished British geneticist and author Steve Jones, each cell in the body contains about six feet of DNA, and if it could somehow be all joined together, would stretch to the moon and back 8,000 times (Jones, 1993).

DARWIN AND THE THEORY OF EVOLUTION

Charles Darwin (1809–1882) was a British naturalist who brought in the era of modern biology with his book *On the Origin of Species by Means of Natural Selection* first published in 1859. Darwin was just 22 years old when he sailed from England on H.M.S. Beagle in 1831. The main mission of the voyage, which lasted five years, was to chart the geological features of the South American coastline – although Darwin's task as ship's naturalist was to study animal life and collect new specimens of fauna and flora. During the journey which also visited Tenerife, Cape Verde, Brazil, and the Galapagos Islands, Darwin became fascinated by the great diversity of life he came across, especially the way it was perfectly adapted to the environment. On the Galapagos, for example, he found 14 different types of finch which all had similar features, yet each bird had a beak uniquely adapted to its own habitat and food source. After completing the voyage in 1836, Darwin wrote an account of his journey, and reflected on what he had observed. He came to realize that the diversity could be explained if all animals had arisen from a common ancestor, but in doing so became slightly modified over time, enabling them to become better adapted to their ecological niche. Later, in 1844, Darwin began formulating his ideas into a more coherent theory that would explain all diversity as resulting from the process of evolution.

It has been said that nothing in biology makes sense except in the light of evolution (Dobzhansky, 1973), but during the mid-nineteenth century Darwin's ideas were highly controversial and widely regarded as blasphemous. In the book of Genesis, for example, the Bible decrees that every species, including man, had been created by the divine hand of God, and unaltered since the dawn of creation. Indeed, if there was any single belief that characterized the Victorian era it was this Christian one. Darwin was well aware of the contentious nature of his theory and spent more than 20 years working on his ideas before daring to publish them. Even then, he was prompted to do so by the work of a young naturalist called Alfred Wallace who had formulated a similar theory. The impact of Darwin's work was enormous. Not only did *The Origin of the Species* prove surprisingly popular (it sold out immediately and went through five editions in Darwin's life), it also prompted religious, academic and popular debate. By the end of the nineteenth century, the theory of evolution had become accepted by much of the scientific community and general public. In doing so, it had changed man's conception of himself and provided one of the great unifying theories of biology.

The suggestion that living things change with time, which is the fundamental notion of evolution, did not originate with Darwin, but he was the first to provide a convincing empirical theory to describe how it occurred. The mechanism Darwin developed to explain evolution was natural selection which was based on two simple concepts: competition and variation. The idea of competition derived from Darwin's observation that all living creatures produce more offspring than are needed to replace their parents. This creates a situation where there are too many individuals for the finite amount of resources that exist for them, yet Darwin had also observed that animal populations remain relatively stable and do not expand beyond certain limits. From this, he reasoned, the consequence of increased numbers of offspring and limited resources must be that all creatures are thrown into competition with each other.

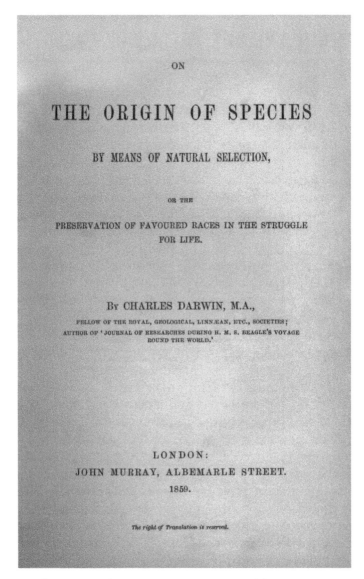

Figure 14.1   *On the Origin of the Species by Means of Natural Selection*
Source: Wikiklaas/Wikimedia commons

The second aspect of natural selection is that all individual members of a species show great variation in their physical characteristics. Humans may look similar, yet we are all different in terms of physique, strength, intelligence etc. One consequence of this variability, Darwin realized, is that some individuals will be better suited (or adapted) to their environments than others. For all living organisms this is important because the members who are best adapted will be the ones more likely to reproduce, thereby passing similar characteristics on to their offspring. This is the principle of selection from which Darwin's cousin Herbert Spencer coined the expression *the survival of the fittest*. However, Darwin's most important insight into natural selection was that over the course of many generations, the process would cause changes in the body form. To give an example: because ancestral giraffes had a liking for feeding in tall trees, natural selection would favour the development of long necks. Following this argument to its logical conclusion, it can be argued that if enough changes take place, natural selection will eventually lead to the development of a new species.

Although Darwin described the process of evolution, he did not explain how inheritance worked. Genes had not been discovered in the nineteenth century, and the lack of knowledge concerning the mechanisms of inheritance provided an obstacle to his evolutionary theory. In fact, the solution to this problem had been formulated in 1865 by a young Augustinian monk living in Bohemia called Gregor Mendel, but his work had been largely ignored and soon forgotten until it was rediscovered around 1900. Mendel had provided the rules of genetic inheritance that Darwin's theory needed in order to explain how natural selection might operate. Darwin died in 1882 and never knew of Mendel's legacy to biology – although curiously Mendel knew of Darwin's work (Fairbanks, 2020). By the time of his death, Darwin had gained recognition and fame. He was given a state funeral and buried in Westminster Abbey close to Sir Isaac Newton (Desmond & Moore, 1991).

KEY TERMS: *evolution, natural selection, competition, variation*

THE WORK OF GREGOR MENDEL

The idea that inheritance occurs through 'transmissible units' was first formulated in a paper by the Augustinian monk Gregor Mendel in 1865 who lived in a monastery in Brno, Moravia (now in the Czech Republic). Prior to this, scientists believed that inheritance was a blending process where 'bloods' of the parents were mixed together in their offspring. However Mendel disproved this theory in a number of experiments using the humble garden pea plant. This choice of vegetable was fortuitous. Firstly, pea plants are simple to breed since they have both male and female organs, making it easy to fertilize a female flower with pollen taken from a male stamen. This also allowed Mendel to cross different plants or self-fertilize the same one – a situation enabling a variety of breeding experiments to be undertaken. Secondly, the traits that Mendel examined, such as the size of the plant (e.g. tall versus dwarf), the colour of its seed (yellow versus green), or the seed texture (smooth versus wrinkled) were dichotomous, meaning that plants either had one trait or the other and there was no in-between trait. Thus, Mendel avoided many of the complexities associated with animal breeding where inherited characteristics (such as size) are not dichotomous but quantitative (i.e. measured in varying amounts). Most important of all, by looking at dichotomous traits it was easy to count the number of times they occurred in each generation. Although the ratios were simple, they enabled Mendel to gain a remarkable insight into genetic inheritance.

In one of his studies, Mendel crossed tall pea plants some five to six feet in height with dwarf plants which were about one foot high. The results showed that all the offspring (called the F1 or first filial generation) were tall. All the dwarf plants had disappeared from the new generation. However, when Mendel self-bred these plants to produce the F2 generation, he got a different set of results. Whilst three-quarters of

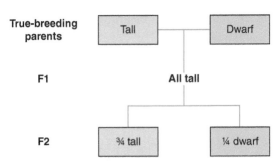

Figure 14.2   The effects of crossing true-breeding pea plants with smooth and wrinkled seeds
Source: Wickens (2009)

the F2 offspring were tall, the remainder were dwarf. Clearly, the factor causing short-ness had not been lost in the F1 generation after all. Rather it had been suppressed by the dominant taller plants. Mendel obtained similar results with other characteristics: smooth seeds were dominant over wrinkled, yellow seeds dominant over green, and red flowers dominant over white. And in addition, this type of experiment always showed that the F1 generation gave rise to only one type of trait, whereas the F2 gen-eration generated two traits in the ratio of three to one. The consistency of these results showed that some basic law of inheritance was at work.

To explain these findings, Mendel saw it was necessary to assume that each plant contained two 'factors' (now called **genes**) which would produce the trait in question (say the height of the plant). One of these factors was provided by the male and the other by the female. Importantly, this insight recognised that each parent carried two 'genes', but transmitted only one to its offspring. However this does not answer the question of why Mendel obtained his ratios of tall and short plants. To answer this, Mendel suggested that the factors (i.e. genes) controlling size in pea plants come in two forms. Today, genes that produce the same trait, but have different variants, are called alleles (a good example of an inherited trait in humans influenced by alleles is eye colour). Thus, Mendel realized that whilst there was one gene controlling size, this came in different forms which meant that plant size could be either tall or short. But if this was the case then why were all pea plants in the F1 generation tall when they con-tained both alleles? Mendel's explanation was insightful and ingenious: alleles could be dominant or recessive. In the case of height for pea plants, when the two different alleles came together, the allele for tallness would dominate over the dwarf one.

To illustrate these principles, assume Mendel began his experiments by crossing 'true' or homozygous tall plants (only containing the genes TT) with homozygous dwarf plants (containing dd genes). When these plants are bred, all plants in the F1 generation are tall because they all contain the allele combination of Td, where the T allele is dominant over the d allele. But why does the F2 generation always produce the 3:1 ratio? To see what happens refer to Figure 14.3. It shows that when the F1 hybrids all containing Td are bred together, the resulting plants will contain an assortment of allele combinations. Assuming that each plant can only randomly pass one allele to its progeny, then this will produce three possible types of plants (TT, Td and dd) in the proportions 1:2:1. Since T is the dominant allele, then both TT and Td combinations will grow to be tall plants, whereas the dd plant will be a dwarf. As a result of breeding F1 hybrids, therefore, one would expect to obtain three tall plants and only one dwarf in the F2 generation.

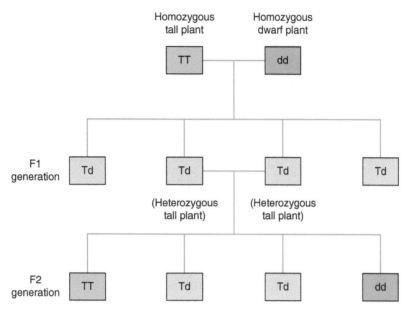

Figure 14.3   The effects of dominant and recessive alleles on the crossing of pea plants
Source: Wickens (2009)

It should be noted that whilst all the traits examined by Mendel were caused by single genes, the majority of human traits are controlled by a combination of many different genes. Furthermore, not all alleles operate in a dominant or recessive fashion. Some alleles, for example, are additive, meaning that they each contribute something to the offspring, whereas others have interactive effects with each other, or may even cancel each other out. Mendel's choice of the simple pea plant had nonetheless provided him with an excellent means of describing in detail the basic laws of inheritance. His work on plant breeding would last 15 years, finishing in 1868 when he was elected as the monastery's abbot. After his death in 1884, Mendel's pea garden was destroyed, along with his notebooks, papers and scientific records. The only record of the work was his forgotten paper from 1865 (Henig, 2000).

KEY TERMS: *genes, alleles, dominant and recessive genes*

THE CHROMOSOMAL BASIS OF INHERITANCE

Although Mendel's paper was sent to academic institutions throughout Europe, the importance of his findings was not recognized. Despite this, important advances were taking place in the late nineteenth century that were supporting Mendel's conception of genetic inheritance. In 1875 Oscar Hertwig became the first person to observe by microscope the process of fertilization (using transparent sea urchin eggs) with the coming together of the sperm and ovum. He also noticed the nuclei

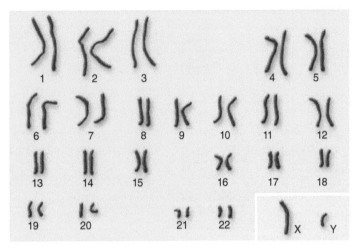

Sex chromosomes

Figure 14.4   The variety of life: The 23 pairs of chromosomes
Source: U.S. National Library of Medicine in Gaskin (2021)

of these two cells fused together to make one, which then initiated the beginning of new cell division and growth. This was a remarkable discovery for several reasons – not least because it showed that the nucleus provided the key to understanding inheritance. Four years later, Walther Flemming discovered tiny rod-like structures inside the nucleus that were later called chromosomes. These existed in pairs, consistent with Mendel's idea that two separate factors were involved in genetic transmission. This idea was confirmed in 1883 when Edouard van Beneden observed the chromosomes from sperm and ovum mix together during fertilization. He also realized that whilst most bodily cells housed pairs of chromosomes in their nuclei, the sperm and ovum contained only single chromosomes, but when the chromosomes came together during fertilization, they formed new pairs. Again this was consistent with Mendel's theory.

Finally, in 1900, the importance of Mendel's work was brought to the attention of the wider scientific community when three scientists (Hugo de Vries, Carl Correns and Erich von Tschermak) independently verified several of Mendel's experimental findings and tracked down his original paper. In doing so, they ushered in the modern age of genetics. Soon afterwards, the American geneticist Walter Sutton proposed that Mendel's factors (or genes) were located on chromosomes, with inheritance being the result of single chromosomes from each parent coming together in the fertilized egg. The ancient notion that traits were transmitted along 'bloodlines' had finally been disproved. Instead, traits were transmitted by indivisible genetic particles that maintained their identity whilst being shuffled into new combinations during fertilization. The secret of life lay with genes.

KEY TERM: *chromosomes*

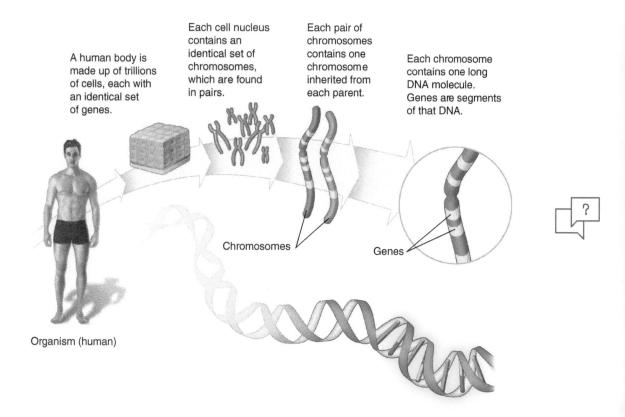

A human body is made up of trillions of cells, each with an identical set of genes.

Each cell nucleus contains an identical set of chromosomes, which are found in pairs.

Each pair of chromosomes contains one chromosome inherited from each parent.

Each chromosome contains one long DNA molecule. Genes are segments of that DNA.

Chromosomes

Genes

Organism (human)

Figure 14.5   Organisms are made up of cells, each of which contains an identical set of genes
Source: Carolina Hrejsa/Body Scientific Intl. in Gaskin (2021)

A CLOSER LOOK AT GENES

So what do genes look like? To answer this, we must examine the composition of chromosomes in more detail. As already mentioned, almost every cell in the body has in its nucleus a set of 23 paired chromosomes (or put another way, a total of 46). These rod-like type structures are comprised of a protein matrix holding in place a long and unique double-stranded chemical, coiled up in a tightly twisted strand. This is called **deoxyribonucleic acid** (DNA). Although the existence of DNA was first detected by Friedrich Miescher in 1869 (who called it nuclein), it was not until 1953 when its molecular structure was elucidated by James Watson and Francis Crick, that the secrets of genetic transmission were unlocked. For this discovery, one of the greatest scientific achievements of the twentieth century, Watson and Crick (along with Maurice Wilkins) were awarded the Nobel Prize in Physiology or Medicine in 1962. An account of how the DNA molecule was deciphered is given by Watson (1968) in *The Double Helix*.

DNA is made up of two chains, composed of phosphate and a sugar called deoxyribose, that swivel around each other in the shape of the double helix (see Figure 14.6). Holding the two strands together as they wind around each other are

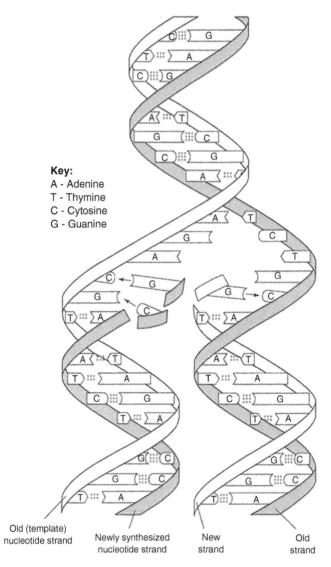

Key:
A - Adenine
T - Thymine
C - Cytosine
G - Guanine

Old (template)
nucleotide strand

Newly synthesized
nucleotide strand

New
strand

Old
strand

Figure 14.6   The DNA molecule
Source: Wickens (2009)

pairs of simple molecules, like the rungs of a ladder, called bases. DNA contains four base types: adenine (A), guanine (G), cytosine (C) and thymine (T), which are also referred to as nucleotides when attached to a sugar and phosphate. Because the four bases are held together by weak hydrogen bonds, the two strands making up the DNA can easily 'unzip' and separate. This is a unique feature of DNA and necessary if it is to make copies of itself. In doing this, the bases are also selective in their bonding: A only bonds with T, and C only bonds with G. Consequently, when the strands of DNA unwind, each nucleotide can only act as a template for its corresponding base. When the bases are joined again, the result is a new 'zipped up' strand that is identical to the old one. It follows, therefore, that DNA has the remarkable property of being able to duplicate itself which is a vital requirement for creating new cells and ultimately a new organism. In fact, millions of cells in the human body are dividing every second, and every minute many miles of new DNA are being produced (Jones, 1993, p. 91).

		U		C		A		G		
U	UUU	Phenylalanine	UCU	Serine	UAU	Tyrosine	UGU	Cysteine	U
	UUC		UCC		UAC		UGC		C
	UUA	Leucine	UCA		UAA**	Stop Codon	UGA**	Stop Codon	A
	UUG		UCG		UAG**	Stop Codon	UGG	Tryptophan	G
C	CUU	Leucine	CCU	Proline	CAU	Histidine	CGU	Arginine*	U
	CUC		CCC		CAC		CGC		C
	CUA		CCA		CAA	Glutamine	CGA		A
	CUG		CCG		CAG		CGG		G
A	AUU	Isoleucine	ACU	Threonine	AAU	Asparagine	AGU	Serine	U
	AUC		ACC		AAC		AGC		C
	AUA		ACA		AAA	Lysine	AGA	Arginine	A
	AUG	Methionine (start codon)	ACG		AAG		AGG		G
G	GUU	Valine	GCU	Alanine	GAU	Aspartate	GGU	Glycine	U
	GUC		GCC		GAC		GGC		C
	GUA		GCA		GAA	Glutamate	GGA		A
	GUG		GCG		GAG		GGG		G

Figure 14.7   The codons that make up the genetic code
Source: Cook et al. (2021)

Yet DNA does more than simply make copies of itself: it also contains the basic physical and functional units of heredity, or genes, most of which serve as blueprints to make proteins (although some genes code for other molecules such as RNA). Put simply, genes are long sequences of bases that lie between the two spiralling chains forming the helical shape of DNA. Although the alphabetic is very simple (A, T, G and C), there are astronomical numbers of these bases on each strand of DNA, making the story (i.e. the genetic code) incredibly complex. It is estimated that the 23 pairs of chromosomes making up the human genome contain over 3,000 million base pairs – which is about 6.5 million base pairs for each chromosome. To put this figure into perspective, the 1969 edition of the *Encyclopaedia Britannica*, which also consisted of 23 volumes, contained 200 million letters. If we equate a letter with a base, then this would fill about three chromosomes. Incredibly, to enable over 3,000 million base pairs to exist, each cell of the body contains about 6 feet of DNA crammed into a nucleus that is 0.005 mm in diameter (Robinson & Spock, 2009).

It may also come as a surprise to learn that the exact number of genes in the human genome is not known for certain. The Human Genome Project (completed in 2003) estimated that we have between 20,000 and 25,000 genes, although recent estimates for protein-encoding genes put the figure at around 21,000 (Willyard, 2018). These genes vary in size from around 500 bases to a massive 2 million bases. But how do we recognize a segment of DNA as a gene? The answer lies in certain triplet sequences of bases known as codons which provide a code for the cell to manufacture an amino acid (see Figure 14.7). It is also these **amino acids** which are the structural units making up a protein. Or put more precisely, **proteins** are essentially long chains of amino acids. Although there are huge numbers of different proteins in the human body,[2] all are composed from just 20 types of amino acid, which are derived from a code of just 3 consecutive DNA bases (e.g. CGA or TGG). In total, there are 64 possible triplets within our DNA that specify all amino acids, with a few codons also providing 'punctuation' for start and stop signals. To recapitulate: a gene is a sequence of codons for all the amino acids which are needed to create a protein.

One of the most surprising aspects of our DNA is that less than 5% of it is composed of functioning genes. Thus, most of it appears to be redundant. If we could somehow enter this genetic world and walk along our chromosomes, jumping from base to base, we would find most of our DNA is actually composed of endless repeats of the same 'nonsense' message, often in the form of five or six bases repeated next to each other (such as ACCTGACCTG). These bases may also be interspersed with simpler repeated sequences, such as the two bases C and A that are multiplied many thousands of times, and at other locations along the chromosome, long and complicated sequences occur whose message, if meaningful, remains unknown. It is only when we come across a sequence of codons that we will have found a gene – a site where a number of other chemical events are likely to be taking place. The terrain of the chromosome is a curious and still largely mysterious world.

KEY TERMS: *genes, deoxyribonucleic acid (DNA), bases, nucleotides, codons, amino acids, proteins*

WHY ARE WE ALL DIFFERENT?

Why is it that human beings who share the same genome of around 25,000 genes are individually unique? The answer is we all have slightly different genes which have evolved into different variants. These are known as alleles. Consequently, some genes located at the same position on a chromosome, and serving the same function, may come in different forms – which will cause their expression to be modified slightly. In fact, any two people will differ in about one base per thousand, which means that there are about 3 million differences in their genetic messages. Even monozygotic twins (who develop from the same fertilized egg) have infrequent genetic differences due to mutations occurring during development and gene copy-number variation (Bruder et al., 2008). Although these differences may be small (most of us are over 99% genetically similar) they provide us with our unique individuality.

Alleles have come about through chance alterations taking place in the structure of bases during evolution, and their effects will depend on where they occur in the gene. If changes occur in the non-functional part of the gene, there will be no effect on

---

[2]Interestingly, the number of proteins in the human body is not known (Ponomarenko et al., 2016), with some estimates putting the figure at between 80,000 and 400,000 (Schröder, 2017) which is far greater than the number of genes. This is because proteins can undergo a number of transformations after they have been synthesized.

the individual. But if a base change takes place in an important codon that encodes for an amino acid, then the outcome could be significant. It may, for example, be sufficient to determine our skin colour, ear lobe length or blood type. Or worse, it may cause an incurable degenerative disease. Multiple alleles have been found for about half of all human genes. The number of potential allele combinations is so vast that everyone alive today is genetically different from each other, and from every person who has ever lived (Rutherford, 2016).

KEY TERM: *alleles*

HOW ARE PROTEINS MADE?

The DNA forming the genetic code for making proteins is locked away in the cell's nucleus. However, protein manufacture takes place in the cell's cytoplasm. This means the genetic information must be able to leave the nucleus. But how does this occur? The answer lies with another type of nucleic acid called **messenger ribonucleic acid** (mRNA). This is similar to DNA except it is single-stranded, contains the sugar ribose (instead of deoxyribose), and uses the base uracil instead of thymine. It is also much shorter than DNA, ranging from less than 100 base nucleotides to no more than a few thousand base pairs. This small size also allows mRNA to move freely out of the nucleus. But before this occurs, the mRNA has to first copy part of the gene's base sequence in an operation known as transcription (Figure 14.8). This process begins when an enzyme called RNA polymerase 'unzips' parts of the DNA, allowing the mRNA to make a complementary copy. Once this has taken place, the mRNA leaves the nucleus to seek out a

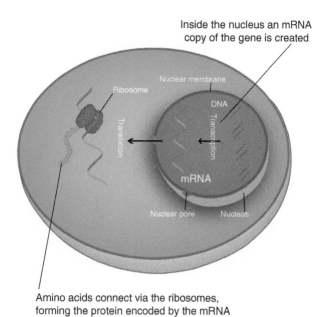

Figure 14.8   Transcription (to RNA) and translation (to proteins)
Source: Cook et al. (2021)

ribosome in the cell which is like a work bench where the assembly of the protein will take place. **Ribosomes** are found in large numbers floating within the cytoplasm or attached to the endoplasmic reticulum. In fact, some cell types may contain a few million ribosomes, although several thousand is more typical. They are also particularly abundant in neurons (Stoykova et al., 1985).

The main component of ribosomes is **ribosomal RNA** (rRNA). This not only provides an anchor for the mRNA, but once the mRNA and rRNA become attached, the ribosome also moves along the mRNA strand by a distance of one (three-letter) codon notch. This brings a new codon into the processing area. At this point, a third type of RNA becomes involved in the protein manufacture. This process involves **transfer RNA** (tRNA), i.e. a short, single-stranded molecule, found throughout the cytoplasm, which is responsible for transporting a single amino acid to the ribosome. The tRNA also has a base structure that is complementary to the codon that codes for the amino acid in the mRNA. As the ribosome exposes the mRNA's codons one at a time, the tRNA becomes attached to its exposed bases, whilst at the same time adding the appropriate amino acid to the growing protein strand. This process is called translation (Figure 14.9).

Once a codon has been matched with an amino acid, a peptide bond is created that links the newly formed amino acid with the next one in the chain. Then the next codon is exposed and the process repeated until all the bases in the mRNA transcript are filled. At this point a new protein composed of a polypeptide chain of amino acids is created. The construction of a protein is a very efficient process with amino acids being incorporated into polypeptide chains at a rate of about 100 per second. It takes less than a minute to make an average protein. Our bodies are continually having to manufacture proteins, and it has been estimated that more than 1 million peptide bonds are made every second in most cells. This high rate of synthesis is required because the human body contains tens of thousands of different proteins that are continually being broken down and replaced every day (Biever et al., 2019).

KEY TERMS: *mRNA (messenger ribonucleic acid), transcription, ribosomes, rRNA (ribosomal ribonucleic acid), tRNA (transfer ribonucleic acid), translation, peptide bond*

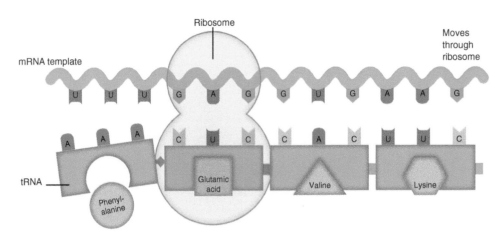

Figure 14.9   Translation of mRNA into a polypeptide chain
Source: Cook et al. (2021).

THE IMPORTANCE OF PROTEINS

To understand why genes are so important, we have to appreciate the nature of the molecules they make – namely proteins. These molecules are vital constituents of all living things from bacteria to man, without which life could not exist. Proteins are large, complex molecules that consist of amino acid chains, but a more important characteristic of proteins is their shape. After the protein has left the ribosome, it is folded into a configuration that is determined by the sequencing of its amino acids. Part of a chain may coil into a helix, other segments lock into rigid rods, and other parts form clefts or flexible swivels. This twisting and folding creates a great variety of complex three-dimensional configurations – and it is this characteristic which enables proteins to serve such a wide range of biological functions. Remarkably, it has been estimated that a single cell may contain up to 42 million protein molecules (Ho et al., 2018). Most proteins also have a limited lifetime, with some being made, carrying out their function and being destroyed within a few days or weeks. It can be seen, therefore, that cells are essentially factories for making proteins. In the case of neurons, proteins are used to make receptors, ion channels, uptake pumps and some neurotransmitters, as well as providing the main constituents of intracellular structures such as the microtubules and Golgi bodies etc. In the body, proteins provide connective tissue and muscle, whilst others act as antibodies, or carriers that transport chemical substances around the body (e.g. hemoglobin). A large number of hormones are also peptides or proteins.

Another important function of proteins is their role as enzymes that carry out almost all of the chemical reactions in cells. Most enzymes are folded to form a cleft that is able to hold a small molecule such as sugar. When a chemical binds to the enzyme in this way, it typically causes a structural modification in the protein, which causes it to speed up a chemical reaction. One example is the enzyme adenylyl cyclase which converts ATP (the cells' main energy source) into the second messenger cAMP. Another important chemical reaction involving proteins is phosphorylation which involves the addition or removal of phosphate from the molecule. This simple chemical modification alters the shape and function of the protein and it plays an important role in a variety of neurochemical processes. For example, protein phosphorylation may inactivate a neurotransmitter, cause an ion channel to open, or produce activational changes in a receptor. Moreover, it should not be forgotten that enzymes also assist with the formation of new molecules by reading the genetic information stored in DNA.

It can be difficult for a student to scale down to the molecular level and visualize the size of proteins. But to give some idea of the scale we are talking about: one of the smallest objects to the naked eye is a grain of salt which is about half a millimetre or 500 microns. The cell body of a neuron can vary from 4 to 100 microns, while an axon may be two or three times this length (although it is much smaller in diameter). If one can imagine around 42 million proteins making up and working within a nerve cell, far beyond our power of eyesight, then one can get some idea of their miniscule existence. Yet in terms of the molecular world, proteins are large structures, and for this reason they are sometimes called macromolecules.

KEY TERMS: *proteins, amino acid chains, enzymes, phosphorylation*

SINGLE GENES AND BEHAVIOUR

Single gene disorders, otherwise known as monogenic diseases, arise from modifications of a single gene. Although most are rare, they affect millions of people worldwide. Scientists currently estimate that over 10,000 of human diseases are monogenic, and new ones continue to be described in the medical literature. According to the World Health Organization, the global prevalence of all single gene diseases at birth is approximately 1 in every 100, although certain populations may show a higher incidence of particular disorders than the general population (an example was Tay-Sachs disease which used to be more common in people of Ashkenazi Jewish descent) (Nelson, 2021). Single gene disorders are nearly always inherited in the way described by Mendel. Consequently, they are also known as Mendelian diseases. These illnesses run in families and, as we will see, are either autosomal dominant, autosomal recessive, or sex-linked (autosomal simply means a chromosome that is not a sex chromosome). Examples of some monogenic conditions, not discussed further in this chapter, include: thalassaemia, which is a blood-related genetic disorder linked to haemoglobin dysfunction; cystic fibrosis, where the individual produces a very thick mucus, along with other body secretions, making them prone to lung infections; and the a forementioned Tay-Sachs disease, where the affected person produces harmful quantities of a fatty substance called ganglioside that accumulates in the brain's nerve cells.

AN AUTOSOMAL DOMINANT ILLNESS: HUNTINGTON'S DISEASE

One single gene disorder already mentioned in this book is **Huntington's disease** which causes degeneration of the brain, particularly the striatum, leading to deterioration of movement, temperament and cognition. Huntington's disease is an example of autosomal dominant disorder which means if a person inherits a copy of the mutated gene (from either parent) it will always cause the disease. The chances of inheriting Huntington's disease if one parent carries the mutated gene are 50%, and this can be understood by using Mendel's laws (see Figure 14.10). For example, if we assume the carrier parent has a mutated allele along with a normal one (Hh), and the other parent has two normal alleles (hh), then the offspring will inherit one of four possible combinations of paired alleles. In effect, the offspring will inherit a normal h allele from the unaffected parent, but will have a 50% chance of inheriting the H allele from the carrier parent. Put another way, 50% of the possible gene combinations in the offspring will carry the dominant (mutated) gene.

Another disorder that can be caused by a mutated dominant gene (although there are many genetic variants) is spinocerebellar ataxia, characterized by the slow degeneration of certain areas of the brain, including the cerebellum which results in poor motor coordination along with speech impairment and abnormal eye movements. Like Huntington's disease, many people with the disorder are not aware that they

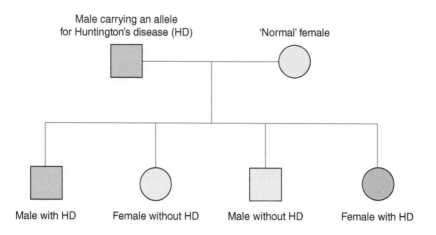

If one parent is a carrier of Huntington's disease then approximately
50% of the offspring will inherit the disease

Figure 14.10   The inheritance of Huntington's disease
Source: Wickens (2009)

carry the faulty gene until middle age, after which they have children who are at risk of developing the illness. This form of ataxia is particularly insidious since in many cases an afflicted person retains full mental capacity but progressively loses their physical control (Paulson, 2009).

KEY TERMS: *Huntington's disease, autosomal dominant disorder, spinocerebellar ataxia*

KEY THINKER 14.1

GEORGE HUNTINGTON

George Huntington was born in 1850, into a family of physicians who had practised for several generations on Long Island, New York. It is clear he was destined to follow his forefathers into medicine, for as a young boy he would accompany his father in his horse drawn carriage on his professional rounds. It was during this time that he would first come across the disease that today bears his name, and it was to make an enduring impression on him. As Huntington would later write: 'We suddenly came upon two women, mother and daughter, both tall, thin, almost cadaverous, both bowing, twisting, grimacing. I stared in wonderment. What could it mean? My father paused to speak with them and we passed on. Then my medical instruction had its inception. From this point on, my interest in the disease has never wholly ceased.'

(Continued)

After receiving his medical training at Columbia University in the city of New York, Huntington returned home in 1871 to assist his father. He soon turned his interest towards the strange disease that was characterized by irregular, spasmodic and involuntary movements of the trunk and limbs which he knew was always fatal. He also closely examined the medical notes that had been compiled by his father and grandfather who had also studied several families with the disease. It was apparent they were all ancestors of one Jeffrey Francis who had emigrated from England in 1634. Although it was clear the disease was inherited in some way, Huntington's great insight was to realize the nature of its transmission.

A few months later, he moved to a practice in Pomeroy, Ohio. Soon after, aged just 20 years, he presented a short paper on Sydenham's chorea to a medical conference, and in its final seven paragraphs outlined a condition which he called 'hereditary chorea'. Describing chorea as the 'dancing propensities of those ... affected' in whom there 'seems to exist some hidden power, something that is playing tricks, as it were, upon the will', he also noted that the disease 'seems to obey certain fixed laws'. Although Huntington was unaware of the existence of genes, he recognized the disease was always passed on to a child by an afflicted parent. Yet the inheritance was not inevitable. As Huntington put it: 'When either or both the parents have shown manifestations ... one or more of the offspring almost invariably suffer from the disease ... but if by any chance these children go through a life without it, the thread is broken ...' In effect, he had described an illness with an autosomal dominant mode of genetic transmission for the first time.

Huntington was not the first to observe this disease. There were a few reports of a similar illness by physicians of earlier times, and an account by Charles Waters had even appeared in a medical textbook of 1842. The disease was also known to many generations of families in colonial New England, some of whom were regarded as witches and publicly burnt to death. The same fate also befell the victims of the infamous Salem Witch Trials of 1692 and 1693 in Massachusetts. Again, some were probably sufferers of the illness. Interestingly, Huntington believed the disease could be traced to six individuals who had migrated from the small village of Bures in Suffolk, although others have attributed it to Puritans who sailed on the Mayflower, emigrating from England to America in the latter part of the seventeenth century.

Huntington moved back to the state of New York in 1874, and would practise medicine there until his retirement in 1915. He never held any academic or hospital position, and did not write any more medical papers. Said to be a humorous and modest man who enjoyed hunting, drawing and playing the flute, he seemed be much loved by his patients. He died from pneumonia in 1916 at the age of 66 years.

AN AUTOSOMAL RECESSIVE ILLNESS: PHENYLKETONURIA

Another single gene defect is **phenylketonuria** (PKU) which affects about one child in every 10,000. Individuals with this condition do not produce a liver enzyme called phenylalanine hydroxylase which is responsible for turning the amino acid phenylalanine into tyrosine. Phenylalanine is found in many foods, especially those high in protein such as eggs, milk, nuts and meat, and if it is not metabolized, will build up in the liver and pass into the bloodstream. This can then enter the developing brain and cause serious neural damage. If left untreated, PKU can impair intellectual development, resulting in severe mental retardation, behavioural problems and epilepsy. Even with treatment, it is estimated that 90% of patients with early onset phenylketonuria display white matter lesions in the brain which are most marked in the parietal and occipital lobes, although they can also extend into the frontal cortex and subcortical areas (Anderson & Leuzzi, 2009; Christ et al., 2006). There is also a reduction in volume of grey matter structures such as the motor cortex and thalamus (Pérez-Dueñas et al., 2006).

PKU is an autosomal recessive disorder caused by an allele found on chromosome 12. Being recessive, this means that for a child to be affected, they must inherit two copies of the allele – one from both parents. People who inherit one copy of the allele are unaffected by the disorder, although they remain carriers and

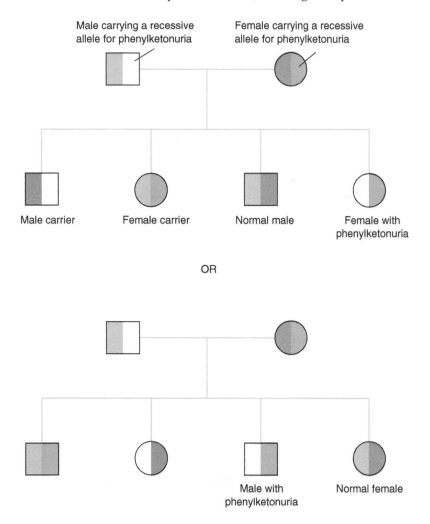

Figure 14.11   The inheritance of phenylketonuria
Source: Wickens (2009)

can pass it on to their offspring. It may come as a surprise to learn that about 1 person in 50 carries the faulty gene, which means that 1 in 2,500 couples (50 × 50) have the potential to produce a child with PKU. But on closer inspection, even assuming both parents are carriers, they still only have a 25% of producing a child with the disorder. To understand why we can again refer to Mendelian laws of inheritance see Figure 14.11. For example, if each parent carries a mutant allele and a normal allele it can be seen that the only combination that produces PKU will occur with a 1 in 4 probability.

Fortunately, PKU can be detected soon after birth by a simple blood test which has become standard practice in hospitals. Once detected, interventions can be undertaken to lessen the effects of the disorder. Phenylalanine is one of the ten essential amino acids that the body cannot manufacture by itself, and consequently the supply of this substance must come from the diet. Thus, by restricting its dietary intake, the build-up of phenylalanine and its metabolic products can be prevented, and providing the diet is initiated early enough in life, many individuals develop normally and have normal IQs (Al Hafid & Christodoulou, 2015). This example also shows that genetic predisposition (i.e. genotype) can be strongly modified by the effects of the environment (i.e. phenotype). Indeed, one should never forget that there are often complex and subtle interactions between genes and environmental factors.

KEY TERMS: *phenylketonuria, autosomal recessive disorder*

X-LINKED INHERITANCE

The third type of Mendelian inheritance occurs when a gene is carried on the X chromosome. Males and females differ in only one chromosome, i.e. males having XY sex chromosomes and females XX (see also Chapter 8). It follows, therefore, that males must always inherit their Y chromosome from the father, and their X chromosome from the mother. A woman's inheritance of two X chromosomes is usually beneficial since it provides protection against harmful genes. This is because if she carries a faulty gene on one of her X chromosomes, it will often have its harmful effects reversed by a normal gene on the other X chromosome. Consequently, X-linked recessive conditions can only occur in females when there are copies of the faulty gene on both X chromosomes, but in males there only needs to be a single copy of a faulty gene on the X chromosome for it to operate, as there is no corresponding gene on the Y chromosome to counteract its effects. This results in a situation where the female can unknowingly carry a mutant gene on a X chromosome and pass it on to her son who will express the trait.

Sex-linked conditions are therefore more common in males. In fact, if the mother carries a mutation on one of her X chromosomes, even if it is recessive, the risk of inheritance for the male is 50%, but a female carrying the same recessive gene on one of her own X chromosomes will be unaffected. Although it is possible for a female to inherit an X-linked mutated gene from both their father (he will always have the trait in question) and mother, this is rare unless the faulty gene is common in a population. One such example is the gene that causes a deficiency of the enzyme glucose-6-phosphate dehydrogenase (G6PD) which is found in certain African-American and Mediterranean populations.

Over 100 genes are known to be X-linked in humans, including red-green colour blindness, Duchenne muscular dystrophy and haemophilia A. In red-green colour blindness, a person cannot distinguish between shades of red and green despite having normal visual acuity. The cause of this disorder resides on the long arm of the X chromosome, which contains several genes that make the light-sensitive pigment called rhodopsin found in the photoreceptors of the eye. The chromosome contains a gene for the red-sensitive pigment, and up to three genes for the green-sensitive pigment. Genetic analysis shows that this type of colour blindness is normally associated with an altered number of genes encoding for these colour-sensitive pigments. Red-green colour blindness affects about 8% of human males and 0.6% of females of Northern European ancestry (Sharpe et al., 1999).

Duchenne muscular dystrophy is a disease that leads to progressive weakening of the muscles, often appearing before the age of six years, and causing death by early adulthood. The mutation produces alterations in a protein called *dystrophin* that helps keep muscle cells intact, and it occurs at a rate of around 1 per 3,500 male births, but only 1 in 50,000,000 females (Falzarano et al., 2015). In about a third of cases it can arise as a new mutation in embryonic development. Young men with Duchenne muscular dystrophy do not normally produce offspring, so the gene typically dies out in the male line, although it continues to pass through generations of females. The *dystrophin* gene consists of around 2 million base pairs which accounts for over 1% of the X chromosome.

SPECIAL INTEREST 14.1

HAEMOPHILIA AND THE FALL OF THE RUSSIAN ROYAL FAMILY

Haemophilia is caused by a mutation on the X chromosome which results in a clotting factor of the blood to be partly or completely missing. Consequently a patient with haemophilia will bleed far longer than is normal after a cut or injury. The earliest descriptions of this disorder are found in Jewish texts including the Talmud from the 2nd century AD that exempted boys from circumcision if two previous brothers had died from bleeding following the operation. After this, haemophilia appears to have been largely forgotten until 1803 when a physician from Philadelphia, Dr John Conrad Otto, described a familial bleeding disease that was inherited through the female line, but only affected males. There are now known to be several types of the disease, with haemophilia A making up about 80% of all cases. It occurs in around 1 in 5,000 males. Female haemophilia can exist but is extremely rare.

(Continued)

Haemophilia is sometimes known as 'the royal disease' because of its prevalence among the royalty of Europe. It appears to have begun with Queen Victoria of England, who would pass the mutation on to various royal households in Europe via two of her daughters. This would also dramatically alter the course of Russian and world history. In 1853 Queen Victoria gave birth to her youngest son Leopold. He provided the first clue that Victoria was carrying the haemophilia gene for he bled profusely even after small cuts and grazes. Leopold was to die at the age of 30 when he fell and suffered a brain haemorrhage. Unfortunately, two of Queen Victoria's daughters, Princess Alice and Princess Beatrice, were also unknowingly carriers of haemophilia, and they would pass it on when marrying into German royal households. But the most famous affected individual was Tsarevich Alexis born in 1904, the son of Tsar Nicholas II of Russia who had married Alexandra, daughter of Princess Alice. In their desperation to treat their son, the Tsar turned to the Siberian monk Rasputin who had arrived in St Petersburg in 1903 claiming spiritual healing powers. Rasputin did indeed appear to have a mysterious ability to heal Alexis, which some believe was due to hypnosis. Whatever his secret, Rasputin gained influence at the Russian court despite tales of sexual profligacy and debauchery. His power increased so much that by 1915 he was taking a role in the selection of cabinet ministers and military decisions – an involvement that greatly discredited the Russian monarchy. Eventually a group of nobles assassinated Rasputin in 1916, although it was too late to save the Tsar and his family from the communist revolution which was to destroy their lives a few months later.

Today, many people with haemophilia lead relatively normal lives. Haemophilia can be managed by transfusions of fresh plasma or injections of the appropriate clotting factor. But both therapies are relatively expensive. In 1984, a breakthrough occurred when the structure of the gene producing haemophilia A was characterized and cloned. This led to the availability of recombinant (genetically engineered) clotting factors which proved safer and cheaper. However the great hope lies with gene therapy. That is, one day it will be possible to inject new genetic material into the person, which will correct the faulty gene, leading to proper production of the blood clotting factors. Clinical trials are currently underway to explore this possibility (Rai & Malik, 2016).

THE GENETIC INFLUENCE ON BEHAVIOUR

The relationship between genes and behaviour, sometimes known as the nature–nurture debate, is much more complicated than the one between genes and disease. There are several reasons for this. One is that genes do not control behaviour directly, but instead encode all the molecular products that build and govern the functioning of the brain (or our bodies) through which behaviour is expressed. Examples of such genes are those that make ion channels, receptors, neurotransmitters, and all the other synaptic machinery. Looked at this way, genes do not cause behaviour, but they certainly have a bearing upon it. Consequently, our genetic inheritance (genotype) may give us certain dispositions to act in certain ways, but ultimately our behaviour (phenotype) is shaped by the interaction of gene and environment. Indeed, even the most stereotypical or instinctive behaviour can be modified by experience, and every learned skill is influenced by innate factors. Another reason why this genetic–behavioural relationship is not simple lies with the complexity of the two variables.

Although Mendelian single-gene inheritance can be important for understanding certain types of disease, it is clear that human traits and behaviour do not follow the simple patterns of single-gene inheritance. Rather, it is likely there are large numbers of genes that can influence any one type of behaviour.

One of the first scientists to investigate the complexities of human inheritance was Darwin's cousin, Francis Galton, who coined the terms *nature* and *nurture*, and developed specialized statistical techniques to explore the subject mathematically. To give an example, in 1875 Galton used correlation to study the inheritance of height, and found a positive relationship between the heights of parents and their children (i.e. as the height of the parent increased so did that of the child). Yet the relationship was not perfect, with taller parents sometimes having smaller children and vice versa. Galton concluded that traits such as height (he also applied the same concepts to intelligence) were not inherited in a dichotomous way – rather they exhibited continuous variation. Clearly, if our height was due to a single dominant gene, as occurred with Mendel's tall and dwarf pea plants, then only two heights would be possible. The fact that there is a great variation in human height shows that its genetic basis is much more complex.

After the rediscovery of Mendel's work in 1900, a heated scientific conflict arose between those defending Mendelian inheritance which advocated dichotomous variation, and those favouring Galton who believed genes produced traits with continuous variation. This debate was resolved by R. A. Fisher in 1918 who demonstrated both positions could be reconciled. Fisher showed that a continuous trait such as height was explainable if a large number of Mendelian factors (i.e. genes) each made a small contribution to tallness. In fact, we now know that there are about 700 genetic variants known to affect height, each of them usually producing a small effect of less than a millimetre (Marouli et al., 2017). In addition to this, environmental factors such as nutrition and exercise significantly contribute to height. Fisher also realized that two or more genes working together combined to produce a trait in a population that followed a probability function called a normal distribution which resembles a bell-shaped curve. In essence, Fisher's theory shows that complex traits are influenced by many genes, but each gene in still inherited according to Mendel's laws.

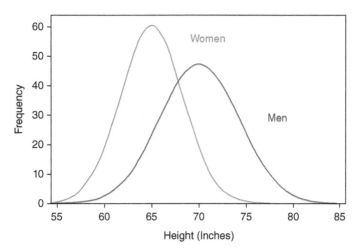

Figure 14.12   Normal distributions for male and female height

But of course human behaviour is a much more complex phenotype than height, as shown by the endless number of ways we behave. Behavioural geneticists now believe that most human traits, whether a predisposition to obesity or homosexuality, or the inheritance of personality traits such as aggressiveness or depression, are likely to be influenced by numerous genes, sometimes numbering several hundred, spread over many chromosomes. For example, it has been estimated that intelligence is influenced by over 500 genes (Hill et al., 2018) and up to 600 genes may contribute towards schizophrenia (Harrison, 2015). Despite this, few would deny the importance of environmental factors such as prenatal influences, learning, and socioeconomic forces in their expression. Clearly, we must accept a multifactorial model of inheritance, with the assumption that no single gene is responsible for the behaviour in question. Due to the complex genetic nature of human beings, and their interaction with unlimited environmental factors, many geneticists regard genes as providing a certain probability that a behaviour or trait will occur. Or put another way, there is a 'probablistic bias' towards a condition appearing as a result of genetic and environmental interaction (Toates, 2007).

But how can we tease out the interaction of genetic and environmental influences in our behaviour? Mendel was fortunate in choosing pea plants that had a simple dichotomous trait. However, as Galton showed, this approach will not work for human behaviour which is far too complex for this type of analysis. Fortunately, there are a number of methods that can be used, including twin and adoption studies in humans, and selective breeding and transgenic manipulation in animals. It is to these methods we now turn.

KEY TERMS: *nature–nurture debate, genotype, phenotype, normal distribution*

TWIN AND ADOPTION STUDIES

One way of assessing the heritability, or the percentage variation, of a given trait that can be attributed to genetic factors is to compare the behaviour of monozygotic (identical) and dizygotic (fraternal) twins. The reasoning is easy to understand: if identical twins are more similar for a given behavioural trait than fraternal twins, then this implies that inheritance plays a more important role in its expression. This is because identical twins share all, or nearly all, of their genetic material, whilst fraternal twins share on average 50% of their genes (see Boomsma et al., 2002). The influence of this inheritance on behaviour can be measured by the concordance rate. Put simply, twins will be concordant for a given trait if both express it, and discordant if they don't. Thus, if concordance rates, which are expressed as percentages, are higher in a group of identical twins compared to non-identical ones, this shows a greater genetic influence on that trait. As we have seen, Huntington's disease which is due to a single dominant gene, has a concordance of 100% in identical twins, but 50% in fraternal twins. In the case of phenylketonuria, the respective percentages are 100% and 25%.

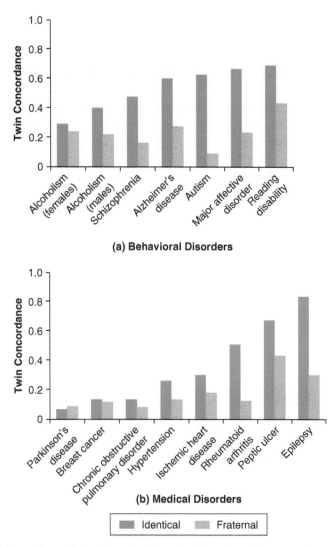

Figure 14.13   Twin studies of behavioural and medical disorders. The concordance of (a) behavioral disorders, and (b) medical disorders in identical and fraternal twins. Concordance is the proportion of twin pairs in which both twins have the disorder. Note the greater concordance in identical twins and the generally higher concordance for behavioral disorders than for medical disorders.

Source: Garrett and Hough (2021), from Plomin, R., Owen, M. J., & McGuffin, P. (1994). The genetic basis of complex human behavior. *Science*, 264, p. 1734. © 1994 American Association for the Advancement of Science. Reprinted with permission from AAAS.

When we look at human behaviour with its far more varied and complex genetic influences, the concordance rates along with heritability estimates[3] show greater variability. For example, according to most estimates, the heritability for intelligence is around 50%, although this can vary across the life span, increasing from about 20% in infancy to 80% in later adulthood (Plomin & Deary, 2015). But whatever figure we choose to accept, it is important not to lose sight of the fact that the environment plays an important role in shaping our intellectual abilities. Indeed, socioeconomic status, education, malnutrition and disease are just a few of the factors that can shape

---

[3]Heritability estimates are a more complex calculation, often calculated by using either correlation and regression methods, or analysis of variance.

our level of intelligence (Oommen, 2014). Some other estimates of heritability by behavioural geneticists are also of interest. For example, the heritability of schizophrenia has been estimated to be 60–90% (Tsuang et al., 1999), 37–46% for depression (Corfield et al., 2017), and 50–60% for male homosexuality (Baily & Pillard, 1991; Whitam et al., 1993).

Despite this, there are several problems associated with using concordance rates as a measure of genetic heritability. Most obvious is the likelihood that identical twins will share the same environment, including parental upbringing and schooling, which could just as equally explain their similar patterns of behaviour. In addition, identical twins are more likely to spend time together, and be treated as a 'pair' by family and friends. Both these factors would be likely to inflate the estimates of genetic influence (Schönemann, 1997). A way around this problem would be to study twins who were separated early in life and then reared apart in different types of environment. If the similarity in concordance continues to persist under these circumstances, then the heritability argument for behavioural traits would be much more convincing.

KEY TERMS: *heritability, twins, concordance rate*

THE MINNESOTA STUDY OF TWINS REARED APART

Despite the difficulties of finding identical twins who have been adopted at an early age and raised in different families, such pairs exist, and they have provided psychologists with fascinating insights into behavioural genetics. In some cases the findings have been truly remarkable. In 1979 Thomas Bouchard, working at the University of Minnesota, came across an account in his local newspaper of a pair of identical twins (Jim Springer and Jim Lewis) who had been separated three weeks after their birth and reunited again at the age of 39. In terms of facial appearance the two men looked quite distinct with their differing hair styles, but in terms of behaviour and the events of their life, they shared many uncanny similarities. Both were called James by their adoptive parents, although each preferred Jim. As schoolchildren they enjoyed woodworking, were better at maths than English, and each had a childhood pet dog called Toy. As they grew older, both drove Chevrolets, took part in stock car racing, and were employed in security work. They smoked heavily and always took their holidays in Florida. Each had a workshop in the basement of their house where one built miniature picnic tables and the other rocking chairs. The coincidences also extended to their wives and children. Each had been married twice, with both their first wives being called Linda and their second named Betty. Jim Lewis and Jim Springer also each had a son called James Alan (or James Allan in Springer's case), and both had similar medical histories with an identical pulse and blood pressure rate, as well as haemorrhoids.

The discovery of the 'Jim twins' inspired Bouchard to set up the Minnesota Study of Identical Twins Reared Apart (MISTRA) in 1979, which he would lead until 2000. The aim of this programme was to assess the relative contributions of genetic and environmental factors to the physical, mental and personality traits that characterize human individuality. In doing this, it also studied identical twins reared together, as well as dizygotic twins reared together and those reared apart. Over its duration, MISTRA would obtain a registry of over 8,000 identical and dizygotic twins, with a database containing information on over 120 pairs of identical twins reared in different environments. Each of these pairs also agreed to participate in an extensive number of personality and cognitive tests which lasted around 50 hours in total. In the process, each subject answered around 15,000 questions and provided a full medical history.

One of the key behavioural traits examined was personality. Participants were given the Minnesota Multiphasic Personality Inventory – a test containing 567 items that measured personality on five main scales, which usually took around two hours to complete. The results showed that identical twins reared apart had scores comparable with identical twins reared together (Bouchard et al., 1990). In other words, they had similar personalities regardless of environment. However, the dizygotic twins reared apart or together showed far greater difference, in their personality scores than would be expected by their genetic variation, and randomly selected individuals produced no statistically reliable correlation on these tests. From all the data gathered, Bouchard estimated that genetic factors account for about 40–50% of the variance in the 'big five' personality traits (extraversion, agreeableness, openness, conscientiousness and neuroticism) frequently used by psychologists (Bouchard, 1994).

Another trait examined by Boucher was intelligence which he measured by using the Wechsler Adult Intelligent Scale. He found the average correlation for twins reared apart was 0.70, and 0.85 for those reared together. This is a high correlation and appears to show that genetic factors are the most important determinant of intelligence. Indeed, Bouchard estimated the heritability of intelligence to be around 70% (Bouchard et al., 1990; McGue et al., 1993). These types of scores have also been replicated by others. For example, a twin study that looked at pairs with high cognitive ability (selected from 11,000 twin pairs) showed the heritability of intelligence to be over 50% (Haworth et al., 2009). It is claimed that this type of variance, sometimes described as a general cognitive factor (g), is found in a broad range of cognitive abilities, although it may change across the life span (Deary et al., 2009).

THE PROBLEM WITH TWIN STUDIES

A comprehensive review of the 30-year history of the MISTRA programme has been written by Nancy Segal who worked on the project for several years (Segal, 2012), and she concludes that identical twins reared apart are as similar to each other as identical twins reared together. This she argues includes personality traits, intelligence, other interests, and social attitudes. In short, Segal believes this provides strong evidence that such behaviours are strongly genetic.

But is this really the case? There is room for doubt since Bouchard's conclusions have been criticized by some, most notably the clinical psychologist Jay Joseph (2003, 2015) who claims to have discovered 22 invalidating issues and biases associated with the MISTRA study. Amongst his claims is that nearly all the twins reared apart actually had frequent or regular contact, or a close emotional bond with each other. Moreover, he argues that the Minnesota researchers biased their findings, but denied independent reviewers access to their raw data. Joseph also points out that the supposedly 'spooky' similarities of some reunited twins prove nothing about genetic influences, since an identical twin pair are inevitably the same age and sex, similar in physical appearance, and usually grow up (even if apart) in similar cultural and socioeconomic environments. For Joseph, it is clear that family, social, cultural, economic and political environments, and not genetics, are the main causes of differences in human behaviour.

Whether one accepts Joseph's arguments or not, it is often overlooked that genetic and environmental factors can interact in many subtle ways. For example, evidence shows that people with similar genetic endowments seek out similar environments and experiences. Thus, genetically similar individuals may be more likely to seek out the same type of friends, have the same interests, or become involved in the same social events. Because individuals are likely to seek outlets for their innate tendencies regardless of what environment they are reared in, this may mean that one will never be able to provide a definite or undisputed estimate of heritability for any given trait (Felson, 2014). But even if such factors could be controlled, there are some researchers who argue that the concept of heritability which uses a single percentage derived from twin studies is basically nothing more than a statistical fallacy with no meaning or relationship to the underlying DNA (Leo, 2003; Pam et al., 1996).

It should not be forgotten that these types of studies potentially have many serious and sinister ramifications. For example, in the case of intelligence, a belief in genetic inheritance could be used to justify elitist or racial streaming in schooling by those responsible for social and educational policy (see Howe, 1997). There are also those who point out that even if intelligence is largely inherited, this means little since the environment still plays an important role – and, of course, this is the one factor we can improve further to the benefit of all. When looked at this way, we can see the deeper problems associated with estimates of heritability (Kaplan, 2012; Kendler et al., 2015).

SELECTIVE BREEDING FOR BEHAVIOUR

Alternative techniques can be used to manipulate and assess the heritability of behavioural traits in animals. One method that has been used since the time of the Agricultural Revolution about 12,000 years ago is to breed plants and animals with desirable characteristics. This is called selective breeding (also known as artificial selection) and it involves choosing parents with a chosen trait to breed together, thereby producing offspring with the same or even improved characteristics. For example, wild cattle and sheep have long legs for speed and large horns for defence, yet the domestic versions of these animals today look very different, with their large bodies for meat and wool, short legs and typically small or non-existent horns. The domestication of dogs may go back even further, with evidence showing this process began prior to Neolithic times some 20,000 and 40,000 years ago (Botigué et al., 2017). Since then dogs have been bred for many traits. Some have been selected for fighting (e.g. pit bull terriers), to aid hunting (e.g. terriers) or for controlling flocks of animals (e.g. sheep dogs). But the same technique can also be used experimentally. The rationale is simple: if a behaviour is influenced by genetic factors then it should be possible to produce it through selective breeding.

In psychology, a classic example of this approach was undertaken by Robert Tryon (1940) who selected rats for their maze-learning ability (see Figure 14.14). Tyron was interested in determining whether intelligence was inherited, and he began examining the performance of a large group of rats on a 17-choice maze task. After this initial stage, he interbred the animals that had shown the best maze scores and those with the worst scores. Thus, he began to create a group of maze-bright rats, and maze-dull animals. Tyron continued this selection procedure for 21 generations. His work soon showed that the two groups differed significantly in their ability to learn the maze. In fact, after seven generations, the distribution of the error scores no longer overlapped between the groups, and the rats continued to show this difference over subsequent generations.

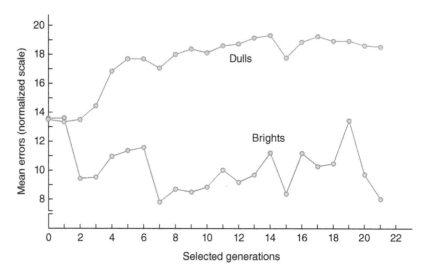

Figure 14.14   Graph showing the results of Tryon's selective breeding for maze-bright and maze-dull rats

Source: Wickens (2009)

These maze-bright and maze-dull strains of rat have been maintained since the 1940s and are still available for experimentation (Robinson & Kerkut, 2013). A key issue is whether there is a biological factor in the brain's biochemistry that could explain the differences between the maze-bright and maze-dull rats. One chemical which has been implicated in several maze studies is the enzyme that breaks down acetylcholine called **acetylcholinesterase** (AChE). Levels of this enzyme have been found to be higher in the brains of the maze-bright rats. This finding suggests that maze-bright rats produce more acetylcholine – although when a group of rats were selectively bred for high AChE activity, they actually proved to be poor on the maze task (Rosenzweig et al., 1958).

Tryon's work would appear to show that maze ability is inherited. Moreover, genetic factors have been shown to be important in many other types of learning, including active and passive avoidance, operant conditioning and discrimination learning (Bovet, 1977). But this conclusion highlighting the over-riding importance of inheritance is premature. For example, Cooper and Zubek (1958) housed their maze-bright and maze-dull rats in enriched or impoverished conditions. They found that if the maze-dull animals were reared in an enriched environment, they performed in a similar way to the maze-bright rats. Thus the enriched condition had no effect on the maze-bright rats, but it greatly improved the performance of the maze-dull animals. Interestingly, the difference between the two groups also diminished when both were raised in the restricted environment. These results show that the 'genetic predisposition' for maze learning is only manifested under certain environmental conditions. Perhaps the most important conclusion to be derived from this research is that genotype-environmental interaction lies at the heart of all behaviour and is complex (Dick, 2011).

KEY TERMS: *selective breeding, maze-bright and maze-dull rats, acetylcholinesterase (AChE)*

SELECTIVE BREEDING FOR ALCOHOL USE

Another area of research where selective breeding has been used to examine the genetic contribution to behaviour is alcohol abuse. This has become a popular subject in behavioural genetics, not least because understanding the relative impact of genetic predisposition and environment on alcohol use has implications for controlling its sale and how we treat its associated diseases. Clearly, the causes of alcohol drinking are complex (Sudhinaraset et al., 2016). There are personality and social factors at play which attract people to alcohol, and it is clear that high levels of stress can often encourage drinking for its feelings of pleasure and relaxation. But still, some people appear to be more vulnerable to alcohol abuse than others, which supports the idea that genetic factors are involved. This has also been supported by recent twin studies. For example, in a comprehensive meta-analysis of alcohol use disorders which looked at 13 twin studies and 5 adoption studies, involving over 38,000 subjects, it was estimated that alcohol misuse was approximately 50% heritable (Verhulst et al., 2015).

Selective breeding for alcohol use was initiated in the 1940s, when Jorge Mardones at the University of Chile began producing two strains of rats that differed in their alcohol consumption. Although most rats will not drink alcohol when given a choice between alcohol and water, some do, and these can be bred together. The two groups were called the UChA and UChB strains (A stands for 'abstainer' and B for 'bibulous'), which consume low and high levels of alcohol respectively. These rats have now been bred for over 70 generations (Quintanilla et al., 2006), and if given a choice between water and a solution containing 10% alcohol, the UChB rats exhibit a strong preference for the latter. It should be noted that these are not the only strains used in alcohol research, for there are at least 6 different genetically selected alcohol preferring and non-preferring rat lines around the world (Ciccocioppo, 2013).

So what are the genetic and biochemical differences that explain the variation in alcohol consumption between the UChA and UChB strains? One difference is that the alcohol-preferring rats metabolize alcohol faster than the non-preferring rats, which makes them more tolerant to this drug. The key to this improved alcohol metabolism lies with an enzyme in the liver called **alcohol dehydrogenase**. The genetics of alcohol dehydrogenase are complex as there are three classes of gene which produce this enzyme (abbreviated as *ALDH1*, *ALDH2* etc.) and several different variants in each class. But it has been found that the alcohol-preferring rats inherit a more efficient version of the *ALDH2* gene than the abstaining animals. This means, in effect, the abstaining (non-tolerant) rats have less active alcohol dehydrogenase, which causes increased elevations of a metabolite called acetaldehyde after alcohol ingestion. It has also been estimated that the *ALDH2* genotype predicts 40–60% of the alcohol consumption in these animals (Quintanilla et al., 2006).

Another strain of rat, called alcohol-preferring, has been bred at the University of Indiana – which also voluntarily drinks alcohol to high intoxicating levels (McBride et al., 2013). In fact, under certain conditions, their behaviour can result in blood alcohol concentrations of 200 mg/100 ml which readily produces motor impairment and sedation – a level that results in serious intoxication and 'loss-of-control' drinking in humans (McBride et al., 2014). These rats also demonstrate physical signs of withdrawal when the alcohol is removed, and show increased metabolic tolerance to alcohol which causes them to exhibit fewer adverse behavioural effects after consuming high amounts compared to control animals.

One of the most significant findings to emerge from an examination of these alcohol-preferring rats is that they have significantly lower levels of **serotonin** and its metabolite 5-HIAA in many regions of the brain, including the cortex, hippocampus and nucleus accumbens (Murphy et al., 1987). As a result of this decreased serotonergic activity, there is a compensatory increase (or upregulation) of 5-HT_{1A} receptors – especially in the hippocampus and frontal cortex (Lumeng et al., 1993). In addition to serotonin, there are also lower baseline levels of **dopamine** in the frontal cortex, nucleus accumbens and striatum in the alcohol-preferring rats (Ma & Zhu, 2014). This is functionally important, for when these animals are injected with alcohol, they show an increased level of dopamine – with the amount of its elevation predicting subsequent alcohol-drinking behaviour (Katner & Weiss, 2001). These studies suggest that alcohol-induced increases in dopamine release play a significant role in the animal's drinking behaviour. This is believed to be particularly important in the **nucleus accumbens** where the effects of alcohol on dopamine are likely to be highly pleasurable (Yan, 1999).

KEY TERMS: *alcohol-preferring and non-preferring rat, alcohol dehydrogenase, serotonin, dopamine, nucleus accumbens*

THE HUNT FOR GENES: LINKAGE MAPPING AND GENOME-WIDE ASSOCIATION

If alcoholic abuse, or any other behavioural trait, has a genetic basis, then it would be extremely useful to identify the genes involved and determine their location in the human genome. There are a number of approaches a geneticist can use to do this, but one of the earliest was linkage mapping. This works on the simple tendency for genes and other genetic markers to be inherited together because of their proximity to each other on the chromosome. We have seen in the previous chapter, for example, that the genes that cause haemophilia and red-green colour blindness lie close together on the X chromosome. Consequently, both genes tend to get inherited together. Similarly, in the hunt for genes linked to alcohol abuse, researchers can attempt to discover their location in the genome by finding a genetic marker (typically a large region of identifiable DNA) that is co-inherited and runs through families who have members with drinking problems. Although this approach does not allow for the precise localization of the gene in question to be identified, it does enable the investigator to narrow it down. This method is particularly useful when an illness or condition is due to a single gene. Indeed, James Gusella used a type of linkage analysis to localize the huntingtin gene to the short arm of chromosome 4 in 1983 (see Chapter 13).

The first linkage studies examining alcohol dependence were undertaken by the Collaborative Study on the Genetics of Alcoholism in the USA, which analysed 987 individuals from 105 alcohol problematic families with 291 DNA markers (Reich et al., 1998). Extracting DNA from blood samples, they found linkages to regions on chromosomes 1 and 7, with some support for a linkage to a region on chromosome 2. A second study provided evidence that alcohol misuse was associated with regions on chromosome 4 in the general vicinity of the alcohol dehydrogenase genes, as well as a region encoding a subunit of the GABA-A receptor (Long et al., 1998). These latter findings have been replicated in other studies (e.g., Foroud et al., 2010). But whilst these studies provide an important first step towards identifying the genes involved in alcoholism, the main drawback is that linkage studies can only highlight broad regions of the genome which may contain many hundreds of genes (Edenberg & Foroud, 2013).

A more recent development is the genome-wide association study. Unlike linkage analysis which requires some prior knowledge about the neurobiology underlying the behaviour or disease in question, genome-wide association examines the entire genome of individuals without any prior hypothesis of where the genes may be located (Bush & Moore, 2012). The ability to look at the whole genome of large groups of individuals has only been made possible with advances in DNA technology over the last 20 years or so. Researchers usually obtain DNA from a blood sample or from cells collected from the inside of the mouth, and then extract the genetic material using a commercial kit. It is analysed with specially designed glass chips containing large numbers of probes that detect single nucleotide polymorphisms (SNPs). These are normally fairly long stretches of DNA which only vary in terms of a single nucleotide (or base) between individuals. Occurring in both genes (when they become alleles) and

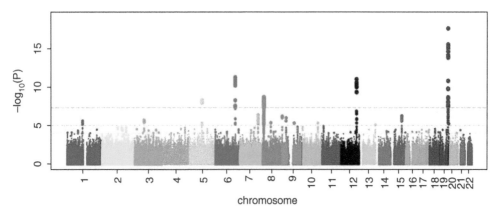

Figure 14.15   An illustration of a Manhattan plot depicting several strongly associated risk loci

Source: Ikram M. K., Xueling, S., Jensen, R. A., Cotch, M. F., Hewitt, A.W., Ikram, M. A., et al. (2010) Four Novel Loci (19q13, 6q24, 12q24, and 5q14) Influence the Microcirculation In Vivo. *PLoS Genet* 6(10): e1001184. https://doi.org/10.1371/journal.pgen.1001184

non-coding DNA, they are the most common type of genetic variation among people. But more importantly, when an SNP is found on a chromosome, it can also act as a biological marker. And if certain SNPs are known to be associated with a trait, then scientists may examine stretches of DNA near those SNPs in an attempt to identify the gene or genes responsible. The results are presented as a Manhattan plot where the strength of association with the trait in question is represented on the vertical axis, and the location of individual single nucleotide polymorphisms on each chromosome on the horizontal axis (Gibson, 2010; Visscher et al., 2012).

The first genome-wide association study to examine the genetic basis of alcohol misuse was undertaken by Johnson et al. (2006) who analysed 104,268 single nucleotide polymorphisms from 120 patients. This identified 51 gene loci which surprisingly included genes for making proteins known as cell adhesion molecules that maintain tissue structure and function. The next major study was undertaken in Germany by Treutlein et al. (2009) who examined 487 alcohol-dependent patients. This again identified stretches of DNA encoding for cell adhesion molecules, as well as the DNA containing the genes for making alcohol dehydrogenase. These first two reports have since been supplemented with at least 16 more studies, resulting in a somewhat confusing array of potential DNA regions being correlated with alcohol misuse – although most have highlighted the DNA containing the genes for alcohol dehydrogenase (Tawa et al., 2016).

One of the criticisms of genome-wide association studies is they only identify a region of the chromosome linked to a trait and not the actual gene itself. This raises the possibility that the suspected genes may be simply 'tagging along' with the true genetic culprits. Another difficulty is that most of the single nucleotide polymorphisms that have been identified in alcoholic individuals are associated with only a small increased risk of the disease. And somewhat frustratingly, the relatively few large studies undertaken so far have produced varied and differing results (Tam et al., 2019). Clearly, genome-wide association testing is still in its infancy, expensive to run and labour intensive, but the field is rapidly expanding and is expected to become much more feasible in the near future. Although the first genome-wide association studies were concerned with identifying genetic risk factors for disease (Hirschhorn & Daly, 2005), they are increasingly being used to study psychiatric disorders and many types of behavioural trait (Reynolds et al., 2021).

KEY TERMS: *linkage mapping, genome-wide association study, single nucleotide polymorphisms, Manhattan plot*

GENETIC ENGINEERING AND TRANSGENIC ANIMALS

Identifying the genes involved in a character trait such as alcohol abuse is one thing, but it doesn't tell us what these genes actually do. Genes, of course, are the blueprints for making proteins. But how do we determine the function of those proteins? Although this type of puzzle has proven difficult to solve in the past, a powerful method for assessing gene function has been developed in recent years through

genetic engineering which involves the direct manipulation of an organism's genes using biotechnology. In its basic form, this either requires making new copies or versions of the gene which are then implanted into another organism, or by inactivating specific genes already present in the genome. An animal that carries a foreign gene that has been deliberately inserted into its genetic material is known as a transgenic animal – and in neuroscience these creatures have already been put to many uses. They have, for example, been used to study the function of genes in degenerative diseases and tailored to address many specific biological questions. The products of genetic engineering have also been utilized in the development of new therapies and drugs to treat human diseases (Park et al., 2008; Watt & Driskell, 2010).

The beginnings of this genetic revolution took place in the 1960s when scientists discovered restriction enzymes that 'cut' DNA with precision at a specific base sequence. These enzymes were first found in bacteria, where they were used to disable the DNA of invading viruses. However, researchers soon realized they could be used experimentally as 'molecular scissors' to create snippets of DNA. That is, DNA could be extracted from a living organism and put into a test tube with restriction enzymes to create lots of DNA fragments. Within a decade of their discovery, geneticists had discovered hundreds of restriction enzymes, enabling them to make many different types of DNA fragment. Today, over 3,000 restriction enzymes have been identified and well over 600 are commercially available for experimental purposes.

By themselves, lots of DNA snippets floating around in a test tube have little use, but a few years after restriction enzymes were discovered, geneticists found ways of joining those bits of DNA together. This technology began in 1971 when American biochemist Paul Berg managed to insert genetic material taken from a bacterium into the DNA of a virus. The DNA of both these organisms existed as closed loops in their natural state, but after being severed with a restriction enzyme, the loops became linear strands of DNA. At this point, Berg made the ends of the strands 'sticky' with two other enzymes, causing them to rejoin into loops again, but in such a way that they combined DNA from each source. Berg's gene-splicing procedure had created the first DNA made up of genetic material from different organisms. This has since become known as **recombinant DNA**.

A more astonishing feat occurred in 1973 when Herbert Boyer and Stanley Cohen took DNA from a toad, and placed it in the DNA of an Escherichia coli (E. coli) bacterium. After this, every time the E.coli divided, the 'foreign' DNA was copied and passed into the new generation of cells. This was the first living organism to be transgenically modified, thereby opening the door to genetic engineering and laying the foundations for gene therapy and the emergence of the biotechnology industry. The next step was to insert new sequences of DNA into more complex creatures such as mammals, in order to create transgenic animals for experimental purposes. This became a reality in 1974 when Rudolf Jaenisch created the first transgenic mouse by introducing foreign DNA into the genome of early progenitor cells developing in the embryo by using a retrovirus as a carrier (Jaenisch & Mintz, 1974). Although these mice were the first transgenic mammals in history, it would take several more years before they were capable of passing their transgene on to their offspring. But this would be successfully undertaken by Gordon and Ruddle in 1981, who microinjected foreign DNA into the fertilized egg of a mouse, and after it replicated, put it back into the ovaries of a recipient female. At this point different strains of animal could be successfully bred.

KEY TERMS: *genetic engineering, transgenic animals, restriction enzymes, recombinant DNA*

KNOCKOUT MICE AND GENE THERAPY

One consequence of this technology was the development of knockout mice in 1989 (see Bevan, 2010) which were purposefully bred to lack a certain gene – a procedure that would enable researchers to examine its function. The logic is simple: by causing

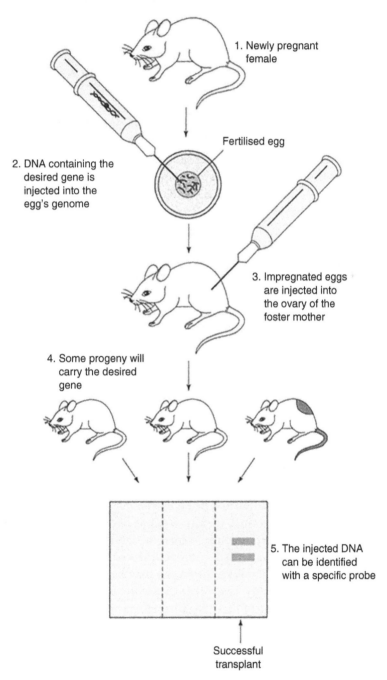

1. Newly pregnant female

Fertilised egg

2. DNA containing the desired gene is injected into the egg's genome

3. Impregnated eggs are injected into the ovary of the foster mother

4. Some progeny will carry the desired gene

5. The injected DNA can be identified with a specific probe

Successful transplant

Figure 14.16 The production of transgenic mice using the DNA microinjection method
Source: Wickens (2009)

a specific gene to be inactive, and observing the differences between these animals and normal ones, the gene's role can be assessed and understood better. Researchers were quick to realize the potential of the knockout mouse. Mice act as a good analogue for most human biological processes since we share about 99% of the same genes (Capecchi, 1994), and to date about 11,000 genes have been 'knocked out' in mice. This accounts for roughly half of the mouse genome, enabling the functions of thousands of proteins to be analysed. Millions of knockout mice are used in experiments each year (Hall et al., 2009; Spencer, 2012). Similar experimental technologies also exist for inserting new genes into a genome, or modifying ones already there (Bouabe & Okkenhaug, 2013).

Transgenic mice have been used to elucidate the role of abnormal proteins such as the amyloid and tau in Alzheimer's disease (Ke et al., 2012; Sasaguri et al., 2017). But similar transgenic models are especially effective at examining illnesses caused by a single mutation such as Huntington's disease. One of the most interesting findings to emerge from this work is that 'knockout mice' that lack both copies of the huntingtin gene do not complete embryonic development and die within 7–8 days (Duyao et al., 1995). Thus, the htt protein clearly plays a critical role in early foetal development. However, knockout mice engineered to carry only one deleted htt gene appear perfectly normal. This is a curious finding because people with Huntington's disease also inherit just one mutated gene (they would only inherit two genes if both parents had the disease). Thus, their mutated gene must be functioning differently from the 'knocked out' one in the mouse. This has raised speculation that the mutated gene, or its protein, in Huntington's disease might be taking on a completely new property, which produces a toxic outcome (this is called a *gain of function*) and is not a simple loss of its effect (Saudou & Humbert, 2016).

A variant of this procedure is the use of gene therapy that one day is likely to use genes to treat or prevent disease. Although the first successful nuclear gene transfer in humans was performed in May 1989, in an attempt to provide immunotherapy for patients with advanced melanoma (Rosenberg et al., 1990), the procedure is still in its experimental stages. Nonetheless, there are a number of clinical trials around the world taking place using gene transplantation, and there is great hope that in the future this technique may allow doctors to treat a wide range of disorders by inserting a gene into a patient's cells instead of using drugs or surgery. Again, one illness that would appear to readily lend itself to this type of manipulation is Huntington's disease. Indeed, the Dutch company Unique is actively involved in this quest and running preliminary trials whose therapeutic goal is to inhibit the production of the mutant huntingtin protein by the selective knocking out of its gene. They have already reported some success in reducing the amount of mutant potent in the striatum, and whilst there is a long way to go, their results appear promising.

KEY TERMS: *knockout mice, gene therapy*

THE PROMISE OF STEM CELLS

Although the use of recombinant DNA technology to understand of how genes contribute to behaviour and disease provides a great challenge, with many benefits, not least the possibility of successful forms of gene therapy, there is arguably a technique with even greater potential for research purposes and treating a variety of medical conditions. This is the production and use of human stem cells – primitive undifferentiated cells that have the potential to become any other type of cell in the body. In effect, stem cells are cells that do not yet have a specific role, but under the right conditions can be manufactured into a cell of one's choosing such as a muscle cell a red blood cell or a neuron.

The first stem cells were discovered by Cambridge scientists Martin Evans and Matt Kaufman in the late 1970s, when they identified pluripotent cells (i.e. cells with the capacity to give rise to all other cell types) in mice blastocysts – a small bundle of cells that forms about four to five days after fertilization which then goes on to become the embryo. In 1986, Evans was able to introduce new genes into cultured stem cells and inject them into the embryo, thereby allowing transmission of the artificially induced mutation into future generations of mice. But a more significant advance took place in 1998 when the American James Thompson was able to extract stem cells from human embryonic tissue, which opened up the possibility of their use in human medical research.

This breakthrough was largely made redundant, however, when it became clear that stem cells could be produced from mature cells – that is, by taking formed adult cells from the skin, muscle and other body parts, and by using the right chemical signals, transform them back into stem cells resembling those found in the embryo (Takahashi et al., 2007). These are called induced pluripotent stem cells and they have greatly opened up the possibilities of stem cell research, enabling the development of an unlimited source of almost all the types of human cell needed for therapeutic purposes. Not surprisingly, this has generated great excitement, especially in regard to the use of stem cells for the treatment of myriad different diseases and degenerative conditions. These include Parkinson's and Alzheimer's disease, spinal cord injury, stroke, cerebral palsy, amyotrophic lateral sclerosis, along with the restoration of vision and other neurological disabilities (Takagi, 2016; Ul Hassan et al., 2009).

KEY TERMS: *pluripotent cells, blastocysts, induced pluripotent stem cells*

STEM CELLS AND PARKINSON'S DISEASE

One illness that is an attractive candidate for stem cell-based therapy is Parkinson's disease. As we saw in the previous chapter, its core pathology involves the loss of highly specialized dopamine neurons in a relatively small area of the brain (the substantia nigra pars compacta) which causes degeneration of the nigrostriatal pathway. The result is a marked loss of dopamine in the caudate nucleus and putamen. Although this disease can be treated in its early stages with dopaminergic drugs, this does not halt or delay the degenerative process which continues unabated to produce progressive motor impairment. One potential approach to treating Parkinson's, therefore, would be to take embryonic stem cells from mouse or human tissue, and then transform them into dopamine-containing neurons, which could be transplanted into the brain to replenish the lost material.

One of the first attempts to use stem cells in an experimental model of Parkinson's disease was undertaken by Anders Björklund in Sweden, who induced neural stem cells grown in culture to differentiate into primitive dopaminergic neurons, which were then implanted into the striatum of adult rats that had received lesions of the substantia nigra (Bjorklund et al., 2002). Although most of the animals over the course of 90 days showed some new growth of dopamine neurons along with behavioural improvement, the results were largely disappointing because a high percentage of the cells died or transformed into other types. Even more worrying was the discovery that about a quarter of these rats also developed brain tumours.

The first studies using primates were performed at the University of Kyoto in Japan. This involved transplanting embryonic stem cells into the putamen of a small group of cynomolgus monkeys with substantia nigra lesions (Takagi et al., 2005). The results were very encouraging since a clear behavioural improvement in the stem cell-transplanted monkeys compared to controls was observed after 10 weeks of recovery. The effectiveness of the transplant was further confirmed when, at 14 weeks, positron emission tomography was used to show an increase in ^{18}F-fluorodopa uptake (which measures the uptake of dopamine into the axon's endings) in the putamen of the treated animals. But once again there were some drawbacks which limited the success of the study. Most notable was the poor survival of the cells. Although the researchers transplanted 300,000–600,000 cells into each side of the brain in each monkey – the survival rate for the grafted cells was only 1.3–2.7%.

A number of research groups around the world have now begun to undertake stem cell work, with improved techniques and more promising results (Barker et al., 2017). One centre where this has taken place is Harvard University which has implanted nigral-lesioned monkeys with dopamine neurons derived from primate skin cells. In 2015, the researchers reported positive results with their procedure. Not only was there a gradual increase of functional motor improvement in the animals over a two-year period without the need for immunosuppression, but also post-mortem analyses showed a robust survival of the transplanted dopaminergic neurons and extensive outgrowth into the putamen (Hallet et al., 2015).

A further study was undertaken in Kyoto, which this time importantly used stem cells taken from human tissue (fibroblast skin cells) and were transformed into dopamine progenitor cells. When these cells were transplanted into the striatum of macaque monkeys with substantia nigra lesions, they produced dopamine resulting in significant behavioural improvement. These implanted cells survived for two years, during which time they continued to improve the motor deficits, and did not cause any side effects. Histological examination showed that these dopaminergic neurons had formed dense neurites (small projections from the cell body likely to form into dendrites and axons) that were growing into the host striatum (Kikuchi et al., 2017).

In July 2018, the Kyoto researchers announced plans to begin human clinical trials for the treatment of Parkinson's disease. The idea was for each patient to receive 4.8 million human-derived dopaminergic progenitor cells, which were to be implanted into the putamen via stereotaxic surgery. Patients would then be observed for two years with motor, cognitive and psychiatric assessments, along with brain-scanning procedures to monitor the graft. The researchers also announced that seven mid-stage Parkinson patients had been recruited to the study – and the first operation would be performed in October 2018, with the remaining operations planned to take place by 2022 (Fan et al., 2020). However, this is only the beginning, for this Japanese trial is likely to be soon repeated in a number of other centres including those in Europe and the US (Barker et al., 2017). These are exciting times for brain research, and perhaps in the next edition of this book, the results from these studies will be reported.

THE EXCITING NEW WORLD OF EPIGENETICS

It may come as a surprise to learn that genes are not static or unchanging units of inheritance, but capable of altering their expression, or biologic effects, without change occurring to their underlying DNA sequence. This phenomenon is known as epigenetics (the Greek prefix epi means *over* and *above*) and it literally refers to a branch of genetics which is 'above' or 'beyond' what might be regarded as traditional genetics. The term 'epigenetics' was coined by the British developmental biologist Conrad H. Waddington in 1956, who showed that embryonic fruit flies could exhibit different thorax and wing structures as adults, simply by changing the temperature in which they grew, or exposing them to certain chemicals (Noble, 2015). In effect, their genetic inheritance remained unchanged, but the expression of the fruit flies' DNA was modified during development. Another way of putting this is to say that whilst traditional genetics explain the way the DNA sequences in our genes are passed from one generation to the next, epigenetics describe the way the genes are read and used. Although there have been concerted efforts to unravel the epigenetic mechanisms of fruit flies and other simple creatures, there has also been a growing realization that human genes can also be modified as a result of similar developmental influences. In short, the behavioural effects of our genetic inheritance are more than just the sum of our genes (see Carey, 2012).

One of the most influential studies to demonstrate this was reported by Lumey et al. (2007) who examined the descendants of those who had survived the six-month Dutch Hunger Winter of 1944 and 1945. This situation was brought about when the Nazis, intent on punishing the people of the Netherlands for helping the Allies, blocked the import of food supplies which plunged much of the country into famine. In fact, by the time the Netherlands was liberated in May 1945, more than 20,000 people had died of starvation. However, the famine did not just affect those who managed to survive the ordeal – it also affected the offspring of women who were pregnant during this period. As adults, the offspring not only had higher levels of fatty acids and low-density cholesterol, but also suffered from a higher incidence of obesity, diabetes and schizophrenia. Moreover, by the time they reached 68 years old, there was a 10% greater chance of mortality. Although these individuals had led nutrient-rich lives, their prenatal exposure in the womb to the famine had seemingly affected their DNA in some way.

The mechanism by which epigenetic modifications take place is a matter of some debate, but increasing evidence, at least in the Dutch Hunger Winter cohort, points to the likelihood of DNA methylation whereby methyl groups (essentially carbon bonded to three hydrogen atoms) become attached to the DNA – which, in turn, alters or silences the affected gene. In an attempt to identify the genes that have been affected in this way, a Dutch research team led by Bastiaan Heijmans was able to examine blood samples taken from individuals who had been prenatally exposed to the famine (Tobi et al., 2018). By taking advantage of powerful genome-wide mapping technology, the researchers were able to show that a number of genes had increased numbers of methyl groups. These importantly included the PIM3 gene linked to body mass index, the PFKFB3 gene linked to glycolysis, and the METTL8 gene linked to adipogenesis. All of these alterations would have had a silencing effect on the gene and a marked effect on lowering the body's metabolism, predisposing the person to weight gain.

Another area of research has shown that the effects of stress can likewise be passed into future generations. For example, Yehuda et al. (2000, 2005) performed a longitudinal study involving 38 pregnant women who were close to the World Trade Centre on 9/11. Not only did some of this cohort go on to develop posttraumatic stress disorder, but the researchers also found that these women had significantly lower cortisol levels in their saliva. About a year later, the researchers measured cortisol levels in the children, and found that those with the traumatized mothers also had lower levels of cortisol. Following up these findings, Yehuda and her colleagues were also able to show that these children subsequently exhibited an increased startle response when shown frightening stimuli. This was also related to the stage of pregnancy – for the greatest startle responses were obtained from children who were in their second or third trimester during the World Trade Centre attacks.

In addition to DNA methylation, there are also other possible modifications that can alter or silence gene function – one of which is histone modification. Histones are 'ball-like' alkaline proteins that are found on the surface of DNA (they help to fit the DNA inside the nucleus), and it appears that if they squeeze DNA tightly enough, then it cannot be 'read' by the messenger RNA. In addition, histones are believed to be inherited along with the DNA.

Epigenetics is one of the fastest-moving fields in biology today and it promises greater insight into a wide range of illnesses, disorders and behaviours. These include, for example, various illnesses such as heart disease, cancer and immune dysfunction, along with psychiatric illness, intelllectual disability, and neurobehavioural illnesses such as autism and attention deficit hyperactivity disorder. The number of agents that are suspected or known to give rise to epigenetic effects are also diverse. These include heavy metals, pesticides, diesel exhaust, tobacco smoke, hormones, radioactivity, viruses, bacteria and basic nutrients (Weinhold, 2006). All in all, the emergence of epigenetics is enabling us to think of DNA, inheritance and development in a radically different way.

KEY TERMS: *epigenetics, DNA methylation, histone modification*

SUMMARY

Life on Earth has existed for around 3.5 billion years, and during this time the laws of evolution (first described by Darwin) have resulted in many life forms, including *Homo sapiens* who made their first appearance in Africa about 200,000 years ago. Human beings have a genome of 23 paired chromosomes which contain around 25,000 genes. Every person has two copies of each gene, one inherited from each parent, which are essentially coded instructions that control the production of proteins within a cell.

The laws of genetic inheritance were first established by Gregor Mendel in 1865 working with pea plants, who also recognized that genes (which he called 'factors') came in different forms (alleles) which were either dominant or recessive. Genes are passed into offspring by gamete cells (in humans these are the sperm and egg) which contain unpaired chromosomes, and then become paired during fertilization.

A significant scientific advance took place in 1954 when James Watson and Francis Crick described the molecular structure of deoxyribonucleic acid (**DNA**) which is tightly coiled up inside our chromosomes. DNA is made up of two chains of deoxyribose that swivel around each other in a shape of a double helix. Between the two chains are pairs of bases (adenine, guanine, cytosine, and thymine) like the rungs of a ladder. Genes are essentially long sequences of bases (the largest human gene contains over 2 million bases) that contain codons (specific triple bases) that can code for individual amino acids. These are also the 'building blocks' of proteins – large complex molecules that play many critical roles in the body. The synthesis of proteins takes place when messenger ribonucleic acid (**mRNA**) carries a transcript from the DNA (in the nucleus) to a ribosome located in the cytoplasm. Here, amino acids are brought to the transcript by transfer ribonucleic acid (**tRNA**), forming a chained molecule joined by peptide bonds and a protein constructed.

Some genetic conditions are caused by a single dominant mutation whereby if someone inherits the gene they will inevitably develop the illness. One such condition is Huntington's disease caused by a mutation occurring on chromosome 4 which makes the protein **huntingtin**. Other conditions such as phenylketonuria are caused by recessive alleles which means two copies of the gene have to be inherited to develop the illness. A third type of single gene disorder is X-linked inheritance where the mutation is carried on the X chromosome. These conditions, which are more common in males, include haemophilia and colour blindness. However most behaviours of interest to the psychologist are caused by multiple genes, whose expression can be modified by environmental influences. The sum of all genetic information that a person inherits is called the genotype, but the totality of gene and environmental influences that becomes expressed is called the phenotype. One way of measuring the relative influence of gene and environmental influences on human behaviour is by measuring the rate of concordance in identical (monozygotic) and non-identical (dizygotic) twins. It is generally accepted that the higher the concordance in identical twins, the more likely the condition is determined by genetic factors.

Experimental strategies can also be used to measure the impact of genetic influences on behaviour, including selective breeding to produce a certain trait (e.g. for alcohol preference) or by the creation of genetically engineered **transgenic animals** in which the genome has been modified in some way (e.g. a certain gene may be 'knocked out' or another added). The latter technique also has therapeutic promise in the form of gene therapy which may one day be able to treat a range of different diseases. Another technique with great promise is the production of **stem cells** which have the potential to become any type of cell in the body. These are already being used experimentally and beginning to be utilized in the treatment of degenerative diseases such as Parkinson's disease. Another exciting development in genetic research, with potential for a greater understanding of behaviour, is the field of epigenetics, which shows that gene expression can be influenced by prenatal events that do not involve changes in the underlying DNA sequence.

GO ONLINE

TEST YOUR UNDERSTANDING OF THIS CHAPTER AND VISIT HTTPS://STUDY.SAGEPUB.COM/WICKENS TO ACCESS INTERACTIVE 'DRAG AND DROP' LABELLING ACTIVITIES AND A FLASHCARD GLOSSARY.

MULTIPLE CHOICE QUESTIONS

Answer the questions below to test your understanding of this chapter's Learning Objectives. You'll find the answers at the end of the chapter.

1. A codon (specific 3 base sequence of DNA) is a code for making which of the following?

    a. individual amino acids
    b. proteins
    c. ribosomes
    d. peptide bonds

2. Which of the following is known to be an X-linked inherited condition?

    a. Huntington's disease
    b. phenylketonuria
    c. haemophilia
    d. cystic fibrosis

3. Who set up the Minnesota Study of Twins Reared Apart programme in 1979?

    a. James Gusella
    b. Thomas Bouchard
    c. Martin Evans
    d. James Thompson

4. Rats that have been selectively bred to prefer alcohol have lower levels of which brain neurotransmitter?

    a. acetylcholine
    b. GABA
    c. glycine
    d. serotonin

5. Restriction enzymes are used to do which of the following?

    a. stop the transcription of DNA into RNA
    b. cut DNA at certain known points in its base sequences
    c. 'unstick' bits of recombinant DNA
    d. inhibit the function of ribosomes

6. Where were stem cells originally found?

    a. in blastocysts
    b. in bone marrow
    c. in the lining of the nose
    d. in skin

FURTHER READING

Flint, J., Greenspan, R. J., & Kendler, K. S. (2020). *How genes influence behavior*. Oxford University Press.
A well-written textbook which provides an accessible introduction to a variety of genetic approaches to understanding a wide range of disorders including alcoholism and intelligence.

Goodsell, D. S. (1996). *Our molecular nature: The body's motors, machines and messages.* Copernicus.
A nicely illustrated book that will help any student learn more and visualize the molecular nature of their body.

Hahn, P. D. (2019). *Madness and genetic determinism: Is mental illness in our genes?* Palgrave Macmillan.
A thought-provoking book on psychiatric genetics with some interesting chapters on twin studies.

Hosken, D. J., Hunt, J., & Wedell, N. (Eds.). (2019). *Genes and behaviour: Beyond nature–nurture.* John Wiley.
An excellent introduction to the nature–nurture debate written by a group of leading researchers providing an up-to-date synopsis of how far we've come and where we are headed.

Joseph, J. (2003). *The gene illusion.* PCCS Books.
A book that provides a strong rebuttal to the idea that genetic factors play an important role in psychiatric disorders, personality, intelligence and socially acceptable behaviour. Also provides a good critique of twin studies in psychological research.

Kim, Y.-K (Ed.). (2009). *Handbook of behavioral genetics.* Springer.
A comprehensive and detailed overview of behavioural genetics written by leading experts in the field with a good historical focus of the field.

Mukherjee, M. (2017). *The Gene: An intimate history.* Scribner.
An easy to read and amusing history of genetic research which also paints a fascinating vision of humanity's past and its possible future.

Plomin, R. (2019). *Blueprint: How DNA makes us who we are.* Allen Lane.
Written by a leading behavioural geneticist, this book makes a strong although personal case for the importance of genes in behaviour.

Plomin, R., Defries, J. C., Knopik, V. S., & Neiderhiser, J. M. (2013). *Behavioral genetics.*.Worth Publishers.
A leading textbook, now in its sixth edition which provides a clear overview of how genetics and the environment affect animals and human behaviour.

Watson, J. (2017). *DNA: The story of the genetic revolution.* Arrow Books.
The remarkable story of DNA from its discovery over 50 years ago to the present day.

GLOSSARY

Absorptive phase. The phase of metabolism that occurs during and immediately after a meal in which insulin is released by the pancreas gland. It contrasts with the post-absorptive phase where glucagon is secreted by the pancreas gland.

Acetylcholine (Ach). An excitatory neurotransmitter that is used at the neuromuscular junction, in ganglia of the autonomic nervous system, and throughout the brain.

Acetylcholinesterase (AchE). An enzyme found in the synapse that inactivates acetylcholine.

Action potential. Otherwise known as the nerve impulse. It is produced by a brief change in the voltage across the axon membrane due to the flow of certain ions into and out of the neuron.

Adenosine. A chemical which has a variety of roles in the nervous system including that of an inhibitory neurotransmitter at some sites.

Adenosine triphosphate (ATP). A molecule which is the main source of energy in the cells of all living organisms.

Adenylyl cyclase. Membrane-bound enzyme that in some neurons is activated by G proteins to catalyze the synthesis of cAMP (a second messenger) from ATP.

Adrenaline. Also known as epinephrine. A substance that acts as both a hormone (released from the adrenal glands) and a neurotransmitter in certain regions of the brain.

Agnosia. A partial or complete inability to perceive sensory information which is not explainable by deficits in basic sensory processing such as blindness.

Agonist. A drug which mimics or facilities the action of a given neurotransmitter – normally by acting on its receptor.

Agraphia. A difficulty or inability to write, although reading (alexia) is often unimpaired.

Akinesia. Absence or poverty of movement.

Alcohol dehydrogenase. An enzyme found in the liver (and lesser extent the stomach) that metabolizes alcohol.

Alexia. An inability to read although the person has no visual deficits.

Allele. A variant form of a gene.

Alpha motor neuron. A neuron which arises from the ventral horn of the spinal cord and whose activation contributes to muscle contraction.

Alzheimer's disease. A degenerative disease of the brain, especially the cerebral cortex and hippocampus, characterized by amyloid plaques and neurofibrillary tangles.

Amino Acids. A group of simple carbon-based compounds that can be linked together by peptide bonds to make larger and more complex molecules called proteins.

Amnesia. A partial or total loss of memory.

Amphetamine. A stimulant which facilitates the release of catecholamines such as noradrenaline and dopamine from nerve endings.

Amygdala. A group of nuclei located in the anterior part of the medial temporal lobe which forms an important part of the limbic system.

Amyloid. A protein that forms the main constituent of neuritic plaques which are found in high amounts in Alzheimer's disease, which is derived from the much larger beta amyloid precursor protein.

Amyloid cascade theory. The theory that the deposition of amyloid is the critical factor in the development of neural degeneration associated with Alzheimer's disease.

Amyloid precursor protein. A 695 amino acid protein that is found in the cells of the brain and certain tissues of the body.

Androgen. A steroid male sex hormone which includes testosterone.

Angular gyrus. A region of the posterior parietal lobe, bordering the primary visual cortex, where damage can lead to reading problems and word blindness.

Anomia. A difficulty in finding the 'right' word, especially when naming objects, which is associated with Broca's aphasia.

Anosmia. An inability to detect certain smells.

Antagonist. A drug which opposes or inhibits the effects of a particular neurotransmitter – normally by competing at a receptor site.

Anterior thalamus. A group of thalamic nuclei which forms an important link in the circuitry of the limbic system. It receives input from the hippocampus and sends output to the cingulate gyrus.

Anterograde amnesia. An inability to create new memories following an insult or injury to the brain.

Anterolateral pathway. A sensory pathway conveying somatosensory information to the brain mainly concerned with relaying pain and temperature information. It also forms an ascending white tract of fibres in the spinal cord known as the anterolateral system.

Aphagia. Cessation of eating. Most notably known to be one consequence of damage to the lateral hypothalamus.

Aphasia. An inability to produce or comprehend language.

Aplysia. A large marine snail that has provided a simple animal model by which to examine the synaptic basis of learning and memory.

Apolipoprotein E gene. A gene which comes in three different forms (alleles) one of which have been linked with late-onset Alzheimer's disease.

Apoptosis. The process of programmed cell death that occurs when cells are no longer needed or have started to function abnormally.

Apraxia. An inability to make voluntary movement in the absence of paralysis or other peripheral motor impairment.

Arcuate fasciculus. A neural pathway that connects Wernicke's area with Broca's area, with damage to this structure causing conduction aphasia.

Artificial Intelligence. The use of computer systems to simulate and model human intelligence.

Asomatognosia. An inability to detect tactile information from one's own body.

Astereognosis. An inability to recognize objects by touch.

Ataxia. An impairment of muscle co-rdination which is often associated with damage to the cerebellum and basal ganglia.

Auditory cortex. Located in the temporal cortex adjacent to the planum temporale which receives sound input from the medial geniculate body of the thalamus.

Autonomic nervous system. The part of the peripheral nervous system controlling the autonomic functions of the body, primarily through its action on glands and the smooth muscles of internal organs. It has two divisions – the sympathetic and parasympathetic systems.

Autoreceptors. Receptors located on the presynaptic neuron whose main function is to regulate the amount of neurotransmitter release.

Autosomal dominant inheritance. Essentially means if one inherits the gene, then one will inherit the characteristic. A prime example of this type of inheritance is Huntington's disease.

Axon. A long thin extension that arises from the nerve cell body and carries the nerve impulse to the axon terminal where neurochemicals are released.

Axon hillock. A cone-shaped area where the axon joins the cell body, and the critical site where depolarization needs to take place for the action potential to be formed.

Balint's syndrome. A disorder associated with bilateral damage of the parietal lobes which produces optic ataxia, paralysis of eye fixation, and simultanagnosia.

Basal forebrain. A region of the brain that lies anterior and below the striatum which forms part of the limbic system.

Basal ganglia. A group of subcortical nuclei and interconnected pathways which are important for movement and contain the caudate nucleus, putamen and globus pallidus.

Basal nucleus of Meynert. A nucleus located in the basal forebrain which innervates the cerebral cortex with cholinergic fibres.

Basilar membrane. A stiff elongated structure found in the cochlea of the inner ear which holds the organ of Conti.

Benzodiazepines. A class of drugs which are used for their anxiolytic and sleep-inducing properties including Valium and Librium.

Beta-adrenergic receptor. A class of noradrenergic (NA) receptor that is linked to the cAMP second messenger system.

Biochemistry. The branch of science that investigates the chemical processes within cells and living organisms.

Bipolar cells. Interneurons found in the retina and other sensory systems that have axon-like processes at both ends of their cell body.

Bipolar depression. A psychiatric disorder characterized by periods of depression and euphoria – sometimes known as manic depression.

Blindsight. The ability of 'blind' subjects with visual cortex damage to accurately point towards or track objects in their environment.

Blood–brain barrier. A barrier formed by tightly packed cells in the capillaries, and their covering by astrocytes (glia cells), which prevents the passage of many harmful substances into the brain.

Bradykinesia. Slowness and poverty of movement and speech.

Brainstem. The old part of the brain that arises from the spinal cord which includes the medulla oblongata, pons and midbrain. It is also contains the reticular formation.

Broca's aphasia. A form of aphasia characterized by slow and poor speech articulation which also lacks the intonation and inflection of normal language.

Broca's area. A region of the posterior frontal cortex, located close to the face area of the primary motor cortex, involved in the production of speech. It is normally dominant (bigger) in the left hemisphere.

Cannon–Bard theory. A theory proposed by Walter Cannon and Philip Bard that views emotional stimuli as events which trigger feelings and physical reactions at the same time.

Capsaicin. An active ingredient found in chilli peppers which has also been used to understand the receptor basis of pain.

Catastrophic-dysphoric reaction. Feelings of despair, hopelessness and anger that are sometimes observed in people with damage to the left hemisphere.

Catecholamines. A class of monoamines that contain a catechol nucleus which includes noradrenaline and dopamine.

Caudate nucleus. A large bilateral C-shaped grey mass sitting below the cerebral cortex which forms the striatum along with the putamen.

Central nervous system. The brain and spinal cord.

Central nucleus of the amygdala. The main output post of the amygdala with projections to the brainstem and hypothalamus.

Cerebellum. A large brain structure meaning 'little brain' located at the back of the brainstem (near the pons) and predominantly involved in motor co-ordination.

Cerebral cortex. The six-layer covering of the cerebral hemispheres, with an outer appearance of various distinct gyri and fissures, which is responsible for our higher cognitive functions, consciousness and self-volition.

Cerebrospinal fluid (CSF). The fluid that fills the ventricles of the brain and the subarachnoid space surrounding the brain and spinal cord.

Cholecystokinin (CCK). A hormone secreted by the duodenum that regulates gastric mobility and is involved in the satiation of hunger. It is also found in the brain where it may have a neurotransmitter function.

Cholinesterase inhibitor. A drug that inhibits the enzyme acetylcholinesterase which breaks down acetylcholine. These drugs are commonly used to treat the early stages of Alzheimer's disease.

Chromosome. A long strand of DNA, coupled with protein, that acts as a carrier for genetic information. Human beings have 23 pairs of chromosomes which are found in the nucleus of nearly every cell in the body.

Cingulate cortex. A large arc of 'old' limbic cortex that lies above and spans the corpus callosum which receives input from the cerebral cortex and thalamus.

Clinical neuropsychology. A branch of psychology that examines the behaviour of brain damaged individuals. A clinical neuropsychologist is also concerned with the diagnosis and treatment of those with brain disorders and injury.

Cochlea. A small bony chamber of the inner ear which houses the basilar membrane that is crucial for hearing.

Cochlea nerve. Cranial nerve eight (CN VIII) projecting from the ear to the brain.

Cochlea nuclei. A small nucleus found in the medulla which receives input from the cochlea nerve.

Codon. A sequence of three bases in DNA which provides a code for making an amino acid.

Cognitive-arousal theory. A theory proposed by Stanley Schachter and Jerome Singer which maintains that in order to experience an emotion an individual has to experience physiological arousal and be able to attribute that arousal to an appropriate stimulus.

Cognitive neuroscience. A discipline which rose to prominence in the 1980s, which predominantly uses brain scanning techniques such as fMRI to examines cognitive and mental processes.

Cognitive reserve. The idea that increased mental activity early in life may increase the brain's resilience to later neural degeneration and dementia.

Commissurotomy. Another name for the surgical operation in which the corpus callosum is severed thereby disconnecting the two cerebral hemispheres.

Computerized axial tomography (CAT). A non-invasive scanning technique that takes detailed three-dimensional pictures of brain structure by computer analysis of X-rays taken at different points and planes around the head.

Conduction aphasia. A language disturbance caused by damage to the arcuate fasciculus which connects Wernicke's and Broca's areas, characterized by an inability to fluently repeat words and sentences.

Cones. A photoreceptor found in the retina which is responsible for fine detailed vision and colour. There are three types of cone with sensitivities to wavelengths of light roughly corresponding to blue, green and red.

Corpus callosum. A broad thick band of around 20 million axon fibres which provides a channel for communication between the two cerebral hemispheres.

Cortical module. In the primary visual cortex a module is a cube-like unit which consists of two ocular dominance columns, a range of orientation detectors, and two cylindrical colour processing blobs. Other types of module probably exist throughout the cerebral cortex.

Corticospinal pathway. The motor pathway originating in the motor cortex (and surrounding areas) of the cerebral cortex, and terminating in the grey matter of the spinal cord. The majority of its axons cross in the medulla to influence the opposite (contralateral) side of the body.

Cortisol. A glucocorticoid hormone released by the adrenal glands, vital for life, and secreted in higher amounts during times of prolonged stress.

Creutzfeldt-Jacob disease. A form of dementia caused by an infectious agent that has some similarities with bovine spongiform encephalopathy.

Cutaneous senses. Sense information from the skin.

Cyclic AMP. A chemical involved in many biochemical reactions of the cell including a role as a second messenger – one function of which is to cause the opening of ion channels following certain types of receptor activation.

Cytochrome blobs.   Peg-like structures found in the primary visual cortex, which are stained by the enzyme cytochrome oxidase and have an important role in colour processing.

Declarative memory.   A type of memory that can be voluntarily 'declared' to consciousness and verbally expressed. In effect, it refers to an ability to recount what one knows.

Deep cerebellar nuclei.   A group of three nuclei (fastigal, interposed and dentate) within the cerebellum which receive input from the Purkinje neurons of the cerebellar cortex, and together provide the sole output of the cerebellum.

Delta-9-tetrahydrocannabinol (THC).   The main psychoactive ingredient in marijuana.

Dendrite.   Tree-like branched extensions of the neuron's body that typically contains large numbers of neurotransmitter receptors.

Deoxyribonucleic acid (DNA).   A long nucleic acid composed of two helical strands (made from the sugar deoxyribose and phosphate) and four bases (adenine, thymine, cytosine, and guanine) which houses the genes necessary for genetic inheritance.

Dermatome.   An area of skin whose sensory fibres all innervate the same dorsal root.

Diabetes mellitus.   A disease caused by the pancreas gland secreting insufficient amounts of insulin which is a hormone enabling the uptake of glucose into cells. Consequently, untreated diabetics have high levels of blood sugar.

Diencephalon.   The part of the forebrain that contains the thalamus and hypothalamus.

Dizygotic twins.   Twins that develop from two different eggs, and thus two different sperms, which makes them genetically different. Sometimes called fraternal twins.

Dopamine.   A neurotransmitter that makes up about 80% of the catecholamine content of the brain which is predominantly found in the striatum, nucleus accumbens, amygdala and frontal cortex.

Dopamine theory of schizophrenia.   The idea that schizophrenia is due to increased dopaminergic activity in the brain.

Dorsal.   An anatomical term that refers to structures towards the back of the body, or the top of the brain (e.g. the dorsal fin of a fish is located on its back or upper surface).

Dorsal-column medial-lemniscus pathway. A pathway carrying cutaneous (touch) information from the spinal cord to the ventral posterior nucleus of the thalamus via the medial lemniscus.

Dorsal columns.   White matter of the dorsal spinal cord containing ascending axons to the brain.

Dorsal raphe.   A nucleus found in the upper brainstem, which along with the medial raphe, provides the forebrain with its serotonergic innervation.

Dorsal roots.   Bundles of peripheral nerves providing sensory information that enter the dorsal (towards the back) part of the spinal cord.

Dorsolateral frontal cortex.   A region of the frontal lobes lying above the orbital frontal region which receives input from dorsomedial thalamus. It is associated with executive functions including working memory.

Dorsomedial thalamus.   A large nucleus of the thalamus which relays information from the limbic system, particularly the amygdala and entorhinal cortex, to the frontal lobe.

Dual-centre set-point theory of hunger.   A theory developed in the 1950s that viewed the lateral hypothalamus as being the initiator of hunger and feeding, and the ventromedial hypothalamus as the satiety centre.

Duodenum.   The first part of the small intestine which also includes the pancreatic duct.

Dyskinesia.   A category of movement disorders characterized by involuntary muscle movements.

Dyslexia.   A term that refers to a group of reading disorders of varying severity.

Dystonia. Lack of muscle tone.

Edinger-Westphal nucleus. A small nucleus in the midbrain that sends fibres into the parasympathetic nervous system which controls contraction of the pupil.

Electroencephalogram (EEG). An apparatus that enables the gross electrical activity of the brain to be recorded from electrodes placed on the scalp.

Endorphin. A natural opiate neuropeptide used as a chemical messenger often released in response to pain or stress.

Engram. Another term for the anatomical, biochemical and/or physiological site of memory.

Entorhinal cortex. A form of transitional cortex found on the medial surface of the temporal lobes that provides the main neural gateway to the hippocampus.

Epinephrine. An American term for adrenaline.

Equipotentiality. The idea that all parts of the association cerebral cortex play an equal role in the storage of memories. This view contrasts with the theory that different parts of the cerebral association cortex have highly specialized functions.

Excitatory postsynaptic potential. A small change in the electrical potential of a neuron towards a positive direction, produced by excitatory neurotransmitters, that increases the likelihood of an action potential.

Exocytosis. A form of active transport that involves the fusion of the vesicles with the cellular membrane in the axon terminals leading to neurotransmitter release.

Extrapyramidal system. The motor system of the brain whose output fibres to the spinal cord do not cross in the pyramidal region of the medulla. The term is commonly used to refer to the cerebellum, basal ganglia and an array of brainstem nuclei.

Fight-or-flight response. A pattern of physiological responses (e.g. increased heart rate, faster respiration, pupil dilation etc.) produced by the sympathetic nervous system that helps mobilize the body's resources to threat.

Follicle stimulating hormone. A hormone released by the anterior pituitary gland that causes maturation of the ovarian follicle and the secretion of oestrogen and progesterone.

Forebrain. A term that refers to all of the brain tissue lying above the midbrain, including the hypothalamus, thalamus, basal ganglia, limbic system and neocortex.

Fornix. A long arching fibre tract that extends from the hippocampus to the mammillary bodies, anterior thalamus and hypothalamus.

Fovea. A pit in the centre of the retina containing colour-sensitive cones where visual acuity is at its greatest.

Free nerve ending. Small diameter nerve endings (also known as naked endings) which act as pain receptors in the skin.

Free radicals Highly reactive and short-lasting breakdown products of oxygen which contain an unpaired outer electron, believed to be involved in ageing and certain types of degenerative disease.

Frontal lobe. The front portion of the cerebral cortex which contains several important anatomical areas including the orbitofrontal and dorsolateral regions, Broca's area, and primary motor cortex.

GABA. The abbreviation for gamma-Aminobutyric acid – an amino acid neurotransmitter that is the most common inhibitory substance in the CNS.

Gamma motor neuron. A nerve cell located in the ventral horn of the spinal cord that innervates muscle spindles.

Ganglion cells. Neurons whose cell bodies form the final output of the retina and whose axons give rise to the optic nerve.

Gate control theory of pain. A theory proposed by Melzack and Wall which views pain as being modified by a gate mechanism located in the spinal cord, whose functioning can also be modified by brain activity.

Genes. A long sequence of paired bases found in DNA that contain various codons, and which acts as a functional unit to make one or more proteins.

Genetic engineering. A group of techniques, including the formation of transgenic animals, that involve altering the natural state of an organism's genome.

Genetics. The scientific study of genes and inheritance.

Gigantocellular tegmental field. An area of the medullary reticular formation involved in sleep, which contains large neurons and whose axons innervate the thalamus and cerebral cortex.

Glial cells. The supporting cells of the CNS that also help maintain the functioning of neurons. In the brain these consist of astrocytes, oligodendrocytes and microglial cells.

Globus pallidus. Part of the basal ganglia involved in movement which receives input from the striatum and whose main output goes to the ventral lateral nucleus of the thalamus and motor cortex.

Glucagon. A hormone released by the pancreas gland which acts on the liver to convert glycogen into glucose

Glutamate. An amino acid which is the major excitatory neurotransmitter in the CNS.

Glycogen. A stored form of sugar, found mainly in the liver, which can be converted into glucose by the pancreatic hormone glucagon.

Gonadotropin releasing hormone. A releasing factor secreted by the hypothalamus which acts on the anterior pituitary gland to help secrete luteinizing hormone, and follicle stimulating hormone.

G-protein. A type of protein which is often likened to a switch. Some G proteins are attached to certain types of neurotransmitter receptor, where they activate a cascade of chemical events inside the cell, including the formation of cAMP (a second messenger).

Growth hormone. A hormone produced by the anterior pituitary which stimulates growth during development. It is also secreted in adults, reaching its peak levels about an hour after falling asleep.

Gyri. The raised ridges of the cerebral cortex (the fissures between the gyri are called sulci) which provide helpful landmarks in the identification of various cortical areas.

Hebbian synapse. A hypothetical synapse that is strengthened every time a presynaptic and postsynaptic neuron fire together, which is believed to be an important mechanism in the neural basis of learning and memory.

Hemiplegia. Paralysis or loss of muscle tone of one half of the body.

Heschl's gyrus. Part of the temporal lobe containing the primary auditory cortex.

Hippocampus. A complex brain structure located in the medial temporal cortex composed of folded primitive three-layered cortical tissue (archicortex). The hippocampal formation consists of the subiculum, the hippocampus proper, and dentate gyrus. Regarded as part of the limbic system, it is most strongly implicated in memory.

Homeostasis. The requirement of the body to maintain a consistent internal environment, despite exposure to various chemical changes and external fluctuations.

Homovanillic acid (HVA). A breakdown product of dopamine that is found in the cerebrospinal fluid.

Hormone. Chemical messengers that are secreted directly into the blood, sometimes from endocrine glands, where they are transported to their target of action.

Huntingtin. The abnormal protein produced by the gene that is responsible for causing Huntington's disease.

Huntington's disease. A genetic disorder, inherited in an autosomal dominant manner, which leads to degeneration of the basal ganglia – normally in middle age. The mutation is caused by an excess number of the triple base CAG repeats in the gene which is located on chromosome 4.

Hyperphagia. Excessive eating and weight gain, as seen, for example, following lesions of the ventromedial hypothalamus

Hypothalamic-pituitary-adrenal axis. This term refers to a complex set of interactions and feedback loops between the hypothalamus, pituitary and adrenal glands. More specifically, it involves the anterior pituitary gland secreting adrenocorticotropic hormone (ACTH) into the blood, which stimulates the adrenal cortex to release glucocorticoids such as cortisol.

Hypothalamus.   A small but hugely important collection of various nuclei lying just below the thalamus, which governs a wide range of homeostatic processes and species typical behaviours. The hypothalamus is also involved in the regulation of the autonomic nervous system, and exerts executive control over the pituitary gland.

Implicit memory.   A type of memory which involves no explicit or conscious intention to learn or memorize.

Inferior colliculi.   Small protrusions found near the upper surface of the midbrain that relay auditory information from the ears to the medial geniculate nucleus.

Inhibitory postsynaptic potential.   A small change in the electrical potential of a neuron towards a negative direction, produced by inhibitory neurotransmitters, that decreases the likelihood of an action potential.

Insulin.   A hormone released by the pancreas gland that enables glucose to enter the cells of the body. It plays an important role in allowing nutrients to be quickly stored after a meal.

Interneuron.   A type of neuron, typically with a short axon, that is located within a given nucleus or structure.

Interstitial nuclei of the anterior hypothalamus.   In humans, these form four small cell groups which are located in the anterior preoptic region of the hypothalamus. Two of these nuclei (INAH 2 and 3) have been shown to be larger in the male.

Inverse agonist.   A drug that produces a neurochemical or behavioural effect opposite to that of a normal agonist.

Ion channel.   A specialized protein complex in the plasma membrane of neurons that allow certain ions, most notably sodium, potassium and calcium, to pass into the cell. Ion channels can be voltage dependent (i.e. they open when the membrane potential reaches a certain level), or neurotransmitter dependent (i.e. they open when the neurotransmitter activates the cell).

Ionotropic receptor.   A receptor complex where the binding site for a neurotransmitter and the ion channel form part of the same unit (e.g. the GABA receptor). Activation of the receptor leads directly to a configurational change in the shape of the channel that allows ions to pass through.

James–Lange theory.   A theory which holds that emotions result initially from physiological reactions involving the autonomic nervous system to events prior to mental interpretation.

Ions.   Atoms (or sometimes molecules) which have lost or gained an electron, which then alters their electrical charge (i.e. they become positively or negatively charged). Ions are particularly important in the formation and transmission of the nerve impulse.

Klinefelter's syndrome.   A genetic condition where males inherit an extra X chromosome (YXX) resulting in increased feminization.

Korsakoff's syndrome.   A syndrome whose main feature is anterograde amnesia, due to thiamine deficiency brought on by chronic alcoholism. Traditionally, it has been associated with damage to the mammillary bodies and dorsomedial thalamus.

Kuru.   A rare form of brain degeneration which is transmitted by ingesting a infectious protein (prion) found in contaminated brain tissue. It is associated with the practice of cannibalism.

Lateral geniculate nucleus.   A region of the thalamus that receives input from the optic nerve and projects to the primary visual cortex.

Lateral hypothalamus.   A region of the hypothalamus that has been implicated in a wide range of fundamental behaviours, including feeding, aggression, sleeping, waking and motivation.

Lateral superior olive.   A nucleus located in the medulla which receives auditory information from both ears and is important in identifying a sound's location.

Leptin.   A hormone manufactured and secreted by adipose cells that communicates to the brain how much fat is being stored. It also appears to be involved in the regulation of food intake.

Leydig cells   The cells in the testes that produce testosterone.

Limbic system. A group of interconnected brain regions that includes an arc of phylogenetically old cortex at the base of the cerebrum, and several other regions, including the hippocampus amygdala, fornix, mammillary bodies, hypothalamus and anterior thalamus.

Locus coeruleus. A dark blue pigmented nucleus in the pons region of the brainstem which is the main origin of noradrenaline containing neurons in the forebrain.

Long term potentiation. A stable and enduring increase in the excitability of a neuron due to its repeated activation by high-frequency stimulation, which is believed to underlie the neural basis of learning and memory.

Luteinizing hormone. A hormone released by the anterior pituitary gland that causes ovulation (the release of the egg from the ovary) and the development of the follicle into a corpus luteum. In males, luteinizing hormone stimulates the Leydig cells to produce testosterone.

Magnetic resonance imaging (MRI). A non-invasive scanning technique that measures the magnetic resonance of hydrogen atoms in the brain, induced by a strong magnetic field and radio waves, to build up a detailed three-dimensional image of brain structure.

Mammillary bodies. Two nuclei located in the posterior region of the hypothalamus which receives a large input from the hippocampus via the fornix.

Materialism. A philosophical position holding that nothing but physical matter exists which also supports the idea that all mental states are the result of material interactions.

Mechanoreceptor. A receptor whose primary function is to detect stretching and pressure movements of the skin.

Medial forebrain bundle. A large bundle of fibres that courses through the lateral regions of the hypothalamus which interconnects regions of the forebrain with midbrain.

Medial geniculate bodies. A region of the thalamus that receives information from the inferior colliculus and sends output to the auditory cortex located in the temporal lobe.

Medial hypothalamus. This part of the hypothalamus contains several important regions, including ventromedial, dorsolateral and arcuate nuclei (the latter being connected with the pituitary gland) and is involved with motivation – especially feeding, emotion and aggression.

Medial prefrontal cortex. The region of the prefrontal cortex that lies adjacent to the cingulate gyrus.

Medial preoptic area. An area of the anterior hypothalamus implicated in sexual behaviour, temperature regulation and sleep.

Medial septum. A nucleus found in the limbic system (close to the hypothalamus) which sends cholinergic fibres into the hippocampus.

Medial temporal lobes. A complex area of the brain which includes the hippocampus, amygdala and surrounding regions of the cortex, including the subiculum, entorhinal cortex and perirhinal cortex.

Medulla oblongata. The part of the brainstem which emerges from the spinal cord. It is the origin of several cranial nerves, and contains centres for vital functions such as respiration, sneezing, vomiting and swallowing.

Melatonin. The hormone released by the pineal gland which plays an important role in the regulation of the body's circadian rhythms.

Mesofrontal dopamine pathway. The dopamine projection arising from the ventral tegmental area that passes to the frontal cortex.

Mesolimbic dopamine pathway. The dopamine projection arising from the ventral tegmental area that passes to parts of the limbic system including the nucleus accumbens.

Messenger RNA. A single stranded nucleic acid that transcribes the genetic message from DNA and transports it into the cytoplasm for protein synthesis.

Metabotropic receptor. A receptor linked to a G-protein, which initiates a number of chemical events inside the neuron, including the activation of second messengers, which leads to the opening of certain ion channels.

Microglia. Glia cells that act as phagocytes (part of the immune system) in the CNS.

Millisecond. One thousandth of a second.

Mitochondria. Organelles in the cytoplasm of the cell responsible for generating adenosine triphosphate (ATP) which is used as energy to drive a wide variety of chemical reactions.

Molecular biology. The branch of science that investigates the structure and interactions of molecules within the cell including enzymes, nucleic acids and proteins.

Monoamine. A class of neurotransmitters that contain an amine in their chemical structure which includes serotonin, dopamine, noradrenaline.

Monoamine oxidase (MAO). An enzyme found in neurons and glial cells that breaks down and inactivates monoamine neurotransmitters.

Monoamine oxidase inhibitors. Chemicals that inhibit the action of monoamine oxidase, thereby increasing the amount of monoamines in the synapse, which have been shown to be effective antidepressants.

Monoamine theory of depression. The hypothesis that depression is due to a synaptic deficiency, or under-activity of one or more monoamines in the brain (especially noradrenaline and/or serotonin).

Monozygotic twins. Genetically identical twins who develop from the same egg.

Motor cortex. The region of the cerebral cortex, located in the precentral gyrus of the posterior frontal cortex, which is topographically organized and sends its fibres into the corticospinal tracts to produces voluntary muscle movement.

Motor end plate. The specialized site on a muscle fibre which receives input from a motor nerve ending.

Muscle spindles. Long thin fibrous capsules that lie embedded between muscle cells, which provide information about stretching to neurons located in the spinal cord.

Myelin. The fatty sheath that covers and insulates the axon produced by the extensions of certain glial cells (oligodendroglia in the CNS, and Schwann cells in the peripheral nervous system).

Myofibrils Small thin fibres within individual muscle cells, made up of short segments called sarcomeres, which contain fine filaments of actin and myosin.

Naloxone. An opiate antagonist.

Narcolepsy. A condition where the person is suddenly overcome by bouts of intense sleepiness which is typically accompanied by a loss of muscle tone (cataplexy).

Negative feedback. An important mechanism in homeostasis and most hormone systems. It refers to the process by which a physiological variable, or hormone, once it reaches a certain level, feeds back to decrease its own activity or production.

Neocortex. The most recently evolved part of the brain consisting of six layers which forms the 'crumpled' outer surface of the cerebral cortex.

Neuritic plaques. Extracellular microscopic discs composed largely of amyloid which are one of the defining pathological features of Alzheimer's disease.

Neurofibrillary tangles. Tangles of fine fibres or neuronal filaments, made from tau protein, which are predominantly found in the cytoplasm of cortical nerve cells and are a distinguishing feature of Alzheimer's disease.

Neuromuscular junction. This is the synapse that exists between the motor neuron and the motor end plate of skeletal muscle which uses acetylcholine as its neurotransmitter.

Neuron. Essentially a specialized cell for generating and conducting electrical information which forms the fundamental unit of the nervous system. Also called a nerve cell.

Neuropeptide Y. A peptide which acts as a neurotransmitter in the hypothalamus and is involved in the regulation of feeding behaviour.

Neuropeptides. Chemical messengers which are composed of amino acids or small proteins. They are typically involved in slow-onset but long-lasting modulation of synaptic transmission.

Neuroscience. A discipline that encompasses a broad range of fields concerned with the structure and functioning of neurons and their systems, including molecular and cell biology, anatomy, biochemistry, physiology and psychology.

Neurotransmitter. A chemical that is released by an axon terminal into a synapse following the arrival of a nerve impulse, and which diffuses in the synapse to bind (attach itself) to receptors of another nerve cell, muscle fibre, or some other structure.

Nigral-striatal pathway. A dopaminergic pathway that extends from the substantia nigra to the striatum which shows marked degeneration in Parkinson's disease.

Nociceptor. Another name for a pain receptor.

Nodes of Ranvier. A small gap in the myelin sheath surrounding the axon, where the action potential is renewed by the process of saltatory conduction.

Noradrenaline. A catecholaminergic neurotransmitter, also known as norepinephrine, found in the brain and the sympathetic division of the autonomic nervous system.

Nucleus accumbens. A major component of the ventral striatum which receives a dopaminergic projection from the ventral tegmentum, involved in signalling reward or possibly stimulating feelings of pleasure.

Nucleus of the solitary tract. A nucleus located in the medulla which receives information from the stomach, duodenum, liver and tongue.

Nucleus raphe magnus. One of the raphe nuclei which has descending projections to the spinal cord and is involved in gate control of pain processing.

Obsessive-compulsive disorder. Classified as an anxiety disorder where the person is afflicted with uncontrollable thoughts (obsessions) and engages in seemingly senseless rituals (compulsions).

Ocular apraxia. An inability to voluntarily shift attention to a new visual stimulus. It is a symptom of Balint's syndrome and associated with damage to occipital-parietal regions of the brain.

Olfactory bulb. The first area of the brain to receive olfactory information from the nose.

Olfactory epithelium. A layer of tissue in the nasal cavity containing olfactory receptors

Olfactory tract. The main pathway arising from the olfactory bulb which forms the lateral and medial olfactory stria.

Oligodendroglia. A type of glia cell with many branches that wraps around axons to form the myelin sheath.

Opiate. A drug with similar properties to opium including morphine and heroin.

Molecular biology. The branch of science that investigates the structure and interactions of molecules within the cell including enzymes, nucleic acids and proteins.

Optic chiasm. The point on the underside of the brain, just anterior to the pituitary gland, where the two optic nerves join, and where the majority of fibres cross to the opposite side of the brain.

Optic radiations. The axon fibres that project from the dorsal lateral geniculate region of the thalamus to the primary visual cortex.

Orbitofrontal region. The part of the prefrontal cortex that lies above the eyes which receives information from the dorsomedial thalamus.

Orexins. Also known as hypocretins, orexins are hypothalamic neuropeptides (produced by the lateral hypothalamus and perifornical region) which have an important role in the regulation of sleep and arousal states.

Organ of Conti. A structure found in the cochlear of the inner ear which houses specialized sensory hairs forming part of the basilar membrane that turns sound into neural impulses.

Otolith organs. The otolith organs are found under the semicircular canals of the inner ear which convey information about head movement to the brain.

Oval window. The part of the cochlea which is hit by the small bone called stapes to transmit sound.

Ovulation. The monthly process in which a mature ovum (egg) is released by the ovaries into the upper fallopian tubes. At this point fertilization can occur if the ovum is impregnated by a sperm cell.

Pancreas gland.   An endocrine gland located in the duodenum which releases insulin and glucagon.

Papez circuit.   A limbic system circuit, first described by James Papez in 1937, which connects the hypothalamus, thalamus, cingulate gyrus and hippocampus. Believed to be important in emotion and certain aspects of memory processing.

Parahippocampal gyrus.   A region of the limbic cortex adjacent to the hippocampus which can be regarded as a continuation of the cingulate gyrus.

Parasympathetic nervous system.   A major branch of the autonomic nervous system (along with the sympathetic nervous system) whose main function is to conserve and restore the body's resources (i.e. reduce arousal).

Parietal lobe.   The part of the cerebral cortex directly behind the central fissure (i.e. the frontal lobe) and above the Sylvian fissure (i.e. temporal lobe).

Parkinson's disease.   A brain disorder caused by degeneration of cells in the substantia nigra leading to poverty of movement, tremor and rigidity.

Periamygdaloid cortex.   Part of 'old' cortex close to the amygdala and a site known to process olfactory information.

Periaqueductal grey area.   The area that surrounds the cerebral aqueduct in the midbrain. It is the major centre through which the hypothalamus enacts behaviours critical to the survival of the self and of the species.

Peripheral nervous system.   All the nerves and neurons beyond the brain and spinal cord including the autonomic nervous system and somatic nervous system.

Perirhinal cortex.   A region of the limbic cortex lying underneath the anterior parts of the hippocampus.

Pharmacology.   The scientific study of drugs and their effects on the body.

Philosophy.   A word that means love of wisdom, philosophy generally tackles subjects that are not amenable to scientific investigation such as the nature of logic, truth, reality and beauty.

Phenylketonuria.   A hereditary disorder that can lead to brain damage caused by a recessive gene which causes the absence of phenylalanine hydroxylase (an enzyme that converts phenylalanine into tyrosine).

Physiological psychology.   A branch of neuroscience that studies the physiological causes of behaviour. Traditionally this subject has been associated with brain lesioning along with electrical recording and stimulation.

Pineal gland.   A small gland which in humans is located behind the third ventricle in an area known as the epithalamus. It secretes the hormone melatonin responsible for the regulation of circadian rhythms.

Pituitary gland.   Sometimes referred to as the master endocrine gland, the pituitary is connected to the hypothalamus and consists of two lobes – the anterior and posterior. The former is connected to the hypothalamus by blood vessels, whilst the latter contains many nerve endings.

Place cells.   Neurons found in the hippocampus that become highly active when the animal is in a particular location. They appear to be important for spatial navigation and forming a cognitive map of the environment.

Planum temporale.   A region of the temporal lobe that is part of Wernicke's area lying adjacent to the primary auditory cortex, which is generally found to be larger on the left side of the brain.

Pons   The region of the brainstem above the medulla and lying below the midbrain. It contains a number of important nuclei including the locus coeruleus and the raphe.

Pontine nucleus.   A large nucleus found in the pons which receives motor input from the cerebral cortex and sends projections to the cerebellum.

Positron emission tomography (PET).   A non-invasive technique for examining brain function in humans that measures the brain's metabolic activity by use of short- lasting radioactive substances (usually 2-deoxyglucose) which emits subatomic particles called positrons.

Prefrontal cortex.   The most anterior region of the frontal lobes consisting of association cortex which receives input from multiple regions of the brain. It contributes to a wide variety of executive functions, including focusing attention and setting goals.

Premotor area. An area of the cerebral cortex located just in front of the primary motor cortex involved in the initiation and selection of movement.

Primary visual cortex. An area in the occipital lobes, in the vicinity of the calcarine fissure, which receives visual information from the lateral geniculate thalamus.

Prion. A protein that is capable of self-replication and acts as an infectious agent responsible for several types of degenerative brain diseases.

Procedural memory. A type of memory that is 'remembered' when an individual performs an action (such as riding a bike). Unlike declarative memory, it is not affected by damage to the hippocampus.

Proprioceptive senses. Sense information from the joints and muscles.

Prosopagnosia. The inability to identify people by sight of their faces, although other features such as their voice can be recognized.

Proteins. A class of large molecules composed of smaller chains of amino acids that have a wide range of functions in the body and are vital for life.

Psychiatry. A branch of medicine concerned with the understanding and treatment of mental illness.

Pulvinar region. A large thalamic nucleus overhanging the superior colliculus and geniculate bodies, believed to be involved in vision and possibly speech.

Putamen. A large round structure that connects with the caudate nucleus to form the striatum.

Pyramidal system. A large system of fibres originating in the motor regions of the cerebral cortex which form the pyramidal tracts that project to the spinal cord. Also known as the corticospinal tract.

Raphe nuclei. A group of nuclei located in the medulla, pons and midbrain. Of particular importance are the dorsal and median raphe which together account for about 80% of the serotonin found in the forebrain.

Receptive field. The receptive field is a portion of sensory space that can elicit neuronal responses when stimulated. In vision, this is the part of the visual world, whereas with touch it may be the mechanical pressure on a receptor or nerve ending.

Receptor. In neuroscience, a receptor is a specialized protein molecule, most often found in the membrane of a neuron, muscle or endocrine organ, which is sensitive to a specific neurochemical, which in turn typically causes some chemical or voltage effect inside the cell.

Recessive gene. A gene that does not express its characteristics unless it is present in a 'double dose'. That is, a copy has to be inherited from both parents.

Recombinant DNA. Genetic material made outside the living cell by splicing two or more pieces of DNA from different sources to create a combination of genes not normally found in nature.

Red nucleus. A large nucleus located in the midbrain tegmentum that receives inputs from the cerebellum and motor areas of the cerebral cortex, and which in turn sends axons to the spinal cord via the rubrospinal tract.

Resting potential. The membrane potential of a neuron when it is at rest, and not being altered by excitatory or inhibitory postsynaptic potentials. The resting potential inside a neuron is generally around –70mV compared to its outside.

Reticular activating system. A network of neurons located in the brain stem that ascend primarily to the thalamus and cortex, and whose activation is responsible for the desynchronized cortical EEG patterns that regulate waking and sleep.

Reticular formation. A complex network of dispersed nuclei and fibre tracts which extend throughout the core of the brainstem to the thalamus. It is involved in a wide range of functions including those that are vital for life.

Retrograde amnesia. An impairment of memory for information that was acquired prior to the onset of amnesia.

Reuptake. The reabsorption of a neurotransmitter into a neuron by a special transporter protein that is normally found in the membrane of presynaptic neurons.

Ribonucleic acid (RNA). A single stranded nucleic acid that contains the sugar ribose. There are three main types of RNA (messenger, transfer and ribosomal), all of which are involved in protein synthesis.

Ribosomes. Spherical structures found in the cytoplasm of the cell, sometimes likened to work benches, where the production of proteins takes place.

Saccadic eye movements. Involuntary, rapid and small movements of the eyes that are used to monitor our visual surroundings.

Saltatory conduction. The means by which the action potential is propagated down the axon from one node of Ranvier to the next.

Schachter–Singer theory. A theory which holds that emotion results from physiological arousal which has to be cognitively interpreted within the context of each situation before the emotional experience occurs.

Schizophrenia. A severe mental illness, classified as a psychosis, which is typically characterized by hallucinations, delusions, incoherent thought, paranoia and emotional withdrawal.

Second messenger. An intracellular signalling molecule that acts to transmit signals from a receptor to a target. One example is cAMP which is synthesized after a neurotransmitter binds to certain a G protein-linked receptor, which then causes protein phosphorylation (i.e. the opening) of ion channels.

Semicircular canals. A group of three looping chambers in the inner ear whose main function is to relay information regarding rotational movement of the head to the brain.

Sensory-specific satiety. The tendency to get bored eating one type of food if consumed over a long period.

Septum. A subcortical structure found in the midline of the brain, some of which partitions the two lateral ventricles, that also contains a cluster of septal nuclei with connections to the hippocampus, amygdala and hypothalamus.

Serotonin A monoamine neurotransmitter, also called 5-hydroxytryptamine (5-HT), which is implicated in a wide range of functions including mood, cognition, reward and arousal.

Serotonin uptake blocker. A class of drug that includes fluoxetine (Prozac) which selectively blocks the reuptake of serotonin from the synaptic cleft.

Sexually dimorphic nucleus. A nucleus found in the preoptic area of the anterior hypothalamus that is larger in males than in females. In humans these are also known as the interstitial nuclei.

Sleep cycle. A sequence of four slow wave sleep stages that progress from predominantly theta activity (4–7 Hz) to delta activity (1–4 Hz), followed by a period of REM sleep. Each cycle lasts for about 90 minutes.

Slow wave sleep. Sleep characterized by slower EEG brain waves than those found in waking, made up predominantly of delta activity (1–4 Hz).

Sodium/potassium pump. A transport mechanism within the plasma membrane of a neuron that regulates the concentration of sodium and potassium ions inside and outside the neuron.

Somatic nervous system. A division of the peripheral nervous system that controls skeletal muscles, and which also sends sensory input from the skin, muscle, tendons joints etc. to the spinal cord and brain.

Somatosensory cortex. A band of tissue in the post-central gyrus of the parietal lobes, adjacent to the primary motor cortex, which receives touch, pain and temperature information. It also obtains motor feedback from the muscles.

Spinoreticular tract. The part of the anterolateral pathway conveying pain and temperature information from the spinal cord to the reticular formation.

Spinotectal tract. The part of the anterolateral pathway conveying pain and temperature information from the spinal cord to the upper brainstem (tectum).

Spinothalamic tract. The part of the anterolateral pathway conveying pain and temperature information from the spinal cord to the thalamus.

Splenium. The rear part of the corpus callosum which transfers visual information between the hemispheres.

Spongiform encephalopathy. A group of transmissible progressive and invariably fatal neurodegenerative diseases caused by infectious proteins (prions). Human examples include Jacob-Creutzfeldt disease and Kuru.

Stem cells. A primitive and undifferentiated cell (first discovered in the early embryo) with the unique ability of being able to develop into just about any other type of cell, including neurons.

Stereochemical theory of olfaction. The theory that there are different types of olfactory receptor which distinguish between smells.

Striatum. An important component of the basal ganglia that is composed of the caudate nucleus and putamen, and so called because of its striped appearance. It is one of the key areas of the brain that regulates movement.

Subiculum. An area of limbic cortex in the parahippocampal gyrus that innervates the hippocampal formation which is important for memory.

Substantia gelatinosa. An area of the spinal cord containing cell bodies and inter neurons.

Substantia nigra. A dark pigmented nucleus found in the midbrain tegmentum composed of two regions: the pars compacta and the pars reticulata. The pars compacta is notable for sending dopaminergic fibres to the striatum, and it also shows marked degeneration in Parkinson's disease.

Subthalamic nucleus. A nucleus involved in motor behaviour that lies below the thalamus, which receives input from the striatum, and innervates the globus pallidus and substantia nigra.

Superior colliculi. Bump-like protrusions in the roof of the midbrain which receives input from the optic nerve, and are important in the orientation of the head and eyes.

Supplementary motor cortex. An area lying anterior and adjacent to the upper part of the primary motor cortex, which is involved in the sequencing of goal-directed movements.

Suprachiasmatic nucleus. A tiny nucleus lying just above the optic chiasm in the medial hypothalamus which acts as a biological clock and is important in the regulation of circadian rhythms.

Sympathetic nervous system. A major branch of the autonomic nervous system (along with the parasympathetic nervous system) whose main function is to mobilize the body's resources for fight or flight (i.e. increase arousal).

Synapse. A point of contact, tiny gap, or junction that provides the site of transmission (chemical or electrical) between a nerve and its effector, such as another neuron or muscle cell.

Synaptic vesicles. Protective sacs that store molecules of neurotransmitter in the endings of axons.

α-Synuclein. A small protein which has been implicated in some forms of Parkinson's disease.

Tau. A protein that is found in neurofibrillary tangles.

Temporal lobe. The area of the cerebral cortex lying below and lateral to the Sylvian fissure and parietal lobe.

Testosterone. The main sex hormone produced by the male gonads, or testes. It has organizational effects on the body and central nervous system during foetal and pubertal development, and activational effects on certain types of behaviour in adulthood.

Thalamus. An egg-shaped mass of nuclei located just above the hypothalamus which functions as the principle relay station for sensory information going to the cerebral cortex, and is also crucially involved in regulating its electrical activity.

Thermoreceptors. Receptors that detect temperature at low levels of activity and pain at higher intensities.

Tolerance. Drug tolerance occurs when the repeated use of a substance leads to that agent producing less of an effect than it did initially which may be a causal factor in addiction. The reasons for drug tolerance are complex and include biological causes (pharmacokinetic and pharmacodynamic) as well as behavioural causes.

Transfer RNA. The single-stranded nucleic acid that is responsible for bringing amino acids found in the cytoplasm to the ribosome for protein synthesis.

Transgenic animals. Animals that have been genetically engineered or modified using DNA from another organism.

Trunk. The central portion of corpus callosum situated between the anterior 'genu' and the more posterior 'splenium'.

Turner's syndrome. A condition in which the female inherits only one X chromosome and does not develop functional ovaries.

Ventral tegmental area (VTA). An area of the midbrain which receives input from the medial forebrain bundle and is the main source of dopaminergic neurons to the forebrain.

Ventricles. The hollow spaces in the brain that contain cerebrospinal fluid. In humans these consist of the two lateral ventricles: the 3rd ventricle and the 4th ventricle.

Ventromedial hypothalamus. A large nucleus in the hypothalamus which has been shown to be important in feeding and female sexual behaviour.

Viscera. Another term for the main internal organs of the body.

Visual cortex. A region of the occipital lobes which is the primary cortical region and receives, integrates and processes visual information from the eyes.

Vomeronasal organ. A sensory organ found in reptiles and most mammals (including humans) that responds to certain types of olfactory information, including pheromones.

Wernicke's aphasia. A language impairment characterized by fluent and meaningless speech, and poor language comprehension.

Wernicke's area. A region of auditory association cortex in the temporal lobes that is involved in language comprehension and the production of meaningful speech.

Working memory. A form of short-term memory that is able to concurrently hold information whilst we process other information or perform a task. Also known as an executive function.

REFERENCES

Abadie, P., Baron, J. C., Bisserbe, J. C., Boulenger, J. P., Rioux, P., Travère, J. M., Barré, L., Petit-Taboué, M. C., & Zarifian, E. (1992). Central benzodiazepine receptors in human brain: Estimation of regional Bmax and KD values with positron emission tomography. *European Journal of Pharmacology*, 213, 107–115.

Abraira, V. E., & Ginty, D. D. (2013). The sensory neurons of touch. *Neuron*, 79, 618–639.

Adams, J., & Dudek, S. (2005). Late-phase long-term potentiation: Getting to the nucleus. *Nature Reviews Neuroscience*, 6, 737–743.

Adelmann, P. K., & Zajonc, R. B. (1989). Facial efference and the experience of emotion. *Annual Review of Psychology*, 40, 249–280.

Adinoff, B. (2004). Neurobiologic processes in drug reward and addiction. *Harvard Review of Psychiatry*, 12, 305–320.

Adkins-Regan, E. (1988). Sex hormones and sexual orientation in animals. *Psychobiology*, 16, 335–347.

Adolphs, R., Cahill, L., Schul, R., & Babinsky, R. (1997). Impaired declarative memory for emotional material following bilateral amygdala damage in humans. *Learning and Memory*, 4, 291–230.

Adolphs, R., Tranel, D., Damasio, H., & Damasio, A. R. (1994). Impaired recognition of emotion in facial expressions following bilateral damage to the human amygdala. *Nature*, 372, 669–672.

Afif, J. A. & Kim, J. C. (2018). Hippocampal projections to the anterior olfactory nucleus differentially convey spatiotemporal information during episodic odour memory. *Nature Communications*, 9, DOI: 10.1038/s41467-018-05131-6

Afifi, A. K., & Bergman, R. A. (2005). *Functional neuroanatomy*. McGraw-Hill.

Aggleton, J. (2014). Looking beyond the hippocampus: Old and new neurological targets for understanding memory disorders. *Proceedings of the Royal Society B: Biological Sciences*, 281, 20140565. http://doi.org/10.1098/rspb.2014.0565

Aggleton, J. P., McMackin, D., Carpenter, K., Hornak, J., Kapur, N., Halpin, S., Wiles, C. M., Kamel, H., Brennan, P., Carton, S., & Gaffan, D. (2000). Differential cognitive effects of colloid cysts in the third ventricle that spare or compromise the fornix. *Brain*, 123, 800–815.

Aghajanian, G. K., Foote, W. E., & Sheard, M. H. (1968). Lysergic acid diethylamide: Sensitive neuronal units in the midbrain raphe. *Science*, 161, 706–708.

Aghajanian, G. K., & Marek, G. J. (1999a). Serotonin and hallucinogens. *Neuropsychopharmacology*, 21, 16S–23S.

Aghajanian, G. K., & Marek, G. J. (1999b). Serotonin–glutamate interactions: A new target for antipsychotic drugs. *Neuropsychopharmacology*, 21, S122–S133.

Agid, Y., Javoy-Agid, F., & Panksepp, J. (1987). Biochemistry of neurotransmitters in Parkinson's disease. In C. D. Marsden & S. Fahn (Eds.), *Movement disorders 2* (pp. 166–230). Butterworth.

Ahima, R. S. (2008). Revisiting leptin's role in obesity and weight loss. *Journal of Clinical Investigation*, 118, 2380–2383.

Ajina, S., & Bridge, H. (2017). Blindsight and unconscious vision: What they teach us about the human visual system. *The Neuroscientist*, 23, 529–541. https://doi.org/101177/1073858416673817

Akhmedov, K., Kadakkuzha, B. M., & Puthanveettil, S. (2014). Aplysia ganglia preparation for electrophysiological and molecular analyses of single neurons. *Journal of Visualized Experiments: JoVE*, 83, e51075. https://doi.org/10.3791/51075

Al Hafid, N., & Christodoulou, J. (2015). Phenylketonuria: A review of current and future treatments. *Translational Pediatrics*, 4, 304–317.

Alexander, A. L., Lee, J. E., Lazar, M., & Field, A. S. (2007). Diffusion tensor imaging of the brain. *Neurotherapeutics*, 4, 316–329.

Alexander, S. P. H. (2009). Glutamate. In L. R. Squire (Ed.), *Encyclopaedia of neuroscience* (Vol. 1) (pp. 885–894). Academic Press.

Allard, M., L'ebre, V., & Robine, J. M. (1998). *Jeanne Calment: From Van Gogh's time to ours*. Freeman.

Allee, W. C., Collias, N. E., & Lutherman, C. Z. (1939). Modification of the social order in flocks of hens by the injection of testosterone propionate. *Physiological Zoology*, 12, 412–440.

Allen, J. S., Damasio, H., & Grabowski, T. J. (2002). Normal neuroanatomical variation in the human brain: An MRI-volumetric study. *American Journal of Physical Anthropology*, 118, 341–358.

Allen, L. S., Hines, M., Shryne, J. E., & Gorski, R. A. (1988). Two sexually dimorphic cell groups in the human brain. *Journal of Neuroscience*, 9, 497–506.

Allouche, S., Noble, F., & Marie, N. (2014). Opioid receptor desensitization: Mechanisms and its link to tolerance. *Frontiers in Pharmacology*, 5, 1–20. https://doi.org/10.3389/fphar.2014.00280

Aminoff, E. M., Kveraga, K., & Bar, M. (2013). The role of the parahippocampal cortex in cognition. *Trends in Cognitive Science*, 17, 379–390.

Amoore, J. E., Johnston, J. W., & Rubin, M. (1964). The stereochemical theory of odor. *Scientific American*, 210, 42–49.

Anand, B. K., & Brobeck, J. R. (1951). Hypothalamic control of food intake. *Yale Journal of Biological Medicine*, 24, 123–140.

Anand, B. K., China, G. S., Sharma, K.N., Dua, S., & Singh, B. (1964). Activity of single neurons in the hypothalamic feeding centres: Effects of glucose. *American Journal of Physiology*, 207, 1146–1154.

Anderson, A. K., & Phelps, E. A. (2001). Lesions of the human amygdala impair enhanced perception of emotionally salient events. *Nature*, 41(1), 305–309.

Anderson, I. M., Haddard, P. M., & Scott, J. (2012). Bipolar disorder. *British Medical Journal*, 345, e8508. https://doi.org/10.1136/bmj.e8508

Anderson, K. E., Eberly, S., Marder, K. S., Oakes, D., Kayson, E., Young, A., & Shoulson, I.; for the PHAROS Investigators. (2019). The choice not to undergo genetic testing for Huntington disease: Results from the PHAROS study. *Clinical Genetics*, 96, 28–34.

Anderson, P. J., & Leuzzi, V. (2009). White matter pathology in phenylketonuria. *Molecular Genetics and Metabolism*, 99(Suppl. 1), S3–S9.

Andrade, P. E., & Bhattacharya, J. (2003). Brain tuned to music. *Journal of the Royal Society of Medicine*, 96, 284–287.

André, V. M., Cepeda, C., & Levine, M. S. (2010). Dopamine and glutamate in Huntington's disease: A balancing act. *CNS Neuroscience and Therapeutics*, 16, 163–178.

Andreano, J. M., & Cahill, L. (2009). Sex influences on the neurobiology of learning and memory. *Learning and Memory*, 16, 248–266.

Andreasen, N. C. (1988). Brain imaging: Applications in psychiatry. *Science*, 239, 1381–1388.

Anglada-Huguet, M., Vidal-Sancho, L., Cabezas-Llobet, N., Alberch, J., & Xifró, X. (2017). Pathogenesis of Huntington's Disease: How to fight excitotoxicity and transcriptional dysregulation. *Huntington's Disease – Molecular Pathogenesis and Current Models*. Advance online publication. https://doi.org/10.5772/66734

Angulo, M. C., Kozlov, A. S., Charpak, S., & Audinat, E. (2004). Glutamate released from glial cells synchronizes neuronal activity in the hippocampus. *Journal of Neuroscience*, 24, 6920–6927.

Anisfeld, M. (1996). Only tongue protrusion modelling is matched by neonates. *Developmental Review*, 16, 149–161.

Annese, J., Schenker-Ahmed, N. M., Bartsch, H., Maechler, P., Sheh, C., Thomas, N., Kayano, J., Ghatan, A., Bresler, N., Frosch, M. P., Klaming, R., & Corkin, S. (2014). Postmortem examination of patient H.M.'s brain based on histological sectioning and digital 3D reconstruction. *Nature Communications*, 5, 1–9. https://doi.org/10.1038/ncomms4122

Apkarian, A. V. (2011). The brain in chronic pain. *Pain Management*, 1, 577–586.

Aqrabawi, A. J., & Kim, J. C. (2018). Hippocampal projections to the anterior olfactory nucleus differentially convey spatiotemporal information during episodic odour memory. *Nature Communications*, 9, 1–10. https://doi.org/10.1038/s41467-018-05131-6

Arana, G. W., Baldessarini, R. J., & Ornsteen, M. (1985). The dexamethasone suppression test for diagnosis and prognosis in psychiatry: Commentary and review. *Archives of General Psychiatry*, 42, 1193–1204.

Archer, J. (1994). Testosterone and aggression. *Journal of Offender Rehabilitation*, 21, 3–39.

Archer, J. (2006). Testosterone and human aggression: An evaluation of the challenge hypothesis. *Neuroscience and Biobehavioral Reviews*, 30, 319–345.

Ardekani, B. A., Figarsky, K., & Sidtis, J. J. (2013). Sexual dimorphism in the human corpus callosum: An MRI study using the OASIS brain database. *Cerebral Cortex*, 23, 2514–2520.

Arendt, J. (2009). Managing jet lag: Some of the problems and possible new solutions. *Sleep Medical Reviews*, 13, 249–256.

Armando, M., Papaleo, F., & Vicari, S. (2012). COMT implication in cognitive and psychiatric symptoms in chromosome 22q11 microdeletion syndrome: A selective review. *CNS and Neurological Disorders Drug Targets*, 11, 273–281.

Armstrong, R. A. (2011). The pathogenesis of Alzheimer's disease: A reevaluation of the 'amyloid cascade hypothesis'. *International Journal of Alzheimer's Disease*, 2011, 630865. https://doi.org/10.4061/2011/630865

Arnáiz, E., & Almkvist, O. (2003). Neuropsychological features of mild cognitive impairment and preclinical Alzheimer's disease. *Acta Neurologica Scandinavica*, 107, 34–41.

Arnold, A. P. (2009). The organizational-activational hypothesis as the foundation for a unified theory of sexual differentiation of all mammalian tissues. *Hormones and Behavior*, 55, 570–578.

Arora, J., Pugh, K., Westerveld, M., Spencer, S., Spencer, D. D., & Constable, R.T. (2009). Language lateralization in epilepsy patients: fMRI validated with the Wada procedure. *Epilepsia*, 50, 2225–2241.

Arora, S. (2006). Role of neuropeptides in appetite regulation and obesity – A review. *Neuropeptides*, 40, 375–401.

Arroll, B., Macgillivray, S., Ogston, S. ..., & Crombie, I. (2005). Efficacy and tolerability of tricyclic antidepressants and SSRIs compared with placebo for treatment of depression in primary care: A meta-analysis. *Annals of Family Medicine*, 3, 449–456.

Arts, N. J. M., Walvoort, S. J. W., & Kessels, R. P. C. (2017). Korsakoff's syndrome: A critical review. *Neuropsychiatric Disease and Treatment*, 13, 2875–2890.

Asberg, M. (2006). Neurotransmitters and suicidal behavior: The evidence from cerebrospinal fluid studies. *Annals of the New York Academy of Sciences*. Advance online publication. https://doi.org/10.1111/j.1749-6632.1997.tb52359.x

Asberg, M., Traskman, L., & Thorén, P. (1976). 5-HIAA in the cerebrospinal fluid: A biochemical suicide predictor? *Archives of General Psychiatry*, 33, 1193–1197.

Aschoff, J. (1967). Comparative physiology: Diurnal rhythms. *Annual Review of Physiology*, 25, 581–600.

Aschoff, J., Hoffman, K., Pohl, H., & Wever, R. (1975). Re-entrainment of circadian rhythms after phase-shifts of the zeitgerber. *Chronobiologia*, 2, 23–78.

Aserinsky, E., & Kleitman, N. (1953). Regularly occurring periods of eye motility and concomitant phenomena. *Science*, 118, 273–274.

Ashton, H. (1992). *Brain function and psychotropic drugs*. Oxford University Press.

Ashton, R. (2002). *This is heroin*. Sanctuary House.

Assefa, S. Z., Diaz-Abad, M., Wickwire, E. M., & Scharf, S. M. (2015). The functions of sleep. *AIMS Neuroscience*, 2, 155–171.

Avramopoulous, D. (2009). Genetics of Alzheimer's disease: Recent advances. *Genome Medicine*, 1, 34. https://doi.org/10.1186/gm34

Ax, A. (1953). The physiological differentiation between fear and anger in humans. *Psychomatic Medicine*, 15, 433–442.

Ayuso-Mateos, J. L. (2000). *Global burden of bipolar disorder in the year 2000*. World Health Organization. Global Burden of Disease.

Azevedo, F. A., Carvalho, L. R., Grinberg, L. T., Farfel, J. M., Ferretti, R. E. L., Leite, R. E. P., Filho, W. J., Lent, R., & Herculano-Houzel, S. (2009). Equal numbers of neuronal and nonneuronal cells make the human brain an isometrically scaled-up primate brain. *Journal of Comparative Neurology*, 513, 532–541.

Baddeley, A. D. (1986). *Working memory*. Clarendon Press.

Baddeley, A. D., & Hitch, G. (1974). Working memory. *Psychology of Learning and Motivation*, 8, 47–89.

Bae, B. I., Xu, H., Igarashi, S., Fujimuro, M., Agrawal, N., Taya, Y., Hayward, S. D., Moran, T. H., Montell, C., Ross, C. A., Snyder, S. H., & Sawa, A. (2005). p53 mediates cellular dysfunction and behavioral abnormalities in Huntington's disease. *Neuron*, 47, 29–41.

Bager, P., Nielsen, N. M., Bihrmann, K., Frisch, M., Hjalgrim, H., Wohlfart, J., Koch-Henriksen, N., Melbye, M., & Westergaard, T. (2004). Childhood infections and risk of multiple sclerosis. *Brain*, 127, 2491–2497.

Bahrick, A. S. (2008). Persistence of sexual dysfunction side effects after discontinuation of antidepressant medications: Emerging evidence. *The Open Psychology Journal*, 1, 42–50.

Baik, J. H. (2013). Dopamine signaling in reward-related behaviors. *Frontiers in Neural Circuits*, 7, 152. https://doi.org/10.3389/fncir.2013.00152

Bailer, U. F., & Kaye, W. H. (2011). Serotonin: Imaging findings in eating disorders. *Current Topics in Behavioral Neuroscience*, 6, 59–79.

Bailey, C. H., & Chen, M. (1983). Morphological basis of long-term habituation and sensitization in Aplysia. *Science*, 220, 91–93.

Bailey, C. H., & Chen, M. (1988). Morphological basis of short-term habituation in Aplysia. *Journal of Neuroscience*, 8, 2452–2459.

Bailey, C. H., Kandel, E. R., & Harris, K. M. (2015). Structural components of synaptic plasticity and memory consolidation. *Cold Spring Harbour Perspectives in Biology*, 7, a021758. https://doi.org/10.1101/cshperspect.a021758

Bailey, J. M., & Pillard, R. C. (1991). A genetic study of male sexual orientation. *Archives of General Psychiatry*, 48, 1089–1096.

Bailey, J. M., Pillard, R. C., Neale, M. C., & Agyei, Y. (1993). Heritable factors influencing sexual orientation in women. *Archives of General Psychiatry*, 50, 217–223.

Bailey, J. M., Vasey, P. L, Diamond, L. M., Breedlove, S. M., Vilain, E., & Epprecht, M. (2016). Sexual orientation, controversy, and science. *Psychological Science in the Public Interest*, 17, 45–101.

Baird, A. D., Wilson, S. J., Bladin, P. F., Saling, M. M., & Reutens, D. C. (2007). Neurological control of human sexual behaviour: Insights from lesion studies. *Journal of Neurology, Neurosurgery and Psychiatry*, 78, 1042–1049.

Baizer, J. S., Ungerleider, L. G., & Desimone, R. (1991). Organization of visual inputs to the inferior temporal and posterior parietal cortex in macaques. *Journal of Neuroscience*, 11, 168–190.

Ball, N., Teo, W. P., Chandra, S., & Chapman, J. (2019). Parkinson's Disease and the environment. *Frontiers in Neurology*,

10, 218. https://doi.org/10.3389/fneur.2019.00218

Ballesteros-Yáñez, I., Castillo, C. A., Merighi, S., & Gessi, S. (2018). The role of adenosine receptors in psychostimulant addiction. *Frontiers in Pharmacology*, 8, 1–18. https://doi.org/10.3389/fphar.2017.00985

Ballinger, E. C., Ananth, M., Talmage, D. A., & Role, L. W. (2016). Basal forebrain cholinergic circuits and signaling in cognition and cognitive decline. *Neuron*, 91, 1199–1218.

Balthazart, J. (2011). Minireview: Hormones and human sexual orientation. *Endocrinology*, 152, 2937–2947.

Bandelow, B., & Michaelis, S. (2015). Epidemiology of anxiety disorders in the 21st century. *Dialogues in Clinical Neuroscience*, 17, 327–335.

Banerjee, N. (2014). Neurotransmitters in alcoholism: A review of neurobiological and genetic studies. *Indian Journal of Human Genetics*, 20, 20–31.

Banich, M. T. (2004). *Cognitive neuroscience and neurophysiology*. Houghton Mifflin.

Banich, M. T., & Compton, R. J. (2018). *Cognitive neuroscience*. Cambridge University Press.

Bao, A.-M., & Swaab, D. F. (2019). The human hypothalamus in mood disorders: The HPA axis in the center. *IBRO Reports*, 6, 45–53.

Barbas, H. (2007). Specialized elements of orbitofrontal cortex in primates. *Annals of the New York Academy of Sciences*, 1121, 10–32.

Barbey, A. K., Koenigs, M., & Grafman, J. (2013). Dorsolateral prefrontal contributions to human working memory. *Cortex*, 49, 1195–1205.

Barbin, J., Seetha, V., Casillas, J. M., Paysant, J., & Pérennou, D. (2016). The effects of mirror therapy on pain and motor control of phantom limb pain in amputees: A systematic review. *Annals of Physical and Rehabilitation Medicine*, 59, 270–275.

Bard, P. (1934). On emotional expression after decortication with some remarks on certain theoretical views. *Psychological Review*, 41, 309–329.

Bard, P., & Mountcastle, V. B. (1948). Some forebrain mechanisms involved in the expression of rage with special reference to suppression of angry behaviour. *Research Association into Research for Nervous Mental Disease*, 27, 362–404.

Bardell, A., Lau, T., & Fedoroff, J. P. (2011). Inappropriate sexual behavior in a geriatric population. *International Psychogeriatrics*, 23, 1182–1188.

Barker, R. A., Parmar, M., Studer, L., & Takahashi, J. (2017). Human trials of stem cell-derived dopamine neurons for Parkinson's disease: Dawn of a new era. *Cell Stem Cell*, 21, 569–573.

Barlow, D. (2000). Unraveling the mysteries of anxiety and its disorders from the perspective of emotion theory. *The American Psychologist*, 55, 1247–1263.

Barlow, H. B. (1982). David Hubel and Torsten Wiesel: Their contributions towards understanding the primary visual cortex. *Trends in Neurosciences*, 5, 145–152.

Barlow, L. A. (2015). Progress and renewal in gustation: New insights into taste bud development. *Development*, 142, 3620–3629.

Barnes, J. (2013). *Essential biological psychology*. SAGE.

Baron-Cohen. S., Burt, L., Smith-Laittan, F., Harrison, J., & Bolton, J. (1996). Synaesthesia: Prevalence and familiarity. *Perception*, 25, 1073–1079.

Baron-Cohen, S., Johnson, D., Asher, J., Wheelwright, S., Fisher, S. E., Gregersen, P. K., & Allison, C. (2013). Is synaesthesia more common in autism? *Molecular Autism*, 4, 40. https://doi.org/10.1186/2040-2392-4-40

Bartoshuk, L. M. (1978). History of taste research. In E. C. Carterette & M. P. Friedman (Eds.), *Handbook of perception: Vol. VIA. Tasting and smelling* (pp. 3–18). Academic Press.

Basbaum, A. I., & Fields, H. L. (1978). Endogenous pain control mechanisms: Review and hypothesis. *Annals of Neurology*, 4, 451–462.

Bastian, A. J. (2011). Moving, sensing and learning with cerebellar damage. *Current Opinion in Neurobiology*, 21, 596–601.

Bastian, A. J., Martin, T. A., Keating, J. G., & Thach, W. T. (1996). Cerebellar ataxia: Abnormal control of interaction torques across multiple joints. *Journal of Neurophysiology*, 76, 492–509.

Bathina, S., & Das, U. N. (2015). Brain-derived neurotrophic factor and its clinical implications. *Archives of Medical Science*, 11, 1164–1178.

Batra, R. (2014). In M. J. Aminoff & R. B. Daroff (Eds.), *Encyclopedia of neurological sciences*. Elsevier.

Batrinos, M. L. (2012). Testosterone and aggressive behavior in man. *International Journal of Endocrinology and Metabolism*, 10, 563–568.

Batten, S. R., Pomerleau, F., Quintero, J., Gerhardt, G. A., & Beckmann, J. S. (2018). The role of glutamate signaling in incentive salience: Second-by-second glutamate recordings in awake Sprague-Dawley rats. *Journal of Neurochemistry*, 145, 276–286.

Baumeister, A. A. (2013). The chlorpromazine enigma. *Journal of the History of the Neurosciences*, 22, 14–29.

Baxter, L. R. (1995). Neuroimaging studies of human anxiety disorders. In F. Bloom & J. R. Kupfer (Eds.), *Psychopharmacology: The fourth generation of progress* (pp. 1287–1299). Raven Press.

Baylor, D. A. (1987). Photoreceptor signals and vision: Proctor lecture. *Investigations in Ophthalmology and Visual Science*, 28, 34–49.

Beach, F. A. (1940). Effects of cortical lesions upon the copulatory behavior of male rats. *Journal of Comparative Psychology*, 29, 193–239.

Bean, B. (2007). The action potential in mammalian central neurons. *Nature Review Neuroscience*, 8, 451–465.

Bear, M. F., Connors, B. W., & Paradiso, M. A. (1996). *Neuroscience: Exploring the Brain*. Williams and Wilkins.

Beard, E., Brown, J., Kaner, E., West, R., & Michie, S. (2017). Predictors of and reasons for attempts to reduce alcohol intake: A population survey of adults in England. *PLoS One*, 12, e0173458. https://doi.org/10.1371/journal.pone.0173458

Beaumont, G. (1991). The use of benzodiazepines in general practice. In L. Hindmarch, G. Beaumont, S. Brandon & B. E. Leonard (Eds.), *Benzodiazepines: Current concepts* (pp. 141–152). John Wiley.

Bechara. A,. Damasio, H., Tranel, & Damasio, A. R. (1997). Deciding advantageously before knowing an advantageous strategy. *Science*, 275, 1293–1295.

Becker, J. B., Breedlove, S. M., Crews, D., & McCarthy, M. M. (Eds.). (2002). *Behavioral endocrinology*. MIT Press.

Beecher, H. K. (1959). *Measurements of subjective responses*. Oxford University Press.

Beevor, C. E., & Horsley, V. (1890). A record of the results obtained by electrical stimulation of the so-called motor cortex and internal capsule in an orang-outang (*simian astyrus*). *Philosophical Transactions*, B181, 120–158.

Behrens, P. F., Franz, P., Woodman, B., Lindenberg, K. S., & Landwehrmeyer, G. B. (2002). Impaired glutamate transport and glutamate-glutamine cycling: Downstream effects of the Huntington mutation. *Brain*, 125, 1908–1922.

Beinfeld, M. C., & Palkovits, M. (1981). Distribution of cholecystokinin (CCK) in the hypothalamus and limbic system of the rat. *Neuropeptides*, 2, 123–129.

Bekris, L. M., Yu, C. E., Bird, T. D., & Tsuang D. W. (2010). Genetics of Alzheimer disease. *Journal of Geriatric Psychiatry and Neurology*, 23, 213–227.

Bellenguez, C., Grenier-Boley, B., & Lambert, J.-C. (2020). Genetics of Alzheimer's disease: Where we are, and where we are going. *Current Opinion in Neurobiology*, 61, 40–48.

Belluzzi, J. D., & Stein, L. (2001). Reinforcement: Neurochemical substrates. In N. J. Smelser & P. B. Bates (Eds.), *International encyclopedia of the social and behavioral sciences* (pp. 12996–12999). Pergamon.

Benabid, A. L., Pollak, P., Louveau, A., Henry, S., & de Rougemont, J. (1987). Combined (thalamotomy and stimulation) stereotactic surgery of the VIM thalamic nucleus for bilateral Parkinson disease. *Applied Neurophysiology*, 50, 344–346.

Benington, J. H., & Heller, H. C. (1995). Restoration of brain energy metabolism as the function of sleep. *Progress in Neurobiology*, 45, 347–360.

Bennett, D. A., Beckett, L. A., Murray, A. M., Shannon, K. M., Goetz, C. G., Pilgrim, D. M., & Evans, D. A. (1996). Prevalence of Parkinsonian signs and associated mortality in a community population of older people. *New England Journal of Medicine*, 334, 71–76.

Benowitz, N. L. (2009). Pharmacology of nicotine: Addiction, smoking-induced disease, and therapeutics. *Annual Review of Pharmacology*, 49, 57–71.

Bentsen, M. A., Mirzadeh, Z., & Schwartz, M. W. (2019). Revisiting how the brain senses glucose – and why. *Cell Metabolism*, 29, 11–17.

Benveniste, H. (2018). The brain's waste-removal system. *Cerebrum: The Dana Forum on Brain Science, 2018*, cer-09-18.

Berenbaum, S. A. (2001). Cognitive function in congenital adrenal hyperplasia. *Endocrinology and Metabolism Clinics of North America*, 30, 173–192.

Berger, R. J., & Phillips, N. H. (1995). Energy conservation and sleep. *Behavioral Brain Research*, 69, 65–73.

Bernhardt, P. C., Dabbs, J. M., Fielden, J. A., & Lutter, C. D. (1998). Testosterone changes during vicarious experiences of winning and losing among fans at sporting events. *Physiology and Behavior*, 65, 59–62.

Bernheimer, H., Birkmayer, W., Hornykiewicz O., Jellinger, K., & Seitelberger F. (1973). Brain dopamine and the syndromes of Parkinson and Huntington: Clinical, morphological and neurochemical correlations. *Journal of the Neurological Sciences*, 20, 415–455.

Berridge, K. C., & Kringelbach, M. L. (2015). Pleasure systems in the brain. *Neuron*, 86, 646–664.

Berridge, K. C., & Robinson, T. E. (2016). Liking, wanting and the incentive-sensitization theory of addiction. *The American Psychologist*, 71, 670–679.

Bevan, M. J. (2010). The earliest knockouts. *Journal of Immunology*, 184, 4585–4586.

Bever, T., & Chiarello, R. J. (1974). Cerebral dominance in musicians and nonmusicians. *Journal of Neuropsychiatry and Clinical Neurosciences*, 21, 94–97.

Bianconi, E., Piovesan, A., Facchin, F., Beraudi, A., Casadei, R., Frabetti, F., Vitale, L., Pelleri, M. C., Tassani, S., Piva, F., Perez-Amodio, S., Strippoli P., & Canaider, S. (2013). An estimation of the number of cells in the human body. *Annals of Human Biology*, 40, 463–471.

Biever, A., Donlin-Asp, P. G., & Schuman, E. M. (2019). Local translation in neuronal processes. *Current Opinion in Neurobiology*, 57, 141–148.

Bischoff-Grethe, A., & Arib, M. A. (2001). Brain imaging and synthetic PET. In M. A. Arib & J. S. Grethe (Eds.), *Computing the brain: A guide to neuroinformatics* (pp. 103–113). Academic Press.

Bishop, K. M., & Wahlsten, D. (1997). Sex differences in the human corpus callosum: Myth or reality? *Neuroscience and Biobehavioral Reviews*, 21, 581–601.

Bittar, R. G., Kar-Purkayastha, I., Owen, S. L., Bear, R. E., Green, A., Wang, S., & Aziz, T. Z. (2005). Deep brain stimulation for pain relief: A meta analysis. *Journal of Clinical Neuroscience*, 12, 515–519.

Bjorklund, L. M., Sánchez-Pernaute, R., Chung, S., Andersson, T., Chen, I. Y. C., McNaught, K. S. P., Brownell, A.-L., Jenkins, B. G., Wahlestedt, C., Kim, K.-S., & Isacson, O. (2002). Embryonic stem cells develop into functional dopaminergic neurons after transplantation in a Parkinson rat model. *Proceedings of the National Academy of Sciences of the USA*, 99, 2344–2349.

Blacker, D., & Tanzi, R. E. (1998). The genetics of Alzheimer disease: Current status and future prospects. *Archives of Neurology*, 55, 294–296.

Blanchard, R. (2001). Fraternal birth order and the maternal immune hypothesis of male homosexuality. *Hormones and Behavior*, 40, 105–114.

Blanchard, R. (2008). Review and theory of handedness, birth order, and homosexuality in men. *Laterality*, 13, 51–70.

Blass, E. M., Anderson, D. R., Kirkorian, H. L., Pempek, T., Price, I., & Koleini, M. F. (2006). On the road to obesity: Television viewing increases intake of high-density foods. *Physiology and Behavior*, 88, 597–604.

Blessed, G., Tomlinson, B. E. & Roth, M. (1968). The association between quantitative measures of dementia and senile change in cerebral gray matter of elderly subjects. *British Journal of Psychiatry*, 114, 798–811.

Bleys, D., Luyten, P., Soenens, B., & Claes, S. (2018). Gene-environment interactions between stress and 5-HTTLPR in depression: A meta-analytic update. *Journal of Affective Disorders*, 226, 339–345.

Bliss, T. V. P., & Lomo, T. (1973). Long-lasting potentiation of synaptic transmission in the dentate area of the anaesthetized rabbit following stimulation of the perforant path. *Journal of Physiology (London)*, 232, 331–356.

Blood, A. J., & Zatorre, R. J. (2001). Intensely pleasurable responses to music correlate with activity in brain regions implicated in reward and emotion. *Proceedings of the National Academy of Sciences of the USA*, 98, 11818–11823.

Bloomfield, M. A. P., Ashok, A. H., Volkow, N. D., & Howes, O. D. (2016). The effects of Δ 9-tetrahydrocannabinol on the dopamine system. *Nature*, 539, 369–377.

Bloomfield, M. A. P., Hindocha, C., Green, S. F., Wall, M. B., Lees, R., Petrilli, K., Costello, H., Ogunbiyi, M. O., Bossong, M. G., & Freeman, T. P. (2019). The neuropsychopharmacology of cannabis: A review of human imaging studies. *Pharmacology and Therapeutics*, 195, 132–161.

Boatman, D., Gordon, B., Hart, J., Selnes, O., Miglioretti, D., & Lenz, F. (2000). Transcortical sensory aphasia: Revisited and revised. *Brain*, 123, 1634–1642.

Boese, A. (2007). *Elephants on acid and other bizarre experiments*. Harvest.

Boesveldt, S., Postma, E. M., Boak, D., Welge-Luessen, A., Schöpf, V., Mainland, J. D., Martens, J., Ngai, J., & Duffy, V. B. (2017). Anosmia: A clinical review. *Chemical Senses*, 42, 513–523.

Bogaert, A. F. (2006). Biological versus nonbiological older brothers and men's sexual orientation. *Proceedings of the National Academy of Sciences of the USA*, 103, 10771–10774.

Bogaert, A. F., & Skorska, M. N. (2020). A short review of biological research on the development of sexual orientation. *Hormones and Behavior*, 119, 104659. https://doi.org/10.1016/j.yhbeh.2019.104659

Bohbot, V. D., Allen, J. J. B., Dagher, A., Dumoulin, S. O., Evans, A. C., Petrides, M., Kalina, M., Stepankova, K., & Nadel, L. (2015). Role of the parahippocampal cortex in memory for the configuration but not the identity of objects: Converging evidence from patients with selective thermal lesions and fMRI. *Frontiers in Human Neuroscience*, 9, 1–17. https://doi.org/10.3389/fnhum.2015.00431

Bon, C. L. M., & Garthwaite, J. (2003). On the role of nitric oxide in hippocampal long term potentiation. *Journal of Neuroscience*, 23, 1941–1948.

Bondy, C. A. (2007). Care of girls and women with Turner syndrome: A guideline of the Turner Syndrome Study Group. *Journal of Clinical Endocrinology and Metabolism*, 92, 10–25.

Bonnett, M. H., & Arand, D. L. (1996). The consequences of a week of insomnia. *Sleep*, 19, 453–461.

Boomsma, D., Busjahn, A., & Peltonen, L. (2002). Classical twin studies and beyond. *Nature Reviews: Genetics*, 3, 872–882.

Booth, D. A. (1990). Sensory influences on food intake. *Nutrition Reviews*, 48, 71–77.

Booth, M. (2003). *Cannabis: A history*. Bantam Books.

Borbély, A. (1986). *Secrets of sleep*. Penguin.

Borchelt, D. R., Ratovitski, T., van Lare, J., Lee, M. K., Gonzales, V., Jenkins, N. A., Copeland, N. G., Price, D. L., & Sisodia, S. S. (1997). Accelerated amyloid deposition in the brains of transgenic mice coexpressing mutant presenilin 1 and amyloid precursor proteins. *Neuron*, 19, 939–945.

Border, R., Johnson, E. C., Evans, L. M., Smolen, A., Berley, N., Sullivan, P. F., & Keller, M. C. (2019). No support for historical candidate gene or candidate gene-by-interaction hypotheses for major depression across multiple large samples. *American Journal of Psychiatry*, 176, 376–387.

Borg, W. P., Sherwin, R. S., During, M. J., Borg, M. A., & Shulman, G. I. (1995). Local ventromedial hypothalamus glucopenia triggers counterregulatory hormone release. *Diabetes*, 44, 180–184.

Borsook, D., Moulton, E. A., Schmidt, K. F., & Becerra, L. R. (2007). Neuroimaging revolutionizes therapeutic approaches to chronic pain. *Molecular Pain*, 3(25). doi:10.1186/1744-8069-3-25

Bos, N. P. A., & Mirmiran, M. (1990). Circadian rhythms in spontaneous neuronal discharges of the cultured suprachiasmatic nucleus. *Brain Research*, 511, 158–162.

Botigué, L. R., Song, S., Scheu, A., Gopalan, S., Pendleton, A. L., Oetjens, M., Taravella, A. M., Seregély, T., Zeeb-Lanz, A., Arbogast, R. M., Bobo, D., Daly, K., Unterländer, M., Burger, J., Kidd, J. M., & Veeramah, K. R. (2017). Ancient European dog genomes reveal continuity since the Early Neolithic. *Nature Communications*, 8, 16082. https://doi.org/10.1038/ncomms16082

Bouabe, H., & Okkenhaug, K. (2013). Gene targeting in mice: A review. *Methods in Molecular Biology*, 1064, 315–336.

Bouchard, C., Tremblay, A., Després, J. P., Nadeau, A., Lupien, P. J., Thériault, G., Dussault, J., Moorjani, S., Pinault, S., & Fournier, P. G. (1990). The response to over-feeding in identical twins. *New England Journal of Medicine*, 322, 1477–1482.

Bouchard, T. J. (1994). Genes, environment, and personality. *Science*, 264, 1700–1701.

Bouchard, T. J., Lykken, D. T., McGue, M., Segal, N. L., & Tellegen, A. (1990). Sources of human psychological differences: The Minnesota study of twins reared apart. *Science*, 250, 223–228.

Bouret, S. G., Draper, S. J., & Simerly, R. B. (2004). Trophic action of leptin on hypothalamic neurons that regulate feeding. *Science*, 304, 108–110.

Bourin, M. (2015). Animal models for screening anxiolytic-like drugs: A perspective. *Dialogues in Clinical Neuroscience*, 17, 295–303.

Bovet, D. (1977). Strain differences in learning in the mouse. In A. Olivierio (Ed.), *Genetics, environment and intelligence* (pp. 79–92). Elsevier.

Bowers, J. S. (2017). Grandmother cells and localist representations: A review of current thinking. *Language, Cognition and Neuroscience*, 32, 257–273.

Boyce, P., & Barriball, E. (2010). Circadian rhythms and depression. *Australian Family Physician*, 39, 307–310.

Boydell, J., & Murray, R. (2003). Urbanisation, migration and risk of schizophrenia. In R. Murray, P. B. Jones, E. Susser, J. van Os & M. Cannon (Eds.), *The epidemiology of schizophrenia* (pp. 49–67). Cambridge University Press.

Boynton, G., & Hegdé, J. (2004). Visual cortex: The continuing puzzle of area V2. *Current Biology*, 14, R523–R524.

Braak, H., Thal, D. R., Ghebremedhin, E., & Del Tredici, K. (2011). Stages of the pathologic process in Alzheimer disease: Age categories from 1 to 100 years. *Journal of Neuropathology and Experimental Neurology*, 70, 960–969.

Bradbury, T. N., & Miller, G. A. (1985). Season of birth in schizophrenia: A review of evidence, methodology, and etiology. *Psychological Bulletin*, 98, 569–594.

Bradley, R. M. (2007). Historical perspectives. In R. M. Bradley (Ed.), *The role of the nucleus of the solitary tract in gustatory processing* (pp. 1–11). CRC Press.

Brand, M., Kalbe, E., Fujiwara, E., Huber, M., & Markowitsch, H. (2003). Cognitive estimation in patients with probable Alzheimer's disease and alcoholic Korsakoff patients. *Neuropsychologia*, 41, 575–584.

Brandler, W. M., & Paracchini, S. (2014). The genetic relationship between handedness and neurodevelopmental disorders. *Trends in Molecular Medicine*, 20, 83–90.

Bray, G. A., & York, D. A. (1979). Hypothalamic and genetic obesity in experimental animals: An autonomic and endocrine hypothesis. *Physiological Review*, 59, 719–809.

Breedlove, S. M., Rosenzweig, M. R., & Watson, N. V. (2007). *Biological psychology*. Sinauer.

Breiter, H. C., Etcoff, N. L., Whalen, P. J., Kennedy, W. A., Rauch, S. L., Buckner, R. L., Strauss, M. M., Hyman, S. E., & Rosen, B. R. (1996). Response and habituation of the human amygdala during visual processing of facial expression. *Neuron*, 17, 875–887.

Breslin, P. A. S. (2013). An evolutionary perspective on food and human taste. *Current Biology*, 23, R409–R418.

Brett, J., & Murnion, B. (2015). Management of benzodiazepine misuse and dependence. *Australian Prescriber*, 38, 152–155.

Briggs, F., & Usray, W. M. (2011). Corticogeniculate feedback and visual processing in the primate. *Journal of Physiology*, 589, 33–40.

Brisch, R., Saniotis, A., Wolf, R., Bielau, H., Bernstein, H. G., Steiner, J., Bogerts, B., Braun, A. K., Jankowski, Z., Kumaritlake, J., Henneberg, M., & Gos, T. (2014). The role of dopamine in schizophrenia from a neurobiological and evolutionary perspective: Old fashioned, but still in vogue. Frontiers in Psychiatry, 5, 47. https://doi.org/10.3389/fpsyt.2014.00047

Brodmann, K. (1912). Neue ergebnisse uber die vergleichene histolgische localisation der grosshirmrinde mit besonderer Berucksichtigung des Stirnhirms. *Anatomischer Anzeiger*, 41, 157–216.

Bronstein, A. M., Patel, M., & Arshad, Q. (2014). A brief review of the clinical anatomy of the vestibular-ocular connections – how much do we know? *Eye*, 29, 163–170.

Brookshire, R. (2007). *Introduction to neurogenic communication disorders*. Mosby Elsevier.

Brown, A. S., Begg, M. D., Gravenstein, S., Schaefer, C. A., Wyatt, R. J., Bresnahan, M., Babulas, V. P., & Susser, E. S. (2004). Serologic evidence of prenatal influenza in the etiology of schizophrenia. *Archives of General Psychiatry*, 61, 774–780.

Brown, P. K., & Wald, G. (1964). Visual pigments in single rods and cones of the human retina: Direct measurements reveal mechanisms of human night and color vision. *Science*, 144, 45–52.

Brown, R. E. (2020). Donald O. Hebb and the Organization of Behavior: 17 years in the writing. *Molecular Brain*, 13, 55. https://doi.org/10.1186/s13041-020-00567-8

Brownell, W. E. (1997). How the ear works – nature's solution for listening. *The Volta Review*, 99, 9–28.

Bruder, C. E., Piotrowski, A., Gijsbers, A. A., Andersson, R., Erickson, S., de Ståhl, T. D., Menzel, U., Sandgren, J., von Tell, D., Poplawski, A., Crowley, M., Crasto, C., Partridge, E. C., Tiwari, H., Allison, D. B., Komorowski, J., van Ommen, G.-J. B., Boomsma, D. I., Pedersen, N. L., . . . Dumanski, J. P. (2008). Phenotypically concordant and discordant monozygotic twins display different DNA copy-number-variationprofiles. *American Journal of Human Genetics*, 82, 763–771.

Brundin, P., & Wyse, R. K. (2019). The linked clinical trials initiative (LCT) for Parkinson's disease. *European Journal of Neuroscience*, 49, 307–315.

Bub, D. N., Arguin, N., & Lecours, A. R. (1993). Jules Dejerine and his interpretation of pure alexia. *Brain and Language*, 45, 531–559.

Buchanan, T. W., Tranel, D., & Adolphs, R. (2009). The human amygdala in social function. In P. W. Whalen & L. Phelps (Eds.), *The human amygdala* (pp. 289–320). Oxford University Press.

Buckner, R. L., Krienen, F. M., Castellanos, A., Diaz, J. C., & Yeo, B. T. T. (2011). The organization of the human cerebellum estimated by intrinsic functional connectivity. *Journal of Neurophysiology*, 106, 2322–2345.

Bunner, K. D., & Rebec, G. V. (2016). Corticostriatal dysfunction in Huntington's disease: The basics. *Frontiers in Human Neuroscience*, 10, 317. https://doi.org/10.3389/fnhum.2016.00317

Burdakov, D., Luckman, S. M., & Verkhratsky, A. (2005). Glucose-sensing neurons of the hypothalamus. *Philosophical Transactions of the Royal Society B*, 360, 2227–2235.

Burman, D. D. (2019). Hippocampal connectivity with sensorimotor cortex during volitional finger movements: Laterality and relationship to motor learning. *PLoS One*, 14(9), e0222064. https://doi.org/10.1371/journal.pone.0222064

Burns, J., Job, D., Bastin, M. E., Whalley, H., Macgillivray, T., Johnstone, E. C., & Lawrie, S. M. (2003). Structural disconnectivity in schizophrenia: A diffusion tensor magnetic resonance imaging study. *British Journal of Psychiatry*, 182, 439–443.

Burton, L. A., Henninger, D., & Hafetz, J. (2005). Gender differences in relations of mental rotation, verbal fluency, and SAT scores to finger length ratios as hormonal indexes. *Developmental Neuropsychology*, 28, 493–505.

Burton, E. J., Barber, R., Mukaetova-Ladinska, E. B., Robson, J., Perry, R. H., Jaros, E., Kalaria, R. N., & O'Brien, J. T. (2009). Medial temporal lobe atrophy on MRI differentiates Alzheimer's disease from dementia with Lewy bodies and vascular cognitive impairment: A prospective study with pathological verification of diagnosis. *Brain*, 132, 195–203.

Burton, R., Henn, C., Lavoie, D., O'Connor, R., Perkins, C., Sweeney, K., Greaves, F., Ferguson, B., Beynon, C., Belloni, A., Musto, V., Marsden, J., & Sheron, N. (2017). A rapid evidence review of the effectiveness and cost-effectiveness of alcohol control policies: An English perspective. *The Lancet*, 389, 1558–1580.

Bush, W. S., & Moore, J. H. (2012). Chapter 11: Genome-wide association studies. *PLoS Computational Biology*, 8(12), e1002822. https://doi.org/10.1371/journal.pcbi.1002822

Bushdid, C., Magnasco, M. O., Voshall, L. B., & Keller, A. (2014). Humans can discriminate more than 1 trillion olfactory stimuli. *Science*, 343, 1370–1372.

Bushnell, M. C., Duncan, G. H., Hofbauer, R. K., Ha, B., Chen, J. I., & Carrier, B. (1999). Pain perception: Is there a role for primary somatosensory cortex? *Proceedings of the National Academy of Sciences of the USA*, 96, 7705–7709.

Butters, N. (1984). Alcoholic Korsakoff syndrome: An update. *Seminars in Neurology*, 4, 226–244.

Byne, W., Tobet, S., Mattiace, L. A., Lasco, M. S., Kemether, E., Edgar, M. A., Morgello, S., Buchsbaum, M. S., & Jones, L. B. (2001). The interstitial nuclei of the human anterior hypothalamus: An investigation of variation with sex, sexual orientation, and HIV status. *Hormones and Behavior*, 40, 86–92.

Cahill, L., Haier, R. J., Fallon, J., Alkire, M. T., Tang, C., Keator, D., Wu, J., & McGaugh, J. L. (1996). Amygdala activity at encoding correlated with long-term, free recall of emotional information. *Proceedings of the National Academy of Sciences*, 93, 8016–8021.

Caire, M. J., Reddy, V., & Varacallo, M. (2020). Physiology, synapse. In StatPearls [Internet]. StatPearls Publishing. https://www.ncbi.nlm.nih.gov/books/NBK526047/

Calne, D. B., & Langston, J. W. (1983). Aetiology of Parkinson's disease. *The Lancet*, 2 (8365–8366), 1459–1467.

Campbell, S. S., & Tobler, I. (1984). Animal sleep: A review of sleep duration across phylogeny. *Neuroscience and Biobehavioral Reviews*, 8, 269–300.

Campfield, L. A., & Smith, F. J. (1990). Transient declines in blood glucose signal meal initiation. *International Journal of Obesity*, 14, 31–41.

Cannon, J. R., Tapias, V., Na, H. M., Honick, A. S., Drolet, R. E., & Greenamyre, J. T. (2009). A highly reproducible rotenone model of Parkinson's disease. *Neurobiological Disease*, 34, 279–290.

Cannon, W. B. (1927). The James-Lange theory of emotions: A critical examination and an alternative theory. *American Journal of Psychology*, 39, 106–124.

Cannon, W. B., & Washburn, A. L. (1912). An explanation of hunger. *American Journal of Physiology*, 29, 441–454.

Cantor, J., Blanchard, R., Paterson, A. D., & Bogaert, A. F. (2002). How many gay men owe their sexual orientation to fraternal birth order? *Archives of Sexual Behavior*, 31, 63–71.

Capaday, C., Ethier, C., Van Vreeswijk, C., & Darling, W. G. (2013). On the functional organization and operational principles of the motor cortex. *Frontiers in Neural Circuits*, 7, 66. https://doi.org/10.3389/fncir.2013.00066

Capecchi, M. R. (1994). Targeted gene replacement. *Scientific American*, 270(3), 52–59.

Caporro, M., Haneef, Z., Yeh, H. J., Lenartowicz, A., Buttinelli, C., Parvizi, J., & Stern, J. M. (2012). Functional MRI of sleep spindles and K-complexes. *Clinical Neurophysiology*, 123, 303–309.

Cappelletti, M., & Wallen, K. (2016). Increasing women's sexual desire: The comparative effectiveness of estrogens and androgens. *Hormones and Behavior*, 78, 178–193.

Cardno, A. G., Marshall, E. J., Coid, B., Macdonald, A. M., Ribchester, T. R., Davies, N. J., Venturi, P., Jones, L. A., Lewis, S. W., Sham, P. C., Gottesman, I. I., Farmer, A. E., McGuffin, P., Revely, A. H., & Murray, R. M. (1999). Heritability estimates for psychotic disorders: The Maudsley twin psychosis series. *Archives of General Psychiatry*, 56, 162–168.

Carere, C., Ball, G. F., & Balthazart, J. (2007). Sex differences in projections from pre-optic area aromatase cells to the periaqueductal gray in Japanese quail. *Journal of Comparative Neurology*, 500, 894–907.

Carew, T. J., Pinsker, H. M., & Kandel, E. R. (1972). Long-term habituation of a defence withdrawal reflex in Aplysia. *Science*, 175, 451–454.

Carey, N. (2012). *The epigenetics revolution*. Icon Books.

Carhart-Harris, R. L., Muthukumaraswamy, S., Roseman, L., Kaelen, M., Droog, W., Murphy, K., Tagliazucchi, E., Schenberg, E. E., Nest, T., Orban, C., Leech, R., Williams, L. T., Williams, T. M., Bolstridge, M., Sessa, B., McGonigle, J., Sereno, M. I., Nichols, D., Hellyer, P. J., . . . Nutt, D. J. (2016). Neural correlates of the LSD experience revealed by multimodal neuroimaging. *Proceedings of the New York Academy of Sciences of the USA*, 113, 4853–4858.

Carlezon, W. A., Devine, D. P., & Wise, R. A. (1995). Habit-forming actions of nomifensine in nucleus accumbens. *Psychopharmacology*, 122, 194–197.

Carlson, A. J. (1912). The relation between the contractions of the empty stomach and the sensation of hunger. *American Journal of Physiology*, 31, 175–192.

Carlsson, A., & Lindqvist, M. (1963). Effect of chlorpromazine or haloperidol on the formation of 3-methoxtyramine and normetanephrine in mouse brain. *Acta Pharmacologica et Toxicologica* 20, 140–144.

Carmo, C., Naia, L., Lopes, C., & Rego, A. C. (2018). Mitochondrial dysfunction in Huntington's disease. *Advances in Experimental and Medical Biology*, 1049, 59–83.

Carr, G. V., & Lucki, I. (2011). The role of serotonin receptor subtypes in treating depression: A review of animal studies. *Psychopharmacology*, 213, 265–287.

Carreiro, A. L., Dhillon, J., Gordon, S., Higgins, K. A., Jacobs, A. G., McArthur, B. M., Redan, B. W., Rivera, R. L., Schmidt, L. R., & Mattes, R. D. (2016). The macronutrients, appetite, and energy intake. *Annual Review of Nutrition*, 36, 73–103.

Caruana, F., Avanzini, P., Gozzo, F., Francione, S., Cardinale, F., & Rizzolatti, G. (2015). Mirth and laughter elicited by electrical stimulation of the human anterior cingulate cortex. *Cortex*, 71, 323–331. https://doi.org/10.1016/j.cortex.2015.07.024.

Casalone, C., & Hope, J. (2018). Atypical and classic bovine spongiform encephalopathy. *Handbook of Clinical Neurology*, 153, 121–134.

Caspers, S., Zilles, K., Laird, A. R., & Eickhoff, S. B. (2010). ALE meta-analysis of action observation and imitation in the human brain. *NeuroImage*, 50, 1148–1167.

Caspi, A., Sugden, K., Moffitt, T. E., Taylor, A., Craig, I. W., Harrington, H., McClay, J., Mill, J., Martin, J., Braithwaite, A., & Poulton, R. (2003). Influence of life stress on depression: Moderation by a polymorphism in the 5-HTT gene. *Science*, 301, 386–389.

Cassanari, V., & Pagni, C. A. (1969). *Central pain: A neurosurgical survey*. Harvard University Press.

Castellucci, V. F., & Schacher, S. (1990). Synaptic plasticity and behavioral modifications in the marine mollusk Aplysia. *Progress in Brain Research*, 86, 105–115.

Catani, M. (2017). A little man of some importance. *Brain*, 140, 3055–3061.

Catani, M., & Mesulam, M. (2008). The arcuate fasciculus and the disconnection theme in language and aphasia: History and current state. *Cortex*, 44, 953–961.

Caulo, M., Van Hecke, J., Toma, L., Ferretti, A., Tartaro, A., Colosimo, C., Romani, G. L., & Uncini, A. (2005). Functional MRI study of diencephalic amnesia in Wernicke-Korsakoff syndrome. *Brain*, 128, 1584–1594.

Caviston, J. P., & Holzbaur, E. L. (2009). Huntingtin as an essential integrator of intracellular vesicular trafficking. *Trends in Cell Biology*, 19, 147–155.

Celec, P., Ostatnikova, D., & Hodosy, J. (2015). On the effects of testosterone on brain behavioral functions. *Frontiers in Neuroscience*, 9, 1–17. https://doi.org/10.3389/fnins.2015.00012

Cerminara, N. L., & Apps, R. (2011). Behavioural significance of cerebellar modules. *Cerebellum*, 10, 484–494.

Chai, L. R., Matter, M. G., Blank, I. A., Fedorenko, E., & Bassett, D. S. (2016). Functional network dynamics of the language system. *Cerebral Cortex*, 26, 4148–4159.

Chalmers, D. J. (2010). *The character of consciousness*. Oxford University Press.

Chan, O., & Sherwin, R. S. (2014). Is there cross talk between portal and hypothalamic glucose-sensing circuits? *Diabetes*, 63, 2617–2619.

Chan, S.-H., Ryan, L., & Bever, T. G. (2013). Role of the striatum in language: Syntactic and conceptual sequencing. *Brain and Language*, 125, 283–294.

Chatzittofis, A., Nordstrom, P., Hellström, C., Arver, S., Åsberg, M., & Jokinen, J. (2013). CSF 5-HIAA, cortisol and DHEAS levels in suicide attempters. *European Neuropsychopharmacology*, 23, 1280–1287.

Chaudhari, N., & Roper, S. D. (2010). The cell biology of taste. *Journal of Cell Biology*, 190, 285–296.

Chauvel, P. Y., Rey, M., Buser, P., & Bancaud, J. (1996). What stimulation of the supplementary motor area in humans tells about its functional organization. *Advances in Neurology*, 70, 199–209.

Chemelli, R. M., Wilioe, J. T., & Sinton, C. M. (1999). Narcolepsy in orexin knockout mice: Molecular genetics of sleep regulation. *Cell*, 98, 437–451.

Chen, H., & Ritz, B. (2018). The search for environmental causes of Parkinson's disease: Moving forward. *Journal of Parkinson's Disease*, 8, S9–S17.

Chen, I., & Lui, F. (2020). Neuroanatomy, neuron action potential. In StatPearls [Internet]. StatPearls Publishing. https://www.ncbi.nlm.nih.gov/books/NBK546639/

Chen, J. Y., Wang, E. A., Cepeda, C., & Levine, M. S. (2013). Dopamine imbalance in Huntington's disease: A mechanism for the lack of behavioral flexibility. *Frontiers in Neuroscience*, 7, 114. https://doi.org/10.3389/fnins.2013.00114

Chen, W. W., Zhang, X., & Huang, W. J. (2016). Role of physical exercise in Alzheimer's disease. *Biomedical Reports*, 4, 403–407.

Chen, X. Q., & Mobley, W. C. (2019). Exploring the pathogenesis of Alzheimer disease in basal forebrain cholinergic neurons: Converging insights from alternative hypotheses. *Frontiers in Neuroscience*, 13, 446. https://doi.org/10.3389/fnins.2019.00446

Chi, J. G., Dooling, E. C., & Gilles, F. H. (1977). Left, right asymmetries of the temporal speech areas of the human fetus. *Archives of Neurology*, 34, 346–348.

Childress, A. R., McLellan, T., & O'Brien, C. P. (1986). Abstinent opiate abusers exhibit conditioned craving, conditioned withdrawal and reductions in both through extinction. *British Journal of Addiction*, 81, 655–660.

Cho, K. (2001). Chronic 'jet lag' produces temporal lobe atrophy and spatial cognitive deficits. *Nature Neuroscience*, 4, 567–568.

Cho, K., Ennaceur, A., Cole, J. C., & Suh, C. K. (2000). Chronic jet lag produces cognitive deficits. *Journal of Neuroscience*, 20, RC66.

Choi, I. H., Kim, K. H., Jung, H., Yoon, S. J., Kim, S. W., & Kim, T. B. (2011). Second to fourth digit ratio: A predictor of adult penile length. *Asian Journal of Andrology*, 13, 710–714.

Chokroverty, S., & Montagna, P. (2009). Sleep, breathing and neurological disorders. In S. Chokroverty (Ed.), *Sleep disorders medicine* (pp. 436–498). Saunders Elsevier.

Chong, K. K., Dunlap, A. G., Kacsoh, D., B., & Liu, R. C. (2019). Experience-dependent coding of frequency-modulated trajectories by offsets in auditory cortex. bioRxiv. https://doi.org/10.1101/613448

Choquet, H., & Meyre, D. (2011). Genetics of obesity: What have we learned? *Current Genomics*, 12, 169–179.

Chouinard, P. A., & Paus, T. (2006). The primary motor and premotor areas of the human cerebral cortex. *The Neuroscientist*, 12,143–152.

Chow, M. S., Wu, S. L., Webb, S. E., Gluskin, K, & Yew, D. T. (2017). Functional magnetic resonance imaging and the brain: A brief review. *World Journal of Radiology*, 9, 5–9.

Christ, S. E., Steiner, R. D., Grange, D. K., Abrams, R. A., & White, D. A. (2006). Inhibitory control in children with phenylketonuria. *Developmental Neuropsychology*, 30, 845–864.

Christensen, P. B., Jensen, T. S., Tsiropoulos, I., Sorensen, T., Kjar, M., Hojer-Pedersen, E., Rasmussen, M. J. K., & Lehfeldt, E. (1998). Mortality and survival in myasthenia gravis: A Danish population based study. *Journal of Neurology, Neurosurgery and Psychiatry*, 64, 78–83.

Christian, C. A., Herbert, A. G., Holt, R. L., Peng, K., Sherwood, K. D., Pangratz-Fuehrer, S., Rudolph, U., & Huguenard, J. R. (2013). Endogenous positive allosteric modulation of GABAA receptors by diazepam binding inhibitor. *Neuron*, 78, 1063–1074.

Christiansen, T. (2020). *Morphine overdose: Signs, symptoms and treatment*. The Recovery Village. https://www.therecoveryvillage.com/morphine-addiction/morphine-overdose/

Chung, W. C., De Vries, G. J., & Swaab, D. F. (2002). Sexual differentiation of the bed nucleus of the stria terminalis in humans may extend into adulthood. *Journal of Neuroscience*, 22, 1027–1033.

Ciccarone, D. (2011). Stimulant abuse: Pharmacology, cocaine, methamphetamine, treatment, attempts at pharmacotherapy. *Primary Care*, 38, 41–58.

Ciccocioppo, R. (2013). Genetically selected alcohol preferring rats to model human alcoholism. *Current Topics in Behavioral Neurosciences*, 13, 251–269.

Cipriani, A., Furukawa, T. A., Salanti, G., Chaimani, A., Atkinson, L. Z., Ogawa, Y., Leucht, S., Ruhe, H. G., Turner, E. H., Higgins, J. P. T., Egger, M., Takeshima, N., Hayasaka, Y., Imai, H., Shinohara, K., Tajika, A., Ioannidis, J. P. A., & Geddes, J. R. (2018). Comparative efficacy and acceptability of 21 antidepressant drugs for the acute treatment of adults with major depressive disorder: A systematic review and network meta-analysis. *The Lancet*, 391(10128), 1357–1366.

Cipriani, A., Furukawa, T. A., Salanti, G., Geddes, J. R., Higgins, J. P. T., Churchill, R., Watanabe, N., Nakagawa, A., Omori, I. M., McGuire, H., Tansella, M., & Barbui, C. (2009). Comparative efficacy and acceptability of 12 new-generation antidepressants: A multiple-treatments meta-analysis. *The Lancet*, 373, 746–758.

Cirelli, C., Gutierrez, C. M., & Tononi, G. (2004). Extensive and divergent effects of sleep and wakefulness on brain gene expression. *Neuron*, 41, 35–43.

Clark, D. L., Boutros, N. N., & Mendez, M. F. (2005). *The brain and behavior*. Cambridge University Press.

Clark, J. T., Kalra, P. S., Crowley, W. R., & Kalra, S. P. (1984). Neuropeptide Y and human pancreatic polypeptide stimulate feeding behavior in rats. *Endocrinology*, 115, 427–429.

Clarke, P. M. R., Henzi, S. P., & Barrett, L. (2012). Estrous synchrony in a nonseasonal breeder: Adaptive strategy or population process? *Behavioral Ecology*, 23, 573–581.

Coenen, V. A., Schmuacher, L. V., Kaller, C., Schlaepfer, T. E., Reinacher, P. C., Egger, K., Urbach, H., & Reisert, M. (2018). The anatomy of the human medial forebrain bundle: Ventral tegmental area connections to reward-associated subcortical and frontal lobe regions. *NeuroImage: Clinical*, 18, 770–783.

Cohen, A. J. (1992). Fluoxetine-induced yawning and anorgasmia reversed by cyproheptadine treatment. *Journal of Clinical Psychiatry*, 53, 174.

Cohen, N. J., & Corkin, S. (1981). The amnesic patient H.M.: Learning and retention of a cognitive skill. *Society for Neuroscience Abstracts*, 7, 235.

Cohen, N. J., & Squire, L. R. (1980). Preserved learning and retention of pattern-analysing skill in amnesia: Dissocia-

of knowing how and knowing that. *Science*, 210, 207–210.

Cola-Conde, C. J., Marty, G., Maestu, F., Ortiz, T., Munar, E., Fernandez, A., Roca, M., Rossello, J., & Quesney, F. (2004). Activation of the prefrontal cortex in the human visual aesthetic perception. *Proceedings of the National Academy of Sciences of the USA*, 101, 6321–6325.

Colcombe, S. J., Erickson, K. I., Scalf, P. E., Kim, J. S., Prakash, R., McAuley, E., Elavsky, S., Marquez, D. X., Hu, L., & Kramer, A. K. (2006). Aerobic exercise training increases brain volume in aging humans. *Journal of Gerontology: Series A: Biological Sciences and Medical Sciences*, 11, 1166–1170.

Coleman, D. L. (1973). Effects of parabiosis of obese with diabetes and normal mice. *Diabetologia*, 9, 294–298.

Coleman, D. L. (1978). Obese and diabetes: Two mutant genes causing diabetes-obesity syndromes in mice. *Diabetologia*, 14, 141–148.

Collet, C., Vernet-Maury, E., Delhomme, G., & Dittmar, A. (1997). Autonomic nervous system response patterns specificity to basic emotions. *Journal of the Autonomic Nervous System*, 62, 45–57.

Collings, V. B. (1974). Human taste response as a function of locos of stimulation on the tongue and soft palate. *Perception and Psychophysics*, 16, 169–174.

Combarieu, J. (1910). *Music, its laws and evolution*. Cornell University Library.

Conrad, C. D. (2008). Chronic stress-induced hippocampal vulnerability: The glucocorticoid vulnerability hypothesis. *Reviews in Neuroscience*, 19, 395–411.

Contet, C., Kieffer, B. L., & Befort, K. (2004). Mu opioid receptor: a gateway to drug addiction. *Current Opinion in Neurobiology*, 14, 370–378.

Cook, N., Shepherd, A., & Boore, J. (2021). *Essentials of anatomy and physiology for nursing practice* (2nd ed.). SAGE.

Cookson, M. R. (2003). Pathways to Parkinsonism. *Neuron*, 37, 7–10.

Cooper, R. M., & Zubek, J. P. (1958). Effects of enriched and restricted early environments on the learning ability of bright and dull rats. *Canadian Journal of Psychology*, 12, 159–164.

Cooper, S. J. (2005). Donald O. Hebb's synapse and learning rule: A history and commentary. *Neuroscience and Biobehavioral Reviews*, 28, 851–874.

Coppen, E. M., & Roos, R. A. C. (2017). Current pharmacological approaches to reduce chorea in Huntington's disease. *Drugs*, 77, 29–46.

Corballis, M. C. (2003). From mouth to hand: Gesture, speech, and the evolution of right-handedness. *Behavioral and Brain Sciences*, 26, 199–208.

Coren, S., Ward, L. M., & Enns, J. T. (2004). *Sensation and perception*. John Wiley.

Corfield, E. C., Yang, Y., Martin, N. G., & Nyholt, D. R. (2017). A continuum of genetic liability for minor and major depression. *Translational Psychiatry*, 7, e1131. https://doi.org/10.1038/tp.2017.99

Corkin, S. (1984). Lasting consequences of bilateral medial temporal lobectomy: Clinical course and experimental findings in HM. *Seminars in Neurology*, 4, 249–259.

Corkin, S. (2002). What's new with amnesic patient H.M.? *Nature Reviews Neuroscience*, 3, 153–160.

Corkin, S. (2013). *Permanent present tense: The man with no memory and what he taught the world*. Allen Lane.

Corkin, S., Milner, B., & Rasmussen, T. (1970). Somatosensory thresholds: Contrasting effects of post-central and posterior parietal lobe excisions. *Archives of Neurology*, 23, 41–58.

Corrow, S. L., Dalrymple, K. A., & Barton, J. J. S. (2016). Prosopagnosia: Current perspectives. *Eye Brain*, 8, 165–175.

Corti, O., Lesage, S., & Brice, A. (2011). What genetics tells us about the causes and mechanisms of Parkinson's disease. *Physiological Review*, 91, 1161–1218.

Costafreda, S. G., Brammer, M. J., David, A. S., & Fu, C. H. (2008). Predictors of amygdala activation during the processing of emotional stimuli: A meta-analysis of 385 PET and fMRI studies. *Brain Research Reviews*, 58, 57–70.

Cotzias, G. C., Van Woert, M. H., & Schiffer, L. M. (1967.) Aromatic acid amino acids and modification of Parkinsonism. *New England Journal of Medicine*, 276, 374–379.

Coupland, C., Hill, T., Morriss, R., Moore, M., Arthur, A., & Hippisley-Cox, J. (2018). Antidepressant use and risk of adverse outcomes in people aged 20–64 years: Cohort study using a primary care database. *BMC Medicine*, 16, 1–24. https://doi.org/10.1186/s12916-018-1022-x

Courtiol, E., & Wilson, D. A. (2015). The olfactory thalamus: Unanswered questions about the role of the mediodorsal thalamic nucleus in olfaction. *Frontiers in Neural Circuits*, 9, 1–8.

Cowan, W. M. (1978). Preface. In W. M. Cowan, Z. W. Hall, & E. R. Kandel (Eds.), *Annual review of neuroscience* (Vol. 1). Annual Reviews.

Coyle, J. T. & Schwarcz, R. (1976). Lesion of striatal neurons with kainic acid provides a model for Huntington's chorea. *Nature*, 263, 244–246.

Craufurd, D., MacLeod, R., Frontali, M., Quarrell, O., Bijlsma, E. K., Davis, M., Hjermind, L. E., Lahiri, N., Mandich, P., Martinez, A., Tibben, A., & Roos, R. A.; Working Group on Genetic Counselling and Testing of the European Huntington's Disease Network (EHDN). (2015). Diagnostic genetic testing for Huntington's disease. *Practical Neurology*, 15, 80–84.

Creese, I., Burt, D. R., & Snyder, S. (1976). Dopamine receptor binding predicts clinical and pharmacological properties of antischizophrenic drugs. *Science*, 194, 481–483.

Crick, F. (1994). *The astonishing hypothesis*. Scribner.

Crick, F., & Mitchison, G. (1983). The function of dream sleep. *Nature*, 304, 111–114.

Crocq, M.-A. (2007). Historical and cultural aspects of man's relationship with addictive drugs. *Dialogues in Clinical Neuroscience*, 9, 355–361.

Cross, A. J., Crow, T. J., & Owen, F. (1986). Post-mortem studies of dopaminergic function in schizophrenia. In G. N. Woodruff, J. A. Poat, & P. J. Roberts (Eds.), *Dopaminergic systems and their regulation* (pp. 273–284). Palgrave Macmillan.

Crow, T. J. (1985). The two-syndrome concept: Origins and current status. *Schizophrenia Bulletin*, 11, 471–485.

Cryan, J. F., & Sweeney, F. F. (2011). The age of anxiety: Role of animal models of anxiolytic action in drug discovery. *British Journal of Pharmacology*, 164, 1129–1161.

Cuellar, A. K., Johnson, S. L., & Winters, R. (2005). *Clinical Psychology Review*, 25, 307–339.

Culliton, B. J. (1976). Psychosurgery: National commission issues surprisingly favorable report. *Science*, 194, 299–301.

Cummings, D. E., Purnell, J. Q., Frayo, R. S., Schmidova, K., Wisse, B. E., & Weigle, D. S. (2001). A preprandial rise in plasma ghrelin levels suggests a role in meal initiation in humans. *Diabetes*, 50, 1714–1719.

Curran, H. V., Freeman, T. P., Mokrysz, C., Lewis, D. A., Morgan, C. J. A., & Parsons, L. H. (2016). Keep off the grass? Cannabis, cognition and addiction. *Nature Reviews Neuroscience*, 17, 293–306.

Curtis, C. E., & D'Esposito, M. (2003). Persistent activity in the prefrontal cortex during working memory. *Trends in Cognitive Sciences*, 7, 415–423.

Curzon, G. (1990). How reserpine and chlorpromazine act: The impact of key discoveries on the history of psychopharmacology. *Trends in Pharmacological Sciences*, 11, 61–63.

Cytowic, R. E. (1993). *The man who tasted shapes*. Putnam.

Czeisler, C. A., Duffy, J. F., Shanahan, T. L., Brown, E. N., Mitchell, J. F., Rimmer, D. W., Ronda, J. M., Silva, E. J., Allan, J. S., Emens, J. S., Dijk, D. J., & Kronauer, R. E. (1999). Stability, precision and near 24 hour period of the human circadian pacemaker. *Science*, 284, 2177–2181.

Daae, E., Feragen, K. B., Waehre, A., Nermoen, I., & Falhammar, H. (2020). Sexual orientation in individuals with congenital adrenal hyperplasia: A systematic review. *Frontiers in Behavioral Neuroscience*, 14, 38. https://doi.org/10.3389/fnbeh.2020.00038

Dabbs, J. M., Frady, R. L., Carr, T. S., & Besch, N. F. (1987). Saliva testosterone and criminal violence in young adult prison inmates. *Psychosomatic Medicine*, 49, 174–182.

Dabbs, J. M., & Morris, R. (1990). Testosterone, social class, and antisocial behavior in a sample of 4,462 men. *Psychological Science*, 1, 209–211.

Dalrymple, K. A., Corrow, S., Yonas, A., & Duchaine, B. (2012). Developmental prosopagnosia in childhood. *Cognitive Neuropsychology*, 29, 393–418.

Damasio, A. R. (2000). A neural basis for sociopathy. *Archives of General Psychiatry*, 57, 128–129.

Damasio, A. R., Tranel, D., & Damasio, H. (1990a). Individuals with sociopathic behavior caused by frontal damage fail to respond autonomically to social stimuli. *Behavioral Brain Research*, 41, 81–94.

Damasio, A. R., Tranel, D., & Damasio, H. (1990b). Face agnosia and the neural substrates of memory. *Annual Review of Neuroscience*, 13, 89–109.

Damasio, H., Grabowski, T., Frank, R., Galaburda, A. M., & Damasio, A. R. (1994). The return of Phineas Gage: Clues about the brain from the skull of a famous person. *Science*, 264, 1102–1105.

Damasio, H. C. (1991). Neuroanatomy of the frontal lobes in vitro: A comment on methodology. In H. S. Levin, H. M. Eisenberg, & A. L. Benton (Eds.), *Frontal Lobe Function and Dysfunction* (pp. 92–121). Oxford University Press.

Damassa, D. A., Smith, E. R., Tennent, B., & Davidson, J. M. (1977). The relationship between circulating testosterone levels and male sexual behavior in rats. *Hormones and Behavior*, 8, 275–286.

Dang-Vu, T. T., Schabus, M., Desseilles, M., Sterpenich, V., Bonjean, M., & Maquat, M. (2010). Functional neuroimaging insights into the physiology of human sleep. *Sleep*, 33, 1589–1603.

Daniel, D. G., Weinberger, D. R., Jones, D. W., Zigun, J. R., Coppola, R., Handel, S., Bigelow, L. B., Goldberg, T. E., Berman, K. F., & Kleinman, J. E. (1991). The effect of amphetamine on regional cerebral blood flow during cognitive activation in schizophrenia. *Journal of Neuroscience*, 11, 1907–1917.

Daniel, R., & Pollmann, S. (2014). A universal role of the ventral striatum in reward-based learning: Evidence from human studies. *Neurobiology of Learning and Memory*, 114, 90–100.

Daniel, T. A., Katz, J. S., & Robinson, J. L. (2016). Delayed match-to-sample in working memory: A BrainMap meta-analysis. *Biological Psychology*, 120, 10–20.

Darke, S., & Zador, D., (2014). Fatal heroin "overdose": A review. *Addiction*, 91, 1765–1772.

Darwin, C. R. (1859). *On the origin of species by means of natural selection.* John Murray.

Das, P., Rai, A., Chopra, A., & Dewan, V. (2012). Sertraline-induced hypersexuality in a patient taking bupropion. *The Primary Care Companion for CNS Disorders*, 14(2), PCC.11l01232. https://doi.org/10.4088/PCC.11l01232

Dauer, W., & Przedborski, S. (2003). Parkinson's disease: Mechanisms and models. *Neuron*, 39, 889–909.

Daum, I., Schugens, M. M., Ackerman, H., Lutzenberger, W., Dichgans, J., & Birbaumer, N. (1993). Classical conditioning after cerebellar lesions in humans. *Behavioral Neuroscience*, 107, 748–756.

Davidson, J. M. (1980). The psychobiology of sexual experience. In J. M. Davidson & R. J. Davidson (Eds.), *The psychobiology of consciousness* (pp. 271–332). Plenum Press.

Davidson, J. M., Camargo, C. A., & Smith, E. R. (1979). Effects of androgens on sexual behavior of hypogonadal men. *Journal of Clinical Endocrinology and Metabolism*, 48, 955–958.

Davies, A. (2018). When do babies smile? The Bump. https://www.thebump.com/a/when-do-babies-smile

Davies, J., Rae, T. C., & Montagu, L. (2017). Long-term benzodiazepine and Z-drugs use in England: A survey of general practice. *British Journal of General Practice*, 67, e609–e613. https://doi.org/10.3399/bjgp17X691865

Davis, H. P., Rosenzweig, M. R., Becker, L. A., & Sather, K. J. (1988). Biological psychology's relationships to psychology and neuroscience. *American Psychologist*, 43, 359–371.

Davis, J., Eyre, H., Jacka, F. N., Dodd, S., Dean, O., McEwen, S., Debnath, M.,

McGrath, J., Maes, M., Amminger, P., McGorry, P. D., Pantelis, C., & Berk, M. (2016). A review of vulnerability and risks for schizophrenia: Beyond the two hit hypothesis. *Neuroscience and Biobehavioral Reviews*, 65, 185–194.

Davis, J. D., Campbell, C. S., Gallagher, R. J., & Zurakov, M. A. (1971). Disappearance of a humoral satiety factor during food deprivation. *Journal of Comparative and Physiological Psychology*, 75, 476–482.

Davis, K. L., Kahn, R. S., Ko, G., & Davidson, M. (1991). Dopamine in schizophrenia: A review and reconceptualization. *American Journal of Psychiatry*, 148, 1474–1486.

Davis, M. (1992). The role of the amygdala in fear and anxiety. *Annual Review of Neuroscience*, 15, 353–375.

Dayalu, P., & Albin, R. L. (2015). Huntington disease: Pathogenesis and treatment. *Neurologic Clinics*, 33, 101–114.

de Lecea, L., Kilduff, T. S., Peyron, C., ... Sutcliffe, J. G. (1998). The hypocretins: Hypothalamus-specific peptides with neuroexcitatory activity. *Proceedings of the National Academy of Sciences of the USA*, 95, 322–327.

de Melo Coelho, F. G., Vital, T. M., Stein, A. M., Arantes, F. J., Rueda, A. V., Camarini, R., Teodorov, E., & Santos-Galduróz, R. F. (2014). Acute aerobic exercise increases brain-derived neurotrophic factor levels in elderly with Alzheimer's disease. *Journal of Alzheimer's Disease*, 39, 401–408.

de Oliveira-Souza, R. (2012). The human extrapyramidal system. *Medical Hypotheses*, 79, 843–852.

de Oliveira-Souza, R., Paranhos, T., Moll, J., & Grafman, J. (2019). Gender and hemispheric asymmetries in acquired sociopathy. *Frontiers in Psychology*, 10, 346. https://doi.org/10.3389/fpsyg.2019.00346

De Rijk, M. C., Tzourio, C., Breteler, M. M., Dartigues, J. F., Amaducci, L., Lopez-Pousa, S., Manubens-Bertran, J. M., Alperovitch, A., & Rocca, W. A. (1997). Prevalence of parkinsonism and Parkinson's disease in Europe: The EUROPARKINSON Collaborative Study. European Community Concerted Action on the epidemiology of Parkinson's disease.

Journal of Neurology, Neurosurgery, and Psychiatry, 62, 10–15.

De Valois, R. L., & De Valois, K. K. (1988). *Spatial vision*. Oxford University Press.

De Vries, T. J., & Shippenberg, T. S. (2002). Neural systems underlying opiate addiction. *Journal of Neuroscience*, 22, 3321–3325.

Dean, D. C., Jerskey, B. A., Chen, K., Protas, H., Thiyyagura, P., Roontiva, A., O'Muircheartaigh, J., Dirks, H., Waskiewicz, N., Lehman, K., Siniard, A. L., Turk, M. N., Hua, X., Madsen, S. K., Thompson, P. M., Fleisher, A. S., Huentelman, M. J., Deoni, S. C., & Reiman, E. M. (2014). Brain differences in infants at differential genetic risk for late-onset Alzheimer disease: A cross-sectional imaging study. *JAMA Neurology*, 71, 11–22.

Deary, I. J., Johnson, W., & Houlihan, L. M. (2009). Genetic foundations of human intelligence. *Human Genetics*, 126, 215–232.

Deary, I. J., Pattie, A., & Starr, J. M. (2013). The stability of intelligence from age 11 to age 90 years: The Lothian birth cohort of 1921. *Psychological Science*, 24, 2361–2368.

Deecke, L., & Kornhuber, H. H. (1978). An electrical sign of participation of the mesial 'supplementary' motor cortex in human voluntary finger movement. *Brain Research*, 159, 473–476.

DeFries, J. C., & Alarcón, M. (1996). Genetics of specific reading disability. *Mental Retardation and Developmental Disabilities Research Reviews*, 2, 39–47.

Dejean, C., Sitko, M., Giardeau, P., Bennabi, A., Caillé, S., Cador, M., Boraud T., & Le Moine, C. (2017). Memories of opiate withdrawal emotional states correlate with specific gamma oscillations in the nucleus accumbens. *Neuropsychopharmacology*, 42, 1157–1168.

Delgado, P. L. (2000). Depression: The case for a monoamine deficiency. *The Journal of Clinical Psychiatry*, 61, 7–11.

Dement, W. C. (1976). *Some must watch while some must sleep*. San Francisco Book Company.

Dement, W. C., & Kleitman, N. (1957). Cyclic variations in EEG during sleep and their relation to eye movements, body motility and dreaming. *Electroen-*

cephalography and Clinical Neuropsychology, 9, 673–690.

Démonet, J. F., Taylor, M. J., & Chaix Y. (2004). Developmental dyslexia. *Lancet.* 363(9419), 1451–1460.

Deneau, G., Yanagita, T., & Seevers, M. H. (1969). Self-administration of psychoactive substances by the monkey. *Psychopharmacologia*, 16, 30–48.

Deng, H., Xiao, X., & Wang, Z. (2016). Periaqueductal gray neuronal activities underlie different aspects of defensive behaviors. *Journal of Neuroscience*, 36, 7580–7588.

Derlet, R. W., Tseng, J. C., & Albertson, T. E. (1992). Potentiation of cocaine and d-amphetamine toxicity with caffeine. *The American Journal of Emergency Medicine*, 10, 211–216.

Desmond, A., & Moore, J. (1991). *Darwin.* Michael Joseph.

Dessens, A. B., Slijper, F. M. E., & Drop, S. L. S. (2005). Gender dysphoria and gender change in chromosomal females with congenital adrenal hyperplasia. *Archives of Sexual Behavior*, 34, 389–397.

DeTure, M. A., & Dickson, D. W. (2019). The neuropathological diagnosis of Alzheimer's disease. *Molecular Neurodegeneration*, 14, 32. https://doi.org/10.1186/s13024-019-0333-5

Deutsch, J. A., & Gonzalez, M. F. (1980). Gastric nutrient content signals satiety. *Behavioral and Neural Biology*, 30, 113–116.

Devane, W. A., Hanus, L., Breuer, A., Pertwee, R. G., Stevenson, L. A., Griffin, G., Gibson, D., Mandelbaum, A., Etinger, A., & Mechoulam, R. (1992). Isolation and structure of a brain constituent that binds to the cannabinoid receptor. *Science*, 258, 1946–1949.

Devlin, J. T., Raley, J., Tunbridge, E., Lanary, K., Floyer-Lea, A., Narain, C., Cohen, I., Behrens, T., Jezzard, P., Matthews, P. M., & Moore, D. R. (2003). Functional asymmetry for auditory processing in human auditory cortex. *Journal of Neuroscience*, 23, 11516–11522.

DeWitt, I., & Rauschecker, J. P. (2013). Wernicke's area revisited: Parallel streams and word processing. *Brain and Language*, 127, 181–191.

Dewsbury, D. A. (1991). 'Psychobiology'. *American Psychologist*, 46, 198–205.

Dharmarajan, T. S., & Gunturu, S. (2009). Alzheimer's disease: A healthcare burden of epidemic proportion. *American Health and Drug Benefits*, 2, 39–47.

Di Chiara, G., & Imperto, A. (1988). Drugs abused by humans preferentially increase synaptic dopamine concentrations in the mesolimbic system of freely moving rats. *Proceedings of the National Academy of Sciences*, 85, 5274–5284.

Diamond, M. C., Scheibel, A. B., Murphy, G. M., & Harvey, T. (1985). On the brain of a scientist: Albert Einstein. *Experimental Neurology*, 88, 198–204.

Dichter, G. S. (2012). Functional magnetic resonance imaging of autism spectrum disorders. *Dialogues in Clinical Neuroscience*, 14, 319–351.

Dick, D. M. (2011). Gene-environment interaction in psychological traits and disorders. *Annual Review of Clinical Psychology*, 7, 383–409.

Dickson, D. W. (2018). Neuropathology of Parkinson disease. *Parkinsonism and Related Disorders*, 46(Suppl. 1), S30–S33.

Dickson, D. W., Crystal, H. A., Bevona, C., Honer, W., Vincent I., & Davies P. (1995). Correlations of synaptic and pathological markers with cognition of the elderly. *Neurobiology of Aging*, 16, 285–298.

Dimitrijevic, M. R., Gerasimenko, Y., & Pinter, M. M. (1998). Evidence for a spinal central pattern generator in humans. *Annals of the New York Academy of Sciences*, 860, 360–376.

DiNuzzo, M., & Nedergaard, M. (2017). Brain energetic during the sleep-wake cycle. *Current Opinion in Neurobiology*, 47, 65–72.

Dittmann, R. W., Kappes, M. E., & Kappes, M. H. (1992). Sexual behavior in adolescent and adult females with congenital adrenal hyperplasia. *Psychoneuroendocrinology*, 17, 153–170.

Dityatev, A. E., & Bolshakov, V. Y. (2005). Amygdala, long-term potentiation, and fear conditioning. *The Neuroscientist*, 11, 75–88.

Dobzhansky, T. (1973). Nothing in biology makes sense except in the light of evolution. *American Biology Teacher*, 35, 125–129.

Donovan, C. M., & Bohland, M. A. (2009). Hypoglycemic detection at the portal vein. *Diabetes*, 58, 21–23.

Dorsey, E. R., Sherer, T., Okun, M. S., & Bloem, B. R. (2018). The emerging evidence of the Parkinson pandemic. *Journal of Parkinson's Disease*, 8, S3–S8.

Doya, K. (1999). What are the computations of the cerebellum, the basal ganglia and the cerebral cortex? *Neural Networks*, 12, 961–974.

Doyon, J., Bellec, P., Amsel, R., Penhune, V., Monchi, O., Carrier, J., Lehéricy, S., & Benali, H. (2009). Contributions of the basal ganglia and functionally related brain structures to motor learning. *Behavioral Brain Research*, 199, 61–75.

Drachman, D. A., & Leavitt, J. (1974). Human memory and the cholinergic system: A relationship to ageing? *Archives of Neurology*, 30, 113–121.

Driver, J., & Mattingley, J. B. (1998). Parietal neglect and visual awareness. *Nature Neuroscience*, 1, 17–22.

Dronkers, N. F., Wilkins, D. P., Van Valin, R. D., & Jaeger, J. J. (2004). Lesion analysis of the brain areas involved in language comprehension. *Cognition*, 92, 145–177.

Dror, O. E. (2013). The Cannon-Bard thalamic theory of emotions: A brief genealogy and reappraisal. *Emotion Review*, 6, 13–20.

Duarte, A., Henson, R. N., Knight, R. T., Emery, T., & Graham, K. S. (2010). Orbito-frontal cortex is necessary for temporal context memory. *Journal of Cognitive Neuroscience*, 22, 1819–1831.

Dubin, A. E., & Patapoutian, A. (2010). Nociceptors: The sensors of the pain pathway. *Journal of Clinical Investigation*, 120, 3760–3772.

Dudel, J. (1978). Excitation of nerve and muscle. In R. F. Schmidt (Ed.), *Fundamentals of neurophysiology* (pp. 19–71). Springer-Verlag.

Dumas, E. O., & Pollock, G. M. (2008). Opioid tolerance development: A pharmacokinetic/pharmacodynamic perspective. *The AAPS Journal*, 10, 537–551.

Dutton, D. G., & Aron, A. P. (1974). Some evidence for heightened sexual attraction under conditions of high anxiety. *Journal of Personality and Social Psychology*, 30, 510–517.

Duyao, M. P., Auerbach, A. B., Ryan, A., Persichetti, F., Barnes, G. T., McNeil, S. M., Ge, P., Vonsattel, J. P., Gusella, J. F., & Joyner, A. L. (1995). Inactivation of the mouse Huntington's disease gene homologue Hdh. *Science*, 269, 407–410.

Duyckaerts, C., Delatour, B., & Potier, M.-C. (2009). Classification and basic pathology of Alzheimer's disease. *Acta Neuropathologica*, 118, 5–36.

Eastman, C. I., & Burgess, H. J. (2009). How to travel the world without jet lag. *Sleep Medicine Clinics*, 4, 241–255.

Eaton, W. W., Anthony, J. C., Gallo, J., Cai, G., Tien, A., Romanoski, A., Lyketsos, C., & Chen, L.-S. (1997). Natural history of DIS/DSM major depression: The Baltimore ECA follow-up. *Archives of General Psychiatry*, 54, 993–999.

Eaton, W. W., Bienvenu, O. J., & Miloyan, B. (2018). Specific phobias. *The Lancet Psychiatry*, 5, 678–686.

Ebbinghaus, H. (1885). *Memory: A contribution to experimental psychology*. (H. A. Ruger & C. E. Bussenius, Trans. 1913.) Teachers College, Columbia University.

Ebner, T. J., Hendrix, C. M., & Pasalar, S. (2009). Past, present, and emerging principles in the neural encoding of movement. *Advances in Experimental and Medical Biology*, 629, 127–137. https://doi.org/10.1007/978-0-387-77064-2_7

Eccles, J. (1965). *The brain and unity of conscious experience*. Cambridge University Press.

Edenberg, H. J., & Foroud, T. (2013). Genetics and alcoholism. *Nature Reviews Gastroenterology & Hepatology*, 10, 487–494.

Ednick, M., Cohen, A. P., McPhail, G. L., Beebe, D., Simakajornboon, N., & Amin, R. S. (2009). A review of the effects of sleep during the first year of life on cognitive, psychomotor, and temperament development. *Sleep*, 32, 1449–1458.

Eggers, C., Dano, R., Schill, J., Fink, G. R., Timmermann, L., Voltz, R., Golla, H., & Lorenzl, S. (2018). Access to end-of life Parkinson's disease patients through patient-centered integrated healthcare.

Frontiers in Neurology, 9, 627. https://doi.org/10.3389/fneur.2018.00627

Eichenbaum, H. (2002). *The cognitive neuroscience of memory: An introduction.* Oxford University Press.

Eichenbaum, H., & Cohen, N. J. (2001). *From conditioning to conscious recollection: Memory systems of the brain.* Oxford University Press.

Eickhoff, S. B., Grefkes, C., Fink, G. R., & Zilles, K. (2008). Functional lateralization of face, hand, and trunk representation in anatomically defined human somatosensory areas. *Cerebral Cortex*, 18, 2820–2830.

Einstein, A. (1954). In C. Seelig (Ed.) & S. Bargmann (Trans.), *Ideas and opinions.* Crown.

Eklund, A., Nicholls, T. E., & Knutson, H. (2016). Cluster failure: Why fMRI inferences for spatial extent have inflated false-positive rates. *Proceedings of the National Academy of Sciences of the USA*, 113, 7900–7905.

Ekman, P., & Friesen, W. V. (1978). *The facial action coding system.* Consulting Psychologists Press.

Ekman, P., Levenson, R. W., & Frieson, W. V. (1983). Autonomic nervous system activity distinguishes among emotions. *Science*, 221, 1208–1210.

Eldridge, L. L., Knowlton, B. J., Furmanski, C. S., Bookheimer, S. Y., & Engel, S. A. (2000). Remembering episodes: A selective role for the hippocampus during retrieval. *Nature Neuroscience*, 33, 1149–1152.

Elliott, R. (2003). Executive functions and their disorders. *British Medical Bulletin*, 65, 49–59.

Ellison-Wright, I., & Bullmore, E. (2009). Meta-analysis of diffusion tensor imaging studies in schizophrenia. *Schizophrenia Research*, 108, 3–10.

Elsinga, P. H., Hatano, K., & Ishiwata, K. (2006). PET tracers for imaging of the dopaminergic system. *Current Medicinal Chemistry*, 13, 2139–2153.

Emad-ul-Haq, Q., Hussain, M., Aboalsamh, H., Bamatraf, S., Malik, A. S., & Amin, H. U. (2019). A review on understanding brain, and memory retention and recall processes using EEG and fMRI techniques. *Neurons and Cognition.* arXiv preprint arXiv:1905.02136. https://www.researchgate.net/publication/332897858_A_Review_on_understanding_Brain_and_Memory_Retention_and_Recall_Processes_using_EEG_and_fMRI_techniques

Emery, A. E. H., & Mueller, R. F. (1992). *Elements of medical genetics.* Churchill Livingstone.

Empson, J. (1993). *Sleep and dreaming.* Harvester Wheatsheaf.

Eom, T., Han, S. B., Kim, J., Blundon, J. A., Wang, Y.-D., Anderson, K., Kaminski, D. B., Sakurada, S. M., Pruett-Miller, S. M., Horner, L., Wagner, B., Robinson, C. G., Eicholtz, M., Rose, D. C., & Zakharenko, S. S. (2020). Schizophrenia-related microdeletion causes defective ciliary motility and brain ventricle enlargement via microRNA-dependent mechanisms in mice. *Nature Communications*, 11, 912. https://doi.org/10.1038/s41467-020-14628-y

Epstein, A. N., Nicolaidis, S., & Miselis, R. (1975). The glucoprivic control of food intake and the glucostatic theory of feeding behavior. In G. J. Mogenson & F. R. Calarasu (Eds.), *Neural integration of physiological mechanisms and behavior* (pp. 148–168). Toronto University Press.

Erickson, K. I., Voss, M. W., Prakash, R. S., Basak, C., Szabo, A., Chaddock, L., Kim, J. S., Heo, S., Alves, H., White, S. M., Wojcicki, T. R., Mailey, E., Vieira, V. J., Martin, S. A., Pence, B. D., Woods, J. A., McAuley, E., & Kramer, A. F. (2011). Exercise training increases size of hippocampus and improves memory. *Proceedings of the National Academy of Sciences of the USA*, 108, 3017–3022.

Ericsson, K. A., & Kintsch, W. (1995). Long-term working memory. *Psychological Reviews*, 102, 211–245.

Esdin, J., Pearce, K., & Glanzman, D. L. (2010). Long-term habituation of the gill-withdrawal reflex in Aplysia requires gene transcription, calcineurin and L-type voltage-gated calcium channels. *Frontiers in Behavioral Neuroscience*, 4, 181. https://doi.org/10.3389/fnbeh.2010.00181

Eslinger, P. J., & Damasio, A. R. (1985). Severe disturbance of higher cognitive function after bilateral frontal lobe ablation: Patient EVR. *Neurology*, 35, 1731–1741.

España, R. A., & Scammell, T. E. (2011). Sleep neurobiology from a clinical perspective. *Sleep*, 34, 845–858.

Estes, W. K., & Skinner, B. F. (1941). Some quantitative properties of anxiety. *Journal of Experimental Psychology*, 29, 390–400.

Estrada-Sánchez, A. M., & Rebec, G. V. (2012). Corticostriatal dysfunction and glutamate transporter 1 (GLT1) in Huntington's disease: Interactions between neurons and astrocytes. *Basal Ganglia*, 2, 57–66.

Evans, K. C., Berger, E. P., Cho, C. G., Weisgraber, K. H., & Lansbury, P. T. (1995). Apolipoprotein E is a kinetic but not a thermodynamic inhibitor of amyloid formation: Implications for the pathogenesis and treatment of Alzheimer disease. *Proceedings of the National Academy of Sciences*, 92, 763–767.

Everson, C. A., & Toth, L. A. (2000). Systemic bacterial invasion induced by sleep deprivation. *American Journal of Physiology*, 278, R905–R916.

Eyding, D., Lelgemann, M., Grouven, U., Harter, M., Kromp, M., Kaiser, T., Kerekes, M. F., Gerken, M., & Wieseler, B. (2010). Reboxetine for acute treatment of major depression: Systematic review and meta-analysis of published and unpublished placebo and selective serotonin reuptake inhibitor controlled trials. *British Medical Journal*, 12(341), c4737. https://doi.org/10.1136/bmj.c4737

Fahn, S. (2015). The medical treatment of Parkinson disease from James Parkinson to George Cotzias. *Movement Disorders*, 30, 4–18.

Fairbanks, D. J. (2020). Mendel and Darwin: Untangling a persistent enigma. *Heredity*, 124, 263–273.

Falzarano, M. S., Scotton, C., Passarelli, C., & Ferlini, A. (2015). Duchenne muscular dystrophy: From diagnosis to therapy. *Molecules*, 20, 18168–18184.

Fan, Y., Winanto, Ng, S. Y. (2020). Replacing what's lost: A new era of stem cell therapy for Parkinson's disease. *Translational Neurodegeneration*, 9(2), 1–10. https://doi.org/10.1186/s40035-019-0180-x

Farah, M. J. (1989). The neural basis of mental imagery. *Trends in Neurosciences*, 12, 395–399.

Faurie, C., & Raymond, M. (2004). Handedness frequency over more than ten thousand years. *Proceedings of the Royal Society of London B*, 271, S43–S45.

Fayez, A., Croft, P., Langford, R. M, Donaldson, L. J., & Jones, G. T. (2016). Prevalence of chronic pain in the UK: A systematic review and meta-analysis of population studies. *British Medical Journal Open*, 6, e010364. https://doi.org/10.1136/bmjopen-2015-010364

Feldman, R. S., Meyer, J. S., & Quenzer, L. F. (1997). *Principles of neuropsychopharmacology*. Sinauer.

Felson, J. (2014). What can we learn from twin studies? A comprehensive evaluation of the equal environments assumption. *Social Science Research*, 43,184–199.

Fendrich, R., Wessinger, C. M., & Gazziniga, M. S. (2001). Speculations on the neural basis of islands in blindsight. *Progress in Brain Research*, 134, 353–366.

Ferguson, C. P., & Pigott, T. A. (2000). Anorexia and bulimia nervosa: Neurobiology and pharmacotherapy. *Behavior Therapy*, 31, 237–263.

Fergusson, D., Doucette, S., Glass, K. C., Shapiro, S., Healy, D., Hebert, P., & Hutton, B. (2005). Association between suicide attempts and selective serotonin reuptake inhibitors: Systematic review of randomised controlled trials. *British Medical Journal*, 330, 396. https://doi.org/10.1136/bmj.330.7488.396

Ferrante, R. J., Gutekunst, C. A., Persichetti, F., McNeil, S. M., Kowall, N. W., Gusella, J. F., MacDonald, M. E., Beal, M. F., & Hersch, S. M. (1987). Heterogeneous topographic and cellular distribution of Huntingtin expression in the normal human neostriatum. *Journal of Neuroscience*, 17, 3052–3063.

Ferrante, R. J., Kowall, N. W., Cipolloni, P. B., Storey, E., & Beal, M. F. (1993). Excitotoxin lesions in primates as a model for Huntington's disease: Histopathologic and neurochemical characterization. *Experimental Neurology*, 119, 46–71.

Ferraz, C. R., Arrahman, A., Xie, C., Casewell, N. R., Lewis, R. J., Kool, J., & Cardoso, F. C. (2019). Multifunctional toxins in snake venoms and therapeutic implications: From pain to haemorrhage and necrosis. *Frontiers in Ecology and Evolution*, 7, 218. https://doi.org/10.3389/fevo.2019.00218

Ferré, S. (2010). Role of the central ascending neurotransmitter systems in the psychostimulant effects of caffeine. *Journal of Alzheimer's Disease*, 20, S35–S49.

Ferré, S. (2016). Mechanisms of the psychostimulant effects of caffeine: Implications for substance use disorders. *Psychopharmacology*, 233, 1963–1979.

Ferreira-Vieira, T. H., Guimaraes, I. M., Silva, F., & Ribeiro, F. M. (2016). Alzheimer's disease: Targeting the cholinergic system. *Current Neuropharmacology*, 14, 101–115.

Ferretti, A., Caulo, M., Del Gratta, C., Di Matteo, R., Merla, A., Montorsi, F., Pizzella, V., Pompa, P., Rigatti, P., Rossini, P. M., Salonia, A., Tartaro, A., & Romani, G. L. (2005). Dynamics of male sexual arousal: Distinct components of brain activation revealed by fMRI. *NeuroImage*, 26, 1086–1096.

Ferri, C. P., Prince, M., Brayne, C., Brodaty, H., Fratiglioni, L., Ganguli, M., Hall, K., Hasegawa, K., Hendrie, H., Huang, Y., Jorm, A., Mathers, C., Menezes, P. R., Rimmer, E., Scazufca, M. & Alzheimer's Disease International. (2005). Global prevalence of dementia: A Delphi consensus study. *The Lancet*, 366, 2112–2117.

Fibiger, H. C., Phillips, A. G., & Brown, E. E. (1992). The neurobiology of cocaine-induced reinforcement. In G. E. W. Wolstenholme (Ed.), *Cocaine: Scientific and social dimensions. Ciba foundation symposium 166* (pp. 96–111). John Wiley.

Fiedorowicz, J. G., & Swartz, K. L. (2004). The role of monoamine oxidase inhibitors in current psychiatric practice. *Journal of Psychiatric Practice*, 10, 239–248.

Fielden, J., Lutter, C., & Dabbs, J. (1994). *Basking in glory: Testosterone changes in world cup soccer fans*. Psychology Department, Georgia State University.

Fields, H. (1999). Pain: An unpleasant topic. *Pain*, 82(Suppl. 1), S61–S69.

Filipski, E., Delaunay, F., King, V.M., Wu, M. W., Claustrat, B., Gréchez-Cassiau, A., Guettier, C., Hastings, M. H., & Francis, L. (2004). Effects of chronic jet lag on tumor progression in mice. *Cancer Research*, 64, 79–85.

Finger, S. (1994). *Origins of neuroscience*. Oxford University Press.

Finger, S. (2000). *Minds behind the brain*. Oxford University Press.

Fisher, M. (1971). Psychosis in the offspring of schizophrenic monozygotic twins and their normal co-twins. *British Journal of Psychiatry*, 118, 43–52.

Fishman, I., Linke, A. C., Hau, J., Carper, R. A., & Müller A.-X. (2018). Atypical functional connectivity of amygdala related to reduced symptom severity in children with autism. *Journal of the American Academy of Child and Adolescent Psychiatry*, 57, 764–774.

Fitzgerald, M. J. T., Gruener, G., & Mtui, E. (2012). *Clinical neuroanatomy and neuroscience*. Elsevier.

Fleisher, A. S., Chen, K., Liu, X., Roontiva, A., Thiyyagura, P., Ayutyanont, N., Joshi, A. D., Clark, C. M., Mintun, M. A., Pontecorvo, M. J., Doraiswamy, P. M., Johnson, K. A., Skovronsky, D. M., & Reiman, E. M. (2011). Using positron emission tomography and Florbetapir F18 to image cortical amyloid in patients with mild cognitive impairment or dementia due to Alzheimer disease. *Archives of Neurology*, 68, 1404–1411.

Fletcher, J. M., Lalor, S. J., Sweeney, C. M., Tubridy, N., & Mills, K. H. (2010). T cells in multiple sclerosis and experimental autoimmune encephalomyelitis. *Clinical and Experimental Immunology*, 162, 1–11.

Fletcher-Watson, S., & Happé, F. (2019). *Autism: A new introduction to psychological theory and current debate*. Routledge.

Flint, J., & Kendler, K. S. (2014). The genetics of major depression. *Neuron*, 81, 484–503.

Floresco, S. B. (2015). The nucleus accumbens: An interface between cognition, emotion, and action. *Annual Review of Psychology*, 66, 25–52.

Floyd, J. A., Janisse, J. J., Jenuwine, E. S., & Ager, J. W. (2007). Changes in REM-sleep percentage over the adult lifespan. *Sleep*, 30, 829–836.

Foer, J., & Siffre, M. (2008). Caveman: An interview with Michel Siffre. *Cabinet Magazine*, 30, 1–6. www.cabinetmagazine.org/issues/30/foer.php

Foroud, T., Edenberg, H., & Crabbe, J. C. (2010). Genetic research: Who is at risk for alcoholism? *Alcohol Research and Health: The Journal of the National Institute on Alcohol Abuse and Alcoholism*, 33, 64–75.

Förstl, H., & Kurz, A. (1999). Clinical features of Alzheimer's disease. *European Archives of Psychiatry and Clinical Neuroscience*, 249, 288–290.

Foster, D. H. (2011). Color constancy. *Vision Research*, 51, 674–700.

Francis, P. T., Palmer, A. M., Snape, M., & Wilcock, G. K. (1999). The cholinergic hypothesis of Alzheimer's disease: A review of progress. *Journal of Neurology, Neurosurgery and Psychiatry*, 66, 137–147.

Frank, G. K. W. (2015). Advances from neuroimaging studies in eating disorders. *CNS Spectrums*, 20, 391–400.

Frank, G. K. W., Shott, M. E., & DeGuzman, M. C. (2019). Recent advances in understanding anorexia nervosa. *F1000Research*, 8, 1–7. https://doi.org/10.12688/f1000research.17789.1

Frank, M. G. (2006). The mystery of sleep function: Current perspectives and future directions. *Reviews in the Neurosciences*, 17, 375–392.

Fratiglioni, L., & Wang, H. X. (2000). Smoking and Parkinson's and Alzheimer's disease: Review of the epidemiological studies. *Behavioral Brain Research*, 113, 117–120.

Frayling, T. M., Timpson, N. J., Weedon, M. N., Zeggini, E., Freathy, R. M., Lindgren, C. M., Perry, J. R. B., Elliott, K. S., Lango, H., Rayner, N. W., Shields, B., Harries, L. W., Barrett, J. C., Ellard, S., Groves, C. J., Knight, B., Patch, A.-M., Ness, A. R., Ebrahim, S., . . . McCarthy, M. I. (2007). A common variant in the FTO gene is associated with body mass index and predisposes to childhood and adult obesity. *Science*, 316, 889–894.

Frederikse, M. E., Lu, A., Aylward, E., Barta, P., & Pearlson, G. (1999). Sex differences in the inferior parietal lobe. *Cerebral Cortex*, 9, 896–901.

Freed, C. R., Zhou, W., & Breeze, R. E. (2011). Dopamine cell transplantation for Parkinson's disease: The importance of controlled clinical trials. *Neurotherapeutics: the Journal of the American Society for Experimental Neurotherapeutics*, 8, 549–561.

Freedman, M. S., Lucas, R. J., Soni, B., von Schantz, M., Muñoz, M., David-Gray, Z., & Foster, R. (1999). Regulation of mammalian circadian behavior by non-rod, non-cone, ocular photoreceptors. *Science*, 284, 502–504.

Frenois, F., Stinus, L., Di Blasi, F., Cador, M., & Le Moine, C. (2005). A specific limbic circuit underlies opiate withdrawal memories. *Journal of Neuroscience*, 25, 1366–1374.

Frias, B., & Merighi, A. (2016). Capsaicin, nociception and pain. *Molecules*, 21(6), 797. https://doi.org/10.3390/molecules21060797

Fried, I., Wilson, C. L., MacDonald, K. A., & Behnke, E. J. (1998). Electric current stimulates laughter, *Nature*, 391, 650.

Friedman, J. M. (2019). Leptin and the endocrine control of energy balance. *Nature Metabolism*, 1, 754–764.

Fu, Y., Matta, S. G., Gao, W., Brower, V. G., & Sharp, B. M. (2000). Systemic nicotine stimulates dopamine release in nucleus accumbens: Re-evaluation of the role of N-Methyl-D-aspartate receptors in the ventral tegmental area. *Journal of Pharmacology and Experimental Therapeutics*, 294, 458–465.

Fujiwara, H., Hasegawa, M., Dohmae, N., Kawashima, A., Masliah, E., Goldberg, M. S., Shen, J., Takio, K., & Iwatsubo, T. (2002). Alpha-Synuclein is phosphorylated in synucleinopathy lesions. *Nature Cell Biology*, 4, 160–164.

Fuller, P. M., Saper, C. B., & Lu, J. (2007). The pontine REM switch: Past and present. *Journal of Physiology*, 584, 735–741.

Funahashi, S. (2001). Neuronal mechanisms of executive control by the prefrontal cortex. *Neuroscience Research*, 39, 147–165.

Funahashi, S., Bruce, C. J., & Goldman-Rakic, P. S. (1989). Mnemonic coding of visual space in the 'monkey's dorsolateral prefrontal cortex. *Journal of Neurophysiology*, 61, 331–349.

Funkenstein, D. (1955). The physiology of fear and anger. *Scientific American*, 192, 74–80.

Furlan, M., Smith, A. T., & Walker, R. (2015). Activity in the human superior colliculus to endogenous saccade preperation and execution. *Journal of Neurophysiology*, 114, 1048–1058.

Fuster, J. M. (2004). Upper processing stages of the perception-action cycle. *Trends in Cognitive Science*, 8, 143–145.

Fuxe, K., Marcellino, D., Borroto-Escuela, D. O., Guescini, M., Fernández-Dueñas, V., Tanganelli, S., Rivera, A., Ciruela, F., & Agnati, L. F. (2010). Adenosine–dopamine interactions in the pathophysiology and treatment of CNS disorders. CNS *Neuroscience and Therapeutics*, 16(3), e18–e42. https://doi.org/10.1111/j.1755-5949.2009.00126.x

Gabrieli, J. D., Brewer, J. B., Desmond, J. E., & Glover, G. H. (1997). Separate neural bases of two fundamental memory processes in the human medial temporal lobe. *Science*, 276, 264–266.

Gajdusek, D. C., Gibbs, C. J., & Alpers, M. (1967). Transmission and passage of experimental 'kuru' to chimpanzees. *Science*, 155, 212–214.

Galaburda, A. M. (1993). Neurology of developmental dyslexia. *Current Opinion in Neurobiology*, 3, 237–242.

Galaburda, A. M., & Livingstone, M. (1993). Evidence for a magnocellular deficit in developmental dyslexia. *Annals of the New York Academy of Sciences*, 682, 70–82.

Gallese, V., Fadiga, L., Fogassi, L., & Rizzolatti, G. (1996). Action recognition in premotor cortex. *Brain*, 119, 593–609.

Gallopin, T., Fort, P., Eggermann, E., Cauli, B., Luppi, P.H., Rossier, J., Audinat, E., Mühlethaler, M., & Serafin, M. (2000). Identification of sleep-promoting neurons in vitro. *Nature*, 404, 922–925.

Galton, C. J., Patterson, K., Graham, K., Lambon-Ralph, M. A., Williams, G., Antoun, N., Sahakian, B. J., & Hodges, J. R. (2001). Differing patterns of temporal atrophy in Alzheimer's disease and semantic dementia. *Neurology*, 57, 216–225.

Garcia-Romeu, A., Kersgaard, B., & Addy, P. H. (2016). Clinical applications of hallucinogens. *Experimental and Clinical Psychopharmacology*, 24, 229–268.

Gardener, H., Spiegelman, D., & Buka, S. L. (2009). Prenatal risk factors for autism: Comprehensive meta-analysis. *The British Journal of Psychiatry*, 195, 7–14.

Gardner, R. C., Burke, J. F, Nettiksimmons, J., Goldman, S., Tanner, C. M., & Yaffe, K. (2015). Traumatic brain injury in later life increases risk for Parkinson disease. *Annals of Neurology*, 77, 987–995.

Garn, S. M., Burdi, A. R., Babler, W. J., & Stinson, S. (1975). Early prenatal attainment of adult metacarpal-phalangeal rankings and proportions. *American Journal of Physical Anthropology*, 43, 327–332.

Garrett, B. (2011). *Brain & behavior: An introduction to biological psychology* (3rd ed.). SAGE.

Garrett, B. (2015). *Brain and behavior: An introduction to biological psychology* (4th ed.). SAGE.

Garrett, B., & Hough, G. (2018). *Brain and behavior: An introduction to behavioral neuroscience* (5th ed.). SAGE.

Garrett, B., & Hough, G. (2021). *Brain and behavior: An introduction to behavioral neuroscience* (6th ed.). SAGE.

Gaskin, S. (2021). *Behavioral neuroscience.* SAGE.

Gauthier, L. R., Charrin, B. C., Borrell-Pagès, M., Dompierre, J. P., Rangone, H., Cordelières, F. P., De Mey, J., MacDonald, M. E., Lessmann, V., Humbert, S., & Saudou, F. (2004). Huntingtin controls neurotrophic support and survival of neurons by enhancing BDNF vesicular transport along microtubules. *Cell*, 118, 127–138.

Gawda, B., & Szepietowska, E. M. (2013). Semantic and affective verbal fluency:

Sex differences. *Psychological Reports*, 113, 1258–1268.

Gazzaniga, M., & LeDoux, J. (1978). *The integrated mind*. Springer.

Gazzaniga, M. S. (1970). *The bisected brain*. Appleton-Century.

Gazzaniga, M. S. (1989). Organization of the human brain. *Science*, 245, 947–952.

Gazzaniga, M. S. (2002). The split-brain revisited. *Scientific American*, 12(1), 27–31.

Gazzaniga, M. S. (2011). *Who's in charge? Free will and the science of the brain*. Robinson.

Gazzaniga, M. S., Fendrich, R., & Wessinger, C. M. (1994). Blindsight reconsidered. *Current Directions in Psychological Science*, 3, 93–96.

Gazzaniga, M. S., Ivry, R. B., & Mangum, G. R. (2002). *Cognitive neuroscience* (2nd ed.). Norton.

Gazzaniga, M. S., Ivry, R. B., & Mangun, G. R. (2009). *Cognitive neuroscience* (3rd ed.). Norton.

Gegenfurtner, K. R. (2003). Cortical mechanisms of colour vision. *Nature Reviews Neuroscience*, 4, 563–572.

Georgopoulos, A. P. (1994). New concepts in generation of movement. *Neuron*, 13, 257–268.

Gerak, L. R., Galici, R., & France, C. P. (2009). Self administration of heroin and cocaine in morphine-dependent and morphine-withdrawn rhesus monkeys. *Psychopharmacology*, 204, 403–411.

Gerloff, C., Corwell, B., Chen, R., Hallett, M., & Cohen, L. G. (1997). Stimulation over the human supplementary motor area interferes with the organization of future elements in complex motor sequences. *Brain*, 120, 1587–1602.

Gervais, M., & Wilson, D. S. (2005). The evolution and functions of laughter and humor: A synthetic approach. *Quarterly Review of Biology*, 80, 395–430.

Geschwind, N. (1965). Disconnexion syndromes in animals and man, *Brain*, 88, 585–644.

Geschwind, N. (1967). Wernicke's contribution to the study of aphasia, *Cortex*, 3, 449–463.

Geschwind, N. (1972). Language and the brain. *Scientific American*, 226, 76–83.

Geschwind, N., & Levitsky, W. (1968). Human brain: Left-right asymmetries in temporal speech region. *Science*, 161, 186–187.

Gibbs, J., Young, R. C., & Smith, G. P. (1973). Cholecystokinin decreases food intake in rats. *Journal of Comparative Physiology and Psychology*, 84, 488–495.

Gibson, G. (2010). Hints of hidden heritability in GWAS. *Nature Genetics*, 42, 558–560.

Giedd, J. N., Blumenthal, J., Jeffries, N. O., Castellanos, F. X., Liu, H., Zijdenbos, A., Paus, T., Evans, A. C., & Rapoport, J. L. (1999). Brain development during childhood and adolescence: A longitudinal MRI study. *Nature Neuroscience*, 2, 861–863.

Giedd, J. N., Raznahan, A., Mills, K. L., & Lenroot, R. K. (2012). Review: Magnetic resonance imaging of male/female differences in human adolescent brain anatomy. *Biology of Sex Differences*, 3(1):19. https://doi.org/10.1186/2042-6410-3-19.

Gilman, P. K. (2007). Tricyclic antidepressant pharmacology and therapeutic drug interactions updated. *British Journal of Pharmacology*, 151, 737–748.

Gilpin, N. W., & Koob, G. F. (2008). Neurobiology of alcohol dependence. *Alcohol Research and Health*, 31, 185–195.

Gjerris, A., Werdelin, L., Rafaelson, O. J., Alling, C., & Christensen, N. J. (1987). CSF dopamine increased in depression: CSF dopamine, noradrenaline and their metabolites in depressed patients and controls. *Journal of Affective Disorders*, 13, 279–286.

Glanzman, D. L. (2009). Habituation in Aplysia: The Cheshire cat of neurobiology. *Neurobiology of Learning and Memory*, 92, 147–154.

Gleitman, L., & Papafragou, A. (2005). Language and thought. In K. J. Holyoak & R. G. Morrison (Eds.), *The Cambridge handbook of thinking and reasoning* (pp. 663–661). Cambridge University Press.

Glenner, G. G., & Wong, C. W. (1984). Alzheimer's disease: Initial report of the purification and characterization of a novel cerebrovascular amyloid protein. *Biochemistry and Biophysics Research Communication*, 120, 885–890.

Glennon, R. A., Titeler, M., & McKenney, J. D. (1984). Evidence for 5-HT2 involvement in the mechanism of action of hallucinogenic events. *Life Sciences*, 35, 2505–2511.

Gloor, P. (1990). Experimental phenomena of temporal lobe epilepsy. Facts and hypotheses. *Brain*, 113, 1673–1694.

Glover, G. H. (2011). Overview of functional magnetic resonance imaging. *Neurosurgery Clinics of North America*, 22, 133–139.

Glynn, I. (1999). *An anatomy of thought*. Oxford University Press.

Goate, A., Chartier-Harlin, M. C., Mullan M., ... & Hardy, J. (1991). Segregation of a missense mutation in the amyloid precursor protein gene with familial Alzheimer's disease. *Nature*, 349, 704–706.

Goetz, C. G. (2011). The history of Parkinson's disease: Early clinical descriptions and neurological therapies. *Cold Spring Harbor Perspectives in Medicine*, 1, a008862. https://doi.org/10.1101/cshperspect. a008862

Gogtay, N., Giedd, J. N., Lusk, L., Hayashi, K. M., Greenstein, D., Vaituzis, A. C., Nugent, T. F., Herman, D. H., Clasen, L. S., Toga, A. W., Rapoport, J. L., & Thompson, P. M. (2004). Dynamic mapping of human cortical development during childhood through early adulthood. *Proceedings of the National Academy of Sciences of the USA*, 101, 8174–8179.

Golbe, L. I. (1995). Genetics of Parkinson's disease. In J. M. Ellenberg, W. C. Koller, & J. W. Langston (Eds.), *Etiology of Parkinson's disease* (pp. 115–140). Marcel Dekker.

Golbe, L. I., Di Iorio, G., Bonavita, V., Miller, D. C., & Duvoisin, R. C. (1990). A large kindred with autosomal dominant Parkinson's disease. *Annals of Neurology*, 27, 276–282.

Golbe, L. I., & Leyton, C. E., (2018). Life expectancy in Parkinson's disease. *Neurology*, 91, 991–992.

Goldberg, M. E., & Hudspeth, A. J. (2000). The vestibular system. In E. R. Kandel, J. H. Schwartz & T. M. Jessell (Eds.), *Principles of neural science* (4th ed.). McGraw-Hill.

Goldey, K. L., & van Anders, S. M. (2014). Sexual modulation of testosterone: Insights for humans from across species. *Adaptive Human Behavior and Physiology*, 1, 93–123.

Goldson, E., & Kelly, D. P. (2008). Developmental-behavioral aspects of chronic conditions. In M. L. Wolraich, D. D. Drotar, & E. C. Perrin (Eds.), *Developmental-behavioral pediatrics* (pp. 301–404). Elsevier.

Goldstein, E. B. (2020). *The mind: Consciousness, prediction and the brain*. MIT Press.

Goldstein, K. (1952). The effect of brain damage on personality. *Psychiatry*, 15, 41–45.

Gomez-Isla, T., Price, J. L., McKeel, D. W., Jr, Morris, J. C., Growdon, J. H., & Hyman, B. T. (1996). Profound loss of layer II entorhinal cortex neurons occur in very mild Alzheimer's disease. *Journal of Neuroscience*, 16, 4491–4500.

Gonzalez, M. F., & Deutsch, J. A. (1981). Vagotomy abolishes cues of satiety produced by stomach distension. *Science*, 212, 1283–1284.

Goodale, M. A., & Milner, A. D (1992). Separate visual pathways for perception and action. *Trends in Neurosciences*, 15, 20–25.

Goodale, M. A., & Milner, A. D. (2004). *Sight unseen*. Oxford University Press.

Goodman, J., McIntyre, C., & Packard, M. G. (2017). Amygdala and emotional modulation of multiple memory systems. In B. Ferry (Ed.), *The amygdala – Where emotions shape perception, learning and memories* (pp. 215–234). IntechOpen.

Goodnick, P. J., & Goldstein, B. J. (1998). Selective serotonin reuptake inhibitors in affective disorders: I. Basic pharmacology. *Journal of Psychopharmacology*, 12, S5–S20.

Gorski, R. A. (1974). The neuroendocrine regulation of sexual behavior. In G. Newton & A. H. Riesen (Eds.), *Advances in psychobiology* (Vol. 2, pp. 1–58). John Wiley.

Gorski, R. A., Gordon, J. H., Shryne, J. E., & Southam, A. M. (1978). Evidence for a morphological sex difference within the medial preoptic area of the rat brain. *Brain Research*, 148, 333–346.

Gossop, M. (2017). *Living with drugs*. Routledge.

Gothelf, D., Eliez, S., Thompson, T., Hinard, C., Penniman, L., Feinstein, C., Kwon, H., Jin, S., Jo, B., Antonarakis, S. E., Morris, M. A., & Reiss, A. L. (2005). *COMT* genotype predicts longitudinal cognitive decline and psychosis in 22q11.2 deletion syndrome. *Nature Neuroscience*, 8, 1500–1502.

Gottesman, I. I. (1991). *Schizophrenia genesis*. Freeman.

Gouchie, C., & Kimura, D. (1991). The relationship between testosterone levels and cognitive ability patterns. *Psychoneuroendocrinology*, 16, 323–334.

Gover, T. D., & Abrams, T. W. (2009). Insights into a molecular switch that gates sensory neuron synapses during habituation in Aplysia. *Neurobiology of Learning and Memory*, 92, 155–165.

Gowing, L., Farrell, M., Ali, R., & White, J. M. (2016). Alpha2-adrenergic agonists for the management of opioid withdrawal. *Cochrane Database of Systematic Reviews*, 2016(5), CD002024. https://doi.org/10.1002/14651858.CD002024.pub5

Goy, R. W., Barkowitch, F. B., & McBair, M. C. (1988). Behavioral masculinisation is independent of genital masculinisation in prenatally androgenised female rhesus monkeys. *Hormones and Behavior*, 22, 552–571.

Grafe, L. A., & Bhatnagar, S. (2018). Orexins and stress. *Frontiers in Neuroendocrinology*, 51, 132–145. https://doi.org/10.1016/j.yfrne.2018.06.003

Graham, R. B. (1990). *Physiological psychology*. Wadsworth.

Graus, Y. M. F., & De Baets, M. H. (1993). Myasthenia gravis: An autoimmune response against the acetylcholine receptor. *Immunologic Research*, 12, 78–100.

Graybiel, A. M., & Grafton, S. T. (2015). The striatum: Where skills and habits meet. *Cold Spring Harbor Perspectives in Biology*, 7(8), a021691. https://doi.org/10.1101/cshperspect.a021691

Graziadei, P. P. C. (1977). Functional anatomy of the mammalian chemoreceptor system. In D. Müller-Schwarze & M. M. Mozell (Eds.), *Chemical signals in vertebrates* (pp. 435–454). Plenum Press.

Greenfield, S. (2000). *The human brain: A guided tour*. Phoenix.

Greicius, M. D., Krasnow, B., Boyett-Anderson, J. M., Eliez, S., Schatzberg, A. F., Reiss, A. L., & Menon, V. (2003). Regional analysis of hippocampal activation during memory encoding and retrieval: fMRI study. *Hippocampus*, 13, 164–174.

Griessner, J., Pasieka, M., Böhm, V., Grössl, F., Kaczanowska, J., Pliota, P., Kargl, D., Werner, B., Kaouane, N., Strobelt, S., Kreitz, S., Hess, A., & Haubenska, W. (2021). Central amygdala circuit dynamics underlying the benzodiazepine anxiolytic effect. *Molecular Psychiatry*, 26(2), 534–544. https://doi.org/10.1038/s41380-018-0310-3

Griffiths, R. R., Bigelow, G. E., & Henningfield, J. E. (1980). Similarities in animal and human drug-taking behavior. In N. K. Mello (Ed.), *Advances in substance abuse* (Vol. 1, pp. 1–90). JAI Press.

Grigg-Damberger, M. M., & Wolfe, K. M. (2017). Infants sleep for brain. *Journal of Clinical Sleep Medicine*, 13, 1233–1234.

Grill, H. J., & Kaplin, J. M. (2002). The neuroanatomical axis for control of energy balance. *Frontiers in Neuroendocrinology*, 23, 2–40.

Grimbos, T., Dawood, K., Burriss, R. P., Zucker, K. J., & Puts, D. A. (2010). Sexual orientation and the second to fourth finger length ratio: A meta-analysis in men and women. *Behavioral Neuroscience*, 124, 278–287.

Groiss, S. J., Wojtecki, L., Südmeyer, M., & Schnitzler, A. (2009). Deep brain stimulation in Parkinson's disease. *Therapeutic Advances in Neurological Disorders*, 2, 20–28.

Groves, P. M., & Rebec, G. V. (1992). *Introduction to biological psychology*. Wm. C. Brown.

Guadalupe, T., Willems, R. M., Zwiers, M. P., Arias Vasquez, A., Hoogman, M., Hagoort, P., Fernandez, G., Buitelaar, J., Franke, B., Fisher, S. E., & Francks, C. (2014). Differences in cerebral cortical anatomy of left- and right-handers. *Frontiers in Psychology*, 5, 261. https://doi.org/10.3389/fpsyg.2014.00261

Gusella, J., Wexler, N., Conneally, P. M., Naylor, S. L., Anderson, M. A., Tanzi, R. E., Watkins, P. C., Ottina, K., Wallace, M. R., Sakaguchi, A. Y., Young, A. B., Shoulson, I., Bonilla, E., & Martin, J. B. (1983). A polymorphic DNA marker genetically linked to Huntington's disease. *Nature*, 306, 234–238.

Gustavsson, A., Svensson, M., Jacobi, F., Allgulander, C., Alonso, J., Beghi, E., Dodel, R., Ekman, M., Faravelli, C., Fratiglioni, L., Gannon, B., Jones, D. H., Jennum, P., Jordanova, A., Jönsson, L., Karampampa, K., Knapp, M., Kobelt, G., Kurth, T., . . . Olesen, J.; CDBE2010Study Group. (2011). Cost of disorders of the brain in Europe 2010. *European Journal of Neuropsychopharmacology*, 21, 718–779.

Gutekunst, C. A., Li, S. H., Yi, H., Mulroy, J. S., Kuemmerle, S., Jones, R., Rye, D., Ferrante, R. J., Hersch, S. M., & Li, X. J. (1999). Nuclear and neuropil aggregates in Huntington's disease: Relationship to neuropathology. *Journal of Neuroscience*, 19, 2522–2534.

Haber, S. N. (2016). Corticostriatal circuitry. *Dialogues in Clinical Neuroscience*, 18, 7–21.

Hain, T. C. (2019). Otoliths. http://doi. dizziness-and-balance.com/disorders/bppv/otoliths.html

Hajima, S. V., Van Haren, N., Cahn, W., Koolschijn, P. C., Hulshoff Pol H. E., & Kahn, R. S. (2013). Brain volumes in schizophrenia: A meta-analysis in over 18 000 subjects. *Schizophrenia Bulletin*, 39, 1129–1138.

Halaas, J. L., Gajiwala, K. S., Maffai, M., Cohen, S. L., Chait, B. T., Rabinowitz, D., Lallone, R. L., Burley, S. K., & Friedman, J. M. (1995). Weight-reducing effects of the plasma protein encoded by the obese gene. *Science*, 269, 543–546.

Hall, B., Limaye, A., & Kulkarni, A. B. (2009). Overview: Generation of gene knockout mice. *Current Protocols in Cell Biology*, 44, 245–261. https://doi.org/10.1002/0471143030.cb1912s44

Hall, W., & Weier, M. (2017). Lee Robins' studies of heroin use among US Vietnam veterans: Robins' heroin studies of Vietnam veterans. *Addiction*, 112, 176–180. https://doi.org/10.1111/add.13584

Hallett, M. (2016). Physiology of free will. *Annals of Neurology*, 80, 5–12.

Hallett, P. J., Deleidi, M., Astradsson, A., Smith, G. A., Cooper, O., Osborn, T. M., Sundberg, M., Moore, M. A., Perez-Torres, E., Brownell, A. L., Schumacher, J. M., Spealman, R. D., & Isacson, O. (2015). Successful function of autologous iPSC-derived dopamine neurons following transplantation in a non-human primate model of Parkinson's disease. *Cell Stem Cell*, 16, 269–274.

Halpern, A. R., & Zatorre, R. J. (1999). When that tune runs through your head: A PET investigation of auditory imagery for familiar melodies. *Cerebral Cortex*, 9, 697–704.

Halpern, D. F. (2004). A cognitive-process taxonomy for sex differences in cognitive abilities. *Current Directions in Psychological Science*, 13, 135–139.

Halpern, D. F. (2011). *Sex differences in cognition*. Routledge.

Hamer, D. H., Hu, S., Magnuson, V. L., Hu, N., & Pattatucci, A. M. (1993). A linkage between DNA markers on the X chromosome and male sexual orientation. *Science*, 261, 321–327.

Hampton, S. M., Morgan, L. M., Lawrence, N., Anastasiadou, T., Norris, F., Deacon, S., Ribeiro, D., & Arendt, J. (1996). Postprandial hormone and metabolic responses in simulated shift work. *Journal of Endocrinology*, 151, 259–267.

Hancock, S., & McKim, W. (2017). *Drugs and behavior*. Pearson.

Handler, C. M., & Fierson, W. M. (2011). Learning disabilities, dyslexia, and vision. *Pediatrics*, 127, e818–e856. https://doi.org/10.1542/peds.2010-3670

Harasty, J., Double, K. L., Halliday, G. M., Kril, J. J., & McRitchie, D. A. (1997). Language-associated cortical regions are proportionally larger in the female brain. *Archives of Neurology*, 54, 171–176.

Hardingham, N., Dachtler, J., & Fox, K. (2013). The role of nitric oxide in pre-synaptic plasticity and homeostasis. *Frontiers in Cellular Neuroscience*, 7, 190. https://doi.org/10.3389/fncel.2013.00190

Hariri, A. R., Tessitore, A., Mattay, V. S., Fera, F., & Weinberger, D. R. (2002). The amygdala response to emotional stimuli:

A comparison of faces and scenes. *NeuroImage*, 17, 317–323.

Harlow, J. M. (1848). Passage of an iron rod through the head. *Boston Medical Surgery Journal*, 39, 389–393.

Harrison, P. J. (2015). Recent genetic findings in schizophrenia and their therapeutic relevance. *Journal of Psychopharmacology*, 29, 85–96.

Hart, B. L. (1967). Testosterone regulation of sexual reflexes in spinal male rats. *Science*, 155, 1283–1284.

Hartmann, E., Chung, R., & Draskoczy, P. R. (1971). 6-Hydroxdopamine: Effects on sleep in the rat. *Nature*, 233, 425–427.

Hasselmo, M. E. (2006). The role of acetylcholine in learning and memory. *Current Opinion in Neurobiology*, 16, 710–715.

Hastings, M. H., Maywood, E. S., & Brancaccio, M. (2018). Generation of circadian rhythms in the suprachiasmatic nucleus. *Nature Reviews Neuroscience*, 19, 453–469.

Hatcher, J. M., Pennell, K. D., & Miller, G. W. (2008). Parkinson's disease and pesticides: A toxicological perspective. *Trends in Pharmacological Sciences*, 29, 322–329.

Hatta, T. (2007). Handedness and the brain: A review of brain-imaging techniques. *Magnetic Resonance in Medical Sciences*, 6, 99–112.

Hattori, N., & Mizuno, Y. (2017). Twenty years since the discovery of the parkin gene. *Journal of Neural Transmission*, 124, 1037–1054.

Haworth, C. M., Wright, M. J., Martin, N. W., Martin, N. G., Boomsma, D. I., Bartels, M., Posthuma, D., Davis, O. S., Brant, A. M., Corley, R. P., Hewitt, J. K., Iacono, W. G., McGue, M., Thompson, L. A., Hart, S. A., Petrill, S. A., Lubinski, D., & Plomin, R. (2009). A twin study of the genetics of high cognitive ability selected from 11,000 twin pairs in six studies from four countries. *Behavior Genetics*, 39, 359–370.

Hay, P., Mitchison, D., Collado, A. E. L., González-Chica, D. A., Stocks, N., & Touyz, S. (2017). Burden and health-related quality of life of eating disorders, including Avoidant/Restrictive Food Intake Disorder (ARFID), in the Australian population. *Journal of Eating Disorders*, 5,

321. https://doi.org/10.1186/s40337-017-0149-z

Hayward, V. (2018). A brief overview of the human somatosensory system. In S. Papetti & S. Charalampos (Eds.), *Musical haptics* (pp. 29–48). Springer Open.

Heal, D. J., Smith, S. L., Gosden, J., & Nutt, D. J. (2013). Amphetamine past and present – a pharmacological and clinical perspective. *Journal of Psychopharmacology*, 27, 479–496.

Healy, D. (1997). *The anti-depressant era*. Harvard University Press.

Heath, R. G. (1972). Pleasure and brain activity in man: Deep and surface electroencephalograms during orgasm. *Journal of Nervous and Mental Disorders*, 154, 3–18.

Hebb, D. O. (1949). *The organisation of behavior*. John Wiley.

Hécaen, H., & Angelergues, R. (1964). Localization of symptoms in aphasia. In A. V. S. DeRueck & M. O'Connor (Eds.), *Disorders of language* (pp. 223–256). Churchill.

Heckman, M. A., Weil, J., & De Meija, E. G. (2010). Caffeine (1, 3, 7-trimethylxanthine) in foods: A comprehensive review on consumption, functionality, safety, and regulatory matters. *Journal of Food Science*, 75, R77–R88.

Heilman, K. M. (2006). Aphasia and the diagram makers revisited: An update of information processing models. *Journal of Clinical Neurology*, 2, 149–162.

Heimer, L., & Larsson, K. (1967). Impairment of mating behavior in male rats following lesions in the preoptic-anterior hypothalamic continuum. *Brain Research*, 3, 248–263.

Hempal, H., O'Bryant, S. E., Molinuevo, J. L., Zetterberg, H., Masters, C. L., Lista, S., Kiddle, S. J., Batrla, R., & Blennow, K. (2018). Blood-based biomarkers for Alzheimer disease: Mapping the road to the clinic. *Nature Reviews, Neurology*, 14, 639–652.

Hendler, R. A., Ramchandani, V. A., Gilman, J., & Hommer, D. W. (2013). Stimulant and sedative effects of alcohol. *Current Topics in Behavioral Neuroscience*, 13, 489–509.

Henig, R. M. (2000). *A monk and two peas: The story of Gregor Mendel and the discovery of genetics*. Houghton Mifflin.

Henke, K., Buck, A., Weber, B., & Wieser, H. G. (1997). Human hippocampus establishes associations in memory. *Hippocampus, 7*, 249–256.

Hennenlotter, A., Dresel, C., Castrop, F., Ceballos-Baumann, A. O., Wohlschläger, A. M., & Haslinger, B. (2009). The link between facial feedback and neural activity within central circuitries of emotion-new insights from botulinum toxin-induced denervation of frown muscles. *Cerebral Cortex, 19*, 537–542.

Hennenlotter, A., Schroeder, U., Castrop, F., Haslinger, B., Stoecker, D., Lange, K. W., & Ceballos-Baumann, A. O. (2005). A common neural basis for receptive and expressive communication of pleasant facial affect. *NeuroImage, 26*, 581–591.

Henschen, S. E. (1926). On the function of the right hemisphere of the brain in relation to the left in speech, music and calculation. *Brain, 49*, 110–123.

Hepper, P. G., Shahidullah, S., & White, R. (1991). Handedness in the human fetus. *Neuropsychologia, 29*, 1107–1111.

Herculano-Houzel, S. (2009). The human brain in numbers: A linearly scaled-up primate brain. *Frontiers in Human Neuroscience, 3*, 1–11. https://doi.org/10.3389/neuro.09.031.2009

Heriot, A. (1955). *The castrati in opera*. Secker and Warburg.

Herkenham, M., Lynn, A. B., Johnson, M. R., Melvin, L. S., de Costa, B. R., & Rice, K. C. (1991). Characterization and localization of cannabinoid receptors in rat brain: A quantitative in vitro autoradiographic study. *Journal of Neuroscience, 11*, 563–583.

Hernán, M. A., Olek, M. J., & Ascherio, A. (2001). Cigarette smoking and the incidence of multiple sclerosis. *American Journal of Epidemiology, 154*, 69–74.

Hersch, S. M., Rosas, D., & Ferrante, R. J. (2011). Neuropathology and pathophysiology of Huntington's disease. In R. L. Watts, D. G. Standaert, & J. A. Obeso (Eds.), *Movement disorders* (Chapter 34). McGraw-Hill.

Heston, L. L. (1970). The genetics of schizophrenia and schizoid disease. *Science, 167*, 249–256.

Heymsfield, S. B., Greenberg, A. S., Fujioka, K., Dixon, R. M., Kushner, R., Hunt, T., Lubina, J. A., Patane, J., Self, B., Hunt, P., & McCamish, M. (1999). Recombinant leptin for weight loss in obese and lean adults: A randomized, controlled, dose-escalation trial. *Journal of the American Medical Association, 282*, 1568–1575.

Hickey, P., & Stacy, M. (2012). Adenosine A2A antagonists in Parkinson's disease: What's next?. *Current Neurology and Neuroscience Reports, 12*, 376–385.

Hickok, G., & Poeppel, D. (2007). The cortical organization of speech processing. *Nature Reviews Neuroscience, 8*, 393–402.

Higgs, S., Cooper, A., & Lee, J. (2020). *Biological psychology*. SAGE.

Hill, K., Mann, L., Laws, K. R., Stephenson, C. M., Nimmo-Smith, I., & McKenna, P. J. (2004). Hypofrontality in schizophrenia: A meta-analysis of functional imaging studies. *Acta Psychiatrica Scandinavca, 110*, 243–256.

Hill, W. D., Arslan, R. C., Xia, C., Luciano, M., Amador, C., Navarro, P., Hayward, C., Nagy, R., Porteous, D. J., McIntosh, A. M., Deary, I. J., Haley, C. S., & Penke, L. (2018). Genomic analysis of family data reveals additional genetic effects on intelligence and personality. *Molecular Psychiatry, 23*, 2347–2362.

Hille, B. (2001). *Ion channels of excitable membranes*. Sinauer.

Hillhouse, T. M., & Porter, J. H. (2015). A brief history of the development of antidepressant drugs: From monoamines to glutamate. *Experimental and Clinical Psychopharmacology, 23*, 1–21.

Hines, M. (2006). Prenatal testosterone and gender-related behavior. *European Journal of Endocrinology, 155*(Suppl. 1), S115–S121.

Hines, M., Armed, F., & Hughes, L. I. A. (2003). Psychological outcomes and gender-related development in complete androgen-insensitivity syndrome. *Archives of Sexual Behavior, 32*, 93–101.

Hines, M., Constantinescu, M., & Spencer, D. (2015). Early androgen exposure and human gender development. *Biology of Sex*

Differences, 6, 3. https://doi.org/10.1186/s13293-015-0022-1

Hirnstein, M., & Hugdahl, K. (2014). Excess of non-right-handedness in schizophrenia: Meta-analysis of gender effects and potential biases in handedness assessment. *British Journal of Psychiatry*, 205, 260–267.

Hirnstein, M., Hugdahl, K., & Hausmann, M. (2019). Cognitive sex differences and hemispheric asymmetry: A critical review of 40 years of research. *Laterality: Asymmetries of Body, Brain and Cognition*, 24, 204–252.

Hirschhorn, J. N., & Daly, M. J. (2005). Genome-wide association studies for common diseases and complex traits. *Nature Reviews Genetics*, 6, 95–108.

Ho, B., Baryshnikova, A., & Brown, G.W. (2018). Unification of protein abundance datasets yields a quantitative Saccharomyces cerevisiae proteome. *Cell Systems*, 6, 192–205.

Hobson, J. A. (1989). *The dreaming brain*. Penguin.

Hobson, J. A., McCarley, R. W., & Wzinski, P. W. (1975). Sleep cycle oscillation: Reciprocal discharge by two brainstem neuronal groups. *Science*, 189, 55–58.

Hodge, C. W., Samson, H. H., & Chappelle, A. M. (1997). Alcohol self-administration: Further examination of the role of dopamine receptors in the nucleus accumbens. *Alcoholism: Clinical and Experimental Research*, 21, 1083–1091.

Hoffman, A. (2005). *LSD: My problem child*. MAPS.org.

Hoffman, L. A., & Vilensky, J. A. (2017). Encephalitis lethargica: 100 years after the epidemic. *Brain*, 140, 2246–2251.

Hoffner, G., Kahlem, P., & Djian, P. (2002). Perinuclear localization of huntingtin as a consequence of its binding to microtubules through an interaction with beta-tubulin: Relevance to Huntington's disease. *Journal of Cell Science*, 115, 941–948.

Hohmann, G. W. (1966). Some effects of spinal cord lesions on experienced emotional feelings. *Psychophysiology*, 3, 143–156.

Hökfelt, T. (2009). Looking at neurotransmitters in the microscope. *Progress in Neurobiology*, 90, 101–118.

Holland, P. C., & Petrovich, G. D. (2005). A neural systems analysis of the potentiation of feeding by conditioned stimuli. *Physiology & Behavior*, 86, 747–761.

Holstege, G. (1991). Descending motor pathways and the spinal motor system: Limbic and non-limbic components. *Progress in Brain Research*, 87, 307–421.

Holstein, G. R. (2012). The vestibular system. In J. Mai & G. Paxinos (Eds.), *The human nervous system* (pp. 1239–1269). Academic Press.

Holtzheimer, P. E., & Nemeroff, C. B. (2006). Future prospects in depression research. *Dialogues in Clinical Neuroscience*, 8, 175–189.

Holtzman, S. G. (1990). Caffeine as a model drug of abuse. *Trends in Neurosciences*, 11, 355–356.

Homayoun, H., & Moghaddam, B. (2007). NMDA receptor hypofunction produces opposite effects on prefrontal cortex interneurons and pyramidal neurons. *Journal of Neuroscience*, 27, 11496–11500.

Honea, R., Crow, T. J., Passingham, D., & MacKay, C. E. (2005). Regional deficits in brain volume in schizophrenia: A meta-analysis of voxel-based morphometry studies. *American Journal of Psychiatry*, 162, 2233–2245.

Hoon, M., Okawa, H., Della Santina, L., & Wong, R. O. (2014). Functional architecture of the retina: Development and disease. *Progress in Retinal and Eye Research*, 42, 44–84.

Hooper, R. (2007, July 2) Yawning may boost brain's alertness. *New Scientist*.

Horne, J. (1978). A review of the biological effects of total sleep deprivation in man. *Biological Psychology*, 7, 55–102.

Horne, J. (1988). *Why we sleep*. Oxford University Press.

Hosak, L. (2013). New findings in the genetics of schizophrenia. *World Journal of Psychiatry*, 3, 57–61.

Howe, M. J. A. (1997). *IQ in question: The truth about intelligence*. SAGE.

Howes, O., McCutcheon, R., & Stone, J. (2015). Glutamate and dopamine in schizophrenia: An update for the 21st century. *Journal of Psychopharmacology*, 29, 97–115.

Howes, O. D., Kambeitz, J., Kim, E., Stahl, D., Slifstein, M., Abi-Dargham, A., & Kapur, S. (2012). The nature of dopamine dysfunction in schizophrenia and what this means for treatment. *Archives of General Psychiatry, 69,* 776–786.

Howes, O. D., & Kapur, S. (2009). The dopamine hypothesis of schizophrenia: Version III – The final common pathway. *Schizophrenia Bulletin, 35,* 549–562.

Howes, O. D., Williams, M., Ibrahim, K., Leung, G., Egerton, A., McGuire, P. K., & Turkheimer, F. (2013). Midbrain dopamine function in schizophrenia and depression: A post-mortem and positron emission tomographic imaging study. *Brain, 136,* 3242–3251.

Howland, R. H. (2015). Buspirone: Back to the future. *Journal of Psychosocial Nursing and Mental Health Services, 53,* 21–24.

Hruby, A., & Hu, F. B. (2015). The epidemiology of obesity: A big picture. *Pharmacoeconomics, 33,* 673–689.

Hser, Y. I., Hoffman, V., Grella, C. E., & Anglin, M. D. (2001). A 33-year follow-up of narcotics addicts. *Archives of General Psychiatry, 58,* 503–508.

Huang, A. R., Strombotne, K. L., Horner, E. M., & Lapham, S. J. (2018). Adolescent cognitive aptitudes and later-in-life Alzheimer disease and related disorders. *Journal of the American Medical Association. 1*(5), e181726. https://doi.org/10.1001/jamanetworkopen.2018.1726

Hubel, D. H. (1995). *Eye, brain and vision.* Scientific American Library.

Hubel, D. H., & Wiesel, T. N. (2005). *Brain and visual perception: The story of a 25-year collaboration.* Oxford University Press.

Hudspeth, A. J. (1983). Mechanoelectrical transduction by hair cells in the acousticolateralis sensory system. *Annual Review of Neuroscience, 6,* 187–215.

Hudspeth, A. J. (2000). Hearing. In E. R. Kandel, H. Schwartz, & T. M. Jessell (Eds.), *Principles of neural science.* McGraw-Hill.

Hugdahl, K., Thomsen, T., & Ersland, L. (2006). Sex differences in visuo-spatial processing: An fMRI study of mental rotation. *Neuropsychologia, 44,* 1575–1583.

Hunt, D. M., Dulai, K. S., Bowmaker, J. K., & Mollon, J. D. (1995). The chemistry of John Dalton's color blindness. *Science, 267,* 984–988.

Huntington Study Group. (2006). Tetrabenazine as antichorea therapy in Huntington disease: a randomized controlled trial. *Neurology, 66,* 366–372.

Huntington's Disease Collaborative Research Group (1993). A novel gene containing a trinucleotide repeat that is expanded and unstable on Huntington's disease chromosomes. *Cell, 72,* 971–983.

Huntley, J. D., & Howard, R. J. (2010). Working memory in early 'Alzheimer's disease: A neuropsychological review. *International Journal of Geriatric Psychiatry, 25,* 121–132.

Huppert, F. A., & Piercy, M. (1979). Normal and abnormal forgetting in organic amnesia: Effect of locus of lesion. *Cortex, 15,* 385–390.

Hurley, K. M., Herbert, H., Moga, M. M., & Saper, C. B. (1991). Efferent projections of the infralimbic cortex of the rat. *Journal of Comparative Neurology, 308,* 249–276.

Huron, D. (2001). Is music an evolutionary adaptation? *Annals of the New York Academy of Sciences, 930,* 43—61.

Hurvich, L. M., & Jameson, D. (1957). An opponent-process theory of color vision. *Psychological Review, 64,* 384–404.

Hyman, S. E. (2005). Neurotransmitters. *Current Biology, 15,* R154–R158.

Iinytska, O., & Argyropoulus, G. (2008). The role of the agouti-related protein in energy balance regulation. *Cellular and Molecular Life Sciences, 65,* 2721–2731.

Ingalhalikar, M., Smith, A., Parker, D., Satterthwaite, T. D., Elliott, M. A., Ruparel, K., Hakonarson, H., Gur, R. E., Gur, R. C., & Verma, R., (2014). Sex differences in the structural connectome of the human brain. *Proceedings of the National Academy of Sciences of the USA, 111,* 823–828.

Ingalls, A. M., Dickie, M. M., & Snell, G. D. (1950). Obese, a new mutation in the house mouse. *Journal of Heredity, 41,* 317–318.

Ingólfsson, H. I., & Andersen, O. S. (2011). Alcohol's effects on lipid bilayer properties. *Biophysics Journal, 101,* 847–855.

Inouye, S., & Kawamura, H. (1979). Persistence of circadian rhythmicity in a mammalian hypothalamic "island" containing the suprachiasmatic nucleus. *Proceedings of the National Academy of Sciences, 76*, 5692–5966.

Irimia, A., Maher, A. S., Rostowsky, K. A., Chowdhury, N. F., Hwang, D. H., & Law, E. M. (2019). Brain segmentation from computed tomography of healthy aging and geriatric concussion at variable spatial resolutions. *Frontiers in Neuroinformatics, 13*, 9. https://doi.org/10.3389/fninf.2019.00009

Irwin, M. (2015). Why sleep is important for health: A psychoneuroimmunology perspective. *Annual Review of Psychology, 66*, 143–172.

Iseki, K., Hanakawa, T., Shinozaki, J., Nankaku, M., & Fukuyama, H. (2008). Neural mechanisms involved in mental imagery and observation of gait. *NeuroImage, 41*, 1021–1031.

Iurato, S. (1967). *Submicroscopc structure of the inner ear*. Pergamon.

Ivanov, A., & Ashton-Jones, G. (2001). Local opiate withdrawal in locus coeruleus neurons in vitro. *Journal of Neurophysiology, 85*, 2388–2397.

Iversen, L. L. (2003). Cannabis and the brain. *Brain, 126*, 1252–1270.

Izquierdo, I., Cammarota, M., Da Silva, W. C., Bevilaqua, L. R., Rossato, J. I., Bonini, J. S., Mello, P., Benetti, F., Costa, J. C., & Median, G. H. (2008). The evidence for hippocampal long-term potentiation as a basis of memory for simple tasks. *Anais da Academia Brasileira da Ciencias, 80*, 115–127.

Jablensky, A. (2010). The diagnostic concept of schizophrenia: Its history, evolution and future prospects. *Dialogues in Clinical Neuroscience, 12*, 271–287.

Jablensky, A., Sartorius, N., Emberg, G., Anker, M., Korten, A., Cooper, J. E., Day, R., & Bertelsen, A. (1992). Schizophrenia: Manifestations, incidence and course in different cultures. A World Health Organisation 10 country study. *Psychological Medicine Monograph Supplement, 20*, 1–97.

Jackson, M. (2014). Evaluating the role of Hans Selye in the modern history of stress. In D. Cantor & E. Ramsden (Eds.), *Stress, shock, and adaptation in the twentieth century* (pp. 1–34). University of Rochester Press.

Jackson, S. E., Llewellyn, C. H., & Smith, L. (2020). The obesity epidemic – Nature via nurture: A narrative review of high-income countries. *SAGE Open Medicine, 8*, 2050312120918265. https://doi.org/10.1177/2050312120918265

Jackson, W. J., Buccafusco, J. J., Terry, A. V., Turk, D. J., & Rush, D. K. (1995). Velnacrine maleate improves delayed matching performance by aged monkeys. *Psychopharmacology, 119*, 391–398.

Jacobs, B., Schall, M., & Scheibel, A. B. (1993). A quantitative dendritic analysis of Wernicke's area in humans. II. Gender, hemispheric, and environmental factors. *Journal of Comparative Neurology, 327*, 97–111.

Jacobs, B. L., van Praag, H., & Gage, F. H. (2000). Adult brain neurogenesis and psychiatry: A novel theory of depression. *Molecular Psychiatry, 5*, 262–269.

Jacobs, L. F., Gaulin, S. J. C., Sherry, D. F., & Hoffman, G. E. (1990). Evolution of spatial cognition: Sex-specific patterns of spatial behavior predict hippocampal size. *Proceedings of the New York Academy of Sciences, 87*, 6349–6352.

Jaenisch, R., & Mintz, B. (1974). Simian virus 40 DNA sequences in DNA of healthy adult mice derived from preimplantation blastocysts injected with viral DNA. *Proceedings of the National Academy of Sciences of the USA, 71*, 1250–1254.

Jaillard, A., Martin, C. D., Garambois, K., Lebas, J. F., & Hommel, M. (2005). Vicarious function within the human primary motor cortex? A longitudinal fMRI stroke study. *Brain, 128*, 1122–1138.

James, S. M., Honn, K. A., Gaddermmedi, S., & Van Dongen, H. P. A. (2017). Shift work: Disrupted circadian rhythms and sleep – implications for health and well-being. *Current Sleep Medical Reports, 3*, 104–112.

Jäncke, L. (2018). Sex/gender differences in cognition, neurophysiology, and neuroanatomy. *F1000Research, 7*, F1000 Faculty Rev-805. https://doi.org/10.12688/f1000research.13917.1

Jardemark, K., Wadenberg, M.-L., Grillner, P., & Svensson, T. H. (2002). Dopamine D3 and D4 receptor antagonists in the treatment of schizophrenia. *Current Opinion in Investigational Drugs*, 3, 101–105.

Jaskiw, G., & Kleinman, J. (1988). Postmortem neurochemistry studies in schizophrenia. In S. C. Schulz & C. A. Tamminga (Eds.), *Schizophrenia: A scientific focus* (pp. 209–216). Oxford University Press.

Javitt, D. C. (2010). Glutamatergic theories of schizophrenia. *The Israeli Journal of Psychiatry and Related Sciences*, 47, 4–16.

Jay, S. M., Lamond, N., Ferguson, S. A., Dorrian, J., Jones, C. B., & Dawson, D. (2007). The characteristics of recovery sleep when recovery opportunity is restricted. *Sleep*, 30, 353–360.

Jeanmonod, D., Magnin, M., & Morel, A. (1993). Thalamus and neurogenic pain: Physiological, anatomical and clinical data. *Neuroreport*, 4, 475–478.

Jenkins, I. H., Jahanshahi, M., Jueptner, M., Passingham, R. E., & Books, D. G. (2000). Self-initiated versus externally triggered movements: II. The effect of movement predictability on regional cerebral blood flow. *Brain*, 123, 1216–1228.

Jeon, T. Y., Lee, S., Kim, H. H., Kim, Y. J., Lee, J. G., Jeong, D. W., & Kim, Y. J. (2010). Long-term changes in gut hormones, appetite and food intake 1 year after subtotal gastrectomy with normal body weight. *European Journal of Clinical Nutrition*, 64, 826–831.

Jeune, B., Robine, J. M., Young, R., Desjardins, B., Skytthe, A., & Vaupel, W. (2010). Jeanne Calment and her successors: Biographical notes on the longest living humans. In H. Maier, J. Gampe, B. Jeune, J. M. Robine, & J. Vaupel (Eds.), *Supercentenarians, demographic research monographs* (pp. 285–323). Springer-Verlag.

Jewitt, D. C., Cleary, J., Levine, A. S., Schaal, D. W., & Thompson, T. (1992). Effects of neuropeptide Y on food-reinforced behavior in satiated rats. *Pharmacology, Biochemistry and Behavior*, 42, 207–212.

Jobard, G., Crivello, F., & Tzourio-Mazoyer, N. (2003). Evaluation of the dual route theory of reading: A metanalysis of 35 neuroimaging studies. *NeuroImage*, 20, 693–712.

Johnson, C., Drgon, T., Liu, Q. R., Walther, D., Edenberg, H., Rice, J., Foroud, T., & Uhl, G. R. (2006). Pooled association genome scanning for alcohol dependence using 104,268 SNPs: Validation and use to identify alcoholism vulnerability loci in unrelated individuals from the collaborative study on the genetics of alcoholism. *American Journal of Medical Genetics*, 141B(8), 844–853.

Johnson, K. O. (2001). The roles and functions of cutaneous mechanoreceptors. *Current Opinion in Neurobiology*, 11, 455–461.

Joiner, W. J. (2016). Unraveling the evolutionary determinants of sleep. *Current Biology*, 26, R1073–R1087.

Jones, B. (1979). Elimination of paradoxical sleep by lesions of the pontine gigantocellular tegmental field in the rat. *Neuroscience Letters*, 13, 285–293.

Jones, B. (2011). Neurobiology of waking and sleeping. *Handbook of Clinical Neurobiology*, 98, 131–149.

Jones, B. (2018). The mysteries of sleep and waking unveiled by Michel Jouvet. *Sleep Medicine*, 49, 14–19.

Jones, D. T., & Reed, R. R. G. (1989). An olfactory neuron specific G protein involved in odorant signal transduction. *Science*, 244, 790–795.

Jones, H. S., & Oswald, I. (1968). Two cases of health insomnia. *Electroencephalography and Clinical Neurophysiology*, 24, 378–380.

Jones, S. (1993). *The language of the genes.* Flamingo.

Joseph, J. (2003). *The gene illusion.* PCCS Books.

Joseph, J. (2015). *The trouble with twin studies.* Routledge.

Joslyn, W. D. (1973). Androgen-induced dominance in infant female rhesus monkeys. *Journal of Child Psychology and Psychiatry*, 14, 137–145.

Jouvet, M. (1962). Recherches sur les structures nerveuses et les mécanismes responsables des différentes phases du sommeil physiologique. *Archives of Italian Biology*, 100, 125–206.

Jouvet, M. (1967). Neurophysiology and the states of sleep. *Science*, 163, 32–41.

Jouvet, M. (1972). The role of monoamines and acetylcholine-containing neurons in the regulation of the sleep-waking cycle. *Ergebnisse der Physiologie*, 64, 166–307.

Jouvet, M. (1979). What does a cat dream about? *Trends in Neurosciences*, 2, 280–282.

Jouvet, M., & Delorme, F. (1965). Locus coeruleus et sommeil paradoxal. *Comptes Rendus Société de Biologie*, 159, 895–899.

Jouvet, M., & Renault, J. (1966). Insomnie persistante apres lesions des noyaux du raphe chez le chat. *Comptes Rendus de la Société de Biologie (Paris)*, 160, 1461–1465.

Jung, J., Cloutman, L. L., Binney, R. J., & Lambon Ralph, M. A. (2017). The structural connectivity of higher order association cortices reflects human functional brain networks. *Cortex*, 97, 221–239.

Kaas, J. H. (2012). Somatosensory system. In J. K. Mai & G. Paxinos (Eds.), *The human nervous system* (pp. 1074–1109). Academic Press.

Kaas, J. H., & Hackett, T. A. (2000). Subdivisions of auditory cortex and processing streams in primates. *Proceedings of the National Academy of Sciences of the USA*, 97, 11793–11799.

Kachian, Z. R., Cohen-Zimerman, S., Bega, D., Gordon, B., & Grafman, J. (2019). Suicidal ideation and behavior in Huntington's disease: Systematic review and recommendations. *Journal of Affective Disorders*, 250, 319–329.

Kalakoski, V., & Saariluoma, P. (2001). Taxi drivers' exceptional memory of street names. *Memory & Cognition*, 29, 634–638.

Kallmann, F. J. (1952). Twin and sibship study of overt male homosexuality. *American Journal of Genetics*, 4, 136–146.

Kamegai, J., Tamura, H., Shimizu, T., Ishii, S., Sugihara, H., & Wakabayashi, I. (2001). Chronic central infusion of ghrelin increases hypothalamic neuropeptide Y and agouti-related protein mRNA levels and body weight in rats. *Diabetes*, 50, 2438–2443.

Kandel, E. R. (2012). The molecular biology of memory: cAMP, PKA, CRE, CREB-1, CREB-2 and CPEB. *Molecular Brain*, 5, 1–12. https://doi.org/10.1186/1756-6606-5-14.

Kandel, E. R. (2016). Eric Kandel. In T. D. Albright & L. R. Squire (Eds.), *The history of neuroscience in autobiography* (Vol. 9, pp. 166–219). Society for Neuroscience.

Kandel, E. R., Dudai, Y., & Mayford, M. R. (2014). The molecular and systems biology of memory. *Cell*, 157, 163–186.

Kang, D. W., Lee, C. U., & Lim, H. K. (2017). Role of sleep disturbance in the trajectory of Alzheimer's Disease. *Clinical Psychopharmacology and Neuroscience*, 15, 89–99.

Kanwisher, N. (2010). Functional specificity in the human brain: A window into the functional architecture of the mind. *Proceedings of the National Academy of Sciences of the USA*, 107, 11163–11170.

Kanwisher, N., McDermott, J., & Chun, M. M. (1997). The fusiform face area: A module in human extrastriate cortex specialised for face perception. *Journal of Neuroscience*, 17, 4302–4311.

Kaplan, J. S. (2012). The effects of shared environment on adult intelligence: A critical review of adoption, twin, and MZA studies. *Developmental Psychology*, 48, 1292–1298.

Kapp, B. S., Frysinger, R. C., Gallagher, M., & Haselton, J. R. (1979). Amygdala central nucleus lesions: Effects on heart rate conditioning in the rabbit. *Physiology and Behaviour*, 23, 1109–1117.

Kapp, B. S., Pascoe, J. P., & Bixler, M. A. (1984). The amygdala: A neuroanatomical systems approach to its contributions to aversive conditioning. In N. Butters & L.R. Squire (Eds.), *The neuropsychology of memory* (pp. 473–488). The Guilford Press.

Kapur, S., & Seeman, P. (2002). NMDA receptor antagonists ketamine and PCP have direct effects on the dopamine D(2) and serotonin 5-HT(2) receptors-implications for models of schizophrenia. *Molecular Psychiatry*, 7, 837–844.

Kar, S. K., & Jain, M. (2016). Current understandings about cognition and the neurobiological correlates in schizophrenia. *Journal of Neurosciences in Rural Practice*, 7, 412–418.

Karama, S., Lecours, A. R., Leroux, J.-M., Bourgouin, P., Beaudoin, G., Joubert, S.,

& Beauregard, M. (2002). Areas of brain activation in males and females during viewing of erotic film excerpts. *Human Brain Mapping*, 16, 1–13.

Kargieman, L., Riga, M. S., Artigas, F., & Celada, P. (2012). Clozapine reverses phencyclidine-induced desynchronization of prefrontal cortex through a 5-HT1A receptor-dependent mechanism. *Neuropsychopharmacology*, 37, 723–733.

Katner, S. N., & Weiss, F. (2001). Neurochemical characteristics associated with ethanol preference in selected alcoholpreferring and -nonpreferring rats: A quantitative microdialysis study. *Alcoholism: Clinical and Experimental Research*, 25, 198–205.

Katzman, R. (1976). The prevalence and malignancy of Alzheimer's disease: A major killer. *Archives of Neurology*, 33, 217–218.

Katzman, R., Terry, R., DeTeresa, R., Brown, T., Davies, P., Fuld, P., Renbing, X., & Peck, A. (1988). Clinical, pathological, and neurochemical changes in dementia: A subgroup with preserved mental status and numerous neocortical plaques. *Annals of Neurology*, 23,138–144.

Kavanau, J. L. (2006). Is sleep's "supreme mystery" unraveling? An evolutionary analysis of sleep encounters no mystery; nor does life's earliest sleep, recently discovered in jellyfish. *Medical Hypotheses*, 66, 3–9.

Kaye, W. H., Greeno, C. G., Moss, H., Fernstrom, J., Fernstrom, M., Lilenfeld, L. R., Weltzin, T. E., & Mann, J. J. (1998). Alterations in serotonin activity and psychiatric symptoms after recovery from bulimia nervosa. *Archives of General Psychiatry*, 55, 927–935.

Kaye, W. H., Jimmerson, D. C., Lake, C. R., & Ebert, M. H. (1985). Altered norepinephrine metabolism following longterm weight recovery in patients with anorexia nervosa. *Psychiatry Research*, 14, 333–342.

Kaye, W. H., Wagner, A., Fudge, J. L., & Paulus, M. (2011). Neurocircuity of eating disorders. *Current Topics in Behavioral Neurosciences*, 6, 37–57.

Kaye, W. H., Wierenga, C. E., Bailer, U. F., Simmons, A. N., & Bischoff-Grethe, A. (2013). Nothing tastes as good as skinny feels: The neurobiology of anorexia nervosa. *Trends in Neurosciences*, 36, 110–120. https://doi.org/10.1016/j.tins.2013.01.003

Ke, Y. D., Suchowerska, A. K., van der Hoven, J., De Silva, D. M., Wu, C. W., van Eersel, J., Ittner, A., & Ittner, L. M. (2012). Lessons from tau-deficient mice. *International Journal of Alzheimer's Disease*, 2012, 873270. https://doi.org/10.1155/2012/873270

Kebabian, J. W., & Calne, D. B. (1979). Multiple receptors for dopamine. *Nature*, 277, 93–96.

Kee, N., Teixeira, C. M., Wang, A. H., & Frankland, P. W. (2007). Preferential incorporation of adult-generated granule cells into spatial memory networks in the dentate gyrus. *Nature Neuroscience*, 10, 355–362.

Kelesidis, T., Kelesidis, I., Chou, S., & Mantzoros, C. S. (2010). Narrative review: The role of leptin in human physiology: emerging clinical applications. *Annals of Internal Medicine*, 152, 93–100.

Kellendonk, C., Simpson, E. H., & Kandel, E. R. (2009). Modelling cognitive endophenotypes of schizophrenia in mice. *Trends in Neurosciences*, 32, 347–358.

Kellner, M. (2010). Drug treatment of obsessive-compulsive disorder. *Dialogues in Clinical Neuroscience*, 12,187–197.

Keltner, D., & Ekman, P. (2000). Facial expression of emotion. In M. Lewis & J. Haviland-Jones (Eds.), *Handbook of emotions* (pp. 415–432). The Guildford Press.

Kenborg, L., Rugbjerg, K., Lee, P.-C., Ravnskjær, L., Christensen, J., Ritz, B., & Lassen, C. F. (2015). Head injury and risk for Parkinson disease: Results from a Danish case-control study. *Neurology*, 84, 1098–1103.

Kendell, R. E., & Adams, W. (1991). Unexplained fluctuations in the risk for schizophrenia by month and year of birth. *British Journal of Psychiatry*, 158, 758–763.

Kendler, K. S., Gatz, M., Gardner, C. O., & Pedersen, N. L. (2006). A Swedish national twin study of lifetime major depression. *American Journal of Psychiatry*, 163, 109–114.

Kendler, K. S., Turkheimer, E., Ohlsson, H., Sundquist, J., & Sundquist, K. (2015). Family environment and the malleability of cognitive ability: A Swedish national home-reared and adopted-away cosibling control study. *Proceedings of the National Academy of Sciences of the USA*, 112, 4612–4617.

Kendrick, K. M., & Baldwin, B. A. (1987). Cells in temporal cortex of conscious sheep can respond preferentially to the sight of faces. *Science*, 236, 448–450.

Kernell, D. (2016). *Colours and colour vision: An introductory survey*. Cambridge University Press.

Kerr, G. W., McGuy, A. C., & Wilkie, S. (2001). Tricyclic antidepressant overdose: A review. *Emergency Medical Journal*, 18, 236–241.

Kertesz, A. (1979). *Aphasia and associated disorders*. New York: Grune and Stratton.

Kessler, R. C. (2012). The costs of depression. *Psychiatric Clinics of North America*, 35, 1–14.

Kestler, L. P., Walker, E., & Vega, E. M. (2001). Dopamine receptors in the brains of schizophrenia patients: A meta-analysis of the findings. *Behavioral Pharmacology*, 12, 355–371.

Kety, S. S., Rosenthal, D., Wender, P. H., & Schesinger, F. (1968). The types and prevalence of mental illness in the biological and adoptive families of adopted schizophrenics. *Journal of Psychiatric Research*, 6, 345–362.

Khajehei, M., & Behroozpour, E. (2018). Endorphins, oxytocin, sexuality and romantic relationships: An understudied area. *World Journal of Obstetrics and Gynaecology*, 7, 17–23.

Kieffer, B. L., & Gavériaux-Ruff, C. (2002). Exploring the opioid system by gene knockout. *Progress in Neurobiology*, 66, 285–306.

Kikuchi, T., Morizane, A., Doi, D., Magotani, H., Onoe, H., Hayashi, T., Mizuma, H., Takara, S., Takahashi, R., Inoue, H., Morita, S., Yamamoto, M., Okita, K., Nakagawa, M., Parmar, M., & Takahasi, J. (2017). Human iPS cell-derived dopaminergic neurons function in a primate Parkinson's disease model. *Nature*, 548, 592–596.

Killcross, S., Robbins, T. W., & Everett, B. J. (1997). Different types of fear-conditioned behavior mediated by separate nuclei within amygdala. *Nature*, 388, 377–380.

Kim, J., & Gorman, J. M. (2005). The psychobiology of anxiety. *Clinical Neuroscience Research*, 4, 335–347.

Kim, S., Jeneson, A., van der Horst, A. S., Frascino, J. C., Hopkins, R. O., & Squire, L. R. (2011). Memory, visual discrimination performance, and the human hippocampus. *Journal of Neuroscience*, 31(7), 2624–2649.

Kim, W. B., & Cho, J.-H. (2017). Encoding of discriminative fear memory by input-specific LTP in the amygdala. *Neuron*, 95, 1129–1146.

Kimura, D. (1992). Sex differences in the brain. *Scientific American*, 267, 80–87.

Kimura, D. (1999). *Sex and cognition*. MIT Press.

Kinsey, A. C., Pomeroy, W. B., & Martin, C. E. (1948). *Sexual behavior in the human male*. Saunders.

Kissileff, H. R., Pi-Sunyer, F. X., Thornton, J., & Smith, G. P. (1981). C-terminal octapeptide of cholecystokinin decreases food intake in man. *American Journal of Clinical Nutrition*, 34, 154–160.

Klee, W. A., & Nirenberg, M. (1974). A neuroblastoma times glioma hybrid cell line with morphine receptors. *Proceedings of the National Academy of Sciences*, 71, 3474–3477.

Klein, A. P., Ulmer, J. L, Quinet, S. A., Mathews, V., & Mark. L. P. (2016). Nonmotor functions of the cerebellum: An introduction. *American Journal of Neuroradiology*, 37, 1005–1009.

Klein, S. B., & Thorne, B. M. (2007). *Biological psychology*. Worth.

Kleinhans, N. M., Johnson, L. C., Richards, T., Mahurin, R., Greenson, J., Dawson, G., & Aylward, E. (2009). Reduced neural habituation in the amygdala and social impairments in autism spectrum disorders. *American Journal of Psychiatry*, 166, 467–475.

Klüver, H., & Bucy, P. C. (1938). An analysis of certain effects of bilateral temporal lobectomy in the rhesus monkey with special reference to "psychic blindness". *Journal of Psychology*, 5, 33–54.

Knecht, S., Kunesch, E., & Schnitzler, A. (1996). Parallel and serial processing of haptic information in man: Effects of parietal lesions on sensorimotor hand function. *Neuropsychologia*, 34, 669–687.

Knuepfer, M. M. (2003). Cardiovascular disorders associated with cocaine use: Myths and truths. *Pharmacology and Therapeutics*, 97, 181–222.

Kobesova, A., & Kolar, P. (2014). Developmental kinesiology: Three levels of motor control in the assessment and treatment of the motor system. *Journal of Bodywork and Movement Therapies*, 18, 23–33.

Kocabicak, E., Tan, S. K., & Temel, Y. (2012). Deep brain stimulation of the subthalamic nucleus in Parkinson's disease: Why so successful? *Surgical Neurology International*, 3, S312–S314.

Kodama, T., Takahashi, Y., & Honda, Y. (1990). Enhancement of acetylcholine release during paradoxical sleep in the dorsal tegmental field of the brain stem. *Neuroscience Letters*, 114, 277–282.

Kodamo, Y., Zhao, C.-M., Kulseng, B., & Chen, D. (2010). Eating behavior in rats subjected to vagotomy, sleeve gastrectomy, and duodenal switch. *Journal of Gastrointestinal Surgery*, 14, 1502–1510.

Kogan, M. D., Vladutiu, C. J., Schieve, L. A., Ghandour, R. M., Blumberg, S. J., Zablotsky, B., Perrin, J. M., Shattuck, P., Kuhlthau, K. A., Harwood, R. L., & Lu, M. C. (2018). The prevalence of parent-reported autism spectrum disorder among US children. *Pediatrics*, 142, e20174161. https://doi.org/10.1542/peds.2017-4161

Kojima, M., Hosoda, H., Date, Y., Nakazato, M., Matsuo, H., & Kangawa, K. (1999). Ghrelin is a growth-hormone-releasing acylated peptide from stomach. *Nature*, 402, 656–660.

Kojima, M., & Kangawa, K. (2005). Ghrelin: Structure and function. *Physiological Reviews*, 85, 495–522.

Kolb, B., & Whishaw, I. Q. (2015). *Fundamentals of human neuropsychology*. Worth.

Konen, C. S., & Kastner, S. (2008). Two hierarchically organized neural systems for object information in human visual cortex. *Nature Neuroscience*, 11, 224–231.

Konopka, R. J., & Benzer, S. (1971). Clock mutants of Drosophilia melanogaster. *Proceedings of the National Academy of Sciences*, 68, 2112–2116.

Koob, G. F., & Bloom, F. E. (1988). Cellular and molecular mechanisms of drug dependence. *Science*, 242, 715–723.

Koob, G. F., & Goeders, N. E. (1989). Neuroanatomical substrates of drug self-administration. In J. M. Leibman & S. J. Cooper (Eds.), *Neuropharmacological basis of reward* (pp. 214–263). Oxford University Press.

Koob, G. F., & Le Moal, M. (2006). *Neurobiology of addiction*. Elsevier.

Koob, G. F., Maldonado, R., & Stinus, L. (1992). Neural substrates of opiate withdrawal. *Trends in Neurosciences*, 15, 186–191.

Koop, L. K., & Tadi, P. (2020). Neuroanatomy, sensory nerves. In *StatPearls* (pp. 1–9). StatPearls Publishing.

Koopman, P., Gubbay, J., Vivian, N., Goodfellow, P., & Lovell-Badge, R. (1991). Male development of chromosomally female mice transgenic for Sry. *Nature*, 351, 117–121.

Koopmans, H. S. (1981). The role of the gastrointestinal tract in the satiation of hunger. In L. A. Cioffi, W. P. T. James, & T. B. van Itallie (Eds.), *The body weight regulatory system* (pp. 45–55). Raven Press.

Kornek, B., & Lassmann, H. (2003). Neuropathology of multiple sclerosis – new concepts. *Brain Research Bulletin*, 61, 321–326.

Kornhuber, H. H., & Deeke, L. (1965). Changes in the brain potential in voluntary movements and passive movements in man: Readiness potential and reafferent potentials. *Pflügers Archives*, 284, 1–17.

Koscik, T., O'Leary, D., Moser, D. J., Andreasen, N. C., & Nopoulis, D. (2009). Sex differences in parietal lobe morphology: Relationship to mental rotation performance. *Brain and Cognition*, 69, 451–459.

Kosonogov, V., De Zorzi, L., Honoré, J., Martínez-Velázquez, E. S., Nandrino, J. L., Martinez-Selva, J. M., & Sequeira, H. (2017). Facial thermal variations: A new marker of emotional arousal. *PLoS One*, 12, e0183592. https://doi.org/10.1371/journal.pone.0183592

Kosten, T. R., & George, T. P. (2002). The neurobiology of opioid dependence: Implications for treatment. *Science and Practice Perspectives*, 1, 13–20.

Koulack, D., & Goodenough, D. R. (1976). Dream recall and dream recall failure: An arousal-retrieval model. *Psychological Bulletin*, 83, 975–984.

Kozio, L. F., Budding, D., Andreasen, N., Budding, D., Andreasen, N., D'Arrigo, S., Bulgheroni, S., Imamizu, H., Ito, M., Manto, M., Marvel, C., Parker, K., Pezzulo, G., Ramnani, N., Riva, D., Schmahmann, J., Vandervert, L., & Yamazaki, T. (2014). Consensus paper: The cerebellum's role in movement and cognition. *Cerebellum*, 13, 151–177.

Krank, M. D., & Perkins, W. L. (1993). Conditioned withdrawal elicited by contextual cues for morphine administration. *Psychobiology*, 21, 113–119.

Krantz, J. (2009). *Experiencing sensation and perception*. Pearson Education.

Krause, A. J., Simon, E. B., Mander, B. A., Greer, S. M., Saletin, J. M., Goldstein-Piekarski, A. N., & Walker, M. P. (2017). The sleep-deprived human brain. *Nature Reviews Neuroscience*, 18, 404–418.

Krekelberg, B. (2010). Saccadic suppression. *Current Biology*, 20, R228–R229.

Kreuz, L. E., & Rose, R. M. (1972). Assessment of aggressive behavior and plasma testosterone in a young criminal population. *Psychosomatic Medicine*, 34, 321–332.

Kril, J. J., & Harper, C. G. (2012). Neuroanatomy and neuropathology associated with Korsakoff's syndrome. *Neuropsychology Review*, 22, 72–80.

Kringelbach, M. L. (2005). The human orbitofrontal cortex: Linking reward to hedonic experience. *Nature Reviews Neuroscience*, 6, 691–702.

Kristensen, P., Judge, M. E., Thim, L., Ribel, U., Christjansen, K. N., Wulff, B. S.,

Clausen, J. T., Jensen, P. B., Madsen, O. D., Vrang, N., Larsen, P. J., & Hastrup, S. (1998). Hypothalamic CART is a new anorectic peptide regulated by leptin. *Nature*, 393, 72–76.

Krüger, J. (1981). The difference between x- and y-type responses in ganglion cells of the cat's retina. *Vision Research*, 21, 1685–1687.

Kruijver, F. P., Zhou, J. N., Pool, C. W., Hofman, M. A., Gooren, L. J., & Swaab, D. F. (2000). Male-to-female transsexuals have female neuron numbers in a limbic nucleus. *Journal of Clinical Endocrinology and Metabolism*, 85, 2034–2041.

Kuffler, S. W. (1953). Discharge patterns and functional organization of the mammalian retina. *Journal of Neurophysiology*, 16, 37–68.

Kuhn, R. (1958). The treatment of depressive states with G22355 (imipramine hydrochloride). *American Journal of Psychiatry*, 115, 459–464.

Kulkarni, B., Bentley, D. E., Elliott, R., Youell, P., Watson, A., Derbyshire, S. W., Frackowiak, R. S., Friston, K. J., & Jones, A. K. P. (2005). Attention to pain localization and unpleasantness discriminates the functions of the medial and lateral pain systems. *European Journal of Neuroscience*, 21, 3133–3142.

Kullmann, D. M. (2011). What's wrong with the amygdala in temporal lobe epilepsy? *Brain*, 134, 2800–2801.

Kumar, S., & Sagili, H. (2014). Etiopathogenesis and neurobiology of narcolepsy: A review. *Journal of Clinical and Diagnostic Research*, 8, 190–195.

Kurihara, K., & Kashiwayanagi, M. (1998). Introductory remarks on unami taste. *Annals of the New York Academy of Sciences*, 855, 393–397. https://doi.org/10.1111/j.1749-6632.1998.tb10597.x

Kurth, F., Jancke, L., & Luders, E. (2017). Sexual dimorphism of Broca's region: More gray matter in female brains in Brodmann areas 44 and 45. *Journal of Neuroscience Research*, 95, 626–632.

Kushida, C. A., Littner, M. R., Morgenthaler, T., Alessi, C. A., Bailey, D., Coleman, J., Jr, Friedman, L., Hirshkowitz, M., Kapen, S., Kramer, M., Lee-Chiong, T., Loube, D. L., Owens, J., Pancer, J. P.,

& Wise, M. (2005). Practice parameters for the indications for polysomnography and related procedures: An update for 2005. *Sleep*, 28, 499–521.

Lacoste-Utamsing, M. C., & Holloway, R. L. (1982). Sexual dimorphism in the human corpus callosum. *Science*, 216, 1431–1432.

Lamb, T. D. (2015). Why rods and cones? *Eye*, 30, 179–185.

Lanciego, J, L., Luquin, N., & Obeso, J. A. (2012). Functional neuroanatomy of the basal ganglia. *Cold Spring Harbor Perspectives in Medicine*, 2(12), a009621. https://doi.org/10.1101/cshperspect.a009621

Lane, R. D., & Nadel, L. (Eds.). (2002). *Cognitive neuroscience of emotion*. Oxford University Press.

Lang, A. E., & Obeso, J. A. (2004). Challenges in Parkinson's disease: Restoration of the nigrostriatal dopamine system is not enough. *The Lancet Neurology*, 3, 309–316.

Lang, P. J. (1994). The varieties of emotional experience: A meditation on James-Lange theory. *Psychological Review*, 101, 211–221.

Langbehn, D. R., Hayden, M. R., & Paulsen, J. S., & the PREDICT-HD Investigators of the Huntington Study Group. (2010). CAG-repeat length and the age of onset in Huntington disease (HD): A review and validation study of statistical approaches. *American Journal of Medical Genetics*, 153B9(2), 397–408.

Langer, S. Z. (2008). Presynaptic autoreceptors regulating transmitter release. *Neurochemistry International*, 52, 26–30.

Langevin, J. P. (2012). The amygdala as a target for behavior surgery. *Surgical Neurology International*, 3(Suppl. 1), S40–S46.

Langston, J. W. (2002). Parkinson's disease: Current and future challenges. *NeuroToxicology*, 23, 443–450.

Langston, J. W., Ballard, P., Tetrud, J., & Irwin, I. (1983). Chronic parkinsonism in humans due to a product of meperidine analog synthesis. *Science*, 219, 979–980.

Lanteaume, L., Khafa, S., Régis, J., Marquis, P., Chauvel, P., & Bartolomei, F. (2007). Emotion induction after direct intrace-rebral stimulations of human amygdala. *Cerebral Cortex*, 17, 1303–1313.

Larsen, J. P., Høien, T., Lundberg, I., & Ødegaard, H. (1990). MRI evaluation of the size and symmetry of the planum temporale in adolescents with developmental dyslexia. *Brain and Language*, 39, 289–301.

Larson, M. E., & Lesné, S. E. (2012). Soluble Aβ oligomer production and toxicity. *Journal of Neurochemistry*, 120, 125–139.

Lashley, K. S. (1950). In search of the engram. *Symposium for the Society of Experimental Biology*, 4, 454–482.

Latesh, M. L. (2008). *Neurophysiological basis of movement*. Human Kinetics.

Lau, H. C., Rogers, R. D., & Passingham, R. E. (2006). On measuring the perceived onsets of spontaneous actions. *Journal of Neuroscience*, 26, 7265–7271.

Laurin, D., Verreault, R., Lindsay, J., MacPherson, K., & Rockwood, K. (2001). Physical activity and risk of cognitive impairment and dementia in elderly persons. *Archives of Neurology*, 58, 498–504.

Lavie, P. (1996). *The enchanted world of sleep*. Yale University Press.

Lavie, P., Pratt, H, Scharf, B., Peled, R., & Brown, J. (1984). Localised pontine lesion: Nearly total absence of REM sleep. *Neurology*, 34, 118–120.

Lawrence, D., & Kuypers, H. (1968). The functional organisation of the motor system in the monkey. *Brain*, 91, 1–36.

Le, A. D., Poulos, C. X., & Cappel, H. (1979). Conditioned tolerance to the hypothermic effect of alcohol. *Science*, 206, 1109.

Le Merrer, J., Becker, J. A. J., Befort, K., & Kieffer, B. L. (2009). Reward processing by the opioid system of the brain. *Physiological Review*, 89, 1379–1412.

LeDoux, J. E. (1995). Emotion: Clues from the brain. *Annual Review of Psychology*, 46, 209–235.

LeDoux, J. E. (1998). *The emotional brain*. Weidenfeld and Nicolson.

LeDoux, J. E. (2003). The emotional brain, fear and the amygdala. *Cellular and Molecular Neurobiology*, 23, 727–738.

LeDoux, J. E. (2012). Rethinking the emotional brain. *Neuron*, 73, 653–676.

LeDoux, J. E., Iwata, J., Cicchetti, P., & Reis, D. J. (1988). Different projections of the central amygdaloid nucleus mediate autonomic and behavioral correlates of conditioned fear. *Journal of Neuroscience*, 25, 17–29.

LeDoux, J. E., Sakaguchi, A. A., & Reis, D. J. (1984). Subcortical efferent projections of the medial geniculate nucleus mediate emotional responses conditioned to acoustic stimuli. *Journal of Neuroscience*, 4, 683–698.

Lee, D. J., Chen, Y., & Schlaug, G. (2003). Corpus callosum: Musician and gender effects. *NeuroReport*, 14, 205–209.

Lee, M. G., Hassani, O. K., & Jones, E. (2005). Discharge of identified orexin/hypocretin neurons across the sleep-waking cycle. *Journal of Neuroscience*, 25, 6716–6720.

Lees, A. J. (1986). L-dopa treatment of Parkinson's disease. *Quarterly Journal of Medicine*, 230, 535–547.

Legrain, V., Iannetti, G. D., Plaghki, L., & Mouraux A. (2011). The pain matrix reloaded: A salience detection system for the body. *Progress in Neurobiology*, 93,111–124.

Lemmer, B. (2009). Discoveries of rhythms in human biological functions: A historical review. *Chronobiology International*, 26, 1019–1068.

Lemon, R. N. (2008). An enduring map of the motor cortex. *Experimental Physiology*, 93(7), 798–802.

Lenzenweger, M. F. (1998). Schizotypy and schizotypic psychopathology: Mapping an alternative expression of schizophrenia liability. In M. F. Lenzenweger & R. H. Dworkin (Eds.), *Origins and development of schizophrenia: Advances in experimental psychopathology* (pp. 93–121). American Psychological Association.

Leo, J. (2003). Essay review: The fallacy of the 50% concordance rate for schizophrenia in identical twins. *Human Nature Reviews*, 3, 406–415.

Leonard, C. T. (1998). *The neuroscience of human movement*. Mosby.

Lepage, M., Habib, R., & Tulving, E. (1998). Hippocampal PET activations of memory encoding and retrieval: The HIPER Model. *Hippocampus*, 8, 313–322.

Leslie, M. (2019). Talk to the hand: Scientists try to debunk the myth that finger length can reveal personality and health. *Biology*. Advance online publication.

https://doi.org/10.1126/science.aay2735

Leucht, S., Cipriani, A., Spineli, L., Mavridis, D., Orey, D., Richter, F., Samara, M., Barbui, C., Engel, R. R., Geddes, J. R., Kissling, W., Stapf, M. P., Lässig, B., Salanti, G., & Davis, J. M. (2013). Comparative efficacy and tolerability of 15 antipsychotic drugs in schizophrenia: A multiple-treatments meta-analysis. *The Lancet*, 382, 951–962.

Leung, L. C., Wang, G. X., Madelaine, R., Skariah, G., Kawakami, K., Deisseroth, K., Urban, A. E., & Mourrain, P. (2019). Neural signatures of sleep in zebrafish. *Nature*, 571, 198–204.

LeVay, S. (1993). *The sexual brain*. MIT Press.

LeVay, S. (2016). *Gay, straight, and the reason why: The science of sexual orientation*. Oxford University Press.

Levenson, W. R., Ekman, P., Heider, K., & Friesen, W. V. (1992). Emotion and autonomic nervous system activity in the Minangkabu of West Sumatra. *Journal of Personality and Social Psychology*, 62, 972–988.

Leventhal, A. G., Thompson, K. G., Liu, D., Zhou, Y., & Ault, S. J. (1995). Concomitant sensitivity to orientation, direction, and color of cells in layers 2, 3, and 4 of monkey striate cortex. *Journal of Neuroscience*, 15, 1808–1818.

Levine, J. (2001). *Purple haze: The puzzle of consciousness*. Oxford University Press.

Levinthal, C. (1988). *Messengers of paradise: Opiates and the brain*. Doubleday.

Levitan, I. B., & Kacmarek, L. K. (2015). *The neuron: Cell and molecular biology*. Oxford University Press.

Levy, J., & Heller, W. (1992). Gender differences in human neuropsychological function. In A. A. Gerall, H. Moltz, & I. L. Ward (Eds.), *Sexual differentiation: Handbook of behavioral neurology* (pp. 245–274). Plenum Press.

Levy-Lahad, E., Wasco, W., Poorkaj, P., Romano, D. M., Oshima, J., Pettingell, W. H., Yu, C. E., Jondro, P. D., Schmidt, S.D., & Wang, K. (1995). Candidate gene for the chromosomal 1 familial Alzheimer's disease locus. *Science*, 269, 973–937.

Lewis, M. B., & Bowler, P. J. (2009). Botulinum toxin cosmetic therapy correlates with a more positive mood. *Journal of Cosmetic Dermatology*, 8, 24–26.

Lewy, A. J., Wehr, T. A., Newsome, D. A., & Markey, S. P. (1980). Light suppresses melatonin secretion in humans. *Science*, 210, 1267–1269.

Li, J. Z., Bunney, B. G., Meng, F., Hagenauer, M. H., Walsh, D. M., Vawter, M. P., Evans, S. J., Choudary, P. V., Cartagena, P., Barchas, J. D., Schatzberg, A. F., Jones, E. G., Myers, R. M., Watson, S. J., Jr, Akil, H., & Bunney, W. E. (2013). Circadian patterns of gene expression in the human brain and disruption in major depressive disorder. *Proceedings of the National Academy of Sciences of the USA*, 110, 9950–9955.

Li, M.-D. (2011). Leptin and beyond: An odyssey to the central control of body weight. *Yale Journal of Biology and Medicine*, 84, 1–7.

Li, W., Ma, L., Yang, G., & Gan, W. (2017). REM sleep selectively prunes and maintains new synapses in development and learning. *Nature Neuroscience*, 20, 427–437.

Liang, K., Wei, L., & Chen, L. (2017). Exocytosis, endocytosis, and their coupling in excitable cells. *Frontiers in Molecular Neuroscience*, 10, 109. https://doi.org/10.3389/fnmol.2017.00109

Libet, B. (2004). *Mind time*. Harvard University Press.

Lickey, M. E., & Gordon, B. (1991). *Medicine and mental illness*. Freeman.

Liechti, M. E. (2017). Modern clinical research on LSD. *Neuropsychopharmacology*, 42, 2114–2127.

Lilly, R., Cummings, J. L., Benson, D. F., & Frankel, M. (1983). The human Kluver-Bucy syndrome. *Neurology*, 33, 141–145.

Lin, L., Faraco, J., Li, R., Kadotani, H., Rogers, W., Lin, X., Qiu, X., de Jong, P. J., Nishino, S., & Mignot, E. (1999). The sleep disorder canine narcolepsy is caused by a mutation in the hypocretin (orexin) receptor 2 gene. *Cell*, 98, 365–376.

Linden, A. M., Schmitt, U., Leppä, E., Wulff, P., Wisden, W., Lüddens, H., & Korpi, E. R. (2011). Ro 15-4513 antagonizes alcohol-induced sedation in mice through $\alpha\beta\gamma2$-type GABA(A) receptors. *Frontiers in Neuroscience*, 5, 3. https://doi.org/10.3389/fnins.2011.00003

Lindsley, D. B., Bowden, J., & Magoun, H. W. (1949). Effect upon the EEG of acute injury to the brainstem activating system. *Clinical Neuropsychology*, 1, 475–486.

Lindvall, O. (1989). Transplantation into the human brain: Present status and future possibilities. *Journal of Neurology, Neurosurgery and Psychiatry*, 52(Suppl.), 39–45.

Lisman, J., Yasuda, R., & Raghavachari, S. (2012). Mechanisms of CaMKII action in long-term potentiation. *Nature Reviews Neuroscience*, 13, 169–182.

Liu, X. H., Morris, R., Spiller, D., White, M., & Williams, G. (2001). Orexin a preferentially excites glucose-sensitive neurons in the lateral hypothalamus of the rat in vitro. *Diabetes*, 50, 2431–2437.

Livingstone, M. S., & Hubel, D. S. (1984). Anatomy and physiology of a color system in the primate visual cortex. *Journal of Neuroscience*, 4, 309–356.

Livingstone, M. S., & Hubel, D. S. (1988). Segregation of form, colour, movement and depth: Anatomy, physiology and perception. *Science*, 240, 740–749.

Lliff, J. J., Wang, M., Liao, Y., Plogg, B. A., Peng, W., Gundersen, G. A., Benveniste, H., Vates, G. E., Deane, R., Goldman, S. A., Nagelhus, E. A., & Nedergaard, M. (2012). A paravascular pathway facilitates CSF flow through the brain parenchyma and the clearance of interstitial solutes, including amyloid β. *Science Translational Medicine*, 4, 147ra111. https://doi.org/10.1126/scitranslmed.3003748

Llinás, R. R., Walton K. D., & Lang E. J. (2004). Cerebellum. In G. M. Shepherd (Ed.), *The synaptic organization of the brain* (pp. 271–310). Oxford University Press.

Lodge, D., & Mercier, M. S. (2015). Ketamine and phencyclidine: The good, the bad and the unexpected. *British Journal of Pharmacology*, 172, 4254–4276.

Logue, A. W. (1986). *The psychology of eating and drinking*. Freeman.

Lokhorst, G.-J. C., & Kaitaro, T. T. (2001). The originality of Descartes' theory about the pineal gland. *Journal of the History of the Neurosciences*, 10, 6–18.

Long, J. C., Knowler, W. C., Hanson, R. L., Robin, R. W., Urbanek, M., Moore, E., Bennett, P. H., & Goldman, D. (1998). Evidence for genetic linkage to alcohol dependence on chromosomes 4 and 11 from an autosome-wide scan in an American Indian population. *American Journal of Medical Genetics*, 81, 216–221.

Long, M. A., Jutras, M. J., Connors, B. W., & Burwell, R. D. (2005). Electrical synapses coordinate activity in the suprachiasmatic nucleus. *Nature Neuroscience*, 8, 61–66.

Lopez, M. S., Tovar, S., Vazquez, M. J., Williams, L. M., & Diéguez, C. (2007). Peripheral tissue-brain interactions in the regulation of food intake. *Proceedings of the Nutritional Society*, 66, 131–155.

López-Muñoz, F., & Alamo, C. (2009). Monoaminergic neurotransmission: The history of the discovery of antidepressants from 1950s until today. *Current Pharmaceutical Design*, 15, 1563–1586.

Lopez-Quintero, C., Pérez de los Cobos, J., Hasin, D. S., ... Blanco, C. (2011). Probability and predictors of transition from first use to dependence on nicotine, alcohol, cannabis, and cocaine: Results of the National Epidemiologic Survey on Alcohol and Related Conditions (NESARC). *Drug and Alcohol Dependence*, 115(1–2), 120–130.

Lorenzetti, V., Cousijn, J., Solowij, N., Garavan, H., Suo, C., Yücel, M., & Verdejo-García, A. (2016). The neurobiology of cannabis use disorders: A call for evidence. *Frontiers in Behavioral Neuroscience*, 10, 86. https://doi.org/10.3389/fnbeh.2016.00086

Loring, D. W., & Meador, K. J. (2019). History of the Wada test. In W. B. Barr & L. A. Bieliauskus (Eds.), *The Oxford handbook of history of clinical neuropsychology* (pp. 1–19). Oxford University Press.

Lu, H.-C., & Mackie, K. (2016). An introduction to the endogenous cannabinoid system. *Biological Psychiatry*, 79, 516–525.

Lu, J., Greco, M. A., Shiromani, P., & Saper, C. B. (2000). Effect of lesions of the ventrolateral preoptic nucleus on NREM and REM sleep. *Journal of Neuroscience*, 20, 3830–3842.

Lu, X. Y., Nicholson, J. R., Akil, H., & Watson, S. J. (2001). Time course of short-term and long-term orexigenic effects of agouti-related protein (86-132). *NeuroReport*, 12, 1281–1284.

Lucking, C., Dürr, A., Bonifati, V., Vaughan, J., De Michele, G., Gasser, T., Harhangi, B. S., Meco, G., Denèfle, P., Wood, N. W., Agid, Y., & Brice, A.; French Parkinson's Disease Genetics Study Group; European Consortium on Genetic Susceptibility in Parkinson's Disease. (2000). Association between early onset Parkinson's disease and mutations in the parkin gene. *New England Journal of Medicine*, 342, 1560–1567.

Luders, E., Rex, D. E., Narr, R. P., Woods, R. P., Jancke, L., Thompson, P. M., Mazziotta, J. C., & Toga, A. W. (2003). Relationships between sulcal asymmetries and corpus callosum size: Gender and handedness effects. *Cerebral Cortex*, 13, 1084–1093.

Lue, L. F., Kuo, Y. M., Roher, A. E., ... & Rogers, J. (1999). Soluble amyloid beta peptide concentration as a predictor of synaptic change in Alzheimer's disease. *American Journal of Pathology*, 155, 853–862.

Lumeng, L., Murphy, J. M., McBride, W. J., & Li, T. K. (1993). Genetic influences on alcohol preference in animals. In H. Begleter & B. Kissin (Eds.), *The genetics of alcoholism* (pp. 165–201). Oxford University Press.

Lumey, L. H., Stein, A. D., Kahn, H. S., ... & Susser, E. (2007). Cohort profile: The Dutch Hunger Winter families study, *International Journal of Epidemiology*, 36, 1196–1204.

Luo, D. G., Xue, T., & Yau, K. W. (2008). How vision begins: An odyssey. *Proceedings of the National Academy of Sciences of the USA*, 105, 9855–9862.

Lüscher, C., & Malenka, R. C. (2012). NMDA receptor-dependent long-term potentiation and long-term depression (LTP/LTD). *Cold Spring Harbor Perspectives in Biology*, 4(6), a005710. https://doi.org/10.1101/cshperspect.a005710

Lyamin, O., Pryaslova, J., Kosenko, P., & Siegel, J. (2007). Behavioral aspects of sleep in bottlenose dolphin mothers and their calves. *Physiology and Behavior*, 92, 725–733.

Lysaker, P. H., Pattison, M. L., Leonhardt, B. L., Phelps, S., & Vohs, J. L. (2018). Insight in schizophrenia spectrum disorders: Relationship with behavior, mood and perceived quality of life, underlying causes and emerging treatments. *World Psychiatry*, 17, 12–23.

Ma, H., & Zhu, G. (2014). The dopamine system and alcohol dependence. *Shanghai Archives of Psychiatry*, 26, 61–68.

Maccioni, R. B., Farías, G., Morales, I., & Navarrete, L. (2010). The revitalized tau hypothesis on Alzheimer's disease. *Archives of Medical Research*, 41, 226–231.

MacCulloch, R. D., Murphy, R. W., Kupriyanova, L. A., & Darevsky, I. S. (1997). The Caucasian rock lizard *Lacerta rostombekovi*: A monoclonal parthenogenetic vertebrate. *Biochemical Systematics and Ecology*, 25, 33–37.

Mackie, K. (2006). Mechanisms of CB1 receptor signaling: Endocannabinoid modulation of synaptic strength. *International Journal of Obesity*, 30, S19–S23.

MacLean, P. D. (1990). *The triune brain in evolution*. Plenum Press.

Macmillan, M. (1996). Phineas Gage: A case for all reasons. In C. Code, C.-W. Wallesch, Y. Joanette, & A. Roch (Eds.), *Classic cases in neuropsychology* (pp. 243–262). Psychology Press.

Maes, M., & Meltzer, H. Y. M. (1995). The serotonin hypothesis of major depression. In F. Bloom & D. Kupher (Eds.), *Psychopharmacology: The fourth generation of progress* (pp. 933–944). Raven Press.

Maess, B., Koelsch, S., Gunter, T. C., & Friederici, A. D. (2001). Musical syntax is processed in Broca's area: An MEG study. *Nature Neuroscience*, 4, 540–545.

Maguire, E. A., Frackowiak, R. S. J., & Frith, C. D. (1997). Recalling routes around London: Activation of the right hippocampus in taxi drivers. *Journal of Neuroscience*, 17, 7103–7110.

Maguire, E. A., Gadian, D. G., Johnsrude, I. S., Good, C. D., Ashburner, J., Frackowiak, R. S., & Frith, D. (2000). Navigation-related structural change in the hippocampi of taxi drivers. *Proceedings of the National Academy of Sciences*, 97, 4398–4403.

Makin, S. (2015). The schizophrenia spectrum. *Scientific American Mind*, 26, 16–17. https://doi.org/10.1038/scientificamericanmind1115-16

Makin, S. (2018). The amyloid hypothesis on trial. *Nature*, 559, S4–S7.

Malaspina, D., Harlap, S., Fennig, S., Heiman, D., Nahon, D., Feldman, D., & Susser, E. S. (2001). Advancing paternal age and the risk of schizophrenia. *Archives of General Psychiatry*, 58, 361–367.

Malenka, R. C., & Bear, M. F. (2004). LTP and LTD: An embarrassment of riches. *Neuron*, 44, 5–21.

Malik, A. R., & Willnow, T. E. (2019). Excitatory amino acid transporters in physiology and disorders of the central nervous system. *International Journal of Molecular Sciences*, 20(22), 5671. https://doi.org/10.3390/ijms20225671

Manasco, H. M. (2014). *Introduction to neurogenic communication disorders*. Jones & Barlett.

Mangalore, R., & Knapp, M. (2007). Cost of schizophrenia in England. *Journal of Mental Health Economics and Policy*, 10, 23–41.

Manning, J. T. (2002). *Digit ratio: A pointer to fertility, behavior and health*. Rutgers University Press.

Manning, J. T. (2007). *The finger ratio*. Faber and Faber.

Manning, J. T., Churchill, A. J. G., & Peters, M. (2007). The effects of sex, ethnicity, and sexual orientation on self-measured digit ratio (2D:4D). *Archives of Sexual Behavior*, 36, 223–233.

Manning, J. T., Scutt, D., Wilson, J., & Lewis-Jones, D. I. (1998). The ratio of 2nd to 4th digit length, a predictor of sperm numbers and concentrations of testosterone, luteinizing hormone and oestrogen. *Human Reproduction*, 13, 3000–3004.

Mansvelder, H. D., & McGehee, D. S. (2002). Cellular and synaptic mechanisms of nicotine addiction. *Journal of Neurobiology*, 53, 606–617.

Manto, M., Bower, J. M, Conforto, A. B., Delgado-García, J. M., da Guarda, S. N., Gerwig, M., Habas, C., Hagura, N., Ivry, R. B., Mariën, P., Molinari, M., Naito, E., Nowak, D. A., Oulad Ben Taib, N., Pelisson, D., Tesche, C. D., Tilikete, C., & Timmmann, D. (2012). Consensus paper: Roles of the cerebellum in motor control – the diversity of ideas on cerebellar involvement in movement. *Cerebellum*, 11, 457–487.

Margolis, E. B., Hjelmstad, G. O., Wakakao, F., & Fields, H. L. (2014). Direct bidirectional μ-opioid control of midbrain dopamine neurons. *Journal of Neuroscience*, 34, 14707–14716.

Marie, D., Jobard, G., Crivello, F., Perchey, G., Petit, L., Mellet, E., Joliot, M., Zago, L., Mazoyer, B., & Tzourio-Mazoyer, N. (2015). Descriptive anatomy of Heschl's gyri in 430 healthy volunteers, including 198 left-handers. *Brain Structure and Function*, 220, 729–743.

Mark, V. H., & Ervin, E. R. (1970). *Violence and the brain*. Harper and Row.

Markianos, M., Botsis, A., & Arvanitis, Y. (1992). Biogenic amine metabolites in plasma of drug-naive schizophrenic patients; Associations with symptomatology. *Biological Psychiatry*, 32, 288–292.

Marouli, E., Graff, M., Medina-Gomez, C., Lo, K.S., Wood, A.R., Kjaer, T.R., Fine, R.S., Lu, Y., Schurmann, C., Highland, H.M., Rüeger, S., Thorleifsson, G., Justice, A.E., Lamparter, D., Stirrups, K.E., Turcot, V., Young, K.L., Winkler, T.W., Esko, T., . . . Lettre, G. (2017). Rare and low-frequency coding variants alter human adult height. *Nature*, 542, 186–190.

Marshall, G. D., & Zimbardo, P. G. (1979). Affective consequences of inadequately explained physiological arousal. *Journal of Personality and Social Psychology*, 37, 970–988.

Marshall, J. C., & Newcombe, F. (1973). Patterns of paralexia: A psycholinguistic approach. *Journal of Psycholinguistic Research*, 2, 175–199.

Marshall, J. F., Turner, B. H., & Teitelbaum, P. (1971). Sensory neglect produced by lateral hypothalamic damage. *Science*, 174, 523–525.

Martel, M. M., Gobrogge, K. L., Breedlove, S. M., & Nigg, J. T. (2008). Masculinized finger-length ratios of boys, but not girls, are associated with Attention-Deficit/Hyperactivity Disorder. *Behavioral Neuroscience*, 122, 273–281.

Martin, G. N. (2006). *Human neuropsychology*. Prentice Hall.

Martin, P. (2002). *Counting sheep: The science and pleasures of sleep and dreams*. HarperCollins.

Martin, R. A. (2001). Humour, laughter and physical health: Methodological issues and research findings. *Psychological Bulletin*, 127, 504–519.

Martin, R. A., & Kuiper, N. A. (1999). Daily occurrence of laughter: Relationships with age, gender, and type a personality. *Humor: International Journal of Humor Research*, 12, 355–384.

Martin, S. M., Manning, J. T., & Dorwick, C. F. (1999). Fluctuating asymmetry, relative digit length and depression in men. *Evolution and Human Behavior*, 20, 203–214.

Martinez, L. M., & Alonso, J.-M. (2003). Complex receptive fields in primary visual cortex. *Neuroscientist*, 9, 317–331.

Martini, F. (1988). *Fundamentals of anatomy and physiology* (4th ed.). Prentice Hall.

Martorana, A., Esposito, Z., & Koch, G. (2010). Beyond the cholinergic hypothesis: Do current drugs work in Alzheimer's disease? *CNS Neuroscience and Therapeutics*, 16, 235–245.

Mashour, G. A., Walker, E. E., & Martuza, R. L. (2005). Psychosurgery: Past, present and future. *Brain Research Reviews*, 48, 409–419.

Masland, R. H. (2001). The fundamental plan of the retina. *Nature Neuroscience*, 4, 877–886.

Masters, W. H., Johnson, V. E., & Kolodny, R. C. (1995). *Human sexuality*. HarperCollins.

Matsuda, L. A., Lolait, S. J., Brownstein, M. J., Young, A. C., & Bonner, T. I. (1990). Structure of a cannabinoid receptor and functional expression of the cloned cDNA. *Nature*, 346, 561–564.

Matsuhashi, M., & Hallet, M. (2008). The timing of the conscious decision to move. *European Journal of Neuroscience*, 28, 2344–2351.

Matthes, H. W., Maldonado, R., Simonin, F., Valverde, O., Slowe, S., Kitchen, I., Befort, K., Dierich, A., Le Meur, M., Dollé, P., Tzavara, E., Hanoune, J., Roques, B. P., & .Kieffer, B. L. (1996). Loss of morphine-induced analgesia, reward effect and withdrawal symptoms in mice lacking the μ-opioid-receptor gene. *Nature*, 383, 819–823.

Mattison, J. A., Colman, R. J., Beasley, T. M., Allison, D. B., Kemnitz, J. W., Roth, G. S., Ingram, D. K., Weindruch, R., de Cabo, R., & Anderson, R. M. (2017). Caloric restriction improves health and survival of rhesus monkeys. *Nature Communications*, 8, 14063. https://doi.org/10.1038/ncomms14063

May, P. J. (2006). The mammalian superior colliculus: Laminar structure and connections. *Progress in Brain Research*, 151, 321–378.

Mayer, D. J. (1979). Endogenous analgesia systems: Neural and behavioral mechanisms. In J. J. Bonica, J. C. Liebeskind & D. Albe-Fessard (Eds.), *Advances in pain research and therapy* (Vol. 3). Raven Press.

Mayer, D. J., Wolfe, T. H., Akil, H., Carder, B., & Liebeskind, J. C. (1971). Analgesia from electrical stimulation in the brainstem of the rat. *Science*, 174, 1351–1354.

Mayer, J. (1953). Glucostatic mechanism of regulation of food intake. *New England Journal of Medicine*, 249, 13–16.

Mayer, J., & Marshall, N. B. (1956). Specificity of gold thioglucose for ventromedial hypothalamic lesions and hyperphagia. *Nature*, 178, 1399–1400.

Mayeux, R., & Stern, Y. (2012). Epidemiology of Alzheimer's disease. *Cold Spring Harbor Perspectives in Medicine*, 2(8), a006239. https://doi.org/10.1101/cshperspect.a006239

Mazur, A., & Booth, A. (1998). Testosterone and dominance in men. *Behavioral and Brain Sciences*, 21, 353–397.

Mazzawi, T., Bartsch, E., Benammi, S., Ferro, R. M. C., Nikitina, E., Nimer, N., Ortega, L. J., Perrotte, C., Pithon, J. V., Rosalina, S., Sharp, A., Stevano, R., Hatlebakk, J. G., & Hausken, T. (2019). Gastric emptying of low- and high-caloric liquid meals measured using ultrasonography in healthy volunteers. *Ultrasound International Open*, 5(1), E27–E33. https://doi.org/10.1055/a-0783-2170

Mazziotta, J. C., Phelps, M. E., Carson, R. E., & Kuhl, D. E. (1982). Tomographic mapping of human cerebral metabolism: Auditory stimulation. *Neurology*, 32, 921–937.

Mazzocco, M. M. M., Bhatia, N. S., & Lesniak-Karpiak, K. (2006). Visuospatial skills and their association with math performance in girls with fragile X or Turner syndrome. *Child Neuropsychology*, 12, 87–110.

Mazzolini, R. G. (1991). Schemes and models of the thinking machine. In P. Corsi (Ed.), *The enchanted loom: Chapters in the history of neuroscience* (pp. 68–143). Oxford University Press.

Mbugua, K. (2003). Sexual orientation and brain structures: A critical review of recent research. *Current Science*, 84, 173–178.

McBride, W. J., Kimpel, M. W., McClintick, J. N., Ding, Z. M., Hauser, S. R., Edenberg, H. J., Bell, R. L., & Rodd, Z. A. (2013). Changes in gene expression within the ventral tegmental area following repeated excessive binge-like alcohol drinking by alcohol-preferring (P) rats. *Alcohol*, 47, 367–380.

McBride, W. J., Rodd, Z. A., Bell, R. L., Lumeng, L., & Li, T. K. (2014). The alcohol-preferring (P) and high-alcohol-drinking (HAD) rats – animal models of alcoholism. *Alcohol*, 48, 209–215.

McCarley, R. W. (1995). Sleep, dreams, and states of consciousness. In P. M. Conn (Ed.), *Neuroscience in Medicine* (pp. 623–646). Lippincott.

McCarley, R. W., Greene, R. W., Rainnie, D., & Portas, C. M. (1995). Brainstem modulation and REM sleep. *Seminars in the Neurosciences*, 7, 341–354.

McCarley, R. W., & Hobson, J. A. (1975). Neuronal excitability modulations over the sleep cycle: A structured and mathematical model. *Science*, 189, 58–60.

McCarthy, R. A., & Warrington, E. K. (1990). *Cognitive neuropsychology*. Academic Press.

McLean, D., Forsythe, R. G., & Kapkin, I. A. (1983). Unusual side effects of clomipramine associated with yawning. *Canadian Journal of Psychiatry*, 28, 569–570.

McClintock, M. K. (1971). Menstrual synchronicity and suppression. *Nature*, 229, 244–245.

McComas, A. J. (2011). *Galvani's spark*. Oxford University Press.

McCorry, L. K. (2007). Physiology of the autonomic nervous system. *American Journal of Pharmaceutical Education*, 71(4), 78. https://doi.org/10.5688/aj710478

McCoy, N. L., & Pinto, L. (2002). Pheromonal influences on sociosexual behavior in young women. *Physiology and Behavior*, 75, 367–375.

McCutcheon, R. A., Abi-Darghan, A., & Howes, O. D. (2019). Schizophrenia, dopamine and the striatum: From biology to symptoms. *Trends in Neurosciences*, 42, 205–220.

McDonald, A. J. (1998). Cortical pathways to the mammalian amygdala. *Progress in Neurobiology*, 55, 257–332.

McDonald, C., Grech, A., Toulopoulou, T., Schulze, K., Chapple, B., Sham, P., Walshe, M., Sharma, T., Sigmundsson, T., Chitnis, X., & Murray, R. M. (2002). Brain volumes in familial and nonfamilial schizophrenic probands and their unaffected relatives. *American Journal of Medical Genetics*, 114, 616–625.

McGinty, D. J., & Sterman, M. B. (1968). Sleep suppression after basal forebrain lesion in the cat. *Science*, 160, 1253–1255.

McGrath, J., Saha, S., Chant, D., & Welham, J. (2008). Schizophrenia: A concise overview of incidence, prevalence, and mortality. *Epidemiologic Reviews*, 30, 67–76.

McGrath, J. J., Petersen, L., Agerbo, E., Mors, O., Mortensen, P. B., & Pederson, C. B. (2014). A comprehensive assessment of parental age and psychiatric disorders. *Journal of the American Medical Association*, 71, 301–309.

McGreal, S. A. (2012). The spirituality of psychedelic drug users. *Psychology Today*. https://www.psychologytoday.com/ie/blog/unique-everybody-else/201212/blog/unique-everybody-else/201212/

the-spirituality-psychedelic-drug-users?collection=129216

McGue, M., Bouchard, T. J., Iacono, W. G., & Lykken, D. T. (1993). Behavioral genetics of cognitive ability: A life-span perspective. In R. Plomin & G. E. McClearn (Eds.), *Nature, nurture & psychology* (pp. 59–76). American Psychological Association.

McKenna, P. J., & Bailey, P. E. (1993). The strange story of clozapine. *British Journal of Psychiatry*, 162, 32–37.

McLean, C. A., Cherny, R. A., Fraser, F. W., Fuller, S. J., Smith, M. J., Beyreuther, K., Bush, A. I., & Masters, C. L. (1999). Soluble pool of Abeta amyloid as a determinant of severity of neurodegeneration in Alzheimer's disease. *Annals of Neurology*, 46, 860–866.

McLelland, T. M., Caldwell, J. A., & Lieberman, H. R. (2016). A review of caffeine's effects on cognitive, physical and occupational performance. *Neuroscience and Biobehavioral Reviews*, 71, 294–312.

McManus, C. (2002). *Right hand, left hand*. Weidenfeld and Nicolson.

McManus, C. (2019). Half a century of handedness research: Myths, truths; fictions, facts; backwards, but mostly forwards. *Brain and Neuroscience Advances*, 3, 2398212818820513. https://doi.org/10.1177/2398212818820513

McNamara, P., Durso, R., & Auerbach, S. (2002). Dopaminergic syndromes of sleep, mood and mentation: Evidence from Parkinson's disease and related disorders. *Sleep and Hypnosis*, 4, 119–131.

Meador, K. J., Loring, D. W., Lee, G. P., Nichols, M. E., Moore, E. E., & Figueroa, R. E. (1997). Level of consciousness and memory during the intracarotid sodium amobarbital procedure. *Brain & Cognition*, 33, 178–188.

Meddis, R. (1977). *The sleep instinct*. Routledge.

Medical Research Council. (1965). Clinical trial of the treatment of depressive illness. *British Medical Journal*, i, 881–886.

Medland, S. E., Duffy, D. L., Wright, M. J., Geffen, G.M., & Martin, N. G. (2006). Handedness in twins: Joint analysis of data from 35 samples. *Twin Research and Human Genetics*, 9, 46–53.

Medland, S. E, Duffy, D. L, Wright, M. J., et al. (2009). Genetic influences on handedness: Data from 25,732 Australian and Dutch twin families. *Neuropsychologia*, 47, 330–337.

Mehta, R., Khan, S., & Mallick, B. N. (2018). Relevance of deprivation studies in understanding rapid eye movement sleep. *Nature and Science of Sleep*, 10, 143–158.

Meissner, C., Recker, S., Reiter, A., Friedrich, H.J., & Oehmichen, M. (2002). Fatal versus non-fatal heroin 'overdose': Blood morphine concentrations with fatal outcome in comparison to those of intoxicated drivers. *Forensic Science International*, 130, 49–54.

Meldrum, D. R., Morris, M. A., & Gambone, J. C. (2017). Obesity pandemic: Causes, consequences, and solutions – but do we have the will? *Fertility and Sterility*, 107, 833–839.

Meltzer, H. Y., Li, Z., Kaneda, Y., & Ichikawa, J. (2003). Serotonin receptors: Their key role in drugs to treat schizophrenia. *Progress in Neuropsychopharmacology and Biological Psychiatry*, 27, 1159–1172.

Melzack, R. (1992). Phantom limbs. *Scientific American*, 266, 120–126.

Melzack, R., & Wall, P. D. (1988). *The challenge of pain*. Penguin.

Mendell, L. M. (2014). Constructing and deconstructing the gate theory of pain. *Pain*, 155, 210–216.

Mendez, M. F. (2000). Mania in neurologic disorders. *Current Psychiatry Reports*, 2, 440–445.

Mendoza, J. E., & Foundas, A. L. (2008). *Clinical neuroanatomy: A neurobehavioral approach*. Springer.

Mennella, J. A., Jagnow, C. P., & Beauchamp, G. K. (2001). Prenatal and postnatal flavor learning by human infants. *Pediatrics*, 107, E88. https://doi.org/10.1542/peds.107.6.e88

Merali, Z., McIntosh, J., & Anisman, H. (1999). Role of bombesin-related peptides in the control of food intake. *Neuropeptides*, 33, 376–386.

Mercuri, N. B., & Bernardi, G. (2005). The 'magic' of l-dopa: Why is it the gold standard Parkinson's disease therapy? *Trends in Pharmacological Sciences*, 26, 341–344.

Messias, E., Chen, C.-Y., & Eaton, W. W. (2007). Epidemiology of schizophrenia: Review of findings and myths. *Psychiatric Clinics of North America*, 30, 323–338.

Mesulam, M. M. (1998). From sensation to cognition. *Brain*, 121, 1013–1052.

Mesulam, M. M., Thompson, C. K., Weintraub, S., & Rogalski, E. J. (2015). The Wernicke conundrum and the anatomy of language comprehension in primary progressive aphasia. *Brain*, 138, 2433–2437.

Metea, M. R., & Newman, E. A. (2006). Glial cells dilate and constrict blood vessels: A mechanism of neurovascular coupling. *Journal of Neuroscience*, 26, 2862–2870.

Meunier, M., Bachevalier, J., Mishkin, M., & Murray, E. A. (1993). Effects on visual recognition of combined and separate ablations of the entorhinal and perirhinal cortex in rhesus monkeys. *Journal of Neuroscience*, 13, 5418–5432.

Meunier, M., & Barbeau, E. (2013). Recognition memory and the medial temporal lobe: From monkey research to human pathology. *Revue Neurologique*, 169, 459–469.

Meyer-Bahlburg, H. F. (1984). Psychoendocrine research on sexual orientation. Current status and future options. *Progress in Brain Research*, 61, 375–398.

Milad, M. R., & Rauch, S. L. (2012). Obsessive-compulsive disorder: Beyond segregated corticostriatal pathways. *Cognition in Neuropsychiatric Disorders*, 16, 43–51.

Miller, B., Messias, E., Miettunen, J., Alaräisänen, A., Järvelin, M. R., Koponen, H., Räsänen, P., Isohanni, M., & Kirkpatrick, B. (2010). Meta-analysis of paternal age and schizophrenia risk in male versus female offspring. *Schizophrenia Bulletin*, 37, 1039–1047.

Miller, B. L., & Cummings, J. L. (Eds.). (2017). *The human frontal lobes: Functions and disorders*. The Guilford Press.

Miller, B. L., Cummings, J. L., McIntyre, H., Ebers, G., & Grode, M. (1986). Hypersexuality or altered sexual preference following brain injury. *Journal of Neurology, Neurosurgery, and Psychiatry*, 49, 867–873.

Miller, D., & Halpern, D. (2013). The new science of cognitive sex differences. *Trends in Cognitive Sciences*, 18, 37–45. https://doi.org/10.1016/.tics.2013.10.011

Miller, J. L., Tamura, R., Butler, M., Kimonis, V., Sulsona, C., Gold, J. A., & Driscoll, D. J. (2017). Oxytocin treatment in children with Prader-Willi Syndrome: A double-blind, placebo-controlled, crossover study. *American Journal of Medical Genetics*, 173, 1243–1250.

Milner, B. (1970). Memory and the medial temporal regions of the brain. In D. H. Pribram & D. E. Broadbent (Eds.), *Biology of memory* (pp. 29–50). Academic Press.

Milner, B., Corkin, S., & Teuber, H.-L. (1968). Further analysis of the hippocampal amnesic syndrome: 14-year follow-up study of HM. *Neuropsychologia*, 6, 317–338.

Mind. (2020). https://www.mind.org.uk/information-support/types-of-mental-health-problems/statistics-and-facts-about-mental-health/how-common-are-mental-health-problems/

Mink, J. W. (1999). Basal ganglia. In M. J. Zigmond, F. E. Bloom, S. C. Landis, J. L. Roberts, & L. R. Squire (Eds.), *Fundamental neuroscience* (pp. 951–972). Academic Press.

Mishkin, M. (1978). Memory in monkeys severely impaired by combined but not separate removal of the amygdala and hippocampus. *Nature*, 273, 297–298.

Mishkin, M., & Delacour, J. (1975). An analysis of short-term visual memory in the monkey. *Journal of Experimental Psychology: Animal Behavior Processes*, 1, 326–334.

Mishra, A., Chaturvedi, P., Datta, S., Sinukumar, S., Joshi, P., & Garg, A. (2015). Harmful effects of nicotine. *Indian Journal of Medical and Paediatric Oncology*, 36, 24–31.

Misra, M., & Klibanski, A. (2014). Endocrine consequences of anorexia nervosa. *The Lancet Diabetes & Endocrinology*, 2, 581–592.

Misra, M., Prabhakaran, R., Miller, K., Tsai, P., Lin, A., Lee, N., Herzog, D. B., & Klibanski, A. (2006). Role of cortisol in menstrual recovery in adolescent girls with anorexia nervosa. *Pediatric Research*, 59, 598–603.

Missale, C., Nash, S. R., Robinson, S. W., Jaber M., & Caron, M. G. (1998). Dopamine receptors: From structure to function. *Physiological Reviews*, 78, 189–225.

Mitchell, A. S., & Chakraborty, S. (2013). What does the mediodorsal thalamus do? *Frontiers in Systems Neuroscience*, 7, 1–19. https://doi.org/10.3389/fnsys.2013.00037

Mitchell, A. S., Czajkowski, R., Zhang, N., Jeffery, K., & Nelson, A. J. D. (2018). Retrosplenial cortex and its role in spatial cognition. *Brain and Neuroscience Advances*, 2, 2398212818757098. https://doi.org/10.1177/2398212818757098

Mithen, S. (2005). *The singing Neanderthals: The origins of music, language, mind and body*. Weidenfeld & Nicolson.

Moayedi, M., & Davis, K. D. (2013). Theories of pain: From specificity to gate control. *Journal of Neurophysiology*, 109, 5–12.

Mobbs, D., Greicius, M. D., Abdel-Azin, E., Menon, V., & Reiss, A. L. (2003). Humor modulates the mesolimbic reward centres. *Neuron*, 40, 1041–1048.

Mochel, F., & Haller, R. G. (2011). Energy deficit in Huntington's disease: Why it matters. *Journal of Clinical Investigation*, 12, 493–499.

Moerel, M., De Martino, F., & Formisano, E. (2014). An anatomical and functional topography of human auditory cortical areas. *Frontiers in Neuroscience*, 8, 225. https://doi.org/10.3389/fnins.2014.00225

Moghaddam, B., & Javitt, D. C. (2012). From revolution to evolution: The glutamate hypothesis of schizophrenia and its implication for treatment. *Neuropsychopharmacology*, 37, 4–15.

Mohr, J. P., Pessin, M. S., Finkelstein, S., Funkenstein, H. H., Duncan, G. W., & Davis, K. R. (1978). Broca aphasia: Pathological and clinical. *Neurology*, 28, 311–324.

Mölbert, S. C., Thaler, A., Mohler, B. J., Streuber, S., Romero, J., Black, M. J., Zipfel, S., Karnath, H. O., & Giel, K. E. (2018). Assessing body image in anorexia nervosa using biometric self-avatars in virtual reality: Attitudinal components rather than visual body size estimation are distorted. *Psychological Medicine*, 48, 642–653.

Moller, A. R. (2000). *Hearing: Its physiology and pathophysiology*. Academic Press.

Monaghan, E., & Glickman, S. (1992). Hormones and aggressive behavior. In J. Becker, S. Breedlove & D. Crews (Eds.), *Behavioral endocrinology* (pp. 262–286). MIT Press.

Money, J., & Ehrhardt, A. A. (1972). *Man and woman, boy and girl: Differentiation and dimorphism of gender identity from conception to maturity*. Johns Hopkins University Press.

Money, J., & Ehrhardt, A. E. (1996). *Man & women, boy & girl: Gender identity from conception to maturity*. Johns Hopkins University Press.

Money, J., Schwartz, M., & Lewis, V. G. (1984). Adult erotosexual status and fetal hormonal masculinzation and demasculinization. *Psychoneuroendocrinology*, 9, 405–414.

Mongeau, R., Blier, P., & Montigny, C. (1997). The serotonergic and noradrenergic systems of the hippocampus: Their interactions and the effects of antidepressant treatments. *Brain Research Reviews*, 23, 145–195.

Montague, C. T., Farooqi, I. S., Whitehead, J. P., Soos, M. A., Rau, H., Wareham, N. J., Sewter, C. P., Digby, J. E., Mohammed, S. N., Hurst, J. A., Cheetham, C. H., Earley, A. R., Barnett, A. H., Prins, J. B., & O'Rahilly, S. (1997). Congenital leptin deficiency is associated with severe early-onset obesity in humans. *Nature*, 387, 903–908.

Moore, D. J., West, A. B., Dawson, V. L., & Dawson, T. M. (2005). Molecular pathophysiology of Parkinson's disease. *Annual Review of Neuroscience*, 28, 57–87.

Moore, R. Y. (1996). Neural control of the pineal gland. *Behavioral Brain Research*, 73, 125–130.

Moore, R. Y., & Eichler, V. B. (1972). Loss of circadian adrenal corticosterone rhythm following suprachiasmatic lesions in the rat. *Brain Research*, 42, 201–206.

Mordes, J. P., el Lozy, M., Herrera, M. G., & Silen, W. (1979). Effects of vagot-

omy with and without pyloroplasty on weight and food intake in rats. *American Journal of Physiology*, 236, R61–R66.

Moreira, A. L. R., Van Meter, A., Genzlinger, J., & Youngstrom, E. A. (2017). Review and meta-analysis of epidemiologic studies of adult bipolar disorder. *Journal of Clinical Psychiatry*, 78, e1259–e1269.

Moreira, P. S., Marques, P., Soriano-Mas, C., Magalhães, R., Sousa, N., Soares, J. M., & Morgado, P. (2017). The neural correlates of obsessive-compulsive disorder: A multimodal perspective. *Translational Psychiatry*, 7, e1224. https://doi.org/10.1038/tp.2017.189

Mori, F., Nishie, M., Kakita, A., Yoshimoto, M., Takahashi, H., & Wakabayashi, K. (2006). Relationship among α-synuclein accumulation, dopamine synthesis, and neurodegeneration in Parkinson disease substantia nigra. *Journal of Neuropathology & Experimental Neurology*, 65, 808–815.

Moriyoshi, K., Masu, M., Ishii, T., Shigemoto, R., Mizuno, N., & Nakanishi, S. (1991). Molecular cloning and characterization of the rat NMDA receptor. *Nature*, 354, 31–37.

Morken, F., Helland, T., Hugdahl, K., & Specht, K. (2017). Reading in dyslexia across literacy development: A longitudinal study of effective connectivity. *NeuroImage*, 144, 92–100.

Moroz, L. L. (2011). Aplysia. *Current Biology*, 21, R60–R61.

Morris, H., & Wallach, J. (2014). From PCP to MXE: A comprehensive review of the non-medical use of dissociative drugs. *Drug Testing and Analysis*, 6, 614–632.

Morris, R. G., Garrud, P., Rawlins, J. N., & O'Keefe, J. (1982). Place navigation impaired in rats with hippocampal lesions. *Nature*, 297, 681–683.

Morris, R. G. M., Anderson, E. G., Lynch, G. S., & Baudry, M. (1986). Selective impairment of learning and blockade of long-term potentiation by an N-methyl-D-aspartate receptor antagonist, AP5. *Nature*, 319, 774–776.

Morton, D. L., Sandhu, J. S., & Jones, A. K. P. (2016). Brain imaging of pain: State of the art. *Journal of Pain Research*, 9, 613–624.

Moscovitch, M., Nadel, L., Winocur, G., Gilboa, A., & Rosenbaum, R. S. (2006). The cognitive neuroscience of remote episodic, semantic and spatial memory. *Current Opinion in Neurobiology*, 16, 179–190.

Muckli, L. (2010). What are we missing here? Brain imaging evidence for higher cognitive functions in primary visual cortex V1. *International Journal of Imaging Systems and Technology*, 20, 131–139. https://doi.org/10.1002/ima.20236

Mukund, K., & Subramaniam, S. (2019). Skeletal muscle: A review of molecular structure and function, in health and disease. *Wiley Interdisciplinary Reviews in System Biology and Medicine*, 12, e1462. https://doi.org/10.1002/wsbm.1462

Muller, D. B., Baglietto, L., Manning. J. T., McLean, C., Hopper, J. L., English, D. R., Giles, G. G., & Severi, G. (2012). Second to fourth digit ratio (2D:4D), breast cancer risk factors, and breast cancer risk: A prospective cohort study. *British Journal of Cancer*, 107, 1631–1636.

Muller, T. D., Nogueiras, R., Andermann, M. L. ... & Tschöp, M. H. (2015). Ghrelin. *Molecular Metabolism*, 4, 437–460.

Münch, M., & Bromundt, V. (2012). Light and chronobiology: Implications for health and disease. *Dialogues in Clinical Neuroscience*, 14, 448–453.

Munévar, G. (2012). *The myth of dual consciousness in the split brain: Contrary evidence from psychology and neuroscience.* International Conference on Brain-Mind Proceedings, BMI Press.

Muntean, B. S., Dao, M. T., & Martemyanov, K. A. (2019). Allostatic changes in cAMP system drive opioid-induced adaptation in striatal dopamine signalling. *Cell Reports*, 29, 946–960.

Murphy, J. M., McBride, W. J., Lumeng, L., & Li, T. K. (1987). Contents of monoamines in forebrain regions of alcohol-preferring rats (P) and nonpreferring rats. *Pharmacology, Biochemistry and Behavior*, 26, 389–392.

Murray, E. A., & Mishkin, M. (1998). Object recognition and location memory in monkeys with excitotoxic lesions of the amygdala and hippocampus. *Journal of Neuroscience*, 18, 6568–6582.

Murrough, J. W., Yaqubi, S., Sayed, S., & Charney, D. S. (2015). Emerging drugs for the treatment of anxiety. *Expert Opinion on Emerging Drugs*, 20, 393–406. https://doi.org/10.1517/14728214.2015.1049996

Muschamp, J. W., & Carlezon, W. A. (2013). Roles of nucleus accumbens CREB and dynorphin in dysregulation of motivation. *Cold Spring Harbor Perspectives in Medicine*, 3, a012005. https://doi.org/10.1101/cshperspect.a012005

Musser, K. T., & McGurk, S. R. (2004). Schizophrenia. *The Lancet*, 363, 2063–2072.

Mustanski, B. S., DuPree, M. G., Nievergelt, C. M., Bocklandt, S., & Hamer, D. H. (2005). A genomewide scan of male sexual orientation. *Human Genetics*, 116, 272–278.

Nagappan, P. G., Subramaniam, S., & Wang, D. (2017). Olfaction as a soldier – a review of the physiology and its present and future use in the military. *Military Medical Research*, 4, 9. https://doi.org/10.1186/s40779-017-0119-4

Nagatsu, T., & Sawada, M. (2009). L-dopa therapy for Parkinson's disease: Past, present, and future. *Parkinsonism and Related Disorders*, 15, S3–S8.

Nakazato, M., Murakami, M., Kojima, D. M., Matsuo, H., Kangawa, K., & Matsukura, S. (2001). A role for ghrelin in the central regulation of feeding. *Nature*, 409, 194–198.

Namba, K., Kitaichi, N., Nishida, T., & Taylor, A. W. (2002). Induction of regulatory T cells by the immunomodulating cytokines α-melanocyte-stimulating hormone and transforming growth factor-β2, *Journal of Leukocyte Biology*, 72, 946s–952.

Nasios, G., Dardiotis, E., & Messinis, L. (2019). From Broca and Wernicke to the neuromodulation era: Insights of brain language networks for neurorehabilitation. *Behavioral Neurology*, 2019, 9894571. https://doi.org/10.1155/2019/9894571

National Health Service (NHS). (2003). Health survey for England – 2003.

https://digital.nhs.uk/data-and-information/publications/statistical/health-survey-for-england

National Health Service (NHS). (2019). Statistics on obesity, physical activity and diet, England, 2019. https://digital.nhs.uk/data-and-information/publications/statistical/statistics-on-obesity-physical-activity

National Institute on Drug Abuse. (2018). What are the treatments for heroin use disorder? https://www.drugabuse.gov/publications/research-reports/heroin/what-are-treatments-heroin-use-disorder

Nauta, W. J .H. (1946). Hypothalamic regulation of sleep in rats: Experimental study. *Journal of Neurophysiology*, 9, 285–316.

Navarro, M., Carrera, M. R., Fratta, W., Valverde, O., Cossu, G., Fattore, L., Chowen, J. A., Gomez, R., del Arco, I., Villanua, M. A., Maldonado, R., Koob, G. F., & Rodriguez de Fonseca, F (2001). Functional interaction between opioid and cannabinoid receptors in drug self-administration. *Journal of Neuroscience*, 21, 5344–5350.

Neafsey, E. J. (1993). Frontal cortex, the mind and the body. *Psycoloquy*, 4, 15.

Neergaard, L. (2007, July 3). Cut a nerve and hunger goes away? *The Olympian*.

Negus, S. S., & Rice, K. C. (2009). Mechanisms of withdrawal-associated increases in heroin self-administration: Pharmacologic modulation of heroin vs food choice in heroin-dependent rhesus monkeys. *Neuropsychopharmacology*, 34, 899–911.

Nehlig, A. (1999). Are we dependent upon coffee and caffeine? A review on human and animal data. *Neuroscience and Biobehavioral Reviews*, 23, 563–576.

Nelson, C. A., Zeenah, C. H., & Fox, N. A. (2019). How early experience shapes human development: The case of psychosocial deprivation. *Neural Plasticity*, 2019, 1676285. https://doi.org/10.1155/2019/1676285

Nelson, D. (2021). New effort to discover genetic causes of single-gene disorders. https://www.biostat.washington.edu/news/stories/new-effort-discover-genetic-causes-single-gene-disorders

Nelson, E. L., Campbell, J. M., & Michel, G. F. (2013). Unimanual to bimanual: Tracking the development of handedness from 6 to 24 months. *Infant Behavior and Development*, 36, 181–188.

Nelson, J. C., & Spyker, D. A. (2017). Morbidity and mortality associated with medications used in the treatment of depression: An analysis of cases reported to U.S. Poison Control Centers, 2000-2014. *American Journal of Psychiatry*, 174, 438–450.

Nelson, R. J. (Ed.). (2001). *The somatosensory system: Deciphering the brain's own body image*. CRC Press.

Nestler, E. J. (2004). Historical review: Molecular and cellular mechanisms of opiate and cocaine addiction. *Trends in Pharmacological Sciences*, 25, 210–217.

New York Times. (2018). 11 things we'd really like to know: Will we ever cure Alzheimer's? *New York Times*. https://www.nytimes.com/2018/11/19/health/dementia-alzheimers-cure-drugs.html

Nguyen, T. (2010). Total number of synapses in the human neocortex. *Undergraduate Journal of Mathematical Modelling: One + Two*, 3, 1–14. http://doi.org/10.5038/2326-3652.3.1.26

Nichols, T. R. (2018). Distributed force feedback in the spinal cord and the regulation of limb mechanics. *Journal of Neurophysiology*, 119, 1186–1200.

Nicoll, R. A. (2017). A brief history of long-term potentiation. *Neuron*, 93, 281–290.

Nieuwenhuys, R. (2011). The structural, functional, and molecular organization of the brainstem. *Frontiers in Neuroanatomy*, 5, 33. http://doi.org/10.3389/fnana.2011.00033

Nihonmatsu. I., Ohkawa, N., Saitoh, Y., Okubo-Suzuki, R., & Inokuchi, K. (2020). Selective targeting of mRNA and the following protein synthesis of CaMKIIα at the long-term potentiation-induced site. *Biology Open*, 9, bio042861. http://doi.org/10.1242/bio.042861

Niimi, M., Sato, M., & Taminato, T. (2001). Neuropeptide Y in central control of feeding and interactions with orexin and leptin. *Endocrine*, 14, 269–273.

Nimkarn, S., & New, M. I. (2010). Congenital adrenal hyperplasia due to 21-hydroxylase deficiency: A paradigm for prenatal diagnosis and treatment. *Annals of the New York Academy of Sciences*, 1192, 5–11.

Niu, H., Alvarez-Alverez, I., Gullien-Grima, F., & Aguinaga-Ontoso, I. (2017). Prevalence and incidence of Alzheimer's disease in Europe: A meta-analysis. *Neurología*, 32, 523–532.

Noble, D. (2015). Conrad Waddington and the origin of epigenetics. *Journal of Experimental Biology*, 218, 816–818.

Noda, H. (1975). Discharges in relay cells of the lateral geniculate nucleus of the cat during spontaneous eye movements in light and darkness. *Journal of Physiology*, 250, 579–595.

Nolte, J. N. (2008). *The human brain: An introduction to its functional anatomy*. Mosby.

Nord, M., & Farde, L. (2010). Antipsychotic occupancy of dopamine receptors in schizophrenia. *CNS Neuroscience and Therapeutics*, 17, 97–103.

Norman. A. B., Tabet, M. R., Norman, M. K., Fey, B. K., Tsibulsky, V. L., & Millard, R. W. (2011). The affinity of D2-like dopamine receptor antagonists determines the time to maximal effect on cocaine self-administration. *Journal of Pharmacology and Experimental Therapeutics*, 338, 724–728.

Nottebohm, F., & Arnold, A. P. (1976). Sexual dimorphism in vocal control areas of the songbird brain. *Science*, 194, 211–213.

Nowliss, G. H., & Frank, M. E. (1977). Qualities in hamster taste: Behavioral and neural evidence. *Olfaction Taste Proceedings. International Symposium*, 6, 241–248.

Nunez, J. (2008). Morris water maze experiment. *Journal of Visualised Experiments*, 19, 897. https://doi.org/10.3791/897

Nutt, D. J., & Malizia, A. L. (2001). New insights into the role of the GABAA-benzodiazepine receptor in psychiatric disorder. *British Journal of Psychiatry*, 179, 390–396.

Nuttall, F. Q. (2015). Body mass index: Obesity, BMI, and health: A critical review. *Nutrition Today*, 50, 117–128.

Obata, K. (2013). Synaptic inhibition and γ-aminobutyric acid in the mammalian central nervous system. *Proceedings of the Japan Academy. Series B, Physical and Biological Sciences*, 89, 139–156.

Ockenburg, S. (2019). The serotonergic transporter gene and depression. *Psychology Today*. https://www.psychologytoday.com/gb/blog/the-asymmetric-brain/201905/the-serotonin-transporter-gene-and-depression

O'Connor, D. B., Archer, J., & Wu, F. C. W. (2004). Effects of testosterone on mood, aggression, and sexual behavior in young men: A double-blind, placebo-controlled, cross-over study. *Journal of Clinical Endocrinology and Metabolism*, 89, 2837–2845.

O'Connor, D. H., Wittenberg, G. M., & Wang. S. S. (2005). Graded bidirectional synaptic plasticity is composed of switch-like unitary events. *Proceedings of the National Academy of Sciences of the USA*, 102, 9679–9684.

O'Doherty, J., Rolls, E. T., Francis, S., Bowtell, R., McGlone, F., Kobal, G., Renner B., & Ahne, G. (2000). Sensory-specific satiety-related olfactory activation of the human orbitofrontal cortex. *NeuroReport*, 11, 893–897.

O'Dowd, A. (2017). Spending on junk food advertising is nearly 30 times what government spends on promoting healthy eating. *British Medical Journal*, 359, j4677. https://doi.org/10.1136/bmj.j4677

Office for National Statistics. (2017). Alcohol-specific deaths in the UK: Registered in 2017. https://www.ons.gov.uk/peoplepopulationandcommunity/healthandsocialcare/causesofdeath/bulletins/alcoholrelateddeathsintheunitedkingdom/registeredin2017

Ogawa, S., Olazabal, U. E., Parhar, I. S., & Pfaff, D. W. (1994). Effects of intrahypothalamic administration of antisense DNA for progesterone receptor mRNA on reproductive behavior and progesterone receptor immunoreactivity in female rat. *Journal of Neuroscience*, 14, 1766–1774.

Ogden, J. A., & Corkin, S. (1991). Memories of H.M. In W. C. Abraham (Ed.), *Memory mechanisms: A tribute to G.V. Goddard* (pp. 195–215). Lawrence Erlbaum.

Ojemann, G. A. (1975). The thalamus and language. *Brain and Language*, 2, 1–120.

Ojemann, G. A. (2010). Cognitive mapping through electrophysiology. *Epilepsia*, 51, 72–75.

Ojemann, G. A., Ojemann, J., Lettich, E., & Berger, M. (1989). Cortical language localization in left, dominant hemisphere: An electrical stimulation mapping investigation in 117 patients. *Journal of Neurosurgery*, 71, 316–326.

O'Keefe, J., & Conway, D. H. (1978). Hippocampal place units in the freely moving rat: Why they fire when they fire. *Experimental Brain Research*, 31, 573–590.

O'Keefe, J., & Dostrovsky, J. (1971). The hippocampus as a spatial map: Preliminary evidence from unit activity in the freely moving rat. *Brain Research*, 34, 171–175.

O'Keefe, J., & Nadel, L. (1978). *The hippocampus as a cognitive map*. Oxford University Press.

Olds, J. (1958). Satiation effects in self-stimulation of the brain. *Journal of Comparative and Physiological Psychology*, 51, 675–678.

Olds, J., & Milner, P. (1954). Positive reinforcement produced by electrical stimulation of septal area and other regions of the rat brain. *Journal of Comparative and Physiological Psychology*, 47, 419–427.

Olds, M. E., & Forbes, J. L. (1981). The central basis of motivation: Intracranial self-stimulation studies. *Annual Review of Psychology*, 32, 523–574.

Oliveira-Maia, A. J., Roberts, C. D., Simon, S. A., & Nicolelis, M. A. (2011). Gustatory and reward brain circuits in the control of food intake. *Advances and Technical Standards in Neurosurgery*, 36, 31–59.

Ooki, S. (2014). An overview of human handedness in twins. *Frontiers in Psychology*, 5, 10. https://doi.org/10.3389/fpsyg.2014.00010

Oommen, A. (2014). Factors affecting intelligence quotient. *Journal of Neurology and Stroke*, 1(4), 00023. https://doi.org/10.15406/jnsk.2014.01.00023

Ornstein, R. (1988). *Psychology*. Harcourt, Brace & Jovanovich.

Ortega-de San Luis, C., & Ryan, T. J. (2018). United states of amnesia: Rescuing memory loss from diverse conditions. *Disease Models & Mechanisms*, 11(5), dmm035055. https://doi.org/10.1242/dmm.035055

Oscar-Berman, M. (2012). Function and dysfunction of prefrontal brain circuitry in alcoholic Korsakoff's syndrome. *Neuropsychology Review*, 22, 154–169.

O'Sullivan, M., Brownsett, S., & Copeland, D. (2019). Language and language disorders: Neuroscience to clinical practice. *Practical Neurology*, 19, 380–388.

Oswald, I., & Adam, K. (1980). The man who had not slept for 10 years. *British Medical Journal*, 2, 1684–1685.

Outhoff, K. (2010). The pharmacology of anxiolytics. *South African Family Practice*, 52, 99–105.

Owen, M. J., & Doherty, J. L. (2016). What can we learn from the high rates of schizophrenia in people with 22q11.2 deletion syndrome? *World Psychiatry*, 15, 23–25.

Pahapill, P. A., & Lozano, A. M. (2000). The pedunculopontine nucleus and Parkinson's disease. *Brain*, 123, 1767–1783.

Paintal, A. S. (1954). A study of gastric stretch receptors: Their role in the peripheral mechanism of satiation of hunger and thirst. *Journal of Physiology*, 126, 255–270.

Pakkenberg, B., Pelvig, D., Marner, L., Bundgaard, M. J., Gundersen, H. J., Nyengaard, J. R., & Regeur, L. (2003). Ageing and the human neocortex. *Experimental Gerontology*, 38, 95–99.

Palmer, J. D. (1975). Biological clocks of the tidal zone. *Scientific American*, 232, 70–79.

Pam, A., Kemker, S. S., Ross, C. A., & Golden, R. (1996). The 'equal environments assumption' in MZ–DZ twin comparisons: An untenable premise of psychiatric genetics? *Acta Geneticae Medicae et Gemellologiae: Twin Research*, 45, 349–360.

Panda, S., Sato, T. K., Castrucci, A. M., Rollag, M. D., DeGrip, W. J., Hogenesch, J. B., Provencio, I., & Kay, S. A. (2002). Melanopsin (*opn4*) requirement for normal light-induced circadian phase shifting. *Science*, 298, 2213–2216.

Pandi-Perumal, S. R., Zisapel, N., Srinivasen, V., & Cardinali, D. P. (2005). Melatonin and sleep in an aging population. *Experimental Gerontology*, 40, 911–925.

Panikkath, R., Panikkath, D., Mojumba, D., & Nugent, K. (2014). The alien hand syndrome. *Baylor University Medical Centre Proceedings*, 27, 219–220.

Panksepp, J. (1972). Hypothalamic radioactivity after intragastric glucose-14 C in rats. *American Journal of Physiology*, 223, 396–401.

Panlilo, L. V., & Goldberg, S. R. (2007). Self-administration of drugs in animals and humans as a model and an investigative tool. *Addiction*, 102, 1863–1870.

Papez, J. (1937). A proposed mechanism of emotion. *Archives of Neurology and Psychiatry*, 38, 725–743.

Paradisi, I., Hernández, A., & Arias, S. (2008). Huntington disease mutation in Venezuela: Age of onset, haplotype analyses and geographic aggregation. *Journal of Human Genetics*, 53, 127–135.

Parakh, K., Sakhuja, A., Bhat, U., & Ziegelstein, R. C. (2008). Platelet function in patients with depression. *Southern Medical Journal*, 101, 612–617.

Park, I.-H., Arora, N., Huo, H., Maherali, N., Ahfeldt, T., Shimamura, A., Lensch, M. W., Cowan, C., Hochedlinger, K., & Daley, G. Q. (2008). Disease-specific induced pluripotent stem cells. *Cell*, 134, 877–886.

Park, S. M., & Kim, K. S. (2013). Proteolytic clearance of extracellular α-synuclein as a new therapeutic approach against Parkinson disease. *Prion*, 7, 121–126.

parkinsons.org.uk (2018). *The incidence and prevalence of Parkinson's in the UK*. 1–6.

Parkkinen, L., O'Sullivan, S. S, Collins, C., Petrie, A., Holton, J. L., Revesz, T., & Lees A. J. (2011). Disentangling the relationship between Lewy bodies and nigral neuronal loss in Parkinson's disease. *Journal of Parkinson's Disease*, 1, 277–286.

Pasick, A. (2000). The yawning orgasm and other antidepressant side effects. www.contac.org/contaclibrary/medications6.htm

Passie, T., Halpern, J. H., Stichtenoth, D. O., Emrich H.M., & Hintzen, A. (2008). The pharmacology of lysergic acid diethylamide: A review. *CNS Neuroscience and Therapeutics*, 14, 295–314.

Patrick, G. T. W., & Gilbert, J. A. (1896). On the effects of loss of sleep. *Psychological Review*, 3, 469–483.

Patterson, R. D., Uppenkamp, S., Johnsrude, I. S., & Griffiths, T. D. (2002). The processing of temporal pitch and melody information in auditory cortex. *Neuron*, 36, 767–776.

Paulesu, E., Démonet, J.-F., Fazio, F., McCrory, E., Chanoine, V., Brunswick, N., Cappa, S. F., Cossu, G., Habib, M., Frith, C. D., & Frith, U. (2001). Dyslexia: Cultural diversity and biological unity. *Science*, 291, 2165–2167.

Paulesu, E., Frith, U., Snowling, M., Gallagher, A., Morton, J., Frackowiak, R. S., & Frith, C. D. (1996). Is developmental dyslexia a disconnection syndrome? Evidence from PET scanning. *Brain*, 119, 143–157.

Paulson, H. L.(2009). The spinocerebellar ataxias. *Journal of Neuro-Ophthalmology*, 29, 227–237.

Paulson, P. E., Camp, D. M., & Robinson, T. E. (1991). Time course of transient behavioral depression and persistent behavioral sensitization in relation to regional brain monoamine concentrations during amphetamine withdrawal in rats. *Psychopharmacology*, 103, 480–492.

Pelc, N. J. (2014). Recent and future directions in CT imaging. *Annals of Biomedical Engineering*, 42, 260–268.

Pendergrast, M. (2013). *For God, country and Coca-Cola: The definitive history of the great American soft drink and the company that makes them*. Basic Books.

Penfield, W. (1975). *Mystery of the mind*. Princeton University Press.

Penfield, W., & Boldrey, E. (1937). Somatic motor and sensory representation in *The cerebral cortex of man* as studied by electrical stimulation. *Brain*, 60, 389–443.

Penfield, W., & Rasmussen, T. (1950). *The cerebral cortex of man*. Macmillan.

Penfield, W., & Roberts, L. (1959). *Speech and brain mechanisms*. Princeton University Press.

Penfield, W., & Welch, K. (1951). The supplementary motor area of the cerebral cortex: A clinical and experimental study. *A.M.A. Archives of Neurology and Psychiatry*, 66, 289–317.

Penhune, V. B., & Steele, C. (2012). Parallel contributions of cerebellar, striatal and M1 mechanisms to motor sequence learning. *Behavioral Brain Research*, 226, 579–591.

Penke, L., Muñoz Maniega, S., Murray, C., Gow, A. J., Hernández, M. C., Clayden, J. D., Starr, J. M., Wardlaw, J. M., Bastin, M. E., & Deary, I. J. (2010). A general factor of brain white matter integrity predicts information processing speed in healthy older people. *Journal of Neuroscience*, 30, 7569–7574.

Perälä, J., Suvisaari, J., Saarni, S., Kuoppasalmi, K., Isometsä, E., Pirkola, S., Partonen, T., Tuulio-Henriksson, A., Hintikka, J., Kieseppä, T., Härkänen, T., Koskinen, S., & Lönnqvist, J. (2007). Lifetime prevalence of psychotic and bipolar I disorders in a general population. *Archives of General Psychiatry*, 64, 19–28.

Peralta, V., deLeon, J., & Cuesta, M. J. (1992). Are there more than two syndromes in schizophrenia? *British Journal of Psychiatry*, 161, 335–343.

Pereira, A. C., Huddleston, D. E., Brickman, A. M., Sosunov, A. A., Hen, R., McKhann, G. M., Sloan, R., Gage, F. H., Brown, T. R., & Small, S. A. (2007). An *in vivo* correlate of exercise-induced neurogenesis in the adult dentate gyrus. *Proceedings of the National Academy of Sciences of the USA*, 104, 5638–5643.

Peretz, I., & Coltheart, M. (2003). Modularity of music processing. *Nature Neuroscience*, 6, 688–691.

Peretz, I., & Zatorre, R. J. (2005). Brain organization for music processing. *Annual Review of Psychology*, 56, 89–114.

Peretz, I. (2006). The nature of music from a biological perspective. *Cognition*, 100, 1–32.

Pérez-Dueñas, B., Pujol, J., Soriano-Mas C., Ortiz, H., Artuch, R., Vilaseca, M. A., & Campistol, J. (2006). Global and regional volume changes in the brains of patients with phenylketonuria. *Neurology*, 66, 1074–1078.

Perls, T., Alpert, L., & Fretts, R. (1997). Middle-aged mothers live longer. *Nature*, 389, 133.

Perls, T. T., Bochen, K., Freeman, M., Alpert L., & Silver, M. H. (1999). The New England Centenarian Study: Validity of reported age and prevalence of centenarians in an eight town sample. *Age and Ageing*, 28, 193–197.

Pert, C. B., & Snyder, S. H. (1973). Properties of opiate-receptor binding in rat brain. *Proceedings of the National Academy of Sciences of the USA*, 70, 2243–2247.

Peters, M., Manning, J. T., & Reimers, S. (2007). The effects of sex, sexual orientation, and digit ratio (2D:4D) on mental rotation performance. *Archives of Sexual Behavior*, 36, 251–260.

Peters, R. H., & Gunion, M. W. (1980). Finickiness in VMH rats also results from the lesions, not just from obesity. *Physiological Psychology*, 8, 93–96.

Peterson, A. C. (1976). Physical androgyny and cognitive functioning in adolescence development. *Developmental Psychology*, 12, 524–533.

Peterson, R. L., & Pennington, B. F. (2012). Developmental dyslexia. *The Lancet*, 379, P1997–P2007.

Peyron, R., Laurent, B., & García-Larrea, L. (2000). Functional imaging of brain responses to pain: A review and meta-analysis (2000). *Neurophysiological Clinics*, 30, 263–288.

Pezawas, L., Meyer-Lindenberg, A., Drabent, E.M., Verchinski, B. A., Munoz, K. E., Kolachana, B. S., Egan, M. F., Mattay, V. S., Hariri, A. R., & Weinberger, D. R. (2005). 5-HTTLPR polymorphism impacts human cingulate-amygdala interactions: A genetic susceptibility mechanism for depression. *Nature Neuroscience*, 8, 828–834.

Pfaff, D. W., & Schwartz-Giblin, S. (1988). Cellular mechanisms of female reproductive behaviors. In E. Knobil & J. D. Neill (Eds.), *The physiology of reproduction* (pp. 1487–1568). Raven Press.

Pfaff, D. W., Arnold, A., Etgen, A., Fahrbach, S., & Rubin, R. (Eds.). (2002). *Hormones, brain, and behavior*. Academic Press.

Pflug, A., Gompf, F., Muthuraman, M., Groppa, S., & Kell, C. A. (2019). Differential contributions of the two human cerebral hemispheres to action timing. *eLife*, 8, e48404. https://doi.org/10.7554/eLife.48404

Pfohl, B., & Winokur, G. (1983). The micropsychpathology of hebephrenic/catatonic schizophrenia. *Journal of Nervous and Mental Disease*, 171, 296–300.

Phelps, E. A., Labar, K. S., Anderson, A. K., O'Connor, K. J., Fulbright, R. K., & Spencer, D. D. (1998). Specifying the contributions of the human amygdala to emotional memory: A case study. *Neurocase*, 4, 527–540.

Phelps, E. A., & LeDoux, J. E. (2005). Contributions of the amygdala to emotion processing: From animal models to human behavior. *Neuron*, 48, 175–187.

Philips, A. G., & Fibiger, H. C. (1989). Neuroanatomical basis of intracranial self-stimulation: Untangling the Gordian knot. In J. M. Leibman & S.J. Cooper (Eds.), *The neuropharmacological basis of reward* (pp. 66–105). Clarendon Press.

Philips, D. P., Semple, M. N., Calford, M. B., & Kitzes, L. M. (1994). Level-dependent representation of stimulus frequency in cat primary auditory cortex. *Experimental Brain Research*, 102, 210–226.

Phillips, R. G., & LeDoux, J. E. (1992). Differential contribution of amygdala and hippocampus to cued and contextual fear conditioning. *Behavioural Neuroscience*, 106, 274–285.

Phillipou, A., Rossell, S. L., Castle, D. J., & Castle, D. J. (2014). The neurobiology of anorexia nervosa: A systematic review. *Australian and New Zealand Journal of Psychiatry*, 48, 128–152.

Philpott, C. M., Bennett, A., & Murty, E. G. (2008). A brief history of olfaction and olfactometry. *Journal of Laryngology and Olfactometry*, 122, 657–662.

Phoenix, C. H., Goy, R. W., Gerall, A. A., & Young, W. C. (1959). Organising action of prenatally administered testosterone propionate on the tissues mediating mating behaviour in the female guinea pig. *Endocrinology*, 65, 269–382.

Piccolino, M. (1997). Luigi Galvani and animal electricity: Two centuries after the foundation of electrophysiology. *Trends in Neurosciences*, 20, 443–448.

Pickles, J. (2013). *An introduction to the physiology of hearing*. Brill.

Pidoplichko, V. I., Noguchi, J., Areola, O. O., Liang, Y., Peterson, J., Zhang, T., & Dani, J. A. (2004). Nicotinic cholinergic synaptic mechanisms in the ventral tegmental area contribute to nicotine addiction. *Learning and Memory*, 11, 60–69.

Pinel, P. J. (2011). *Biopsychology*. Pearson.

Pinker, S. (1997). *How the mind works*. Penguin.

Piven, J. (1997). The biological basis of autism. *Current Opinion in Neurobiology*, 7, 708–712.

Plack, C. J. (2014). *The sense of hearing*. Psychology Press.

Plaza, M., Gatignol, P., Leroy, M., & Duffau, H. (2009). Speaking without Broca's area after tumor resection. *Neurocase*, 15, 294–310.

Pleger, B., Blankenburg, F., Ruff, C. C., Driver, J., & Dolan, R. J. (2008). Reward facilitates tactile judgments and modulates hemodynamic responses in human primary somatosensory cortex. *Journal of Neuroscience*, 28, 8161–8168.

Pleger, B., & Villringer, A. (2013). The human somatosensory system: From perception to decision making. *Progress in Neurobiology*, 103, 76–97.

Plomin, R., & Deary, I. (2015). Genetics and intelligence differences: Five special findings. *Molecular Psychiatry*, 20, 98–108.

Plomin, R., DeFies, J., Knopik, V. S., & Neiderhiser, J. M. (2013). *Behavioral genetics*. Worth.

Polymeropoulos, M. H., Higgins, J. J., Golbe, L. I., Johnson, W. G., Ide, S. E., Di Iorio, G., Sanges, G., Stenroos, E. S., Pho, L. T., Schaffer, A. A., Lazzarini, A. M., Nussbaum, R. L., & Duvoisin, R. C. (1996). Mapping of a gene for Parkinson's disease to chromosome 4q21-q23. *Science*, 274, 1197–1199.

Ponomarenko, E. A., Poverennaya, E. V., Ilgisonis, E. V., Pyatnitskiy, M. A., Kopylov, A. T., Zgoda, V. G., Lisitsa, A. V., & Archakov, A. I. (2016). The size of the human proteome: The width and depth. *International Journal of Analytical Chemistry*. https://doi.org/10.1155/2016/7436849

Pons, T. P., Garraghty, P. E., & Ommaya, A. K. (1991). Massive cortical reorganization after sensory deafferentation in adult macaques. *Science*, 252, 1857–1860.

Porter, R. H., Cernoch, J. M., & McLaughlin, F. J. (1983). Maternal recognition of neonates through olfactory cues. *Physiology of Behaviour*, 30, 151–154.

Portnow, L. H., Vaillancourt, D. E., & Okun, M. S. (2013). The history of cerebral PET scanning: From physiology to cutting-edge technology. *Neurology*, 80, 952-956.

Prange, A. J., Jr, Wilson, I. C., Lynn, C. W., Alltop, L. B., & Stikeleather, R. A. (1974). L-Tryptophan in mania. Contribution to a permissive hypothesis of affective disorders. *Archives of General Psychiatry*, 30, 56–62.

Preller, K. H., Herdener, M., Pokorny T., Planzer, A., Kraehenmann, R., Stämpfli, P., Liechti, M. E., Seifritz, E., & Vollenweider, F. X. (2017). The fabric of meaning and subjective effects in LSD-induced states depend on serotonin 2A receptor activation. *Current Biology*, 27, 451–457.

Prendergast, M. A., Terry, A. V., Jr, Jackson, W. J., Marsh, K. C., Decker, M. W., & Arneric, S. P. (1997). Improvement in accuracy of delayed recall in aged and non-aged, mature monkeys after intramuscular or transdermal administration of the CNS nicotinic receptor agonist ABT-418. *Psychopharmacology*, 130, 276–284.

Prentice, K. J., Gold, J. M., & Buchanan, R. W. (2008). The Wisconsin Card Sorting impairment in schizophrenia is evident in the first four trials. *Schizophrenia Research*, 106, 81–87.

Preskorn, S. H. (2007). The evolution of antipsychotic drug therapy: Reserpine, chlorpromazine, and haloperidol. *Journal of Psychiatric Practice*, 13, 253–257.

Prete, G., D'Ascenzo, S., Laeng, B., Fabri, M., Foschi, N., & Tommasi, L. (2015). Conscious and unconscious processing of facial expressions: Evidence from two split-brain patients. *Journal of Neuropsychology*, 9, 45–63.

Price, D. (2002). Brain mechanisms of persistent brain states. *Journal of Musculoskeletal Pain*, 10, 73–83.

Price, D. D. (1988). *Psychological and neural mechanisms of pain*. Raven Press.

Price, D. L., Tanzi, R. E., Borchelt, D. R., & Sisodia, S. S. (1998). Alzheimer's disease: Genetic studies and transgenic studies. *Annual Review of Genetics*, 32, 461–493.

Priller, C., Bauer, T., Mitteregger, G., Krebs, B., Kretzschmar, H. A., & Herms, J. (2006). Synapse formation and function is modulated by the amyloid precursor protein. *Journal of Neuroscience*, 26, 7212–7221.

Printzlau, F., Wolstencroft, J., & Skuse, D. H. (2017). Cognitive, behavioral, and neural consequences of sex chromosome aneuploidy. *Journal of Neuroscience Research*, 95, 311–319.

Proske, U., & Gandevia, S. C. (2012). The proprioceptive senses: Their roles in signaling body shape, body position and movement, and muscle force. *Physiological Review*, 92, 1651–1697.

Provine, R. R. (1989). Contagious yawning and infant imitation. *Bulletin of the Psychonomic Society*, 27, 125–126.

Provine, R. R. (2001). *Laughter*. Penguin.

Provine, R. R. (2005). Yawning. *American Scientist*, 93, 532–539.

Provine, R. R., Tate, B. C., & Geldmacher, L. L. (1987). Yawning: No effect of 3–5% CO2, and exercise. *Behavioral and Neural Biology*, 48, 382–393.

Public Health England. (2016). The public health burden of alcohol and the effectiveness and cost-effectiveness of alcohol control policies: An evidence review. PHE publications gateway number 2016490. https://www.gov.uk/government/publications/the-public-health-burden-of-alcohol-evidence-review

Public Health England. (2017). Statistics on obesity, physical activity and diet, England 2017. https://www.gov.uk/government/statistics/statistics-on-obesity-physical-activity-and-diet-england-2017

Pukkala, E., Aspholm, R., Auvinen, A., Eliasch, H., Gundestrup, M., Haldorsen, T., Hammar, N., Hrafnkelsson, J., Kyyrönen, P., Linnersjö, A., Rafnsson, V., Storm, H., & Tveten, U. (2002). Incidence of cancer among Nordic airline pilots over five decades: Occupational cohort study. *British Medical Journal*, 325(7364), 567. https://doi.org/10.1136/bmj.325.7364.567

Purtell, L., Sze, L., Loughnan, G., Smith, E., Herzog, H., Sainsbury, A., Steinbeck, K., Campbell, L. V., & Viardot, A. (2011).

In adults with Prader-Willi syndrome, elevated ghrelin levels are more consistent with hyperphagia than high PYY and GLP-1 levels. *Neuropeptides*, 45, 301–307.

Purves, D., Augustine, G. J., Fitzpatrick, D., Hall, W. C., LaMantia, A.-S., McNamara, J. O., & White, L. E. (Eds.). (2008). *Neuroscience*. Sinauer.

Qualls-Creekmore, E., & Münzberg, H. (2018). Modulation of feeding and associated behaviors by lateral hypothalamic circuits. *Endocrinology*, 159, 3631–3642.

Quinn, N., & Schrag, A. (1998). Huntington's disease and other choreas. *Journal of Neurology*, 245, 709–716.

Quintanilla, M. E., Israel, Y., Sapag A., & Tampier, L. (2006). The UChA and UChB rat lines: Metabolic and genetic differences influencing ethanol intake. *Addiction Biology*, 11, 310–323.

Rai, P., & Malik, P. (2016). Gene therapy for hemoglobin disorders – a mini-review. *Journal of Rare Diseases Research and Treatment*, 1, 25–31.

Rainville, P., Duncan, G. H., Price, D. D., Carrier, B., & Bushnell, M. C. (1997). Pain affect encoded in human anterior cingulate but not somatosensory cortex. *Science*, 277, 968–971.

Raisman, G., & Field, P. M. (1973). Sexual dimorphism in the neuropil of the preoptic area of the rat and its dependence on neonatal androgen. *Brain Research*, 54, 1–29.

Rajmohan, V., & Mohandras, E. (2007). The limbic system. *Indian Journal of Psychiatry*, 49, 132–139.

Ralph, M. R., Foster, R., Davis, F., & Menaker, M. (1990). Transplanted suprachiasmatic nucleus determines circadian period. *Science*, 247, 975–978.

Ramachandran, V. S., & Blakeslee, S. (1998). *Phantoms in the brain*. Fourth Estate.

Ramachandran, V. S., & Hubbard, E. M. (2001). Psychological investigations into the neural basis of synaesthesia. *Proceedings of the Royal Academy of London*, 268, 979–983.

Ramachandran, V. S., & Hubbard, E. M. (2003). Hearing colors, tasting shapes. *Scientific American*, 288, 52–59.

Ramachandron, V. S., & McGeoch, P. D. (2007). Occurrence of phantom genitalia after gender reassignment surgery. *Medical Hypotheses*, 69, 1001–1003.

Ramnani, N. (2006). The primate cortico-cerebellar system: Anatomy and function. *Nature Reviews Neuroscience*, 7, 511–522.

Ramus, F., Rosen, S., Dakin, S. C., Day, B. L., Castellote, J. M., White, S., & Frith, U. (2003). Theories of developmental dyslexia: Insights from a multiple case study of dyslexic adults. *Brain*, 126, 841–865.

Ranganath, C., Cohen, M. X., Dam, C., & D'Esposito, M. (2004). Inferior temporal, prefrontal, and hippocampal contributions to visual working memory maintenance and associative memory retrieval. *Journal of Neuroscience*, 24, 3917–3925.

Ranganath, C., & Ritchey, M. (2012). Two cortical systems for memory-guided behaviour. *Nature Reviews Neuroscience*, 13, 713–726.

Rantamäki, T., & Yalcin, I. (2019). Depression and antidepressant action – from molecules to networks. *Cell Tissue Research*, 377, 1–4.

Rapoport, J. (1989). *The boy who couldn't stop washing*. Fontana.

Rapoport, M., van Reekum, R., & Mayberg, H. (2000). The role of the cerebellum in cognition and behavior: A selective review. *Journal of Neuropsychiatry and Clinical Neurosciences*, 12, 193–198.

Rapport, R. (2005). *Nerve endings: The discovery of the synapse*. Norton.

Rasch, B., & Born, J. (2013). About sleep's role in memory. *Physiological Reviews*, 93, 681–766.

Rasmussen, T., & Milner, B. (1977). The role of early left brain damage in determining lateralization of cerebral speech functions. *Annals of the New York Academy of Sciences*, 299, 355–369.

Rassnick, S., Pulvirenti, L., & Koob, G. F. (1992). Oral ethanol self-administration in rats is reduced by the administration of dopamine and glutamate receptor antagonists into the nucleus accumbens. *Psychopharmacology*, 109, 92–98.

Rathakrishnan, B. G., Doraiswamy, P. M., & Petrella, J. R. (2014). Science to practice: Translating automated brain MRI volumetry in Alzheimer's disease from research to routine diagnostic use in the work-up of dementia. *Frontiers in Neurology*, 4, 216. https://doi.org/10.3389/fneur.2013.00216

Rattenborg, N. C., de la Iglesia, H. O., Kempenaers, B., Lesku, J. A., Meerlo, P., & Scriba, M. F. (2017). Sleep research goes wild: New methods and approaches to investigate the ecology, evolution and functions of sleep. *Philosophical Transactions of the Royal Society* B, 372, 20160251. http://doi.org/10.1098/rstb.2016.0251

Raynor, H. A., Niemeier, H. M., & Wing, R. R. (2006). Effect of limiting snack food variety on long-term sensory-specific satiety and monotony during obesity treatment. *Eating Behaviors*, 7, 1–14.

Rechtschaffen, A., Bergmann, B. M., Everson, C. A., Kushida, C. A., & Gilliland, M. A. (1989). Sleep deprivation in the rat: X. Integration and discussion of the findings. *Sleep*, 12, 68–87.

Rechtschaffen, A., Gilliland, M. A., Bergmann, B. M., & Winter, J. B. (1983). Physiological correlates of prolonged sleep deprivation in rats. *Science*, 221, 182–184.

Reich, T., Edenberg, H. J., Goate, A., Williams, J. T., Rice, J. P., Van Eerdewegh, P., Foroud, T., Hesselbrock, V., Schuckit, M. A., Bucholz, K., Porjesz, B., Li, T. K., Conneally, P. M., Nurnberger, J. I., Jr, Tischfield, J. A., Crowe, R. R., Cloninger, C. R., Wu, W., Shears, S., . . . Begleiter, H. (1998). Genome-wide search for genes affecting the risk for alcohol dependence. *American Journal of Medical Genetics*, 81, 207–215.

Reisi, P., Ghaedamini, A. R., Golbidi, M., Shabrang, M., Arabpoor, Z., & Rashidi, B (2015). Effect of cholecystokinin on learning and memory, neuronal proliferation and apoptosis in the rat hippocampus. *Advanced Biomedical Research*, 4, 227.

Reitz, C. (2012). Alzheimer's disease and the amyloid cascade hypothesis: A critical review. *International Journal of Alzheimer's Disease*, 2012, 1–11.

Relkin, E. M., & Doucet, J. R. (1997). Is loudness simply proportional to the auditory nerve spike count? *The Journal of the Acoustic Society of America*, 101, 1735–2740.

Resnick, S. M., Berenbaum, S. A., Gottesman, I. I., & Bouchard, T. J. (1986). Early hormonal influences on cognitive functioning in congenital adrenal hyperplasia. *Developmental Psychology*, 22, 191–198.

Reul, J. M., Labeur, M., Grigoriadis, D. D., De Souza, E.B., & Holsboer, F. (1994). Hypothalamic-pituitary-adrenocortical axis changes in the rat after long term treatment with the reversible monoamine oxidase-A inhibitor Moclobemide. *Neuroendocrinology*, 60, 509–519.

Reul, J. M., Stec, I., Soder, M., & Holsboer, F. (1993). Chronic treatment of rats with the antidepressant amitriptyline attenuates the activity of the hypothalamic-pituitary-adrenocortical system. *Endocrinology*, 133, 312–320.

Reynolds, T., Johnson, E. C., Huggett, S. B., Bubier, J. A., Palmer, R. H. C., Agrawal, A., Baker, E. J., & Chesler, E. J. (2021). Interpretation of psychiatric genome-wide association studies with multispecies heterogeneous functional genomic data integration. *Neuropsychopharmacology*, 46, 86–97.

Ribot, T. (1881). *Les maladies de la mémoire*. Alcan. [*Diseases of memory* (1882), English translation, Kegan Paul, Trench & Co.]

Ricciarelli, R., & Fedele, E. (2017). The amyloid cascade hypothesis in Alzheimer's disease: It's time to change our mind. *Current Neuropharmacology*, 15, 926–935.

Richter, C. (1967). Sleep and activity: Their relation to the 24 hour clock. *Proceedings of the Association for Research in Nervous and Mental Diseases*, 45, 8–27.

Risch, N., Herrell, R., Lehner, T., Liang, K. Y., Eaves, L., Hoh, J., Griem, A., Kovacs, M., Ott, J., & Merikangas, M. R. (2009). Interaction between the serotonin transporter gene (5-HTTLPR), stressful life events, and risk of depression: A meta-analysis. *Journal of the American Medical Association*, 301, 2462–2471.

Risenhuber, M., & Poggio, T. (1999). Hierarchical models of object recognition in cortex. *Nature Neuroscience*, 2, 1019–1025.

Ritchie, S. J., Cox, S. R., Shen, X., Lombardo, M. V., Reus, L. M., Alloza, C., Harris, M. A., Alderson, H. L., Hunter, S., Neilson, E., Liewald, D. C. M., Auyeung, B., Whalley, H. C., Lawrie, S. M., Gale, C. R., Bastin, M. E., McIntosh, A. M., & Deary, I. J. (2018). Sex differences in the adult human brain: Evidence from 5216 UK biobank participants. *Cerebral Cortex*, 28, 2959–2975.

Rizzi, L., Rosset, I., & Roriz-Cruz, M. (2014). Global epidemiology of dementia: Alzheimer's and vascular types. *BioMed Research International*, 2014, 908915, https://doi.org/10.1155/2014/908915

Rizzolatti, G., Fadiga, L., Fogassi, L., & Gallese, V. (1996). Premotor cortex and the recognition of motor actions. *Cognitive Brain Research*, 3,131–141.

Rizzolatti, G., Fogassi, L., & Gallese, V. (2001). Neurophysiological mechanisms underlying the understanding and imitation of action. *Nature Reviews Neuroscience*, 2, 661–670.

Rizzolatti, G., & Kalaska, J. F. (2013). Voluntary movement: The parietal and premotor cortex. In E. R. Kandel, J. H. Schwartz, T. M. Jessel, S. A. Siegelbaum, & A. J. Hudspeth (Eds.), *Principles of neural science* (pp. 865–893). McGraw-Hill.

Robertson, S. D., Matthies, H. J., & Galli, A. (2009). A closer look at amphetamine induced reverse transport and trafficking of the dopamine and norepinephrine transporters. *Molecular Neurobiology*, 39, 73–80.

Robins, L. N., Helzer, J. E., & Hesselbrock, M. (2010). Vietnam veterans three years after Vietnam: How our study changed our view of heroin. *The American Journal of Addictions*, 19, 203–211.

Robinson, R., & Kerkut, G. A. (Eds.). (2013). *Genetics of the Norway rat: International series of monographs in pure and applied biology*. Pergamon.

Robinson, T. E., & Berridge, K. C. (1993). The neural basis of drug craving: An incentive sensitization theory of addiction. *Brain Research Reviews*, 18, 247–291.

Robinson, T. R., & Spock, L. C. (2009). *Genetics for dummies*. John Wiley.

Robson, P. (1999). *Forbidden drugs*. Oxford University Press.

Rodier, P. M. (2000). The early origins of autism. *Scientific American*, 282(2), 56–63.

Rodriguez, I. (2004). Pheromone receptors in mammals. *Hormones and Behavior*, 46, 219–230.

Rodriguez, J. S., & Paule, M. G. (2009). Working memory delayed response tasks in monkeys. In J. J. Buccafusco (Ed.), *Methods of behavior analysis in neuroscience* (Chapter 12). CRC Press.

Roeder, F., Orthner, H., & Müller, D. (1972). The stereotaxis treatment of pedophilic homosexuality and other sexual deviations. In E. Hitchcock, L. Laitinen, & K. Vaernet (Eds.), *Psychosurgery* (pp. 87–111). Thomas.

Roffwarg, H. P., Muzio, J. N., & Dement, W. C. (1966). Ontogenetic development of the human sleep-dream cycle. *Science*, 152, 604–619.

Rogalsky, C., Matchin, W., & Hickok, G. (2008). Broca's area, sentence comprehension, and working memory: An fMRI study. *Frontiers in Human Neuroscience*, 2, 14. https://doi.org/10.3389/neuro.09.014.2008

Rogen, M. T., Stubli, U. V., & LeDoux, J. E. (1997). Fear conditioning induces associative long term potentiation in the amygdala. *Nature*, 390, 604–607.

Rogers, A. E. (2008). The effects of fatigue and sleepiness on nurse performance and patient safety. In R. G. Hughes (Ed.), *Patient safety and quality: An evidence-based handbook for nurses* (Chapter 40). Agency for Healthcare Research and Quality. https://www.ncbi.nlm.nih.gov/books/NBK2645/

Rogers, P. J., & Blundell, J. E. (1980). Investigation of food selection and meal parameters during the development of dietary induced obesity. *Appetite*, 1, 85.

Roland, P. E. (1993). *Brain activation*. John Wiley.

Roland, P. E., Larsen, B., Lassen, N. A., & Skinhøj, E. (1980). Supplementary motor area and other cortical areas in organization of voluntary movements in man. *Journal of Neurophysiology*, 43, 118–136.

Rolls, B. J., Rolls, E. T., Rowe, E. A., & Sweeney, K. (1981). Sensory specific satiety in man. *Physiology and Behavior, 27*, 137–142.

Rolls, B. J., Van Duijvenvoorde, P. M., & Rolls, E. T. (1984). Pleasantness and food intake in a varied four course meal. *Appetite, 5*, 337–348.

Rolls, E. T. (1999). *The brain and emotion*. Oxford University Press.

Rolls, E. T. (2006). Brain mechanisms underlying flavour and appetite. *Philosophical Transactions of the Royal Society of London B, Biological Sciences, 361*(1471), 1123–1136.

Rolls, E. T., & Grabenhorst, F. (2008). The orbitofrontal cortex and beyond: From affect to decision-making. *Progress in Neurobiology, 86*, 216–244.

Rolls, R. (2005). *Classic case studies in psychology*. Hodder Arnold.

Roos, R. A. (2010). Huntington's disease: A clinical review. *Orphanet Journal of Rare Diseases, 5*, 40. https://doi.org/10.1186/1750-1172-5-40

Rosales-Lagarde, A., Armony, J. L., Del Río-Portilla, Y., Trejo-Martínez, D., Conde, R., & Corsi-Cabrera, M. (2012). Enhanced emotional reactivity after selective REM sleep deprivation in humans: An fMRI study. *Frontiers in Behavioral Neuroscience, 6*, 25. https://doi.org/10.3389/fnbeh.2012.00025

Rosas, H. D., Salat, D. H, Lee, S. Y., Zaleta, A. K., Pappu, V., Fischl, B., Greve, D., Hevelone, N., & Hersch, S. M. (2008). Cerebral cortex and the clinical expression of Huntington's disease: Complexity and heterogeneity. *Brain, 131*, 1057–1068.

Rose, R. M., Bernstein, L. S., & Gordon, T. P. (1975). Consequences of social conflict on plasma testosterone levels in rhesus monkeys. *Psychomatic Medicine, 37*, 50–62.

Rose, S. (2003). *The making of memory*. Bantam Books.

Rosen, V. (2018). One brain. Two minds? Many questions. *Journal of Undergraduate Neuroscience Education, 16*, R48–R50.

Rosenberg, S. A., Aebersold, P., Cornetta, K., Kasid, A., Morgan, R. A., Moen, R., Karson, E. M., Lotze, M. T., Yang, J. C., Topalian, S. L., Merino, M. J., Culver, K.,

Miller, A. D., Blaese, R. M., & Anderson, W. F. (1990). Gene transfer into humans – immunotherapy of patients with advanced melanoma, using tumor-infiltrating lymphocytes modified by retroviral gene transduction. *New England Journal of Medicine, 323*, 570–578.

Rosenheck, R., Evans, D., Herz, L., Cramer, J., Xu, W., Thomas, J., Henderson, W., & Charney, D. (1999). How long to wait for a response to Clozapine: A comparison of time course of response to clozapine and conventional antipsychotic medication in refractory schizophrenia. *Schizophrenia Bulletin, 25*, 709–719.

Rosenzweig, M. R., Bennett, E. L., & Diamond, M. C. (1972). Brain changes in response to experience. *Scientific American, 226*, 22–29.

Rosenzweig, M. R., Krech, D., & Bennett, E. L. (1958). Brain chemistry and adaptive behavior. In H. F. Harlow & C. N. Woolsey (Eds.), *Biological and biochemical bases of behavior* (pp. 367–400). Wisconsin University Press.

Roses, A. D. (1995). Apolipoprotein E and Alzheimer's disease. *Scientific American*, Sept/Oct, 16–25.

Rosling, A. M., Sparén, P., Norring, C., & von Knorring, A.-L. (2011). Mortality of eating disorders: A follow-up study of treatment in a specialist unit 1974–2000. *The International Journal of Eating Disorders, 44*, 304–310.

Ross, E. D. (2010). Cerebral localization of functions and the neurology of language: Fact versus fiction or is it something else? *The Neuroscientist, 16*, 222–243.

Ross, G. W., Abbott, R. D., Petrovitch, H., Morens, D. M., Grandinetti, A., Tung, K. H., Tanner, C. M., Masaki, K. H., Blanchette, P. L., Curb, J. D., Popper, J. S., & White, L. R. (2000). Association of coffee and caffeine intake with the risk of Parkinson disease. *Journal of the American Medical Association, 283*, 2674–2679.

Ross, R. S., LoPresti, M. L., Schon, K., & Stern, C. E. (2013). Role of the hippocampus and orbitofrontal cortex during the disambiguation of social cues in working memory. *Cognitive, Affective and Behavioral Neuroscience*, 13, 900–915. https://doi.org/10.3758/s13415-013-0170-x

Rossetti, Y., Pisella, L., & McIntosh, R. D. (2017). Rise and fall of the two visual systems theory. *Annals of Physical and Rehabilitation Medicine*, 60, 130–140.

Rosvold, H. E., Mirsky, A. F., & Pribram, K. H. (1954). Influence of amygdalectomy on social behaviour in monkeys. *Journal of Comparative and Physiological Psychology*, 47, 173–178.

Routh, V. H., Hao, L., Santiago, A. M., Sheng, Z., & Zhou, C. (2014). Hypothalamic glucose sensing: Making ends meet. *Frontiers in Systems Neuroscience*, 8, 236. https://doi.org/10.3389/fnsys.2014.00236

Rouw, R., Scholte, S., & Colizoli, O. (2011). Brain areas involved in synaesthesia: A review. *Journal of Neuropsychology*, 5, 214–242.

Roy, A., De Jong, J., & Linnoila, M. (1989). Cerebrospinal fluid monoamine metabolites and suicidal behavior in depressed patients: A 5-year follow-up study. *Archives of General Psychiatry*, 46, 609–612.

Roze, E., Cahill, E., Martin, E., Bonnet, C., Vanhoutte, P., Betuing, S., & Caboche, J. (2011). Huntington's disease and striatal signaling. *Frontiers in Neuroanatomy*, 5, 55. https://doi.org/10.3389/fnana.2011.00055

Rüb, U., Vonsattel, J. P. G., Heinsen, H., & Korf, H. W. (2015). *The neuropathology of Huntington's disease: Classical findings, recent developments and correlation to functional neuroanatomy*. Springer.

Rubens, A. B., & Benson, D. F. (1971). Associative visual agnosia. *Archives of Neurology*, 24(4), 305–316.

Ruesink, G. B., & Georgiadis, J. R. (2017). Brain imaging of human sexual response: Recent developments and future directions. *Current Sexual Health Reports*, 9, 183–191.

Ruigrok, A. N. V., Salami-Khorshidi, G., Lai. M.-C., Baron-Cohen, S., Lombardo, M. V., Tait, R. J., & Suckling, J. (2014). A meta analysis of sex differences in brain structure. *Neuroscience and Biobehavioral Reviews*, 39, 34–50.

Ruscio, A. M., Stein, D. J., Chiu, W. T., & Kessler, R. C. (2010). The epidemiology of obsessive-compulsive disorder in the National Comorbidity Survey Replication. *Molecular Psychiatry*, 15, 53–63.

Russ, T. C. (2018). Intelligence, cognitive reserve, and dementia: Time for intervention? *Journal of the American Medical Association*, 1(5), e181724. https://doi.org/10.1001/jamanetworkopen.2018.1724

Russek, M. (1971). Hepatic receptors and the neurophysiological mechanisms controlling feeding behaviour. In S. Ehrenpreis (Ed.), *Neurosciences research* (Vol. 4, pp. 213–282). Academic Press.

Russell, M. J., Switz, G. M., & Thompson, K. (1980). Olfactory influences on the human menstrual cycle. *Pharmacology, Biochemistry and Behavior*, 13, 737–738.

Rutherford, A. (2016). *A brief history of everyone who ever lived: The stories in our genes*. Weidenfeld & Nicolson.

Rutlidge, L. L., & Hupka, R. B. (1985). The facial feedback hypothesis: Methodological concerns and new supporting evidence. *Motivation and Emotion*, 9, 219–240.

Saalmann, Y. B. (2014). Intralaminar and medial thalamic influence on cortical synchrony, information transmission and cognition. *Frontiers in Systems Neuroscience*, 8, 83. https://doi.org/10.3389/fnsys.2014.00083.

Sabesan, R., Schmidt, B. P., Tuten, W. S., & Roorda, A. (2016). The elementary representation of spatial and color vision in the human retina. *Science Advances*, 2(9), e1600797. https://doi.org/10.1126/sciadv.1600797

Sack, A. T., & Schuhmann, T. (2012). Hemispheric differences within the fronto-parietal network dynamics underlying spatial imagery. *Frontiers in Psychology*, 3, 214. https://doi.org/10.3389/fpsyg.2012.00214

Sacks, O. (1985). *The man who mistook his wife for a hat*. Picador.

Sacks, O. (1990). *Awakenings*. Picador.

Saha, G. (2005). *Basics of PET imaging: Physics, chemistry and regulations*. Springer.

Saha, S., Chant, D., & McGrath, J. (2007). A systematic review of mortality in schizophrenia: Is the differential mortality gap worsening over time? *Archives of General Psychiatry*, 64, 1123–1131.

Sakai, K., Hikosaka, O., Miyauchi, S., Takino, R., Tamada, T., Iwata, N. K., & Nielsen, M. (1999). Neural representation of a rhythm depends on its interval ratio. *Journal of Neuroscience*, 19, 10074–10081.

Sakurai, T., Amemiya, A., Ishii, M., Matsuzaki, I., Chemelli, R. M., Tanaka, H., Williams, S. C., Richardson, J. A., Kozlowski, G. P., Wilson, S., & Yanagisawa, M. (1998). Orexins and orexin receptors: A family of hypothalamic neuropeptides and G protein-coupled receptors that regulate feeding behavior. *Cell*, 92, 573–85.

Salgado, S., & Kaplitt, M. G. (2015). The nucleus accumbens: A comprehensive review. *Stereotactic and Functional Neurosurgery*, 93, 75–93.

Salk, R. H., Hyde, J. S., & Abramson, L. Y. (2017). Gender differences in depression in representative national samples: Meta-analyses of diagnoses and symptoms. *Psychological Bulletin*, 143, 783–822.

Samii, A., Nutt, J. G., & Ransom, B. R. (2004). Parkinson's disease. *The Lancet*, 363, 1783–1793.

Sánchez, A., Sänchez-Campillo., J., Moreno-Herrero, D., & Rosales, V. (2014). 2D:4D values are associated with mathematics performance in business and economics students. *Learning and Individual Differences*, 36, 110–116.

Sanyal, S., & Van Tol, H. H. (1997). The role of dopamine D4 receptors in schizophrenia and antipsychotic action. *Journal of Psychiatric Research*, 31, 219–232.

Saper, C. B., Fuller, P. M., Pedersen, N. P., Lu, J., & Scammell, T. E. (2010). Sleep state switching. *Neuron*, 68, 1023–1042.

Saper, C. B., Scammell, T. B., & Lu, J. (2005). Hypothalamic regulation of sleep and circadian rhythms. *Nature*, 437, 1257–1263.

Sapolsky, R. M. (2004). *Why zebras don't get ulcers*. Holt.

Sara, S. (2009). The locus coeruleus and noradrenergic modulation of cognition. *Nature Reviews Neuroscience*, 10, 211–223.

Sara, S. J. (2017). Sleep to remember. *Journal of Neuroscience*, 37, 457–463.

Sasaguri, H., Nilsson, P., Hashimoto, S., Nagata, K., Saito, T., De Strooper, B., Hardy, J., Vassar, R., Winblad, B., & Saido, T. C. (2017). APP mouse models for Alzheimer's disease preclinical studies. *The EMBO Journal*, 36, 2473–2487.

Satoh, N., Ogawa, Y., Katsuura, G., Tsuji, T., Masuzaki, H., Hiraoka, J., Okazaki, T., Tamaki, M., Hayase, M., Yoshimasa, Y., & Nakao, K. (1997). Pathophysiological significance of the obese gene product, leptin, in ventromedial hypothalamus (VMH)-lesioned rats: Evidence for loss of its satiety effect in VMH-lesioned rats. *Endocrinology*, 138, 947–954.

Saudou, F., & Humbert, S. (2016). The biology of huntingtin. *Neuron*, 89, 910–926.

Saur, D., Kreher, B. W., Schnell, S., Kümmerer, D., Kellmeyer, P., Vry, M. S., Umarova, R., Musso, M., Glauche, V., Abel, S., & Weiller, C. (2008). Ventral and dorsal pathways for language. *Proceedings of the National Academy of Sciences of the USA*, 105, 18035–18040.

Savic, I., Berglund, H., Gulyas, B., & Roland, P. (2001). Smelling of odorous sex hormone-like compounds causes sex-differentiated hypothalamic activations in humans. *Neuron*, 31, 661–668.

Sawa, A., & Snyder, S. H. (2002). Schizophrenia: Diverse approaches to a complex disease. *Science*, 296, 692–695.

Sayo, A., Jennings, R. G., & Van Horn, J. D. (2012). Study factors influencing ventricular enlargement in schizophrenia: A 20 year follow-up meta analysis. *NeuroImage*, 59, 154–167.

Scammell, T. E., Jackson, A. C., Franks, N. P., Wisden, W., & Dauvilliers, Y. (2019). Histamine: Neural circuits and new medications. *Sleep*, 42(1), zsy183. https://doi.org/10.1093/sleep/zsy183

Schachter, S., & Singer, J. E. (1962). Cognitive, social and physiological determinants of emotional state. *Psychological Review*, 69, 379–399.

Schapira, A. H. (1994). Evidence for mitochondrial dysfunction in Parkinson's disease: A critical appraisal. *Movement Disorders*, 9, 125–138.

Scheckel, C., & Aguzzi, A. (2018). Prions, prionoids and protein misfolding disorders. *Mature Reviews Genetics*, 19, 404–418.

Schildkraut, J. J. (1965). The catecholamine hypothesis of affective disorders: A review of supporting evidence. *American Journal of Psychiatry*, 122, 509–522.

Schinazi, V. R., Nardi, D., Newcombe, N. S., Shipley, T. F., & Epstein, R. A. (2013). Hippocampal size predicts rapid learning of a cognitive map in humans. *Hippocampus*, 23, 515–528.

Schlaepfer, T. E., Harris, G. J., Tien, A. Y., Peng, L., Lee, S., & Pearlson, G. D. (1995). Structural differences in the cerebral cortex of healthy female and male subjects: A magnetic imaging study. *Psychiatry Research*, 21, 581–601.

Schlaug, G., Jancke, L., Huang, Y., & Steinmetz, H. (1995). In vivo evidence of structural brain asymmetry in musicians. *Science*, 267, 699–701.

Schliebs, R., & Arendt, T. (2006). The significance of the cholinergic system in the brain during aging and in Alzheimer's disease. *Journal of Neurotransmission*, 113, 1625–1644.

Schmid, Y., & Liechti, M. E. (2018). Long-lasting subjective effects of LSD in normal subjects. *Psychopharmacology*, 235, 535–545.

Schmitz, A. (2016). Benzodiazepine use, misuse, and abuse: A review. *The Mental Health Clinician*, 6, 120–126.

Schneps, M. (2015, January). Dyslexia can deliver benefits. *Scientific American Mind*, 26, 24–25.

Schnupp, J., Nelken, I., & King, A. (2011). *Auditory neuroscience*. MIT Press.

Schobel, S. A., Kelly, M. A., Corcoran, C. M., Van Heertum, K., Seckinger, R., Goetz, R., Harkavy-Friedman, J., & Malaspina, D. (2009). Anterior hippocampal and orbitofrontal cortical structural brain abnormalities in association with cognitive deficits in schizophrenia. *Schizophrenia Research*, 114, 110–118.

Schoenen, J., & Grant, G. (2004). Spinal cord connections. In G. Paxinos & J. K. Mai (Eds.), *The human nervous system*. Academic Press.

Schönemann, P. H. (1997). On models and muddles of heritability. *Genetica*, 99, 97–108.

Schramm, E., Klein, D. N., Elsaesser, M., Furukawa, T. A., & Domschke, K. (2020). Review of dysthymia and persistent depressive disorder: History, correlates, and clinical implications. *The Lancet Psychiatry*, 7, 801–812.

Schröder, T. (2017). The protein puzzle. Max Planck Research, 17, 54–59. https://www.mpg.de/11447687/W003_Biology_medicine_054-059.pdf

Schroll, H., & Hamker, F. H. (2013). Computational models of basal-ganglia pathway functions: Focus on functional neuroanatomy. *Frontiers in Systems Neuroscience*, 7, 122. https://doi.org/10.3389/fnsys.2013.00122

Schulte, J., & Littleton, J. T. (2011). The biological function of the Huntingtin protein and its relevance to Huntington's disease pathology. *Current Trends in Neurology*, 5, 65–78.

Schultz, W. (2007). Multiple dopamine functions at different time courses. *Annual Review of Neuroscience*, 30, 259–288.

Schumann, C. M., Hamstra, J., Goodlin-Jones, B. L., Lotspeich, L. J., Kwon, H., Buonocore, M. H., Lammers, C. R., Reiss, A. L.., & Amaral, D. G. (2004). The amygdala is enlarged in children but not adolescents with autism; the hippocampus is enlarged at all ages. *Journal of Neuroscience*, 24, 6392–6401.

Schwartz, J. R., & Roth, T. (2008). Neurophysiology of sleep and wakefulness: Basic science and clinical implications. *Current Neuropharmacology*, 6, 367–378.

Schwartz, M. W., & Seeley, R. J. (1997). The new biology of body weight regulation. *Journal of the American Dietetic Association*, 97, 54–58.

Schwartz, W. J., & Gainer, H. (1977). Suprachiasmatic nucleus: Use of 14-C labelled deoxyglucose uptake as a functional marker. *Science*, 197, 1089–1091.

Scorziello, A., Borzacchiello, B., Sisalli, M. J., Di Martino, R., Morelli, M., & Felicielo, A. (2020). Mitochondrial homeostasis and signaling in Parkinson's disease. *Frontiers in Aging Neuroscience*, 12, 100. https://doi.org/10.3389/fnagi.2020.00100

Scoville, W. B., & Milner, B. (1957). Loss of recent memory after bilateral hippocampal lesions. *Journal of Neurology, Neurosurgery and Psychiatry*, 20, 11–21.

Seeman, P., & Kapur, S. (2000). Schizophrenia: More dopamine, more D2 receptors. *Proceedings of the National Academy of Sciences of the U S A*, 97, 7673–7675.

Segal, N. L. (2012). *Born together – reared apart*. Harvard University Press.

Segraws, R. T. (2008). Antidepressant-induced orgasm disorder. *Journal of Sex and Marital Therapy*, 21, 192–201.

Seibt, J., Dumoulin, M. C., Aton, S. J., & Frank, M. G. (2012). Protein synthesis during sleep consolidates cortical plasticity in vivo. *Current Biology*, 22, 676–682.

Seibt, J., & Frank, M. G. (2019). Primed to sleep: The dynamics of synaptic plasticity across brain states. *Frontiers in Systems Neuroscience*, 13, Article 2. https://doi.org/10.3389/fnsys.2019.00002

Selkoe, D. J., & Hardy, J. (2016). The amyloid hypothesis of Alzheimer's disease at 25 years. *EMBO Molecular Medicine*, 8, 595–608.

Semmes, J. (1960). *Somatosensory changes after penetrating brain wounds in man*. Harvard University Press.

Seoane-Collazo, P., Martinez-Sánchaez, N., Millbank, E., & Contreras, C. (2020). Incendiary leptin. *Nutrients*, 12(2), 472. https://doi.org/10.3390/nu12020472

Sergent, J., Ohta, S., & MacDonald, B. (1992). Functional neuroanatomy of face and object processing: A positron emission tomography study. *Brain*, 115, 15–36.

Serrano-Pozo, A., Frosch, M. P., Masliah, E., & Hyman, B. T. (2011). Neuropathological alterations in Alzheimer disease. *Cold Spring Harbor Perspectives in Medicine*, 1, a006189. https://doi.org/10.1101/cshperspect.a006189

Seuntjens, W. (2010). The hidden sexuality of the yawn and future of chasmology. In O. Walusinski (Ed.), *The mystery of yawning in physiology and disease*. Karger.

Sham, P. C., O'Callaghan, E., Takei, N., Murray, G. K., Hare, E. H., & Murray, R. M. (1992). Schizophrenia following pre-natal exposure to influenza epidemics between 1939 and 1960. *British Journal of Psychiatry*, 160, 461–466.

Sharma, K. (2019). Cholinesterase inhibitors as Alzheimer's therapeutics. *Molecular Medicine Reports*, 20, 1479–1487.

Sharma, S. K., Klee, W., & Nirenberg, M. (1975). Dual regulation of adenylate cyclase accounts for narcotic dependence and tolerance. *Proceedings of the National Academy of Sciences*, 72, 3092–3096.

Sharpe, L. T., Stockman, A., & Nathans, J. (1999). Opsin genes, cone photopigments, color vision and colorblindness. In K. Gegenfurtner & L. T. Sharpe (Eds.), *Color vision: From genes to perception*. Cambridge University Press.

Shaw, P. J., Cirelli, C., Greenspan, R., & Tononi, G. (2000). Correlates of sleep and waking in Drosophilia melanogaster. *Science*, 287, 1834–1837.

Shaywitz, B. A., Shaywitz, S. E., Pugh, K. R., & Gore, J. C. (1995). Sex differences in the functional organisation of the brain for language. *Nature*, 373, 607–609.

Shaywitz, S. E., & Shaywitz, B. A. (2005). Dyslexia (specific reading disability). *Biological Psychiatry*, 57, 1301–1309.

Sheldon, C. A., Malcolm, G. L., & Barton, J. J. S. (2008). Alexia with and without agraphia: An assessment of two classical syndromes. *Canadian Journal of Neurological Science*, 35, 616–624.

Shepherd, G. (1991). *Foundations of the neuron doctrine*. Oxford University Press.

Sherin, J. E., Elmquist, J. K., Torrealba, F., & Saper, C. B. (1998). Innervation of histaminergic tuberomammillary neurons by GABAergic and galaninergic neurons in the ventrolateral preoptic nucleus of the rat. *Journal of Neuroscience*, 18, 4705–4721.

Sherin, J. E., Shiromani, P. J., McCarley, R. W., & Saper, C. B. (1996). Activation of ventrolateral preoptic neurons during sleep. *Science*, 271, 216–219.

Sherrington, R., Rogaev, E. I., Liang, Y., Rogaeva, E. A., Levesque, G., Ikeda, M., Chi, H., Lin, C., Li, G., Holman, K., & St George-Hyslop, P. H. (1995). Cloning of a gene bearing missense mutations in early-onset familial Alzheimer's disease. *Nature*, 375, 754–760.

Sherry, D. F., Jacobs, L. F., & Gaulin, S. J. C. (1992). Spatial memory and adaptive specialization of the hippocampus. *Trends in Neurosciences*, 15, 298–303.

Shimizu, N., Oomura, Y., Novin, D., Grijalva, C. V., & Cooper, P. H. (1983). Functional correlations between lateral hypothalamic glucose-sensitive neurons and hepatic portal glucose-sensitive units in the rat. *Brain Research*, 265, 49–54.

Shukla, A. K., & Kumar, U. (2006). Positron emission tomography: An overview. *Journal of Medical Physics*, 31, 13–21.

Shulman, L. M., & Spritzer, M. D. (2014). Changes in the sexual behavior and testosterone levels of male rats in response to daily interactions with estrus females. *Physiology and Behavior*, 133, 8–13.

Shulman, R. G. (2013). *Brain imaging*. Oxford University Press.

Siegel, R. K., & Jarvik, M. E. (1975). Drug-induced hallucinations in animals and man. In R. K. Siegel & L. J. West (Eds.), *Hallucinations: Behavior, experience, and theory*. John Wiley & Sons.

Siegel, S. (1976). Morphine analgesic tolerance: Its situation specificity supports a Pavlovian conditioning model. *Science*, 193, 323–325.

Siegel, S. (1984). Pavlovian conditioning and heroin overdose: Reports by overdose victims. *Bulletin of the Psychonomic Society*, 22, 428–430.

Siegel, S. (2016). The heroin overdose mystery. *Current Directions in Psychological Research*. Advance online publication. https://doi.org/10.1177/0963721416664404

Siegel, S., Hinson, R. E., & McCully, J. (1982). Heroin "overdose" death: Contribution of drug-associated environmental cues. *Science*, 216, 436–437.

Sieradzan, K. A., Mechan, A. O., Jones, L., … & Mann, D. M. (1999). Huntington's disease intranuclear inclusions contain truncated, ubiquitinated huntingtin protein. *Experimental Neurology*, 156, 92–99.

Siffre, M. (1975). Six months alone in a cave. *National Geographic*, 147, 426–435.

Silbersweig, D. A., Stern, E., Frith, C., Cahill, C., Holmes, A., Grootoonk, S., Seaward, J., McKenna, P., Chua, S. E., Schnorr, L., & Frackowiak, R. S. J. (1995). A functional neuroanatomy of hallucinations in schizophrenia. *Nature*, 378, 176–179.

Silventoinen, K., Rokholm, B., Kaprio, J., & Sørensen, T. I. A. (2010). The genetic and environmental influences on childhood obesity: A systematic review of twin and adoption studies. *International Journal of Obesity*, 34, 29–40.

Simeon, D. (2004). Depersonalisation disorder: A contemporary overview. *CNS Drugs*, 18, 343–354.

Simmons, D., & Self, D. W. (2009). Role of mu and delta opioid receptors in the nucleus accumbens in cocaine-seeking behavior. *Neuropsychopharmacology*, 34, 1946–1957.

Simner, J., Mulvenna, C., Sagiv, N., Tsakanikos, E., Witherby, S. A., Fraser, C., Scott, K., & Ward, J. (2006). Synaesthesia: The prevalence of atypical crossmodal experiences. *Perception*, 35, 1024–1033.

Simon, S. A., de Araujo, I. E., Gutierrez. R., & Nicolelis, M. A. (2006). The neural mechanisms of gustation: A distributed processing code. *Nature Reviews Neuroscience*, 7, 890–901.

Simonyan, K. (2019). Recent advances in understanding the role of the basal ganglia. *F1000Research*, 8, 1–9. https://doi.org/10.12688/f1000research.16524.1

Singer, B. F., Bryan, M. A., Popov, P., Robinson, T. E., & Aragona, B. J. (2017). Rapid induction of dopamine sensitization in the nucleus accumbens shell induced by a single injection of cocaine. *Behavioral Brain Research*, 324, 66–70.

Singh, D., Vidaurri, M., Zambarano, R. J., & Dabbs, J. M. (1999). Lesbian erotic role identification: Behavioral, morphological, and hormonal correlates. *Journal of Personality and Social Psychology*, 76, 1035–1049.

Sinha, R., Sarkar, S., Khaitan, T., & Dutta, S. (2017). Duchenne muscular dystrophy: Case report and review. *Journal of Family Medicine and Primary Care*, 6, 654–656.

Skene, D. J., Lockley, S. W., & Arendt, J. (1999). Melatonin in circadian sleep disorders in the blind. *Biological Signals and Receptors*, 8, 90–95.

Skene, D. J., Lockley, S. W., Thapan, K., & Arendt, J. (1999). Effects of light on human circadian rhythms. *Reproduction Nutrition Development*, 39, 295–304.

Skibicka, K. P., & Dickson, S. (2013). Enteroendocrine hormones – central effects on behavior. *Current Opinion in Pharmacology*, 13, 977–982.

Slaby, A. E. (1995). Suicide as an indicum of biologically-based brain disease. *Archives of Suicide Research*, 1, 59–73.

Slater, C. R. (2017). The structure of human neuromuscular junctions: Some unanswered molecular questions. International *Journal of Molecular Sciences*, 18, 2183. https://doi.org/10.3390/ijms18102183

Slotnick, S. (2013). *Controversies in cognitive neuroscience*. Palgrave Macmillan.

Slough, C., Masters, S. C., Hurley, R. A., & Taber, K. H. (2016). Clinical positron emission tomography (PET) neuroimaging: Advantages and limitations as a diagnostic tool. *Journal of Neuropsychiatry and Clinical Neuroscience*, 28, 67–71.

Smink, F. R. E., van Hoeken, D., Oldehinkel, A. J., & Hoek, H. W. (2014). Prevalence and severity of DSM-5 eating disorders in a community cohort of adolescents. *The International Journal of Eating Disorders*, 47, 610–619.

Smit, E. A., & Sadakata, M. (2018). The effect of handedness on spatial and motor representation of pitch patterns in pianists. *PLoS One*, 13(5), e0195831. https://doi.org/10.1371/journal.pone.0195831

Smith, A. P. (2002). Effects of caffeine on human behavior. *Food and Chemical Toxicology*, 40, 1243–1255.

Smith, C., & Lapp, L. (1991). Increases in the number of REMs and REM density following an intensive learning period. *Sleep*, 14, 325–330.

Smith, D., Dempster, C., Glanville, J., Freemantle, N., & Anderson, I. (2002). Efficacy and tolerability of Venlafaxine compared with selective serotonin reuptake inhibitors and other antidepressants: A meta-analysis. *British Journal of Psychiatry*, 180, 396–404.

Smith, E. E., & Jonides, J. (1998). Neuroimaging analyses of human working memory. *Proceedings of the National Academy of Sciences of the U S A*, 95, 12061–12068.

Smith, E. S., & Lewin, G. R. (2009). Nociceptors: A phylogenetic view. *Journal of Comparative Physiology. A, Neuroethology, Sensory, Neural, and Behavioral Physiology*, 195, 1089–1106.

Smith, G. P. (2012). Cholecystokinin and treatment of meal size: Proof of principle. *Obesity*, 14(Suppl. 4), 168S–170S.

Smith, K. S., Berridge, K. C., & Aldridge, J. W. (2011). Disentangling pleasure from incentive salience and learning signals in brain reward circuitry. *Proceedings of the National Academy of Sciences of the U S A*, 108, E255–E264.

Snowden, R., Snowden, R. J., Thompson, P., & Troscianko, T. (2012). *Basic vision: An introduction to visual perception*. Oxford University Press.

Snowdon, D. (2001). *Aging with grace*. Fourth Estate.

Snyder, S. H. (1973). Amphetamine psychosis: A 'model' schizophrenia mediated by catecholamines. *American Journal of Psychiatry*, 130, 61–67.

Snyder, S. H. (1986). *Drugs and the brain*. Scientific American Library.

Snyder, S. H. (2009). Neurotransmitters, receptors, and second messengers galore in 40 years. *Journal of Neuroscience*, 29, 12717–12721.

Snyder, S. H., & Pasternak, G. W. (2003). Historical review: Opioid receptors. *Trends in Pharmacological Sciences*, 24, 198–205.

Soares, J. M., Marques, P., Alves, V., & Sousa, N. (2013). A hitchhiker's guide to diffusion tensor imaging. *Frontiers in Neuroscience*, 7, 31. https://doi.org/10.3389/fnins.2013.00031

Solomon, S. G., & Lennie, P. (2007). The machinery of colour vision. *Nature Reviews Neuroscience*, 8, 276–286.

Somers, V. K., Dyken, M. E., Mark, A. L., & Abboud, A. S. (1993). Sympathetic-nerve activity during sleep in normal subjects. *New England Journal of Medicine*, 328, 303–307.

Sommer, I. E. C., Aleman, A., Bouma, A., & Kahn, R. S. (2004). Do women really have more bilateral language representation than men? A meta-analysis of functional imaging studies. *Brain*, 127, 1845–1852.

Spaniol, J., Davidson, P. S., Kim, A. S., Han, H., Moscovitch, M., & Grady, C. L. (2009). Event-related fMRI studies of episodic encoding and retrieval: Meta-analyses using activation likelihood estimation. *Neuropsychologia*, 47, 1765–1779.

Spaulding, W. D., Silverstein, S. M., & Menditto, A. A. (2017). *The schizophrenia spectrum*. Hogrefe Publishing.

Specht, K. (2020). Current challenges in translational and clinical fMRI and future directions. *Frontiers in Psychiatry*, 10, 924. https://doi.org/10.3389/fpsyt.2019.00924

Spencer, G. (2012). Background on mouse as a model organism. National Human Genome Research Institute. https://www.genome.gov/10005834/background-on-mouse-as-a-model-organism

Sperry, R. W. (1964). The great cerebral commissure. *Scientific American*, 210, 42–48.

Sperry, R. W. (1974). Lateral specialisation in the surgically separated hemispheres. In F. O. Schmidt & F. G. Worden (Eds.), *The neurosciences: Third study program*. MIT Press.

Spetter, M. S., de Graaf, C., Mars, M., Viergever, M. A., & Smeets, P. A. (2014). The sum of its parts—effects of gastric distension, nutrient content and sensory stimulation on brain activation. *PLoS One*, 9(3), e90872. https://doi.org/10.1371/journal.pone.0090872

Springer, S. P., & Deutsch, G. (1989). *Left brain, right brain*. Freeman.

Squire, L. R. (1987). *Memory and the brain*. Oxford University Press.

Squire, L. R. (1992). Declarative and nondeclarative memory: Multiple brain systems supporting learning and memory. *Journal of Cognitive Neuroscience*, 4, 232–243.

Squire, L. R. (2004). Memory systems of the brain: A brief history and current perspective. *Neurobiology Learning and Memory*, 82, 171–177.

Squire, L. R., Amaral, D. G., Zola-Morgan, S., Kritchevsky, M., & Press, G. (1989). Description of brain injury in amnesic patient N.A. based on magnetic resonance imaging. *Experimental Neurology*, 105, 23–25.

Squire, L. R., & Moore, R. Y. (1979). Dorsal thalamic lesion in a noted case of human memory dysfunction. *Annals of Neurology*, 6, 503–506.

Stahl, S. M. (1996). *Essential psychopharmacology*. Cambridge University Press.

Stahl, S. M. (2000). *Essential psychopharmacology*. Cambridge University Press.

Stahl, S. M. (2013). *Stahl's essential psychopharmacology*. Cambridge University Press.

Stanford, S. C. (1996). Prozac: Panacea or puzzle? *Trends in Pharmacological Sciences*, 17, 150–154.

Stanley, B. G., Magdalain, W., Seirafi, A., Thomas, W. J., & Leibowitz, S. F. (1993). The perifornical area: The major focus of (a) patchily distributed hypothalamic neuropeptide Y-sensitive feeding system(s). *Brain Research*, 604, 304–317.

Starr, C., & Taggart, R. (1989). *Biology: The unity and diversity of life*. Brooks/Cole.

Stein, D. J., Costa, D. L. C., Lochner, C., Miguel, E. C., Janardhan Reddy, Y. C., Shavitt, R. G., van den Heuvel, O. A., & Simpson, B. (2019). Obsessive-compulsive disorder. *Nature Reviews Diseases Primers*, 5, 52. https://doi.org/10.1038/s41572-019-0102-3

Stein, J. (2001). The magnocellular theory of developmental dyslexia. *Dyslexia*, 7, 12–36.

Stein, J. (2014). Dyslexia: The role of vision and visual attention. *Current Developmental Disorders Reports*, 1, 267–280.

Stein, J. (2019). The current status of the magnocellular theory of developmental dyslexia. *Neuropsychologia*, 130, 66–77.

Stein, J. F., & Stoodley, C. J. (2006). *Neuroscience: An introduction*. Wiley.

Steiner, H., & Tseng, K. Y. (Eds.). (2016). *Handbook of basal ganglia structure and function*. Academic Press.

Steketee, J. D., & Kalivas, P. W. (2011). Drug wanting: Behavioral sensitization and relapse to drug-seeking behavior. *Pharmacological Reviews*, 63, 348–365.

Stellar, E. (1954). The physiology of motivation. *Psychological Review*, 61, 5–22.

Stemmler, G. (2004). Physiological processes during emotion. In P. Philippot & R. S. Feldman (Eds.), *The regulation of emotion*. Lawrence Erlbaum.

Stephan, F. K., & Zucker, I. (1972). Circadian rhythms in drinking behaviour and locomotor activity of rats are eliminated by hypothalamic lesions. *Proceedings of the National Academy of Sciences*, 60, 1583–1586.

Steriade, M., Datta, S., Pare, D., Oakson, G., & Dossi, R. C. (1990). Neuronal activities in brainstem cholinergic nuclei related to tonic activation processes in thalamocortical systems. *Journal of Neuroscience*, 10, 2541–2559.

Stickgold, R., Hobson, J. A., Fosse, R., & Fosse, M. (2001). Sleep, learning, and dreams: Off-line memory reprocessing. *Science*, 294, 1052–1057.

Stickgold, T., James, L., & Hobson, J. A. (2000). Visual discrimination requires sleep after training. *Nature Neuroscience*, 3, 1237–1238.

Stifani, N. (2014). Motor neurons and the generation of spinal motor neuron diversity. *Frontiers in Cellular Neuroscience*, 8, 293. https://doi.org/10.3389/fncel.2014.00293

Stochholm, K., Bojesen, A., Jenson, A. S., Juul, S., & Gravholt, C. H. (2012). Criminality in men with Klinefelter's syndrome and XYY syndrome: A cohort study. *British Medical Journal Open*, 2(1), e000650. https://doi.org/10.1136/bmjopen-2011-000650

Stoker, T. B. (2018). Stem cell treatments for Parkinson's disease. In T. B. Stoker & J. C. Greenland (Eds.), *Parkinson's disease: Pathogenesis and clinical aspects*. Codon Publications.

Stoodley, C. J. (2014). Distinct regions of the cerebellum show gray matter decreases in autism, ADHD, and developmental dyslexia. *Frontiers in Systems Neuroscience*, 8, 92. https://doi.org/10.3389/fnsys.2014.00092

Stoodley, C. J., & Stein, J. F. (2011). The cerebellum and dyslexia. *Cortex*, 47, 101–116.

Stoudemire, A. (1998). *Clinical psychiatry for medical students*. Lippincott-Raven.

Stoykova, A. S., Dabeva, M. D., Dimova, R. N., & Hadjiolov, A. A. (1985). Ribosome biogenesis and nucleolar ultrastructure in neuronal and oligodendroglial rat brain cells. *Journal of Neurochemistry*, 45, 1667–1676.

Strack, F., Martin, L. L., & Stepper, S. (1988). Inhibiting and facilitating conditions of the human smile: A non-obtrusive test of the facial feedback hypothesis. *Journal of Personality and Social Psychology*, 54, 768–777.

Strange, B. A., Witter, M. P., Lein, E. S., & Moser, E. I. (2014). Functional organization of the hippocampal longitudinal axis. *Nature Reviews Neuroscience*, 15, 655–669.

Stricker, E. M., Rowland, N., Saller, C. F., & Friedman, M. I. (1977). Homeostasis during hypoglycemia: Central control of adrenal secretion and peripheral control of feeding. *Science*, 196, 79–81.

Strittmatter, W. J., Weisgraber, K. H., Huang, D. Y., Dong, L. M., Salvesen, G. S., Pericak-Vance, M., Schmechel, D., Saunders, A. M., Goldgaber, D., & Roses, A. D. (1993). Binding of human apolipoprotein E to synthetic amyloid beta peptide: Isoform-specific effects and implications for late-onset Alzheimer disease. *Proceedings of the National Academy of Sciences of the U S A*, 90, 8098–8102.

Stuber, G. D., & Wise, R. A. (2016). Lateral hypothalamic circuits for feeding and reward. *Nature Neuroscience*, 19, 198–205.

Stunkard, A. J., Foch, T. T., & Hrubec, Z. (1986). A twin study of human obesity. *Journal of the American Medical Association*, 256, 51–54.

Sudhinaraset, M., Wigglesworth, C., & Takeuchi, D. T. (2016). Social and cultural contexts of alcohol use: Influences in a social-ecological framework. *Alcohol Research: Current Reviews*, 38, 35–45.

Sudhoff, K. (1908). *Ein Beitrag zur Geschichte der Anatomie der mittelater speziell der anatomischen Graphik*. J. A. Barth.

Sullivan, E. V., & Fama, R. (2012). Wernicke's encephalopathy and Korsakoff's syndrome revisited. *Neuropsychology Review*, 22, 69–71.

Sullivan, R. J., & Hagen, E. H. (2002). Psychotropic substance-seeking: Evolutionary pathology or adaptation? *Addiction*, 97, 389–400.

Sulser, F., Vetulani, J., & Mobley, P. (1978). Mode of action of antidepressant drugs. *Biochemical Pharmacology*, 27, 257–261.

Sun, Z. Y., Kloppel, S., Riviere, D., Perrot, M., Frackowiak, R., Siebner, H., & Mangin, J.-F. (2012). The effect of handedness on the shape of the central sulcus, *NeuroImage*, 60, 332–339.

Sveinbjornsdottir, S. (2016). The clinical symptoms of Parkinson's disease. *Journal of Neurochemistry*, 139, 318–324.

Svensson, T. H. (2000). Dysfunctional brain dopamine systems induced by psychotomimetic NMDA-receptor antagonists and the effects of antipsychotic drugs. *Brain Research Reviews*, 31, 320–329.

Swaab, D. F., & Hofman, M. A. (1990). An enlarged suprachiasmatic nucleus in homosexual men. *Brain Research*, 537, 141–148.

Swaab, D. F., & Hofman M. A. (1995). Sexual differentiation of the human hypothalamus in relation to gender and sexual orientation. *Trends in Neurosciences*, 18, 264–270.

Swaab, D. F., Purba, J. S., & Hofman, M. A. (1995). Alterations in the hypothalamic paraventricular nucleus and its oxytocin neurons (putative satiety cells) in Prader-Willi syndrome: A study of five cases. *Journal of Clinical Endocrinology and Metabolism*, 80, 573–579.

Swinburn, B., Egger, G., & Raza, F. (1999). Dissecting obesogenic environments: The development and application of a framework for identifying and prioritizing environmental interventions for obesity. *Preventive Medicine*, 29, 563–570.

Szczepanski, S. M., & Knight, R. T. (2014). Insights into human behavior from lesions to the prefrontal cortex. *Neuron*, 83, 1002–1018.

Szymusiak, R., Alam, N., Steininger, T. L., & McGinty, D. (1998). Sleep-waking discharge patterns of ventrolateral preoptic/anterior hypothalamic neurons in rats. *Brain Research*, 803, 178–188.

Takagi, Y. (2016). History of neural stem cell research and its clinical application. *Neurologia Medico-Chirurgica*, 56, 110–124.

Takagi, Y., Takahashi, J., Saiki, H., Morizane, A., Hayashi, T., Kishi, Y., Fukuda, H., Okamoto, Y., Koyanagi, M., Ideguchi, M., & Hashimoto, H. (2005). Dopaminergic neurons generated from monkey embryonic stem cells function in a Parkinson primate model. *Journal of Clinical Investigation*, 115, 102–109.

Takahashi, K., Tanabe, K., Ohnuki, M., Narita, M., Ichisaka, T., Tomoda, K., & Yamanaka, S. (2007). Induction of pluripotent stem cells from adult human fibroblasts by defined factors. *Cell*, 131, 861–872.

Takeshita, R. S. C., Huffman, M. A., Kinoshita, K., & Becovitch, F. B. (2017). Effect of castration on social behavior and hormones in male Japanese macaques (Macaca Fuscata). *Physiology and Behavior*, 181, 43–50.

Talavage, T. M., Gonzalez-Castillo, J., & Scott, S. K. (2014). Auditory neuroimaging with fMRI and PET. *Hearing Research*, 307, 4–15. https://doi.org/10.1016/j.heares.2013.09.009

Tam, V., Patel, N., Turcotte, M., Bossé, Y., Paré, G., & Meyre, D. (2019). Benefits and limitations of genome-wide association studies. *Nature Reviews Genetics*, 20, 467–484.

Tanabe, S. (2013). Population codes in the visual cortex. *Neuroscience Research*, 76, 101–105.

Tanner, C. M., Ottman, R., Goldman, S. M., Ellenberg, J., Chan, P., Mayeux, R., & Langston, J. W. (1999). Parkinson disease in twins: An etiologic study. *Journal of the American Medical Association*, 281, 341–346.

Tanzi, R. E. (2012). The genetics of Alzheimer disease. *Cold Spring Harbor Perspectives in Medicine*, 2, a006296. https://doi.org/10.1101/cshperspect.a006296

Tanzi, R., George-Hyslop, P., Haines, J., … & Gusella, J. F. (1987). The genetic defect in familial Alzheimer's disease is not tightly linked to the amyloid β-protein gene. *Nature*, 329, 156–157.

Taormina, G., & Mirisola, M. G. (2014). Calorie restriction in mammals and simple model organisms. *BioMed Research International*, 2014, 308690. https://doi.org/10.1155/2014/308690

Tartaglia, N. R., Howell, S., Sutherland, A., Wilson, R., & Wilson L. (2010). A review of trisomy X (47,XXX). *Orphanet Journal of Rare Diseases*, 5, 8. https://doi.org/10.1186/1750-1172-5-8

Tarullo, A. R., Balsam, P. B., & Fifer, W. P. (2011). Sleep and infant learning. *Infant Child Development*, 20, 35–46.

Tauscher, J., Hussain, T., Agid, O., Verhoeff, N. P., Wilson, A. A., Houle, S., Remington, G., Zipursky, R. B., & Kapur, S. (2004). Equivalent occupancy of dopamine D1 and D2 receptors with clozapine: Differentiation from other atypical antipsychotics. *American Journal of Psychiatry*, 161, 1620–1625.

Tawa, E. A., Hall, S. D., & Lohoff, F. W. (2016). Overview of the genetics of alcohol use disorder. *Alcohol and Alcoholism*, 5, 507–514.

Taylor, K. M., Saint-Hilaire, M. H., Sudarsky, L., Simon, D. K., Hersh, B., Sparrow, D., Hu, H., & Weisskopf, M. G. (2016). Head injury at early ages is associated with risk of Parkinson's disease. *Parkinsonism and Related Disorders*, 23, 57–61.

Tecuapetla, F., Patel, J. C., Xenias, H., English, D., Tadros, I., Shah, F., Berlin, J., Deisseroth, K., Rice, M. E., Tepper, J. M., & Koos, T. (2010). Glutamatergic signalling by mesolimbic dopamine neurons in the nucleus accumbens. *Journal of Neuroscience*, 30, 7105–7110.

Teitelbaum, P., & Epstein, A. (1962). Recovery of feeding and drinking after lateral hypothalamic lesions. *Psychological Reviews*, 69, 74–90.

Terzian, H., & Ore, G. D. (1955). Syndrome of Klüver and Bucy: Reproduced in man by bilateral removal of the temporal lobes. *Neurology*, 5, 373–380.

Teyler T. J., & DiScenna, P. (1987). Long-term potentiation. *Annual Review of Neuroscience*, 198, 131–161.

Thaker, V. V. (2017). Genetic and epigenetic causes of obesity. *Adolescent Medicine: State of the Art Reviews*, 28, 379–4–5.

Thakker, M. M. (2011). Histamine in the regulation of wakefulness. *Sleep Medicine Reviews*, 15, 65–74.

Thambisetty, M., Tripaldi, R., Riddoch-Contreras, J., & Resnick, S. M. (2010). Proteome-based plasma markers of brain amyloid-β deposition in non-demented older individuals. *Journal of Alzheimer's Disease*, 22, 1099–1109.

Thannickal, T. C., Moore, R. Y., Nienhuis, R., Ramanathan, L., Gulyani, S., Aldrich, M., & Cornford, M., & Siegel. J. M. (2000). Reduced number of hypocretin neurons in human narcolepsy. *Neuron*, 27, 469–474.

Thompson, R. F. (1993). *The brain: A neuroscience primer*. W.H. Freeman.

Thompson, R. F., & Madigan, S. A. (2005). *Memory: The key to consciousness*. Princeton University Press.

Thompson, T., & Schuster, C. R. (1964). Morphine self-administration, food-reinforced, and avoidance behaviors in rhesus monkeys. *Psychopharmacologia*, 5, 87–94.

Thornton, J., Zehr, J., & Loose, M. D. (2009). Effects of prenatal androgens on rhesus monkeys: A model system to explore the organizational hypothesis in primates. *Hormones and Behavior*, 55, 633–645.

Thrap, W. G., & Sarker, I. N. (2013). Origins of amyloid (beta). *BMC Genomics*, 14(1), 290.

Tick, B., Bolton, P., Happé, F., & Ridsdijk, F. (2016). Heritability of autism spectrum disorders: A meta-analysis of twin studies. *Journal of Child Psychology and Psychiatry, and Allied Disciplines*, 57, 585–595.

Tienari, P., Sorri, A., Lahti, I., … & Moring, J. (1985). The Finnish Adoptive Family Study of Schizophrenia. *Yale Journal of Biology and Medicine*, 58, 227–237.

Tienari, P., Wynne, L.C., Moring, J., Lahti, I., Naarala, M., Sorri, A., Wahlberg, K. E., Saarento, O., Seitamaa, M., Kaleva, M., & Läsky, K. (1994). The Finnish Adoptive Family Study of Schizophrenia: Implications for family research. *The British Journal of Psychiatry*, 164(Suppl. 23), 20–26.

Titeler, M., Lyon, R. A., & Glennon, R. A. (1988). Radioligand binding evidence implicates the brain 5-HT2 receptor as a site of action for LSD and phenylisopropylamine hallucinogens. *Psychopharmacology*, 94, 213–216.

Toates, F. (2007). *Biological psychology*. Prentice Hall.

Tobi, E. W., Slieker, R. C., Luijk, R., Dekkers, K. F., Stein, A. D., Xu, K. M., Slagboom, P. E., van Zwet, E. W, Lumey, L. H., Heijmans, B. T., … Heijmans, B. T.; Biobank-based Integrative Omics Studies Consortium. (2018). DNA methylation as a mediator of the association between prenatal adversity and risk factors for metabolic disease in adulthood. *Science Advances*, 4, eaao4364. https://doi.org/10.1126/sciadv.aao4364

Tobler, I., Franken, P., Tracshel, L., & Borbély, A. A. (1992). Models of sleep regulation in mammals. *Journal of Sleep Research*, 1, 125–127.

Tomlinson, B. E. (1984). The pathology of Alzheimer's disease and senile dementia of Alzheimer type. In D. W. K. Kay & G. D. Burrows (Eds.), *Handbook of studies on psychiatry and old age*. Elsevier.

Tooth, G. C., & Newton, M. P. (1961). *Leucotorny in England and Wales, 1942–1954*. Her Majesty's Stationery Office (HMSO).

Torjesen, P. A., & Sandnes, L. (2004). Serum testosterone in women as measured by an automated immunoassay and a RIA. *Clinical Chemistry*, 50, 578–679.

Torrey, E. F. Bowler, A. E., Taylor, E. H., & Gottesman, I. I. (1994). *Schizophrenia and manic-depressive disorder: The biological roots of mental illness as revealed by a landmark study of identical twins*. Basic Books.

Torterolo, P., Sampogna, S., & Chase, M. H. (2011). A restricted parabrachial pontine region is active during non-rapid eye movement sleep. *Neuroscience*, 190, 184–193.

Trajanovic, N. N., Shapiro, C. M., & Milovanović, S. (2013). Sleep-laughing – hypnogely. *The Canadian Journal of Neurological Sciences*, 40, 536–539.

Tranel, D., Manzel, K., & Anderson, S. W. (2008). Is the prefrontal cortex important for fluid intelligence? A neuropsychological study using Matrix Reasoning. *The Clinical Neuropsychologist*, 22, 242–261.

Trehub, S. E. (2001). Musical predispositions in infancy. *Annals of the New York Academy of Sciences*, 930, 1–16.

Tremblay, P., & Dick, A. S. (2016). Broca and Wernicke are dead, or moving past the classic model of language neurobiology. *Brain and Language*, 162, 60–71.

Trenholm, S., & Krishnaswamy, A. (2020). An annotated journey through modern visual neuroscience. *Journal of Neuroscience*, 40, 44–53.

Treutlein, J., Cichon, S., Ridinger, M., Wodarz, N., Soyka, M., Zill, P., Maier, W., Moessner, R., Gaebel, W., Dahmen, N., Fehr, C., Scherbaum, N., Steffens, M., Ludwig, K. U., Frank, J., Wichmann, H. E., Schreiber, S., Dragano, N., Sommer, W. H., … Rietschel M. (2009). Genome-wide association study of alcohol dependence. *Archives of General Psychiatry*, 66, 773–784.

Trezza, V., Damsteegt, R., Achterberg, E. J., & Vanderschuren, L. J. (2011). Nucleus accumbens μ-opioid receptors mediate social reward. *Journal of Neuroscience*, 31, 6362–6370.

Trouth, A. J., Dabi, A., Solieman, N., Kurukumbi, M., & Kalyanam, J. (2012). Myasthenia gravis: A review. *Autoimmune Diseases*, 2012, 874680. https://doi.org/10.1155/2012/874680

Tryon, R. C. (1940). Genetic differences in maze-learning ability in rats. *Yearbook of the National Society for the Study of Education*, 39, 111–119.

Tsang, Y. C. (1938). Hunger motivation in gastrectomized rats. *Journal of Comparative Psychology*, 26, 1–17.

Tschöp, M., Smiley, D. L., & Heiman, M. L. (2000). Ghrelin induces adiposity in rodents. *Nature*, 407, 908–913.

Tschöp, M., Wawarta, R., Riepl, R. L., Friedrich, S., Bidlingmaier, M., Landgraf, R., & Folwaczny, C. (2001). Post-prandial decrease of circulating human ghrelin levels. *Journal of Endocrinolgical Investigation*, 24, 19–21.

Ts'o, D. Y., Zarella, M., & Burkitt, G. (2009). Whither the hypercolumn? *Journal of Physiology*, 587, 2791–2805.

Tsuang, M. T., Stone, W. S., & Faraone, S. V. (1999). Schizophrenia: A review of genetic studies. *Current Psychiatry Reports*, 1, 20–24.

Tsujino, N., & Sakurai, T. (2013). Role of orexin in modulating arousal, feeding, and motivation. *Frontiers in Behavioral Neuroscience*, 7, 28. https://doi.org/10.3389/fnbeh.2013.00028

Tucker, L. B., Velosky, A. G., & McCabe, J. T. (2018). Applications of the Morris water maze in translational traumatic brain injury research. *Neuroscience and Biobehavioral Reviews*, 88, 187–200.

Turk, I., Dirjec, J., & Kavur, B. (1995). The oldest musical instrument in Europe discovered in Slovenia? *Razprave IV Razreda SAZU*, 36, 287–293.

Turner, A. M., & Greenough, W. T. (1983). Synapses per neuron and synaptic dimensions in occipital cortex of rats reared in complex, social or isolation housing. *Acta Stereologica*, 2(Suppl. 1), 239–244.

Turner, A. M., & Greenough, W. T. (1985). Differential rearing effects on rat visual cortex synapses. 1. Synaptic and neuronal density and synapses per neuron. *Brain Research*, 329, 195–203.

Turner, R. (2016). Uses, misuses, new uses and fundamental limitations of magnetic resonance imaging in cognitive science. *Philosophical Transactions of the Royal Society of London B*, 371, 20150349. https//doi.org/10.1098/rstb.2015.0349

Tyng, C. M., Amin, H. U., Saad, M. N. M., & Malik, A. S. (2017). The influences of emotion on learning and memory. *Frontiers in Psychology*, 8, 1454. https://doi.org/10.3389/fpsyg.2017.01454

Tyrer, P., & Baldwin, D. (2006). Generalised anxiety disorder. *The Lancet*, 368, 2156–2166.

Tzschentke, T. M., & Schmidt, W. J. (2003). Glutamatic mechanisms in addiction. *Molecular Psychiatry*, 8, 373–382.

Uhl, G. R., & Grow, R. W. (2004). The burden of complex genetics in brain disorders. *Archives of General Psychiatry*, 61, 223–229.

Ul Hassan, A., Hassan, G., & Rasool, Z. (2009). Role of stem cells in neurological disorder. *International Journal of Health Sciences*, 3, 227–233.

Ungerleider, L. G., & Haxby, J. V. (1994). "What" and "where" in the human brain. *Current Opinion in Neurobiology*, 4, 157–165.

Ungerleider, L. G., & Mishkin, M. (1982). Two cortical visual systems. In D. J. Ingle, M. A. Goodale & R. J. W. Mansfield (Eds.), *Analysis of visual behavior*. MIT Press.

Ungerstedt, U. (1971). Adipsia and aphagia after 6-hydroxydopamine induced degeneration of the nigrostriatal dopamine system. *Acta Physiologica Scandinavca*, 367, 95–122.

Uno, Y., & Coyle, J. T. (2019). Glutamate hypothesis in schizophrenia. *Psychiatry and Clinical Neurosciences*, 73, 204–215.

Valenstein, E. S. (1986). *Great and desperate cures: The rise and decline of psychosurgery and other radical treatments for mental illness*. Basic Books.

Valla, J., & Ceci, S. J. (2011). Can sex differences in science be tied to the long reach of prenatal hormones? Brain organization theory, digit ratio (2D/4D), and sex differences in preferences and cognition. *Perspectives in Psychological Science*, 6, 134–136.

van der Straten, A. L., Denys, D., & van Wingen, G. A. (2017). Impact of treatment on resting cerebral blood flow and metabolism in obsessive compulsive disorder: A meta-analysis. *Scientific Reports*, 7, 17464. https://doi.org/10.1038/s41598-017-17593-7

Van Dijk, A., Klompamkers, A., & Denys, D. (2008). Role of serotonin in obsessive compulsive disorder. *Future Neurology*, 3(5). https://doi.org/10.2217/14796708.3.5.589

Van Essen, D. C., Anderson, C. H., & Felleman, D. J. (1992). Information processing in the primate visual system: An integrated systems perspective. *Science*, 255, 419–423.

Van Gestel, M. A., Kostrezwa, E., Adam, R. A. H., & Janhunen, S. K. (2014). Pharmacological manipulations in animal models of anorexia and binge eating in relation to humans. *British Journal of Pharmacology*, 171, 4767–4784.

van Wyk, M., Solms, M., & Lipinska, G. (2019). Increased awakenings from nonrapid eye movement sleep explain differences in dream recall frequency in healthy individuals. *Frontiers in Human Neuroscience*, 13, 370. https://doi.org/10.3389/fnhum.2019.00370

Vanderschuren, L. J., & Kalivas, P. W. (2000). Alterations in dopaminergic and glutamatergic transmission in the induction and expression of behavioral sensitization: A critical review of preclinical studies. *Psychopharmacology*, 151, 99–120.

Vann, S. D., Aggleton, J. P., & Maguire, E. A. (2009). What does the retrosplenial cortex do? *Nature Reviews Neuroscience*, 10, 792–802.

Varghese, F. P., & Brown, E. S. (2001). The hypothalamic-pituitary-adrenal axis in major depressive disorder. *The Primary Care Companion to The Journal of Clinical Psychiatry*, 3, 151–155.

Vellutino, F. R., Fletcher, J. M., Snowling, M. J., & Scanlon, D. M. (2004). Specific reading disability (dyslexia): What have we learned in the past four decades? *Journal of Child Psychology and Psychiatry*, 45, 2–40.

Venkatraman, A., Edlow, B. L., & Immordino-Yang, M. H. (2017). The brainstem in emotion: A review. *Frontiers in Neuroanatomy*, 11, 15. https://doi.org/10.3389/fnana.2017.00015

Ventura, A. K. (2017). Does breast feeding shape food preferences? Links to obesity. *Annals of Nutrition and Metabolism*, 70, 8–15.

Verhulst, B., Neale, M. C., & Kendler, K. S. (2015). The heritability of alcohol use disorders: A meta-analysis of twin and adoption studies. *Psychological Medicine*, 45, 1061–1072.

Verstichel, P. (2000). Syndrome amnésique de Korsakoff [Korsakoff amnesia syndrome]. *Presse Medical*, 29, 670–676.

Vesalius, A. (1543). *Vesalius on the Human brain* (being a translation of a Section of the Fabrica of 1543). Welcome Historical Medical Museum. Oxford University Press.

Viaene, A. N., Petrof, I., & Sherman, S. M. (2011). Synaptic properties of thalamic input to the subgranular layers of primary somatosensory and auditory cortices in the mouse. *Journal of Neuroscience*, 31, 12738–12747.

Vickers, C. A., Dickson, K. S., & Wyllie, D. J. (2005). Induction and maintenance of late-phase long-term potentiation in isolated dendrites of rat hippocampal CA1 pyramidal neurones. *Journal of Physiology*, 568, 803–813.

Victor, M., Adams, R. D., & Collins, G. H. (1971). The Wernicke-Korsakoff syndrome. A clinical and pathological study of 245 patients, 82 with post-mortem examinations. *Contemporary Neurology Series*, 7, 1–206.

Villafuerte, G., Miguel-Puga, A., Rodriguez, E. M., Machado, S., Manjarrez, E., & Arias-Carrión, O. (2015). Sleep deprivation and oxidative stress in animal models: A systematic review. *Oxidative Medicine and Cellular Longevity*, 2015, 234952. https://doi.org/10.1155/2015/234952

Vioque, J., Torres, A., & Quiles, J. (2000). Time spent watching television, sleep duration and obesity in adults living in Valencia, Spain. *International Journal of Obesity and Related Disorders*, 24, 1683–1688.

Virtanen, J. O., & Jacobson, S. (2012). Viruses and multiple sclerosis. *CNS and Neurological Disorders Drug Targets*, 11, 528–544.

Visscher, P. M., Brown, M. A., McCarthy, M. I., & Yang, J. (2012). Five years of GWAS discovery. *American Journal of Human Genetics*, 90, 7–24.

Volkow, N. D. (2014). *Heroin: NIDA research report series*. National Institute on Drug Abuse. NIH publication number 15-0165.

Vollenweider, F. X., Vollenweider-Scherpenhuyzen, M. F., Bäbler, A., Vogel, H., & Hell, D. (1998). Psilocybin induces schizophrenia-like psychosis in humans via a serotonin-2 agonist action. *NeuroReport*, 9, 3897–3902.

Vonsattel, J. P., Myers, R. H., Stevens, T. J., Ferrante, R. J., Bird, E. D., & Richardson, E. P. (1985). Neuropathological classification of Huntington's disease. *Journal of Neuropathology and Experimental Neurology*, 44, 559–577.

Voracek, M., & Loibi, L. M. (2016). Scientometric analysis and bibliography of digit ratio (2D:4D) research, 1998–2008. *Psychological Reports*, 104, 922–956.

Wagner, H. (1999). *The psychobiology of human motivation*. Routledge.

Wagner, H. J., Hening, H., Jabs, W. J., … & Wandinger, K. P. (2000). Altered prevalence and reactivity of anti-Epstein-Barr virus antibodies in patients with multiple sclerosis. *Viral Immunology*, 13, 497–502.

Wagner, T. D., & Smith, E. E. (2003). Neuroimaging studies of working memory: A meta-analysis. *Cognitive, Affective and Behavioral Neuroscience*, 3, 255–274.

Walker, D. B., Walker, J. C., Cavner, P. J., Taylor, J. L., Pickel, D. H., Hall, S. B., & Suarez, J. C. (2006). Naturalistic quantification of canine olfactory sensitivity. *Applied Animal Behavior Science, 97*, 241–254.

Walker, M. P., & Strickgold, R. (2004). State-dependent learning and memory consolidation. *Neuron, 44*, 121–133.

Walker, M. P., Brakefield, T., Morgan, A., Hobson, J. A., & Stickgold, R. (2002). Practice with sleep makes perfect: Sleep-dependent motor skill learning. *Neuron, 35*, 205–211.

Wallner, M., & Olson, R. W. (2008). Physiology and pharmacology of alcohol: The imidazobenzodiazepine alcohol antagonist site on subtypes of GABAA receptors as an opportunity for drug development? *British Journal of Pharmacology, 154*, 288–298.

Wamsley, E. J., & Stickgold, R. (2011). Memory, sleep and dreaming: Experiencing consolidation. *Sleep Medicine Clinics, 6*, 97–108.

Wang, A., Costello, S., Cockburn, M., Zhang, X., Bronstein, J, & Ritz, B. (2011). Parkinson's disease risk from ambient exposure to pesticides. *European Journal of Epidemiology, 26*, 547–555.

Wang, Q., Bing, C., Al-Barazanji, K., Mossakowaska, D. E., Wang, X. M., McBay, D. L., Neville, W. A., Taddayon, M., Pickavance, L., Dryden, S., Thomas, M. E., McHale, M. T., Gloyer, I. S., Wilson, S., Buckingham, R., Arch, J. R., Trayhurn, P., & Williams, G. (1997). Interactions between leptin and hypothalamic neuropeptide Y neurons in the control of food intake and energy homeostasis in the rat. *Diabetes, 46*, 335–341.

Wang, X.-S., Armstrong, M. E. G., Cairns, B. J., Key, T. J., & Travis, R. C. (2011). Shift work and chronic disease: The epidemiological evidence. *Occupational Medicine, 61*, 78–89.

Wang, Y. C., McPherson, K., Marsh, T., Gortmaker, S. L., & Brown, M. (2011). Health and economic burden of the projected obesity trends in the USA and the UK. *The Lancet, 378*, 815–825.

Wangensteen, O. H., & Carlson, H. A. (1931). Hunger sensations in a patient after total gastrectomy. *Proceedings of the Society of Experimental and Biological Medicine, 28*, 545–547.

Warburton, H., Turnbull, P. J., & Hough, M. (2005). *Occasional and controlled heroin use. Not a problem?* Joseph Rowntree Foundation.

Warren, M. P. (2011). Endocrine manifestations of eating disorders. *Journal of Clinical Endocrinology, 96*, 333–343.

Warren, N., Siskind, D., & O'Gorman, C. (2018). Refining the psychiatric syndrome of anti-N-methyl-d-aspartate receptor encephalitis. *Acta Psychiatrica Scandinavica, 138*, 401–408.

Watson, J. B. (1913). Psychology as the behaviorist views it. *Psychological Review, 20*, 158–177.

Watson, J. D. (1968). *The double Helix: A personal account of the discovery of the structure of DNA.* Weidenfeld & Nicolson.

Watt, F. M., & Driskell, R. R. (2010). The therapeutic potential of stem cells. *Philosophical Transactions of the Royal Society B, Biological Sciences, 65*(1537), 155–163.

Weaver, D. R. (1998). The suprachiasmatic nucleus: A 25-year retrospective. *Journal of Biological Rhythms, 13*, 100–112.

Webster, D. B. (1992). An overview of mammalian auditory pathways with an emphasis on humans. In D. B. Webster, A. N. Popper & R. R. Fay (Eds.), *The Mammalian auditory pathway: Neuroanatomy.* Springer.

Webster, H. H., & Jones, B. E. (1988). Neurotoxic lesions of the dorsolateral pontomesencephalic tegmentum-cholinergic cell area in the cat. *Brain Research, 458*, 285–302.

Wedekind, C., Seebeck, T., Bettens, F., & Paepke A. J. (1995). MHC-dependent male preferences in humans. *Proceedings of the Royal Society of London B, 260*, 245–249.

Weeks, J. R. (1962). Experimental morphine addiction: Method for autonomic intravenous injections in unrestrained rats. *Science, 138*, 143–144.

Wei, P., Bao, R., Lv, Z., & Jing, B. (2018). Weak but critical links between primary somatosensory centers and motor cortex during movement. *Frontiers in Human Neuroscience, 12*, 1. https://doi.org/10.3389/fnhum.2018.00001

Weinberger, D. R., & Wyatt, R. J. (1982). Brain morphology in schizophrenia: *In vivo* studies. In F. A. Henn & H. A. Nasrallah (Eds.), *Schizophrenia as a brain disease*. Oxford University Press.

Weinberger, N. M. (2004). Music and the brain. *Scientific American*, 291, 88–95.

Weingarten, H. P. (1983). Conditioned cues elicit feeding in sated rats: A role for learning in meal initiation. *Science*, 220, 431–433.

Weinhold, B. (2006). Epigenetics. *Environmental Health Perspectives*, 114, A160–A167.

Weinstein, J. J., Chohan, M. O., Slifstein, M., Kegeles, L. S., Moore, H., & Abi-Darghan, A. (2017). Pathway-specific dopamine abnormalities in schizophrenia. *Biological Psychiatry*, 81, 31–42.

Weiskrantz, L. (1997). *Consciousness lost and found*. Oxford University Press.

Weiskrantz, L. (2010). Looking back: Blindsight in hindsight. *The Psychologist*, 23, 356–358.

Weiskrantz, L., Warrington, E. K., Sander, M. D., & Marshall, J. (1974). Visual capacity in the hemianopic field following a restricted occipital ablation. *Brain*, 97, 709–728.

Weiss, P., H., & Fink, G. R. (2009). Grapheme-colour synaesthetes show increased grey matter volumes of parietal and fusiform cortex. *Brain*, 132, 65–70.

Weitzman, E. D., Czeisler, C. A., Coleman, R. M. Spielman, A. J., Zimmerman, J. C., Dement, W., Richardson, G., & Pollak, P. (1981). Delayed sleep phase syndrome: A chronobiological disorder with sleep onset insomnia. *Archives of General Psychiatry*, 38, 737–746.

Wekerle, H. (1993). Experimental autoimmune encephalomyelitis as a model of immune-mediated CNS disease. *Current Opinion in Neurobiology*, 3, 779–784.

Wellman, P. J. (2000). Norepinephrine and the control of food intake. *Nutrition*, 16, 837–842.

Welsh, D. K., Logothetis, D. E., Meister, M., & Reppert, S. M. (1995). Individual neurons dissociated from rat suprachiasmatic nucleus express independently phased circadian firing rhythms. *Neuron*, 14, 697–706.

Wenk, G. L. (2003). Neuropathologic changes in Alzheimer's disease. *Journal of Clinical Psychiatry*, 64(Suppl. 9), 7–10.

Wenzel, B. M. (1973). Chemoreception. In D. S. Farner, J. R. King & C. Parker (Eds.), *Avian biology* (Vol. 3). Academic Press.

Wenzel, J. M., & Cheer, J. F. (2018). Endocannabinoid regulation of reward and reinforcement through interaction with dopamine and endogenous opioid signaling. *Neuropsychopharmacology*, 43, 103–115.

West, K. E., Jablonski, M. R., Warfield, B., Cecil, K. S., James, M., Ayers, M. A., Maida, J., Bowen, C., Sliney, D. H., Rollag, M. D., Hanifin, J. P., & Brainard, G. C. (2011). Blue light from light-emitting diodes elicits a dose-dependent suppression of melatonin in humans. *Journal of Physiology*, 110, 619–626.

Wever, E. G., & Bray, C. W. (1930). The nature of acoustic response: The relation between sound frequency and frequency of impulses in the auditory nerve *Journal of Experimental Psychology*, 13, 373–387.

Wexler, A. (1996). *Mapping fate*. University of California Press.

Whalen, P. J., Rauch, S. L., Etcoff, N. L., McInerney, S. C., Lee, M. B., & Jenike, M. A. (1998). Masked presentations of emotional facial expressions modulate amygdala activity without explicit knowledge. *Journal of Neuroscience*, 18, 411–418.

Whalley, L. J., Starr, J. M., Athawes, R., Hunter, D., Pattie, A., & Deary, I. J. (2000). Childhood mental ability and dementia. *Neurology*, 55, 1455–1459.

Whitam, F. L., Diamond, M., & Martin, J. (1993). Homosexual orientation in twins; A report on 61 pairs and three triplet sets. *Archives of Sexual Behavior*, 22, 187–202.

Wiberg, A., Ng, M., Al Omran, Y., Alfaro-Almagro, F., McCarthy, P., Marchini, J., Bennett, D. L., Smith, S., Douaud, G., & Furniss, D. (2019). Handedness, language areas and neuropsychiatric diseases: Insights from brain imaging and genetics. *Brain*, 142, 2938–2947.

Wickens, A. P. (1998). *The causes of aging*. Harwood.

Wickens, A. P. (2001). Ageing and the free radical theory. *Respiration physiology*, 128, 379–391.

Wickens, A. P. (2009) *Introduction to biopsychology* (3rd ed.). Pearson.

Wickens, A. P. (2015). *A history of the brain: From stone age surgery to modern neuroscience*. Psychology Press.

Wickens, A. P. (2017a). Five depictions of the brain. *The Psychologist*, 30(April), 30–37.

Wickens, A. P. (2017b). The amygdala. In A. E. Wenzel (Ed.), *The SAGE encyclopedia of abnormal and clinical psychology* (Vol. 1). SAGE. https://sk.sagepub.com/reference/the-sage-encyclopedia-of-abnormal-and-clinical-psychology/i4924.xml?term=amygdala

Wickens, A. P. (2017c). The frontal lobes. In A. E. Wenzel (Ed.), *The SAGE encyclopedia of abnormal and clinical psychology* (Vol. 3). SAGE.

Wickens, A. P. (2017d). The limbic system. In A. E. Wenzel (Ed.), *The SAGE encyclopedia of abnormal and clinical psychology* (Vol. 4). SAGE.

Wickens, A. P. (2017e). The thalamus. In A. E. Wenzel (Ed.), *The SAGE encyclopedia of abnormal and clinical psychology*. SAGE.

Wickens, A. P. (2019a). Sir Henry Dale (1875–1968). *Resonance*, 24(8), 833–845.

Wickens, A. P. (2019b). *Key thinkers in neuroscience*. Routledge.

Wiersma, D., Nienhuis, F. J., Slooff, C. J., & Giel, R. (1998). Natural course of schizophrenic disorders: A 15-year follow up of a Dutch incidence cohort. *Schizophrenia Bulletin*, 24, 75–85.

Wikler, A. (1948). Recent progress in research on the neurophysiologic basis of morphine addiction *The American Journal of Psychiatry*, 105, 329–338.

Wilcock, G. K., Esiri, M. M., Bowen, D. M., & Smith, C. C. (1982). Alzheimer's disease. Correlation of cortical choline acetyltransferase activity with the severity of dementia and histological abnormalities. *Journal of Neurological Science*, 57, 407–417.

Wilding, J. P. H. (2006). Pathophysiology and aetiology of obesity. *Medicine*, 34, 501–505.

Wilkinson, A., Sebanz, N., Mandl, I., & Huber, L. (2011). No evidence of contagious yawning in the red-footed tortoise Geochelone carbonaria. *Current Zoology*, 57, 477–484.

Wilkinson, L. L., & Brunstrom, J. M. (2016). Sensory specific satiety: More than just habituation? *Appetite*, 103, 221–228.

Will, B., Galani, R., Kelche, C., & Rosenzweig, M. R. (2004). Recovery from brain injury in animals: Relative efficacy of environmental enrichment, physical exercise or formal training (1990–2002). *Progress in Neurobiology*, 72, 167–182.

Will, R. G., Ironside, J. W., Zeidler, M., Cousens, S. N., Estibeiro, K., Alperovitch, A., Poser, S., Pocchiari, M., Hofman, A., & Smith, P. G. (1996). A new variant of Creutzfeldt-Jakob disease in the UK. *The Lancet*, 347, 921–925.

Willuhn, I., Wanat, M. J., Clark, J. J., & Phillips, P. E. (2010). Dopamine signaling in the nucleus accumbens of animals self-administering drugs of abuse. *Current Topics in Behavioral Neurosciences*, 3, 29–71.

Willyard, C. (2018). New human gene tally reignites debate. *Nature*, 558, 354–355.

Wilson, R. I., & Nicoll, R. A. (2002). Endocannabinoid signaling in the brain, *Science*, 296, 687–682.

Wilson, T. K., & Tripp, J. (2019). Buspirone. StatPearls Publishing. https://www.ncbi.nlm.nih.gov/books/NBK531477/

Winn, P., Tarbuck, A., & Dunnett, S. (1984). Ibotenic acid lesions of the lateral hypothalamus: Comparison with the electrolytic lesion syndrome. *Neuroscience*, 12, 225–240.

Wise, R. A. (2005). Forebrain substrates of reward and motivation. *Journal of Comparative Neurology*, 493, 115–121.

Wiseman, F. K., Pulford, L. J., Barkus, C., Barkus, C., Liao, F., Portelius, E., Webb, R., Chávez-Gutiérrez, L., Cleverley, K., Noy, S., Sheppard, O., Collins, T., Powell, C., Sarell, C. J., Rickman, M., Choong, X., Tosh, J. L., Siganporia, C., Whittaker, H., T., Stewart, . . . London Down syndrome consortium (2018). Trisomy of human chromosome 21 enhances amyloid-β deposition independently of an extra copy of APP. *Brain*, 141, 2457–2474.

Witelson, S. F., Kigar, D. L., & Harvey, T. (1999). The exceptional brain of Albert Einstein. *The Lancet*, 353, 2149–2153.

Wittchen, H.-U., & Jacobi, F. (2005). Size and burden of mental disorders in Europe — a critical review and appraisal of 27 studies. *European Journal of Neuropsychopharmacology*, 15, 357–376.

Wittchen, H.-U., Jacobi, F., Rehm, J., Gustavsson, A., Svensson, M., Jönsson, B., Olesen, J., Allgulander, C., Alonso, J., Faravelli, C., Fratiglioni, L., Jennum, P., Lieb, R., Maercker, A., van Os, J., Preisig, M., Salvador-Carulla, L., Simon, R., & Steinhausen, H. C. (2011). The size and burden of mental disorders and other disorders of the brain in Europe 2010. *European Neuropsychopharmacology*, 21, 655–679.

Wong-Riley, M. T. T. (1979). Changes in the visual system of monocularly enucleated cats demonstrable with cytochrome oxidase histochemistry. *Brain Research*, 171, 11–28.

Woo Baidal, J. A., Locks, L. M., Cheng, E. R., Blake-Lamb, T. L., Perkins, M. E., & Taveras, E. M. (2016). Risk factors for childhood obesity in the first 1,000 days: A systematic review. *American Journal of Preventative Medicine*, 50, 761–779.

Wood, R. I., & Stanton, S. J. (2012). Testosterone and sport: Current perspectives. *Hormones and Behavior*, 61, 147–155.

Woods, S. C., & D'Alessio, D. A. (2008). Central control of body weight and appetite. *Journal of Clinical Endocrinology and Metabolism*, 93, S37–S50.

Woods, S. C., & Stricker, E. M. (2013). Food intake and metabolism. In L. R. Squire, D. Berg, F. E. Bloom, S. du Lac, A. Ghosh & N. C. Spitzer (Eds.), *Fundamental neuroscience*. Academic Press.

World Drug Report. (2013). United Nations publication, Sales No. E.13.XI.6.

World Health Organization (n.d.). World Obesity Federation. https://www.worldobesity.org/about/about-obesity/prevalence-of-obesity

World Health Organization. (2009). Physical inactivity: A global public health problem. https://www.who.int/diet-physicalactivity/factsheet_inactivity/en/

World Health Organization (2017). WHO report on the global tobacco epidemic, 2017: Monitoring tobacco use and prevention policies. World Health Organization.

World Health Organization (2018). Global status report on alcohol and health 2018. https://www.who.int/publications/i/item/9789241565639

World Health Organization. (2020). https://www.who.int/news-room/fact-sheets/detail/obesity-and-overweight

Worth, A., & Annese, J. (2012). Brain observatory and the continuing study of H.M.: Interview with Jacopo Annese. *Europe's Journal of Psychology*, 8, 222–230.

Wray, N. R., & Visscher, P. M. (2010). Narrowing the boundaries of the genetic architecture of schizophrenia. *Schizophrenia Bulletin*, 36, 14–23.

Wren, A. M., Seal, L. J., Cohen, M. A., Brynes, A. E., Frost, G. S., Murphy, K. G., Dhillo, W. S., Ghatei, M. A., & Bloom, S. R. (2001). Ghrelin enhances appetite and increases food intake in humans. *Journal of Clinical Endocrinology and Metabolism*, 86, 5992.

Wright, J. E., Vogel, J. A., Sampson, J. B., Knapik, J. J., Patton, J. F., & Daniels, W. L. (1983). Effects of travel across time zones on exercise capacity and performance. *Aviation Space Environment Medicine*, 54, 132–137.

Wright, M., Skaggs, W., & Nielsen, F. A. (2016). The cerebellum. *WikiJournal of Medicine*, 3(1), 1–15. https://search.informit.com.au/documentSummary;dn=380776158668038;res=IELHEA

Wu, Y. E., Enoki, R., Oda, Y., Huang, Z. L., Honma, K. I., & Honma, S. (2018). Ultradian calcium rhythms in the paraventricular nucleus and subparaventricular zone in the hypothalamus. *Proceedings of the National Academy of Sciences of the USA*, 115, E9469–E9478.

Xie, L., Kang, H., Xu, Q., Chen, M. J., Liao, Y., Thiyagarajan, M., O'Donnell, J., Christensen, D. J., Nicholson, C., Iliff, J. J., Takano, T., Deane, R., & Nedergaard, M. (2013). Sleep drives metabolic clearance from the brain. *Science*, 342, 373–377.

Yaffe, K., Barnes, D., Nevitt, M., Lui, L. Y., & Covinsky, K. A. (2001). Prospective study of physical activity and cognitive decline in elderly women: Women who walk. *Archives of International Medicine*, 161, 1703–1708.

Yamada, K., Wada, E., & Wada, K. (2000). Bombesin-like peptides: Studies on food intake and social behaviour with receptor knock-out mice. *Annals of Medicine*, 32, 519–529.

Yamadori, A., Osumi, Y., Masuhara, S., & Okubo, M. (1977). Preservation of singing in Broca's aphasia. *Journal of Neurology, Neurosurgery, and Psychiatry*, 40, 221–224.

Yan, Q.S. (1999). Extracellular dopamine and serotonin after ethanol monitored with 5-minute microdialysis. *Alcohol*, 19, 1–7.

Yanagisawa, N. (2018). Functions and dysfunctions of the basal ganglia in humans. *Proceedings of the Japan Academy. Series B, Physical and Biological Sciences*, 94, 275–304.

Yang, Y., & Wang, J. Z. (2017). From structure to behavior in basolateral amygdala-hippocampus circuits. *Frontiers in Neural Circuits*, 11, 86. https://doi.org/10.3389/fncir.2017.00086

Yaskin, V. A. (2011). Seasonal changes in hippocampus size and spatial behavior in mammals and birds. *Biology Bulletin Reviews*, 1, 279. https://doi.org/10.1134/S2079086411030108

Yee, M., Maal-Bared, G., Ting-A-Kee, R., Chwalek, M., Mackay-Clackett, I., Bergamini, M., Grieder, T. E., & van der Kooy, D. (2020). Segregation of caffeine reward and aversion in the rat nucleus accumbens shell versus core. *European Journal of Neuroscience*, 52, 3074–3086.

Yehuda, R., Bierer, L. M., Schmeidler, J., Aferiat, D. H., Breslau, I., & Dolan, S. (2000). Low cortisol and risk for PTSD in adult offspring of holocaust survivors. *American Journal of Psychiatry*, 157, 1252–1259.

Yehuda, R., Engel, S. M., Brand, S. R., Seckl, J., Marcus, S. M., & Berkowitz, G. S. (2005). Transgenerational effects of posttraumatic stress disorder in babies of mothers exposed to the World Trade Center attacks during pregnancy. *Journal of Clinical Endocrinology and Metabolism*, 90, 4115–4118.

Yen, C.-T., & Lu, P.-L. (2013). Thalamus and pain. *Acta Anaesthesiologica Taiwanica*, 51, 73–80.

Yeo, S. S., Chang, P. H., & Jang, S. H. (2013). The ascending reticular activating system from pontine reticular formation to the thalamus in the human brain. *Frontiers in Human Neuroscience*, 7, 416. https://doi.org/10.3389/fnhum.2013.00416

Yetnikoff, L., Lavezzi, H. N., Reichard, R. A., & Zahm, D. S. (2014). An update on the connections of the ventral mesencephalic dopaminergic complex. *Neuroscience*, 282, 23–48.

Yin, H. H. (2014). The basal ganglia in action. *Neuroscientist*, 23, 299–313. https://doi.org/10.1177/1073858416654115

Yoneoka, Y., Takeda, N., Inoue, A., Ibuchi, Y., Kumagai, T., Sugai, T., Takeda, K., & Ueda, K. (2004). Acute Korsakoff syndrome following mammillothalamic tract infarction. *American Journal of Neuroradiology*, 25, 964–968.

Yonker, J. E., Eriksson, E., Nilsson, L.-G., & Herlitz, A. (2006). Negative association of testosterone on spatial visualisation in 35 to 80 year old men. *Cortex*, 42, 376–386.

Yost, W. A. (2009). Pitch perception. *Attention, Perception, & Psychophysics*, 71, 1701–1715.

Youdim, M. B. H., Edmondson, D., & Tipton, K. F. (2006). The therapeutic potential of monoamine oxidase inhibitors. *Nature Reviews Neuroscience*, 7, 295–309.

Young, L. R., & Nestle, M. (2002). The contribution of expanding portion sizes to the US obesity epidemic. *American Journal of Public Health*, 92, 246–249.

Young, W. C., Goy, R. W., & Phoenix, C. H. (1964). Hormones and sexual behavior. *Science*, 143, 212–218.

Youngren, K. D., Inglis, F. M.,, Pivirotto, P. J., Jedema, H. P., Bradberry, C. W., Goldman-Rakic, P. S., Roth, R. H., & Moghaddam, B. (1999). Clozapine preferentially increases dopamine release in the rhesus monkey prefrontal cortex compared with the caudate nucleus. *Neuropsychopharmacology*, 20, 403–412.

Zaidel, E. (1985). Language and the right hemisphere. In D. F. Benson & E. Zaidel (Eds.), *The dual brain: Hemispheric specialization in humans* (pp. 205–231). The Guilford Press.

Zaidi, Z. F. (2010). Gender difference in human brain: A review. *The Open Anatomy Journal*, 2, 37–55.

Zakzanis, K. K. (1998). The subcortical dementia of Huntington's disease. *Journal of Clinical and Experimental Neuropsychology*, 20, 565–578.

Zandi, M. S., Irani, S. R., Lang, B., Waters, P., Jones, P. B., McKenna, P., Coles, A. J., Vincent, A., & Lennox, B. R. (2011). Disease-relevant autoantibodies in first episode schizophrenia. *Journal of Neurology*, 258, 686–688.

Zatorre, R. J., Belin, P., & Penhune, V. B. (2002). Structure and function of auditory cortex: Music and speech. *Trends in Cognitive Sciences*, 6, 37–46.

Zee, P. C., & Manthena, P. (2007). The brain's master circadian clock: Implications and opportunities for therapy of sleep disorders. *Sleep Medicine Review*, 11, 59–70.

Zehra., A., Burns, J., Liu, C. K., Manza, P., Wiers, C. E., Volkow, N. D., & Wang, G.-J. (2018). Cannabis addiction and the brain: A review. *Journal of Neuroimmune Pharmacology*, 13, 438–452.

Zeidman, L. A., Stone, J. L., & Kondziella, D. (2013). New revelations about Hans Berger, father of the electroencephalograph (EEG) and his ties to the Third Reich. *Journal of Child Neurology*, 29, 1–9.

Zeki, S. M. (1993). *A vision of the brain.* Blackwell.

Zeki, S. M., & Shipp, S. (1988). The functional logic of cortical connections. *Nature*, 335, 311–317.

Zhang, G., & Stackman, R. W. (2015). The role of serotonin 5-HT2A receptors in memory and cognition. *Frontiers in Pharmacology*, 6, 225. https://doi.org/10.3389/fphar.2015.00225

Zhang, Y., Proenca, R., Maffei, M., Barone, M., Leopold, L., & Friedman, J. M. (1994). Positional cloning of the mouse obese gene and its human homologue. *Nature*, 372, 425–432.

Zhou, J. N., Hofman, M. A., Gooren, L. J., & Swaab, D. F. (1995). A sex difference in the human brain and its relation to transsexuality. *Nature*, 378, 68–70.

Zielinski, M. R., McKenna, J. T., & McCarley, R. W., (2016). Functions and mechanisms of sleep. *AIMS Neuroscience*, 3, 67–104.

Zigmond, M. J. (1999). Otto Loewi and the demonstration of chemical neurotransmission. *Brain Research Bulletin*, 50, 347–348.

Zihl, J., & Heywood, C. A. (2015). The contribution of LM to the neuroscience of movement vision. *Frontiers in Integrative Neuroscience*, 9, 6. https://doi.org/10.3389/fnint.2015.00006

Zihl, J., von Cramon, D., & Mai, N. (1983). Selective disturbance of movement vision after bilateral brain damage. *Brain*, 106, 313–340.

Zisapel, N., Tarrasch, R., & Laudon. M. (2005). The relationship between melatonin and cortisol rhythms: Clinical implications of melatonin therapy. *Drug Development Reviews*, 65, 119–125.

Zola, S. M., Squire, L. R., Teng, E., Stefanacci, L., Buffalo, E. A., & Clark, R. E. (2000). Impaired recognition memory in monkeys after damage limited to the hippocampal region. *Journal of Neuroscience*, 20, 451–463.

Zoubrinetzky, R., Bielle, F., & Valdois, S. (2014). New insights on developmental dyslexia subtypes: Heterogeneity of mixed reading profiles. *PLoS One*, 9(6), e99337. https://doi.org/10.1371/journal.pone.0099337

Zubenko, G. C., Hughes, H. B., Stiffler, J. S., Zubenko, W. N., & Kaplan, B. B. (2002). Genome survey for susceptibility loci for recurrent, early-onset major depression: Results at 10cM resolution. *American Journal of Medical Genetics*, 114, 413–422.

Zubin, J., & Spring, B. (1977). Vulnerability: A new view of schizophrenia. *Journal of Abnormal Psychology*, 86, 103–126.

Zuccato, C., Tartari, M., Crotti, A., Goffredo, D., Valenza, M., Conti, L., Cataudella, T., Leavitt, B. R., Hayden, M. R., Timmusk, T., Rigamonti, D., & Cattaneo, E. (2003). Huntingtin interacts with REST/NRSF to modulate the transcription of NRSE-controlled neuronal genes. *Nature Genetics*, 35, 76–83.

AUTHOR INDEX

SUBJECT INDEX

Page numbers followed by f, t and n indicate figures, tables and notes, respectively.